Professional Java XML

Kal Ahmed
Sudhir Ancha
Andrei Cioroianu
Jay Cousins
Jeremy Michael Crosbie
John Davies
Kyle Gabhart
Steven Gould
James Hart
Ramnivas Laddad
Sing Li
Brendan Macmillan
Daniel Rivers-Moore
Judy Skubal
Karli Watson
Scott Williams

Wrox Press Ltd. ®

Professional Java XML

Published by Wrox Press Ltd,
Arden House, 1102 Warwick Road, Acocks Green,
Birmingham, B27 6BH, UK
Printed in Canada
ISBN 1-861004-01-X

Trademark Acknowledgements

Wrox has endeavored to provide trademark information about all the companies and products mentioned in this book by the appropriate use of capitals. However, Wrox cannot guarantee the accuracy of this information.

Credits

Authors
Kal Ahmed
Sudhir Ancha
Andrei Cioroianu
Jay Cousins
Jeremy Michael Crosbie
John Davies
Kyle Gabhart
Steven Gould
James Hart
Ramnivas Laddad
Sing Li
Brendan Macmillan
Daniel Rivers-Moore
Judy Skubal
Karli Watson
Scott Williams

Additional Material
Teun Duynstee
Richard Huss

Category Manager
Viv Emery

Technical Architect
James Hart

Technical Editors
Craig A. Berry
Helen Callaghan
Jim Molony
Steve Rycroft
Chanoch Wiggers

Author Agents
Emma Batch
Nicola Phillips

Project Administrator
Simon Brand

Technical Reviewers
Roberto Baglioni
Bob Bell
Yogesh Bhandarkar
Rich Bonneau
Carl Burnham
Chris Crane
Cosmo A Difazio
Kevin Farnham
Joey Frasier
Kyle Gabhart
David Gulbransen
Perrumal K.
Mike Koch
Chris Lightfoot
Alex Linde
Jim MacIntosh
Mark Mamone
Jacob Matthew
Phil Powers De George
Don Reamey
James Scheinblum
Mike Slinn
Gavin Smyth
John Timney
Andrew Watt

Production Coordinator
Tom Bartlett

Figures
Shabnam Hussain

Proofreaders
Christopher Smith
Agnes Wiggers

Cover
Shelley Frazier

Index
Adrian Axinte

About the Authors

Kal Ahmed

Kal has now reached the watershed stage in his life where he has been programming and consulting for more than a third of his time on the planet. Despite the shock of realizing this, he plans to continue putting his experience of Topic Maps, XML, Java, Python, and C++ to the test on a daily basis, in his role as Principal Consultant for Ontopia, a company dedicated to the creation of premium software tools using Topic Map technology.

I would like to dedicate my part of this book to my late father, Hersi Ahmed.

Kal Ahmed co-wrote Chapter 10.

Sudhir Ancha

Sudhir is Senior Software Engineer at Nextel Telecommunications. Prior to working at Nextel, he also worked at MCI WorldCom Telecommunications and Learning Byte International. He has worked on various Telecom Projects and also developed training applications using Java and XML. His areas of interest include Security, Improving Performance, Distributed Computing, and different Internet Technologies. In his free time, he also maintains the site http://www.JavaCommerce.com/.

I would like to thank my parents Krishna Rao and Samba Siva, and my brothers, Sunil Kumar and Naresh Kumar, for their love, support, and encouragement throughout my life. Finally I would like to thank all the developers who have helped create such a beautiful XSLT processor, Xalan.

Sudhir contributed Chapters 7 and 8.

Andrei Cioroianu

Andrei is the founder of Devsphere.com, where he builds Java development tools and offers consulting services. His projects range from applets and desktop applications to servlets and server side frameworks. He has also written articles for the Java Developer's Journal.

Andrei invites you to send comments about Chapter 18 to andreic@ZIPLIP.COM.

Jay Cousins

Jay Cousins is an Analyst/Consultant at RivCom, a consultancy specialising in helping businesses adopt XML technologies for the creation, management, and distribution of information. Jay specializes in information analysis and modeling with a focus on DTD and schema development and the mapping of data structures. Jay has written and developed training materials on XML integration and also for the introduction and use of business models within an organization. He is currently involved in the application and development of NewsML and XML based applications for clients in the UK and USA, the application of Topic Maps, and the use of PRISM metadata. Other interests include information design, the application of the Topic Map paradigm to knowledge management, the Semantic Web, language and communication, and the economics of information.

Jay holds an MSc in Analysis, Design, and Management of Information Systems from the London School of Economics, and a BA in English with Comparative Literature from the University of East Anglia. While at the UEA he also studied at the Universität Salzburg, Austria under the ERASMUS exchange programme. Before joining RivCom, Jay worked as a Research Assistant for the Director of the London School of Economics, and wrote and developed content for the Web and for PR. Private interests include art and literature. Jay lives in the UK.

Jay contributed Chapter 5.

Jeremy Michael Crosbie

Jeremy received his Bachelor of Science degree from the University of California, Irvine. He is a Senior Software Engineer with go2 Systems, Inc., a provider of real-world location-sensitive services through mobile devices, where he manages the middle tier development group as well as designing and developing applications. In past lives, Jeremy has worked in the storage and large-scale server industries. When not developing or writing, Jeremy enjoys listening to jazz as well as studying jazz guitar.

I would like to thank Stephen Patrick without whom my career would not be possible; Jordon Saardchit for introducing me to the Wrox team; Stephen Brown, Michael Callinan, and Scott Spencer for putting up with me the last three years and mentoring an ambitious engineer; my parents, Michael and Karen, for getting me through life and supporting everything I ever wanted to do; and especially my dearest Farrah who's caring and understanding inspires me to do my best.

Jeremy contributed Chapters 2, 11, and 14.

John Davies

John is the Technical Director of Century 24 Solutions (or just "C24"), Ltd., located at http://www.c24solutions.com. It's a London based software house providing Java solutions for the financial sector. C24's latest product, Elektra, designed to provide a single business view of complex financial transactions makes extensive use of distributed Java technologies, XML, and Java3D.

John started in IT in the late 70s in hardware, this followed on with 8080 and Z80 assembler, C, C++ in '87, and finally Java in early '96. He spent over fourteen years as a consultant, ten of them abroad in a variety of countries including the US, Asia, and most of Europe where he learnt a few more languages (spoken). Between work and writing John teaches Java, EJB, and XML for Learning Tree. His hobbies include traveling, photography, classical guitar, piloting small planes, fine wines, good beer, spicy food, and socializing.

I would like to thank fellow Astromony graduate, Steve Miller for proof reading and say "Hi Mum!". Above all, I would like to declare my total love and devotion to my fantastically tolerant wife Rachel, wonderful son Luc, and number 2 ,due late Q1 2001. Rachel et Luc, je vous aime!

John contributed Chapter 3 and can be reached at John.Davies@C24Solutions.com.

Kyle Gabhart

Kyle has recently been hired by Brainbench as a Senior Software Engineer. He has been involved in web development for a little over a year now, and has been immersing himself in Java for most of that time. He has developed and taught a "Fast-Track to Java" course for Oracle DBAs, a two-week boot camp for TXU Electric, as well as having given several presentations for a local Java Users Group. His non-technical speaking experience is even more extensive having competed nationally in both debate and public speaking for three years in high school, and two and a half in college.

Kyle contributed Chapters 12 and 13.

Steven Gould

Steven started "playing" with computers 20 years ago, according to his parents. Little did they know, rather than spending much time playing games, he was more interested in finding out how they worked. He spent numerous hours locked away learning the ins and outs of his early computers, learning BASIC, 6502 assembly language, Z80 assembly language, and Pascal. Steven's hobby led him to pursue his degrees in Computer Science (BSc) and Management Science and Operations Research (MSc).

Steven's unique combination of Operations Research (OR) and Computer Science strategically positioned him in the IT marketplace. After working for Dash Associates in England, he moved to the States in 1993 to pursue his career the other side of the pond. Steven utilized his skills in OR and Computer Science in his first few years in the United States, first as Vice President of Software Development for a start-up optimization company in Knoxville, Tennessee, then at SABRE in Fort Worth, Texas.

Since leaving SABRE, he has focused his efforts on object-oriented design and development in particular using C++ and Java. These have been his fortes in recent years as an Executive Consultant for CGI Information Systems based out of the Dallas, Texas office. While business savvy and management are natural talents for Steven, his passion is to remain technical and "in the trenches". As a result, he has passed up numerous management opportunities to continue to do what he loves to do: write both code and documentation (in the form of articles and books).

I would like to thank my Dad and Mum for teaching me to think and write (respectively!), and Shari and Alex for their support, patience, and understanding while I contributed to this book.

Steven contributed Chapter 4 and can be contacted at steven.gould@cgiusa.com.

James Hart

James Hart is a Technical Architect at Wrox Press, specializing in open source and enterprise Java technologies. His first computer experiences came at the tender age of five, when he watched his father solder together a Sinclair ZX81 on the kitchen table, and a subsequent mis-spent youth playing around on Ataris and Macintoshes was all that was needed to ensure he could never escape the lure of the IT industry, in spite of several attempts to find something better to do with his time. His main hobby is trying to work out if he can justify buying an Apple G4 Cube, when he already owns a G4 tower...

I'd like to thank all the authors who worked on this book, and also particularly the editorial team, Chanoch, Helen, Jim, and Steve, who worked so hard to make sure this book lived up to our expectations. Thanks also to Emma, Nikki, Viv, and Simon, for keeping the world out of our hair while we got on with things, and of course thanks to Chris, for all her support through late nights and deadlines. Couldn't have done it without you.

James was the technical architect for Professional Java XML, and contributed Chapter 22 to the book.

Ramnivas Laddad

Ramnivas is a Sun-Certified Java Architect. He has a Masters in electrical engineering with a specialization in communication engineering. He has been developing software systems involving GUIs, networking, distributed systems, real-time systems, and modelling for the past eight years. He has architected and developed object-oriented software systems in Java for the last four years and in C++ for the last eight years. Working with cool new technologies is his favorite pastime.

Ramnivas lives and works in Silicon Valley, USA. He is a Principal Software Engineer at Real-Time Innovations, Inc, where he leads the development of ControlShell, a component-based programming framework for complex real-time systems. He is a great fan of Indian classical music.

Ramnivas contributed Chapters 17 and 20.

Sing Li

First bitten by the computer bug in 1978, Sing has grown up with the microprocessor revolution. His first PC was a $99 do-it-yourself COSMIC ELF computer with 256 bytes of memory and a 1 bit LED display. For two decades, Sing has been an active author, consultant, speaker, instructor, and entrepreneur. His wide-ranging experience spans distributed architectures, multi-tiered Internet/Intranet systems, computer telephony, call-center technology, and embedded systems. Sing has participated in several Wrox projects in the past, has been working with (and writing about) Java and Jini since their very first alpha releases, and is an active participant in the Jini community.

Sing contributed Chapters 15 and 19 to this book.

Brendan Macmillan

Brendan holds honours degrees and has won prizes in both Computer Science and Law; and also completed a Masters thesis on "Analysis of Melody". He represented Australia in the 1993 World Championships Skeleton Competition at the La Plagne bobsled track, France. He is a great believer in open source software development, as both effective and exhilarating. Presently, he is a PhD candidate at the prestigious School of Computer Science and Software Engineering, Monash University, Australia.

I would like to dedicate these chapters to: T. Tiannii Tang, David Blumberg, Joseph Campbell, and Prometheus, and to the members of the JSX-ideas mailing list.

Brendan contributed Chapters 6 and 16.

Daniel Rivers-Moore

Daniel is Director of New Technologies at RivCom, a UK-based consultancy specializing in helping companies and organizations adopt leading-edge technologies for information management and delivery. Daniel was actively involved from the outset in the development of XML and its related technologies, having been an invited expert to the XML Special Interest Group that assisted the World Wide Web's XML Working Group during the development of the core XML standard. He has served as Joint Project Leader of the STEP/SGML Harmonization initiative for bringing together technical documents with engineering data, and is editor of NewsML, the XML-based standard for the management and delivery of multimedia news.

A founder member of `TopicMaps.org`, Daniel served as chair of the subgroup that developed the XML Topic Maps Conceputual Model. Currently, Daniel is acting steering group chair of Knowledge on the Web (KnoW), a collaborative initiative aimed at furthering the development of the latest generation of Web technologies in the service of knowledge management and knowledge sharing. Daniel has a BA in Philosophy and Psychology from the University of Oxford. He spent the first 15 years of his adult life working in the field of voice and theatre before getting a "real job" in publishing in 1986. Daniel is married and lives in Tetbury, a small market town in the Cotswold district of England.

Daniel contributed the bulk of Chapter 10 and additional material to Chapter 5.

Judy Skubal

Judy has over 12 years experience as a software developer, the last five of which have been focused on SGML and XML application development. She currently works as a System Architect for Telos Corporation in Ashburn, Virginia. When not at work, she has three small children who keep her very busy. Her hobbies include quilting, photography, and recently, learning to play the violin.

I'd like to dedicate my chapter to my children Sara, Timmy, and Jenny. Their curiosity about the world has kept my own curiosity alive. And to my husband Alan, for all the times he has quietly taken on the load so I can do my crazy projects (like this one). I don't say it enough, but his dedication and support make things like this possible for me. Thank you Alan (you're still my rock). And thanks lastly to Mike, for finding a small voice and bringing it forth.

Judy contributed Chapter 21 to the book.

Karli Watson

Karli is an in-house author for Wrox Press with a penchant for multicolored clothing. He started out with the intention of becoming a world-famous nano-technologist, so perhaps one day you might recognize his name as he receives a Nobel Prize. For now, though, Karli's computing interests include all things mobile, and upcoming technologies like C#. He can often be found preaching about these technologies at conferences, as well as after hours in drinking establishments. Karli is also a snow-boarding enthusiast, and wishes he had a cat.

Thanks go to the Wrox team, both for helping me get into writing and then dealing with the consequences with patience and a wry smile. Finally, and most importantly, thanks to my wife Donna for continuing to put up with me.

Karli contributed Chapter 9.

Scott Williams

Scott is a writer and trainer who has been working with Java since its early beta days, and XML since well before it was a spec. He has contributed to several other books on Java, has co-authored numerous articles for Visual Systems Journal, and has spoken at major conferences across North America. He co-founded The Willcam Group in 1988, where he was senior developer and editor of around thirty courses on software development. Most recently he was appointed Director of Technology and Development Training for the Corporate Education Services division of CDI Education Corporation, the largest IT skills development company in Canada.

Scott contributed Chapter 1. He welcomes e-mail at scott.williams@cdilearn.com.

The Xerces Blue
Butterfly, which became
extinct earlier this century,
and after which the Xerces XML
parser is named ...

Table of Contents

Table of Contents

Table of Contents

Table of Contents

Table of Contents

Table of Contents

Table of Contents

The Xerces Blue
Butterfly, which became
extinct earlier this century,
and after which the Xerces XML
parser is named ...

Introduction

Java and XML are in the process of becoming the two key technologies shaping enterprise development today. This book brings together expertise from a wide range of programmers and industry specialists to provide you with the springboard that will take you, your career, and your business into the future of Java and XML working together – portable code, and portable data.

What this Book is About

You will find two essential things in this book. On the one hand you will find complete, clear, and illustrative guides to all the major Java APIs for processing XML, and all the main XML technologies and specifications. On the other hand you'll find in this book a thorough introduction to one of the most exciting areas currently in computer programming and the Internet – web services and XML enabled clients and servers.

The book will answer the burning question: "Why are Java and XML so suited to each other?". For example, a constant theme will be the growing impetus behind the use of XML as a serialization technology that has far-reaching uses beyond those to which Java's native serialization can be put to. Another theme will be how the Java Enterprise platform is already ideally placed with its JSP and Servlets technologies to fully exploit XML as a data transmission format. Furthermore, we have the whole question of where the Internet is going as a system of interrelated resources. The answer may be in adding meaning to these structures, and this brings us to the area of semantics and knowledge management where Java and XML are already key players.

Who Should Use This Book

The answer to this is just about everybody who is interested in developing in an enterprise environment. Java has become the programming language of choice for speaking to and listening to the Internet. XML is about to become the universal language for delivering web content and business information across the Internet.

This book brings together these two enabling technologies and shows you how to develop applications that exploit the best features of each.

This is a book for intermediate to advanced Java programmers, either from an enterprise or core programming background. The book assumes no specific knowledge of any Java XML technologies and will be accessible to any programmer with some foundational background in Java programming.

We start XML at a very easy level, but grow to use a full range of the power of the language; very little XML knowledge is initially assumed.

How this Book is Structured

This book has 22 chapters and 8 appendices. In the following sections we will give you a breakdown of the content of these chapters so that you can plan how to use this book to suit your needs best.

❑ **Chapter 1: XML Basics**
This chapter introduces you to basic XML concepts and techniques. Many complex XML issues are not covered here, but we shall meet XML schemas in Chapter 5, XSLT in Chapter 7, XPath in Chapters 7 and 19, and XLink in Chapter 9. We also provide a range of XML reference materials in the appendices.

❑ **Chapter 2: SAX**
Here we introduce the Simple API for XML Parsing as the standard mechanism for converting structured data from any source into a Java XML representation. We'll also introduce the JAXP 1.1 interfaces to access SAX parser and transformer resources.

❑ **Chapter 3: The DOM**
This chapter looks at the Document Object Model, the generic W3C specification of the XML concept in object-oriented terms. We'll look at the official Java DOM interfaces and how they can be used with JAXP to parse, process, manipulate, and transform XML.

❑ **Chapter 4: JDOM**
In this chapter we look at some of the motivating reasons behind the creation of JDOM and how it is different from, yet works with, both SAX and the DOM. We describe how to obtain the latest JDOM release, and how to build and install it, and then introduce you to a simple JDOM program. This will introduce the basics of JDOM, as well as allow us to test out our installation. We also have a full API reference in Appendix F.

❑ **Chapter 5: XML Schema**
The chapter provides a basic theoretical introduction to XML schemas. It is also a practical guide to the principles and rules involved in creating schemas and instance documents. Worked examples and fragments of XML schema and XML instance documents are freely used to aid explanation. There is schema reference material to back this up in Appendix A.

❑ **Chapter 6: XML-Object Mapping**
Various schemes have been proposed for an XML alternative to Java's binary serialization technology. In this chapter we look at the attractiveness of XML as a serialization format and how we can seamlessly map between Java and XML object representations to make better use of emerging networking protocols like SOAP.

❑ **Chapter 7: Introduction to XSLT**
XSLT is a powerful mechanism for transforming XML into just about anything, including renderable HTML, WML and other data interchange formats. It's also quite complicated and we use this chapter to introduce the main techniques and concepts. It's backed up by a reference in Appendix G.

❑ **Chapter 8: Programming Using XSLT**
Some of the best current XSL transformation tools are Java implementations. In this chapter we show how the power of XSL transformation can be leveraged into Java applications using these tools.

❑ **Chapter 9: Connected XML Data**
To connect XML documents together, we can use standards like XInclude, XLink, XPointer, XBase, and XFI. In this chapter we explore these standards, detailing their syntax and providing examples of their use.

❑ **Chapter 10: Semantic Documents**
Where does the Internet go from here? This chapter looks at the notion of XML documents that encode their own meaning in terms of relationships with other documents and resources. We'll look at both the Resource Description Framework and Topic Maps, and we'll use some of the Java techniques and tools that are emerging to deal with this complex area.

❑ **Chapter 11: Socket I/O**
The world of distributed XML enabled services relies on robust underlying network code. In this chapter we'll explore Java socket networking and develop some example socket servers and clients that talk to each other using XML.

❑ **Chapter 12: Server-Side HTTP**
The web tier could be said to be diverging into either pure presentation or business point-of-presence services. Servlets are ideally placed for the second task. In this chapter we'll look at servlets and their powerful API for dealing with HTTP requests and responses. We build lots of example servlets that process XML over HTTP, and we'll cover dealing with all the essential HTTP headers and response codes.

❑ **Chapter 13: Client-Side HTTP**
This chapter builds on the previous chapter, adding more examples to show how we can leverage the HTTP specification to build powerful Java XML HTTP clients.

❑ **Chapter 14: Server-Side Presentation**
This chapter builds on Chapter 8, showing how we can build flexible and powerful server applications that feed on XML and cater in turn for multiple client types, particularly the diverse range of formats required by wireless devices.

❑ **Chapter 15: Client-Side Presentation**
In this chapter, our focus is on thick client designs – designs that involve significant processing and presentation logic on the client side. Through the analysis of a case study, we will see: why client-side processing is often a good idea in real-world application problem solving; the various technologies that enable client-side XML processing; when it may be appropriate to apply each of the client-side processing technologies.

❑ **Chapter 16: XML Object Persistence**
This chapter builds on the work of Chapter 6 where we worked on the idea of mappings between XML and Java objects. Here we use sophisticated Java techniques to develop a new implementation of XML-Object mapping called Hammer, which solves many of the problems faced by current implementations, specifically in dealing with arbitrary runtime types and reference graphs.

❑ **Chapter 17: XML and Databases**
The key idea in this chapter is that of abstracting away from the notion that XML ever has to exist as text markup on a filesystem. We'll look at a standard technique for generating SAX parse events directly from data sets and how we can then apply Java XSLT transformations to generate HTML dynamically from the data. We'll also look at the early access RowSet implementation of the JDBC Optional Extensions, and a number of other techniques for combining XML with Java data access.

❑ **Chapter 18: Configuration and Deployment**
XML is the ideal configuration language, as evidenced by the complete move to XML for application configuration in the J2EE standard. In this chapter we show how to use Java XML parsers and Java XPath implementations to store and process configuration data. We will develop an intranet-style e-mail application that is completely configured – and dynamically configurable – using XML.

❑ **Chapter 19: XML Protocols and Communications**
One vast application area for XML is in communications, more specifically in the area of application level protocols – protocols that enable applications to talk to one another. In this chapter, we will explore how developments in XML have had a great influence over the design of modern application protocols, and how XML has since evolved to be the language of choice for data encoding within protocols. Specifically, we'll be looking at three protocols which make use of XML for their transport functionality: XML-RPC, SOAP, and BXXP.

❑ **Chapter 20: XML and Messaging**
Many say that messaging middleware will become the main information driver in the enterprise application servers of the future, replacing synchronous request/reply mechanisms such as RMI and CORBA. This chapter will look at the issues in using messaging in XML transactions, and we'll develop a case study using the Java Message Service as a façade to a SOAP request, building on some of the development from the previous chapter.

❑ **Chapter 21: B2B Marketplaces**
A lot of momentum is building towards developing sets of standardized schemas and messaging protocols to facilitate automated business processes over the Internet. In this chapter, we look several of these emerging standards and how the Java platform is ideally placed to drive the machinery behind the scenes.

❑ **Chapter 22: Web Services**
Web services are a way of providing code-level access across the Internet to the sorts of services most commonly provided only via human-usable HTML forms. They're grounded in a suite of technologies, based on standard ways of representing interfaces, and standard ways of accessing services. In this chapter we will look at specifying web services using WSDL documents, how the web service lifecycle works, and how to locate web services using UDDI. We'll develop a full case study using the IBM UDDI4J Java client library.

Appendices

❑ **Appendix A: XML-Related Standards**
We cover XLink, XPointer, XPath, and XML Schema.

❑ **Appendix B: The Simple API for XML**
Full API for SAX version 2.0.

❑ **Appendix C: The W3C Document Object Model**
Full Java bindings reference for the DOM Level 2.

❑ **Appendix D: The Transformation API for XML**
Full API of the transformation interfaces now also included with JAXP.

❑ **Appendix E: JAXP 1.1 API**
Full API of the Java API for XML Processing.

❑ **Appendix F: JDOM API**
Full API of JDOM currently at beta 6.

❑ **Appendix G: XSLT Reference**
We provide a reference listing of XSLT transformation elements and functions.

❑ **Appendix H: Installing Tomcat 3.2.1**
We use Tomcat in many of the chapters. Here we provide setup details for first time users.

The Tools You Need for This Book

In this section we give you some advance warning of the software and tools that you need to develop the main applications in this book.

Java Development Kit JDK 1.3

❑ All the code in the book was tested with JDK1. 3. You will need this version.
http://java.sun.com/j2se

❑ The Java API for XML Processing (JAXP) 1.1 can be downloaded from:
http://java.sun.com/xml/

Apache XML Project

❑ Xerces, an XML parser that implements the DOM, SAX and JAXP APIs:
http://xml.apache.org/xerces-j

❑ Xalan, an XSLT processor that supports the XPath standard:
http://xml.apache.org/xalan-j

❑ Apache SOAP 2.0. Although version 2.1 was available at time of going to press, we found 2.0 to be more stable and better documented so we used this version in the book.
http://xml.apache.org/soap

Jakarta Tomcat 3.2.x

❑ Servlet engine implementing Servlets 2.2. We cover how to set this up in Appendix H.
http://jakarta.apache.org/tomcat

XML Editor

A good XML, XSL, DTD, schema, etc. editor will accelerate your mastery of XML. Although not necessary for the book, we recommend XMLSpy as an excellent all round development tool. You can even configure it to use any Java process to perform XSL transformations:

❑ XMLSpy:
   http://www.xmlspy.com

Other Tools

This covers the main tools you'll need for nearly all the chapters. In addition, certain chapters will require you to download one or two small tools or packages in order to fully implement and test the example code. Full download and deployment details (or clear pointers to existing documentation) are always given.

Conventions

We have used a number of different styles of text and layout in this book to help differentiate between the different kinds of information. Here are examples of the styles we use and an explanation of what they mean.

Code has several styles. If it's a word that we're talking about in the text, for example when discussing a SAX startElement() event, it's in this font. If it's a block of code that you can type as a program and run, then it's in a gray box:

```
public void close() throws UnwantedException
```

Sometimes you'll see code in a mixture of styles, like this:

```
<?xml version 1.0?>
<Invoice>
   <part>
      <name>Widget</name>
      <price>$10.00</price>
   </part>
</invoice>
```

In cases like this, the code with a white background is code we are already familiar with; the line highlighted in gray is a new addition to the code since we last looked at it.

Advice, hints, and background information comes in this type of font.

Important pieces of information come in boxes like this.

Bullets appear indented, with each new bullet marked as follows:

- **Important Words** are in a bold type font
- Words that appear on the screen, in menus like File or Window, are in a similar font to that you would see on a Windows desktop
- Keys that you press on the keyboard like *Ctrl* and *Enter*, are in italics

Customer Support

We've tried to make this book as accurate and enjoyable as possible, but what really matters is what the book actually does for you. Please let us know your views, either by returning the reply card in the back of the book, or by contacting us via e-mail at feedback@wrox.com.

Source Code and Updates

As you work through the examples in this book, you may decide that you prefer to type in all the code by hand. Many readers prefer this because it's a good way to get familiar with the coding techniques that are being used.

Whether you want to type the code in or not, we have made all the source code for this book available at our web site at the following address:

http://www.wrox.com/

If you're one of those readers who likes to type in the code, you can use our files to check the results you should be getting – they should be your first stop if you think you might have typed in an error. If you're one of those readers who doesn't like typing, then downloading the source code from our web site is a must!

Either way, it'll help you with updates and debugging.

Errata

We've made every effort to make sure that there are no errors in the text or the code. However, to err is human, and as such we recognize the need to keep you informed of any mistakes as they're spotted and corrected. Errata sheets are available for all our books at http://www.wrox.com/. If you find an error that hasn't already been reported, please let us know.

Our web site acts as a focus for other information and support, including the code from all our books, sample chapters, previews of forthcoming titles, and articles and opinion on related topics.

Technical Support

If you wish to directly query a problem in the book with an expert who knows the book in detail then e-mail support@wrox.com, with the title of the book and the last four numbers of the ISBN in the subject field of the e-mail. Your message is delivered to one of our support staff, who are the first people to read it. We have files on the most frequently asked questions and will answer anything generally immediately. We answer general questions about the book and the web site.

Deeper queries are forwarded to the technical editor responsible for that book. They have experience with the programming language or particular product and are able to answer detailed technical questions on the subject. Once an issue has been resolved, the editor can post any errata the problem brought to light to the web site.

Finally, in the unlikely event that the editor can't answer your problem, he/she will forward the request to the author. We try to protect the author from any distractions from their main job. However, we are quite happy to forward specific book related requests to them. All Wrox authors help with the support on their books. They will either directly mail the customer with the answer, or will send their response to the editor or the support department who will then pass it on to the reader.

P2P Online Forums

Wrox support doesn't just stop when you finish the book. If you have a question that falls outside the scope of the book, or you have modified book code for you own ends and need some further support, then the P2P forum is available to you at http://p2p.wrox.com/.

P2P is a community of programmers sharing their problems and expertise. A variety of mailing lists cover all modern programming and Internet technologies. Links, resources and archives provide a comprehensive knowledge base. Whether you are an experienced professional or web novice you'll find something of interest here.

The mailing lists are moderated to ensure that messages are relevant and reasonable. This does mean that postings do not appear on the lists until they have been read and approved, but prevents the flow of junk mail that unmoderated lists allow. Anonymous access to the lists is allowed for reading, but registration of at least an email address is required to post messages.

The Xerces Blue
Butterfly, which became
extinct earlier this century,
and after which the Xerces XML
parser is named ...

1

XML Basics

This chapter provides a concise yet thorough overview of XML, from a basic discussion of what XML is, to the creation of documents and document standards, and finally to a discussion of XML namespaces. We'll also briefly cover how syntax is described using EBNF (Extended Backus Naur Form), and look at the formal XML specification from W3C (the World Wide Web Consortium, the organization responsible for the creation of Web-related protocols and specifications, including XML), as the specification is always the final authority on correct XML usage.

The purpose of this chapter is straightforward: to prepare you for the material that follows and to arm you with sufficient understanding of XML to be able to use Java in the development of XML applications.

This chapter isn't for everyone. If you are already working with XML, you can probably skip this chapter completely. Many complex XML issues are not covered here, but we shall meet XML schemas in Chapter 5, XSLT in Chapter 7, XPath in Chapters 7 and 18, and XLink in Chapter 9. For more in-depth XML coverage, see Professional XML, *Wrox Press, ISBN 1-861003-11-0.*

In this chapter we will cover:

- ❑ The syntax of XML and the structure of XML documents
- ❑ XML Metadata and Document Type Definitions (DTDs)
- ❑ Validation of XML against a DTD
- ❑ Namespaces and information sets
- ❑ XML resources

What is XML?

You probably already know the following:

- ❑ XML is the eXtensible Markup Language
- ❑ XML provides a platform-neutral and language-independent means of describing data, making it the perfect complement to Java's own platform-independence
- ❑ XML documents can be validated in a variety of ways to ensure consistent format

Those are the basics. Slightly less obvious are the following:

- ❑ XML is markup – a combination of text (content) and textual codes (tags or markup) that describe the nature of the content
- ❑ XML is extensible, which means that you are not confined to a predefined set of tags; you can define your own to suit your own application
- ❑ Because we define our own tags, we can say that XML provides a syntax for us to create our own markup languages

In the following sections we will address all these points using an example-based approach.

XML is Markup

As a markup language, XML shares some similarities with HTML, with which you are likely already somewhat familiar. Consider the simple HTML example in the listing below, and in the screenshot that follows (this example, and most of those that follow, come from a hypothetical Helpdesk application that we'll refer to occasionally):

```
<html>
<head>
<title>Trouble Ticket Tracker</Title>
</head>
<body><h1>Trouble Ticket 746284</H1>
<p>The importance of this ticket is <b>High</B>
<br>The status of this ticket is: <b>Open</B>
<hr>
Description: Customer cannot install product</body></html>
```

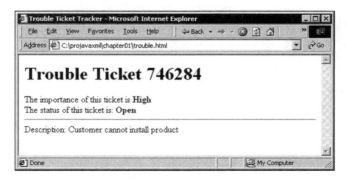

Now consider the following XML document, which encapsulates roughly the same information, and is illustrated the subsequent screenshot:

```
<TroubleTicket ID="746284"
               Importance="High"
               Status="Open">
   <Description>Customer cannot install product</Description>
</TroubleTicket>
```

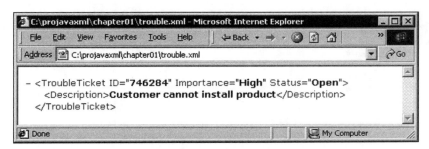

There are many superficial differences between HTML and XML, only some of which are illustrated above. XML is case sensitive, for example, whereas HTML is not. HTML tags can be empty (or standalone) tags like
 (for line break) or <hr> (for horizontal rule) or may be container tags, meaning that they have a start tag, an end tag, and contents between the two, as with the <Title></Title> tags in the example. In XML, on the other hand, all tags are container tags, unless they employ a special syntax; the <br> tag would not be allowed, for example, but <br/> would.

Elements and Attributes: The Structure of Data

Consider the following expanded version of the trouble ticket example we just saw. This simple XML example shows not only that there are items that are characteristics of other items (importance is a characteristic of the trouble ticket, the duration is a characteristic of the call) but also issues like multiplicity (each trouble ticket can consist of multiple calls).

```
<TroubleTicket
   ticketID="T746284"
   Importance="High"
   Status="Open">
   <Description>Customer cannot install product</Description>

   <Call StartTime="02/17/2001 10:35"
      Duration="17"
      HelpAgent="Johnson">
Customer received network errors in installation. Disconnecting
from network caused "Reboot" message. He will reboot and call back.
   </Call>

   <Call StartTime="02/17/2001 11:03"
      Duration="11"
      HelpAgent="Steinberg">
After rebooting, install is successful till point of entering
license number. Customer's license number is incorrect.
   </Call>
</TroubleTicket>
```

When considering the high-level structure of your documents, it is well worth looking at some of the graphical editing and validation tools that are available. The following is the 'Grid view' from XMLSpy (http://www.xmlspy.com), showing more clearly the object model structure of the document:

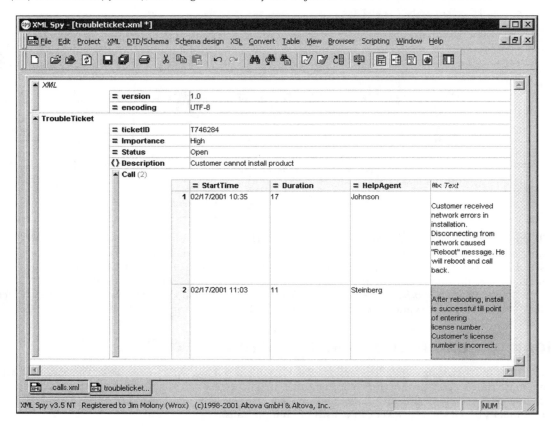

Vocabulary: Elements versus Tags

Many authors and users of XML use the terms **element** and **tag** interchangeably, but the two are not technically the same. Consider the following example:

```
<Description>Customer cannot install product</Description>
```

The above example comprises the Description element. It consists of the <Description> start tag, the </Description> end tag, and the element's content, Customer cannot install product.

If an element has no content, it is said to be an **empty element**. An empty element can be denoted either by a start tag immediately followed by an end tag, or by a start tag on its own, with the name of the tag immediately followed by a "/" character. Both of the following constructs represent an empty element called name:

```
<name></name>
```

```
<name/>
```

XML is eXtensible

As we've seen, in XML we are able to define our own elements, unlike in HTML, where the universe of allowable elements and tags is finite and fixed. This is the extensible nature of XML: we are able to extend and refine our document content and document structure as necessary to meet the changing needs of our application or our problem domain. However, consider the nature of extensibility for a moment. We are able to extend and modify the list of elements we are able to use in our documents – extend the vocabulary we are using – but there are still definite rules to follow – such as the rules we have just seen for forming empty elements. Some rules of structure and syntax are necessary in order to be able to parse the document reliably and make sense of its contents. So what rules are there? This is where we have to leave the freewheeling world of creating elements and content, and start to look at the rigorous world of the XML specification.

The XML Specification

With any technology there has to be a foundation – a set of rules on which software developers can absolutely depend for technical rigor. For XML, that rule of law is laid down in the XML 1.0 Specification, published by W3C. The second edition of the specification has been available since October 2000 and is publicly available at:

http://www.w3.org/tr/2000/rec-xml-20001006

Apart from getting final rulings on what is and is not legal XML, the specification is also useful for context information. If you are interested in gaining more perspective about the creation and objectives of XML, and do not want to read a whole book on the subject, you might find the *"Origin and Goals"* section of the specification useful. In particular, that section itemizes 10 goals for the development of XML that can help explain many of the less obvious design decisions.

Reading the XML Specification

The XML specification itself is rather short, and could be easily printed. But the real power of the specification is when it is read in its HTML version, as it provides so much hyperlinked information. There are four main kinds of information in the specification:

❑ **Narrative**
The specification is fairly terse, but is not devoid of narrative. For my money, the few words of description in the specification are worth their weight in gold – they provide explanation and rationale direct from the creators of XML.

❑ **Productions**
These are the formal rules of the specification, and they are written in a form called Extended Backus Naur Form (EBNF). This is a means of describing a formal syntax or grammar. We'll cover the basics of EBNF in the next section.

❑ **Constraints**
We will shortly be describing what it means for documents to be well-formed or valid. The specification contains a number of well-formedness constraints and validity constraints: additional rules that documents must follow in order to be considered well-formed or valid.

❑ **Examples**
Also worth their weight in gold – they help to explain the rest of the specification.

The Basics of EBNF

The purpose of this section is to give you enough EBNF to get you reading the specification. Actually, although EBNF looks intimidating, there's really very little to it. Let's begin with an example. A well-formed XML document must match the document production in the XML specification. Remember, a production is a formal rule contained in the spec. The "document production" is the formal rule for what constitutes a document. So let's look at that production:

```
document ::= prolog element Misc*
```

The symbol ::= might seem a little foreign to you. Read this symbol as "consists of" or "is defined as". This production basically says that the XML document consists of a prolog, an element (called the **root** element), and any number of miscellaneous items. To fully understand this, we would need to look in turn at the prolog, element, and miscellaneous productions to see how they were formed. But before we do that, a few more general points of interest.

First, if you were reading the HTML version of the specification, you would find that prolog, element, and Misc were all links; selecting the link would take you immediately to that production. That in itself makes it worth using the specification online instead of on paper. The second thing to notice in the above example is that Misc has an asterisk after it. That's a multiplier that says that we can have any number (zero or more) Misc items following the element.

So let's look more rigorously at EBNF. First, the general form of a production is:

```
symbol ::= expression
```

The right hand side expression can take any of the forms in the following table. The letters a, b, and c in the table below are used as placeholders for EBNF symbols like document, prolog, element, etc. The symbols used in the table are similar to the symbols used in regular expressions, which you may be familiar with from your work with operating systems (particularly Unix or Linux) or other programming languages:

a b c	The symbols specified must appear, and must appear in this order
a | b | c	One of these symbols must appear (ia choice)
a*	Zero or more occurrences of a
a+	One or more occurrences of a
a?	Zero or one occurrence of a (optional)
a - b	Anything that matches a, excluding anything that matches b
^a	Anything that does not match a

Note that parentheses can be used to group items, for example (a|b)* would mean any number of occurrences of a or b in any order.

Using EBNF

Let's look at a couple of other productions, just to make sure you're comfortable. Continuing from our first example, let's look at what a `Misc` item is:

```
Misc ::= Comment | PI | S
```

So a `Misc` is any one of a `Comment`, or a `PI`, or an `S`. To understand this one, we must break it down once more, looking at each production in turn. Let's look at `S` which is the production for **whitespace**:

```
S ::= (#x20 | #x9 | #xD | #xA)+
```

The # symbol indicates that we referring to the character with the specified numeric value, so the above production says that whitespace is one or more of the following characters, in any order: the space character (hexadecimal 20), the horizontal tab (hexadecimal 9), the carriage return (hexadecimal D), or the line feed (hexadecimal A).

Well-Formed XML

The XML specification defines a number of constraints – rules that govern the "legality" of the XML document. There are two categories of these constraints: well-formedness constraints and validity constraints. Validity constraints are the more stringent of the two:

❑ To say a document is well-formed is to say that the document conforms to all the well-formedness constraints of the XML specification. These constraints have to do with lexical considerations, syntax, and to some extent the structure of the document as a whole. Well-formedness has nothing to do with content. Well-formedness constraints are identified in the XML specification with the notation [wfc: ...]

❑ To say that an XML document is valid is to say that it is well-formed and that its structure and content – the actual data encapsulated in the document – conforms to the rules laid down in the document's DTD (Document Type Definition). We'll discuss DTDs in much more detail later in this chapter. Validity constraints are identified in the XML specification using the notation [vc: ...]

> **One cannot say that an XML document is valid unless there is a DTD for the document. Moreover, because the requirements for validity are a superset of those for well-formedness, it is perfectly legitimate to say that all valid documents are well-formed. The inverse is not true: one cannot say that all well-formed documents are valid.**

Since the well-formedness constraints form the most basic level of XML syntax, if a document is not well-formed, it is not really an XML document at all. It might be a document, but it's not XML!

17

The Syntax Rules for Well-Formed Documents

We'll consider the requirements for well-formedness in two categories: lexical requirements concerned with syntax, and requirements concerned with document structure. In this section we'll look at the syntax issues. There are only three basic rules for well-formedness:

❑ The contents of the document as a whole must reduce to the document productions as defined in the XML specification. The document production dictates that there must be exactly one "top level" element, called the **root** element, and that all other elements must be subordinate to this root element. This is more to do with structure than syntax, and we'll discuss it in more detail shortly.

❑ All tags must be properly nested. (There's an example illustrating this in the next section, *"Well-formedness and XML Processors".)*

❑ All tags must be properly closed, or must be properly formatted **empty elements**.

The existence of a single root element, and the fact that all other tags must be properly nested implies that the entire document can be represented as a tree structure, with the root element as the root of the tree. We'll pick up on this concept when we discuss the XML Document Object Model (DOM) in Chapter 3.

There are two additional lexical considerations that, though not actually well-formedness constraints, are nonetheless important:

❑ XML is case sensitive everywhere. The <name> tag is not the same as the <Name> tag.

❑ Whitespace is preserved, and passed unchanged to the XML application. This is unlike HTML, in which whitespace is collapsed into a single blank character.

Well-Formedness and XML Processors

The last two requirements seem simple enough, but it is these two that prevent HTML from being well-formed XML. Consider the following document, which we will call overlap.html:

```
<Body>This is <b>bold and <I>italic</B>
and just italic</I> and normal.</Body>
```

This document is rather poorly constructed no matter what our intentions. But in HTML it is at least renderable, as the figure shows.

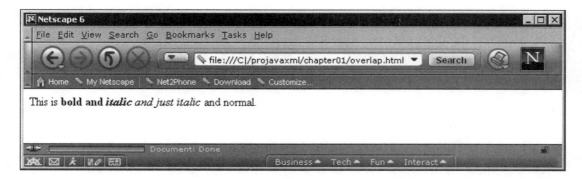

However, look at how Internet Explorer deals with this same document, when we simply rename the file from `overlap.html` to `overlap.xml`.

Microsoft's Internet Explorer incorporates a piece of software called an XML **processor** – literally software that processes or parses XML. In the above screenshot, we've seen how one XML processor handles XML documents that are not well-formed. There are many other processors available; the next screenshot shows another example. This one is the SAXCount command-line tool that comes as part of the Apache Xerces distribution (the parser forms part of the XML4J package inherited from IBM). This tool is written in 100% Java, and in the screenshot we're running it using the java command line:

```
C:\projavaxml\chapter01>echo %classpath%
.;C:\xerces-1_3_0\xerces.jar;C:\xerces-1_3_0\xercesSamples.jar

C:\projavaxml\chapter01>java sax.SAXCount overlap.html
[Fatal Error] overlap.html:1:39: The element type "I" must be terminated by the
matching end-tag "</I>".
org.xml.sax.SAXException: Stopping after fatal error: The element type "I" must
be terminated by the matching end-tag "</I>".
```

The Structure of Well-Formed Documents

Having seen the lexical and syntactic considerations for a well-formed document, it's time to look at the structural considerations.

The Document Production

This is one we've already seen when we were learning EBNF. An XML document consists of three things: the prolog, the root element, and a "miscellaneous" section, which is sometimes referred to as the **epilog**. (Note that the term "epilog" does not appear in the XML specification; it's just a term that is often used to refer to the miscellaneous "stuff" that follows the root element. The term implies – correctly – the positioning of these miscellaneous items after the root element, and is symmetric with the prolog.)

The Prolog

The prolog consists of two main things, both of which are optional: the XML declaration and the DTD – the Document Type Definition. The XML declaration in its simplest form looks as follows:

```
<?xml version="1.0"?>
```

There are few optional attributes we can specify on the XML declaration. We can, for example, specify the encoding to be used in this document (such as UTF-8, UTF-16, etc.). If an XML declaration does not specify an encoding, the document must contain only UTF-8 or UTF-16 character data. (If you are not familiar with UTF-8 and UTF-16 encodings, there are many pertinent resources available on the web. My favorite is at http://www.unicode.org (check the FAQ pages) but there are many others.)

A more substantive attribute on the XML declaration is the standalone flag. This is an attribute that can have a value of yes or no. A document is deemed to be standalone if it makes use of no external markup declarations (this will mean more to you once we've talked about DTDs later in this chapter). The default value is no. The following example shows an XML declaration for a standalone document:

```
<?xml version="1.0" standalone='yes'?>
```

The prolog may also contain the document type definition. We'll revisit this issue later in this chapter in the section *Document Metadata*.

The Root Element

The root element is simply an XML element (we'll talk more about elements shortly) that is the "starting" point for the XML document. There can be only one root element, and it must not appear as the content of any other element. The following is a well-formed XML document representing a trouble ticket consisting only of the XML declaration and the root element. In the following example, our root element is <TroubleTicket>:

```
<?xml version="1.0"?>
<TroubleTicket ticketID="T746284">
    Customer cannot install product
</TroubleTicket>
```

The Epilog

As we saw in our discussion of EBNF, after the root element can come any combination of comments, processing instructions, or whitespace characters. We've already seen what constitutes whitespace, and we'll have more to say about comments and processing instructions shortly.

Elements

The root element, by its very name, is an element. We've seen that the root element can contain other elements. We've also seen that the structure of an element is the start tag, followed by the element content, followed by the end tag, looking somewhat like the following:

```
<name> content </name>
```

We've also seen that empty elements are possible, usually with the following form:

```
<name/>
```

Element Names

Element names can consist of any combination of letters, digits, the hyphen, the underscore, the period, or the colon. Names must begin with a letter, underscore, or colon.

Actually, this definition is a bit naïve, due to the fact that XML supports the Unicode, not just US ASCII. If you interpret the word "letter" to mean just the letters of the Roman alphabet, you'll certainly be safe, but you also will have a more restricted set of name characters to use than the XML specification would otherwise allow. More formally, the name can consist of base characters, ideographics, combining characters, or extenders. For more details on these subsets of the Unicode character set, we refer you to the XML specification, or to the Unicode web site (a fascinating place in its own right) at http://www.unicode.org/.

Element Content

At its simplest, element content can consist of character data or other (nested) elements. We'll also see that the element content can consist of references, CDATA sections, processing instructions, or comments, all of which we'll be examining in due course.

In the following example, the content of the <TroubleTicket> element is the <Description> element, whereas the content of the <Description> element is character data:

```
<TroubleTicket ID="746284"
               Importance="High"
               Status="Open">
  <Description>Customer cannot install product</Description>
</TroubleTicket>
```

Attributes

Look again at our trouble ticket element. It has three attributes, used to further qualify the characteristics of the element:

```
<TroubleTicket
   ID="746284"
   Importance="High"
   Status="Open"
>
  <Description>Customer cannot install product</Description>
</TroubleTicket>
```

The value of an attribute is contained in double quotes (unlike HTML, an attribute value must be in double quotes), and it can consist of virtually any text at all, with the exception of the < and & characters (unless the & introduces a character or entity reference, as we will soon see). Note that to be well-formed, an attribute name may only appear once in the same start-tag or empty-element tag. For example, if we wanted to be able to represent multiple help agents for a given trouble ticket, we could *not* use multiple attributes as in the following:

```
<TroubleTicket ID="746284"
   HelpAgent="Tom" HelpAgent="Martha"
   Status="Open">
</TroubleTicket>
```

Instead, we would use multiple elements, perhaps like the following:

```
<TroubleTicket ID="746284" Status="Open">
   <HelpAgent>Tom</HelpAgent>
   <HelpAgent>Martha</HelpAgent>
</TroubleTicket>
```

Character Data

An element's contents may simply be character data. Valid character data consists of any text that does not contain markup. In particular, the < and & characters are not allowed (again, unless the & introduces a character or entity reference), but we will see in this next section that there are various ways to get around this limitation.

The following is an element containing character data:

```
<Description>Customer cannot install product</Description>
```

CDATA Sections

So what if you really want to use markup in the textual content of an element? For example, we might want to have a <Warning> element, whose contents would be renderable HTML – perhaps something like the following – which is *not* well-formed XML due to the inclusion here of the < character:

```
<Warning>
<hr>Do <STRONG>NOT</STRONG> use function keys!<hr>
</Warning>
```

In cases like this, where we want to include something as character data that would otherwise be illegal in an XML document, we can use a CDATA section. The general format for a CDATA section is as follows:

```
<![CDATA [ text ]]>
```

The text in the general format may contain virtually anything; it does not need to be well-formed XML. We can make our previous example legal using a CDATA section as follows:

```
<Warning>
<![CDATA[<hr>Do <STRONG>NOT</STRONG> use function keys!<hr>]]>
</Warning>
```

Note that CDATA sections cannot be nested one inside the other.

References

References are simply replacements or substitutions that can be used in an XML document. They are similar in some respects to manifest (#define) constants from C or C++, or to "macro" substitutions available in many text editors. The idea will also be familiar users of HTML, where the same general syntax is used for what are commonly called HTML escape sequences.

Character References

Character references are used to represent Unicode characters in either decimal or hexadecimal numbers. They are used to represent characters that may or may not be easily entered from a keyboard, or that may or may not be printable or viewable on the current output device. Character references are introduced by the characters `&#` (for decimal representations) or `&#x` (for hexadecimal representations) and are terminated by a semicolon. Readers familiar with HTML will recognize this syntax as being renderable by most browsers as part of an HTML document as well (in fact, this is also true for the predefined entity references described in the next section). The following table illustrates some simple character reference examples:

Decimal	Hexadecimal	Character	Description
`&#32;`	`&#x20;`		Space
`&#162;`	`&#xA2;`	¢	Symbol for cents
`&#163;`	`&#xA3;`	£	Symbol for British pound
`&#246;`	`&#xF6;`	ö	Letter o with umlaut
`&#169;`	`&#xA9;`	©	Copyright symbol

Entity References

Whereas character references refer to their substitutions by number, entity references refer to their substitutions by name. The following "pre-defined" entity references will be familiar to you if you have worked with HTML escape sequences:

Reference	Character	Description
`&amp;`	&	Ampersand
`&lt;`	<	Less than
`&gt;`	>	Greater than
`&apos;`	'	Apostrophe
`&quot;`	"	Double quote

This table is "complete". In other words, beyond the pre-defined entity references in the above table, we cannot use entities without using a DTD. We'll defer further discussion to the section covering DTDs.

Comments

Comments can appear almost anywhere in an XML document, including the document's prolog. A comment is introduced by the character sequence `<!--` and terminates with the sequence `-->`. The comment can contain any other text, with the exception of `--`. The following example shows two comments, one legal and one illegal:

```
<!-- This is a <<< Legal >>> comment -->
<!-- But -- this is not legal! -->
```

It's worth noting that, due to the disallowance of the `--` character sequence, comments ending in `--->` are not allowed.

Processing Instructions

The last piece of basic XML to cover is the PI – the processing instruction. A PI is interesting, in that its purpose is entirely outside the scope of the XML document. It is intended to allow us to embed, within our XML document, instructions for some external piece of software. The format for a PI is:

```
<?target text ?>
```

The **target** is the name of an application, and can be anything except the letters XML (in any mix of case). The target and the text will both be made available to the application. It's up to the application to then invoke whatever external software is necessary, and pass to it the text of the PI. In this sense it is like an external function call. Other authors have described this as an "application escape" in that it gives an "escape" mechanism to some other application. For example, the PI in the following might be used to perform a database lookup:

```
<Part Number="19354">
  <Description>5mm socket</Description>
  <?DB lookup(part:19354)?>
</Part>
```

For another example, Microsoft, in its script technologies, defines an XML document called a "Script Component File", which may contain a PI of the following form:

```
<?component error="yes" debug="yes" ?>
```

In this case, the PI is being used to turn processing options (error notifications and debugging information) on or off.

Valid XML

The requirement that XML documents be well-formed is meaningful and useful, and is probably enough to ensure that a document can be parsed successfully. But it is generally not enough to ensure that our applications will be able to correctly process the data encapsulated within the document. (In fact, there are significant limitations on DTDs as well – limitations that are largely overcome with the use of schemas. See Chapter 5 for more details.)

For example, there's nothing about well-formedness that will tell users whether the following is legal or not. It is quite possible that we would want the following rejected due to the meaningless attribute values, and perhaps because we only want one <Customer> element associated with each trouble ticket.

```
<TroubleTicket ID="Gone With The Wind"
   HelpAgent="I am not a crook"
   Status="Would you like fries with that?">
   <Customer>Sun Microsystems</Customer>
   <Customer>Microsoft</Customer>
</TroubleTicket>
```

For these and many other sanity and legality checks, we can use the validity constraints defined by the XML specification, and implemented by our creation and use of a DTD.

Document Metadata

Metadata is data about data – information about data. It's not the data itself, it is information – perhaps description information or type information – about the data. We might, for example, want to restrict the values of the `status` attribute of our `<TroubleTicket>` element to one of either `Open` or `Closed`. That rule forms an additional constraint on the data that we consider to be acceptable in our document. We may specify such constraints in the Document Type Definition or DTD.

Location of Metadata

The metadata for our document will be contained in the DTD. There are three choices when it comes to deciding where to put the DTD:

❑   Internal to the document

❑   External to the document, either on the same server or on some other server

❑   Both internal and external, in which case we are said to have an **internal subset** and an **external subset**.

Creating Valid XML Documents

What does it mean, then, to create a valid XML document? It means:

❑   Creating a DTD, or selecting a DTD created by a third party.

❑   Locating the DTD, or, if we are creating it ourselves, deciding where the DTD should be located, as discussed in the previous section. This decision will be governed by common sense criteria such as whether we want to share the DTD with others.

❑   Creating documents that conform to the DTD, either referencing the external DTD or by including it internally, or by using a combination of internal and external subsets.

The first step, creating the DTD, means figuring out what we want in a document, what the rules and constraints will be, and then going ahead and creating the DTD to enforce the decisions we have made. It also means making style decisions – whether a particular characteristic of our data should be modeled as an attribute or element, for example. The next major section, *Markup Declarations in DTDs,* covers how to do this in detail.

The Prolog Revisited: Locating the DTD

The prolog, in addition to the XML declaration, may contain the document declaration and the DTD. The simplest form of the document declaration is as follows, which simply says that we are about to create a `TroubleTicket` document, and further that the root element of the document is the `<TroubleTicket>` element:

```
<!DOCTYPE TroubleTicket>
```

If the DTD is contained in a separate file, we may reference that file as follows:

```
<!DOCTYPE TroubleTicket SYSTEM "TroubleTicket.dtd">
```

The filename specified as the value of the SYSTEM ID is actually a URI, and may be either relative, as in the example above (in which case it is relative to the location of the document from which it is referenced), or absolute.

> *A URI is a Uniform Resource Identifier. URI is a generic concept -- literally just a way of identifying a resource. In the words of the IETF (the Internet Engineering Task Force – the organization that manages the standards and protocols of the Internet), a URI is "a string of characters for identifying an abstract or physical resource". You are undoubtedly already familiar with a special kind of URI: the URL, or Uniform Resource Locator. A URL is a URI in which the location and means of accessing the resouce on the internet are both explicitly defined. For now you will lose little rigor if you just pretend that URIs are the same as URLs. A URN, or Uniform Resource Name, is another form of URI. The URN is different in that it names a resource rather locates it; it is (potentially at least) the responsiblity of a third party agency to locate the resource being named. A URN is also meant to be a persistent identifier: even if the location changes, the name need not necessarily change with it. URNs are not widely used at this point and are still the subject of debate and development.*
>
> *If you find this worth further investigation, you can check out the following:*
>
> > *URIs at http://www.ietf.org/rfc/rfc2396.txt*
> > *URLs at http://www.ietf.org/rfc/rfc1738.txt*
> > *URNs at http://www.ietf.org/rfc/rfc2141.txt*

Don't be confused by the word SYSTEM. It does not refer to a "system file" in the sense of operating system, or a "system file" as opposed to an "application file". The value of the SYSTEM ID simply refers to a file. As an alternative to the SYSTEM ID, as above, we may have a PUBLIC ID, which currently is rarely, if ever, used. The intent of the PUBLIC ID is to provide a mechanism for referencing widely accessible standard document information (in other words something broadly and publicly available, accepted, and understood, as opposed to something more specific to the software system within which we are working). Such standards are not yet commonplace in the XML world, though they are available in other contexts. One context you will come across PUBLIC IDs is in HTML, however. Note the use of a PUBLIC ID in the following sample:

```
<!DOCTYPE HTML PUBLIC "-//W3C//DTD HTML 3.2 Final//EN">
```

The Prolog and the Internal DTD Subset

In addition to declaring the root element name and the SYSTEM (or PUBLIC) ID, the document declaration may include formal markup declarations itself, which taken together are called the internal subset. The full DTD is the combination of the internal and external subsets. The format for the DOCTYPE declaration for internal declarations is as follows:

```
<!DOCTYPE name
[
markup declarations here
]>
```

An example for our trouble ticket document might look like the following – and don't worry if you don't understand all that's in here, that's the whole point of the next section!

```
<!DOCTYPE TroubleTicket
[
<!ELEMENT TroubleTicket (#PCDATA)>
<!ATTLIST TroubleTicket ticket:ID ID #IMPLIED
                        Importance CDATA #IMPLIED
                        Status (Open|Closed|Cancelled) #REQUIRED
]>
```

Markup Declarations in DTDs

The DTD itself consists primarily of constraints – additional rules that we want to ensure apply to a given document before we decide whether or not the document is valid. Such constraints can generally be applied both to elements and to attributes. In addition to these constraints, a DTD can declare named entities and can provide the parsing – the inclusion – of external files to create what is essentially a compound document.

The following declarations are used to declare elements, attributes, entities, and notations. We'll take a look at each one in turn:

```
<!ELEMENT ...  >
<!ATTLIST ...  >
<!ENTITY ...  >
<!NOTATION ...  >
```

Elements

When elements are declared, we are declaring both their name and what they may contain – their **content model**. Keep in mind that what we are declaring is an **element type**; the content of the document will contain actual elements, but the DTD defines the element type. The content model determines what contents – if any – are valid for this element. The general format for an element declaration is:

```
<!ELEMENT name content-model >
```

The name of the element conforms to the rules we have previously discussed. The content-model describes the content that we will consider valid. Unless the content-model consists of the single keyword EMPTY or ANY, it must be enclosed in parentheses.

The content model can be any of the following:

Content Model	Description
EMPTY	The element is empty and must be formatted as an empty element. Note that empty elements can still have attributes.
#PCDATA	The element can have textual content – character data – but no child elements.
Element content	The element can have child elements but no character data of its own.
Mixed content	The element can have a mixture of child elements and character data.
ANY	The element can have any content at all. This essentially says that the content must be well-formed XML, but that there are no other constraints.

EMPTY and ANY are very straightforward. The following two examples illustrate the declaration of an element with an empty content model and one allowing any content. Elements with element content or mixed content require a bit more investigation:

```
<!ELEMENT PrimaryHelpAgent EMPTY>
<!ELEMENT OtherInfo ANY>
```

> The **ANY** content model is certainly easy to use, and is a "quick and dirty" way of declaring your element content models. But its usefulness is open to debate. The purpose of the DTD is to add clarity and rigor to your documents, and it's difficult to see how the widespread use of **ANY** contributes to that effort.

Textual Content

The following example declares an element to have a strictly textual – character data – content model:

```
<!ELEMENT Description (#PCDATA)>
```

PCDATA stands for Parsed Character data. It is essentially just text – character data. The word "parsed" is simply an indication that the XML processor does actually parse the data (for example to expand entity references). Note that even though #PCDATA is a single "keyword", it still must be contained within parentheses in the specification of the content-model.

Element Content

When the content of an element is in turn other elements, there are three pieces of information that we must supply as part of the content model:

- ❑ Which elements are valid as child elements of this element
- ❑ What multiplicity these child elements may have (how many instances of the child element there may be)
- ❑ The sequence or ordering of child elements

If you are familiar with EBNF (or you read the EBNF summary earlier in this chapter) the means describing the above three points in your DTD will seem quite familiar to you.

The general rules are as follows:

- ❑ To indicate multiple alternate elements, separate them with an "or" bar |
- ❑ To indicate a sequence of elements (in which ordering is significant) use commas instead of "or" bars to separate the child elements
- ❑ Indicate multiplicity using the standard EBNF characters:

*	For any number, zero or more
+	For any number, but at least one
?	For zero or one for an optional element)

❑ Use parentheses to group elements together. Multiplicity indicators can be applied to individual elements, or to element groupings

Consider the following examples. In the first example, the <TroubleTicket> consists of an optional Description, followed by exactly one <Customer>, <Product> and <Incident> element, in that order.

```
<!ELEMENT TroubleTicket (Description? , Customer, Product, Incident)>
```

In the following, the <Customer> element contains one or more <Contact> elements:

```
<!ELEMENT Customer (Contact+)>
```

In the following, the <Incident> element contains any number – zero or more – <Call> elements. The <Call> element, in turn, contains any number of <Note> elements:

```
<!ELEMENT Incident (Call*)>
<!ELEMENT Call (Note*)>
```

It's interesting to note that there is no way in XML of indicating exactly one each of multiple elements where ordering is not important.

Note that parentheses are necessary in all models of element content. In particular, even if only one instance of a single element is legal, the parentheses are still necessary. Thus the parentheses are necessary in the following:

```
<!ELEMENT TroubleTicket (Description)>
```

Mixed Content

It is often desirable for an element to be able to contain a combination of child elements and character data – this is the mixed content model. In the case of mixed content, we can only specify which child elements are acceptable; we cannot indicate multiplicity, nor can we specify an ordering. The format for the declaration of an element with a mixed content model is as follows, where elements is a list of the names of valid child elements, separated by "or" bars (note that the asterisk is mandatory):

```
<!ELEMENT name (#PCDATA | elements… )*>
```

For example, in the following, the <Customer> element can contain character data, with optionally any number of <Contact> child elements:

```
<!ELEMENT Customer (#PCDATA | Contact)*>
```

It's interesting, perhaps, to note that child elements are an optional component of a mixed content model. What this implies is that an element that contains only character data – no child elements – is technically a special case of a mixed content model. We feel that this special case arises often enough, and is distinct enough in data modeling terms, that we have chosen to introduce it in this chapter as a separate content model.

> The difference between mixed content and **ANY** may not be obvious at first. The difference is that with mixed content we specify which child elements are acceptable. When we use the **ANY** content model, we are saying that anything at all is acceptable – as long as it is well-formed XML.

Attributes

As you know, elements can have attributes. Using our DTD, we can set constraints on what attributes are acceptable for a given element, whether attributes are optional or required, and we can provide a default value. To a limited extent we can also put constraints on the values of attributes. We do all this with the ATTLIST declaration, which takes the following general form:

```
<!ATTLIST element-name attribute-name type default>
```

In the following example, the <Product> element is declared to have three attributes, one of which is required:

```
<!ATTLIST Product Name CDATA #IMPLIED
                  Rev CDATA #FIXED "1.0"
                  Code CDATA #REQUIRED>
```

CDATA is an attribute type. It is also possible for attribute values to be enumerated, which gives us a high degree of control over their values. There are also a variety of tokenized values: ID and IDREF/IDREFS, ENTITY and ENTITIES, and NMTOKEN and NMTOKENS. We'll take a look at each of these in turn, after first taking a look at how we constrain default values.

Default Attribute Values

There are four possibilities for default values, as shown in the table:

#REQUIRED	This is the simplest. A value must be provided for this attribute.
#IMPLIED	Almost as straightforward. A value may be provided or not, and if it is not, there is no default value.
value	Well, maybe this is simplest. The value supplied here is the default value.
#FIXED value	In this case the attribute's value, if supplied, must match the default value specified in the ATTLIST; if not supplied, the attribute value defaults to that specified in the ATTLIST.

Consider again the ATTLIST declaration:

```
<!ATTLIST Product Name CDATA #IMPLIED
                  Rev CDATA #FIXED "1.0"
                  Code CDATA #REQUIRED>
```

The following would all validate:

```
<Product Name="MedEvac" Rev="1.0" Code="537010502" />
<Product Rev="1.0" Code="537010502" />
<Product Code="537010502" />
```

The following would not validate because the `Rev` attribute value provided is not the `#FIXED` default:

```
<Product Rev="2.0" Code="537010502" />
```

CDATA Attributes

This is the simplest type for an attribute. `CDATA` in this context simply means character data. Any text from the allowable character set will be considered valid. The only restriction is that, as usual, the value cannot contain markup. (In particular, the < character is not valid, and, as usual, the & is not valid unless introducing a reference.)

> Don't confuse **CDATA** attributes with **CDATA** sections (remember, those were the ones using the syntax `<![CDATA [text]]>`). **CDATA** attributes cannot contain markup; those other **CDATA** sections can contain anything at all.

NMTOKEN, NMTOKENS

Specifying an attribute to be of type `NMTOKEN` instead of `CDATA` adds just one more constraint to an attribute: that the value of the attribute must consist only of the characters allowable in an XML name, as previously discussed in this chapter (such as letters, digits, the hyphen, the underscore, the period, or the colon, with the proviso that "letter" in Unicode is a broader character set than many of us are used to). In particular, the value may not contain whitespace; it must be one "token". If the attribute is declared to be of type `NMTOKENS` (plural) then the value may consist of multiple tokens, separated by whitespace, each one conforming to the rules for a single `NMTOKEN`.

The following example shows a use of the `NMTOKEN` attribute type:

```
<!ATTLIST TroubleTicket ticketID ID #IMPLIED
                        PrimaryHelpAgent NMTOKEN #IMPLIED>
...
<TroubleTicket ticketID="T746284"
    PrimaryHelpAgent="Melissa">
```

The following variation uses `NMTOKENS`:

```
<!ATTLIST TroubleTicket ticketID ID #IMPLIED
                        PrimaryHelpAgent NMTOKENS #IMPLIED>
...
<TroubleTicket ticketID="T746284" PrimaryHelpAgent="Melissa Price">
```

Enumerations

Enumerated attributes are almost as simple, and are very powerful. An enumeration is simply a list of the possible values for the attribute. All the possibilities for default values identified in the previous section apply to enumerated types as well. All of the following would be appropriate declarations:

```
<!ATTLIST Contact Status (Primary|Alternate) "Alternate" >
<!ATTLIST TroubleTicket Status (Open|Closed|Cancelled) #REQUIRED
                        SpecialReports (Summary|Detailed) #IMPLIED>
```

Notice the use of #IMPLIED in the above example. This is an optional attribute that takes no default value if it is not supplied. In our example system, this is due to the fact that special reports are not always necessary for a trouble ticket. If they are desired for a specific ticket, they can be supplied either in summary or detailed form.

ID, IDREF Attributes

Attributes of type ID or IDREF seem to be quite confusing to newcomers to XML, but I think this is unnecessary. The key step, however, is to understand the *intent* of these attribute types; the syntax will follow.

The intent of an ID attribute, as the name implies, is to *uniquely* identify an element within a document. For example, we might have a document representing a project team. The document might contain elements like <ProjectLeader>, <TeamMember>, etc. However, each of those elements might have an attribute like EmployeeNumber that we would like to constrain to be unique across all the elements in the document. We can do so by declaring the attribute to be of ID type, with one small glitch: the value for an attribute of ID type must begin with a letter, underscore, or colon. Note also that an attribute of type ID must be declared with a default of either #IMPLIED or #REQUIRED.

Consider the following example, taken from our help desk application. The premise in this example is that we now have two types of tickets: trouble tickets, and tickets for consulting services. However, we want to make sure that the ticket ID is unique, across all tickets. Note that we've added a letter to the beginning of the ticketID values to make them legal.

```
<!DOCTYPE TicketSet
[
<!ELEMENT TicketSet (TroubleTicket|ConsultingTicket)*>
<!ELEMENT TroubleTicket EMPTY>
<!ATTLIST TroubleTicket ticketID ID #IMPLIED>
<!ELEMENT ConsultingTicket EMPTY>
<!ATTLIST ConsultingTicket ticketID ID #IMPLIED>
]>

<TicketSet>
   <TroubleTicket ticketID="T746284" />
   <ConsultingTicket ticketID="T19834" />
   <TroubleTicket ticketID="T321234" />
</TicketSet>
```

We can do a check that the file is valid using an XML editor like XMLSpy (it evens makes a pleasant chiming sound when the green tick on the bottom left corner appears!):

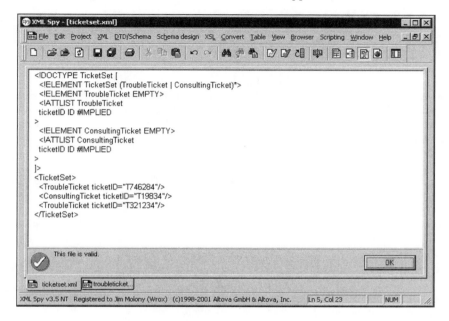

Note that the ID attribute values would still have to be unique, even if the names of the attributes were different. Consider the following modified example DTD:

```
<!DOCTYPE TicketSet
[
<!ELEMENT TicketSet (TroubleTicket|ConsultingTicket)*>
<!ELEMENT TroubleTicket EMPTY>
<!ATTLIST TroubleTicket troubleID ID #IMPLIED>
<!ELEMENT ConsultingTicket EMPTY>
<!ATTLIST ConsultingTicket consultingID ID #IMPLIED>
]>
```

In this case, even though the attributes have different names (and are in different elements) they must still have unique values. (From a style perspective, it would be best not to mislead the reader in this way; since ID attribute values must be unique, it would be best to have the same attribute name, and preferably one with the letters "ID" somewhere in the name.) The following document would not validate:

```
<TicketSet>
    <TroubleTicket troubleID="T746284" />
    <ConsultingTicket consultingID="T19834" />
    <TroubleTicket troubleID="T19834" />
</TicketSet>
```

So that's what ID is all about – now what about IDREF? Just as the word "ID" indicates that we are identifying something, the word "IDREF" implies that we will be referring to a value of type ID. Consider the following XML fragment:

```
The current ticket is <Ticket ticketID="T19834">T19834</Ticket>.
```

The `ticketID` attribute on the `<Ticket>` element refers back to the `ticketID` in some other element, thus making a logical connection between the two elements. The declaration of the `<Ticket>` element might look like this:

```
<!ELEMENT Ticket (#PCDATA)>
<!ATTLIST Ticket ticketID IDREF #REQUIRED>
```

It may not be obvious why you would want to create such a connection in a static or freestanding document. However, in the context of this book, where we are discussing the programmatic creation and manipulation of XML documents, it's not at all difficult to see the benefit. Remember – when you are structuring your XML, you are trying to model as completely as possible the real nature of the data. If the data really does have a connection in real life, it is a Good Thing to have a mechanism like `ID`/`IDREF` to model that connection.

Finally, `IDREFS` behaves exactly the same way as `IDREF`, except that multiple references are possible. Again, consider an XML fragment:

```
The outstanding tickets are <Ticket ticketIDs="T746284 T19834 T5736234">T746284,
T19834 and T5736234</Ticket>.
```

Now the corresponding declaration of the `<Ticket>` element might look like this:

```
<!ELEMENT Ticket (#PCDATA)>
<!ATTLIST Ticket ticketIDs IDREFS #REQUIRED>
```

Entities

We have already seen simple use of entities, including character entities where the character is referenced either numericall (`&#169;` for the copyright symbol) or symbolically (`&amp;` for the ampersand symbol). In addition to these, there are general entities for defining replacement text for use in the XML document, parameter entities (both internal and external) for defining replacement text for use within the DTD itself, and external unparsed entities for referencing external data in a variety of forms.

General Internal Entities

These are very simple to declare in the DTD. Consider the following:

```
<!ENTITY copy "This text is protected by &#169; copyright ">
```

This text could then be placed anywhere in our document by using the construction `&copy;`

External Parsed Entities

The general entities just discussed are internal: they are defined entirely within the DTD and available for use within the XML document. General entities have an external form as well, as follows:

```
<!ENTITY CustomerContent SYSTEM "CustomerContent.xml">
```

In this case, the `CustomerContent.xml` file contents will be inserted wherever this entity is referenced, perhaps as in the following:

```
<Customer>
&CustomerContent;
</Customer>
```

It's interesting to note that if general internal entities are similar to `#define` in C (manifest constants), then external parsed entities are similar to `#include` (source file inclusion).

Parameter Entities

Parameter entities provide us with a means of performing textual substitution within the DTD itself. This can be useful for text that you find yourself repeating frequently in your DTD. In our help desk DTD for example, the phrases `CDATA #IMPLIED` and `CDATA #REQUIRED` are used quite frequently in the definition of our attributes – as they are in many DTDs. To create parameter entities to assist us here, we use syntax almost identical to that of general entities, except that for the use of a `%` sign in the entity definition, and a use of `%` instead of `&` in our use of the entity. Consider the following:

```
<!ENTITY % AttImp "CDATA #IMPLIED">
<!ENTITY % AttReq "CDATA #REQUIRED">
```

These can now be used in attribute declarations, as in the following:

```
<!ATTLIST Product Name %AttImp;
                  Rev CDATA #FIXED "1.0"
                  Code %AttReq;>
```

As a matter of style, it's worth noting that unbridled use of parameter entities can make your DTDs, the syntax for which is already a little cryptic and intimidating, even less clear. Once you are used to reading DTDs, phrases like `CDATA #IMPLIED` will be second nature; a token like `%AttImp` will have you scrambling through the DTD looking for parameter entity declarations. As always, keep maintainability and readability in mind when creating your DTD. If well-chosen parameter entity names increase the maintainability and readability of your document, go ahead and use them; if they do not, then don't.

Parameter entities declared in the external subset of your DTD may only be referenced in the external subset. Parameter entities declared in the internal subset may only replace complete declarations (e.g. a complete `ATTLIST` or `ELEMENT` declaration). The example above, in which the replaced text `CDATA #IMPLIED` is a partial declaration, must appear in the external subset.

Notations

Notations provide a mechanism by which we can associate external programs with certain types of content. This is similar, in principal at least, to the mechanism by which HTML browsers associate plugins with various MIME types. The MIME type is the analog to our XML notation declaration. Another analogy would be to the association that Microsoft Windows makes between certain filename extensions and certain handler programs. In that case, the filename extension would correspond to our XML notation.

Notation Declaration

The syntax for a notation declaration is simple, as shown in the following example, which associates the notation `rm` with the Real Player program from Real Networks:

```
<!NOTATION rm SYSTEM "realplayer.exe">
```

External Unparsed Entities

Notations can be used, for example, in external unparsed entities, as in the following example. You'll note that the syntax is almost identical to that for external parsed entities, with the addition of an `NDATA` clause. The `NDATA` keyword must precede the name of a notation that has already been declared – the `rm` notation in this case.

```
<!ENTITY video SYSTEM "videotest.rm" NDATA rm>
```

Entity Attributes

One way in which external parsed entities can be referenced is as the value of an attribute declared to be of type `ENTITY`, as follows:

```
<!ATTLIST tester demo ENTITY #IMPLIED>
```

A possible use of this would then be the following – note that even though this is an entity reference, we do not use the `&;` syntax. The reason for that should be clear: the `&;` syntax is usually necessary to distinguish this entity reference from the surrounding text or markup. In this case, that distinction is being made by the declaration of the attribute to be of `ENTITY` type.

```
<tester demo="video">
```

It can be tricky to see how all these pieces go together, so here they are in a complete example:

```
<!DOCTYPE tester
[
<!NOTATION rm SYSTEM "file:///C:\temp\realplayer.exe">
<!ENTITY video SYSTEM "videotest.rm" NDATA rm>
<!ELEMENT tester EMPTY>
<!ATTLIST tester demo ENTITY #IMPLIED>
]>
<tester demo="video"/>
```

Enumerated Attributes with Notations

One final use of notations is with a special type of enumerated attribute. Instead of the general case of enumerated types we discussed earlier in this chapter, this further restricts the possible values for the attribute to the set of notations previously declared in the DTD. The "textbook" example for this is with the use of audio formats. The following example puts these pieces together:

```
<!DOCTYPE clip
[
<!NOTATION rm SYSTEM "realplayer.exe">
<!NOTATION au SYSTEM "audioshop.exe">
<!ELEMENT clip EMPTY>
<!ATTLIST clip format NOTATION (au|rm) #REQUIRED
               file CDATA #REQUIRED>
]>
<clip format="au" file="demo.au"/>
```

XML Namespaces

XML namespaces are a fairly simple solution to two very simple problems. The first problem is one that is undoubtedly already familiar to you – the problem of name conflicts. Think of any program of reasonable size that you have written: did you ever have two variables in the program with the same name? Of course you did. The number of variables called simply i, or counter, or number, or some such name, is undoubtedly large. Additionally, consider data elements in Java classes – an element called number in an Address class might refer to the street number, while number in a Team class might mean the number of team members. Name conflicts in programming languages like Java are resolved using scope rules.

In XML, name conflicts are resolved in two ways. When drawing an analogy between data encapsulated in an XML document and a data element in a Java class, the best analog to the data element might be an XML attribute. In that case, the "scope" of the attribute's name is simply the element that it describes. The rules in this case are clear: no two attributes in the same element may have the same name, and there is no conflict between two attributes of the same name if they appear in different elements. If, however, two elements have the same name, the conflict is resolved using XML namespaces.

Name conflicts in XML can occur remarkably easily. The most obvious case is simply that we want to use the same element name more than once to mean different things. In our help desk example, it is easy to imagine that in tracking call information we would want a Note element as a child of several different elements – <TroubleTicket>, <Incident> and <Call> for example – and have them mean different things, process them differently, and display them differently.

It's conceivable that when the document is entirely under your control, you would be able to avoid such conflicts – though it may be inconvenient to do so if the "perfect" name for an element is also the "perfect" name for another element. A less obvious but more common problem arises when we are using more than one vocabulary, one or both of which is under someone else's control. Then two different DTD authors, unknown to one another, might inadvertently cause a name conflict, and this is bound to happen sooner rather than later. (See the section *"Namespace Syntax and the DTD"* for more on this.)

Namespace Syntax

Namespace syntax is really very simple – though a couple of points are confusing the first time you see them. The syntax must accomplish two objectives: must allow us to distinguish between namespaces, and must afford us a mechanism to guarantee (and hopefully manage) their uniqueness within the document.

The Namespace Prefix

The syntax for distinguishing between different namespaces is extremely simple. Instead of simply using an element name like <Name> we use the following form:

```
<prefix:Name>
```

The rules for constructing the prefix and the name are the same as for normal XML names, except that, for obvious reasons, neither may contain a colon. Consider the following example that makes use of two <Note> elements in different contexts:

```
<TroubleTicket>
   <Note>Can't Martha take this ticket?</Note>
   <Incident>
      <Note>This is a recurring problem</Note>
   </Incident>
</TroubleTicket>
```

We can distinguish between the two <Note> elements using namespace prefixes as follows:

```
<TroubleTicket>
   <Ticket:Note>Can't Martha take this ticket?</Ticket:Note>
   <Incident>
      <Incident:Note>This is a recurring problem</Incident:Note>
   </Incident>
</TroubleTicket>
```

Notice that the first prefix is Ticket, not TroubleTicket, which implies that this namespace is related to tickets in general, and not just to trouble tickets.

Attributes can be qualified with a prefix, just as elements can:

```
<TroubleTicket
   ticket:ID="T746284"
   Importance="High"
   Status="Open">
```

The xmlns Attribute

Earlier, we said that the namespace syntax has to allow us to distinguish between namspaces, and must help us guarantee uniqueness within the document. The prefix mechanism we've just seen certainly helps us distinguish between namespaces. The problem now is how to manage our prefixes and guarantee their unique interpretation. The xmlns attribute (xmlns standing for XML namespaces), which can be used on any element, allows us to do just this. The value of the xmlns attribute must be a string that is unique within the document. The intent of the namespace specification authors is that the value of the attribute would be a URI which refers to the person or organization that is somehow in "control" of the namespace (perhaps the organization which authored the DTD). (If you've forgotten what a URI is, refer back to the section *"The Prolog Revisited: Locating the DTD".)*

There is currently no formal requirement that the URI actually refer to any specific kind of document or resource.

```
<Ticket:Note xmlns:Ticket="http://www.cdilearn.com/xml/ticket">
   Can't Martha take this ticket?</Ticket:Note>
```

This is the one part of the namespace syntax that seems confusing to newcomers. Consider the ordering of elements – when we use a prefix, it looks like this, with the prefix coming before the colon:

```
prefix:Name
```

However, in declaring the prefix, we use the following, with the prefix coming after the colon:

```
xmlns:prefix="URI"
```

In use, the prefix becomes a placeholder for the URI referenced in the xmlns attribute's value – that URI is called the namespace name. Try not to confuse the namespace name with the namespace prefix – it will make reading any of the specifications extremely confusing!

Local Names and Universal Names

Think about this for a minute. Within one document, validating XML processors will ensure that we do not declare two elements of the same name. And within one element, we know that we cannot have two attributes of the same name. These are called local names. Hence, the Name part of the prefix:Name construct is called a local name. But consider the combination of prefix and name. Since the prefix, as we have said, is merely a placeholder for the URI, and the URI must be unique, the combination of prefix and name is guaranteed to be unique – and hence is referred to in the namespace specification as a universal name. It should be unique within the universe of the Internet.

The xmlns Attribute and its Containing Element

There is a "cascading effect" to the xmlns attribute. If a certain prefix is used in an element or attribute, and that element does not have a corresponding xmlns attribute that declares that prefix, then the parent element is checked. If the parent does not, the parent's parent is checked, and so on. It is customary, therefore, for the root element to declare the namespace prefixes used in the document:

```
<TroubleTicket
    xmlns:ticket="http://www.cdilearn.com/xml/ticket"
    ticket:ID="T746284"
    Importance="High"
    Status="Open">
```

Setting a Default Namespace

If we have a majority of tags from the same namespace, we may wish to avoid the use of prefixes all over the place, and yet still maintain the rigor afforded by the use of a namespace declaration. We can do so by providing a default namespace declaration. Note that in the following, we are declaring two namespaces in the <TroubleTicket> root element: one with a prefix, and one without:

```
<TroubleTicket
    xmlns="http://www.cdilearn.com/xml/troubleticket"
    xmlns:ticket="http://www.cdilearn.com/xml/ticket"
    ticket:ID="T746284"
    Importance="High"
    Status="Open">
```

In the above example, any unprefixed elements or attributes will belong to the default namespace.

Note that using a default namespace and using no namespace are not the same thing. Some people do talk of having a "default" namespace consisting of all names unqualified by a prefix, without the benefit of a default (unnamed) xmlns declaration. This may be aesthetically tempting but it is technically incorrect. When there is no default xmlns declaration, names unqualified by a prefix are in no namespace at all.

Namespace Syntax and the DTD

It's important to notice that the namespace conventions, by virtue of the syntax chosen (particularly the use of the colon to separate the prefix and the name of the element or attribute) imply that there is nothing about namespaces that violates any of the "traditional" XML rules. In other words, you can use namespaces with existing XML parsers and other XML software, which may or may not be "namespace-aware". This was quite important, since the XML specification and the XML namespace specification are two different specifications, with the former predating the latter. The consequence is that the attribute associated with your namespaces must be declared in your DTD, as in the following:

```
<!ATTLIST TroubleTicket
    xmlns:ticket CDATA #FIXED "http://www.cdilearn.com/xml/ticket"
    ticket:ID ID #IMPLIED
    Importance CDATA #IMPLIED
    Status (Open|Closed|Cancelled) #REQUIRED>
```

The declaration of the default namespace – the use of the xmlns attribute with no prefix declaration – should be acceptable with all current parsers, as the xmlns attribute itself, by definition, belongs to no namespace at all. However, some older, non-namespace-aware parsers may require an additional line, like the one highlighted below, for compatibility. This is inconvenient, but poses no real technical hurdle. (Since the inclusion of a line such as that highlighted below is benign even for newer parsers, the inclusion of such a line is, perhaps, a good safe habit to get into.)

```
<!ATTLIST TroubleTicket
    xmlns CDATA #FIXED "http://www.cdilearn.com/xml/troubleticket"
    xmlns:ticket CDATA #FIXED "http://www.cdilearn.com/xml/ticket"
    ticket:ID ID #IMPLIED
    Importance CDATA #IMPLIED
    Status (Open|Closed|Cancelled) #REQUIRED>
```

This leads to two somewhat inconvenient points about the use of namespaces with DTDs:

❑   The use of namespaces with a DTD is tedious, because defining a namespace requires modification of the declarations for all elements and attributes in that namespace. This is inconvenient (to say the least) but is not insurmountable.

❑   The second issue is that we can only reference one external DTD in our document. That means that there is no way to "combine" or "merge" two document types. At the beginning of this section on namespaces we were careful to say that we might have name collisions between two XML "vocabularies" but we didn't say between two DTDs, and now you see why. Any "merging" of document types would be accomplished only as part of a manual process of merging vocabularies defined in separate DTDs.

When you read about XML stylesheets and schemas, later in this book, you'll also see that these must also be "namespace aware".

Application and Effective Use of XML

At the beginning of this section, we mentioned that XML namespaces solve two simple problems. The first is that of dealing with element name collisions – the desire to use two elements of the same name to mean different things within one document. That argument is usually pretty compelling for most people, with one small exception: attribute names are guaranteed to be unique within an element anyway, so why would anyone ever want to associate an attribute with a namespace? The answer is not one of syntax, but of application. In the XML namespace specification, these two issues are called "collision and recognition". So far, we've only talked about collision. So what is recognition all about? Consider the example of our <Contact> element:

```
<Contact
        Status="Primary"
        Name="Ann McKinsey"
        Phone="417-555-9318"
        Fax="417-555-9319"
        Email="Ann.McKinsey@InteSteel.com"
    />
```

Within this one element, there are actually three kinds of information:

❑   Information that is uniquely relevant – locally relevant – to this element (the status of the contact as a primary or alternative contact)

❑   Information that helps identify and locate a person (name, phone, fax)

❑   Information that is related to Internet connectivity and communication (the email address)

It is very possible that a downstream application would want to handle these three kinds of information in different ways. Personal information might be used to look up a record in a database of some sort, or the phone number might be tied to an auto-dialer, or the fax number might be linked to some sort of fax software. The e-mail address might be tied to an e-mail client of some sort, perhaps to do an automatic mailing or to check for validity of the e-mail address. Phone numbers and e-mail addresses might be subjected to sanity checks of various sorts. The important thing is that an application might want to do any of these things – a sanity check on a phone number, for example – regardless of whether the phone number appears in a <Contact> element representing a person, or a <Supplier> element representing a company or organization, or a <Support> element representing mechanisms for obtaining technical support.

We might use namespaces to facilitate such downstream capabilities by reconstructing our <Contact> element as follows:

```
<Contact
    Status="Primary"
    PersonalIdentifiers:Name="Ann McKinsey"
    PhoneNumber:Phone="417-555-9318"
    PhoneNumber:Fax="417-555-9319"
    InternetResource:Email="Ann.McKinsey@InteSteel.com"
    />
```

XML Information Set

The **XML Information Set (Infoset)** specification is one of the shorter, but more interesting, members of the XML pantheon of specifications. Think for a minute of what the XML 1.0 specification gives us. It allows us to create an XML document (well-formed, valid, or both) and via the DTD it gives us a way of describing, in great syntactic detail, what we mean by a valid document. The DTD is a concrete physical representation of what constitutes a valid document; the XML Infoset specification gives us a means of describing an abstract logical representation of an XML document. Where the DTD deals with elements and attributes, the Infoset deals with **information items**. There is a data model implicit in any XML document and any XML DTD; the XML InfoSet provides an explicit description of that data model.

At the time of writing, the XML Infoset specification is still a work in progress, and is officially still a "Working Draft" (most recently dated December 20, 2000, with a subsequent invitation for further comment and discussion). The intent of the Infoset specification is to provide a reference model – a theoretical model – that can be used and relied upon by the authors of other specifications. It is, for example, compatible with XML 1.0 and is interoperable with such other specifications as theW3C's DOM Level 1 (which is available at http://www.w3.org/tr/rec-dom-level-1).

Infoset Information Items

The most basic building block in the XML Infoset is the information item. There are actually seventeen different kinds of information items defined in the Infoset specification:

Information Item	Description
Document	There can be only one of these
Element	One for each element in the document – including one for the document element
Attribute	One for each attribute of the element – whether the attribute is specified or defaulted
Processing instruction	One for each processing instruction
Unexpanded entity reference	One for each unexpanded general entity reference in the element ("unexpanded" meaning its form prior to its being replaced with its replacement text)
Character	One for each character in the textual content of the document – including characters in CDATA sections
Comment	One for each comment in the document
DTD	There can only be one of these, and then only if the document has a DTD
Internal Entity	One for each general entity declared in the DTD, plus one for each of the predefined entities – lt, gt, amp, apos, and quot
External entity	One for each external general entity in the DTD plus one for the document entity itself
Unparsed entity	One for each unparsed general entity in the DTD

Information Item	Description
Notation	One for each notation in the DTD
Entity start marker and end marker	These essentially "bracket" the expanded general entity
Namespace	One for each namespace for each element
CDATA start marker and end marker	Similar to the entity start markers and end markers, these two "bracket" a CDATA section. It's interesting to note that the Infoset working group, at time of this writing, is considering dropping these two information items since, by virtue of the "special" nature of the CDATA section, the start and end markers are essentially irrelevant.

The Attribute Information Item

It's worth taking a look at one of these information items, to give you an idea of what is involved. Looking at one is sufficient to get the idea; you can refer to the specification itself for details on the others. The attribute information item has seven properties:

❑   The namespace name of the attribute, if it has one. (Remember that the namespace name is the value – the URI – of the appropriate xmlns attribute; it is not the namespace prefix.)

❑   The local name of the attribute

❑   The namespace prefix, if there is one

❑   The value of the attribute, in a normalized form

❑   A flag indicating whether this attribute value was specified in the document, or was defaulted

❑   An indicator of the attribute type (ID, IDREF, CDATA)

❑   The owner element – in other words, the element that contains this attribute

As you can see, the specification of this information item goes beyond what one would see just by looking at the attribute in the document. It carefully encapsulates all the information about the attribute, whether that information is explicitly stated in the text attribute or not, and does so in a predictable and reliable way.

What the Infoset Is and Is Not

It's also important to realize what the Infoset is not. It is not an API. It does not specify any particular kind of processing behavior, and is unlikely to be implemented uniformly in any discrete set of tools. It is, as we said earlier, an explicit description of a data model. So what good is that? It turns out that the InfoSet brings two major advantages to the XML table.

First, the Infoset gives the document designer an alternative starting point. Instead of beginning with documents and syntax and building a DTD (not a great sequence of steps to follow), or beginning with a DTD and building documents (a much better sequence), a designer can now first focus on the data model instead. What is the real nature of the information you are trying to capture in your documents? Once this question has been answered in some sort of detail the Infoset can be built as a precursor to other meta-documents (including the DTD).

Second, the Infoset provides a consistent theoretical foundation for those who are creating other XML specifications. It has been said that the development of the DOM standard (the Document Object Model, discussed in detail in Chapter 3) would have proceeded much more smoothly had the Infoset already existed. More importantly perhaps, it has been said that subtle discrepancies between specs like those for DOM and for other XML technologies like XPath could have been avoided if Infoset had already existed.

For these reasons, the Infoset is a slightly esoteric but meaningful addition to XML specification set, and is likely to increase in importance as the need grows for more portable and more meaningful descriptions of our data.

Working with XML

So far what we've been talking about is XML itself, how to create XML documents, how to create the DTD to guarantee our documents are valid, and so on. The rest of the book is concerned with the creation of software that will work with our XML documents: reading, manipulating, and generating XML. The XML 1.0 specification outlines the bare bones of a software architecture that is used to work with XML. It can be summed up in a couple of sentences and is beautiful in its simplicity. It describes the function of two pieces of software:

❑   The **XML processor** – commonly called the parser – is a piece of software that must do two things: must read the XML document, and must provide access to the document contents in some sort of predictable, rigorous way (for example, by way of an accepted API).

❑   The **XML application** makes use of the services of the XML processor to work with the information encapsulated in the XML document.

Some software packages that we might consider to be applications – Microsoft's Internet Explorer, for example – have an embedded XML processor.

From a software developer's perspective there is another simple distinction between application and processor. In a typical software development situation the processor is a piece of software we will acquire somewhere, whereas the application is software that we ourselves will create.

XML Processors

XML processors come in two flavors: **validating** and **non-validating**. Their different behaviors are what their names imply. Many newcomers prefer non-validating parsers because they report fewer errors, and let you "get away with" more in your XML documents. However, most programmers quickly grow to prefer – and even to depend on – the rigor of a validating processor.

Validating Processors

The behavior of a validating processor is simple and predictable – if a little annoying to the newcomer. The validating processor must read and process every part of the document, including the DTD, and must read and process all parsed external entities. In other words, it must read and process everything the document author built as part of the document, whether part of the same file (entity) or not. The view of the validating processor is "complete". Validating processors are also extremely picky in that they (at user option) report violations of rules expressed in the document's DTD, along with violations of any of the validity constraints defined in the XML specification. It is the thoroughness of the validating processor that makes it so useful to you as a programmer.

It must also be said, however, that all this functionality comes with a cost. The thoroughness of the validating parser can make it cumbersome for large documents. And the fact that the validating parser will normally terminate its processing upon encountering violations of validity constraints (among other things) makes it extremely frustrating to use on poorly constructed documents. In many situations it would be useful to check for well-formedness first, and validity second.

Non-validating Processors

The rules for non-validating processors are not quite as clear-cut. The following are the basic rules for non-validation processors:

❏ They must check the document entity, including the internal DTD subset (if it exists) for well-formedness.

❏ They do not check the document for validity.

❏ The may or may not read external entities.

It's that last characteristic that causes so much trouble for users of non-validating processors. An external parsed entity may – and often will – have an impact on whether the rest of the document is valid or even well-formed. So although we say that the non-validating processor checks for well-formedness, the fact that it does not read external entities means that we really cannot rely on its judgment in this regard.

The Application

The application component of the software system is what we tend to call the "useful" software. The processor component is not "useless" software, but perhaps we could call it the "prerequisite" software. The processor exists so that the application can focus on its own purpose (accounting, order entry, database management, among others) without worrying about the details of processing the contents of the XML document. We don't have much else to say about the application in this section, but it is the programming of the application (which in turn will make use of the services of the processor) that is the subject of much of the rest of this book.

The Relationship Between Application and Processor

Some people tend to see this as a hierarchy, with the XML document at the bottom of the hierarchy, then the XML processor, then the application, and then the end-user at the top of the hierarchy, as in the diagram.

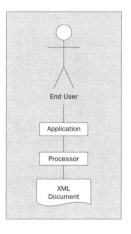

This hierarchical view is accurate from a logical perspective, at least for applications that involve a user-interface and interaction with a user. The physical perspective, however – how the software is actually put together and how it works together – is quite different. The next illustration shows the physical structure of the software.

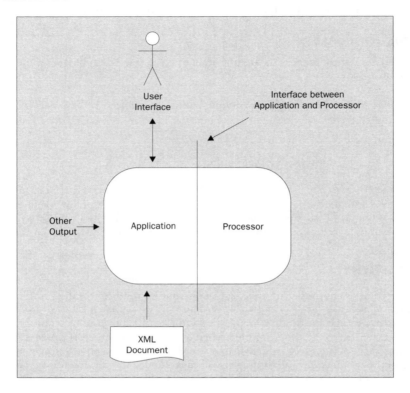

This diagram also highlights two other key points:

- ❑ The actual I/O – whether reading an XML document file, providing output (textual or otherwise, XML or otherwise), or interacting with the user through some other user interface – is all the responsibility of the application. The application makes use of the services of the processor.

- ❑ The interface between the application and the processor is of key importance.

For portable, extendable, adaptable software, standardized interfaces between application and processor will be essential, and yet the XML specification itself sets no limitations on the characteristics of this interface; the work of creating standard interfaces between application and processor is left to other specifications.

In particular, the processor may:

- ❑ Operate on the XML document as a stream of data, reporting items of significance to the application as it encounters them in the stream. This is the approach of the SAX XML parser, which we'll see in detail in the next chapter.

- ❑ Construct a logical tree representing the contents of the entire XML document, and provide an API through which the application can read and potentially manipulate the tree. This is the approach of the DOM parser, which we'll see in Chapter 3.

A Production XML System

The following diagram illustrates a simple software system that we currently use in a production environment, based on XML and Java. The application is a web-based training engine being used in a commercial training school. The engine is implemented as a Java servlet. The student information (name, academic record, etc.) is stored in XML form, as is the training material itself. The student information is used for authentication purposes (to make sure only authorized students receive the materials), for historical purposes (so that students can "pick up where they leave off") and for administrative purposes (school administrators produce a number of historical and statistical reports). On the training material side, when a page of information is requested, the appropriate XML document is read, is converted to HTML and sent to the student for display on a standard web browser.

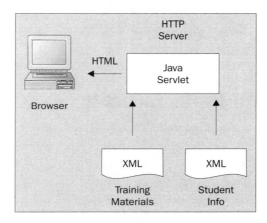

XML Tools and Information

There are, of course, unending numbers of sites on the Internet with information on software packages, white papers, and XML information in general. Here are a few good starting points:

The first place for any XML investigation, and to catch up on current standards and developments, is **W3C** at:

> http://www.w3.org/

There are also two other sites for good general purpose information:

OASIS, the **Organization for the Advancement of Structured Information Standards** is an international consortium dedicated to the creation of portable specifications and standards of various sorts, and as such has an active interest in XML. The organization sponsors an excellent information site at:

> http://www.xml.org/

James Tauber has been involved with XML since 1996 and is currently a representative to the W3C. He maintains a very complete repository of information at:

> http://www.xmlinfo.com/

General XML Software

There are many other web sites with information on XML software of all kinds: editors, utilities, parsers, etc.

O'Reilly and Associates sponsors and hosts a site at:

http://www.xml.com/

James Tauber and Linda van den Brink maintain a well-established and well-regarded site at:

http://www.xmlsoftware.com

Other sites that you might find useful in this regard are:

http://www.xmldir.com/
http://www.xmlpitstop.com/

TroubleTicket.xml in its Entirety

The following is a complete listing of the trouble ticket example we've been working on throughout the chapter. Remember that all the code in this book is available for download from the Wrox web site.

```
<?xml version="1.0"?>

<!DOCTYPE TroubleTicket
[
<!ELEMENT TroubleTicket (Description|Customer|Product|Incident)*>
<!ATTLIST TroubleTicket
    xmlns:ticket CDATA #FIXED "http://www.cdilearn.com/xml/ticket"
    xmlns:PhoneNumber CDATA #FIXED "http://www.cdilearn.com/xml/phonenumbers"
    xmlns:InternetResource CDATA #FIXED
"http://www.cdilearn.com/xml/internetresources"
    ticket:ID ID #IMPLIED
    Importance CDATA #IMPLIED
    Status (Open|Closed|Cancelled) #REQUIRED
    SpecialReports (Summary|Detailed) #IMPLIED
    PrimaryHelpAgent NMTOKEN #IMPLIED>
<!ELEMENT Description (#PCDATA)>
<!ELEMENT Customer (#PCDATA | Contact)*>
<!ATTLIST Customer
    Name CDATA #IMPLIED
    ID CDATA #IMPLIED>
<!ELEMENT Contact EMPTY>
<!ATTLIST Contact
    Status (Primary|Alternate) #FIXED "Primary"
    Name CDATA #IMPLIED
    PhoneNumber:Phone CDATA #IMPLIED
    PhoneNumber:Fax CDATA #IMPLIED
    InternetResource:Email CDATA #IMPLIED>
<!ELEMENT Product EMPTY>
```

```
<!ATTLIST Product
   Name CDATA #IMPLIED
   Rev CDATA #FIXED "1.0"
   Code CDATA #REQUIRED>
<!ELEMENT Incident (Call*)>
<!ELEMENT Call (#PCDATA | Note)*>
<!ATTLIST Call
   Type CDATA #IMPLIED
   StartTime CDATA #IMPLIED
   Duration CDATA #IMPLIED
   HelpAgent CDATA #IMPLIED>
<!ELEMENT Note (#PCDATA)>
]>

<TroubleTicket
   xmlns="http://www.cdilearn.com/xml/troubleticket"
   xmlns:ticket="http://www.cdilearn.com/xml/ticket"
   xmlns:PhoneNumber="http://www.cdilearn.com/xml/phonenumbers"
   xmlns:InternetResource="http://www.cdilearn.com/xml/internetresources"
   ticket:ID="T746284"
   Importance="High"
   Status="Open"
   PrimaryHelpAgent="Melissa">

   <Description>Customer cannot install product</Description>

   <Customer
      Name="International Steel"
      ID="1573">
      <Contact
         Status="Primary"
         Name="Ann McKinsey"
         PhoneNumber:Phone="417-555-9318"
         PhoneNumber:Fax="417-555-9319"
         InternetResource:Email="Ann.McKinsey@InteSteel.com"
      />
   </Customer>

   <Product Name="MedEvac" Rev="1.0" Code="537010502" />

   <Incident>
      <Call
         Type="Inbound"
         StartTime="02/17/2001 10:35"
         Duration="17"
         HelpAgent="Johnson">
      Customer received network errors in installation. Disconnectgin
      from network caused "Reboot" message. He will reboot and call back.
      <Note>This customer is using abusive language</Note>
      </Call>

      <Call
         Type="Inbound"
         StartTime="02/17/2001 11:03"
         Duration="11"
         HelpAgent="Steinberg">
      After rebooting, install is successful till point of entering
      license number. Customer's license number is incorrect.
      </Call>
   </Incident>

</TroubleTicket>
```

49

Summary

In this chapter we've tried to give you a "soup to nuts" introduction to XML. This isn't a book about XML, though; instead, it's a book about XML and Java. As such, the purpose of this chapter was to prepare you for what follows. At this point, we've covered the following in some detail:

- ❑ What XML is all about, and why it is important
- ❑ The structure of XML documents, including the prime importance of elements and attributes
- ❑ What the XML specification contains and how to read it
- ❑ Well-formed and valid XML
- ❑ Document metadata and the DTD
- ❑ XML Namespaces
- ❑ The XML Information Set
- ❑ Working with XML, including the roles of, and relationships between, the XML processor and application

You now have sufficient experience with XML to make good use of the rest of the book. The last section of this chapter, in which we discussed the processor and application, is a great lead-in to what follows – in particular the next two chapters, in which we discuss SAX and DOM – the two most common and most important APIs for accessing and processing XML documents.

The Xerces Blue
Butterfly, which became
extinct earlier this century,
and after which the Xerces XML
parser is named ...

2

SAX

This chapter introduces SAX, the "Simple API for XML Parsing". Prior to the introduction of SAX, a number of XML parsers were developed to provide an event-based means of parsing a document. However, the number of parsers grew, and so did the frustration of many a developer attempting to support them all.

The SAX initiative was borne out of the need for a common API for all event-based parsers. A number of event-driven XML parsers had been developed, all with their own APIs, leading to a proliferation of standards. To resolve this problem, a group of developers on the XML-DEV mailing list defined SAX 1.0, and it was released in May of 1998. When namespaces were added to the XML specification, it was apparent that the SAX API needed to be augmented to support them. SAX 2.0 was then released, improving on the previous version with the addition of namespace provision as well as other features that were deemed necessary as the use of SAX 1.0 proliferated.

Chapter Requirements

In order to get the most out of this chapter, you will need to download and install the following items:

- ❑ The Java 2 SDK, (Standard Edition version 1.2 or better) available at http://java.sun.com/j2se
- ❑ The Java API for XML Parsing (JAXP) version 1.1, available at http://java.sun.com/xml/
- ❑ **The Ælfred Parser,** available at http://www.opentext.com/services /content_management_services/xml_sgml_solutions.html#aelfred_and_sax
- ❑ **The Apache Xerces-Java Parser version 1.3.0**, available at http://xml.apache.org/xerces-j
- ❑ **The SAX 2.0 API** (optional). While the packages above contain all of the standard SAX classes, you may wish to have only the SAX 2.0 classes and interfaces instead of the extra baggage that comes with the others (this is available at http://www.megginson.com/SAX/Java).

Why SAX?

SAX, as mentioned earlier, is an API to be implemented by event-based XML parsers. In an event-based model, as the parser moves through the document, events such as the beginning of an element or the end of the document are reported via callbacks to an event handler. In this type of design there is an object that can fire events and there are listeners able to handle those events. These listeners implement an interface that the firing object understands, and then register with that object as being able to handle the events generated.

Once an event occurs, the object notifies each listener registered to handle that event by calling the appropriate method defined in the interface. There are analogies to the Event Delegation model employed in the AWT for handling user events, where a window detects a button click and notifies the interested parties that a button click has occurred. The same happens in event-driven parsing. When the parser encounters, for instance, the beginning of an element, the event is passed along to the registered object to handle.

To get an idea of what is happening as a SAX parser parses a document we'll use the example below.

```
<?xml version="1.0"?>
  <xmlDocument>
    <heading>This is my XML document</heading>
    That is all.
  </xmlDocument>
```

If we were to parse this document using SAX, the following events, in order, would be fired:

```
startDocument()
startElement(): xmlDocument
startElement(): heading
characters(): This is my XML document
endElement(): heading
characters(): That is all
endElement(): xmlDocument
endDocument()
```

This example also demonstrates that SAX parsing is serial. It does not define a context for events – in other words, there is no way to determine parent/child relationships. If you wanted find out if the <heading> element was found directly after the <xmlDocument> element, it would be your responsibility as the developer to code this into your application.

The Design of SAX

This section gives an overview of the SAX package and its design. We will be looking more carefully at each class and interface throughout the chapter, but for now the diagram below illustrates the class design of the SAX 2.0 package:

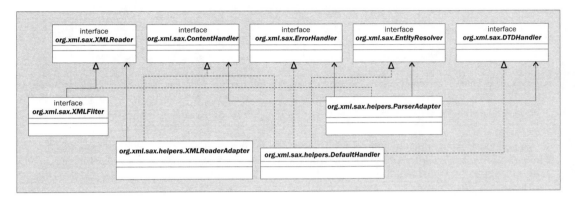

These interfaces and classes represent the core of SAX. The `org.xml.sax.XMLReader` class is where most of the work is done. This is the first step the application needs to make in order to call itself a SAX parser. This interface defines methods used by calling programs to parse a document.

The `org.xml.sax.XMLFilter` interface builds on the `XMLReader` interface. Like the base interface, it generates events to be handled. However an `XMLFilter` can be used to create a chain of event handlers by passing events from itself to its parent.

The `org.xml.sax.ContentHandler` interface is where most developers spend their time. This is where all events are handled. Continuing with the AWT analogy, when we want to intercept mouse clicks we implement the `java.awt.event.MouseListener` interface. When we want to intercept SAX events, we implement the `ContentHandler` interface.

The `org.xml.sax.ErrorHandler` , `org.xml.sax.EntityResolver`, and `org.xml.sax.DTDHandler` are handlers for errors, entities, and DTD-specific events, respectively. We will look at these later.

The `org.xml.sax.helpers.DefaultHandler` is a concrete class that implements the `ContentHandler`, `ErrorHandler`, `EntityResolver`, and `DTDHandler` interfaces. Rather than having to define separate classes for each type of handler, this class allows you to extend it and override only those methods you are interested in. By default, all of the methods are implemented to do nothing. This is like the `java.awt.event.MouseAdapter` class that implements the `MouseListener` interface to simplify mouse-handling code.

The last two classes allow SAX 1.0 parsers to generate SAX 2.0 events and vice-versa. For the former it uses the `org.xml.sax.helpers.ParserAdapter` class, which uses each handler interface since it has to adapt SAX1 events for SAX2. For the latter you would use the `org.xml.sax.XMLReaderAdapter`.

The Exceptions

The exceptions in the SAX package are as follows:

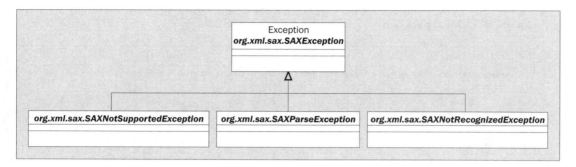

As you can see, each specialized exception extends the `org.xml.sax.SAXException` class. The `SAXNotSupportedException` is thrown when the `XMLReader` class recognizes a feature or property but cannot perform the appropriate operation. We will look at the `XMLReader` class in depth later in this chapter.

The `SAXParseException` is thrown when a general parsing error occurs, such as an invalid element.

The `SAXNotRecognizedException` is thrown when the `XMLReader` being used does not recognize the feature or property being set. Features and properties are used to customize the behavior of your SAX parser, though many are parser-specific and not supported by all implementers. We will look at features and properties later in the chapter.

Differences between SAX 1.0 and SAX 2.0

This section will explain how to use SAX with Java. While SAX 2.0 will be the focus of this section, care will be taken to explain the SAX 1.0 equivalents for those who must use a SAX 1.0 parser. Rather than spend time explaining all of the differences between SAX 1.0 and SAX 2.0, I will explain the important ones, pointing out differences in the examples to come; the remainder are available in Appendix B.

Many of the differences between the versions are due to the support for namespaces in SAX 2.0. The original XML 1.0 recommendation did not specify namespaces, and thus support in SAX 1.0 does not exist (XML namespaces have since been added to the XML 1.0 Recommendation). For this reason, many of the interface and class names have been changed while the methods have remained quite similar, so that those still using SAX 1.0 will not have any trouble if they decide to use SAX 2.0. Another addition is support for skipped entities, but we will discuss this later.

SAX Parsers

SAX 1.0 parsers implement the `org.xml.sax.Parser` interface:

```
package org.xml.sax;

import java.io.IOException;

public interface Parser {
    public void parse(InputSource is) throws SAXException, IOException;
    public void parse(String systemId) throws SAXException, IOException;

    public void setDocumentHandler(DocumentHandler handler);
    public void setDTDHandler(DTDHandler handler);
    public void setEntityResolver(EntityResolver resolver);
    public void setErrorHandler(ErrorHandler handler);
    public void setLocale(java.util.Locale locale) throws SAXException;
}
```

SAX 2.0 parsers implement the `org.xml.sax.XMLReader` interface:

```
package org.xml.sax;

import java.io.IOException;

public interface XMLReader {
    public ContentHandler getContentHandler();
    public DTDHandler getDTDHandler();
    public EntityResolver getEntityResolver();
    public ErrorHandler getErrorHandler();
    public boolean getFeature(String name)
        throws SAXNotRecognizedException, SAXNotSupportedException;
    public Object getProperty(String name)
        throws SAXNotRecognizedException, SAXNotSupportedException;

    public void parse(InputSource is) throws SAXException, IOException;
    public void parse(String systemId) throws SAXException, IOException;

    public void setContentHandler(ContentHandler handler);
    public void setDTDHandler(DTDHandler handler);
    public void setEntityResolver(EntityResolver resolver);
    public void setErrorHandler(ErrorHandler handler);
    public void setFeature(String name, boolean value)
        throws SAXNotRecognizedException, SAXNotSupportedException;
    public void setProperty(String name, Object value)
        throws SAXNotRecognizedException, SAXNotSupportedException;
}
```

The difference between the two interfaces isn't that obvious, but that is not to say that the conversion from SAX 1.0 to SAX 2.0 is simple. Obviously, the method signatures are such that developers need to take namespaces into account in SAX 2.0. Also, the interfaces are named quite differently and they are not directly compatible with each other.

SAX 2.0 includes getter methods for the various handler types unlike SAX 1.0 where once the handler was set there was no way to determine what object was being used to handle a particular set of events. SAX 2.0 also introduces the notion of properties and features allowing developers to customize the behavior of the parser. We will look at some of these properties and features later in the chapter.

The `parse()` methods have largely remained the same in SAX 2.0. The first `parse()` method accepts an `org.xml.sax.InputSource` object, which is really nothing more than a wrapper around the classes available in the `java.io` package. It acts as a helper to the parser more than providing anything useful for the developer. If you wish to have the parser read a file called `foobar.xml`, you could use the following bit of code:

```
import org.xml.sax.InputSource;
import java.io.FileReader;
...

InputSource is  = new InputSource(new FileReader("foobar.xml"));
parser.parse(is);
...
```

The second `parser()` method takes a URI as a parameter. So, if your document is located on a web site at http://foobarbaz.com, you would instantiate a parser as below:

```
parser.parse("http://foobarbaz.com/index.html");
```

The `InputSource` class also provides a constructor that accepts URIs as arguments, but that is just an extra step that can be skipped by using the methods provided by the `Parser` and `XMLReader` interfaces.

In the interest of clarity, I will use the term "parser" to refer to both SAX 1.0 and SAX 2.0 parsers. If the need arises to demonstrate differences between the two, then the appropriate term will be used.

Event Handlers

In addition to the parser, the interfaces of the handlers for the callbacks generated by the parser have also changed due to the introduction of namespaces. In SAX 1.0, handlers for parser events implement the `DocumentHandler` interface. The SAX 2.0 equivalent is the `ContentHandler` interface. With the exception of the addition of two methods in the `ContentHandler` interface, you will notice the method names are the same between SAX 1.0 and SAX 2.0. However, notice that explicit use of namespaces appears in the argument lists of the `ContentHandler` methods.

```
package org.xml.sax;

// the SAX 1.0 handler interface
public interface DocumentHandler {
  public void setDocumentLocator (Locator locator);

  public void startDocument () throws SAXException;
  public void endDocument () throws SAXException;

  public void startElement (String name, AttributeList atts)
     throws SAXException;
  public void endElement (String name) throws SAXException;
```

```
   public void characters (char ch[], int start, int length)
      throws SAXException;
   public void ignorableWhitespace (char ch[], int start, int length)
      throws SAXException;
   public void processingInstruction (String target, String data)
      throws SAXException;
}
```

While the following listing is the SAX 2.0 interface:

```
package org.xml.sax;

// the SAX 2.0 handler interface
public interface ContentHandler {

   public void setDocumentLocator (Locator locator);

   public void startDocument () throws SAXException;
   public void endDocument()  throws SAXException;

   public void startPrefixMapping (String prefix, String uri)
      throws SAXException;

   public void endPrefixMapping (String prefix) throws SAXException;

   public void startElement (String namespaceURI, String localName,
                             String qName, Attributes atts)
      throws SAXException;
   public void endElement (String namespaceURI, String localName,
                           String qName)
      throws SAXException;

   public void characters (char ch[], int start, int length)
      throws SAXException;

   public void ignorableWhitespace (char ch[], int start, int length)
      throws SAXException;

   public void processingInstruction (String target, String data)
      throws SAXException;

   public void skippedEntity (String name)
      throws SAXException;
}
```

As mentioned before, a good analogy between handlers and parsers is the relationship between AWT GUI components and event listeners. If you think of the parser as a Button and the handler as an `ActionListener`, it may help to see how the SAX classes interact.

> *One important difference between listeners in the AWT and SAX handlers is that AWT components allow multiple listeners to be registered with them. In SAX, only one class can be registered as a handler for a given instance of a parser, although the `org.xml.sax.XMLFilter` class can simulate multiple handlers.*

When a `java.awt.Button` is created, it registers classes that implement the `java.awt.ActionListener` interface. As important events occur in a Button's lifetime (such as the button being pushed), the Button calls the `actionPerformed()` method of the registered listener. For a SAX parser, as important events occur (such as the beginning of the document) the appropriate method is called on the registered handler (in this case the `startDocument()` method).

DTDHandler

An interesting interface you may find useful is the `org.xml.sax.DTDHandler`. It is a bit of a misnomer because it doesn't report all the events related to a DTD, only NOTATION, ENTITY, and ENTITIES. As we will see, the SAX2-ext package has a much richer set of interfaces for dealing with DTDs.

```
package org.xml.sax;

public interface DTDHandler
{
  public void notationDecl(String name, publicId, String systemId);
  public void unparsedEntityDecl(String name, String publicId,
    String systemId, String notationName);
}
```

The first method handles NOTATION-type declarations. As you learned in the previous chapter, a NOTATION specifies how to handle a piece of non-XML data. For instance, in the example below:

```
<!NOTATION jpeg SYSTEM "jpeg viewer">
```

states that all elements notated with "jpeg" should be viewed with "jpeg viewer". The NOTATION declaration is coupled with the notion of unparsed entities, since NOTATIONs are used to describe such elements. An unparsed entity (such as non-XML data) is declared as follows:

```
<!ENTITY logo SYSTEM
      "http://www.wrox.com/mypicture.jpeg" NDATA jpeg>
```

This specifies that the `<http://www.wrox.com/mypicture.jpeg>` element can be handled with the jpeg notation.

EntityResolver

In the case where a developer is interested in external entities, the `org.xml.sax.EntityResolver` interface is what they can use to resolve them. It contains one method: `resolveEntity()`, which takes two arguments: the public identifier (set to `null` if none is available) and the system identifier. Note that the top-level document entity does not fire this event, which includes any entities referenced within the DTD.

Using the SAX 2.0 API with SAX 1.0 Parsers

If you are forced to use a SAX 1.0 parser but still wish to use SAX 2.0, have no fear. The developers of the SAX 2.0 API, in their infinite wisdom, provided a helper class for those who must use a SAX 1.0-compliant parser. The `org.xml.sax.helpers.ParserAdapter` class takes a `Parser` and makes it act like an `XMLReader`, including support for namespaces.

The `ParserAdapter` class is essentially an implementation of the `XMLReader` class, so I will not list the API here. The important difference is the constructor, which takes as an argument an implementation of the `org.xml.sax.Parser` class. All of the other methods of this class implement the XMLReader interface to provide the feel of using a SAX 2.0 parser. A limitation to consider is that skipped entities are not reported, due to SAX 1.0 not reporting such information, but all namespace events are reported.

The opposite is also possible whereby a SAX 2.0 parser can be made to behave as a SAX 1.0 parser. The org.xml.sax.helpers.XMLReaderAdapter class was created just for that reason. It simply does the opposite of the org.sax.helpers.ParserAdapter class, in which SAX 1.0-specific events are fired from a SAX 2.0-compliant parser.

SAX2 Properties and Features

When SAX2 introduced the XMLReader interface, it also introduced two new methods: setProperty() and setFeature(). This allowed users of the parser to customize the behavior of their parsers. Although different vendors will add their own properties and features, there are a few that a parser is required to recognize but not necessarily implement. If you attempt to set an unknown property or features, a SAXNotSupportedException is thrown.

Features can be turned on and off, thus only a Boolean value needs to be supplied. Properties differ in that classes may be used to implement a property, therefore an object is passed as an argument.

Features

Below are the core features and properties:

❑ http://xml.org/sax/features/validation – Turns validation on or off. If true, a DTD/schema must be present

❑ http://xml.org/sax/features/external-general-entities – Includes external general entities in parsing if set to true, otherwise it does not include them

❑ http://xml.org/sax/features/external-parameter-entities – Includes external parameter entities in parsing if set to true, otherwise does not include them

❑ http://xml.org/sax/features/namespaces – If set to true, support for namespaces is activated and the namespace-specific portions of SAX are utilized, for example the beginPrefixMapping() event is fired

❑ http://xml.org/sax/features/namespace-prefixes – Reports the prefixed names and attributes for namespace declarations

❑ http://xml.org/sax/features/string-interning – If set to true, all prefixes, element and attribute names, and namespace URIs are internalized using the java.lang.String.intern() method. This is used to take advantage of the String class's pooling behavior for performance reasons.

Properties

Here are the properties:

❑ http://xml.org/sax/properties/dom-node – If SAX is being used as a DOM iterator, then the applicable DOM node is returned. (You will learn more about the DOM in the next chapter.)

❑ http://xml.org/sax/properties/xml-string – This is the literal String that was the source for the current event (this property is read-only).

SAX Parsers

This section introduces you to the most common APIs available for using SAX parsers.

Xerces

The Xerces project was started by the Apache Foundation to create an XML API for both DOM and SAX. If you look at the API, you will notice it contains a number of classes and packages. However, the only classes we need to be concerned with, in order to use SAX, can be found in the `org.apache.xerces.parsers` package. The remaining classes are mostly there for DOM support.

Xerces really provides nothing more than an implementation of the SAX APIs. In the latest version as of this writing – 1.3.0 – both SAX 1.0 and SAX 2.0 interfaces are supported.

Obtaining a SAX Parser with Xerces

The code below shows an example of the use of Xerces to get a SAX parser.

```
import org.apache.xerces.parsers.SAXParser;
import org.xml.sax.Parser;
import org.xml.sax.XMLReader;

public class XercesExample {
  public static void main(String[] args) {

    // obtain a SAX 1.0 parser
    Parser parser = new SAXParser();

    // obtain a SAX 2.0 parser
    XMLReader reader = new SAXParser();
  }
}
```

This code in and of itself does not do anything except create a new `SAXParser` instance. You may have noticed something interesting about the `SAXParser` class: we used the same constructor to create a SAX 2.0 parser as we did to create a SAX 1.0 parser. This is because the `SAXParser` class implements both the `Parser` and `XMLReader` interfaces defined in SAX 1.0 and SAX 2.0, respectively.

Crimson

Crimson, which is based on the Project X parser from Sun, provides a SAX parser implementation and is currently the default parser used in JAXP (discussed later). Like Xerces, it simply implements the `XMLReader` interface, providing an implementation of the SAX APIs.

Obtaining a Parser with Crimson

Shown below is the code necessary to instantiate the Crimson implementation of SAX:

```
import org.apache.crimson.parser.XMLReaderImpl;
import org.xml.sax.XMLReader;

public class TestCrimson {
  public static void main(String[] args) throws Exception {
    XMLReader reader = new XMLReaderImpl();
  }
}
```

As you can see, much like Xerces, Crimson simply provides an implementation of SAX with no bells and whistles attached.

Ælfred

Yet another SAX parser is the Ælfred parser, written by the foremost figure in SAX, David Megginson, prior to the SAX API being conceived. As such, it has its own non-SAX event-driven API hinting at the beginnings of what later became SAX. Once SAX1 was finalized, Ælfred was rewritten to include support for SAX 1.0. Since Ælfred's proprietary API does not offer anything beyond what SAX is capable of, it will not be discussed in this chapter.

What is interesting about Ælfred is its efficiency: it is quite fast and has a very small memory footprint. Unlike the others, which consume a fair amount of memory resources, Ælfred makes an ideal candidate for use within browser applets. Since using an applet incorporating a SAX parser requires the download of the parser's .jar file, you want that file to be as small as possible – XML is a means to an end here, not the central feature behind the application.

Ælfred, despite being a great quick-and-dirty parser, suffers from some shortcomings:

❏   It is not fully XML-conformant

❏   Does not provide validation

❏   Does not natively support SAX 2.0

An example of Ælfred not being XML-conformant is in the case of attributes. In XML, attributes for an element have to be unique for a document to be well-formed, meaning no two attributes can have the same name. Ælfred does not check for this condition and is thus considered non-compliant as all parsers, validating or not, must report errors related to the well-formedness of a document (see http://www.w3.org/TR/2000/REC-xml-20001006#proc-types).

Obtaining a Parser with Ælfred

The code below demonstrates how to instantiate a parser using Ælfred. We first instantiate the natively-supported SAX 1.0 parser and then wrap Ælfred using the org.xml.sax.helpers.ParserAdapter class to generate SAX 2.0 events.

```
import com.microstar.xml.SAXDriver;
import org.xml.sax.XMLReader;
import org.xml.sax.Parser;
import org.xml.sax.helpers.ParserAdapter;
```

```
public class AelfredExample {
  public static void main(String[] args) throws Exception {

    // instantiate a SAX 1.0 parser
    Parser SAX 1.0Parser = new SAXDriver();

    // instantiate a SAX 2.0 parser
    XMLReader SAX 2.0Parser = new ParserAdapter(new SAXDriver());
  }
}
```

JAXP

JAXP, like Xerces, is an API that supports using both DOM and SAX APIs. However, rather than provide a pure implementation of the SAX API, JAXP adds one extra layer of abstraction. Instead of accessing the SAX APIs directly, JAXP offers a framework independent of the chosen parser.

JAXP uses the **factory** design pattern, which is used throughout the standard Java API. A factory is a class used to create related objects, just as an automobile factory is tooled to create parts related to a car. In the case of JAXP, the factory pattern in used to create objects related to parsing XML.

In JAXP the SAXParserFactory class provides the newSAXParser(), which creates a new instance of a SAX2 parser. In addition, the factory class provides methods to set whether the parser is validating and namespace aware, and also methods to discover these properties.

In order to change the parser that is returned by the factory class you would simply change the factory that produces the parser. The parser factory is set by the javax.xml.parsers.SAXParserFactory system variable, which can be set at run time.

The object returned by the newSAXParser() method is of type SAXParser, which defines methods used for parsing. The class merely encapsulates any SAX parser and abstracts parsers from the developer so that any JAXP-compliant parser can be substituted according to business or operational needs.

Once you have obtained a parser and passed it the relevant file, and a "listener" to report events to has been set up, you can set the parser to parse() and the content handler will take over. As each event occurs, the code written into the relevant callback will be executed so that the document will be dealt with appropriately. This should work whether you are extracting data from an XML document, creating a new subdocument, or whatever else you are trying to achieve.

The developers of JAXP also provide a default implementation of this class. In order to use it, you must call the static method newInstance() of the class to obtain the default instance.

Finally, the SAXParser class encapsulates the org.xml.sax.XMLReader interface rather than implements it. At first glance it seems natural to want to implement the interface, but if you consider the previous SAX version, it is not possible to do this and maintain backward compatibility. JAXP is provided to abstract the manner in which parsing is performed, by providing its own interface.

Below is an outline of the `javax.xml.parsers.SAXParserFactory` class to detail the methods of the class, including the exceptions thrown.

```
public abstract class SAXParserFactory {

   protected SAXParserFactory ();

   public static SAXParserFactory newInstance();

   // the factory method
   public abstract SAXParser newSAXParser()
      throws ParserConfigurationException, SAXException;

   public void setNamespaceAware(boolean awareness);
   public void setValidating(boolean validating);
   public boolean isNamespaceAware();
   public boolean isValidating();

   public abstract void setFeature(String name, boolean value)
      throws ParserConfigurationException,
             SAXNotRecognizedException,
             SAXNotSupportedException;

   public abstract boolean getFeature(String name)
      throws ParserConfigurationException,
             SAXNotRecognizedException,
             SAXNotSupportedException;
}
```

The other methods will be discussed later, but the two most important methods here are `newInstance()` and `newSAXParser()`. The `newInstance()`, as mentioned earlier, returns an instance of a `javax.xml.parsers.SAXParserFactory` class. The class only knows how to create one type of SAX parser, as well as set properties for that parser.

> *It should be noted that there are compatibility issues with JAXP and JDK v1.2.2, in particular a "nonfatal internal JIT" error. Using JDK1.3 or upgrading to the latest version of HotSpot can avoid this.*

The `newSAXParser()` method returns an instance of a class extending the `javax.xml.parsers.SAXParser` abstract base class. Again, like the `SAXParserFactory` class, there are a number of methods available for enabling validation and namespace support, but these will be discussed later.

The important methods are the many overloaded `parse()` methods made available. There are a total of ten: five originating from the SAX 1.0 API and five that support the SAX 2.0 API. The first argument in each is either of type `java.io.File`, `org.xml.sax.InputSource`, `java.lang.String`, or `java.io.InputStream`. The second argument differs only in either being the SAX 1.0 `org.xml.sax.HandlerBase` or the SAX 2.0 `org.xml.sax.helpers.DefaultHandler` (there are two methods that take three arguments, the third being a system ID used when the `InputStream` is a relative URL). While JAXP1.1 was released to provide support for SAX 2.0, SAX 1.0 methods were left in order to provide backward compatibility, which is why methods are duplicated with the exception of the second argument.

Obtaining a SAX Parser Using JAXP

The following shows how we would obtain a SAX parser using JAXP. We will be compiling this code later on for our example, and if you wish to look at it, it is contained in the code download /ProJavaXML/Chapter02/JAXPExample/:

```
import java.io.FileReader;
import javax.xml.parsers.SAXParser;
import javax.xml.parsers.SAXParserFactory;
import org.xml.sax.InputSource;
import org.xml.sax.helpers.DefaultHandler;

public class JAXPExample {
  public static void main(String[] args) throws Exception{
    SAXParserFactory factory = SAXParserFactory.newInstance();
    SAXParser parser = factory.newSAXParser();
    InputSource is = new InputSource(new FileReader("SAX2.0.xml"));
    parser.parse(is, new DefaultHandler());
  }
}
```

As you can see the code is quite simple. More interesting is the level of abstraction that JAXP affords us: did we allocate a SAX 1.0 parser or a SAX 2.0 parser? By default, JAXP 1.1 will instantiate a SAX 2.0-compliant parser, however nothing precludes the API from creating a SAX 1.0 parser instance instead, as the JAXP API supports SAX 1.0 as well. This will depend entirely on the parser factory assigned.

After the parser is instantiated, we create an InputSource instance. For this example, we provide the file SAX2.0.xml, which contains the XML document shown in the section below, passing it to the parse() method of the javax.xml.parsers.SAXParser class. The second argument is the content or document handler to use for this document.

In this example we have created an org.xml.sax.helpers.DefaultHandler. This class is like the java.awt.event.MouseAdapter class: it provides do-nothing methods for all of the methods of the xxxHandler interfaces.

In the *Event Handlers* section, we discussed the ContentHandler interface. Other types of handlers include DTDHandler, EntityResolver, and ErrorHandler. The use of these handlers will be covered later, but since the DefaultHandler class implements all of these interfaces in one class with empty implementations, we can extend the DefaultHandler class and override the methods you care about.

That can save development time considerably and in the case of JAXP, it is made a requirement.

To run the example, make sure that the jaxp.jar and crimson.jar files are in your classpath and compile the source code above. Make sure the source code above is saved under the file name JAXPExample.java, and compile as follows:

```
javac JAXPExample.java
```

We also need an XML file for the example to parse. Here is SAX2.0.xml, which our JAXPExample class will be parsing:

```
<?xml version="1.0"?>
<article date="02-Dec-2000">
  <headline>SAX 2.0 Released</headline>
  <author>F. Bar</author>
  <body>SAX 2.0 has been released into the public domain</body>
</article>
```

Copy this code into a file and save it as SAX2.0.xml (if using Windows Notepad, be careful to save it under the **All Files** option and not as **Text Documents (*.txt)**), and into the same directory as JAXPExample.class. This code is also available in the code download for this book, in which case you should copy the /JAXPExample/ folder into wherever you are running the code from. For our purposes, in this chapter, this will be /ProJavaXML/Chapter02/. The example can now be run with the following command line:

```
java JAXPExample
```

However, nothing visible will happen unless the XML file being parsed is badly formed, in which case an exception will be thrown. You may wish to experiment with this – try altering the end element in SAX2.0.xml from </article> to <article>. Now run the example again.

In the screenshot below, it is possible to see both the original successful command (which should operate invisibly) and also the errors thrown by our altered XML document:

A great characteristic of the JAXP framework is its flexibility. If we desire to use a parser other than the default, we set the javax.xml.parsers.SAXParserFactory system property to set the fully-qualified class name of a concrete extension of that class. Below, we set the parser for JAXP to use as Xerces, just by setting this property as shown (make sure, however, that xerces.jar is in your classpath):

```
java
-Djavax.xml.parsers.SAXParserFactory=org.apache.xerces.jaxp.SAXParserFactoryImpl
JAXPExample
```

Correct the end element in SAX2.0.xml and run the above command line. It will parse the XML file successfully. Alter the XML file again and re-run the command, and you will see that this time a series of Xerces exceptions are displayed as opposed to the previous Crimson exceptions.

The Xerces API provides classes that support JAXP (in the org.apache.xerces.jaxp package) so we are able to easily switch between the default JAXP parser and Xerces. If you are using a different parser, check with your vendor to see if they offer JAXP support. In the next section you will see how to write your own JAXP-compliant classes for the Ælfred parser, which should give you some insight into how to write these classes for your favorite parser.

Writing JAXP-Compliant Classes

As promised, this section is devoted to writing a JAXP wrapper for an otherwise non-JAXP-compliant parser. In this example, we will use the Ælfred parser but the techniques shown should not differ much for any other parser. We intend to achieve the following goals in this section:

❏   Wrap our implementation into a javax.xml.parsers.SAXParser class

❏   Write a javax.xml.parsers.SAXParserFactory class to provide instances of our parser

The SAXParser Class

The first step is to wrap Ælfred into a SAXParser class. There are seven methods that we need to implement:

❏   The constructor – The base class specifies this as being protected; our implementation must make this constructor public so that it may be instantiated

❏   getParser() – Returns a SAX org.xml.sax.Parser object

❏   getProperty() – Returns the value of the specified property; this is available only for SAX 2.0 parsers

❏   getXMLReader() – Returns a SAX org.xml.sax.XMLReader object

❏   isNamespaceAware() – Declares if the underlying SAX implementation is namespace-aware

❏   isValidating() – Declares if the underlying SAX implementation validates the XML document

❏   setProperty() – Sets a property to the specified value; this is only available in SAX 2.0.

As you can see, there are a few methods that are only available to SAX 2.0 parsers. Since Ælfred is a SAX 1.0 parser by nature, we obviously cannot use these features.

We will proceed step by step, starting with the constructor:

```
package wrox.sax;

import org.xml.sax.helpers.ParserAdapter;
import javax.xml.parsers.SAXParser;
```

```
import org.xml.sax.SAXException;
import org.xml.sax.Parser;
import org.xml.sax.XMLReader;
import org.xml.sax.SAXNotRecognizedException;
import org.xml.sax.SAXNotSupportedException;

import com.microstar.xml.SAXDriver;

public class AelfredSAXParser extends SAXParser {
  private ParserAdapter parserAdapter = null;
  private Parser parser            = null;
  private boolean namespaceAware   = false;
  private boolean validating       = false;

  public AelfredSAXParser() {
    parser = new SAXDriver();
    parserAdapter = new ParserAdapter(parser);
  }
```

Ælfred is not a SAX 2.0-compliant parser, so our first task is to make it one. This is made easy by the inclusion of the `org.xml.sax.helpers.ParserAdapter` class, which takes a SAX 1.0 parser and enables it to fire SAX 2.0 events, as well as provide validation and namespace-specific information.

The next method is the `getParser()` method. It simply returns the parser we instantiated, throwing a `SAXException` if an error occurs:

```
public Parser getParser() throws SAXException {
  return parser;
}
```

This is simple enough and also explains why we keep a reference to the parser once we have allocated it for use by the `ParserAdapter`. While we want to create a SAX 2.0-compliant parser, it doesn't make sense to ignore all SAX 1.0 functionality.

The `getXMLReader()` method is just the SAX 2.0 version of the `getParser()` method:

```
public XMLReader getXMLReader() throws SAXException {
  return parserAdapter;
}
```

This works because the `org.xml.sax.helpers.ParserAdapter` class implements the `org.xml.sax.XMLReader` interface.

The `isNamespaceAware()` and `isValidating()` methods are also easy to implement. SAX 2.0 defines features and properties that enable or disable certain functionalities, such as namespace resolution and validity checking. Since SAX 1.0 did not provide such options, we do not need them and so set them to `false`:

```
public boolean isNamespaceAware() {
  return false;
}

public boolean isValidating() {
  return false;
}
```

As with namespaces and validating parsers, properties are also a feature exclusive to SAX 2.0. No SAX 1.0 properties are defined in the API. However, in case such properties are made available in a new release of Ælfred, we will select and set the properties using the `ParserAdapter` class. A `SAXNotRecognizedException` will be thrown if an unknown property is set or its value requested. A `SAXNotSupported` exception will be thrown if a well-known property is set that is not supported by the parser implementation. These exceptions will both be thrown by this implementation for every call.

```java
public Object getProperty(String name)
    throws SAXNotRecognizedException, SAXNotSupportedException
{
  return parserAdapter.getProperty(name);
}

public void setProperty(String name, Object value)
    throws SAXNotRecognizedException, SAXNotSupportedException
{
  parserAdapter.setProperty(name, value);
}
}
```

And that is it! Now lets go on to implement the `SAXParserFactory`.

SAXParserFactory

Like the `SAXParser` class, this is fairly simple to implement and there are fewer methods that we have to override to create a concrete extension of the `SAXParserFactory` class:

- ❑   `getFeature()` – Returns the state of the requested feature (SAX 2.0)

- ❑   `setFeature()` – Sets the state of a parser feature (SAX 2.0)

- ❑   `newSAXParser()` – Returns an instance of the `SAXParser` supported by this factory

Notice that two of the three methods are specific to SAX 2.0 parsers. The `getFeature()` and `setFeature()` methods have no use in SAX 1.0 parsers, so they will only throw a `SAXNotRecognizedException` when accessed.

```java
package wrox.sax;

import javax.xml.parsers.ParserConfigurationException;
import javax.xml.parsers.SAXParser;
import javax.xml.parsers.SAXParserFactory;

import org.xml.sax.SAXNotRecognizedException;
import org.xml.sax.SAXNotSupportedException;

public class AelfredSAXParserFactory extends SAXParserFactory {
  public AelfredSAXParserFactory() {
    super();
  }

  public boolean getFeature(String name)
      throws ParserConfigurationException,
```

```
                      SAXNotRecognizedException,
                      SAXNotSupportedException
    {
       throw new SAXNotRecognizedException("Feature '" +
                                           name + "' not recognized");
    }

    public void setFeature(String name, boolean value)
        throws ParserConfigurationException,
               SAXNotRecognizedException,
               SAXNotSupportedException
    {
          throw new SAXNotRecognizedException("Feature '" + name +
                                              "' not recognized");
    }
```

The newSAXParser() method is even easier to implement. All we need to do is allocate a new instance of the AelfredSAXParser class and return it:

```
    public SAXParser newSAXParser() {
       return new AelfredSAXParser();
    }
}
```

Now we take our original JAXP example code and make a slight modification:

```
import java.io.FileReader;
import javax.xml.parsers.SAXParser;
import javax.xml.parsers.SAXParserFactory;
import org.xml.sax.InputSource;
import org.xml.sax.helpers.DefaultHandler;

import wrox.sax.SAXParserHandler;

public class AelfredExample {
   public static void main(String[] args) throws Exception{
      SAXParserFactory factory = SAXParserFactory.newInstance();
      SAXParser parser = factory.newSAXParser();
      InputSource is = new InputSource(new FileReader("SAX2.0.xml"));
      parser.parse(is, new DefaultHandler());
   }
}
```

Assuming that the classpath contains jaxp.jar, crimson.jar and aelfred.jar, use the following command line:

```
java -Djavax.xml.parsers.SAXParserFactory=wrox.sax.AelfredSAXParserFactory
AelfredExample
```

The following output will be generated.

```
startDocument
startElement: TestPage
Namespace URI:
characters:
characters:

characters:
startElement: Header
Namespace URI:
characters: My Header
endElement: Header
characters:
characters:

characters:
startElement: Body
Namespace URI:
characters: The body of the text
endElement: Body
characters:
characters:

endElement: TestPage
endDocument
```

And that is all there is to it. If you are having trouble, the code for this example is including the download for this chapter, under /ProJavaXML/Chapter02/AelfredExample/. It boils down to only needing to wrap certain calls around the JAXP framework in order to get your favorite parser to be available through the JAXP API. If you wish to try to implement JAXP for another parser, here are a few parsers to try:

❑ XP by James Clark. It is another SAX 1.0 driver that can be made to work with SAX 2.0. It can be found at http://www.jclark.com/xml/xp.

❑ Ælfred2 is a project that attempts to improve on the original implementation by providing SAX 2.0-compatibility. It is an ongoing project that can be found at http://xmlconf.sourceforge.net/?selected=java.

❑ Oracle has a Java XML toolkit that contains a SAX 2.0-compliant parser (the current beta version). You will need to sign up for a free membership, but you can find the information at http://technet.oracle.com/tech/xml/parser_java2/.

Using SAX

Now, let's actually do something with the SAX parser. For the rest of this section, we will use the following XML document in our examples; this file is the SAX2.0.xml we used earlier.

```
<?xml version="1.0"?>
<article date="02-Dec-2000">
  <headline>SAX 2.0 Released</headline>
  <author>F. Bar</author>
  <body>SAX 2.0 has been released into the public domain</body>
</article>
```

We will also continue to use the JAXP API for parsing this document. Since we have seen above how to instantiate and run a parser, let's look at writing a handler. In each case the handler that we will be developing does not do anything greatly exciting but it will illustrate how each event is captured and responded to. When you come to implementing your own handlers you will be able to substitute relevant code to deal with the content of the document being parsed accordingly.

Writing the DefaultHandler

As mentioned in the JAXP section, the JAXP API's `parse()` method accepts a `DefaultHandler` for parser events, unlike a raw SAX parser that allows the user to set different classes for handlers. As mentioned before, the `org.xml.sax.helpers.DefaultHandler` class is simply an implementation of all of the SAX handlers, including `ErrorHandler`. This actually makes development a lot easier, since we don't need to write empty method implementations for those we do not need.

The code for this section is also supplied in the code download under `/ProJavaXML/Chapter02/DefaultHandler/`.

Let's start off with a simple handler:

```java
package wrox.sax;

import javax.xml.parsers.SAXParser;
import javax.xml.parsers.SAXParserFactory;
import org.xml.sax.Attributes;
import org.xml.sax.Locator;
import org.xml.sax.SAXException;
import org.xml.sax.SAXParseException;
import org.xml.sax.SAXNotRecognizedException;
import org.xml.sax.SAXNotSupportedException;
import org.xml.sax.helpers.DefaultHandler;

// Create a SAX handler to parse through a document
public class SAXParserHandler extends DefaultHandler {
  private Locator locator = null;

  public void startDocument() throws SAXException {
    System.out.println("startDocument");
  }

  public void endDocument() throws SAXException {
    System.out.println("endDocument");
  }

  public void setDocumentLocator(Locator locator) {
    this.locator = locator;
  }

  public void characters(char[] ch, int start, int length)
      throws SAXException
  {
    String charString = new String(ch, start, length);
    System.out.println("characters: " + charString);
  }
```

```java
    public void startElement(String namespaceURI, String localName,
                             String qName, Attributes atts)
      throws SAXException
{
  System.out.println("startElement: " + qName);

  // list out the attributes and their values
  for (int i = 0 ; i < atts.getLength() ; i++) {
    System.out.println("Attribute: " + atts.getLocalName(i));
    System.out.println("\tValue: " + atts.getValue(i));
  }
}

    public void endElement(String namespaceURI, String localName,
                           String qName)
      throws SAXException
{
  System.out.println("endElement: " + qName);
}

    public void ignorableWhitespace (char[] ch, int start, int length)
      throws SAXException
{
  System.out.println(length + " characters of ignorable whitespace");
}

    public void startPrefixMapping(String prefix, String uri)
      throws SAXException
{
  System.out.println("Begin namespace prefix: " + prefix);
}

    public void endPrefixMapping(String prefix) throws SAXException {
  System.out.println("End namespace prefix: " + prefix);
}

    public void processingInstruction(String instruction, String data)
      throws SAXException
{
  System.out.println("Instruction: " + instruction + ", data: " + data);
}

    public void skippedEntity(String name) throws SAXException {
  System.out.println("Skipped entity: " + name);
  }
}
```

Let's go through the methods. The first two, startDocument() and endDocument() are fired at the beginning and the end of the document, respectively. The startElement() event is fired when an open tag is encountered.

The first two arguments, namespaceURI and localName, are used only if the parser being used is namespace-aware. We will discuss namespaces later. The qName argument is the XML 1.0-compliant qualified name of the element. It is available optionally if the parser is namespace-aware.

According to the SAX 2.0.0 API, whether or not any of these values appears depends on the values of two properties. If the `http://xml.org/sax/features/namespaces` *property is* `true`, *the* `namespaceURI` *and* `localName` *arguments are required to be populated, even if no namespace is present. (This is because the Namespaces Specification requires that all elements be part of the "default" namespace if one isn't declared.) If the property is* `false`, *these arguments are optional. If the* `http://xml.org/sax/features/namespace-prefixes` *property is* `true`, *then the* `qName` *argument is required, otherwise it is optional.*

In both Crimson and Xerces, qName always contains the name of the element while the `namespaceURI` and `localName` arguments are populated only if the parser is set to be namespace-aware.

The last argument, `atts`, contains the attributes associated with this element. The `org.xml.sax.Attributes` interface provides methods for accessing attribute values by name or index. SAX 2.0.0 does not define the order in which attributes are listed, so do not assume that attributes will appear indexed by the order of their appearance in the document. If you are writing an application for a known XML document, it is best to reference attributes by name.

With every `startElement()` call in a valid XML document, there is a matching `endElement()` call. The arguments are the same for the `endElement()` method as they are for the `startElement()` call with the exception of the `Attributes` argument being omitted from the `endElement()` method.

While our sample XML document doesn't demonstrate this, you may be wondering about empty elements, such as the XHTML <br/> tag. This element is essentially both the open and close tag, therefore both the `startElement()` and `endElement()` events are fired for this tag with all attributes (if any) associated with it appearing in the `Attributes` argument of the `startElement()` method.

The `characters()` event is fired whenever character data is encountered, including CDATA sections. The arguments of the method provide a character array, the start of the array to be referenced, and the length of the data.

```
public void characters(char[] ch, int start, int length)
   throws SAXException
{
  String charString = new String(ch, start, length);
  System.out.println("characters: " + charString);
}
```

The parameters passed to the method are a character array, and start and length arguments. The characters can be extracted as a string that begins at the `start` position in the array and continues for `length` characters. It should be noted that the character array may contain extraneous characters and so the relevant characters should always be extracted from the array passed to this callback method. Also, the `character()` method may not include all of the data within the tag in the first call; it is quite possible that a large amount of data may be split into a number of calls. How this is done is implementation-dependent.

One interesting method is the `ignorableWhitespace()` method, which according to the SAX 2.0.0 documentation, must be used to report any irrelevant whitespace within an element. Like the characters method it also passes an array together with `start` and `length` arguments to determine the characters in the array that represent ignorable whitespace. The other events will be discussed in the coming sections.

The following code is the driver for our handler:

```
import javax.xml.parsers.SAXParser;
import javax.xml.parsers.SAXParserFactory;

import wrox.sax.SAXParserHandler;

public class SAXMain {
  public static void main(String[] args) throws Exception {
    SAXParserFactory factory = SAXParserFactory.newInstance();
    SAXParser parser = factory.newSAXParser();
    parser.parse("SAX2.0.xml", new SAXParserHandler());
  }
}
```

Now all we have to do is:

❑ Set the classpath

❑ Compile the code

❑ Run the example

So firstly, make sure `jaxp.jar`, `crimson.jar`, and your current directory are in your classpath. Enter the following on your command line, in the directory you intend to run the code from:

```
set classpath=.;C:\jaxp-1.1\jaxp.jar;C:\jaxp-1.1\crimson.jar
```

Obviously the above will differ according to the location of the relevant JAR files on your system.

Next, we compile the code. Create the package for `SAXParserHandler` within the directory you intend to run the code from. Place `SAXParserHandler.java` within it. Back in the directory we are running from, enter the following on the command line.

```
javac SAXMain.java
```

This will compile both `SAXMain` and `wrox.sax.SAXParserHandler`.

Now all we have left to do is run our code:

```
java SAXMain
```

Below is the output we receive:

```
startDocument
startElement: article
Attribute: date
        Value: 02-Dec-2000
characters:
characters:
```

```
characters:
startElement: headline
characters: SAX 2.0 Released
endElement: headline
characters:
characters:

characters:
startElement: author
characters: F. Bar
endElement: author
characters:
characters:

characters:
startElement: body
characters: SAX 2.0 has been released into the public domain
endElement: body
characters:
characters:

endElement: article
endDocument
```

As you can see, the events are fired in the order in which they are encountered by the parser. The `startDocument()` event is fired first, followed by the `startElement` event for `<article>`, listing the attributes for the element as well. Notice that a blank `characters()` event is fired after the `endElement()` event for this tag and that a number of them appear in the output. This is due to the whitespace between the `</article>` and `<headline>` tags.

One would think that this would be considered ignorable whitespace rather than character data; however if you stop to think about it, how do we define what ignorable whitespace is? How do we know whether this space is important to a particular tag?

Look at the following (rather contrived) example of XHTML below:

```
<code><b>int</b> <b>i</b> = 0 </code>
```

The output that this should give is:

```
int i = 0;
```

The space between the `</b>` and open `<b>` tag is, to the reader, obviously significant; but without a DTD, the parser is unable to determine what is ignorable and what is not, so it will report every space as significant. Let's look and see what happens when we add a DTD to our document and set the parser to be validating.

The DTD for our document, `article.dtd` is given below. The syntax should be familiar to you from the previous chapter:

```
<!ELEMENT article (headline, author, body)>
<!ATTLIST article date CDATA #REQUIRED>
<!ELEMENT headline (#PCDATA)>
<!ELEMENT author (#PCDATA)>
<!ELEMENT body (#PCDATA)>
```

We change our XML document to include a declaration for our DTD:

```
<?xml version="1.0"?>
<!DOCTYPE article SYSTEM "article.dtd">
<article date="02-Dec-2000">
  <headline>SAX 2.0 Released</headline>
  <author>F. Bar</author>
  <body>SAX 2.0 has been released into the public domain</body>
</article>
```

We also make an addition to our code to make sure our parser validates the document:

```
import javax.xml.parsers.SAXParser;
import javax.xml.parsers.SAXParserFactory;

import wrox.sax.SAXParserHandler;

public class SAXMain {
    public static void main(String[] args) throws Exception {
        SAXParserFactory factory = SAXParserFactory.newInstance();
        factory.setValidating(true);
        SAXParser parser = factory.newSAXParser();
        parser.parse("SAX2.0.xml", new SAXParserHandler());
    }
}
```

Making sure that the correct classpath is still set, compile and run `SAXMain` again. Compare the output below to what we saw previously:

```
startDocument
startElement: article
Attribute: date
        Value: 02-Dec-2000
0 characters of ignorable whitespace
1 characters of ignorable whitespace
2 characters of ignorable whitespace
startElement: headline
characters: SAX 2.0 Released
endElement: headline
0 characters of ignorable whitespace
1 characters of ignorable whitespace
2 characters of ignorable whitespace
startElement: author
characters: F. Bar
endElement: author
0 characters of ignorable whitespace
1 characters of ignorable whitespace
2 characters of ignorable whitespace
startElement: body
characters: SAX 2.0 has been released into the public domain
endElement: body
0 characters of ignorable whitespace
1 characters of ignorable whitespace
0 characters of ignorable whitespace
endElement: article
endDocument
```

Notice that the empty `characters()` events are no longer here. This is because we made it clear with our DTD that no parsed-character data would appear in any other element except `<headline>`, `<body>` and `<author>`. The parser now knows that only within those elements should a `characters()` event be fired.

Namespaces

So far we have not discussed using namespaces. In fact, the addition of namespaces to XML is the major reason behind SAX 2.0's release. You can use SAX 1.0 with namespaces, but the APIs available do not make namespaces easy to use.

The code for these operations is under `/ProJavaXML/Chapter02/Namespaces/`.

Let's modify our previous example to include namespaces. First the DTD, `article.dtd`:

```
<!ELEMENT news:article (news:headline, news:author, news:body)>
<!ATTLIST news:article date CDATA #REQUIRED>
<!ELEMENT news:headline (#PCDATA)>
<!ELEMENT news:author (#PCDATA)>
<!ELEMENT news:body (#PCDATA)>
```

And then the XML document, `SAX2.0.xml`:

```
<?xml version="1.0"?>
<!DOCTYPE news:article SYSTEM "article.dtd">
<news:article xmlns:news=" http://www.wrox.com/javaxml/sax/news/"
              date="02-Dec-2000">
  <news:headline>SAX 2.0 Released</news:headline>
  <news:author>F. Bar</news:author>
  <news:body>SAX 2.0 has been released into the public domain</news:body>
</news:article>
```

In this document we now have the `news` namespace, which we will use to denote this article as a news article. In order to support namespaces, we need to tell JAXP to enable support for namespaces. We do this with a call the `SAXParserFactory` class, using the `setNamespaceAware()` method:

```
import javax.xml.parsers.SAXParser;
import javax.xml.parsers.SAXParserFactory;

import wrox.sax.SAXParserHandler;

public class SAXMain {
  public static void main(String[] args) throws Exception {
    SAXParserFactory factory = SAXParserFactory.newInstance();
    factory.setValidating(true);
    factory.setNamespaceAware(true);
    SAXParser parser = factory.newSAXParser();
    parser.parse("SAX2.0.xml", new SAXParserHandler());
  }
}
```

The default JAXP parser in the first early access release contains some bugs, so we will take `jaxp.jar` and `crimson.jar` out of our classpath and replace them with `xerces.jar` (the location of this file will obviously depend on where it is on your system). Enter this on the command line you are running the code from.

```
set classpath=.;C:\xerces-1_3_0\xerces.jar
```

We define Xerces as the default parser by entering the following on the command line:

```
java -Djavax.xml.parsers.SAXParserFactory=org.apache.xerces.jaxp.SAXParserFactory
Impl SAXMain
```

The following is the output:

```
startDocument
Begin namespace prefix: news
startElement: news:article
Attribute: date
        Value: 02-Dec-2000
3 characters of ignorable whitespace
startElement: news:headline
characters: SAX 2.0 Released
endElement: news:headline
3 characters of ignorable whitespace
startElement: news:author
characters: F. Bar
endElement: news:author
3 characters of ignorable whitespace
startElement: news:body
characters: SAX 2.0 has been released into the public domain
endElement: news:body
1 characters of ignorable whitespace
endElement: news:article
End namespace prefix: news
endDocument
```

Notice that we are now firing namespace-related events: `startNamespacePrefix()` and `endNamespacePrefix()`. Also notice a curiosity: the `startNamespacePrefix()` event is fired *before* the `startElement()` event, even though the namespace prefix is declared in the element in the document. This seemingly breaks the serial nature of SAX. However, this also makes sense: as an element is part of a namespace, it is necessary to determine the namespace of an element before the name of the element.

Also, notice that the `startElement()` and `endElement()` events return the name of the element, including the namespace prefix. In SAX 1.0, if namespaces were used, this is how element names are specified. In SAX 2.0, the `startElement()` and `endElement()` events enable better support for namespaces. We will change these two events in the `SAXParserHandler` class:

```
public void startElement(String namespaceURI, String localName,
                         String qName, Attributes atts)
    throws SAXException
{
  System.out.println("startElement: \n\tnamespace: " +
                     namespaceURI + "\n\tlocalName: " + localName);

    // list out the attributes and their values
    for (int i = 0 ; i < atts.getLength() ; i++) {
      System.out.println("Attribute: " + atts.getLocalName(i));
      System.out.println("\tValue: " + atts.getValue(i));
    }
}

public void endElement(String namespaceURI, String localName, String qName)
    throws SAXException
{
  System.out.println("endElement: \n\tnamespace: " +
                     namespaceURI + "\n\tlocalName: " + localName);
}
```

Below we see the output once the changes we added have been compiled.

```
startDocument
Begin namespace prefix: news
startElement:
        namespace:  http://www.wrox.com/javaxml/sax/news/
        localName: article
Attribute: date
        Value: 02-Dec-2000
3 characters of ignorable whitespace
startElement:
        namespace:  http://www.wrox.com/javaxml/sax/news/
        localName: headline
characters: SAX 2.0 Released
endElement:
        namespace:  http://www.wrox.com/javaxml/sax/news/
        localName: headline
3 characters of ignorable whitespace
startElement:
        namespace:  http://www.wrox.com/javaxml/sax/news/
        localName: author
characters: F. Bar
endElement:
        namespace:  http://www.wrox.com/javaxml/sax/news/
        localName: author
3 characters of ignorable whitespace
startElement:
        namespace:  http://www.wrox.com/javaxml/sax/news/
        localName: body
characters: SAX 2.0 has been released into the public domain
endElement:
        namespace:  http://www.wrox.com/javaxml/sax/news/
        localName: body
1 characters of ignorable whitespace
endElement:
        namespace:  http://www.wrox.com/javaxml/sax/news/
        localName: article
End namespace prefix: news
endDocument
```

We see now that the URI for the namespace is now printed, with the element of the namespace printed as well.

Processing Instructions

As you have learned in Chapter 1, processing instructions are portions of an XML document that are application-specific: they are essentially ignored by a parser and passed directly to the application. What happens after that point is up to the application. The '<?xml version="1.0"?>' declaration is specifically forbidden by the SAX API to fire a processingInstruction() event, as it is specific to the XML application.

In order to demonstrate how SAX handles processing instructions, we will add one to our sample document. The altered code for this operation is available in the code download under /ProJavaXML/Chapter02/Processing/.

```
<?xml version="1.0"?>
<!DOCTYPE news:article SYSTEM " article.dtd">
<?article-processor destination="news"?>
<news:article xmlns:article="http://www.wrox.com/javaxml/sax/sports/"
              date="02-Dec-2000">
  <news:headline>SAX 2.0 Released</news:headline>
  <news:author>F. Bar</news:author>
  <news:body>SAX 2.0 has been released into the public domain</news:body>
</news:article>
```

The following shows the additional output generated with the additions to the document:

```
startDocument
Instruction: article-processor, data: destination="news"
Begin namespace prefix: article
...
```

Skipped Entities

Entities, as you learned in Chapter 1, are somewhat like constants representing specific pieces of text. While there are predefined entities like < and &, there are many more that can be defined by the user.

The SAX 2.0 API provides the skippedEntity() event to non-validating parsers that do not wish to resolve entities. However, Xerces, Crimson, and Ælfred do not use this event, either when validating or not validating.

The org.xml.sax.Locator Class

While we have seen that the SAX API serially parses a document and fires events as XML elements are encountered, we have not seen how to determine where in the document an event has been fired. This is where the Locator object comes in. As an event is fired, the setDocumentLocator() method may be called on the provided ContentHandler. The Locator class is used to house location data as events are fired. Be aware that your parser may not implement Locators. The SAX documentation states that parser writers are "strongly encouraged" to implement this behavior, though not required.

Error Handlers

Rather than simply throw exceptions that terminate parsing, the SAX framework defines an org.xml.sax.ErrorHandler interface for the developer to have a say in what happens for certain errors. You must set an ErrorHandler for an instance of a parser or undefined behavior may result. The interface is simple, containing only three methods, dealing with exceptions in order of their severity:

❑   warning()

❑   error()

❑   fatalError()

The warning() method is used to report, well, warnings, to the developer. A warning, simply put, is something not defined as an error or fatal error in the XML 1.0 Recommendation. After a warning, the parser is required to continue parsing.

An **error** event is reported when a violation of the XML 1.0 Recommendation occurs from which the parser can recover. An example is the "encoding" attribute of the XML prologue. If an encoding is specified that is not supported by the parser, this is considered an error, since technically the parser can continue. Again, the parser is required to continue parsing after an error is reported.

A **fatal error** is an event from which the parser cannot recover. An example of this is document that is not well-formed. At this point, the parser should stop as it cannot recover. Another example is using an external entity in an attribute value. Unlike the previous two events, the parser is not required to continue parsing after a fatal error has occurred.

For a list of fatal and non-fatal errors, consult the XML 1.0 Recommendation at http://www.w3.org/TR/2000/REC-xml-20001006.

Although we have so far only implemented classes from the interface, we can now add the following methods to the SAXParserHandler class we created earlier. We are able to do this since the org.xml.sax.helpers.DefaultHandler class implements the ErrorHandler interface. The ErrorHandler methods are also a great place to exploit the Locator class, so we will report the location of the error as well.

```
public void error(SAXParseException e) throws SAXException {
   System.err.println("Recoverable error on line " +
                     locator.getLineNumber() + ", column " +
                     locator.getColumnNumber() + "\n\t" +
                     e.getMessage());
}

public void warning(SAXParseException e) throws SAXException {
   System.out.println("Warning on line " +
                     locator.getLineNumber() + ", column " +
                     locator.getColumnNumber() + "\n\t" +
                     e.getMessage());
}

public void fatalError(SAXParseException e) throws SAXException {
   System.err.println("Fatal error on line " +
                     locator.getLineNumber() + ", column " +
                     locator.getColumnNumber() + ":\n\t" +
                     e.getMessage());
     throw e;
}
```

The document below contains a fatal error:

```
<?xml version="1.0"?>
<TestPage>
    <Header>My Header</Header>
    <Body>The body of the text/Body>
</TestPage>
```

Using our error handlers in a SAX parser, we would get the following fatal error message:

```
Fatal error on line 5, column -1:
        Expected "</Body>" to terminate element starting on line 4.
Exception in thread "main" org.xml.sax.SAXParseException: Expected "</Body>" to
terminate element starting on line 4.
        at org.apache.crimson.parser.Parser2.fatal(Parser2.java:3035)
        at org.apache.crimson.parser.Parser2.fatal(Parser2.java:3029)
        at org.apache.crimson.parser.Parser2.maybeElement(Parser2.java:1474)
        at org.apache.crimson.parser.Parser2.content(Parser2.java:1700)
        at org.apache.crimson.parser.Parser2.maybeElement(Parser2.java:1468)
        at org.apache.crimson.parser.Parser2.parseInternal(Parser2.java:499)
        at org.apache.crimson.parser.Parser2.parse(Parser2.java:304)
        at org.apache.crimson.parser.XMLReaderImpl.parse(XMLReaderImpl.java:433)

        at javax.xml.parsers.SAXParser.parse(SAXParser.java:346)
        at JAXPExample.main(JAXPExample.java:14)
```

The code for this section is contained in the code download under
`/ProJavaXML/Chapter02/ErrorHandling/`. We will see the error handlers in action in the next
section while demonstrating the SAX extensions that are available.

The SAX2-ext Package

SAX 2.0 was primarily written to provide better namespace and validation support. Since SAX 1.0
parsers somewhat reported these events, it was easy to adapt a SAX 1.0 parser to SAX 2.0. However
since the release of SAX 2.0 it was decided that other features could be added to enhance SAX.
Unfortunately, there is no way to adapt these events for a SAX 1.0 parser as they were not conceived at
the inception of SAX 1.0. For this reason, the SAX2-ext package was created, which is an optional
package that SAX2 parsers may or may not support. SAX2-ext cannot be used on its own: a SAX2
parser implementing this package is required.

The handlers for these events have been placed in the `org.xml.sax.ext` package. Two have been
defined: `DeclHandler` and `LexicalHandler`.

DeclHandler

`DeclHandler` is used to handle events that occur while parsing the DTD of a document.
It has four methods.

The first method, `elementDecl()`, is fired when an element declaration is encountered. The `name`
argument is the name of the element. There is no concept of namespaces in a DTD therefore there is none
in the fired events. If an element name contains a namespace, it is considered part of the element name.

```
public void elementDecl(String name, String model)
    throws SAXException;
```

The `model` argument describes the type of element. If this is an empty tag, the value of the argument
will be the string `EMPTY`. If the tag may have any type of child element, the value will be `ANY`. If
restrictions are placed on what tags can occur within this element, the value will be the list of elements,
including the parentheses and minus all whitespace.

For example, if we had the following declaration in our DTD:

```
<!ELEMENT menu (desserts|entree|starters)>
```

The value of the model argument would be (desserts|entree|starters).

The attributeDecl() event is fired when an attribute is being declared.

```
public void attributeDecl(String eName, String aName, String type,
                          String valueDefault, String value)
    throws SAXException;
```

The eName argument is the name of the element with which this attribute is associated. The aName attribute is the name of the attribute. The type argument is the type of this attribute, which can be any of the legal attribute types discussed in Chapter 1. The valueDefault argument is either "#FIXED", "#IMPLIED", "#REQUIRED", or null if none of these applies. Finally, the value argument contains the value of the attribute, or null if no value is defined.

The internalEntityDecl() event is fired when an entity is defined from within the DTD. The name argument is the name of the entity, while the value argument contains the replacement text for this entity.

```
public void internalEntityDecl(String name, String value)
    throws SAXException;
```

The externalEntityDecl() event is fired when an external entity is declared in a DTD.

```
public void externalEntityDecl(String name, String publicId,
                               String systemId)
    throws SAXException;
```

The name argument is the name of the external entity. publicID is the public identifier of this external entity, or null if none was declared; and systemID is the system identifier of this external entity.

Lexical Handler

The org.xml.sax.ext.LexicalHandler interface is made available to handle lexical events, such as comments and CDATA sections. Like DeclHandler, support is not required by SAX parsers.

Below is a listing for this class:

```
package org.xml.sax.ext;

import org.xml.sax.SAXException;

public interface LexicalHandler
{
    public void comment(char[] ch, int start, int length)
        throws SAXException;
```

```
    public void startCDATA() throws SAXException;
    public void endCDATA() throws SAXException;

    public void startDTD(String name, String publicID, String systemID)
        throws SAXException;
    public void endDTD() throws SAXException;

    public void startEntity(String name) throws SAXException;
    public void endEntity(String name) throws SAXException;
}
```

The comment() method fires when an XML comment is encountered in the document. It acts much like the characters() and ignorableWhitespace() methods, in that the character array must only be accessed from the index specified by the start argument and only for the length specified in the length argument.

The startCDATA() and endCDATA() events are fired at the beginning and the end of a CDATA section, respectively. Notice that these events do not have any arguments specifying the data within the section. This is because the characters will be part of the characters() event fired while parsing this section.

The startDTD() and endDTD() methods are fired at the beginning and end of a DTD declaration, respectively. The startDTD() event will be fired proceeding any events reported by DeclHandler or DTDHandler and the endDTD() event being fired after all events have been reported. The startDTD() event has three arguments. The name argument contains the document type name, publicID contains the public identifier, if any, for this DTD, and systemID contains the system identifier if one was given.

Finally, the startEntity() and endEntity() events are fired upon the occurrence of *some* external and internal entities. Each method has an argument set to the name of the entity being parsed. All events from DTDHandler or DeclHandler must be nested within these two events, although the events are not required to be in any order.

An example of entities that are not reported are general entities (such as & and <) inside attribute values. The SAX2-ext documentation states that even though a parser may implement the LexicalHandler interface it is not required to support these methods.

Using SAX2-ext

Fortunately, parsers do exist that support the SAX 2.0 extensions. But looking at the XMLReader interface, how do we set a DeclHandler or LexicalHandler? There are methods for setting the ContentHandler and ErrorHandler, but none for these two interfaces. This is because SAX2-ext is an afterthought and if the standard SAX 2.0 APIs contained these methods, it would be assumed that parsers would implement this functionality.

We haven't talked about the setProperty() method of the XMLReader interface because up until now we didn't have to; but this is what we use to set SAX2-ext handlers. The signature for the setProperty() method is shown below:

```
    public void setProperty(String propertyID, Object value)
        throws SAXNotRecognizedException, SAXNotSupportedException;
```

The exceptions thrown have to do with the property name: a SAXNotRecognizedException is thrown if a property name is supplied that the parser does not know about. The SAXNotSupportedException is thrown if a property is given that is known, but that particular property is not supported. Note that both of these exceptions extend SAXException.

The two properties that we are concerned about are http://xml.org/sax/properties/lexical-handler and http://xml.org/sax/properties/declaration-handler. The value supplied to the setProperty() method is a class implementing the respective class, either LexicalHandler or DeclHandler.

Let's create a trivial example to show how these events are fired. We'll start by extending the class we created in the example from the previous sections to implement the LexicalHandler and DeclHandler interfaces. You can find all of the following files in the code download under /ProJavaXML/Chapter02/sax2-ext/, but if you want to build them yourself, you will need to start by adding the following import statements and amend the class declaration to extends:

```
import org.xml.sax.ext.DeclHandler;
import org.xml.sax.ext.LexicalHandler;

...

public class SAXParserHandler extends DefaultHandler
    implements LexicalHandler, DeclHandler
{
```

Now we begin to implement the methods of the LexicalHandler interface; add the following methods:

```
public void comment(char[] ch, int start,
                    int length) throws SAXException {
  String str = new String(ch, start, length);
  System.out.println("Comment: " + str);
}

public void startCDATA() throws SAXException {
  System.out.println("Start of CDATA section");
}

public void endCDATA() throws SAXException {
  System.out.println("End of CDATA section");
}

public void startDTD(String name, String publicID,
                     String systemID) throws SAXException {
  System.out.println("Start of DTD:");
  System.out.println("\tdoctype name: " + name);
  if (publicID != null) {
    System.out.println("\tpublicID: " + publicID);
  }

  if (systemID != null) {
    System.out.println("\tsystemID: " + systemID);
  }
}
```

```
    public void endDTD() throws SAXException {
      System.out.println("End of DTD");
    }

    public void startEntity(String name) throws SAXException {
      System.out.println("Start entity: " + name);
    }

    public void endEntity(String name) throws SAXException {
      System.out.println("End entity: " + name);
    }
```

The following methods implement the methods of `DeclHandler`:

```
    public void elementDecl(String name, String model) throws SAXException {
      System.out.println("Element declaration: " + name);
      System.out.println("\tModel: " + model);
    }

    public void attributeDecl(String eName, String aName, String type,
                              String valueDefault,
                              String value) throws SAXException {
      System.out.println("Attribute declaration");
      System.out.println("\telement name: " + eName);
      System.out.println("\tattribute name: " + aName);
      System.out.println("\ttype: " + type);
      System.out.println("\tattribute default: " + valueDefault);
      System.out.println("\tdefault value: " + value);
    }

    public void externalEntityDecl(String name, String publicID,
                                   String systemID) throws SAXException {
      System.out.println("External Entity Declaration");
      if (publicID != null) {
        System.out.println("\tpublicID: " + publicID);
      }

      if (systemID != null) {
        System.out.println("\tsystemID: " + systemID);
      }
    }

    public void internalEntityDecl(String name,
                                   String value) throws SAXException {
      System.out.println("Internal Entity Declaration");
      System.out.println("\tName: " + name);
      System.out.println("\tValue: " + value);
    }
}
```

Let's modify the example XML documents we have been using so we can see how these events are fired. First is our DTD:

```
<!ELEMENT article (headline, author, body)>
<!ATTLIST article date CDATA #REQUIRED>
<!ELEMENT headline (#PCDATA)>
<!ELEMENT author (#PCDATA)>
<!ELEMENT body (#PCDATA)>
<!ENTITY pubname "The XML News">
<!ENTITY cent SYSTEM "articleEntities.dtd">
```

Here is the `articleEntities.dtd` called out in the last entity declaration. It contains some entity declarations.

```
<!ENTITY cent "&162;"> <!-- the cent sign -->
<!ENTITY pound "&163;"> <!-- pound sign -->
<!ENTITY onefourth "&188;"> <!-- one-fourth fraction -->
```

Finally, here is our XML document, the new improved `SAX2.0.xml`:

```
<?xml version="1.0" ?>
<!DOCTYPE article SYSTEM "article.dtd">
<article date="02-Dec-2000">
  <headline>SAX 2.0 Released</headline>
  <author>F. Bar</author>
  <body>SAX 2.0 has been released into the public domain with the following
    features:
    <!-- use a CDATA section to enumerate the features -->
    <![CDATA[
    ->Namespace support
    ->Fully configurable with the addition of features and properties
    ->Support for skipped entities
    ]]></body>
</article>
```

We will use Xerces on its own for parsing the document.

> **If you look at the source code below, you will see that we are now importing
> `XMLReader`. This is because JAXP has some difficulty supporting the
> `setProperty()` methods in the extended `DefaultHandler`, even though SAX2 and
> Xerces do not. We expect that this is a bug in the JAXP release and will be corrected
> in future releases.**

However, the source code for the main driver routine is as follows:

```
import java.io.FileInputStream;
import org.apache.xerces.parsers.SAXParser;
import org.xml.sax.XMLReader;

import wrox.sax.SAXParserHandler;


import org.xml.sax.InputSource;

public class SAXMain {
  public static void main(String[] args) throws Exception {
    XMLReader parser = new SAXParser();
    SAXParserHandler handler = new SAXParserHandler();

    parser.setProperty("http://xml.org/sax/properties/declaration-handler",
                       handler);
```

```
        parser.setProperty("http://xml.org/sax/properties/lexical-handler",
                            handler);

    parser.setContentHandler(handler);
    parser.setErrorHandler(handler);

    parser.parse(new InputSource(new FileInputStream(args[0])));
    }
}
```

First, note that we expect a command-line argument, which is the name of the file to parse. Also notice the two calls to setProperty() that make our class the handler for lexical and declaration events, respectively. You will need to compile both this class and the SAXParserHandler classes and as usual make sure that Xerces is in your classpath. With the following command line:

```
java SAXMain SAX2.0.xml
```

we get the following output. The newly added sections are highlighted:

```
startDocument
Start of DTD:
        doctype name: article
        systemID: article.dtd
Start entity: [dtd]
Element declaration: article
        Model: (headline,author,body)
Attribute declaration
        element name: article
        attribute name: date
        type: CDATA
    attribute default: #REQUIRED
        default value: null
Element declaration: headline
        Model: (#PCDATA)
Element declaration: author
        Model: (#PCDATA)
Element declaration: body
        Model: (#PCDATA)
Internal Entity Declaration
        Name: pubname
        Value: The XML News
External Entity Declaration
        systemID: articleEntities.dtd
End entity: [dtd]
End of DTD
startElement: article
Attribute: date
        Value: 02-Dec-2000
3 characters of ignorable whitespace
startElement: headline
characters: SAX 2.0 Released
endElement: headline
3 characters of ignorable whitespace
startElement: author
```

```
characters: F. Bar
endElement: author
3 characters of ignorable whitespace
startElement: body
characters: SAX 2.0 has been released into the public domain with the following
    features:

Comment:  use a CDATA section to enumerate the features
characters:

Start of CDATA section
characters:
    ->Namespace support
    ->Fully configurable with the addition of features and properties
    ->Support for skipped entities

End of CDATA section
endElement: body
1 characters of ignorable whitespace
endElement: article
endDocument
```

As we expect, a `startDocument()` event is fired followed by a `startDTD()` event. Interestingly, a `startEntity()` event is fired once the DTD is being processed. XML 1.0 defines external DTDs as a special kind of external entity, therefore it is treated as a pseudo-entity with the name "[dtd]".

Up until the `endDTD()` event, we see all of the events of the `DeclHandler` interface fired. After that, we are back in familiar territory: `startElement()`, `endElement()`, `characters()`, etc. Then we see a `comment()` event fired from the `LexicalHandler` interface closely followed by the start of a CDATA section. A `characters()` event is fired to provide the character data contained within this section. The rest of the events are what we would expect.

You might be wondering when these handlers would ever need to be used. In reality, the only applications that may require these types of handlers are XML development environments. This type of detail can, for instance, allow such an environment to highlight CDATA sections a certain way, or display DTD declarations in a certain manner.

Implementing an Application with SAX

This section will introduce you to using SAX in your applications. Since SAX is an event-based parser and reacts to elements as they are encountered, it is a good choice where input may be incomplete or where only a particular portion of a document may be necessary to satisfy the application.

You may already be familiar with **vCards**. In case you are not, a vCard is a virtual business card that you can send along with your e-mail. Many mail clients like Microsoft Outlook recognize vCards and allow you to import their contents directly into your list of contacts. In addition to a binary vCard, an effort has been made to create an XML representation of vCards. While it is beyond the scope of this chapter to discuss the vCard XML document at length, the last Internet Draft (since expired) can be found at http://www.globecom.net/ietf/draft/draft-dawson-vcard-xml-dtd-02.html. However, we will discuss some of the important elements of the draft.

Let's look at a sample document:

```
<?xml version="1.0"?>
<vCard version="3.0">
  <fn>Jeremy Michael Crosbie</fn>
  <n>
    <family>Crosbie</family>
    <given>Jeremy</given>
  </n>
  <email email.type="INTERNET">jeremycrosbie@somecompany.com</email>
</vCard>
```

First, the root element of a vCard XML document is the, surprisingly enough, <vCard> tag. Within that is a version field, currently at 3.0. Next is the <fn> element, which stands for full name. Beneath that is the <n> tag, which contains name information where I have provided my family and given name. Lastly, we have the <email> tag, which defines the e-mail address as being an Internet e-mail address (others are defined in the DTD). Other elements for telephone numbers and street addresses exist but are ignored for the purposes of this application.

Since our document may contain more than one vCard, another root element is defined for this purpose. As you see below, this is how to form such a document.

```
<?xml version="1.0"?>
<vCardSet name"friends">
  <vCard version="3.0">
    <fn>Jeremy Michael Crosbie</fn>
    <n>
      <family>Crosbie</family>
      <given>Jeremy</given>
    </n>
    <email email.type="INTERNET">jeremycrosbie@somecompany.com</email>
  </vCard>
  <vCard version="3.0">
    <fn>John Coltrane</fn>
    <n>
      <family>Coltrane</family>
      <given>John</given>
    </n>
  </vCard>
</vCardSet>
```

Using this element is fairly self-explanatory. We use the <vCardSet> element as the root in order to group our vCards. The name attribute defines a name for our vCard list, which may be useful for defining group mailing lists or the like. Within this element is any number of <vCard>s.

The Application

Now we are going to discuss how to use SAX and the vCard XML format in an application. Our application will consist of an XML document; let's say a research paper that has been formatted to a custom XML format. The authors of that document as well as references to other authors are stored in vCards that may be scattered throughout the document. Rather than manually search and copy the vCard references, you now have the tools and prowess to use Java and SAX to handle this task.

We are going to augment our discussion of vCards to include namespaces to ensure that no element name collisions occur. We will use the namespace vcf as defined in the Internet Draft for vCards and book for elements of the book we are reading.

Let's start with a sample document, the start of a treatise on jazz music. You can find this in the code download under the name doc.xml:

```xml
<?xml version="1.0"?>
<book:Book xmlns:book="http://www.wrox.com/javaprocompendium"
     xmlns:vcf="http://www.ietf.org/internet-drafts/draft-dawson-vcard-xml-dtd-
02.txt">
  <book:Title>Jazz Today</book:Title>
  <book:Chapter number="1">
    Jazz has evolved for over a century, beginning with the early remnants
    of the blues then evolving into ragtime, swing, bebop, and onward.
    Arguably no one made more of a contribution to jazz than Louis
    Armstrong.
    <vcf:vCard version="3.0">
      <vcf:fn>Louis Armstrong</vcf:fn>
      <vcf:n>
        <vcf:family>Armstrong</vcf:family>
        <vcf:given>Louis</vcf:given>
        <vcf:other>Pops</vcf:other>
      </vcf:n>
    </vcf:vCard>
    Following his lead, John "Dizzy" Gillespie ignited the bebop revolution,
    picking up where Armstrong left off.
    <vcf:vCard version="3.0">
      <vcf:fn>John Gillespie</vcf:fn>
      <vcf:n>
        <vcf:family>Gillespie</vcf:family>
        <vcf:given>John</vcf:given>
        <vcf:other>Dizzy</vcf:other>
      </vcf:n>
    </vcf:vCard>
  </book:Chapter>
</book:Book>
```

We begin by defining the two namespaces we plan to use in this document: the book namespace for the content and the vcf namespace for the vCard information.

Design

Before we start to code, let's take a moment to think about how to design this application. We can think about each element in the document as being a state that our parser moves to. A well-known design pattern for dealing with this type of problem is called the **State** pattern. The state pattern is a good choice for modeling changes in the state of a system, in this case a parser. As we are parsing elements and encounter those that we are interested in, this is akin to changing state. For example, before we begin parsing we are said to be in the **initial state**. When we begin parsing, we will remain in this state until something of interest occurs. At that point, we move on to the next state. The diagram overleaf details the states we move into and what events cause a change in state.

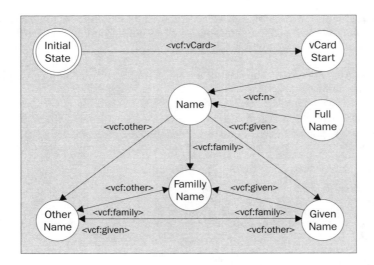

The initial state is denoted by a circle within a circle and represents a starting point. Each transition is directed and is marked with the element that causes the transition. Each transition is determined and well-defined, so for instance if we are in the initial state and a `<vcf:family>` element is encountered this does not cause a state change. The only impetus for a change in the initial state is the `<vcf:vCard>` element. Note that when in the "Other Name" state, for instance, we can go to either the "Family Name" or "Given Name" states. Not shown in the diagram for clarity is the fact that each of the "Name" elements return to the initial state upon the `</vcf:n>` end tag.

A shortcoming of using states is that there is nothing to stop multiple `<vcf:family>` elements from occurring, so we could go from "Given Name" to "Family Name" and then back to "Given Name" using a finite state machine, even though the DTD explicitly disallows this. This is a not something that can be mitigated with any finite state machine so we rely on a document's validity in order for this pattern to work correctly.

Now that we understand the premise, let's look at how we can model this in code. Below is a UML class diagram describing this pattern.

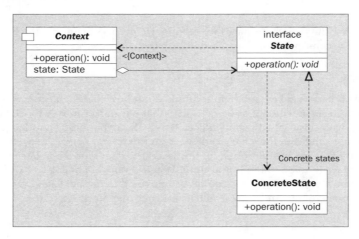

A `Context` contains a reference to a `State` object and passes requests from clients to the current state. A `Context`, as this diagram describes, is an aggregation of different states, which implement the `State` interface. In our design, we are going to have essentially only two states: `InitialState` and `VCardStartState`, since we only care about parsing vCard data.

Other important objects are obviously the parser and the `DisplayFormat` class, which is responsible for printing out the results of the parsing to the screen. We will see these classes shortly.

Implementation

Now let's take a look at what our `DisplayFormat` class is going to look like. The information that is extracted from the document will be held in this class, and this class will then be output to the screen. You can imagine then, that the methods defined in this class will be mutators for a first name, last name, e-mail address and any other name the person referred to is known by. We will also override the `toString()` method and provide a method for clearing the information:

```
public class DisplayFormat {
   private String fullName = null;
   private String givenName = null;
   private String familyName = null;
   private String otherName = null;

   public DisplayFormat() {}

   public void clearDisplay() {
      fullName = null;
      givenName = null;
      familyName = null;
      otherName = null;
   }

   public String getFullName() {
      return fullName;
   }

   public String getGivenName() {
      return givenName;
   }

   public String getFamilyName() {
      return familyName;
   }

   public String getOtherName() {
      return otherName;
   }

   public void setFullName(String fullName) {
      this.fullName = fullName;
   }

   public void setGivenName(String givenName) {
      this.givenName = givenName;
   }
```

```
    public void setFamilyName(String familyName) {
      this.familyName = familyName;
    }

    public void setOtherName(String otherName) {
      this.otherName = otherName;
    }

    public String toString() {
      StringBuffer buf = new StringBuffer(1024);

      buf.append("Full name: " + fullName + "\n");
      buf.append("Family name: " + familyName + "\n");
      buf.append("Given name: " + givenName + "\n");
      buf.append("Other name: " + otherName + "\n");

      return buf.toString();
    }
  }
```

As intimated, this class merely acts as a placeholder for the data we get from the vCards embedded in the document.

The Parser

Now, let's look at our parser. We are only concerned with the startElement() and endElement() methods, so we will extend the org.xml.sax.helpers.DefaultHandler class and override these methods:

```
import org.xml.sax.Attributes;
import org.xml.sax.SAXException;
import org.xml.sax.SAXParseException;
import org.xml.sax.helpers.DefaultHandler;

import java.util.Hashtable;

public class BookParser extends DefaultHandler {
  private State state = null;
  private DisplayFormat format = null;
  private Hashtable prefixes = null;

  public BookParser() {
    state = InitialState.getInstance();
    prefixes = new Hashtable();
    format = new DisplayFormat();
  }
```

We need to implement the SAX methods we will be using for our application. In our case, we need to be aware of what namespaces are currently active so we override the startPrefixMapping() method. As we encounter a namespace, we add it to a hash table for a fast lookup when we encounter elements of that namespace.

```
  public void startPrefixMapping(String prefix,
                                 String namespaceURI) throws SAXException {
    prefixes.put(namespaceURI, prefix);
  }
```

We are also obviously interested in what elements are currently being analyzed so we need to override the startElement() and endElement() methods. You will notice that in the startElement() method we determine what namespace the current element is in by looking it up in the hash table. As we learned earlier, the namespace events associated with an element are fired before the startElement() event so this is safe. Once we determine the namespace of the element we pass on the namespace, element name, attributes, formatting object, and a reference to the handler to the state method handleStartElement(), which handles the input dependent upon the current state. Similar code is provided for the endElement() method.

```java
public void startElement(String namespaceURI, String localName,
                         String qName,
                         Attributes atts) throws SAXException {
   String prefix = (String) prefixes.get(namespaceURI);
   state.handleStartElement(prefix, localName, atts, this, format);
}

public void endElement(String namespaceURI, String localName,
                       String qName) throws SAXException {
   String prefix = (String) prefixes.get(namespaceURI);
   state.handleEndElement(prefix, localName, this, format);
}
```

We also care about the data in between the tags so we need to make sure that we handle character data appropriately, if in the proper state, by overriding the characters() method:

```java
public void characters(char[] chars, int start,
                       int length) throws SAXException {
   String str = new String(chars, start, length);
   state.handleCharacterData(str, format);
}
```

Implementing the State Pattern

As said earlier, each of the handle methods of the State object requires a reference to the content handler. This is so that, as each method of the State object is called, the changeState() method can be called to move to the appropriate state. We will see more about this when we examine how we implement the State pattern.

```java
public void changeState(State state) {
   this.state = state;
}

public void error(SAXParseException e) throws SAXException {
   System.err.println(e.getMessage());
}

public void warning(SAXParseException e) throws SAXException {
   System.err.println(e.getMessage());
}

public void fatalError(SAXParseException e) throws SAXException {
   System.err.println(e.getMessage());
}
}
```

The effect that these methods will have is dependant on the state current at the time. As stated earlier, we only have two states: `InitialState` and `VCardStartState`. Before we get to them, we will define a `State` interface:

```
import org.xml.sax.Attributes;

public interface State {
    public static final String VCARD_PREFIX = "vcf";
    public static final String BOOK_PREFIX = "book";

    public void handleStartElement(String namespacePrefix, String localName,
                                   Attributes atts, BookParser parser,
                                   DisplayFormat format);

    public void handleEndElement(String namespacePrefix, String localName,
                                 BookParser parser, DisplayFormat format);

    public void handleCharacterData(String data, DisplayFormat format);
}
```

The concrete classes are going to contain a `getInstance()` method. Since no internal state is stored in each of these objects, we can save space by only allocating one object for each state. Although the number of states is small, this is good practice in case our application becomes larger. We will use a Singleton pattern for this. The first concrete state class we write is for the `InitialState`. As mentioned earlier, the initial state is the starting state before any parsing is performed. It is there essentially as a placeholder to move to the next appropriate state.

```
import org.xml.sax.Attributes;

public class InitialState implements State {
    private static InitialState state = null;

    protected InitialState() {}
```

Here is where we use the Singleton pattern to make sure only one instance of the `InitialState` class is created:

```
public static InitialState getInstance() {
    if (state == null) {
        state = new InitialState();
    }
    return state;
}
```

In the handler code above we saw references to the `handleStartElement()` method. As you can see in the code below, the initial state examines the namespace currently being used. If we are in the initial state and the prefix being parsed is the vCard namespace, then we change to the `vCardElementState` by calling the `BookParser changeState()` method:

```
    public void handleStartElement(String namespacePrefix, String localName,
                                   Attributes atts, BookParser parser,
                                   DisplayFormat format) {
      if (namespacePrefix.equals(VCARD_PREFIX)) {
        parser.changeState(VCardStartState.getInstance());
      }
    }

    public void handleEndElement(String namespacePrefix, String localName,
                                 BookParser parser, DisplayFormat format) {}

    public void handleCharacterData(String data, DisplayFormat format) {}
}
```

All that happens in this class is that when a start `<vCard>` element is encountered the state is changed to the `VCardStart` state. This is the state that we are in once an element in the `vCard` namespace is encountered while in the initial state. This class is a bit more involved.

First, since this is where the bulk of the state-changing is taking place, we will define a factory that will do a lot of the work for us:

```
public class VCardStateFactory {
  protected VCardStateFactory() {}

  public static State getState(String localName) {
    if (localName.equals("fn")) {
      return VCardFNState.getInstance();
    } else if (localName.equals("n")) {
      return VCardStartState.getInstance();
    } else if (localName.equals("family")) {
      return VCardFamilyNameState.getInstance();
    } else if (localName.equals("given")) {
      return VCardGivenNameState.getInstance();
    } else if (localName.equals("other")) {
      return VCardOtherNameState.getInstance();
    } else if (localName.equals("vCard")) {
      return VCardStartState.getInstance();
    } else {
      return InitialState.getInstance();
    }
  }
}
```

All this class is doing is returning the appropriate state for whatever element name we pass. What is good about this is that our parser still has no idea how states change, so if we ever need to change the way we move between states we don't need to touch the parser code.

Now let's look at the `VCardStartState` class.

```
import org.xml.sax.Attributes;

public class VCardStartState implements State {
  private static VCardStartState state = null;

  protected VCardStartState() {}
```

```
    public static VCardStartState getInstance() {
      if (state == null) {
        state = new VCardStartState();
      }
      return state;
    }
```

All our `handleStartElement()` method needs to do is move to the appropriate state and we do so using our factory:

```
    public void handleStartElement(String namespacePrefix, String localName,
                                   Attributes atts, BookParser parser,
                                   DisplayFormat format) {
      parser.changeState(VCardStateFactory.getState(localName));
    }
```

When we reach the end of an element we may need to change state depending on what the end element is. We will return to the initial state if we are in the vCard namespace and the element is the terminating `</vCard>` element.

```
    public void handleEndElement(String namespacePrefix, String localName,
                                 BookParser parser, DisplayFormat format) {
      if (namespacePrefix.equals(VCARD_PREFIX)) {
        if (localName.equals("vCard")) {
          parser.changeState(InitialState.getInstance());
          System.out.println(format);
          format.clearDisplay();
        }
      }
    }
    public void handleCharacterData(String data, DisplayFormat format) {}
  }
```

As you can see, we have three instance variables: `state`, `format`, and `prefix`. The first two shouldn't need explanation but I'll explain the third. In order to provide the prefixes to the methods of the State classes we need to determine them at the point where they are declared. In order to do this, we create a hash table that contains the URI as a key to be looked up during each event and the prefix as the value.

This makes it easy to determine the prefix for each call as well as being fast. Taking a step back for a minute, it should be becoming clear what this design pattern affords us: the parser class knows nothing about what is going on behind the scenes. All of that logic is contained within the state classes. Below are the implementations of the other state classes, which are used depending on what vCard element is being accessed.

The following four classes each handle their respective elements. Here is VCardFamilyNameState:

```
import org.xml.sax.Attributes;

public class VCardFamilyNameState implements State {
  private static VCardFamilyNameState state = null;

  protected VCardFamilyNameState() {}
```

```
   public static VCardFamilyNameState getInstance() {
     if (state == null) {
       state = new VCardFamilyNameState();
     }
     return state;
   }

   public void handleStartElement(String namespacePrefix, String localName,
                                  Attributes atts, BookParser parser,
                                  DisplayFormat format) {
     parser.changeState(VCardStateFactory.getState(localName));
   }

   public void handleEndElement(String namespacePrefix, String localName,
                                BookParser parser, DisplayFormat format) {
     parser.changeState(VCardStartState.getInstance());
   }

   public void handleCharacterData(String data, DisplayFormat format) {
     format.setFamilyName(data);
   }
}
```

The same is true for VCardFNState:

```
import org.xml.sax.Attributes;

public class VCardFNState implements State {
   private static VCardFNState state = null;

   protected VCardFNState() {}

   public static VCardFNState getInstance() {
     if (state == null) {
       state = new VCardFNState();
     }
     return state;
   }

   public void handleStartElement(String namespacePrefix, String localName,
                                  Attributes atts, BookParser parser,
                                  DisplayFormat format) {
     parser.changeState(VCardStateFactory.getState(localName));
   }

   public void handleEndElement(String namespacePrefix, String localName,
                                BookParser parser, DisplayFormat format) {

     // change back to start state
     parser.changeState(VCardStartState.getInstance());
   }

   public void handleCharacterData(String data, DisplayFormat format) {
     format.setFullName(data);
   }
}
```

The next class is `VCardGivenNameState`, which again changes the state for this particular element:

```java
import org.xml.sax.Attributes;

public class VCardGivenNameState implements State {
  private static VCardGivenNameState state = null;

  protected VCardGivenNameState() {}

  public static VCardGivenNameState getInstance() {
    if (state == null) {
      state = new VCardGivenNameState();
    }
    return state;
  }

  public void handleStartElement(String namespacePrefix, String localName,
                                 Attributes atts, BookParser parser,
                                 DisplayFormat format) {
    parser.changeState(VCardStateFactory.getState(localName));
  }

  public void handleEndElement(String namespacePrefix, String localName,
                               BookParser parser, DisplayFormat format) {
    parser.changeState(VCardStartState.getInstance());
  }

  public void handleCharacterData(String data, DisplayFormat format) {
    format.setGivenName(data);
  }
}
```

And this is the last of the classes that handle the elements within our document, namely
`VCardOtherNameState`:

```java
import org.xml.sax.Attributes;

public class VCardOtherNameState implements State {
  private static VCardOtherNameState state = null;

  protected VCardOtherNameState() {}

  public static VCardOtherNameState getInstance() {
    if (state == null) {
      state = new VCardOtherNameState();
    }
    return state;
  }

  public void handleStartElement(String namespacePrefix, String localName,
                                 Attributes atts, BookParser parser,
                                 DisplayFormat format) {
    parser.changeState(VCardStateFactory.getState(localName));
  }
```

```
    public void handleEndElement(String namespacePrefix, String localName,
                             BookParser parser, DisplayFormat format) {
      parser.changeState(VCardStartState.getInstance());
    }

    public void handleCharacterData(String data, DisplayFormat format) {
      format.setOtherName(data);
    }
  }
```

And finally, we will draw these classes together with our `BookMain` class. `BookMain` simply instantiates an instance of our `BookParser`:

```java
import javax.xml.parsers.SAXParser;
import javax.xml.parsers.SAXParserFactory;
import org.xml.sax.InputSource;
import java.io.FileReader;

public class BookMain {
  public static void main(String[] args) throws Exception {
    SAXParserFactory factory = SAXParserFactory.newInstance();
    SAXParser parser = factory.newSAXParser();
    InputSource is = new InputSource(new FileReader("doc.xml"));
    parser.parse(is, new BookParser());
  }
}
```

To run the example, compile the above classes (these classes are also available in the code download under `/ProJavaXML/Chapter02/vCardApp/`). Next, we'll set our classpath, so, on the command line, navigate to the directory from which you are running the code. On the command line then enter:

```
set CLASSPATH=.;C:\jaxp-1.1\crimson.jar;C:\jaxp-1.1\jaxp.jar
```

Obviously this will depend on where these JAR files are. Now we are ready to run, so simply compile all the files in the directory and run them with:

```
java BookMain
```

The output should look like this:

SAX 2.01

At the time of this writing, a bug-fix pre-release was issued on December 28, 2000. It is hoped by the time of publication that the official release will be available. The list of defects and enhancements forthcoming can be found at http://www.megginson.com/SAX/bugs.html.

Summary

This chapter has dealt wholly with SAX, the Simple API for XML. We have seen why SAX was created and the purpose it serves: to provide a fast, event-driven parsing paradigm. Also, we have seen how SAX works and the relationship between parsers and handlers. I cannot stress enough that the similarities between SAX and the Event Delegation model help us to understand how SAX works.

SAX also offers flexibility and room for future expansion. With the addition of features and properties, a parser is allowed any number of possibilities. One expansion released since SAX 2.0 is the SAX 2.0-ext package, which has handlers for other types of events not covered in the SAX 2.0 release. The beauty of this package is that no changes to the original API are required.

Going further, we have seen how to leverage JAXP to use SAX by decoupling our parser implementation from the API. We have seen how JAXP affords us the flexibility of dynamically assigning the parser implementation we desire rather than choosing at compile time. We have also seen the ease with which we can take any parser and fit it into the JAXP framework, giving us the ability to use our favorite parser with JAXP.

Hopefully, you have seen the power that SAX affords us, and what it can do to enhance your applications. In the next chapter, a new paradigm will be introduced that takes a different approach to parsing XML documents.

The Xerces Blue
Butterfly, which became
extinct earlier this century,
and after which the Xerces XML
parser is named ...

3

The DOM

SAX clearly provides us with a simple way to write a program that can react to data in an XML document at the moment that data is read in. This is great if we're only interested in a few parts of a document, and we know how to locate them within the stream of SAX events, or if we know we're only interested in reading the data in sequence. But if we want programmatic access to the entire document, in a non-linear order, SAX isn't going to provide the complete solution.

The W3C's Document Object Model (DOM) is a specification for a set of interfaces that XML parser vendors can implement in order to provide a model of an XML document as a set of objects. The interface describes methods to access, manipulate and manage the document.

What do we mean by 'manipulate' in this context? Well, if we imagine this chapter represented as an XML document, we would have various elements indicating the sections, their titles, the blocks of code, and the locations of files containing the illustrations. We could, using SAX, perhaps, read through the document and extract all of the level-1 headings for the table of contents. But if we decided we wanted to move one of the sections to the start of the chapter, SAX wouldn't provide any help at all. We could, perhaps, perform the task using string manipulation tools (but Java's not very friendly when it comes to playing with String data), but we'd have to do our own parsing of the XML tags to find the section of text we wanted to move. That defeats one of the main points of XML – having re-usable tools that do all of the hard work for us. So DOM provides us with a way to manipulate XML documents by manipulating the things that make up the document: elements, character data, attributes, and so on. Using DOM, we could move a section by moving the object representing its element. It is, as the title suggests, a model of the document, in object form.

Using the DOM we can build, navigate the structure, add, modify or delete elements and their content. In fact anything in an XML document can be created, updated, read or deleted by using the Object Model: processing instructions, comments, entities, DTDs, and so on; even whitespace.

Unlike SAX, the DOM specification is defined by W3C (http://www.w3.org/tr). Since its beginnings in 1997 there have been 2 main releases (which, defying every convention the IT industry has ever had, the W3C calls "levels") and at the time of writing level 3 is currently being drafted. It is important at this early stage to point out the relationship between the levels. DOM Level 2 does not make Level 1 obsolete; it makes very minor changes, in fact just one or two lines, but adds to the existing functionality. It is similar to the way packages were added to Java 1.0 through version 1.1, 1.2 and 1.3. The core Java functionality remained the same and writing something in Java without using features from 1.0 would be virtually impossible; likewise DOM Level 1 is an essential core part of the DOM specifications at all levels.

Chapter Requirements

The examples in this chapter were compiled and tested using Java 1.3.0, however several of the examples use nothing but Java 1.0 features, but it would be wise to test first if you are using older versions of the JVM (Java Virtual Machine):

❑   The Java API for XML Parsing (JAXP) version 1.1 (Download from http://java.sun.com/xml)

❑   The Apache Xerces-J Parser (for Java) version 1.3.0 (Download from http://xml.apache.org/xerces-j)

History of the DOM

Surprisingly, for a technology that is now virtually ubiquitous in XML processing applications, the DOM came about as a specification to provide portability of dynamic, HTML-embedded, client-side JavaScript code across web browsers, as part of 'dynamic HTML'. The idea was that web page scriptwriters would be able to use a DOM representation of the web page to manipulate the web page as it was displayed in the browser. The DOM provided mappings between the HTML document and objects that could then be used to create, update, read or delete HTML elements dynamically.

W3C then formed a DOM working group. Through new members the DOM was influenced by SGML (Standard Generalized Markup Language), XML's predecessor, as well as several other vendor-specific object models. At the same time, XML was developing and becoming a standard. The DOM, as it was developed, embraced both specific support for HTML documents, and also a generalized interface which could be used to access any XML document's content.

One of W3C's primary objectives was to provide a standard programming interface to the DOM so that it could be used by a variety of languages. The DOM is therefore not specifically designed for use with Java; in fact the canonical definition of the DOM is written in Interface Definition Language (IDL) as defined by the Object Management Group (OMG) in its CORBA 2.2 specification. IDL is a language independent interface specification and therefore can be used to map the interfaces into specific languages. The DOM is thus platform- and language-independent.

The DOM Level 1 Specification (http://www.w3.org/tr/rec-dom-level-1) started in late '97 and was finalized as a W3C "Recommendation" in August 1998 (this is the closest the W3C ever gets to calling something a standard). The last update was made in October 1998. This specification provided a Document class and through the API, methods to populate it. It did not however provide methods to serialize or persist the DOM (that is, to load a file into a DOM, or to output the data in the DOM as a file); this was left to the implementer. Two years later the DOM Level 2 became a recommendation in November 2000. This did not supersede level 1 but added to the existing functionality. There were several new interfaces in this release and one new exception. Functionally, changes included the use of CORBA 2.3.1 IDL mapping and, more importantly for us, the addition of XML namespace handling. On the 1ˢᵗ September 2000 we saw the first working draft of the DOM Level 3 specifications again this builds on level 2 rather than replaces it. There are a few changes to note regarding this specification, but we will address them at the end of this chapter. Both DOM level 2 and 3 were modularized, splitting different elements of the specification into independent sections. This allows vendors to implement just the core DOM functionality, and provide other elements as optional features where appropriate. The relevant specifications can be found at the following locations:

DOM module	Location of specification
DOM Level 2 Core	http://www.w3.org/TR/DOM-Level-2-Core
DOM Level 2 Events	http://www.w3.org/TR/DOM-Level-2-Events
DOM Level 2 Style	http://www.w3.org/TR/DOM-Level-2-Style
DOM Level 2 Traversal and Range	http://www.w3.org/TR/DOM-Level-2-Traversal-Range
DOM Level 2 Views	http://www.w3.org/TR/DOM-Level-2-Views

DOM Level 3 has similar URLs (change Level-2 in the URL for Level-3), but there is one new addition to Level 3: the long-awaited *DOM Level 3 Content Models and Load and Save*, at http://www.w3.org/TR/DOM-Level-3-Content-Models-and-Load-Save.

What is the DOM?

The DOM is an Application Programming Interface (API) for HTML and XML documents. It is not an implementation but simply a package of Java interfaces defining the API. Implementations of the interface are provided by parser vendors, browser manufacturers, and so on. The DOM closely resembles the structure of the documents it models; let's take a look at a simple example.

```
<wml>
  <card id="Wrox1" ontimer="#Chapter3">
    <timer value="20"/>
    <p>
      <img src="wroxlogo.wbmp" alt="Welcome to Wrox"/>
    </p>
  </card>

  <card id="Chapter3" title="XML Pro Ch.3">
    <p>The DOM</p>
  </card>
</wml>
```

This is WML (Wireless Markup Language), an HTML-like markup language used by WAP (Wireless Application Protocol) devices. It is also perfectly valid XML. We won't go into WML in detail here, but briefly for those interested, this first displays the wroxlogo image (or the "alt" text if images are not supported) on the WAP device for 2 seconds. It will then advance to the "Chapter3" card displaying "The DOM" under the title.

The DOM represents this WML document like this:

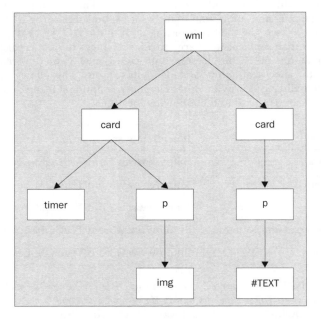

The DOM Document appears to have a tree-like structure (albeit upside down here). In fact it is closer to a forest in that it can contain many trees. There is however nothing in the specification to the effect that documents must be implemented as trees or a forest. In fact there is nothing in the specification that defines the relationship between objects in the structure; for this reason we should avoid a direct association with terms like tree, grove or forest. The specification refers to the term "structure model" to describe the tree-like representation of a document. An important property of the structure model is structural isomorphism, that is, any DOM implementation will represent any given document using the same structure model, objects and relationships.

From the perspective of our application, we see each of the rectangles in the model as a **Node**. We can ask a node to give us a reference to its children, or its parent – so, if we had a reference to the first card node, we could access its parent, the wml node, or its children, the timer and p nodes.

Remember, the DOM only specifies those interfaces that can be used to manage XML or HTML documents. Each DOM application is free to maintain documents in any convenient representation, as long as the interfaces shown in this specification are supported.

Further reading about the DOM in general can be found at http://www.w3.org/tr/rec-dom-level-1/introduction.html.

DOM Level 1

There are two main parts to the DOM Level 1 specification: the DOM Core that describes interfaces for accessing XML, and the HTML specific DOM API that extends the Core providing more specific interfaces for HTML. We're really only interested in the XML core here. Let's have a look at the Java interface mapping provided by the W3C DOM Level 1 specification.

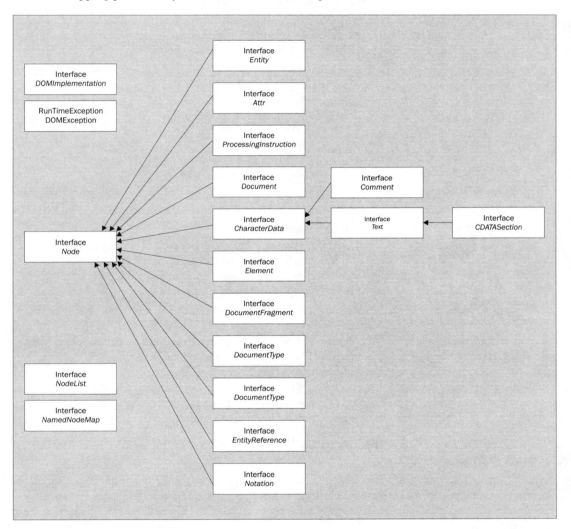

Node

Node is by far the most important interface in the DOM. As you can clearly see from the UML diagram above the large majority of interfaces implement Node, and two of the three that don't relate to it directly.

There are 13 different Node types, defined by extended interfaces which provide additional functionality (above and beyond that common to all nodes) specific to the type of node in question.

For all nodes, you can use the Node interface's `getNodeType()` method to return the `Node` type, which is a short integer matching one of the following constants, also defined in `Node`:

`getNodeType() ==`	Node Represents	`instanceof`
Node.ELEMENT_NODE	An XML element.	Element
Node.ATTRIBUTE_NODE	An attribute on an XML element.	Attr
Node.TEXT_NODE	Any text not contained within an XML tag: includes comments, marked CDATA sections, and element content.	Text
Node.CDATA_SECTION_NODE	A section marked up by [CDATA:[...]] notation.	CDATASection
Node.ENTITY_REFERENCE_NODE	A reference to an entity. By accessing its children you can get at the nodes making up the entity itself.	EntityReference
Node.ENTITY_NODE	An entity. The children of the entity will also be available through any entity references which point to this entity.	Entity
Node.PROCESSING_INSTRUCTION_NODE	An XML processing instruction, such as the <?xml ... ?> instruction.	Processing Instruction
Node.COMMENT_NODE	An XML Comment.	Comment
Node.DOCUMENT_NODE	The XML Document as a whole. This will have the root element as one of its children, but may also have comments, processing instructions, and so on.	Document
Node.DOCUMENT_TYPE_NODE	A <!DOCTYPE ... > declaration.	DocumentType
Node.DOCUMENT_FRAGMENT_NODE	A piece of XML which, alone, does not necessarily represent a complete, valid XML document.	DocumentFragment
Node.NOTATION_NODE	Notations, like entities, are declared in a DTD, and represent additional information about external entities, or processing applications.	Notation

Navigation Methods

All nodes have methods which allow you to navigate the DOM structure. The following 5 methods return single Nodes. They all return null if there is no corresponding node.

Node Method	Notes
getParentNode()	Returns the parent of the node
getFirstChild()	Returns the first child node in left to right order
getLastChild()	Returns the last child node
getPreviousSibling()	Returns the previous node at the same level
getNextSibling()	Returns the next node at the same level

getChildNodes() belongs to the Navigation set, but differs from these methods in that it returns a NodeList, which represents an ordered list of Node objects. The following code snippet demonstrates the typical way of using getChildNodes() and NodeList.

```
NodeList kids = root.getChildNodes();

if(kids != null) {
    for (int k=0; k<kids.getLength(); k++) {
        Node node = kids.item(k);
        // Do something with node.
    }
}
```

A NodeList is a fairly simple interface, which only defines these two methods: getLength() and item(). The item() method is very forgiving, and will simply return null if the index passed is out of range, rather than throwing an exception.

Node Information Methods

There are several methods provided by a node for accessing the crucial properties of the node: the data it contains.

getNodeName() will return the name of the node as a String. Each type of Node returns slightly different types of data for this method. The most common type of Node, an Element, returns the element's tag name, for example. Here's what will be returned by each node type:

Node Type	Node Name
Element	The tag name
Attr	The name of the attribute
Text	The literal text: '#text'
CDATASection	The literal text: '#cdata-section'
EntityReference	The name of the referenced entity
Entity	The name of the entity
ProcessingInstruction	The target of the processing instruction
Comment	The literal text: '#comment'
Document	The literal text: '#document'
DocumentType	The document-type's name
DocumentFragment	The literal text: '#document-fragment'
Notation	The name of the notation

getNodeValue() and setNodeValue() are most commonly used for Attr, Text and CDATASection nodes; in these cases they set or return the data corresponding to the tag (which is usually one of the things we are most concerned with when processing XML). The value is passed as a String, in both cases. However, again, since these methods are defined by the Node interface, they are available in every node type. Here's what is returned by each type of node:

Node Type	Node Value
Element	null
Attr	Value or attribute
Text	Content of the text node
CDATASection	Content of the CDATA Section
EntityReference	null
Entity	null
ProcessingInstruction	Entire content excluding the target
Comment	Content of the comment
Document	null
DocumentType	null
DocumentFragment	null
Notation	null

getAttributes() is used to access a node's attributes. Obviously, only an element node has attributes, but this method is defined in the Node interface, so is available on all node types, but will return null if there are no attributes available. If there are attributes, they will be returned in the second of the DOM's node collections: the NamedNodeMap, which is a hash table of sorts. It is used in various situations where an collection of nodes are guaranteed to have unique names, such as the set of attributes belonging to a single element, or the entities declared in a document's type. The NamedNodeMap has five methods:

NamedNodeMap Method	Notes
getNamedItem(String name)	Returns the item from the map with the given name, or null if no such item exists.
setNamedItem(Node arg)	Unlike most hash tables, we don't need to specify a key, since the key is implicit in the node we pass the method (it is the node's name). This will silently replace any node already held in the map with that name.
removeNamedItem(String name)	Removes the named node from the map. A DOMException is thrown if the item was not present in the map.
item(long index)	Each item in the map is assigned a sequential index, although the order in which these indexes are allocated to the nodes should not be seen as significant. This is simply to allow us to loop through the map accessing every member using a convenient method. Null is returned if the index is out of range.
getLength()	Returns the number of items in the map.

`getOwnerDocument()` returns the document that this `Node` belongs to, or `null` if the `Node` is a `Document` or a `DocumentType` which is not used with any document yet.

It's often a source of confusion to DOM newcomers that attributes are not actually child nodes of elements. An attribute node is actually a separate root in the DOM node forest, and it normally has a text node as a child. However, it's possible for an attribute to contain entity references or other complex node data. Since attributes, in spite of this complexity, are normally treated as simple name-value pairs, convenience methods such as these have been created to allow access to attributes through a friendly API.

The last of the information methods, `hasChildNodes()`, returns `true` if the current `Node` has any child nodes.

Node Manipulation Methods

The following four methods can be used to manipulate the child nodes of the node they are called on:

Node Method	Notes
`insertBefore(Node newChild, Node refChild)`	Inserts the `newChild` before the `refChild` in the ordered list of children. A `DOMException` is thrown if `refChild` isn't a child of the node. The method returns the same node as is inserted.
`replaceChild(Node newChild, Node oldChild)`	Removes `oldChild` from its position in the parent node's list of children, and replaces it with the `newChild`. Returns the `oldChild` node. Again, a `DOMException` is thrown if the node to be replaced isn't one of the parent's children.
`removeChild(Node oldChild)`	Attempts to remove the specified node from the parent node's children. Returns the node which has been removed, or throws a `DOMException` if the node is not one of the parent's children.
`appendChild(Node newChild)`	Adds `newChild` to the end of the parent node's child list.

There are some additional requirements placed on all of these methods: you can't give some nodes certain types of nodes as children (for example, you can't have an element as a child of an attribute), and you can't make a node a child of a node of which it is already a parent. These sorts of operations will throw a `DOMException`.

Also, we can't just instantiate `Node` objects – remember, `Node` is an interface. We must use a factory method to ask the underlying implementation to provide us with a new `Node` object. A `DOMException` will also be thrown if we try to give a node a child node which wasn't created from the correct factory. There is one method available on any node that can furnish us with a valid node for these purposes:

`cloneNode()` returns a duplicate of the node. It takes a single boolean parameter, and passing `true` will recursively clone the node's children as well; passing `false` will clone only the node itself (and its attributes, if it is an element). The new `Node` has no parent, but belongs to the same document.

The other node creation methods all belong to the largest of the `Node` sub-interfaces, `Document`.

Document

Most of the methods added to the Node interface by Document are createXXX() methods, where XXX is the type of node to be created.

Document Method	Notes
createElement(String tagName)	Creates an element with the given tag name.
createDocumentFragment()	Creates a new document fragment.
createTextNode(String data)	Creates a text node, initialized with the data passed in as a String.
createComment(String data)	Creates a comment node, initialized with the data passed in as a String.
createCDATASection(String data)	Creates a CDATA node, initialized with the data passed in as a String.
createProcessingInstruction(String target, String data)	creates a Processing Instruction node with the specified target and data.
createAttribute(String name)	Creates an empty attribute with the given name.
createEntityReference(String name)	Creates a reference to the specified entity.

The returned nodes do not have a parent, so can be added to the node tree using the methods we looked at before, subject to the constraints on what type of node can be a child of what other type.

getDocType() returns the document's doctype attribute, whose value is either null or a DocumentType object.

The last of the three non-node interfaces in the DOM, DOMImplementation, provides methods for performing operations that are independent of any particular instance of the document object model. You can obtain an object which implements this interface from a Document by calling the getImplementation() method.

getDocumentElement() is one of the most important methods in the Document interface, and is used to return the root element of the document. A Document typically has several child nodes – processing instructions, comments, a DocumentType, and so on, but we are almost always most interested in the root element of the XML.

Finally getElementByTagName() will return a NodeList of all the elements in the document, in document order, that match the passed tag name. The special value "*" matches all tags.

Element

Element is by far the most common of nodes. While it is possible to access a lot of the features of an element through methods in the Node interface, the Element interface extends this to provide us with even more specialized functionality.

getTagName() returns the name of the element – the same as the Node interface's getNodeName() method, but more explicit.

Elements also have a `getAttribute()` method, which takes a string as a name, and returns the value of the named attribute, or `null` if it doesn't exist. This is a shorthand for using the `getAttributes()` `.getNamedItem().getValue()` combination provided in the `Node` interface.

Similarly, a `setAttribute()` method, which takes two strings as arguments, one for the attribute name, and one for the value, saves you the effort of creating a new `Attr` node, obtaining the element's attribute map, and putting the attribute object into it.

Finally, `removeAttribute()` removes an attribute with the name we pass in as a string.

The following three methods are similar to the above versions, except they either take or return an `Attr` (Attribute) instead of the string representation.

```
getAttributeNode(String name)
setAttributeNode(Attr newAttr)
removeAttributeNode(Attr oldAttr)
```

`getElementsByTagName()` will, as for the `Document` interface, return a `NodeList` of elements that match the passed tag name, only this time only traversing the element's children, rather than the entire document.

Attr

The other `Node` sub-interfaces are relatively simple compared with `Element`; `Attr`, for example has a `get/setValue()`, and only a simple `getName()` (to create an attribute with a different name you have to make a new node).

Parsing and Transforming with JAXP

JAXP (The Java API for XML Processing), which we met in the last chapter, provides a mechanism for us to access DOM implementations. As with SAX, JAXP sits on top of the parser and hides parser-specific interfaces from the application. It provides a standard for XML to DOM I/O, an area still undefined in the DOM specifications.

Sun's JAXP reference implementation uses Apache's Crimson, which was derived from the Java Project X parser from Sun, as its default XML parser. However, the pluggable architecture of JAXP allows any conformant implementation to be used, including Apache's other parser, Xerces.

It is important to note that DOM level 1 and 2 do not specify a means of reading or writing XML from a file into or out of a DOM. To do this we have three simple choices:

❑ Write file/stream I/O ourselves. This is not hard to do, but unless you have a very specific case it's a bit like re-inventing the wheel.

❑ Use a custom DOM library, often supplied by DOM vendors. This has up until recently been the most common method.

❑ Use JAXP to abstract either of the previous options by using a generic interface to the parser.

The lack of what would seem a vital feature in DOM is a result of its origins. It was designed to model existing HTML documents in browsers but not to read them in and write them out (the browser was supposed to read the document in, and there was no need to write it back out again). File I/O has traditionally been very machine-dependent and avoiding this part of the specification has avoided issues with operating system I/O.

Since we covered direct access to SAX parser factories in the previous chapter, we'll now take a look at the more general JAXP notions of creating and transforming objects using the abstract document builder factory and transformer factory classes.

Reading XML into a DOM using JAXP

We mentioned above that JAXP comes with a default implementation, which therefore simplifies the process. We will, however demonstrate how to change this in order to use a different implementation. To read XML into a DOM using JAXP requires three simple steps.

❑   Get a new DocumentBuilderFactory instance.

❑   Use the DocumentBuilderFactory to create a DocumentBuilder.

❑   Use the DocumentBuilder to create the Document either as a new document or from an existing file or stream of data.

It is the DocumentBuilderFactory that we access in the first instance, which provides us with an underlying implementation from a specific parser. Firstly let's take a look at the simple, default case:

```
import javax.xml.parsers.*;

public class JAXPDOMTest {

  public static void main(String[] args) {

    DocumentBuilderFactory dbf = DocumentBuilderFactory.newInstance();
    DocumentBuilder db = dbf.newDocumentBuilder();
    Document doc = db.newDocument();

  }
}
```

At the end of the program, doc is now a new "virgin" DOM Document.

In fact, we can use one of six different methods in DocumentBuilder for creating DOM Documents.

DocumentBuilder Method	Notes
newDocument()	Creates a blank document.
parse(File f)	Parses the given file.
parse(InputSource is)	Parses the specified SAX input source (org.xml.sax.InputSource).
parse(InputStream is)	Parses XML data from the specified input stream.
parse(InputStream is, String systemId)	Parses XML data from the specified input stream, passing in a URI which should be used to resolve relative URIs.
parse(String uri)	Parses XML data from the specified URI.

The underlying implementation is totally hidden from us. All of these methods return an object which implements the document interface, so we can then proceed to use all of the methods discussed above to process the parsed data. How the parser goes about providing this is not our concern.

In order to change the default parser we have a few options. One is to change one of the system properties read by JAXP. In this case, JAXP looks to the `javax.xml.parsers` `.DocumentBuilderFactory` property to locate a parser which provides an implementation. There are three easy ways to change this setting. One is to specify the value on the command line when we execute our Java code, using the `-D` tag to define a property value. For example, to tell JAXP to use Xerces' implementation instead of Crimson's, you would use the following command line option when you called the `java` run-time up:

```
-Djavax.xml.parsers.DocumentBuilderFactory=org.apache.xerces.jaxp.DocumentBuilderF
actoryImpl
```

A default value for the property can be set by creating a file in your `%JAVA_HOME%\jre\lib` directory called `jaxp.properties`, which contains the line:

```
javax.xml.parsers.DocumentBuilderFactory=org.apache.xerces.jaxp.DocumentBuilderFac
toryImpl
```

or an equivalent specifying another parser's JAXP implementation.

Alternatively, we can read the value from our own properties file, using code like this:

```
FileInputStream fin = new FileInputStream( "wrox.properties" );
Properties props = new Properties();
Props.load(fin);
Fin.close();

String parserOfTheMonth = props.getProperty("DOMParser");
System.setProperty("javax.xml.parsers.DocumentBuilderFactory", parserOfTheMonth );
```

The property is checked when we call the `DocumentBuilderFactory`'s static `newInstance()` method. This class, provided by the JAXP distribution, is actually an abstract class, and what is returned is actually an instance of a concrete subclass. It locates the class to instantiate by checking the property setting.

If there is no specified value for this property, JAXP 1.1 uses the JAR services API to look for a JAR file on the classpath which contains a file in its `META-INF/services` directory with the name `javax.xml.parsers.DocumentBuilderFactory`, and reads the content of that file to obtain the name of an implementing class. If that doesn't work, JAXP has one last default, which is to look for the Crimson parser class (`org.apache.crimson.jaxp.DocumentBuilderFactoryImpl`).

Writing XML out from a DOM using JAXP

Writing XML out is slightly harder. However, JAXP 1.1 provides a mechanism which we can use to do this without having to use any parser-specific calls. We need to use a **Transformer**, which, as with the `DocumentBuilder` comes from a factory. We create a new `Transformer` from a `TransformerFactory` and then use this `Transformer` to write the DOM Document to the output. As you may guess from the name, a `Transformer` object can do much more than simply take a DOM object and output its contents: it can also be used to apply transformations to the data held in a DOM, or in a file. We'll come back to transformers again in detail in chapter 8: *Programming With XSLT*.

There is one last thing to note here and that is that the method we use, transform(), takes wrapper objects, Source and Result. We have to wrap the DOM Document in a Source object and similarly the output stream or file in a Result. Here is the basic code required to output the contents of the Document doc to the output stream System.out:

```
TransformerFactory transformerFactory = TransformerFactory.newInstance();
Transformer transformer = transformerFactory.newTransformer();
transformer.transform(new DOMSource(doc), new StreamResult(System.out));
```

What we've done here is to create a new factory instance (which again is provided by a concrete implementation, not by the JAXP class itself), and use that factory to create a Transformer object and then finally call the Transformer's transform() method with our wrapped parameters.

The StreamResult class passed to transform() as the second argument is the source of flexibility here. In fact, the StreamResult is a specialized subclass of the more general Result class. There are three subclasses of Result: DOMResult, SAXResult and StreamResult. The first two are for sending the output (result) directly to a new DOM or SAX parsing process. StreamResult provides constructors that take the following parameters, representing different output targets:

- java.io.File
- java.io.OutputStream
- java.lang.String (representing a URI)
- java.io.Writer

Building a DOM Tree

In this example, we'll show how to use the core DOM API and the JAXP factory classes to create and print out an XML document:

```java
import org.w3c.dom.*;

import javax.xml.parsers.*;
import javax.xml.transform.*;
import javax.xml.transform.stream.*;
import javax.xml.transform.dom.*;

import java.io.PrintWriter;
import java.io.IOException;

public class CreatePresident
{
    public static void main( String[] args )
    {
        Document doc;

        Element president;
        Element person;
        Element firstName;
        Element surname;
```

First we create a new document:

```
try
{
                // Create a new Document using JAXP
    DocumentBuilderFactory dbf = DocumentBuilderFactory.newInstance();
    DocumentBuilder db = dbf.newDocumentBuilder();
    doc = db.newDocument();
```

We'll start by creating a `Person`:

```
    person = doc.createElement("Person");

    //Now create the "<FirstName>" element
    firstName = doc.createElement("FirstName");

    // Create a Text node "George" and add it to the "FirstName" tag
    firstName.appendChild( doc.createTextNode("George") );

    // Add the "<FirstName>" element to "<Person>"
    person.appendChild(firstName);

    // Same as above
    surname = doc.createElement("Surname");
    surname.appendChild( doc.createTextNode("Bush") );
    person.appendChild(surname);

    president = doc.createElement("President");

    // Set the "Country" attribute in "<President>"
    president.setAttribute("Country","US");
    president.appendChild( person );

    // Add everything to the XmlDocument (doc)
    doc.appendChild( president );
```

Now we can use JAXP to output the `Document` to `System.out`.

```
TransformerFactory tFactory = TransformerFactory.newInstance();
    Transformer transformer = tFactory.newTransformer();
    transformer.transform(new DOMSource(doc), new
      StreamResult(System.out));
}
catch( ParserConfigurationException pcEx )
{
    System.out.println("ParserConfigurationException: " +
      pcEx.getMessage());
    pcEx.printStackTrace();
}
catch( TransformerConfigurationException tcEx )
{
    System.out.println("TransformerConfigurationException: " +
      tcEx.getMessage());
    tcEx.printStackTrace();
}
catch( TransformerException tEx )
{
```

```
                System.out.println("TransformerException: "+tEx.getMessage());
                tEx.printStackTrace();
            }
        }
    }
```

Compile this and run it and you should get this result:

```
Command Prompt                                                    _ □ X

C:\projavaxml\chapter03>echo %classpath%
.;C:\jaxp-1.1\jaxp.jar;C:\jaxp-1.1\xalan.jar

C:\projavaxml\chapter03>javac CreatePresident.java

C:\projavaxml\chapter03>java CreatePresident
<?xml version="1.0" encoding="UTF-8"?>
<President Country="US"><Person><FirstName>George</FirstName><Surname>Bush</Surn
ame></Person></President>
C:\projavaxml\chapter03>_
```

Something that may appear strange with the output is that it is not very well formatted. We tend to get used to writing XML documents in pretty, human-readable forms like this:

```
<?xml version="1.0" encoding="UTF-8"?>

<President Country="US">
  <Person>
    <FirstName>George</FirstName>
    <Surname>Bush</Surname>
  </Person>
</President>
```

If it were formatted like this, we would in fact be introducing extra whitespace, whitespace we never told the DOM tree it should contain. Whitespace in XML is significant and these two versions of XML are not the same. In fact parsing in the two different versions would result in two different DOM models. This distinction can be disabled when parsing by calling the DocumentBuilderFactory's setIgnoringElementContentWhitespace() method before we obtain a DocumentBuilder from it, passing in the parameter true.

Working Inside the Tree

We have now managed to create a DOM tree with predefined data and then transform it into a StreamResult to System.out. How would we read one in from an existing XML document? Well, again we have to leave the DOM Level 1 specification and use additional classes. Below we use JAXP 1.1, this time to create a Document from an external source:

```
import org.w3c.dom.*;

import javax.xml.parsers.*;
import javax.xml.transform.*;
import javax.xml.transform.stream.*;
import javax.xml.transform.dom.*;
```

```
import java.io.File;
import java.io.FileInputStream;
import java.io.FileNotFoundException;
import java.net.URL;

public class ReadXML
{
   public static void main( String[] args )
   {
      Document doc = null;
      boolean validation = true;

      if( args.length == 0 )
      {
         System.out.println("Usage:\tReadXML filename.xml");
         return;
      }

      String source = args[0];

      try
      {
         System.out.println( "Reading from "+source );
```

I have used `DocumentBuilderFactory`'s `setValidating()` to switch parser validation to `false` or "off". If this property is set to `true`, documents will be validated against a DTD or schema.

```
DocumentBuilderFactory dbf = DocumentBuilderFactory.newInstance();
dbf.setValidating(false);
DocumentBuilder db = dbf.newDocumentBuilder();
doc = db.parse(source);
```

doc now contains a DOM object representing the structure of the parsed XML. We'll now stamp our mark on the document's content, and re-output it to the screen in a modified form. First, we need to get hold of the document's root element:

```
Node root = (Node)doc.getDocumentElement();
```

Then we need to create a new element which we can add to the DOM tree.

```
Element info = doc.createElement("Info");

info.setAttribute("Date",(new java.util.Date()).toString() );
root.appendChild( info );

System.out.println("Done, here's the modified XML output: -\n");
```

The output code is the same as before:

```
            TransformerFactory tFactory = TransformerFactory.newInstance();
            Transformer transformer = tFactory.newTransformer();
            transformer.transform(new DOMSource(doc), new
                StreamResult(System.out));
        }
        catch( FileNotFoundException fnfEx )
        {
            System.out.println(source+" was not found");
        }
        catch( Exception ex )
        {
            ex.printStackTrace();
            System.out.println( ex.getMessage() );
        }
    }
}
```

Working with NodeList and Node Attributes

The above example is intended to demonstrate the reading of a file into a DOM Document. Below is a more complex example that takes a DOM Document and displays it as a javax.swing.JTree. JTree provides a perfect structure for displaying a DOM model. In this example we will read in the document and iterate through it reading the type of nodes and adding them to the JTree with extra information depending on their type. Later in this chapter we will discover a much easier way of "iterating" through the DOM tree using DOM level 2 Iterators and TreeWalkers.

```
import org.w3c.dom.*;

import javax.xml.parsers.*;
import javax.xml.transform.*;
import javax.xml.transform.stream.*;
import javax.xml.transform.dom.*;

import javax.swing.*;
import javax.swing.tree.*;
import javax.swing.event.*;
import java.awt.*;
import java.awt.event.*;
import java.util.*;
import java.io.*;
import java.net.*;

public class XML2JTree extends JPanel
{
    private         JTree    jTree;
    private static  JFrame   frame;

    public static final int FRAME_WIDTH = 640;
    public static final int FRAME_HEIGHT = 480;

    public XML2JTree(Node root)
    {
```

There are several ways of constructing a `JTree`, for the example we have used a Java `TreeModel` (in the `DefaultTreeModel`). The `DefaultTreeModel` takes a `TreeNode` in its constructor and for this we have passed a `DefaultMutableTreeNode` generated from our DOM model. The `TreeNode` passed to the `DefaultTreeModel` therefore represents the root of the DOM model being displayed.

```
DefaultMutableTreeNode treeRoot = createTreeNode(root);
DefaultTreeModel dtModel = new DefaultTreeModel(treeRoot);

jTree = new JTree(dtModel);
```

The following lines simply set up the style and look of the `jTree` as it is displayed.

```
jTree.getSelectionModel().setSelectionMode(
    TreeSelectionModel.SINGLE_TREE_SELECTION);
jTree.putClientProperty("JTree.lineStyle", "Angled");
jTree.setShowsRootHandles(true);
```

Editing is turned off but this example could be extended to provide `Node` editing features.

```
jTree.setEditable(false);
```

This creates the `JScrollPane` that we are going to use but the Java code below overrides one of the `JScrollPane` methods (`getPreferredSize()`) in order to fix the size of the pane. There are several ways of doing this; if this was not done the scrollable area of the screen would depend on the size of the XML being displayed.

```
JScrollPane jScroll = new JScrollPane()
{
    // This keeps the scrollpane a reasonable size
    public Dimension getPreferredSize()
    {
        return new Dimension( FRAME_WIDTH-20, FRAME_HEIGHT-40 );
    }
};

jScroll.getViewport().add(jTree);

JPanel pal = new JPanel();
panel.setLayout(new BorderLayout());
panel.add("Center", jScroll);
add("Center", panel);
}
```

That's it for the GUI code. We simply need to write the method which takes a DOM `Node`, and builds a `TreeNode` out of it. Our implementation takes a DOM `Node` and recurses through the children until each one is added to a `DefaultMutableTreeNode`. This can then be used by the `JTree` as a tree model.

```
protected DefaultMutableTreeNode createTreeNode( Node root )
{
    DefaultMutableTreeNode dmtNode = null;

    String type = getNodeType(root);
    String name = root.getNodeName();
    String value = root.getNodeValue();

    String displayString = "["+type+"] --> "+name+"="+value;
```

The following displays the attributes if there are any:

```
NamedNodeMap attribs = root.getAttributes();
if(attribs != null )
{
   for( int i = 0; i < attribs.getLength(); i++ )
   {
      Node attNode = attribs.item(i);
      String attName = attNode.getNodeName().trim();
      String attValue = attNode.getNodeValue().trim();

      if(attValue != null)
      {
         if (attValue.length() > 0)
         {
            displayString += " ("+attName+"=\""+attValue+"\")";
         }
      }
   }
}
dmtNode = new DefaultMutableTreeNode(displayString);
```

If there are any children and they are non-`null` then we recurse. This "weeds" out the blank lines that would actually be the carriage-returns used when beautifying the XML. Strictly speaking we should display these, but we aren't interested in them in this example.

```
if(root.hasChildNodes())
{
   NodeList childNodes = root.getChildNodes();
   if(childNodes != null)
   {
      for (int k=0; k<childNodes.getLength(); k++)
      {
         Node nd = childNodes.item(k);
         if( nd != null )
         {
            // A special case could be made for each Node type.
            if( nd.getNodeType() == Node.ELEMENT_NODE )
            {
               dmtNode.add(createTreeNode(nd));
            }
            String data = nd.getNodeValue();
            if(data != null)
            {
               data = data.trim();
               if( data.length() > 0)
               {
                  dmtNode.add(createTreeNode(nd));
               }
            }
         }
      }
   }
}
return dmtNode;
}
```

Finally, we have a simple method that returns a displayable string given a `NodeType` from the input `Node`:

```java
public String getNodeType(Node node) {
   String type;
   switch (node.getNodeType()) {
      case Node.ELEMENT_NODE:
         type = "Element";
         break;
      case Node.ATTRIBUTE_NODE:
         type = "Attribute";
         break;
      case Node.TEXT_NODE:
         type = "Text";
         break;
      case Node.CDATA_SECTION_NODE:
         type = "CData section";
         break;
      case Node.ENTITY_REFERENCE_NODE:
         type = "Entity reference";
         break;
      case Node.ENTITY_NODE:
         type = "Entity";
         break;
      case Node.PROCESSING_INSTRUCTION_NODE:
         type = "Processing instruction";
         break;
      case Node.COMMENT_NODE:
         type = "Comment";
         break;
      case Node.DOCUMENT_NODE:
         type = "Document";
         break;
      case Node.DOCUMENT_TYPE_NODE:
         type = "Document type";
         break;
      case Node.DOCUMENT_FRAGMENT_NODE:
         type = "Document fragment";
         break;
      case Node.NOTATION_NODE:
         type = "Notation";
         break;
      default:
         type = "Unknown"
         break;
      }
   return type;
}
```

That constitutes a usable class if we want to embed a `JTree` of a DOM tree into an application. To simplify testing, however, we add a `main()` method which instantiates our XML `JTree`, and displays it in an application window.

```java
public static void main(String[] args)
{
   Document doc = null;

   // Just check we have the right parameters first.
   if( args.length < 1 )
   {
```

```
            System.out.println( "Usage:\tXML2JTree filename.xml" );
            return;
        }
        String filename = args[0];
```

`frame` is the actual "window" that appears on the screen, it will have the title "XML to Java" and will start up in the center of the screen. It is important to set the size of the frame in Swing due to the undefined defaults of various operating systems.

```
        // Create a frame to "hold" our class
        frame = new JFrame("XML to JTree");

        Toolkit toolkit = Toolkit.getDefaultToolkit();
        Dimension dim = toolkit.getScreenSize();
        int screenHeight = dim.height;
        int screenWidth = dim.width;

        frame.setBounds( (screenWidth-FRAME_WIDTH)/2,
            (screenHeight-FRAME_HEIGHT)/2, FRAME_WIDTH, FRAME_HEIGHT );

        frame.setBackground(Color.lightGray);
        frame.getContentPane().setLayout(new BorderLayout());
```

Finally we give the frame an icon and add a default listener to the window so that it "dies" when we click on the close icon.

```
        frame.setIconImage(toolkit.getImage("Wrox.gif"));

        // Add a WindowListener so that we can close the window
        WindowListener wndCloser = new WindowAdapter()
        {
            public void windowClosing(WindowEvent e)
            {
                exit();
            }
        };
        frame.addWindowListener(wndCloser);
```

This is the JAXP part, we could use any loader here to read the XML into the DOM.

```
        try
        {
            DocumentBuilderFactory dbf = DocumentBuilderFactory.newInstance();
            dbf.setValidating(false);  // Not important for this demo

            DocumentBuilder db = dbf.newDocumentBuilder();
            doc = db.parse(filename);
        }
        catch( FileNotFoundException fnfEx )
        {
```

```
            // Display a "nice" warning message if the file isn't there.
            JOptionPane.showMessageDialog(frame, filename+" was not found",
                "Warning", JOptionPane.WARNING_MESSAGE);

            System.out.println();
            exit();
        }
        catch( Exception ex )
        {
            JOptionPane.showMessageDialog(frame, ex.getMessage(), "Exception",
                                    JOptionPane.WARNING_MESSAGE);

            ex.printStackTrace();
            exit();
        }

        Node root = (Node)doc.getDocumentElement();

        frame.getContentPane().add(new XML2JTree( root ),
            BorderLayout.CENTER);

        frame.validate();
        frame.setVisible(true);
    }
```

Providing a method inside our code to finish the application is often preferable to simply calling `System.exit()` in multi-threaded applications, as it provides a single point of exit from the application where we can release resources and close opened files.

```
    private static void exit()
    {
        System.out.println("Graceful exit");
        System.exit(0);
    }
}
```

I have used the previous simple XML example to demonstrate the output. Note the extra comment and CDATA lines to help vary the `Node` types:

```
<?xml version="1.0" encoding="UTF-8"?>
<President Country="US">
    <!--This is an XML comment-->
    <![CDATA[This can contain almost <anything>]]>
    <Person>
        <FirstName>George</FirstName>
        <Surname>Bush</Surname>
    </Person>
</President>
```

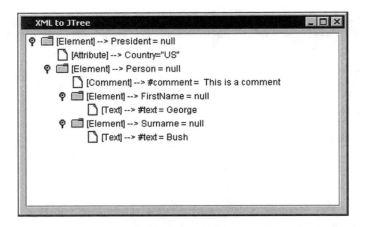

> An important feature of the DOM worth noting is that text inside an element is considered a child of the element rather than the value of the element. This may seem rather confusing at first, given the example **<H1>Header</H1>** will result in an element whose name is **H1** and value is **null**. It will have a child of type **Text** whose name will be **#text** and value **Header**.
>
> It is also worth noting that this is different from the way JDOM works (as we'll see in the next chapter).

As you iterate through the DOM you will be able to identify the type of Node by using the getNodeType() method. You can either use this or instanceof to downcast Node objects to the appropriate sub-interface of Node. If node.getNodeType() returns Node.TEXT_NODE you can then cast the node to Text:

```
if (node.getNodeType() == Node.TEXT_NODE)
{
Text tNode = (Text) node;
   // Code specific to a Text [Node]
}
```

It is often possible to navigate through the Document using the methods of Node alone. The majority of the functionality of Node and its sub-interfaces lies in the Node interface.

Lastly, before we leave DOM Level 1 and move on to Level 2, there is a method in the Document object that deserves a little more attention: getElementsByTagName(). Given a large DOM Document it is often difficult to find the element we actually need; often the Element or Node we are looking for almost becomes hidden by the volume of others. Using getElementsByTagName() is quite simple. Imagine a large document with a number of nodes:

```
<MajorBank Office="London ">
   <!-- Foreign Exchange trades -->
<Trade Type="ForEx">
   <ID>FX20010205-463</ID>
   <Amount>15000000</Amount>
   <Currency>USD</Currency>
```

```
    <BUY/>
    <Term>SPOT</Term>
    <Rate>1.47545</Rate>
    <!-- Lots more details -->
  <Trade>
  <Trade Type="ForEx">
    <ID>FX20010205-469</ID>
    <Amount>6500000</Amount>
    <Currency>EUR</Currency>
    <BUY/>
    <Term>1 Week</Term>
    <Rate>1.57349</Rate>
    <!-- Lots more details -->
  </Trade>
  <!-- Lots more Trades -->
  </MajorBank>
```

This document might be transmitted as part of a trading system in a large bank trading foreign currencies. From the masses of data, we want to list the actual trades. To do that we could do the following:

```
NodeList nl = doc.getElementsByTagName("Trade");
int len = nl.getLength();

for (int i = 0; i < len; i++)
{
    Node n = nl.item(i);
    if( isMyTrade( n ) )
        processMyTrade( n );
}
```

getElementsByTagName() then is a useful method for finding elements in a document: we can obtain the elements we are interested in in a useful collection form, which we can use to iterate through the nodes and investigate them one at a time.

DOM Level 2

DOM Level 2, being a more recent specification than level 1, has notably less implementations supporting it. Vendors providing either compliant or pre-release implementations, at the time of writing, include Oracle (http://technet.oracle.com/tech/xml), Apache (http://xml.apache.org), and obviously Sun (http://www.java.sun.com/xml).

As we mentioned at the beginning of the chapter, DOM Level 2 is an extension of DOM Level 1: it doesn't deprecate the DOM Level 1 interfaces and methods, and a DOM Level 2 parser has to be DOM Level 1 compliant.

The main changes added are to support namespaces. The interfaces we have been using have had the following significant changes made to them:

❑ **Attr**: The Attr interface has a new getOwnerElement() method.

❑ **Document**: The Document interface has five new methods: importNode(), which is used to transfer a node owned by a different document into the document, getElementById(), which allows you to access elements within a validated XML document which make use of ID attributes, and several methods which update level 1 methods with namespace support: createElementNS(), createAttributeNS(), and getElementsByTagNameNS().

131

❑ **NamedNodeMap**: The `NamedNodeMap` interface has three new methods, all relating to namespace support: `getNamedItemNS()`, `setNamedItemNS()`, and `removeNamedItemNS()`.

❑ **Node**: The `Node` interface has two new methods: `isSupported()` and `hasAttributes()`. Three new attributes relating to namespaces have been added, two are read-only (`namespaceURI` and `localName`), and `prefix`, which is read-write. This maps into five new `get` and `set` methods.

❑ **Element**: The `Element` interface has eight new methods: six namespace enablers for old favorites: `getAttributeNS()`, `setAttributeNS()`, `removeAttributeNS()`, `getAttributeNodeNS()`, `setAttributeNodeNS()`, `getElementsByTagNameNS()`, and one new method, in namespace and non-namespace versions: `hasAttribute()` and `hasAttributeNS()`.

Additional modules in DOM Level 2

In addition to the changes to the Core, DOM Level 2 has been segmented into 14 modules. It is possible for an implementation to conform to DOM Level 2, or to a set of DOM Level 2 modules. The 14 modules are:-

❑ Core module

❑ XML module

❑ HTML module
(Note: At time of writing, this module is not yet a W3C Recommendation.)

❑ Views module

❑ Style Sheets module

❑ CSS module

❑ CSS2 module

❑ Events module

❑ User interface Events module

❑ Mouse Events module

❑ Mutation Events module

❑ HTML Events module

❑ Range module

❑ Traversal module

In order to demonstrate some of the new features of DOM level 2, such as `TreeWalkers`, `Iterators and NodeFilters` etc., it will be necessary to leave Sun's JAXP implementation. We will use Apache's Xerces.

Apache Xerces (at version 1.3 and 2.0 alpha at the time of writing) supports XML 1.0 recommendation as well as XML Schema and DOM Level 1 and 2. This and other Apache packages are provided under Apache's license and are open source. You can obtain a copy of Xerces at http://xml.apache.org. Version 1.3 will be sufficient for all our examples.

Leaving the new namespace methods until later, some interesting new methods have been added to `Document` and `Node`.

Document

In `Document`:

```
public Element getElementById(String elementId)
```

will only work if the DOM implementation has information on which attributes are of type ID (defined by a DTD or a schema), simply using `"ID"` will not work unless you define it as an `ID`. A `null` is returned if the `Element` is not found or ID has not been defined.

Node

In `Node`, the new method:

```
public boolean isSupported(String feature, String version)
```

returns `true` if the feature and version are supported, for example:

```
if (!doc.isSupported("Traversal", "2.0")) {
    throw new MyException("Traversal is not supported" );
}
```

This enables us to continue to use a parser-neutral interface such as JAXP, and use this method call to determine if the parser JAXP has furnished us with can support the operations we wish to perform.

Also, the following method for querying the existence of attributes of a node has been added:

```
public boolean hasAttributes()
```

The method could have been rather useful in the previous example. For instance, we used the following in our previous implementation:

```
NamedNodeMap attribs = root.getAttributes();
if(attribs != null ) {
    ...
}
```

This could have become:

```
if(root.hasAttributes()) {
    ...
}
```

One method we've not mentioned before has been moved in DOM Level 2. The `normalize()` method used to be in the `Element` class and has been moved to `Node` in DOM Level 2. `normalize()` can be used to ensure that the DOM view of a document is the same as if it were saved and re-loaded, collapsing whitespace between elements in non-mixed content elements, and turning empty start-tag end-tag pairs into proper empty element tags. For example:

```
<Document>
    <p>Some text
    </p>
    <Data></Data>
</Document>
```

After `normalize()` will result in:

```
<Document> <p>Some text </p> <Data/> </Document>
```

It is probably worth noting at this point that if `<Data>` and `</Data>` were on separate lines the extra line and spaces are recognized by the parser and passed to the DOM. The `Data` element then has a valid non-null `Text` node as a child. Normalizing it will not therefore shorten it to `<Data/>`.

Element

Apart from several new namespace methods that we will cover shortly, there are two new methods for Attributes, `hasAttribute(String)` that returns `true` if the element has a child attribute of that name, and a namespace version `hasAttributeNS()`.

Attr

`Attr` has one new attribute: `ownerElement`, can be obtained by the new method `getOwnerElement()`. It will return `null` if the attribute is unused.

DOMException, DocumentType, NamedNodeMap

There are other minor changes, including several new `DOMException` types, and new namespace methods in `NamedNodeMap`.

Using Namespaces

The W3C Namespace recommendation can be found at http://www.w3.org/tr/rec-xml-names. The Namespace methods generally include "NS" in their name, for example `createElementNS()` or `getAttributeNS()`.

Here's some namespace oriented XML:

```xml
<?xml version='1.0' encoding='UTF-8'?>

<DOMExample>

    <book xmlns="http://www.wrox.com/book-titles">
        <title price="$59.95">Professional Java XML</title>
        <chapter title="The DOM">
            <author title="Mr." name="John Davies"/>
        </chapter>
    </book>

    <order xmlns:html="http://www.c24solutions.com">
        <name html:class="H1">Steve Miller</name>
    <payment type="credit" html:class="H3">Paid</payment>
    <html:a href="/jsp/prebookings?order-ref=0527658">Check order</html:a>
    <date location="London" html:class="H3">2001-07-21</date>
     </order>

</DOMExample>
```

The first <book> section has a default namespace; this means that it, and all its child elements, defaults to belonging to that namespace without having to be explicitly identified as such. You can read each element as meaning 'book, in the Wrox book-titles sense of the word', and 'chapter, in the Wrox book-titles sense of the word'.

The second <order> section defines a "prefixed" namespace, in this case with the defined prefix html. In order to use it we refer to the namespace prefix when we want to specify that an element or attribute belongs to that namespace, as for example in the first <name> element where the attribute class is part of the html namespace (which we have declared as meaning the namespace called http://www.c24solutions.com).

Notice that some of the elements don't actually belong to a namespace at all: DOMExample, order, payment and date all belong to no namespace at all. They are unqualified element names.

We can use some of the new namespace methods to query the namespace URI and search for elements with specified namespace URIs.

```
import org.w3c.dom.*;

import javax.xml.parsers.*;

import java.io.*;
import java.net.URL;

public class NamespaceDemo
{
    public NamespaceDemo(String filename)
    {
        Document doc = null;

        try
        {
```

We've covered this area before: we simply read the file into the DOM, this time using a File class.

```
DocumentBuilderFactory dbf = DocumentBuilderFactory.newInstance();
dbf.setNamespaceAware (true);
DocumentBuilder db = dbf.newDocumentBuilder();
doc = db.parse(new File(filename));

String wrox = "http://www.wrox.com/book-titles";
String local = "a";
String c24 = "http://www.c24solutions.com";

System.out.println("Elements in the "+wrox+" namespace...");
```

Now, we use the namespace version of getElementsByTagName(). The first argument is used to specify the URI that defines the namespace we want our elements to belong to. The second specifies the element name we're interested in. We want all of the wrox namespace elements, so we use the wildcard, *. Then we iterate through the returned NodeList, displaying the results.

```
NodeList nl = doc.getElementsByTagNameNS(wrox,"*");
for(int i=0; i<nl.getLength(); i++)
{
    Node n = nl.item(i);
    System.out.println(n.getNodeName());
}
```

This time, using the same method, we use the wildcard for the namespace URI (we don't care which namespace the returned elements are from), but we pass in a specific value for the element local name (the name without any prefix). Again, we iterate through the `NodeList`, displaying the names of the nodes we have found.

```
System.out.println("\nElements with a local name of "+local+"...");
nl = doc.getElementsByTagNameNS("*",local);
for(int i=0; i<nl.getLength(); i++)
{
    Node n = nl.item(i);
    System.out.println(n.getNodeName());
}
```

Finally, let's look for attributes belonging to a specific namespace. This time we get all the elements in the document using `getElementsByTagName("*")`, and look for the specified attributes (those in the c24 namespace):

```
System.out.println("\nAttributes in the "+c24+" namespace...");
nl = doc.getElementsByTagName("*");
for(int i=0; i<nl.getLength(); i++)
{
    if( nl.item(i) instanceof Element )
    {
```

Remembering that the actual text inside an `Element` is the first child of the `Element`, not the `Element` itself:

```
// Save the text part
Text t = (Text) nl.item(i).getFirstChild();

// Search for particular attributes, no wildcards here!
Element e = (Element) nl.item(i);
```

We are now iterating through all of the elements, we have saved the text part (whether it exists or not) and are now looking to see if the element has an attribute called `class` in the c24 namespace.

```
Attr a = e.getAttributeNodeNS(c24,"class");
```

If anything other than `null` is returned, it is what we are looking for so we display it, putting the actual value of the attribute into element tags.

```
if( a != null )
{
    String val = a.getNodeValue();
    System.out.println("<"+val+">" + t.getNodeValue()+
        "</"+val+">");
}
        }
    }
} .
catch ( Exception e )
{
```

```
            // We should really have more Exception types here
            System.out.println( "Exception: "+e.getMessage() );
          e.printStackTrace();
          }
      }
    public static void main( String[] args )
    {
        NamespaceDemo nsd = null;

        if( args.length >= 1 )
            nsd = new NamespaceDemo( args[0] );
        else
            System.out.println("Usage: NamespaceDemo file.xml");
    }
  }
```

Running this gives the following output:

Additional DOM Level 2 Interfaces

Let's now take a look at some of the other 14 modules in the DOM level 2 specifications. The W3C have defined a set of interfaces to view and track updates, specify styling, traverse and specify ranges. A DOM implementation must implement the hasFeature(feature, version) method of the core DOMImplementation class as well as the isSupported(feature, version) method in Node. If the result of either method is true then the implementation supports this feature. For example, if we wish to use the DOM level 2 Views module we can first test whether our DOM implementation supports Views or not. This is done by calling isSupported("Views", "2.0") on the Document. The reason for this technique is that the implementation is loaded at run-time and we might not know which implementation we are actually going to be using. The second parameter is the level supported, level 2 in this case.

DOM Events

It's possible that we might want to associate certain nodes within our document with various user-actions. For example, if somebody clicks on a screen representation of a node, we may want to trigger loading of a different document. This is the principle behind hyperlinks. DOM Events provide a mechanism for us to register certain event listeners with a node, and then to have a user interface, or other client of the DOM, trigger the firing of these events. Alternatively, we may have a display component showing an on-screen representation of the data in the DOM. We might need to update this display if the data in the DOM is changed, but the UI needs to receive some notification that a change has taken place. DOM events provide a mechanism for events in this direction as well.

This is implemented if `isSupported("Events","2.0")` returns `true`. Apache Xerces provides a basic implementation of DOM Level 2 Events.

This package has seven interfaces and one exception:

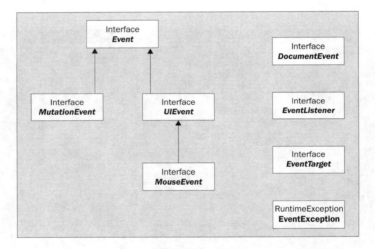

The diagram above demonstrates the class relationships in the events package.

The `DocumentEvent` interface provides methods to create an `Event`. The implementation of the `Document` normally implements this interface as well. `EventTarget` is implemented by all nodes (the `Node` implementation itself), this provides methods to add and remove an `EventListener`. So, if a user viewing a screen `View` changes a document's `Node`, an `Event` is created using the `Document`'s `createEvent()` method, this is then dispatched to the changed `Node` using `Node`'s `dispatchEvent()`. If the `Node` has a registered `EventListener` then they will be called to process the user's `Event`.

`MutationEvent`, `UIEvent` and `MouseEvent` have extra information more applicable to user interfaces, x and y position (for `MouseEvents`), previous and new values (for `MutationEvent`).

Lastly, before we leave this section it is worth mentioning the three types of `Event` processing. These can be defined in `initEvent()`:

❑   **Bubbling**: Where the `Event` is sent to the parent `Node` and then on to the parent's parent's `Node` etc. after the `EventTarget` has handled the `Event`: it bubbles up through the DOM tree, all the way to the document level.

- ❑ **Cancelable**: Where after the `EventTarget` has handled the `Event` it can be canceled to prevent default handling associated with the `Event`.

- ❑ **Capturing**: Where the `Event` can be handled by one of the `EventTarget`'s "ancestors" (parent, or parent's parent etc.) before the `EventTarget`, this stops it from propagating from one consumer to another.

Traversal

We've had to build a lot of very similar boilerplate code in our examples to walk through a DOM tree, processing the nodes we are interested in. The DOM Traversal APIs provide mechanisms for parser vendors to supply implementations which make these common tasks much simpler.

The `TreeWalker`, `NodeIterator`, and `NodeFilter` interfaces provide easy-to-use, robust, selective traversal of a DOM Document. `NodeIterators` and `TreeWalkers` provide different ways of representing the nodes of a DOM Document. A `NodeIterator` presents a flattened view of the Document (or of a Node and its sub-tree), the result is an ordered sequence of nodes. Due to the flat nature of the result iterators see no hierarchy and consequently only have methods to move forward and backward, not up and down. On the other hand, a `TreeWalker` maintains the hierarchical representation of the DOM Document or sub-Node. `TreeWalkers` are therefore generally better for tasks in which the structure of the document around selected nodes will be manipulated. Conversely `NodeIterators` are better for tasks that focus on the content of each selected node.

The Traversal API is implemented if `isSupported("Traversal", "2.0")` returns `true`. Again, Xerces 1.3 provides such an implementation.

The `Traversal` package defines four interfaces:

Interface	Purpose
`DocumentTraversal`	Implemented by `Document`, this interface defines two methods for creating `NodeIterator` and `TreeWalker` from a `Node` in the `Document`. They both take an instance of a `NodeFilter`.
`NodeIterator`	Similar to the `java.util.Iterator` interface, this interface defines `nextNode()` and `previousNode()`. Both return `null` if there are no more members in that set. The other methods are `getRoot()` (as defined at creation), two `NodeFilter` related methods `getWhatToShow()` and `getFilter()`, `getExpandEntityReferences()` and `detach()` which releases resources and renders the `NodeIterator` unusable.
`TreeWalker`	More powerful than the `NodeIterator`, this definition provides an interface that, when implemented, can be "walked" through the nodes of the passed Node tree. Methods like `parentNode()`, `firstChild()`, `lastChild()`, `nextSibling()`, `previousSibling()`, `nextNode()` and `previousNode()` provide movement in almost every direction possible from the current `Node`, incidentally set (and got) by `setCurrentNode()` and `getCurrentNode()`. All movement methods return `null` if no `Node` is available in that direction.

Table continued on following page

Interface	Purpose
NodeFilter	Can be used to precisely filter the Nodes an iterator or walker will consider. A number of parameters can be set when defining the NodeIterator or TreeWalker: SHOW_ALL, SHOW_ELEMENT, SHOW_ATTRIBUTE, SHOW_TEXT, SHOW_CDATA_SECTION, SHOW_ENTITY_REFERENCE, SHOW_PROCESSING_INSTRUCTION, SHOW_COMMENT, SHOW_DOCUMENT, SHOW_DOCUMENT_TYPE, SHOW_DOCUMENT_FRAGMENT, SHOW_NOTATION
	There is only one defined method, acceptNode() that returns either FILTER_ACCEPT, FILTER_REJECT or FILTER_SKIP.

Traversal Example

Let's see these in practice, I've used the following hierarchy for demonstrating the TreeWalker and NodeIterator:

```
<FamilyTree name="The British Royal Family">
    <Person born="1926" name="Queen Elizabeth II"
          spouse="Philip">
        <Person born="1948" name="Charles, Prince of Wales" spouse="Diana">
            <Person born="1982" name="Prince William"/>
            <Person born="1984" name="Prince Henry of Wales"/>
        </Person>
        <Person born="1950" name="Anne, Princess Royal" spouse="Mark"
              spouse2="Tim">
            <Person born="1977" name="Peter Phillips"/>
            <Person born="1981" name="Zara Phillips"/>
        </Person>
        <Person born="1960" name="Andrew, Duke of York" spouse="Sarah">
            <Person born="1988" name="Princess Beatrice of York"/>
            <Person born="1990" name="Princess Eugenie of York"/>
        </Person>
        <Person born="1964" name="Edward, Earl of Wessex" spouse="Sophie"/>
    </Person>
</FamilyTree>
```

The code below will not work with Sun's JAXP 1.1 as supplied. You should use Apache's Xerces 1.3 implementation, which we saw earlier, since it supports Traversal: Ensure that the xerces.jar file is available on your classpath at compile and runtime, and use one of the techniques detailed at the start of the chapter to ensure that the JAXP DocumentBuilderFactory loads up Xerces, not Crimson, at runtime.

```
import org.w3c.dom.*;
import org.w3c.dom.traversal.*;

import javax.xml.parsers.*;

import java.io.*;
import java.net.URL;
```

```
public class TraversalDemo
{
  public TraversalDemo(String filename)
  {
    Document doc = null;
    NodeIterator iter = null;
    TreeWalker walker = null;

    try {
      DocumentBuilderFactory dbf = DocumentBuilderFactory.newInstance();
      DocumentBuilder db = dbf.newDocumentBuilder();

      doc = db.parse(new File(filename));

      // Check if Traversals are supported
      if( doc.isSupported("Traversal", "2.0" ) )
      {

        // first we try the NodeIterator
        System.out.println("Members of the royal family with children...\n");
```

Now, we set up the `NodeIterator` with a "`MyParentFilter`". `MyParentFilter` filters out everything except Nodes representing parents: it is only interested in `Person` nodes with children.

```
        iter = ((DocumentTraversal)doc).createNodeIterator( doc,
          NodeFilter.SHOW_ALL, new MyParentFilter(), true );

        Node n;
        while ((n = iter.nextNode()) != null)
        {
          Element e = (Element ) n;
          System.out.println(e.getAttribute("name") +
              " ("+e.getAttribute("born")+")");
        }

        System.out.println("\nLooking for Princess Anne...");
```

Next we set up a `TreeWalker` that just looks at "Person" Nodes. We then check each of these until we find "Anne".

```
        walker = ((DocumentTraversal)doc).createTreeWalker( doc,
          NodeFilter.SHOW_ALL, new MyPersonFilter(), true );

        // Stroll through the Nodes looking for "Anne"
        while((n = walker.nextNode()) != null)
        {
          Element e = (Element ) n;
          String name = e.getAttribute("name");
          if( name.indexOf("Anne") != -1 )
              break;
          System.out.println("Skipping "+name);
        }
```

Right, now that we've got the "Anne" Node let's take a look at the various methods of `TreeWalker` and see what they return. The Nodes in the DOM have the same relationship as the family they represent, therefore the children of the "Anne" Node, for example, should print out the real child's names of Princess Anne:

```
                Element anne = (Element) walker.getCurrentNode();
                System.out.println( "Found \""+anne.getAttribute("name")+"\"\n" );

                walker.setCurrentNode(anne);
                Element pSibling = (Element) walker.previousSibling();

                walker.setCurrentNode(anne);
                Element nSibling = (Element ) walker.nextSibling();

                walker.setCurrentNode(anne);
                Element fChild = (Element ) walker.firstChild();

                walker.setCurrentNode(anne);
                Element lChild = (Element ) walker.lastChild();

                walker.setCurrentNode(anne);
                Element pNode = (Element ) walker.previousNode();

                walker.setCurrentNode(anne);
                Element nNode = (Element ) walker.nextNode();

                System.out.println(
                    "PreviousSibling=\""+pSibling.getAttribute("name")+"\"" );
                walker.setCurrentNode(anne);
                System.out.println( "NextSibling = \""+
                    nSibling.getAttribute("name")+"\"" );
                walker.setCurrentNode(anne);
                System.out.println( "firstChild = \""+fChild.getAttribute("name")+
                    "\"" );
                walker.setCurrentNode(anne);
                System.out.println( "LastChild = \""+lChild.getAttribute("name")+
                    "\"" );
                walker.setCurrentNode(anne);
                System.out.println( "PreviousNode = ""+pNode.getAttribute("name")+
                    "\"" );
                walker.setCurrentNode(anne);
                System.out.println( "NextNode = \""+nNode.getAttribute("name")+
                    "\"" );
            }
            else
            {
                System.out.println("Sorry but Traversal is not implemented");
            }

        }
        catch ( Exception e )
        {
            // We should really have more Exception types here
            System.out.println( "Exception: "+e.getMessage() );
        }
    }
    public static void main( String[] args )
    {
        TraversalDemo nsd = new TraversalDemo( args[0] );
    }
}
```

Let's look at our filter implementations. We have two `NodeFilter` classes, the first `MyParentFilter`, will only accept or "show" Nodes where the Node has child Nodes (that is, children in this example) and is of type "Person". The second class, `MyPersonFilter`, simply accepts any Node with the name "Person".

```java
class MyParentFilter implements NodeFilter
{
  public short acceptNode(Node n)
  {
    if( n.hasChildNodes() && n.getNodeName().equals("Person"))
        return FILTER_ACCEPT;
    return FILTER_SKIP;
  }
}

class MyPersonFilter implements NodeFilter
{
  public short acceptNode(Node n)
  {
    if( n.getNodeName().equals("Person"))
      return FILTER_ACCEPT;
    return FILTER_SKIP;
  }
}
```

Run this and you'll get the output:

```
Command Prompt

C:\projavaxml\chapter03>echo %classpath%
.;C:\xerces-1_3_0\xerces.jar

C:\projavaxml\chapter03>javac TraversalDemo.java

C:\projavaxml\chapter03>java TraversalDemo familytree.xml
Members of the royal family with children...

Queen Elizabeth II (1926)
Charles, Prince of Wales (1948)
Anne, Princess Royal (1950)
Andrew, Duke of York (1960)

Looking for Princess Anne...
Skipping Queen Elizabeth II
Skipping Charles, Prince of Wales
Skipping Prince William
Skipping Prince Henry of Wales
Found "Anne, Princess Royal"

PreviousSibling="Charles, Prince of Wales"
NextSibling = "Andrew, Duke of York"
firstChild = "Peter Phillips"
LastChild = "Zara Phillips"
PreviousNode = "Prince Henry of Wales"
NextNode = "Peter Phillips"

C:\projavaxml\chapter03>
```

For reference and for those not too familiar with the British royal family, below is a simple family tree.

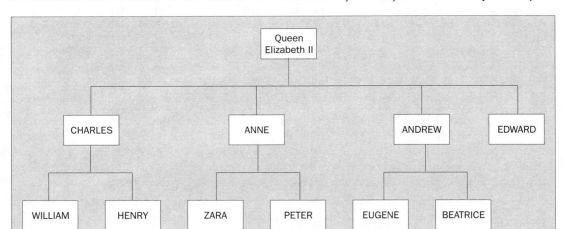

Ranges

A range identifies a range of content in a DOM Document, DocumentFragment or Attr. It is contiguous in the sense that it can be characterized as selecting all of the content between a pair of boundary-points in the underlying XML document.

Ranges are implemented if isSupported("Range", "2.0") returns true. This is the last of the modules which Xerces 1.3 implements.

Ranges defines two interfaces:

❑   DocumentRange: Implemented by Document, this interface defines one simple method, createRange().

❑   Range: An interface defining methods for interacting with a specific range of data.

If we take an XML document, such as this presidential example from earlier in the chapter, a range would appear as a continuous section of the document, as if we had clicked and dragged across the document in a text editor. The bold characters here, for example, represent a range:

```
<President Country="US">
    <Person>
        <FirstName>George</FirstName>
        <Surname>Bush</Surname>
    </Person>
</President>
```

The area selected is a range, whether it covers element, attribute or node boundaries or not.

Most of the methods in the Range interface only take a Node, but setStart() and setEnd() take offsets too. The example above would represent a case where offset would be needed due to the fact that the range boundaries are not on node boundaries.

- ❏ setStart(Node,int offset)

- ❏ setEnd(Node,int offset)

- ❏ setStartBefore(Node)

- ❏ setStartAfter(Node)

- ❏ setEndBefore(Node)

- ❏ setEndAfter(Node)

- ❏ selectNode(Node)

- ❏ selectNodeContents(Node)

We can find the nearest common parent, getCommonAncestorContainer() (<Person> in the above example – it is the smallest element which completely contains the range) and enquire about range start and end points. These methods all return the corresponding node and offset set in the above methods.

- ❏ getStartContainer()

- ❏ getStartOffset()

- ❏ getEndContainer()

- ❏ getEndOffset()

Finally we can compare and manipulate the range

- ❏ collapse(): Collapses a Range onto one of its boundary-points.

- ❏ compareBoundaryPoints(short how, Range r): Compares the boundary-points of two ranges in a document.

- ❏ deleteContents(): Removes the contents of a Range from the containing document or document fragment without returning a reference to the removed content.

- ❏ extractContents(): Moves the contents of a Range from the containing document or document fragment to a new DocumentFragment.

- ❏ cloneContents(): Duplicates the contents of a Range.

- ❏ insertNode(Node): Inserts a node into the Document or DocumentFragment at the start of the Range.

- ❏ surroundContents(Node): Re-parents the contents of the Range to the given node and inserts the node at the position of the start of the Range.

- ❏ cloneRange(): Produces a new Range whose boundary-points are equal to the boundary-points of the Range.

So, to go back to our example:

```
<President Country="US">
    <Person>
        <FirstName>George</FirstName>
        <Surname>Bush</Surname>
    </Person>
</President>
```

The startpoint of our range is in the first text node (the one containing the word George), and has an offset of 2 (the number of characters before it within the node). The endpoint, on the other hand, can be described in two ways. It is either in the second text node, and has an offset of 4, or it is in the <Surname> element node, and it has an offset of 1 (the number of child nodes before it beneath the Surname element). The difference between these two endpoints can't be seen in the document text, but can be seen if we look at a diagram of the DOM tree:

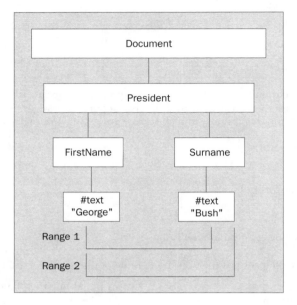

In this diagram, both of these different Ranges are illustrated. The start-points of each Range are the same, as we said: in the first text node, offset by two characters. But range 1's endpoint has been set to be in the second text node, with an offset of 4: it is inside the text node, immediately after the last character. Range 2 has had its endpoint defined as being inside Surname, with an offset of 1. It is immediately after the end of the text node, and contains the entire text node object.

If we were to remove range 1 from this DOM, the contents of the first text node would be changed to read simply "Ge", and the contents of the second text node would be reduced to an empty string. If we were to remove range 2 from the document, the same thing would happen to the first text node, but the second text node would be completely removed: it would no longer exist.

DOM Level 3

At the time of writing, DOM Level 3 is just a proposal, a "working draft". It has been available since September 2000 and is, as yet, unchanged. There are several additions to the DOM Core as well as minor changes proposed to DOM Level 2 Events and Views. The biggest addition, so far, is a specification for content models, and load and save, one of the biggest omissions from existing specifications and one of the main drives behind JAXP. The 7 new interfaces in this area are:

`DOMImplementationLS`	A new `DOMImplementation` interface that provides the factory methods for creating the objects required for loading and saving from files or streams etc.
`DOMBuilder`	A parser interface similar to the `DocumentBuilder` in JAXP.
`DOMInputSource`	Encapsulates information about the source of the XML to be loaded. Since the DOM specification is designed for languages other than Java this has to be generic. This is again similar to JAXP's `Source` class.
`DOMEntityResolver`	During loading, provides a way for applications to redirect references to external entities, again another interface designed to provide a generic API across all languages.
`DOMBuilderFilter`	Provides the ability to examine and optionally remove `Element` nodes as they are being processed during the parsing of a document. This is an interesting addition in that a filter could be used to construct a DOM containing only a subset of the whole document, saving both memory and parsing time.
`DOMFormatter`	Provides for the actual formatting of DOM data into the output format. Similar to serialization classes in most existing implementations.
`DOMWriter`	An interface for writing out DOM documents. The form in which the data from the DOM will be written is controlled by a `DOMFormatter`, and the destination for the data is a `DOMOutputStream`.

To keep up to date in the latest level 3 drafts you can refer to W3C's site at http://www.w3.org/TR. There are no current full implementations of this proposed specification yet and it would be unwise to provide examples on a subject that is likely to change. Of the new feature proposed the most interesting would probably be the `DOMBuilderFilter`. It will be interesting to watch this space as JAXP and JDOM both vie for a place in the Java core specification.

Summary

In this chapter we started off looking at the history of the DOM, how it started from HTML browsers and what it was originally designed for. We then went in to more detail of interfaces and methods defined by DOM Level 1. We saw that most of the DOM functionality we will ever need is already in DOM level 1 and for this reason it has been built on rather than replaced.

We then moved on to JAXP and saw how it provided a standard for reading and writing DOM Documents from Java Files and streams, an area left wide open by both DOM level 1 and 2.

After looking at some examples we moved on to the DOM Level 2 packages or modules and saw how several of the areas that proved awkward to program using DOM level 1 had been standardized in level 2. This provided powerful new interfaces like `TreeWalkers` and `NodeIterators`. We used these in examples and provided `NodeFilters` to narrow our search through the nodes. We finished DOM level 2 by looking at the other modules like ranges.

Finally we took a brief look at the DOM Level 3 working draft as it stands today.

The Xerces Blue
Butterfly, which became
extinct earlier this century,
and after which the Xerces XML
Parser is named ...

4

JDOM

Since we have already covered SAX and DOM you very well may be wondering, "What? Another API for manipulating XML documents?" On the surface, you would be correct; JDOM is just that. However, JDOM wasn't created to be just another API for XML document manipulation, JDOM provides a Java-centric, object-oriented approach to XML document manipulation. In addition, it does away with some of the inconsistencies in APIs that exist between parsers by providing adapters that account for these differences.

In this chapter we begin by looking at some of the motivating reasons behind the creation of JDOM and how it is different from, yet works with, both SAX and DOM. We describe how to obtain the latest JDOM release, and how to build and install it, and then introduce you to a simple JDOM program. This will introduce the basics of JDOM, as well as allow us to test out our installation.

The next section then goes into more detail about JDOM by looking at the packages and main classes that make up the JDOM API. Using this knowledge we will be better suited to dive into some examples that illustrate practical applications of JDOM.

We'll conclude this chapter with a discussion of what lies in the future for JDOM, and give some pointers to where you can find more information.

What is JDOM?

The JDOM API was designed by Brett McLauglin and Jason Hunter, with James Duncan Davidson, author of the JAXP specification, providing additional support and feedback in its development. According to the JDOM mission statement, JDOM was designed to:

- ❑ Make manipulating XML documents in Java "as simple as Java itself".

- ❑ Provide an object-oriented and Java-oriented approach to manipulating XML documents.

- ❑ Feel natural to Java programmers, by making use of objects and collections rather than unnecessarily complex XML-centric APIs.

- ❑ Require a minimal learning curve, meaning that Java programmers don't need to understand the details of XML.

Officially, according to the JDOM FAQ (http://www.jdom.org/docs/faq.html), JDOM is not an acronym, which ensures that it complies with Sun's trademark policies restricting the use of the "Java" trademark in product or API names. Unofficially, you can think of it as meaning something like "Java Document Object Model". JDOM defines an API for Java, and in spite of the name similarity JDOM is neither built on, nor modeled after, DOM. In fact, JDOM is only loosely tied to XML and could, in theory, be used to represent any hierarchical document. As such, it can quite accurately and appropriately be described as *a* document object model, even though it is not an implementation of *the* World Wide Web Consortiums (W3C) Document Object Model.

Possibly one of the best things about JDOM is that it is "free" in more ways than one. Not only is it an open source API, it also uses an Apache-style license – the only modification being that acknowledgement of the use of JDOM is made optional. This allows developers to use JDOM in their products without requiring that they release their own products as open source software provided all other terms of the license are adhered to. The fact that it is open source also means that it is able to adopt new standards for things like SAX and DOM more quickly than a proprietary alternative.

Why the Need for Another API for XML?

While JDOM is designed to work with both SAX and DOM, it is not simply an abstraction layer on top of such APIs. Instead, it is designed as a lightweight means of creating and manipulating XML documents without the weaknesses of either SAX or DOM.

SAX offers a fast and powerful API – provided you are interested in parsing and processing XML documents in an event-driven way. DOM, on the other hand, provides a very flexible API allowing you to do pretty much anything (valid) with the XML document at the expense of having to have the entire document loaded in memory as long as the application is running, a slow start-up time, and a (relatively) complex process for document manipulation.

JDOM makes a compromise between these two approaches and then some. It provides a fast, efficient means of manipulating XML documents, an approach that is also much more object-oriented and Java-centric than either SAX or DOM. In addition, by making JDOM open source software it attempts to provide quicker time-to-market support for new standards and emerging specifications.

JDOM also integrates well with both SAX and DOM. In fact, to build a JDOM Document object you can either build it from scratch using JDOM objects, or you can build it indirectly, which includes using a SAX parser or building the document from a DOM document. Although JDOM is often used in conjunction with SAX, DOM, or both, it can also be used on its own with no support from either. In addition, JDOM has been designed to support the run-time plug-in of any DOM or SAX parser.

JDOM also supports easy conversion from a JDOM Document into a DOM document or a set of SAX events. It does not totally replace the need for SAX or DOM, but instead complements them by simplifying XML document manipulation for Java programmers.

When to Use JDOM, SAX or DOM?

DOM was designed to provide a common object model for use across scripting languages. Therefore developers are able to use the same document object model in any language. SAX, on the other hand, addresses the problems raised by DOM in having to store the entire XML document in memory. To do so, it takes a different approach to parsing and manipulating an XML document. By handling the document linearly SAX does not require that the entire XML document be read in or stored in memory in its entirety before it can be read and processed, which makes it possible to handle larger XML documents without putting excessive stress on the host machine.

This does, however, require that we re-think the way we handle an XML as we move from an object oriented to an event stream oriented style of data access. On the whole, applications of SAX and DOM are well separated, there are relatively few types of applications that are well suited to being re-modeled using the event-driven approach and vice versa.

Like DOM, JDOM attempts to provide an intuitive document object model. Rather than having to learn a new style of programming such as DOM requires, however, JDOM provides a much more Java oriented solution. Like SAX it does not require documents to be fully loaded, but it does not impose an event-driven model. As a result, JDOM is a more Java focused approach to XML document manipulation. An XML document is modeled in JDOM using collections of Java objects.

While JDOM is very powerful and easy to use, it may not solve all XML manipulation problems. For example, even though JDOM could be used to translate an XML document from one XML schema to another schema, this type of task is better handled via XSLT. It is possible to integrate JDOM with something like the Apache Xalan XSLT processor by using org.jdom.XMLOutputter to output to an java.io.OutputStream which can then be piped into Xalan's XSLT processor. However, we're getting ahead of ourselves here: we'll look at the org.jdom.XMLOutputter class in detail later in this chapter.

One of the stated goals of JDOM is to "solve 80% of the problems with 20% of the effort" – an idea generally known as the Pareto Principal.

There are basically three ways to create a JDOM Document object:

- ❑ Indirectly from a DOM document using the DOMBuilder class. This approach is most useful when integrating JDOM with another application that has already constructed an org.w3c.dom.Document DOM document object.

- ❑ Indirectly using SAX and the SAXBuilder class. Due to the speed of SAX, this is the preferred way of reading and parsing an XML file to create a JDOM Document.

- ❑ Directly by building a JDOM Document using JDOM classes. This is most likely if you are creating an XML document from scratch.

We will see examples of each of these approaches throughout the remainder of this chapter.

It is also worthwhile noting at this point that JDOM can output its XML document in a variety of ways. The primary means of output supported by the core JDOM package are as follows:

- ❑ Output as a DOM object.
- ❑ Output as a series of SAX events.
- ❑ Output as an XML document (typically to a file or output stream).

In order to see most easily the results of our programs, we will be using the final approach throughout this chapter. That is, we will be outputting our JDOM documents as XML output, either to the console or to a file. One of the examples will also demonstrate outputting a DOM document.

In addition to the above output forms, you can also write your own class to output a JDOM Document or individual JDOM components in any other format.

Before we dive into the details of the JDOM API, we must download and install JDOM.

Downloading and Installing JDOM

As of the time of this writing, JDOM is still undergoing beta testing. The following section is based on the beta release of JDOM and the details are therefore subject to change before the final release. For the most up-to-date information on the current release, refer to the JDOM web site at: http://www.jdom.org/.

Minimum Requirements

Before downloading and installing JDOM, you should check that you have a recent version of the Java Development Kit for your platform. Java2 – version 1.2 or 1.3 – is recommended, although JDK 1.1 is also supported.

Currently the only part of the Java 2 API that JDOM uses is the Collections API. If you are using JDK 1.1, it is recommended that you upgrade to Java 2. Otherwise you may need to download and install collections.jar from Sun's web site (at http://java.sun.com/products/javabeans/infobus/).

Alternatively, if you download the entire JDOM source tree – see below for details – you will find collections.jar in the jdom/lib/ directory. The only problem with this approach is that the collections.jar file contains the Collections classes in the com.sun.java.util.collections package, and not the java.util package as in Java 2. To address this JDOM comes with some special JDOM build scripts – build11.bat and build11.sh – that perform a modified build.

Since the Java 2 SDK 1.2 is now widely in use, and Java 2 SDK 1.3 has been released, in the remainder of this chapter we'll assume that you are using either one of these.

Obtaining the JDOM Distribution

There are several ways to obtain a JDOM distribution. JDOM developers will prefer to access the latest release of the source code by CVS (Concurrent Versions System), which we will discuss in a moment. The site also provides a web interface for downloading beta (milestone) releases, public releases – there are none at the time of writing, and there is also a repository where the source code, as well as user guides, tutorials, READMEs and any and all other resources can be found.

Ant build files are provided to assist compilation of the source code. Ant is a build tool like make and gnumake but with the added benefit of platform independence. Configuration files are specified in XML format and are then mapped to a specific OS by the class that implements the command. For more information on Ant, refer to http://jakarta.apache.org/ant/.

Downloading JDOM Through the Web

By far the simplest way to download JDOM is via the web interface at http://www.jdom.org. Simply select the latest download. The only drawback with this is that downloading using this method is relatively slow.

You may download binary distributions through this interface as well as source code via the repository.

Obtaining the Source Code Directly from CVS

The latest information on accessing the JDOM source code from CVS can always be found at the JDOM web site (http://www.jdom.org); however, the basic steps are as follows.

> *CVS automatically controls versioning of software and allows access via the Internet. One of its main benefits is the ability to merge changes from multiple sources to the same file. CVS for windows is available direct from the download section of the JDOM site or direct from CVSHome.org.*

Open a command window (whether UNIX terminal window or a DOS command prompt) and navigate to the directory where you would like to download the source code to. Log into the JDOM CVS server anonymously, using:

```
cvs -d :pserver:anonymous@cvs.jdom.org:/home/cvspublic login
```

When prompted for a password, enter "anonymous" (no quotes). You can now obtain the latest JDOM distribution, using:

```
cvs -d :pserver:anonymous@cvs.jdom.org:/home/cvspublic co jdom
```

This will copy the jdom module from the JDOM CVS server onto your local machine.

JDOM Source Directory Structure

After downloading and uncompressing a JDOM source snapshot, you should have a directory tree similar to the following:

```
jdom/
    etc/
    lib/
        bin/
    samples/
        CVS/
        sax/
            CVS/
    src/
        java/
            org/
                jdom/
                    adaptors/
                    input/
                    output/
```

The `src/` directory is the main directory containing the JDOM source files. The `samples/` directory contains the source files for some sample JDOM programs. When getting started with JDOM it is often useful to refer to these to see how the authors intended JDOM to be used.

The `lib` and `etc` directories contain additional files used by JDOM. The `lib` directory stores the Ant, Xerces and Java Collections JAR files. The Java Collections JAR is only required when using version 1.1 of the JDK and implements the Java 2 Collections API – it is not required when using JDK 1.2 or later since Java 2 contains the Collections API.

Ant is required to build the JDOM JAR file and finally, the Xerces JAR is an XML parser available from the Apache Organization (at http://xml.apache.org/), and is used by JDOM as the default SAX and DOM parser. Bear in mind, however, that a version-compatible Xerces parser is included in your JDOM installation, so you should not have to download this software separately.

Building and Installing JDOM

Now that we have downloaded and uncompressed the source files, we can compile the JDOM JAR. To simplify building of JDOM, the JDOM team has provided build scripts. These simply act as a wrapper around Ant, and ensure that the environment is initialized as required. You can see the cross-platform build instructions in the Ant build file, `build.xml` in the root JDOM directory.

Though the steps are the same under different platforms thanks to the use of Ant, the path syntax varies slightly between UNIX and Microsoft Windows. Just to be clear, we describe how to build JDOM on both a UNIX platform as well as a Microsoft Windows platform.

Building Under UNIX

To illustrate compilation of JDOM under UNIX, we assume that the JDK is already installed in `/opt/jdk1.3`, you are using the Bourne Shell (or equivalent), and you have uncompressed the JDOM source files into `/opt/jdom`.

Note that to install and build in a directory such as `/opt/jdom` may require that you have root permissions on your system. If you do not have root permissions, then install and build JDOM in a directory in which you do have permission, for example, your home directory.

Set up your Java environment

Depending on your installation, this may already have been done. You should have an environment variable JAVA_HOME set to point to your root JDK directory, and the Java compiler, `javac`, should be in your PATH. If this is already done, you can skip this step.

To set up your environment, type the following:

```
JAVA_HOME=/opt/jdk1.3
PATH=$PATH:$JAVA_HOME/bin
export JAVA_HOME PATH
```

Run the build.sh Script.

This can be done by typing:

```
cd /opt/jdom
sh ./build.sh
```

This will start the build process. The output will be something like the following:

```
$ cd /opt/jdom
$ ./build.sh
JDOM Build System
------------------

Building with classpath
/opt/jdk1.3/lib/tools.jar:./lib/xerces.jar:./lib/ant.jar:/opt/jdk1.3/lib/dev.jar:

Starting Ant...

Buildfile: build.xml

init:
----------- JDOM 1.0beta5 [2000] ------------

prepare:
    [mkdir] Created dir: /opt/jdom/build

prepare-src:
    [mkdir] Created dir: /opt/jdom/build/src
    [mkdir] Created dir: /opt/jdom/build/classes
  [copydir] Copying 31 files to /opt/jdom/build/src

collections:

compile:
    [javac] Compiling 31 source files to /opt/jdom/build/classes

package:
      [jar] Building jar: /opt/jdom/build/jdom.jar

BUILD SUCCESSFUL

Total time: 25 seconds
```

As you can see from this output, the `jdom.jar` file has been created in the `build` directory beneath the root JDOM installation directory, `/opt/jdom`.

Building Under Microsoft Windows

To illustrate compilation of JDOM under DOS or Microsoft Windows, we assume that the JDK is already installed in `C:\jdk1.3`, and you have uncompressed the JDOM source files into `C:\jdom`.

Set Up Your Java Environment

Depending on your installation, this may already have been done. You should have an environment variable `JAVA_HOME` set to point to your root JDK directory, and the Java compiler, `javac`, should be in your `PATH`. If this is already done, you can skip this step.

To set up your environment, open up an MS-DOS command window and type the following:

```
set JAVA_HOME=C:\jdk1.3
set PATH=%PATH%;%JAVA_HOME%\bin
```

Note that you can also set these environment variables globally either through the Control Panel (in Windows NT and Windows 2000), or by editing `autoexec.bat` in earlier versions. Any of these approaches will work just fine.

Run the build.bat Script

In the same command window type:

```
C:\>cd jdom

C:\jdom\>build
```

This will start the `build` process. The output will be similar to the UNIX output shown above except for the paths used.

As you should see from the output of the `build` command, the `jdom.jar` file is created in the `build` directory beneath the root JDOM installation directory, `c:\jdom`.

Build Options

As described above, the `build` command with no command line options is used to build the main `jdom.jar` file. The `build` command also supports several other useful options. The following options can be given on the same line and immediately following the `build` command:

❏   `package` – This is the default if no options are given. It builds the main `jdom.jar` file in the `build` directory.

❏   `javadoc` – Builds the latest JDOM API documentation in `build/apidocs/`. Although this is available on the JDOM web site, you can generate your own local copy of this documentation and ensure that it is the most up to date.

❏   `samples` – Builds the JDOM sample programs in the `build/samples/` folder.

❏   `compile` – Compiles the JDOM source files beneath the `build` directory. This option does *not* generate the JAR file.

❏   `clean` – Removes the entire `build` subdirectory, removing all class files, jar files, and any other temporary files created by running other `build` commands. It is generally a good idea to run this option before rebuilding JDOM if you have just updated the source files directly from CVS.

❏   `usage` – Does not "build" anything as such, just lists the available options for the `build` command.

Setting Your Classpath

To use JDOM, you will need to add the JDOM classes to your Java classpath. The preferred way to do this is to add the `jdom.jar` file to your classpath.. Alternatively, you can add the `build/classes/` directory beneath the JDOM installation directory to your classpath..

In addition to adding the JDOM class files to your classpath,, you also should add the Xerces JAR file that comes with JDOM – it should be in the `lib` directory of your JDOM installation. When you add the `xerces.jar` file to your classpath, be sure to add it at the beginning of your classpath and certainly *before* any other XML-related libraries.

If an older version of `xerces.jar` occurs earlier in your classpath than the `xerces.jar` file that comes with JDOM, then you may encounter a `java.lang.NoSuchMethodError` or `java.lang.NoClassDefFoundErrors` when trying to use JDOM in a program. This is because JDOM supports the SAX 2.0 and DOM 2.0 specifications and this requires up-to-date versions of the SAX and DOM classes – these are included in the version of Xerces that comes with JDOM.

Finally, if you want to run the JDOM samples you should add the `build/classes/` directory of your JDOM installation to your classpath..

To summarize these, let us assume that you want to add each of these to your classpath. Then under UNIX (Bourne Shell), you could use:

```
CLASSPATH=/opt/jdom/build/classes:$CLASSPATH
CLASSPATH=/opt/jdom/lib/xerces.jar:/opt/jdom/build/jdom.jar:$CLASSPATH
export CLASSPATH
```

Alternatively, under DOS or Microsoft Windows, you could use:

```
set CLASSPATH=c:\jdom\build\classes;%CLASSPATH%
set CLASSPATH=c:\jdom\lib\xerces.jar;c:\jdom\build\jdom.jar;%CLASSPATH%
```

Now that you have built JDOM and set up your environment, we can test the installation by running some of the sample programs that come with JDOM.

Testing Your JDOM Installation

The JDOM distribution comes with several sample JDOM programs, illustrating a variety of applications of JDOM. We'll see a few JDOM programs ourselves later in this chapter, but it is worthwhile browsing the samples to at least get familiar with what is there.

Whilst being informative, the samples also are useful for testing your JDOM installation. We'll run one of these, the WarReader, later in this section. We'll conclude this section with a look at some of the common problems you may run into when testing your JDOM installation.

To run any of the JDOM samples, you must have already compiled these by building the samples as described earlier. The sample class files, as well as some sample XML input files, will then be beneath the `build/classes/` subdirectory of your JDOM installation.

There is also a JDOM test suite under development; however, at the time of this writing, this does not come with the full JDOM source code distribution. If you're interested in this, then you can download it from the JDOM web site.

The WarReader Sample Program

The WarReader sample program takes one command line argument, the name of a web application definition file – usually called `web.xml`. The WarReader then reads the specified web application file and displays some summary information about the web application including a list of the registered servlets, any roles defined and whether the web application is distributed.

The following illustration shows the results of running this sample program under UNIX. Beginning from the JDOM installation directory – in this case, `/opt/jdom/` – we change into the `build/classes/` subdirectory. Here you will see a variety of sample XML files, as well as the `samples` subdirectory containing the JDOM samples class files.

```
$ pwd /opt/jdom
$ cd build/classes
$ echo $CLASSPATH
/opt/jdom/lib/xerces.jar:/opt/jdom/build/jdom.jar:/opt/jdom/build/classes
```

By passing the single argument `web.xml` to the WarReader program (make sure that this file is in your directory), we see the desired output.

```
$ java samples.WarReader web.xml
This WAR has 2 registered servlets:
        snoop for SnoopServlet (it has 0 init params)
        file for ViewFile (it has 1 init params)
This WAR contains 3 roles:
        manager
        director
        president
This WAR is distributed
$
```

As we can see from the above output, the sample `web.xml` file contains two registered servlets (`SnoopServlet` and `ViewFile`), three roles (`manager`, `director`, and `president`) and the WAR file in question is distributed.

In windows, navigate to `C:\jdom\build\classes` and call

```
java samples.WarReader web.xml
```

and you will get a similar output.

Common Configuration Problems

As described in the earlier section, *Setting Your Classpath*, you need to ensure that the `xerces.jar` file included with the JDOM download is in your classpath before any other XML-related classes. Older versions of Xerces, as well as some other XML libraries, support DOM Level 1 and SAX 1.0. JDOM, however, supports DOM Level 2 and SAX 2.0 and must be able to find the related classes.

For other frequently asked questions, refer to the JDOM FAQ at http://www.jdom.org/docs/faq.html.

Writing a First JDOM Program

Now that we have installed, configured, and tested our JDOM installation, it's about time we write our first JDOM program. We begin by looking at the basics of JDOM, including how to build a simple JDOM Document from scratch using only JDOM objects, and how to use the XMLOutputter class to output the XML representation of this document.

All JDOM programs utilize the Document class defined in org.jdom.Document. This class represents an XML document in JDOM. A valid XML document must have a root element, which we create by instantiating a new JDOM Element object and can optionally have a DOCTYPE. In the example below we will use these two classes to define a simple JDOM Document.

The JDOM XMLOutputter class, which is defined in org.jdom.output.XMLOutputter is a commonly used utility that "converts" the JDOM Document into XML. We shall use this to output our simple JDOM Document to screen.

Introducing the HelloWorld Program

As is traditional when learning any new language or API, we shall write a simple "Hello World" program. This program will produce the following output:

```
<?xml version="1.0" encoding="UTF-8"?>
<GREETING>Hello World!</GREETING>
```

This is a simple, yet valid XML document. Below we list the program to produce this output using JDOM.

```
import org.jdom.Element;
import org.jdom.Document;
import org.jdom.output.XMLOutputter;

public class HelloWorld {
  public static void main(String[] args) {
    // Create a root Element for the Document
    Element root = new Element("GREETING");

    root.setText("Hello World!");

    // Create a new document using the root element just created
    Document doc = new Document(root);

    try {
      // Output the new document (doc) to System.out
      XMLOutputter outputter = new XMLOutputter();
      outputter.output(doc, System.out);
    } catch (Exception e) {
      System.err.println(e);
    }
  }
}
```

The first three lines import the required JDOM classes: Element, Document, and XMLOutputter as discussed previously. The next few lines you'll recognize as standard Java. Within the main() method, the first line creates a new Element with the name GREETING. This is responsible for producing the <GREETING></GREETING> tags in the eventual XML output.

The next line initializes the element text. That is the text that appears between the <GREETING></GREETING> tags. In this case, this text is "Hello World". The third line of code in main() creates a new JDOM Document and initializes it with the root element just created.

Finally, the code in the try-catch block creates a new XMLOutputter object, then uses it to output the JDOM Document just created – in the variable, doc – as an XML document to the standard output stream, System.out.

Compiling and Running HelloWorld

Now that we have introduced the HelloWorld.java JDOM program, go ahead and compile it using:

```
>javac HelloWorld.java
```

Now, when you run the HelloWorld program you should see the desired output. A sample of the output generated by compiling and running the HelloWorld program under UNIX is shown below.

```
> java HelloWorld
<?xml version="1.0" encoding="UTF-8"?>
<GREETING>Hello World!</GREETING>
>
```

As you can see from the above, HelloWorld generated the required XML output.

JDOM Object Model & API Overview

One of the original goals of JDOM was to define a document object model that felt "natural" to Java programmers. In this section, we will see that the JDOM API has a very clean and simple design. So much so that only a basic understanding of XML is required in order to be effective with JDOM. We'll look at the four packages that make up JDOM, and look at the main classes and interfaces in each package.

If you haven't already done so by now, it is probably worthwhile compiling the latest JDOM API documentation directly from the source code we downloaded earlier. See the section, *Build Options*, earlier in this chapter for details on generating the JDOM API documentation. As we go through the JDOM API at a high level and discuss the different classes, you can view the JDOM documentation to help get a better understanding of the classes.

The JDOM API is broken down into four basic packages:

❑ **The main JDOM package** (org.jdom). This contains the main JDOM component classes including Document, Element, DocType and so on.

❑ **JDOM input package** (org.jdom.input). This package contains helper classes used to construct a JDOM Document from existing XML sources. The main two classes of interest allow us to build a JDOM Document using a DOM parser, or a SAX parser.

❑ **JDOM output package** (org.jdom.output). The output package contains helper classes for converting from a JDOM Document into some other representation of an XML document. It includes classes to output a DOM document, generate a series of SAX events, and one to output XML directly.

❑ **JDOM DOM adapters** (org.jdom.adapters). Unfortunately not all DOM implementations have a consistent interface. The adapters package addresses this problem by giving a common interface to some of the more widely used DOM implementations.

Below we'll discuss the purpose of each of these packages and look at the main classes and/or interfaces in each package.

The org.jdom Package

The primary JDOM classes can be found in the main org.jdom package. We use these classes to construct a JDOM Document from scratch, or to manipulate an existing JDOM Document. They represent the main XML constructs in an XML document.

Probably the most important class in this package is the Document class, so we will begin by looking at that class, and then look at some of the other important and the more frequently used classes in this package.

The Document Class

The Document class defines the JDOM representation of an XML document. Although up until now we have been talking somewhat generically about a JDOM Document, the concrete definition of it exists in the org.jdom package. In constructing a Document object generally we must specify a root Element and, optionally, a DocType. We will look at these classes in more detail below.

In addition to holding a DocType, and root Element object, a Document can also hold ProcessingInstructions and Comments. The Document class has methods that deal with all four of these components.

In addition to instantiating a JDOM Document directly, a Document object also can be created from a DOM document or by using a SAX parser to parse an XML file. No matter how the Document object is built, its representation is not tied to any particular parser.

The DocType Class

An XML document can have a DOCTYPE associated with it. This is modeled in JDOM using a DocType object. A DocType object can be associated with a Document when the Document is first constructed, or later specified using the Document.setDocType method. The DocType object for a Document can be retrieved using the Document.getDocType method.

A DocType object has three parts of interest: the name of the element being constrained, a public ID and a system ID. For example, consider the following DOCTYPE statement.

```
<!DOCTYPE web-app
    PUBLIC "-//Sun Microsystems, Inc.//DTD Web Application 2.2//EN"
           "http://java.sun.com/j2ee/dtds/web-app_2.2.dtd">
```

The element being constrained here is a web-app document. The public ID is given immediately after the keyword PUBLIC, and the system ID is the URL of the DTD describing a valid web-app document.

161

When constructing a `DocType` object, three public constructors are available. The most basic takes a single argument specifying the element name. The second public constructor takes two arguments: the element name, as well as the system ID. The third public constructor allows us to specify all three parts of the `DOCTYPE`: the element name, the public ID, and the system ID. There is also a fourth constructor that is protected and can therefore only be used by derived classes.

Methods are available in the `DocType` class to get and set each of the components that make up a `DOCTYPE` declaration. The following example illustrates creating a new `DocType` object representing the above `DOCTYPE`, then getting and outputting its components.

```
import org.jdom.DocType;
...
// Create new DocType object
DocType docType
    = new DocType("web-app",
                  "-//Sun Microsystems, Inc.//DTD Web Application 2.2//EN",
                  "http://java.sun.com/j2ee/dtds/web-app_2.2.dtd");

System.out.println("Element: " + docType.getElementName());
System.out.println("Public ID: " + docType.getPublicID());
System.out.println("System ID: " + docType.getSystemID());
...
```

Inserting this code into a program, then compiling and running it should give the following output:

```
Element: web-app
Public ID: -//Sun Microsystems, Inc.//DTD Web Application 2.2//EN
System ID: http://java.sun.com/j2ee/dtds/web-app_2.2.dtd
```

The Namespace Class

The JDOM `Namespace` class represents an XML namespace. Since JDOM is fully namespace aware, it handles many of the details for us. For a namespace prefix to be used, it must be mapped in the XML document to a URI using `xmlns:[prefix]` attribute. This mapping of namespace prefixes to URIs is handled by JDOM during output.

Additionally, namespaces are recognized and correctly preserved during input too. Although namespaces are a DOM Level 2 addition, JDOM supports namespaces even with a DOM Level 1 parser.

The `Namespace` class implements a factory for obtaining a reference to a `Namespace` object. This way new namespace objects are only created when needed.

Additionally, namespaces are passed as optional parameters to most `Element` and `Attribute` manipulation methods, as we shall see below. In the following section we will see an example of creating a new `Element` object using a namespace.

One final note worth making is although the `Namespace` class itself does not implement `java.io.Serializable`, `Elements` and `Attributes` containing `Namespaces` can be serialized. This is because the `Element` and `Attribute` classes handle serialization of their `Namespaces` manually. When objects of these classes are deserialized, the classes use the static `Namespace.getNamespace()` methods to ensure that there is only one unique `Namespace` object for any unique prefix-URI pair. This is done for improved efficiency.

The Element Class

Every JDOM `Document` object has a root `Element` object. This represents the main XML element contained within the document. This root element encloses the main body of the XML document. It, in turn, can contain other XML elements including other "sub-elements", comments, CDATA sections, processing instructions and text.

An `Element` object, also part of the `org.jdom` package, defines the behavior of an XML element. It is a very frequently used component in JDOM. We can get and set the `Elements` textual context, its attributes and its child elements.

JDOM `Elements` are namespace-aware. Although we looked at the JDOM `Namespace` previously, it is worthwhile noting that all methods that operate on an `Element` object and its `Attributes` can be invoked with a single `String` name (in the default namespace), or the `String` local name of the `Element` and a `Namespace` object.

There are two types of constructors with public access for creating a new `Element` object – one that takes a name as an argument, and another that takes a local name and a namespace (several ways of specifying the namespace are available). Examples of these are shown below:

```
...
// Create a new Element without specifying a namespace
Element element = new Element("myElement");

// Create a new Element with a namespace
Namespace namespace
          = Namespace.getNamespace("prefix",
                                    "http://www.mydomain.com/sample");
Element element = new Element("myElement", namespace);
...
```

Similarly, namespaces can be used when getting or removing an `Elements` attribute, and children.

Although you may be tempted to use namespaces by naming elements something like `"myNamespace:myElement"`, the JDOM `Element` class won't allow it. `Element` names cannot contain colons. The correct way to specify a namespace for an element is as shown in the second example above: get the `Namespace` object first, and then use this when creating the `Element`.

An `Element` may have textual content associated with it. To access the text within an `Element` object, there are two accessors and one mutator as follows:

```
...
// Get the text contained in this element with all whitespace preserved
String text = element.getText();

// Get the text contained in this element with all whitespace normalized
String trimmedText = element.getTextTrim();

// Set this elements text to the given string
element.setText(newTextString);
...
```

The functionality of the `getText()` and `setText()` methods is as expected – they get and set the text contained within the `Element` object.

The `getTextTrim()` method warrants a little more attention. It is essentially a helper method that normalizes the whitespace. That is, it removes any leading or trailing whitespace, and replaces multiple whitespace characters with a single space within the text. This method is useful in situations where the multiple spaces are unimportant. `getText()` does not do this by default because, according to the XML 1.0 specifications, tools such as JDOM must preserve all whitespace. It is then up to the application reading or manipulating the XML to determine whether or not the whitespace is important.

Occasionally `Elements` have attributes associated with them. For example, in the XML below the element `Employee` has an attribute `EmpID` with a value of `"ABC1234"`.

```
<Employee EmpID="ABC1234"/>
```

Several methods are available to access an `Element`'s attributes. `getAttribute()` retrieves a JDOM `Attribute` object representing a named attribute. There is a second `getAttribute()` method that takes a `Namespace` as its second argument. To get a list of all the `Attributes` attached to an `Element`, we can use the `getAttributes()` method.

Alternatively, we can retrieve the value of a specific, named attribute using the `getAttributeValue()` methods (with and without a `Namespace` argument). For example, if the `element` variable represents the above XML element, then the following line would output `"ABC1234"`.

```
System.out.println(element.getAttributeValue("EmpID"));
```

Many XML elements have sub-elements, and other child objects. For example, in the following XML, the `Book` element has three children. The first is a comment, and the next two are other elements.

```
<Book>
  <!-- This is a sample comment -->
  <Title>Pro Java XML</Title>
  <Publisher>Wrox Press</Publisher>
</Book>
```

JDOM provides several methods allowing us to access an `Element`'s children. To access a named child, use the `getChild()` methods that returns the child `Element`. The `Element` class also provides helper methods to return the text of a child `Element` – these methods are named, `getChildText()` and `getChildTextTrim()`. As with retrieving the text from an `Element` using the `getTextTrim()` method, the `getChildTextTrim()` methods normalize whitespace.

Finally, we can retrieve a `List` of all immediate children of an `Element` using the `getChildren()` methods. The `List` returned is a `java.util.List`. To manipulate the children of this element, simply manipulate the `List` object itself. Note that if the `Element` has no children, then the `List` returned would be empty. However, it can still be manipulated using the usual Java 2 `List` methods.

For example, to insert a new child element as the second child in the element use the following:

```
List children = element.getChildren();
children.add(1, new Element("elementName"));
```

Remember that the index is zero based, so the second item in the list has an index of 1.

That's all that is involved. The new child will be added to this `Element` as the second child `Element`.

The Attribute Class

We mentioned earlier that `Elements` can have attributes. We looked at the `Element.getAttribute()` methods that return an `Attribute` object, and the `Element.getAttributes()` method that returns a `List` of attributes.

The `Attribute` class models an XML attribute. It has three public constructors that allow us to create a new named attribute and assign it an initial value. The first constructor does not place the attribute in a namespace. The other constructors place the attribute in a namespace specified either using a `Namespace` object, or using a namespace prefix and URI.

The `Attribute` class has various methods that allow us to get and set information about the attribute, including its value, name, namespace and namespace information, and its parent `Element`.

When retrieving the value of an `Attribute`, the `Attribute` class also provides several helper methods that convert the attributes value from the default `String` value into one of the native types: `boolean`, `double`, `float`, `int`, or `long`. These methods are `getBooleanValue()`, `getDoubleValue()`, `getFloatValue()`, `getIntValue()`, and `getLongValue()` respectively. If the attribute value cannot be converted into the required native Java type then each of these methods will throw a JDOM `DataConversionException` exception.

Other Classes

We have looked in some detail at some of the most frequently used classes in the main `org.jdom` package. Other classes in this package include:

❏ `ProcessingInstruction` – this models an XML Processing Instruction (PI). The methods in this class provide access to the target of the PI as well as its data.

❏ `Entity` – models an XML entity.

❏ `CDATA` – models an XML CDATA section. The `getText()` method returns the text from within the CDATA section.

❏ `Comment` – models an XML comment. The `getText()` method returns the comment text. It can be changed using the `setText()` method.

❏ `Verifier` – this class is a little different to the other classes described in this section in that all its methods are static. The methods in the `Verifier` class provide a number of helper functions to help verify valid XML components. The methods help valid the different components against what is considered "legal" according to the XML specifications. It does not currently perform validation of a `Document` against a DTD or Schema.

That concludes our look at the main `org.jdom` package. The only other classes in this package define various exceptions used within JDOM. Next we will go on to look at the `org.jdom.input` package.

The org.jdom.input Package

The `org.jdom.input` package defines classes used to construct a JDOM `Document` from external sources. There are two main classes of interest to us: the `DOMBuilder` and `SAXBuilder` classes. We'll look at these in more detail below. In addition, there is also a helper class `BuilderErrorHandler` which implements the `org.xml.sax.ErrorHandler` interface to provide a SAX error handler.

At the time of writing, these were the only classes in this package, although it is possible that others may be added in the future.

The SAXBuilder Class

The SAXBuilder class, as its name suggests, uses a SAX parser to build a JDOM Document. Building a JDOM Document in this way is essentially a two-step process. Firstly we create a new instance of a SAXBuilder object. We then invoke one of the build methods to read the XML input and build a JDOM Document object.

To create a new SAXBuilder object four different constructors are available. The default constructor creates a new SAXBuilder using the default SAX parser – Xerces – and with validation turned off. This will be sufficient for most purposes. The other three constructors allow us a little more control over which SAX parser to use and whether validation should be on or off. After construction of a SAXBuilder object, validation can be enabled and disabled using the setValidation() method.

After creating a SAXBuilder object, we optionally can initialize it with a custom DTD handler, Entity resolver, XML filter, and error handler. This is done using the setDTDHandler(), setEntityResolver(), setXMLFilter(), and setErrorHandler() methods respectively.

Once we have created a SAXBuilder object and initialized it as required, we can use it to build a JDOM Document. There are seven different publicly accessible build() methods available. The main difference between the seven build() methods lies in where the XML input is to come from. It can come from a variety of sources including one specified by a java.io.File, java.io.InputStream, java.io.Reader, a URI specified as a string, or a java.net.URL.

SAX parsers tend to be very fast compared to DOM parsers. As a result, when we need to read in XML and generate a JDOM Document, the SAXBuilder should be our first choice. If, for whatever reason, you prefer not to use the Xerces parser, then you can always substitute in a third party SAX parser instead. Simply pass the name of the SAX Driver class to the SAXBuilder constructor when creating the builder. Make sure that the classes required by the alternate parser are available in your classpath.

An alternative to the SAXBuilder is the DOMBuilder. We look at this next.

The DOMBuilder Class

The DOMBuilder class is intended to allow us to build a JDOM Document from a pre-existing DOM document. For example, when our application or component needs to interface with another application which already has available a DOM document. Using the DOMBuilder class, we can build a JDOM Document from the DOM document, and then manipulate the new JDOM Document as necessary.

The use of the DOMBuilder class involves many the same steps as when using a SAXBuilder. That is, we first create a new instance of a builder object, in this case DOMBuilder. We then invoke one of the build() methods to read the XML input and build a JDOM Document object.

There are four different constructors available for creating a new DOMBuilder object. The default constructor creates a new DOMBuilder using Xerces as its parser. This will be sufficient for most purposes, however the other three constructors allow you more control in selecting a DOM parser – actually a DOM adapter – and allow you to enable or disable validation. We will look at DOM adapters in more detail in the section titled, *The org.jdom.adapters Package*.

Having created a DOMBuilder object, we can now use it to build a JDOM Document from an existing DOM document object using one of the DOMBuilder.build methods. This build() method is just like the SAXBuilder.build() methods except that it takes as a single argument as its input, an org.w3c.dom.Document object.

It is also possible to construct a JDOM `Element` object directly from a DOM element (`org.w3c.dom.Element`) object using one of the alternate `DOMBuilder.build()` methods.

An important note: if you look at the API documentation for the `DOMBuilder` class, you will see three additional `DOMBuilder.build()` methods. Each of these takes a single argument, either a `java.io.File`, `java.io.InputStream`, or a `java.net.URL`, and builds a JDOM `Document`.

The `DOMBuilder` class is intended primarily as a way of generating a JDOM `Document` from a pre-existing DOM document. These other methods are provided as a means of cross-checking the `SAXBuilder.build()` methods.

> To generate a JDOM `Document` from an XML input source using a DOM parser is going to be slow. Instead, you should always choose a SAX parser to parse XML.

The only real exception to this rule is if you are trying to validate the correct operation of the `SAXBuilder` class, for example, when debugging `SAXBuilder` and/or a SAX parser implementation.

The org.jdom.adapters Package

Whereas SAX defines a standard API for accessing any SAX-compliant parser, this is not the case with DOM: not all DOM parsers were created equal and not all have the same API. The interface and classes in the `org.jdom.adapters` package address this problem by defining a common `DOMAdapter` interface. This defines a wrapper for obtaining a DOM document object from any DOM parser.

The class hierarchy for this package is illustrated below.

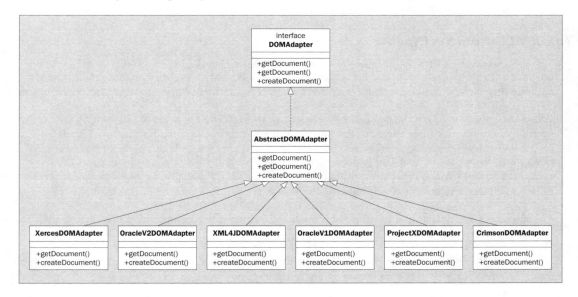

The `AbstractDOMAdapter` class is an abstract implementation of the `DOMAdapter` interface. It is the base class from which all other DOM adapter classes are derived. The JDOM API contains implementations of DOM adapter classes for the most popular DOM parsers including Xerces from Apache (the default parser), Crimson DOM parser (also from Apache), Project X from Sun, and Oracle Version 1 and Version 2 DOM parsers. No matter which adapter we use to build a JDOM `Document` the resulting `Document` is not tied to the adapter or parser used to generate it.

In general, you'll rarely need to use any of these classes directly unless you are developing a DOM adapter for a currently unsupported DOM parser, or are developing or debugging one of the existing DOM adapter classes. To use a specific DOM parser, we simply specify the name of the adapter class when we instantiate a `DOMBuilder` or `DOMOutputter` object. The details of the individual DOM parser implementation are then hidden from us in the appropriate adapter class.

This concludes our look at the input side of JDOM, the part that generates JDOM `Document` objects for us. Some of the later examples in this chapter will make use of these classes to read XML documents. We now go on to look at the output side of JDOM.

The org.jdom.output Package

The `org.jdom.output` package includes the classes responsible for outputting a JDOM `Document` in a variety of different forms. At the time of writing three main output forms were supported: XML, DOM, and SAX. Support for these are implemented in the `XMLOutputter`, `DOMOutputter`, and `SAXOutputter` classes respectively. Below we look at each of these classes in turn.

The most common uses for these output classes – to output an entire document – are not too different from their input counterparts, the `SAXBuilder` and `DOMBuilder` classes. To output an entire JDOM `Document` using any of these output classes first we must instantiate the required "outputter" class. Then we invoke the required `output()` method to output the document in the required form.

The XMLOutputter Class

The `XMLOutputter` class is perhaps the most useful output class and is especially useful for debugging purposes. It can be used to dump out, in XML, an entire JDOM `Document` or individual JDOM components such as `Element`, `Comment`, `CDATA`, `Entity`, and `ProcessingInstruction` objects.

When instantiating a new `XMLOutputter` object, we can select what level of indentation we require, whether we want new lines added to the output, and what character encoding to use. The default constructor assumes no indentation and no new lines, and uses the default character encoding. All whitespace from the element text is preserved. The default constructor generally outputs the most compact form of XML output, even though it may not be easily readable by humans. We humans tend to like whitespace in the form of indentation and new lines.

To generate XML output in a more human readable format, it is recommended that we use the two, or three argument constructor.

- ❏ For the first parameter, specify the level of indentation as a `String`, for example, a `String` consisting of two spaces is usually a good start.
- ❏ The second parameter determines whether new lines should be printed or ignored. Pass in a value of `true` to output new lines.
- ❏ The third parameter is optional and specifies the character encoding to use.

It is worth noting at this point some of the characteristics of the output generated using the XMLOutputter class. We can see examples of most of these throughout this chapter.

❑ The XML declaration is always output on its own line.

❑ ProcessingInstructions are always output on their own lines.

❑ Empty elements are printed as a single empty element tag. For example, the "distributed" Element containing no text and no children – such as in a web application – would be output as <distributed/>.

❑ Text-only Elements are printed as the text content between a start and end tag. For example, a title Element containing the text "JDOM" would be output as <title>JDOM</title>.

❑ The setIndent() methods can be used to enable/disable output of indentation and set the indentation string to use.

❑ The setNewlines() method can be used to determine whether or not to output newlines or suppress them.

❑ Other set methods are available to allow finer grain control over the output.

Below is an example of a document output using the default XMLOutputter. Note, for this document, the lack of space and new lines. In fact, in this case, the output really appears on just two "lines". We have had to split it in order to display it on the printed page. This output is still valid XML and is readable by humans. However, the structure of the document is not at all clear.

```
<?xml version="1.0" encoding="UTF-8"?>
<web-app><servlet><servlet-name>snoop</servlet-name><servlet-class>
SnoopServlet</servlet-class></servlet><servlet><servlet-name>file</
servlet-name><servlet-class>ViewFile</servlet-class><init-param><pa
ram-name>initial</param-name><param-value>1000</param-value><descri
ption>The initial value for the counter  <!-- optional --></descrip
tion></init-param></servlet><distributed /><security-role><role-nam
e>manager</role-name><role-name>director</role-name><role-name>pres
ident</role-name></security-role></web-app>
```

Compare this to the output of the same document generated using an XMLOutputter created using two-space indentation and with new lines enabled. That is, with an XMLOutputter created using:

```
new XMLOutputter("  ", true);
```

Even though this was generated from the same JDOM Document object, note how much more readable this output is.

```
<?xml version="1.0" encoding="UTF-8"?>
<web-app>
  <servlet>
    <servlet-name>snoop</servlet-name>
    <servlet-class>SnoopServlet</servlet-class>
  </servlet>
  <servlet>
    <servlet-name>file</servlet-name>
    <servlet-class>ViewFile</servlet-class>
    <init-param>
```

```
          <param-name>initial</param-name>
          <param-value>1000</param-value>
          <description>
            The initial value for the counter        <!-- optional -->
          </description>
        </init-param>
      </servlet>
      <distributed />
      <security-role>
        <role-name>manager</role-name>
        <role-name>director</role-name>
        <role-name>president</role-name>
      </security-role>
  </web-app>
```

The DOMOutputter Class

To output a JDOM Document as a DOM document (that is, an org.w3c.dom.Document), we can use the DOMOutputter class. There are two constructors available. The default constructor uses the default DOM adapter – XercesDOMAdapter. Alternatively, we can specify a DOM adapter class to select a specific DOM adapter.

Once we have a DOMOutputter object, we can use it to generate a DOM Document (org.w3c.dom.Document) object from a JDOM Document object. Additionally, we can use the DOMOutputter object to generate DOM Element (org.w3c.dom.Element) objects from JDOM Element objects, as well as DOM Attribute (org.w3c.dom.Attr) objects from JDOM Attribute objects.

The DOMOutputter class is most useful when your JDOM program needs a DOM Document object to pass to another program.

The SAXOutputter Class

The SAXOutputter class provides a means of generating a series of SAX2 events from a JDOM Document just as if a SAX parser were reading an XML representation of the Document.

As of this writing there are a small number of SAX callback functions not fully implemented. Refer to the most up-to-date JDOM API documentation on the SAXOutputter class to see a current list of these. The most notable callbacks not currently implemented include the DTDHandler and ErrorHandler callbacks. At this point, it is not possible to access notations and unparsed entity references in a DTD from a JDOM Document, therefore the DTDHandler callbacks have not been implemented. Additionally, the ErrorHandler callbacks are not implemented since they are supposed to be invoked when the document is parsed and the JDOM Document has already been parsed and should be valid.

When constructing a new SAXOutputter object, we must specify a SAX ContentHandler (actually an org.xml.sax.ContentHandler) as a minimum. We can, optionally, also specify a SAX ErrorHandler (org.xml.sax.ErrorHandler), DTDHandler (org.xml.sax.DTDHandler), and EntityResolver (org.xml.sax.EntityResolver) when creating a SAXOutputter object.

Once we have a SAXOutputter object, we can invoke the output() method, passing it the JDOM Document object we wish to output.

Clearly the SAXOutputter class is most useful when our JDOM program needs to fire off SAX events that are to be handled by other programs.

Putting It All Together

Now that we have explored the JDOM API in detail, we can bring together what we learned in some more advanced and interesting examples. The first example shows how to use the SAXBuilder to read an XML document, and prints some summary information about the document. The second example illustrates the same thing but using a DOMBuilder to build a JDOM Document from a DOM document. We should get the same results when running these two example programs with the same input!

The third example shows how we can build a JDOM Document using the core JDOM components. It also illustrates the use of the XMLOutputter class to output the results to the screen.

Using SAXBuilder

In this first example, we use the SAXBuilder class to read in a user-specified XML document and build a JDOM Document. We will then output some summary information about the XML document that has been read.

The SAXBuilderDocumentDump program shown below takes a single command line argument – the name of an XML file to read. It starts by instantiating a new SAXBuilder object using the default SAX parser. This SAXBuilder object is then used to read the XML file specified and build a JDOM Document representation of it, stored in the local variable doc.

```
import java.util.List;
import org.jdom.DocType;
import org.jdom.Document;
import org.jdom.Element;
import org.jdom.input.SAXBuilder;
import org.jdom.output.XMLOutputter;

public class SAXBuilderDocumentDump {
  public static void main(String[] args) {

    if (args.length != 1) {
      System.out.println("Usage: SAXBuilderDocumentDump <XMLFile>");
      return;
    }
    // Create a new SAXBuilder using the default SAX parser
    //   (with no validation -- the default)
    SAXBuilder builder = new SAXBuilder();
```

From this JDOM Document object we obtain the document type, which may be null if no DOCTYPE is specified in the XML input file, and the root element:

```
    try {
      //  create a new JDOM Document from the command line argument
      Document doc = builder.build(args[0]);

      DocType docType = doc.getDocType();
      Element root = doc.getRootElement();
```

A summary of the XML file is then output, including the name of the file read, information about its document type (if any is available), and information about its root element.

```
        System.out.println("Input file: " + args[0]\n);

        System.out.print("Document type: ");
        if (null == docType) {
          System.out.println("none specified");

        } else {
          System.out.println();
          System.out.println("  Name: " + docType.getElementName());
          System.out.println("  Public ID: " + docType.getPublicID());
          System.out.println("  System ID: " + docType.getSystemID());
        }

        System.out.println();
        System.out.println("Root element:");
        System.out.println("  Name: " + root.getName());
        System.out.println("  Text (trimmed): '" + root.getTextTrim() +"'");

        List attributes = root.getAttributes();
        System.out.println("  Number of attributes: " + attributes.size());

        List children = root.getChildren();
        System.out.println("  Number of (immediate) children: " +
                          children.size());
      } catch (Exception e) {
        System.err.println(e);
      }
    }
  }
}
```

If we create the following sample file as test input, `fibo.xml`:

```
<?xml version="1.0" encoding="UTF-8"?>
<Fibonacci_Numbers>
  <fibonacci index="0">0</fibonacci>
  <fibonacci index="1">1</fibonacci>
  <fibonacci index="2">1</fibonacci>
  <fibonacci index="3">2</fibonacci>
  <fibonacci index="4">3</fibonacci>
  <fibonacci index="5">5</fibonacci>
  <fibonacci index="6">8</fibonacci>
  <fibonacci index="7">13</fibonacci>
  <fibonacci index="8">21</fibonacci>
  <fibonacci index="9">34</fibonacci>
  <fibonacci index="10">55</fibonacci>
</Fibonacci_Numbers>
```

We can then run SAXBuilderDocumentDump specifying fibo.xml as a parameter. Below is the output that is generated:

```
Input file: fibo.xml

Document type: none specified

Root element:
  Name: Fibonacci_Numbers
  Text (trimmed): ''
  Number of attributes: 0
  Number of (immediate) children: 11
```

As you'll see from the above output, fibo.xml has no document type, a root element named Fibonacci_Numbers with no text content, no attributes and eleven children.

To illustrate some of the other features, consider the web application specification file, web.xml, shown below as input.

```xml
<?xml version="1.0" encoding="ISO-8859-1"?>
<!DOCTYPE web-app
    PUBLIC "-//Sun Microsystems, Inc.//DTD Web Application 2.2//EN"
    "http://java.sun.com/j2ee/dtds/web-app_2.2.dtd">

<web-app>
    <servlet>
        <servlet-name>snoop</servlet-name>
        <servlet-class>SnoopServlet</servlet-class>
    </servlet>
    <servlet>
        <servlet-name>file</servlet-name>
        <servlet-class>ViewFile</servlet-class>
    </servlet>
    <servlet-mapping>
        <servlet-name>snoop</servlet-name>
        <url-pattern>/Snoop</url-pattern>
    </servlet-mapping>

    <distributed/>

    <security-role>
      <role-name>manager</role-name>
      <role-name>director</role-name>
      <role-name>president</role-name>
    </security-role>
</web-app>
```

Running SAXBuilderDocumentDump with web.xml as its parameter generates the following output. From the output we can see that this XML input file has a document type specified which, as you can see, refers to the Web Application 2.2 specifications. The root element is named web-app. It has no textual content, no attributes and five children. Once again, we can verify this information by taking a quick look at the input file, web.xml.

```
Input file: web.xml

Document type:
  Name: web-app
  Public ID: -//Sun Microsystems, Inc.//DTD Web Application 2.2//EN
  System ID: http://java.sun.com/j2ee/dtds/web-app_2.2.dtd

Root element:
  Name: web-app
  Text (trimmed): ''
  Number of attributes: 0
  Number of (immediate) children: 5
```

Notice how simple SAXBuilderDocumentDump was as a result of using JDOM. The SAXBuilder hides all the complexities of SAX by handling SAX events and catching any SAXExceptions, which it converts to JDOMExceptions.

Our next example program illustrates the use of the DOMBuilder class to generate a JDOM Document.

Using DOMBuilder

The DOMBuilder class allows us to create a JDOM Document object from a pre-existing DOM Document. To illustrate this we need a means of creating a DOM Document to begin with. In this example, we'll use a SAXBuilder, as before, to read an XML file and create a JDOM Document, then use a DOMOutputter to output this to a DOM Document. We can then use this DOM Document as the input to a DOMBuilder object.

Though this may seem a little convoluted when you think that the DOMBuilder class can directly read an XML file, it does serve to illustrate two important points in one example. Firstly, it illustrates the use of the DOMOutputter class to create a DOM Document object. Secondly, it illustrates the use of the DOMBuilder to create a JDOM Document from a DOM Document.

Additionally, recall that using the DOMBuilder to read an XML input source is inefficient. DOM parsers are much slower than SAX parsers at reading an XML input source.

As with the SAXBuilderDocumentDump program we read in a user-specified XML document, but in this example we use it to build a DOM Document. We then use a DOMBuilder object to convert the DOM Document into a JDOM Document. Again, we'll output some summary information about the XML document read. We can verify that this information is the same as the information output by our SAXBuilderDocumentDump program.

The DOMBuilderDocumentDump program shown below consists of two (static) methods: main() and getDOMDocument(). The getDOMDocument() method uses a SAXBuilder to read the specified XML file, and demonstrates how to output a DOM org.w3c.dom.Document object from a JDOM Document object.

```
import java.io.File;
import java.util.List;

import org.jdom.DocType;
import org.jdom.Document;
import org.jdom.Element;
import org.jdom.JDOMException;
```

```
import org.jdom.input.DOMBuilder;
import org.jdom.input.SAXBuilder;
import org.jdom.output.DOMOutputter;
import org.jdom.output.XMLOutputter;

public class DOMBuilderDocumentDump {
  static org.w3c.dom.Document getDOMDocument(String filename)
    throws JDOMException {

    // Create a new SAXBuilder to read the XML file
    SAXBuilder builder = new SAXBuilder();

    Document jdomDoc = builder.build(filename);

    // Create a new DOMOutputter object
    DOMOutputter outputter = new DOMOutputter();

    // Output this JDOM Document as a DOM Document
    return outputter.output(jdomDoc);
  }
```

Since this is just a demonstration program getDOMDocument() uses an external XML file as its input source. In a more practical situation, we might obtain a DOM Document from another program.

The DOMBuilderDocumentDump program takes a single command line argument – the name of an XML file to read. It starts by calling the getDOMDocument() method to read the specified file and generate a DOM Document.

```
public static void main(String[] args) {
  // Check that the user entered one argument (the name
  //  of an XML file to read)
  if (args.length != 1) {
    System.out.println("Usage: DOMBuilderDocumentDump <XMLFile>");
    return;
  }

  org.w3c.dom.Document domDoc;
  try {
    // Output status information
    System.out.println("Input file: " + args[0]);
    System.out.println();

    // Get a DOM Document.
    domDoc = getDOMDocument(args[0]);

  } catch (JDOMException ex) {
      System.out.println("Unable to get a valid DOM Document from " +
                          args[0]);
      ex.printStackTrace();
      return;
  }
```

The main() method then uses this DOM Document as input to a DOMBuilder object that then generates a JDOM Document representation of the DOM Document:

```
// We now have a valid DOM Document

try {
    // Create a new DOMBuilder using the default DOM parser
    DOMBuilder builder = new DOMBuilder();

    // Read the DOM document, and create a new JDOM Document from it
    Document doc = builder.build(domDoc);
```

From this JDOM Document object we obtain the document type and root element. A summary of the XML file is then output including the name of the file read, information about its document type, and information about its root element.

```
    DocType docType = doc.getDocType();
    Element root = doc.getRootElement();

    // Output summary information about the document
    System.out.print("Document type: ");
    if (null == docType) {
        System.out.println("none specified");

    } else {
        System.out.println();
        System.out.println("  Name: " + docType.getElementName());
        System.out.println("  Public ID: " + docType.getPublicID());
        System.out.println("  System ID: " + docType.getSystemID());
    }

    System.out.println();
    System.out.println("Root element:");
    System.out.println("  Name: " + root.getName());
    System.out.println("  Text (trimmed): '" + root.getTextTrim() +"'");

    List attributes = root.getAttributes();
    System.out.println("  Number of attributes: " + attributes.size());

    List children = root.getChildren();
    System.out.println("  Number of (immediate) children: " +
                        children.size());

    } catch (Exception e) {
        e.printStackTrace();
    }
  }
}
```

Below is a sample of the output from running this program using the XML input file we used with our previous example, SAXBuilderDocumentDump. The output shown below was generated using the input file, fibo.xml.

```
Input file: fibo.xml

Document type: none specified

Root element:
  Name: Fibonacci_Numbers
  Text (trimmed): ''
  Number of attributes: 0
  Number of (immediate) children: 26
```

Compare this with the output from our previous program. As we can see, it is the same as the output from SAXBuilderDocumentDump, much as expected. The output should be the same, given the same input.

In our next example, we look at using JDOM components to build and manipulate a JDOM Document that is then used to output XML.

Manipulating JDOM Components

In our final example of JDOM, we illustrate the manipulation of a JDOM Document and its components. You may already be familiar with the Servlet 2.2 specification. It defines a web application as consisting of a collection of servlets, JSPs, and other web components ordered in such a way that they can be deployed in a compliant web container. The deployment descriptor is a file called web.xml, and this defines certain properties of the web application in a standard format.

In this example, we provide a WebApp class that can be used to build a web application deployment descriptor programmatically. It uses JDOM to do the document manipulation and creation of the XML output. The main methods provided by the WebApp class are as follows:

- ❑ WebApp constructor – Two forms are available: one that assumes the default 2.2 DOCTYPE, and another that allows us to override the default and provide our own DOCTYPE information.

- ❑ output() – Two forms of the output() method are provided: the first supports output to an OutputStream, the second to a Writer.

- ❑ getDisplayName() / setDisplayName() – These methods allow us to get and set the web applications display name property.

- ❑ addServlet() – This method allows us to add a servlet definition to the web application. This allows us to specify a servlet name, and the class in which the servlet is implemented.

- ❑ addServletMapping() – This method allows us to add a servlet mapping to the web application. A servlet mapping maps a virtual URL to a specific servlet.

Since this class is intended to illustrate manipulation of XML using JDOM, it does not support every aspect of the Servlet 2.2 specifications and it doesn't provide for all the functionality we might eventually want. However, it is sufficiently complete so as to provide a usable class, as well as to demonstrate XML manipulation with JDOM.

The `main()` method illustrates the sample use of this class to build a web application definition, and output it to the standard output stream (`System.out`). The web application it builds is given a display name of "**Sample Web Application**", has two servlets registered (`myServlet` and `mySecondServlet`) and two servlet mappings defined, one for each servlet.

Below is the `WebApp.java` class file, in its entirety:

```java
import java.io.IOException;
import java.io.OutputStream;
import java.io.OutputStreamWriter;
import java.io.Writer;

import java.util.Iterator;
import java.util.List;

import org.jdom.DocType;
import org.jdom.Document;
import org.jdom.Element;
import org.jdom.output.XMLOutputter;

public class WebApp {
  private static String DEFAULT_DOCNAME = "web-app";
  private static String DEFAULT_PUBLIC_ID =
                  "-//Sun Microsystems, Inc.//DTD Web Application 2.2//EN";
  private static String DEFAULT_SYSTEM_ID =
                       "http://java.sun.com/j2ee/dtds/web-app_2_2.dtd";
```

The `main()` method creates an object of type `WebApp`, which it then loads with the web application name, before mapping a servlet (`com.myCompany.myPackage.myServletClass`) to its URL on the server (`/myServletURL`). We then do this for a second servlet, `com.myCompany.myPackage.mySecondServletClass` using methods defined in just a moment. We then output the document to the system output stream:

```java
public static void main(String[] args) {
  WebApp webApp = new WebApp();

  webApp.setDisplayName("Sample Web Application");
  webApp.addServlet("myServlet",
                    "com.myCompany.myPackage.myServletClass");
  webApp.addServletMapping("myServlet", "/myServletURL");

  webApp.addServlet("mySecondServlet",
                    "com.myCompany.myPackage.mySecondServletClass");
  webApp.addServletMapping("mySecondServlet", "/mySecondServletURL");

  try {
    webApp.output(System.out);

  } catch (Exception ex) {
      System.out.println(ex);
  }
}
```

The doc property of the class holds the web application Document. The default constructor creates a new web application object with the default document name (web-app), and default public and system IDs for the web application 2.2 specifications using the static variable values as above

```
private Document doc;

public WebApp() {
  this(DEFAULT_DOCNAME, DEFAULT_PUBLIC_ID, DEFAULT_SYSTEM_ID);
}
```

A second constructor is given that allows us to specify a document name, and alternative public and system IDs given in the docName, publicID, and systemID parameters:

```
public WebApp(String docName, String publicID, String systemID) {
  doc = new Document(new Element("web-app"));
  doc.setDocType(new DocType(docName, publicID, systemID));
}
```

The output() method outputs the current web application document in its XML format to the given output stream:

```
public void output(OutputStream os) throws IOException {
  XMLOutputter outputter = new XMLOutputter("  ", true);
  outputter.output(doc, os);
}
```

The setDisplayName() and getDisplayName() methods wrap the given string in a <display-name> element, and return the appropriate value, respectively. Web application deployers can optionally use this value to identify the application:

```
public String getDisplayName() {
  Element displayName = doc.getRootElement().getChild("display-name");
  if (displayName == null) {
    return "";
  }
  return displayName.getText();
}

public void setDisplayName(String appName) {
  Element displayName = doc.getRootElement().getChild("display-name");

  if (displayName == null) {
    displayName = insertBefore("servlet",
                               new Element("display-name"));
  }

  displayName.setText(appName);
}
```

The `addServlet()` method takes the servlet class name and the "friendly" name for the servlet and place them in the `web.xml` file.

```
public void addServlet(String servletName, String servletClass) {
  Element servlet = new Element("servlet");
  servlet.addContent(new Element("servlet-name").setText(servletName));
  servlet.addContent(new Element("servlet-class").setText(servletClass));
  insertBefore("servlet-mapping", servlet);
}
```

Notice the shorthand form for adding child elements that we have used here. We can also do this by adding children to a list and using the `setChildren()` method.

To illustrate the effect of this method, passing the values `com.myCompany.myPackage.myServletClass` and `myServlet` will create the following sub-tree:

```
<servlet>
  <servlet-name>myServlet</servlet-name>
  <servlet-class>
    com.myCompany.myPackage.myServletClass
  </servlet-class>
</servlet>
```

Web applications define a system for mapping a URL that maps to a servlet call:

```
public void addServletMapping(String servletName, String servletUrl) {
  Element servletMapping = new Element("servlet-mapping");
  servletMapping.addContent(
                    new Element("servlet-name").setText(servletName));
  servletMapping.addContent(
                    new Element("url-pattern").setText(servletUrl));
  insertBefore("mime-mapping", servletMapping);
}
```

Finally, we define a helper method, `insertBefore()` that will insert a given `Element` before the first occurrence of the given tag whose name is specified as a string:

```
private Element insertBefore(String tag, Element element) {
  // Get a list of existing children
  List children = doc.getRootElement().getChildren();
  if (children.isEmpty()) {
    doc.getRootElement().addContent(element);
  } else {
    int position = 0;
    Iterator it = children.iterator();

    while (it.hasNext()) {
      if (((Element)it.next()).getName().equals(tag)) {
        break;
      }
      position++;
    }
```

```
            children.add(position, element);
        }

        return element;
    }
}
```

In the case of web applications, the order of the web-app children is important. The private method insertBefore() in the WebApp class helps with this ordering. It also demonstrates the insertion of new Elements in a specific place in the root Elements list of children. Note how this can be done using the native java.util.List – part of the Java 2 Collections API.

If we were to compile and run this example, we should get the following output:

```
<?xml version="1.0" encoding="UTF-8"?>
<!DOCTYPE web-app PUBLIC "-//Sun Microsystems, Inc.//DTD Web Application 2.2//EN"
"http://java.sun.com/j2ee/dtds/web-app_2_2.dtd">
<web-app>
  <display-name>Sample Web Application</display-name>
  <servlet>
    <servlet-name>myServlet</servlet-name>
    <servlet-class>
      com.myCompany.myPackage.myServletClass
    </servlet-class>
  </servlet>
  <servlet>
    <servlet-name>mySecondServlet</servlet-name>
    <servlet-class>
      com.myCompany.myPackage.mySecondServletClass
    </servlet-class>
  </servlet>
  <servlet-mapping>
    <servlet-name>myServlet</servlet-name>
    <url-pattern>/myServletURL</url-pattern>
  </servlet-mapping>
  <servlet-mapping>
    <servlet-name>mySecondServlet</servlet-name>
    <url-pattern>/mySecondServletURL</url-pattern>
  </servlet-mapping>
</web-app>
```

I will take it as read that you can see how this could be applied to create XML files dynamically; in the above example we have done half of the necessary work to create a deployment tool for web applications.

The Future of JDOM

When you started reading this chapter you may have been thinking, "Why should I learn about an API which hasn't reached version 1.0 yet?" That would have been a fair question. Hopefully now that you've made it this far, you have a much better understanding of what JDOM is, how it differs from SAX and DOM, and where and when you could use it. Hopefully, you'll agree just how useful it is for XML document manipulation.

For JDOM version 1.0, the major planned changes will include:

❑ Memory and performance optimizations.

❑ Support for inline entities.

❑ Support for inline DTDs.

❑ Adoption of JDOM as a Java extension.

However, perhaps the most significant of these will be the fact that JDOM is being put through the **Java Community Process** (JCP) as a **Java Specification Request** (JSR). This will establish JDOM as an industry standard and positions it well for later inclusion into the core JDK at some point in the future, which is a move that Sun Microsystems has expressed a desire for.

Since the JCP requires certain mandatory review periods, it is expected that this will be completed in the third quarter of 2001 at the very earliest. Still, this does not stop us using JDOM today and getting a head start on a future standard! We've already seen just how powerful it is for XML document manipulation.

In JDOM version 2.0 we hope to see support for XPath, localization of strings, in-memory validation, deferred building – so that not all of a document must be in memory at once – and XSLT support. For the most up-to-date list of up-coming additions and changes to JDOM, refer to the TODO.TXT file that comes with the JDOM distribution.

Get Involved

Finally, if you're interested in seeing JDOM progress more quickly then join the development effort. As an open source development project, it relies on the support and involvement of developers like you. To find out how to get involved in the project, check out the JDOM web site and sign up for one of the mailing lists.

Further Reading

For more information on JDOM, refer to any of the following resources.

❑ **The JDOM home page** is the best place to start for information on JDOM, or to download the latest release. http://www.jdom.org/.

❑ **JDOM Frequently Asked Questions (FAQ)** – available at http://www.jdom.org/docs/faq.html. These also contain some useful troubleshooting tips, and describe common problems you may encounter when you start working with JDOM. Read them!

❑ **JDOM discussion lists** – available from the JDOM web site. Perhaps the most useful for you as a JDOM developer is the jdom-interest mailing list. It has a low-to-medium traffic volume – typically 5-10 messages a day. Archives of the messages posted are also available online. Before posting a question, especially if you are new to JDOM, please be sure to read the FAQs first. You'll be amazed at how often the same questions come up time and time again!

❑ **JavaWorld** – available at http://www.javaworld.com/. In May and July 2000, Jason Hunter and Brett McLaughlin – the "fathers of JDOM" – wrote a two-part series on JDOM entitled, "Easy Java/XML integration with JDOM", which is available here.

Summary

In this chapter we looked at what JDOM is, and how it differs from – and complements – SAX and DOM. The main point to remember is that JDOM does not replace SAX or DOM and is not an XML parser. Instead, JDOM provides a Java-centric, object-oriented approach to XML document manipulation. In fact, due to the design of JDOM it is not limited to XML and could equally well be applied to any hierarchical document structure.

We then looked at how to obtain the latest release of the JDOM source files, and how to install and build the main `jdom.jar`. We introduced a simple HelloWorld JDOM program.

After looking at the JDOM API in more detail, we used some of what we'd learned to create some more sophisticated examples. These demonstrated the ease of use and power of JDOM in manipulating XML documents. We then finished up with a look at some of the expected additions to JDOM in the upcoming releases.

Hopefully, by now, you have a good understanding JDOM and where it can best be used. In the next chapter, we will take a look at XML Schemas and their uses.

The Xerces Blue
Butterfly, which became
extinct earlier this century,
and after which the Xerces XML
parser is named ...

5

XML Schemas

"XML Schemas express shared vocabularies and allow machines to carry out rules made by people. They provide a means for defining the structure, content and semantics of XML documents."

(W3C© Architecture Domain, XML Schema – http://www.w3.org/XML/Schema)

Quoting the opening sentence from the W3C XML Schema page is a good way to introduce this chapter, because it captures many of the key issues involved in data interchange – the human-machine interface, the ability to define a common language, and the requirement for structured content with defined semantics. As a 'mission statement' it explicitly states the purpose of XML Schema, and implicitly indicates the limitations of the existing way of defining an XML document's structure – the **Document Type Definition** (DTD).

These limitations include the fact that DTDs only supports ten data types (compared to XML Schema's 40 plus) and that DTDs are written in non-XML syntax (increasing the burden on the programmer). For a simple application this is not a problem and to criticise DTDs for these limitations is as unfair as criticising HTML for lacking the structural integrity of XML; DTDs and HTML perform the function they are intended to.

XML Schema is powerful because it offers the developer a lot more features and versatility for solving problems:

❑ Improved data management capability because of the ability to extend and restrict datatypes

❑ The ability to create user-defined datatypes

❑ An object-oriented nature intuitive to object-oriented programmers

It also holds out many other benefits in terms of greater power to manipulate the data elements, and to create the ordering and content that an application problem demands. It does this by controlling data sequence, applying keys, or using the substitution mechanism.

This chapter aims to provide an introduction to XML Schema – to introduce the key concepts, and to apply them as we build a schema and steadily improve it by using the features of XML Schema. To do this we will use real-world scenarios. Through this approach, we hope to ground this introduction to the application of XML Schema in some of the data-modeling problems that we all face and try to solve every day.

The XML Schema Candidate Recommendation specification (issued 24 October 2000) consists of three parts: XML Schema Part 0: Primer, XML Schema Part 1: Structures, and XML Schema Part 2: Data types.

❑   The Primer – Provides an illustrated explanation of the specification.

❑   Part 1 – Defines XML Schema in terms of the schema structural components. These are the building blocks of a schema from the abstract model to the individual attribute, element, and data type definitions that are provided by the XML Schema specification.

❑   Part 2 – Data types in XML Schema are defined and explained, from the built-in primitive and derived data types, to the methods for extending those data types, and then finally to the methods for creating and defining user-defined data types.

> **For a more in-depth understanding of the XML Schema Candidate Recommendation, there is no substitute for reading these three parts. More information can be found at the W3C Home Page: http://www.w3.org/XML/Schema.**

This chapter will cover two main objectives:

❑   The first is a basic theoretical introduction to XML Schema to provide background – why is an XML schema language required, how is that language structured, and how is its data defined?

❑   The second is a practical guide to the principles and rules involved in creating schemas and instance documents. Worked examples and fragments of XML Schema and XML instance documents are freely used to aid explanation.

To achieve this, the chapter is broken down into two sections. The first covering the background, and the second discussing the theory and practice of XML Schema.

The first section discusses:

❑   The W3C's vision for the Web and XML Schema's place in the XML Activity

❑   The limitations of the DTD as a framework for establishing the content model of an XML document (in terms of the structure and data it can model)

❑   A comparison between the DTD and the capabilities offered by XML Schema

The second section explains the specification in detail. Explanation is blended with illustrative examples, and the focus is on providing a clear presentation of the key constructs and concepts that are required to understand and use XML Schema. We will begin with a basic DTD and its conversion into an XML Schema. Then, as we delve deeper into the XML Schema specification, we will use further worked examples to demonstrate the capabilities of XML Schema for giving us greater ability to model our data. The examples will become gradually more complex as we work through the chapter and add more to the sample schema that we are building.

XML Schema: a Thread in the Web

XML Schema has to be understood within the context of the W3C's XML Activity and the goals of the W3C itself. The W3C describes its mission as promoting the interoperability and technical evolution of the Web in order to make the Web a 'robust, scalable, and adaptive infrastructure' for the exchange of data in a 'world of information'. The W3C intends to achieve this mission by articulating a process based on three long-term goals for the Web ('Universal Access', the 'Semantic Web', and the creation of a 'Web of Trust') and the expression of a design architecture that inherits the Internet's design principles of 'Interoperability', 'Evolution', and 'Decentralization'.

> **Full descriptions of the W3C's Web Goals and Design Principles of the Web may be found on the 'About the World Wide Web Consortium' pages on the W3C's web site at http://www.w3.org/Consortium/**

Put simply, the role of the W3C can be described as one of conceptualization and realization – of producing the ideas, developing the technology, and creating the standards that will make this vision of the Web work. To achieve this goal, the W3C's efforts are constituted into various Activities grouped under specific domains – the **Architecture Domain**, **User Interface Domain**, **Technology and Society Domain**, and the **Web Accessibility Initiative**.

XML Schema is part of the W3C's **XML Activity** in the Architecture Domain. As part of the XML Activity, XML Schema is a component part of the W3C's phased delivery and implementation of an interoperable, scalable, and semantic Web architecture. XML Schema is important to achieving this goal because it provides an advanced mechanism for the description and specification of the structural and data constraints of an XML document, and XML is central to achieving the vision of a semantic Web and the free interchange of data between organisations and people.

Extensible Markup Language (XML) and the XML Activity

The XML Activity is responsible for the W3C's development of XML. XML is an **application profile** of the **Standardized General Markup Language (SGML)** (ISO 8879), a technical term meaning that it offers a subset of SGML's capabilities.

> *XML borrows from the features of SGML. As an application profile, XML is a subset of SGML, meaning that it only includes those capabilities of SGML that are necessary for XML to perform its task of publishing structured information. The 'simplification' process that underlay the creation of XML removed the cost and complexity involved in an SGML implementation. In essence, XML can be considered a scaled-down version of SGML.*

SGML is a **meta language** from which other markup languages are derived. SGML is a rich and powerful syntax that enables data to be stored independently of the application domain and application logic (simply put, software and vendor-neutral). However, this is achieved at the expense of great complexity. SGML is still used for industrial-strength publishing solutions by major corporations, but for smaller publishing requirements it is inappropriate.

XML resolves this issue by providing a less complicated and more economic alternative for publishing information. In the web context, HTML works brilliantly, but it can be badly formed and still be read by a browser (this laxness was intentional and formed part of the impetus that helped to spread the Web). It is not realistic to allow this laxness when exchanging data, and XML addresses this need.

187

Visit **http://www.w3.org/XML/Activity.html** for further information about the W3C's XML Activity.

Structured Data and Common Semantics

As an encoding syntax, XML is both human-readable and machine-readable and offers an extensible and user-defined format for marking up and structuring information. The machine-readable part of XML is the markup that it is intended to be read and interpreted by the application processing the document.

To illustrate, consider the XML markup in the first example below. The markup `<MyElement>` is machine-readable and, depending how the `<MyElement>` element type is defined, tells the application how to process `<MyElement>` and the constraints that apply to its contents. `My content` is the element content and is human-readable – it is the data itself, the information that is of meaning to the human who will read and interpret it, and realize that `My content` is a piece of data defined by `<MyElement>`.

```
<MyElement>My content</MyElement>
```

We can extend this in the second example; here `<MyElement>` is now defined as `<TelephoneNumber>`. Also, we have specified a data type `xsd:integer` , which dictates what **type** of information can be held in the content. `My content` is now an integer string representing the value of this element – `0207123456`. The application knows that the element must hold an integer value, which a human can interpret as a telephone number.

```
<TelephoneNumber type="xsd:integer">0207123456</TelephoneNumber>
```

Common semantics are central to maintaining the integrity of data during interchange and ensuring that both sender and recipient understand the data as meaning the same thing. XML achieves this by preserving data structure through enforceable content models with defined data types, delivering semantic and structural validity when the XML is parsed and processed.

Spreadsheets, algorithms, and documents – anything that is dependent on a particular sequence or hierarchy for the preservation and communication of its intended meaning can be considered structured information. The consequences for economic analysis of, say, swapping the values of an import/export balance statement from 40/60 to 60/40 by incorrectly restructuring a document after processing hardly need be stated. XML facilitates the transfer of data because it supplies the extensibility, the ability to support local or international use of data, and the platform independence that contribute to preserving data structure and meaning.

An XML document defined according to a DTD can be validated against the structure defined for that class of XML documents, by using a validating XML parser. The DTD defines the sequential ordering and nesting of an XML document's component elements, as well as defining the data types that the document may legitimately contain within its element or attribute content. A DTD is used to define the content model of an XML document associated with it, and so can be used to define the content model of a whole class of documents, as well as to validate whether a document conforms to the structure prescribed for it by its governing DTD.

DTDs versus XML Schema: Why Do We Need an XML Schema?

The DTD was inherited from XML's parent, the Standardized General Markup Language (SGML) (ISO 8879). As an application profile of SGML, XML offers a subset of SGML's capabilities in a simplified format that removes much of the complexity of SGML.

However, XML's DTD mechanism for expressing document structure has limitations when structuring a document. Although the DTD specifies markup and data constraints, its capabilities for doing so are limited.

Specifically, a DTD has the following limitations:

❑ DTDs are written in their own syntax, which is not XML syntax.

❑ DTDs do not support namespaces.

❑ DTDs offer limited capability for the sophisticated expression of data types beyond declaring basic formats such as #PCDATA, CDATA, or ANY.

❑ DTDs offer limited capability for data type extension or for explicitly defining relationships between data types and elements.

❑ DTDs have limited capacity to specify exact constraints on a data type. It is not possible to exactly specify the value or occurrence of an element if you wish to, (for instance, should you wish it to occur exactly three times and have a minimum inclusive value of 12 and a maximum exclusive value of 25).

To illustrate, imagine a scenario where telephone numbers are being entered into the database for an inner London telephone directory. With a DTD we can specify the element recording this value as being #PCDATA (parsed character data), or we could restrict its content to numerical tokens by declaring it as NMTOKENS, and we are able to specify a single, an optional, a one or more, or a zero or more occurrence of this element. In the example below we provide a DTD element declaration for `<TelephoneDirectory>` and `<TelephoneNumber>`. We specify the `<TelephoneNumber>` element type as being of #PCDATA and declare that the `<TelephoneDirectory>` element must contain zero or more `<TelephoneNumber>` elements:

```
<!ELEMENT TelephoneNumber (#PCDATA)>
<!ELEMENT TelephoneDirectory (TelephoneNumber)*>
```

Using XML Schema, we can exactly specify the minimum and maximum number of `<TelephoneNumber>` elements that `<TelephoneDirectory>` can contain, and we can define `<TelephoneNumber>` more precisely – for example, we can stipulate that `<TelephoneNumber>` can only contain ten characters and that the first four in that sequence must be 0207. We do this by using a regular expression (a more advanced feature covered later in the chapter).

In the example of an XML Schema declaration of these elements below, we declare that `<TelephoneDirectory>` will record a minimum of zero and a maximum of 100 telephone numbers. `<TelephoneNumber>` is declared as being of type xsd:string (we could use xsd:integer, but if we wish to record a dash in our telephone number (for example, 0207-123456) then this would prevent us doing so:

```
<xsd:element name="TelephoneNumber" type="xsd:string" />
<xsd:element name="TelephoneDirectory ref="TelephoneNumber" minOccurs="0"
maxOccurs="100" />
```

As this basic example shows, XML Schema offers greater precision than is possible with a DTD.

To illustrate this, consider the sample DTD `TelephoneDirectory.dtd`, and the accompanying XML document instance `TelephoneDirectory.xml`.

TelephoneDirectory.dtd and TelephoneDirectory.xml

`TelephoneDirectory.dtd` presents the content model of a basic telephone directory with a simple element hierarchy and data structure. The listing below illustrates the data that a `<TelephoneDirectory>` must contain. The listing helps to show how the elements are nested within each other to create a tree structure, each branch of which carries its own leaves of data:

`TelephoneDirectory.dtd`, is used to define the structure of the `TelephoneDirectory.xml` instance document that follows. Note that although the `<CommercialDirectory>` appears more complicated than the `<PrivateDirectory>` they are actually quite similar and both make use of the `address` parameter entity in the construction of their content model. All of the data is `#PCDATA` to simplify the example.

```
<?xml version="1.0" encoding="UTF-8"?>

<!-- ENTITY declarations -->
<!ENTITY % address " (Street+, City, PostalCode, Country?)">

<!--compound ELEMENT declarations -->
<!ELEMENT TelephoneDirectory (TitlePage, ContentsPage, DirectoryInformation,
ClassifiedDirectory, Index)>
<!ELEMENT ContentsPage (ContentsEntry)+>
<!ELEMENT ClassifiedDirectory (PrivateDirectory, CommercialDirectory)>
<!ELEMENT PrivateDirectory (PrivateEntry)+>
<!ELEMENT PrivateEntry (Name, Address, TelephoneNumber+)>
<!ELEMENT CommercialDirectory (CommercialEntry)+>
<!ELEMENT CommercialEntry (CompanyName,
                           Address,
                           TelephoneNumber+,
                           Fax?,
                           WebSite?)>
<!ELEMENT Index (IndexEntry)+>
<!ELEMENT Name (Surname, ChristianName+)>

<!-- simple ELEMENT declarations -->
<!ELEMENT TitlePage (#PCDATA)>
<!ELEMENT Address (%address;)>
<!ELEMENT ContentsEntry (#PCDATA)>
<!ELEMENT DirectoryInformation (#PCDATA)>
<!ELEMENT IndexEntry (#PCDATA)>
<!ELEMENT Surname (#PCDATA)>
<!ELEMENT ChristianName (#PCDATA)>
<!ELEMENT CompanyName (#PCDATA)>
<!ELEMENT Street (#PCDATA)>
<!ELEMENT City (#PCDATA)>
<!ELEMENT PostalCode (#PCDATA)>
<!ELEMENT Country (#PCDATA)>
<!ELEMENT TelephoneNumber (#PCDATA)>
<!ELEMENT Fax (#PCDATA)>
<!ELEMENT WebSite (#PCDATA)>
```

This DTD will validate the instance of `TelephoneDirectory.xml` that follows:

```xml
<?xml version="1.0" encoding="UTF-8"?>
<!DOCTYPE TelephoneDirectory SYSTEM
"C:\ProJavaXML\Chapter05\TelephoneDirectory\TelephoneDirectory.dtd">
<TelephoneDirectory>
  <TitlePage>ABC Private and Commercial Telephone Directory</TitlePage>
  <ContentsPage>
    <ContentsEntry>Directory Information</ContentsEntry>
    <ContentsEntry>Classified Directory</ContentsEntry>
    <ContentsEntry>Private Directory</ContentsEntry>
    <ContentsEntry>Commercial Directory</ContentsEntry>
    <ContentsEntry>Index</ContentsEntry>
  </ContentsPage>
  <DirectoryInformation/>
  <ClassifiedDirectory>
    <PrivateDirectory>
      <PrivateEntry>
        <Name>
          <Surname>Smythe</Surname>
          <ChristianName>James</ChristianName>
        </Name>
        <Address>
          <Street>WestLea</Street>
          <City>London</City>
          <PostalCode>E4 12CN</PostalCode>
        </Address>
        <TelephoneNumber>0208123456</TelephoneNumber>
      </PrivateEntry>
    </PrivateDirectory>
    <CommercialDirectory>
      <CommercialEntry>
        <CompanyName>Eastern Cleaning District Supplies</CompanyName>
        <Address>
          <Street>Upper Paddock Street</Street>
          <City>London</City>
          <PostalCode>WC1 2AB</PostalCode>
        </Address>
        <TelephoneNumber>0207123456</TelephoneNumber>
        <Fax>0207123457</Fax>
        <WebSite>www.easterncleaning.co.uk</WebSite>
      </CommercialEntry>
    </CommercialDirectory>
  </ClassifiedDirectory>
  <Index>
    <IndexEntry>Eastern Cleaning District Supplies Ltd. </IndexEntry>
    <IndexEntry>Smythe, James. </IndexEntry>
    <IndexEntry>et cetera</IndexEntry>
  </Index>
</TelephoneDirectory>
```

`TelephoneDirectory.dtd` is simple. The address entity enables the reuse of the repeatable address component for the private and commercial entries. `TelephoneDirectory.dtd` structures the data and does what it is intended, but it also raises questions. We can see that the bulk of the data – held in the private and commercial directories – differs in structure but is of a similar type. By capturing the data type we can use this as a base from which to create and derive other data that is of the 'telephone directory' type.

For now, however, let's take a look at how the schema that describes our `TelephoneDirectory.xml` document might look. We will not get too caught up into the minutiae of complex and simple types at present, but we will take a look at how XML Schemas can reuse types and elements, and also how they can be more precise in defining these types and their occurrences:

```xml
<?xml version="1.0" encoding="UTF-8"?>
<xsd:schema xmlns:xsd="http://www.w3.org/2000/10/XMLSchema"
            elementFormDefault="qualified">
  <xsd:complexType name="AddressType">
    <xsd:sequence>
      <xsd:element ref="Street" maxOccurs="unbounded"/>
      <xsd:element ref="City"/>
      <xsd:element ref="PostalCode"/>
      <xsd:element ref="Country" minOccurs="1"/>
    </xsd:sequence>
  </xsd:complexType>
```

Here it is possible to see where we have defined `AddressType` as a complex type. We can now reuse it in the instance of both `PrivateEntryType` and `CommercialEntryType`. `AddressType` ensures that the following elements will appear in the following order and only in the following occurrences:

- Any number of `<Street>` elements
- A single `<City>` element
- A single `<PostalCode>` element
- A `<Country>` element, which must occur at least once

```xml
<xsd:element name="ChristianName" type="xsd:string"/>
<xsd:element name="City" type="xsd:string"/>
<xsd:complexType name="ClassifiedDirectoryType">
  <xsd:sequence>
    <xsd:element name="PrivateDirectory" type="PrivateDirectoryType"/>
    <xsd:element name="CommercialDirectory"
                 type="CommercialDirectoryType"/>
  </xsd:sequence>
</xsd:complexType>
<xsd:complexType name="CommercialDirectoryType">
  <xsd:sequence maxOccurs="unbounded">
    <xsd:element name="CommercialEntry" type="CommercialEntryType"/>
  </xsd:sequence>
</xsd:complexType>
<xsd:complexType name="CommercialEntryType">
  <xsd:sequence>
    <xsd:element ref="CompanyName"/>
    <xsd:element name="Address" type="AddressType"/>
    <xsd:element ref="TelephoneNumber" maxOccurs="unbounded"/>
    <xsd:element ref="Fax" minOccurs="0"/>
    <xsd:element ref="WebSite" minOccurs="0"/>
  </xsd:sequence>
</xsd:complexType>
```

Here we see the definition of `CommercialEntryType`, which contains, among other things, an `<Address>` element that we have previously defined as `AddressType`.

```xsd
<xsd:element name="CompanyName" type="xsd:string"/>
<xsd:element name="ContentsEntry" type="xsd:string"/>
<xsd:complexType name="ContentsPageType">
  <xsd:sequence maxOccurs="unbounded">
    <xsd:element ref="ContentsEntry"/>
  </xsd:sequence>
</xsd:complexType>
<xsd:element name="Country" type="xsd:string"/>
<xsd:element name="DirectoryInformation" type="xsd:string"/>
<xsd:element name="Fax" type="xsd:string"/>
<xsd:complexType name="IndexType">
  <xsd:sequence maxOccurs="unbounded">
    <xsd:element ref="IndexEntry"/>
  </xsd:sequence>
</xsd:complexType>
<xsd:element name="IndexEntry" type="xsd:string"/>
<xsd:complexType name="NameType">
  <xsd:sequence>
    <xsd:element ref="Surname"/>
    <xsd:element ref="ChristianName" maxOccurs="unbounded"/>
  </xsd:sequence>
</xsd:complexType>
<xsd:element name="PostalCode" type="xsd:string"/>
```

Below, we are reusing the `AddressType` in `PrivateEntryType`. `PrivateEntryType` is itself a complex type, however. It is through the use and reuse of these types that we can create building blocks of code that can be implemented in our XML schemas.

```xsd
<xsd:complexType name="PrivateDirectoryType">
    <xsd:sequence maxOccurs="unbounded">
      <xsd:element name="PrivateEntry" type="PrivateEntryType"/>
    </xsd:sequence>
</xsd:complexType>
<xsd:complexType name="PrivateEntryType">
    <xsd:sequence>
      <xsd:element name="Name" type="NameType"/>
      <xsd:element name="Address" type="AddressType"/>
      <xsd:element ref="TelephoneNumber" maxOccurs="unbounded"/>
    </xsd:sequence>
</xsd:complexType>
<xsd:element name="Street" type="xsd:string"/>
<xsd:element name="Surname" type="xsd:string"/>
<xsd:element name="TelephoneDirectory">
    <xsd:complexType>
      <xsd:sequence>
        <xsd:element ref="TitlePage"/>
        <xsd:element name="ContentsPage" type="ContentsPageType"/>
        <xsd:element ref="DirectoryInformation"/>
        <xsd:element name="ClassifiedDirectory"
                     type="ClassifiedDirectoryType"/>
        <xsd:element name="Index" type="IndexType"/>
      </xsd:sequence>
    </xsd:complexType>
</xsd:element>
<xsd:element name="TelephoneNumber" type="xsd:string"/>
<xsd:element name="TitlePage" type="xsd:string"/>
<xsd:element name="WebSite" type="xsd:string"/>
</xsd:schema>
```

Consider also the name elements – we have a private name and a company name. Both are data of the type 'name', but this data type is not made explicit. If name were a data type, then we could use this as a base from which we could derive private and commercial variants of the name data type. We could take an existing data structure and extend or restrict it to meet the individual needs of each application context.

XML Schema compensates for the shortcomings of the DTD by providing more rigorous procedures for constraining XML documents in terms of how markup is used and how the component parts of an XML document structure fit together. It also facilitates the definition of the structure, semantics, and contents of an XML document and so addresses many of the weaknesses of DTDs that have been identified in this chapter so far:

- ❑ XML Schemas are themselves XML documents.

- ❑ XML Schema supports namespaces and allows for multiple namespace inclusion.

- ❑ XML Schema offers rich data typing. In addition to providing built-in and primitive data types, XML Schema offers a mechanism for extending and deriving data types, opening up more flexibility and scope for the schema author.

- ❑ XML Schema provides modularity. Model and attribute groups introduce modularity, make relationships between content items explicit, and facilitate reuse of schema components and schemas themselves.

XML Schemas are themselves XML documents – An XML Schema is written using XML syntax and so is itself an XML document that can be validated. A schema's semantics are defined using a fixed vocabulary of elements and attributes, which constitute the schema for XML Schema. A valid XML Schema must conform to the 'schema for XML Schema', often shorthanded to the 'schema for schema'.

This is a slightly confusing phrase but it simply means that for an XML Schema to be valid then the elements and attributes that it contains must come from the parent schema. The use of XML syntax for expressing schema is powerful for several reasons. Firstly, it means an XML Schema author doesn't have to learn a DTD-specific syntax for writing schemas. Secondly, it provides a more expressive and rigorous language for defining XML documents and the constraints that apply to them. Thirdly, it enables the use of standard XML editing tools and environments for creating and validating instances of XML Schema documents.

XML Schema supports namespaces and allows for multiple namespace inclusion – By supporting namespaces, XML Schema allows additional namespaces to be imported into an XML Schema document instance. This allows data types defined in other namespaces to be imported into an XML Schema, complementing XML Schema's data typing capability. Using namespaces enables elements defined in external namespaces to be reused in the schema that is importing them, saving the author the need to 'reinvent the wheel'.

The use of the namespace prefix distinguishes an element as originating from a different namespace. Imported namespaces are declared in the schema element, and the namespaces are referenced during validation of the schema. The namespace prefix prevents naming collisions occurring if elements from different namespaces happen to have the same name, and this makes it possible to use elements of the same name but with different content.

XML Schemas offers rich data typing – XML Schema's inclusion of built-in and primitive data types provide data typing far in excess of the parameter entity construction of DTDs. XML Schema elements have two data types – complex and simple. Simple data types cannot contain other elements in their content or have attributes. Complex data types can contain other subelements as content and carry attributes. New data types can be derived from existing data types, with the ability to rigorously establish the data's values and the lexical representation of those values by restricting the facets that the data types are allowed to have.

XML Schemas provide modularity – XML Schema's provision of group constructs to allow the modeling of attribute and model groups offer a substantial improvement over parameter entities as a method of incorporating repeatable constructs. Modularity also introduces the ability for inheritance and object reuse. An example of this would be using the substitution mechanism of XML Schema to replace an element with another element or a group of elements specified as a substitution group.

Taken together, the benefits of an XML Schema offer the XML author greater control and flexibility than is possible by using a DTD. In the next section we work through the construction of an XML Schema using a new example, this time a document for expressing a legal contract.

XML Schema: Theory and Practice

This section explains what is involved in constructing an XML Schema by combining theoretical explanation with practical worked examples. Schema element, attribute, and type concepts will be explained and their use illustrated.

We will begin by using `contract.dtd` as the data model for a `contract.xsd` XML Schema document, providing an XML instance document conforming to this XML Schema, `contract.xml`. Using this fictional `contract.xsd` as a working example, we will work through the XML Schema specification, moving from simple to more advanced XML Schema features.

```
<?xml version="1.0" encoding="UTF-8"?>
<!-- ENTITY declarations -->
<!ENTITY % address " (OfficeNumber, Street+, City, Country?, Telephone+, Fax?,
Email?)">
<!--compound ELEMENT declarations -->
<!ELEMENT Contract (Title, Parties, ContractAgreement)>
<!ELEMENT ContractAgreement (ContractBody, Authorisation)>
<!ELEMENT ContractBody (Terms+, Conditions+, ContractText?)>
<!ELEMENT Contractor (Name, %address;)>
<!ELEMENT Contractee (Name, %address;)>
<!ELEMENT Parties (Contractor, Contractee)>
<!-- simple ELEMENT declarations -->
<!ELEMENT Authorisation (#PCDATA)>
<!ATTLIST Authorisation
  authorisationCode CDATA #IMPLIED
>
<!ELEMENT City (#PCDATA)>
<!ELEMENT Conditions (#PCDATA)>
<!ELEMENT ContractText (#PCDATA)>
<!ELEMENT Country (#PCDATA)>
<!ELEMENT Email (#PCDATA)>
<!ELEMENT Fax (#PCDATA)>
<!ELEMENT Name (#PCDATA)>
<!ELEMENT OfficeNumber (#PCDATA)>
<!ELEMENT Street (#PCDATA)>
<!ELEMENT Telephone (#PCDATA)>
<!ELEMENT Terms (Term+)>
<!ELEMENT Term (#PCDATA)>
<!ELEMENT Title (#PCDATA)>
```

Now consider this basic schema used to represent the DTD, which we will call `contract.xsd`. Take a moment to read through it:

```xml
<?xml version="1.0" encoding="UTF-8"?>
<xsd:schema xmlns:xsd="http://www.w3.org/2000/10/XMLSchema"
            elementFormDefault="qualified">
  <xsd:element name="Contract">

    <xsd:annotation>
      <xsd:documentation>
        An XML Schema for a simple contract
      </xsd:documentation>
    </xsd:annotation>

    <xsd:complexType>
      <xsd:sequence>
        <xsd:element ref="Title"/>
        <xsd:element name="Parties" type="PartiesType"/>
        <xsd:choice>
          <xsd:element name="ContractAgreement"
                       type="ContractAgreementType"/>
          <xsd:element name="ClassifiedContractAgreement"
                       type="ClassifiedContractType"/>
        </xsd:choice>
      </xsd:sequence>
    </xsd:complexType>
  </xsd:element>

  <xsd:complexType name="AuthorisationType">
    <xsd:simpleContent>
      <xsd:restriction base="xsd:string">
        <xsd:attribute name="authorisationCode">
          <xsd:simpleType>
            <xsd:restriction base="xsd:string">
              <xsd:pattern value="[A-Z]{4}\s\d{3}-\d{3}"/>
            </xsd:restriction>
          </xsd:simpleType>
        </xsd:attribute>
      </xsd:restriction>
    </xsd:simpleContent>
  </xsd:complexType>

  <xsd:element name="Conditions" type="xsd:string"/>

  <xsd:complexType name="ContractAgreementType">
    <xsd:sequence>
      <xsd:element name="ContractBody" type="ContractBodyType"/>
      <xsd:element name="Authorisation" type="AuthorisationType"/>
    </xsd:sequence>
  </xsd:complexType>

  <xsd:complexType name="ContractBodyType">
    <xsd:sequence>
      <xsd:element name="Terms" type="TermsType" maxOccurs="unbounded"/>
      <xsd:element ref="Conditions" maxOccurs="unbounded"/>
      <xsd:element ref="ContractText" minOccurs="0"/>
    </xsd:sequence>
  </xsd:complexType>

  <xsd:element name="ContractText" type="xsd:string"/>
```

```xml
<xsd:complexType name="ContractorType">
  <xsd:sequence>
    <xsd:element name="Name" type="NameType"/>
    <xsd:element name="Address" type="AddressType"/>
    <xsd:element name="Contact" type="ContactType"/>
  </xsd:sequence>
</xsd:complexType>

<xsd:complexType name="AddressType">
  <xsd:sequence>
    <xsd:element name="Office" type="xsd:string"/>
    <xsd:element name="Street" type="xsd:string" maxOccurs="3"/>
    <xsd:element name="City" type="xsd:string"/>
    <xsd:element ref="Province" minOccurs="0"/>
    <xsd:element name="Code" type="CodeType"/>
    <xsd:element ref="Country" minOccurs="0"/>
  </xsd:sequence>
</xsd:complexType>

<xsd:element name="Province">
  <xsd:complexType>
    <xsd:choice>
      <xsd:element name="County" type="xsd:string"/>
      <xsd:element name="State" type="xsd:string"/>
    </xsd:choice>
  </xsd:complexType>
</xsd:element>

<xsd:complexType name="CodeType">
  <xsd:choice>
    <xsd:element name="PostCode" type="xsd:string"/>
    <xsd:element name="ZipCode" type="xsd:integer"/>
  </xsd:choice>
</xsd:complexType>

<xsd:complexType name="ContactType">
  <xsd:choice>
    <xsd:element name="ContactMethod" type="ContactMethodType"/>
    <xsd:element name="PersonalClientMethod"
                 type="PersonalClientContactMethodType"/>
  </xsd:choice>
</xsd:complexType>

<xsd:complexType name="ContactMethodType">
  <xsd:annotation>
    <xsd:documentation>U
      Use the preferred contact attribute to identify the preferred
      method of contacting the addressee
    </xsd:documentation>
  </xsd:annotation>

  <xsd:sequence>
    <xsd:element name="Email" type="xsd:string" minOccurs="0"/>

    <xsd:element name="Fax" type="xsd:string" minOccurs="0"/>
```

```xsd
        <xsd:element name="Telephone">
          <xsd:complexType>
            <xsd:simpleContent>
              <xsd:extension base="xsd:integer">
                <xsd:attribute name="IntCode" type="xsd:string"/>
              </xsd:extension>
            </xsd:simpleContent>
          </xsd:complexType>
        </xsd:element>

    </xsd:sequence>

    <xsd:attribute name="PreferredContact" type="xsd:string"/>
</xsd:complexType>

<xsd:complexType name="PersonalClientContactMethodType">
  <xsd:annotation>
    <xsd:documentation>
      Use the Duration attribute to indicate the number of months
      of the client relationship in figures
    </xsd:documentation>
  </xsd:annotation>

  <xsd:complexContent>
    <xsd:extension base="ContactMethodType">
      <xsd:sequence>
        <xsd:element name="MobilePhone" type="xsd:integer"/>
      </xsd:sequence>
      <xsd:attribute name="Duration" type="xsd:integer"/>
    </xsd:extension>
  </xsd:complexContent>

</xsd:complexType>

<xsd:element name="Country">
  <xsd:simpleType>
    <xsd:restriction base="xsd:string">
      <xsd:enumeration value="UK"/>
      <xsd:enumeration value="USA"/>
    </xsd:restriction>
  </xsd:simpleType>
</xsd:element>

<xsd:complexType name="PartiesType">
  <xsd:sequence>
    <xsd:element name="Contractor" type="ContractorType"/>
    <xsd:element name="Contractee" type="ContractorType"/>
  </xsd:sequence>
</xsd:complexType>

<xsd:element name="Term" type="xsd:string"/>

<xsd:complexType name="TermsType">
  <xsd:sequence>
    <xsd:element ref="Term" maxOccurs="unbounded"/>
    <xsd:element ref="PaymentTerm" maxOccurs="0"/>
  </xsd:sequence>
</xsd:complexType>

<xsd:element name="Title" type="xsd:string"/>
```

```
<xsd:complexType name="ClassifiedContractType" final="restriction">
  <xsd:complexContent>
    <xsd:extension base="ContractAgreementType">
      <xsd:sequence>
        <xsd:element ref="LegalClassification"/>
        <xsd:element ref="CodeOrKeyword" minOccurs="2" maxOccurs="2"/>
      </xsd:sequence>
    </xsd:extension>
  </xsd:complexContent>

</xsd:complexType>
<xsd:element name="LegalClassification" type="LegalClassificationType"/>

<xsd:simpleType name="LegalClassificationType">
  <xsd:restriction base="LegalClassifiersType">
    <xsd:minLength value="1"/>
    <xsd:maxLength value="3" fixed="true"/>
  </xsd:restriction>
</xsd:simpleType>

<xsd:simpleType name="LegalClassifiersType">
  <xsd:list itemType="LegalKeywordsType"/>
</xsd:simpleType>

<xsd:simpleType name="LegalKeywordsType">
  <xsd:restriction base="xsd:string">
    <xsd:enumeration value="conveyancing"/>
    <xsd:enumeration value="contract"/>
    <xsd:enumeration value="partnership"/>
    <xsd:enumeration value="commercial"/>
    <xsd:enumeration value="private"/>
    <xsd:enumeration value="etcetera…"/>
  </xsd:restriction>
</xsd:simpleType>

<xsd:element name="CodeOrKeyword" type="CodeOrKeywordCodeType"/>

<xsd:simpleType name="CodeOrKeywordCodeType">
  <xsd:union memberTypes="LegalKeywordsType ListLegalCodeType"/>
</xsd:simpleType>

<xsd:simpleType name="ListLegalCodeType">
  <xsd:list itemType="LegalCodeType"/>
</xsd:simpleType>
<xsd:element name="LegalCode" type="LegalCodeType"/>

<xsd:simpleType name="LegalCodeType">
  <xsd:restriction base="xsd:integer">
    <xsd:pattern value="\d{6}"/>
  </xsd:restriction>
</xsd:simpleType>

<xsd:simpleType name="Settlement">
  <xsd:restriction base="xsd:string"/>
</xsd:simpleType>
```

```
<xsd:simpleType name="NameType">
  <xsd:restriction base="xsd:string"/>
</xsd:simpleType>

<xsd:element name="PaymentTerm">
  <xsd:complexType mixed="true">
    <xsd:sequence>
      <xsd:element name="DebtorName" type="NameType"/>
      <xsd:element name="DebtorAddress" type="AddressType"/>
      <xsd:element name="CreditorName" type="NameType"/>
      <xsd:element name="CreditorAddress" type="AddressType"/>
      <xsd:element name="Amount" type="xsd:string"/>
      <xsd:element name="SettlementPeriod" type="Settlement"/>
      <xsd:element name="SettlementDate" type="Settlement"/>
    </xsd:sequence>
  </xsd:complexType>
</xsd:element>
</xsd:schema>
```

Below is `contract.xml`, an XML instance document conforming to the class of XML documents that are defined by `contract.xsd`.

```
<?xml version="1.0" encoding="UTF-8"?>
<Contract xmlns:xsi="http://www.w3.org/2000/10/XMLSchema-instance"
xsi:noNamespaceSchemaLocation="C:\ProJavaXML\Chapter05\contract\contract.xsd">
  <Title>
    Contract to exchange data between American Data, Inc.
     and European Data Ltd.
  </Title>

  <Parties>
    <Contractor>
      <Name>American Data, Inc.</Name>
      <Address>
        <Office>12 Columbus House</Office>
        <Street>Columbus Avenue</Street>
        <City>San Francisco</City>
        <Province>
          <State>CA</State>
        </Province>
        <Code>
          <ZipCode>1234567</ZipCode>
        </Code>
        <Country>USA</Country>
      </Address>
      <ContactMethod PreferredContact="Telephone">
        <Telephone>123456789</Telephone>
      </ContactMethod>
    </Contractor>

    <Contractee>
      <Name>European Data Ltd.</Name>
      <Address>
        <Office>No 1 Queen's Gardens</Office>
```

```
            <Street>Hyde Park</Street>
            <City>London</City>
            <Code>
              <PostCode>W1 11H</PostCode>
            </Code>
            <Country>UK</Country>
          </Address>
          <ContactMethod PreferredContact="Telephone">
            <Telephone>0207123456</Telephone>
          </ContactMethod>
        </Contractee>
      </Parties>

      <ContractAgreement>
        <ContractBody>
          <Terms>
            <Term>Exchange of data relating to x,y, and z.</Term>
            <Term>All accounts to be settled within 30 days</Term>
          </Terms>
          <Conditions>That all data is to be structured</Conditions>
          <ContractText>This contract establishes...</ContractText>
        </ContractBody>
        <Authorisation authorisationCode="LONSF"/>
      </ContractAgreement>
    </Contract>
```

The first thing to focus on is the schema declaration in `contract.xsd`:

```
<?xml version="1.0" encoding="UTF-8"?>
<xsd:schema xmlns:xsd="http://www.w3.org/2000/10/XMLSchema"
            elementFormDefault="unqualified">
  <xsd:element name="Contract">
<!-- Rest of schema -->
</xsd:schema>
```

Firstly, the schema is an XML document and it is written in XML syntax, beginning and closing with a `schema` element, and so conforming to the constraints of well-formed XML. The schema declaration contains the reference to the XML Schema namespace and the namespace prefix of `xsd` has been applied. All elements in this schema, identified by the `xsd:` prefix, are drawn from the XML Schema namespace, and will be validated against the schema that defines this namespace – the 'schema for XML Schema'. The `xsd` prefix is used to identify the XML Schema namespace by convention and, indeed, another prefix could be used if desired, or it could be removed altogether, and the schema would still be valid. Using it, though, clearly identifies elements qualified with the `xsd` prefix in the schema as belonging to the XML Schema and not being the schema author's own creation.

The `xmlns` attribute is used to set a default namespace for the schema – during validation, it identifies the namespace, or namespaces if more than one has been set (for example, because elements and attributes in the schema come from more than one namespace), where the definitions for the elements, attributes, and types used in the schema can be found.

Next, the `elementFormDefault` attribute value is set to `unqualified`, which simply means that only the global elements in this XML Schema must be qualified by a namespace. If this namespace is qualified with a namespace prefix when referenced, then the namespace prefix will have to be used. (The namespace prefix is optional unless elements from different namespaces have the same name, in which case its use is required to avoid naming clashes during validation). If set to `unqualified`, then only the global element declarations would have to be qualified and the local element declarations would not have to be. Global elements are always qualified.

Using `qualified` introduces the complexity of namespaces, but it protects against the need to monitor for an element's declaration changing from local to global should this happen in a schema where the `elementFormDefault` is set to `unqualified`.

> *If an element is declared globally, then it is declared in the body of the XML document. If an element is declared locally, then it is declared within the body of another element declaration.*

Next, we turn to the declaration of the XML instance document:

```
<Contract xmlns:xsi="http://www.w3.org/2000/10/XMLSchema-instance"
xsi:noNamespaceSchemaLocation="C:\ProJavaXML\Chapter05\contract\contract.xsd">
<-- Rest of XML document -->
</Contract>
```

Note in the contract element declaration that the `xsi` prefix for the XML Schema namespace for instances has been imported. `xsi` is a namespace where attributes defined by *Part 1: Structures* for direct use in XML documents are located. The `xsi` namespace defines four attributes:

- ❑   `xsi:type` – this allows an element in a schema to explicitly assert its type

- ❑   `xsi:null` – used to indicate that an element's content is missing or 'null' and for defining an empty element (its use does not prohibit empty elements having attributes)

- ❑   `xsi:schemaLocation` and `xsi:noNamespaceSchemaLocation` – which are used to indicate to a processor where schema documents for use during validation are located, although the processor is not required to locate these schemas when assessing the document

In this declaration `xsi:noNamespaceSchemaLocation` tells us that the `contract.xsd` schema is 'noNamespace', meaning that `contract.xsd` is not defining a namespace but only a schema, and indicates to the processor where the schema is located – the 'SchemaLocation' is at `C:\ProJavaXML\Chapter05\contract\contract.xsd`. (Obviously, this will reflect the location of the schema in different implementations.) `xsi:schemaLocation` is used to identify the default namespace of an XML instance document and carries two values – one providing the location of the namespace and a second providing the location of a schema document.

If `contract.xsd` had used the `targetNamespace` attribute in the schema declaration of `contract.xsd`, then this schema would have a namespace, and, (depending on whether the `elementFormDefault` was set to `qualified` or `unqualified`) the elements declared within the schema would have had to use the namespace prefix specified for the schema to qualify them when used or referenced locally within the schema document. This issue is discussed later in the chapter.

Now that we have considered a basic schema declaration and an example of an XML instance document conforming to that schema, we move on to a more in-depth look at specific aspects to the XML Schema specification. We will go on to look at some aspects of the following:

❏ Schema components

❏ Datatypes

❏ Namespaces

❏ Incorporating multiple schemas in a single schema instance

❏ Advanced features of XML Schema

❏ Parsing and processing an XML document

Schema Structure: Schema Components

Structurally, a schema is built from blocks known as **schema components**. An XML Schema consists of twelve XML Schema components that are classified under **primary**, **secondary**, and **helper** categories.

❏ Primary components are simple type and complex type definitions, and element and attribute declarations.

❏ Secondary components are attribute group, identity-constraint, and model group definitions, and also notation declarations.

❏ Helper components are used to form parts of other components; they include annotations, model groups, particles, and wildcards. Unlike primary and secondary components, helper components cannot be named and independently accessed. Helper components are context dependent; their meaning reflects the context of their use and so they have a local meaning rather than a global meaning that applies throughout the whole schema.

This hierarchy is illustrated in the diagram below:

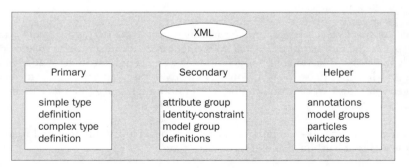

It is worth holding this architectural hierarchy in mind when writing a schema, because it provides a natural sequence with which to conceptualize a data structure and to visualize how this data will be broken down. Our working model, `contract.xsd`, begins by illustrating the primary components and evolves as we move through the schema specification.

Primary Components

This section details element and attribute declaration before exploring complex type and simple type definition.

Element and Attribute Declaration

Elements are declared in XML Schema using the element `<element>`. An element declaration in XML Schema carries a **name** and a **type**:

- ❏ **name** is used to identify the element and to provide a mechanism by which that element can be referenced when required.

- ❏ **type** indicates the data type of the element. Depending on the complexity of the element being declared, the type will either give the built-in data type to which the element's content must conform, or provide the name of another data type of which this element is a member or is a derivative of.

In the example from `contract.xsd` below, `<Authorization>` is declared to be of data type `xsd:string`. The `string` data type is declared as originating from the `xsd` namespace (the use of namespaces will be explained in the next section) and is used to replace the `#PCDATA` of the DTD.

```
<xsd:element name="Authorization" type="xsd:string"/>
```

In a DTD, the occurrence value of an element is indicated by use of an operator. The operators allow the following constraints on element occurrence to be set. (The symbol is given after the definition):

- ❏ Optional (`?`)
- ❏ Zero-or-more (`*`)
- ❏ One-or-more (`+`)
- ❏ Exactly once (no operator)

XML Schema can specify occurrence more rigorously by using the `minOccurs` and `maxOccurs` attributes to specify the number of times that an element may occur. `minOccurs` and `maxOccurs` both have a default value of `1`. If a value of `0` is given to the `minOccurs` attribute of an element, then it specifies that the element's presence is optional. Both `minOccurs` and `maxOccurs` can carry any positive integer value, and `maxOccurs` can be set to `unbounded`, enabling an element to be repeated as many times as is required.

If required, `<Authorization>` can now be specified as occurring at the required frequency. In the example below this is at least once and at most three times:

```
<xsd:element name="Authorization" type="xsd:string"
             minOccurs="1"
             maxOccurs="3"/>
```

In this example, however, it is required to occur exactly three times:

```
<xsd:element name="Authorization" type="xsd:string"
             minOccurs="3"
             maxOccurs="3"/>
```

Element declarations can use the `ref` attribute in place of the `name` attribute, in order to reference an existing element declaration rather than repeat it. Generally, the `ref` attribute must reference a globally declared element or attribute.

Global declarations are those given within the schema element, and are not nested within another element declaration or type definition; declarations of this latter type are considered **local**.

In the example element declaration using reference below, the `<Authorization>` element is referenced:

```
<xsd:element ref="Authorization"/>
```

Note that because no occurrence indicator attribute has been specified the occurrence of `<Authorization>` here will be determined by the default value of the `minOccurs` and `maxOccurs` attributes, which is 1. If we wanted to define a new default value for this element's occurrence, then we are able to – and that is a strong advantage of an XML Schema compared with a DTD.

Note also that when an element is referenced by another element, its occurrence is specified locally when it is referenced and not in its global element declaration. This is illustrated in an excerpt from `contract.xsd` below:

```
<!-- Rest of XML Schema -->
<xsd:complexType name="ContractBodyType">
  <xsd:sequence>
    <xsd:element name="Terms" type="TermsType" minOccurs="2" maxOccurs="2"/>
    <xsd:element ref="Conditions" maxOccurs="unbounded"/>
    <xsd:element ref="ContractText" minOccurs="0"/>
  </xsd:sequence>
</xsd:complexType>

<xsd:complexType name="TermsType">
  <xsd:sequence>
    <xsd:element ref="Term" minOccurs="1" maxOccurs="1"/>
  </xsd:sequence>
</xsd:complexType>

<xsd:element name="Term" type="xsd:string"/>
<!-- Rest of XML Schema -->
```

The `ContractBodyType` is composed of a sequence of three elements – `Terms`, `Conditions`, and `ContractText`, the occurrence of which is specified in their local declaration within `ContractBodyType`. The `Terms` element is declared as being of the data type `TermsType`. Both `TermsType` and the `Term` element are declared globally, and both have their frequency declared locally when they are used in the construction of data types. Note how the schema has created the data type of `Term` and used it as the basis for extension in order to create the `<Terms>` element, which is a holder for individual terms and so in reality is a data type of type term itself.

Now, if we look at `contract.xml` again, we can see how this affects the document:

```
<!-- Rest of XML document -->
<ContractBody>
    <Terms>
      <Term>Exchange of data relating to x,y, and z.</Term>
      <Term>All accounts to be settled within 30 days</Term>
    </Terms>
```

```
        <Conditions>That all data is to be structured</Conditions>
        <ContractText>This contract establishes...</ContractText>
    </ContractBody>
    <!-- Rest of XML document -->
```

The element `Term` has been used to create a data type, `TermsType`, and when we wish to specify the exact number of individual instances of `Term` it holds, then this can be specified exactly, as can the occurrence of the containing `Terms` element within the contract body. To illustrate, we change the occurrence values specified by `TermsType` and `Terms` below from unbounded to 2 and 1 respectively. This schema must now have two `Terms` elements, and each `Terms` element may only contain one `Term` – anything else would throw an error during validation. We are now able to exert far greater control over the occurrence of `Terms` in our legal contract than was possible using a DTD.

```
    <!-- Rest of XML document -->
    <ContractBody>
        <Terms>
            <Term>Exchange of data relating to x,y, and z.</Term>
        </Terms>
        <Terms>
         <Term>All accounts to be settled within 30 days</Term>
        </Terms>
        <Conditions>That all data is to be structured</Conditions>
        <ContractText>This contract establishes...</ContractText>
    </ContractBody>
    <!-- Rest of XML document -->
```

The attribute Element

The procedure for declaring an **attribute** is similar to that for declaring an element, but the syntax for specifying an attribute's occurrence differs because an attribute's default occurrence is strictly optional and cannot be specified as 0 or unbounded in the way that the occurrence of an element can. If the attribute is required then its `use` attribute is given the value `required`.

The `use` attribute is also used to define whether an attribute's value is fixed or can vary. If the value is variable, then the `value` attribute is used to give that value. This is illustrated by two variant attribute declarations for the `authorizationCode` attribute of the `<Authorization>` element. In this example, `authorizationCode` is required, and so the `use` attribute carries this value.

```
    <xsd:attribute name="authorizationCode" type="CDATA" use="required" />
```

In this next example, however, `authorizationCode`'s default value of optional has not been overridden and still applies. However, the `use` attribute indicates that the attribute's value is `fixed`. The `value` attribute shows that this value has been set at the string LASF 333-679. When validated, any value other than the string "LASF 333-679" for this attribute would produce an error, ensuring the data robustness of a document instance conforming to this schema.

```
    <xsd:attribute name="authorizationCode"
                    type="CDATA"
                    use="fixed"
                    value="LASF 333-679"/>
```

The attributeGroup Element

The `<attributeGroup>` element is used to declare a set of attributes, which occur together in several complex types. By declaring the group in this way, you can reference the members from the complex type definitions that require that particular group of attributes. An example is given below:

```
<xsd:complexType>
   <xsd:sequence>

<!--  element declarations -->
   </xsd:sequence>
   <xsd:attributeGroup ref="myAttGroup"/>
</xsd:complexType>

<xsd:attributeGroup name="myAttGroup">
  <xsd:attribute name="attA" type="xsd:string" />
  <xsd:attribute name="attB" type="xsd:string" />
  <xsd:attribute name="attC" type="xsd:string" />
</xsd:attributeGroup>
```

Empty Element Declaration

To define an element as **empty** in XML Schema (so that its values are carried by the element's attributes), it must be explicitly declared as such. This is done by declaring it as a complex type with `<xsd:attribute>` only and no `<xsd:element>` as its content.

```
<xsd:element name="emptyElement">
   <xsd:complexType>
      <xsd:attribute name="myAttributeName" type="myAttributeType"/>
   </xsd:complexType>
<xsd:element/>
```

Type Definitions: Complex Type and Simple Type

A **declaration** serves two purposes: it declares the **definition** of an information item and associates a name with this information item. A declaration is used during validation to check for correspondence between schema components and the information items or nodes that they are declared to conform to.

> *An information item is one of the terms used to define the information that may be contained in an XML document. See the XML Information Set: http://www.w3.org/TR/xml-infoset/ to learn more.*

Definition in XML Schema is said to refer to the definition of schema components that may be used as parts of other schema components. More plainly, it is used to define the parts of a part-whole relationship. XML Schema has two principal types of definition – **complex type** and **simple type**. These definitions are created by **restricting** or **extending** other type definitions. That is to say, taking a base type and either restricting or extending the facets that it can have.

The type definition being restricted or extended by this process is always referred to as the **base type definition**, and this process of creating or deriving new types from old types is called **derivation**.

Restriction works by reducing the number of facets that the derived type can have or inherit from its base type. For example, a base type has facets of A and B with respective values of {1,2} and {3,4}, while the restricted type can only offer facet A with a respective value of {2}. Extension is the opposite to restriction, adding to the base catalogue of facets and values. The chapter will provide examples of using both methods for type definition.

Simple Type Definitions – Built-in and User-Derived Data Types

Simple type definitions are used to define the data types of elements and attributes, thus creating the basic type definitions from which complex types can be created. XML Schema *Part 2: Datatypes* defines two simple types that fall into two categories – **built-in** and **user-derived**.

- ❑ Built-in data types are defined in the XML Schema specification and are either **primitive** (they exist in their own right and are not defined in terms of other data types) or **derived** (data types that are defined in terms of other data types).

- ❑ User-derived data types are defined by a schema author and will be particular to the schema that creates them, or to any schema that includes them by reference.

The power of XML Schema's ability to derive data types is augmented by the constraints that XML Schema is able to exert over the creation of new simple types. The derivation mechanism gives the schema author more control over the restrictions that they can impose on the base data types available to them.

The simple type definition achieves this because it defines the set of constraints that apply to the strings that represent the values of a simple type, and provides information about the values that these strings encode after they have been **normalized**. A simple type definition, therefore, reflects the **normalized value** rather than the **initial value** of the element or attribute that it defines.

To explain this distinction, the normalized value is the sequence of characters that compose a string after the whitespace has been removed, according to the value expressed by the `whiteSpace` facet of the simple type definition. Before normalization, the sequence of characters composing a string is called the initial value of the string. The `whiteSpace` facet can have the three values of `preserve`, `collapse`, and `replace` as specified in the XML 1.0 specification.

Refer to Appendix A for the built-in simple types of XML Schema. The schema author can derive a new simple type by restricting an existing base type definition of a built-in primitive or user-derived simple type. This means that the new type's range of values will be a subset of the values of the base type.

Before going further it is useful to explore the scope of the `<restriction>` element in constraining the facets of a simple type. XML Schema defines fifteen facets for simple types. These facets and a description of their use are given in the table below.

Simple Type facet	Scope of use
length	Constrains the length of a simple type in terms of the number of units of length that it can have; the units of length can be characters, octets, or list items the simple type is allowed to contain
minLength	Constrains the minimum number of units of length that a simple type can have for its value
maxLength	Constrains the maximum number of units of length that a simple type can have for its value
pattern	Constrains the literals composing the value of a facet to a pattern defined by a regular expression

Simple Type facet	Scope of use
enumeration	Constrains the value of a facet to specific values
whiteSpace	Constrains the value of a facet according to the rules for whitespace normalization as defined in the XML 1.0 specification
maxInclusive	Constrains the value of a facet to a specific inclusive upper bound
maxExclusive	Constrains the value of a facet to a specific exclusive upper bound
minInclusive	Constrains the value of a facet to a specific inclusive lower bound
minExclusive	Constrains the value of a facet to a specific exclusive lower bound
precision	Constrains the value of a facet to a specific maximum number of decimal digits
scale	Constrains the value of a facet to a specific maximum number of decimal digits in the fractional part
encoding	Constrains the literals of data types derived from the binary data type to a specific form
duration	Constrains the value of a facet to a particular duration of time
period	Constrains the value of a facet to a specific frequency of recurrence

The choice of which facets can be applied to a base type when deriving a new simple type is defined by the XML Schema specification, and depends on the data type of the base type. This is an obvious restriction given the scope of data types and the range of facets that XML Schema offers – a precision facet would not be applicable to a Boolean primitive data type.

To illustrate this by example, let's consider the facets enumeration and pattern. These are chosen because they illustrate how XML Schema can be used to create a set of fixed string values for an element, and to determine the pattern to which the string expressing an element's value must conform.

The enumeration Element

By creating a new simple type, using the enumeration facet, we can specify that the only values the element carries are those that we explicitly enumerate. To illustrate this, we create a new Country simple type for our contract.xsd, restricting the base type string by enumerating the values that this new simple type can carry to the strings UK and USA:

```
<!-- Rest of XML schema -->
<xsd:element name="Country">
<xsd:simpleType>
  <xsd:restriction base="xsd:string" >
    <xsd:enumeration value="UK"/>
    <xsd:enumeration value="USA"/>
  </xsd:restriction>
</xsd:simpleType>
<!-- Rest of XML schema -->
```

The revised fragment from `contract.xml` shows the difference. Not only is the schema author able to specify what value is enumerated, but the enumeration restriction ensures that if these values are not given, then an error would be thrown during validation.

```
<!-- Rest of XML document -->
<Parties>
  <Contractor>
    <Name>American Data, Inc.</Name>
    <Office>12 Columbus House</Office>
    <Street>Columbus Avenue</Street>
    <City>San Francisco</City>
    <Country>USA</Country>
    <Telephone>123456789</Telephone>
  </Contractor>

  <Contractee>
    <Name>European Data Ltd.</Name>
    <Office>No 1 Queen's Gardens</Office>
    <Street>Hyde Park</Street>
    <City>London</City>
    <Country>UK</Country>
    <Telephone>0207123456</Telephone>
  </Contractee>
</Parties>
<!-- Rest of XML document -->
```

The pattern Element

The `pattern` facet allows us to specify that a value must always conform to a certain pattern of characters. Instances of where such patterns are critical could include a library indexing system, an address code, or access codes. The pattern facet uses a regular expression language (similar to Perl) and supports Unicode characters.

> *A table of regular expression examples can be found in Appendix D of the Primer from the XML Schema Candidate Recommendation specification.*

Let's consider a scenario where we want to restrict the value of the `<AuthorizationCode>` element to a pattern where the regular expression `[A-Z]{4}\s\d{3}-\d{3}` resolves to '4 upper case characters followed by a whitespace followed by 3 digits followed by a hyphen followed by another 3 digits' – for example, the sequence LASF 123-456. The attribute content model allows an optional `simpleType` in its content model and so this restriction is possible. We specify `xsd:string` as the base type of our attribute and restrict it to the sequence we want by using the `pattern` facet. This is illustrated in the fragments from `contract.xsd` below:

```
<!-- Rest of XML schema -->
<xsd:complexType name="AuthorizationType">
    <xsd:simpleContent>
        <xsd:restriction base="xsd:string">
    <xsd:attribute name="authorizationCode">
        <xsd:simpleType>
            <xsd:restriction base="xsd:string">
        <xsd:pattern value="[A-Z]{4}\s\d{3}-\d{3}"/>
        </xsd:restriction>
```

```
        </xsd:simpleType>
      </xsd:attribute>
      </xsd:restriction>
   </xsd:simpleContent>
</xsd:complexType>
<!-- Rest of XML schema -->
```

And this is `contract.xml`:

```
<Authorization authorizationCode="LASF 123-456">
  Authorised by...
</Authorization>
```

Remember that simple types are the building blocks of the XML Schema. A simple type is used to specify the parameters of the possible values for a data type but it does no more than that. Decisions concerning issues such as which value is used and the sequential ordering of particles are decided by the other schema components that are using the simple types as their base type.

Simple Type Varieties

In the simple type examples given so far, we have only been concerned with simple types of a variety XML Schema defines as **atomic**. XML Schema allows three varieties of simple types to be defined: **atomic, list**, and **union**.

Atomic

An atomic simple type definition is a restriction of one of XML Schema's primitive built-in data types, meaning that when we create a new simple type definition of the atomic variety we can only restrict it by the facets applicable to that primitive built-in type. The consequence of this is that the content of an atomic simple type is considered to comprise one semantic meaning and is not semantically divisible.

In a simple type definition of atomic type the string "A B C" would only be interpreted as a single string of three letters and two whitespace characters, and would not be interpreted as three semantic units separated by whitespace.

List

Defining a simple type to be of the **list** variety, enables the interpretation of element content as a list of **tokens** and gives meaning to each token within the simple type's content. A list type's content is considered a sequence of atomic types, and each clearly divisible part of the characters contained within is considered a semantic unit in its own right. Occurring in a list type, the string "A B C" would consist of three semantic units. "A B C" becomes interpreted as "A *and* B *and* C". A list type can only be derived from an atomic type whose lexical space allows whitespace.

XML Schema has three built-in derived simple types that are list types, NMTOKENS, IDREFS, and ENTITIES. XML Schema also allows the creation of new list types, but explicitly limits this to derivation from existing atomic types and disallows their creation from other list types or complex types.

A new list type is created by using the xsd:list element with the itemType attribute specifying the simple type definition to which each of the tokens within the list must conform. When defining new list types, the length, minLength, maxLength, and enumeration facets can be applied to restrict the base type.

In summary, creating a list type consists of three steps:

❑ Locate or create the required base type (this must be a simple type)

❑ Derive a list type from the base type

❑ Restrict the list type to the desired specification

To illustrate, consider a scenario within contract.xsd. Suppose we wish to classify a contract according to a legal keyword that describes the legal area that the contract covers.

❑ First, we define our legal keywords in a LegalKeywordsType derived from the atomic base type xsd:string.

❑ Then we make a list of these legal keywords by creating a list type called LegalClassifiersType that specifies LegalKeywordsType as the value of its itemType attribute.

❑ We then decide to limit the length of keywords that the list can contain. To do this, we create a simple type called LegalClassification that restricts LegalClassifiersType, and specify the minimum and maximum lengths of the list that we require, which, in this instance, is one and three respectively.

The resulting fragment from the XML instance document is shown below – a LegalClassification element containing a list of two legal keywords from the enumerated values specified by LegalKeywordsType within the list length constraints specified.

```
<!-- Rest of XML schema -->
<xsd:element name="LegalClassification" type="LegalClassificationType"/>
<xsd:simpleType name="LegalClassificationType">
  <xsd:restriction base="LegalClassifiersType">
    <xsd:minLength value="1"/>
    <xsd:maxLength value="3"/>
  </xsd:restriction>
</xsd:simpleType>
<xsd:simpleType name="LegalClassifiersType">
  <xsd:list itemType="LegalKeywordsType"/>
</xsd:simpleType>
<xsd:simpleType name="LegalKeywordsType">
  <xsd:restriction base="xsd:string">
    <xsd:enumeration value="conveyancing"/>
    <xsd:enumeration value="contract"/>
    <xsd:enumeration value="partnership"/>
    <xsd:enumeration value="commercial"/>
    <xsd:enumeration value="private"/>
    <xsd:enumeration value="etcetera…"/>
  </xsd:restriction>
</xsd:simpleType>
<!-- Rest of XML schema -->
```

Union

By defining a simple type to be of the list variety, a schema author can ensure that its element or attribute content will not be processed as a single atomic string, with one semantic meaning, but will be processed as a sequence of multiple instances of one atomic type. Defining a simple type to be of the **union** variety means that the schema author can define both atomic and list types as the valid content of an element or an attribute. This is because a union type can contain either a single semantic value *or* a list of multiple instances of semantic values. XML Schema has no built-in union types and so they must always be derived.

A union type is defined using the `<xsd:union>` element, either declaring the types inside the union or specifying them using the optional `memberTypes` attribute. The values of the `memberTypes` attribute are a whitespace-separated list of the types that we wish to include in the union.

The example below illustrates creating a union type for `UnionNumberType` using member types of `StringNumberType` and `IntegerNumberType`. `ListIntegerType` has been derived as a list type and so is able to hold multiple atomic values, unlike `IntegerNumberType`, which can only hold one single value. The `UnionNumberType` can carry either a string, restricted to one of the enumerated values specified for it, or a list of the range of integer values that it is given:

```
<!-- Rest of XML schema -->
<xsd:simpleType name="UnionNumberType">
  <xsd:union memberTypes="StringNumberType ListIntegerNumberType"/>
</xsd:simpleType>

<xsd:element name="StringNumber" type="StringNumberType"/>
<xsd:simpleType name="StringNumberType">
  <xsd:restriction base="xsd:string">
    <xsd:enumeration value="one"/>
    <xsd:enumeration value="two"/>
    <xsd:enumeration value="three"/>
  </xsd:restriction>
</xsd:simpleType>
<xsd:simpleType name="ListIntegerNumberType">
  <xsd:list itemType="IntegerNumberType"/>
</xsd:simpleType>
<xsd:simpleType name="IntegerNumberType">
  <xsd:restriction base="xsd:integer"/>
</xsd:simpleType>

<xsd:element name="IntegerNumber" type="IntegerNumberType"/>
<xsd:element ref="StringNumber"/>
<xsd:element name="ListNumber" type="ListIntegerNumberType"/>
<xsd:element name="UnionNumber" type="UnionNumberType" maxOccurs="2"/>
<!-- Rest of XML schema -->
```

And here is a fragment from `number.xml`, demonstrating the result of such an application of the schema:

```
<!-- Rest of XML document -->
  <IntegerNumber>123</IntegerNumber>
  <StringNumber>one</StringNumber>
  <ListNumber>123 123</ListNumber>
  <UnionNumber>one</UnionNumber>
  <UnionNumber>123 456 789</UnionNumber>
<!-- Rest of XML document -->
```

To illustrate a more complicated example of a union type we will return to our example `contract.xsd`. Imagine a scenario where we want the ability to classify our legal contract by multiple legal keywords or by numeric codes, but what we want to specify particularly is the pattern that those codes can take.

To do this, we create a `CodeOrKeywordCodeType` union, and use this as the base type of the `<CodeOrKeywordCode>` element that will appear in the XML document. We specify `CodeOrKeywordCode`'s occurrence in the XML instance as exactly 2, providing one element for keywords and one for codes in the document. We set a constraint on the pattern facet of `LegalCodeType` to the pattern `\d{6}` (a sequence of six digits), and then derive a list type from it to enable more than one code to appear in the instance document.

We leave the occurrence of the legal keywords as once, although if we wished to specify more then we could do so (as we did with `LegalClassificationType` earlier in the chapter) by specifying the length of the list.

If our schema instance document allows us to have more than one instance of `CodeOrKeywordCode`, as this fragment does, then the `CodeOrKeywordCode` instance containing keywords must come first (unless this requirement is overridden using the `xsi:type` attribute) because `LegalKeywordsType` was specified first, before `ListLegalCodeType`, when the member types were declared.

```xml
<!-- Rest of XML schema -->
<xsd:complexType name="ClassifiedContractType">
    <xsd:complexContent>
        <xsd:extension base="ContractAgreementType">
      <xsd:sequence>
       <xsd:element ref="LegalClassification"/>
       <xsd:element ref="CodeOrKeyword" minOccurs="2" maxOccurs="2"/>
      </xsd:sequence>
      </xsd:extension>
    </xsd:complexContent>
</xsd:complexType>
<!-- Rest of XML schema cut -->
<xsd:element name="CodeOrKeyword" type="CodeOrKeywordCodeType"/>
    <xsd:simpleType name="CodeOrKeywordCodeType">
        <xsd:union memberTypes="LegalKeywordsType ListLegalCodeType"/>
    </xsd:simpleType>
    <xsd:simpleType name="ListLegalCodeType">
        <xsd:list itemType="LegalCodeType"/>
    </xsd:simpleType>
    <xsd:element name="LegalCode" type="LegalCodeType"/>
    <xsd:simpleType name="LegalCodeType">
        <xsd:restriction base="xsd:integer">
      <xsd:pattern value="\d{6}"/>
        </xsd:restriction>
    </xsd:simpleType>
<!-- Rest of XML schema -->
```

And here is `contract.xml` implementing this change:

```xml
<!-- Rest of XML document -->
<ClassifiedContractAgreement>
  <ContractBody>
    <Terms>
      <Term>Exchange of data relating to x,y, and z.</Term>
      <Term>All accounts to be settled within 30 days</Term>
    </Terms>
```

```
      <Conditions>That all data is to be structured</Conditions>
      <ContractText>This contract establishes...</ContractText>
    </ContractBody>
    <Authorization authorizationCode="LASF 123-456">Authorised by...</Authorization>
    <LegalClassification>commercial contract</LegalClassification>
    <CodeOrKeyword>contract</CodeOrKeyword>
    <CodeOrKeyword>123456 123456</CodeOrKeyword>
  </ClassifiedContractAgreement>
  <!-- Rest of XML document -->
```

If the values that CodeOrKeyword can contain must change, then updating our schema to conform to the new requirements is straightforward. We can either go back to our original definitions to edit those, or we can override them by restricting the original type definitions and creating new values in addition to the ones that they already have.

Complex Types

A complex type definition defines the elements and attributes that can compose the content model of a complex type.

A complex type definition can be created by:

❑   Restricting a complex base type definition

❑   Extending a simple or complex base type definition

❑   Restricting the ur-type definition

Complex types can contain elements, other complex types, and attributes, either declaring them within the complex type or referencing them. Note that when an element is referenced then its occurrence is given in the location from which it is referenced and not in the element itself. This ensures that the element's occurrence reflects the local context of its use rather than the global context of the global declaration that made it available throughout the schema.

It is important not just to think of a complex type as an elaborate element declaration, but also in its structural function as a **model group** schema component. To return to the component hierarchy of XML Schema, a complex type is not just a **primary** schema component; the model group that it embodies is also a **helper** schema component.

In XML Schema a model group consists of a **compositor**, **particles**, and an optional **annotation** element. The compositor element is used to indicate how the particles that make up the content of a group model's type definition are to be included when the model group is interpreted by the application and expanded to create a new model group.

There are three compositor elements:

❑   <sequence> means that the elements in a model group must appear in the order in which they are expressed by the model group

❑   <choice> means that exactly one of the model group's elements must be used in the model group

❑   <all> specifies that all of the elements in a group can appear once or not at all, and that no constraint applies to the order in which they appear

The `<annotation>` element is optional and is primarily used to contain the `<documentation>` and `<appinfo>`. `<documentation>` is used to provide human-readable information for documentation purposes, while `<appinfo>` is used to provide machine-readable information for the application processing the schema instance document. The `<annotation>` element can be used at the beginning of `<complexType>`, `<simpleType>`, `<schema>`, and `<attribute>` elements.

Here is another look at the beginning of `contract.xsd`, demonstrating how this element is used:

```
<?xml version="1.0" encoding="UTF-8"?>
<xsd:schema xmlns:xsd="http://www.w3.org/2000/10/XMLSchema"
elementFormDefault="qualified">
  <xsd:element name="Contract">
    <xsd:annotation>
      <xsd:documentation>
        An XML Schema for a simple contract
      </xsd:documentation>
    </xsd:annotation>
          <xsd:complexType>
      <xsd:sequence>
        <xsd:element ref="Title"/>
        <xsd:element name="Parties" type="PartiesType"/>
        <xsd:element name="ContractAgreement" type="ContractAgreementType"/>
      </xsd:sequence>
    </xsd:complexType>
  <!-- Rest of XML schema -->
```

Finally, a complex type can be defined **anonymously**. An anonymous type definition can be identified by the absence of a `type` attribute in an element declaration, or by a simple or complex type with no name. XML Schema uses the `type` attribute to declare the type of a schema component and also as a mechanism for referencing other types during schema construction. This practice is not required, though, and in situations where a `type` (complex or simple) is either seldom used or requires little restriction, then the use of anonymous types can simplify a schema and reduce the need to name and reference.

To illustrate the use of complex types, consider this `Address` construct for inclusion in `contract.xsd`. `Address` is a complex type consisting of six elements. The `minOccurs` and `maxOccurs` facet attributes are used to show that `<Street>` can only appear twice, and that `<Country>` is optional. Two complex types are used by the `<AddressType>`, `<Province>`, and `<CodeType>`, each containing a `<choice>` compositor that allows one of its elements to be chosen.

`<Province>` is an anonymous type whose child elements of `<County>` and `<State>` allow for international naming conventions to describe the geographical area, just as `<Code>` provides the variants of `<PostCode>` and `<ZipCode>` to give the postal code. Note the use of the two different methods by which `<Province>` and `<Code>` are included:

`<Province>` is included by reference, and by contrast, `<Code>` is included by declaring it as an element of type `<CodeType>`.

```
<!-- Rest of XML schema -->
<xsd:complexType name="AddressType">
  <xsd:sequence>
    <xsd:element name="Office" type="xsd:string"/>
    <xsd:element name="Street" type="xsd:string" maxOccurs="3"/>
    <xsd:element name="City" type="xsd:string"/>
```

```
            <xsd:element ref="Province" minOccurs="0"/>
            <xsd:element name="Code" type="CodeType"/>
            <xsd:element ref="Country" minOccurs="0"/>
        </xsd:sequence>
    </xsd:complexType>

    <xsd:element name="Province">
        <xsd:complexType>
            <xsd:choice>
                <xsd:element name="County" type="xsd:string"/>
                <xsd:element name="State" type="xsd:string"/>
            </xsd:choice>
        </xsd:complexType>
    </xsd:element>
    <xsd:complexType name="CodeType">
        <xsd:choice>
            <xsd:element name="PostCode" type="xsd:string"/>
            <xsd:element name="ZipCode" type="xsd:integer"/>
        </xsd:choice>
    </xsd:complexType>
    <!-- Rest of XML schema -->
```

And here is the `address` construct from our `contract.xml` document:

```
    <!-- Rest of XML document -->
    <Contractee>
      <Name>European Data Ltd.</Name>
        <Address>
            <Office>No 1 Queen's Gardens</Office>
            <Street>Hyde Park</Street>
            <City>London</City>
            <Code>
                <PostCode>W1 11H</PostCode>
            </Code>
            <Country>UK</Country>
        </Address>
    <!-- Rest of XML document cut-->
    </Contractee>
    <!-- Rest of XML schema -->
```

Both `<Province>` and `<CodeType>` are complex types, but the anonymous complex type `<Province>` can be included by simple reference, whereas the named complex type `<Code>` has to be referenced as a type and then declared as an element.

In case you are wondering, `<Province>` is declared anonymously because of the simplicity of its content model – no constraints are specified and the context of its use is local within `<AddressType>` rather than being globally accessed throughout the document. `<Code>` is also simple but it contains two base types, because a 'code' model should offer reuse possibilities, in case we might want to use it as a globally accessible base type for deriving other code formats and using them elsewhere in the schema.

The `<ContactMethod>` complex type provides a reusable group model that allows a combination of `<Email>`, `<Fax>`, or `<Telephone>` contact details to be given, with an optional `PreferredContact` attribute available to give the preferred method of contact. The purpose of the `PreferredContact` attribute is given by using the `<xsd:documentation>` subelement of the `<xsd:annotation>` element, included within the complex type definition of `<ContactMethod>`.

```
<!-- Rest of XML schema -->
<xsd:complexType name="ContactMethodType">
  <xsd:annotation>
    <xsd:documentation>Use the preferred contact attribute to identify the
preferred method of contacting the addressee</xsd:documentation>
  </xsd:annotation>
  <xsd:sequence>
    <xsd:element name="Email" type="xsd:string" minOccurs="0"/>
    <xsd:element name="Fax" type="xsd:string" minOccurs="0"/>
    <xsd:element name="Telephone" type="xsd:integer"/>
  </xsd:sequence>
  <xsd:attribute name="PreferredContact" type="xsd:string"/>
</xsd:complexType>
<!-- Rest of XML schema -->
```

These changes would affect our XML document as follows:

```
<ContactMethod PreferredContact="Telephone">
  <Telephone>0207123456</Telephone>
</ContactMethod>
```

Adding an Attribute – Extending a Simple Type by Creating a Complex Type

As explained above, the rules for creating simple elements and attributes prohibit the addition of an attribute to a simple type. If you need to add an attribute to a simple data type, though, deriving a complex type from the simple type, and extending the simple type during derivation to add an attribute to its properties can accomplish this. The `<xsd:simpleContent>` and `<xsd:extension>` elements are wrapped in an anonymous `<xsd:complexType>` element.

The `<xsd:simpleContent>` element indicates that the content model of the element we are creating only contains character data and does not contain any elements. In the example below, we revise the `<TelephoneNumber>` element of `contract.xsd` to add an attribute to hold the international dialling code.

```
<!-- Rest of XML schema -->
<xsd:element name="Telephone" >
  <xsd:complexType>
    <xsd:simpleContent>
      <xsd:extension base="xsd:integer">
        <xsd:attribute name="IntCode" type="xsd:string"/>
      </xsd:extension>
    </xsd:simpleContent>
  </xsd:complexType>
</xsd:element>
<!-- Rest of XML schema -->
```

An XML fragment illustrates the effect:

```
<ContactMethod PreferredContact="Telephone">
  <Telephone IntCode="+44">0207123456</Telephone>
</ContactMethod>
```

This derivation method enables us to add an attribute to our simple type and keep the element content as a simple type. Extension can also be used for complex type derivation, as we shall see below.

Using Extension for Complex Type Derivation

The previous example illustrated using the <xsd:extension> element to extend a simple type. For deriving new complex types from other complex types, <xsd:extension> can also be used to add new elements and attributes to existing complex type definitions. The structure used to achieve this is similar to that used for extending the simple type. Instead of a <xsd:simpleContent> element a <xsd:complexContent> element is used, explicitly indicating that the base type is complex. Again, the base attribute of <xsd:extension> names the type being extended. When extending a complex type the base type's content model is treated as though present in the derivation, and new elements and attributes are simply added at the end of the existing content model where required.

In the example below we create <PersonalClientContactMethod>, using <ContactMethod> as an extension base and adding a <MobilePhone> element and a Duration attribute, the purpose of which is described in the <Documentation> element. The <ContactType> element can be modified using the Choice compositor – this enables the user to choose between standard and personal contact records. contract.xsd revised in light of this change illustrates an instance of this:

```xml
<!-- Rest of XML schema -->
<xsd:element name="Contact" type="ContactType"/>
<!-- Rest of XML schema cut-->
<xsd:complexType name="ContactType">
  <xsd:choice>
    <xsd:element name="ContactMethod" type="ContactMethodType"/>
    <xsd:element name="PersonalClientMethod"
                 type="PersonalClientContactMethodType"/>
  </xsd:choice>
</xsd:complexType>
<!-- Rest of XML schema cut -->
<xsd:complexType name="PersonalClientContactMethodType">
  <xsd:annotation>
    <xsd:documentation>
      Use the Duration attribute to indicate the number of months
      of the client relationship in figures
    </xsd:documentation>
  </xsd:annotation>
  <xsd:complexContent>
    <xsd:extension base="ContactMethodType">
      <xsd:sequence>
        <xsd:element name="MobilePhone" type="xsd:integer"/>
      </xsd:sequence>
      <xsd:attribute name="Duration" type="xsd:integer"/>
    </xsd:extension>
  </xsd:complexContent>
</xsd:complexType>
<!-- Rest of XML schema -->
```

We can see this implemented in the following sample XML:

```xml
<Contact>
  <PersonalClientMethod Duration="14">
    <Telephone>0123456789</Telephone>
    <MobilePhone>000123456</MobilePhone>
  </PersonalClientMethod>
</Contact>
```

219

Mixed Content – Handling with a Complex Type

A data model might often require a situation where we need a mixed content model that allows text to appear between interchangeable elements. A typical example of this need to include markup and text within the same element might be an e-commerce situation, where a customer buys something online.

Bills and associated correspondence will be automatically generated and then personalized to match the details of the individual customer. A billing letter template can be created and order details from the online form fed into corresponding elements interspersed throughout the text before the letter is finally processed. The <BillingOrder> element would need to contain boilerplate text and the relevant <Price>, <CustomerName>, <OrderDate> – among other elements.

XML Schema uses the complex type to deliver mixed content by applying the mixed attribute and setting its Boolean value to true. The XML Schema mixed content model is more rigorous than it was in XML 1.0 because the order and number of child elements appearing in the mixed model is constrained to match the order and number of child elements as defined in the XML Schema. (In XML 1.0 the sequence and number of elements in a mixed model is not constrained and so elements can appear in any order and in any number.)

To illustrate, let us consider a <PaymentTerm> element for our contract.xsd. In this scenario, a term for a contract consists of generic data that delimits the actual contract term, and variable data that customizes the term and makes it relevant to the individual contract requirement, for example, a payment term where settlement dates are variable and must be specified, and where the contract parties to whom the payment terms apply need to be specifically identified.

The variable information in the sample <PaymentTerm> can be captured inside elements, and our sample <PaymentTerm> takes the following format:

```
<PaymentTerm>
  That <DebtorName>J.James</DebtorName>
  of <DebtorAddress> … </DebtorAddress>

  agrees to pay <CreditorName>ABC Ltd</CreditorName >
  of <CreditorAddress> … </CreditorAddress>

  the sum of <Amount>One hundred pounds</Amount>
  within <SettlementPeriod>thirty days</SettlementPeriod>
  or by the <SettlementDate>29 February</SettlementDate>
  whichever is the soonest.
</PaymentTerm>
```

The code for <PaymentTerm> is shown below. <PaymentTerm> is defined as a complex type, setting the mixed attribute to true. The other elements are included in the sequence in which they must appear, ensuring that when we validate our <PaymentTerm> its contents will be in the correct sequential order.

The debtor name, creditor name, and address constructs reuse the existing name and address types, but because they create new elements of these data types specifically labelled debtor and creditor, they clearly distinguish debtor from creditor information. The <Settlement> element is used as the base type for expressing the settlement date and period. <PaymentTerm> is added to the <TermsType> datatype and classified as having optional occurrence.

In the fragment from `contract.xml` revised to reflect this change, we can see that the structural integrity of the data has been maintained within the text. XML Schema is much more specific in this respect than XML itself – unlike XML, XML Schema insists that the order and number in which elements appear in a content model must be reflected in the XML instance document, and this is assessed at validation.

```xml
<!-- Rest of XML schema -->
<xsd:complexType name="TermsType">
  <xsd:sequence>
    <xsd:element ref="Term" maxOccurs="unbounded"/>
    <xsd:element ref="PaymentTerm" maxOccurs="0"/>
  </xsd:sequence>
</xsd:complexType>

<xsd:simpleType name="Settlement">
  <xsd:restriction base="xsd:string"/>
</xsd:simpleType>

<xsd:element name="PaymentTerm">
  <xsd:complexType mixed="true">
    <xsd:sequence>
      <xsd:element name="DebtorName" type="NameType"/>
      <xsd:element name="DebtorAddress" type="AddressType"/>
      <xsd:element name="CreditorName" type="NameType"/>
      <xsd:element name="CreditorAddress" type="AddressType"/>
      <xsd:element name="Amount" type="xsd:string"/>
      <xsd:element name="SettlementPeriod" type="Settlement"/>
      <xsd:element name="SettlementDate" type="Settlement"/>
    </xsd:sequence>
  </xsd:complexType>
</xsd:element>
<!-- Rest of XML schema -->
```

And below is the fragment of `contract.xml` where this construct appears:

```xml
<Terms>
  <Term>Exchange of data relating to x,y, and z.</Term>
  <Term>All accounts to be settled within 30 days</Term>
  <PaymentTerm>
    That <DebtorName>American Data, Inc.</DebtorName>
    of <DebtorAddress>
        <Office>12 Columbus House</Office>
        <Street>Columbus Avenue</Street>
        <City>San Francisco</City>
        <Province>
        <State>CA</State>
      </Province>
      <Code>
        <ZipCode>1234567</ZipCode>
      </Code>
    </DebtorAddress>
    agrees to pay <CreditorName>European Data Ltd. Ltd</CreditorName>
    of <CreditorAddress>
        <Office>No 1 Queen's Gardens</Office>
        <Street>Hyde Park</Street>
```

```
            <City>London</City>
            <Code>
              <PostCode>W1 11H</PostCode>
            </Code>
         </CreditorAddress>
      the sum of <Amount>One hundred pounds</Amount>
      within <SettlementPeriod>thirty days </SettlementPeriod>
      or by the <SettlementDate>29 February</SettlementDate>
      whichever is the soonest.
    </PaymentTerm>
  </Terms>
```

Using Restriction for Complex Type Derivation

A complex type can also be derived by restriction. Unlike restricting a simple type, where the simple type's range of values is restricted, complex type restriction restricts the range of the base complex type's declarations. The complex type derived by restriction offers the same components as its base but restricts the range of values that the base type can offer.

To illustrate, consider the complex type definition for <AddressType> where a maximum of three <Street> elements can occur.

```
<!-- Rest of XML schema -->
<xsd:complexType name="AddressType">
  <xsd:sequence>
    <xsd:element name="Office" type="xsd:string"/>
    <xsd:element name="Street" type="xsd:string" maxOccurs="3"/>
    <xsd:element name="City" type="xsd:string"/>
    <xsd:element ref="Province" minOccurs="0"/>
    <xsd:element name="Code" type="CodeType"/>
    <xsd:element ref="Country" minOccurs="0"/>
  </xsd:sequence>
</xsd:complexType>
<!-- Rest of XML schema -->
```

To derive a new complex type for <AddressType> with the restriction that only two <Street> elements can be given, we restrict the value of the maxOccurs attribute for <Street> in the derived <RestrictedAddressType> to two as follows. To do this the <xsd:complexContent> element is used in conjunction with an <xsd:restriction> element:

```
<xsd:complexType name="RestrictedAddressType">
  <xsd:complexContent>
    <xsd:restriction base="AddressType">
      <xsd:sequence>
    <xsd:element name="Office" type="xsd:string"/>
    <xsd:element name="Street" type="xsd:string" maxOccurs="2"/>
    <xsd:element name="City" type="xsd:string"/>
    <xsd:element ref="Province" minOccurs="0"/>
    <xsd:element name="Code" type="CodeType"/>
    <xsd:element ref="Country" minOccurs="0"/>
      </xsd:sequence>
    </xsd:restriction>
  </xsd:complexContent>
</xsd:complexType>
```

Mechanisms for Controlling Type Derivation and Use

As the explanation of complex and simple types has made apparent, the type construction of XML Schema offers ample scope for the derivation and use of types. However, there may be occasions when it is desirable to limit this scope for derivation and use, and XML Schema provides this with the `final` attribute.

An instance of this could be with the `ClassifiedContractType` in `contract.xsd`, where the classification system depends on exactly two `<CodeOrKeyword>` elements and between one and three enumerated values for `<LegalClassification>` being used.

```xml
<!-- Rest of XML schema -->
<xsd:complexType name="ClassifiedContractType" final="restriction">
  <xsd:complexContent>
    <xsd:extension base="ContractAgreementType">
      <xsd:sequence>
        <xsd:element ref="LegalClassification"/>
        <xsd:element ref="CodeOrKeyword" minOccurs="2" maxOccurs="2"/>
      </xsd:sequence>
    </xsd:extension>
  </xsd:complexContent>
</xsd:complexType>
<xsd:element name="LegalClassification" type="LegalClassificationType"/>
<xsd:simpleType name="LegalClassificationType">
  <xsd:restriction base="LegalClassifiersType">
    <xsd:minLength value="1"/>
    <xsd:maxLength value="3" fixed="true"/>
  </xsd:restriction>
</xsd:simpleType>
<!-- Rest of XML schema -->
```

To control type derivation, we can use the `final` attribute. The `final` attribute is used with the `<xsd:simpleType>` and `<xsd:complexType>` elements and it has three values:

❑ `restriction` – this value prevents a type being derived by restriction

❑ `extension` – this prevents a type being extended

❑ `#all` – this value prevents any derivation of a type at all

To illustrate, applying the `final` attribute with a `restriction` value to the `complexType` `ClassifiedContractType` would prevent its value being restricted – the occurrence of `<CodeOrKeyword>` could not be restricted from its value of two to a lower figure. A `finalDefault` attribute, which has the same values as the `final` attribute, can be applied to the `<xsd:schema>` element, with the effect of applying the designated restriction on change to every element in the schema document.

Using the `fixed` attribute with its value set to `true` can control a simple type's use and derivation. `fixed` is applied to the individual facet value declarations of a simple type and its use prevents that facet value being changed. `fixed` only fixes the value of the individual facet to which it is applied and does not prevent the simple type being modified by the addition or amendment of other facet declarations. Applying `fixed` to the simple type `<LegalClassificationType>` in the example above protects the value of the `maxLength` facet, but the value of the `minLength` facet could be changed if this `<LegalClassificationType>` were used as a base type for derivation.

Using the block attribute can control the use of derived types and substitution groups to replace types. block has the same three possible values as the final attribute and it will block the replacement of one type by another type, derived by the value given for block. In other words, if the value of block is restriction, then the type that carries the block attribute cannot be replaced by a type that has been derived from that type by restriction.

To illustrate, consider how we restricted the <AddressType> element to change the occurrence of <Street> from three to two. By applying the block attribute with a value of restriction to an instance of the <AddressType> element, the substitution of <AddressType> by <RestrictedAddressType> would be prevented – but only the substitution by <RestrictedAddressType>. If <AddressType> had also been extended, then the <ExtendedAddressType> could replace the blocked <AddressType> unless the value of the block attribute was changed from restriction to extension, in which case it would block the replacement of <AddressType> by <ExtendedAddressType>.

A blockDefault attribute can be applied to the schema with the same global effect given by the finalDefault attribute. A good example of using the block attribute to prevent type replacement by substitution groups or derived types can be seen in the schema declaration of the XML Schema itself where the value of blockDefault is given #all.

Ur-Type Definition

There is actually a third definition type in XML Schema, and that is the **ur-type definition**. The ur-type definition lies at the top of the type definition hierarchy of every XML Schema.

Unlike all other type definitions, which are an extension or restriction of other type definitions, the ur-type is a distinguished type definition that is present as the root type definition in the schema. To use an object-oriented analogy, the ur-type definition is the superclass. As anyType, the ur-type definition can function as both a simple and a complex type, and so restrictions of it can be either simple or complex:

```
<xsd:element name="myElement">
   <xsd:complexType>
      <xsd:complexContent>
         <xsd:restriction base="xsd:anyType">
            <xsd:attribute name="myAttributeName" type="myAttributeType"/>
         </xsd:restriction>
      </xsd:complexContent>
   </xsd:complexType>
</xsd:element>
```

To illustrate the power of the ur-type, in the example above xsd:anyType is being used as the restriction base of a complexType element. <xsd:anyType> is an abstraction of the ur-type base from which all simple and complex types are derived and so by using this restriction base we are placing no constraints on the attributes that <myElement> can have.

xsd:anyType can literally be used as though it were any other type; because it has no constraints, an element of type xsd:anyType can have any value. To illustrate this point, the built-in data types of XML Schema are restrictions of anySimpleType, which is itself a simple restriction of the ur-type definition.

Secondary Components and Helper Components

Secondary schema components are attribute group, identity-constraint, model group definitions, and also notation declarations. **Helper** components are used to form parts of other components; they include annotations, model groups, particles, and wildcards. Some of these concepts have already been introduced – the concept of a model group and the purpose of the <annotation> element have already been discussed. Particles, wildcards, identity-constraint, substitution, and attribute groups are explained in more depth below.

Model Groups, Particles, and Wildcards

In this section we discuss how the XML Schema grammar or language specifies constraints on how schema components are structured, and the form in which they are allowed to appear when they appear in a schema instance. This is a logical necessity without which a schema could not be validated and would, effectively, be worthless as a representation of data.

The three compositors sequence, choice, and all are used to specify the constraints that determine how a group of elements collected together to create a **model group** is ordered and used in a complex type model definition. To illustrate, consider the use of all.

In the example below, the <drawing> element consists of a list of <circle>, <rectangle>, and <square> elements in a complex type constrained by the model group component all. The <drawing> can contain either all of the elements in any order or none of them.

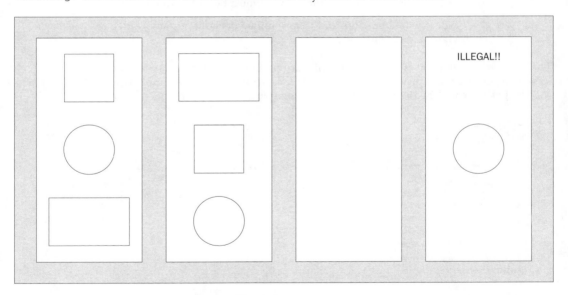

The term **particle** in XML Schema is used to refer to the content of an element. Model groups, the declarations of elements, the constraints placed on occurrence (for example the number of items a List type can have in its content or the maximum number of times that an element can appear), can all be considered as particles, and are used during validation to ensure that a complex type definition conforms to the constraints specified by its content model.

The **wildcard** particle is different from the other particles because it is specifically used to validate element and attribute information items by using their namespace URI, rather than the name under which the element is declared in the schema. The wildcard complex type provides namespace and processContents attributes and optional annotation.

The namespace attribute is used to specify the namespace to be used during validation and can have the values of:

❑ ##any – the namespace is not specified

❑ ##other – specifies that the namespace is not the target namespace of the element's originating schema; for example, if an element were imported from a schema, then using ##other would prevent the validation of that element by its 'ancestor' schema

❑ ##targetNamespace – the target namespace of the element's schema

❑ ##local – used to identify the namespace of the schema in which the element is, or the value of the URI itself

The processContents attribute provided by the wildcard schema component offers three values for the degree of processing to be applied to an element that is being assessed by a processor:

❑ strict – the element being assessed must have an xsi:type attribute and it must be valid

❑ skip – the only constraint is that the element must be well-formed XML

❑ lax – validate where possible and where unique declarations are available; otherwise ignore elements

The <xsd:any> element is used to hold wildcard particles for elements, with the <xsd:anyAttribute> used to hold wildcards for attributes. In the example below, <myElement> is specified as validated by the locally declared namespace:

```
<xsd:element name="myElement">
    <xsd:complexType>
      <xsd:sequence>
        <xsd:any namespace="##local" processContents="lax">
          <xsd:annotation>
            <xsd:documentation>Validation of this element has been set to
lax</xsd:documentation>
          </xsd:annotation>
        </xsd:any>
      </xsd:sequence>
    </xsd:complexType>
</xsd:element>
```

Identity-Constraint

Schema component **Identity-constraints** are used to associate a name with a unique identity and so enable the referencing of schema components. There are three identity-constraint categories:

- ❑ `unique` – an identity definition that asserts the uniqueness of an element and so enables the element's content to be accessed by an XPath expression. When an XPath expression is evaluated, the tuples (the ordered sets of values) returned by the identity of the element being assessed are compared against the constraints that define the identity as defined in the value held by the XPath expression. If the values match, the element can be reliably referenced as the item of information that the XPath statement identifies.

- ❑ `key` – applies the same level of identity definition given by `unique`, but `key` also asserts that the information item selected by the XPath expression must have tuples as its Identity-constraint. Using tuples means that the uniqueness of identity for an item can be more rigorously defined.

- ❑ `keyRef` – is used to assert that the values of the tuples selected for evaluation by the XPath statement are equivalent to their value after they have been evaluated by the XPath statement. In other words, to ensure that the value of the `keyRef` corresponds to the value that is being referenced by it.

Identity-constraints function by using XPath expressions to select the element information items to which the identity-constraint applies; if the conditions of the expression are not met, then the identity constraint will not be valid. Taken together, the three categories are used to establish uniqueness by identifying an element or attribute that is being used by a schema component, and providing the facility of constraining identity to ensure that these elements can be uniquely identified, thereby ensuring the validity of the element making use of them.

Identity-constraint enables unique identity to be given within the scope that it is specified. An example of using identity-constraint is in an element whose group model consists of several complex types, and where it is necessary to ensure that the elements being used are exactly identified to ensure the required element with the required characteristics is used.

Substitution and Substitution Groups

The substitution group mechanism of XML Schema enables an element to be substituted for another element, and we have already seen its use with the attribute group. Elements can be specified for substitution as well. Elements in a substitution group must be of the same type or derived from the type of the element (known as the **head element**) that they are to substitute. The head element must also be a globally declared element.

If an element in the substitution group is not derived from the same type as the head element, then it must be declared using the `xsi:type` attribute (more about the use of this attribute is explained in the section on *Advanced XML Schema Features* below). This works by employing the `substitutionGroup` attribute and giving this attribute the name of the head element. The example below illustrates this mechanism. `ChristianName` and `Surname` are declared as a substitution group for `Name`.

```
<xsd:element name="ChristianName"
             type="xsd:string"
             substitutionGroup="Name" />
<xsd:element name="Surname" type="xsd:string" substitutionGroup="Name" />
```

Substitution of an element can be made obligatory by using the abstract attribute of an element. A reason for this could be a frequently changing value. In such a case it might be desirable to modify the substitution group and use the substituted element as a placeholder for that dynamic value.

If the Boolean value of an abstract attribute of an element is set to true, then that element's use in an instance document is forbidden and it has to be replaced by the substitution group defined for it. Setting the abstract of Name to true would oblige its substitution by the substitution group declared above.

```
<xsd:element name="Name" type="xsd:string" abstract="true" />
```

If a type is declared as abstract, then the type that is to substitute it must be derived from it. To allow the substituting type to appear in an instance document (or any element that is defined by the type declared as abstract) then the substitute must use the xsi:type attribute, and the value of xsi:type must be that of a type derived from the type declared abstract.

Consider an example consultant.xsd schema where LegalConsultant and PRConsultant are derived from the type Consultant and Consultant is declared as an abstract type. HRConsultant is not derived from but is defined as a Consultant type. Before HRConsultant can appear in an instance document, HRConsultant must be given the xsi:type attribute and that attribute must reference a type that is derived from the Consultant type (for example LegalConsultant) and so be able to substitute it.

Using Namespaces in XML Schema

At its most basic, an XML Schema declaration will take the following form, incorporating the namespace for XML Schema:

```
<?xml version="1.0" encoding="UTF-8"?>
<xsd:schema xmlns:xsd="http://www.w3.org/2000/10/XMLSchema" >

    <!--  schema component declarations here -->

</xsd:schema>
```

XML Schema uses the namespace mechanism for qualifying attribute and element names. The schema element is the root element of every schema document, and the namespaces that qualify the schema are declared within it.

The <xsd:schema> element defines this as a schema document conforming to the W3C's XML Schema specification. The location of this schema and its associated prefix is then given in the namespace declaration xmlns:xsd. The xmlns attribute is used to identify a default namespace for a schema, and its use explicitly states which namespace(s) apply to a schema. Associating a namespace prefix with xmlns enables the association of a schema component with a namespace, enabling that component's validation against the constraints defined for it in its namespace.

Other attributes can be applied to a schema declaration, and they play a crucial role during validation:

❑   xmlns – used to set a default namespace for a schema. By providing a default namespace, elements and attributes belonging to this namespace do not have to be prefixed by a namespace prefix, (although a prefix can be used if desired, and may be required to avoid naming clashes when elements with the same name from different namespaces are included in a single document instance).

- ❑ `targetNamespace` – used to define the namespace that is being described by an XML Schema

- ❑ `elementFormDefault` – this has two values; `qualified` and `unqualified`. It is used to specify whether locally defined elements have to be qualified or not. The default value is `unqualified`, meaning they are not. If the value is set to `qualified` then elements defined locally also have to be qualified. Globally defined elements are always qualified. The `qualified` and `unqualified` values are used to indicate whether element values are qualified by default in a namespace.

- ❑ `attributeFormDefault` – identical to `elementFormDefault` but applies to attributes

- ❑ `finalDefault` and `blockDefault` – already described in the section above

How a schema is qualified will have consequences for the structure of schemas and the instance documents that conform to them. We will consider these now by giving a series of sample declarations for our `contract` XML Schema. To remind us, we provide it in its basic form, in which it references the schema for XML Schema. The `elementFormDefault` attribute is set to `qualifed`, meaning that local elements and attributes must be qualified by namespaces as well as the global elements and attributes:

```
<xsd:schema xmlns:xsd="http://www.w3.org/2000/10/XMLSchema
elementFormDefault="qualified">"
```

Setting a Target Namespace and Unqualified Local Element Declarations

We begin by setting a `targetNamespace` for `contract.xsd`. This states that a namespace is being defined by this schema and it provides the location of that namespace. We will use the `xmlns` attribute to set this as a default namespace for the schema. Logically, as we are using this schema to define a namespace, we have to do this – elements being defined in this schema are now defining a namespace and that namespace has to, therefore, become a default namespace of the schema. We associate the `con` prefix with this default namespace for clarity so we can see at a glance which namespace elements in our schema come from:

```
<xsd:schema xmlns:xsd=http://www.w3.org/2000/10/XMLSchema
targetNamespace="C:\ProJavaXML\Chapter05\contract\contract"
xmlns="C:\ProJavaXML\Chapter05\contract\contract" elementFormDefault="qualified">
```

The consequences of this schema declaration are illustrated through the `contract.xsd` schema fragment below. The `<Contract>` element and the `PartiesType` type have been defined by using elements defined in the XML Schema namespace. By setting a `targetNamespace`, elements defined within that schema are accordingly subject to that namespace, which has to be referenced when the schema is validated.

When elements defined in the namespace are used, then their namespace has to be referenced during validation. Using the `con` prefix makes this clear in the example below:

```
<!-- Rest of XML schema -->
<xsd:element name="Contract">
  <xsd:annotation>
    <xsd:documentation>Illustrates the need to qualify local element and attribute
declarations when elementFormDefault is set to 'qualified'</xsd:documentation>
  </xsd:annotation>
  <xsd:complexType>
    <xsd:sequence>
      <xsd:element ref="con:Title"/>
      <xsd:element name="Parties" type="con:PartiesType"/>
```

```
        <xsd:choice>
          <xsd:element name="ContractAgreement" type="con:ContractAgreementType"/>
          <xsd:element name="ClassifiedContractAgreement"
type="con:ClassifiedContractType"/>
        </xsd:choice>
      </xsd:sequence>
    </xsd:complexType>
  </xsd:element>
<!-- Rest of XML schema cut -->
  <xsd:complexType name="PartiesType">
<!-- Rest of XML schema -->
```

Remember that elements associated with the default namespace of a schema do not have to be identified with a prefix unless one is defined for the default namespace in the schema declaration. For example, if the xmlns:xsd declaration were changed to xmlns, then the xsd prefix could be removed from all schema elements defined in this namespace and the schema would still validate.

Introducing a `targetNamespace` as you develop your schema has the consequence of requiring that elements defined in the schema be qualified by a default namespace if you are to reference them locally inside the schema. The schema document would have to be checked and rewritten accordingly.

The schema declaration:

```
<xsd:complexType name="PartiesType">
    <xsd:sequence>
      <xsd:element name="Contractor" type="ContractorType"/>
      <xsd:element name="Contractee" type="ContractorType"/>
    </xsd:sequence>
  </xsd:complexType>
```

would be legal before a `targetNamespace` was added. It would still be legal even with a `targetNamespace`, providing that when the `targetNamespace` and the accompanying `xmlns` namespace declaration were added, a prefix was not specified. If, however, a namespace prefix was specified at this point, (in this example, the prefix is `con`), then the local declarations and references would have to be qualified by the `con` prefix accordingly. The `PartiesType` declaration above would have to be amended to reflect this and so read:

```
<xsd:complexType name="PartiesType">
    <xsd:sequence>
      <xsd:element name="Contractor" type="con:ContractorType"/>
      <xsd:element name="Contractee" type="con:ContractorType"/>
    </xsd:sequence>
  </xsd:complexType>
```

The effect of applying a `targetNamespace` to a schema on an instance XML document conforming to that schema is shown by the declaration for `contract.xml` below.

The original declaration:

```
<?xml version="1.0" encoding="UTF-8"?>
<Contract xmlns:xsi="http://www.w3.org/2000/10/XMLSchema-instance"
xsi:noNamespaceSchemaLocation="C:\ProJavaXML\Chapter05\contract\contract.xsd">
```

is now no longer applicable, because since setting the `targetNamespace`, the schema has defined a namespace and so that namespace is referenced by an XML instance document conforming to this schema. The namespace defined by `contract.xsd` is set as the default namespace of the `contract.xml` instance document using the `xmlns` attribute. The `noNamespaceLocation` attribute is replaced by the `schemaLocation` attribute, which is used to indicate where the schema is located. Note that it contains a pair of values – the first identifying the namespace, the second identifying where the schema document is. The `xsi` namespace is imported, enabling the use of `xsi` attributes:

```
<?xml version="1.0"?>
<Contract xmlns="C:\ProJavaXML\Chapter05\contract\contract"
xmlns:xsi="http://www.w3.org/2000/10/XMLSchema-instance"
xsi:schemaLocation="C:\ProJavaXML\Chapter05\contract\contract.xsd >
</Contract>
```

The problem with setting a target namespace is that many XML documents do not use namespaces, and so their elements are unqualified and cannot be validated by a schema with a target namespace. To validate an unqualified element in an instance document, the schema being used to validate it cannot have a target namespace. The type of XML document that your schema will be validating has to be considered before you set a target namespace for the schema.

Qualified Local Declarations

Qualifying local declarations for attributes and elements can be done by setting the `elementFormDefault` and `attributeFormDefault` values to `qualified`. (Individual elements or attributes can also be set as `qualified`, even when the `elementFormDefault` and `attributeformDefault` values are set to `unqualified`, by using the `form` attribute of the individual element or attribute and setting its value to `qualified`.)

In the example below, the namespace prefix `con` clearly illustrates the difference between a local and global declaration of qualifying local declarations, and so the impact of qualifying local declarations on the structure of your schema:

```
<!-- Rest of XML schema -->
<xsd:schema targetNamespace="C:\ProJavaXML\Chapter05\contract\contract.xsd"
xmlns:con=" C:\ProJavaXML\Chapter05\contract\contract.xsd"
xmlns:xsd="http://www.w3.org/2000/10/XMLSchema" elementFormDefault="qualified">
  <xsd:element name="Contract">
    <xsd:annotation>
      <xsd:documentation>An XML Schema for a simple contract</xsd:documentation>
    </xsd:annotation>
    <xsd:complexType>
      <xsd:sequence>
        <xsd:element ref="con:Title"/>
        <xsd:element name="Parties" type="con:PartiesType"/>
        <xsd:choice>
          <xsd:element name="ContractAgreement" type="con:ContractAgreementType"/>
          <xsd:element name="ClassifiedContractAgreement"
type="con:ClassifiedContractType"/>
        </xsd:choice>
      </xsd:sequence>
    </xsd:complexType>
  </xsd:element>
<!-- Rest of XML schema -->
```

Note that the namespace prefix specified in the schema is not reflected in the XML instance, because it is not appended to the name given to the elements that will be used in the instance, only to the elements that are being used to define them in the schema. The elements in the XML instance are *implicitly* identified as belonging to this schema namespace. To *explicitly* identify every element in the XML instance as belonging to the default namespace, apply the default namespace prefix to the namespace declaration in the instance document:

```
<con:Contract xmlns:con="C:\ProJavaXML\Chapter05\contract\contract"
xmlns:xsi="http://www.w3.org/2000/10/XMLSchema-instance"
xsi:schemaLocation=" C:\ProJavaXML\Chapter05\contract\contract
C:\ProJavaXML\Chapter05\contract\contract.xsd >

<con:Title>Sample Contract</con:Title>
    <con:Parties>
    <!-- et cetera -->
</con:Contract>
```

Qualifying Attributes in XML Schema

The rules for qualifying attributes differ from those for qualifying elements because the W3C's *Namespaces in XML* specification does not allow namespaces for attributes to be given by default.

> For more information see the W3C's *Namespaces in XML*:
> **http://www.w3.org/TR/REC-xml-names/**

If an attribute has to be qualified, then the namespace prefix has to be given explicitly. If the `attributeFormDefault` for the instance document has been set to `unqualified`, an individual attribute can be made to override this global declaration at the local level. It does this by qualifying itself using the `form` attribute and setting this value to `qualified`.

This solves the problem of how to qualify an attribute whose use is required when the `attributeFormDefault` has been set to `unqualified`. In the example below, the `form` attribute is applied to the `PreferredContact` attribute of `<ContactMethod>` from the `contract.xsd` schema in order to qualify it:

```
<xsd:attribute name="PreferredContact" type="CDATA" use="required"
form="qualified"/>
```

Advanced XML Schema Features

The XML Schema specification is comprehensive and there is only limited scope to explore advanced features from XML Schema. In particular, we consider:

❑ Those mechanisms that enable the inclusion, substitution, and redefinition of schema components to facilitate definition and type reuse – focusing on `xsi:type`, `xsi:include`, and `xsd:redefine`

❑ Setting an attribute's or element's uniqueness within a certain scope

Using the xsi:type

XML Schema allows the derivation of new types from existing types and the definition of elements according to existing types. The `xsi:type` allows a type to be replaced by a type derived from it in an XML instance document, by explicitly defining this as the type of the element. In `contract.xsd`, the `<LegalClassification>` element is of the `LegalClassificationType` defined in that schema. This type is derived from `LegalClassifiersType`:

```xml
<!-- Rest of XML schema -->
<xsd:element name="LegalClassification" type="LegalClassificationType"/>
  <xsd:simpleType name="LegalClassificationType">
    <xsd:restriction base="LegalClassifiersType">
      <xsd:minLength value="1"/>
      <xsd:maxLength value="3" fixed="true"/>
    </xsd:restriction>
  </xsd:simpleType>
  <xsd:simpleType name="LegalClassifiersType">
    <xsd:list itemType="LegalKeywordsType"/>
  </xsd:simpleType>
<!-- Rest of XML schema -->
```

Using the `xsi:type` attribute enables the substitution of this derived type in an XML instance document where `<LegalClassification>` would normally be expected to appear:

```xml
<LegalClassification xsi:Type="LegalClassifiersType" > commercial contract
</LegalClassification>
```

Using xsd:include

Constructing a schema by including schema components from multiple documents enables the schema author to reuse type definitions and model groups and apply them in different contexts, adapting them as necessary. To include a schema component contained in another schema document, we use the `<include>` element, declaring it after the schema declaration at the top of the schema. The `schemaLocation` attribute of `<include>` is used to give the URI of the included schema, while its optional `<annotation>` child element can be used to provide relevant documentation or application information if required.

There are restrictions to using `<include>`, however. The target namespace(s) of the schema(s) from which schema component(s) are being included must match the target namespace of the schema in which they are being included. If a schema document that is itself composed of schema components from multiple schema instance documents is being referenced, then only that schema needs to be referenced and not the child schemas from which it is composed.

To illustrate, we take the `<Term>` elements from our `contract.xsd` and place them in a separate `term.xsd` schema. We ensure that both schemas have a common `targetNamespace`, and then use the `<include>` element to include the `<Term>` definitions in our `contract` schema. `<annotation>` is used to document the inclusion:

```xml
<xsd:include schemaLocation="http://www.myCompany.com/term.xsd">
  <xsd:annotation>
    <xsd:documentation>The term.xsd schema contains further predefined terms
applicable to our contracts</xsd:documentation>
  </xsd:annotation>
</xsd:include>
```

If we need to include schema components from a schema that does not share a common target namespace with the including schema, then the `<xsd:import>` element must be used instead of the `<xsd:include>` element. The namespace attribute of `xsd:import` is used to identify the URI of the target namespace of the imported schema component and the `schemaLocation` attribute is used to provide a location for the schema that corresponds to that namespace. The imported namespace is also declared in the schema declaration of the including schema and associated with a prefix, that prefix being used for the imported elements to enable them to be associated with their defining schema during validation when the schema is assessed.

`<xsd:import>` must be the first child element declared in the schema, and there are also restrictions on the components that can be imported – only globally declared elements and named types can be imported; locally declared elements and anonymous types cannot be. Imported complex types can be used as base types for derivation in the including schema, and the `<xsd:import>` mechanism can be used to import 'Type Libraries' – schemas of existing schema component definitions that can be reused and facilitate schema production.

Using xsd:redefine

The `<xsd:redefine>` element allows the schema author to redefine the definitions and declarations of simple and complex types, and model and attribute groups, that have been included in a schema from an external schema. `<xsd:redefine>` is similar to `<xsd:include>` in that it requires the external schema to have the same target namespace as the schema that is including it, and `<xsd:redefine>` also uses the same extension structure as `<xsd:include>`, but it differs from `<xsd:include>` in several important ways.

Firstly, an `<xsd:redefine>` element allows a new type to have the same name as the base type from which it is being derived without throwing an error. The construct for redefinition is illustrated below when a new element for `<CompanyContactNumber>` is defined for our `ContactMethod` type:

```
<xsd:redefine schemaLocation="http://www.myCompany.com/externalschema.xsd">
<xsd:complexType name="ct:ContactMethod">
   <xsd:complexContent>
     <xsd:extension base="ct:ContactMethod">
       <xsd:sequence>
          <xsd:element name="CompanyContactNumber" type="xsd:integer"/>
       </xsd:sequence>
     </xsd:extension >
   </xsd:complexContent>
</xsd:complexType>
</xsd:redefine>
```

Once a type has been redefined, though, that redefinition applies across the whole schema document and so any schema component using the redefined type is liable to be affected by the redefinition. This global effect of redefining a type could lead to conflict if the extension applied to the redefined type has already been applied by other types elsewhere in the schema, that are derived from the newly redefined base type. Consequently, the XML Schema specification advises caution when using `<xsd:redefine>`.

Defining Uniqueness by Using the ID Attribute

Like XML, XML Schema enables the identity of elements to be defined using ID, IDREF, and IDREFS. XML provides these as attributes. XML Schema supports ID by providing it as a simple type from which attributes can be declared. This is a more powerful and flexible construct for defining ID than in XML because XML Schema's typing allows ID to be applied to attributes and elements and their content, whereas in XML ID can only be applied *as* an attribute.

Validation

During parsing an XML instance document will be assessed against its schema to check that it conforms to the constraints specified for it by the schema. At this point the processing does two things – **schema validation** and the addition of **infoset contributions**.

Schema Validation and Infoset Contributions

During schema validation the parser checks that the XML instance document conforms to the schema and/or the namespace that has been specified for the XML instance by either the `xsi:schemaLocation` or the `xsi:noNamespaceSchemaLocation` attribute in the XML document's declaration. (Remember that these attributes provide hints for the processor and that it is not obliged to use them during assessment. It is possible that the processing application may have specified its own schema to use during schema validation.) During processing, the processor records the checking that it has done and any errors that it has encountered. Each element in the document is examined for conformance to the constraint rules specified in the schema, beginning with the root element and proceeding methodically throughout the document until schema validation has been completed.

When testing an element for conformance, the processor locates the element's schema declaration and verifies that the value of the namespace specified by the `targetNamespace` attribute in the schema reflects the element's namespace URI. If the schema does not have a `targetNamespace` attribute and is a 'noNamespace' schema, then the processor makes sure that the element being validated is not qualified by a namespace.

Providing that an error is not thrown at this point, the processor ensures that the type of each element corresponds to that specified for it in the schema, or in the XML instance document if the `xsi:type` attribute has been used. If the `xsi:type` has been used, then the processor will ensure that the substitution is legitimate and does not contravene a block on substitution if this has been specified by a `block` attribute in the element's declaration.

The validation of the element complete, the processor then makes the necessary infoset contributions. Each schema component contains information that is used when processing the XML instance – for example, information about the types and default values – which are not expressed in the XML instance itself but which will possibly be required for subsequent processing of the XML instance. To make sure that this information is available as part of the post-schema-validation infoset used during subsequent processing, the infoset contributions have to be made during conformance checking as the XML instance is validated against its schema.

The attributes and contents of each element are then checked for conformance to the constraints specified by the element's content model. Simple type elements will be checked to ensure that their content is of the correct type and that they contain no elements or attributes (excluding valid attribute additions to simple types).

Complex type elements are validated to ensure that they conform to the constraints of their constituent elements and attributes (for example, that required attributes are present, that elements in mixed content text are in the correct sequence, or that any substitutions made are permissible). The same process is then applied to subelements as the structural hierarchy of the elements in the XML instance document is progressively processed (wildcards allow processing to be `lax`, `skip`, or `strict`) and validation is complete.

The choice of parser to use when parsing your XML file depends on the context:

❑ The Simple API for XML (SAX) is a reactive, event-driven, serial-access protocol for accessing XML documents, and would typically be used for reading a stream of XML data.

❑ The W3C's Document Object Model (DOM) is a language-independent interface that creates a tree representation of the XML document and allows it to be manipulated by the user.

Unlike SAX, DOM makes two passes over the data – the first to place it in memory, and the second to manipulate it. DOM is slower because of this, and so where speed is required SAX is a better option because it is fast and less memory intensive, making SAX more suitable for server applications and network programs that must handle a large data stream and respond to events as they are encountered during processing. Using DOM, though, is a better option when you need to manipulate the data.

With DOM an object model of the XML document is created and the user can randomly access the tree to manipulate the data objects and add, remove, or modify the data objects as required. DOM enables an XML document to be modified or a new XML document to be created, and can output the document in XML, or other forms, including HTML. The characteristics and performance traits of SAX and DOM, though, mean that the choice of which to use will be influenced by the processing requirements of the application.

Schema validators are available from a variety of sources listed on the W3C's site at http://www.w3.org/XML/Schema.html, with implementations available in C, C++, and Java from Oracle and Apache.

Summary

In this chapter we have considered the background surrounding the XML Schema and the W3C's XML Activity. We saw that XML Schema has various operational advantages over DTD.

We then went on to examine the actual features of the schema itself. In particular, we looked at primary and secondary components; the use of simple and complex types and how new types may be restricted or derived from them. We also looked at secondary components and helper components, including particles and wildcards, identity constraints, substitution and substitution groups.

Next, we looked at more aspects of the creation of XML schemas, including the setting of namespaces and the qualification of attributes, and how we could reference schemas from within schema document instances. We surveyed a few of the advanced features of the XML Schema, in particular the use of <xsi:type>, <xsd:include>, and <xsd:redefine>. We also touched on the use of ID in defining uniqueness in document instances. And finally, we briefly touched on the parsing and processing of XML documents defined by XML Schema.

One chapter, though, cannot hope to do justice to the XML Schema specification, although this chapter has elaborated the basic primary components and provided an introduction into the concepts involved in building an XML Schema. Many of XML Schema's advanced features have not been explored, but it is difficult to elaborate a technical specification approaching almost 400 pages in one chapter. For someone wishing to really understand the XML Schema there is really no shortcut to reading the *Primer* and at least looking at *Structures* and *Datatypes*, the URLs to which are provided in the introductory section above.

The Xerces Blue
Butterfly, which became
extinct earlier this century,
and after which the Xerces XML
parser is named ...

6

XML-Object Mapping

So far, we've looked at the data structures that XML documents can encapsulate, and we've looked at how DTDs and schemas can constrain those structures. We've also looked at some programming APIs that allow us to read the data from an XML document into our programs, and in some cases, output data from our programs as XML.

As object-oriented Java programmers, however, we often need to think in terms of abstraction. We don't want to tie our code to a specific parser, so we use an abstraction API such as JAXP. We don't want to tie ourselves to a specific version of DOM (**Document Object Model**), so we build classes that wrap up our DOM-specific calls. What if we decide we don't want our application to be tied to an XML representation of data? Or, perhaps, what if our application is currently tied to some other representation, and we want to be able to switch to XML?

In this chapter, we're going to take a slight step back and think about exactly how data inside our programs (encapsulated in objects), and data in XML documents (encapsulated in elements and attributes) are similar, and how they differ. We'll look at what the differences that do exist mean for us when we want to move data seamlessly from one form to the other.

Mappings

An **XML-Object Mapping**, in the context of this book, is a description of a transformation of information from in-memory Java objects into an XML document, and vice versa. We use the term "mapping" to mean a bi-directional one-to-one mapping; it must be reversible (enough information must be transferred in order to reconstruct the original by performing the mapping in the opposite direction). This reversibility requires a one-to-one mapping (When you map object A into XML document A, then when you map it back you get object A back; when you map object B into XML, you must get a different XML document: if it also mapped to document A, when we mapped it back, we'd get object A, not object B. So the mapping must be one-to-one).

In fact, this is what many XML-enabled applications do, with handwritten code for the transformation in each direction; however, a systematic and regular mapping can be easily automated, encapsulating the mapping process in a simple piece of re-usable logic, so that we don't have to re-implement it in every object we want to use the mapping on. So, what we mean by a mapping is a set of rules for translating an object into an XML document, and an XML document into objects, that follows these rules.

However, because the complete range of representations of XML and Java objects are so different (we'll go into exactly how and why they're different in a moment), we cannot describe one single mapping in which every possible XML construct has a representation in Java object form, and every possible object construct has a representation in XML form. As we'll see, we must choose an abstract domain – select a subset that can represent the kind of information of interest to us. This is really independent of both XML and Java objects.

Broadly speaking, the possible domains are split into three areas; **Documents** – textual documents that can be logically marked up in XML, **data** (in the sense of structured sets of typed information, such as that found in a database); or even **objects**.

Note that the object domain encompasses more than Java objects, as we may want to communicate with other object-oriented languages apart from Java, whether to interface with legacy systems, have cross-platform compatibility, or to allow other software to interface with it should it become (or when it becomes) a legacy piece of software itself. Further, recent developments have seen databases incorporate many object-orientated ideas, such as inheritance of types and polymorphism. In addition, traditional RDBS have also incorporated XML API access to their data. Thus, we mean "objects" in a generic, interoperable sense, not tied down specifically to *Java* objects.

Our choice of abstract domain then determines the subset of constructs of XML documents that will mark up the information, and the subset of Java objects that will hold the information, available on each side of the mapping. We do not necessarily completely cover all possible constructs in either the XML or Java object domain.

For **documents**, practically all of XML is covered; but this maps back and forth to only a tiny sub-set of Java objects (note the arrow, indicating the transformations in both directions):

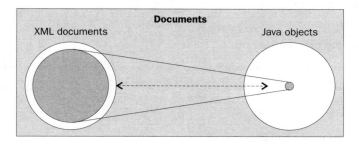

For **data**, both domains are moderately restricted (though in quite different ways):

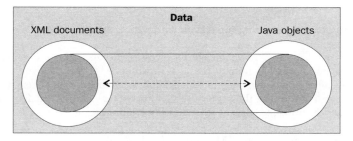

For **objects**, the XML domain is slightly more restricted than it is for data, but the Java object domain is almost completely covered:

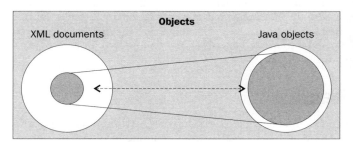

Note that the mechanism for constraining information, or specifying a subset of it, is called "typing". For java objects, classes define this typing; for XML, it is typically performed by DTDs or Schema. Once we have established the XML-Object mapping in this way, we can use it to transform information in both directions – from Object-to-XML, and from XML-to-Object. We derive both transformations from the one canonical mapping.

The benefits to establishing this mapping include access to the XML in an object-oriented way while maintaining platform independent cross-compatible data format that XML offers. In addition, XML data is human readable, self-documenting marked up information, ever more so when there is a DTD or schema to validate the information.

Other good reasons to be able to look at and understand the information:

- ❑ For debugging ("Sunlight is the best disinfectant.")
- ❑ To help describe what and how a program works
- ❑ To analyze the data with statistical profilers
- ❑ To allow simple conversion of data into another format. The problems of reverse-engineering communications protocols and file formats are legion

Further good reasons for being able to edit the information are that we can then:

- ❑ Make corrections and additions
- ❑ Recover corrupted data
- ❑ Create test cases for a program
- ❑ Rapidly prototype by creating input data with a tool, or by hand

Note that both persistence and data interchange are processes of translating in-memory objects into a serial stream form or flat file and back. The difference is that persistence is over time, and data interchange is over space. Of course, Java already has an excellent serialization mechanism, using `ObjectOutputStream` and `ObjectInputStream`, used for just those purposes, by providing an automatic file format for applications to save objects, and which forms the basis of RMI and Jini communications.

To summarize, the special thing about XML is that the data values themselves are human readable and editable (in theory at least), and their nature and the purpose to which they are put is self-documenting. That is, the information is "marked up". Furthermore, because it has become a standard lingua franca, many applications are already able to speak and understand it – and a related consequence is that many tools are available to edit, display, parse and translate it. Finally, because XML is "extensible", we can more easily cope with changing information structures, as the document evolves. If we can make data available as XML, it can be translated and used as a data source for a vast range of other programs. Automated mapping is the bridge.

Mapping in Practice

Let's take a look at an example of what we mean by an XML-object mapping. In fact, we've already met one such mapping – DOM. When an XML Parser generates a DOM tree, it is generating objects whose data is an in-memory representation of the XML document, corresponding to the document in structure and content. We can also look at another example, the following XML document:

```
<person>
  <name>Fred</name>
  <age>45</age>
</person>
```

Is mapped to java using the following code:

```
Person person = new Person();
person.name = "Fred";
person.age = 45;
```

As the example shows, an XML-Object mapping is between values, but there is another level of mapping, between types – a DTD-Class mapping (or perhaps a Schema-Class mapping). Here is a conceptual diagram of the relationships:

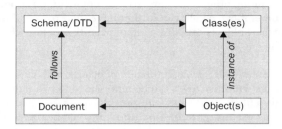

Here is the previous XML-Object mapping example's related DTD to Class mapping. First the DTD:

```
<!ELEMENT person (name, age)>
<!ELEMENT name (#PCDATA)>
<!ELEMENT age (#PCDATA)>
```

And here is the class definition that matches that DTD:

```
class Person {
   String name;
   int age;
}
```

Note that XML and objects are "values", whereas DTDs and classes are "types". They are quite distinct concepts, at different levels as are the corresponding XML-Object and DTD-Class mappings.

XML-Object mapping is a way of converting XML documents into a group of objects, and vice versa. Since data in a Java program is typically stored in objects, the code in the preceding chapters on SAX, DOM and JDOM can do precisely this. That is, the programs define a way to transform objects into an XML document when they write the XML, and the reverse transformation of parsing the XML document back into objects, when they read the XML.

The implementation of DOM maps the XML onto a tree of various types of Node objects, variously representing tags, attributes, text and so on. JDOM maps in a similar way. While this is an accurate and general representation of the XML document, in object-modeling terms this can be quite restrictive. Unless our application really is dealing with XML documents as entities, we will often want the data to be stored in our own objects, representing concepts of use to us in writing our logic, and possessing methods that make sense in the context of our application.

The manual writing of custom code to write and parse XML is a lot of work; thus, the focus of this chapter is on tools that automate the process of XML-Object mapping. In order to do this, we need to look more closely at XML and Java objects, and how one can be represented by the other; that is, the possible mappings between them.

Objects to XML

What are objects, and how can we represent objects in XML? XML can represent hierarchical information, with tags containing other tags. Similarly, through composition, an object can have children stored in its data members, which can further have their own children – which resembles this hierarchical structure. Further, objects can also contain primitive fields, which cannot contain anything other than their value – the end of the line.

XML can represent this apparently hierarchical structure of objects, with tags containing other tags. Thus, tags can represent object fields. Primitive fields can be represented in two ways: as attributes, or as tags containing only character data (that is, not containing any other tags, or "mixed content"). We saw such character data in our mapping example: `<age>45</age>`. It could be represented in attributes as: `<person age="45" />`. Note that neither can contain anything other than their value – just like primitives.

This is very similar to the attributes of XML. XML also has leaf nodes, which are nodes containing pure character data. In the example we gave earlier, we mapped the primitive data members of our class into character data within elements of the XML.

Although objects can represent hierarchical information, with objects containing other objects by composition, we need to be careful: objects are more powerful than this. The composition of objects is not the same as the strict containment of XML: the objects themselves are not contained, but are merely **references** to those objects. This distinction is important, because it allows an object to be referred to by more than one object. It also allows circular references, where two objects refer to each other, for example, or even an object referring to itself.

An example of a multiple reference is a many-to-one relationship between things, such as many employees having the same supervisor. Imagine a sequence of employee tags, each of which needs to refer to the same supervisor. Unless we make a separate copy of the supervisor tag for each employee, we can't represent the relationships with this structure. Sometimes, making the copies is in fact the neatest solution; but of course the clever thing to do is to just reverse the relationship, to list the supervisor tags first, and the employees within each one, so that it becomes one-to-many. The real problem is many-to-many relationships, where this trick doesn't work. For example, if each employee has more than one supervisor.

So, while XML nested tags represent a data structure which can be drawn as a tree with a root element, and its trunk splitting into branches pointing to its immediate children, and so on out to the leaves, an object that contains references to other objects can form part of a complex, non-hierarchical structure that is not a tree, but rather a more general form which mathematicians calls a graph.

Since neither multiple references nor circular references can be represented in XML with nested tags, we must define another way to represent these relationships. One example is the ID and IDREF attribute types of DTDs. However, note that IDREF references to IDs are not typed – a pair of them can be used to reference any tag from any other tag, without causing invalidity. Contrast this with the validity checks on what tags can be contained within other tags.

From the viewpoint of Java objects, this distinction between "containment" and "references" is illusory, as all composition in Java is in fact by reference. The result is that DTDs can only validate the structure of tags when they happen to form the strict containment hierarchies of tree structures. That is, the limitation is not really at the level of XML, but at the DTD level. That is, not a problem of values, but of types.

Another complication is that part of the value of an object is its type, or class, which is not fixed until run-time. That is, a field of compile-time type `Object` can hold an actual object of any run-time type (or run-time "class", as the Java Language Specification prefers it). Thus, it is not possible to know what type of object it holds, until run-time. Thus, the XML needs to state the run-time type of the object, and not the type of the field containing it. Now, XML is fully capable of representing these values; the problem is in type validity with respect to a DTD. To do this, the DTD needs to know the run-time types permissible for each field. This requires its compile time type of the field, and its subclasses, and if it is an interface, a list of types (classes) implementing it. While this can be done using parameter entities and the choice operator ("|"), it is quite awkward.

On a completely different level, there is also the hierarchy of classes, and a further hierarchy of inner classes, not to mention the directory-based hierarchy of packages, all of which *are* strictly contained.

> *Incidentally, the limited form of multiple inheritance permitted when implementing and extending interfaces is not strict containment, since more than one interface can be inherited or extended. Therefore, this is not quite a tree. But since cycles are not permitted, it is still a limited form of graph. The rather prosaic name for this in-between data structure is a "DAG" – a Directed Acyclic Graph.*

To summarize, although references and therefore graphs can be represented in XML, *typed* references are an insurmountable problem for DTDs to validate them. On the other hand, run-time types can be both represented in XML and validated by DTDs, albeit awkwardly.

XML to Objects

What is XML, and how can we represent XML as objects? The DOM is a completely general way to faithfully map any well-formed XML into objects. This includes XML used to mark up "documents – or "document-centric" XML; but it goes further than this, because it does in fact completely cover the XML domain, and so maps every XML construct to Java objects – including even those that mark-up text (like HTML) and Processing Instructions and even XML comments, which generally are not part of the document markup.

We saw this complete set of data describing an XML document referred to in Chapter 1 as the infoset. In order to represent the complete infoset of any XML document in objects, you need a set of classes like the DOM. Note that these pre-set DOM classes are a tiny sub-set of all possible Java classes. However, for documents, it is not possible to do all that much better from this, as documents don't map very intimately to objects. They are very different kinds of things.

It is worth noting that this generality of the DOM means that it can also map other kinds of information into objects – specifically, XML that marks up data ("data-centric") or objects ("object-centric"). Unfortunately, this very generality means that the information will not be made accessible in a contextual way – DOM document cannot define behavior. However, DOM is very good at representing data-centric information

Applications that use XML to represent data centric information can therefore devolve responsibility for maintaining the data structure to the document. Since an XML's structure can be rigidly defined, the application need not hold that information. This provides the benefit of reduced error checking, since the XML document can also specify more exactly data types, which also facilitates automatic type conversion.

Mapping in Theory

A mapping is an isomorphism – a point-to-point correspondence between two objects or concepts. I point at my nose; you point at yours, and so we know we are isomorphic. Like a street map of a city, we can identify an intersection on the map, and also visit the physical intersection, as one corresponds to the other.

Because XML and objects belong to discrete models – documents and in-memory data – we must consider how to anchor the end-points of the mapping in the XML and the objects. What exactly are we mapping from (what aspects); and what are we mapping to? When we have defined these two end-points, and the mapping between them, we can convert back and forth between XML and objects with ease.

The approach we take to defining these end points varies with our focus: Do we want to work with arbitrary XML? Or is our interest in data, such as that stored in a database? Or are we interested in arbitrary objects? That is, **documents**, **data** or **objects**. Perhaps surprisingly, these different perspectives require quite different approaches. First, let's look at arbitrary XML; that is, document type XML.

Document-Centric XML

We can define "document-centric" XML (as distinct from "data-centric" XML), as permitting mixed content with order significance, and as having an irregular structure, which carries important information. These are important to be able to mark up text and documents.

> *While the term "document-centric XML" is in common usage, this definition is adapted from "XML and Databases", by Ronald Bourret, and is available at:*
> http://www.rpbourret.com/xml/XMLAndDatabases.htm

Perhaps the most defining characteristic of "document-centric" XML is that it permits mixed content typical of marked-up text, as in XHTML:

```
<h1>
  In document-centric XML, a tag can contain both
  <i>tags</i>
  and
  <i> text</i>.
That is, mixed content.
</h1>
```

A DTD sufficient for this particular fragment is:

```
<!ELEMENT h1 (#PCDATA | i )*>
<!ELEMENT i (#PCDATA)>
```

The point is that the element <h1> can contain both the <i> tag and PCDATA text.

Mixed content is a common requirement in XML when it is used to mark up text for presentation. As the example shows, the basic idea of mixed content is that an element can contain both elements and text. The text forms a stream that overlaps many different elements. This text stream is actually important in and of itself as a piece of data and its structure is not defined by contained element. The structure of these elements helps us interpret parts of it.

Regarding the other two characteristics of order and irregular structure: note that this underlying stream of text makes the order of the tags very important, as reordering them would corrupt the fragment of the text within them. And, finally, note also that the existence of the contained tags is of course very important, as they communicate important information to better define the data.

In contrast, XML without mixed content forms a tree, with strict containment – that is, text only occurs in the leaves of the tree, and there can be no conceptual flow between different levels of tags. An example of XML in which tags can contain either other tags or text, but not mixed, is from the initial example:

```
<person>
  <name>Fred</name>
  <age>45</age>
</person>
```

And the corresponding DTD:

```
<!ELEMENT person (name, age)>
<!ELEMENT name (#PCDATA)>
<!ELEMENT age (#PCDATA)>
```

The text, in isolation, is meaningless. Only the structure gives it meaning.

Further, arbitrary XML also includes all legal XML, such as processing instructions, comments, and even DTD fragments and so on. A mapping from this to objects could be called XML-complete, because of this coverage.

Firstly, we have already seen a tool that can map between document-centric arbitrary XML and objects: DOM. The DOM specification defines the mapping between XML documents and a set of pre-defined objects, and JDOM defines a similar mapping. It is worth pointing out that this is very XML-based, in that all possible XML (within the definition of well-formedness) is mapped to a subset of objects – it cannot map other objects back to XML, simply because they are not part of the mapping.

This seems a fairly shallow kind of mapping, as all the classes used are generic and none are specific to the actual XML at hand. However, this is not the only way to perform such a mapping. XMLC is a tool that provides a slightly deeper kind of mapping, by creating some Java classes based on the XML, to provide alternative access points to the DOM objects.

XMLC

XMLC is the Enhydra application server's XML presentation compiler. Lutris Enhydra is a suite of server-side development tools and an application server, but we shall only be looking at the XMLC utility here. As at the time of writing, it is in version 2.0, and available for download at: http://xmlc.enhydra.org/

XMLC provides programmatic access points into an XML document's content. The person writing the XML document adds information that defines elements whose content is modifiable. The XML document defines the mapping, as well as being the data that is compiled into classes. These objects, when instantiated, can be used to modify the content of the document and then write the XML back out again:

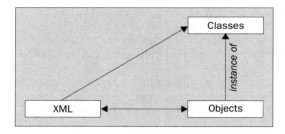

The element whose value is to be mapped is given an `id` attribute. The value of the `id` attribute then becomes the name of a field that will hold the content, as the following example shows. We begin by creating the XML document:

```
<html>
<head>
  <title id="title">-- content here --</title>
</head>
<body>
  <p id="content">-- content here --</p>
</body>
</html>
```

The `-- content here --` sections here should not be strictly necessary but XMLC compiles away any empty elements and this stops that.

Secondly, we compile this XML document into a class with XMLC. XMLC generates a class, whose constructor builds the DOM tree for the document "by hand", and also sets the value of the special fields, one for each element marked with an `id` attribute. In this example, we have marked both the title and a paragraph within the body of the HTML that represents the content of the HTML. The name of the field is "`element`" followed by the value of the `id` attribute.

Once we have classes that represent the data, we no longer require the XML document as the data and the access points to it are encapsulated in Java files produced. Let's see how this is translated to code by XMLC.

Installing the XMLC Utility

XMLC was written for a UNIX environment; however, there is a `bash` emulator called CygWin for Windows users. `bash` is a UNIX command line interface somewhat like the (DOS) Command Prompt. You can download CygWin from the same site as XMLC or directly from `http://sources.redhat.com/ cygwin/`. The installation for CygWin is quite simple and instructions are provided on the download page. UNIX users should be fairly comfortable with installing XMLC, and so we will only provide instructions for installation on Windows systems. We're using the version of the tools obtained from the Enhydra site.

Note that although a UNIX environment is needed to compile the classes, they are pure Java classes so they can be used on any system where a JVM is installed. The compiler expects JDK1.1.7B according to the documentation, although the system works fine with JDK1.3.

To install the bash emulator unzip the `cygnutools.zip` file directly into the root directory for the system drive, usually C:. This will create the following four directories:

```
C:\usr\
C:\bin\
C:\tmp\
C:\enhydra\
```

`C:\enhydra\` is the launch point for the emulator; in order to start it, click either `C:\enhydra\EnhydraShell_95_98` or `C:\enhydra\EnhydraShell_NT` as appropriate. A command line window will then open as follows:

```
EnhydraShell_NT                                                    _ □ ×

C:\enhydra>echo off

Welcome to The Enhydra Development Environment.
Many thanks to the Cygnus group for the GNU tools...

Enhydra$
```

Many of the commands that work in a Command Prompt will also work here. The first differences to notice is that UNIX uses a root by which all files are references as opposed to starting with drive letter. The second is that the file separator is the "/" character. As a result a path of

`C:\jdk1.3\bin\java`

has been converted to the UNIX environment as:

`//C/jdk1.3/bin/java`

We can now go ahead and install XMLC. Once you have downloaded XMLC unzip it; we will assume that it has been unzipped to `C:\java\`, this will create a sub folder called `xmlc2.0\` that will contain the XMLC distribution.

We install XMLC by invoking a file called `xmlc-config` which can be found in the root directory for the distribution from within the bash shell. To do so, start CygWin if it is not already running. `xmlc-config` must be invoked from the root directory for XMLC as it depends on this starting point to locate the executable and other resources it needs to run. We first change the working directory to `C:\java\xmlc2.0` as follows:

```
Enhydra$ cd //c/java/xmlc2.0
Enhydra$
```

You can list the files in this directory by entering the `dir` command or `ls`. This will give the following output:

```
Enhydra$ ls
READMEXMLC      dist        lib         xmlc-config
bin             doc
Enhydra$
```

You can see that `xmlc-config` is here, we can install it with the following command:

```
Enhydra$ bash xmlc-config -java //c/jdk1.3/bin/java -javac //c/jdk1.3/bin/javac
```

This informs XMLC that it can find `javac` and `java` in the directories listed. It will use these to compile and run the files. We should now be able to use XMLC to compile the file above.

Assuming that the HTML above has been stored in `C:\projavaxml\Chapter06\xmlc` and named `SimpleHtmlDoc.html`, we can compile the file as follows: we must first change the working directory so that we are in the same folder as the file using the `cd` command:

```
Enhydra$ cd //c/projavaxml/Chapter06/xmlc
```

To compile `SimpleHtmlDoc.html` we run the following command:

```
Enhydra$ //c/java/xmlc2.0/bin/xmlc -keep SimpleHtmlDoc.html
```

The `-keep` option instructs XMLC not to delete the Java source code. This will then create both a class file and a Java source file. Let's look at the code that is generated (formatted for readability):

```
import org.w3c.dom.*;
import org.enhydra.xml.xmlc.XMLCError;
import org.enhydra.xml.xmlc.XMLCUtil;
import org.enhydra.xml.xmlc.dom.XMLCDomFactory;

public class SimpleHtmlDoc
   extends org.enhydra.xml.xmlc.html.HTMLObjectImpl
   implements org.enhydra.xml.xmlc.XMLObject,
             org.enhydra.xml.xmlc.html.HTMLObject {
```

You can see that we will be using the DOM classes to hold the data in memory. XMLC does not do away with DOM but rather hides the DOM usage from us in intuitive method names. The two id attributes we defined `content` and `title` have been translated into properties, named `$elementContent` and `$elementTitle`. Dollar signs precede the property names in order to reduce the chance of collisions with existing variables, should we extend the class, or wish to edit it.

```
   private int $elementId_content = 8;
   private int $elementId_title = 3;

   private org.enhydra.xml.lazydom.html.HTMLBRElementImpl $element_Content;
   private org.enhydra.xml.lazydom.html.HTMLTitleElementImpl $element_Title;
```

Next come several properties that determine the formatting type, and inheritance chain, and include information about the source document and output Java file names. A static class initializer sets some defaults.

There are three constructors; the first is the default, no-argument constructor which simply calls the `buildDocument()` helper method, which build and populates the DOM `Document` object that holds the data for this object. The second takes a boolean argument `buildDom` which determines whether `buildDocument()` is called. A third document clones the `SimpleHtmlDoc` passed as an argument to it:

```
public SimpleHtmlDoc() {
  buildDocument();
}

public SimpleHtmlDoc(boolean buildDOM) {
  if (buildDOM) {
    buildDocument();
  }
}

public SimpleHtmlDoc(SimpleHtmlDoc src) {
  setDocument((Document)src.getDocument().cloneNode(true),
                      src.getMIMEType(),
                      src.getEncoding());
                      syncAccessMethods();
}
```

Notice that `buildDocument()` has public access so it can be called at a later point if the constructor was called with an argument of false:

```
public void buildDocument() {
  lazyDocument =
(org.enhydra.xml.lazydom.html.LazyHTMLDocument)(
    (org.enhydra.xml.xmlc.dom.lazydom.LazyDomFactory)
      fDOMFactory).createDocument(fTemplateDocument);

  lazyDocument.setPreFormatOutputOptions(fPreFormatOutputOptions);
  setDocument(lazyDocument, "text/html", null);
}
```

The `setDocument()` method, defined in the `HTMLObjectImpl` that this class extends, then calls the `buildTemplateSubDocument()` method. This method then creates each element, assigning with their value, and populates the document with them:

```
private static void
buildTemplateSubDocument(
                org.enhydra.xml.lazydom.LazyDocument document,
                org.w3c.dom.Node parentNode) {

Node $node0, $node1, $node2, $node3, $node4;
Element $elem0, $elem1, $elem2, $elem3;
Attr $attr0, $attr1, $attr2, $attr3;

$elem1 = document.getDocumentElement();
((org.enhydra.xml.lazydom.LazyElement)$elem1).makeTemplateNode(1);

((org.enhydra.xml.lazydom.LazyElement)$elem1)
                                    .setPreFormattedText("<HTML>");

$elem2 = document.createTemplateElement("HEAD", 2, "<HEAD>");
$elem1.appendChild($elem2);
```

```
    $elem3 = document.createTemplateElement("TITLE", 3,
                                    "<TITLE id=\"title\">");
    $elem2.appendChild($elem3);


    $attr3 = document.createTemplateAttribute("id", 4);
    $elem3.setAttributeNode($attr3);
    $node4 = document.createTemplateTextNode("title", 5, "title");
    $attr3.appendChild($node4);

    $node4 = document.createTemplateTextNode("HelloWorld 0.8.3",
                                    6,
                                    "HelloWorld 0.8.3");


    $elem3.appendChild($node4);

    $elem2 = document.createTemplateElement("BODY", 7, "<BODY>");
    $elem1.appendChild($elem2);

    $elem3 = document.createTemplateElement("BR", 8, "<BR id=\"content\">");
    $elem2.appendChild($elem3);


    $attr3 = document.createTemplateAttribute("id", 9);
    $elem3.setAttributeNode($attr3);

    $node4 = document.createTemplateTextNode("content", 10, "content");
    $attr3.appendChild($node4);

    $elem3 = document.createTemplateElement("BR", 11, "<BR>");
    $elem2.appendChild($elem3);
}
```

Two methods are available to get the content of the HTML document, getElementContent() and getElementTitle(). The basis for this is not that we include content in the document that can be used to create the required content, but rather to allow us load a document into an instance of SimpleHtmlDoc. This is done by passing an instance of Node to the syncWithDocument() method shown last.

```java
public org.w3c.dom.html.HTMLBRElement getElementContent() {
  if (($element_Content == null) && ($elementId_content >= 0)) {
    $element_Content =
      (org.enhydra.xml.lazydom.html.HTMLBRElementImpl)
        lazyDocument.getNodeById($elementId_content);
  }
  return $element_Content;
}

public org.w3c.dom.html.HTMLTitleElement getElementTitle() {
  if (($element_Title == null) && ($elementId_title >= 0)) {
    $element_Title =
      (org.enhydra.xml.lazydom.html.HTMLTitleElementImpl)
        lazyDocument.getNodeById($elementId_title);
  }
  return $element_Title;
}
```

We can set the content of the `<title>` and `<body>` elements with the `setTextTitle()` and `setTextContent()`

```
public void setTextTitle(String text) {
  if (($element_Title == null) && ($elementId_title >= 0)) {
    $element_Title =
      (org.enhydra.xml.lazydom.html.HTMLTitleElementImpl)
        lazyDocument.getNodeById($elementId_title);
  }
  doSetText($element_Title, text);
}

protected void syncWithDocument(Node node) {
  if (node instanceof Element) {
    String id = ((Element)node).getAttribute("id");
    if (id.length() == 0) {
    } else if (id.equals("content")) {
      $elementId_content = 8;
      $element_Content =
        (org.enhydra.xml.lazydom.html.HTMLBRElementImpl)node;

    } else if (id.equals("title")) {
      $elementId_title = 3;
      $element_Title =
        (org.enhydra.xml.lazydom.html.HTMLTitleElementImpl)node;

    }
  }

  Node child = node.getFirstChild();
  while (child != null) {
    syncWithDocument(child);
    child = child.getNextSibling();
  }
 }
}
```

The `syncWithDocument()` method checks that the `Node` passed to it is an element (rather than a processing instruction or a comment) and then iterates through its children, calling the `syncWithDocument()` method on each of those.

The compiled class also inherits a special `toDocument()` method, which serializes the DOM to XML, and so completes the mapping. We can test this simply with the following Java class, `simpleTest`. Once the work has been done, this stage is very straightforward. We instantiate `SimpleHtmlDoc`, set the text content for the title and content and output the result to a file.

```
public class simpleTest {

  public static void main(String[] args) {

    SimpleHtmlDoc simpleDocument = new SimpleHtmlDoc();

    simpleDocument.setTextDynamicTitle("My Dynamic Title");
    simpleDocument.setTextDynamicContent("My dynamic Content");

    System.out.println(simpleDocument.toDocument());

  }
 }
```

The result is as shown below:

There is a slightly different naming convention for span tags, which can be used to mark arbitrary sections of text.

> *XMLC also has several other features, which are covered at*
> http://staff.plugged.net.au/dwood/xmlc/dynamic.html

Note that everything is done strictly in terms of the DOM – that is the tree that is built, and the specially marked nodes are not stored separately but are in the DOM tree, and an internal reference is maintained to access them directly. The underlying DOM tree is complete, and the access points provided by XMLC are strictly in addition to it. Thus, the objects returned by these access methods are just ordinary DOM objects, and can be manipulated as DOM objects normally are. These access points are thus the only things provided by XMLC in terms of a more specific mapping.

Using XMLC As a Template Tool

XMLC's primary usefulness is in creating a class that represents a template XML document. We first define a template XML document and mark sections to request access to the element's content. From the class generate, we can instantiate objects in order to manipulate them and the document, allowing us to dynamically generate XML documents based on the template, like a form letter, with blank fields. The static parts can include graphics, color and layout, as well as boilerplate text.

The basic idea is a tradeoff: compiling the class from reading the XML is relatively slow, but writing out the XML again is relatively fast. Once the XML is compiled to a class, the data at access points can be changed and the new XML quickly written out.

This simplifies access to the XML document and defines intuitive access methods into sections of the document. In a way, XML is like an ancient tape drive, where you must read the whole thing in sequentially, and write in a similar fashion, from start to finish in one continuous stream. XMLC gives us a random access to it, like RAM or a disk drive, so that you can read and write just the specific part you need to change.

This provides a performance gain only when we're working within an XML template: that is, the XML is mostly static layout, and only particular parts (the access points) require dynamic data. By pre-compiling the DOM tree creation, XMLC cuts short the parsing step, so that we can update just a specific part – piecemeal – similarly to how SQL updates a database. XMLC provides additional access points for the things that we often want to change, like a custom index. This gives performance slightly closer to that of the fine-grained access of databases. Though of course, the XML is still actually being written out as a whole – XMLC only cuts short the parsing phase.

Another strength related to the use of templates is that a programmer can modify just those indicated points, by accessing Java objects, without needing to see or think about the layout. Similarly, the graphic artist who designed the layout can continue to work purely with graphic tools, and not worry about embedded code. Similar benefits may also hold for the writer of the boilerplate text.

This tool is an alternative to embedded approaches, such as JSP (Java embedded in HTML) and servlets (HTML embedded in Java). Such embedding can be confusing. There is a fundamental mismatch, as position in a markup language usually indicates layout, whereas position in Java means order of execution. It's often best to keep them separated. The only contract required between these two parties is agreement on the ID attributes used to indicate the access points, and what sort of nodes can go at those ID locations.

Even if the XML is changed completely, so long as the contract is kept and the ID attributes retain their name, if XMLC is used to compile an entirely new class to represent it, the access methods will remain exactly the same as before. The Java code will still work. A nice side effect is that a compile time error will result if the contract is broken, making debugging easier.

Summary of the mapping

The mapping between XML and classes is based on the DOM specification. The access point layer is defined by the XML author with an id attribute, and specifies the element that will be accessed, and the name of the generated access point.

The mapping is to a class or type. The object end-point is anchored by defining the API of the class – that is, the access methods and their names. The XML end-point is anchored by the ID id attributes. The way these end-points are mapped is defined by the DOM and its nodes. However, note that the mapping is set by the XML end-point, and the object side is determined entirely from this, as the diagram at the beginning of this section on XMLC shows.

Because XMLC is built upon DOM, it is XML-complete, and can represent any XML whatsoever. This includes "document-centric" XML, with mixed content of tags and raw text together, order significance and irregular structure.

Incidentally, XMLC's architecture, which consists of building on top of the DOM, is an especially useful approach, since a great many other tools also do this. This makes the DOM a kind of in-memory lingua franca for XML, which can be modified piecemeal, and yield much better performance than writing and reading actual XML documents or streams in between the tools. That is, the in-memory DOM tree of Java objects really is a Random Access Device. Any API that can handle DOM Node objects can be used in conjunction with XMLC.

Data-Centric XML

"Data-centric" XML (as distinct from document-centric XML above) is XML that marks up data. We can define it as not permitting mixed content, its order is not significant and it has a regular, predictable structure.

Firstly, the lack of mixed content means that the XML forms a tree, with strict containment – that is, text only occurs in the leaves of the tree, and there can be no conceptual flow between different levels of tags.

Secondly, order is not significant. The meaning of the XML would be unaltered if the age came before the name – order is not (or at least, should not) be significant in data-centric XML. Unfortunately, it does become awkward to represent this in a DTD, especially for larger numbers of contained tags, as DTDs were not designed for this usage.

Thirdly, the structure is regular, as the reading application will expect these two fields, if it is mapping them to a class or database table. The structure does not convey information in itself.

Data-centric XML carries structured data, and so already resembles objects – it has its complex (or compound) types, like classes; and it also has simple types, like the Java primitives `int` and `boolean`. The defining characteristics are:

❑ No mixed content

❑ Primitive types

❑ Compound types

❑ No typed references (which object-centric XML requires, as we will see in the next section)

We can also have references (multiple and cyclic) in data-centric XML, such as those described by the ID and IDREF attribute types of DTDs, therefore represent graphs in general. Although databases usually do support *typed* references, DTDs do not (at least, at present). That is, they do not support constraints on what tag can be referenced from where, in the way that what tags can be contained by other tags are constrained, as discussed in the earlier "*Objects to XML*" section.

However, this lack of typed references is not so serious for marked up data. Since the information is rigidly structured this structure is generally known to the application, and it need not be validated by the DTD. However, it does mean that the self-documentation aspect of the data is incomplete, which is not ideal for reverse engineering, interoperability and coping with evolving applications and so on.

Fortunately, references in data-centric XML are comparatively rare in practice. While the references can, and often are, present in the underlying data source, extracted data is more commonly in the form of a tree (tables are a form of a data tree; that is, we have a table that contains rows that contain data elements) than as a graph – from classical taxonomy to the Java class hierarchy.

This is partly because when stored in a database, each reference requires an additional `select` command to access the data from a table, imposing a performance hit on references, which discourages their use. This is fortunate, as tree structures can be represented entirely as nested tags, which is much simpler and more human readable than when they contain `ID` and `IDREF` type attributes.

JAXB (The API Formerly Known As Adelard)

JAXB (Java API for XML Binding), formerly know as Adelard, is one of Sun's planned extensions to Java 2 platform, designed to provide automated XML to Object mapping. It is expected that it will be released as a preview technology some time in spring of 2001. While it originally had intended to make use of schemas as a basis, at the time of writing, the absence of a finalized XML Schema specification from the W3C means that it currently plans to simulate some of the features of XML Schema by supplementing DTDs with a "binding schema", which is a schema-like document.

Although very little information is available about it, Sun's JABX/Adelard project will become the standard for data-centric XML - when and if it is released. Despite the current uncertainty over its details, and when and if it will be available, it is well worth considering as an example of the issues in implementing an XML-Object mapping for data-centric XML.

JAXB generates and compiles new classes based on a mapping described by the DTD, and objects belonging to these new classes can automatically map their data to and from XML. This mapping of classes to XML is also called marshalling. These two levels are represented by a modified version of the diagram we saw earlier:

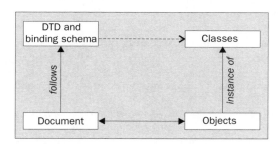

The difference with the earlier mapping for document-centric XML, is that the top arrow is now one way only: JAXB can derive classes from a DTD and a binding schema document, but not vice versa.

In order to define the binding, and once the DTD has been written, the DTD is compiled into a schema type document that can then be edited to add the bindings that DTD cannot define. The binding schema, together with the DTD, will then be mapped to Java classes therefore defining the XML-Object mapping. This also means that a particular JAXB mapping will not handle any XML – only XML that conforms to the compiled DTD.

There is also some debate as to whether JAXB will support the full range of DTDs, or some subset. Apart from the mixed content constraint, a further subset is likely, considering some of the surprising complexities of DTD-class mapping possible.

On the object side, JAXB can only map XML to those classes which it itself compiled. However, the objects in question are not application classes, but JAXB classes. This is similar in some ways, then, to the DOM. Because the objects do not have any methods from the application, they are pure data objects, from the application's perspective. This is not usually the way we like to work in object-oriented programming (objects are data plus behavior).

However, as data objects, the generated classes can be passed around as arguments, or incorporated into user objects by composition. They can also be extended, so that they become part of user objects themselves, and special pains have been taken in the JAXB specifications to allow this to work. However, this requires user objects to be designed with JAXB as their foundation. Although this kind of problem has been addressed for years in the context of IDLs (Interface Definition Language for CORBA and other interoperability mechanisms), anyone who has worked with IDL will admit it tends to be awkward.

The benefits of JAXB are similar to those of XMLC above. JAXB automates the parsing and outputting of documents, a significant benefit, as well as automating the marshalling and unmarshalling of objects to XML. Ultimately, we don't have to worry about XML from within our programs at all.

Binding Schema

The binding schema makes up for the shortfall between DTD and XML Schema by specifying how the XML tags are to be mapped into objects. A tool is provided to automatically generate a default binding schema from the DTD, which we can then edit. Although details are not yet available, it would seem necessary that all of these must be correct:

❏ All attributes are mapped to primitive types or Strings

❏ All tags with only character data are mapped to primitive types or Strings

❏ All tags containing other tags (compound types) must be mapped to classes.

The assumption here must be that tags with mixed content (character data and tags) will be disallowed.

However, it is simply not possible to infer the possible primitive types from a DTD – it does not even contain any sample values (for example: we might guess that character data of "100" is a numeric field, but there's no way to know this from just the DTD). The choice of any primitive type must therefore be made manually. It is quite possible that JAXB does not support this degree of mapping to primitive types, and instead maps all attribute values and character data simply to strings. In fact, this course is suggested by the `ShoeOrder` example which was given in the original data binding design note on Sun's Java Community Process site, and which we will be looking at a little later on. However, this would throw the work of parsing Strings to `int`, `double` and other primitive types back onto the user, who must then also address the problems of parsing values like `NaN`, and ensuring that precision is exactly preserved.

The JAXB specification is being developed under the Java Community Process under Java Specification Request number 31 (JSR-31), XML Data Binding. The JSR homepage is at http://java.sun.com/aboutJava/communityprocess/jsr/jsr_031_xmld.html, and provides information on the status of the specification, and also a link to the original data binding white paper, "An XML Data-Binding Facility for the Java Platform ", at http://java.sun.com/xml/jaxp-docs-1.0.1/docs/bind.pdf.

Using XML Schema would make things a lot easier, mainly because it supports the definition of primitive types explicitly! This was the long-held plan for JAXB, but XML Schema has been repeatedly delayed, and the need to release JAXB has forced this route to be abandoned. Also, DTDs are a ubiquitous standard at this point and are stable, whereas XML Schema are in limited use, and may well change considerably before their final approval, as they have already. The Schema specification is also quite weighty and complex, not to mention controversial in some circles, which may hamper its widespread adoption. However, it is expected that when XML Schema is released, that JAXB will be adapted to support it.

DTD-Class Mapping

There are a number of common constructs in DTDs that do not map obviously to classes. These are problems for any data-centric DTD-class mapping, though it is not clear how or if JAXB will deal with them. These are some examples of fairly simple DTD elements which can cause such problems:

```
<!ELEMENT Sequence (A,B,C)>
<!ELEMENT Choice (A|B|C)>
<!ELEMENT Number (A*,B+,C?)>
<!ELEMENT CompoundExpression ((A,B,C)|(C,B,AD))>
```

Let's take these in turn.

Sequences: (A,B,C)

Firstly, this aspect of DTDs is not properly a part of data-centric XML. Of course, the tags will be laid down in a specific order; it is just that these are not significant. The fields of a class have no defined order; however, the getters and setters of JAXB could in fact be imposing an order on the elements internally – for example, by accessing an array, or vector of values – instead of using fields for the values. Or the ordering could simply be imposed by the marshalling logic.

Choices: (A|B|C)

The "|" operator corresponds to type substitution in Java, which is possible with interfaces and supertypes. For example:

```
class Choice {
  ChoiceI choiceI;
}
interface ChoiceI {}
class A implements ChoiceI {}
class B implements ChoiceI {}
class C implements ChoiceI {}
```

Thus, just as a <Choice> tag can hold a <A>, <B> or <C> tag, a Choice object field of type Choice can hold an object of type A, B or C. However, it seems unlikely that JAXB has actually implemented this functionality. Note that these interfaces would be used purely as markers, for type substitutability, and not contain any method definitions.

Number: (A*,B+,C?)

Arrays are the natural way to represent multiple values in Java, especially as they are strongly typed. This may be how JAXB will implement this aspect of DTDs, using perhaps indexed getter and setter methods. The "?" may be adequately represented by a reference field which either contains an object, or null, but primitives can't make this distinction.

```
class Number {
  A[] aArray;
  B[] bArray;
  C c;
}
```

However, the internal implementation shouldn't worry us; we should concentrate on the API exposed in the form of getters and setters.

Compound Expressions: ((A,B,C)|(C,B,AD))

The trouble with compound expressions is that they require the creation of intermediate anonymous types. Note that both Choice and Number also require extra interfaces and array objects to be created that don't correspond to tags in the DTD. The present example above could be deconstructed into:

```
<!ELEMENT Compound (Anonymous1|Anonymous2)>
<!ELEMENT Anonymous1 (A,B,C)>
<!ELEMENT Anonymous2 (C,B,AD)>
```

Now, two anonymous classes can be created which implement the Compound interface.

```
class Compound {
  CompoundI compoundI;
}
interface Compound I {}
class Anonymous1 implements Compound I{
  A a;
  B b;
}
class Anonymous2 implements CompoundI {
  C c;
  D d;
}
```

Note also that in the preceding examples, the tag name has been assumed to coincide with a class name. However, it is much more likely that JAXB will follow the Schema lead, and use field names as the tag names, and associate a type (class) with them in the binding schema.

Implementation

The foregoing has been about the mapping used by JAXB; we now turn to how JAXB will be implemented in practice, and how to use it. First, here is some example XML and compiled code, taken from pages 2 and 5 respectively from the design note "An XML Data-Binding Facility for the Java Platform": http://java.sun.com/xml/jaxp-docs-1.0.1/docs/bind.pdf.

In the example, a typical XML document conforming to an unspecified DTD or schema is shown, as follows:

```
<ShoeOrder id="4040458" style="Sandal">
  <color>Brown</color>
  <size>9 1/2</size>
  <width>AA</width>
</ShoeOrder>
```

The associated XML Schema (not given here, as JAXB now uses its "binding schema") specifies the allowable values for color, size and width; but most interesting are the id and style attributes, which are of types ID and IDREF, respectively. That is, the id="4040458" makes this tag something that can be referred to from another tag, while the style="Sandal" actually does refer to some other tag. This implies that JAXB can deal with arbitrary graphs of data. However, as discussed previously, neither DTDs nor XML Schema are sufficiently powerful to constrain the types of the tags referenced.

A class, describing objects that could hold the data from such a document, is later then shown:

```
public class ShoeOrder {
  public ShoeOrder(String id, Style style, String color, String size, String
width);

  public String getId();
  public void setId(String id);

  public Style getStyle()
  public void setStyle(Style style);
```

```
    public String getColor();
    public void setColor(String color);

    public String getSize();
    public void setSize(String size);

    public String getWidth();
    public void setWidth(String width);

    public void marshal(OutputStream out) throws IOException;
    public static ShoeOrder unmarshal(InputStream in) throws IOException;
}
```

Note the use of getters and setters: these are used to access the fields of the data object. When JAXB was to perform extensive range validation of data, this programmatic indirection was important to allow the values to be checked for every update. It is possible that if the getters and setters of JavaBeans are to be used for validation, the constrained properties API of JavaBeans could be used for validation.

However, now that range validation is not part of the first version of JAXB, the package would seem to be much easier to use if the data fields were simply made public, in the normal way. Arguably, this would also be more logical, because they really are public, since they come from open, human readable XML.

Almost all the accessors use `Strings`, and not primitives, even when it might be appropriate (that is `int` for `id`). The one exception is the `Style` object, which would be the one referred to in the XML as "Sandal". One curious thing about this is how JAXB knows that this is the type of object referred to, as it is not indicated in the XML Schema. It may be that it is simply inferred from the name of the attribute: that is, the first letter of "style" is simply pushed to uppercase, to form the class name "`Style`". A related issue is where this `style` tag appears in the XML. It is often natural to nest it within the parent tag, inline; however, all such tags referenced could alternatively be lumped together into a preamble.

Note also the `marshal` method is used serialize the object to XML in an output stream, and the `unmarshal` method creates an instance of the class from XML in an input stream (which is why it is static).

These are some possible reasons for the use of getters and setters:

❑   For ease of retrofitting range validation in future releases

❑   For ordered tags to be represented in classes, without implementing them in fields

Another thing to note is that the compiler generates parameterized types: JAXB has parameterized types in the limited sense that the `unmarshal()` from XML method of the compiled class has the correct compile time return type for that class. This is in contrast to Java's own serialization mechanism, which requires a cast from `Object` to the correct type. This minor benefit of JAXB is entirely due to JAXB compiling code: if we wrote the classes by hand, we typically would do just the same thing. Note that this may not be true in the final JAXB implementation – this opinion is derived from the `ShoeOrder` example class above. If the final version, for example, generates classes which inherit their marshaling and unmarshaling capabilities from a superclass, rather than it being generated by the JAXB compiler, this facility will be lost.

When writing to or reading from XML, JAXB objects appear to take the stream for the XML as an argument. This is in contrast to Java's own serialization mechanism, which extends streams, and so already has a stream, and need not be supplied one.

Conclusions on JAXB

Historically, the central theme of JAXB was validation, in terms of allowable ranges of values, but that was when it planned to use XML Schema. With the switch to DTDs, this becomes impractical. This is probably a good thing, as XML-Object mapping and range validation are quite distinct tasks, and it is probably beneficial to concentrate on one such task at a time, rather than attempting to serve two masters.

Should we use JAXB?

❑ The launch date has been delayed many times, and it appears to not actually exist yet.

❑ Manually editing a binding schema seems very awkward. Another language to learn?

❑ Getters and setters are an awkward and unnecessary way to access data.

❑ Pure data objects, lacking methods, are not ideal for object oriented programming.

At present, it appears that JAXB will not be a successful technology.

Object-Centric XML

We have been talking about "data-centric" and "document-centric" markup, terms which are relatively well understood. But for the purposes of this discussion, it is important to note that we haven't yet described a mapping which is capable of writing any Java object out into an XML document. For this purpose, we need to introduce a new concept – **Object-centric** XML.

"Object-centric" XML exists completely in the object domain – that is, any object can be mapped to and from XML. Because the XML and object domains are so different, this total coverage of the object domain means that the XML domain will not be totally covered: in fact, the mapping will be between objects and some specialized object markup language, an XML application designed to describe such object graphs.

Complete coverage of the object domain requires our mapping to be aware of two specific features which object data structures possess: run-time types and graphs (typed references). A mapping that does not cater for these features will not generate XML that can be used to re-create the original objects correctly. This is in addition to the primitive types and complex/compound/structured types (classes) of "data-centric" XML. It's all about types.

SOAP (Simple Object Access Protocol)

SOAP is primarily a Web services protocol employing XML over HTTP, like RPC-XML, so it has transport and method-invocation components – we'll be looking at these in detail later in Chapter 19. At the heart of it is an object encoding protocol, which is why we are interested in it. Though SOAP is far from being a WWW Consortium recommendation – it is merely a "note" – since it is pivotal for Microsoft's .NET strategy, and has recently received an endorsement from the OASIS ebXML consortium, it is likely to be important in the future. But quite apart from this, it is the only well-known standard that can actually map arbitrary object graphs to XML. Note that it only specifies the mappings: at present no Java implementation fully automates XML-Object mapping, and none address Schema-Class mapping at all.

Type and variable handling in SOAP relies heavily on XML schemas. Unfortunately, the XML Schema specifications have changed significantly since the last release of SOAP (version 1.1, 8 May 2000), making most of the examples given in the specifications incompatible with the current version of XML Schema. Since the original examples are available in the SOAP specifications, we attempt to provide something more here, by trying update SOAP to the current XML Schema.

SOAP borrows from XML Schema the inheritance mechanism and the related run-time typing, which can be used for polymorphism. Unfortunately, XML schemas do not support multiple inheritance in any way, and so cannot represent Java interfaces.

Although SOAP adds to all the primitive XML schema data types the ability to reference, and to be referenced using the uriReference and ID types respectively, unfortunately, just as in XML Schema, these are not typed references; so while it is possible to represent graphs in SOAP, it is not possible to validate their structure with respect to a schema. This is a serious flaw, since validation of structure is perhaps the fundamental purpose of using types in documents such as schemas or DTDs.

SOAP also adds to XML schemas a comprehensive array typing mechanism which can represent all possible Java array types – indeed, it is significantly more powerful than this.

To complete this brief overview, the following is an example of a complete SOAP message, with the section of interest highlighted – the object encoding protocol section, with the GetLastTradePriceResponse element (the transport and method-invocation components are covered in Chapter 19):

```
HTTP/1.1 200 OK
Content-Type: text/xml; charset="utf-8"
Content-Length: nnnn

<SOAP-ENV:Envelope
   xmlns:SOAP-ENV="http://schemas.xmlsoap.org/soap/envelope/"
   SOAP-ENV:encodingStyle="http://schemas.xmlsoap.org/soap/encoding/"/>
   <SOAP-ENV:Body>
      <m:GetLastTradePriceResponse xmlns:m="Some-URI">
         <Price>34.5</Price>
      </m:GetLastTradePriceResponse>
   </SOAP-ENV:Body>
</SOAP-ENV:Envelope>
```

Note the m namespace. It seems superfluous, but this is one method for indicating the schema that defines the types for these XML values. It is a bit like a Java import statement. Specifying it in an attribute of the GetLastTradePriceResponse confines its effect to this tag and its contents.

Java's int, boolean and other primitive types are "simple" types in SOAP, whereas classes and arrays are "compound" types – they are types that can contain more than one thing. Classes contain fields, which are accessed by name (which must be unique). Arrays contain elements, which don't have a name – they are accessed by their ordinal position (which is, by nature unique).

Strings are ambivalent in SOAP. Though they are really objects, they are also treated as primitives for convenience, in both Java and in SOAP. Java overloads "+" for concatenation of strings, and automatically creates objects from string literals. In SOAP, they are "simple" types, and yet can also be referenced with id and href. SOAP also treats arrays of bytes in this way, which Java does not.

263

Here is the initial XML-Object mapping example again, with the XML Schema based declaration of SOAP:

```
<person>
  <name>Fred</name>
  <age>45</age>
</person>

<element name="person">
  <complexType>
    <element name="name" type="SOAP-ENC:string"/>
    <element name="age" type="xsd:int"/>
  </complexType>
</element>
```

This schema fragment uses an **anonymous type**, in that the type is both defined and used at once, like an anonymous class in Java. The only thing differing from a pure XML Schema, is the SOAP-ENC:string. All this does is add in the reference attributes. The SOAP-ENC namespace refers to http://schemas.xmlsoap.org/soap/encoding/ (and the full schema is available at that address).

Every tag is the name of a field, unless it is accessed by ordinal position (like an array). Each tag also has a type. This can be specified within the tag itself as a run-time type. It can also be implied in other ways: from the schema or from the basetype of an array. The run-time class can be a subtype – that is, the schema is like a class definition, which specifies the compile-time type of a field, whereas the explicit type given in a tag is the run-time type of the object.

Run-time types

Classes define the contents of objects – they are very much a typing mechanism. Just as primitive types describe whether the value of a field is a boolean or an int, a class defines what an object can contain, in terms of its fields, and their type. Note especially that an object field of a particular type can also hold objects which are sub-types (or sub-classes) of that field. An immediate example is a Vector, which can contain objects of class Object – which includes all possible objects, since they are all sub-classes of Object. This is related to the concept of "substitutability", that one type can take the place of another in such circumstances. For example, a subclass type can take the place of the superclass type, but not the other way around. This polymorphism is a very useful side-effect of inheritance, and one that XML Schema and SOAP support.

To illustrate this, we will first define a base class, and derive two further types from it (closely based on the example in section 4.1 of the "XML Schema Part 0: Primer"). The idea is that an Address is a generic idea, but that US and UK addresses differ principally in having a Zip codes and postcodes, respectively:

```
<schema targetNamespace="http://www.example.com/IPO"
    xmlns="http://www.w3.org/2001/XMLSchema"
    xmlns:ipo="http://www.example.com/IPO">

  <complexType name="Address">
    <sequence>
      <element name="name"   type="string"/>
      <element name="street" type="string"/>
      <element name="city"   type="string"/>
    </sequence>
  </complexType>
```

The US address, with state and Zip code. Note that its extension base is the generic address:

```
<complexType name="USAddress">
  <complexContent>
    <extension base="ipo:Address">
      <sequence>
        <element name="state" type="ipo:USState"/>
        <element name="zip"   type="positiveInteger"/>
      </sequence>
    </extension>
  </complexContent>
</complexType>
```

The UK address, with just a postcode. Again, the extension base is the generic address:

```
<complexType name="UKAddress">
  <complexContent>
    <extension base="ipo:Address">
      <sequence>
        <element name="postcode" type="ipo:UKPostcode"/>
      </sequence>
    </extension>
  </complexContent>
</complexType>
```

Next, we define a type that can use the above types:

```
<complexType name="PurchaseOrderType">
  <sequence>
    <element name="shipTo"   type="ipo:Address"/>
    <element name="billTo"   type="ipo:Address"/>
  </sequence>
</complexType>
</schema>
```

Finally, having declared all the types, here is some XML that illustrates the actual polymorphism:

```
<ipo:purchaseOrder
  xmlns:xsi="http://www.w3.org/1999/XMLSchema-instance"
  xmlns:ipo="http://www.example.com/IPO">

  <shipTo exportCode="1" xsi:type="ipo:UKAddress">
    <name>Helen Zoe</name>
    <street>47 Eden Street</street>
    <city>Cambridge</city>
    <postcode>CB1 1JR</postcode>
  </shipTo>

  <billTo xsi:type="ipo:USAddress">
    <name>Robert Smith</name>
    <street>8 Oak Avenue</street>
    <city>Old Town</city>
    <state>PA</state>
    <zip>95819</zip>
  </billTo>
</ipo:purchaseOrder>
```

We use the xsi ("XML Schema instance") namespace for xsi:type, since the XML is the instance (or value) of the type. The <shipTo> and <billTo> elements are constrained by the Schema to be of type USAddress or UKAddress (or, the supertype, Address). In the example, shipTo is of type UKAddress, and billTo is of type USAddress. If these run-time types were omitted – that is, if there was no xsi:type attribute then these fields would default to the static compile-time type of Address.

Incidentally, XML schemas use the name of a field as an element name, and the type of it in an attribute. This isn't really right, as the content (the tags permitted inside) is determined by the element name and attributes, rather than the element name alone. It therefore would be more logical to have the runtime type as the element name, which then would naturally determine the element content. However, using the fieldname as the element name allows for easy compatibility with existing data-centric XML, which is statically typed and so does not require run-time types to be stated.

Interestingly, SOAP does provide the ability to use the run-time type as the element name, which is necessary for arrays, since they don't have a field name to serve as the element name. However, this can't be used to reverse the roles in general, because there is then no way to represent the field name when it is present, as a name attribute could.

Unfortunately, this is the only kind of substitutability of *types* that XML Schema, and therefore SOAP, permits. Although this inheritance from a single superclass maps accurately onto Java superclasses, there is no equivalent to Java interfaces. For the purposes of substitution, Java interfaces are a kind of multiple-inheritance mechanism, for they allow an object of a class which implements several interfaces to be held by a field of any of those interface type – and not just of its superclasses.

Typed References

SOAP uses href attributes of type uriReference, to refer to id attributes, of type ID; thus mixing conventions from both DTDs and HTML. However, these are not typed:

```
<greeting id="String-0">Hello</greeting>
<salutation href="#String-0"/>
```

```
<element name="greeting" type="SOAP-ENC:string"/>
<element name="salutation" type="SOAP-ENC:string"/>
```

Note the # prefix of href to indicate that the reference is within the same document. Note that some type safety can be provided by the convention of using values for the type attributes in the same way as the above incorporate string. However, this convention is not maintained by the specification, nor enforced.

So, while arbitrary graphs can be represented, these are not typed references – all the validation power of a schema goes out the window if any object whatsoever can be brought in by an untyped reference. For example, a Person object might be needed, but a Car object referenced instead.

It is curious that XML schemas make these two omissions (interfaces and typed references) when they have enough features to fill several hundreds of pages of specifications. Perhaps it is because it attempts to serve three masters (objects with inheritance and polymorphism, data with validation of ranges etc., and documents with DTD emulation, that it does not serve objects on their own in an ideal fashion.

Arrays

Array types have a very complete specification in SOAP, representing not just multi-dimensional arrays; and arrays of arrays; but also multi-dimensional arrays of multi-dimensional arrays. That is, in Java you can say:

```
Object [][][] a = new Object[1][1][1] { new Object[1][1] };
```

This creates a three-dimensional array, whose sole element is another two-dimensional array. SOAP can represent this as a single type rather than a composite:

```
Object[1,1][1,1,1]
```

that is, reading right-to-left (the opposite of Java), a three-dimensional array [,,], of a two-dimensional array [,], of basetype Object (assuming an appropriate Schema definition of Object). This reverse ordering makes some sense, as we read towards the base type. This is a stronger array definition than Java has – although it is unclear in what circumstances this would be useful.

Note that this means that Java classes are not sufficiently strong to ensure that the types specified by SOAP are maintained by the objects.

Because this array typing is purely a feature of SOAP, we must use the encoding namespace to refer to it. This is conventionally bound to SOAP-ENC. In the following example (taken from the SOAP specifications), in an array of integers there are two types: a compile-time type from the schema fragment, of SOAP-ENC:Array, and also a run-time type of xsd:int[2].

```
<element name="myFavoriteNumbers" type="SOAP-ENC:Array"/>
<myFavoriteNumbers SOAP-ENC:arrayType="xsd:int[2]">
  <number>3</number>
  <number>4</number>
</myFavoriteNumbers>
```

An example of a multi-dimensional array, where one of the types of the array is given as the element name:

```
<SOAP-ENC:Array SOAP-ENC:arrayType="xsd:string[2,3]">
  <item>r1c1</item>
  <item>r1c2</item>
  <item>r1c3</item>
  <item>r2c1</item>
  <item>r2c2</item>
  <item>r2c3</item>
</SOAP-ENC:Array>
```

Aside from the types of arrays, array content is also considered. A sub-range of an array can be represented using an offset and a length; and a sparse array can be represented by specifying just the specific values present. This amounts to a naive compression scheme, which sounds attractive, but is probably not worth the extra complication.

Implementations

There are several implementations of SOAP available, but at the time of writing, none of them have fully implemented the encoding scheme, which is the aspect of interest for this chapter. For example, at the time of writing, the latest release of **Apache SOAP**, (based on the IBM SOAP4J code, which was donated) version 2.1 (of 5 Feb 2001), did not implement id and href – the crucial feature for object graphs – nor multi-dimensional arrays. This appears to be due to a general focus on the transport and method invocation aspects of SOAP, and so the less pressing work on encoding is deferred, leaving it to users to perform the encoding manually. To check the current status of the Apache SOAP implementation, you can look at http://xml.apache.org/soap/features.html

Conclusions on SOAP

SOAP basically borrows all the XML Schema typing mechanisms, adding only the arrays and facilitating references. The great potential of the Class-Schema mapping is that we could in principle create the SOAP-style Schema from classes automatically, and vice versa. With similar tools available for other languages, we could have automatic cross-language interoperability.

However, this utopia is a little flawed: while the above certainly will make it tremendously easier to transfer data across languages, it does not address the related but different problem of transporting data across applications. It is highly unlikely that any two applications will store their data in objects in exactly the same way, especially across languages, whose idioms may suggest quite different approaches. Therefore, some extra level of mapping is required. One solution to this, an "Abstract Data Layer", is discussed in Chapter 16 "*XML-Object Mapping and Peristence*", where an implementation is also given.

Note further, that if we compile classes automatically from the schema, then there will be pure data objects, as with JAXB, and in general we will still need to move that data into our own objects, where we have the specific methods to deal with them. That is, assuming an object oriented approach is appropriate for the task.

JSX: Java Serialization to XML

In the meantime, another object-centric XML-Object mapping project is fully implemented. **JSX (Java Serialization to XML)** implements run-time types and typed references, and also mimics Java's own serialization mechanism, meaning that it can map any object graph to XML – including those classes which customize their serialization format to some extent. However, it does not include any mapping from classes to DTD or Schema.

Its use is as simple as Java's own serialization. Following is an array of arrays example:

```
class Array {
  int[][] i = { {11,12,13}, {21,22,23} };
  static public void main(String arg[]) throws java.io.IOException {
    new JSX.ObjOut().writeObject(new Array());
  }
}
```

Note that `IOException` can be thrown. This produces:

```
<Array>
  <ArrayOf-ArrayOf-int obj-name="i" length="2">
    <ArrayOf-int length="3"
      a0="11"
      a1="12"
      a2="13"/>
    <ArrayOf-int length="3"
      a0="21"
      a1="22"
      a2="23"/>
  </ArrayOf-ArrayOf-int>
</Array>
```

An example of nested objects and references:

```
class Vertex {
  String text;
  Vertex left;
  Vertex right;
  public Vertex(String text) { this.text = text; }
  static public void main(String[] arg) throws java.io.IOException {
    String a = "one";
    String b = "two";
    Vertex vertex = new Vertex(a);
    vertex.left = new Vertex(b);
    vertex.right = new Vertex(b);
    vertex.left.left = vertex;
    vertex.left.right = vertex;
    new JSX.ObjOut().writeObject(vertex);
  }
}
```

The resulting serialization:

```
<Vertex
  text="one">
  <Vertex obj-name="left"
    text="two">
    <alias-ref obj-name="left" alias="0"/>
    <alias-ref obj-name="right" alias="0"/>
  </Vertex>
  <Vertex obj-name="right"
    text-alias="3"/>
</Vertex>
```

The `alias` names are assigned by counting from the first object (starting from 0). Since both `String` and `Vertex` instances are objects, the text `two` is the fourth object - number 3, counting from 0.

Deserialization - transforming the XML back to objects is the same in principle as for Java's own serialization. Note that `ClassNotFoundException` can be thrown if the target class is not in the classpath of the deserializer (exactly as in Java serialization):

```
class JSXTest {
  public static void main(String[] args) throws java.io.IOException,
      ClassNotFoundException {
    new JSX.ObjOut().writeObject( new JSX.ObjIn().readObject() );
  }
}
```

This code reads from System.in and writes to System.out, and is used like this:

```
java JSXTest < vertex.xml
```

JSX is available at http://www.csse.monash.edu.au/~bren/JSX/.

The big advantage over existing mechanisms is that it works with any pre-existing classes, just as serialization does. There is no need to use getters or setters (as JAXB does). Of course, there is no reason in principle why this project could not map to the SOAP XML format, instead of its own XML format.

Summary

We discussed in this chapter the general problem of mapping data between XML and objects. In particular, we discussed how three different kinds of data information require three different approaches:

- **Document-centric XML** is XML that marks up documents. We can define it as permitting mixed-content, as order significant, and as having an irregular structure, that therefore carries important information. These are important to be able to mark up text and documents.

- **Document-centric mapping** is complete over the document domain. It can include anything (mixed XML element content in particular). Example tools that take this approach are DOM and XMLC.

- **Data-centric XML** is XML that marks up data. We can define it as not permitting mixed content, in which order is not significant, and as having a regular, predictable structure. It can include references, and represent graphs.

- **Data-centric mapping** is complete over the data domain, defined by XML Schema or DTD + supplementary schema. It treats data as a tree, with strict containment. It includes primitive and compound types. JAXB might be a way to tackle this kind of XML mapping.

- **Object-centric XML** is XML that marks up objects. It is similar to data-centric XML, in that mixed content is not permitted and order is not significant; but its structure is not necessarily predictable, and often carries important information in its own right. This is partly the role of run-time typing and typed references.

- **Object-centric mapping** is complete over the object domain. It includes run-time typing and typed references. SOAP is an example of this kind of mapping.

Object-centric XML is an application of XML which we have established especially for the purposes of this chapter. In mapping objects into XML, we need to map:

- ❑ **Primitives**: `int`, `boolean`, `double`, etc – we must establish an unambiguous text representation

- ❑ **Objects**: collections of primitives and other objects, including arrays – we must establish a means to map these into tags and attributes

- ❑ **Run-time types**: part of the value of an object is its class –In some way we must store this as an attribute to indicate type

- ❑ **References**: multiple and circular references are what make object graphs more complex – we must use references to represent these in some way

In order to understand how we are mapping object data to XML data and vice versa, we need to establish a base domain which restricts what kinds of XML, or what kinds of objects, the mapping is valid for. We might distinguish such a domain by applying the criteria below:

- ❑ An XML-Object mapping is in both directions

- ❑ The document domain is restricted by well-formedness and validity with respect to DTD or Schema definitions

- ❑ The data domain is restricted by Schema definitions (or perhaps a DTD plus a binding specification)

- ❑ The object domain is restricted by class definitions

- ❑ The Schema-Class mapping may be to classes, from classes, or in both directions

Finally, we may need to build code around the actual objects that are mapped to XML. This may be because our classes have evolved, or because we need to communicate with another application that uses different names. One way to do this with minimum impact is to use an Object-Object mapping – that is, to simply copy all the fields across to another object, with different names. This is somewhat similar to the "Adapter" Design Pattern, but applied to data rather than code. One danger with this approach is that separate code is needed for the mappings in each direction, and so maintenance is a little more difficult. A better approach is to specify a mapping in one place, and use an Object-Object mapping tool to derive the mappings in each direction from it.

Another approach to changing field names is instead to perform an XML-XML mapping. That is, to transform the XML into another XML document. This could be applied to translate files of legacy data to the new format which we can map into objects, or to insert a transformation phase in between sending and receiving XML from another application. For the latter use, we need to provide transformations in both directions, with the attendant problems of duplication, as above. That said, the ideal tool for such XML-XML mappings is the eXtensible Stylesheet Language for Transformations, XSLT – the subject of the next chapter.

The Xerces Blue
Butterfly, which became
extinct earlier this century,
and after which the Xerces XML
parser is named ...

7

Introduction to XSLT

In this chapter we are going to look at the eXtensible Stylesheet Language (XSL) and its associated XML transformation engine, the eXtensible Stylesheet Language for Transformations (XSLT).

An elegant feature of XSLT is that it can be used programmatically to convert, query, format, sort, and output document data in just about any format, and is itself specified using the syntax of XML. We therefore have both object type (the XML document) and the processing language (XSLT) adhering to the same internationally recognized validation and representation standards. XSLT inherits all the advantages of XML as a format for transmission between networked computers, and this provides Java programmers with a new set of powerful tools for working with XML in a portable and dynamic fashion.

We will be looking at XSLT transformations using Java in the next chapter. Here we will be putting in the groundwork to get you working with XSLT and using it to manipulate XML data.

In covering the foundations of XSLT we will:

- ❑ Start off with the main components of an XSL document

- ❑ Develop an example source XML document and illustrate the basic XSLT mechanisms

- ❑ Learn how to specify and apply XSL templates

- ❑ Introduce the XPath expression syntax and show how it is used to extend the range of XSLT directives

- ❑ Show how to use more advanced features to facilitate creating new XML documents from old

- ❑ Cover the fundamental expression types, formatting instructions, and conditional processing

XSLT Transformations Overview

In this age of information, it is becoming necessary to make your data available in many different formats, the number of which is steadily increasing. This is partly due to the growing variety of client devices and also the current focus on B2B communications, making it necessary to provide a means for accessing new data formats such as XML and WML.

The potential for transformation is something that sets XML apart from other data formats such as HTML, PDF, and postscript, and indeed data stored in a database. In these formats, an in-depth knowledge of the data and its structure is required for data extraction and transformation. In addition, HTML documents are hardly ever well-formed and this makes reliable data manipulation unviable. We can also use XSLT features to query and extract information from XML documents, instead of merely using them for presentation purposes.

Let's look at several scenarios where XSLT transformations can be useful:

❑ Data extraction.

❑ Serving data clients with differing data needs (for example WML, XML, or HTML) from the same source. There is a potential for a large amount of work in this area as B2B communications and the number of alternative data delivery formats increases.

❑ Content provided by different sources can be seamlessly integrated using XSLT into a data service, whether a web site, an intranet site, a device access service, and so on.

We'll start off with the basics.

A Simple XSLT Transformation

XSLT is based on **templates**: a stylesheet specifies a match against an element in the document to be transformed and when one of these elements is encountered, a transformation is carried out according to the template. For our example we will consider an XML that stores call records for a telephone service provider. The company keeps records in an XML format as specified in the following DTD:

```
<!ELEMENT PHONE_RECORDS ( CALL)* >

<!ELEMENT CALL ( FROM, DATE, TIME, DESTINATION, DURATION, CALL_PROMOTION?)>

<!ELEMENT FROM ( #PCDATA ) >
<!ELEMENT DATE ( #PCDATA ) >

<!ELEMENT TIME EMPTY >
<!ATTLIST TIME
    HOUR NMTOKEN #REQUIRED
    MINUTE NMTOKEN #REQUIRED
>

<!ELEMENT DESTINATION ( #PCDATA ) >
<!ATTLIST DESTINATION
    CITY NMTOKEN #REQUIRED
    COUNTRY NMTOKEN #REQUIRED
    STATE NMTOKEN #IMPLIED >
```

```
<!ELEMENT DURATION EMPTY >
<!ATTLIST DURATION
   HOURS NMTOKEN #REQUIRED
   MINUTES NMTOKEN #REQUIRED >


<!ELEMENT CALL_PROMOTION ( #PCDATA ) >
```

The root element of the phone record document is the `<PHONE_RECORDS>` element (see the example listing below) and it includes the following child nodes:

❑ Each call is enclosed with a `<CALL></CALL>` tag pair.

❑ The `<FROM>` element indicates the source telephone number from which the call was made.

❑ The `<DATE>` and `<TIME>` elements indicate the date and time the call was made. The `<TIME>` element also has `HOUR` and `MINUTE` attributes to provide information about when the call was made.

❑ The `<DESTINATION>` element contains details about the phone number called and has attributes describing the `STATE`, `CITY`, and `COUNTRY` called.

❑ The duration of the call in seconds is recorded in the `<DURATION>` element with attributes `HOURS` and `MINUTES`.

❑ Special rates are denoted by the `<CALL_PROMOTION>` tag; in this example the special promotion entitled the caller to half price calls to from the US to Europe. We have denoted this with `HALF_PRICE` in the document below, `calls.xml`:

```xml
<?xml version="1.0"?>
<!DOCTYPE PHONE_RECORDS SYSTEM "calls.dtd">

<PHONE_RECORDS>

  <!-- Call Record 1 -->
  <CALL>
    <FROM>703-433-5678</FROM>
    <DATE>5/5/2000</DATE>
    <TIME HOUR="19" MINUTE="32"/>
    <DESTINATION STATE="California"
                 CITY="Sunnyvale"
                 COUNTRY="US">
    510-798-8390</DESTINATION>
    <DURATION HOURS="1" MINUTES="15"/>
  </CALL>

  <!-- Call Record 2 -->
  <CALL>
    <FROM>703-374-2363</FROM>
    <DATE>5/15/2000</DATE>
    <TIME HOUR="20" MINUTE="15"/>
    <DESTINATION  CITY="Birmingham"
                 COUNTRY="UK">
    44-121-739-4294</DESTINATION>
    <DURATION HOURS="0" MINUTES="30"> </DURATION>
    <CALL_PROMOTION>HALF_PRICE</CALL_PROMOTION>
  </CALL>

</PHONE_RECORDS>
```

For our first task we are commissioned to make this data available in a web browser as shown in the screenshot below:

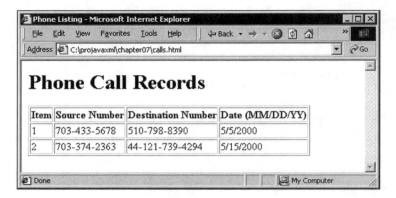

We will now begin to develop an XSLT stylesheet to convert our XML file into the HTML document shown in the screenshot above. The stylesheet for this example can be created in four steps explained below. We'll first have a glance at the full file.

The Full Stylesheet

Shown below is the completed stylesheet, `calls.xsl`. We will now explain each part of the stylesheet to show how we arrived at this final document.

```
<?xml version="1.0"?>
<xsl:stylesheet
  xmlns:xsl="http://www.w3.org/1999/XSL/Transform"
  version="1.0">

<xsl:template match="PHONE_RECORDS">
  <html><head> <title>Phone Listing</title> </head>
  <body>
     <h1>Phone Call Records</h1>
     <table border="1">
      <th>Item</th>
        <th>Source Number</th>
        <th>Destination Number</th>
        <th>Date (MM/DD/YY)</th>

      <xsl:apply-templates/>

     </table>
  </body> </html>
</xsl:template>

<xsl:template match="CALL">
  <tr>
     <td><xsl:number/></td>
     <td><xsl:value-of select="FROM"/></td>
     <td><xsl:value-of select="DESTINATION"/></td>
     <td><xsl:value-of select="DATE"/></td>
  </tr>
</xsl:template>

</xsl:stylesheet>
```

The Header

All XSLT stylesheets begin with a header. This header includes a declaration that specifies the XML version being used (as required by the XML specification) and may optionally include a declaration of the character encoding used. The XML version we are using is 1.0.

The **namespace** for XSLT stylesheets is declared as http://www.w3.org/1999/XSL/Transform. The root element is the `<xsl:stylesheet>` tag and it has two required attributes: the version to use (currently 1.0) and the namespace declaration as shown above.

> Note that the stylesheet name space URI is just a distinct, standardiszed name. The contents of this location are of no interest or relevance.

This stylesheet, and in fact each and every one of our stylesheets, will therefore begin with the following lines:

```
<?xml version="1.0"?>
<xsl:stylesheet xmlns:xsl="http://www.w3.org/1999/XSL/Transform" version="1.0">
```

The Main Template

The next step is to find each of the `<CALL>` elements in the `<PHONE_RECORDS>` element, and process them. In our example, we want to publish only the FROM, DESTINATION, and DATE elements. The rest of the XML elements need not be processed. To control which elements need to be processed, we use **templates**.

> The primary XML processing feature in XSLT is to apply "template" procedures to matching XML elements in the source document. An XSLT template directive is specified with the **`<xsl:template>`** element.

The `<xsl:template>` instruction uses an optional attribute match that specifies the element type that the template should be applied to. XSLT is based on the idea of context: the element type specified by the match attribute gives the context for any transformation carried out. This means that all matching nodes are specified in relation to the current node, similar to the relative path specifications within a web site. The default match for a template (if match is not specified) is the root of the document.

The `<xsl:apply-templates/>` declaration causes all matching templates to be processed and their output to be inserted at this point in the output document. If `<xsl:apply-templates/>` is called without any match attribute then template rules defined for all the children of the current context node will be executed.

This works much like a function or a call to a program method: each call to `<xsl:apply-templates/>` will transfer control to other templates that process the appropriate nodes (specified by the match attribute) before passing control back to the calling rule. For our example, we will start with the first template rule which we want to apply to the root `<PHONE_RECORDS>` element.

When `<xsl:apply-templates>` is called, the rules defined for the child elements of `<PHONE_RECORDS>` are called in turn. We have one top-level template rule for the `<CALL>` element, which is a child element of `<PHONE_RECORDS>` element. After the template rule for the `<CALL>` element is completely processed, control returns to the parent element, `<PHONE_RECORDS>`. Then the next template rule in `<PHONE_RECORDS>` is processed, and so on.

Let's have another look at the top-level template:

```
<xsl:template match="PHONE_RECORDS">
  <html><head> <title>Phone Listing</title> </head>
  <body>
      <h1>Phone Call Records</h1>
      <table border="1">

        <th>Item</th>
        <th>Source Number</th>
        <th>Destination Number</th>
        <th>Date (MM/DD/YY)</th>

    <xsl:apply-templates/>

      </table>
  </body> </html>
</xsl:template>
```

This template defines the top-level structure of the resulting document. We create a table that has four headers, Item, Source Number, Destination Number, and Date. As we will see in a moment, if an element is not part of the XSL namespace (tags prefixed with xsl:) the element will not be processed by XSLT. In other words, the elements not beginning with xsl: will be directly copied to the output.

For example, if the <PHONE_RECORDS> element had two child elements <CALL> and <COMPANY> then, by calling <xsl:apply-templates/> without any arguments from the template for <PHONE_RECORDS>, the rules for <CALL> and <COMPANY> get processed in turn. Template rules can be applied specifically to <CALL> elements by declaring them as follows: <xsl:apply-templates match="CALL"/>. The match attribute can also be generalized using powerful XPath expressions, but we'll get to those later in the chapter.

Specifying the Remaining Templates

Continuing with our example, we have declared the <xsl:apply-templates/> in the rule for the <PHONE_RECORDS> element. The next task is to insert the result of applying the template rules found in the remanider of this context. The data we require will be found within the <FROM>, <DESTINATION>, and <DATE> elements, which are all child elements of the <CALL> element. Also, we need to generate a serial number to be displayed under the Item column. For providing this functionality we will be using the <xsl:number> generator described more precisely below.

We will create a new row for each data item or call. Let's see what this looks like again:

```
<xsl:template match="CALL">
  <tr>
    <td><xsl:number/></td>
    <td><xsl:value-of select="FROM"/></td>
    <td><xsl:value-of select="DESTINATION"/></td>
    <td><xsl:value-of select="DATE"/></td>
  </tr>
</xsl:template>
```

The match attribute here specifies that this template should be applied to each top-level <CALL> element.

Generating Sequences

The `<xsl:number>` instruction is an XSLT function that generates a sequence of identifiers. By specifying it as just `<xsl:number/>` we using it in its simplest form. `<xsl:number>` offers many other features, for example:

❑ The sequence need not always start at 1, it can be easily configured to be a different number

❑ A separate condition can be specified and, on its occurrence, the sequence number can be reset

Sequences can be shown in other formats like Roman numerical, alphabetical order, etc.

Apart from `xsl:number`, the only other processing instruction inside this template is `<xsl:value-of select=Expression>`, which inserts the string value of the resulting expression into the output document. Where `Expression="tagname"`, this inserts, as a string, the contents of the first `<tagname>` element encounted as a child at the current node. In our case, this inserts the **contents** of the `<FROM>` node in place of the `<xsl:value-of/>` instruction. The contents of the first FROM node in the first call element are just `703-433-5678`.

Let's now see XSLT in action.

Using Xalan 2.0 to Generate Output

There are many Java XSLT processors available that implement the XSLT specification. Two of the better known ones are Saxon and Xalan.

> *Saxon can be downloaded from http://users.iclway.co.uk/mhkay/saxon while Xalan and Xerces can be downloaded from the Apache Foundation at http://xml.apache.org and a version is also available in the JAXP download from http://java.sun.com/xml.*

Most of the examples provided in this chapter were tested with Xalan 2.0. They should also work with Saxon without any problems, since both implement the complete XSLT 1.0 specification.

In order to try this XSLT code out you will need to download Xerces as well, which Xalan uses as a SAX 2.0 parser internally. You will need to place `xalan.jar` and `xerces.jar` in your classpath.

You can test the examples given in the remainder of the chapter using Xalan from the Windows command prompt or using a Unix shell. You could also use an XML editor like XMLSpy, which needs MSXML 3.0 for its XSLT processing (we'll show how later). Here's the syntax for Xalan from the command line:

```
> java org.apache.xalan.xslt.Process -in calls.xml -xsl calls.xsl -out calls.html
```

Omitting the -out parameter and its filename will cause the output to be printed to stdout. For the current example, to generate output, execute the above command from the command prompt:

```
C:\projavaxml\chapter07>echo %classpath%
.;C:\xalan-j_2_0_0\bin\xalan.jar;C:\xerces-1_3_0\xerces.jar

C:\projavaxml\chapter07>java org.apache.xalan.xslt.Process -in calls.xml -xsl ca
lls.xsl -out calls.html

C:\projavaxml\chapter07>type calls.html
<html>
<head>
<META http-equiv="Content-Type" content="text/html; charset=UTF-8">
<title>Phone Listing</title>
</head>
<body>
<h1>Phone Call Records</h1>
<table border="1">
<th>Item</th><th>Source Number</th><th>Destination Number</th><th>Date (MM/DD/YY
)</th>

<tr>
<td>1</td><td>703-433-5678</td><td>
    510-798-8390</td><td>5/5/2000</td>
</tr>

<tr>
<td>2</td><td>703-374-2363</td><td>
    44-121-739-4294</td><td>5/15/2000</td>
</tr>

</table>
</body>
</html>

C:\projavaxml\chapter07>_
```

If you have a browser capable of performing XSLT transformation such as Internet Explorer 5.5, then it's also possible to view the output directly by adding the stylesheet reference in the XML file. If you wish to do so, you should add the following declaration directly after the xml declaration as shown below:

```
<?xml version="1.0"?>
<?xml-stylesheet type="text/xsl" href="calls.xsl"?>
<!-- remainder of file goes here -->
```

> This feature is also useful when processing XSL files with XSLT parsers. Instead of providing a reference to an XSL file externally, it can be retrieved from the source XML document.

Declaring Variables

Like other languages, in XSLT variables become handy when the same text needs to be used multiple times while creating the output. Variables needs to initialized only once and they can be used anywhere in the stylesheet.

> **In XSLT, once a value has been assigned to a variable, the variable cannot be updated.**

Variables are defined using `<xsl:variable>` element. Variable can be initialized in any of the following three ways:

1. If the content of the `<xsl:element>` element is empty, and the `select` attribute holds an expression, the value of the variable is the result of evaluating the expression:

```
<xsl:variable name='jcom' select="position()" />

<xsl:variable name='jcom' select="XSLT Tutorial" />
```

2. If the content of the `<xsl:variable>` is not empty, and there is no `select` attribute, the value of the variable is set to the content of the element:

```
<xsl:variable name='jcom'>XSLT Tutorial</xsl:variable >
```

3. Finally if there is neither any content nor a `select` attribute, the variable is initialized to an empty string:

```
<xsl:variable name='jcom'/>
```

To obtain the value of the variable we precede the name of the variable by dollar sign. For example once the variable `jcom` is initialized using any of the above instructions, by placing `$jcom` elsewhere in the stylesheet, it will be substituted with the actual value of `jcom`.

The following example shows how variables can be used in stylesheets. This stylesheet prints the FROM and `<DESTINATION>` phone numbers when the `<DESTINATION>` phone number has `8384` as part of the number:

```
<xsl:stylesheet xmlns:xsl = "http://www.w3.org/1999/XSL/Transform"
    version = "1.0" >
  <xsl:template match = "*" >
      Printing name() : <xsl:value-of select = "name()" />
      Printing local-name() : <xsl:value-of select = "local-name()" />
      Printing namespace-uri():
      <xsl:value-of select = "namespace-uri()" />
      <xsl:apply-templates />
  </xsl:template>
</xsl:stylesheet>
```

Note how using `$dest` simplified the usage of `<xsl:if>` condition. More details about how to use `<xsl:if>` and `contains()` function are given later in this chapter.

Merging Multiple Stylesheets

If the XML files are large or the sequence of expressions for obtaining required output from the XML file is complex, then it becomes necessary to split the XSLT stylesheets into multiple files. It's also a useful methodology where the logic that has been implemented in one stylesheet can be reused. There are two ways in which this can be done, **importing** and **including**.

Importing Stylesheet Using <xsl:import>

Stylesheets can be imported using the <xsl:import> tag. The syntax for <xsl:import> is

```
<xsl:import href=uri-reference />
```

where the `href` attribute refers to the URI of the stylesheet. One example of the <xsl:import> element is shown below:

```
<xsl:stylesheet version="1.1"
    xmlns:xsl="http://www.w3.org/1999/XSL/Transform">
    <xsl:import href="address.xsl"/>
    <xsl:import href="billing.xsl"/>
    <!-- rest of the child elements -->
</xsl:stylesheet>
```

Here the stylesheet is importing two external stylesheets, `address.xsl` and `billing.xsl`.

The following apply when the imported stylesheets conflict with directives in the existing stylesheet (the one which is importing other stylesheets). In any such conflict, the rules in the **existing stylesheet** take precedence. If there is a conflict between imported stylesheets, the **last one imported** (`billing.xsl` in the example above) takes precedence.

It is an error for a stylesheet to directly or indirectly import itself. The <xsl:import> element can only be the child of an <xsl:stylesheet> element. In addition, the <xsl:import> element's children must precede all other children of the <xsl:stylesheet> element, including any <xsl:include> elements.

Including Stylesheets using <xsl:include>

Including a stylesheet is similar to copying the text from another stylesheet to the current stylesheet. Unlike <xsl:import>, in <xsl:include> the templates and other rules have higher precedence in the including stylesheet than those imported using <xsl:import>. Including a stylesheet is equivalent to actually implementing these templates in the parent stylesheet.

The syntax for <xsl:include> element is:

```
<xsl:include href=uri-reference />
```

The `href` attribute provides the URI of the stylesheet to include. One example for <xsl:include> is as follows:

```
<xsl:stylesheet version="1.1"
      xmlns:xsl="http://www.w3.org/1999/XSL/Transform">
   <xsl:import href="areamap.xsl"/>
   <xsl:include href="zipcode.xsl"/>
   <!-- rest of the customer.xsl elements -->
</xsl:stylesheet>
```

In the above XSL file, we are developing a stylesheet called `customer.xsl` to show all the customer records. We are importing the `areamap.xsl` stylesheet file and **including** a `zipcode.xsl` stylesheet file. Let's assume both `areamap.xsl` and `zipcode.xsl` have a template to format the Zip code. The one in the `areamap.xsl` file displays Zip code as *****-**** where the stars are characters (example 22102-1936) using the following template rule:

```
<xsl:template match="ZIPCODE">
  <xsl:value-of select="ZipMain"/>-
  <xsl:value-of select="ZipExtension"/>
</xsl:template>
```

The Zip code function in `zipcode.xsl` displays Zip code as ***** Ext: **** (example 22102 Ext: 1936):

```
<xsl:template match="ZIPCODE">
  <xsl:value-of select="ZipMain"/> Ext:
  <xsl:value-of select="ZipExtension" />
</xsl:template>
```

Now since both the templates are available from the current stylesheet `customer.xsl`, the question arises as to which one is executed. If the current stylesheet itself has the required template rule defined, then the template rule in the **current** stylesheet takes precedence. Otherwise the last **included** stylesheet takes precedence. Finally, if a template rule is not defined in either of these, parent and the included stylesheets, then the template rule defined in the last **imported** stylesheet takes precedence.

So finally for the above example, if there's a `ZIPCODE` template in `customer.xsl` then it gets executed, otherwise the `ZIPCODE` in `zipcode.xsl` gets executed. Finally if the rule is not found in either of these, then the template rule defined in `areamap.xsl` would be executed.

An `<xsl:include>` element can occur anywhere as child of an `<xsl:stylesheet>` element after the last `<xsl:import>` element (if any). As far as the processing engine is concerned, there is no difference between an included rule and a rule that's physically present. Both imported and included stylesheets retain their base URI. So anything that involves referencing a relative URI is done relative to the original URI of the imported stylesheet.

> *A good idea is to split stylesheets into "standard" and special templates. The standard stylesheet can be quickly sent over the network to a consumer, which can request the specifal functionality only if it is necessary within the document being processed.*

Before we begin looking at how templates work in more detail, we need to tackle XPath and its ability to specify more precisely what we can do with the `match` attribute in an `<xsl:template>`. There are two intuitive terms that we should define more exactly, the **context node** and the **location path**.

The **context node** is the node in the source XML document currently being processed. So in our phone listing example, when we declare `<xsl:template match="CALL">`, the context is the current `<CALL>` element being processed. Each `<CALL>` has its own subtree of elements. Similarly if we declare `<xsl:template match="/">`, the context is the root of the document. Most of the time in this document when we refer to it as current "context", we are actually referring to the context node or current node.

A **location path** is used to set the context to the node to be processed. For example when we declare `<xsl:template match="CALL">`, the context is set to the `<CALL>` element using a location path of `match="CALL"`. Similarly, the context can be set to the root node by using a location path of `match="/"`. These are simplified versions of what we can do with XPath expressions, which we'll talk about next.

Using XPath Expressions

XPath expressions are used to refer to elements and attributes in an XML tree, both in absolute terms starting from the root element, and in relative terms according to the current, or context, node. During the development of XSLT, a specification, known as XPointer, for defining linking between XML documents was developed. Both XPointer and XSLT needed a way to point to various parts of a document. XSLT needed it to select parts of the document to apply templates, and XPointer for referencing one part of a document from another. The solution was to provide a common syntax and semantics that both XSLT and XPointer could use. This new subset was called XPath.

XPath expressions are primarily used for specifying locations, although XPath can also be used for string and numerical expression evaluation. A location path is built up using the XPath syntax to select a set of nodes in the document. Location paths can be defined either absolutely or relatively. Relative paths are defined relative to the context node. The root node is the default context node.

Location paths can be defined using either **abbreviated** syntax or **non-abbreviated** syntax. Abbreviated syntax is the most commonly used format and is easy to write. Non-abbreviated syntax must be used in special situations where more selective and expressive criteria are required. XPath also provides a set of **functions** like position(), which help in creating more useful expressions. The next few examples explain how different XPath expression can be used with different select and match attributes to narrow the search for the required node. Initially we will be considering abbreviated syntax.

Selecting Nodes Hierarchically

The forward slash / is the absolute location path and always points to the root element of the XML document. The root element need not always be the start element or the one provided as DOCTYPE in the XML document. It's the absolute root of the entire document. For example the following stylesheet selects the values for all the elements under the PHONE_RECORDS element:

```
<?xml version="1.0"?>
<xsl:stylesheet xmlns:xsl="http://www.w3.org/1999/XSL/Transform"
                version="1.0">
<xsl:template match="/">
   <xsl:apply-templates select="PHONE_RECORDS"/>
</xsl:template>
</xsl:stylesheet>
```

XPath also allows us to navigate through the tree to deeper path matches. The / character when used between two element names indicates hierarchy from left to right. For example if we specify a path of CALL/DATE, this specifies any <DATE> elements that are children of a <CALL> element. In the example below we will show this in use:

```
<?xml version="1.0"?>
<xsl:stylesheet xmlns:xsl="http://www.w3.org/1999/XSL/Transform"
   version="1.0">

<xsl:template match="PHONE_RECORDS">
  <html><body>
      <xsl:apply-templates/>
  </body></html>
</xsl:template>
```

```
<!-- Print call dates in bold -->
<xsl:template match="CALL/DATE">
        <b><xsl:value-of select="text()"/></b>
</xsl:template>

</xsl:stylesheet>
```

If none of the <CALL> elements has a <DATE> child element, then the internal part of the <xsl:template> will not be evaluated. However, the other elements of the <CALL> record will be evaluated. If we modify the calls.xml file so that the second call has no DATE, the output from this stylesheet will be as follows:

```
<html><body>
  703-433-5678
 <b>5/5/2000</b>
  510-798-8390

  703-374-2363
  44-121-739-4294
  HALF_PRICE
</body></html>
```

Notice that the last set does not have a date value (since none exists in the modified XML file). Also in the output you will notice that values for all the elements in calls.xml have been displayed. The reason being that from the template rule for match="PHONE_RECORDS", a call was made to <xsl:apply-templates> without any select criteria, which means to apply template rules to all the text nodes under the root. Also, the default template rule for a text node is to display the value of the text node. As a result, values for all the elements are mapped to the output document.

The same example can also be written this way:

```
<?xml version="1.0"?>
<xsl:stylesheet xmlns:xsl="http://www.w3.org/1999/XSL/Transform"
                version="1.0">

<xsl:template match="/">
   <html><body>
        <xsl:apply-templates/>
   </body> </html>
</xsl:template>

<!-- Print call dates in bold -->
<xsl:template match="PHONE_RECORDS/CALL/DATE">
        <b><xsl:value-of select="text()"/></b>
</xsl:template>
</xsl:stylesheet>
```

Here the template rule is applied first at the document root node level and then special rules are applied for elements under the <PHONE_RECORDS> element. If we want to make all the <DATE> elements that are found within the <PHONE_RECORDS> appear in bold, whether or not they are the child nodes of a <CALL> element, we could use the wildcard *. For example, the above template can be written:

```
<xsl:template match="PHONE_RECORDS/*/DATE">
        <b><xsl:value-of select="text()"/></b>
</xsl:template>
```

It is also possible to select <DATE> elements at multiple levels. This can be done by preceding the element with //. For example the attribute match="PHONE_RECORDS//DATE" selects all <DATE> elements at any level under <PHONE_RECORDS> element.

Usage of // is generally discouraged and should be restricted to the cases when it's really required. This is for reasons of efficiency.

Selecting Node Values

If you want the <xsl:apply-templates> instruction to process only certain child elements, you can specify this in the select parameter of the <apply-templates> element. For example to select only the <FROM> element from the call record, <xsl:apply-templates> would be called with its select attribute set to select="FROM".

For example the following stylesheet select.xsl:

```
<?xml version="1.0"?>
<xsl:stylesheet xmlns:xsl="http://www.w3.org/1999/XSL/Transform" version="1.0">

<xsl:template match="PHONE_RECORDS">
  <html><body>
      <xsl:apply-templates/>
  </body> </html>
</xsl:template>

<!-- Selecting the list of Source Phone Numbers -->

<xsl:template match="CALL">
  <xsl:apply-templates select="FROM"/>
</xsl:template>

</xsl:stylesheet>
```

will give this output:

```
<html><body>
   703-433-5678
   703-374-2363
</body></html>
```

The select attribute follows the same patterns as the match attribute of the <xsl:template> element. When select="FROM" is called, the value of the <FROM> element from the current context node is returned.

Another way of selecting the value of a particular element is by using <xsl:value-of> element. The following steps provide the same output as above:

```
<xsl:template match="CALL">
    <xsl:value-of select="FROM"/>
</xsl:template>
```

The `<xsl:value-of>` directive is normally used in situations where you need to copy the content of an element directly into the output. The value of a given element is the concatenation of any parsed character data between the start and end tags of the element.

The complete syntax for `<xsl:value-of>` is:

```
<xsl:value-of select=Expression disable-output-escaping="yes"|"no"/>
```

The `disable-output-escaping` parameter indicates whether special characters such as <, >, etc. need to be output as they are, or escaped and therefore represented as `&lt;` and `&gt;`. Default is `no`, which means that the < and > characters can be output as is. Any and all XPath Expressions may be used as the value of an element's select attribute. The example given at the start of this chapter in `calls.xsl` shows how to use the `<xsl:value-of>` element.

Selecting Attribute Values

Let's use XPath to change the presentation of our phone listing, adding the time when the call was made in the `HH:MM` format (hour:minutes). In the example, the hour and minute are declared as attributes like this: `<TIME HOUR="19" MINUTE="32"> </TIME>`. Here's how we want our phone listing to look:

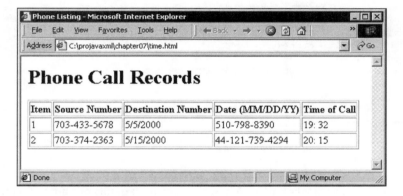

> **Attribute values are selected in XPath by placing @ in front of the attribute name.**

By specifying `select="@HOUR"`, we obtain the value of HOUR relative to the `<TIME>` context. So the element `<TIME HOUR="19" MINUTE="32"></TIME>` will result in the number 19 being output.

Let's modify our current XSL file to include both hour and minute information. Since HOUR and MINUTE are declared as attributes, a different template rule is required to retrieve these values. Here's what our `time.xsl` XSL file is going to look like. First, let's look at a slightly updated top-level template from our first `calls.xsl` stylesheet:

```
<xsl:template match="PHONE_RECORDS">
  <html><head> <title>Phone Listing</title> </head>
  <body>
      <h1>Phone Call Records</h1>
      <table border="1">
         <th>Item</th>
         <th>Source Number</th>
         <th>Destination Number</th>
         <th>Date (MM/DD/YY)</th>
        <th>Time of Call</th>

      <xsl:apply-templates/>

      </table>
  </body> </html>
</xsl:template>
```

And here are our adjusted templates for the new time-friendly output:

```
<xsl:template match="CALL">
  <TR>
   <td><xsl:number/></td>

   <xsl:for-each select="FROM|DESTINATION|DATE">
      <td><xsl:value-of select="."/></td>
   </xsl:for-each>
   <td><xsl:apply-templates select="TIME"/></td>
  </TR>
</xsl:template>

<xsl:template match="CALL/TIME">
    <xsl:value-of select="@HOUR"/>:
    <xsl:value-of select="@MINUTE"/>
</xsl:template>
```

To liven things up a bit, we'll take a diversion to see the output of this transformation in XMLSpy (which we met in Chapter 1). You will need to ensure that you have the MSXML 3.0 parser utility installed on Windows. Create the files calls.xml and time.xsl, and set calls.xml to be the file to apply XSL to in your **Project Properties**:

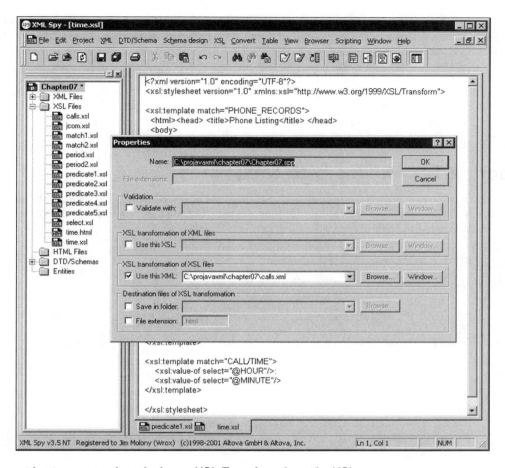

Then with `time.xsl` selected, choose **XSL Transform** from the **XSL** menu:

The <TIME> element does not have any content (only the two attributes, HOUR and MINUTE). So we need to specify a template for it, otherwise nothing will be displayed. The template for the <TIME> element is called by adding the line <xsl:apply-templates select="TIME"/>, within the template for the <CALL> element.

The <TIME> template match attribute will attempt to match instances of CALL/TIME, since we want to include the value of the <TIME> element. Next, by calling select="@HOUR" and select="@MINUTE" the new time format can be constructed. (Notice the : after the end of <xsl:value-of select="@HOUR"/> line.) For this example we will display time in the HH:MM format.

Selecting Text Nodes with text()

The text() function selects the text node that is the child of the context node. The text between the start tag of the context node and the start of the next tag is selected. For example, if the context node has a child element as follows:

```
<Element1>Element Value
    <Child1>Child Text</Child1>
<Element1>
```

then when text() function is called on the <Element1>, then the value returned is Element Value.

Text nodes are processed by default and their text value is printed out. For example, if the stylesheet is written as:

```
<?xml version="1.0"?>
<xsl:stylesheet
  xmlns:xsl="http://www.w3.org/1999/XSL/Transform" version="1.0">

  <xsl:template match="CALL">
      <xsl:apply-templates select="FROM" />
  </xsl:template>
</xsl:stylesheet>
```

then even though the corresponding template rule for <xsl:apply-templates select="FROM" /> is not defined in the stylesheet, the output will be the list of all FROM phone numbers. The reason for this is that for text nodes there is a hidden default template rule declared as:

```
<xsl:template match="text()">
  <xsl:value-of select="."/>
</xsl:template>
```

The text() function is also useful when data from multiple elements needs to be constructed in the output document. In the following example we retrieve values of <NUMBER>, <DESTINATION>, and <DATE>from the <CALL> element. A two-step process is used, with two discrete templates as follows:

```
<xsl:template match="CALL">
    <xsl:apply-templates select="FROM|DESTINATION|DATE"/>
</xsl:template>

<xsl:template match="FROM|DESTINATION|DATE">
  <xsl:value-of select="text()"/>
</xsl:template>
```

The first template rule is activated and processed when the <CALL> element is encountered. Inside <CALL>, <xsl:apply-templates> is executed with the match criteria FROM|DESTINATION|DATE. This means we activate the second template defined to process these three elements, when any one of the elements is encountered while iterating though <CALL> element. Inside the new template created to process these three elements, the value of each of the elements is selected using the text() function and processed to the output document. When the above template rule is applied on the calls.xml document, the output is:

```
703-433-5678
5/5/2000
510-798-8390

703-374-2363
5/15/2000
44-121-739-4294
```

This shows that text for all three elements has been selected and written to output.

Using <xsl:for-each>

The same template rule declared in the above step can be combined into one single template rule, by using the XSLT function <xsl:for-each>. Instead of calling the second template rule for each of the valid elements FROM|DESTINATION|DATE, the <xsl:for-each> function iterates through each of these elements inside the same template rule for the <CALL> element.

Here's how <xsl:for-each> can be used to combine the above two template rules into a single template:

```
<xsl:template match="CALL">
  <xsl:for-each select="FROM|DESTINATION|DATE">
    <xsl:value-of select="text()"/>
  </xsl:for-each>
</xsl:template>
```

The output will be same in both the scenarios. Also note that in the above expressions we are using | to specify multiple elements. Here | represents the boolean expression or and the expression is evaluated true even when only one of the elements satisfies the select criteria.

The select attribute needs to have a valid expression. <xsl:for-each> is similar to the Java for construct. The complete syntax for <xsl:for-each> element is:

```
<xsl:for-each select="Expression">
    <xsl:sort>*
          template body
</xsl:for-each>
```

The declaration for <xsl:for-each> is pretty straightforward. The select attribute accepts an XPath expression. A set of sorting rules can be defined, which can help in sorting the results based on values from one of the elements or show results in ascending or descending order. A separate section later in this chapter explains more details about the sorting rules that can be applied in templates. Next the rest of the template body, in this case <xsl:value-of select="text()"/>, is declared.

Two other ways of selecting text are using single or double period. A single period . indicates the current node. For example, for selecting the value of <FROM>, <DATE> and <DESTINATION> elements for the current call records, the template rule can be defined as:

```
<xsl:template match="CALL">
   <xsl:for-each select="FROM|DESTINATION|DATE">
   <xsl:value-of select="." />
   </xsl:for-each>
</xsl:template>
```

where, using the <xsl:value-of> function, the value of the current element represented by . is selected and written to output. Please note that using a single period character for selecting the value of the current node is quite different from just using text(). The text() function only selects the text from the end tag of the current element till the start tag of next element. For example, say the stylesheet is defined as follows:

```
<?xml version="1.0"?>
<xsl:stylesheet
   xmlns:xsl="http://www.w3.org/1999/XSL/Transform" version="1.0">
   <xsl:template match="PHONE_RECORDS">
          <xsl:value-of select="text()"/>
   </xsl:template>
</xsl:stylesheet>
```

The output contains no text since the <PHONE_RECORDS> element does not have any text nodes. It does have a couple of child nodes, which in turn have child nodes. But the text() function does not retrieve text from these elements. Now define the template rule as follows:

```
<?xml version="1.0"?>
<xsl:stylesheet
   xmlns:xsl="http://www.w3.org/1999/XSL/Transform" version="1.0">
   <xsl:template match="PHONE_RECORDS">
       <xsl:value-of select="."/>
   </xsl:template>
</xsl:stylesheet>
```

Then the output is:

```
703-433-5678
 5/5/2000
 510-798-8390

703-374-2363
 5/15/2000
 44-121-739-4294
 HALF_PRICE
```

The explanation for this is that . selects all the values of the currently matched element, which includes values of all the subelements too.

A double period . . is used to represent the parent of the current node. Here's an example that illustrates how to use the double period. Suppose the template rule has been defined as follows:

```
<xsl:template match="CALL">
   <xsl:apply-templates select="DESTINATION/@CITY"/>
</xsl:template>
```

```
<xsl:template match="DESTINATION/@CITY">
   <xsl:value-of select=".."/>
   <xsl:value-of select="."/>
</xsl:template>
```

Then the output is:

```
510-798-8390
Sunnyvale

44-121-739-4294
Birmingham
```

Which indicates for the second template rule, both the values have been selected. First . selects the value of the current node which is the CITY attribute, and then . . selects the parent element of CITY attribute which is the <DESTINATION> phone number element.

Narrowing the Search Using Predicates

Predicates are used to narrow the node search results while using XPath expressions. They are useful in determining various conditions like:

❑   If the value of an attribute or element matches a given string

❑   Whether a given node exists at a particular position in the result tree

❑   If an element contains a particular child, attribute, or other required node

Predicates are declared within square brackets [ ] and are appended at the end of the location path expression. Each predicate contains a boolean expression which is compared against the required node value. Here are couple of examples that will explain how to use predicates while creating templates. In our phone records example, let's assume we want to retrieve only calls which have been made to the UK. The template rule can be defined as follows:

```
<xsl:template match="PHONE_RECORDS">
    <xsl:apply-templates select="CALL/DESTINATION/@COUNTRY[.='UK']" />
</xsl:template>
```

The output when this template rule is executed is UK. So from the list only one matching node is selected. In the above template, . returns the value of the context node, where the context node is set to CALL/DESTINATION/@COUNTRY.

The operators <, >, >=, <=, =, != are supported in predicates. Since it is not possible to use double quotes inside select expressions, only single quotes are used.

On the same subject, it's not possible to have reserved characters like < and > in predicates, although we can use them with appropriate escaping. These should be replaced by special characters like < and > inside predicates. For example, the following template rule selects all calls made after 20:00hrs:

```
<xsl:template match="PHONE_RECORDS">
    <xsl:apply-templates select="CALL/TIME/@HOUR[.&gt;19]"/>
</xsl:template>
```

Since our example `calls.xml` file has only a single record for a call made after 8 PM, the output will be just one number 20. Notice how > has been used instead of > inside the predicate.

For the following template rule, only call records that have the STATE attribute in the destination element are selected:

```
<xsl:template match="PHONE_RECORDS">
   <xsl:apply-templates select="CALL[DESTINATION/@STATE]" />
</xsl:template>
```

When the above template rule is executed, the output will be:

```
703-433-5678
5/5/2000
510-798-8390
```

Only one of the call records, the one with a STATE attribute, is selected. The other call record returns `false` on this expression and so it is ignored.

Boolean Expressions

Predicates can also contain compound boolean expressions. For example, if we want the search criteria to be either that a <DESTINATION> element should have the STATE attribute, or that a <CALL> element has a <CALL_PROMOTION> element, then the template rule can be declared as follows:

```
<xsl:template match="PHONE_RECORDS">
   <xsl:apply-templates select="CALL[DESTINATION/@STATE | CALL_PROMOTION]"/>
</xsl:template>
```

Notice the | condition in between the XPath subexpressions. When either one of these expressions return `true`, then the entire call record will be selected. When the above template rule is executed, the output will be:

```
703-433-5678
5/5/2000
510-798-8390

703-374-2363
5/15/2000
44-121-739-4294
HALF_PRICE
```

Notice that data for both the elements has been selected. Remember that the <DESTINATION> element in the first <CALL> element has the STATE attribute but does not have the <CALL_PROMOTION> child. The second <CALL> element has <CALL_PROMOTION> but does not match the first pattern. When iterating through each call record, both the call records satisfy at least one of the conditions defined in the predicate. If instead of | in the above predicate, we used "and", then none of the call records would be selected, since none of them satisfy both the conditions.

Wild Cards

The XPath expressions can also have wild card characters along with the predicates. For example, to select all CALL records that have the <CALL_PROMOTION> child, the template rule can be defined as follows:

```
<xsl:template match="PHONE_RECORDS">
   <xsl:apply-templates select="*[CALL_PROMOTION]" />
</xsl:template>
```

The output for above template rule will be:

```
703-374-2363
5/15/2000
44-121-739-4294
HALF_PRICE
```

Only the elements for the second call record are selected, since only the second call record has the <CALL_PROMOTION> element.

Multiple Predicates

XPath expressions can also contain more than one predicate in a single expression. For example to select a call record with <DESTINATION> number 510-798-8390, and STATE attribute California, the template rule can be defined as:

```
<xsl:template match="PHONE_RECORDS">
<xsl:apply-templates
   select="CALL/DESTINATION[.='510-798-8390']/@STATE[.='California']"/>
</xsl:template>
```

In the above expression we have two predicates. Only when the first predicate returns true will the next predicate expression be executed. Since there's only one call record in our calls.xml document matching this, there will be only single string output called California. This feature is useful when different states in different countries have same area code for the phone number.

Predicates can also use XPath functions. For example if we wish to select only the first <CALL>, then the template rule can be declared as follows:

```
<xsl:template match="PHONE_RECORDS">
      <xsl:apply-templates select="CALL[position()=1] " />
</xsl:template>
```

Here we are using one of the XPath functions, position(), which returns the number assigned to the node in the list when processing a list of nodes, with the first node numbered as 1. The position() method is an XPath function which is quite different from the XSLT function <xsl:number> we have already met. The <xsl:number> function (in its simplest use) simply increments every time it is invoked.

Selecting Nodes using Axes

Up to this point we've been selecting nodes using abbreviated path expressions. They are simpler to write and preferable to use most of the time. But there are situations when more flexibility is required. This extra functionality is provided by a non-abbreviated location path. In general every location path has the following structure:

```
axisname :: nodetest [predicate]
```

The `axisname` provides the direction to travel from the current context node, and `nodetest` provides information about which nodes need to included in the direction specified by the `axisname`. The optional `predicate` is used to narrow the search criteria.

In an abbreviated location path, the `axisname :: nodetest` form is derived internally by the XSLT parser from an XPath expression, and the corresponding logic is applied to the source document. For example, the XPath expression `select="CALL/DESTINATION"` is resolved internally by XSLT processor as `select="child::CALL/child::DESTINATION"`.

But on the other hand, predicates are free to use non-abbreviated syntax, since they themselves form part of the XPath expression. For example, it is perfectly valid to declare:

```
<xsl:apply-templates select="*[child::CALL_PROMOTION]"/>
```

Generally, unless the extra functionality provided by a non-abbreviated location path is required, these are avoided both for ease of code maintenance and readability. Also, non-abbreviated expressions are not allowed as part of `match` attributes in templates. For example you cannot replace this template rule:

```
<xsl:template match="CALL/DESTINATION" />
```

with this one:

```
<xsl:template match="child::CALL/child::DESTINATION" />
```

The XSLT processor would throw an exception if this expression is used as part of a `match` attribute.

Using Axes

Non-abbreviated location paths provide the extra functionality needed for navigating in different directions while selecting nodes. We talk about directions through the document in terms of various **axes**, such as the set of ancestor nodes, the sets of siblings in each direction, and so on.

To explain the various axis names that are available and the nodes they return, let's consider a simple XML file as follows:

```
<?xml version="1.0" ?>

<L0>
   <L11 attr_11_1="" attr_11_2="">
      <L111/>
      <L112
       attr_112_1=""
```

```
                attr_112_2=""
                attr_112_3=""/>
         </L11>
         <L12 attr_12_1="">
             <L121 attr_121_1=""/>
             <L122 attr_122_1=""/>
             <L123 attr_123_1=""/>
         </L12>
         <L13>
            <L131 attr_131_1=""/>
         </L13>
    </L0>
```

It can be represented in the form of a tree as follows.

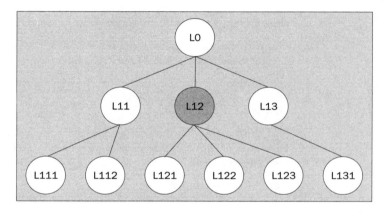

Assuming the current context node is L12, the following table lists various valid axis names and the node that is selected when each of these axis name is applied on the current (shaded) context node (L12). The dark circle is the current context node. Nodes are shown in the order they are selected, starting with the first selected node.

Axis Name	Selects...	Node Selected (Selection order)
ancestor	The parent of the context, its parent's parent and so on until until the root is reached..	L0
ancestor-or-self	The same set as above, plus itself	L0, L12
attribute	The attributes of the context node, if the context node is a element.	attr_12_1
child	Immediate children of the context node.	L121, L122, L123
descendant	All the children of the context node including children's children till the very end leaf node. The descendent axis will never consider values for attributes and namespace nodes.	L121, L122, L123

Table continued on following page

Axis Name	Selects...	Node Selected (Selection order)
descendant-or-self	Selects all descendants and also includes the context node.	L12, L121, L122, L123
following	All nodes in the remainder of the document tree that start after the end of context.	L13, L131
following-sibling	All nodes that start after the end of the context node and have the same parent as the current node.	L13, L131
namespace	If the current node is an element, then all the namespace nodes that are in scope for that element are selected, else its empty.	
parent	The parent of the current node. If the current node is root, then parent is empty.	L0
preceding	Selects all nodes that appear before the start of the context node, excluding ancestors of the context node.	L11, L111, L112
preceding-sibling	Selects all nodes that start before the context node and have the same parent as the context node.	L11, L111, L112
self	Current (context) node.	L12

Here are some examples using our `calls.xml` file as an example.

Example Using child

In the following template, `child::DESTINATION` selects the `<DESTINATION>` element of each CALL record:

```
<xsl:template match="PHONE_RECORDS">
   <xsl:apply-templates select="CALL" />
</xsl:template>

<xsl:template match="CALL">
   <xsl:value-of select="child::DESTINATION" />
</xsl:template>
```

This is equivalent to selecting the `<DESTINATION>` element value by specifying it as:

```
<xsl:value-of select="DESTINATION" />
```

When the above template rule is executed the output is the list of all the Destination numbers as follows:

```
510-798-839
044-121-739-4294
```

Example Using attribute

In the following template rule, the value of the COUNTRY attribute is selected and displayed in output:

```
<xsl:template match="PHONE_RECORDS">
   <xsl:apply-templates select="CALL" />
</xsl:template>

<xsl:template match="CALL">
    <xsl:value-of select="child::DESTINATION/attribute::COUNTRY"/>
</xsl:template>
```

The above expression is also equivalent to:

```
<xsl:value-of select="DESTINATION/@COUNTRY"/>
```

The output after executing the above template is a list of all COUNTRY names as follows:

```
US
UK
```

Example Using ancestor

The ancestor axis selects the list of all ancestors for the context node. Consider the following template rules:

```
<xsl:template match="PHONE_RECORDS">
   <xsl:apply-templates select="CALL[position()=1]" />
</xsl:template>


<xsl:template match="CALL[position()=1]">
   <xsl:apply-templates
      select="DESTINATION/ancestor::*"
      mode = "listdetails"/>
</xsl:template>

<xsl:template match = "*" mode = "listdetails" >
      <xsl:value-of select = "concat(name(),'{',text(),'}')" /> -
</xsl:template>
```

All the ancestors of the <DESTINATION> element of the first <CALL> record are selected. The elements selected are, in order, the <PHONE_RECORDS> element, and then the <CALL> element at position 1. After selecting each element, the template rule to display selected node name and text is called with the mode attribute listdetails.

The value printed in this template rule is the current node name and its value. Here's the part which prints this value:

```
<xsl:value-of select = "concat(name(),'{',text(),'}')" />
```

The format is ElementName { Element Value }. The entire string is displayed as one, using one of the XPath functions concat(), which concatenates a set of strings and displays it as one single string.

299

The syntax of the `concat()` function is:

```
string concat(string str1)
string concat(string str1, string str2)
```

The `concat()` function can take any number of string arguments and it returns a concatenation of all the strings.

For both `<PHONE_RECORDS>` and `<CALL>` elements, there won't be any values in the output within braces since neither `<PHONE_RECORDS>` nor `<CALL>` have any `text()` nodes:

Finally, this is the string which appears in the output document:

```
PHONE_RECORDS{} - CALL{} -
```

The reason there's no text between `{}` is because neither `<PHONE_RECORDS>` nor `<CALL>` elements have any text nodes. They have a couple of child nodes, but the `text()` function does not consider any text from child nodes. The element names as are displayed in the order they were selected and retrieved by the particular axis name.

Also for the last template rule to display the selected node name and text, we are using the `mode` attribute. Since the match attribute for this template is `*`, this template rule will always be called. To restrict when it's called, the `mode` attribute is used. This template rule will be executed only when the `mode` attribute is set to `listdetails` from the calling template. We will see a bit more about `mode` later in the chapter.

Example Using ancestor-or-self

With some slight changes to above template rule we can also check the values returned by the `ancestor-or-self` axis. Instead of using `ancestor`, if the axis name is changed to `ancestor-or-self`, then the output will be:

```
PHONE_RECORDS{} - CALL{} - DESTINATION{510-798-8390}
```

This time the `<DESTINATION>` element itself is also selected, since the `ancestor-or-self` axis is supposed to select both the ancestor nodes and also the context node itself. Since the `<DESTINATION>` element contains contains valid text nodes, the value of the text, which is the destination number, is displayed inside the braces.

Example Using descendant

The `descendant` axis is used to select the child elements right till the last child or leaf node. For example in the following template:

```
<xsl:template match="PHONE_RECORDS">
  <xsl:for-each select="descendant::CALL">
   <xsl:value-of select="FROM" />
  </xsl:for-each>
</xsl:template>
```

For each of the `<CALL>` records that are descendents of `<PHONE_RECORDS>` elements, the `<FROM>` number is selected and processed to output as follows:

```
703-433-5678
703-374-2363
```

Example Using preceding

Suppose while processing each of the elements defined inside a <CALL> element, at some point we wish to know what elements have already been processed prior to the current element. This is where the preceding axis is helpful. Starting from the context node, it lists all the elements that have been processed before reaching the current element. In this example we will use the second CALL to calculate what elements have already been processed.

Here's what the template rule looks like:

```
<xsl:template match="PHONE_RECORDS">
    <xsl:apply-templates select="CALL[position()=2]" />
</xsl:template>

<xsl:template match="CALL[position()=2]">
    <xsl:apply-templates select="DESTINATION/preceding::*" mode = "listdetails" />
</xsl:template>

<xsl:template match = "*" mode = "listdetails" >
        <xsl:value-of select = "concat(name(),'{',text(),'}')" /> -
</xsl:template>
```

We are trying to retrieve the list of all elements that have already been processed, before starting to process the DESTINATION element in the second CALL record. After executing the above template rule, the output will be:

```
CALL{} - FROM{703-433-5678} - DATE{5/5/2000} - TIME{} -
DESTINATION{510-798-8390} - DURATION{} - FROM{703-374-2363} - DATE{5/15/2000} -
TIME{} -
```

From the example we can see that all elements of the first CALL record have been selected, including the <CALL> element of the first call record, right up to the <TIME> element of the second call record.

Example Using parent

The parent axis is used for determining if the parent element of the current node has a particular type or value. For example, say it becomes necessary to start processing a child element, but then to process the entire parent element only if one of the child elements satisfies some required criteria. For example, say we wish to include only <CALL> records that a have <CALL_PROMOTION> child. Here's what the template rule would look like:

```
<xsl:template match="/PHONE_RECORDS">
        <xsl:apply-templates select="//CALL_PROMOTION" />
</xsl:template>

<xsl:template match="CALL_PROMOTION">
    <xsl:value-of select="parent::CALL"/>
</xsl:template>
```

First the <CALL_PROMOTION> elements inside the entire document are retrieved starting from the root element <PHONE_RECORDS>. After each <CALL_PROMOTION> element is retrieved, its entire parent element, which is the entire <CALL> element, is selected by using the parent axis. The CALL elements, which don't have a <CALL_PROMOTION> child are never considered and are never included in output.

301

Abbreviated Syntax

For quick reference here's a list of the full syntax for some of the common abbreviated expressions.

Abbreviated Syntax	Full Syntax
`fieldname`	`child::fieldname`
`@fieldname`	`attribute::fieldname`
`.` (period character)	`self::node()`
`..` (double period)	`parent::node()`
`//`	`/descendant-or-self::node()`

Any one of these can be used to create the expressions for retrieving required data from source files.

Expressions Types

In all the expressions we have seen in this chapter so far, the output has always been a **node-set**. XPath expressions can be one of these:

❑ **Node-set**
A node-set represents a set of nodes that have been selected from the source document matching a required condition. The nodes in a node-set are not restricted to be of a single element type. When a node-set is evaluated, then the result is `false` if empty, otherwise `true`. We use this feature most of the time while creating predicates. The **number** of nodes in the resultant node-set can be calculated using the `count()` function.

❑ **Boolean**
Boolean values are obtained by comparing values using operators such as = and !=. A boolean can have only two values, either `true` or `false`.

❑ **Number**
An XPath number is a double precision 64-bit floating-point number. Unlike in most other programming languages, XPath does not use scientific notation for floating numbers, either for input or output. For example, you need to write 1000000, not 1.0E6. To print a number in scientific format, you can use the XPath `format-number()` function.

The following set of functions and operators can be used with numeric values:

❑ Numerical comparision and equality operators < ,<= ,> ,>= ,= ,!=

❑ Multiplicative and addition operators *, `div`, `mod`, +, -

❑ Unary minus operator -

❑ The `number()` function, which can convert from any value to a number

❑ The `string()` and `format-number()` functions, which convert a number to a string

❑ The `boolean()` function, which converts a number to a boolean

❑ The `round()`, `ceil()` and `floor()`, which convert a number to a integer

❑ The `sum()` function, which computes the numeric sum of the nodes

String Type

A string value in XPath is a sequence of zero or more characters, created using the same Unicode (UTF) characters that are allowed in the XML file. A string can never be `null`: it defaults to the zero length string. A string can be compared using = and ! = operators. When it's required to convert strings from lowercase to uppercase or vice-versa, the `translate()` function can be used. The total length of a string can be determined by using the `string-length()` function. This function returns the total number of XML characters that are present in the current string.

Any of the valid XPath data types can be converted to a string using the `string()` function. The following rules apply when converting an object to a string using the `string()` function:

❑   If the node-set is converted to string, then the value of the first node in the node-set is considered. If the value is empty then an empty string is returned.

❑   A number is converted to string using the following rules:

    ❑   NaN (Not a Number) is converted to the string NaN. A NaN results when an attempt is made to convert a non-numeric string value into a number.

    ❑   Positive infinity (1 div 0) is converted to the string Infinity

    ❑   Negative infinity (-1 div 0) is converted to string Infinity

    ❑   Non integers (numbers that have decimal values) are converted to the English text form, with a decimal point included in the text, with at least one digit before and after the decimal point. For negative numbers, a minus sign is paced in front of the resultant string.

❑   Boolean values are converted to the string true or false.

Applying Template Rules

Here we take a more in-depth look at the template rules. Through the chapter we've been looking at lots of simple examples. The basic laws of how template rules are applied can be explained quite simply. XSLT stylesheet transformations are applied on a tree constructed from the data provided in the XML file. For our phone records example, the tree is constructed in memory as follows:

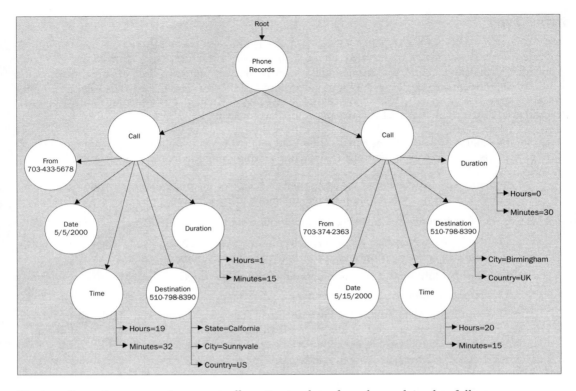

The transformation process is conceptually quite simple and can be explained as follows:

❑ The process begins by traversing the document tree, attempting to find a single matching rule for each visited node.

❑ Once the rule is found, the body of the rule is instantiated. XSLT processing instructions in the body of the rule use the matching node as the context. In our example processing begins as soon as the root node is encountered.

❑ Further processing is specified with the `<xsl:apply-templates>` element. The nodes to process are specified via the `match` attribute. If the `match` attribute is omitted, processing continues at the next element that has a matching template defined for it. In our example when `<xsl:apply-templates>` is encountered, the processor processes the template rules defined for the child elements which for our example are the `<CALL>` ones.

❑ The same process is repeated for all template rules defined for all the child elements.

The exact order of templates does not have to match the order of elements in the source file. The complete syntax for `<xsl:template>` element is as follows:

```
<xsl:template
    match = pattern
    name = qname
    priority = number
    mode = qname>
    <xsl:param>*
        template body
</xsl:template>
```

Definitions for each of these attributes to `<xsl:template>` elements are as follows:

❑ `match`
    The pattern or the XPath expression that determines whether this template this template rule needs to be executed or not. If this parameter is missing, then the template name attribute needs to have a valid value.

❑ `name`
    Used to provide a name to the template. One of the attributes, `name` or `match`, should be specified.

❑ `xsl:param`
    Paramaters can be directly passed to templates from other templates.

The following example shows how to use the `name` attribute and `<xsl:param>` directive:

```xml
<?xml version="1.0"?>
<xsl:stylesheet xmlns:xsl="http://www.w3.org/1999/XSL/Transform"
    version="1.0" >

<xsl:template name="show_heading">
  <xsl:param name="heading" />
  <xsl:value-of select="$heading" />
</xsl:template>

<xsl:template match="PHONE_RECORDS">
  <xsl:call-template name="show_heading">
     <xsl:with-param name="heading">
       <strong><xsl:value-of select="$heading" /></strong>
   </xsl:with-param>
   </xsl:call-template>
</xsl:template>

<xsl:stylesheet
```

From the template rule for `<PHONE_RECORDS>`, we invoke a second template rule whose name is `show_heading`. To this template rule we are passing an extra parameter called `heading`, which has the value to be shown as `<strong>` text. When the template rule with name `show_heading` is invoked, the parameter return value for `heading` is retrieved and it's shown in the output embedded within the `<strong>` tag.

❑ `mode`
    This attribute is useful when same content needs to be shown differently at different times.

❑ `priority`
    The `priority` attribute has a positive or negative value, helping to choose between multiple competing templates that match with the same node.

Priority

We'll look at priority in a little more depth. Here are couple of factors that provide information about how much priority is given to each template:

❑ First preference is given to all templates that have a qualifying match attribute.

❑ From this list we select the templates that have the same mode as the one used on the call to the <xsl:apply-templates> element. If the <xsl:apply-templates> element does not have a mode attribute, then the selected templates should not have a mode attribute.

❑ From a list of templates, we select those that have the highest **import** precedence. All the rules that we looked at previously in xsl:import, xsl:include are considered.

❑ If there is still a choice, we select the one with the numerically highest priority.

If there are still matching nodes, then templates are given priority based on the patterns used to select the node. The higher the priority number of the match expression, the more preference it gets:

❑ The patterns node(), text(), and * are not very good for selecting nodes precisely. They match any nodes that match the given expression. They have a low priority of -0.5

❑ Patterns of the form nspc:* select only nodes within a particular namespace. So they are given priority 0.25

❑ Patterns of the form CALL or @STATE are most commonly used to select nodes. They are given priority 0.0

❑ Patterns that have predicates like CALL[DESTINATION/@STATE] or CALL/TIME/@HOUR[.>19] are more precise in selecting the right type of node. These are given a priority greater then 0.

❑ The default priority is 0.5.

❑ When there are multiple patterns inside one template rule, each separated by |, like this one [CALL/DATE | CALL/DESTIONATION/@STATE], then each pattern is evaluated separately and sum of all their priorities is the priority of the current expression.

If after performing all the above priority checks, there are still templates with the same priorities, then the XSLT processor can either choose the one that appears last in the stylesheet, or report a error.

Creating Result Trees

Let's assume at some point we need to create a well-formed XML file instead of the HTML files we have been creating so far. Suppose we want to transform our original XML document so that CALL has the following format in the output document:

```
<CALL
    FROM="703-433-5678"
    DESTINATION ="510-798-8390"
    DURATION_HOURS="1"
      DURATION_MINUTES="15"
/>
```

If we had to write the output using `<xsl:value-of>` function, the template rule would be as follows:

```
<!-- Incorrect -->
<xsl:template match="CALL">
  <CALL
      FROM="<xsl:value-of select="child::FROM"/>"
      DESTINATION="<xsl:value-of select="DESTINATION"/>"
      DURATION_HOURS ="<xsl:value-of select="DURATION/@HOURS"/>"
      DURATION_MINUTES="<xsl:value-of select="DURATION/@MINUTES"/>"
  />
</xsl:template>
```

But there is a problem. Attribute fields may not contain the reserved characters < and > in XML, and as XSLT files are XML documents, this will be rejected. For this reason, an alternative solution is provided in the XSLT language. Here's the correct way to write the above template rule:

```
<xsl:template match="CALL">
<CALL
      FROM="{child::FROM}"
      DESTINATION="{DESTINATION}"
      DURATION_HOURS="{DURATION/@HOURS}"
      DURATION_MINUTES="{DURATION/@MINUTES}"
/>
</xsl:template>
```

The value that the expression evaluates to is substituted inside the braces. {DESTINATION} is equivalent to writing `<xsl:value-of select="DESTINATION"/>`.

After executing this template rule on the `calls.xml` file, and wrapping this in a CALLS element, the final output will be will be:

```
<CALLS>
<CALL FROM="703-433-5678"
      DESTINATION="510-798-8390"
      DURATION_HOURS="1"
      DURATION_MINUTES="15" />

<CALL FROM="703-374-2363"
      DESTINATION="44-121-739-4294"
      DURATION_HOURS="0"
      DURATION_MINUTES="30" />
</CALLS>
```

We can place any valid location steps (XPath expressions) within a pair of braces. For example, both these lines give the same output and are perfectly valid:

```
DURATION_MINUTES="{DURATION/@MINUTES}"
```

or

```
DURATION_MINUTES="{child::DURATION/attribute::MINUTES}"
```

It is also valid to combine an attribute value template with literal data or other attribute value templates. For example, while generating the phone listings for each destination, say we want to give a hyperlink to the city map for the destination number. The desired output phone listing is shown below:

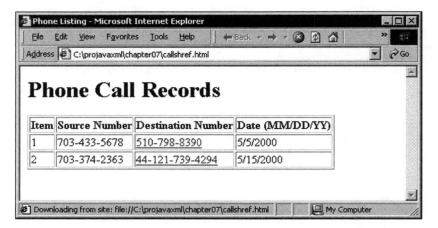

The hyperlink can be generated in the template rule for the <CALL> element using the following rule:

```
<A HREF =
    "http://www.worldmaps.com/map/{DESTINATION/@COUNTRY}/{DESTINATION/@CITY}.html"
>
    <xsl:value-of select="DESTINATION"/>
</A>
```

Notice how multiple attribute value templates are combined along with the literal string. The final output string that will be generated after applying the above rule on calls.xml is as follows:

```
<A href="http://www.worldmaps.com/map/US/Sunnyvale.html"> 510-798-8390</A>
```

The attribute value templates, referenced using {}, cannot be used as the value of a select or match attribute, an xmlns: attribute, an attribute that evaluates to the name of another XSL instruction element, or the attribute of an immediate child of <xsl:stylesheet>.

The <xsl:element> and <xsl:attribute> Elements

We can also use a combination of the <xsl:element> and <xsl:attribute> elements to create the same hyperlink. We will assume the desired output should appear as follows in the output:

```
<A href="http://www.worldmaps.com/map/US/Sunnyvale.html"> 510-798-8390</A>
```

Here the element name is A, its single attribute is href, and the attribute's value is:

```
"http://www.worldmaps.com/map/" + CountryName + "/" + cityname + ".html"
```

Here is the template rule that generates this hyperlink code:

```
<xsl:element name="a">
  <xsl:attribute name="href">
        http://www.worldmaps.com/map/<xsl:value-of
            select="DESTINATION/@COUNTRY"/>/<xsl:value-of
            select="DESTINATION/@CITY"/>.html
  </xsl:attribute>
  <xsl:value-of select="DESTINATION"/>
</xsl:element>
```

The value of the name attribute provided in <xsl:element> becomes the element name for the final output. In this case it's <a>. The value of the name attribute provided in <xsl:attribute> becomes the attribute name for the resultant name, here it is href. The entire text between the start and end tags for <xsl:attribute> becomes the new inserted attribute value. For the current example, it's the entire URL, that refers to the city map.

It is perfectly acceptable to combine the attribute element with other content within <xsl:element> in order to generate child elements as shown here:

```
<xsl:template match="CALL">
  <xsl:element name="CALL_RECORD">
    <xsl:attribute name="Date">
      <xsl:value-of select="DATE"/>
    </xsl:attribute>
    <FROM><xsl:value-of select="FROM" /> </FROM>
    <DESTINATION
        DURATION_HOURS="{DURATION/@HOURS}"
        DURATION_MINUTES="{DURATION/@MINUTES}"
    >
    <xsl:value-of select="DESTINATION/@CITY" />
    </DESTINATION>
  </xsl:element>
</xsl:template>
```

This example combines <xsl:element>, <xsl:attribute>, and {} together. For each new <CALL> element, a new element is created in the output with name <CALL_RECORD>. The date on which the call was made is added as an attribute to this new element. In the remaining part of this template rule, <NAME> and <DESTINATION> are added as subelements of <CALL_RECORD>.

Below is the output for one of the <CALL> elements when this template rule is applied on calls.xml:

```
<CALL_RECORD Date="5/5/2000">
  <FROM>703-433-5678</FROM>
  <DESTINATION DURATION_MINUTES="15" DURATION_HOURS="1">
    Sunnyvale</DESTINATION>
</CALL_RECORD>
```

Using `<xsl:text>`

So far we have been inserting literal text in the output. The text output matches exactly that of the text in the stylesheet. Another way of displaying the same text is by using `<xsl:text>`. The complete syntax for the `<xsl:text>` element is:

```
<xsl:text
   disable-output-escaping = "yes" | "no">
   <!-- Content: #PCDATA -->
</xsl:text>
```

Here's a example of using `<xsl:text>`:

```
<h1><xsl:text>Phone Call Records</xsl:text></h1>
```

The actual text to be included in the output is included between start and end elements of the `<xsl:text>` element. Using the `disable-output-escaping` attribute, the output-escaping feature can be switched off. This option allows you to include special characters in the output. For example, say you want to display the text as >><<HELLO>><< in the output.

If you try to display this text literally inside the stylesheet:

```
<!-- Incorrect -->
<xsl:template match="CALL">
  >><<HELLO>><<
</xsl:template>
```

the processor will report an error, since this breaks the well formedness of the XML. Next if we try to display this text using `&lt;` and `&gt;` like this:

```
<xsl:template match="CALL">
  &gt;&gt;&lt;&lt;HELLO&gt;&gt;&lt;&lt;
</xsl:template>
```

The output escaping means that the output will still have `&lt;` and `&gt;` in it; they will not be converted to their respective characters. Now, if you use `<xsl:text>` with escaping disabled, like this:

```
<xsl:template match="CALL">
<xsl:text disable-output-escaping="yes">
  &gt;&gt;&lt;&lt;HELLO&gt;&gt;&lt;&lt;
</xsl:text>
</xsl:template>
```

This code will print >><<HELLO>><< to the output.

Another major advantages of using `<xsl:text>` element is that whitespace is preserved. This feature is quite useful where formatting is an important part of the output.

Using the <xsl:processing-instruction> element

The <xsl:processing-instruction> element is useful for simply creating a processing instruction in the output document. A processing instruction in an XML documents has two parts, target and content:

```
<?target content?>
```

The syntax for an <xsl:processing-instruction> element is:

```
<xsl:processing-instruction name="target">
   <!-- template content  -->
</xsl:processing-instruction>
```

Where target is given as the value for the name attribute of <xsl:processing-instruction> specified using the name attribute and content becomes the text between the start and end tags of the <xsl:processing-instruction> in the final output.

For example, if we need to generate processing instruction in the following format in the output:

```
<?javac src=generatereport.java ?>
```

then the following xsl:processing-instruction needs to be included in the stylesheet:

```
<xsl:processing-instruction name="javac">
   src="generatereport.java"
</xsl:processing-instruction>
```

The value of the name attribute, which is javac, is assigned to the target field. The content between the start and end tags of the <xsl:processing-instruction> element, which is src="generatereport.java", is assigned to the content field in the processing instruction finally generated as output.

The content of the processing instruction can be set using an <xsl:value-of> element if required. For example, to get the charge for each call made, we can create a template as shown below:

```
<xsl:template match="CALL">
  <xsl:processing-instruction name="getprice">
    DESTINATION=<xsl:value-of select="DESTINATION"/>
  </xsl:processing-instruction>
</xsl:template>
```

When this template rule is applied to calls.xml the output will be:

```
<?getprice DESTINATION=510-798-8390?>
<?getprice DESTINATION=44-121-739-4294?>
```

Copying Nodes Using <xsl:copy>

The <xsl:copy> element provides an easy way to copy the current node. It creates a shallow copy of the current node in the output tree, plus all the namespace nodes visible at that point in the source. <xsl:copy> by default does not copy attributes and subelements of the current node or element.

For example, this stylesheet creates a copy of the current XML document:

```
<?xml version="1.0"?>
<xsl:stylesheet xmlns:xsl="http://www.w3.org/1999/XSL/Transform" version="1.0">
    <xsl:template match="@*|node()">
        <xsl:copy>
            <xsl:apply-templates select="@*|node()"/>
        </xsl:copy>
    </xsl:template>
</xsl:stylesheet>
```

@* is the abbreviated syntax for attribute::*, which indicates that it should match all attributes.

Here is another example for the <xsl:copy> element. Suppose we decide that only the <FROM> and <DESTINATION> elements should be copied to the output exactly as they appear in the source document, including the start and the end tags. Here's the template that does this:

```
<xsl:template match="FROM|DESTINATION">
  <xsl:copy>
    <xsl:for-each select="@*">
      <xsl:copy />
    </xsl:for-each>
    <xsl:apply-templates />
  </xsl:copy>
</xsl:template>
```

When this template rule is applied to the XML document, the <FROM> and <DESTINATION> elements will be copied to the output, along with their attributes. The inside <xsl:for-each> element handles attributes. When this template rule is applied on calls.xml the output looks like this:

```
<FROM>703-433-5678</FROM>
5/5/2000
<DESTINATION STATE="California"
    CITY="Sunnyvale"
    COUNTRY="US">
    510-798-8390
</DESTINATION>
 5/5/2000

<FROM>703-374-2363</FROM>
5/15/2000
<DESTINATION
    CITY="Birmingham"
    COUNTRY="UK">
    44-121-739-4294
</DESTINATION>
5/15/2000
HALF_PRICE
```

Notice that both the <FROM> and <DESTINATION> elements have been copied entirely along with their attributes. For the remaining elements (<DATE> and <CALL_PROMOTION>), the default template rule is applied and only the PCDATA for these elements is returned.

XSLT also provide function called <xsl:copy-of> which does a deep copy of the current node to the output. The difference between <xsl:copy> and <xsl:copy-of> is, when a node is copied using xsl:copy-of then descendents are also copied. The complete syntax for <xsl:copy-of> is:

```
<xsl:for-each select="Expression">
```

where the Expression gives access to the node-set or other value whose output needs to be copied to output. For example in the above example, for each node, we were iterating through all the attributes to copy them to output using the following lines:

```
<xsl:for-each select="@*">
    <xsl:copy/>
</xsl:for-each>
```

Let's create an example where the output should have only <CALL> elements that have the <CALL_PROMOTION> subelement. One of the ways to do this one is by using predicates since these are allowed as part of a match attribute's value. For example the following template rule is activated only when the <CALL> element has a <CALL_PROMOTION> subelement:

```
<xsl:template match="CALL[CALL_PROMOTION]">
```

In all there will be three templates for this stylesheet. The first template matches the root element and makes sure only CALL elements that have the CALL_PROMOTION child are selected. The second template selects all the nodes of the current element, including the attributes, and invokes an additional template with the mode attribute set to showdata. The third template is the same as the first one shown in this section and is capable of copying the entire stylesheet, as it is, to output. To control the call, the mode attribute is used and only when mode is set as showdata will this template be activated and copy the contents of the current element to output. Here's how the complete stylesheet looks:

```
<?xml version="1.0"?>
<xsl:stylesheet xmlns:xsl="http://www.w3.org/1999/XSL/Transform"
    version="1.0">

<xsl:template match="PHONE_RECORDS">
    <xsl:apply-templates select="CALL[CALL_PROMOTION]" />
</xsl:template>

<xsl:template match="CALL[CALL_PROMOTION]">
    <xsl:apply-templates select="@*|node()" mode="showdata" />
</xsl:template>

<xsl:template match="@*|node()" mode="showdata">
  <xsl:copy>
     <xsl:apply-templates select="@*|node()"/>
  </xsl:copy>
</xsl:template>

</xsl:stylesheet>
```

When this stylesheet is executed using Xalan on `calls.xml`, as we did earlier in the chapter, the output will be as follows:

```
Command Prompt                                                          _ □ ×

C:\projavaxml\chapter07>echo %classpath%
.;C:\xalan-j_2_0_0\bin\xalan.jar;C:\xerces-1_3_0\xerces.jar

C:\projavaxml\chapter07>java org.apache.xalan.xslt.Process -in calls.xml -xsl mode.xsl
<?xml version="1.0" encoding="UTF-8"?>

    <FROM>703-374-2363</FROM>
    <DATE>5/15/2000</DATE>
    <TIME>2015</TIME>
    <DESTINATION>BirminghamUK
    44-121-739-4294</DESTINATION>
    <DURATION>030</DURATION>
    <CALL_PROMOTION>HALF_PRICE</CALL_PROMOTION>


C:\projavaxml\chapter07>
```

So you can see that the entire call record that has the CALL_PROMOTION child is copied to output.

Formatting Output Conditionally Using mode

Modes are useful when you want to include the same content from the source document in the output document multiple times. If the data is to be displayed in the same format, we could implement a template that would achieve this, but if the data should be output differently depending on the position in the document, we would need to use another technique. For example, let's say that while processing the <CALL> element, the names of the table headers should be directly taken from element names and that, from the second column, the element values should be displayed.

The screenshot below shows how the final screen should look. Notice that the table headers correspond to the element names and that the header columns have a different background color. Here's where the mode attribute comes in. In one mode we can display the table header, and in the other mode we can display the element values:

The stylesheet for providing this capability can be developed in five steps.

1. Create a Template Rule to Process the Root Node

The `<HTML>` and `<body>` tags need to be initialized once only. Here's how the template rule for the root node looks:

```
<xsl:template match="/">
  <html>
    <head><Title>Phone Records</Title></head>
    <body>
      <h1>Phone Call Records</h1>
      <xsl:apply-templates/>
    </body>
  </html>
</xsl:template>
```

2. Create a Template Rule for the <PHONE_RECORDS> Element

Here's how the template looks at the `<PHONE_RECORDS>` level. We wish to process the entire document, so we specify a match for the `PHONE_RECORDS` element. Since the entire data from the XML file is encapsulated in a table we define the table at this level and then continue to process the document:

```
<xsl:template match="PHONE_RECORDS">
  <table border="1" cellspacing="0">
    <xsl:apply-templates
          select="CALL[position()=1]/*" mode="ShowHeader"/>
    <xsl:apply-templates/>
  </table>
</xsl:template>
```

Here `position()=1` refers to the first index position of the node in the collection of matching nodes returned. So for the expression above this would match the first `CALL` element of the child nodes of the `PHONE_RECORDS` element. Notice that we have used the `mode` attribute here. The `select` expression indicates that when the first `<CALL>` child of `<PHONE_RECORDS>` is being processed it should apply the mode `ShowHeader`.

3. Declare the Default Template for the <CALL> Element

In the final output we want only three elements to be shown in each row, `<FROM>`, `<DESTINATION>`, and `<DATE>`, so the default template rules will be as follows:

```
<xsl:template match="CALL">
  <tr>
    <xsl:apply-templates select="FROM|DESTINATION|DATE"/>
  </tr>
</xsl:template>
```

4. Specify the Default No-Mode Template

Here is the template that is applied when none of the mode attributes match and current match is for one of these three elements `<FROM>`, `<DESTINATION>`, and `<DATE>`:

```
<xsl:template match="FROM|DESTINATION|DATE">
  <td><xsl:value-of select="."/></td>
</xsl:template>
```

We merely select the value of each of these elements and send it to the output.

5. Specify the ShowHeader Mode Template

This template is defined for the `ShowHeader` mode. If you remember, this occurs at the first occurrence of a `<CALL>` child element in the `<PHONE_RECORDS>` element. So this template rule is executed once only. We set the header here:

```
<xsl:template match="FROM|DESTINATION|DATE" mode="ShowHeader">
  <th bgcolor="#F2F2F2">
    <xsl:value-of select="name(.)"/>
  </th>
</xsl:template>
```

The `name()` function selects the element name of the element that the expression given within its brackets evaluates to. In this instance we have specified the current element and so for each occurrence of the `<FROM>`, `<DESTINATION>`, and `<DATE>` elements, its name will be output. For each element a new table header is added with the element `<th bgcolor="#F2F2F2">`.

That finishes all the five steps required for creating the stylesheet. Here is the completed stylesheet:

```
<xsl:stylesheet version="1.0"
                xmlns:xsl="http://www.w3.org/1999/XSL/Transform">
  <xsl:template match="/">
    <html>
      <head><Title>Phone Records</Title></head>
      <body>
        <h1>Phone Call Records</h1>
        <xsl:apply-templates/></body>
    </html>
  </xsl:template>

  <xsl:template match="PHONE_RECORDS">
    <table border="1" cellspacing="0">
      <xsl:apply-templates
          select="CALL[position()=1]/*" mode="ShowHeader"/>
      <xsl:apply-templates/>
    </table>
  </xsl:template>

  <xsl:template match="CALL">
    <tr>
      <xsl:apply-templates select="FROM|DESTINATION|DATE"/>
    </tr>
  </xsl:template>

  <xsl:template match="FROM|DESTINATION|DATE">
    <td><xsl:value-of select="."/></td>
  </xsl:template>

  <xsl:template match="FROM|DESTINATION|DATE" mode="ShowHeader">
    <th bgcolor="#F2F2F2">
      <xsl:value-of select="name(.)"/>
    </th>
  </xsl:template>
</xsl:stylesheet>
```

Notice that as well as calling the `ShowHeader` mode template we then call a general apply templates with no match attribute given. This will mean that the first `<CALL>` subtree will be processed twice: once to generate the table headers and the second time to produce `<CALL>` details.

Sorting Output Data

XSLT also provides powerful built-in capabilities for sorting the results before sending them to the output. The XSL instruction used to provide this capability is `xsl:sort`. Here's the syntax for `xsl:sort`:

```
<xsl:sort
   select = "Expression"
   order = { "ascending" | "descending" }
   case-order = { "upper-first" | "lower-first" }
   data-type = { "text" | "number" | qname }
   lang = { language-code } />
```

These break down into the following controls:

select	This can be a valid XPath expression including the match expression. The default is the string value of the current node.
order	Indicates whether nodes need to be processed in ascending or descending order. The default is ascending order.
case-order	When strings with equal precedence exist, this parameter indicates whether upper-case needs to be given higher preference or should it be given to lower-case text. The default is language dependent.
data-type	Defines whether the values need to be sorted alphabetically or numerically, or using a user-defined data type. The default is to sort alphabetically.
lang	Defines the language whose preferences need to be used. The default depends on the current processing environment.

Another common rule is: if `xsl:sort` is used along with `xsl:if`, then `xsl:if` needs to be declared first. Here's how the XSL code would look, if we wanted to sort by the DESTINATION city:

```
<?xml version="1.0"?>
<xsl:stylesheet xmlns:xsl="http://www.w3.org/1999/XSL/Transform" version="1.0">

   <xsl:template match="/PHONE_RECORDS">
   <html><head> <title>Phone Listing</title> </head>
   <body>
      <h1>Phone Call Records</h1>
      <table border="1">
   <tr>
      <th>Source Number</th>
      <th>Destination Number</th>
      <th>Date (MM/DD/YY)</th>
      <th>City</th>
      <th>Country</th>
   </tr>
```

```
    <xsl:for-each select="CALL">
      <xsl:sort select="DESTINATION/@CITY" order="descending" />
      <tr>
      <td><xsl:value-of select="FROM"/></td>
      <td><xsl:value-of select="DESTINATION"/></td>
      <td><xsl:value-of select="DATE"/></td>
      <td><xsl:value-of select="DESTINATION/@CITY"/></td>
      <td><xsl:value-of select="DESTINATION/@COUNTRY"/></td>
      </tr>
    </xsl:for-each>


    </table>
    </body> </html>
  </xsl:template>
</xsl:stylesheet>
```

Sorting can also be done at multiple levels by specifying sort statements one after another with ascending preference order. For example, if instead of just sorting by city, we also want to sort listing by COUNTRY name, then the instructions can be written this way:

```
<xsl:sort select="DESTINATION/@COUNTRY" order="descending" />
<xsl:sort select="DESTINATION/@CITY" order="ascending" />
```

Here's how the output document is going to look when multiple sorting instructions are specified in the XSLT file:

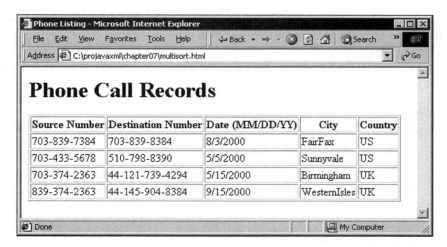

First the phone listings are sorted by country name, and then they are sorted by city name.

Implementing Conditional Logic

There are two instructions in XSLT that support conditional processing in a template: `<xsl:if>` and `<xsl:choose>`. The `<xsl:if>` instruction provides simple if-then conditionality; the `<xsl:choose>` instruction supports selection from multiple possible values.

Conditional Processing Using `<xsl:if>`

The `<xsl:if>` condition is similar to the `if` condition in Java. First the expression is evaluated to a boolean. If the result is `true`, then the conditions specified in `<xsl:if>` are executed. Otherwise they are ignored.

The syntax for `<xsl:if>` condition is:

```
<xsl:if test=boolean expression>
      template body
</xsl:if>
```

Here's an example that uses, `<xsl:if>`. Suppose we wish to print call destination numbers to the output in alternating colors. We can use `<xsl:if>` to evaluate the current position and check if it's odd or even. In this example, at every odd position, we print the destination phone number in blue:

```
<xsl:template match="/PHONE_RECORDS">
<html><body>
    <xsl:for-each select="CALL/DESTINATION" >
       <xsl:if test="position() mod 2 = 0">
          <xsl:value-of select="text()"/><br/>
       </xsl:if>

       <xsl:if test="position() mod 2 > 0">
          <font color="blue">
            <xsl:value-of select="text()"/>
          </font><br/>
       </xsl:if>
    </xsl:for-each>
</body></html>
</xsl:template>
```

The resultant output after executing the above stylesheet is:

```
<html> <body>
<font color="blue">510-798-8390</font>
<br>44-121-739-4294<br>
</body> </html>
```

This indicates that an element at an odd position in the node-set is displayed in blue. While creating the validation conditions using `<xsl:if>`, any of the operators like <, <=, >, >=, =, !=, *, div, mod, +, - and functions that are allowed on XPath data types can be used.

Conditional Processing Using <xsl:choose>

The `<xsl:choose>` instruction is similar to `<xsl:if>`, except that it caters for multiple test conditions on an expression. The syntax for `<xsl:choose>` is as follows:

```
<xsl:choose>
    <xsl:when test=boolean expression 1>
        Case 1 Template Body
    </xsl:when>

    <xsl:when test=boolean expression 2>
        Case 2 Template Body
    </xsl:when>

    <xsl:otherwise>
        default template body
    </xsl:otherwise>
</xsl:choose>
```

Similarly to `<xsl:if>`, `<xsl:when>` is evaluated to a Boolean and if the result is `true`, then any instructions inside `<xsl:when>` are executed. `<xsl:when>` is more like the `switch` statement in Java. If none of the expressions satisfy the `<xsl:when>` conditions, then the instructions inside `<xsl:otherwise>` get executed.

For example, in the above example for `<xsl:if>`, say we had to declare `<xsl:if>` twice, first to check if the current position was odd, and the second to check if it was even. Both these steps can be combined into one using `<xsl:choose>` as follows:

```
<xsl:choose>
    <xsl:when test="position() mod 2 = 0">
        <xsl:value-of select="text()"/><br/>
    </xsl:when>
    <xsl:otherwise>
        <font color="blue">
            <xsl:value-of select="text()"/>
        </font><br/>
    </xsl:otherwise>
</xsl:choose>
```

As with `<xsl:if>`, while creating the validation conditions using `<xsl:when>`, any of the operators like <, <=, >, >=, =, !=, *, div, mod, +, - and functions that are allowed on XPath expressions can be used here.

Formatting Output Using <xsl:output>

For reasons of simplicity, in all the examples in this chapter where we are showing output, we are not printing the heading that is generated at the top of the output file when the stylesheet is parsed using the XSLT parser. For example, using Xalan, by default the following header will be generated:

```
<?xml version="1.0" encoding="UTF-8"?>
```

If the stylesheet had <html> element declarations, then the XSLT parser is capable of interpreting that the output is going to be a HTML file and it will print the following heading in the output file,

```
<META http-equiv="Content-Type" content="text/html; charset=UTF-8">
```

These were the default headings. It's also possible to specify the expected output format through the XSL file. This capability is provided by the <xsl:output> directive. The complete syntax for <xsl:output> is as follows:

```
<xsl:output
    method = "xml" | "html" | "text" | qname
    version = nmtoken
    encoding = "encoding_name"
    omit-xml-declaration = "yes" | "no"
    standalone = "yes" | "no"
    doctype-public = "PUBLIC_ID"
    doctype-system = "SYSTEM_ID"
    cdata-section-elements = "element_name1 element_name2"
    indent = "yes" | "no"
    media-type = string />
</xsl:output>
```

Here are the details of each attribute in the <xsl:output> element:

❑   method
    This attribute specifies details about the format of the final output document. The default
    value for this attribute is "xml". If the root element of the output document is set to <html>,
    then the method attribute has its value set to "html". This ensures that the text() method
    outputs only the contents of the text nodes in the output. The entire markup tags are stripped
    and plain text is printed out. It's also possible to have a custom value for the method attribute.
    For example if the final output document is to be WML (Wireless Markup Language), then the
    expected root element is <wml>. So the value of the method attribute is specified as "wml".

❑   version
    A optional value that specifies the output device version. Most of the times this does not have
    any effect on the output.

❑   encoding
    The encoding format like UTF-8, UTF-16, or ISO-8859-1 that needs to be used while
    creating the output.

❑   omit-xml-declaration
    The XML declaration at the top of the output document can be completely disabled by
    providing value to this attribute as yes.

❑   standalone
    The default XML declaration has a standalone attribute. This attribute in the stylesheet is
    used to set the standalone attribute of the XML declaration.

❑   doctype-public and doctype-system
    These attributes are used to set the DOCTYPE of the final output document. These parameters
    play very useful roles when documents in other formats like WML need to be generated using
    XSL stylesheets. If the value for these attributes is provided as follows:

```
<xsl:output
  method="wml"
    omit-xml-declaration="no"
    doctype-public="-//WAPFORUM//DTD WML 1.1//EN"
    doctype-system="http://www.wapforum.org/DTD/wml_1.1.xml" />
```

then in the final output document, the heading is printed as follows:

```
<?xml version="1.0" encoding="UTF-8"?>

    <!DOCTYPE wml
    PUBLIC "-//WAPFORUM//DTD WML 1.1//EN"
    "http://www.wapforum.org/DTD/wml_1.1.xml">
```

This is the expected WAP file-heading format (except the encoding type). If there's any variation from this one, then the WAP browser may not interpret the WAP file correctly. Notice how the DOCTYPE and PUBLIC attributes are generated dynamically using the parameters specified in the <xsl:element> declarations.

❑ cdata-section-elements
   A whitespace seperated list of element names in the result tree whose contents needs to be shown in output using CDATA sections instead of character references.

❑ indent
   If this attribute has value set as yes, then the XSLT processor can add extra whitespace in the output, to make the output document look more presentable. This feature is optional and may not be supported by all XSLT parsers.

❑ media-type
   The MIME type of the output document like text/html, text/xml, and more.

By setting these different attributes to an <xsl:element>, the output format can specified.

Summary

In this chapter we have covered most of the important elements that are used for creating XSLT sylesheets. XSLT, together with XPath, provides a rich set of functions, which are useful in creating more flexible and powerful XML transformation solutions. This chapter can act as foundation for creating XSLT stylesheets and after completing this chapter you should now be able to refer with confidence to XSLT reference guides such as *"XSLT Programmer's Reference"*, Wrox Press, ISBN 1-861003-12-9, and include the new functions in your stylesheets.

We have also laid the groundwork for leveraging the power of XSLT from within Java. In the next chapter we will be explaining how XSLT features can be directly used within the Java programming environment, along with how to use some of the latest Java XSLT processors.

The Xerces Blue
Butterfly, which became
extinct earlier this century,
and after which the Xerces XML
parser is named ...

8

Programming Using XSLT

We have covered the use of XSLT in the previous chapter, and have outlined how it came it be. However, so far, we have not looked at how we can make use of XSLT stylesheets to allow dynamic transformation of content from within Java programs. While the technology is powerful on its own, it becomes more powerful when used within programs such as will be shown in this chapter.

The thing is that writing programs to manipulate XML in Java is actually quite hard. Java doesn't handle XML data structures very naturally: it handles objects, and at a push, arrays of objects. But the highly structured tree of XML is not easily handled in Java code. XSLT, on the other hand, is a language entirely designed to handle XML trees as a fundamental data structure. You can consider XSLT's role in handling XML data as similar to that of SQL in handling relational tables of data: it has a syntax specifically designed for the problem. And just as we use SQL to write commands to extract data from databases for use in our programs, we can use XSLT to write commands to extract data from XML for use in our code.

In fact, since the XSLT specification was finalized, XSLT and Java have been integrated together ever more closely. Several XSLT parsers have been developed for use with the Java language for processing XML files, although the way that this has been done and the way they are used varies. Fortunately, many of the later parsers have used the Transformation API for XML (TrAX), which was specified as part of JAXP, but, like SAX or DOM, provides a uniform API to enable Java programmers to access the functionality of XSLT processors.

In this chapter we will be covering in depth the use of the Xalan XSLT parser developed by the Apache Software Foundation, and explain and show the use of the TrAX API. We will also investigate XSLTC, a parser with a very different approach, released by Sun Microsystems, which converts XSLT Stylesheets into class files for easy usage at run-time.

Processing XSL Stylesheets

Xalan, previously known as LotusXSL, was developed in IBM Development Labs under the leadership of Scott Boag. Later it was handed over to the Apache Foundation for subsequent development and support as an open source product. There have been considerable changes in this API since then and it has gained more popularity among Java developers. With feedback from numerous users using this parser, Xalan has gone through many changes and has become an increasingly stable and effective parser. As of this writing, Xalan is in version 2.0.

TrAX Overview

As of version 2.0 of Xalan, it has been modified to use the **Transformations API for XML (TrAX)** interfaces. TrAX allows developers to produce XSLT-based applications that are not tied to particular XSLT implementations. The specification for TrAX is being developed through Sun's Java Community Process as part of JAXP 1.1, and is contained in the package javax.xml.transform. Currently two XSLT processors fully implement TrAX: Xalan 2.0 (http://xml.apache.org/xalan-j/), and Saxon 6.1 (http://users.iclway.co.uk/mhkay/saxon/). We actually made use of TrAX in Chapter 3, *The DOM*, to output the contents of our DOM trees. Then, we used a null transformer: a Transformer object that actually applied no transformation rules to the document being passed through it. Now, we're going to look at how we can use the TrAX API to create transformers which are much more powerful.

TrAX works as follows: Like all JAXP interfaces, TrAX employs an abstract factory. The basic class for creating any transformation objects is javax.xml.transform.TransformerFactory, which is an abstract class and cannot be instantiated using a constructor. Instead a new instance of a concrete TransformerFactory is obtained by using the static newInstance() method of the TransformerFactory class.

When the method newInstance() is invoked, TrAX does the same checks as the other JAXP 1.1 factories. It looks in the javax.xml.transform.TransformerFactory system property, checks jaxp.properties in your jre/lib directory, and also tries using the JAR service API. Finally, it will default to trying the Xalan 2.0 implementation. In Xalan, the class that implements TransformerFactory is org.apache.xalan.processor.TransformerFactoryImpl.

The system property javax.xml.transform.TransformerFactory can be specified at the command prompt as follows:

```
java -Djavax.xml.transform.TransformerFactory=
org.apache.xalan.processor.TransformerFactoryImpl StreamInputExp
```

Of course, since the returned object extends and implements the abstract TransformerFactory class, we don't need to know what actual type the run-time implementation has at compile time. In our Java code a new instance of the TransformerFactory can be instantiated as follows:

```
TransformerFactory tFactory = TransformerFactory.newInstance();
```

And what does a `TransformerFactory` make? `Transformers`, naturally. A transformer is obtained by calling the factory's `newTransformer()` method, either with no arguments, to create a `null` transformer, or with a source representing a way to access an XSLT stylesheet, to create a transformer which will apply the transformation that stylesheet describes. To apply the transformation, the transformer's `transform()` method is called, passing in a source and a result, and the data from the source is transformed, and fed to the result object.

The way TrAX handles input sources and results for output is important, so let's take a look at this in a little detail:

For sending input (either inputting a style-sheet when constructing a `Transformer`, or when providing an input for a transformation process), one of these classes derived from `javax.xml.transform.Source` is used:

❑   `javax.xml.transform.stream.StreamSource`

❑   `javax.xml.transform.sax.SAXSource`

❑   `javax.xml.transform.dom.DOMSource`

For returning output, one of these classes derived from `javax.xml.transform.Result` is used:

❑   `javax.xml.transform.stream.StreamResult`

❑   `javax.xml.transform.sax.SAXResult`

❑   `javax.xml.transform.dom.DOMResult`

The following sections explain how to use each of these derived classes for providing input and output.

Using StreamSource and StreamResult

The `javax.xml.transform.stream.StreamSource` class is useful when XML markup (XML or XSL data) is available through any of the following classes or its derivatives,

❑   `java.io.File`

❑   `java.io.InputStream`

❑   `java.io.Reader`

❑   `java.lang.String` (File name or URL where the file exists)

In cases where the XML markup was read from either `java.io.InputStream` or `java.io.Reader` then you should also set the `SystemID` which essentially identifies the location from where the source document was loaded initially (used to resolve relative URLs within the source). If the XML markup was read from either `java.io.File` or `java.lang.String`, then `SystemID` is automatically set to the location from where the file was read. If there are any relative URI's in the input document, then they are resolved using the `SystemID`. In the `StreamSource` class, `SystemID` can be set using the `setSystemID(String)` function.

A `StreamResult` class, which writes the output data into a stream, can be constructed from the following classes or their derivatives:

❑   `java.io.File`

❑   `java.io.OutputStream`

❑   `java.io.Writer`

The following example shows how to use `StreamSource` and `StreamResult`:

```java
import javax.xml.transform.TransformerFactory;
import javax.xml.transform.Transformer;
import javax.xml.transform.stream.StreamSource;
import javax.xml.transform.stream.StreamResult;
import javax.xml.transform.TransformerException;
import javax.xml.transform.TransformerConfigurationException;

// Imported java classes
import java.io.FileOutputStream;
import java.io.FileNotFoundException;
import java.io.IOException;

public class StreamInputExp
{
  public static String XSL_SOURCE_FILE = "calls.xsl";
  public static String XML_SOURCE_FILE = "calls.xml";
  public static String OUTPUT_FILE = "calls.html";

  public static void main(String[] args)
  {
    try {
        TransformerFactory tFactory = TransformerFactory.newInstance();
        StreamSource xslStreamSource = new StreamSource(XSL_SOURCE_FILE);

        StreamSource xmlStreamSource = new StreamSource(XML_SOURCE_FILE);

        Transformer transformer = tFactory.newTransformer(xslStreamSource);
        transformer.transform(xmlStreamSource,
                    new StreamResult(new FileOutputStream(OUTPUT_FILE)));

          System.out.println("Ouput is in " + OUTPUT_FILE);
      } catch(Exception e) {
        e.printStackTrace();
      }
    }
  }
}
```

First a new instance of `TransformerFactory` is initialized from the `TransformerFactory` class by calling the static method `newInstance()`.

In this example we will be using one of the `StreamSource` constructors which accepts the name of the file or URI as parameter. It's initialized from the filename or URI provided in the variable `XSL_SOURCE_FILE` using the following constructor:

```java
StreamSource xslStreamSource = new StreamSource(XSL_SOURCE_FILE);
```

As we have explained above, for this constructor the SystemID is automatically set to the location or URL from where the source file is being loaded. So if the input file has any relative URI's, then they will be resolved using the SystemID provided. Using a similar constructor we create a StreamSource for the XML source file on which transformations need to be applied. The name of the XML source file is provided in the variable XML_SOURCE_FILE, and it's initialized using the constructor:

```
StreamSource xmlStreamSource = new StreamSource(XML_SOURCE_FILE);
```

At this point, no files have been read. The StreamSource object will make the data in the source it wraps available when it is passed to a processing method, such as the newTransformer() or transform() methods.

The next step is to apply the transformation rules defined in XSL source file on the XML source file. We use the factory's newTransformer() method to create a new transformer implementation, initialized from our XML document's source:

```
Transformer transformer = tFactory.newTransformer(xslStreamSource);
```

After the new transformation class is initialized, we can perform the transformation, and send the result to a file. The transform function is invoked on the current transformer class as follows:

```
transformer.transform(xmlStreamSource,
            new StreamResult(new FileOutputStream(OUTPUT_FILE)));
```

Using one of the StreamResult class constructors, a new instance of the StreamResult class is constructed in the above function and the output is written to the file specified by file name given in the variable OUTPUT_FILE.

The complete source code for this example should be saved in StreamInputExp.java. Let's now run it, and see how the output is written. To compile this file, you need to download and JAXP 1.1, if you haven't done so already, and set up the required files in classpath. At compile time, you only need to refer to classes in the jaxp.jar file included in the JAXP distribution, so the command:

```
javac -classpath C:\jaxp-1.1\jaxp.jar StreamInputExp.java
```

should suffice for compilation. However, at run-time, this isn't enough. jaxp.jar doesn't contain any implementation classes, and you'll run into a NoClassDefFound error very quickly indeed if you run the example with the same classpath setting. You'll need to include the xalan.jar file included in the distribution as well, but Xalan relies on being able to access an XML parser (it uses JAXP to obtain a SAX parser, so you can use any JAXP-compliant parser), so you should also add crimson.jar to the list. So, to run the code, the minimal classpath is:

```
java -cp C:\jaxp-1.1\jaxp.jar;C:\jaxp-1.1\xalan.jar;C:\jaxp-1.1\crimson.jar
StreamInputExp
```

Of course, if you change your system properties so that JAXP uses Saxon as the TrAX implementation, or Xerces for SAX support, you will need to replace crimson.jar and/or xalan.jar with the JAR files containing the appropriate tools. Assuming you have a copy of Xerces 1.3 in the indicated location, for example, the following should also work, with Xalan relying on Xerces for its XML parsing support:

```
java -cp C:\jaxp-1.1\jaxp.jar;C:\jaxp-1.1\xalan.jar;C:\xerces-1_3_0\xerces.jar
-Djavax.xml.parsers.SAXParserFactory=org.apache.xerces.jaxp.SAXParserFactoryImpl
StreamInputExp
```

329

In order to test this example out we will use an XML file and a Stylesheet from Chapter 7, `calls.xml` and `calls.xsl`. The source code for these is shown below. First, `calls.xml`:

```xml
<?xml version="1.0"?>
<!DOCTYPE PHONE_RECORDS SYSTEM "calls.dtd">

<PHONE_RECORDS>

  <!-- Call Record 1 -->
  <CALL>
    <FROM>703-433-5678</FROM>
    <DATE>5/5/2000</DATE>
    <TIME HOUR="19" MINUTE="32"/>
    <DESTINATION STATE="California"
                 CITY="Sunnyvale"
                 COUNTRY="US">510-798-8390
    </DESTINATION>
    <DURATION HOURS="1" MINUTES="15"/>
  </CALL>

  <!-- Call Record 2 -->
  <CALL>
    <FROM>703-374-2363</FROM>
    <DATE>5/15/2000</DATE>
    <TIME HOUR="20" MINUTE="15"/>
    <DESTINATION  CITY="Birmingham"
                 COUNTRY="UK">44-121-739-4294
    </DESTINATION>
    <DURATION HOURS="0" MINUTES="30"> </DURATION>
    <CALL_PROMOTION>HALF_PRICE</CALL_PROMOTION>
  </CALL>

</PHONE_RECORDS>
```

and now `calls.xsl`:

```xml
<?xml version="1.0"?>
<xsl:stylesheet xmlns:xsl="http://www.w3.org/1999/XSL/Transform" version="1.0">

<xsl:template match="PHONE_RECORDS">
  <html><head> <title>Phone Listing</title> </head>
  <body>
      <h1>Phone Call Records</h1>
      <table border="1">

       <th>Item</th>
       <th>Source Number</th>
       <th>Destination Number</th>
       <th>Date (MM/DD/YY)</th>

  <xsl:apply-templates/>
      </table>
  </body> </html>
</xsl:template>
```

```
<xsl:template match="CALL">
  <tr>
     <td><xsl:number/></td>
     <td><xsl:value-of select="FROM"/></td>
     <td><xsl:value-of select="DESTINATION"/></td>
     <td><xsl:value-of select="DATE"/></td>
  </tr>
</xsl:template>

</xsl:stylesheet>
```

The output from this executing this code will be same as that produced in Chapter 7. Here is the resulting HTML viewed in a web browser:

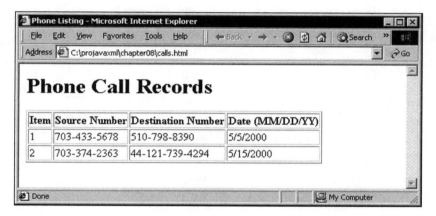

Using SAXSource and SAXResult

In the previous example, we relied on the Transformer to create an XML parser and read in the data from the input source we handed it. Sometimes, however, we want to have a little more control over this parsing process. Maybe we already have a SAX parser in our application, and don't want the overhead of creating another. Maybe we want to ensure that certain features are supported by the parser and switched on before the data is read into the XSLT processor. In these situations, we can use a SAXSource to wrap a SAX 2.0 parser implementation.

At the other end of the transformation process, a SAXResult lets us plug in a SAX ContentHandler to react to SAX events fired by the result as it reads the XML data output by the XSLT processor.

A javax.xml.transform.sax.SAXSource can be constructed using any of the following three constructors:

- ❑ SAXSource()
- ❑ SAXSource(XMLReader reader, InputSource inputSource)
- ❑ SAXSource(InputSource inputSource)

For the first constructor, without any arguments, it will create a SAXSource representing an empty XML document.

When the second constructor is used, the org.xml.sax.XMLReader class provided in the argument will be handed a ContentHandler on behalf of the transformer, and the transformer will then call its parse() method, handing it the InputSource we specify with the other argument. This will cause it to parse the input source, calling the various SAX event methods on the ContentHandler: this gives the XSLT processor the chance to read in and act upon the data from the source.

For the third constructor, the default org.xml.sax.XMLReader class is created using the org.xml.sax.helpers.XMLReaderFactory class. This XMLReader object will act in the same way as the specified XMLReader in the previous constructor.

The example shown below shows how to change the body of our earlier example to use SAXSource and SAXResult:

```
TransformerFactory tFactory = TransformerFactory.newInstance();

Transformer transformer = tFactory.newTransformer(new
                                StreamSource(XSL_SOURCE_FILE));

XMLReader reader = XMLReaderFactory.createXMLReader();

Serializer serializer = SerializerFactory.getSerializer
                (OutputProperties.getDefaultMethodProperties("html"));

serializer.setOutputStream(new FileOutputStream(OUTPUT_FILE));

transformer.transform(
            new SAXSource(reader, new InputSource(XML_SOURCE_FILE)),
            new SAXResult(serializer.asContentHandler()));
```

The output after executing this code is similar to the output from the previous example. In the same way as in the previous example, a new instance of TransformerFactory is initialized from the TransformerFactory class by calling the static method newInstance(). And from the TransformerFactory class a new instance of the Transformer class is created, also passing the StreamSource with a reference to our XSL source file. After this step is executed, the Transformer class is ready to apply XSLT transformations, using the rules defined in the source XSL file.

> There's nothing to stop us from using a SAXSource to read in the XSLT transformation file as well, of course.

Next a new instance of XMLReader is created using the XMLReaderFactory class. It's possible to use the JAXP SAXParserFactory to obtain an XMLReader, if you'd rather use the JAXP property system to locate a parser, using the following lines instead:

```
SAXParserFactory spf = SAXParserFactory.newInstance();
XMLReader reader = spf.newSAXParser().getXMLReader();
```

In either case, we should obtain a working XMLReader, without having to know which parser we're talking to.

Using the XMLReader and the XML source code encapsulated in a single object using InputSource, a new instance of SAXSource is created.

To handle the result of the transformation, we make use of a class provided by Xerces: an XML serializer, which is capable of outputting XML data as formatted text. We use one of its default rendering modes: HTML, and tell it to serialize its output to a file, specified by the OUTPUT_FILE variable.

This serializer can act as a ContentHandler for an XMLReader implementation. The SAXResult class acts as a socket into which we can plug a ContentHandler, which will expose the result of the XSLT transformation as if it were an XMLReader, calling the event handlers on the ContentHandler. So, we can use this to interface the XSLT processor to the Xerces serializer.

The complete code is saved in the file SAXInputExp.java in the source code directory:

```java
import javax.xml.transform.*;
import javax.xml.transform.sax.*;

import org.xml.sax.InputSource;
import org.xml.sax.XMLReader;
import org.xml.sax.ContentHandler;
import org.xml.sax.ext.LexicalHandler;
import org.xml.sax.SAXException;
import org.xml.sax.helpers.XMLReaderFactory;

import javax.xml.transform.stream.StreamSource;
import javax.xml.transform.stream.StreamResult;

import org.apache.xalan.serialize.SerializerFactory;
import org.apache.xalan.serialize.Serializer;
import org.apache.xalan.templates.OutputProperties;

import java.io.FileOutputStream;
import java.io.IOException;

public class SAXInputExp
{
    public static String XSL_SOURCE_FILE = "calls.xsl";
    public static String XML_SOURCE_FILE = "calls.xml";
    public static String OUTPUT_FILE = "calls.html";

    public static void main(String[] args)
    {
      try
      {
        TransformerFactory tFactory = TransformerFactory.newInstance();

        Transformer transformer =  tFactory.newTransformer(
                                      new StreamSource(XSL_SOURCE_FILE));

        XMLReader reader = XMLReaderFactory.createXMLReader();

        Serializer serializer = SerializerFactory.getSerializer
                      (OutputProperties.getDefaultMethodProperties("html"));

        serializer.setOutputStream(new FileOutputStream(OUTPUT_FILE));
```

```
            transformer.transform(new SAXSource(reader,
                            new InputSource(XML_SOURCE_FILE)),
                            new SAXResult(serializer.asContentHandler()));

            System.out.println("Ouput is in " + OUTPUT_FILE);
    }
    catch(Exception exp)
    {
        exp.printStackTrace();
    }
    }
}
```

One of the main advantages of using SAXResult is its ability to allow other content handlers to be the receivers of the output from the transformations. For example, if we have a class called PhoneListingsProcessor which implements the org.xml.sax.ContentHandler interface, then we can change the last line of our code to:

```
transformer.transform(new SAXSource(reader,
                            new InputSource(XML_SOURCE_FILE)),
                            new SAXResult(new PhoneListingsProcessor()));
```

When the transform() method is executed, the output data is passed on to PhoneListings Processor. Next the PhoneListingsProcessor class prints out the start elements, end elements and character data by executing the parser used by org.xml.sax.ContentHandler in the same order that the output has been retrieved. Its functionality is pretty much similar to feeding a normal, valid XML file into SAX parser.

Using DOMSource and DOMResult

The DOMSource class allows an org.w3c.dom.Node to be used as the source of the input tree. Any of the nodes derived from org.w3c.dom.Node are valid input, but the most common will be Document.

The DOMResult class allows an org.w3c.dom.Node to be specified to which result DOM nodes will be appended. If an output node is not specified, the transformer will use newDocument() to create an output org.w3c.dom.Document node. If a node is specified, it should be one of org.w3c.dom.Document, org.w3c.dom.Element, or org.w3c.dom.DocumentFragment.

Specification of any other node type is implementation dependent and undefined by this API. If the result is an org.w3c.dom.Document, the output of the transformation must have a single element root to set as the document element. If your transformation doesn't generate data conforming to this pattern, you can use a DocumentFragment to capture this result.

In the following example we can see the use of the DOMSource and DOMResult classes:

```
import javax.xml.transform.TransformerFactory;
import javax.xml.transform.Transformer;
import javax.xml.transform.dom.DOMSource;
import javax.xml.transform.dom.DOMResult;
import javax.xml.parsers.DocumentBuilder;
import javax.xml.parsers.DocumentBuilderFactory;
```

```java
import javax.xml.transform.stream.StreamSource;
import javax.xml.transform.TransformerException;
import javax.xml.transform.TransformerConfigurationException;

import org.w3c.dom.Document;
import org.w3c.dom.Node;
import org.apache.xalan.serialize.Serializer;
import org.apache.xalan.serialize.SerializerFactory;
import org.apache.xalan.templates.OutputProperties;

// Imported Java classes
import java.io.FileOutputStream;
import java.io.FileNotFoundException;
import java.io.IOException;

public class DOMInputExp
{
  public static String XSL_SOURCE_FILE = "calls.xsl";
  public static String XML_SOURCE_FILE = "calls.xml";
  public static String OUTPUT_FILE = "calls.html";


    public static void main(String[] args)
    {
      try
      {
          TransformerFactory tFactory = TransformerFactory.newInstance();

          Transformer transformer = tFactory.newTransformer(new
                                       StreamSource(XSL_SOURCE_FILE));

      // Initializing Document object from XML source file
          DocumentBuilderFactory domFactory = DocumentBuilderFactory.newInstance();
          DocumentBuilder domBuilder = domFactory.newDocumentBuilder();
          Document document = domBuilder.parse(XML_SOURCE_FILE);

          DOMSource domSource = new DOMSource(document);
          domSource.setSystemId(XML_SOURCE_FILE);

          DOMResult domResult = new DOMResult();

          transformer.transform(domSource, domResult);

          Serializer serializer = SerializerFactory.getSerializer
                        (OutputProperties.getDefaultMethodProperties("html"));

          serializer.setOutputStream(new FileOutputStream(OUTPUT_FILE));
          serializer.asDOMSerializer().serialize(domResult.getNode());

          System.out.println("Ouput is in " + OUTPUT_FILE);
    }
    catch(Exception exp)
    {
        exp.printStackTrace();
    }
    }
}
```

335

We create a new instance of `TransformerFactory` and using this class a new instance of `Transformer` class is created. So far this should be familiar to you. The next three steps are used to initialize `org.w3c.dom.Document` from the input XML file. We use the `DocumentBuilderFactory` class to create a new instance of `DocumentBuilder`. Next by passing the XML source file URL a new `Document` class is initialized.

Next, using the current `org.w3c.dom.Document` as a parameter, a `DOMSource` object is created and initialized. Next an empty `DomResult` object is created. The results after the transformation process will be stored in this class.

Finally, using the current transformer class, transformation is applied on the `DOMSource` object, and the rules defined in `XSL_SOURCE_FILE` will be applied on the DOM tree inside the `DOMSource` object.

The results after applying the transformations are stored in `DomResult` object. We use the `Serializer` class as before, this time handing it the output node from the result object, which it will then iterate through, format and print to the specified output stream.

Not all `Factory` implementations implement all the SAX, DOM and Stream features. To check if a particular feature is supported, you can use the `FEATURE` field of each class type. For example to check if the current XSLT processor supports both `SAXSource` and `SAXResult`, we can check:

```
if (tFactory.getFeature(SAXSource.FEATURE) &&
    tFactory.getFeature(SAXResult.FEATURE))  {
  // SAX features are supported
}
```

Similarly, the availability of `DOMSource` and `DOMResult` can be verified using:

```
if (tFactory.getFeature(DOMSource.FEATURE) &&
    tFactory.getFeature(DOMResult.FEATURE))  {
  // DOM features are supported.
}
```

As long as the transformer factory implementation supports a particular feature, the input and output does not necessarily have to be of the same type. For example it is not required that if input is `StreamSource`, then output should be `StreamResult`.

Xalan's Architecture

TrAX provides nice high-level tools for applying a transformation to XML and processing the result. But sometimes we need more functionality than is exposed through the TrAX interfaces.

Most of the core API for Xalan can be divided into four modules. Some of these modules implement the functionality required for using the TrAX interfaces declared under `javax.xml.transform`, while others implement functionality we can only access by talking directly to Xalan's internal API. The four modules are explained in the following sections. Please note we have tried to give an overview of each of the modules in Xalan. The details of internal functionality of Xalan product were kept to a minimum and only those details that are useful in writing programs using Xalan, are covered. Details about the design of Xalan as a processor are beyond the scope of this chapter.

Process Module (org.apache.xalan.processor)

When XSLT transformations need to be applied using TrAX interfaces, the classes under this package act as the starting point. The `org.apache.xalan.processor.TransformerFactoryImpl` implementation under this package implements the `javax.xml.transform.TransformerFactory` abstract class, and we've been using it in all our previous examples.

So when JAXP is used for processing XSLT stylesheets and no other value has been specified for the `javax.xml.transform.TransformerFactory` system property, then the default `TransformerFactory` class returned on executing the `newInstance()` static method is `org.apache.xalan.processor.TransformerFactoryImpl`.

After the `TransformerFactoryImpl` is instantiated, a new instance of `org.apache.xalan.processor.StylesheetHandler` is created which implements the `ContentHandler` interface and acts as the content handler for the parse events encountered when reading in the stylesheet. Adapters are used to map whichever input source type we hand the parser to this model. The `StylesheetHandler` constructs a schematic representation of the XSL stylesheet.

As we have explained in chapter 7, `xsl:stylesheet` can have only a limited set of top level elements like `xsl:template`, `xsl:include`, `xsl:import`, `xsl:output`, `xsl:param`, etc. Also `xsl:template` can have only a restricted set of elements like `xsl:apply-templates`, `xsl:call-template`, `xsl:number`, `xsl:if`, `xsl:copy`, `xsl:choose` etc. The DTD for all the allowed elements at a particular level is defined at http://www.w3.org/TR/xslt#dtd.

In Xalan the above hierarchy is defined in `org.apache.xalan.processor.XSLTElementDef`. The `StylesheetHandler` passes the events on to the appropriate `XSLTElementProcessor` for the given event, according to the rules defined in `XSLTElementDef` that is associated with the event.

Finally, using both `org.apache.xalan.processor.XSLTElementDef` to define elements, and `org.apache.xalan.processor.XSLTAttributeDef` to define attributes, the schematic model for the current XSL stylesheet is constructed. Both these classes hold the allowed namespace, local name, and type of element or attribute. The final schema is stored in an `org.apache.xalan.processor.XSLTSchema`.

Finally as a recap, the main goal of this module is to read the XSLT input from any of these sources, which can be a file, or byte stream, or stream of SAX events, or DOM tree; and to make the structure of the source document readily available, in a set of objects that represents schema of all the elements and other nodes. This internal representation is like a proprietary document object model.

Templates Module (org.apache.xalan.templates)

The primary purpose of this module is to hold stylesheet data, not to perform procedural tasks associated with the construction of the data. Neither does it perform tasks associated with the transformation itself. The classes under this package implement the `javax.xml.transform.Templates` interface of the TrAX API.

The base class of all template objects that are associated with an XSLT element is the `org.apache.xalan.templates.ElemTemplateElement`. An `ElemTemplateElement` also knows its position in the source stylesheet – the line and column numbers of the element declaration in the source document. They are useful only for error and reporting purposes, and is not same as the result returned from using XPath's `position()` function. `ElemTemplateElement` also implements the `org.apache.xml.utils.PrefixResolver` class and can answer questions about current namespace nodes.

Next the main stylesheet which has details about all the nodes in the input source document excluding all the imports is created using `org.apache.xalan.templates.Stylesheet` which extends `org.apache.xalan.templates.ElemTemplateElement`. `ElemTemplateElement` is the base class for all template objects and using various classes like:

- `org.apache.xalan.templates.KeyDeclaration` (for xsl:key)

- `org.apache.xalan.templates.ElemVariable` (for xsl:variable and xsl:param)

- `org.apache.xalan.templates.ElemTemplate` (for xsl:template)

- `org.apache.xalan.templates.ElemAttributeSet` (for representing attributes associated with element)

and similar other classes. Each of the stylesheet elements are saved in the `Stylesheet` class.

Finally `org.apache.xalan.templates.StylesheetComposed` is created which includes the current stylesheet and also has includes and import methods resolved. The root of the Stylesheet is represented by `org.apache.xalan.templates.StylesheetRoot` and has all the imported `StylesheetComposed` objects.

Transformer Module (org.apache.xalan.transformer)

The Transformer module implements the classes required for performing runtime transactions. The Transformer module is in charge of run-time transformations. The `org.apache.xalan.transformer.TransformerImpl` class implements the TrAX Transformer interface, `javax.xml.transform.Transformer`.

This package also provides the class which handles the results of stylesheet processing. During transformation, the processor sends a stream of SAX events, which are dispatched by an `org.apache.xalan.transformer.ResultTreeHandler`. This wraps whatever actual `Result` object is handling the result, and provides a single point for the transformer process to call to 'write' the results of processing.

`TransformerImpl`, with the help of a `StyleSheetRoot` object, starts processing the source tree (or it can also provide a `ContentHandler` reference for handling SAX parse events using the `SourceTree Handler`), and completes the transformation process. The transformer module completes most of the transformation process, but element level operations are generally performed by template modeule objects in an `execute()` method. Each of the template objects like `ElemVariable`, `ElemTemplate` and others which extend `ElemTemplateElement` implement the `execute()` method, and from this method events like `processingInstruction`, `characters`, `startElement`, `endElement` and others are invoked using the `org.apache.xalan.transformer.ResultTreeHandler`.

Leaving these there are couple of classes in this package which help in implementing the XSLT language specifications while performing the transformation on the source and creating the result tree, like `Counter` and `CountersTable` classes for generating the counter used by `xsl:number`, and Key management classes `KeyIterator`, `KeyManager`, and `KeyTable` used by `xsl:key`, etc.

This module also includes functionality beyond that required to provide a TrAX interface. These are not necessarily part of the `org.apache.xalan.transformer` package, but represent other modules that act on the result trees, like:

❑   `Serializer` which allows turning a tree or set of events into a stream of XML, HTML, or plain text.

❑   `Stree` module, which helps in implementing read-only `DOM2.0` interfaces, and provides more details on implementing faster transforms like document order indexes. This module also tries to implement incremental transformation, like reading only partial nodes into memory from the entire source document, but the trade-off for this approach is that it involves creating new threads inside the parser. In most server side applications it is preferred not to use threads – the EJB specification discourages usage of threads from individual programs. So this approach of loading only partial nodes might not be successfully used.

❑   `Extensions` module allows Java code and script to be called from within a style sheet. The extensions module is covered in more detail later in this chapter.

XPath Module (org.apache.xpath)

The XPath module helps in executing XPath expressions from the Java code. First the XPath strings are compiled into expression trees, and then these expressions are executed using the XPath `execute(..)` function. This module resides outside the `org.apache.xalan` package indicating it as a separate independent package. It's got only a small dependency on the Xalan `Utils` module. XPath includes a couple of other modules, which handle XPath axes (`org.apache.xpath.axes`), XPath functions (`org.apache.xpath.functions`), XPath operations (`org.apache.xpath.operations`) and different XPath data types (`org.apache.xpath.objects`) like Boolean, String, NodeSet, etc. Details about XPath axes and various XPath functions, objects and data types were explained in chapter 7.

Most of these submodules are used internally. The idea is to keep the usage of XPath expressions simple. The user has to pass only the XPath Expressions to be executed, call the `execute()` method and get the correct result back. The `XPathAPI` class works as a wrapper around the low-level classes and does most of the internal initialization required for executing an XPath expression to give the resultant output. This does involve some initializations and so using the low-level classes directly may give slightly better performance – but beware, as always, when using internal APIs, since you're tying yourself not only to a specific processor, but also to a specific version..

Developing Applications Using XSLT Parser

To this point, we have seen how to apply simple transformations and output the resultant data. While explaining about `StreamSource` and `StreamResult` we took an XSLT file and an XML file, and through the code, we applied the rules defined in XSLT file on the XML file and got back the result. The result was stored in a HTML file.

In the next few sections we will be looking at various other features that Xalan provides when applying XSLT transformations.

Passing Parameters to Stylesheets

Just like stylesheet variables, parameters are accessed in a stylesheet by preceding the parameter name with a $ sign. For example, to access the `pageheadingParam` parameter from a stylesheet the declaration will be as follows:

```
<xsl:template match="/PHONE_RECORDS">
  <html><head> <title>Phone Listing</title> </head>
  <body>
      <h1><xsl:value-of select="$pageheadingParam"/></h1>
      <table border="1">
        <tr>
          <td><b>Item</b></td>
          <td><b>Source Number</b></td>
          <td><b>Destination Number </b></td>
          <td><b>Date (MM/DD/YY)</b></td>
          <td><b>Time (HH:MM)</b></td>
        </tr>
        <xsl:apply-templates/>
        </table>
  </body> </html>
</xsl:template>
```

Here the heading of the output page is generated dynamically by passing the parameter `pageheading Param` to the stylesheet.

Parameters can be passed to stylesheets while applying transformation both from the command line and from inside Java code. When executing Xalan from the command prompt, parameters are passed to stylesheet using the `-param` option. Here's how we can pass parameters to `callsparam.xsl` file. When the parameters string contains spaces, you should place it within double quotes (" ").

```
java org.apache.xalan.xslt.Process -in calls.xml -xsl callsparam.xsl -out
PhoneListing.html -param pageheadingParam "Welcome to Online Phone Listings"
```

This entire command should be typed on one line. Here's what the output page looks like:

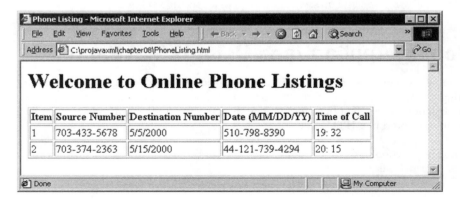

The heading parameter `Welcome to Online Phone Listings` was passed as a parameter to the stylesheet. The same can be done from Java code programmatically using the `setParameter()` method on a transformer object. Syntax for this function is as follows:

```
setParameter(String paramName, java.lang.Object value)
```

Here's some example code, which shows how a parameter can be passed to a stylesheet using TrAX. The name of the parameter to be passed is `pageheadingParam`:

```
TransformerFactory tFactory = TransformerFactory.newInstance();
Transformer transformer = tFactory.newTransformer(
                               new StreamSource(XSL_SOURCE_FILE));

transformer.setParameter("pageheadingParam", "Welcome to Online Phone Listings");

StreamSource xmlStreamSource = new StreamSource(XML_SOURCE_FILE);

transformer.transform(xmlStreamSource,
        new StreamResult(new FileOutputStream(OUTPUT_FILE)));

transformer.setParameter("pageheadingParam", "Online Phone Listings");

transformer.transform(xmlStreamSource,
        new StreamResult(new FileOutputStream(OUTPUT_FILE_OTHER)));
```

One more thing to notice in the above listing is, we have created the `transformer` object only once and reused it to recreate two different output files. Only the value of the parameter `pageheadingParam` had to be changed. So we are using the same `transformer` object twice.

Remember that creating a `transformer` involves a lot of operations, like reading the XSLT data from the source and re-initializing the `XSLTSchema` in memory and lots of initialization operations after that.

If the same source document is used multiple times, remember:

❑   Don't reinitialize the `Transformer` object multiple times

❑   Don't perform the same transformations repeatedly – instead store the result

Using Associated Stylesheets

If the stylesheet is declared as part of the XML, using the `getAssociatedStylesheet()` method of the `TransformerFactory` class allows us to obtain a transformer for the document's associated stylesheet.

Here's the code, which retrieves the stylesheet declared inside the XML file and applies the parameter `pageheadingParam` to the stylesheet:

```
// Take the default stylesheet
String media= null;
String title = null;
String charset = null;
```

```
TransformerFactory tFactory = TransformerFactory.newInstance();
Source stylesheet = tFactory.getAssociatedStylesheet(
        new StreamSource(XML_SOURCE_FILE),media, title, charset);

Transformer transformer = tFactory.newTransformer(stylesheet);

transformer.setParameter("pageheadingParam", "Welcome to Online Phone Listings");

StreamSource xmlStreamSource = new StreamSource(XML_SOURCE_FILE);

//Writing output
transformer.transform(xmlStreamSource,
            new StreamResult(new FileOutputStream(OUTPUT_FILE)));
```

We reference the stylesheet in the XML document follows:

```
<?xml-stylesheet type="text/xsl" href="callsparam.xsl" ?>
```

Executing XPath Expressions

Xalan also provides a mechanism to execute XPath expressions programmatically from our code. Classes under the package `org.apache.xpath` provide this functionality. The `org.apache.xpath.XPathAPI` class works like a kind of wrapper around the low-level classes and does most of the internal initialization required for executing an XPath expression and to give the resultant output.

We can optimize XPath expressions by pre-compiling the XPath expressions using the low-level API, and then using these compiled XPath expressions over and over.

The steps involved in executing XPath expressions and getting back resultant data using Xalan programmatically is fairly simple, since the `org.apache.xpath.XPathAPI` class hides most of the complexities involved in setting namespaces and other minor details. The XPathAPI class provides different functions using which the result after executing the XPath expression can be retrieved in either of these formats:

❑ A single node implementing the interface `org.w3c.dom.Node`

❑ An ordered list of nodes, implementing the interface `org.w3c.dom.NodeList`, which represents a collection of nodes

❑ An iterator implementing the interface `org.w3c.dom.traversal.NodeIterator`, from which the rest of the resultant nodes can be retrieved by iterating through the entire list

Here's some code which uses the XPathAPI class,

```
import javax.xml.parsers.DocumentBuilder;
import javax.xml.parsers.DocumentBuilderFactory;
import javax.xml.transform.Transformer;
import javax.xml.transform.TransformerFactory;
import javax.xml.transform.dom.DOMSource;
import javax.xml.transform.stream.StreamResult;
import org.apache.xpath.XPathAPI;
import org.w3c.dom.traversal.NodeIterator;
import org.xml.sax.InputSource;
```

```java
import java.io.FileInputStream;
import java.io.FileNotFoundException;
import java.io.StringWriter;

import org.w3c.dom.Node;
import javax.xml.transform.OutputKeys;
import org.w3c.dom.Document;

public class XPathExpressions
{
  public static String XML_FILE_NAME = "calls.xml";
  public static String XPATH_EXPRESSION = "/PHONE_RECORDS/CALL[1]/DESTINATION";

  public static void main (String[] args) throws Exception
  {
      InputSource in = new InputSource(new FileInputStream(XML_FILE_NAME));
      DocumentBuilderFactory dfactory = DocumentBuilderFactory.newInstance();
      Document doc = dfactory.newDocumentBuilder().parse(in);

      TransformerFactory tFactory = TransformerFactory.newInstance();
      Transformer transformer = tFactory.newTransformer();

      // Avoids printing <?XML ..> each time the transformer is called
      transformer.setOutputProperty(OutputKeys.OMIT_XML_DECLARATION, "yes");

      NodeIterator nodeIterator = XPathAPI.selectNodeIterator(
              doc, XPATH_EXPRESSION);

      Node currentNode;
      StringWriter finalResult = new StringWriter();
      StreamResult resultWrapper = new StreamResult(finalResult);
      while ((currentNode = nodeIterator.nextNode())!= null)
      {
          // Serializing data to StringWriter class
          transformer.transform(new DOMSource(currentNode),
            resultWrapper);
      }
      System.out.println(finalResult.toString());
  }

}
```

The initial process followed is pretty much same as previous ones. A `Transformer` is initialized from the `Transformerfactory` class – this is a simple null transformer which we'll use to output the results of our XPath query without transforming them, although we set one of its output properties so that it omits an XML declaration from the output. From the XML source file URL a new `Document` is initialized. We'll execute the XPath query on this document object.

In this example we will be using the `selectNodeIterator()` function from the `XPathAPI` class which accepts a reference to the context node and the XPath expression to be applied. In our current example, this function will be called as follows,

```java
NodeIterator nodeIterator = XPathAPI.selectNodeIterator(
        doc, XPATH_EXPRESSION);
```

343

The `doc` variable is a reference to the current `Document` object and the `XPATH_EXPRESSION` variable has the actual XPath expression to be applied. The result after executing this function is a `NodeIterator` class, using which each of the nodes from the resultant nodeset is retrieved and the data for each node is serialized to the `StringWriter` class by applying the null transformation. The resultant output can be retrieved in the string format by calling the `toString()` method on the `StringWriter` class.

Finally we have the result after executing the XPath expression. The usage of low level XPath API calls that involve using the `org.apache.xpath.XPath` class directly is required only when you need more flexibility while applying XPath expressions.

Chaining Output Across Multiple Transformations

Often the logic to be implemented for retrieving the result data gets quite complicated and it is then often a mistake to include formatting information with it. We therefore need a way to separate the two. This is where the chaining feature of XSLT comes into help. We can implement one stylesheet which retrieves the data we are interested in, and a second which formats the data in an output template.

In this mode, the output generated by executing one XSLT transformation becomes the input for another XSLT stylesheet transformation and the final output is the result of applying the last XSLT transformation. There's no limit to the number of transformations that can be chained together.

To test this, we will use our tried and tested `calls.xml` file. The expected output from executing this code will be same HTML file as always, however we will enforce separation of logic and formatting.

We will use two stylesheets to achieve this. The first (`ListingLogic.xsl`) generates the table data having FROM, DESTINATION and DATE information:

```
<?xml version="1.0"?>
<xsl:stylesheet xmlns:xsl="http://www.w3.org/1999/XSL/Transform" version="1.0">

<xsl:template match="/PHONE_RECORDS">
      <phone_listing>
      <xsl:apply-templates/>
  </phone_listing>
</xsl:template>

<xsl:template match="CALL">
  <tr>
    <td><xsl:number/></td>
    <xsl:apply-templates select="FROM|DESTINATION|DATE"/>
  </tr>
</xsl:template>

<xsl:template match="FROM|DESTINATION|DATE">
  <td><xsl:value-of select="text()"/></td>
</xsl:template>

</xsl:stylesheet>
```

This XSL file does not have any real HTML tags or other `<table>` tags. All it generates is the tags having the data. Here's the output from the first XSL file:

```
<phone_listing>
    <tr>
        <td>1</td>
        <td>703-433-5678</td>
        <td>510-798-8390</td>
        <td>5/5/2000</td>
    </tr>

    <tr>
        <td>2</td>
        <td>703-374-2363</td>
        <td>44-121-739-4294</td>
        <td>5/15/2000</td>
    </tr>
</phone_listing>
```

Notice that there is not a single `<html>` or `<table>` tag. Apart from the parent tag `<phone_listing>` which was generated to aid in processing this output in the next template, the only other tags we have are `<tr>` and `<td>` tags. In HTML, each `<td>` generates a new cell and each `<tr>` generates a new row in the output. So at this point we have two rows with four columns each filled with data. There is no other information like where these rows will be placed, how the final page looks like etc. This is an intermediate output and this tree becomes the input for the second XSL file (`ListingGui.xsl`):

```
<?xml version="1.0"?>
<xsl:stylesheet xmlns:xsl="http://www.w3.org/1999/XSL/Transform" version="1.0">

  <xsl:template match="phone_listing">
      <html><head> <title>Phone Listing</title> </head>
      <body>
       <h1>Phone Call Records</h1>
       <table border="1">
      <tr>
      <td align="center"><b>Item</b></td>
      <td align="center"><b>Source Number</b></td>
      <td align="center"><b>Destination Number </b></td>
      <td align="center"><b>Date (MM/DD/YY)</b></td>
    </tr>
      <!-- The table having exact listing values will be substituted here -->
      <xsl:apply-templates select="@*|node()"/>

        </table>
      </body> </html>
</xsl:template>

<!-- Copy the contents from previous transformation as it is
     They will be substituted in between the tables
  -->
<xsl:template match="@*|node()">
  <xsl:copy>
    <xsl:apply-templates select="@*|node()"/>
  </xsl:copy>
</xsl:template>


</xsl:stylesheet>
```

To aid in processing the template in the second XSL file, in the output from first XSL file a new element called <phone_listing> is added, which is added as the root element for the current tree.

The second XSL file `ListingGui.xsl` is the one, which adds the <html> and <table> tags and creates the final output. The second XSL file starts by matching with the <phone_listing> element, which essentially was the output from previous transformation, using the following template rule:

```
<xsl:template match="phone_listing">
```

All the text that needs to appear above the listing data, including the table header, is placed here directly. Next, at the location where the listing data generated needs to be placed, the call to a new template rule is declared:

```
<xsl:apply-templates select="@*|node()"/>
```

Here for the select attribute we are using XPath expression @*|node() where @* indicates to select any attribute and node() indicates to select any element. So the final result after executing this template will be all the elements and attributes available in the input tree will be copied to output directly.

This template rule is implemented in the same XSL file as follows:

```
<xsl:template match="@*|node()">
  <xsl:copy>
    <xsl:apply-templates select="@*|node()"/>
  </xsl:copy>
</xsl:template>
```

When this template rule is executed, all the output from previous XSL file is copied into the new location, except the <phone_listing> element, since we are currently processing its child elements.

So at this stage, for the output from second XSL file, we have added the <html> and <table> header tags and the data inside the table. What's missing are the closing tags for the </html>, </table> tags etc. so these are added here, after the template rule for copying data from the previous transformation.

We have completed the first steps required for implementing the chaining process. What remains is implementing the chaining of these stylesheets through Java code.

Xalan provides two different ways of implementing stylesheet chaining. The first approach is to use multiple Transformer objects with the output of one Transformer object given as input to the second Transformer object and so on. This approach is also called the pipe mechanism. In this scenario, the Transformer object which receives the input becomes the content handler for the previous Transformer object instance. The very first Transformer object becomes the content handler for the XMLReader, which is used to parse the input document.

The second approach is to have multiple instances of the org.xml.sax.XMLFilter class, with the first one declared the parent of the second XMLFilter object, the second one declared the parent of the third XMLFilter object and so on. XMLReader is set as the parent for the very first instance of XMLFilter object.

The following example explains how to chain output using pipes. As explained above, when using the piping model, output from one `Transformer` object is sent as input to another `Transformer` object. The second `Transformer` object becomes the content handler for the previous `Transformer` object.

Continuing with our calls example, we have two XSL files, `ListingLogic.xsl` and `ListingGui.xsl` where the output from `ListingLogic.xsl` needs to be provided as input to `ListingGui.xsl`. For each of these XSL files, a `TransformerHandler` instance is created from the `SAXTransformer Factory` class. These classes, from the `javax.xml.transform.sax` package, wrap `Transformers` such that they can act as a `ContentHandler` for a set of SAX events, apply the transformation to the XML these events describe, and fire SAX events out the other end describing the result of the transformation to another `ContentHandler`.

We will be using the capability of the `SAXResult` object to allow other content handlers to be the receivers of the output from the transformations. First of all, we create two source objects representing the two input XSLT files, and then generate our two `SAXTransformerHandlers` from them:

```
TransformerFactory tFactory = TransformerFactory.newInstance();
SAXTransformerFactory saxTFactory = ((SAXTransformerFactory) tFactory);

StreamSource listingLogicSource = new StreamSource(LOGIC_XSL_FILE);
StreamSource guiSource     = new StreamSource(GUI_XSL_FILE);

TransformerHandler saxTfHandler1 =
            saxTFactory.newTransformerHandler(listingLogicSource);

TransformerHandler saxTfHandler2 =
            saxTFactory.newTransformerHandler(guiSource);
```

The next step is to create an `XMLReader` which will read in the input XML file, and start off our chain. The `saxTfHandler1` is then made the `ContentHandler` for the reader. This means all the SAX parse events that are generated while parsing the content will handled by `saxTfHandler1`. For `saxTfHandler1`, `saxTfHandler2` is set as the content handler. They are set as follows:

```
XMLReader reader = XMLReaderFactory.createXMLReader();
reader.setContentHandler(saxTfHandler1);
saxTfHandler1.setResult(new SAXResult(saxTfHandler2));
```

After this step a `Serializer` class is initialized, allowing the final output to be written to a file, and this `Serializer` class is set as content handler for `saxTfHandler2` using a `SAXResult` class.

```
Serializer serializer = SerializerFactory.getSerializer
            (OutputProperties.getDefaultMethodProperties("html"));

serializer.setOutputStream(new FileOutputStream(OUTPUT_FILE));
tHandler2.setResult(new SAXResult(serializer.asContentHandler()));
```

To this point we have not applied any transformations on the source XML file. We have been initializing the XSLT schema in memory and setting up the transformation process. The real transformation process takes place once we call the parse method on the `XMLReader` class.

```
reader.parse(new InputSource(INPUT_XML_FILE));
```

The final output will be a complete HTML document, which has both phone listings and proper headings, displayed in tabular form.

347

Using Extensions in Stylesheets

While creating XSLT stylesheets the task becomes easier if we are able to use another language like Java or JavaScript as part of the stylesheet and substitute the output from the external program as part of output from the stylesheet. This is where the extension mechanism provided in stylesheets comes in.

According to the XSLT specifications there are no hard and fast rules to indicate which extensions need to be provided as part of the XSLT processor implementation, but it does provide a mechanism to verify if a particular extension is provided in the current implementation. The extensions provided here differ from implementation to implementation.

Continuing with our Xalan usage, in this section we will be explaining various extension mechanisms that have been provided with Xalan. Most of the extensions provided here are also supported in other XSLT processors like Saxon and XT (http://www.jclark.com/xml/xt.html). With slight variation in how the namespaces are declared, the extensions should work fine with very minor changes to stylesheets.

XSLT allows two kinds of Extensions: Extension Elements and Extension Functions.

Extension Elements

If the element is prefixed by a namespace which has been designated as an extension namespace, then that element is considered as an extension element. Normally elements that are prefixed by a default namespace are copied to the result tree (output) directly. In the case of extension elements, they normally perform some action. It's not mandatory for an extension element to always return a valid value. It can also return `null` if there's nothing to return. If an extension element returns any value, then it gets copied to the result tree directly.

A namespace is designated as an extension namespace by using an `extension-element-prefixes` attribute. It can be declared either at `xsl:stylesheet` element level, if the same namespace prefix needs to be accessible globally, or it can be declared as an attribute of a literal result element or extension element.

Multiple namespaces can be declared as extension prefixes by declaring them in the same line separated by whitespace. For example the following lines designate `extension1` and `extension2` as extension element prefixes:

```
<xsl:stylesheet
   ...
   xmlns:extension1="urn:extension-1-namespace"
   xmlns:extension2="urn:extension-2-namespace"
   extension-element-prefixes="extension1 extension2"
>
```

It is considered an error if `extension-element-prefixes` has a string in its list and there's no namespace declaration for this string. Also the `extension-element-prefixes` are valid only for elements declared within the current stylesheet or within the current element subtree (if declared at element level). These prefixes do not apply to any imported or included stylesheets.

The default namespace (declared by using an attribute of the form `xmlns="urn:some-namespace"`) may be designated as an extension namespace by including `#default` in the list of namespace prefixes.

By default namespace declarations are included in the transformation output. This can be avoided by adding the prefix name in the list of values for `exclude-result-prefixes`. For example to stop printing the namespace declarations of both `extension1` and `extension2` to the output, it can be declared as:

```
<xsl:stylesheet
    .........
    xmlns:extension1="urn:extension-1-namespace"
    xmlns:extension2="urn:extension-2-namespace"
    extension-element-prefixes="extension1 extension2"
    exclude-result-prefixes = "extension1 extension2
>
```

There is no effect on how extension elements are processed by avoiding the namespaces being printed to output. It's done mostly to hide the namespaces that are used internally within a stylesheet or to reduce the length of output content.

Extension elements declared within the extension namespace need to be mapped to a specific implementing class or script. We'll look at how this is accomplished later.

Extension Functions

Extension functions are mostly used to pass arguments to an extension implementation and insert the value returned from the extension implementation. For example, this extension function call:

```
<xsl:value-of select="listingExtension:getLocaleDate( DATE, TIME/@HOUR,
TIME/@MINUTE)"/>
```

could access this extension implementation:

```
function getLocaleDate(callDate, callHour, callMinute)
{
   var currentDate = new Date(callDate);
   currentDate.setUTCHours(callHour);
   currentDate.setUTCMinutes(callMinute);
   if (timeZone == "GMT") {
    return currentDate.toGMTString();
   }
   else {
       return currentDate.toLocaleString();
   }
}
```

which is written using JavaScript. The way to embed JavaScript into a Stylesheet is explained in the next section.

349

The parameters passed to an extension can be any of the valid XSLT data types. When the extension function is written in Java, objects of the following Java classes will be passed to the extension function.

XSLT Data Type	Java Data Type
Node-Set	`org.w3c.dom.traversal.NodeIterator`
String	`java.lang.String`
Boolean	`java.lang.Boolean`
Number	`java.lang.Double`
Result Tree Fragment	`org.w3c.dom.DocumentFragment`

Extension elements, which are implemented using Java, can also access certain items in the XSLT environment through the `org.apache.xalan.extensions.ExpressionContext` interface.

Two more elements, which are required for declaring extension elements and extension functions in the stylesheet, are `lxslt:component` and `lxslt:script` where the `lxslt` namespace refers to:

```
xmlns:lxslt="http://xml.apache.org/xslt"
```

Please note that this namespace declaration is Xalan-specific. For other XSLT processors the namespace will be different. In Xalan, the `lxslt` namespace provides support for both `lxslt:component` and `lxslt:script`.

Within the scope of this `lxslt` namespace, the syntax for `lxslt:component` is:

```
<lxslt:component
    prefix="prefix_extension"
    elements="element1 element 2 element3 .... elementn"
    functions="func1 func2 func3 .... funcn"
    <lxslt:script>
        . . .
    </lxslt:script>
</lxslt:component>
```

For each of the `extension-element-prefixes`, there needs to be one `lxslt:component` element, with that namespace prefix as the value for the `prefix` attribute in the `lxslt:component` element. Each of the values given for the `elements` attribute separated by whitespace are extension elements (the names are given here without the namespace prefix). Similarly each of the values given for `functions` attribute separated by whitespace are extension functions (again, no namespace prefixes are used).

There's no limit to the number of elements and functions each `lxslt:component` can have. The only limitation is on `lxslt:script`. There can be only one `lxslt:script` for each `lxslt:component` and this script element is the one which implements all the functionality for extension elements and functions.

`lxslt:script` can be declared in either Java or Javascript (or any other scripting language supported through BSF – the Bean Scripting Framework). The syntax for `lxslt:script` when it's declared using JavaScript is:

```
<lxslt:script lang="javascript">
    <!-- script implementation-->
</lxslt:script >
```

In future there is a plan to support a src feature which will have reference to external JavaScript file which has the required implementation. This will avoid having lot of code in the XSL Stylesheet file. As of version 2.0, this feature is not yet supported in Xalan.

```
<lxslt:script
    language="javascript"
    src="LisitingRoutines.js"
</lxslt:script>
```

When using the Java language for our extensions, the lxslt:script element can refer to the class which contains the necessary implementation using an lxslt:script element like this:

```
<lxslt:script lang="javaclass" src="full_classname" />
```

So to provide a class name, declare it as:

```
<lxslt:script lang="javaclass" src="com.jcom.util.ListingPosition"/>
```

Extension elements and functions written in Java are loaded and handled directly by Xalan. Many other scripting languages are supported through Bean Scripting Framework (BSF). BSF allows other scripting languages to be incorporated into Java applications and applets. Through BSF the following scripting languages are supported for creating extensions:

- ❏ Javascript
- ❏ NetRexx
- ❏ BML
- ❏ JPython
- ❏ Jacl
- ❏ JScript
- ❏ VBScript

For running the JavaScript examples provided with this chapter the following files need to be in your classpath: bsf.jar (distributed as part of Xalan) and js.jar (which can be downloaded from http://www.mozilla.org/rhino/). For other scripting languages that are supported and the files required for supporting these languages, please visit http://xml.apache.org/xalan-j/ for more details. Also for more details about the BSF project please visit http://oss.software.ibm.com/developerworks/projects/bsf.

Creating Extensions Using JavaScript

Let's get started with our first example, which uses both extension elements and extension functions implemented using Javascript. In all the extension examples provided in this chapter we will be using the same calls.xml file (as ever). Most of the examples provided here can be run direct from the prompt like this one:

```
java org.apache.xalan.xslt.Process -in calls.xml -xsl javascript_calldetails.xsl -
out Listing.html
```

although the effect would be the same if we were to execute them from within code.

In this example we will be using a JavaScript function to print the date in an expanded form, which means that the date and time, which were declared in the XML file as:

```
<TIME HOUR="19" MINUTE="32"> </TIME>
<DATE>5/5/2000</DATE>
```

will be printed in output as:

Fri, 05 May 2000 19:32:00 GMT

The final output expected after executing the transformations on `calls.xml` is as shown in this figure,

The stylesheet for this example can be created in four easy steps.

Step 1

The very first step is to initialize the `xsl:stylesheet` element with the necessary namespace references. In this example we will be using one extension prefix called `listingExtension`. Here's what the `xsl:stylesheet` element looks like:

```
<?xml version="1.0"?>
<xsl:stylesheet
    xmlns:xsl="http://www.w3.org/1999/XSL/Transform"
    version="1.0"
    xmlns:lxslt="http://xml.apache.org/xslt"

    xmlns:listingExtension=
                "http://www.wrox.com/xslt/phonedetails"

    extension-element-prefixes="listingExtension"
    exclude-result-prefixes="listingExtension"
>
```

A couple of things about the above declaration: first we declared, `xmlns:lxslt` so that we can use the `lxslt:component` element to create the script inside the stylesheet. Next we create a new extension namespace called `listingExtension`. Then we added the name of this extension in the list of valid extensions defined by `extension-element-prefixes`. Next, we don't want our custom namespace declaration to appear in the output, so we hide it by adding the extension name in the list of values for the `exclude-result-prefixes` attribute.

Step 2

The steps required for printing out the results to the output start from this step. Let's first declare our JavaScript declaration. We will be having one `lxslt:component` element in our code. The prefix for this one is going to be our one and only extension element, `listingExtension`. To show how to declare both extension elements and extension functions within the same `lxslt:component` element, we have taken one extension element, `setTimeZone`, and another extension function, `getLocaleDate`. If required, in real life, the `currentTimeZone` value can also be passed as a parameter to the `getLocaleDate()` function, avoiding another call to set the time-zone. The opening `lxslt:component` tag therefore looks like this:

```
<lxslt:component prefix="listingExtension"
                 elements="TimeZone"
                 functions="getLocaleDate">
```

Next comes the implementation of the `TimeZone` element. In our JavaScript function we have one local variable called `currentTimeZone`. The time-zone sent through the `TimeZone` element is stored in this local variable. We start the `lxslt:script` element like this:

```
<lxslt:script lang="javascript">

    var currentTimeZone;
```

When we use the `TimeZone` element in our stylesheet, it will look like this:

```
<listingExtension:TimeZone zone="GMT"/>
```

When the XSLT processor encounters this, it will recognize that the prefix means this is an extension element, and it will identify the `lxslt:component` element which provides the extension in question. It will then call the script contained within the `lxslt:script` element, looking for a function with the signature:

```
TimeZone(xslProcessorContext, elem)
```

The name of the function is the name of the element, and the two arguments are objects, the first representing the XSL processor itself, and the second representing the element which led to this function being called.

The value of the attribute `zone` we set on the `TimeZone` element can be accessed inside our script using the `getAttribute("attributename")` method on the element object we were given. We can then store the value in the local variable. From this element, we don't want to return anything, so we return `null` at the end of this method. Here's what the code looks like:

```
function TimeZone(xslProcessorContext, elem) {
    CurrentTimeZone=new String(elem.getAttribute("zone"));
    return null;
}
```

The function is simply implemented as a function of the appropriate name. Our `getLocaleDate()` extension function takes three parameters: date, hour and minute. This function uses the `currentTimeZone` variable set previously by the `TimeZone` element. If the time-zone is set as GMT, then the JavaScript function `toGMTString()` is executed, else `toLocaleString()` is executed, and the time is converted to the local time-zone and returned back to the calling method:

```
function getLocaleDate(callDate, callHour, callMinute) {
    var currentDate = new Date(callDate);
    currentDate.setUTCHours(callHour);
    currentDate.setUTCMinutes(callMinute);
    if (currentTimeZone == "GMT") {
        return currentDate.toGMTString();
    } else {
        return currentDate.toLocaleString();
    }
}
```

Step 3

This step is a simple one which we've done before. In this step we start to build the actual stylesheet, and create a template to match all <CALL> elements inside the <PHONE_RECORDS> element. The only new code implemented here is to call the `listingExtension:TimeZone` element. If the `listingExtension` namespace was not declared with the extension element prefix, then `TimeZone` element would have been directly copied to output. But since it is declared as an extension element prefix, it's going to invoke the `TimeZone` extension element method. The call to this element here will invoke the function we built in step 2.

Here's what the complete template rule looks like:

```
<xsl:template match="/PHONE_RECORDS">
  <html><head> <title>Phone Listing</title> </head>
  <body>
     <h1>Phone Call Listings</h1><hr size="1" />
  <listingExtension:TimeZone zone="GMT"/>
        <xsl:apply-templates select"CALL" />
  </body> </html>
</xsl:template>
```

Step 4

Finally in this section, we will be implementing the template rule in the stylesheet, which will traverse through all the <CALL> elements and print details about each phone call. The values for the <FROM> and <DESTINATION> elements are printed directly using the `xsl:value-of` element. For getting the value of the date, the `getLocaleDate()` extension function is called within the `listingExtension` namespace. Again since `listingExtension` is declared as an extension element prefix, it will execute the corresponding `getLocaleDate()` code in the extension function implementation which was implemented in Step 2. Also while invoking the `getLocaleDate()` function values for DATE element and HOURS and MINUTE attributes of TIME element are retrieved and passed as parameters, just like for a normal XSLT function.

The final output from getLocaleDate() is the completed date. Using the xsl:value-of element, the result from the getLocaleDate() is extracted and printed to output. The final step is to output values for the duration of the call. HOURS and MINUTES attributes are retrieved using DURATION/@HOURS and DURATION/@MINUTES and printed to output in the HH:MM format. Here's how the complete code for this template rule looks:

```
<xsl:template match="CALL">

  <p><b>FROM : </b>
     <xsl:value-of select="FROM"/><br/>
  <b>DESTINATION : </b>
     <xsl:value-of select="DESTINATION"/><br/>

  <b>DATE : </b>
     <xsl:value-of select="
         listingExtension:getLocaleDate(string(DATE),
            string(TIME/@HOUR), string(TIME/@MINUTE))"/><br/>

  <b>DURATION : </b>
      <xsl:value-of select="DURATION/@HOURS" /> Hours
     ,<xsl:value-of select="DURATION/@MINUTES" /> Minutes

  </p><hr size="1" />
</xsl:template>
```

That completes the steps required for embedding JavaScript code inside an XSLT stylesheet and invoking these functions from other templates. We have also seen how we can implement both extension elements and extension functions inside the lxslt:component and lxslt:script elements.

Creating Extension Elements Using Java

In the previous example we have seen how to create extension elements using JavaScript. In this section we will show you how to create extension elements and functions using Java and pass parameters to the Java code.

In this section we will be accessing the Java class using the src attribute in the lxslt:script element as follows:

```
<lxslt:script lang="javaclass" src=" ListingPosition"/>
```

Our intention this time is to create the same phone listing, with columns as Item, FROM, DESTINATION and DATE. Previously we were displaying the item number using xsl:number. In this example the xsl:number functionality is replaced by our ListingPosition class.

The ListingPosition class has three main functions: start(), getValue() and increment(), and a single variable: currentPosition. The default value for the currentPosition variable is 0. Here's how the stylesheet elements and functions in ListingPosition class relate to one another:

Stylesheet Element	ListingPosition Action
start	Passes initial value for currentPosition variable by calling start() method in ListingPosition class
increment	Increments value of currentPosition variable by calling increment() method in ListingPosition class
getValue()	Returns current value of currentPosition variable by calling getValue() method in ListingPosition class

To accommodate these changes in the stylesheet start and increment will be declared as elements and getValue() will be declared as a function, since it's not changing anything in the class file. Here's how the lxslt:component element looks after making these changes:

```
<lxslt:component prefix="positionIndicator"
                 elements="start increment" functions="getValue">
   <lxslt:script lang="javaclass" src="com.jcom.util.ListingPosition"/>
</lxslt:component>
```

We are using positionIndicator as the extension prefix for this instance of lxslt:component. The Java source code for ListingPosition is fairly simple. The main thing to notice is how the start() method retrieves the value from the DOM element passed as parameter. Also notice how each of the functions in the class are invoked from Java code when the corresponding element or function prefixed with extension namespace, is activated or declared in Stylesheet. Here's the source code for ListingPosition:

```
Public class ListingPosition {

  Int currentPosition = 0;

  Public void start(
     org.apache.xalan.extensions.XSLProcessorContext context,
     org.w3c.dom.Element elem) {
       CurrentPosition = getIntValue(elem.getAttribute("value"));
  }

  public int getPosition() {
    return currentPosition;
  }

  public void increment(
     org.apache.xalan.extensions.XSLProcessorContext context,
     org.w3c.dom.Element elem) {
       currentPosition = currentPosition +
                         getIntValue(elem.getAttribute("value"));
  }

  private int getIntValue(String varValue){
    int tmpInt;
```

```
    try {
      tmpInt = Integer.parseInt (varValue);
    }
    catch (NumberFormatException exp){
      exp.printStackTrace ();
      tmpInt = 0;
    }
    return tmpInt;
  }
```

Each of the extension functions need to be provided with two parameters. They are current context, represented by an XSLProcessorContext, and the current element, represented by org.w3c.dom.Element. This is used for retrieving attributes and their values declared for this element.

From the XSL stylesheet, just before calling the <xsl:apply-templates/> method to iterate through all the <CALL> elements, we make a call to the start() method in the ListingPosition class. This is done as follows:

```
....
<positionIndicator:start value="1"/>
<xsl:apply-templates/>
....
```

That initializes the counter variable inside the ListingPosition class as 1. The start element is prefixed by the positionIndicator string, since for the current instance of lxslt:component inside which ListingPosition class is declared as script, we are using positionIndicator as the extension prefix.

Next, while displaying the call records, wherever a position needs to be shown, we make a call to the getPosition() method and at the end of iterating through one <CALL> element, call the increment() method. This is implemented as follows:

```
<xsl:template match="CALL">
  <TR>
   <td><xsl:value-of
             select="positionIndicator:getPosition()"/></td>
   <xsl:for-each select="FROM|DESTINATION|DATE">
      <td><xsl:value-of select="text()"/></td>
   </xsl:for-each>
  </TR>
  <positionIndicator:increment value="1"/>
</xsl:template>
```

In the above code, every time a call is made to the increment() function, the value is passed as 1. So the internal counter in ListingPosition class will be incremented by 1.

Redirecting Output to Multiple Files

This extension is quite useful when the resultant output from applying transformations on the XML file needs to be split into multiple files. For example, suppose there's already a pre-existing software package which generates a huge XML file which has phone call records from different area codes all dumped into a single XML file. It becomes tough if the calls to different area codes need to be split manually. In scenarios like these, this particular extension for writing output to multiple files could be useful since transformations can be applied to the XML file using an XSLT parser, and output can be split into multiple files. In Xalan this functionality is provided through one of the extension classes: `org.apache.xalan.lib.Redirect`.

There are two ways a Java class can be declared and accessed globally. One is by using `lxslt:component` and `lxslt:script`. The other way is to use abbreviated syntax. In abbreviated syntax, the class name is declared to be associated with a namespace and is accessed globally using that namespace. In this example, we will declare the namespace for the `org.apache.xalan.lib.Redirect` class as `xmlns:redirect`, and access this class globally direct using `redirect` as a prefix.

To apply this extension in a stylesheet, the following namespaces need to be declared either at `xsl:stylesheet` element level or at individual element level:

```
xmlns:lxslt="http://xml.apache.org/xslt"
xmlns:redirect="org.apache.xalan.lib.Redirect"
extension-element-prefixes="redirect"
```

You can either just use `redirect:write`, in which case the file will be opened and immediately closed after the write, or you can bracket the write calls by `redirect:open` and `redirect:close`, in which case the file will be kept open for multiple writes until the close call is encountered. The following examples show both these scenarios.

First we will be using only `redirect:write` and create a separate `.html` file for every call. Note that, every time a `redirect:write` is invoked on the file, if the file already exists, all the previous contents of the file will be lost and a new file will be created. Normally in a `PhoneListing`, there will be lots of calls from the same `<FROM>` number. To make it simple we will be creating a new HTML file for every `<FROM>` number. To see how different files are generated, one having a list of hyperlinks to all other newly generated HTML files, one for each call record, we can run this example from command prompt as follows:

```
java -in calls.xml -xsl Redirect_MultipleFiles.xsl -out CallsList.html
```

When it is executed, there will be links in the `CallsList.html` file to all other newly created files.

The logic used is fairly simple. While traversing each of the `<CALL>` elements, in the current output file, the `<FROM>` number is added with a hyperlink to a file called `<FROM>` + `".html"`. This is done as follows:

```
<xsl:template match="CALL">
  <xsl:element name="a">
    <xsl:attribute name="href">
      <xsl:value-of select="FROM"/>.html
    </xsl:attribute>
    <xsl:value-of select="FROM"/>
  </xsl:element><p />
```

Within the same template rule, all other <CALL> element details are retrieved and are written to output within the <redirect:write/> block. This is done as follows:

```
<redirect:write file ="{FROM}.html" >

  <html>
    <body>
      <p>
        <b>FROM : </b> <xsl:value-of select="FROM"/><br />
        <b>DESTINATION :</b><xsl:value-of select="DESTINATION"/><br />
        <b>DATE : </b><xsl:value-of select="DATE" /> ,
          <xsl:value-of select="TIME/@HOUR" />:
          <xsl:value-of select="TIME/@MINUTE" /> <br />
        <b>DURATION:</b><xsl:value-of select="DURATION/@HOURS" /> Hours,
          <xsl:value-of select="DURATION/@MINUTES" /> Minutes
      </p>
      <hr size="1" />
      <a href="MultipleFile.html">Back to main index </a>
    </body>
  </html>
</redirect:write>
</xsl:template>
```

In the above stylesheet the filename is generated using "{FROM}", which is equivalent to declaring it as <xsl:value-of select="FROM">. This has been explained in Chapter 7.

The rest of the steps are fairly simple. Text from each of the elements FROM, DESTINATION, DATE and DURATION (HOUR and MINUTE attributes) are selected and written to output. At the bottom of the template before closing the file, a hyperlink to the main file CallsList.html is provided for easy navigation. This entire sequence is embedded with <redirect:write> element.

The output in the main file will be like this:

```
<html><head><title>Phone Listing</title></head>
<body><h1>Phone Call Records</h1>

<a href="703-433-5678.html">703-433-5678</a><p></p>
<a href="703-374-2363.html">703-374-2363</a><p></p>

</body></html>
```

Next in the above example, if the file attribute redirect:write element is given a static file name like:

```
<redirect:write file ="AllListings.html">
```

and the main template rule from where xsl:apply-templates is called on the <CALL> elements nests it within redirect:open and redirect:close, as shown below:

```
<xsl:template match="/PHONE_RECORDS">
    <redirect:open file =" AllListings.html" />
        <xsl:apply-templates select="CALL"  />
    <redirect:close file ="AllListings.html" />
</xsl:template>
```

in this case all the call details will be written to the single file AllListings.html.

Making Database Calls Through Stylesheets

Xalan provides database query capabilities through the extension API implemented in the package `org.apache.xalan.lib.sql`. One of the main classes in this package is the `XConnection` class. By following these steps queries can be performed on a database using the `XConnection` class, and the resultant data can be retrieved.

❏ Using any one of the different constructors provided for `XConnection` class a new connection to the database is obtained.

❏ A `query()` is executed on the connection. When the `query()` method is called, a new instance of `XStatement` is created. `XStatement` executes the query and retrieves the `Resultset`. From this result set a new `RowSet` object is created. This `Rowset` object returns an array of column-header elements, and a single row element. Using the same rowset object again and again, all the row information is retrieved.

❏ Once all the usage for the connection is done, the database connection can be closed using the `close()` method.

The example provided in this chapter has been tested with an Oracle database. But there's no restriction on which database to use as long as a new connection can be established with the database using any one of the constructors provided for the `XConnection` class. The entire stylesheet for this application is developed in the following four steps.

Step 1

We will be using `org.apache.xalan.lib.sql.XConnection` a couple of times in this example. So, using the abbreviated syntax, a new namespace is declared for this class as follows:

```
xmlns:sql="org.apache.xalan.lib.sql.XConnection"
extension-element-prefixes="sql"
```

Next, the query to be executed is defined in the variable `query`. The query that needs to be executed is:

```
select CALL_FROM, CALL_DESTINATION, TO_CHAR(CALL_DATE, 'MM/DD/YYYY') from
PHONE_LISTING_TABLE
```

A new template rule is defined which starts acting on the root node.

The constructor we will be using in this example is:

```
XConnection(java.lang.String driver, java.lang.String dbURL, java.lang.String
user, java.lang.String password)
```

When using Java extension functions, the syntax to invoke the constructor of a class from a stylesheet is:

```
JavaClassPrefix:new(args)
```

The current prefix for XConnection is `"sql"`. So using the above syntax the constructor for an XConnection class is invoked with other required arguments. If successful, a new connection is created and stored in the variable `dbConn` using the following declaration:

```
<xsl:variable name="dbConn"
   select="sql:new('oracle.jdbc.driver.OracleDriver',
                   'jdbc:oracle:thin:@aucdb.javacommerce.com:1625:auc',
                   'secureuser', 'securepwd')"/>
```

Step 2

The query() method can be executed on the XConnection object as follows,

```
<xsl:variable name="table" select="sql:query($dbConn, $query)"/>
```

At this point we have a rowset object identified by $table/row-set. Let's start building our output table. The very first thing to do is set up the table (HTML output) headers. We need to show three elements: FROM, DESTINATION and DATE. Traversing through the column-headers element set as follows we can retrieve all the column names:

```
<xsl:for-each select="$table/row-set/column-header">
   <xsl:variable name="columnName" select="@column-label"/>
</xsl:for-each>
```

But this one is going to give the actual database column names: CALL_FROM, CALL_DESTINATION and CALL_DATE. So we need to perform an xsl:choose operation and map them to the correct column headings. This step is done as follows:

```
<xsl:choose>
  <xsl:when test="$columnName='CALL_FROM'">FROM</xsl:when>
  <xsl:when test="$columnName='CALL_DESTINATION'">DESTINATION</xsl:when>
  <xsl:otherwise>DATE</xsl:otherwise>
</xsl:choose>
```

Step 3

After all the column headers are displayed, the next step is to iterate through all the row elements and retrieve each row. To select each row, we call xsl:apply-templates next with its select attribute as the starting row of the resultant row-set subtree:

```
<xsl:apply-templates select="$table/row-set/row"/>
```

The new template which is called when apply-templates is called is:

```
<xsl:template match="row">
   <TR><xsl:apply-templates select="col"/></TR>
</xsl:template>
```

This template rule handles each row element. The next step is to retrieve data from each of the columns associated with each row. So again xsl:apply-templates is invoked with its select attribute as col, which will activate this template rule which processes each column:

```
<xsl:template match="col">
   <TD><xsl:value-of select="text()"/></TD>
</xsl:template>
```

Finally the text associated with each row is printed in the table.

Step 4

Now we are done with retrieving all the data from the database. It's time to close the connection. This is done by calling the `close()` method:

```
<xsl:value-of select="sql:close($dbConn)"/>
```

That completes all the steps required for make a SQL query and retrieving data from the database.

Translets

Now, having looked at Xalan for most of the chapter, let's move away from Apache projects. In this section we will be explaining how to use one of the Sun's Microsystems tools, the **XSLT compiler**. The main functionality of this compiler is that it takes an XSLT file as input and produces a class file as output. This step is known as compiling the stylesheet and the output is known as a **translet**. Once this class file has been generated from a stylesheet, it can be reused multiple times and parsing the same stylesheet is not required – the stylesheet itself is no longer even required. There are a couple of advantages to using translets. The most prominent ones are speed and size. The size of a translet is much smaller when compared to traditional XSLT engines that are used to parse XSL files, since the generated translet class stands alone, and only contains the exact functionality needed to perform the stylesheet transformation, so doesn't require the full power of an XSLT processor. Since the step of processing the stylesheet is performed at compile-time in translets, performance is increased considerably.

The main limitation of translets is that they don't support the complete XSLT specification, implementing only partial features, which are sufficient for most simple XSLT projects. For information about which features are supported and to download XSLT Compiler, you should visit http://www.sun.com/software/xml/developers/xsltc/.

The XSLT Compiler uses the **Byte Code Engineering Library (BECL)** developed by Markus Dahm. You need to download the latest BECL jar file from http://www.inf.fu-berlin.de/~dahm/JavaClass/downloads.html, and keep it in your classpath when running the compiler.

Setting up XSLT Compiler on your machine is fairly simple. It needs the following files to be in the classpath:

❑ `xsltcrt.jar`, `xsltc.jar` and `xml.jar` (These are part of XSLTC distribution)

❑ `BCEL.jar` (Byte Code Engineering Library)

This can be accomplished, however, by simply setting up an environment variable, `XSLT`, on your system, pointing to the directory containing the XSLTC distribution.

You should add the XSLTC distribution's `bin` directory to your `PATH` environment variable as well.

Next, to compile your stylesheet, go to the folder where your stylesheet exists. Then, supposing your stylesheet's name is `phones.xsl`, type the following command at the command prompt:

```
xsltc phones.xsl
```

That line should generate a file called `phones.class` in the same folder.

Note that no .java file is generated: XSLTC doesn't create Java source code and compile it (note that you don't need tools.jar on your classpath), instead building Java bytecode directly using the BCEL. It is a true XSLT-to-bytecode compiler.

Next to apply transformation on XML file (say calls.xml) type the following at command prompt:

```
xslt calls.xml phones
```

This executes the phones.class translet's transformation on the calls.xml file. Notice we specify the class using its class identity, not the name of the file.

If your XML file is at a remote location, for example it exists at http://www.javacommerce.com/phone.xml, then at the command prompt specify the XML file name using the -u (URL) switch as follows:

```
xslt -u http://www.javacommerce.com/phone.xml calls
```

Translets implement the Translet interface, which is as follows:

```
public interface Translet {
    public void transform(DOM document, TransletOutputHandler handler)
            throws TransletException;

    public void transform(DOM document, TransletOutputHandler[] handlers)
            throws TransletException;

    public void transform(DOM document, NodeIterator iterator,
                        TransletOutputHandler handler)
            throws TransletException;

    public Object addParameter(String name, Object value);
}
```

So, to make use of a translet through this interface, we would first need to instantiate it, then we can set parameters using the addParameter() method, and then we can apply the transformation to a DOM object, with the result being passed to a TransletOutputHandler.

However, these DOM and TransletOutputHandler classes are very translet-specific (although they do have hooks which can allow us to attach them to standard SAX parsers and ContentHandlers), so a utility class called ProcessTranslet is provided in the translets folder in the source directory which simplifies this process. To use this program from your Java code, just perform the following steps:

```
ProcessTranslet processTranslet = new ProcessTranslet();

processTranslet.setXMLFileName("http://www.javacommerce.com/phone.xml");
processTranslet.setStyleSheetClassName("callsparam");
// This will overwrite the current heading in Stylesheet
processTranslet.setParameter(
                "pageheadingParam", "New Page Heading");
System.out.println(processTranslet.applyTransformation());
```

The output from the applyTransformation() method will be the resultant XML output as a string after applying transformations.

Summary

That completes the chapter on applying XSLT transformations from within our own programs. Xalan has been one of the first to implement TrAX API and other vendors are slowly moving towards this too. We have covered most of the topics and options that are currently supported by Apache's implementation, including the mechanisms provided for building our own extensions to XSLT.

Finally, we looked at Sun's XSLTC compiler, which allows us to treat XSLT files as sourcecode for Java classes which we can make use of in our own programs.

The Xerces Blue
Butterfly, which became
extinct earlier this century,
and after which the Xerces XML
parser is named ...

9

Connected XML Data

With any traditional data storage convention there will often be situations when a single repository is unsuitable for storing any and all data. Similarly, when you store information in XML, you will generally want to generate multiple interrelated files rather than one enormous file. For example, let's say you have an XML representation of a catalog of books. These books may divide up into several categories, such as computing, science fiction, romance, etc. Although each book has identical characteristics (perhaps including an attribute to specify its category) a 'flat' XML layout containing all books may result in a huge file. In cases such as this, it is often preferable to place each category into a separate file.

However, this immediately raises questions. If we have several interrelated files, how do we specify the relationships between them? In the above example we end up with several files that are individually easier to maintain, but what do we do when we want to perform an operation on every book regardless of category, or to add a category, and so on? Here, as we will see later in this chapter, a W3C standard comes to our rescue: **XInclude**. This standard allows us to create XML files that 'include' external XML data, that is, declare that a certain file (or portion of a file) should be included at a certain point in a parent file. This can shorten files and allow simple reuse of data.

There are many more situations where relationships between XML files are important. There may be logical links between sections of one XML file and another; perhaps one document includes a citation of another, for example. In situations like this we have another standard to draw on: **XLink**. Like HTML hyperlinks XLinks allow resources to be linked in some way, although as we will see later in the chapter XLink provides much more freedom than HTML hyperlinks.

Both XInclude and XLink require a method of specifying locations within XML files. As we saw in the last two chapters, XPath allows us to do this. However, XPath only allows us to specify locations by node (although it can result in complex node sets). In order to get greater flexibility it is useful to gain a finer granularity than this, down to characters within elements. To do this we use an extension of XPath, known as **XPointer**. XPointer also allows us to specify ranges of data by their start and end points, which can be useful with contextual links, to name but one example.

Another standard that is used by XLink (which is much simpler than XPointer) is **XBase**, which allows us to simply define relative addresses between XML files stored at the same location. This allows simpler URI addressing, as we will see.

These four standards together allow us to define complex relationships between XML data. There is also a fifth standard that comes under the 'connected XML umbrella', which allows us to manipulate and distribute sub-sections of XML documents independently of their parent documents while keeping their required structure. This standard is called **XFI**, or **XML Fragment Interchange**.

In this chapter we will take a look at each of these five standards, detailing their syntax and providing examples of their usage. We will start with the underlying standard, XPointer, before moving on to the standards that make use of it.

> **Before we start, though, there is some important information to point out. None of these standards have yet reached the stage of being a W3C Recommendation. This means that although they are jammed full of useful techniques that could provide new ways of exploiting XML content, there is as yet little support for them. The reason for this is that changes are possible across the board, and an implementation that conforms to these standards may well be broken when the standards are updated. However, it is still worth getting a feel for these standards, as their core values are likely to remain unchanged, and they certainly do have great potential.**

XPointer

XPointer, as already mentioned, is an extension of XPath that allows greater flexibility when accessing XML documents. Specifically, XPath only allows you to access information on a node by node basis. For example, in the following XML:

```
<List>
   <Item id="item1">Sausages</Item>
   <Item id="item2">Beans</Item>
   <Item id="item3">Fried Egg</Item>
   <Item id="item4">Chips</Item>
</List>
```

XPath can specify whole elements, such as:

```
<List>
   <Item id="item1">Sausages</Item>
   <Item id="item2">Beans</Item>
   <Item id="item3">Fried Egg</Item>
   <Item id="item4">Chips</Item>
</List>
```

No finer granularity is possible. However, XPointer allows us to dig down into character content. We could, for example, specify:

```
<List>
    <Item id="item1">Sausages</Item>
    <Item id="item2">Beans</Item>
    <Item id="item3">Fried Egg</Item>
    <Item id="item4">Chips</Item>
</List>
```

That is, a single word in the content of an element. Using the XPointer syntax this could be specified in a URI reference, perhaps using XLink (see later) to link to the above text from elsewhere, such as from an <EggType> element in a separate XML document.

When we talk about **location** in XPath we invariably mean a node (and remember that XPath can return several nodes, in a **location set**). When we use XPointer the term location can correspond to a lower level of granularity. Specifically, XPointer locations can mean **points** or **ranges** as well as nodes. A point is the lowest level location possible in an XML document, such as "the position just before the 'F' of 'Fried' in the <Item> element with an ID of item3" in the above example.

A **point** is defined by two parameters: a **containing node** and a non-negative **index** integer. So, for the text node point mentioned above (just before Fried) we can say that the containing node is the third <Item> child of <List>, and the index is zero.

Note that points can exist in nodes that aren't of type text. For example, we could have a point that had <List> as its containing node. In this case the index is either zero, which would mean that the point refers to the location just before the first contained node, or *n* (where *n* is less than or equal to the total number of children of the container node, in this example 4), which would mean that the point refers to the location just after the *n*th contained node.

A **range** is defined by two points, such that the text 'Fried' in the above example can be specified as a range. Ranges always consist of two points, the beginning and end points of the range. Ranges can contain XML structure and content, which is why we can specify points in container elements. We could, for example, specify "the range between the start of the <Item> element with an ID of item3 and the start of the <Item> element with an ID of item4" and get the same result as for the XPath example above. It is possible to have a range whose start and end points are the same. In this case the range is known as a **collapsed range**.

The XPointer specification also defines **covering ranges** for each location type. A covering range is a range type location that includes a given location, which is calculated in a different way depending on the location type. The following list shows how covering ranges are calculated for different location types:

❑ Point – the covering range is a collapsed range at the point location

❑ Range – the covering range is identical to the range

❑ Attribute or Namespace location – a range spanning the string value of the location (may span more characters than the location itself)

❑ Root location – the covering range spans all children of the root

❑ Other – the covering range covers the node containing the location, or that *is* the location (if the location type is node)

Types of XPointer

There are three types of XPointer that you can use:

❑   Full

❑   Bare Name

❑   Child Sequence

Full XPointer expressions use the most complex syntax, and will be covered in a moment. **Bare Name** and **Child Sequence** XPointers are much simpler, and we can detail their use here. A word of warning – many of XPointer processing applications available on the web don't support full XPointers, which leaves out most of the more interesting functionality. Bear this in mind if you download software to process your XPointer applications!

Bare Name XPointers

These are the simplest type of XPointers, and simply involve pointing at an element with a given ID attribute value. The XPointer used is simply to search for the ID. For example, the following XPointer:

```
menu
```

As we will see later, this is equivalent to the full XPointer syntax xpointer(id("menu")).
This simply points at the element with an ID of menu. For example, this would point to the highlighted section in the following document:

```
<Content>
    <List id="menu">
        <Item id="mitem1">Home</Item>
        <Item id="mitem2">Next</Item>
        <Item id="mitem3">About</Item>
    </List>
    <List id="contributors">
        <Item id="citem1">John</Item>
        <Item id="citem2">Paul</Item>
        <Item id="citem3">George</Item>
        <Item id="citem4">Ringo</Item>
    </List>
</Content>
```

Note that this is really a shorthand for using the XPath id() function. According to the XPointer specification, this syntax is included to encourage the use of ID values in XML documents (as they are likely to survive document transformations and therefore mean that modifications in existing XPointers may be unnecessary) and to provide an analogue to HTML fragment identifiers (bookmarks).

Child Sequence XPointers

This type of XPointer enables you to address elements by their document order position in an XML document. A given element can be identified in a sequence that is equivalent to saying something along the lines of "this element is the third child of the second child of the fifth child of the document element". A child sequence is simply a string that represents this ancestry. The above location can be translated into the following child sequence XPointer:

```
/1/5/2/3
```

The document element is represented by 1, its fifth child by 5, and so on. Each child number is separated from the one before by a forward slash (/). This might point to the highlighted setion of the following document:

```
<Catalogue>
    <Entry id="books">
        ...
    </Entry>
    <Entry id="cds">
        ...
    </Entry>
    <Entry id="records">
        ...
    </Entry>
    <Entry id="dvds">
        ...
    </Entry>
    <Entry id="videos">
        <Item id="video1">
            <Title>Gladiator</Title>
            <Price currency="usd">10.99</Price>
            <Rating>3.5</Rating>
        </Item>
        <Item id="video2">
            <Title>Grosse Point Blank</Title>
            <Price currency="usd">8.99</Price>
            <Rating>4</Rating>
        </Item>
        ...
    </Entry>
</Catalogue>
```

We have the option of combining child sequences with bare names by specifying the **highest level** element by its bare name. For example, if the fifth child of the document element had the ID videos, as in the above example, we could replace the above XPointer with:

```
videos/2/3
```

Full XPointers

Finally, we get to the most complex XPointer format. A full XPointer is made up of one or more sections that are evaluated in order from left to right. Evaluation stops when a section returns a valid XPointer result, such as a node, range, etc.

Each section may be further classified into a scheme. The scheme mechanism provides a general framework for extensibility that can be used for future versions of XPointer, or for other media types that wish to adopt all or part of this specification in defining their own fragment identifier languages.

A scheme instructs the XPointer processor that a given type of resource is being pointed to, and as such will affect the syntax of the pointer itself. Currently there are two schemes available: xmlns and xpointer, where specifying the xpointer scheme means that the resource pointed to is XML. The xmlns scheme is used to declare namespaces prior to XPointer processing, and so it is really a special class of scheme as it doesn't as such specify a resource type to point to.

Sections using `xmlns` will never return a valid XPointer result, so they can be used prior to `xpointer` scheme sections in left to right order without affecting the end result, but instead facilitating the XPointer processing (perhaps by simplifying the syntax required).

Before we move on, let's clarify the above with a qualitative example. Each section in an XPointer follows the following format – the name of the scheme followed by an expression enclosed in brackets:

```
scheme(expression)
```

So the two existing schemes are used as follows:

```
xmlns(expression)
xpointer(expression)
```

Any section can fail in one of the following ways:

❑   If the scheme is unknown

❑   If the scheme is not applicable to the resource being targeted

❑   If no sub-resource is located in the target resource (an empty result is a failure in XPointer; note that this is *not* the case in XPath, where an empty result is valid)

❑   If either the `string-range()` or `start-point()` function is used and fails (see function-specific sections later for details on this)

As already mentioned, an XPointer may be built up of several sections, for example:

```
xmlns(expression1)xpointer(expression2)xpointer(expression3)
```

Here, if `xpointer(expression2)` returns a valid result then `xpointer(expression3)` will not be evaluated. `xpointer(expression2)` is always evaluated, as the `xmlns` section can never return a valid XPointer result. If all sections fail then a **sub-resource error** will be raised. This is one of three XPointer errors that can arise during XPointer processing, the other two being:

❑   **Syntax error** – this error is raised if the syntax of the XPointer used does not comply with the XPointer specification

❑   **Resource error** – this error is raised if a syntactically correct XPointer is used to point into a resource that does not exist or is not well formed

Note that the XPointer specification does not detail how an XPointer processor should deal with these errors if they occur, that is down to the specific implementation.

The xmlns Scheme

This scheme allows us to associate strings with namespaces such that we can refer to them in this shorthand in later XPointer processing. An `xmlns` expression has the following simple syntax:

```
string=namespace
```

For example, we could use the following XPointer section:

```
xmlns(bns=http://www.wrox.com/bookns/)
```

Subsequent XPointer sections could then refer to elements such as `<bns:Book>`.

The xpointer Scheme

An XPointer expression consists of one or more expression parts separated by forward slashes (/), each of which may use the current **context**. Context is an important concept to grasp, but it is really quite simple. A context consists of the following:

❑   A **context location** within the target resource. This may refer to multiple actual locations, such as "all <Item> children of <Menu>".

❑   Two non-negative non-zero integers giving additional information relating to the position of the context node. These are **context size** (which is the total number of locations in the context location), and **context position** (which is the index of the current **context node** among the locations defined by the context location).

❑   Any namespaces in scope.

❑   Any variable definitions in scope.

❑   The set of functions available in the current scheme.

In the XPointer scheme context is always initialized. The context node is initialized to the root node of the document (from which it follows that the context size and position are both 1, as there can be only one root node). Namespaces are initialized as per xmlns scheme declarations, and the set of functions is the complete set of available XPointer and XPath functions. No means of initializing variable definitions is supplied, so this set will initialize to empty.

The first expression part of an XPointer takes this root node context initialization as its reference point (if one is required by the part – as we will see, all except one XPointer function are context insensitive, but many XPath expressions use it). However, each expression part may result in a change in the context, such that subsequent parts will use a new context.

As an example, consider the child sequence XPointer type we looked at earlier (/1/5/2/3), which also makes use of context. Each child number was separated from the previous one by a forward slash. If we take each child number as a separate entity we can see that it operates on the context specified by the preceding part – we specify a child of the current context, which was specified by the previous child number.

Let's break this down into steps to clarify. Initially, the context node is the root. The first integer, 1, simply refers to this node in child sequence syntax. The next step, 5, changes the context node to the fifth child of the root note. This means that the context position will be 5, and the context size will be the total number of children of the root (which will be 5 if the context node is the last child of the root, as in the example XML we showed for this sequence earlier). From here on in, the sequence repeats.

A single expression part may be an XPath expression part, as XPointer includes the complete XPath syntax. In addition, we can use one of the set of functions defined by XPointer as an expression part. Note that these two possibilities together may result in providing XPath expression parts with a context that contains XPointer-specific locations (that is, point and range locations). This won't cause any problems but needs to be borne in mind to prevent logical errors when obtaining your result set.

One modification that has been made in order to make XPointer and XPath work together is that the XPath NodeType enumeration has been extended, now including point and range in addition to node etc. This will allow you to perform XPath node tests including these new location types.

Access to the extra functionality that XPointer provides is achieved using the XPointer function library, which we'll cover shortly.

XPointer Functions

The xpointer scheme adds eight new functions to the XPath set, each of which returns a location set. Remember, in XPointer a location set may include point and range locations as well as node locations, and many of the XPointer functions do just that.

The functions are:

- ❏ range-to()
- ❏ string-range()
- ❏ range()
- ❏ range-inside()
- ❏ start-point()
- ❏ end-point()
- ❏ here()
- ❏ origin()

We'll look at these in order.

range-to()

This function returns a location set of range locations, one for each location in the current context. Each range will span the XML from the starting point of a location to the end point specified by the argument of range-to(). The argument of range-to() is a location set that is evaluated with respect to the current context.

For example, let's select a range that encompasses the second and third <Item> elements of the simple XML document we saw earlier:

```
<List>
    <Item id="item1">Sausages</Item>
    <Item id="item2">Beans</Item>
    <Item id="item3">Fried Egg</Item>
    <Item id="item4">Chips</Item>
</List>
```

We can do this using the IDs for the elements (assuming they are of type id, declared in the DOCTYPE for the XML document that includes the above):

```
xpointer(id("item2")/range-to(id("item3")))
```

We can also do this by element index (here assuming that <List> is the root element, such that the context allows us to use simply Item[2] to refer to the required starting element):

```
xpointer(Item[2]/range-to(Item[3]))
```

Note that counting starts with 1 as the first <Item> element.

Or we can even throw in a more complex XPath relationship:

```
xpointer(Item[2]/range-to(following-sibling::Item[1]))
```

Remember, this function works on every location in the context. This is the same expression as above, only in full XPath notation. The following expression:

```
xpointer(//Item/range-to(.))
```

would return a location set of ranges spanning each `<Item>` element in the document. Recall that the `//Item` merely stands for "all `<item>` elements" regardless of their position in the folder.

string-range()

This function returns zero or more ranges that encompass plain text in an XML document, by means of pattern matching. Apart from being used to specify locations when obtaining string ranges, markup is ignored (this function gives access to the string-values or elements). This means that string ranges can span XML tags, which are ignored.

`string-range()` takes between two and four arguments (the last two are optional):

```
string-range(location set, string, start_index, length)
```

Here, *string* is the string to search for in any text content within the locations specified in location-set. For each match a range is returned from the character specified in *start_index* (which defaults to 1, the first character in the string) and of length *length*. If a length is not specified then the default is 'to the end of *string*'.

If *string* is not found in the target text locations then the XPointer expression containing this function will fail, as detailed earlier.

Going back to our earlier example, we mentioned that we could select the text Fried from the third `<Item>` element:

```
<List>
    <Item id="item1">Sausages</Item>
    <Item id="item2">Beans</Item>
    <Item id="item3">Fried Egg</Item>
    <Item id="item4">Chips</Item>
</List>
```

We can do this using `string-range()` with:

```
xpointer(string-range(//Item, 'Fried'))
```

This would find any occurrence of the string Fried in an `<Item>` element anywhere in the target XML document.

Note that whitespace in string *is matched literally.*

Alternatively we could obtain the first letter of `Fried`:

```
xpointer(string-range(//Item, 'Fried', 1, 1))
```

Perhaps we'd like to be able to change it to `Dried` (although I really hope we wouldn't...).

Or, we could see exactly what was fried by combining this with `range-to()`:

```
xpointer(string-range(//Item, 'Fried', 7, 1)/range-to(.))
```

This would return a range containing `'Egg'`:

```
<Item id="item3">Fried Egg</Item>
```

Note that both the starting index and string length may result in a range outside of the text matched, and even outside of the element, for example:

```
xpointer(string-range(//Item, 'Fried', 1, 14))
```

This would cover:

```
<List>
    <Item id="item1">Sausages</Item>
    <Item id="item2">Beans</Item>
    <Item id="item3">Fried Egg</Item>
    <Item id="item4">Chips</Item>
</List>
```

As mentioned earlier, the intervening markup is ignored.

range()

This function returns a covering range for each location in its location set argument. For example (using our standard XML document):

```
xpointer(range(//Item[2]))
```

will be a range containing the second `<Item>` element, and:

```
xpointer(range(string-range(//Item, 'Fried', 1, 14)))
```

will be a range covering the string range shown at the end of the last section. Here the range function has no effect on the resulting location set.

range-inside()

This function has no effect on point and range locations in its location set argument, but will obtain ranges from node locations. Specifically, it uses each location it is passed as a container node, and returns a range spanning its contents. If the location is a text node then the range will span the contained text, otherwise it will span all children of the node location.

Again, using our example XML:

```
xpointer(range-inside(//Item[2]))
```

will return a string range spanning the text Beans.

start-point()

This returns the starting points of each location in its location set argument. For points this is simply the point itself, for ranges we get the point at the start of the range, and for nodes this is a point just inside the node.

For example:

```
xpointer(start-point(range-inside(//Item[2])))
```

returns a point location just before the text inside the second <Item> element, that is, just before the B of Beans.

If the container node of the result of this function is of type attribute or namespace then the XPointer expression containing the function will fail, as detailed earlier.

end-point()

This operates much like start-point(), except that this function returns the point at the end of a range.

For example:

```
xpointer(end-point(range-inside(//Item[2])))
```

This will return a point location just after the s of Beans.

here()

This function changes the context to the node containing the XPointer. As XPointers can appear within XML documents (in particular in XLinks – see later) it is often necessary to refer to locations within the current document, and often easier to use the XPointer location as a starting point.

For example, a given element may contain the following XPointer:

```
xpointer(here()/range(child::*))
```

which would refer to a range covering all child elements of the element containing the XPointer.

Note that if the XPointer appears inside a text node here() corresponds to the element containing the text node, not the text node itself.

origin()

This function is similar to here() in that it changes the context and requires no arguments. However, its use is more involved and relates directly to XLink usage. It returns the element from where a user initiated traversal of a link. We'll see more information about this function later in the chapter.

XPointer Status

The version of the XPointer specification used here, the most recent at the time of writing, is the Last Call Working Draft dated 8th January 2001. It is possible that changes will be made before this specification becomes a Recommendation, although it is expected that these will be minor.

Unfortunately, I have yet to find an implementation of XPointer that includes all of the syntax. There are a few available that support bare names and child sequences, but none that support the full syntax. Keep an eye on http://www.w3.org/XML/Linking, which lists current implementations (although you may have to check the products themselves too to find out what they support).

XPointer Summary

So far in this chapter we've covered XPointers and their usage. However, XPointer isn't that useful on its own. In order to use XPointers we need to move on and look at the next of the five technologies covered in this chapter – XInclude.

XInclude

XInclude, as mentioned in the introduction to this chapter, is a standard that allows XML documents to include other XML documents at specified locations (which may be inserted in XML or plain text form, that is as a CDATA block).

The intention is that an inclusion processor would move through an XML document, processing inclusions and inserting the relevant data as it goes. This may be a recursive procedure, as inclusions may have inclusions of their own.

Including Resources

Using XInclude is really quite simple – at least, it is if you understand XPointers! All XInclude functionality is held in a single element, `<include>`, which is the sole entry in the XInclude namespace (http://www.w3.org/1999/XML/xinclude). This simple element has two attributes (three if you include the ID type `id` attribute):

❑   `href` – the URI of the resource to include (supports XPointer references within resources).

❑   `parse` – may be `xml` (the default) or `text`. The first specifies that the resource should be included as XML (that is, it should extend the infoset of the containing document) whereas `text` means that the resource should be placed in a text node (which may result in escaping of XML control characters).

So, on with an example! We'll use the XML document we've seen previously, and call it `food.xml`:

```
<?xml version='1.0'?>
<List>
   <Item id="item1">Sausages</Item>
   <Item id="item2">Beans</Item>
   <Item id="item3">Fried Egg</Item>
   <Item id="item4">Chips</Item>
</List>
```

The simplest way to include data is to include a whole resource, that is, a whole XML document. This doesn't even require the use of XPointers. For example, to embed `food.xml` in `menu.xml` we would do the following:

```xml
<?xml version='1.0'?>
<menu>
    <food xmlns:x="http://www.w3.org/1999/XML/xinclude">
        <label>
            Food on offer:
        </label>
        <x:include href="food.xml"/>
    </food>
</menu>
```

If this were processed by an XInclude processor we'd end up with the following XML document:

```xml
<?xml version='1.0'?>
<menu>
    <food xmlns:x="http://www.w3.org/1999/XML/xinclude">
        <label>
            Food on offer:
        </label>
        <List>
            <Item id="item1">Sausages</Item>
            <Item id="item2">Beans</Item>
            <Item id="item3">Fried Egg</Item>
            <Item id="item4">Chips</Item>
        </List>
    </food>
</menu>
```

As you can see, the `<include>` element is replaced by its target.

If we add the `parse="text"` attribute to the `<include>` element then the XML included would be treated as text. Every < would be included as `&lt;`, every > as `&gt;` and so on. For example:

```xml
<?xml version='1.0'?>
<menu>
    <food xmlns:x="http://www.w3.org/1999/XML/xinclude">
        <label>
            Item 3 on our menu:
        </label>
        <Item3>
            <x:include href="food.xml#xpointer(//Item[3])"/>
        </Item3>
    </food>
</menu>
```

would result in:

```xml
<?xml version='1.0'?>
<menu>
    <food xmlns:x="http://www.w3.org/1999/XML/xinclude">
        <label>
            Item 3 on our menu:
        </label>
        <Item3>
            &lt;Item id="item3"&gt;Fried Egg&lt;/Item&gt;
        </Item3>
    </food>
</menu>
```

Remember – the full XPointer syntax is supported.

XInclude Status

At the time of writing, the most recent XInclude specification is a Working Draft dated the 26th of October 2000. However, this is such a simple specification (and, indeed, implementations are readily available – although none of them support full XPointer syntax at the time of writing) that it seems unlikely to change much on its journey to Recommendation status.

For examples of using XInclude see http://msdn.microsoft.com/xml/articles/xml05292000.asp and http://www.ibiblio.org/xml/XInclude/.

XInclude Summary

This XInclude section is fairly brief – but then XInclude is a very simple technology. However, this simplicity doesn't hinder the fact that XInclude can be very useful, particularly for reusing data in multiple places. The proper use of XInclude could also come in very handy for adding 'boilerplate' text to your XML documents.

XBase

XBase is the simplest of the technologies we'll look at in this chapter, and in fact isn't that useful on its own. However, it can be extremely helpful when used with XLink. Put simply, it defines a **base URI** for an element and everything contained by that element. This base URI will then be used to resolve relative links and URI references on attributes of these elements (for more information on URIs and URLs, and the difference between them, see Chapter 1). This can greatly simplify URI references in the document and allows more centralized maintenance of the document especially should the referenced content be moved. The base URI needn't be related to the URI where the XML document itself is located.

Setting a Base URI

Setting base URIs is achieved using an attribute called `xml:base`, which may be added to any element. Any contained elements use the value of this attribute as a reference point for defining URIs, perhaps in `href` attributes. Note that this is of course dependent on the presence of an XBase-aware processor – although in the case of XLink links this is implicit.

For example:

```
<top xml:base="http://www.wrox.com/javaxml/">
  ...
</top>
```

Any elements contained by `<top>` use the URI http://www.wrox.com/javaxml/ as a base reference.

We will see more XBase examples in the XLink section.

XBase Status

The current version of XBase is a Proposed Recommendation dated the 20th of December 2000. Once again, this version is unlikely to undergo any major changes, in part due to the inherent simplicity of XBase.

XBase Summary

As we have seen, XBase provides a method of defining base URIs for elements within our XML documents. In the next section – XLink – it will soon become apparent how useful this can be.

XLink

Today we are so used to HTML hyperlinks that we hardly consider them for what they are any more – nor consider their limitations. XLink is a technology allowing XML structures to define links between resources, which may take a very similar form to HTML hyperlinks. However, the XLink designers have recognized many of the failings of HTML hyperlinks and extended the model, allowing far more flexibility.

HTML hyperlinks have the following characteristics:

❑ They act between two URIs

❑ They are unidirectional (they can only be traversed in one direction)

❑ They are defined at their starting point, within the resource at the starting URI

❑ They are purely navigational links

❑ They are activated by the user

XLinks, on the other hand, have the following characteristics:

❑ They may act between more than two URIs

❑ They may be traversable in more than one direction

❑ They may be defined at either end of their end points or in a separate location altogether

❑ They may represent more complex relationships than simple navigation

❑ They may be activated by means other than user intervention

XLinks come in two flavors: **simple** and **extended**. Simple XLinks conform to the same restrictions as HTML hyperlinks, whereas extended ones extend these capabilities to provide the enhancements outlined above.

Before we start it is worth going over some of the terminology used in XLink.

XLink Terminology

In XLink, a unidirectional link between two resources is known as an **arc**. If the arc definition is contained in one of its target resources then that resource is known as a **local resource**, while a resource included in but not containing the arc definition is a **remote resource**. If the arc points from a local resource to a remote resource then it is an **outbound** arc, and if it points from a remote resource to a local resource it is an **inbound** arc.

It is also possible for an arc to be specified separately from its resources, which are therefore both remote. In this case the arc is a **third-party** arc. Third-party arcs are often held in **linkbases**, which are XML resources that may contain many third-party links and are known (or explicitly pointed out) to XLink processors.

In the following diagram the local resource on the far left defines an outbound and inbound arc, and a linkbase defines a third-party arc between remote resources:

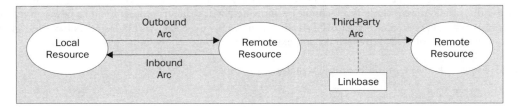

XLink Architecture

The XLink specification details six element types together with nine attributes, which apply to one or more of the elements. The six elements are not elements in their own right, rather you may declare any of your own elements as being one of them using a tenth attribute: `type`. This is possible for any element that has access to the XLink namespace. Note that an XLink type element may double as any other type of attribute, such that you don't have to interrupt the structure of your XML documents. In many cases this functionality may require `DOCTYPE` modifications.

The element types available are:

- ❑   `simple`
- ❑   `extended`
- ❑   `locator`
- ❑   `arc`
- ❑   `resource`
- ❑   `title`

We'll look at these, and the attributes they support in subsequent sections.

Simple XLinks

A simple XLink is, as mentioned, similar to an HTML hyperlink. As such it is declared at its source in a local resource and declares a remote resource URI as its target.

Simple XLinks have the following attributes:

Attribute	Required?	Description
type	Yes	Must be `simple` for simple links.
href	Yes	URI of target resource, supports XPointer syntax.
role	Optional	URI reference describing target remote resource. If for example the resource was an address in XML format then perhaps we could specify an HTML page describing the format of this address, with something like: `http://www.wrox.com/javaxml/address.htm`. The XLink processor might then enable the user to examine the resource specified here for additional information.
arcrole	Optional	URI reference describing relationship between local and remote resource. To follow on from the above, perhaps the address XML file at the target is the office address of a person description in the source document. Here we could provide a description of this relationship: `http://www.wrox.com/javaxml/office.htm`.
title	Optional	Human-readable string describing the link, may be used for example in a pop-up box when the mouse pointer hovers over the link in a browser.
show	Optional	One of `new`, `replace`, `embed`, `other`, or `none`. This attribute specifies what should happen when the link is followed in a browser. `new` means to open a new window; `replace` means to replace the content of the current window; `embed` means to embed the target content in the current window; `other` means that another action is required (and specified elsewhere); and `none` means that no action is specified.
actuate	Optional	One of `onLoad`, `onRequest`, `other`, or `none`. This attribute specifies when the link should be activated. `onLoad` means as soon as the document is loaded; `onRequest` means when the user interacts with the link; `other` means that the timing is specified elsewhere; and `none` means that no timing is specified.

For example, let's say we had a `person.xml` document and an `address.xml` document, and wanted to provide links between them to signify home and office addresses (to follow on from the example in the above table). We'll focus on the following sections of these documents – initially linkless:

```
<People>
   <Person>
      <Name>Bob Smith</Name>
      <Age>32</Age>
      <Occupation>Clerk</Occupation>
   </Person>
   ...
</People>
```

```
<Addresses>
   <Address>
      <DoorNumber>562</DoorNumber>
      <Street>Acacia Avenue</Street>
      <City>London</City>
   </Address>
   <Address>
      <DoorNumber>23</DoorNumber>
      <Street>Oxford Street</Street>
      <City>London</City>
   </Address>
   ...
</Addresses>
```

We might modify the first document to include links to relevant addresses, for example:

```
<People>
   <Person xlink:type="simple" href="addresses.xml#//Address[1]"
           title="Home Address" actuate="onRequest" show="replace"
           role="address.htm" arcrole="home.htm">
      <Name>Bob Smith</Name>
      <Age>32</Age>
      <Occupation xlink:type="simple" href="addresses.xml#//Address[2]"
           title="Work Address" actuate="onRequest" show="replace"
           role="address.htm" arcrole="work.htm">Clerk</Occupation>
   </Person>
   ...
</People>
```

An XLink-aware processor could then create these links.

As another example, consider the following XML:

```
<document xmlns:xlink="http://www.w3.org/1999/xlink">
   This document contains a
   <link xlink:type="simple" href="target.xml" title="Click me"
                            actuate="onRequest" show="replace">
      link
   </link>
   .
</document>
```

Here the text link in the <document> element is where the actual link would be rendered.

The above example could equally have been expressed with an extended link, although the syntax would be very different. Simple links are intended as a shorthand subset of extended links.

Extended XLinks

Extended XLinks are rather more complicated than simple ones, so we'll start with a quick overview of their structure before getting into the proper syntax.

An extended XLink is defined using the following information:

- ❏ Details of each resource involved in the link
- ❏ Details of relationships between resources
- ❏ The characteristics of the link, such as how it may be activated
- ❏ Descriptive information concerning the link, its resources, and the relationships between resources

All of this information is contained in an element with a `type` attribute of `extended`, in the form of attributes and contained elements. Of the contained elements possible, `locator` type elements describe remote resources; `resource` type elements describe local resources; `arc` type elements describe the arcs between resources; and `title` type elements provide human-readable descriptions of the XLink. Next we'll look at each of these elements in turn as we build up an example link.

extended Type Element

Starting from the top, then, we need to declare the XLink namespace such that we can use an `extended` type element. One way of doing this is to enclose link elements in a root, `<ColorLinks>`, say, that sets up this information. We'll place this in our document: `colors.xml`:

```
<ColorLinks xmlns:xlink="http://www.w3.org/1999/xlink">
   . . .
</ColorLinks>
```

Inside this structure we can place our linking elements. For now let's ignore the structure of the XML document containing the links and just place an element used purely for linking in our document, called `<Link>`:

```
<ColorLinks xmlns:xlink="http://www.w3.org/1999/xlink">
    <Link xlink:type="extended">
       . . .
    </Link>
</ColorLinks>
```

`extended` type elements may also have `role` and `title` attributes describing the link via a URI reference and simple text respectively – exactly the function that these attributes had for simple elements. We'll just use `title` here:

```
<ColorLinks xmlns:xlink="http://www.w3.org/1999/xlink">
    <Link xlink:type="extended" title="Fruit">
       . . .
    </Link>
</ColorLinks>
```

Next, we need to add some resources to participate in our link.

resource and locator Type Elements

Each contained `resource` and `locator` type element describes a participating resource. `resource` elements simply enclose the resource they refer to (and the contained text and XML therefore constitutes the resource), and `locator` elements *must* use their `href` attribute to provide the URI of a remote resource (where the URI supports XPointer syntax).

Both resource-locating elements may also have `role` and `title` attributes giving URI and textual information about the resource. Finally, these elements may have `label` attributes for identification purposes. There is no requirement that `label` attributes should be unique – we'll see the consequences of this later.

Let's add some local resources:

```
<ColorLinks xmlns:xlink="http://www.w3.org/1999/xlink">
    <Link xlink:type="extended" title="Fruit">
        <Resource xlink:type="resource" label="c1">
            Orange fruit
        </Resource>
        <Resource xlink:type="resource" label="c2">
            Green fruit
        </Resource>
        <Resource xlink:type="resource" label="c3">
            Red fruit
        </Resource>
        <Resource xlink:type="resource" label="c4">
            All colors of fruit
        </Resource>
    </Link>
</ColorLinks>
```

And some remote resources:

```
<ColorLinks xmlns:xlink="http://www.w3.org/1999/xlink">
    <Link xlink:type="extended" title="Fruit">
        ...
        <Resource xlink:type="resource" label="c4">
            All colors of fruit
        </Resource>
        <Locator xlink:type="locator" label="f1" href="fruit.xml#redapple"/>
        <Locator xlink:type="locator" label="f2" href="fruit.xml#greenapple"/>
        <Locator xlink:type="locator" label="f3" href="fruit.xml#orange"/>
        <Locator xlink:type="locator" label="f2" href="fruit.xml#gooseberry"/>
        <Locator xlink:type="locator" label="f1" href="fruit.xml#strawberry"/>
    </Link>
</ColorLinks>
```

Now we have our resources we need to define relationships between them.

arc Type Elements

Arcs between resources are defined by arc type elements. Each one of these may possess arcrole, title, show, and actuate attributes, which have the same meaning as they have for simple links. In addition they have from and to attributes to specify the arcs themselves. This is achieved using the label values from individual resources. Note that each arc is unidirectional, so to configure a two-way link two arcs are required. Note also that multiple resources may share the same label. In this case the arc element actually defines more than one arc – from each from labeled resource to each to labeled resource.

Again, let's add to our document:

```
<ColorLinks xmlns:xlink="http://www.w3.org/1999/xlink">
    <Link xlink:type="extended" title="Fruit">
        ...
        <Locator xlink:type="locator" label="f1" href="fruit.xml#strawberry"/>
        <Arc xlink:type="arc" from="c1" to="f3" show="replace"
                              actuate="OnRequest"/>
        <Arc xlink:type="arc" from="c2" to="f1" show="replace"
                              actuate="OnRequest"/>
        <Arc xlink:type="arc" from="c3" to="f2" show="replace"
                              actuate="OnRequest"/>
        <Arc xlink:type="arc" from="c4" to="f1" show="replace"
                              actuate="OnRequest"/>
        <Arc xlink:type="arc" from="c4" to="f2" show="replace"
                              actuate="OnRequest"/>
        <Arc xlink:type="arc" from="c4" to="f3" show="replace"
                              actuate="OnRequest"/>
    </Link>
</ColorLinks>
```

We have now set up the following 10 arcs:

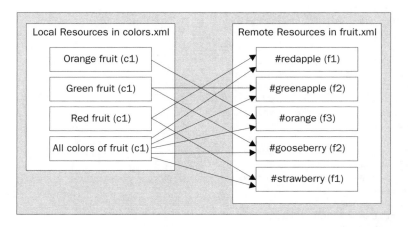

Note that these ten arcs are defined using just six arc type elements.

title Type Elements

`title` type elements can also be contained in `extended` type elements. They are intended to provide information about the link much like `title` attributes, but they differ from these in that they may include additional markup – and even nested links – and not just simple text. We may also use several `title` type elements in a single link, perhaps for different languages.

We could, for example, add the following to the link code we've been assembling here:

```
<ColorLinks xmlns:xlink="http://www.w3.org/1999/xlink">
    <Link xlink:type="extended" title="Fruit">
        ...
        <Arc xlink:type="arc" from="c4" to="f3" show="replace"
                             actuate="OnRequest"/>
        <Title xlink:type="title">
            <h1>Color Links</h1><br/>
            The following is a series of links between colors and fruit that are
            that color:<br/><br/>
        </Title>
    </Link>
</ColorLinks>
```

And with this we've covered all you need to know about extended links.

Extended Link Example

As another example, let's consider a list of people, each with a link to the home page of their employer. We'll create these links external to the people list, which is as follows (`people.xml`):

```
<?xml version='1.0'?>
<People>
    <Person id="p1">
        <FirstName>Karli</FirstName>
        <LastName>Watson</LastName>
        <Employer>Wrox Press Ltd.</Employer>
    </Person>
    <Person id="p2">
        <FirstName>Donna</FirstName>
        <LastName>Watson</LastName>
        <Employer>Agalinks</Employer>
    </Person>
    <Person id="p3">
        <FirstName>Mike</FirstName>
        <LastName>Parry</LastName>
        <Employer>Birmingham University</Employer>
    </Person>
    <Person id="p4">
        <FirstName>Dan</FirstName>
        <LastName>Kenny</LastName>
        <Employer>Birmingham University</Employer>
    </Person>
</People>
```

Next, let's look at the links in our linkbase (we'll talk more about linkbases later, for now it is all right to assume that the links stored here will be created). This file, `linkbase.xml`, has the root element `<Links>` that defines the `xlink` namespace and contains links in `<Link>` elements (of type `extended`). We can define all of the above links using a single `<Link>` element.

The first task is to use XPointer to reference the `<Employer>` elements in `people.xml`. For each of these we use a `<Loc>` element (of type `Locator`), and use a child sequence XPointer of the form ID/childnumber. Next we use more `<Loc>` elements to point at the employer homepages:

```xml
<?xml version='1.0'?>
<Links xmlns:xlink="http://www.w3.org/1999/xlink">
    <Link xlink:type="extended" title="Employer Links">
        <Loc xlink:type="locator"
            href="people.xml#p1/3"
            role="author.html"
            label="r1"/>
        <Loc xlink:type="locator"
            href="people.xml#p2/3"
            role="manager.html"
            label="r2"/>
        <Loc xlink:type="locator"
            href="people.xml#p3/3"
            role="student.html"
            label="r3"/>
        <Loc xlink:type="locator"
            href="people.xml#p4/3"
            role="researcher.html"
            label="r3"/>
        <Loc xlink:type="locator"
            href="http://www.wrox.com/"
            title="Wrox Press Homepage"
            label="r4"/>
        <Loc xlink:type="locator"
            href="http://www.agalinks.com/"
            title="Agalinks Homepage"
            label="r5"/>
        <Loc xlink:type="locator"
            href="http://www.bham.ac.uk/"
            title="Birmingham University Homepage"
            label="r6"/>
```

Next we can define the arcs themselves. This simply involves referencing the `label` attributes of the resources we wish to connect. Note that two of the locators have the same `label` (`r3`). This is because they share the same employer, so we can simplify things and define four links in three arcs:

```xml
        <Arc xlink:type="arc"
            title="Employer Home Page"
            show="New"
            actuate="onRequest"
            from="r1"
            to="r4"/>
        <Arc xlink:type="arc"
            title="Employer Home Page"
            show="New"
            actuate="onRequest"
            from="r2"
            to="r5"/>
```

```
        <Arc xlink:type="arc"
             title="Employer Home Page"
             show="New"
             actuate="onRequest"
             from="r3"
             to="r6"/>
    </Link>
 </Links>
```

Here each arc is defined as one that the user needs to interact with to traverse it, and that will show its result in a new window.

The arcs that this linkbase would create are shown below:

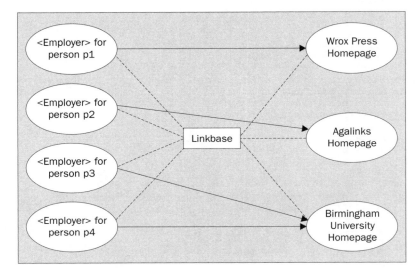

Alternatively, we could embed the link definitions in people.xml, in fact this example could even be achieved using several simple links on <Employer> elements. However, separating the links out like this certainly keeps our original XML uncluttered.

Linkbases

So far we've been using the concept of linkbases storing links without talking about how these will be located by XLink processors. Specific implementations may have set linkbase files that you can modify to define links, but it might be easier in some cases to create your own to keep file sizes smaller and more easily manageable. Again, some implementations may allow you to specify such files and mark them in some way, but XLink also allows you to instruct a processor as to the existence of a linkbase at execution time.

XLink defines a special kind of arc for this purpose. Let's say that in the previous example we want to embed an instruction in people.xml that explicitly says to look for links in our linkbase.xml file. All we need to do is to create an arc from people.xml to linkbase.xml that has a specific arcrole value, namely http://ww.w3.org/1999/xlink/properties/linkbase:

```
<?xml version='1.0'?>
<People xmlns:xlink="http://www.w3.org/1999/xlink">
   <GetLinkBase xlink:type="simple"
                href="linkbase.xml"
                arcrole="http://ww.w3.org/1999/xlink/properties/linkbase"
                actuate="onLoad">
   ...
</People>
```

Here the `actuate` attribute is set to `onLoad` so that the links will be discovered and added immediately. Of course, you may choose to have these added when the user wants them; we can do this using:

```
<GetLinkBase xlink:type="simple"
             href="linkbase.xml"
             arcrole="http://ww.w3.org/1999/xlink/properties/linkbase"
             actuate="onRequest"
             title="Show links">
```

This method of accessing linkbases may be recursive, if a similar link were to appear in `linkbase.xml` for example.

XLink Status

XLink is currently a Proposed Recommendation, the most recent version being that of the 20th of December 2000. PRs occasionally have minor changes before becoming Recommendations, so it is well worth keeping an eye on the W3C site for updates to the information given here.

XLink Summary

XLink provides a way of placing links between XML resources, in a much more flexible way than is possible between HTML documents. Of course, when XHTML usage becomes more popular then this standard may well replace standard HTML links in the long run.

For now, though, the use of XLink is very much a world of potential. As yet there are few working implementations around (and none that support full XPointer addressing), but you can be sure that people are working to change this situation.

XFI – XML Fragment Interchange

Now we come to the final technology covered in this chapter, XFI. XFI is a specification that allows you to send sections of an existing XML document to a receiver. You might not think you need a specification to tell you how to do this, but in reality there is a major stumbling block to consider, namely: how do you describe how the fragment fits into the original document?

For example, consider the `people.xml` file from the last section:

```
<?xml version='1.0'?>
<People>
    <Person id="p1">
        <FirstName>Karli</FirstName>
        <LastName>Watson</LastName>
        <Employer>Wrox Press Ltd.</Employer>
    </Person>
    <Person id="p2">
        <FirstName>Donna</FirstName>
        <LastName>Watson</LastName>
        <Employer>Agalinks</Employer>
    </Person>
    <Person id="p3">
        <FirstName>Mike</FirstName>
        <LastName>Parry</LastName>
        <Employer>Birmingham University</Employer>
    </Person>
    <Person id="p4">
        <FirstName>Dan</FirstName>
        <LastName>Kenny</LastName>
        <Employer>Birmingham University</Employer>
    </Person>
</People>
```

Let's say we wanted to send the entries for two people to someone:

```
<Person id="p2">
    <FirstName>Donna</FirstName>
    <LastName>Watson</LastName>
    <Employer>Agalinks</Employer>
</Person>
<Person id="p3">
    <FirstName>Mike</FirstName>
    <LastName>Parry</LastName>
    <Employer>Birmingham University</Employer>
</Person>
```

The first problem here is that the above section (also known as a **fragment**) doesn't constitute a complete XML document – it has more than one root element. In addition, all other document information is lost (which would include namespace declarations, doctype, entity definitions, etc. should they appear in the source document).

XFI solves this problem by saying that you need to send two pieces of information to exchange a fragment: the fragment body itself, and complete context information. This extra information is known as the **fragment context specification**, or **fcs**.

Fragment Context Specification

A fragment may be located in a document by means of the XML structure surrounding it. Using our last example we can say that the two elements in the fragment are the second and third <Person> children of <People>, or, visually:

```
<People>
   <Person/>
   fragment
</People>
```

We needn't include the <Person> elements after the fragment, this is enough information to locate the fragment.

XFI defines an <fcs> element (from its http://www.w3.org/XML/Fragment/1.0 namespace) that locates a fragment using just this structure, using a <fragbody> element to position it. For example:

```
<f:fcs xmlns:f="http://www.w3.org/XML/Fragment/1.0">
   <People>
      <Person/>
      <f:fragbody fragbodyref="http://www.myserver.com/peoplefragment.xml"/>
   </People>
</f:fcs>
```

Here we use the fragbodyref attribute of <fragbody> to locate the fragment itself, which in this situation would have been extracted to a separate file so that we can locate it using a URI.

<fcs> also possesses some attributes that allow further specification of the context information, shown in the table below:

Attribute	Description
extref	URI reference to the DTD of the source document.
intref	URI reference to any extra internally specified information, such as internal entity references. This may require extracting them to a separate file.
parentref	URI reference to the source document.
sourcelcn	URI reference to the fragment within the source document (would normally be the URI of parentref plus some XPath location information).

All of these attributes are optional.

In addition, it is quite possible that extra namespaces would need to be set up in the <fcs> attribute to match the source declarations. This includes the default namespace for the fragment, which would be set using simply xmlns="URI". Note that this default namespace is the default at the position of the fragment within the source document, which might not necessarily be the same as the default for the source document itself.

Packaging Fragments

As an extension of the above, it is also possible to send a fragment along with its `<fcs>` information in a single file, called a **package**. This is achieved using two extra elements, `<package>` and `<body>`, both from the `http://www.w3.org/XML/Package/1.0` namespace. We use `<package>` as the root element containing both `<fcs>` and `<body>`, and don't need to use the `fragbodyref` attribute of `<fragbody>` as the fragment content is explicit.

For example:

```
<p:package xmlns:p="http://www.w3.org/XML/Package/1.0"
           xmlns:f=" http://www.w3.org/XML/Fragment/1.0">

    <f:fcs>
       <People>
          <Person/>
          <f:fragbody/>
       </People>
    </f:fcs>

    <p:body>
       <Person id="p2">
          <FirstName>Donna</FirstName>
          <LastName>Watson</LastName>
          <Employer>Agalinks</Employer>
       </Person>
       <Person id="p3">
          <FirstName>Mike</FirstName>
          <LastName>Parry</LastName>
          <Employer>Birmingham University</Employer>
       </Person>
    </p:body>

</p:package>
```

XFI Status

The most recent version of the XFI specification is a Working Draft dated the 30th of June 1999. Although this is quite an old specification it seems relatively complete, and it is probably safe to assume that no major changes are forthcoming. The syntax is such that this technology could be put to use relatively easily, without having to resort to third-party implementations.

XFI Summary

This method of exchanging XML data could be very useful for large, multi-author documents as it could significantly reduce network traffic. In addition it is conceivable that XFI could be combined with some sort of locking system, such that sections of a large file could be 'signed out' for editing, and locked so that other authors would be denied access. Whatever happens to this technology (the fact that it is an ageing Working Draft is hardly conducive to using it), it certainly offers some interesting possibilities.

Summary

In this chapter we have seen five XML technologies related to connected XML data:

- ❏ **XPointer** – an extension to XPath allowing addressing of ranges and string data down to the sub-element level

- ❏ **XInclude** – a method of reusing XML data within multiple documents

- ❏ **XBase** – a method of setting the base URI for XML documents

- ❏ **XLink** – a method of linking multiple XML resources in a powerful and flexible way

- ❏ **XFI** – a technique for exchanging fragments of larger XML documents while retaining context

Additionally, we had a look at how we might use these in a series of short examples. In later chapters elements of these specifications will be put to practical use in a Java environment.

The Xerces Blue
Butterfly, which became
extinct earlier this century,
and after which the Xerces XML
parser is named ...

10

Semantic Documents

The evolution of computer science comprises periods of incremental development interspersed with sudden leaps through the introduction of new paradigms. Each paradigm shift brings a different way of seeing things, or a radically new approach to an old problem. Examples of paradigm shifts are:

❏ The emergence of the relational model for databases as a general-purpose mechanism for the storage of structured data

❏ The creation of the World Wide Web as a global network of linked information objects that may be displayed and interacted with by users anywhere in the world

❏ The emergence of XML as a universal syntax for data interchange

This chapter is about a further paradigm shift, which is just beginning to take shape. The new paradigm builds on the XML and Web revolutions, but adds some essential new aspects. It has come to be known as the 'Semantic Web', which could loosely be translated as 'Web of meaning'.
We shall begin by describing briefly what the Semantic Web is supposed to be, and how it differs from what has gone before. Then we shall consider two approaches to building a Semantic Web:

❏ Resource Description Framework (RDF)

❏ XML Topic Maps (XTM).

We shall take a simple example of a set of structured information – an extract from an imaginary XML version of the Wrox Press catalog – and show how this could be translated into the RDF and XTM paradigms. For each of these translations, we shall provide Java code that can be used to automate the translation process. Finally, we shall consider the similarities and differences between the RDF and XTM approaches to building semantic documents, and will say a few speculative words about future directions.

Three Paradigms Compared

If we compare relational databases, the World Wide Web, and XML documents, the most striking thing about them is that they embody three quite distinct structures into which all data is placed. Each structure has its strengths and its shortcomings, and therefore none of the paradigms is set to prevail at the expense of the others. All three coexist and are optimized for different purposes.

Essentially, the three paradigms can be characterized as follows:

❏ The relational database model sees data as composed of sets of 2-dimensional arrays, or tables, with joins between them defined in terms of primary keys identifying particular rows in a table, and foreign keys, linking other table rows to them, either from elsewhere in the same table, or from a different table altogether.

❏ XML sees all data as being expressed through a hierarchy, or tree, of nested elements, where each element may have content comprising text, other elements, or a combination of the two, and also may have properties (or attributes) in the form of name-value pairs associated with it. XML also has the mechanism of ID attributes and IDREF attributes, which are analogous to the primary keys and foreign keys of relational databases, though they are limited to references within the same XML document. The XML paradigm is complemented by a number of additional specifications, including XPointer (http://www.w3.org/TR/xptr) and XLink (http://www.w3.org/TR/xlink), which allow XML elements to be linked to one another across multiple documents.

❏ The World Wide Web sees all data as a globally accessible set of pages, where each page, and optionally each distinct part of the page, can be identified by a Uniform Resource Identifier (URI) which may be either a Uniform Resource Locator (URL) or a Uniform Resource Name (URN). A URL provides the possiblity of accessing the information object directly, through the mechanisms of the Web; the URN provides a persistent globally unique identifier for the information object, but needs to be mapped to a URL or some other access mechanism if the object is to be tracked down and its data made available to the system.

The major strength of the relational paradigm is the ability to manage large quantities of data efficiently, while ensuring data integrity and allowing effective queries into the data. The major strength of the XML paradigm is its ability to handle human-readable information in a hightly structured way, thus providing for the first time a real bridge between documents and data. The major strength of the World Wide Web is its ability to provide universal access and addressability to information of all kinds, regardless of the storage format and the operating systems of the computers on which the information is held.

The relational database paradigm has not gone away with the advent of XML, and XML coexists very happily with the World Wide Web – indeed, XML was designed specifically with the Web in mind, taking an earlier standard (Standard Generalised Markup Language, or SGML, standarized by the International Organization for Standardisation in 1986 as ISO standard number 8870) and adapting it for Web use. The various paradigms coexist, each providing its special strenghts, and much interesting research and development is going into finding optimal ways for them to be used together.

The Semantic Web

Despite the great strengths of the three paradigms we have been discussing, it turns out that there is still something essential that is missing. The missing piece to the puzzle is an effective means of associating meaning with data, in ways that makes information shareable and transferrable across the diversity of systems that make up the World Wide Web.

Even on a local system it is necessary to provide what is known as a 'schema' to describe the structure of a given data set and provide an indication of the intended meaning of each aspect of that structure. Relational databases are described by so-called relational schemas, which show how some view of an information domain translates into a specific set of relational tables. XML documents may likewise be enriched by a description of their internal structure, through a Document Type Definition (DTD) or XML Schema (see Chapter 1 for a full discussion of this).

But when we reach out from our local system and begin doing business and sharing information and data with people and systems from anywhere and everywhere in the entire globe, the problem immediately arises that our schemas and those that govern the data we are receiving from others will not always match. Much effort is currently being put into developing common data models, expressed through shared schemas, that are agreed upon by particular communities of interest within vertical or horizontal industry domains. Such work is extremely important, and enables us to make real progress towards global information sharing and global commerce. But developing shared schemas and agreeing to use them can only push back the boundaries of the problem to a limited extent. Given the diversity of requirements and the essential individuality of human nature, there will always be a variety of schemas in use, and multiple ways of describing the same things. So the fundamental question of meaning remains: how will the system recognize, when two different datasets are received that conform to different data models or schemas, whether or not they in fact describe the same thing?

The problem arises with exchange of information between one time period and another, not just between one place or community of interest and another. As businesses evolve and companies are acquired or spun off, the information models they use to structure their data will inevitably change over time. Yet it is extremely important to be able to look back on past data and be able to combine it with current data, to compare and contrast it in meaningful ways, detecting trends or constants across data that does not conform to a single data model or schema.

This is the essential problem that faces us as we move towards the next generation of Web-based systems. The World Wide Web Consortium (usually referred to by its acronym, W3C – http://www.w3.org/), in its Semantic Web Activity Statement (http://www.w3.org/2001/sw/Activity.html) describes it as follows:

> *The Semantic Web is a vision: the idea of having data on the Web defined and linked in a way that it can be used by machines not just for display purposes, but for automation, integration and reuse of data across various applications. In order to make this vision a reality for the Web, supporting standards, technologies and policies must be designed to enable machines to make more sense of the Web, with the result of making the Web more useful for humans. Facilities and technologies to put machine-understandable data on the Web are rapidly becoming a high priority for many communities. For the Web to scale, programs must be able to share and process data even when these programs have been designed totally independently. The Web can reach its full potential only if it becomes a place where data can be shared and processed by automated tools as well as by people.*

RDF and Topic Maps

The centrepiece of the W3C's proposed approach to the Semantic Web is the specification known as Resource Description Framework, or RDF. However, the activity will include studying how RDF relates to, and how it may be enhanced by, other specifications that address similar or complementary requirements. One of these complementary initiatives is known as Topic Maps. In January 2000, an ISO standard (ISO 13250) under the name **Topic Navigation Maps** was approved. Just over a year later, in February 2001, an independent consortium comprising several members of the Working Group that developed the ISO specification, and others, released an XML-compliant Topic Map specification under the name of **XML Topic Maps**, or **XTM**. The W3C Semantic Web Activity Statement recognizes the close relationship between RDF and XTM, in the following terms:

> *The ISO Topic Map (XTM) community has been finding increasing synergy with the RDF data model. We are hopeful that the markup language background of the Topic Map community will suggest syntax alternatives for graph-oriented data that can be considered for incorporation into RDF and that RDF will be seen to be usable for Topic Map data as well.*

So, let's take a brief look at RDF and XTM in turn, and see how they relate to the issues and requirements we have been discussing in this chapter. Later we'll see some Java implementations for reasoning with these formalisms.

The RDF Data Model and Syntax

We spoke above of the structural paradigms underpinning relational databases, XML documents, and the World Wide Web. RDF is based on yet another structural paradigm, known as a 'directed graph'. Whereas an XML document is fundamentally hierarchical in nature, consisting of nested information objects (XML elements) seated one inside the other, RDF creates a network of connected objects without any single topmost or outermost element.

The objects in a directed graph are called **nodes**, and the links between them are called **arcs**. In the case of RDF, the nodes are **resources** – information objects that can be addressed through URIs. An RDF document consists of a set of **statements** about resources, each of which is sometimes known as a **triple**, because it contains just three components. The components of an RDF statement, or triple, are the **subject**, a **predicate** (a property of that resource) and an **object** (a value of that property).

In the simplest case, the subject is a resource and the object (the value of the specified property of that resource) is a string literal. In its most basic form, RDF can be used to assign a piece of metadata (data about data) to a resource. Let's say that the resource is this chapter, and the metadata we want to assign is the property of author with the value Daniel Rivers-Moore. Supposing that the URI of this chapter were http://www.wrox.com/semanticdocs.doc, the complete RDF statement can be presented in tabular form like this:

Subject	Predicate	Object
http://www.wrox.com/semanticdocs.doc	Author	Daniel Rivers-Moore

Graphically, the same statement could look like this:

The RDF specification provides a basic XML syntax that can be used to serialize this structure, as well as a number of techniques for making the syntactic expression more compact. The full version of the syntax would express the statement like this:

```
<rdf:Description about="http://www.wrox.com/semanticdocs.htm">
  <myschema:Author>Daniel Rivers-Moore</myschema:Author>
</rdf:Description>
```

In order to allow this statement to be parsed without error, the two namespace prefixes `rdf` and `myschema` need to be declared. The `rdf` namespace prefix must be associated with the RDF namespace name, which is the following URI string: http://www.w3.org/1999/02/22-rdf-syntax-ns#. The `myschema` namespace prefix will be associated with a namespace name that is a globally unique identifier (in URI syntax) for a schema that defines the `Author` property. A complete RDF document containing just this item would look like this:

```
<rdf:RDF
 xmlns:rdf="http://www.w3.org/1999/02/22-rdf-syntax-ns#"
 xmlns:myschema="http://www.wrox.com/schema/">
  <rdf:Description about="http://www.wrox.com/semanticdocs.htm">
    <myschema:Author>Daniel Rivers-Moore</myschema:Author>
  </rdf:Description>
</rdf:RDF>
```

As we have said, RDF provides a number of mechanisms for making the syntax more compact. For example, in this case, where there is only one `Author` element, and the value of the author property is a simple string, an attribute may be used instead of a child element as follows:

```
<rdf:RDF
 xmlns:rdf="http://www.w3.org/1999/02/22-rdf-syntax-ns#"
 xmlns:myschema="http://www.wrox.com/schema/">
  <rdf:Description about="http://www.wrox.com/semanticdocs.htm"
    myschema:Author="Daniel Rivers-Moore"/>
</rdf:RDF>
```

For our immediate purpose, the syntactic shorthand is not of any particular interest, as it is more important to see the full structure in order to understand clearly what is happening. Indeed, in many cases, the requirement is not to collapse the syntax, but rather to expand the structure in order to enrich the model of the world that is being represented. For example, rather than considering the author as being adequately represented by a single string, it might be more useful to show that the author is a person, who has a `Name` property which is a string. We might also want to ascribe other properties to the person, such as e-mail address or gender. This can be done as follows:

```
<rdf:RDF
  xmlns:rdf="http://www.w3.org/1999/02/22-rdf-syntax-ns#"
  xmlns:myschema="http://www.wrox.com/schema/">
 <rdf:Description about="http://www.wrox.com/semanticdocs.htm">
  <myschema:Author>
   <rdf:Description about="http://www.rivcom.com/staff/drm">
    <myschema:Name>Daniel Rivers-Moore</myschema:Name>
    <myschema:Email>Daniel.rivers-moore@rivcom.com</myschema:Email>
    <myschema:Gender>male</myschema:Gender>
   </rdf:Description>
  </myschema:Author>
 </rdf:Description>
</rdf:RDF>
```

Note that a single mechanism is being used to assert that Daniel Rivers-Moore is the author of the chapter, and to assert that male is the gender of Daniel Rivers-Moore, despite the fact that the value of the gender property is the simple string male, while the value of the Author property is now a structured object. In both cases, the method is to create a subject-predicate-object triple. The subject is identified through the about attribute of an <rdf:Description> element, the predicate is the name of a child of that element, and the object is the content of that child element, which may itself be either a string or a further <rdf:Description> element. Because RDF is a *resource* description framework, we can only ascribe properties (or predicates) to things that are seen as resources, and are associated with unique URI strings. So, to treat Daniel Rivers-Moore not as a simple string, but as something that can have properties in its own right, we have associated him with a unique URI: http://www.rivcom.com/staff/drm.

Because of the inherent nesting capability of XML, it is very easy to build quite complex structures by treating the objects of triples as subjects in new triples that nest within the first one. But although XML allows nested structures to be used, the same information can be presented as a simple list of triples, as shown in the tabular presentation below:

Subject	Predicate	Object
http://www.wrox.com/semanticdocs.htm	Author	http://www.rivcom.com/staff/drm
http://www.rivcom.com/staff/drm	Name	Daniel Rivers-Moore
http://www.rivcom.com/staff/drm	Email	daniel.rivers-moore@rivcom.com
http://www.rivcom.com/staff/drm	Gender	male

Flattening the structure in this way makes it very easy to manage the information in a relational database environment, with a simple 3-column table structure. Each row of the table can then be expressed as a separate <rdf:Description> element with an about attribute specifying the subject, a single sub-element corresponding to the predicate, with its content being the object.

Equivalent Representations

The meaning of this RDF structure is identical to the meaning of the nested XML structure shown previously. In place of the nesting, we have an exact match between the content of the `<myschema:Author>` element and the values of the `about` attributes of the following three `<rdf:Description>` elements:

```
<rdf:RDF
 xmlns:rdf="http://www.w3.org/1999/02/22-rdf-syntax-ns#"
 xmlns:myschema="http://www.wrox.com/schema/">
  <rdf:Description about="http://www.wrox.com/semanticdocs.htm">
    <myschema:Author>http://www.rivcom.com/staff/drm</myschema:Author>
  </rdf:Description>
  <rdf:Description about="http://www.rivcom.com/staff/drm">
    <myschema:Name>Daniel Rivers-Moore</myschema:Name>
  </rdf:Description>
  <rdf:Description about="http://www.rivcom.com/staff/drm">
    <myschema:Email>Daniel.rivers-moore@rivcom.com</myschema:Email>
  </rdf:Description>
  <rdf:Description about=" http://www.rivcom.com/staff/drm">
    <myschema:Gender>male</myschema:Gender>
  </rdf:Description>
</rdf:RDF>
```

Now that we have a structure in which the content of every element is a simple string, we can use the more compact form of the syntax, with additional attributes in the `<rdf:Description>` elements, instead of using child elements.

```
<rdf:RDF
 xmlns:rdf="http://www.w3.org/1999/02/22-rdf-syntax-ns#"
 xmlns:myschema="http://www.wrox.com/schema/">
  <rdf:Description about="http://www.wrox.com/semanticdocs.htm"
   myschema:Author="http://www.rivcom.com/staff/drm"/>
  <rdf:Description about="http://www.rivcom.com/staff/drm"
   myschema:Name="Daniel Rivers-Moore"/>
  <rdf:Description about="http://www.rivcom.com/staff/drm"
   myschema:Email="daniel.rivers-moore@rivcom.com"/>
  <rdf:Description about="http://www.rivcom.com/staff/drm"
   myschema:Gender="Male"/>
</rdf:RDF>
```

Finally, because the last three `rdf:Description` elements have the same value for their `about` attributes, they can be combined into a single element to give a yet more compact form.

```
<rdf:RDF
 xmlns:rdf="http://www.w3.org/1999/02/22-rdf-syntax-ns#"
 xmlns:myschema="http://www.wrox.com/schema/">
  <rdf:Description about="http://www.wrox.com/semanticdocs.htm"
   myschema:Author="http://www.rivcom.com/staff/drm"/>
  <rdf:Description about="http://www.rivcom.com/staff/drm"
   myschema:Name="Daniel Rivers-Moore"
   myschema:Email="daniel.rivers-moore@rivcom.com"
   myschema:Gender="Male"/>
</rdf:RDF>
```

It is important to note that, as far as an RDF processor is concerned, there is no difference in meaning between the alternative XML structures we have shown. The underlying objects that they represent are triples that associate a subject with an object via a predicate. The subject and objects are nodes, and the predicate is a directed arc that starts at the subject and connects it to the object. Since the object of our first arc is the same as the subject of the other three arcs, the net result of the whole set of triples is a 'directed graph' that can be shown diagrammatically as follows:

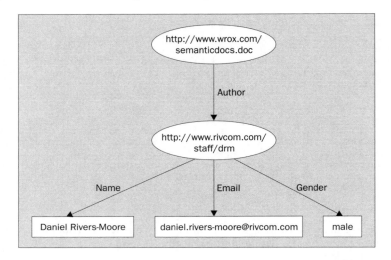

The next enhancement to this structure is to apply a typing mechanism to some of our resources. For example, we might want to say that Daniel Rivers-Moore is a type of person. We already know that the name, e-mail and gender properties are drawn from a particular schema (the one we have been calling myschema, and which is associated with the namespace URI http://www.wrox.com/schema. We now presume that this schema defines an object type called person, that is permitted to have these three properties. We want our RDF statements, and the resulting graph, to indicate explicitly that the resource identified by the URI http://www.rivcom.com/staff/drm is an object of type person.

RDF Types

RDF provides a special type property for this purpose. We shall now add this to our RDF document in shortened syntax, and to our directed graph diagram.

```
<rdf:RDF
 xmlns:rdf="http://www.w3.org/1999/02/22-rdf-syntax-ns#"
 xmlns:myschema="http://www.wrox.com/schema/">
  <rdf:Description about="http://www.wrox.com/semanticdocs.htm"
   myschema:Author="http://www.rivcom.com/staff/drm"/>
  <rdf:Description about="http://www.rivcom.com/staff/drm"
   rdf:type="http://www.wrox.com/schema/Person"
   myschema:Name="Daniel Rivers-Moore"
   myschema:Email="daniel.rivers-moore@rivcom.com"
   myschema:Gender="Male"/>
</rdf:RDF>
```

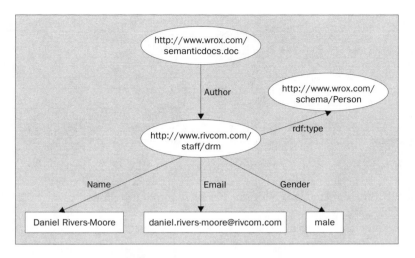

We are now ready to introduce a very important capability of RDF. So far, we have been making statements about resources, which may be simple string literals, or may represent objects of particular types, such as people, or whatever other kinds of thing our schema recognizes. But sometimes, we want to go further and make statements about our statements. For example, we might want to say that the Wrox catalog asserts that Daniel Rivers-Moore is the author of this chapter. In order to do this, we have to treat the whole statement about the authorship of the chapter into a resource in its own right. This is known as **reification**. We reify (or 'make real') the statement, so that we can then say further things about it.

Reification

Reification in RDF is performed by using special built-in types, namely rdf:Statement, rdf:subject, rdf:predicate and rdf:object. To reify the statement that Daniel Rivers-Moore is the author of the Semantic Documents chapter, we create a new resource, whose rdf:subject is the subject of the original statement, whose rdf:predicate is the predicate of the original statement, and whose rdf:object is the object of the original statement, and whose type is rdf:Statement. Here is what that would look like:

```
<rdf:RDF
 xmlns:rdf="http://www.w3.org/1999/02/22-rdf-syntax-ns#"
 xmlns:myschema="http://www.wrox.com/schema/">
  <rdf:Description>
    <rdf:subject resource="http://www.wrox.com/semanticdocs.doc">
    <rdf:predicate resource="http://www.wrox.com/schema/Author"/>
    <rdf:object resource="http://www.rivcom.com/staff/drm"/>
    <rdf:type resource="http://www.w3.org/1999/02/22-rdf-syntax-ns#Statement"/>
  </rdf:Description>
</rdf:RDF>
```

There is no about attribute, because this is not a statement about anything else, but is simply an object in its own right, about which further statements can be made. Suppose I wish to say that this statement is asserted by the Wrox catalog, I can add an additional AssertedBy property (also defined in myschema), which makes this new statement about my original statement:

```
<rdf:RDF
 xmlns:rdf="http://www.w3.org/1999/02/22-rdf-syntax-ns#"
 xmlns:myschema="http://www.wrox.com/schema/">
  <rdf:Description>
    <rdf:subject resource="http://www.wrox.com/semanticdocs.htm"/>
    <rdf:predicate resource="http://www.wrox.com/schema/Author"/>
    <rdf:object resource="http://www.rivcom.com/staff/drm"/>
    <rdf:type
     resource="http://www.w3.org/1999/02/22-rdf-syntax-ns#Statement"/>
    <myschema:AssertedBy resource="http://www.wrox.com/ctlg.doc"/>
  </rdf:Description>
</rdf:RDF>
```

Diagrammatically, the directed graph for this can be depicted as follows:

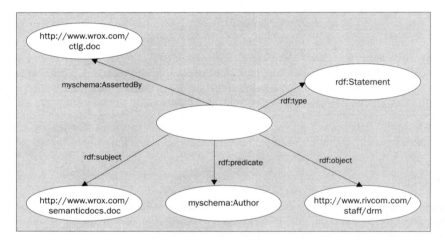

Features of RDF

The above overview of RDF is not complete. There are a few additional constructs, such as allowing resources to be grouped together within containers, and allowing statements to be made about these containers or about their contents. However, we have seen enough to get a sense of RDF's main features and capabilities. Essentially, what RDF allows is the use of a very simple construct – associating three things together in a subject-predicate-object triple – to build up arbitrarily complex directed graphs consisting of nodes and arcs linking those nodes together. Each node is considered to be a resource, and these resources can be typed. Each triple, consisting of two nodes and an arc, makes a statement about a resource by ascribing a property to it, and the property may itself be a string literal or another resource. The triple, or statement, may be 'reified', so that it becomes a node in its own right, and statements can be made about it as an object or subject in its own right.

Lying behind the entire construct is the notion of a schema, which defines the types to which the nodes may belong, and the properties that may be applied to nodes of each particular type. The schema itself is not defined in the RDF specification, though there is a related specification called RDF Schema, which does provide a formal schema-definition mechanism. However, whereas RDF has been approved as a W3C Recommendation, the RDF Schema specification has never moved beyond the stage of being a Candidate Recommendation.

More recently, the W3C has developed another, much fuller, schema specification language called XML Schema (see Chapter 5 for a full description of this) which, at the time of writing, is also a W3C Candidate Recommendation. In addition, there is an XML schema specification language called RELAX (Regular Language for XML) that has been developed by the Japanese Institute for Standardization (JIS) and may at some future point be ratified by ISO as a full international standard. RDF itself, however, is able to work with any schema definition mechanism, since it simply uses URI strings to reference the schema constructs.

All the theory is not much use if there are no tools to work with the RDF framework. In the next section we'll start our Java development by using the Jena toolkit to build an application that will generate our RDF format from the Wrox Catalog XML.

Creating the RDF Catalog with Jena

Jena is an experimental open source toolkit for creating and manipulating RDF models either as a set of RDF triples or as a set of resources with properties. Jena is available for download from http://www.hpl.hp.co.uk/people/bwm/rdf/jena/.

Parsing the Input File

Both the RDF sample code and the XTM sample code presented later in this chapter are built to read data from an XML format document. A sample of the input document is shown below. A parser for this document format is implemented in `semantic.CatalogParser` which uses a SAX parser to parse the XML file format and then generates notification events through the `semantic.CatalogHandler` interface whenever a complete catalog entry is found. We'll get straight on to the main generation code, and leave these two support classes till the end of the chapter (we'll use them again in the Topic Maps section).

Here's the XML for our catalog:

```
<?xml version="1.0" ?>
<catalog
  xmlns="http://namespace.wrox.com/catalog"
  xmlns:xlink="http://www.w3.org/1999/xlink">
  <catalog-entry>
    <contribution xlink:href =
        "http://www.wrox.com/semanticdocs.doc">Semantic Documents</contribution>
    <contributor identity="http://www.rivcom.com/staff/drm">
      <name>Daniel Rivers-Moore</name>
      <email>daniel.rivers-moore@rivcom.com</email>
      <gender type="male"/>
    </contributor>
    <contributor identity="http://www.ontopia.net/people/kal">
      <name>Kal Ahmed</name>
      <email>kal@ontopia.net</email>
      <gender type="male"/>
    </contributor>
  </catalog-entry>
</catalog>
```

407

The RDFHandler

The class semantic.RDFHandler class implements CatalogHandler and maps the catalog and its entries into an RDF model. The RDF model requires the creation of some resources and properties which form the infrastructure of the model. The resource created represents the source catalog file by its URL. The properties created represent the RDF predicates AssertedBy, Author, Name, Email and Gender all of which are defined in the namespace http://www.wrox.com/schema/. This initialization is performed in the startCatalog() function which is invoked by the CatalogParser when the <catalog> tag is found in the input XML file.

The code for the RDFHandler class is shown below:

```
package semantic;

import com.hp.hpl.mesa.rdf.jena.model.*;
import com.hp.hpl.mesa.rdf.jena.mem.*;
import org.xml.sax.SAXException;
import java.io.*;

/**
 * An implementation of the CatalogHandler interface which maps catalog
 * entries into an RDF model.
 * Output is written to an RDF file.
 */
public class RDFHandler implements CatalogHandler {

  /**
   * The RDF model to be populated with catalog data
   */
  protected Model model = new ModelMem();

  /**
   * The namespace and tags for myschema
   */
  protected static final String MYSCHEMA_NS = "http://www.wrox.com/schema/";
  protected static final String ASSERTEDBY_TAG = "AssertedBy";
  protected static final String AUTHOR_TAG = "Author";
  protected static final String NAME_TAG = "Name";
  protected static final String EMAIL_TAG = "Email";
  protected static final String GENDER_TAG = "Gender";

  /**
   * The properties to be used in the RDF model.
   */
  protected Property pAssertedBy;
  protected Property pAuthor;
  protected Property pName;
  protected Property pEmail;
  protected Property pGender;

  /**
   * The Wrox catalog resource
   */
  protected Resource rWroxCatalog;
```

```
/**
 * Initialises the RDF model
 */
public void startCatalog() throws SAXException {
  try {

    // Create properties
    pAssertedBy = model.createProperty(MYSCHEMA_NS, ASSERTEDBY_TAG);
    pAuthor = model.createProperty(MYSCHEMA_NS, AUTHOR_TAG);
    pName = model.createProperty(MYSCHEMA_NS, NAME_TAG);
    pEmail = model.createProperty(MYSCHEMA_NS, EMAIL_TAG);
    pGender = model.createProperty(MYSCHEMA_NS, GENDER_TAG);
    rWroxCatalog =
      model.createResource("http://www.wrox.com/catalog.xml");
  } catch (RDFException ex) {
    throw new SAXException(ex);

  }
}
```

The main processing of the RDFHandler is contained within the addEntry() function. This function is
invoked by the CatalogParser each time a complete <catalog-entry> tag and all of its content has
been processed. The result of the parser is a single ContributionData object and an array of
ContributorData objects. The ContributionData object contains only two public member variables,
name and identity, each of which are String objects. Each ContributorData object contains four
public member variables, name, identity, email and gender all of which are String objects.

The value of the identity member of the ContributionData is used to create an RDF resource which
represents the contribution. Then, for each contributor a resource is created to represent the contributor
and the Name, Email and Gender properties for that resource are added to the model. Each call to the
model.add() function creates an RDF triple using the supplied parameters and adds it to the model.
However, we must explicitly create the RDF triple associating the contributor and the contribution as
we want to be able to reify that statement later. The statement is created in almost the same way, by
passing the appropriate parameters to the model.createStatement() function. The statement thus
created is not automatically added to the RDF model, so we must call model.add() to insert it.
Reifying the statement is then a simple matter of adding a new statement to the RDF model in which
the reified statement is treated as the resource part of the RDF triple:

```
public void addEntry(ContributionData contribution,
                     ContributorData[] contributors) throws SAXException {
  try {
    Resource rContribution = model.createResource(contribution.identity);
    for (int i = 0; i < contributors.length; i++) {

      // Create resource for the contributor
      Resource rContributor =
        model.createResource(contributors[i].identity);

      // Add name, email and gender properties to the contributor resource
      model.add(rContributor, pName, contributors[i].name);
      model.add(rContributor, pEmail, contributors[i].email);
      model.add(rContributor, pGender, contributors[i].gender);
```

```
                // Create a statement that asserts that the contributor authored
                // the contribution resource
                Statement s = model.createStatement(rContribution, pAuthor,
                                                     rContributor);
                model.add(s);

                // Model that the authorship statement is asserted by the catalog
                model.add(s, pAssertedBy, rWroxCatalog);
            }
        } catch (RDFException ex) {
            throw new SAXException(ex);
        }
    }

    public void endCatalog() throws SAXException {
        // Nothing to do here
    }
```

Having created the RDF model in memory, the final step is to serialize the model into XML format. This is simply done by calling the write() method of the model:

```
    /**
     * Write the RDF model to XML serialisation.
     */
    public void write(OutputStream s) throws SAXException, IOException {
        try {
            model.write(new PrintWriter(s));
        } catch (RDFException ex) {
            throw new SAXException(ex);
        }
    }
}
```

Running the Example

We'll use a utility class semantic.SemDoc to run our example programs. This is also given at the end of the chapter. The class contains a simple main() method for running the RDF catalog creator as an application. The application expects three command-line parameters; the class to be used as the catalog handler; the input catalog file to be read and the output file to be written. So to run the RDF mapping we need to execute the command:

> **java semantic.SemDoc semantic.RDFHandler catalog.xml catalog.rdf**

To compile and run the application successfully, you will need to ensure that the jar files jena.jar and xerces.jar (both from the Jena distribution) are both on the classpath of the machine.

Here, for example, is a classpath set up for all the development in the chapter. Note you will need to alter the absolute filenames to suit your system:

> **set classpath=.;C:\jena\lib\jena.jar;C:\tm4j-0_5\jars\tm4j.jar;**
C:\jena\lib\xerces.jar

The output `catalog.rdf` should be as follows:

```
<rdf:RDF
  xmlns:rdf='http://www.w3.org/1999/02/22-rdf-syntax-ns#'
  xmlns:RDFNsId0='http://www.wrox.com/schema/' >
  <rdf:Description rdf:about='http://www.ontopia.net/people/kal'>
    <RDFNsId0:Name>Kal Ahmed</RDFNsId0:Name>
    <RDFNsId0:Email>kal@ontopia.net</RDFNsId0:Email>
    <RDFNsId0:Gender>male</RDFNsId0:Gender>
  </rdf:Description>
  <rdf:Description rdf:about='#RDFAnonId4'>
    <RDFNsId0:AssertedBy rdf:resource='http://www.wrox.com/catalog.xml'/>
  </rdf:Description>
  <rdf:Description rdf:about='http://www.wrox.com/semanticdocs.doc'>
    <RDFNsId0:Author ID='RDFAnonId4'
rdf:resource='http://www.rivcom.com/staff/dm'/>
    <RDFNsId0:Author ID='RDFAnonId9'
rdf:resource='http://www.ontopia.net/people/kal'/>
  </rdf:Description>
  <rdf:Description rdf:about='http://www.rivcom.com/staff/dm'>
    <RDFNsId0:Name>Daniel Rivers-Moore</RDFNsId0:Name>
    <RDFNsId0:Email>daniel.rivers-moore@rivcom.com</RDFNsId0:Email>
    <RDFNsId0:Gender>male</RDFNsId0:Gender>
  </rdf:Description>
  <rdf:Description rdf:about='#RDFAnonId9'>
    <RDFNsId0:AssertedBy rdf:resource='http://www.wrox.com/catalog.xml'/>
  </rdf:Description>
</rdf:RDF>
```

Visualizing the Result

RDFViz (http://www.ilrt.bris.ac.uk/discovery/rdf-dev/rudolf/rdfviz/) is a tool for the visualization of RDF models in the same simple graph notation shown earlier in this section. To generate the graph, simply submit the URL of the RDF file you wish to have processed via the form on the RDFViz web page. The generated graph may then be accessed as a GIF file, as a VRML file or in a number of different graph description formats. The RDFViz tool is also available for download to enable the processing to be run locally. The output of the RDFViz tool is highly useful for examining relatively small RDF files. However, because the tool renders all of the model into a single graphic, the visualization tends to become more difficult to read with increasing size.

We next look at the primary alternative methodology for semantic documents – Topic Maps.

The XTM Conceptual Model and Syntax

Whereas RDF has been developed within the W3C community, Topic Maps have emerged from the SGML community working within the framework of the International Organization for Standardization (ISO). With the publication in February 2001 of XTM version 1.0, Topic Maps can now be expressed in a standardized way in XML syntax, and so become a candidate for use as part of the Semantic Web.

Like RDF, Topic Maps allow arbitrarily complex networks (graphs) to be built out of very simple structures. The arcs in these graphs, however, do not have a specific direction. Rather, the nodes at each end of the arcs are distinguished by their `roles`. Like RDF, Topic Maps recognize the notion of a resource, and identify that resource through the use of a URI. Also like RDF, Topic Maps have the notion of **reification**, which allows things to be said about other things. However, the thing reified in Topic Maps is not a statement but a *subject*, which is defined as 'anything that can be conceived of or spoken about by a human being'.

411

The essential notion of Topic Maps is that a **topic** is a resource that reifies a **subject**, and allows **characteristics** to be assigned to it. The subject may be identified by one or more **subject identifiers**, which are resources, but the subject itself may or may not be a resource. If the subject is not a resource, it is known as a **non-addressable subject**. The characteristics that can be assigned to topics are **names**, **occurrences** and **roles in associations**. Occurrences are resources that are relevant in some way to the subject reified by the topic, and they can be typed – for example as descriptions, definitions, mentions, or any other way in which a resource may relate to a subject. Finally, any assignment of a characteristic to a topic can be related to a **scope**, which is defined as the context within which the assignment is valid.

Scoping is an extremely powerful mechanism, allowing us for example to assign different names to the same topic, where the names are valid in different contexts, or to assert that a given association between topics only applies in particular circumstances. The contexts themselves, which constitute the scopes of the characteristic assignments, are defined as sets of topics.

Comparing RDF and Topic Maps

What RDF and Topic Maps share is the use of a highly generalized mechanism for building up structured networks of relationships between resources, using the mechanisms of typing and reification to provide meaning to those structures. What Topic Maps add to RDF is the ability to reify subjects that are *not* resources (known as non-addressable subjects), and the recognition of contextual dependence, where any aspect of the structure may be applicable only in certain circumstances or for certain purposes.

The following two diagrams, and their accompanying explanations, are drawn from the XTM Conceptual Model. Taken on their own, they of course do not provide a complete picture of XTM, but they do serve to highlight some important structural aspects.

First, let us look at the diagram of the XTM class hierarchy:

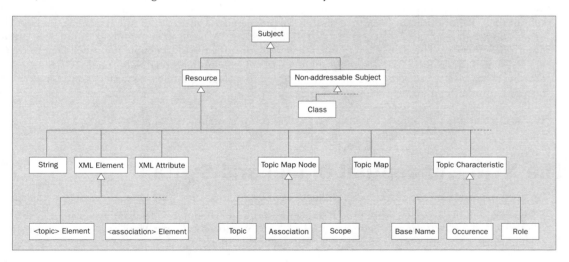

This diagram uses the conventions of UML (Unified Modeling Language) to show a hierarchy of classes and subclasses, starting from the notion of Subject, of which everything else is a subclass. The XTM specification provides the following description of this diagram:

A Subject is anything that can be spoken about or conceived of by a human being. A Resource is a Subject that has identiy within the bounds of a computer system. Any other Subject is known as a Non-addressable Subject. There are many types of Non-addressable Subject. A Class is a Non-addressable Subject. Types of Resource include Sting, XML Element and XML Attribute, as well as Topic Map, Topic Map Node and Topic Characteristic, and many others. Types of XML Element include <topic> *Element and* <association> *Element, and many others. There are just three types of Topic Map Node:* Topic, Association, *and* Scope. *There are just three types of Topic Characteristic:* Base Name, Occurrence, *and* Role.

Now let us look at how topics, resources and subjects relate to one another:

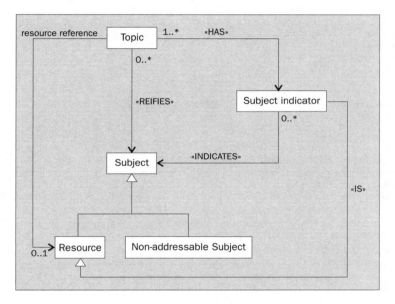

Here too, the conventions of UML (Unified Modeling Language) are being used. This time what is being shown is the relationships between Subjects and Resources. The triangular arrow-heads represent class-subclass relationships, as in the previous diagram. The simple arrows represent other kinds of relationships between objects of the types represented by the rectangles. The numbers beside the arrows represent the number of objects that may be involved in the relationship. If there is no number, the meaning is 'exactly one'. Thus, the central downward arrow means 'Every Topic reifies exactly one Subject, and every Subject may be reified by zero or more Topics.' The XTM specification provides the following description of this diagram:

> **A Topic can have any number of Subject Indicators. A Subject Indicator is a Resource that indicates what Subject is reified by the Topic. If the Subject is itself a Resource, there can be a direct reference from the Topic to that Resource in addition to any references there may be to Subject Indicators.**

Let us see how the information we used in our RDF examples would be approached in an XTM environment.

First, we need topics to reify all the subjects we are interested in. Each topic element will represent a single topic, and we shall give each topic a single name. XTM allows topics to have zero or more names, but where more than one name is provided, scopes should be specified to determine the context within which each name is applicable. In addition to the optional names, each topic element is required to have an id attribute, which can be used to reference it from other elements.

First, let us create a topic that reifies "Daniel Rivers-Moore", and another that reifies the concept of "person". We shall use the <instanceOf> child of the topic element to say that Daniel is an instance of the person class. This is done through the topicRef child of the <instanceOf> element, which has an xlink:href attribute that references the element whose id attribute has the value person. (This mechanism for creating links between one element and another is defined in the W3C's XLink specification, which can be found at http://www.w3.org/TR/xlink.)

```
<topicMap xmlns:xlink="http://www.w3.org/1999/xlink">
  <topic id="drm">
    <instanceOf>
      <topicRef xlink:href="#person"/>
    </instanceOf>
    <baseName>
      <baseNameString>Daniel Rivers-Moore</baseNameString>
    </baseName>
  </topic>
  <topic id="person">
    <baseName>
      <baseNameString>person</baseNameString>
    </baseName>
  </topic>
</topicMap>
```

Though we know from the above that Daniel Rivers-Moore is a person, we do not have any indication of what a person really is (beyond the fact that it has a name which is the string person). Of course, we cannot point to the concept of person directly, to refer the system or the reader to the concept itself, because the concept of person is an abstraction – it is a *non-addressable subject*.

What we can do is use the mechanism of subject indicators. These are resources that indicate what the subject is, in as unambiguous a way as possible.

> **The XTM specification states that 'authors are encouraged to always indicate the subject identity of their topics in the most robust manner possible, in particular through the use of standardized ontologies expressed as published subject indicators'.**
>
> **Similarly, a published subject indicator is 'a subject indicator that is published and maintained at an advertised address for the purpose of facilitating topic map interchange and mergeability'.**

The XTM specification itself provides a small number of published subject indicators that are useful for building topic maps. We shall use the published subject indicator for 'class' in the example that follows.

We shall use as our subject indicator for person, the person entry at http://www.dictionary.com. Actually, this is not ideal, since this entry includes many definitions of person, and we really want a subject indicator that references a definition of the concept of person as we intend it, rather than all the definitions of the word 'person'. In addition to a subject indicator, we can also indicate one or more occurrences of the subject, person. These occurrences can be external or inline. I shall use an inline resource, which will be a resourceData child of the occurrence element. I shall give this occurrence the description type.

For this purpose, we create a new topic for description. Both the person and the description are stated to be classes (the topics are instances of the `class` class, which is identified through the published subject identifier in the XTM specification:

```
<topic id="person">
  <instanceOf>
    <topicRef
     xlink:href="http://www.topicmaps.org/xtm/1.0/core.xtm#class"/>
  </instanceOf>
  <subjectIdentity>
    <subjectIndicatorRef
     xlink:href="http://www.dictionary.com/cgi-bin/dict.pl?term=person"/>
  </subjectIdentity>
  <baseName>
    <baseNameString>person</baseNameString>
  </baseName>
  <occurrence>
    <instanceOf>
      <topicRef xlink:href="#description"/>
    </instanceOf>
    <resourceData>
      The class of human beings.
      Any individual person is an instance of this class.
    </resourceData>
  </occurrence>
</topic>
<topic id="description">
  <instanceOf>
    <topicRef
     xlink:href="http://www.topicmaps.org/xtm/1.0/core.xtm#class"/>
  </instanceOf>
  <subjectIdentity>
    <subjectIndicatorRef
     xlink:href="http://www.dictionary.com/cgi-bin/dict.pl?term=description"/>
  </subjectIdentity>
  <baseName>
    <baseNameString>description</baseNameString>
  </baseName>
  <occurrence>
    <instanceOf>
      <topicRef xlink:href="#description"/>
    </instanceOf>
    <resourceData>
        The class of descriptions. Every description is an
        instance of this class. This class may be used to type
        occurrences that serve as descriptions of topics.
    </resourceData>
  </occurrence>
</topic>
```

Now that I have a topic for Daniel Rivers-Moore, clearly defined as being a person, I shall create a topic for this chapter. Unlike Daniel, who is a non-addressable subject (he does not exist within a computer, or on the Web), this chapter is a resource, and can be addressed directly at a URI. The `subjectIdentiy` of the chapter is therefore defined using a `resourceRef` rather than a `subjectIndicatorRef`:

```
<topic id="semanticdocs">
  <subjectIdentity>
    <resourceRef xlink:href="http://www.wrox.com/semanticdocs.doc">
  </subjectIdentity>
  <baseName>
    <baseNameString>Semantic Documents</baseNameString>
  </baseName>
</topic>
```

We could of course create a topic called `chapter` and say that this is an instance of that class. However, we did not put any type on this resource in the RDF example, so what we now have is sufficient for our purposes, and the next thing to do is to create the authoring relationship between Daniel and the chapter. In RDF, this is a directional arc. In XTM, there is no direction to the relationship, but instead, we create an **association** with two members sub-elements, which references the two topics we wish to associate. The member elements also contain `roleSpec` child elements that point to topics that specify the roles. We therefore create topics for the roles of `author` and `work`, which are referenced from the `<roleSpec>` children the two `<member>` elements:

```
<association id="drm-semdocs">
  <member>
    <roleSpec>
      <topicRef xlink:href="#author"/>
    </roleSpec>
    <topicRef xlink:href="#drm"/>
  </member>
  <member>
    <roleSpec>
      <topicRef xlink:href="#work"/>
    </roleSpec>
    <topicRef xlink:href="#semanticdocs"/>
  </member>
</association>
<topic id="author">
  <instanceOf>
    <topicRef
    xlink:href="http://www.topicmaps.org/xtm/1.0/core.xtm#role"/>
  </instanceOf>
  <baseName>
    <baseNameString>author</baseNameString>
  </baseName>
  <occurrence>
    <instanceOf>
      <topicRef xlink:href="#description"/>
    </instanceOf>
    <resourceData>
      The author role in the association between an author
      and a work.
    </resourceData>
  </occurrence>
</topic>
<topic id="work">
  <instanceOf>
    <topicRef
```

```
         xlink:href="http://www.topicmaps.org/xtm/1.0/core.xtm#role"/>
      </instanceOf>
      <baseName>
        <baseNameString>work</baseNameString>
      </baseName>
      <occurrence>
        <instanceOf>
          <topicRef xlink:href="#description"/>
        </instanceOf>
        <resourceData>
           The work role in the association between an author
           and a work.
        </resourceData>
      </occurrence>
    </topic>
```

The next task is to assign the `Email` and `Gender` properties to `Daniel`. The assignment of properties to topics is done by creating associations between the topic and the property value, where the nature of the associations (and hence the nature of the properties) is determined by the roles. In this case, we shall create a topic for `male`, and an association between `Daniel` and this gender. We shall also create a topic for the e-mail address `daniel.rivers-moore@rivcom.com`. Since this is a string, it can be placed directly inline as the content of a `<resourceData>` sub-element of an occurrence of the topic.

This is something of a shortcut solution. A more rigorous approach would be to create also a special `occurrence` type for this purpose, declaring a published subject identifier for it and referencing this through an `<instanceOf>` sub-element of the occurrence:

```
<!-- The association between Daniel and his gender -->

  <association>
    <member>
      <roleSpec>
        <topicRef xlink:href="#person"/>
      </roleSpec>
      <topicRef xlink:href="#drm"/>
    </member>
    <member>
      <roleSpec>
        <topicRef xlink:href="#gender"/>
      </roleSpec>
      <topicRef xlink:href="#male"/>
    </member>
  </association>

<!-- The association between Daniel and his e-mail address -->

  <association>
    <member>
      <roleSpec>
        <topicRef xlink:href="#person"/>
      </roleSpec>
      <topicRef xlink:href="#drm"/>
    </member>
    <member>
      <roleSpec>
        <topicRef xlink:href="#email"/>
      </roleSpec>
      <topicRef xlink:href="#drm-at-rivcom"/>
    </member>
  </association>
```

417

```
<!-- The male gender -->

  <topic id="male">
    <instanceOf>
      <topicRef xlink:href="gender"/>
    </instanceOf>
    <baseName>
      <baseNameString>male</baseNameString>
    </baseName>
  </topic>

<!-- The class of genders -->

  <topic id="gender">
    <instanceOf>
      <topicRef
       xlink:href="http://www.topicmaps.org/xtm/1.0/core.xtm#class"/>
    </instanceOf>
    <subjectIdentity>
      <subjectIndicatorRef
       xlink:href="http://www.dictionary.com/cgi-bin/dict.pl?term=gender"/>
    </subjectIdentity>
    <baseName>
      <baseNameString>gender</baseNameString>
    </baseName>
    <occurrence>
      <instanceOf>
        <topicRef xlink:href="#description"/>
      </instanceOf>
      <resourceData>The class of genders. Male and female are instances of this
class.</resourceData>
    </occurrence>
  </topic>

<!-- Daniel's email address -->

  <topic id="drm-at-rivcom">
    <baseName>
      <baseNameString>Daniel Rivers-Moore's email address</baseNameString>
    </baseName>
    <occurrence>
      <resourceData>daniel.rivers-moore@rivcom.com</resourceData>
    </occurrence>
  </topic>

<!-- The e-mail role -->

  <topic id="email">
    <baseName>
      <baseNameString>email address</baseNameString>
    </baseName>
    <occurrence>
      <instanceOf>
        <topicRef xlink:href="#description"/>
      </instanceOf>
      <resourceData>
          The email address role in the association between
          a person and their email address.
      </resourceData>
    </occurrence>
  </topic>
```

Our final task is to indicate that the Wrox catalog asserts that Daniel is the author of this chapter. To do this, we have to create a topic that reifies the association, so we can assign characteristics to it. This is done by creating a topic that has the association element as its subject indicator:

```
<topic id="drm-semdocs-association">
  <subjectIdentity>
    <subjectIndicatorRef xlink:href="#drm-semdocs"/>
  </subjectIdentity>
</topic>
```

Now that we have reified the association as a topic, we can assign characteristics to it. The characteristics that are available to us are names, occurrences and roles in associations. Given that we want simply to say that the Wrox catalog asserts that Daniel is the author of this chapter, one way we can do this is simply to use an occurrence subelement in this topic, stating that it occurs in the Word `catalog`.

```
<topic id="drm-semdocs-association">
  <subjectIdentity>
    <subjectIndicatorRef xlink:href="#drm-semdocs"/>
  </subjectIdentity>
  <occurrence>
    <resourceRef xlink:href="http://www.wrox.com/ctlg.doc"/>
  </occurrence>
</topic>
```

Alternatively, we could create a topic for the Wrox catalog itself, and create an association between the Wrox catalog topic and the topic that reifies the authorship association between Daniel and the chapter:

```
<!-- the Wrox catalog -->

<topic id="wrox-catalog">
  <subjectIdentity>
    <resourceRef xlink:href="http://www.wrox.com/ctlg.doc"/>
  </subjectIdentity>
</topic>

<!-- association between Wrox catalog and Daniel-chapter association -->

<association>
  <member>
    <roleSpec>
      <topicRef xlink:href="#asserter"/>
    </roleSpec>
    <topicRef xlink:href="#wrox-catalog"/>
  </member>
  <member>
    <roleSpec>
      <topicRef xlink:href="#assertion"/>
    </roleSpec>
    <topicRef xlink:href="#drm-semdocs-association"/>
  </member>
</association>

<!-- the asserter role -->
```

```
<topic id="asserter">
  <instanceOf>
    <topicRef
     xlink:href="http://www.topicmaps.org/xtm/1.0/core.xtm#role"/>
  </instanceOf>
  <baseName>
    <baseNameString>asserter</baseNameString>
  </baseName>
  <occurrence>
    <instanceOf>
      <topicRef xlink:href="#description"/>
    </instanceOf>
    <resourceData>
      The asserter role in the association between
      a document that makes an assertion and the assertion
      itself.
    </resourceData>
  </occurrence>
</topic>

<!-- the assertion role -->

<topic id="assertion">
  <instanceOf>
    <topicRef
     xlink:href="http://www.topicmaps.org/xtm/1.0/core.xtm#role"/>
  </instanceOf>
  <baseName>
    <baseNameString>assertion</baseNameString>
  </baseName>
  <occurrence>
    <instanceOf>
      <topicRef xlink:href="#description"/>
    </instanceOf>
    <resourceData>
      The assertion role in the association between a
      document that makes an assertion and the assertion itself.
    </resourceData>
  </occurrence>
</topic>
```

Features of Topic Maps

As with RDF, the above account of Topic Maps in general, and XTM in particular, is by no means complete. We have alluded briefly to the powerful notion of *scope* within topic maps, but have not made use of it in the worked examples to show the use of multiple names for the same topic in different scopes, for example. What we have done is to show how a Topic Maps approach would address the same simple set of tasks as we worked through in the RDF examples. It should be clear from this exercise that the Topic Maps approach requires somewhat more work, but that the resulting structure, while perhaps a little more verbose that the RDF structure, is no harder to read, and is quite a lot more informative. It is informative to humans because it includes mechanisms for including descriptions of the meanings of the constructs that are created. It is also more informative to the system, because it requires the explicit identification of topics that provide meanings for the roles that other topics play in associations. In RDF, you simply have a string that identifies a resource or names a property. In Topic Maps, you have a reference to a rich structure that may include substantial documentation, and, yet more importantly, pointers to publicly available definitions of the concepts that are being used.

Another powerful mechanism that XTM provides is a set of precise rules for what to do when bringing together Topic Maps in order to merge them into one. Essentially, if two topics have the same subject, they should be merged, and any redundant duplication between their characteristics eliminated. It may not always be possible to determine whether two topics from different Topic Maps have the same subject, since the subjects may be non-addressable subjects. If two topics with non-addressable subjects have the same subject identifier resource, then they can be deemed to be the same. But *not* having the same subject identifier does not necessarily mean they are not the same.

If I point to the Websters' definition of person, and you to the Oxford English Dictionary definition of person, our subjects may well be the same despite the different resources we chose as our subject identifiers. However, with the use of human intelligence, we can make these merge by creating at third topic that includes *both* these resources as subject identifiers. This topic has to be merged with both the others (since it shares a subject identifier with each), and so constitutes a strong assertion of identity between the subjects you and I were talking about.

The kinds of mechanisms that Topic Maps use explicitly recognize that knowledge and meaning involve human intelligence. Computers can address resources unambiguously, but when it comes to asserting meanings, you can't beat people – or rather, you can beat individual people, by using the results of the collaborative efforts of communities of people. The kinds of resources that a carefully built Topic Map will use as its subject identifiers will be resources that represent well-established or widely shared consensus definitions of the meanings of certain constructs. This is perhaps the closest we can come today to bringing machine intelligence and human intelligence together in constructive synergy, to build 'semantic documents' and the 'Semantic Web'.

As we did before with RDF, we'll now look at a Java solution for generating the topic map from our `catalog.xml` data.

Creating the Catalog Topic Map with TM4J

TM4J is an open-source Java toolkit for creating and manipulating topic maps. The toolkit can be downloaded from the TM4J website, http://www.techquila.com. TM4J makes use of the Apache Xerces XML parser which you will need to download separately from the Apache website at http://xml.apache.org.

The class `topicmap.TopicMapHandler` implements the `CatalogHandler` interface and plugs into the `CatalogParser` developed for the `RDFHandler` in the previous section (but shown at the end of this chapter). The `TopicMapHandler` class performs a mapping from the catalog information extracted by the `CatalogParser` into a topic map form. To achieve the mapping, a number of topics are required to create the initial topic map infrastructure of types and constants. These topics are represented by the class member variables `tDescription`, `tPerson`, `tAuthor`, `tWork`, `tGender`, `tMale`, `tFemale`, `tEmail`, `tAsserter`, `tAssertion` and `tWroxCatalog`.

All of these topics are created in the `startCatalog()` function of the handler as shown below. TM4J provides a factory interface for the creation of all topic map objects and it is this factory object that is initialized first, followed by the `TopicMap` object itself. When creating the infrastructure topics, all of the repetitive code required for creating a topic and setting its type, name, subject indicator, and description occurrence is contained within a separate subroutine, `createTopic()` which in turn calls `createOccurrence()` to set the type and inline data value for the description occurrences. The observant reader of the code will notice that the description of the topic `tDescription` has to be set after the topic itself is created, to avoid trying to type the description occurrence before the value of the typing topic `tDescription` is set.

Here is the `TopicMapHandler` class:

```
package semantic;

import com.techquila.topicmap.*;
import com.techquila.topicmap.utils.*;
import org.xml.sax.SAXException;
import org.apache.xml.serialize.*;
import java.io.*;
import java.net.*;

public class TopicMapHandler implements CatalogHandler {
  protected TopicMapFactory factory;
  protected TopicMap tm;

  // Topic classes:
  Topic tDescription;
  Topic tPerson;
  Topic tAuthor;
  Topic tWork;
  Topic tGender;
  Topic tMale;
  Topic tFemale;
  Topic tEmail;
  Topic tAsserter;
  Topic tAssertion;
  Topic tWroxCatalog;

  protected int topicCount = 1;
  protected String baseURI = "http://www.wrox.com/catalog/xtm-catalog.xtm";

  /**
   * Invoked when the catalog parser determines the start of a catalog listing.
   * Creates the topic map and populates it with the infrastructure topics
   * required to map the catalog entries.
   */
  public void startCatalog() throws SAXException {
    try {
      factory = new TopicMapFactoryImpl();
      tm = factory.createTopicMap();
      tm.setBase(new URL(baseURI));

      // Description
      tDescription = createTopic(
        "description", null, "description",
        "http://www.dictionary.com/cgi-bin/dict.pl?term=description",
        null);
      Occurrence occ =
        createOccurrence(tDescription,
          "The class of descriptions. Every description is " +
          "an instance of this class. This class may be used to type " +
          "occurrences that serve as descriptions of topics.");
      tDescription.addOccurrence(occ);
```

```java
      // Person
      tPerson = createTopic(
         "person", null, "person",
         "http://www.dictionary.com/cgi-bin/dict.pl?term=person",
         "The class of human beings.\nAny individual person is an " +
         "instance of this class.");

      // Author
      tAuthor = createTopic(
         "author", null, "author", null,
         "The author role in the association between an author and a work.");

      // Work
      tWork = createTopic(
         "work", null, "work", null,
         "The work role in the association between an author and a work.");

      // Gender
      tGender = createTopic(
         "gender", null, "gender",
         "http://www.dictionary.com/cgi-bin/dict.pl?term=gender",
         "The class of genders. Male and female are instances of this class.");

      // Male
      tMale = createTopic("male", tGender, "male", null, null);

      // Female
      tFemale = createTopic("female", tGender, "female", null, null);

      // E-mail
      tEmail =  createTopic("email", null, "email", null,
         "The email address role in the association between a person " +
         "and their email address.");

      // Asserter
      tAsserter = createTopic("asserter", null, "asserter", null,
         "The asserter role in the association between a document that " +
         "makes an assertion and the assertion itself.");

      // Assertion
      tAssertion = createTopic("assertion", null, "assertion", null,
         "The assertion role in the association between a document that" +
         "makes an assertion and the assertion itself.");

      // WroxCatalog
      tWroxCatalog = createTopic(
         "wroxcatalog", null, "Wrox Catalog", null, null);
      tWroxCatalog.setSubject("http://www.wrox.com/catalog/catalog.xml");

   } catch (TopicMapProcessingException ex) {
      throw new SAXException(ex);
   } catch (MalformedURLException ex) {
      throw new SAXException(ex);
   }
}

public void endCatalog() throws SAXException {

   // Nothing to do here
}
```

After the infrastructure is created, the main body of processing performed by the `TopicMapHandler` class is to map each catalog entry into a set of topics and associations. This mapping is performed in the `addEntry()` function which is shown below.

One topic is created for the contribution and one for each contributor and one for each contributor's e-mail address. As each topic must be assigned a unique identifier, the processing function makes use of a counter variable, `topicCount`, to generate the identifiers. An 'x' is prepended to the identifier value to avoid creating attribute values which are syntactically incorrect. The identifiers generated must be complete URLs using the base URI of the topic map document – this is taken care of in the `createTopic()` function in most cases, but must be explicitly coded when setting the ID of the contributor-contribution association. All of the associations between contributor and email address, contributor and gender and contributor and contribution are also created in this function. Once again, the repetitive code for creating the association is moved into a separate subroutine, `createAssociation()`.

```java
public void addEntry(ContributionData contribution,
                     ContributorData[] contributors) throws SAXException {
  try {

    // Contribution
    Topic contrib = createTopic("x" + String.valueOf(topicCount++), null,
      contribution.name, null, null);
    contrib.setSubject(contribution.identity);

    for (int i = 0; i < contributors.length; i++) {

      // Author topic
      Topic auth = createTopic("x" + String.valueOf(topicCount++),
        tPerson, contributors[i].name, null, null);

      // E-mail topic
      Topic e = createTopic("x" + String.valueOf(topicCount++), tEmail,
        "Email address of: " + contributors[i].name, null, null);
      Occurrence occ = createOccurrence(null, contributors[i].email);
      e.addOccurrence(occ);

      // Select correct gender topic
      Topic g = null;
      if (contributors[i].gender.equals("male")) {
        g = tMale;
      }
      if (contributors[i].gender.equals("female")) {
        g = tFemale;

        // Author-gender association
      }
      if (g != null) {
        createAssociation(tAuthor, auth, tGender, g);

        // Author/e-mail association
      }
      createAssociation(tAuthor, auth, tEmail, e);

      // Author-contribution association
      Association a = createAssociation(tAuthor, auth, tWork, contrib);
      a.setID(baseURI + "#x" + String.valueOf(topicCount++));
```

```
        // Reify the author-contribution association
        Topic assocTopic =
          factory.createTopic(baseURI + "#x"
                            + String.valueOf(topicCount++));
        assocTopic.addSubjectIndicator(a.getID());

        // Create asserter-assertion association
        createAssociation(tAsserter, tWroxCatalog, tAssertion, assocTopic);
      }
    } catch (TopicMapProcessingException ex) {
      throw new SAXException(ex);
    }
  }
```

The following creates a topic with the specified id, type and name:

```
  public Topic createTopic(String id, Topic type, String baseName,
        String subjectIndicator,
        String description) throws TopicMapProcessingException {
    Topic ret = factory.createTopic(baseURI + "#" + id);
    BaseName bn = factory.createBaseName(null);
    bn.setString(baseName);
    ret.addName(bn);
    if (type != null) {
      ret.addType(type);
    }
    if (subjectIndicator != null) {
      ret.addSubjectIndicator(subjectIndicator);
    }
    if (description != null) {
      Occurrence occ = createOccurrence(tDescription, description);
      ret.addOccurrence(occ);
    }
    return ret;
  }
```

The next method creates an occurrence of the specified type with the specified in-line resource data:

```
  public Occurrence createOccurrence(Topic type, String data) {
    Occurrence ret = factory.createOccurrence(null);
    if (type != null) {
      ret.setType(type);
    }
    if (data != null) {
      ret.setResourceData(data);
    }
    return ret;
  }
```

Here we define a method to create a binary association between two topics, each playing a specific role in the association:

```
public Association createAssociation(Topic role1Type, Topic role1Player,
                                     Topic role2Type, Topic role2Player) {
   Association ret = factory.createAssociation(null);
   Member m1 = factory.createMember(ret, null);
   m1.setRoleSpec(role1Type);
   m1.addPlayer(role1Player);
   Member m2 = factory.createMember(ret, null);
   m2.setRoleSpec(role2Type);
   m2.addPlayer(role2Player);
   tm.addAssociation(ret);
   return ret;
}
```

Finally the output can be written, on request, to an output stream. The output is a serialized XML file conforming to the XTM specification. TM4J provides a flexible output serializer, com.techquila.topicmap.utils.XTMWriter, which generates SAX2 events. This enables the programmer to use whatever standard XML serializer he or she wishes. In this code example, the serializer used is the one from the Apache Xerces toolkit.

```
public void write(OutputStream s) throws SAXException, IOException {
   try {
      OutputFormat format = new OutputFormat();
      format.setIndenting(true);
      format.setIndent(2);
      XMLSerializer ser = new XMLSerializer(s, format);
      TopicMapWalker walker = new TopicMapWalker();
      XTMWriter writer = new XTMWriter();
      writer.setContentHandler(ser.asContentHandler());
      walker.setHandler(writer);
      walker.walk(tm);
   } catch (TopicMapProcessingException ex) {
      throw new SAXException(ex);
   }
}
```

Running the Example

As with the RDF example, the class semantic.SemDoc can be used to run the topic map example. This is done by executing a command such as:

```
> java semantic.SemDoc semantic.TopicMapHandler catalog.xml catalog.xtm
```

To compile and/or run the application successfully, you will need to ensure that the JAR files tm4j.jar (from the TM4J distribution) and xerces.jar (from the Apache Xerces distribution) are both your classpath.

You should see the generated file `catalog.xtm` as follows:

```xml
<?xml version="1.0" encoding="UTF-8"?>
<topicMap xmlns="http://www.topicmaps.org/xtm/1.0/"
  xmlns:xlink="http://www.w3.org/1999/xlink"
xml:base="http://www.wrox.com/catalog/xtm-catalog.xtm">
  <topic id="asserter">
    <baseName>
      <baseNameString>asserter</baseNameString>
    </baseName>
    <occurrence>
      <instanceOf>
        <topicRef xlink:href="#description"/>
      </instanceOf>
      <resourceData>The asserter role in the association between a
        document that makes an assertion and the assertion itself.</resourceData>
    </occurrence>
  </topic>
  <topic id="work">
    <baseName>
      <baseNameString>work</baseNameString>
    </baseName>
    <occurrence>
      <instanceOf>
        <topicRef xlink:href="#description"/>
      </instanceOf>
      <resourceData>The work role in the association between an author
        and a work.</resourceData>
    </occurrence>
  </topic>
  <topic id="wroxcatalog">
    <subjectIdentity>
      <resourceRef xlink:href="http://www.wrox.com/catalog/catalog.xml"/>
    </subjectIdentity>
    <baseName>
      <baseNameString>Wrox Catalog</baseNameString>
    </baseName>
  </topic>

<!--
  Several pages of topics removed for space reasons.
  You could view the generated file by running the code, or look at
  the one in the download samples for this book.
-->

</topicMap>
```

It is possible to view the topic map in a development system such as the empolis K42 product (see http://k42.empolis.co.uk for download and installation instructions). As well as providing an interactive tool for building and editing topic maps, there is the TMV topic map viewer applet. The first view (ALL) allows to view all topics in the topic map:

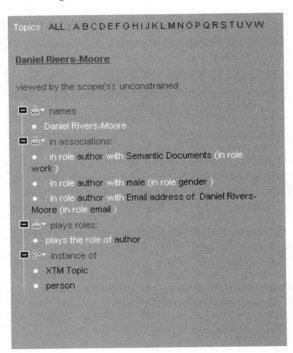

Topics : ALL : A B C D E F G H I J K L M N O P Q R S T U V W

asserter
assertion
author
Daniel Rivers-Moore
description
email
Email address of: Daniel Rivers-Moore
Email address of: Kal Ahmed
female
gender
Kal Ahmed
male
person
Semantic Documents
work
Wrox Catalog
XTM Topic

Selecting a topic allows us to navigate into a tree view of the chosen topic:

Topics : ALL : A B C D E F G H I J K L M N O P Q R S T U V W

Daniel Rivers-Moore

viewed by the scope(s): unconstrained

- ▣ ♣▾ names
  - • Daniel Rivers-Moore
- ▣ ♣▾ in associations:
  - • : in role author with Semantic Documents (in role work)
  - • : in role author with male (in role gender)
  - • : in role author with Email address of: Daniel Rivers-Moore (in role email)
- ▣ ♣▾ plays roles:
  - • plays the role of author
- ▣ ♣▾ instance of
  - • XTM Topic
  - • person

Support Classes

Before we conclude the chapter, we present here the support classes necessary to run the Java RDF and Topic Map tools that we developed earlier.

The CatalogHandler Interface

The `CatalogHandler` interface encapsulates the behaviour of our two different format generators: `RDFHandler`, and `TopicMapHandler` which both implement this interface:

```
package semantic;

import org.xml.sax.SAXException;
import java.io.*;

public interface CatalogHandler {
  public void startCatalog() throws SAXException;
  public void endCatalog() throws SAXException;
  public void addEntry(ContributionData contribution,
                    ContributorData[] contributors) throws SAXException;
  public void write(OutputStream s) throws SAXException, IOException;
}
```

The CatalogParser Class

This class, together with its support classes `ContributionData` and `ContributorData`, is used to handle events generated by the `catalog.xml` data.

```
package semantic;

import org.apache.xerces.parsers.*;
import org.xml.sax.*;
import org.xml.sax.helpers.*;
import java.io.*;
import java.util.*;

public class CatalogParser extends DefaultHandler {
  private static final String CATALOG_NS =
    "http://namespace.wrox.com/catalog";
  private static final String XLINK_NS = "http://www.w3.org/1999/xlink";
  private static final String HREF_ATT = "href";
  private static final String CATALOG_TAG = "catalog";
  private static final String CATALOGENTRY_TAG = "catalog-entry";
  private static final String CONTRIBUTION_TAG = "contribution";
  private static final String CONTRIBUTOR_TAG = "contributor";
  private static final String IDENTITY_ATT = "identity";
  private static final String NAME_TAG = "name";
  private static final String EMAIL_TAG = "email";
  private static final String GENDER_TAG = "gender";
  private static final String TYPE_ATT = "type";
  private static final String GENDER_MALE = "male";
  private static final String GENDER_FEMALE = "female";
```

```
  private SAXParser parser;
  private CatalogHandler handler;
  private StringBuffer data;

  // Members to hold entry data:
  private ContributionData contribution;
  private ContributorData contributor;
  private ArrayList contributors;

  public CatalogParser() {
    parser = new SAXParser();
    parser.setContentHandler(this);
  }

  public void setCatalogHandler(CatalogHandler h) {
    handler = h;
  }

  public void parse(InputSource src) throws SAXException, IOException {
    parser.parse(src);
  }

  public void startElement(String nsURI, String localName, String qName,
                           Attributes atts) throws SAXException {
    if (nsURI.equals(CATALOG_NS)) {
      if (localName.equals(CATALOG_TAG)) {
        handler.startCatalog();
      } else if (localName.equals(CATALOGENTRY_TAG)) {
        contribution = new ContributionData();
        contributors = new ArrayList();
      } else if (localName.equals(CONTRIBUTION_TAG)) {
        contribution.identity = atts.getValue(XLINK_NS, HREF_ATT);
        data = new StringBuffer();
      } else if (localName.equals(CONTRIBUTOR_TAG)) {
        contributor = new ContributorData();
        contributor.identity = atts.getValue("", IDENTITY_ATT);
      } else if (localName.equals(GENDER_TAG)) {
        contributor.gender = atts.getValue("", TYPE_ATT);
      } else {
        data = new StringBuffer();
      }
    }
  }

  public void endElement(String nsURI, String localName,
                         String qName) throws SAXException {
    if (nsURI.equals(CATALOG_NS)) {
      if (localName.equals(CONTRIBUTION_TAG)) {
        contribution.name = data.toString();
      } else if (localName.equals(NAME_TAG)) {
        contributor.name = data.toString();
      } else if (localName.equals(EMAIL_TAG)) {
        contributor.email = data.toString();
      } else if (localName.equals(CONTRIBUTOR_TAG)) {
        contributors.add(contributor);
      } else if (localName.equals(CATALOG_TAG)) {
        handler.endCatalog();
      } else if (localName.equals(CATALOGENTRY_TAG)) {
        ContributorData[] arry = new ContributorData[contributors.size()];
        arry = (ContributorData[]) contributors.toArray(arry);
        handler.addEntry(contribution, arry);
      }
```

```
      }
    }

    public void characters(char[] chars, int start, int len) {
      if (data != null) {
        data.append(chars, start, len);
      }
    }
  }
}

class ContributionData {
  public String identity;
  public String name;
}

class ContributorData {
  public String identity;
  public String name;
  public String email;
  public String gender;
}
```

The SemDoc Utility

This is a command line front end that we used to test our two format handlers:

```
package semantic;

import org.xml.sax.*;
import java.io.*;

public class SemDoc {
  public static void main(String[] args) {
    Class handlerClass;
    CatalogHandler handler;

    if (args.length != 3) {
      usage();
      System.exit(-1);
    }
    try {
      handlerClass = Class.forName(args[0]);
      handler = (CatalogHandler) handlerClass.newInstance();
      File input = new File(args[1]);
      CatalogParser parser = new CatalogParser();
      parser.setCatalogHandler(handler);
      parser.parse(new InputSource(new FileInputStream(input)));
      FileOutputStream output = new FileOutputStream(args[2]);
      handler.write(output);
      System.exit(0);
    } catch (ClassNotFoundException ex) {
      System.out.println("Cannot locate handler: " + args[0]);
      System.exit(-1);
    } catch (ClassCastException ex) {
      System.out.println(args[0] + " is not a CatalogHandler instance.");
      System.exit(-1);
    } catch (InstantiationException ex) {
      System.out.println("Cannot instantiate handler: " + args[0]);
      System.exit(-1);
    } catch (IllegalAccessException ex) {
```

```
      System.out
        .println("Access exception while attempting to instantiate handler: "
                + args[0]);
    } catch (SAXException ex) {
      System.out.println("SAXException while parsing catalog");
      System.out.println(ex.getMessage());
      if (ex.getException() != null) {
        System.out.println("Cause: " + ex.getException().getMessage());
        ex.getException().printStackTrace();
      }
    } catch (FileNotFoundException ex) {
      System.out.println("Cannot find file: " + args[1]);
    } catch (Exception ex) {
      System.out.println(ex.toString()
                      + ": Failure while parsing catalog.");
      ex.printStackTrace();
      System.out.println(ex.getMessage());
    }
    System.exit(-1);
  }

  public static void usage() {
    System.out
      .println("semantic.SemDoc " +
              "handlerClass inputFile outputFile");
  }
}
```

We now turn back to mull over the approaches we have looked at and to summarize the work of the chapter.

The Ingredients of a Solution

The creation of the Semantic Web is something that will take some time. More research and deep thinking need to be done, and more standards and specifications need to be agreed upon to provide a common platform for implementing the results of that research and that thinking. But already today it is possible to identify a few key features of the solution. These can be summarized as follows:

❑ The ultimate meaning of data is only determinable by humans.

❑ Humans do reach consensus on common definitions of underlying concepts that are important to them.

❑ The established consensus on any underlying concept can serve as a reference point in the event of disagreement or misunderstanding in particular cases.

❑ It is not necessary to go back to the consensus statement every time information is exchanged, provided the pointers are available to be followed in case of need.

❑ It is possible to assert equivalences or conversion algorithms between statements that are based on different underlying consensus statements.

❑ The sharing does not have to be universal. If a small community agrees on a lot of shared constructs for use with a particular set of documents, the mappings to their documents can be very simple. On the other hand, if a large community wants to share a wide range of documents, then the mappings will be more complex and will need to relate back to more fundamental and widely shared constructs.

❑ Any document can be a 'semantic document' provided it is possible to establish the links from its constituent information items to the shared constructs in terms of which they can be understood.

It is now not too hard to see how we can put these ingredients together into a recipe for a establishing 'semantic documents' and the 'Semantic Web':

- ❑ We need to have a large number of widely shared sets of definitions enshrining common understanding of sets of useful underlying constructs. These are commonly called taxonomies (classification schemes), or ontologies (formalised statements of the kinds of things that can exist within a particular system or world-view).

- ❑ We need a mechanism for asserting the relationships that exist between the items of information in our documents and the things that are defined in these taxonomies and ontologies.

- ❑ We need a mechanism for asserting the correspondences and differences between items drawn from distinct taxonomies or ontologies.

It is important to note that a 'semantic document' is therefore not a special kind of document. Nothing needs to be done to the document itself in order to make it into a semantic document. The XML family of standards includes the XPointer (http://www.w3.org/TR/xptr) and XLink (http://www.w3.org/TR/xlink) specifications, which allow XML elements to be linked to one another across multiple documents. We can thus establish links between the items in any XML document and other documents, which describe established taxonomies and ontologies, held in some other place on the Web. We can thus add semantic processability to documents to which we have read-only access. Of course, if we are originating documents ourselves, or have the right to edit or modify existing documents, there may be advantages in placing additional semantic markup inline within the document. But this is not required, and in some cases will not be possible. Both RDF and XTM allow these kinds of links to be created, and allow us to provide different kinds of machine-processable semantics to documents.

Summary

In March 2001, the first international Knowledge Technologies Conference took place in Austin Texas, and brought together some 150 people for four days of intensive tutorials, presentations, and working meetings. Both RDF and Topic Maps featured strongly on the programme, as did research into neural science, and how humans come to acquire knowledge in the first place, by making sense of the mass of data that are made available to them through their sense organs. In one interesting remark, Paul Prueitt of OntologyStream, observed that "RDF is essentially an information technology – albeit a very powerful one – since it sees all information in terms of resources that exist within the computer system. Topic Maps, on the other hand, are potentially a knowledge technology in that they recognize that there is something (the 'subject' of the topic) that exists inherently outside the bounds of the system. This is critical in making the leap from an information technology to a knowledge technology in the full sense of the term."

The next two to three years promise to be critical in making a reality out of what has long been a dream. The basic technologies are now in place. As they are developed, refined, and harmonized with one another, we are likely to see something that can credibly be described as 'semantic interoperability on the Web'. The benefits of this achievement, if it is indeed a success, will be considerable.

The Xerces Blue
Butterfly, which became
extinct earlier this century,
and after which the Xerces XML
parser is named ...

11

Socket I/O

The Java sockets API provides a good introduction to networking with Java. XML-enabled applications need to be able to talk to each other over networks and the best way of doing this is by using sockets over TCP/IP. Fair enough, you might think you're not using them because you can't see any mention of sockets in the communications API you're actually using. But in the cases where some other API provides a better abstraction of the problem, or you are forced to use another set of interfaces for security or convenience, it's almost certain that socket-based communication is working in the background.

Working with streams of data is natural to many of the XML processing systems we've already seen in this book, and streams are what we deal with at the socket level. The things that can go wrong at this level are of fundamental importance to the development of distributed XML applications, and so that's why we're covering them at this stage in the book, before you go on to work at protocols higher up in the food chain.

In this chapter we will cover the following:

❑   The `java.net.Socket` and `java.net.SocketServer` classes

❑   Writing socket clients and servers

❑   Basic multithreading issues in server design

❑   Writing an XML socket server and client application parsing streams over TCP/IP

Java Sockets API

Let's compare setting up a Java listening server to setting one up in C. The example below would assume that you have standard UNIX C libraries:

```c
#include <netinet/in.h>
#include <sys/socket.h>
#include <stdio.h>
#include <strings.h>
#include <arpa/inet.h>

int main(int arg, char*argv[])
{
  int fdListen = 0;
  int fdClient = 0;
  struct sockaddr_in serverAddress;
  char buffer(255);

  fdListen = socket(AF_INET, SOCK_STREAM, 0);
  bzero(&serverAddress, sizeof(serverAddress));
  serverAddress.sin_family = AF_INET;
  serverAddress.sin_addr.s_addr = htonl(INADDR_ANY);
  serverAddress.sin_port = htons(13);
  bind(fdListen, (socketaddr*)&serverAddress, sizeof(serverAddress));

  listen(fdListen, 10);

  while (1)
  {
    fdClient = accept(fdListen, (socketaddr*)NULL, NULL);
    printf("Got a connection\n");
    close(fdClient);
  }
}
```

This is the equivalent in Java:

```java
import java.net.ServerSocket;
import java.net.Socket;

public class SocketExample {
  public static void main(String[] args) throws Exception {
    ServerSocket server = new ServerSocket(13);

    while (true) {
      Socket socket = server.accept();
      System.out.println("Got a connection");
      socket.close();
    }
  }
}
```

Aside from the obvious difference in length, the Java code is much easier to read. I won't go into the details of how the above C code works. I hope that it has been enough to show you how powerful Java can be in just a few lines of code.

Connection-Oriented and Connectionless Protocols

When we use the term "socket", we are usually referring to a connection-oriented protocol. What this means is that the transmission of data across a network has a connection on two ends that is persistent throughout a particular transaction. When sending data over a socket, the data is split into packets. A connection-oriented protocol, such as TCP/IP, guarantees that the order in which packets are sent is the order in which they will be received on the other end.

The example above shows how to create a **listening socket**, often referred to as a **server socket**. A server socket is one where a request can be sent for processing. Servers bind to a well-known port, or one that is advertised to have a particular service available. No other server is able to bind to that port while a server is already bound to it. An example is the File Transport Protocol (FTP) application, which is known to run on port 21.

A connectionless protocol is one where no real connection is made between the requestor and handler. As such, communications are not guaranteed to arrive in any predetermined order or even arrive at all. When a client makes a request to a **User Datagram Protocol** (UDP) server, for example, it does not call a `connect()` method of any kind. Instead, it specifies the port and IP address of the server and writes the packet onto the network, hoping it arrives.

The server does not attempt to make any connection with the client, but merely waits for data to arrive on its port and reads that data. There are instances where it makes sense to use UDP over TCP, such as with the Domain Name Service (DNS). In order to find the location of a machine on a network, you would usually need to query several servers. It is much more efficient to send the same packet to any number of destinations than it is to send multiple copies of a packet making multiple connections to multiple servers. When dealing with XML (which is usually transported over HTTP, an application layer on top of TCP/IP, which we cover in the next two chapters) we want our data to arrive and know that it arrived, so we will not delve further into UDP as the details of how it works are beyond the scope of this book.

Creating a Simple Client-Server Application

This section will look into creating a service that handles requests. In the introductory example of this chapter, we saw how to create a basic server. We will look further into the API to see exactly how this works.

The java.net.ServerSocket Class

Key to understanding socket servers is familiarity with the `java.net.ServerSocket` class. This section will describe the constructors and methods of this class.

Constructors

All of the constructors in the `ServerSocket` class take at least one parameter: a port number. The port number is the location on a machine where a service makes itself available to the outside world, listening out for client requests. We locate a machine via its IP address, but we locate a service by its port number. There are port numbers reserved for "standard" services, such as FTP and Telnet. The port range of 0 to 1024 is reserved for such services leaving the rest available for general applications.

The other parameter worth mentioning here is `backlog`. This parameter configures the backlog queue, by determining how many requests to keep waiting before connections are refused. When no backlog parameter is specified, the default is set to 50. Once the queue is full with requests waiting to be serviced, subsequent connections are refused until a request is serviced.

The following are the constructors associated with this class:

```
public ServerSocket(int port) throws IOException

public ServerSocket(int port, int backlog) throws IOException

public ServerSocket(int port, int backlog, java.net.InetAddress address) throws
IOException
```

This final constructor can be used if a server uses multiple IP addresses. If the server wishes to accept only requests made to a particular IP address, this parameter should contain that value. In order to set this parameter, we use the methods of the `java.net.InetAddress` class. For example, if we only want to process requests sent to the IP address `192.168.0.1`, we could do this as follows:

```
InetAddress addr = InetAddress.getByName("192.168.0.1");
ServerSocket server = new ServerSocket(22334, 50, addr);
```

This code creates an instance of an `InetAddress` class by supplying the IP address to the static `InetAddress.getByName()` method. We then pass this value to the appropriate constructor.

Methods

These are the methods associated with the `SocketServer` class:

`public Socket accept() throws IOException`	This method waits for a connection to the server, blocking execution until a connection is made. Interestingly, the port that this socket is bound to is not the same port to which it originally connects. Once the connection is established, it is handed off to another available port.
`public void close() throws IOException`	This method closes the listening socket and cleans up any resources.
`public InetAddress getInetAddress()`	The local address of the server socket is returned by this method.
`public int getLocalPort()`	This method returns the port to which this server is bound.
`public int getSoTimeout() throws IOException`	The SO_TIMEOUT parameter determines the amount of time in milliseconds that the server will listen before it throws an exception. If this value is zero, then the server will wait an arbitrary amount of time. Setting a timeout can prevent a process permanently blocking the process.
`public void setSoTimeout(int timeout) throws SocketException`	This sets the value of the SO_TIMEOUT parameter.

There are two other methods, the protected `implAccept()` method and the `setSocketFactory()` methods. The `implAccept()` method is used by classes that extend the `ServerSocket` class to return their own implementation of the `Socket` class from the `accept()` method. The `setSocketFactory()` method overrides the default server socket factory to return custom server sockets from the constructors.

The java.net.Socket Class

Much like the `ServerSocket` class, the `Socket` class is used to communicate over the network. The difference is that `Socket` simply opens a socket connection to send or receive data, unlike a server that listens for a connection on a socket. While there are a lot of methods in this class, it is beyond the scope of this book to explain every one of them in detail, so we will concentrate on those methods that will be most likely used in the context of this book.

Constructors

We will consider the following constructors in relation to `Socket` class:

`public Socket() throws SocketException`	This creates an unconnected socket.
`public Socket(InetAddress host, int port) throws UnknownHostException, IOException` `public Socket(String host, int port) throws IOException`	These two methods do essentially the same thing; the second is a wrapper for the first, making it simpler to create a socket. The remote host name is specified in the `host` argument, while the port on which to connect is specified in the `port` argument.
`public Socket(InetAddress host, int port, InetAddress localAddress, int localPort) throws IOException`	This method, in addition to connecting the host and port specified in the first two arguments, binds the socket to the specified local address and local port. What normally happens when the local port and address are not specified is that the default local address and any free port are assigned to these values. A client does not often know ahead of time what ports are available, however, if it does need to make use of a specific port you should use this constructor.

Methods

The methods of the `Socket` class are as follows:

`public void close() throws IOException`	This method closes the socket connection, freeing any resources associated with it.
`public InetAddress getInetAddress()`	This returns the `InetAddress` to which this socket is connected.
`public InetAddress getLocalAddress()`	This returns the local address to which this socket is bound. In other words, if this socket was allocated on a machine with IP address `192.168.0.1`, this is what the return value would contain.

Table continued on following page

`public int getLocalPort()`	This returns the local port to which the socket is bound.
`public java.io.OutputStream getOutputStream() throws IOException`	The `getOutputStream()` method returns an output stream to which data can be written. We can use this to construct a more specific IO handler such as a `Reader` or a `Writer`.
`public java.io.InputStream getInputStream() throws IOException`	The `getInputStream()` method returns an input stream on which data can be read. We will be using both of these last two methods quite a bit in our examples to come.
`public int getPort()`	This returns the port on the remote server to which this socket is connected.

Writing a Socket Server

In the beginning of the chapter, we saw how to create a socket server. All it did was bind to a port, and wait for a request. Let's now build on this example to create a server that will return its own local time.

We'll take our original implementation and enhance it a bit. The design we use will help to extend our example further as we get into the chapter.

```java
import java.io.BufferedReader;
import java.io.InputStreamReader;
import java.io.IOException;
import java.io.PrintWriter;
import java.net.ServerSocket;
import java.net.Socket;
import java.text.SimpleDateFormat;
import java.util.Date;

public class SimpleServer {
  public static int DEFAULT_PORT = 22334;
  private Socket request = null;

  public SimpleServer(Socket request) {
    this.request = request;
  }

  public static void main(String[] args) throws Exception {
    ServerSocket server = new ServerSocket(DEFAULT_PORT);
    System.out.println("Server starting");

    while (true) {

      // wait for a client request
      System.out.println("Waiting...\n");
      Socket socket = server.accept();

      System.out.println("Request from client received. Processing request.");
```

```
        // handle the request
        SimpleServer handler = new SimpleServer(socket);
        handler.handleRequest();
    }
}

public void handleRequest() throws IOException {
    Date date = new Date(System.currentTimeMillis());

    SimpleDateFormat formattedDate =
        new SimpleDateFormat("EEE MMM d hh:mm:ss z yyyy");

    PrintWriter pwos = new PrintWriter(request.getOutputStream());

    pwos.println(formattedDate.format(date));
    pwos.flush();
    pwos.close();
    request.close();
    }
}
```

We added a constructor to our class that takes an argument of type `java.net.Socket`; the constructor then stores this socket, which represents a client request.

We also created an instance method for this class, `handleRequest()`. It uses the socket passed in the constructor and handles the request. First, we format the date and time that we will send to the client:

```
public void handleRequest() throws IOException {
    Date date = new Date(System.currentTimeMillis());

    SimpleDateFormat formattedDate =
        new SimpleDateFormat("EEE MMM d HH:mm:ss z yyyy");
```

Now we need to send this data to the client. We do this by getting the socket's input stream. We use a `java.io.PrintWriter` to write out the character data to the socket and then clean up our socket:

```
    PrintWriter pwos = new PrintWriter(request.getOutputStream());

    pwos.println(formattedDate.format(date));
    pwos.flush();
    pwos.close();
    request.close();
    }
```

To run this example, compile this code as follows:

```
javac SimpleServer.java
```

and run it like this:

```
java SimpleServer
```

The program will run, and not much else for now. It won't do anything until it receives a request for a connection. Now, let's look at the client side.

Writing the Client

All the client needs to do is open a connection to the server and read the output. The code is as follows:

```java
import java.io.BufferedReader;
import java.io.InputStreamReader;
import java.io.OutputStream;
import java.io.PrintWriter;
import java.net.Socket;

public class SimpleClient {
  public static void main(String[] args) throws Exception {
    Socket sock = new Socket(args[0], Integer.parseInt(args[1]));

    BufferedReader bris =
      new BufferedReader(new InputStreamReader(sock.getInputStream()));

    String line = null;
    line = bris.readLine();

    System.out.println(line);

    bris.close();
    sock.close();
  }
}
```

The main() method takes two command-line arguments, the IP address of the server, and the port number to connect on. We instantiate a Socket instance with these values:

```java
Socket sock = new Socket(args[0], Integer.parseInt(args[1]));
```

Next, we construct a java.io.BufferedReader to read the result. It is always a good idea to use a BufferedReader when reading character data from any I/O stream, as it is more efficient. After we open the stream, we read the result and print it to the screen.

```java
BufferedReader bris = new BufferedReader(new
InputStreamReader(sock.getInputStream()));

String line = null;
line = bris.readLine();

System.out.println(buffer.toString());
```

We compile our class as follows:

```
javac SimpleClient.java
```

Make sure that you have the server running and open another prompt. Execute the following statement:

```
java SimpleClient 127.0.0.1 22334
```

After less than a second, you should see output similar to the following:

```
Wed Feb 29 21:53:22 GMT 2001
```

A More Robust Server

In the example above, we created a simple server that is able to handle one request at a time. This is hardly acceptable for many applications. We could increase the backlog value so that any number of requests can be queued, but we are still left with the problem of handling requests one at a time. Fortunately, like socket programming, Java makes solving these problems quite simple.

In order to make our server more scalable, we will use the Java threading APIs. First, we will start by implementing the Runnable interface. There is only one method in the Runnable interface, public void run(), that we need to implement. Luckily for us, the design we chose earlier saves us quite a bit of work.

```java
import java.io.BufferedReader;
import java.io.InputStreamReader;
import java.io.IOException;
import java.io.PrintWriter;
import java.net.ServerSocket;
import java.net.Socket;
import java.text.SimpleDateFormat;
import java.util.Date;

public class RobustServer implements Runnable {
  public static int DEFAULT_PORT    = 22334;
  private Socket request            = null;

  public RobustServer(Socket request) {
    this.request = request;
  }

  // the method of the Runnable interface we need to implement
  public void run() {
    try {
      handleRequest();
    } catch(IOException ioe) {
      System.out.println("Error occurred while trying to service request." +
      " Server will now stop");
      System.exit(0);
    }
  }
}
```

We also need to make some slight changes to our main() method:

```java
public static void main(String[] args) throws Exception {
  ServerSocket server = new ServerSocket(DEFAULT_PORT);

  System.out.println("Server starting");
  while (true) {

    System.out.println("Waiting...\n");
    // wait for a client request
    Socket socket = server.accept();

  System.out.println("Request from client received. Processing request.");
    // handle the request
    RobustServer handler = new RobustServer(socket);
    Thread thread = new Thread(handler);
    thread.start();
  }
}
```

443

The handleRequest() method is the same as for the SimpleServer program.

We only needed to add a few lines. The first allocates a new Thread object and takes the handler object as an argument. Notice that the call to the handleRequest() method has now been moved into the run() method. The Thread class has a constructor that takes a class implementing the Runnable interface as an argument, which is what allows us to do this. Secondly, we call the start() method on the thread, which will in turn invoke the run() method of the SimpleServer class in a separate thread. What we have accomplished here is that now our listening socket runs in its own thread. When a request comes in, it hands it to another thread and continues listening rather than performing the work itself. This allows the server to handle a much larger number of requests than before. All we have left to do is compile the new code:

```
javac RobustServer.java
```

We require no changes on the client side, which is the real beauty of client-server programming. To run this example, turn off the SimpleServer and start up your RobustServer. Try the following sequence, which is exactly the same for the client:

```
java SimpleClient 127.0.0.1 22334
```

After less than a second, you should see output similar to the following:

Wed Feb 29 22:12:47 GMT 2001

Other Considerations

Though our server is now more robust, it suffers from the problem of poor scalability. What if we want our server to handle thousands of requests simultaneously? Spawning a new thread every time a new request will soon become a performance bottleneck. Thread pools offer a solution to this problem.

A thread pool creates a specified number of threads at startup and no more. As requests come in, they are placed in a work queue and the threads are notified that work is available to be done. One thread is allowed to grab the unit of work and perform it while the others sleep or perform other work. The advantage of this is that we don't need to create a new thread for every single request. Instead, we create threads that wait for requests to come in with each waiting thread contending for the work.

So far, we have seen how simple it is to write socket-based programs as well as extend them to a multithreaded model. The next section will introduce a sample XML application.

Writing an XML Socket Server

In this section we will develop a client-server XML application. Here is what our application is to do:

❏   The server is responsible for sending certain statistics to connecting clients, such as the IP address of the client, the port number on which the request is being served, and the current date and time on the server.

❏   Our client only cares about what time the server has. We will send a request and ignore everything but the date/time section.

This is a fairly simple application but it should give you a good idea of how we can send XML over sockets.

The XML Document

First we need to know what our document is going to look like. We want each of the elements described before, but we also need some error handling logic. In the case that a server is unable to fulfill the client's request, the header of the `<ServerStats>` element will contain in its `status` attribute the value `error`. The DTD is provided below:

```
<!ELEMENT ServerStats (IPaddress | Port | DateTime)>
<!ATTLIST ServerStats
  status CDATA #REQUIRED
>
<!ELEMENT IPAddress (#PCDATA)>
<!ELEMENT Port (#PCDATA)>
<!ELEMENT DateTime (Date | Time)>
<!ELEMENT Date EMPTY>
<!ATTLIST Date
  month CDATA #REQUIRED
  day CDATA #REQUIRED
  year CDATA #REQUIRED
>
<!ELEMENT Time EMPTY>
<!ATTLIST Time
  hour CDATA #REQUIRED
  minute CDATA #REQUIRED
  second CDATA #REQUIRED
>
```

We only provide the DTD to illustrate what our document should adhere to. Since this DTD is not publicly available, it does not make sense to include it in the XML document itself. Here is a sample document:

```
<?xml version="1.0"?>
<ServerStats status="success">
  <IPAddress>127.0.0.1</IPAddress>
  <Port>22334</Port>
  <DateTime>
    <Date day="28" month="Dec" year="2000" timezone="GMT" />
    <Time hour="21" minute="34" second="12" />
  </DateTime>
</ServerStats>
```

If we do receive an error, the document will look something like this:

```
<?xml version="1.0"?>
<ServerStats status="fail">
</ServerStats>
```

445

The Server

Let's start with our implementation of the server. It is not going to be much different from the server we created earlier; except for the addition of the methods required to send the client the requested information.

```java
import java.io.BufferedReader;
import java.io.InputStreamReader;
import java.io.IOException;
import java.io.PrintWriter;
import java.net.ServerSocket;
import java.net.Socket;
import java.text.SimpleDateFormat;
import java.util.Date;
import java.util.Calendar;
import java.util.GregorianCalendar;

public class XMLServer implements Runnable {
   private Socket request       = null;
   PrintWriter pwos;
   public XMLServer(Socket request) {
     this.request = request;
   }

   //
   // the method of the Runnable interface we need to implement
   public void run(){
     try {
       handleRequest();
     } catch(IOException e) {

       String response = "<?xml version=\"1.0\"?>" +
                         "<ServerStats status=\"fail\"></ServerStats>";

       try {
         pwos = new PrintWriter(request.getOutputStream());
         pwos.println(response);

       } catch(IOException ex) {
         // nothing we can do at this point. We assume the client has
         // disconnected
       } finally {
         if(pwos!=null) pwos.close();
       }
     } finally {
       // make sure the socket actually closes
       try {
         request.close();
       } catch(Exception e) {}
     }
   }

   public static void main(String[] args) throws Exception {
     // we use an argument to the class for the port number
     ServerSocket server = new ServerSocket(Integer.parseInt(args[0]));
```

```
      System.out.println("Server starting");
      while (true) {
        System.out.println("Waiting...\n");
        // wait for a client request
        Socket socket = server.accept();

        System.out.println("Request from client received. Processing request.");
        // handle the request
        XMLServer handler = new XMLServer(socket);
        Thread thread = new Thread(handler);
        thread.start();
      }
    }

  public void handleRequest() throws IOException {
    StringBuffer response = new StringBuffer(1024);

    // start of the response. We assume it is successful
    response.append("<?xml version=\"1.0\"?><ServerStats status=\"success\">");
    response.append("<IPAddress>"
                + request.getLocalAddress().getHostAddress()
                + "</IPAddress>");

    response.append("<Port>" + request.getPort() + "</Port>");


    // get the current date and time
    GregorianCalendar cal = new GregorianCalendar();
    response.append("<DateTime>");
    response.append("<Date day=\"" + cal.get(Calendar.DAY_OF_MONTH)
                + "\" month=\"" + getMonth(cal)
                + "\" year=\""   + cal.get(Calendar.YEAR)
                + "\" />");

    // get the time
    response.append("<Time hour=\"" + cal.get(Calendar.HOUR_OF_DAY)
                + "\" minute=\"" + cal.get(Calendar.MINUTE)
                + "\" second=\"" + cal.get(Calendar.SECOND)
                + "\" />");
    response.append("</DateTime></ServerStats>");

    // now send it over to the client
    PrintWriter pwos = new PrintWriter(request.getOutputStream());
    pwos.println(response.toString());
    pwos.close();
  }

  // Return the month as a String
  private String getMonth(Calendar cal) {
    String month = null;

    switch(cal.get(Calendar.MONTH)) {
      case Calendar.JANUARY: month = "Jan";  break;
      case Calendar.FEBRUARY: month = "Feb"; break;
      case Calendar.MARCH: month = "Mar"; break;
      case Calendar.APRIL: month = "Apr"; break;
      case Calendar.MAY: month = "May"; break;
      case Calendar.JUNE: month = "Jun"; break;
      case Calendar.JULY: month = "Jul"; break;
      case Calendar.AUGUST: month = "Aug"; break;
      case Calendar.SEPTEMBER: month = "Sep"; break;
```

```
        case Calendar.OCTOBER: month = "Oct"; break;
        case Calendar.NOVEMBER: month = "Nov"; break;
        case Calendar.DECEMBER: month = "Dec"; break;
      }
      return month;
    }
}
```

If we compile our server and run it using the following command line:

```
java XMLServer 22334
```

we can run our original client implementation and receive the following output:

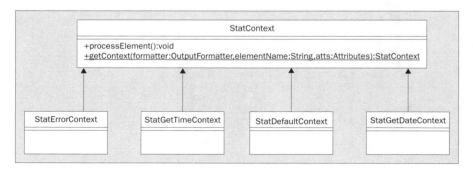

But this isn't quite what we want. We only want our client to parse out the date and time received from the server, and then present this to the user. For that we will need to further develop the client side. We can start with the simple client we developed earlier acting as a skeleton, but we obviously need more complex code to flesh out these bones. Here is what our client needs to do:

❑   The first element will always be `<ServerStats>`. If the status attribute is not equal to `success`, stop parsing and report that an error occurred.

❑   If the element is `<IPAddress>` or `<Port>`, ignore it.

❑   If the element is `<Date>`, then process the `date` and `time` child attributes to retrieve the information.

The Design

We listed the three simple things we need to do with our client, so why not separate these concerns from the main parsing code? We will do so with four "contexts". One context will be for a failed status attribute, one for a successful one, one to ignore uninteresting elements, and another to handle processing the date elements. These contexts will be organized as shown below:

The StatContext class is the abstract base class with a static method that is used to allocate the correct context given the input values. Each extending context should be obvious in its function: the StatDefaultContext will be used for those elements that don't need anything done.

Before we dive into implementation, we have an OutputFormatter class that is passed to the getContext() method that we need to discuss. This class contains the logic used to display the date to our users. Here is its implementation:

```
public class OutputFormatter {
   private String hour = null;
   private String minute = null;
   private String second = null;
   private String day = null;
   private String month = null;
   private String year = null;

   public OutputFormatter() {
   }

   public void setTime(String hour, String minute, String second) {
      this.hour = hour;
      this.minute = minute;
      this.second = second;
   }

   public void setDate(String day, String month, String year) {
      this.day = day;
      this.month = month;
      this.year = year;
   }

   public String toString() {
      StringBuffer buf = new StringBuffer(255);

      buf.append("Today's date: " + day + "-" + month + "-" + year);
      buf.append("\nTime: " + hour + ":" + minute + ":" + second);
      return buf.toString();
   }
}
```

This is a fairly simple object, but it will go a long way in our design if we ever need to extend the object. We will discuss this later. Now, let's look at implementing the contexts we discussed. First, we will start with the base class:

```
import org.xml.sax.Attributes;

public abstract class StatContext {
   public static final String SERVER_STAT = "ServerStats";
   public static final String IP_ADDRESS = "IPAddress";
   public static final String PORT = "Port";
   public static final String DATE = "DateTime";
   public static final String DATE_CHILD = "Date";
   public static final String TIME_CHILD = "Time";
   public static final String STATUS_SUCCESS = "success";
   public static final String STATUS_FAIL = "fail";

   public abstract void processElement();
```

```
    protected StatContext() {
    }

    protected StatContext(OutputFormatter formatter,
                          String elementName,
                          Attributes atts) {
    }

    // Return the appropriate context for the given element
    public static StatContext getContext(OutputFormatter formatter,
                                         String elementName,
                                         Attributes atts) {
      StatContext ctx = null;

      // check the ServerStats element
      if (elementName.equals("ServerStats")) {
        if (atts.getValue("status").equals(STATUS_SUCCESS)) {
          ctx = new StatDefaultContext(formatter, elementName, atts);
        } else {
          ctx = new StatErrorContext(formatter, elementName, atts);
        }

      } else if (elementName.equals(IP_ADDRESS) ||
                 elementName.equals(PORT) ||
                 elementName.equals(DATE)) {
        ctx = new StatDefaultContext(formatter, elementName, atts);

      } else if(elementName.equals(DATE_CHILD)) {
        ctx = new StatGetDateContext(formatter, elementName, atts);

      } else if(elementName.equals(TIME_CHILD)) {
        ctx = new StatGetTimeContext(formatter, elementName, atts);
      }

      return ctx;
    }
}
```

Most of the logic is in the `getContext()` static method. Depending on what element is currently being processed, the correct context will be allocated. Let's look at these contexts.

The StatDefaultContext Class

This is the "do nothing" context we will use when nothing needs to be done. We list it below:

```
import org.xml.sax.Attributes;

public class StatDefaultContext extends StatContext {
  public StatDefaultContext(
    OutputFormatter formatter,
    String elementName,
    Attributes atts) {
  }

  public void processElement() {
  }
}
```

The StatErrorContext Class

We will use this context when the status of the `ServerStats` element is not `success`. We want to stop all parsing, so we will throw a `RuntimeException`:

```java
import org.xml.sax.Attributes;

public class StatErrorContext extends StatContext
{
   public StatErrorContext(OutputFormatter formatter,
                           String elementName,
                           Attributes atts) {

   }

   public void processElement() {
      throw new RuntimeException("An error occurred");
   }
}
```

The StatGetTimeContext Class

Here is where we start doing some of the real work. Below is the code, which is fairly straightforward. The `processElement()` method gets the attributes of the `<Time>` element and sets the values of the `OutputFormatter` object:

```java
import org.xml.sax.Attributes;

public class StatGetTimeContext extends StatContext {
   Attributes atts = null;
   OutputFormatter formatter = null;

   public StatGetTimeContext(OutputFormatter formatter,
                             String elementName,
                             Attributes atts) {
      this.atts = atts;
      this.formatter = formatter;
   }

   public void processElement(){

      formatter.setTime(
        atts.getValue("hour"),
        atts.getValue("minute"),
        atts.getValue("second"));
   }
}
```

The StatGetDateContext Class

Much like the `StatGetTimeContext` class, this one sets values for the `OutputFormatter` class. The code is very much the same, except date values are being set.

```java
import org.xml.sax.Attributes;

public class StatGetDateContext extends StatContext {
  Attributes atts = null;
  OutputFormatter formatter = null;

  protected StatGetDateContext() {
  }

  public StatGetDateContext(OutputFormatter formatter,
      String elementName, Attributes atts) {
    this.atts = atts;
    this.formatter = formatter;
  }

  public void processElement(){
    formatter.setDate(
      atts.getValue("day"),
      atts.getValue("month"),
      atts.getValue("year"));
  }
}
```

Putting It Together

Now that we have seen the basis for our design, let's put it all together. We need to create a handler for the XML parser. We will extend the `org.xml.sax.helpers.DefaultHandler` class to simplify our code:

```java
import org.xml.sax.Attributes;
import org.xml.sax.helpers.DefaultHandler;
import org.xml.sax.SAXException;

public class ServerStatHandler extends DefaultHandler {
  private OutputFormatter formatter = null;

  public ServerStatHandler() {
    formatter = new OutputFormatter();
  }

  public void startElement(String namespaceURI,
                           String localName,
                           String qName,
                           Attributes atts)
    throws SAXException {

    StatContext ctx = StatContext.getContext(formatter, localName, atts);
    ctx.processElement();
  }

  public void endDocument() {
    System.out.println(formatter);
  }
}
```

Our handler is rather simple: the only interesting part is the startElement() method, which hands the work to the StatContext class and then the processElement() method.

Now we have to implement our client. We need to instantiate a parser, set the handler, and run the parser – that's all we have to do:

```
import org.apache.xerces.parsers.SAXParser;
import org.xml.sax.InputSource;
import org.xml.sax.SAXException;
import org.xml.sax.XMLReader;
import java.io.InputStreamReader;
import java.io.IOException;
import java.net.Socket;

public class XMLClient {
  public static void main(String[] args) throws Exception {
    // get a parser
    XMLReader reader = new SAXParser();
    reader.setContentHandler(new ServerStatHandler());

    // open the socket connection
    Socket sock = new Socket(args[0], Integer.parseInt(args[1]));

    // get the InputStream and begin reading
    InputStreamReader isReader = new InputStreamReader(sock.getInputStream());
    InputSource is = new InputSource(isReader);
    reader.parse(is);
    isReader.close();
  }
}
```

Compile the code, make sure the server is still running, and type the following at the command prompt:

```
java XMLClient 127.0.0.1 22334
```

Adjust the IP address and port according to the settings of the server. Here is the sample output:

What we have done here is to move all of our logic out of the parser and into classes that we can extend. We have created an extremely generic client that we can manipulate by changing the StatContext class. This is by no means perfect, however – something to consider, for instance, is deciding at run time which implementation of the StatContext class to run.

Summary

This chapter has focused on socket I/O in Java. We saw how to make a simple client-server program in just a few lines of code. Taking it a step further, we saw how to make our servers more robust, enabling them to handle many more requests that the first version.

In order to tie in how socket I/O can work with XML, we developed a small program that provides some server-side information to a requesting client. Using SAX, the client filtered out details that were not important and instead focused on what the client cared about. Using SAX over socket I/O is a natural choice because it allows the client to read only the data it needs rather than loading the entire document as in the DOM model to only get a few lines of meaningful information.

In the next two chapters, we will move on from sockets to the HTTP protocol. We will look at server-sider and client-side applications that use XML as the top-level transmission format.

The Xerces Blue
Butterfly, which became
extinct earlier this century,
and after which the Xerces XML
parser is named ...

12

Server-Side HTTP

In this chapter we will lay the foundations for building distributed XML applications that use the HTTP protocol as the underlying transport mechanism. We will be particularly looking at servlets as the point of interaction between these applications and the network. Servlets come with extensive HTTP handling features built in, and using these features in several examples will motivate learning about – or refreshing ourselves with – the basic principles of communication over HTTP. Most importantly, we'll be trying to stop thinking about HTTP as simply the protocol used by web browsers to view web sites. As we'll see, HTTP is well suited to the task of building the infrastructure for quite complex distributed XML applications.

This chapter will focus on the server side of HTTP interactions, the types of response packages we can get from HTTP servers, and how servlets can generate these standardized objects. In the next chapter we'll look at the picture from the client's point of view, although there will naturally be one or two points of crossover.

Here's a quick look at the topics we'll cover in this chapter:

- ❑ The Hypertext Transfer Protocol (HTTP)
- ❑ An introduction to servlets and the servlet architecture
- ❑ The `GenericServlet` and `HttpServlet` classes with some examples
- ❑ How to construct a command-line web client capable of sending HTTP requests to the server
- ❑ How to use the command-line client to send XML formatted data to a servlet for processing
- ❑ Parsing XML data on the server and sending XML formatted data to the client

HTTP Basics

HTTP is one of the most commonly used protocols over the Internet. Consequently, a thorough understanding of its capabilities and limitations is necessary for any serious developer designing web-based applications. Most web programming, however, only targets one kind of HTTP client – web browsers – and therefore only makes use of a small part of HTTP's capabilities. To understand how to write the server and client components of an HTTP application, we'll need to take the lid off the protocol a little more. So, what is HTTP? A simple definition would be:

HTTP is stateless application-level protocol based around a request-response system.

What does this mean? First, HTTP is an application-level protocol. That means that it requires an underlying network connection to successfully send and receive requests. Typically, that underlying network protocol is TCP/IP, although this is not mandatory. TCP/IP was developed by the US Department of Defense (DOD) as a part of a research project designed to connect a number of different networks from various vendors together into a cohesive network. We know this system today by a different name, the Internet. The DOD needed this system to be robust and to be capable of recovering from a network failure and the loss of any of the nodes.

Network protocols are often layered on top of each other, with each layer providing additional functionality, and the TCP/IP protocol is no exception. The lowest layer is the **IP protocol**, which stands for **Internet Protocol**. The function of the IP protocol is very basic: it transmits chunks of data from system to system. The IP protocol provides a fast and effective communication layer, but it does nothing to ensure that every packet of data sent is successfully received in the proper order. By itself IP transmissions will drop data packets, deliver partial packets, and even deliver packets out of sequence.

The TCP layer is stacked on top of the IP layer to clean up the mess left in the wake of the IP protocol's transmissions. The **TCP Protocol**, which stands for **Transmission Control Protocol**, creates a virtual connection between the two systems involved in the data transmission and ensures that all packets sent from one machine arrive at the other machine intact and in the proper order. If an error occurs during the exchange, then TCP will detect the error and require that particular data packet to be resubmitted. The combination of these two protocols is a reliable and efficient communication protocol that is vendor-neutral and provides a stable communication layer for other protocols like HTTP to operate on top of.

One of the things that makes HTTP a common choice for developing client-server applications is the widespread use of **HTTP Proxies**. Proxies provide a means for HTTP clients behind a firewall to access HTTP servers outside the firewall. This means that we can deploy applications onto a server anywhere on the internet, and it can be accessed not only by other machines on the open internet, but also inside corporate intranets, University networks, and so on.

HTTP is also a stateless protocol. A protocol's 'statefulness' refers to its ability to remember information from one transmission to another. A **stateful protocol** is one that creates a context composed of the client's previous requests. A **stateless protocol** has no context; each request is an independent connection to the server.

HTTP is a stateless protocol because no memory of the client-server interaction is maintained from one request to another. The file transfer protocol (FTP), to give a counter-example, is stateful – it is built around using a sequence of commands, such as 'change directory', 'tell me what files are in this directory', or 'download the file called `foo.txt` from the current directory'. In order for these commands to make sense, the server has to create a context for each user who is logged in, and remember things like who they are, what privileges they have, and which directory they are currently in. HTTP does not work this way – it is built around commands that require no context on the server at all, such as 'get me the resource called `webpages/info/foo.txt`'.

If it is true that HTTP is a stateless protocol, then how do web sites maintain a dialogue with the user – such as in an online ordering system or shopping cart? Well, that's up to the applications that use HTTP as their communications protocol. For example, web browsers and some web applications use a system of 'cookies' to establish the identity of one client, so the web application knows that the client that asked for resource A one minute ago is the same client that is asking for resource B now. Since we won't necessarily be targeting web browsers, we may want to make use of a different technique for establishing stateful connections between our client and server components. But it is important to remember right from the start that HTTP isn't going to provide the solution for us, we'll have to do some work ourselves. In practice, this means that the client has to identify itself to the server with each request.

We also said that HTTP uses a request/response system. What does this mean? It means that each interaction between a client and a server consists of the client making a request, and the server sending back a response. The server will never initiate an interaction with a client, or send more than one response in reply to a single request (it isn't possible, for example, to ask for several resources to be sent back, or to ask for a resource to be sent to you repeatedly, say once a minute, or the next time it changes). The client will always expect a single response to its requests, signifying the success or failure of the server to carry out the request. Retrieving multiple resources will require the client making multiple requests. Retrieving a resource once a minute will require the client to make a request once every minute, or retrieving the resource whenever it changes will require the client to poll the server from time to time to see if the resource has changed.

> Note that although we said before that HTTP is stateless, it is not necessarily connectionless. HTTP 1.1 (the current version of the specification) allows a client to establish a single connection to the server, over which it can make several sequential requests. HTTP doesn't use this to provide a state mechanism, however, so this does not change the way the protocol works. It simply removes the overhead required to establish a new connection to the server for each new request. In practice this makes very little difference to us as programmers, and simply improves the speed of the protocol.

So now we have a preliminary understanding of what exactly HTTP is. With that understanding, we can move on to a more pragmatic look at the HTTP protocol.

A Typical HTTP Scenario

What happens when I type a **URL (Universal Resource Locator)** such as http://java.sun.com/xml/ into a browser address field and hit Enter? The browser will break up the URL we entered into three components:

- **http::** This sequence identifies the protocol the browser should use to send the request. If it said https:, the browser would use the secure HTTP protocol to connect to the server. In this case, it will use the normal HTTP protocol.

- **//java.sun.com**: Ignoring the "//", which basically just means 'starting from the top of the Internet and working down', this part is of course the address of a server. Any valid address specification will work here – be it a 192.164.84.23-style 'dotted-quad' IP address, or the name of a machine on your local network, or the word localhost, which will resolve to the local machine. We can specify a port number on the host by adding a : (colon) character followed by the port on which the server is running. Since we haven't specified a port here, the browser will assume the default port for an HTTP server, which is 80. (The default for a secure HTTP server, which the browser would use if we had specified https: as the protocol, is 443.)

- **/xml/**: This is the resource identifier, which uniquely identifies the resource that we want to retrieve from the server.

The browser will now create a socket connection to port 80 on the server java.sun.com, and, over this connection, send a request that starts:

```
GET /xml/ HTTP/1.1
```

This, again, has three components:

- **GET**: This is the request method. The client is asking the server to 'get' a resource. There are several other request methods, but GET is the most basic, and the method used by web browsers and other HTTP clients to retrieve content from servers.

- **/xml/**: This is the resource identifier, which was extracted from the URL earlier.

- **HTTP/1.1**: This specifies which version of the HTTP protocol the client is using, in this case version 1.1.

The server will parse this request. Its first task is to look at the resource identifier, and map it somehow to one of the resources which it has available to it. A common way to map the resource is to use a hierarchy of directories, which the web server is told to look in to find resources, although this is by no means the only mapping that is possible. So, the server is looking for a resource called /xml/, which it may well have been told to associate with a particular HTML file. It will look to see if the GET method is an appropriate action to take with this resource (not all resources can be 'got'), and if so, it will build an HTTP response to send back to the browser containing the data from the document, and send it back along the same socket connection that the client used to make the request.

HTTP Request Methods

HTTP defines several methods by which a client may send a request to the server. Each method has a different purpose and provides different functionality. HTTP/1.0 defines three types of request methods: GET, HEAD, and POST. Five additional methods are defined by HTTP/1.1: CONNECT, DELETE, OPTIONS, PUT, and TRACE. We will address several of these request methods over the course of this chapter and the next one, but the two most commonly used methods are GET and POST.

The GET Request Method

The GET request method is the simplest and most commonly used of all the request methods. A GET request method can be used to retrieve either static or dynamic content from a web server. The most common result is for the server to respond to a GET request by sending a static HTML document or image. It is possible, however, to append query parameters to the request URL that the server can then parse and process to build dynamic content to be sent back to the client. You've probably seen a GET request URL such as the following:

http://www.google.com/search?q=Java+XML&start=10

All data immediately after the ? character is known as the query string and, in this case, it is made up of pairs of parameter names and their value separated by the & character. In the string above we have two parameters; q, and start, with respective values Java+XML and 10, heading to the server to be processed. We'll explore this in much greater detail in the next chapter when we discuss the client-side of HTTP.

The POST Request Method

A POST is primarily intended as a means to transmit large amounts of data to the server for processing. Because the POST request method allows the encapsulation of a variety of **MIME (Multi-Purpose Internet Mail Extensions)** data types (text/plain, text/html, image/jpeg to name a few) into the request body, then you as the developer have a great deal of flexibility in what type of data you transmit to the server. You can use POST requests to send text, HTML, binary files, images, serialized Java objects, and a whole range of other data types.

GET vs. POST

Of the eight request methods defined in HTTP/1.1, the GET and POST request methods are easily the most commonly used methods for submitting data to the server. As such, they warrant a closer comparison of their roles.

To submit data with a GET request, we have to use the query string, as we saw above. This places certain restrictions on the sort of uses we can put a GET request to as a means of communicating between a client and a server. For one thing, there's a limit to the amount of data that can be placed into a query string. We're limited to ASCII-format character data, and certain characters have to be encoded because they have special meaning in a URL. It doesn't make sense to encode a large amount of data in this way for sending to the server.

Another restriction on using GET requests for sending data to the server is in their original purpose: to *get* a specific resource. When we talked before about sending a request to java.sun.com to GET /xml/, we can reasonably expect, whenever we send that request, to get Sun's Java and XML homepage. It may not be the same every time we ask for it (it should contain the latest news from Sun about their Java XML projects), but it represents the same resource.

A GET request is a way of asking the server to return you the latest version of a certain resource. Even when we ask for a resource with a query string attached – say, http://www.google.com/search?q=Java+XML, we are asking for the same resource whenever we send it. In this case, we're asking for Google's latest search results for the query 'Java XML'. So, although we are sending data to the server, it is really only data that allows the requested resource to be narrowed down more specifically.

Another property of GET requests is that all of the data that makes up the request is in the URL. If I send you an e-mail containing the URL I gave above, you can use it to request the results of the search on Google yourself.

POST requests, on the other hand, are intended for us to send data to the server – to *post* data to a specific processing resource on the server. Once we've posted the data, the server may set off various actions involving that data, such as storing it, or sending it in an e-mail, or using it to authenticate a credit-card transaction. The response to us having sent the post request will usually be an indication of whether or not processing was successful, rather than a resource that has been specifically located by the request we made. We can send any kind of data at all, including international text, or binary information, and there's no arbitrary limit to the amount of data we can send.

You can look at it as similar to the difference between ordering a catalog, and placing an order from a catalog. To order a catalog from a supplier, we simply send them a short letter saying what kind of catalog we are interested in – much like a GET request. If we send the same letter twice, or three times, we simply end up with several copies of the same catalog. We can give a copy of the letter to a friend, and if they post it, they'll get a copy of the catalog.

Placing an order with the catalog company, on the other hand, is more like a POST request. We'll have to send them our credit card details, and information about what items we want to buy. Unlike with the GET request, however, if we accidentally sent this letter twice, we'd end up placing two orders, which might not be our intention. We could give the letter to our friend to send, but if they sent it, we'd still receive the goods, and get charged for them.

So GET and POST are different animals, and we need to be wary about thinking of the difference between them as simply 'GET for small amounts of data, POST for large amounts of data'.

HTTP Responses

We've talked about requests quite a lot, but we've not looked at the response at all. So, to go back to the example we examined before, how does java.sun.com respond to the request,

```
GET /xml/ HTTP/1.1
```

Well, the first part of its response is the HTTP Status line, which should hopefully look something like:

```
HTTP/1.1 200 OK
```

This will be followed by a set of headers, and the actual response body, both of which we will turn to shortly. The purpose of the status line is to inform the client as to the degree of success that the server had in fulfilling the request the client made. The HTTP status line is, itself, composed of three essential parts: the **HTTP version**, a **status code** and an associated **status message** (in that order). All three of these components are found together, on the very first line of the response the server sends back to the client. Let's look at each of these separately.

HTTP Version

The HTTP version will be normally one of two values: HTTP/1.0 or HTTP/1.1. HTTP/1.1 provides several enhancements over HTTP/1.0, including more request methods, persistent connections, and unlimited query string lengths, to name a few. While the HTTP/1.1 protocol does provide more functionality, there are times when you may wish to restrict your application to using only HTTP/1.0, to ensure maximum compatibility with any client or server. HTTP/1.0 is the lowest common denominator, and allows you to interact with a wider range of services.

HTTP Status Code

The heart the HTTP status line is a three-digit integer known as the status code. The HTTP status code is an integer constant that corresponds to the specific condition of the client's request. The HTTP specification maps each code to a condition. HTTP/1.0 defines 17 possible statuses, while HTTP/1.1 more than doubles that with 39 possible statuses. Here is a list of a few that both versions have in common:

Code	Description
200	The client has issued a successful request and the requested content has been returned.
204	The client should continue to use the previous document, as no updated content exists. This is typically sent when the client has requested updated content by clicking their browser's Refresh button.
301	The document requested has been permanently moved. The new location is specified in the location response header and the client should request that URL to get the content. Browsers will do this automatically.
302	The document requested has been temporarily moved. The new location is specified in the location response header. The client should use this new URL to get the content, but if it needs the resource again should continue to use the original URL.
401	The client has failed to provide the necessary credentials to access a password-protected page.
404	Everyone has seen this status code at one time or another. This status code informs the client that the requested resource does not exist.
500	This status code indicates that the process responsible for providing the resource has crashed and the server doesn't know what to do about it. It may also indicate that part of the web server is malfunctioning.
503	The resource is currently too busy to respond. This could be the result of maintenance, overloaded database connections, or any other inadequate system resource. Web programs can send this code to indicate they are not ready.

These are just a few of the most common HTTP status codes. HTTP 1.0 and 1.1 specifications can be viewed at http://www.cis.ohio-state.edu/htbin/rfc/rfc1945.html and rfc2068.html.

One thing you should notice about the status codes is that they are organized according to the type of information they are returning. HTTP/1.0 defines four status categories, while HTTP/1.1 adds one additional category. These categories are:

Code	Description
100-199	HTTP/1.1 only. These codes are used to transmit any information between the client and server that the end user is not intended to respond to, or even be aware of.
200-299	A successful request!
300-399	The requested resource(s) have moved. A new address is usually provided with these codes.
400-499	Indicates that the client has caused an error.
500-599	Indicates that the server has caused an error.

HTTP Status Message

HTTP also defines a string constant associated with each status code. This constant is a brief (one or two words) text description of the status code. This is simply a helpful hint for human programmers who need to quickly know what a particular status code represents. Clients only pay attention to the three-digit integer, as there is nothing that constrains the server to only return the specific string constant associated with that status code. A server could opt to send back a nonsensical text message, or even no text message at all. For a listing of all the status messages, consult the HTTP RFC resources listed above.

HTTP Response Headers

The status code tells the client whether its request made sense, and whether the server has been able to do anything about it, but it doesn't tell the client a great deal more. Additional meta data about the response is provided in the form of response headers. It is through the response headers that the server communicates such critical information to the client as:

- ❑ What format the content is in
- ❑ How long the client can cache the requested page
- ❑ Where a requested document has been relocated to
- ❑ That the server wants the client to store a cookie

We will now see what possibilities there are. The following is a list, in alphabetical order, of HTTP response headers that we will be using in this chapter and the next one:

Header	Description
Allow	Specifies the request methods (GET, POST, PUT, etc.) supported by the server. This header should be included if the server has to send a 405 (Method Not Allowed) status code. This error message is sent from the server when the client requests a resource from the server, using a request method not supported by that resource.
Cache-Control	HTTP/1.1 only. Informs the client under what circumstances the response body may be cached (caching is performed by clients, as well as intermediate proxy servers, to improve performance and avoid repeatedly requesting the same resource.)
Content-Length	Indicates the total number of bytes the response contains. Omitting this header will prevent an HTTP/1.1-compliant client from maintaining a persistent connection.
Content-Type	Indicates the MIME type of the response body. For a web page, this is usually text/html. We'll look at these in detail in a moment.
Date	The current date and time on the server.
Expires	Indicates the time at which the content expires. This is a further tool for controlling caching, allowing a client to know how long a cached copy of the resource is valid for.
Last-Modified	This header indicates the time the requested resource was last modified. This allows the client to request a document on the condition that it has been changed after a specified time. We'll explore this in greater detail in the next chapter.
Location	Notifies the client of a new address for the requested resource.
Retry-After	Informs the client how soon they can repeat a request. This is typically used in conjunction with a 503 (Service Unavailable) response.
Server	Identifies the name of the host server. The client should use this name in constructing subsequent requests for resources, regardless of the name it originally used to access this resource.

Again, this list only constitutes a handful of the response headers defined by HTTP; but it is a list that you may want to refer to as you go through this chapter.

The HTTP Response Body

The response body is the content or document that the client requested. Depending upon what Content-Type is specified in the response headers, the client will determine how to handle the response body content. In the case of a web browser, if a value of text/html is specified, then the browser will render the HTML content, as you would expect.

Internet Explorer 5.5 displays content specified as text/xml as an XML tree structure, or applies an XSL stylesheet (if one is specified) and display the content as defined by the stylesheet. Netscape 6 will allow you to associate a **CSS (Cascading Style Sheet)** with an XML document directly, but any previous version of Netscape will not recognize an XML document as anything special. You can also tell most browsers that an external application should be invoked to display content of a certain MIME type. The following table shows a list of some of the more common MIME types:

Common MIME Types	Meaning
application/msword	Microsoft Word document
application/pdf	Acrobat PDF document
application/vnd.lotus-notes	Lotus Notes document
application/vnd.ms-excel	Excel spreadsheet
application/zip	Zip archive
audio/basic	Sound file (.au or .snd format)
audio/midi	MIDI sound file
text/css	Cascading Style Sheet
text/html	HTML document
text/xml	XML document
image/jpeg	JPEG image
image/gif	GIF image
video/mpeg	MPEG video file
video/quicktime	QuickTime video file

So long as the server has properly specified what type of content is being sent, then the response body itself will be handled appropriately (provided the client can handle this content type). In our examples we will initially be sending response bodies conforming to the text/html content type, but later in this chapter we will be transmitting text/xml content.

So an HTTP response consists of three things: a status line, one or more response headers, and the response body itself. We will be dealing with each of these components of the response when we get into the example code later in this chapter, but first we need to get a clearer view of the big picture by looking at a typical HTTP scenario.

HTTP Programming

HTTP provides a lot of definitions, but it's up to developers of servers and clients to implement them. It seems like overkill to develop a complete HTTP server from scratch every time we want to build a web application, so it is convenient that web server programmers have often provided hooks that allow us to write programs that act as 'resources' for their servers to serve. In the early days of the web, the standard for processing data retrieved over HTTP was the **Common Gateway Interface (CGI)**. CGI opened the door to the Internet's first web-based applications. Online reservations could be made, database-driven information could be delivered, and goods could be purchased with a click of a button Although CGI was a powerful technology, it was not a friendly one.

CGI has lost the prominent status it once possessed. Now only large corporations, with tons of legacy code that would be too costly to convert, still use CGI for serious applications. Different technologies have emerged, and on the Java platform, the modern equivalent of CGI is provided by two elements of the Java 2 Platform, Enterprise Edition: Java Servlets and JavaServer Pages (JSP).

Java Servlets and JSP are superior technologies to CGI in many ways. They are more efficient than CGI, because a lightweight Java thread is created from within the same JVM process to handle each HTTP request, as opposed to the standard implementation of CGI, which creates a completely new process on the server to handle each request. Servlets and JSPs are much easier to work with than CGI, because they have a much richer infrastructure and more powerful APIs for working with the HTTP protocol. Much of the low-level processing is handled behind the scenes, and a convenient API is provided that allows the Java developer to easily handle HTTP Headers, as well as browser-related data such as HTML forms, cookies, and session data. Also, there are the advantages that come naturally with the Java language: portability, security, and a large library of functionality for handling things like databases, enterprise components, graphics, and, of course, XML.

Introduction to Servlets

A servlet allows us to carry out processing when an HTTP request is received from a client, for a specific resource that the server has been told maps to the servlet. It processes client input and responds appropriately. Servlets are small, poolable Java components that have a number of services provided to them by the server, or "container", they run in. This enables the application programmer to focus on the logic of the application rather than tedious repetitive details to do with the handling the same kind of requests from arbitrary sources.

This logic is written by the servlet programmer within a normal Java class, which extends either the `GenericServlet` or `HttpServlet` classes defined by the Servlet API. By overriding methods defined in these classes, we can write code that will be executed whenever the servlet is requested by a client.

The Role of Servlets in J2EE

One significant concept that J2EE has formalized is the **web container**. You have no doubt heard of, and perhaps have even used, a web server with a J2EE-compliant web container. Some of the more popular industry players are Tomcat, JRun, Resin, and WebSphere. A web container executes within a Java run-time environment and provides the implementation of the Servlet API and support for JavaServer Pages. Web containers work in the background and manage the initialization and invocation of servlets, garbage collection, and pooling. Web containers also provide transaction support and object pooling. For a deeper understanding of Java web containers, you might want to read Chapter 7 of *Professional Java Server Programming: J2EE Edition*, Wrox Press, ISBN 1-861004-65-6.

In order to follow along with the examples in this book, you will need a functioning web container on your system. There are several very good web containers out there that you can use to develop, test, and deploy your servlets onto. Two open source web containers that are excellent are Resin and Apache Tomcat. For this chapter, we will use Jakarta Tomcat from the Apache Foundation (http://jakarta.apache.org). If you do not already have Tomcat 3.2.1 or above installed on your system, you can find installation instructions in Appendix H of this book.

Servlets and HTTP

When compared with CGI, servlets are a dramatic improvement in HTTP-based programming. Unlike CGI, each client request does not result in the server launching another instance of the application. The one exception to this is when the needs of the application demand that only one client be able to access the servlet and its resources at any time. To restrict access to the servlet to one client at a time, the request-handling methods we implement can be declared `synchronized`, or the servlet can implement the `SingleThreadModel` interface (which guarantees that the container will not allow more than one instance of the servlet to be created).

When the server receives a client request, the server checks to see if that servlet is currently in memory. If the servlet is currently in memory, then a new thread is spawned, and the user's request is handled. If the servlet is not in memory, only then is a new instance created.

So how does our client-server paradigm change once servlets are brought into the picture? Very little. The web server maintains a list of URL patterns that map to servlets on the host server. Anytime the client requests a URL that matches one of these patterns, the web server forwards the request to the web container to be handled. The web container then either instantiates a new servlet instance, or creates a new thread for an existing servlet instance to handle the client request.

Most web servers use a default mapping of /servlet or /servlets with respect to the web application root URL to represent a request that should be handled by a specified servlet class. Of course, in an enterprise production environment you will want to write custom mappings to separate various applications and keep things organized and easier to maintain. Once the request is passed to a servlet, the servlet then queries the request object (this object contains the details of the client request, parsed out of the original client request and presented as easily manipulated Java objects) and accesses any server-side resources necessary (databases, other servlets, EJBs, static files, etc.). The servlet then prepares a response to be sent back to the client.

With a clearer idea of how servlets allow us to utilize the HTTP protocol, we can begin to explore the nuts and bolts of the servlet architecture and try out some examples.

The Servlet Architecture

The servlet framework provides an abstraction of the HTTP request-response paradigm that is more powerful and more efficient than CGI. The servlet API provides methods for parsing client requests, creating an HTTP-compliant response, and even handling a user's persistent session. We'll explore these features in greater detail as we learn more about the servlet architecture.

The servlet API is contained in two Java extension packages: javax.servlet and javax.servlet.http. As you might expect, the classes contained in javax.servlet are protocol independent, while the classes contained in javax.servlet.http are specific to the HTTP protocol.

Although the servlets we will be developing will in fact be HTTP-based servlets, we will need several of the interfaces and exceptions defined in the javax.servlet package. As a result we will import both packages into our servlet classes.

The Servlet Interface

Your servlets will, directly or indirectly, implement this interface. The most likely scenario is that you will extend either GenericServlet or HttpServlet.

> *Although more sophisticated J2EE applications will make use of all five methods declared by the interface, for our purposes, we are only concerned with the two most commonly used methods: init() and service(). For a more in depth look at servlets, you can read Chapters 7-10 in* Professional Java Server Programming: J2EE Edition, *Wrox Press, ISBN- 1861004656.*

The figure below provides us with a glimpse of the class hierarchy at the backbone of the servlet framework:

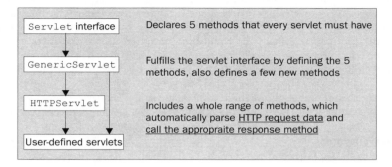

The top-level class is the `Servlet` interface that defines five core methods that are a part of every servlet. These five lifecycle methods are discussed in the next sections.

The init() Method

This method is called only once, when the servlet is first created, and is not called again for subsequent client requests. The signature of the method is:

```
public void init(ServletConfig config) throws ServletException
```

As the name implies, the `init()` method allows the servlet to perform any necessary initialization of variables, objects, and resources that the servlet will use in responding to client requests. The web container also passes a `javax.servlet.ServletConfig` object that may contain default variable values, database parameters, or any number of initialization parameters for the method to use.

The getServletConfig() Method

This method retrieves the container's configuration details:

```
public ServletConfig getServletConfig()
```

You should implement this method to allow other servlets or server-side resources access to the `ServletConfig` object created in the `init()` method.

The service() Method

The signature for this method is:

```
public void service(ServletRequest request, ServletResponse response)
throws ServletException, IOException
```

The `service()` method is the lifeblood of a servlet. It is a servlet's equivalent of the `main()` method. This is the first method called (remember, `init()` is only called once during the lifetime of a servlet) by the web container each time it receives a servlet request. From here, all application logic handled by the servlet begins and ends. As is true with the `main()` method, however, the servlet is free to instantiate objects, call local and remote methods upon those objects, reference static classes and their methods, and make whatever other Java calls are necessary.

469

When the web server receives a client request that maps to a servlet, the container retrieves a thread from the thread pool, or perhaps creates a new thread for that servlet, and calls the service() method to handle the request. When a servlet services a client request, two important objects are passed into the service() method: ServletRequest and ServletResponse. The ServletRequest object contains important information sent by the client that the server uses to fulfill the client request. Likewise the ServletResponse object is there so that the servlet can set parameters and fill the object with data before sending the object back to the container to be forwarded to the client.

Encapsulating the request-response paradigm in an object-oriented framework provides tremendous flexibility and a much more logical mechanism for understanding and fulfilling client-server communication.

The getServletInfo() Method

The signature for this method is:

```
public String getServletInfo()
```

This method should return a String object containing information about this servlet such as the author, creation date, description, or other useful information. This string can then be used by the web container to display a list of all available servlets and their descriptions, or perhaps by a logging utility.

The destroy() Method

The signature for this method is:

```
public void destroy()
```

This method performs the same kind of function as the finalize() method should in Java classes. Here you place any cleanup code that your servlet might need. You could use this method to persist the servlet's state, log useful information about the servlet, close a database connection, unregister the database driver, or even inform another application that this servlet instance is about to be garbage-collected. The container calls this method just before a servlet instance is garbage-collected. Typically this will occur when the web server is shutting down, or when the server is running out of memory. The container will make every effort to wait for active service() threads to finish executing before calling this method.

GenericServlet

Of course, the Servlet interface is of little use without classes to implement it. As you can see from the figure earlier, there is only one class, GenericServlet, in the servlet API that directly implements the Servlet interface. In a sense, the Servlet interface specifies a contract between the web container and the servlet. This way, you could even create an entirely new class of custom servlets and so long as the new class implements the Servlet interface, no changes would need to be made in the web container.

Although you could create a new class of servlets by implementing the Servlet interface, it is more likely that you will simply want to extend GenericServlet either directly, or indirectly (through HttpServlet). The real benefit that GenericServlet provides is that it is a concrete implementation of the Servlet interface. It is important to note, however, that GenericServlet is an abstract class, so it is still necessary to extend this class and override its key methods (init(), service(), etc.). If you extend a class from GenericServlet, or HttpServlet, then you won't have to worry about whether or not your have implemented everything required by the Servlet interface because the GenericServlet class has already fully implemented the interface for you.

Essentially, the GenericServlet class provides a protocol-independent implementation of the Servlet interface. Although the HttpServlet class is the only class that currently extends GenericServlet, the door is wide open to allow other subclasses that handle specific protocols to derive their core structure from the GenericServlet class in the future.

In addition to implementing the methods declared in the Servlet interface, GenericServlet defines a few additional methods of its own. Two additional methods are defined that provide logging capabilities. Those two methods are log(String msg) and log(String msg, Throwable cause). Since HttpServlet extends GenericServlet, any HttpServlet classes that you write will implicitly support these seven methods, allowing you to use them directly, or override them in your own servlets.

Before we move on to discuss the HttpServlet class, let's apply what we know of servlets in a basic example.

Setting up the Environment

We have used the following set up for all the examples in this chapter. The root directory is C:\projavaxml\chapter12. Any files not used in a particular webapp will be stored in this directory. Webapps for each example are in the webapps subdirectory. Classes for each example webapp are in the webapps\example\WEB-INF\classes directory and the web.xml file for the example is in the webapps\example\WEB-INF directory.

Each example will use a <Context> entry in Tomcat's conf\server.xml file so that a URL such as http://localhost:8080/projavaxml/chapter13/example will map to the C:\projavaxml\chapter12\webapps\example directory.

> In general we will give filenames relative to the root folder, for example
> **webapps\example\WEB-INF**, rather than the fully qualified path.

Preparing the Container

Before we can even create the source code for the servlet, we need to prepare the web container and ensure that there is a proper directory structure setup. The Java Servlet Specification 2.2 outlines the directory structure that all Java web applications should comply with. The Java Servlet Specification identifies the following directory structure for a web application with root directory example:

❑   example
      The base directory where JSPs and static HTML pages are normally kept

❑   example/WEB-INF/web.xml
      The deployment descriptor that specifies and configures the servlets

❑   example/WEB-INF/lib
      The directory where JAR files should be stored

❑   example/WEB-INF/classes
      The directory where your class files (in the proper package directory structure) should be stored

Using Tomcat, we can put this directory anywhere we like, and use a <Context> directive in Tomcat's startup script server.xml to map a specified URL to our base directory.

Minimal Servlet Example

Let's test out our understanding of servlets by creating a minimal servlet example, which extends `GenericServlet` and overrides the `service()` method. Since the `service()` method is called directly by the web container when a client request is received, our class can get by without defining any additional methods.

Write the Servlet

With the container's directory structure prepared for a Java web application, it is time to actually write the servlet code. First create a Java class called `MyServlet` in `MyServlet.java` under `webapps\messaging\WEB-INF\classes`. Here is the complete source code for `MyServlet`:

```java
import javax.servlet.*;
import java.io.PrintWriter;
import java.io.IOException;

public class MyServlet extends GenericServlet {
    public void service(ServletRequest request, ServletResponse response)
            throws ServletException, IOException {

        // Set MIME type for the response
        response.setContentType("text/html");

        // Create and obtain a reference to a print writer object
        PrintWriter out = response.getWriter();

        // Add content to the print writer's buffer
        out.println("<!DOCTYPE HTML PUBLIC \"-//W3C//DTD HTML 4.0 "
                + "Transitional//EN\">");
        out.println("<HTML>");
        out.println("<HEAD><TITLE>Simple Servlet</TITLE></HEAD>");
        out.println("<BODY>");
        out.println("<H1>Hello</H1>");
        out.println("</BODY></HTML>");

        // Close the print writer to release those resources
        out.flush();
        out.close();
    }
}
```

Compile the Source

Java servlets use `javac` to compile the source code into a class file just like other Java classes. The only thing you need to do differently is to be sure that `<TOMCAT_HOME>\lib\servlet.jar` is in your classpath. Once you've done that, and assuming that you've set up the directory structure correctly, you should be able to run this command from the `WEB-INF\classes` directory:

```
C:\projavaxml\chapter12\webapps\hello\WEB-INF\classes> javac MyServlet.java
```

Assuming that you entered the code without any errors, this command will compile the source and create a class file called `MyServlet.class`.

In order to test this servlet out, there is one more file that we must create: `web.xml`. It is used to inform the web container certain details about the servlets used in your web application. This file is also referred to as the web application **deployment descriptor**.

Writing the Deployment Descriptor

An important part of the Java Servlet 2.2 specification is the use of an XML file to define properties about each servlet deployed in the web container. This XML file web.xml is also referred to as the deployment descriptor and is used by the container to set a variety of properties for the web application, including: initialization of database resources, passing parameters to be used to initialize a servlet, and specifying a welcome page or error page for the application. Although our very minimal example will not highlight the various ways that the web.xml file can be used in testing, development, and production, it will at least get you in the habit of creating a deployment descriptor for your Java web applications.

Create the web.xml file in the webapps\hello\WEB-INF directory and copy the following code into it:

```
<?xml version="1.0" encoding="ISO-8859-1"?>
<!DOCTYPE web-app
  PUBLIC "-//Sun Microsystems, Inc.//DTD Web Application 2.2//EN"
  "http://java.sun.com/j2ee/dtds/web-app_2.2dtd">

<web-app>
  <servlet>
    <servlet-name>MinExample</servlet-name>
    <servlet-class>MyServlet</servlet-class>
  </servlet>
</web-app>
```

Add the following Context directive to the server.xml file in <TOMCAT_HOME>\conf:

```
<Context
    path="/projavaxml/chapter12/hello"
    docBase="C:/projavaxml/chapter12/webapps/hello"
    debug="1"
    reloadable="true">
</Context>
```

Testing the Servlet

Once you have the servlet successfully compiled and you've created the web.xml file, you are ready to test your servlet. To do this, first start up your web server (for Tomcat, this is the startup.bat or startup.sh script in the \bin directory). When Tomcat is ready, then open a web browser and enter the following URL in the address field:

http://localhost:8080/projavaxml/chapter12/hello/servlet/MyServlet.

Your browser should look like the following:

Now let's examine step by step what happened when your browser accessed the servlet. The first time that MyServlet is called, Tomcat creates an instance of the servlet, and initializes the servlet by first collecting information from the deployment descriptor web.xml and then calling the servlet's init() method. Let's take a closer look at web.xml.

The Deployment Descriptor in More Detail

The first line is an XML declaration specifying the version and encoding of the XML file. This is followed by the document type declaration DOCTYPE specifying the URI for the DTD that this application uses. The J2EE specification declares the web-app_2.2.dtd as the standard DTD for Java Servlets 2.2.

All declarations related to your web application are enclosed within <web-app> tags. To declare properties for a servlet, you enclose parameter/value tag pairs within <servlet></servlet> tags. In this example, the first parameter specifies the servlet's name and the second specifies the servlet's class.

> **The class should be a fully qualified package name. This example uses the default package and therefore only the class name is required.**

```
<web-app>
  <servlet>
    <servlet-name>MinExample</servlet-name>
    <servlet-class>MyServlet</servlet-class>
  </servlet>
</web-app>
```

Our deployment descriptor only specifies two parameter/value pairs for one servlet. If we had multiple servlets in our web application, they would each have their own servlet tag. At startup, the web container assigns these values internally, so any changes to this file would necessitate a restart of the web container before they take effect.

We could also have specified parameter values that would be passed into the init() method of our servlet. The servlet-name parameter functions as an alias, allowing your servlets, JSPs, and HTML pages to refer to the servlet using MinExample rather than the class name, MyServlet.

Another customization we can perform is to use mappings between servlet names and URL paths. If we add the following to our web.xml document at the same level as the servlet directives, then the servlet MyServlet alias MinExample will appear at http://localhost:8080/projavaxml/chapter12/hello/helloservlet:

```
<servlet-mapping>
   <servlet-name>MinExample</servlet-name>
   <url-pattern>/helloservlet</url-pattern>
</servlet-mapping>
```

The Servlet

Since this is the first time that MyServlet has ever been called since Tomcat was started, it will take all appropriate parameters specified in web.xml and pass them to the servlet's init() method. The two parameters we specified are only important to the web container, so Tomcat calls the servlet's init() method and passes a ServletConfig object with only container-specific parameters to initialize the servlet. Since we have not overridden this method in our class, then the init() method defined in GenericServlet is called to initialize our servlet. This is perfectly all right, because even if we had overridden it, the servlet API requires us to call super.init().

The next method called is the service() method. All requests addressed to this servlet are received by the service() method, regardless of the request method used (GET, POST, etc.). This method retrieves the client's request and formulates a response to be sent back to the client. Both the request and response are nicely encapsulated into objects:

```
public void service(ServletRequest request, ServletResponse response)
    throws ServletException, IOException {
```

The first thing we do is set the MIME type for the content that will be sent back to the client. This command will actually set the Content-Type response header that the client receives:

```
response.setContentType("text/html");
```

The next step is to obtain a reference to the PrintWriter attached to the response object so that we can write content to its buffer to be sent back to the client:

```
PrintWriter out = response.getWriter();
```

Next we fill the print writer's buffer with text. The syntax here should feel very comfortable, as it is similar to sending output to the screen. Rather than sending output to System.out.println(), you are sending output to the print writer attached to the response:

```
out.println( "<HTML><HEAD>" );
out.println( "<TITLE>Simple Servlet Example</TITLE>" );
out.println( "</HEAD><BODY>" );
out.println( "<H1>Hello</H1>" );
out.println( "</BODY></HTML>" );
```

Since we are dealing with an I/O stream (the print writer), it is important that we flush the data contained in the buffer and close the object:

```
    out.flush();
    out.close();
}
```

Finally, the response object is sent back to the client through the container, and the client parses the response string and renders the HTML that was sent through the string via the out.println() statements.

HttpServlet

The HttpServlet class extends GenericServlet and provides an HTTP-specific implementation of the Servlet interface. With the previous example, you might be wondering why we even need HttpServlet. Very simply, HttpServlet provides more functionality and allows us to more easily specify the kind of information that we can accept from and send to an HTTP client.

So long as you are developing servlets that will use HTTP as the communication protocol, you will never need to worry about the Servlet interface or the GenericServlet class, except to the extent that HttpServlet derives its form from the Servlet interface, and its substance from its parent.

HttpServlet defines nine methods, and all of them relate to handling user requests via the service() method. Those nine methods are as follows:

```
public void service(ServletRequest request, ServletResponse response)
    throws ServletException, IOException
```

This service() method overrides the service() method defined in GenericServlet. The container calls this method and passes it a ServletRequest and a ServletResponse object. Within the method implementation, these two objects are converted into HTTP-specific objects: HttpServletRequest and HttpServletResponse. The method then calls the overloaded service() method defined within HttpServlet. This method is fully implemented and should never be overridden.

```
protected void service(HttpServletRequest request, HttpServletResponse response)
    throws ServletException, IOException
```

This overloaded method is protected rather than public because it is only intended to be called by the other service() method described above. When it receives a request, it parses the HttpServletRequest object and determines what type of request (GET, POST, etc.) the client issued. Once the request method is determined, then the request is dispatched to another method specifically intended to handle that type of request. This method takes the form doXXX() with the request method named inserted in place of the XXX. This service() method is also fully implemented and should never be overridden.

```
protected void doDelete(HttpServletRequest request, HttpServletResponse response)
    throws ServletException, IOException
```

```
protected void doGet(HttpServletRequest request, HttpServletResponse response)
    throws ServletException, IOException
```

```
protected void doPost(HttpServletRequest request, HttpServletResponse response)
    throws ServletException, IOException
```

```
protected void doPut(HttpServletRequest request, HttpServletResponse response)
    throws ServletException, IOException
```

These four methods correspond to four of the possible HTTP request methods: DELETE, GET, POST, and PUT. In this chapter we will examine doGet() and doPost(). It will be up to you to determine which request methods your application requires. You should then override the doXXX() method associated with the request method your application requires, we will see how to do this in a moment. The two methods you will most commonly override in your own servlets are doGet() and doPost(). The service() methods inherited by your own servlets will properly route the client's requests to the appropriate methods.

```
protected void doOptions(HttpServletRequest request, HttpServletResponse response)
    throws ServletException, IOException

protected void doTrace(HttpServletRequest request, HttpServletResponse response)
    throws ServletException, IOException
```

These two methods are called by the `service()` method to handle client requests that specify the OPTIONS or TRACE methods respectively. Their purpose will be described in the next chapter. These two methods are fully implemented by the `HttpServlet` class and therefore should not be overridden by your servlets.

```
protected long getLastModified(HttpServletRequest request)
```

This method returns the time the requested page was last modified, measured in milliseconds since January 1, 1970 00:00:00 GMT. HTTP 1.1 allows a client to issue a conditional GET request against the server. The client can use the If-Modified-Since request header to indicate that if the resource has been modified since the specified time, then the server should serve a fresh page rather than a cached one. Overriding this method will allow you to control the caching of pages with your servlet's `doGet()` method. We'll take a closer look at this in the next chapter.

Overriding doGet() and doPost()

When a request is received by a class that extends `HttpServlet`, the request first enters the generic `service()` method (inherited by your class from its parent class, `HttpServlet`). This method then transforms the properties of the request object to comply with the `HttpServletRequest` interface and transforms the currently empty response object so that it complies with the `HttpServletResponse` interface.

These objects are then passed to the overloaded HTTP-specific `service()` method mentioned before, which polls the `HttpServletRequest` object to determine what request method the client specified. Upon determining which method the client specified, the request is then dispatched to the appropriate doXXX() method and the `HttpServletRequest` and `HttpServletResponse` objects are passed as well. It is within this method (`doGet()`, `doPost()`, `doPut()`, etc.) that the real handling of the client's request takes place.

If a request is sent to a class that extends `HttpServlet` and the specified request method is not overridden in the derived class, then the default implementation defined in the base class will be used. Two methods defined in `HttpServlet` are already fully implemented: `doTrace()` and `doOptions()`. The default implementation for the other four methods is to return an HTTP error with status code 400 (in the case of HTTP 1.0) or status code 405 (in the case of HTTP 1.1). It is imperative that your servlet classes override any of these four request methods that it needs to handle.

As previously mentioned, the GET and POST request methods are the most commonly used methods. We will not even address any other request methods until the next chapter. Let's take a look at an example of an HTTP servlet that can handle both GET and POST requests.

The GET or POST Example

Very often, you will find that you want to handle a client request regardless of whether they use a GET or POST request method. When this is the case, you can have one doXXX() method call the other. In the following example, we will see an HttpServlet that does just that. We will also see our first example of a servlet examining a request header.

Enter the following Java code into a new file: webapps\getorpost\WEB-INF\classes\GetPostServlet.java:

```java
import javax.servlet.*;
import javax.servlet.http.*;
import java.io.PrintWriter;
import java.io.IOException;

public class GetPostServlet extends HttpServlet {
  public void doGet(HttpServletRequest request,
                    HttpServletResponse response) throws ServletException,
                    IOException {

    // Set MIME type for the response
    response.setContentType("text/html");

    // Create and obtain a reference to a print writer object
    PrintWriter out = response.getWriter();

    // Add content to the print writer's buffer
    out.println("<!DOCTYPE HTML PUBLIC \"-//W3C//DTD HTML 4.0 "
            + "Transitional//EN\">");
    out.println("<HTML>");
    out.println("<HEAD><TITLE>GET or POST Example</TITLE></HEAD>");
    out.println("<BODY>");
    out.println("<H1>HTTP request method: " + request.getMethod()
            + "</H1>");
    out.println("</BODY></HTML>");

    // Close the print writer to release those resources
    out.close();

  }

  public void doPost(HttpServletRequest request,
                    HttpServletResponse response) throws ServletException,
                    IOException {

    // re-route request to doGet()
    doGet(request, response);
  }
}
```

Here is the complete listing for the deployment descriptor:

```
<?xml version="1.0" encoding="ISO-8859-1"?>
<!DOCTYPE web-app
  PUBLIC "-//Sun Microsystems, Inc.//DTD Web Application 2.2//EN"
  "http://java.sun.com/j2ee/dtds/web-app_2.2dtd">

<web-app>
  <servlet>
    <servlet-name>GetOrPost</servlet-name>
    <servlet-class>GetPostServlet</servlet-class>
  </servlet>

</web-app>
```

You're now ready to compile the servlet in the `webapps\getpost\WEB-INF\classes` directory. Refer to the previous example for instructions.

Add a new Context to `server.xml`:

```
<Context
    path="/projavaxml/chapter12/getpost"
    docBase="C:/projavaxml/chapter12/webapps/getpost"
    debug="1"
    reloadable="true">
</Context>
```

Now you're ready to test the servlet. Start up Tomcat and type
`http://localhost:8080/projavaxml/chapter12/getpost/servlet/GetOrPost` in your
browser's address/location box. This request will cause Tomcat to load the servlet and call the
`service()` method, which will in turn route your request to the `doGet()` method (since GET is the
default request method). Your browser window should look something like this:

Remember, that when specifying the servlet name, the web container is case-sensitive.

Generating Post Requests

So we see that the servlet correctly intercepted a GET request, but how do we test to see if the servlet will correctly handle a POST request? There are two ways of doing this. The first, and most common way is to use an HTML form and to specify POST as the request method when you are creating the form. This would be a fine solution, except that we are not prepared to discuss HTML forms until the next chapter.

Our second solution is to use a custom HTTP client that will allow us to specify what request method we wish to use. We will develop the source code for a custom HTTP client. While it might seem like overkill to write a custom HTTP client in order to test your servlet's ability to handle POST requests, it is acceptable because we will be using this utility to test several of the later examples in this chapter and the next.

The BasicHttpGopher Utility

The following source code is a command line BasicHttpGopher utility. It essentially creates a socket connection with a web server (the Tomcat server running on your local machine), sends an HTTP-formatted request, and retrieves an HTTP-formatted response.

The utility is composed of two classes: BasicHttpGopher and BasicSocketConnection. We'll step through the code piece by piece so that you can understand what is going on behind the scenes. You can enter the code as we move through it, or download the source code from the Wrox web site at http://www.wrox.com.

The BasicHttpGopher Class

We'll start out with the declarative part of the class:

```java
import java.io.BufferedReader;
import java.io.IOException;
import java.io.InputStreamReader;

import java.util.ArrayList;

public class BasicHttpGopher {

  private BasicSocketConnection socketConn;
```

Nothing here should be new to you except for the BasicSocketConnection class. The BasicSocketConnection object will handle the underlying network connection that will form the backbone of our HTTP communication. We'll build that class in just a moment.

The main() method

The BasicHttpGopher application is a command line HTTP client, rather than a GUI. The main() method contains the command-line input code, which will dictate the interaction between the user and the application. Here's how the main() method begins:

```java
public static void main(String[] args) {

  // This bufferedreader is set to read Standard Input (keyboard)
  BufferedReader in =
    new BufferedReader(new InputStreamReader(System.in));
```

```
// These variables are used to create the request
String _host, _requestMethod, _url, _version;
int _port;
char ans;
ArrayList headerList;
BasicHttpGopher gopher;
```

The method begins by creating a `BufferedReader` object that wraps an `InputStreamReader` object that wraps a special object of the `System` class, `System.in`, which collects input from the user from the command line. After creating this object, a variety of variables are declared, which will be used to store information received from the user that will then be used as parameters for the `BasicHttpGopher` constructor.

Next, we actually build the command-line interaction between the application and the user. Each question presented to the user relates to some aspect of the request that will be sent to the server.

```
try {
  System.out.print("Host: ");
  _host = in.readLine();
  System.out.print("Port: ");
  _port = Integer.parseInt(in.readLine());
  System.out.print("Request Method: ");
  _requestMethod = in.readLine();
  System.out.print("Request URL: ");
  _url = in.readLine();
  System.out.print("HTTP Version 1.0 or 1.1? ");
  _version = in.readLine();
  System.out.print("Any Request Headers? ");
  ans = (in.readLine()).charAt(0);

  if (ans == 'y' || ans == 'Y') {
    String temp;
    headerList = new ArrayList();
    while (ans == 'y' || ans == 'Y') {
      System.out.print("Request Header and Value: ");
      temp = in.readLine();
      headerList.add(temp);
      System.out.print("Add another request header? ");
      ans = (in.readLine()).charAt(0);
    }

    System.out.println();
    gopher = new BasicHttpGopher(_host, _port, headerList.toArray(),
                          _requestMethod + " " + _url + " HTTP/"
                          + _version);
  } else {
    System.out.println();
    gopher = new BasicHttpGopher(_host, _port,
                          _requestMethod + " " + _url + " HTTP/"
                          + _version);
  }
} catch (IOException ioe) {
  ioe.printStackTrace();
}
}
```

Once the data is collected from the user, then a `BasicHttpGopher` object is instantiated. There are two overloaded constructors. One takes an `Object` array of request headers that we pass in at the prompt, while the other takes no request headers at all.

The Constructors

We start with the constructor that uses no request headers. The constructor will create a `BasicSocketConnection` object, set the connection's request line, check to be sure the host is valid, and then establish the connection with the host, thereby submitting the request.

```
public BasicHttpGopher(String host, int port, String requestLine) {
  socketConn = new BasicSocketConnection(host, port);
  socketConn.setRequestLine(requestLine);
  if (socketConn.checkHost()) {
    socketConn.connect();
  }
}
```

The next constructor accepts an `Object` array of request headers. It looks just like the previous constructor, except that a `for` loop is added that adds the request headers contained in the array to the `BasicSocketConnection` object.

```
public BasicHttpGopher(String host, int port, Object[] requestHeaders,
                       String requestLine) {

  socketConn = new BasicSocketConnection(host, port);
  socketConn.setRequestLine(requestLine);

  int count = requestHeaders.length;
  for (int x = 0; x < count; x++) {
    socketConn.addRequestHeader(requestHeaders[x].toString());
  }
  if (socketConn.checkHost()) {
    socketConn.connect();
  }

  }
}
```

That's all there is to the `BasicHttpGopher` class. Now let's take a look at the real workhorse that operates behind the scenes, the `BasicSocketConnection` class.

The BasicSocketConnection Class

`BasicHttpGopher` relies upon `BasicSocketConnection` to handle the actual communication with the server. As usual, we'll start with the declarative part of the class:

```
import java.net.*;
import java.io.*;
import java.util.ArrayList;

public class BasicSocketConnection {
  private String host;
  private int port;
  private String requestLine;
  private ArrayList requestHeaders;
```

Aside from importing the necessary classes, there are four instance variables that must be declared. Each of the variables relates to a different part of an HTTP request: host, port, request URL, and the request headers.

The Constructor

The `BasicSocketConnection()` constructor takes in only two parameters, the host and the port. The other aspects of the `BasicSocketConnection` object will be set using setter methods that we will create later. So the constructor takes those two parameters, sets the corresponding instance variables, and creates an empty `ArrayList` that can be used to store a list of request headers:

```
public BasicSocketConnection(String host, int port) {
   this.host = host;
   this.port = port;
   requestHeaders = new ArrayList();
}
```

Establishing the Connection

The constructor simply registers the essential properties of a `BasicSocketConnection` object. No connection is established with the server until the `connect()` method is called. Here is the code for that method:

```
public void connect() {
   try {
      Socket gopher = new Socket(host, port);
      callServer(gopher);
   } catch (UnknownHostException uhe) {
      System.out.println("Unknown host: " + host);
      uhe.printStackTrace();
   } catch (ConnectException ce) {
      System.out.println("Connection refused! Are you sure the web "
                       + "server is working properly?");
   } catch (IOException ioe) {
      System.out.println("IOException: " + ioe);
      ioe.printStackTrace();
   }
}
```

The method creates a `Socket` object using the object's host and port and then passes that socket to the `callServer()` method. The rest of the method is simply a series of `catch()` blocks that will diagnose any network problems for you.

Sending the Request

This method actually invokes the command against the server and returns the results to standard output:

```
private void callServer(Socket gopher) throws IOException {
   PrintWriter out;
   BufferedReader in;

   System.out.println("Connecting to " + host + " ...");
   out = new PrintWriter(gopher.getOutputStream(), true);
   in = new BufferedReader(new InputStreamReader(gopher.getInputStream()));
   out.println(requestLine);
   processHeaders(out, requestHeaders);
   out.println();
```

The method begins by declaring an output variable and an input variable. After sending a statement to standard output, the input and output objects are created based on the socket object that was passed into the method. The next step is to send the request line to the server and then to send any request headers to the server. This is handled by the processHeaders() method that we will create very shortly.

At this point, the request has been sent to the server and the response returned to the socket's input stream (which has been wrapped by the BufferedReader object). All that remains is for the data to be retrieved from the stream. That is precisely what happens next:

```
System.out.println("Response from host:" + "\n");

String line;
int lineCount = 0;
int lineMax = 15;

while ((line = in.readLine()) != null) {
  if (lineCount > lineMax) {
    System.out.println("\nPress Return...");
    System.in.read();
    lineCount = 0;
  }   // end if ( lineCount > lineMax )

  System.out.println(line);
  lineCount++;

}

// Close out these resources
out.close();
in.close();
gopher.close();

}
```

This method reads data from the HTTP response sent back from the server one line at a time with the BufferedReader's readLine() method. That line is then displayed by the console through the System.out.println() call. You will notice that there is also an if statement. This simply checks to see how many lines are currently being displayed. Once the lineCount variable reaches the maximum, then a **Press Return...** prompt will be displayed, and the user will be permitted to view the current text before pressing a key to advanced to the next block of the response data. Finally, once all the data has been retrieved from the response buffer, the output stream object, input stream object, and socket object are all closed to release those resources.

Sending the Request Headers

As previously mentioned, there is a special method used to process the request headers. This method is only called once, but by using a separate method, it helps to break down the logic into more manageable parts. This method takes in two parameters: a PrintWriter object and an ArrayList of request headers. Here is the source for the processHeaders() method:

```
private void processHeaders(PrintWriter pw, ArrayList headers) {
  if (headers != null) {
    int count = headers.size();
    for (int i = 0; i < count; i++) {
      pw.println((String) headers.get(i));
    }
  }
}
```

The method begins by checking to be sure that the `ArrayList` actually contains one or more request headers. This check allows us to decouple the `callServer()` method (the method that calls `processHeaders()`) from the specific values contained within the `BasicSocketConnection`'s instance variables. As far as the HTTP request itself is concerned, no special measures need to be taken if there are no request headers. The request architecture is very flexible. The server will look for headers, and if none are returned, it will proceed to process the request or retrieve the optional appended request body in the case of a `POST` request.

Verifying the Host

This method is declared as public so that the class that creates a `BasicSocketConnection` object (which is the `BasicHttpGopher` class in this case) can verify the existence and/or accessibility of the host machine to which the client's request will be sent:

```
public boolean checkHost() {
  try {
    InetAddress.getByName(host);
    return (true);
  } catch (UnknownHostException uhe) {
    System.out.println("Invalid host: " + host);
    return (false);
  }
}
```

The method uses the `InetAddress` class defined in the `java.net` package to attempt to locate the specified host. If the host cannot be found, then an `UnKnownHostExeception` is thrown and the method returns `false`, otherwise, the method returns `true`.

Setting the Request Properties

There are two methods that are used to set the properties of the HTTP request. The use of the first method is mandatory (you cannot make a successful request without it) and the second is optional.

The first method is the `setRequestLine()` method. Without this method, you cannot make a valid request on the server:

```
public void setRequestLine( String requestLine ) {
  this.requestLine = requestLine;
}
```

The request line consists of the request method, the URL, and the HTTP version. This string is constructed by the `BasicHttpGopher` class and passed to this method for a particular `BasicSocketConnection` object.

The next method is the `addRequestHeader()` method. This is an optional method (HTTP does not require requests to contain header parameters) and it allows you to add one or more request headers:

```
public void addRequestHeader( String requestHeader ) {
  requestHeaders.add( requestHeader );
}
```

The `BasicSocketConnection` constructor initialized an empty `ArrayList` called `requestHeaders`. This is the collection that this method stores request headers in.

Note that, strictly speaking, HTTP/1.1 does require one request header – Host: – to be provided, but that it is possible to make a valid HTTP/1.0 request without sending any headers at all.

Helper Methods

Each of the instance members of the BasicSocketConnection class has a getter method in case the calling class should need access to this data. The BasicHttpGopher class does not use them, but they are included here for completeness:

```
    public String getHost() { return(host); }
    public int getPort() { return(port); }
    public String getRequestLine() { return (requestLine); }
    public ArrayList getRequestHeaders() { return requestHeaders; }
}
```

Compiling the Source

Since neither of these applications is dependent upon the web server, there's no reason to compile the class files into your web server's directory structure as we have done with our previous servlet examples. So compile these two files in C:\projavaxml\chapter12. We'll be using this application to test several of the examples in this chapter and the next chapter.

POST Request Example

In our earlier example, the GetPostServlet, we learned that GET is the default request method used by most browsers. There will, however, be times when you want to create different results depending upon the request method sent by the client. We can send various request methods to the server (and thus to our servlets) using the BasicHttpGopher utility. Assuming that you have compiled BasicHttpGopher.java and BasicSocketConnection.java you can test your servlets by sending various request values.

To send a POST request to the BasicHttpGopher, first make sure that Tomcat is running. BasicHttpGopher will send requests to the Tomcat server in the same way your browser does. Next, start BasicHttpGopher from the command line by invoking the class file with the command:

```
java BasicHttpGopher
```

This will start the BasicHttpGopher utility and you will be prompted to provide a series of inputs. Try using the following inputs:

```
Host: localhost
Port: 8080
Request Method: POST
Request URL: /projavaxml/chapter12/getpost/servlet/GetOrPost
HTTP Version 1.0 or 1.1? 1.0
Any Request Headers? n
```

You should get the following result:

```
C:\projavaxml\chapter12>java BasicHttpGopher
Host: localhost
Port: 8080
Request Method: POST
Request URL: /projavaxml/chapter12/getpost/servlet/GetOrPost
HTTP Version 1.0 or 1.1? 1.0
Any Request Headers? n

Connecting to localhost ...
Response from host:

HTTP/1.0 200 OK
Content-Type: text/html
Servlet-Engine: Tomcat Web Server/3.2.1 (JSP 1.1; Servlet 2.2; Java 1.3.0rc3; Wi
java.vendor=Sun Microsystems Inc.)

<!DOCTYPE HTML PUBLIC "-//W3C//DTD HTML 4.0 Transitional//EN">
<HTML>
<HEAD><TITLE>GET or POST Example</TITLE></HEAD>
<BODY>
<H1>HTTP request method: POST</H1>
</BODY></HTML>

C:\projavaxml\chapter12>
```

As you can see from the output, the request object contains the request method sent by the client. If you're still not convinced that we have successfully overridden the doGet() and doPost() methods defined in HttpServlet, try modifying the doPost() method of GetPostServlet with the following code:

```java
public void doPost(HttpServletRequest request,HttpServletResponse response)
    throws ServletException, IOException {

    // Set MIME type for the response
    response.setContentType("text/html");

    // Create and obtain a reference to a print writer object
    PrintWriter out = response.getWriter();

    // Add content to the print writer's buffer
    out.println( "<HTML><HEAD>" );
    out.println( "<TITLE>Get And Post Example</TITLE>" );
    out.println( "</HEAD><BODY>" );
    out.println( "<H1> Congratulations </H1>" );
    out.println( "<H1> This is a POST request.</H1>" );
    out.println( "</BODY></HTML>" );

    // Close the print writer to release those resources
    out.close();
}
```

Once you've made the change, recompile the code into the `webapps\getpost\WEB-INF\classes` directory and test it out with the `BasicHttpGopher` utility.

You could even experiment with using `BasicHttpGopher` to access other web sites on the Internet. If you use http://www.wrox.com/ (or any other host server) instead of `localhost` and you use port 80 instead of 8080 then you can access pages out on the web, pull them down to your local machine and view the status line, response headers, and response body that are normally sent back to the browser.

Outputting XML

If you have been studying this book in sequence, you should have a solid grounding in XML. If you have not and you do not feel comfortable with how to manipulate XML using the SAX and DOM APIs, then you will want to study Chapters 2 and 3 before continuing in this chapter.

Fundamentally, XML is no different from HTML. They are both text-based markup languages that organize information using pre-defined tag sets. Although there are plenty of levels on which they differ, at their core they are both readable text. Both an HTML document and an XML document can be written out as a long string of characters. This is important as this is ultimately how XML is transmitted over HTTP.

Sending XML Formatted Data via POST

Of the various request methods available in HTTP, the one best suited for sending XML-formatted data is the POST request method. This is because POST allows you to append a request body (sometimes called a request entity) in addition to the request headers. Without this aspect, a POST would be no different from a GET request. Put another way, a GET request is an attempt to get the resource specified in the URL, while a POST request posts a request body to the specified resource.

If you look at the previous example where we overrode the `doPost()` method, you will see that it appears no different from the overridden `doGet()` method. This is because a POST request in the absence of a body functions exactly like a GET request. Even when we get into passing parameters from HTML forms in the next chapter, you will see that they both pass parameters and that servlets access their value in the same way. Aside from the ability to send a POST request body, the only way in which they differ is that GET requests send parameters through the URL, while POST requests send parameters through the request body. We'll delve deeper into that in the next chapter. For now, we need to modify our `HttpGopher` and `SocketConnection` classes so that they can handle POST requests with appended request bodies.

Changing the BasicHttpGopher Class

Make the following changes to the `BasicHttpGopher` class, saving it as `HttpGopher`, to allow the inclusion of a file's contents in the request body.

The main() Method

```
public static void main(String[] args) {

  // This bufferedreader is set to read Standard Input (keyboard)
  BufferedReader in =
    new BufferedReader(new InputStreamReader(System.in));
```

```
    // These variables are used to create the request
    String _host, _requestMethod, _url, _version;
    String _fileName = null;
    int _port;
    char ans;
    ArrayList headerList;
    HttpGopher gopher;

    try {
      System.out.print("Host: ");
      _host = in.readLine();
      System.out.print("Port: ");
      _port = Integer.parseInt(in.readLine());
      System.out.print("Request Method: ");
      _requestMethod = in.readLine();

      if (_requestMethod.charAt(0) == 'P'
              || _requestMethod.charAt(0) == 'p') {
        System.out.print("Would you like to append a file to the POST "
                        + "request? ");
        ans = (in.readLine()).charAt(0);
        if (ans == 'y' || ans == 'Y') {
          System.out.print("Enter the path and filename of the file: ");
          _fileName = in.readLine();
        }
      }

      System.out.print("Request URL: ");
      _url = in.readLine();
      System.out.print("HTTP Version 1.0 or 1.1? ");
      _version = in.readLine();
      System.out.print("Any Request Headers? ");
      ans = (in.readLine()).charAt(0);

      if (ans == 'y' || ans == 'Y') {
        String temp;
        headerList = new ArrayList();
        while (ans == 'y' || ans == 'Y') {
          System.out.print("Request Header and Value: ");

          temp = in.readLine();
          headerList.add(temp);
          System.out.print("Add another request header? ");
          ans = (in.readLine()).charAt(0);
        }

        System.out.println();
        gopher = new HttpGopher(_host, _port, headerList.toArray(),
                                _requestMethod + " " + _url + " HTTP/"
                                + _version, _fileName);
      } else {
        System.out.println();
        gopher = new HttpGopher(_host, _port,
                                _requestMethod + " " + _url + " HTTP/"
                                + _version, _fileName);
      }
    } catch (IOException ioe) {
      ioe.printStackTrace();
    }
  }
}
```

These modifications will allow the user to specify a file, the text of which will become the body of the POST request. To accomplish this, we must add: a local variable, _filename; some code to collect the filename from the user (assuming this is a POST request); and a modification to the constructor calls to allow the filename to be passed to the constructor.

The Constructors

There are two constructors for the HttpGopher utility, and both of them take in the minimum information needed to create a valid HTTP request; the server's host and port, and the request line itself. In addition to these three pieces, they both take in a String argument representing a filename. Although both constructors require this argument, it may contain a null string:

```
public HttpGopher(String host, int port, String requestLine,
                  String fileName) {
  socketConn = new SocketConnection(host, port);

  socketConn.setRequestLine(requestLine);

  if (requestLine.charAt(0) == 'P' || requestLine.charAt(0) == 'p') {
    socketConn.setPost(true);
    if (fileName != null) {
      socketConn.setFile(fileName);
    }
  }

  if (socketConn.checkHost()) {
    socketConn.connect();

  }
}
```

```
public HttpGopher(String host, int port, Object[] requestHeaders,
                  String requestLine, String fileName) {
  socketConn = new SocketConnection(host, port);

  socketConn.setRequestLine(requestLine);

  if (requestLine.charAt(0) == 'P' || requestLine.charAt(0) == 'p') {
    socketConn.setPost(true);
    if (fileName != null) {
      socketConn.setFile(fileName);
    }
  }

  int count = requestHeaders.length;
  for (int x = 0; x < count; x++) {
    socketConn.addRequestHeader(requestHeaders[x].toString());
  }
  if (socketConn.checkHost()) {
    socketConn.connect();
  }
}
```

Both constructors make the same changes. A `String` parameter named `filename` is added along with an `if` block that checks the first letter of the request method, the same as the `if` block we added to the `main()` method. If it is a `POST` request, then the `setPost()` method is set to `true` and the filename is set for the `SocketConnection` object using the `setFileName()` method. We'll add both of these methods to the `SocketConnection` class in just a short while.

These changes aren't very interesting until we modify the `BasicSocketConnection` class. All we've done here is allow the user to specify a filename so that the contents of that file can be included in the HTTP request body sent in the `POST` request to the server.

Changing the BasicSocketConnection Class

We'll modify the `BasicSocketConnection` class, saving the result to `SocketConnection.java`, to read the contents of the specified file and append them to the body of a `POST` request. We'll start by adding the necessary variables to the class definition:

```
public class SocketConnection {
  private String      host;
  private int         port;
  private String      requestLine;
  private ArrayList   requestHeaders;
  private boolean     isPost;
  private String      fileName;
```

The `isPost` variable specifies whether or not this is a `POST` request and the `fileName` string stores the file name and the path of the file that should be included in the `POST` request body.

The callServer() Method

This is the method that will do the real work of including the file's contents in the body of the request:

```
private void callServer(Socket gopher) throws IOException {
  PrintWriter out;
  BufferedReader in;

  System.out.println("Connecting to " + host + " ...");

  out = new PrintWriter(gopher.getOutputStream(), true);
  in = new BufferedReader(new InputStreamReader(gopher.getInputStream()));
  out.println(requestLine);

  if (getPost()) {
    ByteArrayOutputStream byteStream = new ByteArrayOutputStream();
    PrintWriter pw = new PrintWriter(byteStream, true);
    if (getFile() != null) {
      BufferedReader fileIn =
        new BufferedReader(new FileReader(fileName));
      String line;
      while ((line = fileIn.readLine()) != null) {
        pw.println(line);
      }
      pw.flush();
```

```
}    // end if ( getFile() != null )
 String len = String.valueOf(byteStream.size());
addRequestHeader("Content-Length: " + len);
processHeaders(out, requestHeaders);
out.println();
out.println(byteStream.toString());
pw.close();
byteStream.close();
} else {
processHeaders(out, requestHeaders);
out.println();
}      // end if ( getPost() )

System.out.println("Response from host:" + "\n");

// Rest of method same as before...
```

If the request is a POST request and a file has been specified, then a ByteArrayOutputStream is created and the contents of the file are fed into the stream using a PrintWriter object. Then, the size of the stream is measured and the Content-Length request header is set with that value. Every POST request with an attached request body is required to include a Content-Length header. Finally, the contents of the stream are added to the socket's output stream.

Helper Methods

Finally, there are a few helper methods that need to be added to round the application out:

```
public boolean getPost() { return isPost; }
public void setPost(boolean flag) { isPost = flag; }
public String getFile() { return fileName; }
public void setFile(String fn) { fileName = fn; }
```

> **Remember to update any references or constructors in BasicHttpGopher and BasicSocketConnection to SocketConnection and HttpGopher.**

Testing the changes

With those changes in place, you should be ready to recompile HttpGopher.java and then run the program.

Try running the program with some of the servlets you've written earlier this chapter. Everything should function the same as before, except that you can now append a file to the request body. The data contained in that file will not appear in any of the responses you receive however, because we have not yet written a servlet capable of reading this data. That is what we will do now.

An XML Messaging Application

Our first step into handling XML within a servlet will be in the form of sending an XML file to the servlet for processing. We will construct a flexible XML-based architecture for a remote content management system. This application will enable the client to send a POST request to the server with XML-formatted data contained within the request body. That data will be extracted by the HttpGopher application from an XML file sitting on the client's machine.

For this example, we will construct a skeletal architecture for a remote content management system. XML-formatted commands will instruct the server to create, remove, modify, or display content records. The particular example we will use for demonstration is a news summary. This is intended to address a real-world problem. Many web sites display the titles and summaries of news items on their front page as a invitation to the full article. This application will provide the framework for a remote management utility in the next chapter that will allow us to add and view news summary items.

The XML will represent a command being sent to the server to manipulate data on the server in some way. To determine which information contained within the XML should be parsed out, the servlet is initialized with certain tag names that will be specified in the application's deployment descriptor web.xml. Initially, our servlet will simply parse out the specified data and return it to the client, but in the next chapter, the servlet will respond to the client's command by modifying an in-memory record of the data.

We can see this in the following diagram:

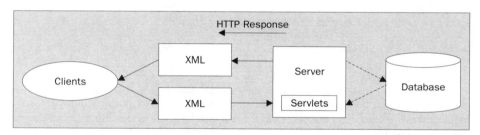

This demonstrates the sort of XML-based client-server messaging system that we have in mind. We'll lay the groundwork for the server side in this chapter and bring it all together with the client side in the next chapter.

To handle the parsing of the XML we will be using JAXP 1.1 for the interface, SAX 2.0 for the underlying parsing routine, and Xerces 1.3 for the parsing engine. If you do not have the necessary JAR files located on your machine and your classpath variable set appropriately, refer back to Chapter 2 for further discussion on SAX and JAXP 1.1.

We'll be creating three classes: SaxServlet, SaxCommand, and CharHelper. SaxServlet is the servlet that will retrieve the XML document from the request body and pass it to SaxCommand to be parsed. SaxCommand will use CharHelper to help in processing the results and passing the parsed data back to the servlet for final processing.

The SaxServlet Class

This class will carry out the requests made by the client. Initially, the application will simply parse out a portion of the data specified in the deployment descriptor and return that to the client.

Start off by creating a Java source file named `SaxServlet.java` in `webapps\messaging\WEB-INF\classes`. This takes care of all the declarations that we will need for the class:

```java
import org.xml.sax.SAXException;
import org.xml.sax.InputSource;
import javax.xml.parsers.*;
import javax.servlet.*;
import javax.servlet.http.*;

import java.io.IOException;
import java.io.PrintWriter;
import java.util.HashMap;
import java.util.Enumeration;

public class SaxServlet extends HttpServlet {
    private static final String PARAM_COMMAND = "CommandType";
    private static final String COMMAND_ATTR = "type";
    private static final String ADD_COMMAND = "add";
    private static final String DELETE_COMMAND = "delete";
    private static final String EDIT_COMMAND = "edit";
    private static final String VIEW_COMMAND = "view";

    private String commandType;
    private HashMap paramValues;
```

We import the necessary packages (including some XML packages that we will be using very soon), and declare a variety of variables that will be used later in the application. The static final variables represent command strings and parameter values that will be used in the application. They are defined here so that name changes don't require you to go back later and comb through the code to find every use of a particular string. The other two variables will be initialized in the constructor.

We should take a moment to examine the `paramValues` HashMap object before going further. This object will be used to store the XML data that is parsed out of the client's request. If you already know about hashmaps, then you can skip this paragraph. The HashMap class belongs to the `java.util` package and is a member of the Collections API. A HashMap object is a data structure that is capable of storing name/value pairs of data. The names are called keys, and every value contained in a HashMap must be mapped to a unique key. Both keys and values are stored as objects of the Object class in a HashMap, so class casting is almost always necessary when retrieving data from a HashMap. Data is not stored in any particular order, and the order may change over time as the contents of the HashMap change. The only thing that is guaranteed is that a valid key will return one, and only one, value from a HashMap. Both keys and values are permitted to be `null` in a HashMap object. Like Vector, HashMap expands automatically to accommodate more data.

Next, we need to initialize the servlet with the names of the XML tags that will be processed later when a client request is received. This initialization takes place in the `init()` method. Parameter name/value pairs are defined in the deployment descriptor `web.xml` and passed to the `init()` method via a ServletConfig object. These name/value pairs are then extracted from the ServletConfig object and stored appropriately. The source for the `init()` method is as following:

```
   public void init() throws ServletException {
     paramValues = new HashMap();

     // retrieve the specified parameter from web.xml
     commandType = getServletConfig().getInitParameter(PARAM_COMMAND);

     // retrieve all initialization parameters from web.xml
     Enumeration enum = getServletConfig().getInitParameterNames();
     String tempName, tempValue;

     // loop through each of the parameters
     while (enum.hasMoreElements()) {
       tempName = (String) enum.nextElement();
       tempValue = getServletConfig().getInitParameter(tempName);

       // store all the values except for the one retrieved earlier
       if (!tempName.equals(PARAM_COMMAND)) {
         paramValues.put(tempValue, null);
       }
     }
   }
```

You'll notice that only one of these parameters was retrieved explicitly by its name, `commandType`. The other parameters are retrieved collectively and each one is stored in the `paramValues HashMap` except for the `commandType` that was explicitly retrieved. By not explicitly retrieving the other parameters, we have created a more flexible architecture in which both the name and number of parameters can be changed without having to modify the servlet. A quick change to the `web.xml` file and a restart of the web container are all that's required. The only constant is the `CommandType` parameter, which we will see later is the cornerstone of the XML message.

Next, we create a method called `parseDocument()` that receives a reference to the request object. Within this method we will obtain a `SAXParser`, through a `SAXParserFactory` and attach it to the input stream of the request object. We haven't seen this yet, but both `GenericServlet` and `HttpServlet` permit you to obtain an input stream from the request object and extract data that has been posted in the request body.

Here's what the code for the `parseDocument()` method looks like:

```
 private void parseDocument(HttpServletRequest request)
         throws ServletException {
   SAXParserFactory factory = SAXParserFactory.newInstance();
   factory.setValidating(false);
   factory.setNamespaceAware(true);
   SaxCommand myHandler = new SaxCommand(commandType, paramValues);

   try {
     SAXParser parser = factory.newSAXParser();
     InputSource is = new InputSource(request.getInputStream());
     parser.parse(is, myHandler);
   } catch (IOException ioe) {
     log("Error attempting to open InputStream " + "on request object.",
         ioe);
   } catch (ParserConfigurationException pce) {
     log("Error attempting to load parser into factory.", pce);
   } catch (SAXException se) {
     log("SAX Exception", se);
   }
 }
```

Most of this code should look pretty familiar, but let's take a notice of a couple of new things. First, we have created a SaxCommand() object, which is referenced by a variable of type DefaultHandler. We haven't gotten to the SaxCommand class yet, but it extends DefaultHandler, which is why we can refer to it with a variable of type DefaultHandler. The DefaultHandler class was introduced in Sax 2.0 in place of individually implementing EntityResolver, DTDHandler, ContentHandler, and ErrorHandler (all of which are essential for SAX parsing).

SaxCommand also defines a single constructor that accepts a string and a HashMap. We pass the commandType string and the parameters HashMap so that when those values are parsed out of the XML, they can be stored in the HashMap with the keys specified in the deployment descriptor. Thus, when the parsing is complete, the HashMap is filled with name key/value pairs based on the keys (XML elements) specified in the deployment descriptor. To change what element values are parsed out, we merely need to change the deployment descriptor and restart the server. Although this application doesn't do anything exciting with the HashMap of values, in the next chapter we will see a more robust XML example in which this technique would be quite useful.

There are two other things to notice about the parseDocument() method. The first is the InputSource that the SAXParser is given to parse. It is an input stream that is opened on the request object by the method getInputStream(). This stream contains any data that was sent in the body of the POST request by the client. The other thing to notice is the log() method used in the three catch() blocks.

The log() method is an overloaded method inherited from GenericServlet. It is overloaded in that you can simply send a string, or you can send a string and an object that extends the Throwable class (the superclass of all exceptions). The target of the log() method is container specific, but Tomcat writes the information to <TOMCAT_HOME>\logs\servlet.log.

The next method we need is processCommand(). It is responsible for processing the value of the type attribute after it has been parsed out of the commandType XML tag. For now, the method does nothing aside from sending a message to the client informing them that the command was successfully received. In the next chapter, however, the role of the processCommand() method will be expanded dramatically.

```java
private String processCommand() {
    String command = (String) paramValues.get(COMMAND_ATTR);
    paramValues.remove(COMMAND_ATTR);

    if (command.equals(ADD_COMMAND)) {
      return "Add Command Received";
    } else if (command.equals(DELETE_COMMAND)) {
      return "Delete Command Received";
    } else if (command.equals(EDIT_COMMAND)) {
      return "Edit Command Received";
    } else if (command.equals(VIEW_COMMAND)) {
      return "View Command Received";
    } else {
      return "Command \'" + command + "\' not understood.";
    }
  }
}
```

Finally, we need the method we are most familiar with: doPost(). For the most part, this method is no different from what it has been with any of our other servlets. The difference occurs in the heart of the method when the parseDocument() and processCommand() methods are called. After this, the HashMap values are pulled out of the HashMap and sent to the client alongside their respective keys. Add this method to complete the SaxServlet source code:

```java
public void doPost(HttpServletRequest request,
                   HttpServletResponse response) throws ServletException,
                   IOException {

    // Set the MIME type for the response
    response.setContentType("text/html");

    // Create and obtain a reference to a print writer object
    PrintWriter out = response.getWriter();

    // Add content to the print writer's buffer
    out.println("<!DOCTYPE HTML PUBLIC \"-//W3C//DTD HTML 4.0 "
            + "Transitional//EN\">");
    out.println("<HTML>");
    out.println("<HEAD><TITLE>XML Messaging (SAX)</TITLE></HEAD>");
    out.println("<BODY>");

    // Only parse the XML file if parameters have been sent to
    // indicate what data to extract
    if (paramValues != null) {

        // Parse the specified values out of the request body
        parseDocument(request);

        // Process the type of command specified
        out.println(processCommand());
        out.println();

        // Loop through the HashMap values returned from the parser
        // and display them to the client
        Object[] keys = paramValues.keySet().toArray();
        int count = keys.length;
        for (int x = count - 1; x >= 0; x--) {
            out.println((String) keys[x] + ": "
                    + (String) paramValues.get(keys[x]));
        }
    }
    out.println("</BODY>");
    out.println("</HTML>");
    out.close();
}
}
```

This method is merely the conductor. After setting up some basic servlet and response object properties, two methods are called in order: parseDocument() and processCommand(). As you saw previously, the parseDocument() method fills the paramValues() HashMap with the data that was parsed out of the XML document by the SaxCommand class. The method then iterates through those values and displays them to the client.

Now that you've got that source code put together, you're ready to build the SaxCommand class. This is where all the actual parsing logic takes place and the HashMap values are filled.

The SaxCommand Class

The single constructor defined in SaxCommand accepts a string (the commandType) and a HashMap (the other elements to parse out of the XML data). SaxCommand will search through the XML document searching for elements that match the values contained in the commandType string and the keys stored in the HashMap.

Let's begin by creating a Java source file named SaxComand.java in the same directory as the SaxServlet source file. Here's the start of the source code:

```
import org.xml.sax.*;
import org.xml.sax.helpers.*;
import javax.xml.parsers.*;
import java.io.*;
import java.util.*;

public class SaxCommand extends org.xml.sax.helpers.DefaultHandler {
  private static final String COMMAND_ATTR = "type";

  private String commandType;
  private HashMap paramValues;
  private Set paramNames;
  private boolean saveData;
  private String key;
```

The first three variables should be familiar to you since you saw them (or at least their counterparts) in the SaxServlet source code. But the other three are unique to this class. The variable paramNames is of type Set and it contains all the keys from the HashMap. paramNames is initialized in the SaxCommand constructor.

The boolean variable saveData is a flag to indicate whether or not the characters being parsed fall within one of the elements that is going to be returned. The key variable is a reference to a particular HashMap key name and is used in conjunction with the saveData variable.

Next we insert the constructor:

```
public SaxCommand(String commandTag, HashMap paramList) {
  commandType = commandTag;
  paramValues = paramList;
  paramNames = paramValues.keySet();
}
```

As mentioned earlier, paramNames is a set of all the keys contained in the paramValues HashMap.

As you know, the SAX API is an event-driven method of parsing an XML document. As the parser encounters structures in the document (processing instruction, beginning of an element, end of an element, character data, etc.) it interprets these as events and invokes a callback method to handle the event. If these methods are not overridden, then a default, empty implementation is used. We will be overriding two such callback methods.

Now we add our first SAX 2.0 method, startElement():

```
public void startElement(String uri, String name, String qualName,
                Attributes attrs) throws SAXException {
```

```
        if (saveData) {
          throw new SAXException("Parsing Error: Cannot nest other "
                              + "elements within CDATA sections.");
        }
        if (paramNames.contains(name)) {
          saveData = true;
          key = name;
        } else if (name.equals(commandType) && (attrs != null)) {
          paramValues.put(COMMAND_ATTR, attrs.getValue(COMMAND_ATTR));
        }
      }
```

When the parser encounters a new tag, it calls `StartElement()`. By overriding it in this class, we substitute our own implementation whenever this event is triggered.

This `startElement()` method compares the tag name for each element to the `Set` of keys contained in `paramNames` and then to the value of `commandType`. If a match is found, the element is flagged for storage, in the case of the `HashMap` keys, or the specified attribute of `commandType` is directly stored in the `HashMap` in the case of a match with the `commandType` variable.

When `SaxCommand` finds a match between the `commandType` value and an element contained in the XML data, then the "type" attribute contained in that element is copied and that name/value pair is stored in the `HashMap` to be retrieved later by the `SaxServlet`.

Because this method is called at the beginning of every XML element, it is important to be sure that we are accessing the proper information and storing only that. If this element's tag name matches the `Set` of keys contained in `paramNames`, then it is flagged for storage using the `saveData` variable. If the `characters()` method is reached before the `startElement()` is reached again, then we have a valid block of data that can be stored in the `HashMap`. Otherwise, we have a nested tag that is not suitable for storage. For simplicity's sake, this parsing algorithm doesn't go any deeper than this. If there is data in the XML file that needs to be parsed out, it cannot be contained within a nested tag. Only simple, single name/value pairs can be stored.

The final method we need is another SAX 2.0 callback method, the `characters()` method.

```
      public void characters(char buf[], int offset,
                            int len) throws SAXException {
        if (saveData) {
          String value = CharHelper.printLine(buf, offset, len);
          if (value != null && value != "") {
            paramValues.put(key, value);
            saveData = false;
          }
        }
      }
    }
```

When the parser encounters character data, it passes those characters in a buffer to this method. If the `saveData` variable has been flagged to `true`, then we know that we are dealing with character data within an element tag that was specified in the deployment descriptor and is expected by `SaxServlet`. If `saveData` is `true`, then the `printLine()` method of the `CharHelper` class is called and the data originally passed by the parser is sent. If the return value from this method is a valid `String` object that contains actual data, then it is stored in the `HashMap` using the `key` variable (this value was set to the tag name earlier in the `startElement()` method).

We have one more class to write, but it's a short one.

The CharHelper Class

The CharHelper class is a general-purpose class that you can use with almost any XML parsing application you write. It has two methods that are helpful for processing character data. The printLine() method iterates through the character buffer calling the getChar() method. The getChar() method properly formats characters for an HTML display. Here is the CharHelper source:

```java
public class CharHelper {

    public static String printLine(char buf[], int offset, int len) {
        StringBuffer newString = new StringBuffer();
        int end = offset + len;
        for (int i = offset; i < end; i++) {
            newString.append(getChar(buf[i]));
        }
        return newString.toString();
    }

    public static String getChar(char c) {
        if (c == '&') {
            return "&amp;";
        } else if (c == '"') {
            return "&quot;";
        } else if (c == '<') {
            return "&lt;";
        } else if (c == '>') {
            return "&gt;";
        } else if (c == '\'') {
            return "&apos;";
        } else if (c < 127) {
            return "" + c;
        } else {
            return "&#" + Integer.toString(c) + ";";
        }
    }
}
```

The class converts characters into ASCII format (the standard format used in HTTP). It acts as a sort of filter that operates character by character.

With those three class files taken care of, it is time to create the two XML files that this application requires. The first is the actual XML file that you will be transmitting to the server.

The command.xml File

Unlike web.xml, there is nothing that dictates what the name of this file should be. This file name only has meaning to the extent that you must be able to identify it to the HttpGopher application, so that the file's contents can be fed into an input stream and transferred to the server in the body of a POST request.

The command.xml file contains two primary components: a command (indicated by <command> tags), and one or more additional elements that contain data that is used to fulfill the command on the server. The final result is an XML-based command that instructs the server (via a servlet) to perform a particular task.

For this example, we will construct an XML-formatted news summary. Create a file called command.xml. It is entirely up to you where you store this file, just be sure that you know the full path to it, or at least the relative path to it from the HttpGopher class file. This is the source code:

```
<?xml version="1.0"?>
<command type="add">
  <news>
    <title>New Chip Doubles Processing Speed</title>
    <byline>Chipworks Inc</byline>
    <content>
      <summary>A new chip has been developed by Chipworks Inc that
        effectively doubles the current upper bounds of
        processing power.
      </summary>
    </content>
  </news>
</command>
```

As you have previously seen, the current implementation does not actually create, edit, or modify database records, but this still gives you an idea of what the entire command would look like and how the servlet would go about processing this data.

The beauty of the way that the SaxServlet class was written is that you have the ability to determine what data contained in the above XML file you want to display, simply by modifying the deployment descriptor. Let's take a look at that right now.

The web.xml File

As you may have already guessed, the deployment descriptor plays a big role in this particular application. Not only will we be defining initialization parameters for our servlet, but also these parameters will actually control what information is extracted from the XML file during parsing and what information is discarded. This introduces a tremendous degree of flexibility that we've not seen with any of our previous servlets!

Create a web.xml file as follows in webapps\messaging\WEB-INF:

```
<?xml version="1.0" encoding="ISO-8859-1"?>
<!DOCTYPE web-app
  PUBLIC "-//Sun Microsystems, Inc.//DTD Web Application 2.2//EN"
  "http://java.sun.com/j2ee/dtds/web-app_2.2dtd">

<web-app>
  <servlet>
    <servlet-name>SaxServlet</servlet-name>
    <servlet-class>SaxServlet</servlet-class>
    <init-param>
      <param-name>CommandType</param-name>
      <param-value>command</param-value>
    </init-param>
    <init-param>
      <param-name>SubItem1</param-name>
      <param-value>title</param-value>
    </init-param>
    <init-param>
      <param-name>SubItem2</param-name>
      <param-value>byline</param-value>
    </init-param>
    <init-param>
      <param-name>SubItem3</param-name>
      <param-value>summary</param-value>
    </init-param>
  </servlet>
</web-app>
```

Servlet initialization parameters are defined within the context of a containing `<servlet>` tag. When the web container is invoking a servlet for the first time, the `web.xml` file is parsed to see if any parameters have been defined for the servlet being loaded. These values are never examined again until after a server restart when the servlet class is invoked again.

As mentioned earlier, the only parameter of these four that is mandatory is the `CommandType` parameter. If you look at `command.xml`, you will see that the `<command>` element is the containing element. Without it, you don't have a command. The other elements are still important, but there is no absolute necessity to declare any of them in the deployment descriptor. Every element contained in the `command.xml` file that is also declared in the deployment descriptor will be processed appropriately. Everything else will be discarded.

It is important to notice that with the exception of the `CommandType` parameter, the actual name of the parameter is entirely irrelevant. What is important is the specified value, which corresponds to an element in `command.xml`. In order to make `SaxServlet` flexible, it was necessary to make the initialization process dynamic rather than static. Consequently, the names of the other parameters make no impact on the servlet's execution.

Finally, add a new Context to `server.xml`:

```
<Context
    path="/projavaxml/chapter12/messaging"
    docBase="C:/projavaxml/chapter12/webapps/messaging"
    debug="1"
    reloadable="true">
</Context>
```

Putting the Application Together

We are finally ready to test the application out. In order to run the application, you should have the following:

- ❏ Source code for `SaxServlet.java`, `SaxCommand.java`, and `CharHelper.java`
- ❏ The `command.xml` file
- ❏ The `web.xml` file
- ❏ Necessary XML class files in your classpath, `xerces.jar` for Xerces-J Parser 1.3
- ❏ Updated and successfully compiled `HttpGopher` and `SocketConnection` class files to `HttpGopher` and `SocketConnection`
- ❏ Tomcat ready to go.

If you've been following along with the examples in this chapter, then you should already have the last two items taken care of.

The next step is to compile the three Java files:

```
C:\projavaxml\chapter12\webapps\messaging\WEB-INF\classes> javac *.java
```

Also be sure that the `web.xml` file is the correct directory `WEB-INF`.

Once everything is ready and your web container is up and running, you are ready to test the application. To begin, fire up the `HttpGopher` application: `java HttpGopher`. When prompted, enter the following information, substituting the appropriate path for the `command.xml` file:

```
Host: localhost
Port: 8080
Request Method: POST
Would you like to append a file to the POST request? y
Enter the path and filename of the file: command.xml
Request URL: /projavaxml/chapter12/messaging/servlet/SaxServlet
HTTP Version 1.0 or 1.1? 1.1
Any Request Headers? n
```

You should receive similar output to this:

```
C:\projavaxml\chapter12>java HttpGopher
Host: localhost
Port: 8080
Request Method: POST
Would you like to append a file to the POST request? y
Enter the path and filename of the file: command.xml
Request URL: /projavaxml/chapter12/messaging/servlet/SaxServlet
HTTP Version 1.0 or 1.1? 1.1
Any Request Headers? n

Connecting to localhost ...
Response from host:

HTTP/1.0 200 OK
Content-Type: text/html
Servlet-Engine: Tomcat Web Server/3.2.1 (JSP 1.1; Servlet 2.2; Java 1.3.0rc3; Wi
ndows 2000 5.0 x86; java.vendor=Sun Microsystems Inc.)

<!DOCTYPE HTML PUBLIC "-//W3C//DTD HTML 4.0 Transitional//EN">
<HTML>
<HEAD><TITLE>XML Messaging (SAX)</TITLE></HEAD>
<BODY>
Add Command Received

title: New Chip Doubles Processing Speed
byline: Chipworks Inc
summary: A new chip has been developed by Chipworks Inc that effectively doubles
  the current upper bounds of processing power.
</BODY>
</HTML>

C:\projavaxml\chapter12>
```

Sending XML-Formatted Data to the Client

There are a variety of benefits to an XML-formatted exchange. One is that XML is an extensible data representation layer than can adapt to a business's or industry's changing needs. Another is that it is a flexible format that any XML-aware client could make use of. This opens the door to a variety of clients having access to the same core data, but having it transformed for them, perhaps through XSLT.

Unlike sending XML-formatted data to the server, sending it back to the client is a breeze. There are two things you need to do to your servlets to send back XML:

❑   Set the response object's `Content-Type` header to `text/xml`

❑   Insert XML tags in the output stream just as you would standard HTML

Here's a quick modification to the `SaxServlet` class that does just that:

```
public void doPost(HttpServletRequest request,HttpServletResponse response )
  throws ServletException, IOException {
// Set the MIME type for the response
response.setContentType("text/xml");

// Create and obtain a reference to a print writer object
PrintWriter out = response.getWriter();

// Add content to the print writer's buffer
out.println( "<?xml version=\"1.0\" encoding=\"utf-8\"?>" );
out.println( "<HTML>" );
out.println( "<HEAD><TITLE>XML Messaging (SAX)</TITLE></HEAD>" );
out.println( "<BODY>" );

//Other code same as before…

}
```

Remember to recompile the code. Test this change out with the HttpGopher and with Internet Explorer 5. Both of them are capable of handling XML-formatted text.

Your output should look something like this:

Summary

In this chapter we have learned the basics of HTTP and Java servlets, and have had our first taste of how to handle XML over HTTP. We've taken the entire trip from sending a GET request to the server, all the way to sending an XML-formatted command to the server, and receiving XML-formatted data back.

With respect to HTTP, we have covered the HTTP status line, status codes, response headers, and the HTTP request body. We have compared the two most common request methods, GET and POST, in some detail, highlighting the strengths and weaknesses of each method. We've explored some of the intricacies of HTTP by developing a powerful command-line client application capable of invoking any type of request method on the server, dispatching request headers, and even sending a document body attached to a POST request.

In the servlet realm, we have experimented with both the GenericServlet class and the HttpServlet class. We've seen how to override methods defined in HttpServlet and provide new implementations of various request methods. We've learned how to pass initialization parameters to our servlets at invocation time. We've also learned how to open an input stream on a request object to allow our servlets to directly process data transferred via a request body.

Finally, we've developed a server-side application capable of receiving XML-formatted messages and returning XML-formatted responses.

In the next chapter, we'll explore the client side of the HTTP equation. We'll study HTTP request headers, learn how to parse XML on the client side, and round out our messaging application to be a full client-server XML command structure.

he Xerces Blue
utterfly, which became
xtinct earlier this century,
nd after which the Xerces XML
arser is named ...

13

Client-Side HTTP

The client-side of the HTTP equation is the side of the Internet that the vast majority of users are most familiar with. Virtually everyone who uses the Internet does so through an Internet browser such as Internet Explorer, Netscape Navigator, or Opera.

We should, however, keep in mind that the exchange of XML data has much wider application than simply enhancing an online shopping experience. We are laying the groundwork for using HTTP as a machine-to-machine protocol in which XML-formatted data is the common medium of exchange. This is particularly pertinent for Business-to-Business (B2B) and Enterprise Application Integration (EAI) development, two areas that are currently receiving a huge amount of attention as businesses strive to link and automate interactions between existing computerized processes.

This chapter builds on the server-side foundations in the previous chapter, where we developed the `HttpGopher` application, a necessary prerequisite for this chapter.

Here's a high-level view of what we'll cover in this chapter:

- ❑ A more detailed look at the HTTP request architecture
- ❑ The capabilities a servlet has for responding to HTTP requests
- ❑ The various kinds of queries that can be sent via an HTTP request
- ❑ The ways that XML data can be sent and received by an HTTP-compliant client
- ❑ A full client-server application that sends XML over HTTP

Setting up the Environment

We have used the following set up for all the examples in this chapter. The root directory is `C:\projavaxml\chapter13`. Any files not used in a particular web application will be stored in this directory. Web apps for each example are in the `webapps` subdirectory. Classes for each example web app are in the `webapps\example\WEB-INF\classes` directory and the `web.xml` file for the example is in the `webapps\example\WEB-INF` directory.

Each example will use a `Context` entry in Tomcat's `conf\server.xml` file so that a URL such as http://localhost:8080/projavaxml/chapter13/example will map to the `C:\projavaxml\chapter13\webapps\example` directory.

> **In general we will give filenames relative to the root folder, for example `webapps\example\WEB-INF`, rather than the fully qualified path.**

See the corresponding section in the previous chapter if you are still not sure about setting up the directory structures for servlet deployment.

HTTP Request Architecture

In order to have a more complete understanding of the HTTP request architecture, it is necessary to stop and examine the three most powerful aspects of the HTTP request: the request method, request headers, and request parameters. We will begin by explaining the function of each of the eight request methods, with special attention being paid to the more commonly used methods.

Next we'll proceed to the topic of request headers, by looking at the headers that are available to HTTP clients and then examining how our servlets can handle those headers.

Finally, we'll conclude our look into the HTTP request architecture by learning about and working with HTTP request parameters. We'll understand the differences between sending parameters via a GET and POST and we'll also take a look at what goes on behind the scenes of an HTML form. Naturally, we'll explore all of this in terms of handling HTTP parameters from within a Java servlet.

> *HTTP 1.0 and 1.1 specifications can be viewed at http://www.cis.ohio-state.edu/htbin/rfc/rfc1945.html and rfc2068.html.*

Let's being by taking a look at the HTTP request methods.

HTTP Request Methods

As mentioned in the previous chapter, HTTP defines specific methods by which a client may send a request to the server. Each method has a different purpose and provides different functionality. HTTP/1.0 defines three types of request methods: GET, HEAD, and POST. Five additional methods are defined by HTTP/1.1: CONNECT, DELETE, OPTIONS, PUT, and TRACE.

CONNECT

The HTTP/1.1 specification in fact reserved the CONNECT method to be implemented at a later date. It will be used for SSL tunneling through proxy servers. Basically, the proxy server opens a connection with the host machine on the specified port and acts as a simple bi-directional tunnel. So long as the SSL communication is maintained, the proxy server will not interfere or perform any cryptographic functions whatsoever.

DELETE

The DELETE method allows a client to request that the server delete a document housed on the server, specifying the document in the Request URI. There is no guarantee that the server will comply with the request, even if the status code returned to the client indicates that the action was successfully completed. The decision to delete the specified document is still reserved by the server. It is preferable to override the doDelete() method within a servlet and require some sort of authorization before performing the requested delete.

HEAD

This is similar to a GET request except that the server never sends a content body as part of the response. This method is used as a way of communicating with the server without actually displaying content to the client. It provides a way for a client to retrieve metadata about a resource, such as the size of a download, without retrieving the specified document. It is also used by some webcrawlers to gather data about a particular URI.

OPTIONS

This is used to query a server about the capabilities it provides. This allows the client to determine what request types are permitted, and if there are any special requirements imposed by the server on certain requests. For example, a client could use the OPTIONS method to determine what request methods are permitted by the server (indicated with an *) or by a particular resource on the server (for example this URI cannot be accessed with anything except for a POST request). A client could also use the OPTIONS method to determine if there are any requirements imposed by the server on requests, such as requiring every request to include a Content-Type header.

PUT

This is the complement of a GET request and stores the content body at the location specified by the Request URI. It is similar to uploading a file with FTP, and like FTP it requires proper authentication. If the specified request URI already exists, then this should be treated as a more recent copy.

TRACE

A useful debugging method capable of tracking the path of a request through firewalls and proxy servers. This can be a valuable aid in debugging complex network problems. Essentially, the TRACE method invokes a remote, application-layer loop-back of the request message. It reveals the request chain that the client's request travels through.

GET and POST

GET and POST will be briefly discussed later in this chapter as they relate to HTML forms. For more discussion of GET and POST, you should read the first section of the previous chapter.

A client's request method is the most important component of a client's request. The method identifies the nature of the request and sends information to the server regarding the purpose of the request and the type of response expected. Although it is a necessary component of a request, merely specifying a request method is not sufficient to invoke a request on the server. A Request URI and HTTP version number are also necessary since version 1.0. To understand this better, read the first section of the previous chapter, and then take a look at the source code for HttpGopher.java.

Two optional, but very powerful components of an HTTP request are the request headers and request parameters. We'll first take a look at request headers and then proceed to explore request parameters.

HTTP Request Headers

In taking a deeper look at the HTTP request paradigm, there is an immense amount of power and flexibility afforded by the use of HTTP request headers. Request headers allow a client to communicate a variety of information to the server that enhances the exchange with the server. The client can use request headers to inform the server what data formats the client can accept, to provide authorization information for access to secure web pages, to return a cookie to the server, and to specify information about the request itself, like the MIME type and size.

In the previous chapter we touched on this subject when we addressed the use of request headers in sending a POST request body. It is necessary to include a Content-Length header to communicate the size of the request body to the server. The If-Modified-Since header was also briefly mentioned. HTTP 1.1 defines over 20 HTTP request headers that an HTTP-compliant client can send. The table below provides a subset of those headers that we will be using in this chapter:

Header	Description
Accept	This header specifies the MIME types that the client is capable of handling. Your servlets can examine this header to determine if the client can handle XML-formatted data. If the client can, then the servlet can send an XML-formatted response.
Content-Length	Only applicable to POST requests, this header identifies the total number of bytes that constitute the POST data. Omitting this header will prevent the server from recognizing an attached request body.
Content-Type	Indicates the MIME type of the request body. This header is generally only useful as part of a POST request to indicate the MIME type of the attached document (request body) or when making PUT requests.
Host	Indicates the host and port of the client. This header was optional in HTTP 1.0, but is standard in HTTP 1.1.
If-Modified-Since	This is an extremely handy request header that is used in conjunction with a GET request. It allows the client to conditionally request data based upon when that data was last modified. We'll see more about this when we explore HTTP request queries.
User-Agent	This header identifies the browser or client making the request. All browsers send this header by default, and it would be a good idea to do the same with any custom client applications that you develop. It certain situations, this can allow for custom content-delivery depending on the specified value.

Handling HTTP Request Headers within a Servlet

Once again, the Java language has spared us the worries of low-level coding with the cleanly designed Java Servlets API that abstracts from the underlying protocol details. The `HttpServletRequest` interface of the `javax.servlet.http` package provides this abstraction. There are four core `public` methods for handling headers, and a handful of short-cut methods for some of the more commonly used request headers. The four main public methods are as follows:

`String getHeader(String name)`	This method returns the value of the named header from the request object, or `null` if the named header does not exist in the request.
`int getIntHeader(String name)`	This method returns the value of the named header provided that a valid integer value can be parsed out of the header value. It can throw a `NumberFormatException`.
`Enumeration getHeaderNames()`	Returns an enumeration of all the header names contained in the request.
`Enumeration getHeaders(String name)`	Returns an enumeration (possibly emtpy) of all the header values contained in the request.

There are also a handful of specialized short-cut methods designed to retrieve the values of some of the more commonly used request headers. These methods are actually inherited from the parent interface `ServletRequest`. Only two of these methods are interesting to us, however, and they are:

`int getContentLength()`	Returns the value of the `Content-Length` header as an integer, or 1 if one is not specified.
`String getContentType()`	Returns the value of the `Content-Type` header as a `String`, or `null` if it is not specified.

Armed with this knowledge, we are ready to take on an example. We'll use a servlet to reveal the typical request headers sent by commercial web browsers.

ShowHeaders Servlet Example

First, let's create a code base and a context for Tomcat. Edit Tomcat's `server.xml` file to add the following context:

```
<Context
    path="/projavaxml/chapter13/showheaders"
    docBase="C:/projavaxml/chapter13/webapps/showheaders"
    debug="1" reloadable="true">
</Context>
```

Create the directory webapps\showheaders\WEB-INF\classes and save the following file there:

```java
import java.io.*;
import javax.servlet.*;
import javax.servlet.http.*;
import java.util.*;

public class ShowHeaders extends HttpServlet {

  public void doGet(HttpServletRequest request,
                    HttpServletResponse response) throws ServletException,
                    IOException {
    PrintWriter out;
    Enumeration headerNames;
    String headerName;

    // Set MIME type for the response
    response.setContentType("text/html");

    // Create and obtain a reference to a print writer object
    out = response.getWriter();

    // Add content to the print writer's buffer
    out.println("<!DOCTYPE HTML PUBLIC \"-//W3C//DTD HTML 4.0"
             + "Transitional//EN\">");
    out.println("<HTML>");
    out.println("<HEAD><TITLE>Request Headers Example</TITLE></HEAD>");
    out.println("<BODY>");
    out.println("<H1 ALIGN=CENTER>Showing HTTP Request Headers</H1>");
    out.println("<BR>");
    out.println("<TABLE BORDER=1 ALIGN=CENTER>");
    out.println("<TR BGCOLOR=\"#CCCCCC\">");
    out.println("<TH>Header Name<TH>Header Value");

    // Retrieve the headers from the request object
    // and add them to the print writer's buffer
    headerNames = request.getHeaderNames();
    while (headerNames.hasMoreElements()) {
      headerName = (String) headerNames.nextElement();
      out.println("<TR><TD>" + headerName + "</TD>");
      out.println("<TD>" + request.getHeader(headerName) + "</TD></TR>");
    }

    // Close any open HTML tags
    out.println("</TABLE>");
    out.println("</BODY>");
    out.println("</HTML>");

    // Close the print writer to release those resources
    out.close();

  }

  public void doPost(HttpServletRequest request,
                     HttpServletResponse response) throws ServletException,
                     IOException {
    doGet(request, response);
  }
}
```

Now let's take a closer look at the key portion of the code:

```
headerNames = request.getHeaderNames();
while (headerNames.hasMoreElements()) {
  headerName = (String) headerNames.nextElement();
  out.println("<TR><TD>" + headerName + "</TD>");
  out.println("<TD>" + request.getHeader(headerName) + "</TD></TR>");
}
```

The code starts by retrieving an `Enumeration` of `String` objects with each object representing the name of a request header sent by the client. Request headers can be thought of as name/value pairs. For every request header name sent to the server, a corresponding value is contained within the request object. To access those values, we must iterate through every request header name and retrieve the corresponding value from the request object. In order to iterate through the enumeration of request header names, we can use the `nextElement()` and `hasMoreElements()` methods together.

> *An `Enumeration` allows you to iterate through its list of objects using the `nextElement()` method. The object maintains a marker representing the current location in the enumeration and each call to `nextElement()` advances the marker to the next record.*

The `hasMoreElements()` method returns a `boolean` primitive of `true` if there are more elements contained in the enumeration, or `false` if the end of the enumeration has been reached. By placing the `hasMoreElements()` method within a `while` loop, we are able to iterate through the enumeration, extracting each request header, and exit the loop when all headers have been processed.

Once we have the iteration loop built, then we need to actually process the request headers themselves. In addition to advancing the marker through the iteration, the `nextElement()` method returns the object contained in the next row. Since all enumeration elements are stored as members of the `Object` class, we will have to cast these elements to type `String` before referencing them with the `headerName` variable. Now that we have a header name, we can proceed to retrieve its corresponding value. To retrieve a request header value, we use the `HttpRequest getHeader()` method and supply it with the name of the request header. The request header name/value pairs are displayed together within an HTML table.

Deployment

Now create the deployment descriptor for the servlet at webapps\showheaders\WEB-INF\web.xml using the following code:

```xml
<?xml version="1.0" encoding="ISO-8859-1"?>
<!DOCTYPE web-app
    PUBLIC "-//Sun Microsystems, Inc.//DTD Web Application
    2.2//EN" "http://java.sun.com/j2ee/dtds/web-app_2.2dtd">

<web-app>
    <servlet>
        <servlet-name>Headers</servlet-name>
        <servlet-class>ShowHeaders</servlet-class>
    </servlet>
    <servlet-mapping>
        <servlet-name>
            Headers
        </servlet-name>
        <url-pattern>
            /headers
        </url-pattern>
    </servlet-mapping>
</web-app>
```

With those two files created, you are ready to compile the servlet and test it. If you need instructions on compiling servlets, see the previous chapter. Once the servlet has successfully compiled, you can test it by starting Tomcat and typing the following URL into your browser's address or location field: http://localhost:8080/projavaxml/chapter13/showheaders/headers. Your browser should display something like this:

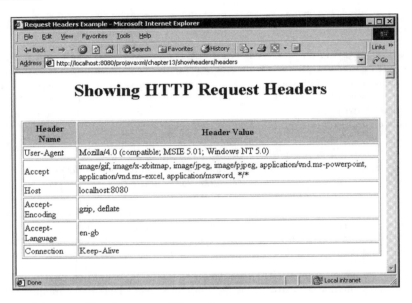

Analysing the ShowHeaders Servlet Example

Let's take a closer look at the headers displayed in this example. IE 5 sends three additional headers that are not mentioned in the list displayed earlier in this chapter. The first header is the Accept-Encoding header that communicates to the server that this client is capable of handling specially encoded data, such as data that has been gzip compressed. The second header, Accept-Language, informs the server of the language the response should be given in. And the third header, Connection, merely specifies that the client is requesting a persistent connection with the server.

Netscape 6 sends additionally the Keep-Alive attribute:

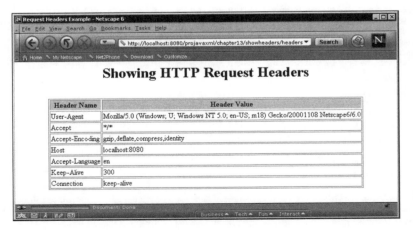

This gives you an idea of what headers are sent back by your web browser, but what does this mean for our own applications? There are two primary ramifications. The first is that our servlets will need to make use of this data when appropriate, and the second is that we should consider including these standard headers in any custom HTTP clients we write.

On the servlet side of things, the standard header that we will find most useful is the `Accept` header. This fundamentally communicates the limitations of the client to the server. Your servlet must produce a response that adheres to one of the specified formats (typically `text/html`, `text/xml`, or `text/wml`). The servlet should also set the `Content-Type` response header to inform the client as to which MIME type the response adheres to. We'll see an example of this later in the chapter.

On the client side of things, careful consideration should be given as to whether your custom client would benefit from sending any of these headers along with its HTTP requests. For our purposes we will send the following request headers: `User-Agent`, `Accept`, and `Host`. The following code snippets show the changes that must be made to the `HttpGopher` class in order to send these headers in every request made by the `HttpGopher` application.

First create a new static method inside your `HttpGopher.java` file:

```
private static void setDefaultHeaders( SocketConnection sc ) {
    sc.addRequestHeader( "User-Agent: Gopher/1.0" );
    sc.addRequestHeader( "Accept: text/html, text/plain, text/xml" );
    sc.addRequestHeader( "Host: " + sc.getHost() + ":" + sc.getPort() );
}
```

Then add a call to this method in each constructor before the `connect()` method is called on the `SocketConnection` object:

```
if ( requestLine.charAt(0) == 'P' || requestLine.charAt(0) == 'p' ){
    socketConn.setPost( true );
    if ( fileName != null )
        socketConn.setFile( fileName );
}
setDefaultHeaders( socketConn );
if ( socketConn.checkHost() ) socketConn.connect();
}
```

Testing the application is simple. Recompile `HttpGopher.java` and invoke the new class file. Enter valid values for each of the parameter requests and you should get a response similar to this one:

```
Command Prompt                                                              _ □ X

C:\projavaxml\chapter13>java HttpGopher
Host: localhost
Port: 8080
Request Method: POST
Request URL: /projavaxml/chapter13/showheaders/headers
HTTP Version 1.0 or 1.1? 1.0
Any Request Headers? n

Connecting to localhost ...
Response from host:

HTTP/1.0 200 OK
Content-Type: text/html
Servlet-Engine: Tomcat Web Server/3.2.1 (JSP 1.1; Servlet 2.2; Java 1.3.0rc3; Windows 2000 5.0 x86;
java.vendor=Sun Microsystems Inc.)

<!DOCTYPE HTML PUBLIC "-//W3C//DTD HTML 4.0Transitional//EN">
<HTML>
<HEAD><TITLE>Request Headers Example</TITLE></HEAD>
<BODY>
<H1 ALIGN=CENTER>Showing HTIP Request Headers</H1>
<BR>
<TABLE BORDER=1 ALIGN=CENTER>
<TR BGCOLOR="#CCCCCC">
<TH>Header Name<TH>Header Value
<TR><TD>User-Agent</TD>
<TD>Gopher/1.0</TD></TR>
<TR><TD>Accept</TD>

Press Return...

<TD>text/html, text/plain, text/xml</TD></TR>
<TR><TD>Host</TD>
<TD>localhost:8080</TD></TR>
</TABLE>
</BODY>
</HTML>

C:\projavaxml\chapter13>_
```

So what have we gained by doing this? First of all, we have given our custom client a unique identifier with the User-Agent header. We can now write custom code into any of our servlets that will cause them to respond in a specialized way whenever an HttpGopher client requests data from the servlet. This opens up a wealth of opportunities for us. If our web resources were capable of responding to requests from browsers and a variety of custom HTTP clients, then it would be very beneficial to be able to distinguish those that provide specialized services.

For example, imagine that we modify the HttpGopher client so that it can receive XHTML text, parse out the tags and only reveal the content contained within the XML tree. Our servlet could examine the User-Agent header and serve up plain XHTML with no images. For another client, our servlet might send standard HTML with images, or perhaps just plain text.

This is not, however predictable with respect to commercial browsers. We've already discussed the usefulness of the Accept-Header, and the Host header is merely a courtesy, as this information can sometimes be difficult to find given the frequent use of request forwarding, and the fact that some machines have multiple hostnames.

Now that you've been exposed to some of the more common request headers and you've had a taste of how and why you they should be handled within your servlets, it's time to explore another aspect of the HTTP request architecture, request parameters.

Sending HTTP Request Parameters

As we have seen in the previous chapter, the GET request method will access a specified resource and return some sort of textual response. While this is handy, we often desire greater control over the specifics of our requests. For example, when you are using a search engine on the web and you are looking for information on Java programming, would you generally prefer that the search engine return a list of 10,000 loosely related items, or a few dozen closely related ones?

It is obvious that most of the time we would prefer fewer items that more closely matched specifically with what we are searching for. So how do we accomplish this feat? Very simply, we pass a list of specific search terms to the search engine and those values are used in collecting a list of potential matches. The way that HTTP accomplishes this task is through the use of HTTP request parameters.

In the world of HTTP, a parameter is essentially a named entity that carries a corresponding value. By default, that value is an empty string "". Since HTTP transmits everything through a character array, all parameters are of type String. You've likely seen a list of parameter name/value pairs before in a web address:

http://www.somewhere.com/serverprogram?id=567&name=value&something=xyz

This will pass the parameters id, name, and something, with their respective values to the server to be processed. There are two special characters that you should take note of in this URL. The first is the question mark ?. This character indicates to the web server that you are going to pass one or more parameters to the specified server resource. Parameter name/value pairs are recognized by a very simple pattern: paramName=value. The first parameter name/value pair appears directly after the ? and any additional parameters are separated by the & characters. As you can see from the above example, the id parameter and its value of 567 appears directly after the ? and the other two parameters are appended by using the & character.

GET vs. POST

Parameters are transmitted differently depending on which request method you are using. This was discussed in detail in the previous chapter under the heading "*GET vs. POST*". As a quick recap, parameters are only appended to the URL when a GET request is issued (like the example above). The POST request encodes the parameters inside the request body.

To experiment with sending parameters to a servlet, we could modify the HttpGopher application to also handle the passing of HTTP parameters, but there is a much easier and more commonly used solution available to us. HTTP parameters are created and passed to the server whenever an HTML form is used.

This brings us to the logical question – how do we handle HTTP parameters within a servlet?

Handling HTTP Request Parameters within a Servlet

The `ServletRequest` API (which is also inherited by the `HttpServletRequest` API) makes handling HTTP parameters in your servlets very simple. The API provides three methods to aid you in handling HTTP parameters:

`String getParameter(String key)`	If the request object contains the parameter specified by the given key (case-sensitive), then that value is returned as a `String` object. If the key is not found, then the method returns `null`.
`String[] getParameterValues(String key)`	Some HTML input elements, like a multi-selection list or a group of check boxes, can return multiple values for the same parameter name. When provided with a valid key, this method will return a `String` array of those values.
`Enumeration getParameterNames()`	This method returns an enumeration of all the parameter names contained in the request object. If there are no parameters, then an empty enumeration is returned.

The API provides two ways of accessing parameter data. You must either know the parameter names, or you can retrieve an `Enumeration` object containing the parameter names and iterate through that list.

One of the nice things about the API, is that you don't mind which request method a form uses; these method calls stay exactly the same. Whether you use them in the servlet's `doGet()` or `doPost()` method you use the same method signature in exactly the same way to access the parameters contained in the request object. To solidify your understanding of how these methods work, let's try a simple example.

FormHandler Servlet Example

Begin by creating a Java class `FormHandler.java` in `webapps\WEB-INF\formhandler\classes`. Here is the complete source code for `FormHandler`:

```java
import javax.servlet.*;
import javax.servlet.http.*;
import java.util.*;
import java.io.*;

public class FormHandler extends HttpServlet {

  public void doGet(HttpServletRequest request, HttpServletResponse response)
      throws ServletException, IOException {

    // Set MIME type for the response
    response.setContentType("text/html");

    // Create and obtain a reference to a print writer object
    PrintWriter out = response.getWriter();
```

```java
      // Add content to the print writer's buffer
      out.println("<!DOCTYPE HTML PUBLIC \"-//W3C//DTD HTML 4.0 "
              + "Transitional//EN\">");
      out.println("<HTML>");
      out.println("<HEAD><TITLE>FormHandler Example</TITLE></HEAD>");
      out.println("<BODY>");
      printParams(out, request);
      out.println("</BODY>");
      out.println("</HTML>");

      // Close the print writer to release those resources
      out.close();

  }


  public void doPost(HttpServletRequest request,
                     HttpServletResponse response) throws ServletException,
                     IOException {

    // Set MIME type for the response
    response.setContentType("text/html");

    // Create and obtain a reference to a print writer object
    PrintWriter out = response.getWriter();

    // Add content to the print writer's buffer
    out.println("<!DOCTYPE HTML PUBLIC \"-//W3C//DTD HTML 4.0 "
            + "Transitional//EN\">");
    out.println("<HTML>");
    out.println("<HEAD><TITLE>FormHandler Example</TITLE></HEAD>");
    out.println("<BODY>");
    printParams(out, request);
    out.println("</BODY>");
    out.println("</HTML>");

    // Close the print writer to release those resources
    out.close();

  }


  private static void printParams(PrintWriter pw, HttpServletRequest req)
          throws ServletException, IOException {
    Enumeration keys = req.getParameterNames();
    String key;
    while (keys.hasMoreElements()) {
      key = (String) keys.nextElement();
      pw.println("<b>Name:</b> " + key + "   <b>Value:</b> "
                  + req.getParameter(key) + "<br>");
    }
  }
}
```

Does the above code look familiar? It should. We created an almost identical `while()` loop when we wrote the `ShowHeaders` servlet earlier on. This is because the Java API considers reusable patterns to be one of the greatest goods. The Servlet API defines several methods which all return an `Enumeration` object to represent a list of related data: `getParameterNames()`, `getParameterValues()`, `getHeaderNames()`, `getHeaderValues()`, and `getInitParameters()` to name a few. Just as we did in the `ShowHeaders` servlet with request headers, this method retrieves an `Enumeration` of all the parameters contained in the servlet, iterates through them using the `nextElement()` method, retrieves the value with a call to `getParameter()`, and exits the loop when `hasMoreElements()` returns `false`.

One more thing to note about the `FormHandler` servlet, is that the `doPost()` method forwards the request to the `doGet()` method. Although you've seen this before, none of the servlets we've developed so far have been built to handle request parameters. Considering the fact that parameters sent via GET requests and those sent via POST requests are transmitted in such different ways, how can we treat them the same? The answer lies in the abstraction provided by the Servlet API, in particular the `ServletRequest` interface.

When a request is forwarded to the web container, then the container processes the request by creating a request object that implements the `HttpServletRequest` interface. That object contains all the relevant information contained within the client's request, such as the request method, headers, parameters, and the request body (in the case of a POST request with an attached request body). So although the container must retrieve this information in different ways (depending on the request method used by the client), the container creates the same object type regardless of the method used. This provides a common interface to access request properties that is not tied to a client's request method.

Now create the `web.xml` file in `webapps\formhandler\WEB-INF\`:

```xml
<?xml version="1.0" encoding="ISO-8859-1"?>
<!DOCTYPE web-app
    PUBLIC "-//Sun Microsystems, Inc.//DTD Web Application
    2.2//EN" "http://java.sun.com/j2ee/dtds/web-app_2.2dtd">

<web-app>
    <servlet>
        <servlet-name>FormHandler</servlet-name>
        <servlet-class>FormHandler</servlet-class>
    </servlet>
    <servlet-mapping>
        <servlet-name>
            FormHandler
        </servlet-name>
        <url-pattern>
            /formhandler
        </url-pattern>
    </servlet-mapping>

</web-app>
```

Add a new context to Tomcat's `server.xml`:

```
<Context
   path="/projavaxml/chapter13/formhandler"
   docBase="C:/projavaxml/chapter13/webapps/formhandler"
   debug="1"
   reloadable="true">
</Context>
```

Compile the servlet in the `webapps\formhandler\WEB-INF\classes` directory. Next, you'll need to create an HTML file named `testForm.html` and save it in `webapps\formhandler`:

```html
<!DOCTYPE HTML PUBLIC "-//W3C//DTD HTML 4.0 Transitional//EN">
<HTML>
<HEAD>
<TITLE>Test Form for Servlet</TITLE>
</HEAD>
<BODY>

<form name= "myForm" method="GET"
   action="formhandler">
  <table width="50%" border="0">
    <tr>
      <td width="41%"><b>First Name</b></td>
      <td width="59%"><input type="text" name="firstName"></td>
    </tr>
    <tr>
      <td width="41%"><b>Last Name</b></td>
      <td width="59%"><input type="text" name="lastName"></td>
    </tr>
    <tr>
      <td width="41%"><b>City</b></td>
      <td width="59%"><input type="text" name="city"></td>
    </tr>
    <tr>
      <td width="41%"><b>State/Province</b></td>
      <td width="59%"><input type="text" name="stateProv"></td>
    </tr>
    <tr>
      <td width="41%"><b>Country</b></td>
      <td width="59%"><input type="text" name="country"></td>
    </tr>
    <tr>
      <td width="41%"><b>E-mail</b></td>
      <td width="59%"><input type="text" name="email"></td>
    </tr>
    <tr>
      <td width="41%"><b> How did you hear about us? </b></td>
      <td width="59%">
        <select name="marketing" size="1">
          <option value="-1">Please select one</option>
          <option value="1">Sun's website</option>
          <option value="2">A friend</option>
          <option value="3">Search engine</option>
```

```
            <option value="4">Other</option>
          </select>
        </td>
      </tr>
      <tr>
        <td width="41%" align="right"> </td>
        <td width="59%">
          <input type="submit" name="Submit" value="Sign-up">
          <input type="reset" name="clear" value="Clear Form">
        </td>
      </tr>
    </table>
  </form>

</BODY>
</HTML>
```

Finally you're ready to test the servlet. Start up Tomcat and open a web browser. Enter the following URL into your browser's address or location field:

http://localhost:8080/projavaxml/chapter13/formhandler/testForm.html

Your browser should look something like this:

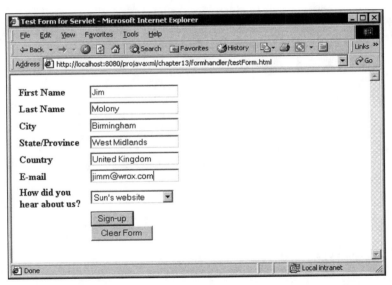

Next you need to fill out the form fields and press the **Sign-Up** button (clicking this button will submit the form to the servlet). The browser will then take the data you entered, attach it to the parameter names specified by the HTML form and send the name/value pairs to the servlet by appending them to the URL. If the method specified by the form was POST instead of GET, then the name/value pairs would be encapsulated in the request body. Either way, the method calls to extract the data go unchanged. So the servlet retrieves the data from the request object and sends back a response similar to the one below:

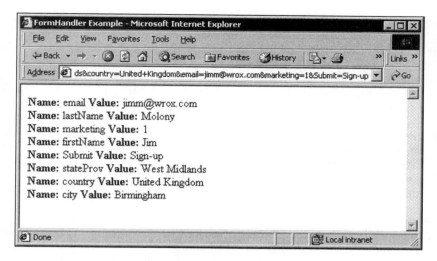

You've successfully handled HTML form data within a Java servlet. Parameters are a tremendous tool, and a very commonly used means of transmitting data within a web application. You've probably worked with them before, but now you have a true understanding of what they are and how to use them within your Java servlets.

If you like, you can even test this out with the `HttpGopher` utility. When you are prompted for the request URL, follow the servlet name, `formhandler`, with a question mark and a parameter and value (`formhandler?name=Elizabeth`). You can append additional parameters by using an `&`. The servlet should return an HTML formatted table of all the request parameters and their values, just as it did when you used the HTML form and sent the request through the browser.

A Closer Look at Query Strings

Although the query string and the request entity body perform identically when processing an HTML form, both of them have significant differences that yield diverse and powerful functionality. In the previous chapter we explored some of the possibilities available when using a request entity body when we read in the contents of an XML document and sent them to the server as a request entity body. Now we're going to take some time to explore the possibilities available to us via the query string.

By convention, the query string is used to send parameters to the server with the pattern: `?param1=value1&param2=value2`. This is a perfectly acceptable use of the query string, but it is also a very limited one. The query string is simply any data after a question mark, following the name of a server-side resource. It is the tail end of a full URL, a string that identifies the location of a resource, and it identifies the precise resource the client is requesting.

For instance, http://www.somewhere.com/catalog?2345 is a perfectly valid way of asking `catalog` to provide you with item 2345. Likewise, http://www.somewhere.com/search?query=banana is no different, the query string is requesting the resource containing the search engine's results for the query banana. It just happens that this query is also in a format that can easily be generated with an HTML form using the GET request method.

So if a query string can simply append an integer like 2345 to the end of a URL, how can we handle this sort of request from within a servlet? The answer is much simpler than you might think. The Servlet API would treat the previous query string ?2345 as a parameter with a null value, just as if the query string had read ?2345= with no value following the equal sign. Within the context of your servlet, this will result in an HTTP parameter named 2345, which contains the value null. Your servlet can simply check for the first parameter, ignore the value, parse the parameter name into an integer, and then proceed to retrieve item 2345 (perhaps from a database or flat file).

Yet another application of this is an XML-oriented one, specifically using XPointer. Imagine that you have a servlet that returns search results as an XML document. Each of the items returned in the results list would naturally contain a URL pointing to the location of that resource. The URL's query string could contain XPointer notation that looked something like search?query=bananas#xpointer(/result[1]), and an XPointer client could extract the specific resources you were looking for.

The list of possibilities could go on and on; no doubt you are already thinking of additional ways to use the query string portion of a URL. The key here is to understand that a query string's capabilities extend far beyond simply taking a list of parameter name/value pairs generated by an HTML form and sending them to the server. The query string is a powerful tool in a web developer's bag of tricks, and it is unfortunate that both it and the request entity body are often marginalized and used only to process HTML forms.

Before you are ready to tackle the full client-server XML messaging application at the end of the chapter, you should get a little more experience under your belt. The next section contains a client-server example that uses several HTTP request queries.

HTTP Request Queries

Now it's time to hone your understanding of the HTTP Request/Response paradigm and make more use of the Servlet API. We'll look at three complete examples that address some of the most common types of queries that web applications are expected to handle. Some of the material will be straightforward, as we have already covered it previously, but some of it will be new. Where new concepts or techniques are used, appropriate descriptions and explanations will be provided.

The following client-server applications will be presented in this section:

❑ Parameter.java
The browser client passes form data to a servlet. The servlet then returns a list of hyperlinks with parameters appended to the URLs. Clicking a link will send a request to the server and a custom message will be returned to the client via the response object.

❑ Parameter2.java
The client issues a conditional GET request on the servlet, only wanting new content if it has been modified since a certain date. The server sends back data based upon the condition set by the client request.

Parameter Servlet Example

This example will involve sending parameters both via a GET request and via a POST request. Two servlets will be used to handle the exchange with the client. The figure describes how the communication between client and server will flow:

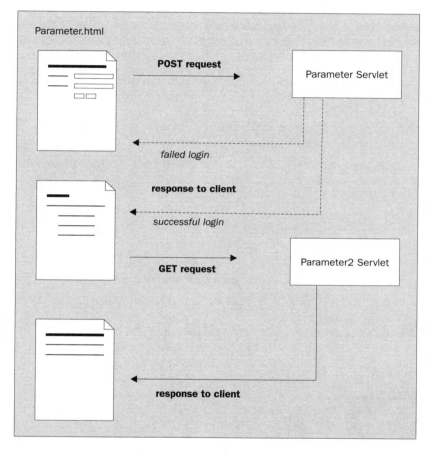

The application will begin with an HTML page parameter.html. This page will contain a form with two fields, username and password. The user will fill these fields out and click a button to submit the form via a POST request. The form will then be handled by a servlet Parameter.java, which will validate the user input. If the user has entered a valid user name and password, then the servlet will send an HTML response back to the client containing three hyperlinks, each with appended parameters. When the user clicks on one of the links, then a second servlet Parameter2.java is called to handle that request and process the parameters sent via the GET request.

The application contains a total of four files: one HTML file, two servlets, and the deployment descriptor. We'll build each component as it appears in the application. The HTML file is first.

The parameter.html Page

This is a very simple page with a very basic HTML form. It is very important to notice that this form uses the POST request method. The form will be transmitting sensitive information (username and password). If the form transmits this data via a GET request, then those parameter values will be appended to the URL. This leaves the username and password of the user clearly visible to all. This information might even be visible by calling up the browser's "History" feature. Sensitive data should always be transmitted via a POST request rather than a GET. Having said that, POST requests are still sent as a stream of characters and they can be "sniffed" by even novice hackers. Therefore, this method should not be used for truly secure data transfer, which requires encryption.

Create a file called parameter.html in the directory webapps\parameter. Enter the following HTML code into the body of that file:

```
<!DOCTYPE HTML PUBLIC "-//W3C//DTD HTML 4.0 Transitional//EN">
<HTML>
<HEAD>
<TITLE>Parameter Tester</TITLE>
</HEAD>
<BODY>
<H1>Servlet Login Via a POST request</H1>

<FORM action="login" method="POST">
<TABLE>
   <TR>
      <TD><B>User Name</B></TD>
      <TD><INPUT type="text" name="name"></INPUT></TD>
   </TR>
   <TR>
      <TD><B>Password</B></TD>
      <TD><INPUT type="password" name="pass"></INPUT></TD>
   </TR>
   <TR>
      <TD></TD>
      <TD><INPUT type="submit" value=" Login "></INPUT>
          <INPUT type="reset" value=" Clear "></INPUT></TD>
   </TR>
</TABLE>
</FORM>

</BODY>
</HTML>
```

Once you have this saved as parameter.html in the directory specified above, then you're ready to move on to the next component. The action of this HTML form is the name login. As we will soon see, there isn't a servlet named login. Instead, there is a Parameter servlet with an alias of login specified in the deployment descriptor.

The Parameter Class

This is the servlet that will handle the form submission made by `parameter.html`. Create a file called `Parameter.java` in the `webapps\parameter\WEB-INF\classes` directory:

```java
import javax.servlet.*;
import javax.servlet.http.*;
import java.util.*;
import java.io.*;

public class Parameter extends HttpServlet {

    // Default Constants
    private static final String DEFAULT_USERNAME = "Donald Duck";
    private static final String DEFAULT_PASSWORD = "quack";

    // Init parameter names
    private static final String PARAM_USERNAME = "name";
    private static final String PARAM_PASSWORD = "pass";

    // Local variables
    private String userName;
    private String password;
```

The default values and parameter names are defined here as constants to make maintaining code as painless as process. If the default values change or one of the parameter names should change, then there is only one place you have to go to make the change – the top of the code.

Clearly in a production environment, we would not want to hard code our username and password, as every time they changed we would be forced to recompile the code. Also, some unscrupulous individual who gained access to the class file could use a decompiler to reconstruct the original source code and discover the username and password. These values are merely provided here as default values. You will want to override these values, especially in a production environment. In just a moment, we will see one way of overriding them, by declaring new values in the deployment descriptor.

Initialize the Servlet

This servlet's primary function is to validate a username and password combination. Rather than relying on hard-coded default values for this validation, the `init()` method will retrieve the values specified in the application's deployment descriptor `web.xml`:

```java
public void init(ServletConfig config) throws ServletException {

    // Always call super.init()
    super.init(config);

    // Retrieve parameters from web.xml
    userName = config.getInitParameter(PARAM_USERNAME);
    password = config.getInitParameter(PARAM_PASSWORD);

    // Use default values if none were specified
    if (userName == null) {
      userName = DEFAULT_USERNAME;
    }
    if (password == null) {
      password = DEFAULT_PASSWORD;
    }

  }
}
```

The `init()` method will scan the `web.xml` file located in the application's `WEB-INF` directory to see if there are any parameters that match the ones specified by the two `getInitParameter()` calls. If there are none, then a `null` string will be returned. The `if` statement will catch this case and set the variables with the default values defined earlier.

Again, understand that this level of security is the sort you might use on a closed network, small company extranet, or any other web-based application requiring a moderate level of security. It should not be used to protect sensitive data such as social security numbers, credit card numbers, or any kind of financial or very private personal information. This sort of data requires a more secure connection such as SSL and the use of encrypted passwords stored in a secure database.

Extract the Form Data

When the user clicks the Submit button, the browser will package up the data entered in the two text fields, encapsulate that information in the request body of a `POST`, and send the request to the server. The web container will then transfer control to the `Parameter` servlet. In order for the servlet to extract the data entered in the form, two `getParameter()` calls must be made. For this class, those calls have been placed within the `checkAccess()` method, which is called from the servlet's `doPost()` method:

```
public boolean checkAccess(HttpServletRequest req)
        throws ServletException {
  if (userName.equals(req.getParameter(PARAM_USERNAME))
        && password.equals(req.getParameter(PARAM_PASSWORD))) {
    return true;
  } else {
    return false;
  }
}
```

This method takes the username and password sent by the client and compares them to the name and password values that were set during the servlet initialization. If they match, then the method returns `true`, otherwise, the method returns `false` and the login fails.

Process the Request

This is the core of the `Parameter` servlet, the `doPost()` method. As previously mentioned, this servlet will only accept `POST` requests, as a `GET` request would create a potential security breach. This method looks very much like our other `doGet()` and `doPost()` methods:

```
public void doPost(HttpServletRequest request, HttpServletResponse response)
      throws ServletException, IOException {
  PrintWriter out;

  // Set MIME type for the response
  response.setContentType("text/html");

  // Create and obtain a reference to a print writer object
  out = response.getWriter();

  // Add content to the print writer's buffer
  out.println("<!DOCTYPE HTML PUBLIC \"-//W3C//DTD HTML 4.0 "
            + "Transitional//EN\">");
  out.println("<HTML>");
  out.println("<HEAD><TITLE>Parameter Example</TITLE></HEAD>");
  out.println("<BODY>");
```

```
            // Check the parameter values sent by the client
            if (checkAccess(request)) {
              out.println("<H1><font color=\"green\">"
                          + "Login Successful!</font></H1>");
              out.println("<H4>  Please select a link to pass"
                          + " parameters to the servlet:</H4>");
              out.println("<BR><UL>");
              out.println("<LI><A HREF=\"styleservlet?color=blue&font=Arial\">"
                          + "A blue background and Arial font</A></LI>");
              out.println("<LI><A HREF=\"styleservlet?color=red&font=Courier\">"
                          + "A red background and Courier font</A></LI>");
              out.println("<LI><A HREF=\"styleservlet?color=green&font=Times\">"
                          + "A green background and Times font</A></LI>");
              out.println("</UL>");
            } else {
              out.println("<H1><font color=\"red\">" + "Login Failed!</font></H1>");
              out.println("<BR>");
              out
                .println("Click <A HREF=\"parameter.html\">here</A> to try again.");
            }   // end if ( checkAccess( request ) )

            // Close any open tags
            out.println("</BODY>");
            out.println("</HTML>");

            // Close the print writer to release those resources
            out.close();
          }
        }
```

After creating the standard HTML output that is used with every servlet response, this method branches off by way of an `if` statement. The `checkAccess()` method is called, and the output sent to the browser is determined based upon whether or not the username and password sent by the client match the values set in the `init()` method. If they do not match, then the client receives an error message and a link to return to the HTML form. If they do match, then the browser displays three hyperlinks that each have parameters appended to the URL's. These hyperlinks all access the same resource, a servlet with a URL `styleservlet` as an alias for the `Parameter2` class. We'll build that servlet now.

The Parameter2 Class

This is the servlet that will handle the GET request made by one of the three hyperlinks sent to the browser by the `Parameter` servlet. We'll start in the usual way by creating the source code beginning with the class outline. Create a file called `Parameter2.java` in the same directory as `Parameter.java`:

The outline of the `Parameter2` class is as follows:

```
import java.io.*;
import java.util.*;
import javax.servlet.*;
import javax.servlet.http.*;

public class Parameter2 extends HttpServlet {

  // Constant values that correspond to request parameter names
  private final static String PARAM_COLOR = "color";
  private final static String PARAM_FONT = "font";
```

The two `String` constants correspond to the names of the two parameters that will be passed by the client. Each of the hyperlinks sent to the client by the `Parameter` servlet contains a `color` parameter and a `font` parameter appended to the URL. When the user clicks one of the links, then the `Parameter2` servlet is called and passed these values. The servlet will then output a page using the specified background color and type font.

Process the Request

This servlet defines only one method, `doGet()`:

```
public void doGet(HttpServletRequest request, HttpServletResponse response)
        throws ServletException, IOException {
    PrintWriter out;

    // Set MIME type for the response
    response.setContentType("text/html");

    // Create and obtain a reference to a print writer object
    out = response.getWriter();

    // Add content to the print writer's buffer
    out.println("<!DOCTYPE HTML PUBLIC \"-//W3C//DTD HTML 4.0"
            + "Transitional//EN\">");
    out.println("<HTML>");
    out.println("<HEAD><TITLE>2nd Parameter Example</TITLE></HEAD>");
    out.println("<BODY BGCOLOR=\"" + request.getParameter(PARAM_COLOR)
            + "\">");
    out.println("<FONT FACE=\"" + request.getParameter(PARAM_FONT) + "\">");
    out.println("<BR>");
    out.println("<H2>Congratulations!</H2>");
    out.println("<P><FONT SIZE=\"+2\">");
    out.println("You have successfully submitted a GET request with"
            + " parameters appended to the query string."
            + " Try pressing your browser's back button and"
            + " selecting a different link.");

    // Close any open HTML tags
    out.println("</FONT>");
    out.println("</P>");
    out.println("</FONT>");
    out.println("</BODY>");
    out.println("</HTML>");

    // Close the print writer to release those resources
    out.close();
    }
}
```

This method extracts the value for the `color` parameter and uses that to set the `BGCOLOR` attribute of the `<BODY>` tag, and then extracts the value for the `font` parameter and uses that to set the font for the entire page's text by wrapping it with a `<FONT>` tag.

Compile the Servlets

Once you finish entering the code for these two servlets, compile the class files. With those class files successfully compiled, you are ready to create the deployment descriptor `webapps\parameter\WEB-INF\web.xml`.

The web.xml Descriptor

The deployment descriptor is important because the values it specifies will establish the username and password that the servlet will recognize.

Create your web.xml as follows

```
<?xml version="1.0" encoding="ISO-8859-1"?>
<!DOCTYPE web-app
    PUBLIC "-//Sun Microsystems, Inc.//DTD Web Application
    2.2//EN" "http://java.sun.com/j2ee/dtds/web-app_2.2dtd">

<web-app>
    <servlet>
        <servlet-name>Login</servlet-name>
        <servlet-class>Parameter</servlet-class>
        <init-param>
            <param-name>name</param-name>
            <param-value>ProJava</param-value>
        </init-param>
        <init-param>
            <param-name>pass</param-name>
            <param-value>August</param-value>
        </init-param>
    </servlet>
    <servlet-mapping>
        <servlet-name>Login</servlet-name>
        <url-pattern>/login</url-pattern>
    </servlet-mapping>

    <servlet>
        <servlet-name>StyleServlet</servlet-name>
        <servlet-class>Parameter2</servlet-class>
     </servlet>
    <servlet-mapping>
        <servlet-name>StyleServlet</servlet-name>
        <url-pattern>/styleservlet</url-pattern>
    </servlet-mapping>

</web-app>
```

Note how we've used servlet-mapping directives to rename our servlets login and styleservlet relative to our base URL. You can opt not to include the two initialization parameters. In their absence, the Parameter servlet will use the default values defined at the beginning of the class file definition.

Now add a new context into the Tomcat server.xml file:

```
<Context
    path="/projavaxml/chapter13/parameter"
    docBase="C:/projavaxml/chapter13/webapps/parameter"
    debug="1"
    reloadable="true">
</Context>
```

That completes the application code. Now it's time to see it in action.

Testing the Parameter Servlet Application

If you've built all four of the files correctly, then the testing process guides itself. Here's a quick checklist before we test the application. Make sure you have:

- ❑ Created `parameter.html` and stored the file at the base of your web application directory
- ❑ Successfully compiled `Parameter.java` and `Parameter2.java` into the directory `WEB-INF\classes`
- ❑ Created the deployment descriptor `WEB-INF\web.xml`
- ❑ Updated `servlet.xml`

If you missed one of those, simply refer to the directions above; otherwise you're ready to test the application. Start up your web server, if it isn't already running, open a web browser and enter the URL http://localhost:8080/projavaxml/chapter13/parameter/parameter.html, and fill in the form with some erroneous username and password:

Upon submitting this form, your browser should generate an error page similar to this one:

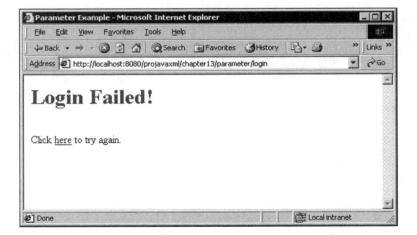

Now try it again with the correct username and password that you specified in the deployment descriptor. If you chose not to include these parameters in the descriptor, then use the default values specified in the `Parameter.java` source code. This time, you should see a screen similar to this one:

If you have difficulty logging in, remember that servlet parameters are case sensitive. Make sure that the data you are entering matches the case of the specified values exactly.

You should now be prompted by your browser to select a link. Selecting one will send a GET request to the `styleservlet` servlet along with the appended parameters. These parameters will be used to render a different style to the response for each link. Try each of them to see how the results change.

Conditional GET Request Example

The HTTP/1.1 specification describes an interesting feature available to GET requests. A request header can be specified that will inform the server to send back a content body in the response only if that body has been modified since the date specified by the request header. That header is the `If-Modified-Since` header, and the request is called a conditional GET request, because it is conditional on the server possessing a more recent copy of the resource.

The Servlets API provides for this feature with a method called `getLastModified()`, defined in the `HttpServlet` class, which returns a long representing the time the resource was last modified measured in milliseconds since January 1, 1970 00:00:00 GMT. The classic implementation of this useful caching feature is for the servlet to set a variable with a timestamp during initialization and to return that value whenever the `getLastModified()` method is called. Since initialization would not occur again until the servlet was reloaded by the server (through reloading, or a server restart) this would accurately reflect the last time the servlet was modified.

Another way to implement a conditional GET request is to pass a filename as a parameter appended to the query string and to return the modification date of the specified file housed on the server. It is this second implementation that we will explore in this next example.

In this example, our custom client application, HttpGopher, will send a conditional GET request to the server along with a file name parameter appended to the URI. If the requested file is a valid one, then the servlet will return the date that the specified file was last modified. At this point, the web server will take over and compare the date specified in the request header with the date returned by the getLastModified() method. If the date returned by the servlet is newer, then the web server will call the servlet's doGet() method to reprocess the request. Otherwise, the server will send back a 304 status code Not Modified. Typically, a browser would know to display the cached version of the page. In our example, the HttpGopher application will merely displayed the status code returned by the server.

The application contains a total of three files: a servlet, the deployment descriptor, and a simple text file to test the application with. We'll start off with the servlet.

The RecentPage Class

This servlet should be saved in a file called RecentPage.java in the webapps\conditional\WEB-INF\classes directory. As usual, we'll start with the class and data member definitions:

```
import java.io.*;
import java.util.*;
import javax.servlet.*;
import javax.servlet.http.*;

public class RecentPage extends HttpServlet {

  private final static String PARAM_FILENAME = "fileName";
  private final static String DIRECTORY =
    "c:\\projavaxml\\chapter13\\webapps\\conditional";

  private File fileObj;
```

This should all be pretty self-explanatory. The first constant is the parameter name that will be passed by the client. The second constant is the directory on the server where the servlet will look for files. And the third member is not a constant, but is merely an instance variable of type File. We'll see how this is used in just a moment.

Process the Request

Since we're talking about a conditional GET request, it's only logical that we would need a doGet() method to handle client requests. Here is the code for that method:

```
public void doGet(HttpServletRequest request, HttpServletResponse response)
    throws ServletException, IOException {
  PrintWriter out;
  String fileName, type;

  // Create and obtain a reference to a PrintWriter object
  out = response.getWriter();

  fileName = request.getParameter(PARAM_FILENAME);
  fileObj = new File(DIRECTORY, fileName);

  if (fileName != null && fileObj.exists()) {
    type = getType(fileObj);
```

```
        if (type == null) {

          // Set the MIME type for the response
          response.setContentType("text/html");

          // Print the standard HTML header info
          printHtmlHeaders(out, "Client Request Error");

          // Begin content for the response body
          out.println("<BODY>");
          out.println("<H1>Invalid Request</H1>");
          out.println("   Specified file was an invalid type.");
          out.println("<BR>");
          out.println("<B>Specified File: </B>" + fileName);
          out.println("<BR>");
          out.println("<B>Valid File Types: </B>");
          out.println("<UL><LI>.txt</LI>");
          out.println("     <LI>.htm or .html</LI>");
          out.println("     <LI>.xml</LI></UL>");

          // Close any open HTML tags
          out.println("</BODY>");
          out.println("</HTML>");

        } else {
          BufferedReader buff;
          String line;

          buff = new BufferedReader(new FileReader(fileObj));

          // Set MIME type for the response
          response.setContentType(type);

          // Send the file to the PrintWriter's buffer
          while ((line = buff.readLine()) != null) {
            out.println(line);
          }

          // Close the BufferedReader
          buff.close();

        }
      } else {

      // Set the MIME type for the response
      response.setContentType("text/html");

      // Print the standard HTML header info
      printHtmlHeaders(out, "Client Request Error");

      // Begin content for the response body
      out.println("<BODY>");
      out.println("<H1>Invalid Request</H1>");
      out.println("<B>The requested resource expects "
                  + "a valid file name parameter.</B>");
```

```
    out.println("<FONT color=\"blue\">You requested the "
            + "following file: " + fileName + "</FONT>");
    out.println("<BR>");
    out.println("   Your request either did not contain "
            + "a file name parameter, ");
    out.println("   or the file name you specified does not exist.");

    // Close any open HTML tags
    out.println("</BODY>");
    out.println("</HTML>");

}
// Close the print writer to release those resources
out.close();
}
```

The logic in this method branches off several times. The first branch checks to be sure that the user has sent a `fileName` parameter and that the specified file exists. If either of these conditions is not met, then the client sent an error message. The next branch is after the file's extension is checked against the known list of extensions that the servlet has been designed to handle. If the extension is invalid, then the servlet replies with an error message and a listing of the acceptable file types. Finally, if a `fileName` parameter has been passed that refers to a valid file on the server and that file is of a type supported by the servlet, then the contents of that file are returned to the client through the output stream.

Determine the File Type

This class contains two helper methods that are called from within `doGet()`. The first is the `getType()` method:

```
private String getType(File fobj) throws IOException {
    String ext, type;

    // Retrieve the file extension from the specified file object
    ext = fobj.getName().substring((fobj.getName()).lastIndexOf('.'));

    // Translate that extension into a valid ContentType
    if (ext.equals(".htm") || ext.equals(".html")) {
      type = "text/html";
    } else if (ext.equals(".txt")) {
      type = "text/plain";
    } else if (ext.equals(".xml")) {
      type = "text/xml";
    } else {
      type = null;
    }

    return type;
}
```

This method parses out the extension for the specified file, compares it against a predefined list of acceptable values and then either returns the corresponding MIME type, or `null` to indicate that the extension is not found in the list.

Format the Response

Due to the various branches contained in the doGet() method, three different responses could potentially be sent back to the client. In an effort to avoid repetitious code, this very simple helper method has been added to print the top portion of the HTML that is the same for every response:

```
private void printHtmlHeaders(PrintWriter pw, String title)
    throws IOException {

    // Add content to the print writer's buffer
    pw.println("<!DOCTYPE HTML PUBLIC \"-//W3C//DTD HTML 4.0"
             + "Transitional//EN\">");
    pw.println("<HTML>");
    pw.println("<HEAD><TITLE>" + title + "</TITLE></HEAD>");
}
```

Return the Modification Date

As previously stated, this method returns the modification date of the specified file rather than the servlet's modification date:

```
public long getLastModified(HttpServletRequest req) {
    fileObj = new File(DIRECTORY, req.getParameter(PARAM_FILENAME));
    if (fileObj.exists()) {
        long time = fileObj.lastModified();
        return time;
    }
    return -1;
}
```

As you can plainly see, the implementation of this method is very simple. A file object is created using the parameter specified and if that file exists, then the file's modification date is returned. The method returns a -1 if the specified file is not valid (this is also what the method returns by default if you do not override the superclass implementation).

The web.xml Descriptor

Here is the deployment descriptor webapps\conditional\WEB-INF\web.xml:

```
<?xml version="1.0" encoding="ISO-8859-1"?>
<!DOCTYPE web-app
    PUBLIC "-//Sun Microsystems, Inc.//DTD Web Application
    2.2//EN" "http://java.sun.com/j2ee/dtds/web-app_2.2dtd">

<web-app>
    <servlet>
        <servlet-name>Condition</servlet-name>
        <servlet-class>RecentPage</servlet-class>
        <init-param>
            <param-name>name</param-name>
            <param-value>ProJava</param-value>
        </init-param>
    </servlet>
    <servlet-mapping>
        <servlet-name>Condition</servlet-name>
        <url-pattern>/condition</url-pattern>
    </servlet-mapping>
</web-app>
```

Note that we map the servlet class to the URL condition.

537

The tester.txt File

Finally, we need a file to test the application with. The client will pass a `fileName` to the servlet and the servlet will search for that file in a specified directory. Assuming that you have copied the servlet exactly as shown above, that directory is `C:\projavaxml\chapter13`.

> *If you need to modify this for your own Windows machine, be sure to use double \ \ in your Java code to express a directory separator. This is necessary because Java reserves the backslash character for special character escape sequences. So in order to express a backslash, you have to use a double slash.*

Here is a simple text file that you can use for testing purposes. Feel free to come up with your own:

```
Howdy Partner!

This is a plain text file.

Thank you, please drive thru.
```

Save this file in whatever directory you specified for the `private static final` variable `DIRECTORY` in the above code.

Test the Application

Naturally, the first step is to compile the servlet. Just like the other servlets we've done, this file will be located in the web application's `classes` directory. Once the servlet has been successfully compiled and the class file is in the correct directory, then you're ready to test it out.

Fire up Tomcat, open a web browser, enter the URL http://localhost:8080/projavaxml/chapter13/conditional /condition?fileName=tester.txt and press *Enter*. You should receive a response similar to this one:

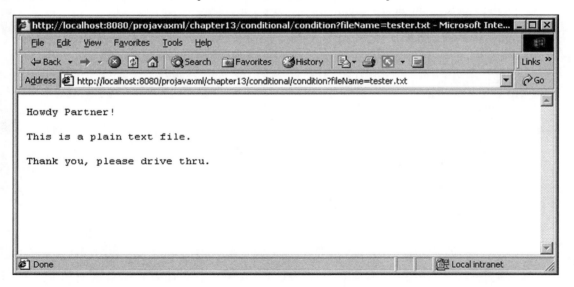

Now try entering an invalid filename to test the servlet's error checking mechanism. You should receive a response similar to this one:

Making a Conditional GET Request

If your servlet is working just fine, then it's time to test the `If-Modified-Since` header. To do this, we will need to abandon the browser and break out the `HttpGopher` utility again. Start up `HttpGopher` and enter the following inputs:

```
Host: localhost
Port: 8080
Request Method: GET
Request URL: /projavaxml/chapter13/conditional/condition?fileName=tester.txt
HTTP Version 1.0 or 1.1? 1.0
Any Request Headers? y
Request Header and Value: If-Modified-Since: Fri, Jan 12 2001 00:12:05 GMT
Add another request header? n
```

Since the above date is a while ago, you should definitely receive the contents of `tester.txt`. Now try this again with tomorrow's date or next year's date. You should get a 304 status code `Not Modified`.

You've successfully performed a conditional GET request on a server-side file. You could write a program that executed every night or once a week that made a conditional GET request against a server, only intending to download the information if it had been modified since the last request. There are dozens of other uses for a conditional GET request. For a B2B application, for example, you might want to poll a site daily or weekly or monthly, for example, to look for changes in pricing. This is a very useful technique for minimising wasted bandwidth and CPU time.

Full Client-Server XML Messaging Application

We've been leading up to it for the past two chapters, and we are now finally ready to tackle the full-blown client-server XML over HTTP messaging application. In this example, we will write a graphical client that will create an XML document and then send a serialized representation of the XML to the server for processing. This is an expansion on the application that concluded Chapter 12. This time, both the client and server will need to parse XML data structures and the transaction layer from the client to the server will use serialized XML streams; the server's responses will be standard I/O streams.

Although the application does use a Java class as a wrapper for the XML tree, the only data being exchanged between the client and server is a serialized stream of XML. This is a very flexible solution. In the future, we could develop multiple clients, on multiple platforms, using various languages, and so long as they were capable of sending and receiving XML data structures, then they would be able to communicate with out any regard for the other vast differences.

As you may recall, the application at the end of Chapter 12 allowed an XML message to be transmitted to the server as an encapsulated POST request body. Those messages took the form of XML-formatted commands and associated data. Those commands involved the management of news summaries that were housed on the server. With this application, the client will provide a more robust user interface in which the client can view records on the server, delete records, and create new records.

The application consists of four files:

- ❑ XmlClient.java
  The application's UI comes via an AWT application. This program sends serialized XML to the servlet for processing. Although it is helpful if you have worked with AWT before, it is not necessary in order for you to learn the XML concepts we will be exploring in this exercise. The application merely provides us with a more robust and user-friendly interface to work with.

- ❑ Command.java
  The Java class that will be serialized and exchanged between the client and server. This class is an XML data wrapper, and it is designed to represent and act upon XML data without the developer needing to worry about the details of that process.

- ❑ XmlServlet.java
  This is a very basic servlet that accepts POST submissions of serialized XML from which it constructs Command objects and processes those commands on behalf of the client.

- ❑ web.xml
  As always, we will write a deployment descriptor for our application.

The XML Data Model

Before we dive into the code, it would be helpful to step back and get a better understanding of the XML data model that the entire application is based upon and driven by.

The XML data structure that we are attempting to model looks like this:

```
<?xml version="1.0" encoding="UTF-8"?>
<command type="add">
    <target>article.txt</target>
    <news>
        <title>XML and Java are sweeping the nation!</title>
        <byline>Clyde Kadiddlehopper</byline>
        <summary>
            XML and Java form a unique technological
            combination that delivers both power and
            flexibility
        </summary>
    </news>
</command>
```

It is a platform-neutral, vendor-neutral model that includes three primary pieces of information:

❑   **A command type**
    add, delete, or view. This instructs the servlet what should be done with the rest of the data contained in the XML command.

❑   **A target file**
    This identifies what file on the server should be affected by this command's execution. In the case of an add command, this file would either be created on the server, or overwritten with the data contained in the XML.

❑   **A news snippet**
    This is the business motivation behind the entire project. A news snippet consists of a title, author, and brief summary describing the entire article. You most often see these snippets, or teasers on the home page of an informational web site. They are dynamic database-driven news snippets designed to attract the user to the full article, and thus to attract them to the entire web site.

This application is intended to be a bare-bones design of an XML-messaging system that is used to remotely manage dynamic content. With that foundation provided, we can turn to the actual coding with a clearer picture of what we intend to create with this application.

The XmlClient Class

Although prior experience with Java AWT applications is helpful, it is not necessary in order for you to benefit from this exercise. The application merely provides us with a portable, robust, easy to use, user interface. Due to the fact that the following source code is GUI intensive, it seems appropriate to take a look at the final product, as this will give you a better idea of how everything fits together. The following screenshot will give you some insight into what we're about to build:

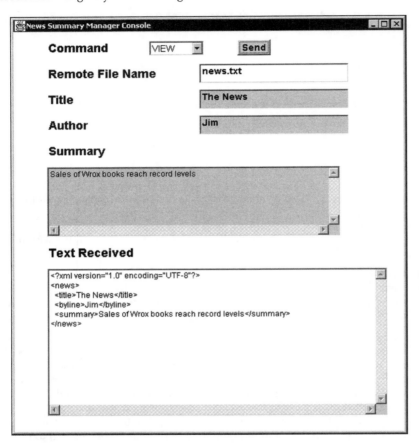

Create a file called XmlClient.java located at C:\projavaxml\chapter13. We'll start off with the import statements, class definition, and variable declarations:

```
mport java.awt.*;
import java.awt.event.*;

import java.net.*;
import java.io.*;

import org.jdom.*;
import org.jdom.output.XMLOutputter;
```

```
public class XmlClient extends Frame implements ActionListener,
        ItemListener {

    private static final String SERVLET_PATH =
      "/projavaxml/chapter13/messaging/xmlservlet";

    private Choice CommandList = null;
    private Button CommandButton = null;
    private Label ReceiveLabel = null;
    private TextArea ReceiveText = null;
    private Label SendLabel = null;
    private TextArea SendText = null;
    private URL currentPage;
    private String protocol;
    private String host;
    private int port;
    private String contentType;
    private Label CommandLabel = null;
    private Panel sendPanel = null;
    private Label FileLabel = null;
    private TextField FileText = null;
    private Label TitleLabel = null;
    private TextField TitleText = null;
    private TextField ByLineText = null;
    private Label ByLineLabel = null;
```

You'll notice that in addition to some of the more standard packages, we have imported the org.jdom package. This is because we will be using the JDOM API for all the parsing required in this application. If you're not familiar with JDOM, you should first read through Chapter 4 before proceeding on. JDOM was chosen for this application because of the robustness of the API. We will be building Document objects, manipulating XML trees, serializing and deserializing XML structures, and a whole array of other tasks that are made so much easier with the JDOM API.

The only other thing worth mentioning is the single constant that our class defines. The SERVLET_PATH variable should reflect the path to your servlet relative to the host address, as this will be used later in establishing a connection with the server.

Responding to User Actions

```
public void actionPerformed(ActionEvent ae) {
    if (ae.getActionCommand().equals("Send")) {
      ReceiveText.setText("");
      sendCommand();
    }
}

public void itemStateChanged(ItemEvent ie) {
    if (CommandList.getSelectedItem().equals("ADD")) {
      TitleText.setEditable(true);
      ByLineText.setEditable(true);
      SendText.setEditable(true);

    } else if (CommandList.getSelectedItem().equals("DELETE")) {
      TitleText.setEditable(false);
      ByLineText.setEditable(false);
      SendText.setEditable(false);
```

```
    } else if (CommandList.getSelectedItem().equals("VIEW")) {
      TitleText.setEditable(false);
      ByLineText.setEditable(false);
      SendText.setEditable(false);

    }
  }
```

The `actionPerformed()` method monitors the **Send** button. When the user clicks this button, then this method calls the `sendCommand()` method, the method that actually contacts the servlet.

The `itemStateChanged()` method makes unavailable those fields that do not pertain to the selection the user just made. For instance, if you choose to view the contents of a file housed on the server, you have no need to enter a title or summary for a new news item.

GUI Component Construction

Each GUI component is constructed by way of a method. This keeps all the GUI controls organized, easy to find, and easy to maintain. These methods should all be pretty self-explanatory:

```
private Label getByLineLabel() {

    if (ByLineLabel == null) {
      ByLineLabel = new java.awt.Label();
      ByLineLabel.setName("ByLineLabel");
      ByLineLabel.setFont(new java.awt.Font("dialog", 1, 18));
      ByLineLabel.setText("Author");
      ByLineLabel.setSize(80, 23);
      ByLineLabel.setForeground(Color.blue);
    }
    return ByLineLabel;
  }

private TextField getByLineText() {

    if (ByLineText == null) {

      ByLineText = new java.awt.TextField(25);
      ByLineText.setName("ByLineText");
      ByLineText.setFont(new java.awt.Font("dialog", 1, 14));
      ByLineText.setSize(200, 23);
    }
    return ByLineText;
  }


private Choice getCommandList() {

    if (CommandList == null) {
      CommandList = new java.awt.Choice();
      CommandList.setName("Command");
      CommandList.setFont(new java.awt.Font("dialog", 0, 14));
      CommandList.setSize(100, 46);
      CommandList.setEnabled(true);
```

```java
    CommandList.addItemListener(this);
    CommandList.add("ADD");
    CommandList.add("DELETE");
    CommandList.add("VIEW");
  }
  return CommandList;
}


private Button getCommandButton() {

  if (CommandButton == null) {
    CommandButton = new java.awt.Button();
    CommandButton.setName("CommandButton");
    CommandButton.setFont(new java.awt.Font("dialog", 1, 14));
    CommandButton.setSize(86, 25);
    CommandButton.setLabel("Send");

    CommandButton.addActionListener(this);
  }
  return CommandButton;
}


private Label getCommandLabel() {

  if (CommandLabel == null) {
    CommandLabel = new java.awt.Label();
    CommandLabel.setName("CommandLabel");
    CommandLabel.setFont(new java.awt.Font("dialog", 1, 18));
    CommandLabel.setText("Command");
    CommandLabel.setSize(105, 23);
  }
  return CommandLabel;
}


private Label getFileLabel() {

  if (FileLabel == null) {
    FileLabel = new java.awt.Label();
    FileLabel.setName("FileLabel");
    FileLabel.setFont(new java.awt.Font("dialog", 1, 18));
    FileLabel.setText("Remote File Name");
    FileLabel.setSize(80, 23);
    FileLabel.setForeground(Color.blue);
  }
  return FileLabel;
}


private TextField getFileText() {

  if (FileText == null) {
    FileText = new java.awt.TextField(25);
    FileText.setName("FileText");
    FileText.setFont(new java.awt.Font("dialog", 1, 14));
  }
  return FileText;
}
```

```java
private Label getReceiveLabel() {
  if (ReceiveLabel == null) {
    ReceiveLabel = new java.awt.Label();
    ReceiveLabel.setName("ReceiveLabel");
    ReceiveLabel.setFont(new java.awt.Font("dialog", 1, 18));
    ReceiveLabel.setText("Text Received ");
    ReceiveLabel.setSize(145, 23);
  }
  return ReceiveLabel;
}
```

```java
private TextArea getReceiveText() {

  if (ReceiveText == null) {
    ReceiveText = new java.awt.TextArea(14, 70);
    ReceiveText.setName("ReceiveText");
  }
  return ReceiveText;
}
```

```java
private Label getSendLabel() {

  if (SendLabel == null) {
    SendLabel = new java.awt.Label();
    SendLabel.setName("SendLabel");
    SendLabel.setFont(new java.awt.Font("dialog", 1, 18));
    SendLabel.setText("Summary");
    SendLabel.setSize(126, 23);
    SendLabel.setForeground(Color.blue);
  }
  return SendLabel;
}
```

```java
private TextArea getSendText() {
  if (SendText == null) {
    SendText = new java.awt.TextArea(6, 60);
    SendText.setName("SendText");
  }
  return SendText;
}
```

```java
private Label getTitleLabel() {

  if (TitleLabel == null) {
    TitleLabel = new java.awt.Label();
    TitleLabel.setName("TitleLabel");
    TitleLabel.setFont(new java.awt.Font("dialog", 1, 18));
    TitleLabel.setText("Title");
    TitleLabel.setSize(80, 23);
    TitleLabel.setForeground(Color.blue);
  }
  return TitleLabel;
}
```

```
  private TextField getTitleText() {
    if (TitleText == null) {
      TitleText = new java.awt.TextField(25);
      TitleText.setName("TitleText");
      TitleText.setSize(200, 23);
      TitleText.setFont(new java.awt.Font("dialog", 1, 14));
    }
     return TitleText;
  }
```

Constructor

Next, we have the constructor:

```
  public XmlClient() {
    try {
      setTitle("News Summary Manager Console");
      setLayout(new FlowLayout(FlowLayout.LEFT, 50, 10));
      setSize(575, 650);
      sendPanel = new Panel(new GridLayout(3, 2, 5, 10));

      add(getCommandLabel(), getCommandLabel().getName());
      add(getCommandList(), getCommandList().getName());
      add(getCommandButton(), getCommandButton().getName());

      sendPanel.add(getFileLabel());
      sendPanel.add(getFileText());

      sendPanel.add(getTitleLabel());
      sendPanel.add(getTitleText());
      sendPanel.add(getByLineLabel());
      sendPanel.add(getByLineText());

      add(sendPanel);
      add(getSendLabel(), getSendLabel().getName());
      add(getSendText(), getSendText().getName());

      add(getReceiveLabel(), getReceiveLabel().getName());
      add(getReceiveText(), getReceiveText().getName());

      addWindowListener(new WinClosing());
      setVisible(true);

    } catch (Throwable Exc) {
      System.out.println(Exc.getMessage());
    }
  }
```

The main() method

This is the main() method:

```
  public static void main(String[] args) {
    XmlClient client = new XmlClient();
  }
```

HTTP Communication

And last, but certainly not least, we have the brains behind the whole application. The sendCommand() method creates a Command object and converts it into a JDOM object, which then outputs a string of pure XML and sends it in the body of a POST request to the server.

```java
private void sendCommand() {
  URLConnection conn;
  ByteArrayOutputStream byteStream;
  BufferedReader in;
  URL servletURL;
  String line;
  Command commandObj = null;
  Document doc = null;
  PrintWriter out;
  XMLOutputter xout;

  try {
    servletURL = new URL("http://localhost:8080" + SERVLET_PATH);

    conn = servletURL.openConnection();
    conn.setUseCaches(false);
    conn.setDoOutput(true);

    if (CommandList.getSelectedItem().equals("ADD")) {
      commandObj = new Command("add", FileText.getText(),
                               TitleText.getText(), ByLineText.getText(),
                               SendText.getText());
      doc = commandObj.toXml();
    } else if (CommandList.getSelectedItem().equals("DELETE")) {
      commandObj = new Command("delete", FileText.getText());
      doc = commandObj.toXml();
    } else if (CommandList.getSelectedItem().equals("VIEW")) {
      commandObj = new Command("view", FileText.getText());
      doc = commandObj.toXml();
    }

    byteStream = new ByteArrayOutputStream(512);

    xout = new XMLOutputter();
    xout.setTrimText(true);
    xout.output(doc, byteStream);

    conn.setRequestProperty("Content-Length",
                            String.valueOf(byteStream.size()));
    conn.setRequestProperty("Content-Type", "multi-part/form-data");

    byteStream.writeTo(conn.getOutputStream());

    in = new BufferedReader(new InputStreamReader(conn.getInputStream()));

    if ((line = in.readLine()) != null) {
      ReceiveText.setText(line + "\n");
```

```
        }
        while ((line = in.readLine()) != null) {
          ReceiveText.append(line + "\n");
        }

        in.close();
      } catch (IOException ioe) {
        ReceiveText.append("\n");
        ReceiveText.append("Error: " + ioe + "\n");
        ioe.printStackTrace();
      } catch (Exception e) {
        ReceiveText.append("\n");
        ReceiveText.append("Error: " + e + "\n");
        e.printStackTrace();
      }
    }
  }
```

This method examines the choice the user made from the Choice box, and creates an appropriate Command object to carry out that function. This Command object then converts itself into a JDOM Document object via the toXml() method defined in the Command class. An XMLOutputter object (defined in the org.jdom.output package) is then used to produce a pure string of XML from the JDOM object. The XMLOutputter writes that string to the byteStream stream. The data is written to a byteStream so that the length of the data can be determined in order to set the Content-Length request header (a requirement for a valid HTTP POST). The byteStream (which now contains the XML string) is then dumped into the output stream retrieved by the URLConnection object.

Closing the Application

In order for the application to recognize that you have clicked the frame's close button, there must be a listener for that event. The WinowListener interface provides a means of listening for the event of a user clicking the close button. Unfortunately, the WindowListener also contains a variety of other methods that we are not interested in. Rather than provide empty implementations for those methods, we can use the WindowAdapter class that has already done that for us. The following class file can either be created separately, or simply added at the bottom of your XmlClient.java file below the XmlClient class definition:

```
class WinClosing extends WindowAdapter {
  public void windowClosing( WindowEvent we ) {
    System.exit(0);
  }
}
```

An object of this class is created in the XmlClient constructor. The line is:

```
addWindowListener( new WinClosing() );
```

This adds a window listener to the frame by creating an object of type WinClosing. Now, when we click the close button on the application window, the windowClosing() method of this class will be called and the application will exit properly.

The Command Class

This class is a helper class that wraps an XML data structure that will be used by both the client and servlet. It is crucial that this be in the classpath for both the client and servlet.

Here's how the class starts:

```
import org.jdom.*;

public class Command {

    private final static String ROOT_EL = "command";
    private final static String ROOT_ATTR = "type";
    private final static String TARGET_EL = "target";

    private final static String NEWS_EL = "news";
    private final static String TITLE_EL = "title";
    private final static String BYLINE_EL = "byline";
    private final static String SUMMARY_EL = "summary";

    private String command;
    private String target;
    private String title;
    private String byLine;
    private String summary;
```

If you turn back and take a look at the XML data structure that this class is intended to model, then the role of each of these variables falls neatly into place. The final static constants are used to allow flexibility in naming conventions (tag and attribute names can easily change), while the standard `String` variables are merely instance variables of every `Command` object.

The Constructors

There are three different methods available for constructing a `Command` object, but they facilitate the creation of only two flavors of `Command` objects. The minimal `Command` object consists of only a `<command>` tag and a `<target>` tag. This type of command is used to instruct the server to display or delete some data. Since the `Command` object is not provided with any new data, the other tags aren't necessary. Here's what the minimal `Command` object looks like as an XML node:

```
<?xml version="1.0" encoding="UTF-8"?>
<command type="delete">
   <target>article.txt</target>
</command>
```

This simply specifies the command type and the affected file. This is obviously provided for by the constructor, which takes in two arguments:

```
public Command(String command, String target) {
   this.command = command;
   this.target = target;
   this.title = null;
   this.byLine = null;
   this.summary = null;
}
```

The more robust XML command with the contained news item is clearly provided for by the constructor with five parameters, but what about the third constructor?

```
public Command(String command, String target, String title,
               String byLine, String summary) {
  this.command = command;
  this.target = target;
  this.title = title;
  this.byLine = byLine;
  this.summary = summary;
}
```

The third constructor parses a JDOM Document object into a Command object. The first two data members are present in every Command object, and the last three will simply contain null values if the Document passed to the constructor only contained the first two members:

```
public Command(Document doc) {
  Element el;
  el = doc.getRootElement();
  if (el.isRootElement() && el.getName().equals(ROOT_EL)) {
    command = el.getAttributeValue(ROOT_ATTR);
    target = el.getChildText(TARGET_EL);

    // getChildText() returns null if the element doesn't exist
    title = el.getChildText(TITLE_EL);
    byLine = el.getChildText(BYLINE_EL);
    summary = el.getChildText(SUMMARY_EL);
  }
}
```

So those three constructors provide for both types of Command objects, and even permit a Document object to be parsed and wrapped by an object of the Command class.

To XML and Back Again

What good would a constructor that can parse a JDOM Document object be without a complementary method that could do the inverse? That is the precise purpose for this method:

```
public Document toXml() {
  Document doc;
  Element commandEl, targetEl, newsEl, titleEl, byLineEl, summaryEl;

  commandEl = new Element(ROOT_EL);
  commandEl.addAttribute(ROOT_ATTR, command);
  targetEl = new Element(TARGET_EL);
  targetEl.addContent(target);
  commandEl.addContent(targetEl);


  if (title != null) {

    // Create the news element
    newsEl = new Element(NEWS_EL);

    // Create the title element
    titleEl = new Element(TITLE_EL);
    titleEl.addContent(title);
```

```
      // Create the byline element
      byLineEl = new Element(BYLINE_EL);
      byLineEl.addContent(byLine);

      // Create the summary element
      summaryEl = new Element(SUMMARY_EL);
      summaryEl.addContent(summary);

      newsEl.addContent(titleEl);
      newsEl.addContent(byLineEl);
      newsEl.addContent(summaryEl);

      commandEl.addContent(newsEl);
    }

    doc = new Document(commandEl);
    return doc;
  }
```

This method creates the first two elements and then checks to see if the `title` element is `null`, if it is, then the root element `commandEl` is fed into a `Document` constructor and the resulting object is then returned to the caller. If `title` is not `null`, then the full XML structure is built before creating the `Document` object.

This method and the complementary constructor are crucial components of this class, because they allow the rest of the application to use `Document` objects as the universal data component. This is particularly valuable in light of the fact that the `Document` class implements the `Serializable` interface. This is what allows the application to serialize `Document` objects and transfer them over HTTP between the client and servlet.

Data Accessors

And no class would be complete without methods to access the data members. Only `get()` methods have been used here, but in a more fully featured version of the application, there would likely be a need for `set()` methods as well.

```
    public String getByLine() {
      return byLine;
    }

    public String getCommand() {
      return command;
    }

    public String getSummary() {
      return summary;
    }

    public String getTarget() {
      return target;
    }

    public String getTitle() {
      return title;
    }
  }
```

This concludes the code for the `Command` class; all that is left is the `XmlServlet` class and the deployment descriptor.

The XmlServlet Class

This servlet is not especially different from the other servlets you've written in this chapter and the previous one, except for the fact that it constructs an object wrapper for the client's request, and interacts with the XML document through the JDOM API and the Command class data wrapper.

As usual, you'll want to store this file in your webapps\messaging\WEB-INF\classes directory for this example. Here is the outline for the XmlServlet class:

```
import java.io.*;
import java.util.*;
import javax.servlet.*;
import javax.servlet.http.*;

import org.jdom.*;
import org.jdom.output.XMLOutputter;
import org.jdom.input.SAXBuilder;

public class XmlServlet extends HttpServlet {
```

Handling the Client's Request

Our dear friend the doPost() method appears once again. We must implement the doPost() method rather than the doGet() method because the only way that an HTTP client can send a serialized java object is by attaching it as a request body to a POST.

```
public void doPost(HttpServletRequest request, HttpServletResponse response)
    throws ServletException, IOException {
  PrintWriter out;
  out = response.getWriter();
  response.setContentType("text/xml");
  processCommand(request, out);
  out.close();
}
```

Processing the Client's Command

Here the servlet creates a SAXBuilder object, opens an InputStream to the client's request, reads the serialized XML into the SAXBuilder's build() method, and then uses the Document object produced to create a Command object. Since the Command object is wrapping the actual XML command, this is the interface that the rest of the method will interact with in order to process the client request.

```
private void processCommand(HttpServletRequest req, PrintWriter out) {
  SAXBuilder builder;
  Document doc;
  Command commandObj = null;
  String param;

  try {
    builder = new SAXBuilder();
    doc = builder.build(req.getInputStream());
    commandObj = new Command(doc);
```

After the `Command` object has been constructed, it is time to process the client's command:

```
param = commandObj.getCommand();
```

As we know from the client we created earlier, there are three possible commands: add, delete, and view. First the add command:

```
if (param.equals("add")) {
   File file;
   BufferedOutputStream buff;
   XMLOutputter xOut;
```

We begin by declaring the objects that we will need. The `Element` object will be used to extract the news element (and its children) from the XML tree. This is the relevant portion of the XML tree that we are interested in persisting. Here's the code that extracts the news element and constructs a new JDOM `Document` from that element:

```
Element el = doc.getRootElement();
el = el.getChild("news");
doc = new Document(el);
```

Now we create the file and the `BufferedOutputStream` to write to that file. The `XMLOutputter` object will be used to write the `Document` object to the stream:

```
file = new File(commandObj.getTarget());
buff = new BufferedOutputStream(new FileOutputStream(file));
xOut = new XMLOutputter("  ", true);
xOut.output(doc, buff);
buff.close();

out.println("Content Successfully Updated!");
} else if (param.equals("delete")) {
   File file;
   file = new File(commandObj.getTarget());
   if (file.exists()) {
      if (!file.delete()) {
         out.println("Error: " + file.getName() + " cannot be deleted!");
      } else {
         out.println(file.getName() + " successfully deleted.");
      }
   } else {
      out.println("Error: " + file.getName() + " does not exist!");
   }
```

Finally there is the `view` command. All this method does is send the request on to the `sendFile()` method:

```
   } else if (param.equals("view")) {
      sendFile(commandObj.getTarget(), out);
   }
} catch (JDOMException jde) {
   out.println("JDOM Error!");
   out.println(jde.getMessage());
} catch (FileNotFoundException fnfe) {
   out.println("Could not find the file!");
   out.println(fnfe.getMessage());
} catch (IOException ioe) {
   out.println(ioe.getMessage());
   out.println("Servlet Error!");
}
}
```

Serving up the Data

This final method is a utility method that simply reads a file from the server into a buffer and sends the results to the client. This functionality is needed a couple of times in the `processCommand()` method, so it saves some coding by placing these calls into a reusable method:

```
private void sendFile(String fileName,
                        PrintWriter pw) throws IOException {
  File file;
  BufferedReader in;
  String line;

  file = new File(fileName);
  if (!file.exists()) {
    pw.println(fileName + " does not exist!");
    return;
  }

  in = new BufferedReader(new FileReader(file));

  while ((line = in.readLine()) != null) {
    pw.println(line);
  }
  in.close();
}
}
```

The web.xml Descriptor

The last file we need to address is the servlet deployment descriptor. Our application doesn't use any initialization parameters, although the application at the end of Chapter 12 provided an excellent example of how you could utilize initialization parameters in an application like this one. All we need for this servlet, however, is a simple web.xml:

```
<?xml version="1.0" encoding="ISO-8859-1"?>
<!DOCTYPE web-app
    PUBLIC "-//Sun Microsystems, Inc.//DTD Web Application
    2.2//EN" "http://java.sun.com/j2ee/dtds/web-app_2.2dtd">

<web-app>
   <servlet>
      <servlet-name>XmlServlet</servlet-name>
      <servlet-class>XmlServlet</servlet-class>
   </servlet>
   <servlet-mapping>
      <servlet-name>XmlServlet</servlet-name>
      <url-pattern>/xmlservlet</url-pattern>
   </servlet-mapping>
</web-app>
```

And, of course, a new Tomcat context in server.xml:

```
<Context
    path="/projavaxml/chapter13/messaging"
    docBase="C:/projavaxml/chapter13/webapps/messaging"
    debug="1"
    reloadable="true">
</Context>
```

Testing the Application

The first step is, of course, to compile the two source files and place their class files in the appropriate directories. Next, be sure that you have all of the utility classes and files ready: the Command class, and the WinClosing class file.

When you've got everything in order, start up your web container, open a command prompt, and start the client XmlClient from the command line. This should bring up the Java AWT frame and you're ready for testing. Experiment with the various features available, especially the following combination: create a news summary by filling in the fields, selecting ADD and clicking the Send button. Next, keep the filename field untouched, and just change the command from ADD to VIEW and click the Send button again. You should see the XML file appear that you just created.

Summary

In the course of these last two chapters we have developed a lightweight, flexible means of transferring simple XML objects that describe instructions and parameters to be carried out by the receiving machine. It is an attempt to standardize the way that distributed computing, and particularly distributed messaging is done.

What we have outlined and hinted at is that HTTP is a universal transportation layer, XML is quickly becoming a universal data standard, and Java maintains a unique place in the industry as the most successful open-source, platform-neutral, programming language. A more dynamic combination simply doesn't exist in the industry today. Although XML claims no allegiance to a particular language, Java is, at least currently, the language best suited to maximize its potential.

The Xerces Blue
butterfly, which became
extinct earlier this century,
and after which the Xerces XML
parser is named ...

14

Server-Side Presentation

Introduction

So far we have learned a lot about the various components of XML: the basics, XSL and XSLT, SAX and DOM views of the XML world, JAXP and JDOM, and some of the capabilities of XML. Any well-formed XML document can be transformed into any other well-formed XML. This turns out to be extremely powerful for many reasons. First, if you are receiving a document in an XML format foreign to your application, it is easy to place a transformation between your application and the other to provide the material in a format your application can understand. Another important use of this transformation process takes advantage of the fact that presentation code can be manipulated in the same manner.

Now, while we concede that there are other consumers besides people, visual presentation is the scope of this chapter. We will, in any case, cover messaging, B2B communication, and Web Services in the last three chapters of this book. For the remainder of the chapter we will concentrate on the problem of serving clients that use differing rendering formats and explore the mechanisms available for dynamically generating server-side content.

We will start off using some of the technologies we have been learning in this book, including XML and XSLT. We will also look at applications developed specifically for this task. You should be familiar with the basics of Java Servlets in order to try out the examples in this chapter.

What we will need

In order to complete the examples make sure you are using the following:

- ❑ Jakarta Tomcat 3.2.1. For information on installing Tomcat, see Appendix H.
- ❑ JAXP 1.1 available at http://java.sun.com/xml/.
- ❑ The UP.SDK 4.1 from OpenWave (formerly Phone.com) available at http://developer.openwave.com/. We have chosen this emulator as it currently offers the most up to date, easy to use, and stable emulator for WML devices.
- ❑ Cocoon 1.8.3 available at http://xml.apache.org/.

Diverse Browsers

In the early days of the Internet, only one graphical browser existed: NCSA Mosaic. That gave birth to the Netscape Navigator browser and later Microsoft's Internet Explorer. Developing for each of these browsers was easy when both, more or less, presented HTML in the same manner. As time went on, the lack of development in web standards, however, led to both manufacturers adding features that web developers wanted, but in different ways. Still, the logic required to handle presenting the same website on all the different desktop web browsers isn't that complex.

Enter the new millennium. A new generation of browsers has entered the market that bears little resemblance to the Netscape and Internet Explorer browsers; these browsers live on wireless devices. These browsers don't even use HTML – they understand languages like WML (WAP's Wireless Markup Language) CHTML (Compiled HTML) and HDML (Handheld Device Markup Language).

Increasingly, devices other than desktop computers are going to be accessing our web sites in the future. Anything from a TV set-top box to an in-car voice-based browser might be logging on in a few years time, so we need to address not only the range of markup standards that exist today, but the possibility of a wide range of future markup languages.

This diversity presents a challenge to the conventional architecture of web sites. Most moderately complex, dynamic web sites employ a **three-tier architecture**, like this:

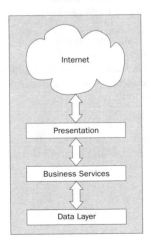

This three-tier model is essentially a **Model-View-Controller** or MVC architecture. From the bottom up, the first layer is the **Data Layer**, which serves as our model, which is essentially a data source holding the data to be displayed to the user. For example, an online bookstore would hold all information about books, customers, and so on here. The next layer is the **Business Services Layer**, which functions as a controller. This layer is responsible for the business logic: calculating orders, validating a credit card number, and submitting the order for processing, ensuring that the model is only manipulated in accordance with business rules (a shipment order is only placed once a credit approval has been received, and so on).

Next is the **Presentation Layer**, the view, responsible for displaying content to a user. This layer is what is directly accessed by client applications, in our case clients communicating over the Internet. The presentation layer uses the business layer to determine, for example, how many books are in stock or how much a given book costs. The result is then displayed.

This architecture means that security is simpler to implement, requiring only that the communication between layers be authenticated in some way. It also means that the architecture is more flexible, allowing substitution of the data source, perhaps to migrate to another platform. We can modify the business logic for a different market, or indeed, modify the presentation logic for an alternative content consumer with minimal effect on the other layers.

In addition, we can add layers as required such as, for example, a data access layer to interface to legacy applications. If we have multiple business logic tiers, we have what is called an **N-tier system**.

Multiple Presentation Layers

The architecture above depicts a site with essentially only one presentation type and is somewhat unrealistic; it is fast becoming inevitable that we will have multiple consumers of our data, both internal to the company and external. In fact, thinking in terms of a single, or primary, consumer can be unhelpful as this can change dramatically and quickly.

One solution, given that we have a layered model such as that above, to meet the needs of multiple client platforms, is to re-implement the presentation tier to provide the specific presentation logic for that platform, talking to our uniform business-tier interface.

This would look more like the following:

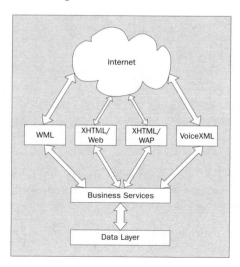

This model is accurate for any site wishing to have both a web and wireless presence. In the future, we can look forward to a possible merging of WML and HTML through the development of XHTML but we will still need to support legacy WML devices.

The problem is that there is a great deal of duplication of effort required to build this sort of system. There are, essentially, two types of presentation logic: there is the general logic concerned with knowing what information to request from the business services at what stage during the user's interaction with the web application, and there is that logic which is concerned with presenting results and options to the user in the format appropriate to their device. The first is largely the same on all devices. The user of the online bookstore must first be shown a catalog page, which gives them the option to look at more details about books, regardless of what browser they are using. This is a form of business logic, which is concerned principally with the user experience of the application, but not the detail of the interface. The second type of logic is specific to each of the platforms, and is concerned with things like how to lay out the information on the user's display, how to present the user with a form, or how to include images in the page.

This duplication is not helpful when we decide to change the layout of our site. We end up having to completely re-code all our presentation tiers, even though a lot of the logic could be shared between them. What we want is something like what we have in our business and data layers: a shared presentation layer that is extensible for additional devices. Given the number of devices to code for, how can we hope to accomplish this?

Fortunately XSLT, when combined with the fact that XML is now the basis of a wide range of presentation formats, gives us the solution to this problem. Below is the architecture that emerges:

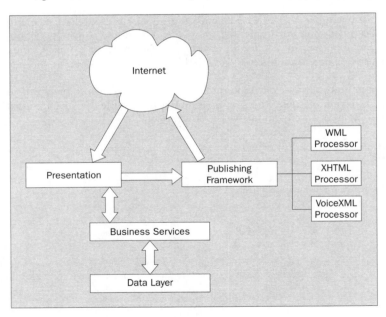

What we have is a publishing framework that sits in between the web server and the client application, which translates requests from the presentation layer. The publishing framework takes the same data in each case and transforms it to the specific needs of the client by applying a stylesheet provided for that purpose.

This ensures that content is left independent of presentation and the presentation is flexible, scalable and maintainable. Our content is completely separate from how it is displayed.

Server-Side Content

While the initial hype that surrounded Java was propelled largely by Applets (browser embedded client-side applications), over time, Java for the client became less of a focus as people shifted their attention toward server-side programming. However, Java is making a client-side comeback, on the same wave as this browser diversification we have been discussing: The Java 2 Platform, Micro Edition, is a version of the Java platform designed for handheld and embedded devices, and creates the possibility of developing applications on the client-side which will run on a wide range of client machines. This would hopefully allow us to develop a different sort of presentation tier altogether: a client-side presentation tier.

However, in spite of this, there are various reasons for applying presentation logic on the server. Firstly, changes to the application can be done centrally on the server and do not have a propagation period as clients upgrade: they are available when the clients next log on. Secondly, we can guarantee that the responsiveness of the application is fairly even across access types – we cannot expect every device accessing the site to have the power required to present the content. Wireless devices have limited bandwidth, processing power, memory, and battery life.

So, in the course of this chapter, we will present several techniques which can be used to develop a maintainable presentation tier for multiple client devices, all based around the idea of using XSLT to transform content into a device-specific form.

XSLT and Servlets

This section will present the use of XSLT with servlets to generate different markup from the same data. In order to achieve the goal of an extensible presentation layer we must:

❑ Create a platform-neutral representation of our data

❑ Create a stylesheet for each platform we plan on supporting

❑ When a device hits our server, determine the device type and generate the content using the appropriate transformation

The Application

In order to better compare the various options available to us, we will take a simple application and implement it in each technology, thus exposing the strengths and weaknesses of each. The application we are going to develop is a demographic questionnaire. Users will be asked a series of questions and their answers will be displayed at the end. The application works by displaying questions to the user and simply repeating the answers back to them.

While simple, the application will address two important issues: generating data dynamically and using forms on a variety of platforms.

Step 1: Platform-Neutral Data

First we need to create a platform-neutral format for our data. Below are the questions and range of answers for the first page of the questionnaire:

```xml
<?xml version="1.0"?>
<questionnaire processor="questionServlet">
    <page>
        <question field="gender" caption="What is your gender?">
            <choice>Male</choice>
            <choice>Female</choice>
        </question>
    </page>
    <page>
        <question field="age" caption="What age range do you fall in?">
            <choice>14-18</choice>
            <choice>19-25</choice>
            <choice>26-40</choice>
            <choice>41+</choice>
        </question>
    </page>
</questionnaire>
```

As you can see the data format has been kept quite simple: a questionnaire consists of one or more pages, each of which consists of one or more questions. Now let's see how we can transform this.

Step 2: User Agent Dependent Styling

We now need to create stylesheets for each of the user-agents we wish to cater for. First is the stylesheet to serve HTML clients:

```xml
<?xml version="1.0" encoding="UTF-8"?>
<xsl:stylesheet version="1.0" xmlns:xsl="http://www.w3.org/1999/XSL/Transform">
<xsl:output method="html" omit-xml-declaration="yes"/>
```

XSLT has the capability of outputting markup for the most common browser formats. Here we specify html-style output as well as instructing the processor to omit the `<?xml version="1.0"?>` declaration (not needed or understood by most browsers) in case it doesn't do this automatically.

Our first template matches the root element, and builds the framework of the web page that will contain our form.

```xml
<xsl:template match="questionnaire">
    <html>
        <head>
            <title>Questionnaire</title>
        </head>
        <body>
            <xsl:element name="form">
                <xsl:attribute name="action">
                    <xsl:value-of select="@processor"/>
                </xsl:attribute>
            </xsl:element>
```

```
                    <xsl:attribute name="method">
                        post
                    </xsl:attribute>
                    <table>
                        <xsl:apply-templates/>
                    </table>
                    <input type="submit"/>
                </xsl:element>
            </body>
        </html>
    </xsl:template>
```

Inside the `<body>` element, we need to instruct the XSLT processor to build us a form element, because the `action` attribute needs to be calculated at run-time: it is obtained from the `<questionnaire>` element's `processor` attribute. The contents of the form element is an HTML table, which will contain the questions, and a submit button. The HTML version of the page ignores the separate pages. Inside the table we perform a template match, which should match the template for each question:

```
    <xsl:template match="question">
        <tr>
            <td>
                <xsl:value-of select="@caption"/>
            </td>
            <td>
                <xsl:element name="select">
                    <xsl:attribute name="name"><xsl:value-of
select="@field"/></xsl:attribute>
                    <xsl:apply-templates/>
                </xsl:element>
            </td>
        </tr>
    </xsl:template>
```

The question template lays out a row of the table, containing two cells. The first cell contains the question's `caption` attribute. The second cell contains an HTML `<select>` element, which again we have to construct by hand, in order to give the element the correct `name` value. Inside the select element we apply templates again, in order to catch each of the contained `choice` elements.

```
    <xsl:template match="choice">
        <option>
            <xsl:value-of select="text()"/>
        </option>
    </xsl:template>
</xsl:stylesheet>
```

The choice elements are simply mapped into an HTML option, containing the text of the original element.

Our WML stylesheet is a bit more complicated. WML has the notion of "cards" which are part of a "deck": a concept foreign to HTML. Since WML has well-defined restrictions on deck size as well as bandwidth a developer will typically combine a number of screens into one deck. In order to do this, we need to think a bit differently than we did with HTML. In addition, WML has a well-defined concept of variables, which are used to store values from forms, and to submit data to the server. So the structure of our WML document will be quite different.

The stylesheet starts, as always, with the stylesheet declaration, but this time we specify more information about the target `doctype`.

```
<?xml version="1.0" encoding="UTF-8"?>
<xsl:stylesheet version="1.0" xmlns:xsl="http://www.w3.org/1999/XSL/Transform">
<xsl:output method="xml" media-type="text/vnd.wap.wml" doctype-public="-
//WAPFORUM//DTD WML 1.1//EN" doctype-
system="http://www.wapforum.org/DTD/wml_1.1.xml"/>
```

Our first template again matches the root element, and all it does is insert the `wml` root element and then apply the next template.

```
<xsl:template match="questionnaire">
    <wml>
        <xsl:apply-templates select="page"/>
    </wml>
</xsl:template>
```

This time we do care about `page` elements: they will constitute our WML cards. We construct each card with an `id` value (which we use for navigation) and a title (which the WAP browser may or may not display for each card). We simply use the XSLT `position()` function to obtain a number for each page, which we use to number the cards. We then apply the other templates and, at the end of the card, we call a special template called `navigate`, which we'll come to later.

```
<xsl:template match="page">
    <xsl:element name="card">
        <xsl:attribute name="id">
            page<xsl:value-of select="position()"/>
        </xsl:attribute>
        <xsl:attribute name="title">
            Questionnaire page <xsl:value-of select="position()"/>
        </xsl:attribute>
        <xsl:apply-templates/>
        <xsl:call-template name="navigate"/>
    </xsl:element>
</xsl:template>
```

The next template to match will be the `question` element, so for each question on a page we write out the question caption, followed by a select box. The select box is virtually identical to the HTML equivalent, except that as well as a name, it has a title:

```
<xsl:template match="question">
    <p>
        <xsl:value-of select="@caption"/>
    </p>
    <p>
        <xsl:element name="select">
            <xsl:attribute name="name"><xsl:value-of
select="@field"/></xsl:attribute>
            <xsl:attribute name="title"><xsl:value-of
select="@field"/></xsl:attribute>
            <xsl:apply-templates/>
        </xsl:element>
    </p>
</xsl:template>
```

The template for choice elements is identical to that from the HTML stylesheet:

```
<xsl:template match="choice">
    <xsl:element name="option">
        <xsl:attribute name="value"><xsl:value-of
select="text()"/></xsl:attribute>
        <xsl:value-of select="text()"/>
    </xsl:element>
</xsl:template>
```

Finally, we need to tell the WML browser how we want to navigate between cards. For all but the last card, we want to have the option of going on to the next card. On the last card, we want to have a submit button.

WML has an element we can use to describe these actions, called the `<do>` element. We will use an `accept`-type `do` element, which presents the user with an option to accept the entries they have made on a particular screen. We model the two different situations using an XSLT `choose` element. First we check to see if the current node is the last node, and if so create an accept action which submits the form to the server. This will ultimately produce WML code that looks something like this:

```
<do type="accept" label="Submit">
    <go href="questionServlet" method="post">
        <postfield name="gender" value="$gender"/>
        <postfield name="age" value="$age"/>
    </go>
</do>
```

To submit data from the form to the server, we need to tell the WML browser what values to submit and what names to give them, using `<postfield>` elements. We obtain all of these by using an XSLT `for-each` loop, which generates a `postfield` element for each question in the questionnaire. The values submitted are the contents of the WML variables, `$gender` and `$age`, which indicate that the post fields should contain the value of the earlier form select boxes with those same names. Here is the XSLT that generates this type of `<do>` element:

```
<xsl:template name="navigate">
    <xsl:choose>
        <xsl:when test="position()=last()">
            <do type="accept" label="Submit">
                <xsl:element name="go">
                    <xsl:attribute name="href">
                        <xsl:value-of select="/questionnaire/@processor"/>
                    </xsl:attribute>
                    <xsl:attribute name="method">post</xsl:attribute>
                    <xsl:for-each select="//question">
                        <xsl:element name="postfield">
                            <xsl:attribute name="name">
                                <xsl:value-of select="@field"/>
                            </xsl:attribute>
                            <xsl:attribute name="value">
                                $<xsl:value-of select="@field"/>
                            </xsl:attribute>
                        </xsl:element>
                    </xsl:for-each>
                </xsl:element>
            </do>
        </xsl:when>
```

In the other case, it's slightly simpler: we simply have to point the user at the next card. We gave each card an ID earlier on, and we can use that as a fragment identifier to tell the browser to look elsewhere in the document. For a card called `page2`, the fragment identifier is `#page2`. We can obtain the number of the next card by adding 1 to the current XSLT `position()`.

```
            <xsl:otherwise>
                <do type="accept" label="Next">
                    <xsl:element name="go">
                        <xsl:attribute name="href"><xsl:value-of
select="concat('#page',position()+1)"/></xsl:attribute>
                    </xsl:element>
                </do>
            </xsl:otherwise>
        </xsl:choose>
    </xsl:template>
</xsl:stylesheet>
```

To give you some idea of what we've done here, here is the result of running each of these stylesheets across the sample data we gave at the beginning. First, the HTML output:

```
<html>
    <head>
        <meta http-equiv="Content-Type" content="text/html; charset=utf-8">
        <title>Questionnaire</title>
    </head>
    <body>
        <form action="questionServlet" method="post">
            <table>
                <tr>
                    <td>What is your gender?</td>
                    <td><select name="gender">
                        <option>Male</option>
                        <option>Female</option>
                            </select></td>
                </tr>
                <tr>
                    <td>What age range do you fall in?</td>
                    <td><select name="age">
                        <option>14-18</option>
                        <option>19-25</option>
                        <option>26-40</option>
                        <option>41+</option>
                            </select></td>
                </tr>
            </table><input type="submit"></form>
    </body>
</html>
```

And second, the WML stylesheet:

```
<?xml version="1.0" encoding="utf-8"?>
<!DOCTYPE wml PUBLIC "-//WAPFORUM//DTD WML 1.1//EN"
                    "http://www.wapforum.org/DTD/wml_1.1.xml">
<wml>
    <card id="page1" title="Questionnaire page 1">
        <p>What is your gender?</p>
        <p>
```

```
            <select name="gender" title="gender">
                <option value="Male">Male</option>
                <option value="Female">Female</option>
            </select>
        </p>
        <do type="accept" label="Next">
            <go href="#page2"/>
        </do>
    </card>
    <card id="page2" title="Questionnaire page 2">
        <p>What age range do you fall in?</p>
        <p>
            <select name="age" title="age">
                <option value="14-18">14-18</option>
                <option value="19-25">19-25</option>
                <option value="26-40">26-40</option>
                <option value="41+">41+</option>
            </select>
        </p>
        <do type="accept" label="Submit">
            <go href="questionServlet" method="post">
                <postfield name="gender" value="$gender"/>
                <postfield name="age" value="$age"/>
            </go>
        </do>
    </card>
</wml>
```

Applying the Transformation

In order to make our application a bit more generic, we create an XSLTServlet class that contains methods used to transform the content using XSLT. The source for this servlet is below:

```
import javax.servlet.*;
import javax.servlet.http.HttpServlet;

import javax.xml.transform.*;
import javax.xml.transform.stream.*;
import org.xml.sax.InputSource;

import java.io.FileInputStream;
import java.io.IOException;

import java.util.Enumeration;
import java.util.Hashtable;

public class XSLTServlet extends HttpServlet {

  private Hashtable transformers   = null;
  private Hashtable contentTypes   = null;
```

The XSLTServlet class will serve as the base class for all our servlets. It contains useful utility methods that will be used as the basis for our application.

The `init()` method loads the transformers we will need for a particular servlet. In our `web.xml` we will specify the stylesheets as well as the users-agents that match them in order to generate the correct markup. Once we retrieve the stylesheet, we instantiate a `javax.xml.transform.Transformer` object to hold the stylesheet. This gives us a performance improvement over re-allocating the transformer each time we need it, but we will need to be a little careful using it in the multi-threaded servlet environment.

```
public void init() throws ServletException {
  super.init();
  ServletConfig config = getServletConfig();
  ServletContext ctx = config.getServletContext();
  transformers = new Hashtable();

  try {
    TransformerFactory factory = TransformerFactory.newInstance();
    Enumeration params = getServletConfig().getInitParameterNames();
```

What we do next is iterate through all of the parameters specified in our deployment descriptor. Each of the stylesheets defined are prefixed by `"xsl"` so we are explicitly looking for those here. We then get the "real" path to each stylesheet from the servlet context, and instantiate a new `javax.xml.transform.Transformer` to pre-load our stylesheets and boost performance a bit.

```
    while (params.hasMoreElements()) {
      String param = (String)params.nextElement();

      if (param.startsWith("xsl")) {
        // create a new transformer and add it to the table
        String userAgent = param.substring(3);
        String xslFilePath = ctx.getRealPath(config.getInitParameter(param));

        StreamSource src = new StreamSource(new FileInputStream(xslFilePath));

        Transformer trans = factory.newTransformer(src);
        addTransformer(trans, userAgent);
      }
    }
  } catch(Exception e) {
    throw new ServletException(e.getMessage());
  }

  getContentTypes(config);
}
```

The private method `getContentTypes()` iterates through all of the transformers that have been added and attempts to match them with the initialization parameters assigning content types to each user agent. If no match is found the content type defaults to `text/html`:

We check through the keys of the transformers table in order to determine the content-types that the application supports. We use this information to retrieve the appropriate transformer:

```
private void getContentTypes(ServletConfig conf) {

  final String DEFAULT_CONTENT_TYPE = "text/html";
  contentTypes = new Hashtable();
  Enumeration list = transformers.keys();
```

```
      while (list.hasMoreElements()) {
        String userAgent = (String)list.nextElement();
        String contentType = conf.getInitParameter("ct" + userAgent);

        // if contentType is null, set to default
        if (contentType == null) {
          contentType = DEFAULT_CONTENT_TYPE;
        }
        contentTypes.put(userAgent, contentType);
      }
    }

    public Transformer getTransformer(String userAgent) {
      return (Transformer) transformers.get(userAgent);
    }

    public void addTransformer(Transformer transformer, String userAgent) {
      transformers.put(userAgent, transformer);
    }

    public String getContentType(String userAgent) {
      return (String) contentTypes.get(userAgent);
    }
```

The `addTransformer()` and `getTransformer()` methods adds a mapping between a browser type and a transformer, and get the transformer associated with a given user agent.

All of the transformation work a servlet will need is contained in the following method. An application passes in the user-agent for the browser making the request. The user-agent is matched against the table of transformers to determine if an appropriate one exists. Since user-agents can vary greatly, what we have done instead is performed a `userAgent.indexOf()` to determine the most closely specified user agent in our table. This is a bit of a kludge but serves our purposes.

A better way to do this would be to define an entire class structure built around determining user-agents and allowing developers to specify new ones through properties files. We will see such an implementation later in the chapter.

```
    public void transform(String userAgent, Source doc, ServletResponse res) throws
  TransformerException, IOException {
      Enumeration list = transformers.keys();
      Transformer transformer = null;
      String agent = null;

      while (list.hasMoreElements()) {
        // if there is a user-agent like this one get the associated transformer
        agent = (String)list.nextElement();

        if ( userAgent.indexOf(agent) != -1 ) {
          transformer = getTransformer(agent);
          break;
        }
      }
```

```
      // if the transformer is null, no matching one found
      if (transformer == null) {
        throw new TransformerException("No transformer for user-agent " +
userAgent);
      }

      // set the appropriate content type
      res.setContentType(getContentType(agent));

      // create the Result object
      StreamResult result = new StreamResult(res.getOutputStream());
      transformer.transform(doc, result);
    }
  }
```

Our questionnaire servlet that will be extending this class appears below. It will use the methods of its parent class to load all of the stylesheets and match them to user agents. It will also be responsible for applying the appropriate transformation for a given user-agent.

```
import java.io.IOException;
import javax.servlet.ServletException;
import javax.servlet.http.HttpServletRequest;
import javax.servlet.http.HttpServletResponse;

import javax.xml.transform.stream.StreamResult;
import javax.xml.transform.stream.StreamSource;

import XSLTServlet;

public class QuestionnaireServlet extends XSLTServlet {
  private StreamSource source  = null;
```

Our `init()` method here doesn't bother with determining the stylesheets. Remember that this is what the base class is for, which is why it is very important that you call `super.init()` in order for those stylesheets to be loaded. But we create a `StreamSource` object around the underlying source document:

```
  public void init() throws ServletException {
    super.init();

    // look for the document we are supposed to load
    String doc = getServletConfig().getInitParameter("doc");
    source = new
StreamSource(getServletConfig().getServletContext().getRealPath(doc));
  }
```

The `doGet()` method simply forwards requests to the `doPost()` method.

```
  public void doGet(HttpServletRequest request, HttpServletResponse response)
throws ServletException, IOException {
    doPost(request, response);
  }
```

Our `doPost()` method is simplified due to the work of the base class. We simply determine the user agent and pass that along to the `transform()` method which will generate the appropriate content:

```
public void doPost(HttpServletRequest request, HttpServletResponse response)
throws ServletException, IOException {
    String userAgent = request.getHeader("User-Agent");

    try {
      transform(userAgent, source, response);
    } catch(Exception e) {
      throw new IOException(e.getMessage());
    }
  }
}
```

Of course, in order to load our stylesheets we need to specify them in the `web.xml` file as shown below:

```
<?xml version="1.0" encoding="ISO-8859-1"?>

<!DOCTYPE web-app
    PUBLIC "-//Sun Microsystems, Inc.//DTD Web Application 2.2//EN"
    "http://java.sun.com/j2ee/dtds/web-app_2_2.dtd">

<web-app>
    <servlet>
        <servlet-name>
      questionnaireServlet
        </servlet-name>
        <servlet-class>
      QuestionnaireServlet
        </servlet-class>
```

We prefix all of our user-agents with `"xsl"` in order to specify that these parameters are the stylesheets for the user-agents.

```
        <init-param>
            <param-name>xslMozilla</param-name>
    <param-value>WEB-INF\xsl\questionnaire_html.xsl</param-value>
        </init-param>

        <init-param>
    <param-name>xslUP</param-name>
    <param-value>WEB-INF\xsl\questionnaire_wml.xsl</param-value>
        </init-param>

        <init-param>
            <param-name>doc</param-name>
    <param-value>WEB-INF\xml\questionnaire_main.xml</param-value>
        </init-param>
```

We also define the content types that are to be used for each of the above user-agents. These are prefixed with "ct".

```
        <!-- define the content type for each of the above user agents -->
        <init-param>
            <param-name>ctMozilla</param-name>
            <param-value>text/html</param-value>
        </init-param>

        <init-param>
            <param-name>ctUP</param-name>
            <param-value>text/vnd.wap.wml</param-value>
        </init-param>

    </servlet>

    <servlet-mapping>
    <servlet-name>questionnaireServlet</servlet-name>
    <url-pattern>/questionnaire</url-pattern>
    </servlet-mapping>

</web-app>
```

The directory structure for our application is then as follows:

```
webapps\
    xslt\
        WEB-INF\
            web.xml
            xml\
                questionnaire_main.xml
            xsl\
                questionnaire_wml.xsl
                questionnaire_html.xsl
            classes\
                XSLTServlet.class
                QuestionnaireServlet.class
```

Setting up the UP.SDK

Installing the OpenWave UP.SDK is quite simple. You can obtain the installation at http://developer.openwave.com/. Upon downloading, execute the file and the installation will begin. The instructions are relatively straightforward.

Step 3: Run the Application

If your `TOMCAT_HOME` and `JAXP_HOME` environment variables are set to point to your Jakarta Tomcat and JAXP directories respectively, this sequence of commands should enable you to compile the servlets:

```
set CLASSPATH=%JAXP_HOME%\jaxp.jar;%JAXP_HOME%\crimson.jar;%JAXP_HOME%\xalan.jar

javac -classpath .;%TOMCAT_HOME%\lib\servlet.jar;%CLASSPATH%
QuestionnaireServlet.java
```

Once the files are compiled, you can deploy the servlets with this command:

```
copy *.java %TOMCAT_HOME%\webapps\xslt\WEB-INF\classes
```

And then start Tomcat with this command:

```
%TOMCAT_HOME%\bin\startup
```

Below we will see what happens when we access the URL of the servlet (http://localhost:8080/xslt/questionnaire) using different user-agents. First, let's look at Internet Explorer, whose user-agent header will match to "Mozilla". Most common web browsers have this in the user agent header, since they share a common ancestry in NCSA Mosaic. This will result in the HTML stylesheet being applied:

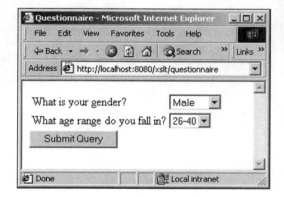

Using OpenWave's SDK, we get the following screens:

 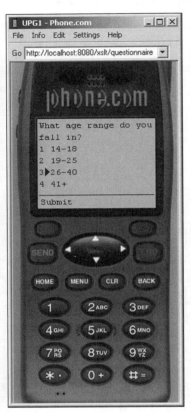

Now, when we submit either form, we get a 404 not found error, which is a result of the fact that we've not created a servlet to process the results. There's a simple reason for this: we haven't extended our XSLT logic to handle anything other than simple form data, so we don't have any way of presenting a simple result page. Our system doesn't lend itself well to dynamically generating content within our servlet before applying the transformation.

Limitations of Our Design

The main problem with our implementation is that, while we can dynamically generate content for different devices, we cannot easily generate that content based on user responses. For example, we have no problem displaying the questions to the user in HTML, WML, or any other markup but we cannot necessarily generate content containing what the user chose as an answer. The problem is generating markup that is dependent upon user input in a platform-independent manner. In other words how can we interact with what the user enters?

Considering what we just implemented, we simply can't do that without a lot of work. How can we create a solution generalized for all platforms? The answer is using a framework that specializes in this very task. In the next section we will look at how we can use XSL/T to generate reactive content that does not rely on the capabilities of the browsing device.

A Framework for Content Generation

Now that we have seen how we can combine XSLT and servlets to generate server-side content for multiple clients, we can look at a package that adds much functionality to the application above, and that has done most of the work towards defining a framework for publishing the data.

Having a better understanding of what is going on under the cover, we can concentrate on the task of communicating the message rather than making sure that all potential clients are served.

Cocoon

Beginning as simply a servlet for generating static XML pages, Cocoon has evolved into a full-featured framework for generating content for multiple platforms. In addition, Cocoon allows us to plug in our own components and customize content generation. However, the built-in functionality should suffice for most needs, and so we will concentrate on covering that.

A Brief Look at Cocoon's Architecture

What Cocoon does that is new is that it defines an additional separation of logic and content. Most systems attempt to separate out the data and the way that it is displayed: separation of content and style. Cocoon separates style into two levels, logic and pure style.

Basically, we first produce the content that will be displayed; this stage may include querying a database and formatting the results into a predetermined DTD format. Once we have the data we apply the page logic to it. This defines the structure that the information will be in on the page. When we have defined the data that will be shown and the way that it is shown, we transform it to the formatting it will be in, whether WML, HTML or some other format. Each transformation is done using stylesheets.

While Cocoon can be used for real-time processing, the complexity involved causes a significant performance penalty on the server. As a result Cocoon is often used as a page compiler to create content offline that is then published to a static site. Once areas and processes that are relatively static (such as defining mappings between user agents and formatting) are laid out, Cocoon can maintain the model for the site.

In the examples below, we will illustrate how all of these functions fit together to generate our content.

Setting Up Cocoon

This section will describe setting up Cocoon for use with Tomcat 3.2.1, which is really only a servlet. More detailed instructions are available at http://xml.apache.org/cocoon/install.html#tomcat.

Once you have downloaded Cocoon, expand the archive. Cocoon has a strange directory arrangement and the best way for us to ensure that everything we need is on the classpath, or otherwise available to the Cocoon web application, is to manually move all the pieces into the right place ourselves. Move the following .jar files from Cocoon's lib directory into Tomcat's lib directory:

- ❏ fop_0_15_0.jar
- ❏ turbine-pool.jar
- ❏ w3c.jar
- ❏ xalan_1_2_D02.jar
- ❏ xml.jar
- ❏ xerces_1_2.jar

A nice feature of this and later versions of Tomcat is that .jar files are automatically loaded when in this directory. Unfortunately, they're loaded in alphabetical order, which means that the Sun parser.jar (which contains Sun's old Project X parser: a DOM Level 1 parser) will be loaded before the Cocoon xerces_1_2.jar (which contains the DOM Level 2 classes). We need Xerces to be loaded first, so we have to rename the xerces_1_2.jar file to something which will load earlier: aaa_xerces_1_2.jar, for example.

In addition, you need to place the cocoon.jar file from Cocoon's bin directory into Tomcat's lib directory as well.

Next we need to define Cocoon's context. In Tomcat's conf directory, we need to modify the server.xml file. Add the following line inside the <ContextManager> element:

```
<Context path="/cocoon" docBase="webapps/cocoon" debug="0" reloadable="true" />
```

This tells Tomcat that any files accessed through a URL containing "/cocoon" are to be passed to the Cocoon servlet and that the URL is mapped to the webapps\cocoon directory. We also specify the debug output level (in this case none) and that the servlet should be checked to see if changes have been made before each access, and if so, reloaded.

Next we need to create the directories we specified in our context. We create the following directories:

- %TOMCAT_HOME%\webapps\cocoon
- %TOMCAT_HOME%\webapps\cocoon\WEB-INF

where TOMCAT_HOME is an environment variable set to the top directory of your Tomcat installation. Now we move the Cocoon descriptors into the appropriate directories. Under the Cocoon directory, we move the src\WEB-INF\web.xml and conf\cocoon.properties to the cocoon\WEB-INF directory we just created under Tomcat. We need to modify the web.xml file slightly to tell it where it can find the cocoon.properties file. The change is noted below.

```
<web-app>
 <servlet>
  <servlet-name>org.apache.cocoon.Cocoon</servlet-name>
  <servlet-class>org.apache.cocoon.Cocoon</servlet-class>
  <init-param>
   <param-name>properties</param-name>
   <param-value>WEB-INF/cocoon.properties</param-value>
  </init-param>
 </servlet>

 <servlet-mapping>
  <servlet-name>org.apache.cocoon.Cocoon</servlet-name>
  <url-pattern>*.xml</url-pattern>
 </servlet-mapping>
</web-app>
```

Hello, World!

To get a feel for Cocoon and how it works we will implement the tried-and-true "Hello, World!" program. Below is a simple Hello World application that illustrates the principles behind Cocoon. Here is the source document we will use, which you should save in the `webapps\cocoon` directory as `helloworld_main.xml`:

```xml
<?xml version="1.0"?>
<?cocoon-process type="xslt"?>
<?xml-stylesheet href="xsl/helloworld_html.xsl" type="text/xsl" media="explorer"?>
<?xml-stylesheet href="xsl/helloworld_wml.xsl" type="text/xsl" media="wap"?>
<page>
    <header>
        <title>Hello, World!</title>
    </header>
    <content>
        <section>Hello, XSLT World!</section>
    </content>
</page>
```

We use three processing instructions: `cocoon-process` and two `xml-stylesheet` instructions. You should be familiar with the latter two but the first is central to how Cocoon operates. Cocoon has a number of built-in processors for manipulating content. The one we use is the XSLT processor. Below that is the stylesheet instruction, which is just as important. The media type specifications of these two stylesheet instructions says that, if the client accessing the page is of type "explorer", the `helloworld_html.xsl` stylesheet should be used to transform the content, while if the client is of type "wap", it should use `helloworld_wml.xsl`. So how does Cocoon determine which media a browser maps to?

In the `cocoon.properties` file there is a section that allows you to define media types and how they apply to different user agents. Below is the default configuration:

```
browser.0 = explorer=MSIE
browser.1 = pocketexplorer=MSPIE
browser.2 = handweb=HandHTTP
browser.3 = avantgo=AvantGo
browser.4 = imode=DoCoMo
browser.5 = opera=Opera
browser.6 = lynx=Lynx
browser.7 = java=Java
browser.8 = wap=Nokia
browser.9 = wap=UP
browser.10 = wap=Wapalizer
browser.11 = mozilla5=Mozilla/5
browser.12 = mozilla5=Netscape6/
browser.13 = netscape=Mozilla
```

We can simply add media types or assign the same ones to different devices as they come along. For example, the "explorer=MSIE" tag indicates that the XSL stylesheet associated to the media type "explorer" should be mapped to those browsers that have the string "MSIE" in their "user-agent" HTTP header.

Moving forward, we now need to define stylesheets. The XSLT is fairly straightforward, but we include a processing instruction that defines the formatter Cocoon is to use for the result. Here's a stylesheet which will generate HTML output. You should save this in a subfolder of your webapps\cocoon directory called xsl, as helloworld_html.xsl:

```xml
<?xml version="1.0"?>
<xsl:stylesheet xmlns:xsl="http://www.w3.org/1999/XSL/Transform" version="1.0">
<xsl:output method="html" indent="no" omit-xml-declaration="yes"/>
    <xsl:template match="/">
    <xsl:processing-instruction name="cocoon-format">
        type="text/html"
    </xsl:processing-instruction>
        <html>
        <xsl:apply-templates />
        </html>
    </xsl:template>
```

We create the HTML <title> element inside of the HTML <head> tag, as would be expected.

```xml
    <xsl:template match="header">
        <head>
            <title><xsl:value-of select="title" /></title>
        </head>
        <xsl:apply-templates select="content"/>
    </xsl:template>
    <xsl:template match="content">
        <body>
            <xsl:apply-templates />
        </body>
    </xsl:template>
```

We create a section heading from our document's <section> tag.

```xml
    <xsl:template match="section">
        <p>
            <h1><xsl:value-of select="."/></h1>
            <xsl:apply-templates select="block"/>
        </p>
    </xsl:template>
```

Finally, we insert the body of our text into the document to be output.

```xml
    <xsl:template match="block" >
        <xsl:value-of select="." />
    </xsl:template>
</xsl:stylesheet>
```

Here is the stylesheet we use for WML, which also goes in the xsl directory, and is called helloworld_wml.xsl. Notice how the processing instruction we define specifies that the output is for WML.

```
<?xml version="1.0"?>
<xsl:stylesheet xmlns:xsl="http://www.w3.org/1999/XSL/Transform" version="1.0">

    <xsl:template match="page">
    <xsl:processing-instruction name="cocoon-format">
        type="text/wml"
    </xsl:processing-instruction>
```

We're only creating a single card in this WML deck. As with our HTML page, we set the title attribute of the <card> element to the title of our document. We also assign an arbitrary value to the id attribute.

```
<wml>
    <xsl:element name="card">
        <xsl:attribute name="title">
            <xsl:value-of select="header/title"/>
        </xsl:attribute>
        <xsl:attribute name="id">top</xsl:attribute>
        <p align="center">
        <xsl:apply-templates />
        </p>
    </xsl:element>
</wml>
</xsl:template>
```

Again, as with our HTML document we want to actually display the title in an obvious manner. Here we use italics.

```
<xsl:template match="header">
    <xsl:apply-templates />
</xsl:template>
<xsl:template match="title">
    <i><xsl:value-of select="."/></i><br />
</xsl:template>
```

Finally, we insert the body of the text into our WML card.

```
<xsl:template match="content">
    <xsl:apply-templates />
</xsl:template>
<xsl:template match="section">
    <xsl:value-of select="."/><br/>
    <xsl:value-of select="block" />
</xsl:template>

</xsl:stylesheet>
```

As you can see these stylesheets are pure XSLT; only the processing instruction specifying the output format is a Cocoon-specific feature, otherwise anyone well versed in XSLT can easily adapt to Cocoon.

581

Now, when we access the XML document via our web browser, or the UP.SDK emulator, we can see that Cocoon applies the appropriate XSLT stylesheet for us:

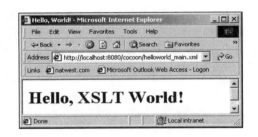

The next section will show how we can leverage Cocoon with our sample application.

Implementing Our Application with Cocoon

We need to change our initial data slightly to create documents that Cocoon can use. We modify the XML file from the sample application as noted below:

```
<?xml version="1.0"?>
<?cocoon-process type="xslt"?>
<?xml-stylesheet href="xsl/questionnaire_html.xsl" type="text/xsl"
media="explorer"?>
<?xml-stylesheet href="xsl/questionnaire_wml.xsl" type="text/xsl" media="wap"?>
<questionnaire processor="questionnaire_main.xml">
    <page>
        <question field="gender" caption="What is your gender?">
            <choice>Male</choice>
            <choice>Female</choice>
        </question>
    </page>
    <page>
```

```
        <question field="age" caption="What age range do you fall in?">
            <choice>14-18</choice>
            <choice>19-25</choice>
            <choice>26-40</choice>
            <choice>41+</choice>
        </question>
    </page>
</questionnaire>
```

The processing instructions added tell Cocoon to process this document using XSLT and apply the correct stylesheet given a particular user-agent. We then change the processor attribute of the questionnaire element to point to the `questionnaire_main.xml` file in order to provide the answer. Looking at this document it is not obvious how we are going to do that, but we will soon see how this can be accomplished.

Our implementation previously was limited by the fact that we could not generate content based on user interaction. Fortunately with Cocoon this is not a problem. Below is the HTML stylesheet used to do exactly that, built around our original HTML XSL stylesheet:

```
<?xml version="1.0"?>
<xsl:stylesheet xmlns:xsl="http://www.w3.org/1999/XSL/Transform" version="1.0">
<xsl:output method="xml" indent="no" omit-xml-declaration="yes"/>

    <xsl:param name="gender"/>
    <xsl:param name="age"/>
```

Here we are using the `<xsl:param>` element to define parameters for use within our stylesheet. In and of themselves they don't do more than define a constant. However a recommended behavior of this element is to allow web servers to pass in variables to a stylesheet, much like a method call. Cocoon implements this behavior, passing in HTTP POST parameters to the stylesheet.

```
    <xsl:template match="questionnaire">

        <xsl:processing-instruction name="cocoon-format">
            type="text/html"
        </xsl:processing-instruction>
```

Here we tell Cocoon to format the output for HTML. This formatting will be applied after the stylesheet has run its course.

```
        <html>
            <head>
                <title>Questionnaire</title>
            </head>
            <body>
```

Now, instead of simply building the form element as before, we need to detect whether the client is returning to this page for the first time, or after they've filled in the form. We can tell by looking to see if the gender and age properties are set. If the user is visiting the page with no values for those parameters, we simply show them the form, using exactly the same template as before:

```
<xsl:choose>
    <xsl:when test="not($gender) and not($age)">
        <xsl:element name="form">
            <xsl:attribute name="action">
                <xsl:value-of select="@processor"/>
            </xsl:attribute>
            <xsl:attribute name="method">post</xsl:attribute>
            <table>
                <xsl:apply-templates/>
            </table>
            <input type="submit"/>
        </xsl:element>
    </xsl:when>
```

If the user has already completed the form, then we return the values of the two parameters instead:

```
    <xsl:otherwise>
        <p>You are <xsl:value-of select="$gender"/></p>
        <p>You are aged <xsl:value-of select="$age"/></p>
    </xsl:otherwise>
</xsl:choose>

        </body>
    </html>
</xsl:template>
```

The rest of the stylesheet is just the other templates for completing the form:

```
<xsl:template match="question">
    <tr>
        <td>
            <xsl:value-of select="@caption"/>
        </td>
        <td>
            <xsl:element name="select">
                <xsl:attribute name="name"><xsl:value-of
select="@field"/></xsl:attribute>
                <xsl:apply-templates/>
            </xsl:element>
        </td>
    </tr>
</xsl:template>
<xsl:template match="choice">
    <option>
        <xsl:value-of select="text()"/>
    </option>
</xsl:template>
</xsl:stylesheet>
```

This may be a bit confusing at first. Remember that our content document specifies that it should be used as the callback document, meaning that once a user has entered a response that document will be used to produce output as well. When an option is selected, say "gender", the parameter declaration in the stylesheet will be populated. What the <xsl:when> element does is test whether or not one of the parameters contains a value, just like an if statement in Java. If not, we display the question to the user since this means the user has yet to answer the questions.

Sample output using Cocoon is shown below:

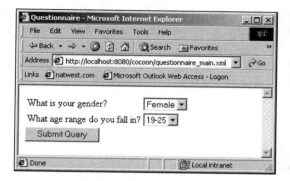
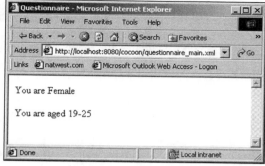

Here is our stylesheet for WML, again based around our previous stylesheet:

```
<?xml version="1.0" encoding="UTF-8"?>
<xsl:stylesheet version="1.0" xmlns:xsl="http://www.w3.org/1999/XSL/Transform">
    <xsl:output method="xml" media-type="text/vnd.wap.wml"
                doctype-public="-//WAPFORUM//DTD WML 1.1//EN"
                doctype-system="http://www.wapforum.org/DTD/wml_1.1.xml"/>
    <xsl:param name="gender"/>
    <xsl:param name="age"/>
```

Again we use the `<xsl:param>` element to define parameters to be passed in.

```
<xsl:template match="questionnaire">
    <xsl:processing-instruction name="cocoon-format">
        type="text/wml"
    </xsl:processing-instruction>
```

This time we specify the output to be prepared for WML-enabled devices when specifying the cocoon-format processing instruction.

As with the HTML stylesheet we test if a value has been set for either the gender or age parameters. If not, this means the user has yet to answer any questions so we display the first question card. We use the same generic template for each card that will generate both questions, as before.

```
<wml>
    <xsl:choose>
        <xsl:when test="not($gender) and not($age)">
            <xsl:apply-templates select="page"/>
        </xsl:when>
```

In the alternative case, we have results to display, so we do so, in a single card deck.

```
<xsl:otherwise>
    <card id="result" title="Questionnaire Results">
        <p>You are <xsl:value-of select="$gender"/>
        </p>
        <p>You are aged <xsl:value-of select="$age"/>
        </p>
    </card>
```

```
                    </xsl:otherwise>
                </xsl:choose>
        </wml>
    </xsl:template>
```

Again, the other templates are exactly as before.

```
    <xsl:template match="page">
        <xsl:element name="card">
            <xsl:attribute name="id">page<xsl:value-of
select="position()"/></xsl:attribute>
            <xsl:attribute name="title">Questionnaire page <xsl:value-of
select="position()"/></xsl:attribute>
            <xsl:call-template name="navigate"/>
            <xsl:apply-templates/>
        </xsl:element>
    </xsl:template>
    <xsl:template match="question">
        <p>
            <xsl:value-of select="@caption"/>
        </p>
        <p>
            <xsl:element name="select">
                <xsl:attribute name="name"><xsl:value-of
select="@field"/></xsl:attribute>
                <xsl:attribute name="title"><xsl:value-of
select="@field"/></xsl:attribute>
                <xsl:apply-templates/>
            </xsl:element>
        </p>
    </xsl:template>
    <xsl:template match="choice">
        <xsl:element name="option">
            <xsl:attribute name="value"><xsl:value-of
select="text()"/></xsl:attribute>
            <xsl:value-of select="text()"/>
        </xsl:element>
    </xsl:template>
    <xsl:template name="navigate">
        <xsl:choose>
            <xsl:when test="position()=last()">
                <do type="accept" label="Submit">
                    <xsl:element name="go">
                        <xsl:attribute name="href">
                            <xsl:value-of select="/questionnaire/@processor"/>
                        </xsl:attribute>
                        <xsl:attribute name="method">post</xsl:attribute>
                        <xsl:for-each select="//question">
                            <xsl:element name="postfield">
                                <xsl:attribute name="name">
                                    <xsl:value-of select="@field"/>
                                </xsl:attribute>
                                <xsl:attribute name="value">
                                    <xsl:value-of select="concat('$',@field)"/>
                                </xsl:attribute>
                            </xsl:element>
```

```
                    <postfield name="result" value="true"/>
                </xsl:for-each>
            </xsl:element>
        </do>
    </xsl:when>
    <xsl:otherwise>
        <do type="accept" label="Next">
            <xsl:element name="go">
                <xsl:attribute name="href">
                    <xsl:value-of select="concat('#page',position()+1)"/>
                </xsl:attribute>
            </xsl:element>
        </do>
    </xsl:otherwise>
    </xsl:choose>
    </xsl:template>
</xsl:stylesheet>
```

Let's look at what we had to do. First we inserted an `<xsl:processing-instruction>` declaration directly inside the match for the root element. Once Cocoon's XSLT processor is done, the result is passed to a Cocoon formatter; this formatter is dependent upon the device displaying it, and we select which formatter applies to our output with this instruction. For example, for HTML formatting we use `"text/html"` for the cocoon-format PI. The WML value is `"text/wml"`.

> *Notice that with the HTML formatter the value corresponds to the MIME-type for HTML whereas for WML this is not the case. In WML the MIME-type is `text/vnd.wap.wml`, which is the MIME-type of the result of Cocoon's formatting a document that indicates the format as being `"text/wml"`. Don't assume that Cocoon's formatters directly correspond to the ultimate target MIME-type.*

Just as we did with the HTML stylesheet, we determine what will display depending upon the value of the gender and age parameters. Below we have screenshots of the resulting output.

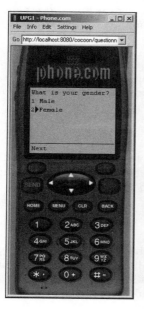
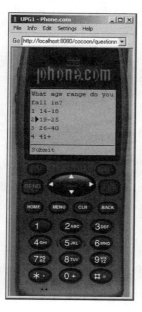

By now you should be seeing how Cocoon leverages XSLT to make a powerful framework. We didn't have to write any custom Java code for any of this: all we need is knowledge of stylesheets and Cocoon takes care of the rest. Unlike our Java implementation, we can very easily generate output that varies depending on what the user enters rather than being limited to posting static data.

Cocoon is a more powerful publishing framework than we have covered here, including a powerful dynamic content generation language (XSP –eXtensible Server Pages), and the ability to take content from a number of different producers, apply contextual presentation logic, and output the same information in a wide variety of formats.

If you have done a "view source" from whatever browser you used to access the samples, you probably noticed that Cocoon places a comment at the end telling you how long it took Cocoon to process your request. Cocoon requires a lot of processing power in order to generate pages. The authors realized this and included a few rather simple mechanisms that make Cocoon perform rather well given the circumstances. The principal mechanism is a cache, which ensures that the same content is not transformed the same way repeatedly.

Cocoon 2

While the current version of Cocoon is extremely powerful, it does have its drawbacks. First, it is based on the DOM API. The Cocoon authors describe this as a "passive" API, essentially meaning that the document must reside in memory before anything can be done with it. Since Cocoon could potentially be processing rather large documents (especially in the case of XSL-Formatting Objects, which can be used to create PDF files, for example) this is obviously a problem.

Rather than use DOM, the designers have elected to use SAX in Cocoon2, which is what they call an "active" API where elements are processed as they are encountered. Cocoon was at first thought to only be a proof-of-concept implementation not thinking it would become what it is today, perhaps being a reason for why SAX was not chosen to begin with.

Using SAX increases performance dramatically: whereas the server had to wait for the document to be loaded into memory before being processed for the client, the server can now process elements and send them to the client as they are parsed increasing response times dramatically.

Sitemaps

A big addition in Cocoon 2 is the concept of sitemaps. A sitemap is a central repository of web information, which is really a step towards having Cocoon manage the entire web site, from its content to the manner in which is retrieved.

Status

Cocoon 2 is still in the alpha stages of development and as of yet is not considered stable. There is a CVS branch you can view if you are curious and wish to look into Cocoon 2. You can find more information on Cocoon 2 at http://xml.apache.org/cocoon/cocoon2.html.

Cocoon Conclusions

We have only touched the tip of the iceberg of Cocoon. A number of other features are available, so many that an entire book could be dedicated to developing applications using them. As such we cannot hope to cover all of them here, but it is hoped that your interest has been piqued to learn more. You are encouraged to go to http://xml.apache.org/cocoon/ to learn more.

Other Content Frameworks

Aside from Cocoon, other frameworks exist that accomplish the same goal. Some are open-source initiatives like Cocoon, others are commercial products.

❑   OracleMobile (http://www.oraclemobile.com/) has an ASP model whereby you develop your site's content in Oracle's MobileXML language. From this language content is generated which is browseable by just about any wireless device.

❑   Aligo's M-1 Server (http://www.aligo.com/) is similar except it is software you buy to plug into your system. It also allows you to develop one set of pages to be displayed on any wireless device as well as web browsers.

❑   Prowler is another open-source initiative (http://www.infozone-group.org/projects_main.html) aimed at providing a foundation for web applications. What sets Prowler apart from something like Cocoon is that it manages almost the entire application. It relies on a four-tier architecture: the data (called resources in Prowler-speak), adapters (which convert XML requests/responses into a format the resource can understand), the repository which contains a root document linking all resources via adapters to one XML document, and at the top is the Prowler API which provides access to the repository in a session and transaction-based manner. Notice we have said nothing of content generation: a framework like Cocoon can sit on top of Prowler and use it to retrieve data.

❑   Enhydra is another open source product (http://www.enhydra.org/), which is really a full enterprise server platform, and so takes in much broader scope than simply content presentation. One of its goals, though, is also to provide unified presentation logic, regardless of the client browser.

❑   Jetspeed is an implementation of an Enterprise Information Portal (EIP). What an EIP does is make applications, databases, and other network resources available to users via a web or wireless browser. Jetspeed also plugs in to content frameworks like Cocoon. Being under the auspices of the Jakarta effort, Jetspeed is an open-source work-in-progress. More information can be found at http://jakarta.apache.org/jetspeed/site/.

Summary

We saw in this chapter the issues involved in server-side content generation and the problems we as developers face in a world of many Internet-ready devices. In the early days it was easy to write content for web-browsers, because only a few different browser flavors existed. Now we have wireless devices of all shapes, sizes, and capabilities we have to worry about.

Our first stab at the solving the problem was to create a framework for handling multiple types of content. We created a basic servlet containing methods used to transform XML into different content-types. This is a good solution for sites that have only static content, but we ran into maintainability issues when we wanted to display content based on user input.

Enter Cocoon: a framework whose purpose is to provide a mechanism for generating multiple markup interpretations of the same content. It is made to do just what we want: take a platform-neutral markup and generate multiple browser-specific documents. What's more is that it does not suffer from the problems of our static-only implementation: it is more than capable of handling dynamic content.

In order to survive in the world of wireless clients, we need to find a way to avoid a maintenance nightmare. The three-tier architecture model does a good job of separating the concerns of the data, business, and content logic but we are left with the problem of generating content for untold numbers of devices. As we've seen over the course of this chapter, XML and XSLT are the key technologies that can help us to ensure that the principles of processing, production, and formatting of content are separated.

The Xerces Blue
Butterfly, which became
extinct earlier this century,
and after which the Xerces XML
parser is named ...

15

Client-Side Presentation Logic

So far in this book, much has been said on the subject of how XML can be used in the design of server-side applications and components within the J2EE context. By performing most of the processing and transformations on the server side, our web-based application and services can be used by a very wide audience via even the most basic HTML browsers. This is possible because the information that is passed between the client and the server in these cases is standard HTML, even though the internal data interchange format may originally have been XML. The server application logic has transformed the data (perhaps using XSLT) to HTML by the time the client accesses the data through a servlet or JSP.

The protocol of choice used between the client and the server is HTTP. In fact, much of the modern corporate intranet infrastructure is optimized and configured for delivering HTTP-based traffic. This architecture reflects a very 'thin' client, basically a browser supporting simple HTML. The diagram overleaf illustrates a standard view of a J2EE application.

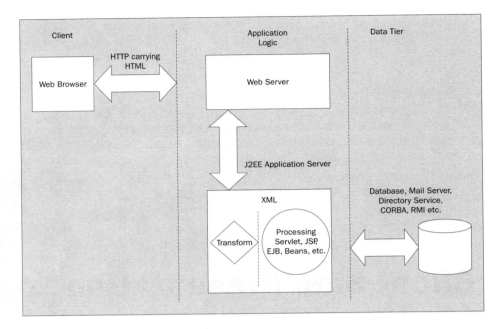

Client–Side XML Processing

In practice, however, there are frequently real-life scenarios where a more proportional sharing of processing between the client and server is necessary. This means that the client will share in the data processing tasks, potentially alleviating the heavy load on the server. In this scenario, the data interchanged between the client and the server is more than HTML. The interchange also contains data that the client can perform processing on. In such a case, the protocol of choice between client and server is still HTTP (as it is still the most widely supported protocol in corporate intranet infrastructures).

This means that we must incorporate an extra data delivery mechanism between the 'medium weight' client and the server. XML, as it turns out, is perfect for satisfying this niche in an interoperable manner. The diagram below illustrates the data flow in these scenarios. We can see the additional transform and processing function that is performed by the client now, something that did not occur in the 'thin' client scenario before.

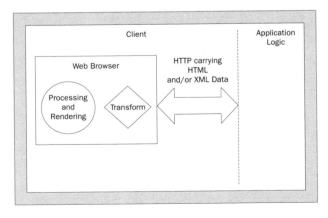

In fact, if we restrict our discussion to a purely Java-based context, the processing and transformation occurring on the client side will be carried out by application logic written in the Java language. As the current processing for automatic XSLT transformation on the browsers is rather patchy at this moment, the client-side processing module is implemented using a Java applet in this context. Appropriately enough, all of the major mainstream browsers now provide full support for Java applets – with most of them at the JDK 1.1 level. This is certainly sufficient to perform highly sophisticated processing on the client side.

Couple this with the fact that most modern-day client machines are actually quite high-powered (fast CPUs with lots of memory), there is even more reason to adopt a 'medium weight' client architecture to offload the processing from the server. The only caveat may be bandwidth restrictions and the presence of firewalls, especially when the client connects to the server via slow links (such as dialup modems). This effectively limits the size of the applet that may be downloaded.

When we combine the universal data encapsulation/expression power of XML with the run-anywhere nature of Java, we have a widely applicable medium weight client architecture that can be deployed in a very wide variety of design scenarios. The diagram below illustrates the 'medium weight' client in the Java context. Especially noteworthy is the ability to have custom application logic (in the form of a downloaded applet) to process XML-based data on the client side.

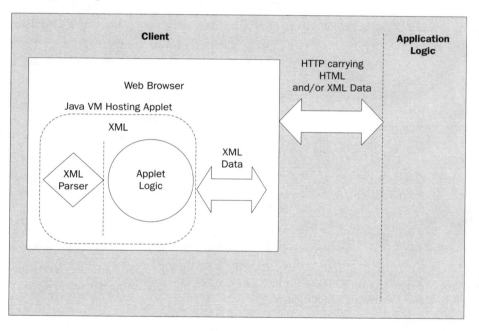

In this chapter, our focus is on these client designs – designs that involve significant processing and presentation logic on the client side. Through the analysis of a case study, we will see:

❑   Why client-side processing is often a good idea in real-world application problem solving

❑   The various technologies that enable client-side XML processing

❑   When it may be appropriate to apply each of the client-side processing technologies

❑   What is involved in enabling client-side XML processing

Along the way, we will also be covering design techniques applicable for client-side Java XML programming. More specifically, we will see:

- ❏ How to get XML data from the server to the client side using proven technology
- ❏ How to access and manipulate the XML data on the client side
- ❏ How to modify the appearance of the client-side XML document, with or without Java

In short, we will see how, as professional Java programmers, we can add value to a web-based application by moving a portion of the presentation logic from server to client. A servlet can be used on the server side to provide this sharing.

In order to be complete, there is one more common architecture, somewhere between the 'thin' and the 'medium weight' client that we must take a look at. In this case, XML data and/or mixed HTML/XML data is sent between the client and the server, but the client takes advantage of the built-in support on the browser for presenting the XML data to the user. For example, IE 5 will handle XSLT stylesheets for transforming XML data into HTML documents. The diagram below illustrates this scenario:

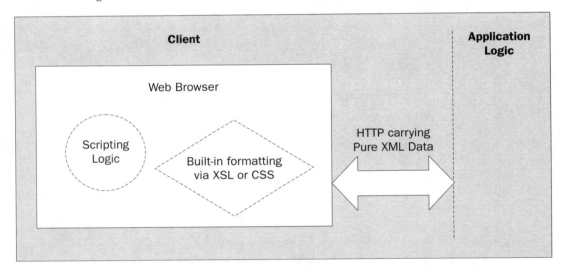

We will conclude this chapter with an examination of the built-in XML handling capabilities within the current breed of mainstream browsers. Obviously, we can also combine these capabilities with client-side custom applet processing functionality.

Getting XML Data to the Client Side: Three Techniques

In order for processing to occur on the client, data must be transferred between the server and the client. We have already established that XML can be used to our advantage for the exchange of structured datasets between client and server. The next question that comes to mind is how the data should be transferred. There are at least three very common techniques:

❑ **One shot:** Deliver the XML data encapsulated in-line with the HTML document

> The limitation of this technique is that the data is essentially static, and cannot be changed without a complete reload of the URL – essentially resetting the processing logic. Updating the data must be done as a reload, and the complete dataset must be transferred all over again.

❑ **Client pull:** Have the client make a connection back to the server

> This is considerably more flexible, and the client has great latitude in optimizing the actual data transferred. However, doing this ad hoc can be problematic because the client needs to make a connection back to the server – and there is no telling whether the connection can in fact be made, due to security restrictions, routing problems, etc.

❑ **In-band client pull:** Have the client request data through a proven HTTP channel

> This is commonly known as HTTP tunneling, and is the preferred way of implementing a client pull. It is sure to work because it uses the same channel that the original HTML page and applet were downloaded through to make a request back to the server for data transfer.

In this chapter, we will be deploying the in-band client pull technique, creating an HTTP tunnel that we can make arbitrary data requests through. We will also be working with several examples where the one-shot technique is used.

Case Study for a Specialized Travel Agency Chain

Our hypothetical customer is a large chain of travel agencies. Each of the travel agents in the chain specializes in his/her own areas. There are agents that specialize in Asia, others that are specialists in Africa, and still others specialize in trips to tropical destinations.

While there are hundreds of agencies in the chain, there is only a single headquarters. Each travel agent has access to a computer that is tied in to the network at the headquarters. Some computers are connected via existing packet switched networks, while others dial in using analog modems to access points provided by the headquarters.

The entire chain of travel agencies is located in a major market. In this market, there is a constant flow of last minute vacancies from tour operators, wholesalers, and distributors that are being sold off (on almost a daily basis) at a fraction of their original cost. These trips may be cancellations, seats that are blocked but unsold, or low season excess. The rationale from the operators and wholesalers is that "getting something for these packages/seats is better than getting nothing at all".

These last minute specials are commonly known as "sell-offs". The headquarters of the travel agency chain receives notification of these sell-offs from the major distributors and operators daily. These notifications used to come in the form of faxes, but with the new e-business system that is installed, they now come into the headquarters in the format of transmitted XML documents.

The agency chain decides to enter the sell-off market. The trick of the trade is to notify the agencies as soon as possible upon the discovery of availability. Since many other independent travel agencies and chains also receive this sell-off information, and are essentially in competition for these sales, timeliness and efficiency are of the essence here.

Our mission is to design a system that will publish information on these sell-offs in the most economical, timely, and efficient way possible. The diagram below lays out the data flow in the system, and where XML may be used for data interchange.

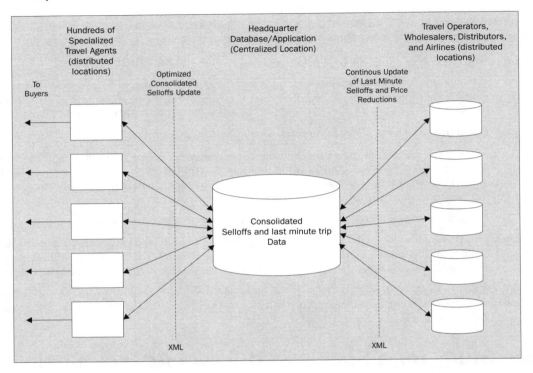

The server in headquarters is mainly a database server, containing an RDBMS that consolidates all the received sell-off specials. There is a desire not to load the server with unnecessary processing since other departments at the headquarters – including the all-important accounting department, also use the very same server.

A Quick Analysis

The restrictive server platform forces us to consider scenarios where processing is off-loaded from the server, and shared by the client machines. Since most of the agencies have acquired their desktop computers recently, most of them have machines that have computing power and memory to spare.

Furthermore, the restrictive budget of the project does not warrant large-scale server-side development and testing. We must keep the server piece of the system relatively simple. Yet, our design must cater for the specialization of the individual travel agents. One design alternative considered is to classify and organize the sell-off information, and then map it to the specialty of each of the travel agencies. Server-side application logic will then customize the delivery of the sell-off information to each connection agency. This approach requires significant database table and query design, as well as server-side programming. It would also definitely exceed the client's anticipated budget.

A large portion of the travel agents are connecting to the headquarters via slow analog modems, and some are on a packet switched network that charges by the data transmitted. Therefore, there is a definite need to optimize on the quantity of data transmitted between the client and server.

Our XML Centric Design

From our analysis, we can conclude that the design must incorporate:

❑   Significant client-side processing of the information, reducing the need for server-side development

❑   Intelligent optimization of the information transmitted between the client and server; ideally only new sell-off information should be transmitted during each update

❑   Customization of presentation according to each travel agency (for example, the specialized tropical travel agencies do not want to sell trips that have a commission of less than $300)

We will satisfy every one of the above requirements with our design. The figure below shows the general approach at a high level:

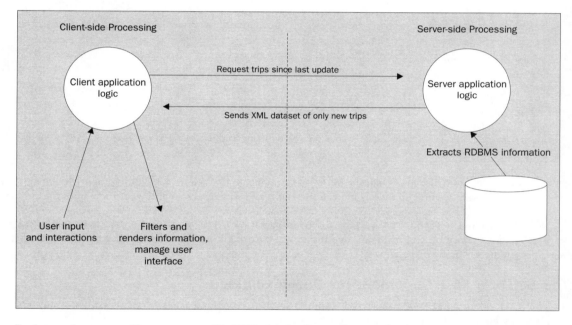

Each travel agency will access a specific URL that loads a web page displaying a customizable applet. The applet is customizable via <param> in the <applet> tag of the HTML page. This applet will contact a servlet at the headquarters to download and display the required information.

The High-Level System View

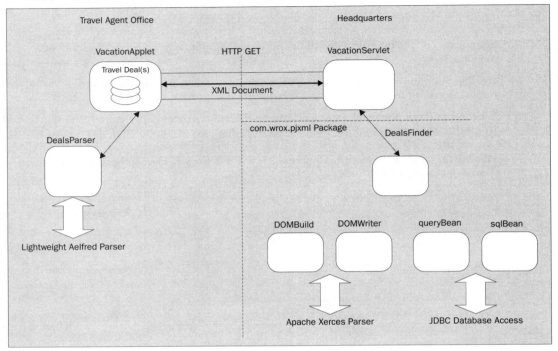

In more detail, the figure above shows all the components of the system – including their class names. The following sections include the description of the client and server classes and what they do in the system.

Note that we use an HTTP GET transaction for information exchange between the client and server. This is necessary in order for the application to work through the firewalls installed at the headquarters and at many of the travel agencies.

The Sell-offs XML Document for Data Exchange

The XML document being transferred from the server to the applet on the client is a list of sell-offs. Here is what an instance of the document may look like:

```
<?xml version="1.0" encoding="UTF-8"?>
<selloff>
  <trip number="31" region="2">
    <startdate>April 15</startdate>
    <duration>1 week</duration>
    <location>Moon Palace in Cancun</location>
    <price commission="400">1899</price>
  </trip>

  <trip number="32" region="1">
    <startdate>June 19</startdate>
    <duration>2 weeks</duration>
    <location>Princeville Hotel in Kauai</location>
    <price commission="700">2699</price>
  </trip>
```

```
    <trip number="33" region="3">
      <startdate>Jan 16</startdate>
      <duration>1 week</duration>
      <location>Calinda in Aruba</location>
      <price commission="300">1299</price>
    </trip>

    <trip number="34" region="2">
      <startdate>May 12</startdate>
      <duration>1 week</duration>
      <location>Westin Regina in Puerto Vallarta</location>
      <price commission="300">1399</price>
    </trip>
  </selloff>
```

We can see here that a `selloff` element consists of multiple `trip` elements. Each trip has a `number` and `region` attribute. The `number` is monotonically increasing as new sell-offs arrives, and is used by the client to download only newer trips.

The `region` is used by the applet for filtering trips. We can also see that a `trip` has `startdate`, `duration`, `location`, and `price` sub-elements. `commission` for a trip is an attribute of the `price` sub-element.

Client-Side Classes

The main user interface is the `VacationApplet` class; this applet will handle user interactions. It allows the user to query the headquarters for the latest sell-off update (fetching only new trip information since the last update). It also presents the travel agency user with specialized filtering capabilities. For example, it can be configured to show only those trips that offer commission of a certain value or above, and it can also show trips by different regions via the user interface.

When the user clicks the Update button, the applet connects to the headquarters computer and makes a call to the servlet via an HTTP GET request. The call sends the highest trip number that it has already received, and the servlet returns a sell-offs XML dataset document consisting of all the new sell-offs that have arrived since the last update.

The customized XML parser for the disconnected dataset that is transmitted from the servlet is called `DealsParser`. This parser will parse the data and create a vector of `TravelDeal` objects that the `VacationApplet` can use to populate its user interface elements.

To parse the XML dataset, it makes use of the Ælfred lightweight SAX2-compliant parser that is obtainable from http://www.opentext.com/microstar.

`TravelDeal` encapsulates a single sell-off. It has a description field that is 'human friendly' and is displayed by the `VacationApplet` in its listbox. It also contains easily accessible commission and region fields used in the intelligent filtering.

The Server-Side Classes

We start with the main driver for the server side code; `VacationServlet`. The servlet does very little other than setting handling the HTTP GET transaction and calling the methods of an embedded up an XMLRPC call by registering an instance of a `DealsFinder` object.

`com.wrox.pjxml.DealsFinder` is essentially a relational-to-XML mapping class. It has one method, `locateDealsXML()`, that is called by the servlet. Given a trip number, it will perform a query on the sell-off database using JDBC to obtain all trips with greater trip numbers (which therefore arrived later) than those in the previous update of the client. This data is then placed into a DOM using a `DOMBuild` instance. The DOM is written out to XML using a `DOMWriter` instance. The output is converted into a `String` and returned as the response to the servlet, which in turn send the XML as a response to the client. There are four more classes concerned with the data source and the two DOM classes mentioned above. We will start with the JDBC classes:

`com.wrox.pjxml.sqlBean` is a JDBC helper class. It manages the connection to and disconnection from the JDBC source. In a production environment, we could modify this class to make use of connection pooling support, etc., supplied by the container. The other JDBC helper class is `com.wrox.pjxml.queryBean`. It has a method that supports query by trip number. It inherits from `sqlBean`.

`com.wrox.pjxml.DOMBuild` uses the DOM support in the Apache Xerces library. It takes the resultset returned from a JDBC query and builds an XML DOM tree with it. The final class, `com.wrox.pjxml.DOMWriter`, is a simple modification of a sample class supplied with Apache Xerces. It writes out a DOM tree as XML. We use this to create the XML string of new trips that is then shipped back to the client.

Filtering Disconnected XML Dataset: VacationApplet

The `VacationApplet` class manages the user interface seen by the travel agency customers. The screenshot below shows how this user interface should look. It makes use of standard Java AWT widgets, enabling it to run on browsers that support the earliest 1.x JDKs.

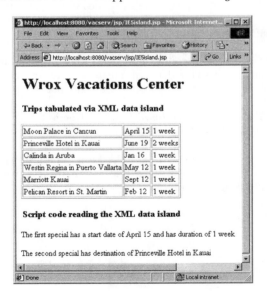

The **Update** button will make the call across to the servlet when clicked, and download any new sell-offs that may be available. All sell-offs are displayed in the list box, when the **All Deals** radio button is selected. Clicking any one of the other radio buttons will display a subset of the sell-offs for that region.

A sample web page that contains the applet can be found in the `projavaxml\Chapter15\vacserv` directory of the distribution. It is called `index.html`:

```html
<html>
    <head>
    </head>
    <body>
        <table width="600">
            <tr><td>
                <center><h1>Wrox Travel Center</h1></center>
            </td></tr>
        </table>
        <applet archive="aelfred.jar"
                code="VacationApplet.class"
                width=600
                height=400>
            <param name="mincomm" value="0">
        </applet>
    </body>
</html>
```

Note that the Ælfred XML parser is downloaded via the `archive` attribute (for more information on AElfred, see Chapter 2 – this assumes that Ælfred is available in the web app). This XML parser library has a very small footprint (23k), very quick to download even over analog modems.

> **AElfred is a freely available, lightweight SAX parser specifically built for Java applet use. Originally created by Microstar, it is now maintained by OpenText. For more information on the AElfred parser, and to obtain documentation, development kit and samples, visit: http://www.opentext.com/services /content_management_services/xml_sgml_solutions.html#aelfred_and_sax**

The parameter called `mincomm` can be used to set filtering based on minimum acceptable commission value for trips (in dollars). Here it is set to 0. As an example, the applet will only display trips with commission greater than (or equal to) $300 if we set it to 300.

You can locate the source of `VacationApplet.java` in the `\vacserc\` directory of the distribution. We will follow it line by line below.

```java
import java.applet.Applet;

import java.awt.*;
import java.awt.event.*;

import java.util.Vector;
import java.net.URL;
import java.io.InputStream;
import java.io.StringWriter;
```

We derive from `Applet` (not `JApplet`), and we implement the `ItemListener` for the radio button selection, and the `ActionListener` to handle the **Update** button click event:

```
public class VacationApplet extends Applet
    implements ItemListener,
      ActionListener {

  static final int LISTWIDTH = 400;
  static final int LISTHEIGHT = 200;
  static final int FONTSIZE = 16;

  private Font myFont;

  private FontMetrics myFM;
  private int numLines = 0;
  private int myLineHeight = 0;

  private int curLineIndex = 1;
```

`curTripNumber` contains the trip number from the last update; it starts at 0:

```
  private int curTripNumber = 0;
  int minCommision = 0;
```

`listNeedUpdate` is used initially to determine if the list has been initialized. This occurs if the user clicks one of the radio buttons without first clicking the **Update** button.

```
  private boolean listNeedUpdate;

  private CheckboxGroup destGroup;
  private Checkbox allClick, mexicoClick, caribClick, hawaiiClick;
  private Button updateButton;

  private Panel clickPanel;
  private List tripList;
```

The `currentRegionFilter` contains the region code for filtering the listbox, depending on the clicked radio button. `curDeals` is a `Vector` of `TravelDeals` instances that is used to populate and filter the listbox. `minCommission` is obtained from the applet parameter `mincom`, and is used to filter the trips in the listbox based on minimum acceptable commission:

```
  public int currentRegionFilter = 0;
  public Vector curDeals = null;
  public int minCommission = 0;

  public void init() {
    super.init();
```

The remainder of the init() methods code sets up the AWT user interface, and obtains the mincomm parameter:

```
        destGroup = new CheckboxGroup();

        allClick = new Checkbox("All Deals");
        allClick.addItemListener(this);
        allClick.setCheckboxGroup(destGroup);

        mexicoClick = new Checkbox("Mexico");
        mexicoClick.addItemListener(this);
        mexicoClick.setCheckboxGroup(destGroup);

        caribClick = new Checkbox("Caribbean");
        caribClick.addItemListener(this);
        caribClick.setCheckboxGroup(destGroup);

        hawaiiClick = new Checkbox("Hawaii");
        hawaiiClick.addItemListener(this);
        hawaiiClick.setCheckboxGroup(destGroup);

        destGroup.setSelectedCheckbox(allClick);

        listNeedUpdate = true;
        tripList = new List();
        tripList.setSize(LISTWIDTH, LISTHEIGHT);
        myFont = new Font("SansSerif", Font.PLAIN, FONTSIZE);
        tripList.setFont(myFont);

        updateButton = new Button("Update");
        updateButton.addActionListener(this);

        clickPanel = new Panel();
        clickPanel.setLayout(new FlowLayout());
        clickPanel.add(allClick);
        clickPanel.add(hawaiiClick);
        clickPanel.add(mexicoClick);
        clickPanel.add(caribClick);
        clickPanel.add(updateButton);

        setLayout(new BorderLayout());
        add("Center", tripList);
        add("North", clickPanel);

        String tpComm = getParameter("mincomm");
        minCommission = Integer.parseInt(tpComm, 10);
    }
```

The locateDealsXML() method is a wrapper method for hiding the details of the HTTP GET transaction. If we assume that the applet is on the localhost at port 8080, the URL that it creates the GET transaction is:

```
http://localhost:8080/vacserv/servlet/locatedeals?tnum=nnn
```

603

where nnn is the latest trip number seen by the client. The application on Tomcat that will hold the application is called /vacserv. The simplest way to do this is to create the following directory structure in the webapps\ directory in Tomcat:

```
webapps\
    vacserv\
        WEB-INF\
            classes\
```

The applet will then read the content of the URL into a String, and return it to the caller. This effectively hides all IO operations from the caller. We also define the methods mentioned earlier for the applet:

```
private String locateDealsXML(int tripNum) {
    String resp;
    URL myURL;
    try {
        URL tpURL = getDocumentBase();
        myURL = new URL(tpURL.getProtocol(),
                        tpURL.getHost(),
                        tpURL.getPort(),
                        "/vacserv/servlet/locatedeals?tnum=" + tripNum);

        InputStream myStream = myURL.openStream();
        StringWriter myWriter = new StringWriter();
        int c;
        while ((c = myStream.read()) != -1)
            myWriter.write(c);
        myWriter.close();
        resp = myWriter.toString();
    } catch (Exception e) {
        resp = e.toString();
    }

    return resp;
}
```

The filterList() method performs filtering on the curDeals vector. It clears the listbox, and repopulates it with a filtered list of deals. The filtering is based on the currentRegionFilter and the minCommission.

```
private void filterList() {
    tripList.removeAll();
    if (currentRegionFilter == 0) {
        for (int i = 0; i < curDeals.size(); i++) {
            TravelDeal tpDeal = (TravelDeal) curDeals.elementAt(i);
            if (tpDeal.getCommission() >= minCommission) {
                tripList.add(tpDeal.getDescription());
            }
        }
    } else {
        for (int i = 0; i < curDeals.size(); i++) {
            TravelDeal tpDeal = (TravelDeal) curDeals.elementAt(i);
```

```
        // System.out.println("the region is " + tpDeal.getRegion());
        if (currentRegionFilter == tpDeal.getRegion()) {
          if (tpDeal.getCommission() >= minCommission) {
            tripList.add(tpDeal.getDescription());
          }
        }
      }
    }
  }
}
```

`updateListData()` is the method that actually makes the call to the server. It passes the result of the call, containing all of the new trips available, in a disconnected XML dataset, into an instance of `DealsParser`. This instance will parse the dataset and create a vector of `TravelDeal` instances.

We then add this new vector of `TravelDeal` instances to the `curDeals` vector – thus expanding the list of available deals:

```
private void updateListData() {
  String dealsXML = locateDealsXML(curTripNumber);
  DealsParser myParser = new DealsParser();
  if (curTripNumber == 0) {
    curDeals = myParser.parse(dealsXML);
  } else {    // curTripNumber != 0
    Vector tpVec = myParser.parse(dealsXML);
    for (int i = 0; i < tpVec.size(); i++) {
      curDeals.addElement(tpVec.elementAt(i));
    }
  }

  curTripNumber = myParser.getMaxTripNumber();
}
```

`itemStateChanged()` is called every time one of the radio buttons is selected or deselected. On a selection, we change the value `currentRegionFilter` and we then refresh the filtered list:

```
public void itemStateChanged(ItemEvent evt) {
  if (evt.getStateChange() == java.awt.event.ItemEvent.SELECTED) {
    if (evt.getSource() == mexicoClick) {
      currentRegionFilter = TravelDeal.MEXICO;
    } else {
      if (evt.getSource() == hawaiiClick) {
        currentRegionFilter = TravelDeal.HAWAII;
      } else {
        if (evt.getSource() == caribClick) {
          currentRegionFilter = TravelDeal.CARIBBEAN;
        } else {
          currentRegionFilter = 0;
        }
      }
    }
  }
```

```
      // System.out.println("Current filter is now " + currentRegionFilter);
      if (listNeedUpdate) {
        updateListData();
        listNeedUpdate = false;
      }
      filterList();
    }
  }
```

`actionPerformed()` is called whenever the **Update** button is clicked. We then make a call to the remote server, and reset the filter list:

```
  public void actionPerformed(ActionEvent evt) {
    updateListData();
    filterList();
    listNeedUpdate = false;
  }
}
```

We will need to create the next class in order to compile the applet, so we will leave that for the moment. The file should be saved in the vacserv\ directory.

Parsing and Converting XML Data: The DealsParser Class

The DealsParser class parses an XML document containing a list of sell-offs and creates a vector of TravelDeal instances. Below is TravelDeals.java, which you can find it in the vacserv\ directory. As you can see, it is a straightforward class containing easily accessible ID, commission, region, and description information.

```
public class TravelDeal {
  public static final int HAWAII = 1;
  public static final int MEXICO = 2;
  public static final int CARIBBEAN = 3;

  private int Region;
  private int Commission;
  private int ID;
  private String Description;

  public TravelDeal(int inID, int inRegion, int inCommission,
                    String inDesc) {
    ID = inID;
    Region = inRegion;
    Commission = inCommission;
    Description = inDesc;
  }
  public void setRegion(int inRegion) {
    Region = inRegion;
  }
  public int getRegion() {
    return Region;
  }
```

```
   public void setCommission(int inComm) {
     Commission = inComm;
   }
   public int getCommission() {
     return Commission;
   }
   public void setID(int inID) {
     ID = inID;
   }
   public int getID() {
     return ID;
   }
   public void setDescription(String inDesc) {
     Description = inDesc;
   }
   public String getDescription() {
     return Description;
   }
}
```

DealsParser performs its work using a SAX2-based parser. In fact, it uses the Ælfred parser in the aelfred.jar file. com.microstar.xml.XmlHandler is the default handler implementation. The com.microstar.xml.XmlParser is the SAX2 parser class itself.

The source of DealsParser.java can be found in the vacserv\ directory of the distribution.

```
import com.microstar.xml.XmlParser;
import com.microstar.xml.XmlHandler;

import java.io.ByteArrayInputStream;
import java.io.InputStream;
import java.util.Vector;
import java.net.URL;

public class DealsParser extends com.microstar.xml.HandlerBase {
```

Note that we inherit from HandlerBase to avoid implementing all the methods of the handler (HandlerBase provides default behavior).

```
private Vector myDeals;
private int maxTripNumber = 0;
private XmlParser parser;

private int curID = 0;
private int curCommission = 0;
private int curRegion = 0;

private String lastParsedText = "";
private String workString = "";
private String curPrice, curLocation, curStartdate, curDuration;

public DealsParser() {
  myDeals = new Vector();
}
```

During parsing, we maintain the trip number of the latest trip. This is used by `VacationApplet` to determine the delta update that it needs whenever it contacts the server. The `getMaxTripNumber()` method allows the `VacationApplet` to obtain this number. Only trips newer than those already sent, as indicated by the `maxTripNumber`, will be included in the sell-off transmission.

```
public int getMaxTripNumber() {
  return maxTripNumber;
}
```

`DumpDeals()` is a debug method used in testing `DealsParser`. It works in conjunction with the `main()` method and parses a `testfile.xml` URL in order to test parsing functionality:

```
public void DumpDeals() {
  TravelDeal curDeal;
  for (int i = 0; i < myDeals.size(); i++) {
    curDeal = ((TravelDeal) myDeals.elementAt(i));
    System.out.println("Deals #" + (i + 1) + " is "
                         + curDeal.getDescription() + "(Comm: $"
                         + curDeal.getCommission() + ", Region:"
                         + curDeal.getRegion() + ")");
  }
}

public static void main(String args[]) {
  DealsParser myParser = new DealsParser();
  URL myURL = null;
  try {
    myURL = new URL("http://localhost:8080/vacdeal/testfile.xml");
  } catch (Exception e) {
    e.printStackTrace();
  }
  myParser.parse(myURL);
  myParser.DumpDeals();
}
```

We have two `parse()` methods. The first one is used by `VacationApplet` and takes the XML to be parsed as a string argument. The second variation parses the XML from a URL. Both of them will instantiate the Ælfred SAX2 parser to perform parsing.

```
public Vector parse(String inXML) {
  try {
    parser = new XmlParser();
    InputStream myInput = new ByteArrayInputStream(inXML.getBytes());

    parser.setHandler(this);

    parser.parse(null, null, myInput, null);
  } catch (Exception se) {
    se.printStackTrace();
  }
  return myDeals;
}
```

```
public Vector parse(URL myURL) {
  try {
    parser = new XmlParser();
    InputStream myInput = myURL.openStream();

    parser.setHandler(this);
    parser.parse(null, null, myInput, null);
  } catch (Exception se) {
    se.printStackTrace();
  }
  return myDeals;
}
```

Here are the handlers for the parser. The general strategy is to collect the subelement and attribute information of the `<trip>` element, and add an entry to the `myDeals` vector whenever we reach an `endElement(</trip>)` on the `<trip>` element.

```
public void attribute(String name, String val, boolean inSpec) {
  if (name.compareTo("number") == 0) {
    maxTripNumber = Integer.parseInt(val, 10);
    curID = maxTripNumber;
  } else if (name.compareTo("region") == 0) {
    curRegion = Integer.parseInt(val, 10);
  } else if (name.compareTo("commission") == 0) {
    curCommission = Integer.parseInt(val, 10);
  }
}
```

The `charData()` method is called whenever character data is parsed by the XML parser. Here, we accumulate the character data in the `lastParsedText` variable.

```
public void charData(char[] ch, int start, int length) {
  int limit = start + length;
  String cdata = "";
  for (int i = start; i < limit; i++) {
    cdata += ch[i];
  }
  lastParsedText = cdata;
}
```

Note that for the handling in `endElement()` for `</trip>`, we:

❑   Format the collected trip description as `workstring`

❑   Create a new `<TravelDeal>` element

❑   Add the new element to `myDeals`

```
public void endElement(String name) {

  if (name.compareTo("startdate") == 0) {
    curStartdate = lastParsedText;
  }
  if (name.compareTo("duration") == 0) {
    curDuration = lastParsedText;
  }
```

```
    if (name.compareTo("location") == 0) {
      curLocation = lastParsedText;
    }
    if (name.compareTo("price") == 0) {
      curPrice = lastParsedText;
    }
    if (name.compareTo("trip") == 0) {
      workString = curLocation + "--" + curStartdate + " for "
                 + curDuration + "--**$" + curPrice + "**";
      myDeals.addElement(new TravelDeal(curID, curRegion, curCommission,
                                        workString));
    }
  }
 }
}
```

These are all the classes on the client. Before you can compile them successfully, however, you must make that the `aelfred.jar` file is in your classpath. You should copy the JAR file the same directory as the applet's classes:

```
> javac -classpath .;.\aelfred.jar VacationApplet.java
```

This completes our examination of the client-side classes. They will all be loaded into the browser from the `vacserv\` directory. Let us turn our attention to the server-side classes.

Supplying XML Data: VacationServlet Classes

The first class we examine is the simplest: the `VacationServlet` class. You can find the source code in the `projavaxml\vacserv\WEB-INF\classes` directory. This servlet class handles the HTTP GET method and supplies an XML document (sell-offs) in return.

```
import javax.servlet.ServletException;
import javax.servlet.http.HttpServlet;
import javax.servlet.http.HttpServletResponse;
import javax.servlet.http.HttpServletRequest;
import javax.servlet.ServletConfig;

import java.io.OutputStream;
import java.io.IOException;

import com.wrox.pjxml.*;

public class VacationServlet extends HttpServlet {

public DealsFinder myFinder;

    public void init(ServletConfig conf) throws ServletException {
myFinder = new DealsFinder();
        myFinder.init();
    }
```

Client calls are received through the HTTP GET method. Here, we extract the `tnum` parameter from the request, and use it to fetch all the trip descriptions that needs to be returned. Most of the work is performed by the `locateDealsXML()` method of the `com.wrox.pjxml.DealsFinder` class.

```
public void doGet(HttpServletRequest req, HttpServletResponse res)
    throws ServletException, IOException  {

  String tripno = req.getParameter("tnum");
  int tripNumber = 0;
  if (tripno != null) {
    try {
      tripNumber = Integer.parseInt(tripno);
    } catch (Exception ex) {
      tripNumber = 0;
    }
  }

  String tpXML = myFinder.locateDealsXML(tripNumber);
  byte[] byteAry = tpXML.getBytes();
  res.setContentLength (byteAry.length);
  OutputStream output = res.getOutputStream();
  output.write (byteAry);
  output.flush ();
}
```

The RDBMS to XML Mapper: DealsFinder Class

The `DealsFinder` class fields the remote call from the `VacationApplet`, and co-ordinates the retrieval of data from the JDBC data source, and the conversion of this data into XML format for the return value. The main purpose of this class is to handle the `locateDealsXML()` method, typically called remotely.

Other than the `VacationServlet` class we have just looked at, the rest of the server-side classes are in a package called `com.wrox.pjxml`. This packaging facilitates the reuse of these classes, for the JSP example that we will be looking at later.

```
package com.wrox.pjxml;

import java.io.ByteArrayOutputStream;
import java.io.PrintWriter;

public class DealsFinder {
  queryBean myQuery;

public DealsFinder() {}
```

The `init()` method makes the required JDBC connection. This is typically called from the `init()` method of a servlet or JSP.

```
public void init() {
  try {
    myQuery = new queryBean();
    myQuery.makeConnection();
  } catch (Exception e) {}
}
```

The `locateDealsXML()` method performs all the necessary co-ordination needed, by making the query via the `getDeals()` method of `queryBean`. It also creates an instance of `DOMBuild`, and uses the `AddATrip()` method to add more nodes to the DOM tree.

```java
public String locateDealsXML(int tripno) {
  DOMBuild myDOM;
  ByteArrayOutputStream myOut = new ByteArrayOutputStream();
  String retVal = "";
  try {
    myDOM = new DOMBuild();

    myQuery.getDeals(""+tripno);

    myDOM.CreateRoot();
    while (myQuery.getNextTrip())   {
      myDOM.AddATrip(myQuery.getColumn("tripno"),
                     myQuery.getColumn("region"),
                     myQuery.getColumn("startdate"),
                     myQuery.getColumn("duration"),
                     myQuery.getColumn("location"),
                     myQuery.getColumn("price"),
                     myQuery.getColumn("commission"));
    }
```

Finally, it asks `DOMBuild` to write the tree out as an XML document in a string:

```java
    myDOM.writeDOMTree(new PrintWriter(myOut));
    retVal = myOut.toString();

    } catch (Exception ex) {
      retVal = ex.toString();
    }
    return retVal;
  }
}
```

RDBMS Query Result to XML: DOMBuild and DOMWriter Classes

The `DOMBuild` and `DOMWriter` classes make extensive use of the Apache Xerces library. Here is the source code to `DOMBuild.java`. This class builds the DOM tree consisting of a root `<sell-off>` element, with a collection of `<trip>` subelements.

```java
package com.wrox.pjxml;

import java.io.IOException;

import org.w3c.dom.Document;
import org.w3c.dom.Node;
import org.w3c.dom.Element;

import org.apache.xerces.dom.DocumentImpl;
import org.apache.xerces.parsers.DOMParser;
import java.io.PrintWriter;
```

```
public class DOMBuild {

   private DocumentImpl myDoc;
   private Element docElement;

   public DOMBuild() {}

   public void CreateRoot() {
     myDoc = new DocumentImpl();
     docElement = myDoc.createElement("sell-off");
     myDoc.appendChild(docElement);
   }
```

`AddATrip()` is the main method in this class, it is called by the `DealsFinder` class to add `<trip>` nodes under the `<sell-off>` root element.

```
public void AddATrip(String tripNum,
                     String region,
                     String startDate,
                     String duration,
                     String location,
                     String price,
                     String commission) {

   Element trip = myDoc.createElement("trip");
   trip.setAttribute("number", tripNum);
   trip.setAttribute("region", region);

   Element sdate = myDoc.createElement("startdate");
   sdate.appendChild(myDoc.createTextNode(startDate));

   Element dur = myDoc.createElement("duration");
   dur.appendChild(myDoc.createTextNode(duration));

   Element loc = myDoc.createElement("location");
   loc.appendChild(myDoc.createTextNode(location));

   Element pr = myDoc.createElement("price");
   pr.setAttribute("commission", commission);
   pr.appendChild(myDoc.createTextNode(price));

   trip.appendChild(sdate);
   trip.appendChild(dur);
   trip.appendChild(loc);
   trip.appendChild(pr);
   docElement.appendChild(trip);
}
```

The `writeDOMTree()` method uses the `DOMWriter` class to create an XML document in a `String` representing the tree.

```
public void writeDOMTree(PrintWriter out)  {
   try {
     DOMWriter.print(out, myDoc);
   } catch (Exception e) { e.printStackTrace(); }
 }
}
```

The DOMWriter class is actually a modification of the DOMWriter.java sample program from the Xerces distribution. The original source can be found in the samples/dom directory of the Xerces distribution. Here, we will detail the simple modifications that had been made to the DomWriter.java file. You can find the modified file in the code/service/webapps/xmlrpc/classes/com/wrox/pjxml directory.

At the very top of the file, we added:

```
package com.wrox.pjxml;
```

We commented out the first two statements in the file to remove further dependencies on packages within the DOMWriter sample that we will not need:

```
//package dom;
//import util.Arguments;
```

Next, we comment out the print() method that we will not use:

```
/** Prints the resulting document tree.

  public static void print(String parserWrapperName, String uri,
                        boolean canonical ) {
...
} // print(String,String,boolean)
*/
```

We added two methods to the class to enable us to use the class on a PrintWriter:

```
public void setWriter(PrintWriter outlet)  {
  out = outlet;
}

public static void print(PrintWriter outlet, Node node) {
  DOMWriter writer;
  try {
    writer = new DOMWriter(false);
    writer.setWriter(outlet);
    writer.print(node);
  } catch ( Exception e ) {
    //e.printStackTrace(System.err);
  }
}
```

Finally, we remove the main() method from the file. This eliminates the reference to external argument processing classes.

Instead of modifying the source code yourself, you can use the modified file provided in the source code distribution.

JDBC Access: SqlBean and QueryBean Classes

The final source files we will look at are the `com.wrox.pjxml.sqlBean` class and the `com.wrox.pjxml.queryBean` class. These are simple JDBC access beans – `sqlBean` handles the connection and disconnection to the JDBC datasource. We're using a simple JDBC to ODBC bridge for our example. We have named the database "travel"; it contains the following data:

tripno	region	startdate	duration	location	price	commission
31	2	April 15	1 week	Moon Palace in Cancun	1899	400
32	1	June 19	2 weeks	Princeville Hotel in Kauai	2699	700
33	3	Jan 16	1 week	Calinda in Aruba	1299	300
34	2	May 12	1 week	Westin Regina in Puerto Vallarta	1399	300
35	1	Sept 12	1 week	Marriott Kauai	2200	600
36	3	Feb 12	1 week	Pelican Resort in St. Martin	1700	400

We simply enter this into a table named "hotdeals" and add the database as an ODBC source. The file is available in the code download as `traveldeals.mdb`. To add a DSN entry in Windows, select the Start | Settings | Control Panel and choose the Data Sources (ODBC) entry, which may be in the Administrative Tools menu. Choose the System DSN tab and select the Add... button. Choose Microsoft Access Driver (.mdb) as the driver and select Finish.

You will be presented with the following:

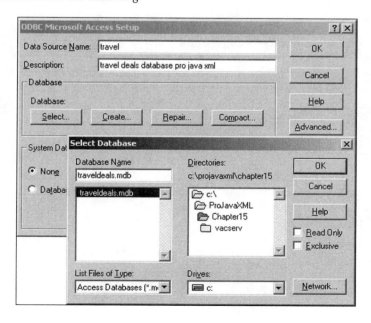

enter "travel" for the **Data Source Name** and a short description of the database. Now select the database from the download code (as shown) and press **OK** through to the finish. This will allow us to refer to the database using the URI jdbc:odbc:travel.

Here is sqlBean.java that uses it:

```
package com.wrox.pjxml;

import java.sql.Connection;
import java.sql.DriverManager;

public class sqlBean  {
   private String myDriver = "sun.jdbc.odbc.JdbcOdbcDriver";
   private String myURL = "jdbc:odbc:travel";

   protected Connection myConn;

   public sqlBean() {}

   public void makeConnection() throws  Exception   {
    Class.forName( myDriver);
    myConn = DriverManager.getConnection(myURL);
   }

   public void takeDown() throws Exception {
    myConn.close();
   }

}
```

queryBean supports the single query method, getDeals(). getNextTrip() is used to iterate through the JDBC Resultset that is returned from this query.

```
package com.wrox.pjxml;

public class queryBean extends sqlBean {
   String myTripQuery = "select * from hotdeals where tripno > ";

   ResultSet myResultSet = null;
   public queryBean() {super();}

   public boolean getDeals(String tripNo) throws Exception {
     String myQuery = myTripQuery + tripNo;
     Statement stmt = myConn.createStatement();
     myResultSet = stmt.executeQuery(myQuery);

     return (myResultSet != null);
   }

   public boolean getNextTrip() throws Exception {
     return myResultSet.next();
   }

   public String getColumn( String inCol) throws Exception {
     return myResultSet.getString(inCol);
   }
}
```

Compiling the Servlet

In order to compile the `VacationServlet`, you must make sure you have `xerces.jar`; it should go without saying that you will need the servlet API jar file in your classpath. First, open a Command Prompt window and change your working directory to the `\vacserv\web-inf\classes\` directory. You should able to compile the servlet using the following line:

```
javac -classpath .;<path_to>\xerces.jar VacationServlet.java
```

On my system `<path_to>` equates to `c:\Xerces\Xerces.jar`

Setting Up Tomcat 3.2.1

Place the files generated in the `webapps\` directory for Tomcat. The complete web application looks like this:

```
webapps\
    vacserv\
        aelfred.jar
        DealsParser.class
        index.html
        TravelDeal.class
        VacationApplet.class
        WEB-INF\
            web.xml
            classes\
                VacationServlet.class
                com\
                    wrox\
                        pjxml\
                            DealsFinder.class
                            DOMBuild.class
                            DOMWriter.class
                            queryBean.class
                            sqlBean.class
```

That means both the client and server are being served from the same web application in Tomcat. There is one file that is left for us to write, the `web.xml` descriptor file that will contain the servlet mapping:

```xml
<?xml version="1.0" encoding="ISO-8859-1"?>

<!DOCTYPE web-app
    PUBLIC "-//Sun Microsystems, Inc.//DTD Web Application 2.2//EN"
    "http://java.sun.com/j2ee/dtds/web-app_2.2.dtd">
<web-app>
  <servlet>
    <servlet-name>
      locatedeals
    </servlet-name>
    <servlet-class>
      VacationServlet
    </servlet-class>
  </servlet>
</web-app>
```

We are assuming that you have modified `tomcat.bat` to include `xerces.jar` as the first entry in Tomcat's classpath.

Testing the End-to-End System

For the system test, start Tomcat from its `bin` directory:

```
tomcat start
```

Next, make sure the server portion is working OK. Start an instance of Internet Explorer, and enter the following URL:

http://localhost:8080/vacserv/servlet/locatedeals?tnum=0

You should see the `<selloff>` XML document with all the trips listed, as shown in the following screenshot; this is what the applet will be working with.

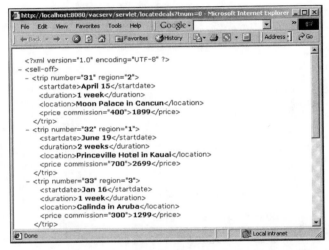

Next, start another instance of Internet Explorer, and enter the following URL:

http://localhost:8080/vacserv/

If everything is configured correctly, you should see the applet running as shown below.

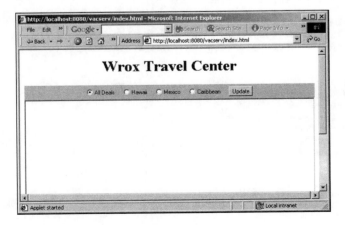

Now, here is the acid test – click the Update button!

This should set the following sequence of events into motion:

- ❏ VacationApplet starts an HTTP GET transaction to contact VacationServlet
- ❏ VacationServlet goes through the JDBC to ODBC bridge and accesses the RDBMS sell-off information
- ❏ VacationServlet builds a DOM tree of the RDBMS information, and creates an XML dataset, which it returns to the VacationApplet for client-side processing
- ❏ VacationApplet receives the disconnected XML dataset and parses it using a SAX2 parser
- ❏ VacationApplet builds an internal Vector of TravelDeal objects and populates the AWT listbox with the list of objects

Whew! No wonder it takes a little while to start up in this test. You should see a display similar to the one below if all goes well.

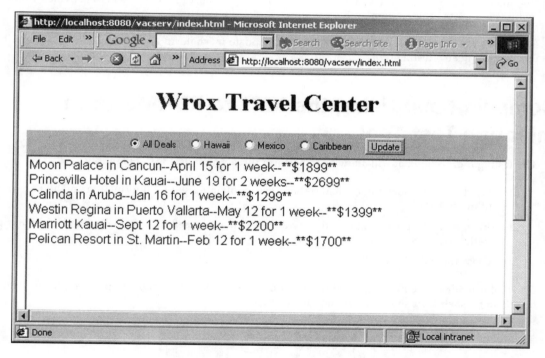

Now, you can try client-side filtering by clicking any of the region filters. Try clicking the Hawaii or Mexico filters and you will see that the displayed list is filtered.

You may also want to modify `index.html` to filter on a different minimum commission level. For example, the following `index.html` will cause the system to only show trips with commission of $300 or more:

```
<html>
  <head>
  </head>
  <body>
    <table width="600">
      <tr><td>
      <center><h1>Wrox Travel Center</h1></center>
      </td></tr>
    </table>
    <applet archive="aelfred.jar" code="VacationApplet.class" width=600
height=400>
<param name="mincomm" value="300">
    </applet>
  </body>
</html>
```

You may want to repeat this test with the Netscape 4.7 and Netscape 6 browsers to convince yourself that this is a cross-browser compatible solution.

Finally, we need to test the optimized incremental update mechanism that is built into the system. For this, we will need a testing tool.

Compiling and Using the XML-to-RDBMS Data Injection Test Tool

The testing tool we look at will allow us to perform three simple RDBMS operations:

❑ Read an XML document called `data1.xml` containing sell-off information and add the trips to the RDBMS

❑ Read an XML document called `data2.xml` containing sell-off information and add the trips to the RDMBS

❑ Clear the RDBMS of all records

The tool provides a GUI consisting of three buttons. Clicking each button will perform the associated task. The finished GUI should resemble the one below:

The testing tool can be found in the `projavaxml\Chapter15\tools` distribution directory. It consists of the following source files:

❑ `TestTool.java`
❑ `HandlerBase.java`
❑ `databaseBean.java`
❑ `sqlBean.java`

We will not examine sqlBean here, since it is the file we created earlier. The program again makes use of the Ælfred SAX2 parser available within the aelfred.jar file.

Here is the databaseBean.java, it has two methods; the first takes sufficient parameters about a sell-off to register it on the database. The second cleans out the whole database. Here is the code for it:

```
import java.sql.Statement;

public class databaseBean extends com.wrox.pjxml.sqlBean {
   String myAppend1 = "insert into hotdeals (startdate, region," +
                      " duration, location, price, commission) values ('";
   String myAppend2 = "','";
   String myAppend3 = "')";

   public queryBean() {super();}

   public boolean addTrip(String startdate,
                          String region,
                          String duration,
                          String location,
                          String price,
                          String commission)
      throws Exception  {

    String myQuery = myAppend1 + startdate + myAppend2 + region + myAppend2 +
                     duration + myAppend2 + location + myAppend2 + price +
                     myAppend2 + commission + myAppend3;
     Statement stmt = myConn.createStatement();
     return (stmt.executeUpdate(myQuery) == 1);

   }

   public void clean()throws Exception {
     Statement stmt = myConn.createStatement();
     stmt.execute("delete from hotdeals");
   }
}
```

Here is ParseHandler.java. The ParseHandler class handles the parsing of the incoming XML data file. Note the inheritance from the default HandlerBase class.

```
class ParseHandler extends com.microstar.xml.HandlerBase {
   String lastParsedText = null;
   String lastParsedStart = null;
   String lastParsedLoc = null;
   String lastParsedDur = null;
   String lastParsedPri = null;
   String lastParsedCom = null;
   String lastParsedRegion = null;
```

Here, we make a connection to the RDBMS:

```
databaseBean myQuery = new databaseBean();

public void startDocument () {
  try {
    myQuery.makeConnection();
  } catch (Exception e) { e.printStackTrace(); }
}
```

The general parsing strategy here is to collect all the fields and attributes of a trip record, and then at the `endElement()` of the `<trip>` element, we add a record to the RDBMS representing the trip.

```
public void endElement (String name) {
  if (name.compareTo("startdate")==0)  {
    lastParsedStart = lastParsedText;
  }
  if (name.compareTo("duration")==0) {
    lastParsedDur = lastParsedText;
  }
  if (name.compareTo("location")==0) {
    lastParsedLoc = lastParsedText;
  }
  if (name.compareTo("price")==0) {
    lastParsedPri = lastParsedText;
  }
  if (name.compareTo("commission")==0) {
    lastParsedCom = lastParsedText;
  }
  if (name.compareTo("region")==0) {
    lastParsedRegion = lastParsedText;
  }

  if (name.compareTo("trip")==0) {
    try {
      myQuery.addTrip(lastParsedStart,
                      lastParsedRegion,
                      lastParsedDur,
                      lastParsedLoc,
                      lastParsedPri,
                      lastParsedCom);

    } catch (Exception e) { e.printStackTrace(); }
  }
}
```

`endDocument()` is an opportune time for taking down the RDBMS connection:

```
public void endDocument() {
  try {
    myQuery.takeDown();
  } catch (Exception e) { e.printStackTrace(); }
}
```

The actual `TestTool` class sets up the GUI, and handles the button selection. It will use an instance of the `ParseHandler` to do the parsing and data injection work. `TestTool` works with two XML files containing sell-off information. You can press one button to inject the first set, and another to inject the second set. The first XML file is `data1.xml`:

```xml
<?xml version="1.0"?>
  <selloff>
    <trip>
      <startdate>April 15</startdate>
      <region>2</region>
      <duration>1 week</duration>
      <location>Moon Palace in Cancun</location>
      <price>1899</price>
      <commission>400</commission>
    </trip>
    <trip>
      <startdate>June 19</startdate>
      <region>1</region>
      <duration>2 weeks</duration>
      <location>Princeville Hotel in Kauai</location>
      <price>2699</price>
      <commission>700</commission>
    </trip>
    <trip>
      <startdate>Jan 16</startdate>
      <region>3</region>
      <duration>1 week</duration>
      <location>Calinda in Aruba</location>
      <price>1299</price>
      <commission>300</commission>
    </trip>
    <trip>
      <startdate>May 12</startdate>
      <region>2</region>
      <duration>1 week</duration>
      <location>Westin Regina in Puerto Vallarta</location>
      <price>1399</price>
      <commission>300</commission>
    </trip>
    <trip>
      <startdate>Sept 12</startdate>
      <region>1</region>
      <duration>1 week</duration>
      <location>Marriott Kauai</location>
      <price>2200</price>
      <commission>600</commission>
    </trip>
    <trip>
      <startdate>Feb 12</startdate>
      <region>3</region>
      <duration>1 week</duration>
      <location>Pelican Resort in St. Martin</location>
      <price>1700</price>
      <commission>400</commission>
    </trip>
</selloff>
```

And `data2.xml`:

```xml
<?xml version="1.0"?>
  <selloff>
    <trip>
      <startdate>Sept 3</startdate>
      <region>2</region>
      <duration>1 week</duration>
      <location>Hyatt Caribe in Cancun</location>
      <price>2399</price>
      <commission>800</commission>
    </trip>
    <trip>
      <startdate>Jan 3</startdate>
      <region>1</region>
      <duration>2 weeks</duration>
      <location>Pono Kai in Kapaa</location>
      <price>3099</price>
      <commission>1000</commission>
    </trip>
    <trip>
      <startdate>Oct 1</startdate>
      <region>3</region>
      <duration>1 week</duration>
      <location>Amsha Paradise in D.R.</location>
      <price>1299</price>
      <commission>300</commission>
    </trip>
    <trip>
      <startdate>July 4</startdate>
      <region>2</region>
      <duration>1 week</duration>
      <location>Krystal in Puerto Vallarta</location>
      <price>2499</price>
      <commission>800</commission>
    </trip>
    <trip>
      <startdate>August 12</startdate>
      <region>1</region>
      <duration>2 weeks</duration>
      <location>Hilton Waikoloa in Hawaii</location>
      <price>4999</price>
      <commission>1200</commission>
    </trip>
    <trip>
      <startdate>Mar 3</startdate>
      <region>3</region>
      <duration>1 week</duration>
      <location>Atlantis in Nassau</location>
      <price>2700</price>
      <commission>800</commission>
    </trip>
  </selloff>
```

Here is the actual implementation of the `TestTool` class:

```
import java.awt.*;
import java.awt.event.*;

import java.io.InputStream;
import java.io.FileInputStream;

import com.microstar.xml.XmlParser;
import com.microstar.xml.XmlHandler;

public class TestTool extends Frame implements ActionListener {
  private Panel basePanel;
  private Button purgeButton;
  private Button inject1Button;
  private Button inject2Button;
  private XmlParser parser;
  private ParseHandler myHandler;

  public TestTool() {
    super("Travel Deals Test Tool");
    purgeButton = new Button("Purge Data");
    inject1Button = new Button("Inject 1st set");
    inject2Button = new Button("Inject 2nd set");

    purgeButton.addActionListener(this);
    inject1Button.addActionListener(this);
    inject2Button.addActionListener(this);
```

This `WindowAdapter()` enables the Close button on the window frame to work.

```
    addWindowListener( new WindowAdapter() {
      public void windowClosing(WindowEvent ev) { System.exit(0); }
    });
    basePanel = new Panel();
    basePanel.setLayout(new FlowLayout());
    basePanel.add(purgeButton);
    basePanel.add(inject1Button);
    basePanel.add(inject2Button);
    add(basePanel);
  }

  private void parseAndAddRecords(String filename) throws Exception {
    parser = new XmlParser();
    InputStream myInput = new FileInputStream(filename);
    myHandler = new ParseHandler();
    parser.setHandler(myHandler);
    parser.parse(null, null,myInput, null);
  }
```

`actionPerformed()` is where the button clicks are handled. Note the direct access to `queryBean`'s methods to purge the RDBMS of all records.

```
public void actionPerformed(ActionEvent evt) {
  try {
    if (evt.getSource() == purgeButton) {
      databaseBean myUtil = new databaseBean();
      myUtil.makeConnection();
      myUtil.clean();
      myUtil.takeDown();
    }
    if (evt.getSource() == inject1Button) {
      parseAndAddRecords("data1.xml");
    }
    if (evt.getSource() == inject2Button) {
      parseAndAddRecords("data2.xml");
    }
  } catch (Exception ex) {
    ex.printStackTrace();
  }
}

public static void main (String args[])
    throws Exception {
  TestTool myTT = new TestTool();
  myTT.pack();
  myTT.show();

}
}
```

While simple, this test tool illustrates the general framework that any XML-to-RDBMS conversion program needs to have. It can serve as a starting point for coding modules that involve such functionality. We have placed all the relevant files in a folder named `projavaxml\Chapter15\tool\`

To properly compile the tool, you need to make sure that you have the `aelfred.jar` file in your classpath, together with `sqlBean`. You can compile the files from the folder they are in using the following commands:

```
set classpath=<path_to>aelfred.jar;%classpath%
set classpath=<path_to>\vacserv\WEB-INF\classes;%classpath%
set classpath=.;%classpath%
javac  TestTool.java
```

The first three lines add `aelfred.jar`, the `com.wrox.pjxml` package (substitute the relevant paths to Ælfred and the `com.wrx.pjxml` package), and the current directory. The final command should then compile the files. Here is the result on my system:

Once the compilation is successful, close any browser with the applet displayed – this will ensure the applet's max trip number is consistent during our test. You can start the `TestTool` using the same command-line window above:

```
java TestTooljava
```

Using this tool, we can simulate the arrival of new sell-off information from tour operators and travel wholesalers for our system. Follow this sequence:

❑ Clicking the Purge Data button to clean the database

❑ Starting up our end-to-end system, and clicking Update – you will see that no trips are displayed

❑ Clicking the Inject 1st set button to inject the first set of data from the `data1.xml` file into the database

❑ Clicking on the Update button on the end-to-end system, to display the set of data

❑ Clicking the Inject 2nd set button to inject the second set of data from the `data2.xml` file into the database

❑ Clicking on the Update button on the end-to-end system to display the new set of data

To confirm that indeed only the newly arrived sell-off list is transmitted between the client and the server, you may want to set up the HTTP Tunneling Monitor program (detailed in Chapter 19). This utility will give you an X-ray view of the XML-based traffic that actually flows between the client and the server.

This concludes our examination of client-side XML filtering and processing enabled by a fully-fledged Java applet and SAX2 parser. We will now check out some of the built-in XML-handling features of the modern day browsers – and see how they may be used for client-side XML presentation.

Built-in XML Presentation Capabilities of Modern Browsers

For most practical intents and purposes, we are talking about either the Netscape Communicator/Navigator or Microsoft's Internet Explorer when we talk about client-side browsing. Surprisingly enough, native support for XML formatting is a relatively recent feature enhancement for both lines of browsers.

Internet Explorer 4.x and 5.x XML Presentation Support

Microsoft has supported the formatting and viewing of XML documents since version 4.x of its browsers. More recently, full XSLT is supported by MSXML. `msxml.dll` is a C++ implementation of XML and XSLT parsing library that IE 5 depends on; it can also be used by third party developer to perform the same tasks.

At the time of writing, the latest version of MSXML is 3.0. If you simply load an XML document into an Internet Explorer version that supports XML formatting, you will see a collapsible tree view of the parsed document:

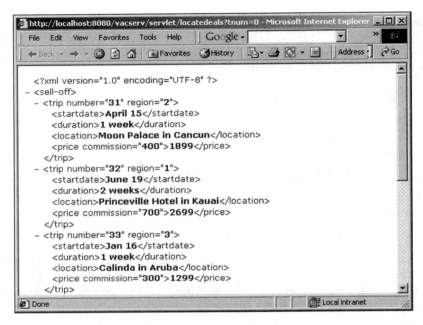

While this can act as a mechanism to check for document well-formedness, it is not too useful for presenting the information contained in the XML to users.

The two most popular ways of formatting XML data for display (using Internet Explorer) are as follows:

❑   XSLT formatting and transformations

❑   XML data islands embedded within the HTML page

XSLT Formatting of XML Data

XSLT formatting of XML data allows us to associate an XSLT stylesheet with a raw XML data file. We have created a JSP that will illustrate how this may be used to format our sell-off information. You can find the source code to this JSP under the \vacserv\jsp directory. It is called IE5xslt.jsp:

```
<?xml version="1.0" ?>
<%@ page language="java"
         import="com.wrox.pjxml.DealsFinder"
         contentType="text/xml" %>

<?xml-stylesheet type="text/xsl" href="tripdeals.xsl" ?>
<%!
      public DealsFinder myFinder;
      public void jspInit() {
        myFinder = new DealsFinder();
        myFinder.init();
      }
```

```
%>
<%
      String myStr = myFinder.locateDealsXML(0);
      int chop = myStr.indexOf(">");
      myStr = myStr.substring(chop + 1);
%>


<%= myStr %>
```

This JSP uses the `DealsFinder` class from the `VacationServlet` to display all the available sell-offs in XML format. Two things to note, that are very important when using JSP to generate XML output for direct consumption by browsers, are:

1. Make sure you use the `contentType` attribute of the page directive to specify the MIME type `text/xml`

2. Make sure that `<?xml version="1.0" ?>` is the very first line in the file with no leading blank space whatsoever.

Failing to ensure that either one of the above is taken care of will render your work very difficult to debug, especially when working with multiple browser versions.

The XSLT stylesheet, `tripdeals.xsl`, contains:

```
<?xml version="1.0" ?>
<xsl:stylesheet xmlns:xsl="http://www.w3.org/TR/WD-xsl" version="1.0">
  <xsl:template match="/">
    <HTML>
      <BODY>
        <TABLE WIDTH="600">
         <TR><TD><H1>Wrox Vacations Center</H1></TD></TR>
         <TR><TD><H2>Client-side XSLT Formatting - JSP Generated XML
Data</H2></TD></TR>
        </TABLE>
        <TABLE BORDER="1">
          <TR>
            <TD><b>Trip Number</b></TD>
            <TD><b>Region</b></TD>
            <TD><b>Location</b></TD>
            <TD><b>Start</b></TD>
            <TD><b>Duration</b></TD>
            <TD><b>Price</b></TD>
          </TR>
          <xsl:for-each select="sell-off/trip">
            <TR>
              <TD><xsl:value-of select="@number"/></TD>
              <TD><xsl:value-of select="@region"/></TD>
              <TD><xsl:value-of select="location"/></TD>
              <TD><xsl:value-of select="startdate"/></TD>
              <TD><xsl:value-of select="duration"/></TD>
              <TD><xsl:value-of select="price"/></TD>
            </TR>
          </xsl:for-each>
        </TABLE>
      </BODY>
    </HTML>
  </xsl:template>
</xsl:stylesheet>
```

This basically formats the XML data in a simple tabular format. We can try it out and see the result with the URL:

http://localhost:8080/vacserv/jsp/IE5xslt.jsp

You should see a result similar to the one below:

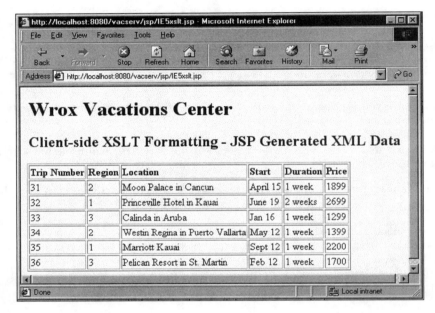

If you try the example with any version of the Netscape browser, you will notice that none of the XML data will be formatted properly. In fact, if we simply want to display of the XML data on IE 5 browsers, we do not even need to write an XSLT stylesheet. There is built-in support for the formatting of an XML data island.

XML Data Island Support

What Microsoft calls "XML data islands" are actually XML document(s) embedded within the flow of HTML. There is a special <XML> tag in Internet Explorer's HTML dialect to support this. We have created a JSP page to demonstrate this capability. Here is IE5island.jsp from the projavaxml\vacserv\jsp directory:

```
<%@ page language="java" import="com.wrox.pjxml.DealsFinder" %>
<%!
public DealsFinder myFinder;
public void jspInit() {
        myFinder = new DealsFinder();
        myFinder.init();
}
%>
<HTML><HEAD></HEAD><TITLE></TITLE>
<BODY>
<XML ID="vacDeals">
<%
```

```
         String myStr = myFinder.locateDealsXML(0);
         int chop = myStr.indexOf(">");
         myStr = myStr.substring(chop + 1); %>
<%= myStr %>
</XML>

<table width="600">
<tr>
<td><H1>Wrox Vacations Center</H1></td>
</tr>
<tr>
<td><H3>Trips tabulated via XML data island</H3></td>
</tr>
</table>

<table datasrc="#vacDeals" border="1">
<tr>
<td><div datafld="location"></div></td>
<td><div datafld="startdate"></div></td>
<td><div datafld="duration"></div></td>
</tr>
</table>
<P>
<table width="600">
<tr>
<td><H3>Script code reading the XML data island</H3></td>
</tr>
</table>

<script>
document.write("The first special has a start date of " +
vacDeals.XMLDocument
        .documentElement
        .childNodes.item(0)
        .childNodes.item(0).text +
" and has duration of " +
vacDeals.XMLDocument
        .documentElement
        .childNodes.item(0)
        .childNodes.item(1).text +
"<P>" );

document.write("The second special has destination of " +
vacDeals.XMLDocument.documentElement.childNodes.item(1).childNodes.item(2).text);
</script>
</BODY>
</HTML>
```

Note that this actually generates an HTML file, and not an XML data set as the previous IE5xslt.jsp did. If you access the URL:

http://localhost:8080/vacserv/jsp/IE5island.jsp

631

you can see how Internet Explorer supports XML data islands, as shown below:

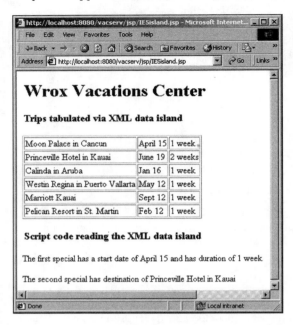

By embedding XML in this fashion, within the <XML> tag, we can use the data island as a data source (via the datasrc attribute) for any data source-aware element. It so happens that <table> is such an element in IE 5. Therefore, the HTML code segment below will display the XML data island in tabular form:

```
<table datasrc="#vacDeals" border="1">
<tr>
<td><div datafld="location"></div></td>
<td><div datafld="startdate"></div></td>
<td><div datafld="duration"></div></td>
</tr>
</table>
```

Another potentially very powerful feature, especially for JavaScript programmers, is that the elements in the XML data island are actually accessible from the Dynamic HTML DOM (Document Object Model). More specifically, JavaScript (or VBScript) code within the HTML page can actually read the elements in the XML document as an extension of the document object model. This enables the script code to read, format, or interpret the XML data. One may use Dynamic HTML to change the presentation (using scripting code) or the user interface, based on the data.

We have a simple script segment within the IE5island.jsp file to demonstrate reading the XML data using script:

```
<script>
document.write("The first special has a start date of " +
               vacDeals.XMLDocument
                      .documentElement
                      .childNodes.item(0)
                      .childNodes.item(0)
```

```
                        .text + " and has duration of " +
                vacDeals.XMLDocument
                    .documentElement
                    .childNodes.item(0)
                    .childNodes.item(1).text + "<P>" );

document.write("The second special has destination of " +
                vacDeals.XMLDocument
                    .documentElement
                    .childNodes.item(1)
                    .childNodes.item(2).text);
</script>
```

This segment reads the element values from the first trip's `startdate`, and the second trip's `destination`.

In-depth coverage of Javascript, IE Dynamic HTML DOM, or IE Dynamic HTML programming is beyond the scope of this section. Interested readers are encouraged to consult Professional Javascript *(ISBN 1-861002-70-X) and* XML IE5 Programmer's Reference *(ISBN 1-861001-57-6) from Wrox for more information.*

Netscape 6 Support for Cascading Style Sheet XML Formatting

Internet Explorer browsers have had various levels of support for XML since the 4.x version. Netscape, on the other hand, provided no native support for formatting of XML-based data until version 6.x. The rendering engine was replaced by a high-performance open source "Gecko engine" technology and support for XML data is now native.

The formatting support at version 6.0 of the browser (the most recent available at the time of writing) is confined to Cascading Style Sheets Level 1, and additionally supporting some Cascading Style Sheets Level 2 features. Support for CSS1 in the formatting of HTML documents has long been standard in both the Microsoft and Netscape browsers. However, support for specific CSS2 features such as tables, and formatting of XML documents, is new for the Netscape 6.0 browser.

Here is a JSP file that utilizes the possibilities offered, called `NScss2.jsp`:

```
<?xml version="1.0" ?>
<%@ page language="java" import="com.wrox.pjxml.*" contentType="text/xml" %>
<?xml-stylesheet type="text/css" href="trip.css" ?>
<triplist>
<title>Wrox Travel Center</title>
<topic>CSS2 Formatting via JSP Generated XML Data</topic>
<%!
public DealsFinder myFinder;
public void jspInit() {
        myFinder = new DealsFinder();
        myFinder.init();
}
%>
<%
    String myStr = myFinder.locateDealsXML(0);
    int chop = myStr.indexOf(">");
    myStr = myStr.substring(chop + 1); %>
<%= myStr %>
</triplist>
```

Again, we are generating an XML document instead of HTML here. Note the way we have included the `<triplist>` outermost element, and added the heading as an additional element. This highlights one of the major differences between XSLT-styled formatting and transformation as opposed to CSS-based formatting. With CSS, the flow and structure of the underlying XML document must be very close to the transformed output. XSLT, on the other hand, allows data to be extracted from the original XML document and displayed in an arbitrary fashion. One will likely find XSLT-based formatting support in a later version of Netscape browser.

The associated stylesheet is now of the `text/css` type, and is called `trip.css`. The CSS2 stylesheet `trip.css` is quite simple:

```
title, topic { display: block }
title { font-family: Times; font-size: 28pt; font-weight: bold }
topic { font-family: Times; font-size: 18pt; margin:20px; }
trip { display: table-row; font-family: Helvetica; font-size: 12pt }
location { display: table-cell }
startdate { display: table-cell }
price { display: table-cell }
duration { display: table-cell }
```

This essentially says that elements `topic` and `titles` are ones that starts a block (like HTML tags `<title>`, `<p>`, etc.), and does not flow in-line (like HTML tags `<b>`, `<i>`, `<font>`, etc.). Tags that start a block will cause any content to be placed in a new block, while tags that flow in-line will not. The rest of the file formats the various elements, and specifies that `location`, `startdate`, and `price` are table cells, while `trip` is a table row.

You can access this JSP page via the URL:

http://localhost:8080/vacserv/jsp/NScss2.jsp

The result should be identical to the screenshot below:

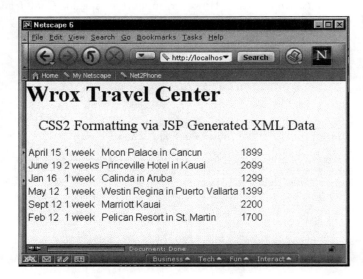

Make sure you use Netscape 6 or higher to access this. If you use Netscape 4 or IE 5, you will not get the desired tabular display – these browsers do not support the table formatting features of CSS2.

> *CSS1 and CSS2 are very complex formatting standards, and an in-depth look at the technology involved is out of the scope of this section. The interested reader is encouraged to delve into the subject further at: http://developer.netscape.com.*

Cross-Browser Solutions

After working through the formatting examples in this section, it should be evident to us that if we use XSLT or the XML data islands to format our XML data for presentation, we would have to be sure that all of our clients are using Internet Explorer browsers. On the other hand, if we use CSS1 or CSS2 for formatting we should make sure that all of our clients are using Netscape browsers.

Of course, we can always duplicate our effort and support both, requiring users of different browsers to use different URLs (or writing intelligent code that will detect the browser being used and re-directing the URL). From this experience, we can safely draw one important conclusion:

> **In order to maintain some sanity in vendor and revision level compatibility as far as browsers are concerned, a client-side XML processing solution using a Java applet is BY FAR the technique of choice.**

Limitation of the One-Shot Approach

It should also be evident that, while transformation and formatting of the XML data on the client side – using native browser support for XSLT or CSS1/CSS2 – will reduce the load on the server, the amount of data manipulation and filtering possible is rather limited. The page of XML data that is generated by the JSP is a static snapshot of all the trips available at the moment of access. Use of XSLT and CSS1/CSS2 only provides a direct mapping of the static data that the page consists of.

It is not possible, for example, to do what we did with the applet-based travel agency example and have an optimized information update mechanism. If we were to use the one-shot approach with static data, the user would have to refresh the page and download the complete list of available trips each and every time. In order to perform intelligent filtering, extensive coding in the scripting language will need to be created to access the object model provided with the browser.

In contrast to our Java applet-based solution, XSLT or CSS1/CSS2 formatting cannot:

- ❑ Perform intelligent interactive filtering (for instance, filtering based on region or commission) without extensive script programming

- ❑ Perform optimized updates of the disconnected data set

Nevertheless, it is important for us to be familiar with these formatting techniques since there can be scenarios where they can be used, alone or in conjunction with Java-based processing or script programming, to solve design problems.

Summary

The benefits of applying Java and XML within a system are certainly not solely restricted to J2EE server-based programming. There are many real-life design scenarios where client-side Java programming and XML processing can be deployed to our advantage. In fact, nearly all contemporary mainstream browsers will support medium weight client designs where significant processing can be performed on the client machine.

In this chapter, we have examined an end-to-end case study in which client-side Java XML processing is a major component in our design strategy.

Our simulation made heavy use of XML as the data interchange format of choice. Along the way, we have gained firsthand design and programming experience in implementing client-side XML processing and presentation, including exposure to:

- ❑   HTTP tunneling
- ❑   Filtering and parsing XML documents
- ❑   Creating applets to handle data display and to access data sources
- ❑   Using a testing tool to ensure that our data is refreshed correctly

Finally, we examined the latest available built-in facilities for handling XML on the mainstream browsers, among which were XSLT, XML data islands, and CSS. These built-in features can be used to our advantage as tools in our arsenal for building effective web application systems.

In the next chapter we will examine other ways to format XML data for graphical presentation. We will be returning to server-side techniques to provide us with a much richer graphical interface, and looking at technologies such as SVG, XSL-FO, and PDF.

he Xerces Blue
utterfly, which became
xtinct earlier this century,
nd after which the Xerces XML
arser is named ···

16

XML Object Persistence

Saving objects in XML form has great advantages in terms of coping with evolution of applications over time, and for interoperability across different applications – and even across different programming languages. But most importantly, it enables us to *see* what we are doing with our data, and to work with it directly, separate from our application. It gives us the power to see, know, and understand the data, and the power to alter, edit, and control that data.

This chapter presents and explains a second generation XML tool that persists arbitrary object graphs to XML automatically. It frees us from the need to write low-level code to parse and write XML, so we can forget about the details of SAX, DOM, and JDOM. The tool marks up the object data with the names used in the source code – that is, the XML attribute and element names are named for the Java field and class names, so that the data is automatically self-describing and self-documented. In this way, it leverages our investment in designing high-quality objects. This is achieved with the very powerful `java.lang.reflection` API, and some surprising techniques for accessing `private` fields.

The tool also implements a technique for evolution of classes and versioning of XML, called an "Abstract Data Layer" (ADL). This encapsulates the relationship between an object and XML, so that they free to evolve independently.

The tool we'll develop is called Hammer, since it's a tool that can be used to knock any shape of object through an XML-shaped hole, and it's also about as versatile and simple to use as the hand tool of the same name.

The previous chapter looked at one end use of XML, of presenting data graphically. This chapter is about infrastructure, and connecting object data into the world of XML, where it can be used by almost anyone, to do almost anything. An immediate example is to just go right ahead and present those objects graphically – it is this kind of interoperability which is perhaps the fundamental triumph of XML.

Another use, of course, is persistence – writing information into a permanent form before it vanishes from memory.

The code in this chapter is ©Brendan MacMillan and is available under the Gnu Public License.

Persistence

Quick, write down what you are thinking! You have just mapped in-memory data into a persistent and human-readable form. This is also called "serializing" because the words are written linearly, one after another), "marshaling" (like a military formation) and "writing".

Reading what you have written maps from the persistent form back into memory – called "deserializing" or "unmarshaling". You could read it back tomorrow, or a year from now – this quality of enduring over time is what earns it the name "persistence".

Someone else could also read it, too; and if the language you choose was a lingua franca, like the American English of this book, then lots of people will be able to. It makes sense to choose a lingua franca for us to communicate, even if it is not the native tongue of either of us, for the sake of this interoperability. Everyone then need only learn one extra language, instead of all the languages of the world. It seems that XML is now established as a lingua franca, and its growth is inevitable. This is why it makes sense to persist to XML.

More formally, persistence is saving and restoring program state, usually to a database of some kind, such as a file, a directory service, or a relational database. In practice, this usually means transferring object data from memory to hard disk, where it can endure beyond termination of its creating program, and even survive the off-switch.

Why Persist?

Data that endures is not just a convenience, but also an important safety feature, especially for applications where the data is the whole point, such as desktop word processors and enterprise banking databases. This can include a kind of meta-persistence, where the sequence of changes is logged, so they can be later reapplied or undone.

We may also wish to persist data that is not the core but incidental to an application, such as configuration information and lists of high-scores. Another use is purely for safety, as for example a number-cruncher whose complex calculations take several days persists the intermediate results. If there is a system crash or power failure, the computation can be restarted from that point on, without losing all the work completed so far – quite like saving our position in an adventure game before tackling the next monster. Or saving a Word document regularly on a Windows machine.

Incidentally, although we talk about persisting objects, we don't really do that. Objects consist of both data and code, but we persist only the data. What we are persisting is state, not objects.

Why Persist to XML?

Given that we want to persist object data, why would we want to persist them it into XML?

A programming tool like XML can be seen as having two sides: an inside and an outside. The inside is the intrinsic qualities of the tool, what it does and how well it works. The outside is how it fits into the rest of the world, its uses and competitors. We will first look at the inside of XML.

XML gives us human-readable, self-documented, marked-up information, that is extensible. These qualities are important for interoperability and evolution of applications. The XML element and attribute names that hold the information also "mark it up". That is, they describe what it is, or document it, and the purpose to which it is to be put – or at least, they should do. In addition, a DTD or Schema, with respect to which the XML is valid, provides a further level of documentation, with such precision that the document can be validated automatically. We can also extend the XML, by adding new attributes and elements. But why are these qualities of human-readability, self-documenting markup and extensibility useful to us?

Human readability and self-documentation facilitate interoperability, because they make it easier to adapt one XML format to another. Data persisted by one application can be read in by another, even if they are written in different programming languages. For example, this helps us to communicate with databases and web-services, and to import legacy data from a retired application. Because human beings write programs, making it human-readable will make it easier for a human to explain the data to a computer.

Human readability and self-documentation also make it easier to read and recover corrupted XML, should any programs mess it up somehow.

The ability to edit the persisted XML provides a short-cut for data-entry and modification. We can use this simply to add and correct data, and also create test cases for application development. Further, it can aid rapid prototyping by allowing us to create data without writing the complete program to generate that data – we need only write the program to read the data. Thus, it can lower the cost of testing out ideas and exploring new approaches.

XML's extensibility facilitates evolution of applications and data format, by making it possible to add new attributes and elements without breaking back-compatibility with existing legacy XML. In comparison with many relational database tables, its fields (character data and attribute values) have variable width, and more fields can be added at any time without breaking well-formedness (though validity with respect to a DTD or XML Schema is another matter).

The openness of human readability, self-documentation, and extensibility eases the hard tasks of understanding, adapting, recovering, and debugging, by helping us to see what is really going on, so we can solve problems effectively – and in programming, as in government, sunlight is the best disinfectant.

The above covers the inside of XML, and some of its most useful inherent qualities. But the outside of XML – its environment – provides the most compelling argument. XML has become very popular, and this has two important consequences: firstly, many tools are available to edit, display, parse, and transform it, and more are being written all the time. Secondly, many applications already read and write XML, so that it is a standard for data interchange – a computer equivalent of a lingua franca. The crucial thing about a universal language like this is that once it gains a foothold, it doesn't make sense for us to speak another language, and so exclude ourselves from the network of communication – even if we find a language with better "inside" qualities. It seems that XML has definitely established this foothold, and is now here to stay.

If we want to communicate with the world, it makes sense to speak XML.

This chapter is about automating the mapping between objects and XML for persistence, and many of the practical issues are shared with any serialization mechanism. Therefore, we can get off to a good start by taking a look at how Java's own serialization mechanism deals with them, before looking at a specific XML mapper.

Java's Own Serialization

Java's serialization mechanism is an automated mapping between Java objects and a binary wire format, that can be used as a persistence mechanism (for example, as an automatic save file format) or to interoperate between applications (for example, it is the basis of RMI and Jini for data interchange between applications). Both are processes of serialization. Apart from writing out binary streams instead of XML, the architecture and design issues are identical to XML-Object mapping.

We will cover here the issues of generic mapping, customization, transient, validation, evolution, and something we will call the **data layer**.

One of the design issues in automatically mapping objects to XML and back again, is whether to use a generic, or custom per object mapping. Generic mapping is when the names of the tags and attributes are taken from the class and field names of the objects automatically, and a custom mapping is when the object itself specifies the mapping. The solution used by Java's own serialization is to be generic by default, but to allow objects to specify their customization. It checks for special methods in the object, and if present calls them to serialize (and deserialize) the object instead of using the generic mapping.

A very common "customization" is to extract only some fields for serialization: those that do not define the object for the purposes of persistence. Depending on the code, this might include run-time or session-based data, such as cached and computed values, graphical presentation details, and incidental associations with other objects. Java's `transient` keyword fulfills this role by marking a field as not for serialization.

These customization techniques can also be used to validate object values when they are deserialized, to check for rogue data, and to compute inferred values and set up caches and so on. Another mechanism is provided for such validation that is triggered only when the entire object graph is deserialized; if the validation is dependent on the values of other objects, it is important that they have already been deserialized. However, there is another catch to this: the triggered code may also compute values derived from the deserialized data, and another object may be dependent on these computed values. But again, the objects cannot predict the order in which they have been deserialized – one of them must be first, but which one? Java solves this by defining an ordering: a priority can be set for each validation, and these will be called in order.

Another issue is the evolution of classes. Over time, fields are added and deleted, or have their name changed; perhaps an implementation changes drastically what data is stored. This issue of evolution is vitally important for persistence, because of its very nature: persistent data endures over time, and so is more exposed to evolution.

Java's own serialization allows new fields to be added; if the values of these fields are not specified in legacy serialized objects, they are set to their default value (`null` or 0 or equivalent). However, fields cannot be deleted, as this would mean throwing information from the serialized format away. Unfortunately, this also prevents fieldnames from being changed, as this looks to the serialization mechanism like the old name being deleted, and a new one created – there is no guaranteed way for Java to infer that these are the "same" field. One workaround is to add "validation" code to transfer the value of the old field to the new one, when deserializing.

There is a related distinction for EJB (Enterprise JavaBeans), which can either be container-managed (generic, and managed by the container of the bean) or bean-managed (customized by the bean itself). Persistence in EJB is more than just a mapping, however, as it also must deal with synchronizing the states of distributed objects, and generally the details of mapping object state to a relational database.

Hammer

Hammer, the tool we're going to develop throughout this chapter, is a very simple tool for automating the mapping between XML and objects – hence the name. It is based on JSX, which we looked at briefly in Chapter 6, and uses the same reflection techniques, so that all application objects can be written to XML and read back again without any coding work apart from a simple call to Hammer.

These are the main features Hammer has:

❑ Comprehensively self-documenting markup in the output – this is discussed below. This is important for providing us with the ability to transform the resulting XML.

❑ Simpler output to write – this is important for parsers to be written in other languages such as C++, Perl, Python, C#, for cross-language interoperability. But mainly, it makes the architecture much easier to follow, for the purposes of illustration in a book.

❑ The format itself is customizable – the code is designed as an object-end and a format-end – as compilers sometimes are. A small collection of methods connect these two ends together, so that a different mapping can be specified by overriding these methods. An XML Schema/SOAP-style format customization class is included as an example of how this is done.

XML Format

There are several possible dialects that can be used to encode objects in XML. All it really needs to do is to be able to mark up the important information: primitive and object values, and their relationships. More specifically, as covered in Chapter 6, *XML-Object Mapping*, an "object-centric" XML format needs to mark up these four aspects of objects:

❑ **Primitives**

❑ **Objects** (including **class instances** and **arrays** of objects and primitives)

❑ **Run-time types**

❑ **Typed references** (including multiple and circular references)

Formal Object Grammar

The following grammar shows the skeletal architecture for how an object graph can be created; it is also the basic architecture for the code that maps object graphs into XML. A later grammar fills in further details of this one, and a final grammar maps them to XML.

Object	→	Array | ClassInstance
Array	→	Value*
ClassInstance	→	Value*
Value	→	Primitive | Object

We begin with an "object" which could be an array or class instance – but not a primitive. Both arrays and class instances contain values, which can be primitives, or other objects. "|" means "or", and "*" means "zero or more". "Object" is bolded to indicate it is the beginning, or root, of the grammar.

643

An object can be an instance of a class or an array – we use the slightly awkward term "class instance" in this formal definition, to differentiate between the former and generic objects. Note that this distinction is part of the run-time type of an object, since a field of compile-time type "Object" could refer to an array or an instance of a class – it cannot be determined at compile time. The other crucial distinction is between primitives and objects, since primitive values cannot contain other types, whereas objects can.

Strings

Strings are ambivalent entities with characteristics of both primitives and objects. They are in fact really objects; but are often treated as primitives for convenience. We do so here, for the sake of readability in the XML; but this minor inconsistency introduces a permanent wrinkle in the neatness of the mapping, which will be noted in the code when it occurs.

Reference Types

This picture is slightly misleading, as objects never actually *contain* other objects, but merely references to them. Thus, we can have multiple references to the same object, and references to a "containing" one. It also opens the possibility of a "null" value – that is, a reference that does not actually refer to anything. We follow the convention (and that is all it is) that the first time an object is encountered, it is written out in full, but subsequent encounters are written as an "alias-reference" to it. These two considerations lead to this line for objects:

```
       Object  →  Null | Alias-reference | String | Array | ClassInstance

        Array  →  Value*

ClassInstance  →  Value*

        Value  →  Primitive | Object
```

Now that we have considered what the XML needs to represent, let's look at the different ways it could be represented in an XML format.

XML Formats

There are many possible ways to represent objects in XML. However, the main differences seem to be in how field names and types are represented – they can be put into element names or attributes. Interesting, this makes four basic possibilities, and there exist mappings that have used each approach. Some other variations are also possible. Consider the following class and example XML representation:

```
class Person {
  String name = "Fred";
  int age = 45;
}
```

```
<Person>
  <String name="name">Fred</String>
  <int name="age">45</int>
</Person>
```

In this format, everything gets a tag – both primitives and objects. Types go to tags (Person, String, int) and names go to attributes (name, age), and values go to content (CDATA content for primitives, and element content for reference types).

XML Schema style

The choice of types going to the tag works especially well for the root tag (which has no name), and for elements of arrays. XML schemas (which SOAP object encoding also uses) have problems with both of these, because they use the name of the field as the tag.

```
<person xsd:type="Person">
  <name xsd:type="String">Fred</name>
  <age xsd:type="int">45</age>
</person>
```

This decision seems to be because it is then possible to have compatibility with legacy XML, by using a schema to define static types for the fields, so we could read something like this with a schema declaring types for person, name, and age:

```
<person>
  <name>Fred</name>
  <age>45</age>
</person>
```

```
<xsd:element name="person" type="Person"/>
<xsd:complexType name="Person">
  <xsd:all>
    <xsd:element name="name" type="xsd:String"/>
    <xsd:element name="age" type="xsd:int"/>
  </xsd:all>
</xsd:complexType>
```

But this approach doesn't completely make sense for objects, which can have run-time types, especially when we consider that the tag name logically defines the type of the element; to have the type information later on, in an attribute, doesn't make as much conceptual sense.

Arrays

Here's our types-as-element names approach applied to an array of Person objects:

```
<ArrayOf-Person length="2">
  <Person>
    <String name="name">Fred</String>
    <int name="age">45</int>
  </Person>
  <Person>
    <String name="name">Fred</String>
    <int name="age">45</int>
  </Person>
</ArrayOf-Person>
```

Note that the array components have no name associated with them. Since SOAP uses field names for tags, this logically would mean that they have no tag name. Since this would not be well-formed XML, SOAP permits dummy tags here (that is, any name at all, which will just be ignore). As an alternative, SOAP also has a special syntax for the tag to indicate the type of the object – in other words, exactly what we have already, but more complex.

The dimensionality and base type of the array are munged to create a new tag for it (ArrayOf-Person), as if it were simply an object belonging to a class of that name. This is what Java does internally, treating arrays as parameterized types. However, hyphens are not legal in Java class names, but perfectly legal in XML tag names, so including the hyphen ensures our generated type won't conflict with any Java types.

Note that the two Person elements don't have a name in the array – they are identified only by ordinal position, which is as it should be. In SOAP, they end up having dummy tag names for this – for allowing types to be used. But in the Hammer encoding scheme, this behavior falls out naturally.

Run-time Types

Unfortunately, specifying the type explicitly as an attribute is not as readable as conventional XML. And yet, the SOAP style has equal trouble; The truth may be that the information required for objects is simply not quite as readable as plain XML. However, SOAP does have an option to omit explicit specification of type, when it can be safely inferred from the Schema. This of course does not apply when the run-time type differs from the compile-time type, and in this case it seems that we simply must sacrifice some readability to be able to markup the polymorphic types of an object-oriented programming language.

Typed References

Finally, we need a way to represent multiple references to the one object, and circular references. The approach is to write out all objects as above, the first time they are referenced. We say the objects are written out "inline". However, note that this representation, though convenient, is quite misleading: they appear to be contained within other tags, when in fact, objects are never actually inside other objects, but are merely referenced from them. Thus, if an object is referenced twice, neither of the references has some special status as the home of the object. However, we represent the objects in the XML format as if this was the case.

The main motivation for this choice is simply that the result is very simple and intuitive when there are no multiple or circular references.

This is how we handle them when they do occur:

```
<ArrayOf-Person length="3">
  <Person>
    <String name="name">Fred</String>
    <int name="age">45</int>
  </Person>
  <alias-ref alias="_[0]"/>
  <null/>
</ArrayOf-Person>
```

The alias attribute of the "alias-ref" tag refers to the object. The convention is that the root object is named "_" by default (as it has no name, not being a field in an object). The "[0]" is the standard indexing syntax used for arrays, so that "_[0]" refers to the first element of the root array.

Note also that this example also demonstrates the encoding of the "null" value for references. The assignment rules of Java mean that any reference field can be set to null. The third component is null, and the array length is now 3, because arrays must always be fully populated. That is, the length and the number of components shown need to agree, and we pad them out with nulls, which is exactly the in-memory representation for arrays.

So, we have here an XML representation of an array of type `Person[]`, containing two references to the same `Person` object, and one `null` reference.

There are a few natural constraints on these aliases:

❑ Aliases can only refer to previously written objects; that is, only back references, not forward or self references.

❑ Only objects can be referenced – class instances, arrays, Strings – not primitives, nulls, or other aliases.

❑ Only objects within the outermost containing tags can be referenced – that is, the tags must be within the same XML document.

Alternative Mapping Strategies

The possibilities for mapping Java field names and run-time types to XML tags and attributes are:

❑ **Field name to tag, and run-time type to attribute** – this is the XML Schema approach (note that where the type can be inferred from the name, using a schema, it may be omitted):

```
<age type="int">45</age>
```

or (if inferring from field name):

```
<age>45</age>
```

❑ **Run-time type to tag, and field name to attribute** – this is the basic Hammer approach:

```
<int name="age">45</int>
```

❑ **Both field name and run-time type as tags** – this is the basic RPC-XML (Remote Procedure Call) approach:

```
<member>
  <name>age</name>
  <value><int>45</int></value>
</member>
```

or, a simpler representation, which creates new tags such as "age" (instead of using all fixed elements as above):

```
<age>
  <int>45</int>
</age>
```

❑ **Both field name and run-time type as attributes** – with the tag representing a fundamental quality, such as whether it is a class instance, array, or primitive – this is basically the KOML (Koala Object Markup Language) approach:

```
<value name="age" type="int">45</value>
```

647

Which is the best approach? For back-compatibility with existing data-centric XML, probably the XML Schema/SOAP pattern. However, the Hammer idea of the element name defining the element, makes more sense conceptually for XML that marks up object state. The remaining two (RPC-XML and KOML) offer much more information about the data which is for our specific purpose here of persistence. The RPC-XML approach of using all fixed elements allows the basic format to be validated with respect to a static DTD or schema – however, it does not allow the structure of the objects themselves to be validated, which would be more useful.

Formal XML Grammar

Having dealt with the object side of the grammar, and then discussed the various possible mappings from this, to a specific XML format, we'll now extend it to actually produce the XML. Separating these two tasks into an object side and an XML side makes it easier for us to adapt the code to generate other formats.

The grammar we now cover uses the basic Hammer mapping, of **run-time** types to element names, and field names to attributes. This grammar can be used as a guide to writing a tool to produce XML from objects, as we shall shortly do. It can also be used to verify whether a particular XML document is valid with respect to this grammar.

Object	→	Null | Alias-reference | String | Array | ClassInstance
Null	→	<null [name="*fieldname*"]/>
Alias-ref	→	<alias-ref [name="*fieldname*"] alias="*aliasName*"/>
String	→	Primitive
Array	→	<*arrayType* [name="*fieldname*"] length="*length*"> Value* </*arrayType*>
ClassInstance	→	<*classType* [name="*fieldname*"]> Value* </*classType*>
Value	→	Primitive | Object
Primitive	→	<*primitiveType* [name="*fieldname*"]> *value* </*primitiveType*>

Like class names, words starting with a capital letter can be expanded further (like Array and ClassInstance) That is, there is a **production rule** (with a →) associated with them, and so they are **non-terminals** – our job isn't finished yet, as they can still be expanded further.

Italicized words *arrayType*, *fieldName*, *length* represent those that are filled in programmatically – these are **terminals**, because they won't be expanded any further by the grammar.

Bracketed text [name="*fieldname*"] is optional – incidentally, the reason that the field name is always optional is because values (object or primitive) can occur in an array, where there is no field name. It is accessible only by its position – that is to say, by its index. Further, the first object – the root – has no container at all, and so no field name.

Words that don't start with a capital will be output directly to XML as is, like name and length. The same is true for spaces and symbols, which are all just plain characters, such as the XML symbols of <, >, =, ", and /. These are also **terminals**. The sole exceptions to this are |, *, [, and] which are used to denote relationships within the grammar.

Breaking and Building an Object

Here we show how the grammar works on a Java object. We show the Java object and class, and then start with the Object non-terminal of the grammar.

On each successive line, we invoke a rule of the grammar above. Note that some steps involve additional information that is not shown in the grammar, such as the name of fields and so on, which the implementing code needs to take care of.

```
class Person {
    String name = "Fred";
    int age = 45;
}
```

Now, let's see what process Hammer (or another implementation of the grammar) would need to take in order to obtain the XML representation of an instance of this Person class. First, we start with the root of the grammar:

```
Object
```

What kind of object is the instance? Naturally, it's an instance of a class.

```
ClassInstance
```

Looking at the production rule for ClassInstance, we obtain the following, filling in the classType with the **run-time** type of the instance:

```
<Person>
    Value*
</Person>
```

The Value* represents the values of the data members of the instance. Our instance has two data members.

```
<Person>
    Value
    Value
</Person>
```

A Value, according to the production in the grammar, is either a Primitive or an Object. In our case, both are primitives (although one is a String, we have said we will treat Strings as primitive types).

```
<Person>
    Primitive
    Primitive
</Person>
```

We now apply the production for `Primitive` to each of the data members of the instance:

```
<Person>
 <String name="name">Fred</String>
 <int name="age">45</int>
</Person>
```

Writing XML

The following diagram represents the recursive algorithm for serializing nested objects. The dotted lines represent leaves in the tree – that is, items that do not contain any further objects, and where the recursion bottoms out, and returns. Note that there are two kinds of object that can contain other objects: class instances and arrays. Class instances contain fields, and arrays contain components. Both are values; and a value may either be a primitive or reference type – which may refer to a null value, a String, a previously serialized object, or a new object inline. If the latter, then the cycle begins again.

The other thing to note about this design is that it has several apparently unnecessary methods. The purpose of these is to provide a hook for subclasses to modify the XML format by overriding them. The basic Hammer format can be changed fairly easily to a SOAP or XML Schema style (which more-or-less simply swap the name and **run-time** type of references); further overriding can create RPC-XML or KOML style encodings (note that the deserialization code cannot accommodate the latter two so easily).

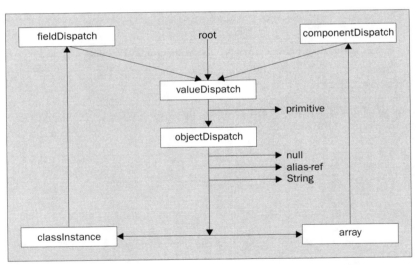

The Out Class

`Out` is responsible for hammering objects out into XML. It is the class that implements the serialization process.

```
package hammer;
import java.lang.reflect.*;

public class Out implements Constants {
  static final String SPACER = " ";
```

We inherit a lot of constant definitions from the `Constants` interface we'll meet later. This allows us to ensure that our serialization and deserialization code understand the same core vocabulary.

```
IdHashtable aliasTable = new IdHashtable();   //==, not .equals()
```

We use a special hashtable which we'll also meet later to store references to all the objects we serialize.

```
public void toXML(Object obj) {
  aliasTable.clear();
  objectDispatch(null, obj, ALIAS_ROOT, "");   //jump in halfway through
}
```

This is the main method in the class, and it simply takes an `Object` reference as an argument, and uses it to start the serialization process. As implemented here, Hammer outputs the serialized data to `System.out`.

```
static final int STATIC_OR_TRANSIENT = Modifier.STATIC | Modifier.TRANSIENT;
```

Front-end: the Object Side

This front-end is the part that that deals with the "object-side" of the mapping to XML. It forwards requests to (actually, just calls methods in) the back-end to write the actual XML. It navigates the object graph recursively, and the above diagram and the initial two initial grammars given above are the rules which it follows.

There are four dispatcher methods which perform this navigation operation. Let's start with the object dispatcher:

```
void objectDispatch(String name, Object obj, String alias,
                    String indent) {
  if (obj==null) {
    nullReference(name, indent);
  } else if (aliasTable.containsKey(obj)) {
    String targetAlias = (String) aliasTable.get(obj);
    aliasReference(name, targetAlias, indent);
  } else {
    aliasTable.put(obj, alias);
    Class runTimeType = obj.getClass();
    String runTimeTypeName = runTimeType.getName();
    if (runTimeType == String.class)
      primitive(runTimeTypeName, name, obj+"", indent);
    else if (runTimeType.isArray())
      array(getArrayTypeName(runTimeType), name,
            Array.getLength(obj)+"", runTimeType, obj, alias, indent);
    else
      classInstance(runTimeTypeName, name, runTimeType, obj,
                    alias, indent);
  }
}
```

The object dispatcher has to work out whether it's dealing with a new instance of a class, a new array, an object it has encountered before, or a `null`. It also has to handle the awkward case of `Strings`, which look like objects, but which it treats as primitives. It gathers information pertaining to each of these possibilities, and passes on responsibility for handling the object to another method, as follows:

Type of Object	Dispatched to
`Null`	`nullReference()`
new class instance (not a `String`)	`classInstance()`
new class instance (`String`)	`primitive()`
new array	`array()`
previously encountered object	`aliasReference()`

This is handled by simple conditional logic. The method takes as its arguments the name of the field that holds the reference to this object, an object that needs to be serialized, an 'alias', which is the unique identifier we assign to each object so that we can create references, and an indent, which is used for pretty formatting.

First the method checks to see if the object is null. This is the trivial case. Then it checks to see if the object has been serialized before; if so, it will be in the hashtable, and the alias that was used to identify that original object is retrieved and used to generate an alias reference. Otherwise, we have a new object. The first thing to do in this case is to put the object into the hashtable with the alias supplied to this method, and then try to work out what sort of object it is. This is done by simply investigating the object's class.

When the program is first called, the object to be serialized is passed to this method, with null as its name (so no name attribute will be added), "_" as its alias, and an empty string as its indent. Later on, other objects are encountered, and this method is called again. This is a recursive approach to serialization.

The `fieldDispatch()` method is called to process all the fields within an object. Its task is to obtain all of the fields (using a class called `MagicClass`, which can see inside even private parts of objects, and which we'll also look at later on), check if they are `static` or `transient` (we're not interested whether they are), gather information about the field and call the `valueDispatch()` method.

```
void fieldDispatch(Class parentRunTimeType, Object obj,
                     String alias, String indent) {
  Class[] interfaces = parentRunTimeType.getInterfaces();
  int i;
  Field[] fields = MagicClass.getAllFields(parentRunTimeType);

  for (i=0; i<fields.length; i++) {
    Field f = fields[i];
    if ((f.getModifiers() & STATIC_OR_TRANSIENT) != 0) continue;
    Class compileTimeType = f.getType();
    String fieldName = f.getName();
    Object fieldValue = null;
    try {
      fieldValue = f.get(obj);
    } catch (IllegalAccessException e) { e.printStackTrace(); }
    valueDispatch(compileTimeType, fieldName,
                  fieldValue, alias+"."+fieldName, indent);
  }
}
```

The key thing to notice here is that, when dispatching the field on to the value processor, it adds the fieldname onto the end of its alias to create the alias for the value the field contains. So, if the field was called name, and belonged to the root object, the alias passed on would be _.name.

One thing that's less obvious is the way that values are retrieved from the field. We need to handle primitive and reference type fields the same, so we want to retrieve the value of the field as an Object, not a primitive. The get() method of the java.lang.reflect.Field class does this by wrapping primitive field values in their object wrapper, allowing us to store the value in a reference of type Object.

componentDispatch() extracts the contents of arrays and does the same thing as fieldDispatch() with the elements:

```
void componentDispatch(Class parentRunTimeType, Object obj,
                       String alias, String indent) {
  Class componentType = parentRunTimeType.getComponentType();
  for (int i=0; i< Array.getLength(obj); i++) {
    valueDispatch(componentType, null, Array.get(obj,i),
                  alias+"["+i+"]", indent);
  }
}
```

This time, when providing each element with an alias, the dispatcher adds an array index to the end of its own alias. So, the third item in an array referred to by the root element's 'friends' field, would be given the alias _.friends[2] (remember the array index starts at zero).

Again, we need to be a little clever about retrieving the elements from the array, since we need an object, not a primitive, so we can handle all array contents the same. We do this by using the java.lang.reflect.Array class get() method, which will wrap up primitives from an array in their object counterpart.

valueDispatch() is called by both componentDispatch() and fieldDispatch() for each element of an array or field of an object, to serialize their contents:

```
void valueDispatch(Class compileTimeType, String name,
                   Object value, String alias, String indent) {
  if (compileTimeType.isPrimitive())
    primitive(compileTimeType.getName(), name, value.toString(), indent);
  else
    objectDispatch(name, value, alias, indent);
}
```

This method's main purpose is to decide whether the contents of the field is a primitive or an object, and hand it over to either the primitive() method (which we saw earlier was used by objectDispatch() to handle Strings), or to objectDispatch(). As we've seen, whether the value was a primitive originally or an object, we have an object passed down to us, so we also need the method that dispatched the request to tell us what the compile-time type of the object was.

Regardless of what the original primitive type was, we're writing its value out to XML, so we convert the object wrapper to a string before handing it over to the primitive() method.

The only other method in this part of the class is a convenience method that builds a unique type-name for an array, according to the rules we specified earlier. This recursively builds up the type name for arrays of arrays, and so on.

```
String getArrayTypeName(Class type) {
  String typeName = "";
  while (type.isArray()) {
    typeName += ARRAY_TYPE_PREFIX;
    type = type.getComponentType();
  }
  return typeName + type.getName();
}
```

Linking Front-end to Back-end

This small group of methods links the front-end to the back-end – that is, the object-side to the XML-side. This architecture allows us to customize the XML format by specifying a different mapping to the back-end, or even to invoke a different back-end altogether, possibly to write a non-XML format, such as a spreadsheet compatible format or LaTeX document format, for example.

But getting back to XML: we discussed various XML formats in the grammar section, and chose the `<runtimeType name="fieldName">`*value*`</runtimeType>` style as providing the most comprehensive self-documentation and greatest clarity. However, this may not turn out to the very best format in general, and probably not optimal for every possible use, and certainly there will be a need from time to time, to interoperate with other formats.

For these reasons, the code has been written with a front-end to handle the object side (the code above), and a back-end to handle the output to the XML side (the code in the following pages). This is the theoretically ideal way to construct compiler-like tools, as the front and back ends can be switched independently, and different versions plugged in.

The following section of code is the connection between the front and back ends. By modifying this code, we can alter the relationship between them, or plug in an entirely different XML end. Instead of literally editing the source code, these methods are designed to be overridden by an extending class, following the **Template Method** design pattern (see *Design Patterns*, Gamma et al. – Addison Wesley, ISBN 0-201633-61-2).

Thus, the methods as they appear here are not useful in themselves – they merely forward the requests from the front-end to the back-end unaltered – but their purpose is to expose this particular step in the code so that they can be overridden by other methods in a subclass, to implement a different mapping. Later, an example is given of this for the XML Schema format.

```
// "Template Method" allows different formatting
void primitive(String type, String name, String value, String indent) {
  primitiveImpl(type, name, value, indent);
}

void nullReference(String name, String indent) {
  nullReferenceImpl(NULL_TYPE, name, indent);
}

void aliasReference(String name, String targetAlias, String indent) {
  aliasReferenceImpl(ALIAS_TYPE, name, targetAlias, indent);
}

void array(String type, String name, String length, Class clazz,
           Object obj, String alias, String indent) {
```

```
        arrayImpl(type, name, length, clazz, obj, alias, indent);
    }

    void classInstance(String type, String name, Class clazz,
                       Object obj, String alias, String indent) {
        classInstanceImpl(type, name, clazz, obj, alias, indent);
    }
```

High-level Back-end

These methods are the last stage that deals with both objects and XML. They define the architectural format of the XML, but not how the detail is actually written. Hence, they are "high-level". They may be overridden by subclasses for the most dramatic changes in the fundamental design of the output format.

Note that the front and back ends are not *entirely* distinct, as classInstanceImpl() and arrayImpl() call methods in the front-end (fieldDispatch() and componentDispatch(), respectively), so that the recursion loop actually spans across the front and back ends. In a sense, therefore, this is still a mix of back and front ends – it is a notoriously difficult task of compiler design to totally separate the two.

The actual code for writing the XML-specific details has been encapsulated into the next section of code, after this one, allowing us to share the logic involved in writing XML elements and attributes between different methods.

```
    void primitiveImpl(String type, String name, String value,
                       String indent) {
        openTag(indent, type, name);
        textContent(value);
        closeTag(type);
        System.out.println();
    }
```

This method is responsible for writing out primitive types. It does so simply by writing out an XML element named after the type of the primitive, with the name of the containing field as an attribute. It then writes the value as element content, and closes the element.

```
    void nullReferenceImpl(String type, String name, String indent) {
        emptyTag(indent, type, name);
        System.out.println();
    }
```

Nulls are written out as an empty tag, called null, with the name of the field that contains it as an attribute. The linking layer passes in the string null as a parameter, which it obtains from the Constants interface.

```
    void aliasReferenceImpl(String type, String name, String targetAlias,
                            String indent)
    {
        emptyTag(indent, type, name, ALIAS_ATTR, targetAlias);
        System.out.println();
    }
```

Aliases are written with another empty tag. This time, as well as passing the type to be the tag name and the containing field name to be written as an attribute, we pass the alias to which this reference points, again to be written as an attribute. Again, the linking layer passes in the string `alias-ref`, which comes from the `Constants` interface as a parameter to be used as the element name.

```
void classInstanceImpl(String type, String name, Class clazz,
                       Object obj, String alias, String indent) {
  openTag(indent, type, name);
  System.out.println();
  fieldDispatch(clazz, obj, alias, indent+SPACER);
  System.out.print(indent);
  closeTag(type);
  System.out.println();
}
```

This method is a little bit more complex, because, as well as writing out the class type as a tag, and adding the name of the enclosing field as an attribute, it has to call back into the front-end to get the `fieldDispatch()` method to analyze the instance's fields. This is where the indent value is increased to ensure that the child elements of the class are indented by one space.

```
void arrayImpl(String type, String name, String length,
               Class clazz, Object obj, String alias, String indent) {
  openTag(indent, type, name, LENGTH_ATTR, length);
  System.out.println();
  componentDispatch(clazz, obj, alias, indent+SPACER);
  System.out.print(indent);
  closeTag(type);
  System.out.println();
}
```

This method is very similar to the `classInstanceImpl()` method, but it has to pass additional information to the open tag to include the array length attribute.

Low-level Back-end: The XML-side

This is the code that actually writes the XML. It is encapsulated into these routines so that it does not clutter up the above high-level routines, and also so that this aspect of the XML format can be altered independently of the overall architecture of the format. For example, these would be the methods to override in order to write out a spreadsheet compatible format, or LaTeX format. (Of course, the same effect would probably be better achieved by using a second tool – such as XSLT – to transform the XML into this format, and so maintain the role of XML as the lingua franca for cross-application data transport.)

Thus, the following methods are workhorses for writing out the actual XML.

All the elements we'll write out have one thing in common: they can all have a name attribute. So, we have methods that can write out start elements and empty elements which have a name attribute (although if `null` is passed as the name value, they don't write out the name attribute), and we also have overloaded versions of these methods that take two extra strings, representing a name and a value for a second attribute. This provides all the functionality we need, but if you were working on a more complex system, you might use DOM to provide this layer. To allow for alternative encodings that use some other default attribute, we have also provided an overridable static block that sets the default attribute to "name".

```
protected static String DEFAULT_ATTR;
static { DEFAULT_ATTR=NAME_ATTR; }

void emptyTag(String indent, String tag, String defaultValue) {
  System.out.print(indent+"<"+tag);
  if (defaultValue!=null)
    System.out.print(" "+DEFAULT_ATTR+"='"+defaultValue+"'");
  System.out.print("/>");
}

void emptyTag(String indent, String tag, String defaultValue,
              String extraAttr, String extraValue) {
  System.out.print(indent+"<"+tag);
  if (defaultValue!=null)
    System.out.print(" "+DEFAULT_ATTR+"='"+defaultValue+"'");
  if (extraValue!=null)
    System.out.print(" "+extraAttr+"='"+extraValue+"'");
  System.out.print("/>");
}
```

The two empty tag methods write out an indented tag with the given name, and add a name attribute if provided. The second overloads the first and can write out a second attribute with the given name and value.

```
void openTag(String indent, String tag, String defaultValue) {
  System.out.print(indent+"<"+tag);
  if (defaultValue!=null)
    System.out.print(" "+DEFAULT_ATTR+"='"+defaultValue+"'");
  System.out.print(">");
}

void openTag(String indent, String tag, String defaultValue,
             String extraAttr, String extraValue) {
  System.out.print(indent+"<"+tag);
  if (defaultValue!=null)
    System.out.print(" "+DEFAULT_ATTR+"='"+defaultValue+"'");
  if (extraValue!=null)
    System.out.print(" "+extraAttr+"='"+extraValue+"'");
  System.out.print(">");
}
```

The open tag methods are almost exactly the same, except they leave the tag open for content to follow, before the close tag method is called:

```
void closeTag(String indent, String tag) {
  System.out.print(indent);
  closeTag(tag);
}
void closeTag(String tag) {
  System.out.print("</"+tag+">");
}
```

One version provides indenting before printing the close tag, the other is intended for printing the close tag on the end of a line.

The following two methods add extra XML capabilities, which could be used to add documentation or additional information to the output XML.

```
void comment(String indent, String commentText) {
  System.out.print(indent+"<!-- "+commentText+" -->");
}
void processingInstruction(String indent, String target, String data) {
  System.out.print(indent+"<?"+target+" "+data+"?>");
}
```

Finally, we have a method that writes out safely escaped text to go inside XML elements:

```
void textContent(String text) {
  char[] ch = text.toCharArray();  //faster processing
  for (int i=0; i<ch.length; i++) {
    switch (ch[i]) {
      case '&': System.out.print("&amp;"); break;
      case '<': System.out.print("&lt;"); break;
      case '>': System.out.print("&gt;"); break;
      case '\"': System.out.print("&quot;"); break;
      default:
        if (ch[i] > '\u007f')
          System.out.print("&#"+Integer.toString(ch[i])+";");
        else
          System.out.print(ch[i]);
    }
  }
}
```

The Constants Interface

The constants used in Out are declared in this interface, so that they can be made available to the deserializer as well.

```
package hammer;

interface Constants {
  static final String NULL_TYPE = "null";

  static final String ALIAS_TYPE = "alias-ref";
  static final String ALIAS_ATTR = "alias";
  static final String ALIAS_ROOT = "_";

  static final String ARRAY_TYPE_PREFIX = "ArrayOf-";
  static final String LENGTH_ATTR = "length";

  static final String TYPE_ATTR = "type";
  static final String NAME_ATTR = "name";
  static final String VERSION_ATTR = "version";
}
```

The IdHashtable Class

This version of a hashtable only sees two keys as the same object if they are the same object – that is, if a==b is true. In contrast, the Java 1.2 Hashtable sees them as identical if they have the same value – this is, if a.equals(b) is true.

This class is required because of a change between Java 1.1 and Java 1.2. In 1.1, Hashtable keys were hashed according to their reference; but in Java 1.2, this was changed to hash according to their value. One clear example of this is when you clone an object – they are different objects, with different references, but their values are the same. The Java 1.2 Hashtable sees them as the same object, but they are not.

```
package hammer;
public class IdHashtable extends java.util.Hashtable {
  public Object put(Object key, Object value) {
    return super.put(new IdObject(key), value);
  }
  public Object get(Object key) {
    return super.get(new IdObject(key));
  }
  public boolean containsKey(Object key) {
    return super.containsKey(new IdObject(key));
  }

  static private class IdObject {
    Object o;
    public int hashCode() { return System.identityHashCode(o); }
    public boolean equals(Object x) { return ((IdObject)x).o == this.o; }
    public IdObject(Object o) { this.o = o; }
  }
}
```

The MagicClass Class

This class does two impossible things – it enables us to access private, protected, and "package" fields; and also to create objects without invoking their constructor. Indeed, they needn't have a no-argument constructor.

The technique used for this magical creator has a wider significance: it is a way to invoke any of the native private methods that do the real work behind the scenes of Java. Basically, this technique completely opens up the insides of Java, so we can do practically anything that Java itself can do.

The first trick is that in Java 1.2, the AccessibleObject was introduced as a superclass of the Field, Method, and Constructor classes in java.lang.reflect. As the code shows, it is simply a matter of using the setAccessible(true) methods to give us access to private, protected, and "package" members. When applied to Field objects, it gives us access to their data. This rather trivial trick seems relatively unknown in the Java developer community, which may be just as well, since it opens up a few security issues. Note that security managers can control which classes are allowed to use this method, so in a JVM that has a security manager in place, this may not work, unless you tweak the security settings.

The second magic trick is an extension of the first: we merely apply it to a Method object that represents the private native method we wish to invoke – in this case, the method that the java.io.ObjectInputStream uses to create new objects. Inspection of the source code for Java (freely available from the Javasoft site), shows numerous examples of such methods, and their use.

Note that it would have been more elegant to subclass `java.lang.Class`; but we cannot, as it is final.

```
package hammer;
import java.lang.reflect.*;  //Method, Field
import java.io.*;  //Serializable interface
import java.util.*;  //Vector

class MagicClass {
    private final static Object[] argValues = new Object[2];
    private final static Class[] argTypes = {Class.class, Class.class};
    private final static Method allocateNewObject;
    static {
      Method m = null;
      try {
        m = java.io.ObjectInputStream.class.getDeclaredMethod(
          "allocateNewObject", argTypes);
        m.setAccessible(true); //the magic paint
      } catch (Exception e) {
        System.err.println(e);
        System.exit(0);
      }
      allocateNewObject = m;
    }
```

This static block gets hold of a reference to the method we're interested in using, and uses the reflection API to make it accessible to our code:

```
static Object newInstance(Class currentClass) {
    argValues[0] = currentClass; //runtime class we want to create.
    argValues[1] = Object.class; //closest non-serializable ancestor.
   try {
     return allocateNewObject.invoke(null, argValues);
   } catch (InvocationTargetException e) { e.printStackTrace(); }
   } catch (IllegalAccessException e) { e.printStackTrace(); }
   }
   return null;
}
```

This is the method that actually creates new objects without using constructors, by invoking the method we borrowed from `ObjectInputStream`:

```
static Field[] getAllFields(Class c) {
   Vector a = new Vector(); //of arrays (don't know how many superclasses)
   int total = 0;
   do {
     Field[] f = c.getDeclaredFields();  //declared in this class
     total += f.length;
     a.add(f);
   } while ( (c = c.getSuperclass()) != Object.class);
   Field[] allf = new Field[total];  //declared in all classes
   int pos = 0;
   for (int i=0; i<a.size(); i++) {
     Field[] thisf = (Field[]) a.elementAt(i);
     System.arraycopy(thisf, 0, allf, pos, thisf.length);
```

```
        pos += thisf.length;
      }
    Field.setAccessible(allf, true);   //the Magic bit
    return allf;
  }
```

This method works its way through all the fields declared in the class passed to it, and its superclasses, and its superclasses' superclasses, and so on, populating a vector with arrays containing the fields it finds. It then adds all these arrays together to build one big array, and then calls the setAccessible() method to make all of them available to us.

```
  static Field getAnyField(Class c, String fieldName)
      throws NoSuchFieldException {
    Field f = null;
    Class initc = c;  //store it for error
    do {
      try {
        f = c.getDeclaredField(fieldName);
      } catch (NoSuchFieldException e) {  //do nothing; it's OK
      }
    } while ( f==null && (c = c.getSuperclass()) != Object.class);
    if (f==null)
      throw new NoSuchFieldException("Can't find the field "
      +((fieldName==null)?"--null value--":"'"+fieldName+"'.\n")
      + "Not in " +initc+ ", or private etc, or in superclasses.");
    try {
      f.setAccessible(true);     //the Magic bit
    } catch (SecurityException e) {
      e.printStackTrace();
    }
    return f;
  }
}
```

This method is used to obtain an accessible reference to a specific field, by again searching up the superclass hierarchy for a class that contains a field of the given name. Again it sets it to be accessible, before returning the field reference.

The above is the complete code for writing out an XML representation of an object graph. Let's test it out. You should have four files in the hammer package: Out.java, MagicClass.java, Constants.java and IdHashtable.java. Now we need to generate a class to serialize some instances of, and a main class that ties it all together. First, let's make a person:

```
public class Person implements java.io.Serializable {

    private int age;
    private String name;
    private Person[] friends;

    public Person(String name, int age) {
        this.age=age;
        this.name=name;
    }
```

```
        public void setFriends(Person[] friends) {
            this.friends=friends;
        }

    }
```

Note that Hammer doesn't require classes to implement `Serializable`, but we do anyway for reasons that will become clear. Now we can create some interrelated objects, and see how Hammer handles them:

```
import hammer.*;
import java.io.ObjectOutputStream;

public class HammerTest {
    public static void main(String[] args) {
        Out out = new Out();

        Person fred = new Person("Fred", 34);
        Person george = new Person("George", 43);
        Person deborah = new Person("Deborah", 28);

        george.setFriends(new Person[] {deborah, fred});
        fred.setFriends(new Person[] {george});
        deborah.setFriends(new Person[] {george});

        out.toXML(fred);
    }
}
```

Now, compiling and running this class with the `hammer` package on the classpath will produce the following output:

```
E:\Java\Hammer>java HammerTest
<Person>
 <int name='age'>34</int>
 <java.lang.String name='name'>Fred</java.lang.String>
 <ArrayOf-Person name='friends' length='1'>
  <Person>
   <int name='age'>43</int>
   <java.lang.String name='name'>George</java.lang.String>
   <ArrayOf-Person name='friends' length='2'>
    <Person>
     <int name='age'>28</int>
     <java.lang.String name='name'>Deborah</java.lang.String>
     <ArrayOf-Person name='friends' length='1'>
      <alias-ref alias='_.friends[0]'/>
     </ArrayOf-Person>
    </Person>
    <alias-ref alias='_'/>
   </ArrayOf-Person>
  </Person>
 </ArrayOf-Person>
</Person>
```

Here's the XML data produced:

```
<Person>
 <int name='age'>34</int>
 <java.lang.String name='name'>Fred</java.lang.String>
 <ArrayOf-Person name='friends' length='1'>
  <Person>
   <int name='age'>43</int>
   <java.lang.String name='name'>George</java.lang.String>
   <ArrayOf-Person name='friends' length='2'>
    <Person>
     <int name='age'>28</int>
     <java.lang.String name='name'>Deborah</java.lang.String>
     <ArrayOf-Person name='friends' length='1'>
      <alias-ref alias='_.friends[0]'/>
     </ArrayOf-Person>
    </Person>
    <alias-ref alias='_'/>
   </ArrayOf-Person>
  </Person>
 </ArrayOf-Person>
</Person>
```

As we can see, the object passed into Hammer is simply referred to as a 'Person' – no name is given, Fred has become anonymous. This is because fred was only the name of the variable in the context of the HammerTest main() method: by the time Hammer got hold of him, he was simply a reference to an object of type Person.

Inside the Person element, we can see elements for the age and name fields, named for their Java type. The friends field is interesting, because it is an array and it contains a reference to one of our two other people. Fred's only friend is George, who we now get a full description of. When we reach his friends array, we find Deborah, who we also are encountering for the first time. Her friends include George, of course, and the circular reference is resolved with an alias-ref element referring to _.friends[0]: the first element of the array called friends which is a member of _, the root element. That points to George.

Just for contrast, we can serialize the same object using Java's serialization system, by doing this:

```java
import java.io.ObjectOutputStream;

public class SerializerTest {
    public static void main(String[] args) {

        ObjectOutputStream objOut;

        try {
            objOut = new ObjectOutputStream(System.out);

            Person fred = new Person("Fred", 34);
            Person george = new Person("George", 43);
            Person deborah = new Person("Deborah", 28);

            george.setFriends(new Person[] {deborah, fred});
            fred.setFriends(new Person[] {george});
            deborah.setFriends(new Person[] {george});
```

```
      objOut.writeObject(fred);
            objOut.flush();
        } catch (Exception e) {
        }
    }
}
```

This results in the following output, as well as a few odd control signals and beeps emanating from the console:

Hopefully this shows that what Hammer's output lacks in brevity it makes up for in style and readability.

We now turn to the other direction of the mapping: parsing the XML, and re-creating the object graph that it represents.

Reading XML

Once we have written an object graph out into XML, we need to be able to read it back in again, and re-create the original object graph (technically, a copy of the graph). Because we start with the XML and move to objects, we are working in the opposite direction from the writing code above, so the architecture is fundamentally different.

In working backwards (from XML to objects), it reads the element names first, and interprets them based on the containing element. Each element represents a value – primitive or object – and is plugged into (or bound to) the appropriate part of the containing object. If the containing element is a class instance, then it is plugged into the field with the name given in the element. If the containing element is an array, then it is plugged into the current ordinal position of the array, as it is filled up. This ability to plug things into objects – to assign values to the fields of class instance objects and to the components of array objects – is accomplished with the reflection API.

However, the reflection mechanism for plugging a value into a class instance object is quite different from plugging it into an array object. It is the same task, but these different containers (class instances and arrays) are accessed in very different ways. The code uses the object-oriented facility of polymorphism, so that we can invoke the same method on each kind of container, but the container implements that method in the appropriate way for it.

We make an abstract class called Container, which declares the bind() method to do this. We then extend it with two classes – ClassInstanceAsContainer and ArrayAsContainer – which implement the bind() method as appropriate for class instances and arrays. And now, whenever we create a new class instance or array, we wrap it in one of the above two classes, and treat them as the same kind of thing. This level of indirection allows us to not worry about the details of the containing element.

If you check the code, you'll also see a `RootAsContainer` – this is because the entire object graph is grown from the very first object, which doesn't actually have a name. The root represents this first object, and although it is a slightly different kind of a thing from class instances or arrays, the same methods need to be invoked on it, so it simplifies the code to include it in the polymorphism.

You'll also see that the same trick is also used for the `deriveValueType()` and `aliasAdd()` methods. The former is used to find out what type the container expects to be plugged in (the reflection API again handles them differently); and the latter is for building the alias. Aliases are the strings we used in writing out the XML for referencing previously written out objects, and are designed to look as much like Java source code as possible. For class instances, the alias is formed by appending `.fieldname` to the current alias; for arrays, it is formed by appending `[index]`. We had to make up a name for the root object, since it doesn't have one. By convention, we are using an underscore ("_") for this, but it could be anything. An example of an alias is `"_[0].name"`, where the root is an array, and the first component is a class instance, which has a field named "name". This alias is a reference to that field.

You may also notice that these containers are also pushed and popped from a stack – this is to cope with nested containers, and is a substitute for recursion.

Recursion

Recursion is often the most natural way to process nested elements, such as tags; and this is how the previous section's code writes out XML. However, for reading XML, we use SAX (via JAXP1.1) to parse it, and this introduces a serious problem for recursion. SAX is, as we've seen, event-driven, which means that we cannot recurse, as we did when writing the XML. Recursion requires a routine to call itself (which can be indirect, by calling another routine that then calls the first one) perhaps many times. The local variables are stored on the program stack for each call; and when the recursion finally "bottoms out" (that is, stops calling itself, and returns), it works its way back out up the stack, and is able to access the state at each previous recursion through the local variables it was using before. Java, of course, does all this automatically for us, and recursion is extremely simple to implement.

Ideally, we would parse nested tags by calling the routine to handle the tag, whenever we saw a tag. If we already happened to be inside the tag routine, then this would be recursive, and the enclosing tag (and all the associated information in local variables) would be saved on the stack while we ran through the same method again but in the context of the nested element.

However, because SAX is event driven, it cannot call us with the next tag, until we have returned control to it, by returning from the tag handler. When we return like this, it pops the stack, and so we cannot recurse (incidentally, we could have used DOM instead to avoid this problem, but that would create the whole DOM tree in memory, which is unnecessary).

Recursion is a funny thing – if you find the above confusing, try tracing the execution of `Out.java` for an array that contains another array. You will have entered several methods twice, before returning from them – but the previous information is not overwritten or lost, but stored on the stack.

Then, follow the execution of one of the SAX routines below – `startElement()`, `characters()`, or `endElement()` – and note that they return before getting another call back. Of course, SAX cannot give us another event unless it is executing. As SAX is not running in a different thread, the only way it can get control back is when we return from the event handler.

However, we still need to process nested tags – if we cannot use Java's stack, we simply use our own, called `nestedContainers`. This is named for the fact that it only need contain tags that can nest – that is, class instances or arrays, the objects that can contain other values.

The In Class

In hammers XML objects in the opposite direction: into object-shaped holes.

```
package hammer;

//using SAX 2.0 from JAXP 1.1
import org.xml.sax.*; //Attr, ContentHandler, Exceptions
import org.xml.sax.helpers.*; //DefaultHandler,
import java.io.IOException;

import java.util.Stack;
import java.util.Hashtable;
import java.lang.reflect.*;

public class In extends DefaultHandler implements Constants {
```

Again, we import the necessary packages, and we implement Constants to obtain access to the string constants Out used to encode the objects as XML. We extend SAX's DefaultHandler: this allows us to simply override the SAX event handling methods we want to intercept, leaving default behavior for all the others we're not interested in.

```
public In() {
  try {
    parser = javax.xml.parsers.SAXParserFactory.newInstance()
                          .newSAXParser();
  } catch (SAXException e) {
    e.printStackTrace();
  } catch (javax.xml.parsers.ParserConfigurationException e) {
    e.printStackTrace();
  }
}
private javax.xml.parsers.SAXParser parser;
protected Stack nestedContainers = new Stack(); //nested tags
private Stack aliasStack = new Stack();  //building names
private Hashtable aliasTable = new Hashtable(); //previous objects
```

The constructor attempts to obtain a JAXP SAX parser instance. As we saw in Chapter 2, this can be any parser that supports the SAX interfaces, meaning we can plug any SAX parser implementation into Hammer to perform this part of the operation.

Apart from the simple constructor, we also have several private data members, including our container stack (which we discussed earlier), a stack we'll use to build alias names, and a hashtable to hold references to objects we've deserialized already so we can resolve references.

```
public Object fromXML() {
  return fromXML(new InputSource(System.in));
}

public Object fromXML(InputSource in) {
  nestedContainers.clear();
  aliasStack.clear();
  aliasStack.push(""); //initialise name building
  aliasTable.clear();
```

```
            nestedContainers.push(new RootAsContainer());  //root is first container
            try {
              parser.parse(in, this);
            } catch (IOException e) { e.printStackTrace();
            } catch (SAXException e) { e.printStackTrace();
            }
            return ((Container)nestedContainers.pop()).container;
        }
```

These two versions of the `fromXML()` method provide In's public API. One takes a SAX
`InputSource`, the other takes no parameters, and simply wraps `System.in`.

The method first initializes the instance variables, puts a representation of the root element onto the
container stack, and kicks off the parsing process. Notice it hands the parser a reference to itself as an
event handler. This will lead to the parser parsing the stream we have given it, and calling methods on this
object whenever elements and so on are encountered. Finally, after the parse has finished, it takes the last
container left on the stack (which should be the completed populated object graph), and returns it.

```
        static final int NESTED_TAGS = 0;
        static final int CHARACTER_DATA = 1;
        static final int EMPTY_TAG = 2;
        int inTag = NESTED_TAGS; //classification of tag
```

When processing SAX events, it pays to know where you are. We're going to keep track of what state
we're in by use of a variable called `inTag`, which will have one of these three values:

Value	Significance	Such As
NESTED_TAGS	We're in a tag that may contain other tags	A class instance or an array
CHARACTER_DATA	We're in a tag that may contain character data	A primitive
EMPTY_TAG	We're in a tag that may not contain anything	A null value or a reference

When we start, we know we're handling an object, so we will be in a `NESTED_TAGS` type tag.

SAX Event Handlers

We're only interested in elements and content, so we only need to implement three SAX event handler
methods. This is the first SAX event handler, for open tags:

```
        public void startElement(String namespaceURI, String localName,
            String rawName, Attributes atts) throws SAXException {
          switch (inTag) {
          case CHARACTER_DATA:
            throw new SAXException(
              "Expected character data, found nested tag: " +
              "<"+rawName+">. Found in object with alias '" +
              aliasStack.peek()+"'");
          case EMPTY_TAG:
            throw new SAXException(
```

```
                    "Expected empty tag, found nested tag: \n"+
                    "<"+rawName+">. Found in object with alias '" +
                    aliasStack.peek()+"'");
        }
        String nameAttr = atts.getValue(NAME_ATTR);
        elementDispatch(localName, nameAttr, atts);
    }
```

Now, depending upon the context (as stored in `inTag`), we react in one of two different ways. We're only expecting to receive this event when we are in an element that can contain other elements, so we throw a `SAXException` if we're not. Alternatively, if we're expecting an element, then we've found one, so we can call the `ElementDispatch()` method. We extract the value of the element's name attribute, if present, and pass it, along with the element's name (which is the run-time type of the data this element represents), and the `Attr` object.

As before, we implement an interface between front and back ends. This is so subclasses can override it, to cater for different XML formats. The intermediate method in this case is `elementDispatch()`, and it forwards calls on unchanged to `elementDispatchImpl()`.

```
//extenders can change this:
  public void elementDispatch(String typeName, String name, Attributes atts) {
    elementDispatchImpl(typeName, name, atts);
  }
```

The following method is the one that actually handles the open tag. We set up first three instance variables, which will store information from the opening tag for later use when primitive data values arrive in the `characters()` method:

```
String primitiveName;
String primitiveValue;
Class primitiveType;
```

`elementDispatchImpl()` investigates each opening tag to determine the type of value it represents (value used here in the sense of our formal grammar):

```
public void elementDispatchImpl(String typeName, String name, Attributes atts) {
    Object obj = null;  //convenience field
//NULL
    if (typeName!=null && typeName.equals(NULL_TYPE)) {
      inTag = EMPTY_TAG;
      ((Container) nestedContainers.peek()).bind(name, null);
      return;
    }
```

If the value is `null`, there's very little for us to do. We don't need to create an object, we just need to register `null` with our container. This is crucial because the array container keeps track of which element we are in by counting the number of times we have bound elements to it. We set the `inTag` value to `EMPTY_TAG` to say we aren't expecting any more data. To bind `null` with the container, we ask the top container on the stack to bind it to the field named in the element's name attribute. Of course, elements don't always have name attributes, but this can only be the case if they are the root object, or an array element, and the behavior in these circumstances isn't dependent on the element having a name. We'll look at how containers handle binding later on.

```
//ALIAS
    if (typeName!=null && typeName.equals(ALIAS_TYPE)) {
      inTag = EMPTY_TAG;
      String alias = atts.getValue(ALIAS_ATTR);
      obj = aliasTable.get(alias);
      ((Container) nestedContainers.peek()).bind(name, obj);
      return;
    }
```

Aliases again are empty tags, so we set the `inTag` value to `EMPTY_TAG`. We then retrieve the alias name from the attributes we've received, and use this to fetch the object referred to from our alias hashtable. This object is then bound to the container in the same way as before.

Now, if we get this far we have an array, a class instance, or a primitive. We need to find out if what we have is a container, or a primitive.

```
//CONTAINER
    Container container = ((Container) nestedContainers.peek());
    Class compileTimeType = container.deriveValueType(name);
    if ( !(compileTimeType.isPrimitive()) )  { //if the container was a class...
      aliasStack.push(aliasStack.peek()+container.aliasAdd(name));
    }
```

First we obtain a reference to the container we're currently in. We use this reference to discover the compile-time type of the field with the name of our current element (compile-time type is good enough, since it will tell us if we're dealing with a primitive). If the compile-time type is not primitive, we are dealing with a reference type – an object. We work out what the alias for the object is (what it will be referred to as by reference tags) using the `aliasStack`. The top item on the stack is the containing object's alias, so we retrieve this, and concatenate it with a string we obtain from our container. If our container is a class instance, this string will be a dot followed by the field name. If its an array, this will be our index enclosed in square brackets.

```
//PRIMITIVE/STRING-AS-PRIMITIVE
    if (compileTimeType.isPrimitive() || compileTimeType==String.class) {
      primitiveType = compileTimeType;
      primitiveName = name;
      primitiveValue = "";
      inTag = CHARACTER_DATA;
      return;
    }
```

This section handles primitives, and also fields where the compile-time type is `String` (we'll come to fields where the run-time type is `String` but the compile-time type isn't next). All we do is populate two of our three state-maintaining variables with the data from this element (the fieldname and the type), and initialize the third, which will store the value.

```
//STRING-AS-OBJECT
    if (typeName.equals(String.class.getName())) {
      primitiveType = String.class;
      primitiveName = name;
      primitiveValue = "";
      inTag = CHARACTER_DATA;
      return;
    }
```

We now check to see if the **run-time** type is String: This would be sufficient, but the previous method is more efficient and in the majority of cases Strings will be stored in fields with compile-time type String (the only other run-time types they could possibly be held in are Object, Comparable, and Serializable). Again, we treat the data the same way.

```
//ARRAY
    if (typeName.startsWith(ARRAY_TYPE_PREFIX)) {
      int length = Integer.parseInt(atts.getValue(LENGTH_ATTR));
      obj = newArrayInstance(typeName, length);
      ((Container) nestedContainers.peek()).bind(name, obj);
      nestedContainers.push(new ArrayAsContainer(obj));
      aliasTable.put(aliasStack.peek(), obj);
      return;
    }
```

Now we check to see if the element's name starts with our array prefix, which is the only way we can tell if we have an array or a class instance. We can now obtain the array's size from the length attribute, and generate a new array object of the correct type and size (using a utility method we'll come to at the end of the class). We can then bind it to the container, add an alias for this object, and a reference to it, to the alias table, and create a new container wrapper around this array, and put it on the container stack. Now, any elements we encounter will bind to this array, not to the container that was on top before.

```
//CLASS INSTANCE
    try {
      obj = MagicClass.newInstance(Class.forName(typeName));
    } catch (ClassNotFoundException e) { e.printStackTrace();
    }
    ((Container) nestedContainers.peek()).bind(name, obj);
    nestedContainers.push(new ClassInstanceAsContainer(obj));
    aliasTable.put(aliasStack.peek(), obj); //store
    }
```

Finally, we get to class instances. We use MagicClass to create us a new instance of the class without using a constructor, and, in the same way as for arrays, register with the container, push this object onto the top of the stack as a new container, and add a reference to it to the alias table.

The next SAX event handler handles characters() events: data from inside elements. In Hammer's world, this is always the value for a primitive type or String.

```
  public void characters(char[] ch, int start, int end)
                throws SAXException {
    String s = new String(ch, start, end);
    if (inTag!=CHARACTER_DATA) {
      if (s.trim().length()!=0)
        throw new SAXException(
          "Only primitives are permitted character data content:\n"+
          "'"+s+"' non-whitespace character data "+
          "found in object with alias '"+ aliasStack.peek()+"'");
    } else {
      primitiveValue += s;  //may be several calls (don't trim)
    }
  }
```

All we do is check that we are expecting character data in the first place (throwing a SAXException if we aren't), and if so, add it to the primitiveValue instance variable. We leave actually binding the primitive to its parent object to the endElement() method.

```java
public void endElement(String namespaceURI, String localName,
                       String rawName) throws SAXException {
  switch (inTag) {
    case EMPTY_TAG:   //emptytag
      break;
    case NESTED_TAGS: //nestable tag
      nestedContainers.pop();
      aliasStack.pop();
      break;
    case CHARACTER_DATA:  //character data
      Object value = null;
      if (primitiveType==String.class) {
        value = primitiveValue;
        aliasTable.put(aliasStack.pop(), primitiveValue); //store
      } else if (primitiveType==char.class) {
        value = new Character(primitiveValue.charAt(0));
      } else {
        try {
          Constructor cons = (Constructor) primCons.get(primitiveType);
          value = cons.newInstance(new Object[] {primitiveValue});
        } catch (InstantiationException e) { e.printStackTrace();
        } catch (IllegalAccessException e) { e.printStackTrace();
        } catch (IllegalArgumentException e) { e.printStackTrace();
        } catch (InvocationTargetException e) { e.printStackTrace();
        }
      }
      ((Container) nestedContainers.peek()).bind(primitiveName, value);
      break;
  }//end switch
  inTag = NESTED_TAGS;
}
```

endElement() is called when the closing tag for an element is encountered. We need to react differently according to what kind of data we expect to have been processing in the enclosed content, so we switch according to the current value of inTag.

If we're ending an empty element, we have nothing to do, since all processing was completed in the startElement() method. If we're ending a container, which may have had other tags inside it, then we're going back up a level, so we must remove the container's entries from the container and alias stacks.

If we're ending a primitive, then the three primitive data fields should now be populated with the primitive's data. We have a String containing the string representation of the primitive's value. We need to turn the primitive into an object to bind it to the container. With Strings, this isn't a problem, they are already in object form. The other primitives need to have wrapper objects constructed. All except char have a constructor on their wrapper class that takes a String as an argument, so we also treat char specially. The others are constructed using the same technique. A reference to the appropriate wrapper class is obtained from a hash table which we populate using the following static block:

```
static Hashtable primCons;
static {
  Class primConsInit[][] = {
    {int.class, Integer.class},
    {double.class, Double.class},
    {boolean.class, Boolean.class},
    {byte.class, Byte.class},
    {short.class, Short.class},
    {long.class, Long.class},
    {float.class, Float.class}
    //"Character" wrapper has no constructor taking a String argument
  };
  primCons = new Hashtable((int)(primConsInit.length/.75));
  Class[] args = {String.class};

  for (int i=0; i<primConsInit.length; i++) {
    try {
      primCons.put(
        primConsInit[i][0],
        primConsInit[i][1].getDeclaredConstructor(args)
      );
    } catch (NoSuchMethodException e) { e.printStackTrace(); }
  }
}
```

This generates a hashtable mapping between the `Class` objects associated with each primitive type and the constructor, which takes a single `String` as an argument. This enables us in the `endElement()` method to invoke this constructor to create a wrapper object for each primitive. This is then bound to the container.

Lastly, we have a block of utility code, which consists of a method to obtain an array with the correct dimensionality and underlying type. To obtain primitive data types, we rely on another static hashtable, this time mapping the names of primitive types to references to primitive `Class` objects.

```
static int arrayTypePrefixSkip = ARRAY_TYPE_PREFIX.length();
static Object newArrayInstance(String arrayTypeName, int length) {
  int index = 0;
  int dimensionality = 0;
  while (arrayTypeName.startsWith(ARRAY_TYPE_PREFIX, index)) {
    dimensionality++;
    index+=arrayTypePrefixSkip;
  }
  String baseTypeName = arrayTypeName.substring(index);
    //NB: baseType!=componentType

  int[] dimensions = new int[dimensionality];
  dimensions[0] = length;
  Class baseType = (Class) primType.get(baseTypeName);
  if (baseType==null)
    try {
      baseType = Class.forName(baseTypeName);
    } catch (ClassNotFoundException e) { e.printStackTrace(); }
  return Array.newInstance(baseType, dimensions);
}

static Hashtable primType;
```

```
    static {
      Object primTypeInit[] = {
          int.class,
          double.class,
          boolean.class,
          char.class,
          byte.class,
          short.class,
          long.class,
          float.class };
      primType = new Hashtable((int)(primTypeInit.length/.75));
      for (int i=0; i<primTypeInit.length; i++) {
        primType.put(primTypeInit[i]+"", primTypeInit[i]);
      }
    }
}
```

That completes the code for In.java. Now we need to implement the supporting Container classes. There is one for the root object, one for arrays, and one for class instances. The need for polymorphism is that both arrays and class instances can contain other values, but Java provides different methods of access to them. Since the request is the same for each type – please bind this value in – but the behavior is different, it is a classic use for polymorphism, which is defined precisely in those terms: the same requests for different types are handled in different ways.

Note that in addition to this, the root of the entire graph is also a kind of a container, and it makes for neater code to treat it as such. The first container on the stack will always be a RootAsContainer, which is pushed and popped by the initial fromXML() method above.

So, first of all, let's define the abstract Container class that we extend to implement the specific behaviors:

```
package hammer;

abstract class Container implements Constants {
  Object container;

  public Container(Object container) { this.container = container; }
  abstract public void bind(String fieldName, Object value);
  abstract public Class deriveValueType(String fieldName);
  abstract public String aliasAdd(String fieldName);
}
```

Containers have three methods, all of which we've seen in action in In. First is the bind() operation, which binds a child with a given name to the containing object. Then there is deriveValuetype(), which gives us the compile-time type for a given field name. Finally there is aliasAdd(), which returns the string that needs to be appended onto a parent container's alias to produce the alias for a container.

Now, let's see how this is implemented for the root container:

```
package hammer;

class RootAsContainer extends Container {
    public RootAsContainer() {
super(null);
    }
```

```
    public void bind(String fieldName, Object value) {
        container = value;  //plug into root
    }
    public Class deriveValueType(String fieldName) {
        return Object.class;  //compile time type of the root
    }
    public String aliasAdd(String fieldName) {
        return ALIAS_ROOT;
    }
}
```

The root will only be called upon to bind a single object: the root element of the XML document. So, the constructor doesn't set the contained object, the bind operation does. The compile-time type is therefore always the class of the contained element, and the alias is always ALIAS_ROOT, which we've defined in Constants as "_". Constants is accessible from this class, incidentally, becaue it is implemented by Container.

Now, the largest and most complex container is the class instance:

```
package hammer;
import java.lang.reflect.*;

class ClassInstanceAsContainer extends Container {
    Class containerClass;  //cache
    public ClassInstanceAsContainer(Object container) {
        super(container);
        containerClass = container.getClass();
    }
}
```

When binding to a class instance, name is significant. We want to bind a value to a specific field of the instance. We rely on MagicClass to obtain a reference to any field for us and open it up so we can access it using the set() method.

```
    public void bind(String fieldName, Object value) {
        try {
            MagicClass.getAnyField(containerClass, fieldName)
                             .set(container, value);
        } catch (NoSuchFieldException e) {  //eg: field evolved out
            e.printStackTrace();
        } catch (IllegalAccessException e) {  //eg: field evolved out
            e.printStackTrace();
        }
    }
```

Obtaining the compile-time type for any field is also achieved through MagicClass.

```
    public Class deriveValueType(String fieldName) {
        try {
            return MagicClass.getAnyField(containerClass, fieldName).getType();
        } catch (NoSuchFieldException e) {
            e.printStackTrace();
            System.exit(0);
        }

        return null; //reachable if runtime exception not caught above
    }
```

Aliases for fields of a class instance must add a dot followed by the fieldname.

```
      public String aliasAdd(String fieldName) {
        return "."+fieldName;
      }
    }
```

Finally, the array container:

```
  package hammer;
  import java.lang.reflect.*;

  class ArrayAsContainer extends Container {
      int index;
      Class valueType;  //cache
      public ArrayAsContainer(Object container) {
          super(container);
          this.index = 0;
          valueType = container.getClass().getComponentType();
      }
      public void bind(String fieldName, Object value) {
          Array.set(container, index++, value);
      }
      public Class deriveValueType(String fieldName) {
          return valueType;
      }
      public String aliasAdd(String fieldName) {
          return "["+index+"]";
      }
```

The only special thing this class is doing is keeping a tally of how many times it has had objects bound to it. The compile-time type of members of an array is always the underlying type of elements of the array, and aliases for array members add the index enclosed in square brackets.

Now, with these five classes in the hammer package, we can write another test class to use In to read in some XML created using Out. We need to modify our Person class so that we can obtain information from a reconstituted instance of the class:

```
  public class Person implements java.io.Serializable {

      private int age = 34;
      private Object name = "Fred";
      private Person[] friends = null;

      public Person(String name, int age) {
          this.age=age;
          this.name=name;
      }

      public void setFriends(Person[] friends) {
  this.friends=friends;
      }

      public String toString() {
        StringBuffer s = new StringBuffer((String) name + ", " + age +
                                          " [friends: ");
```

```
        for (int i = 0; i < friends.length; i++) {
            s.append((String) friends[i].name);
        }
        s.append("]");
        return s.toString();
    }
}
```

Now we can build a `Person` from an XML document generated by `Out` from a `Person` object:

```
import hammer.*;

public class HammerInTest {
 public static void main(String[] args) {
   In in = new In();
   Person somebody = (Person) in.fromXML();

   System.out.println(somebody.toString());

 }
}
```

Since `Out` writes to `System.out` and `In` reads (by default) from `System.in`, we can use redirection to pipe output to or from files, as follows:

```
java HammerTest > fred.xml
java HammerInTest < fred.xml
```

This tells the shell to feed the output of the first program to a file called `fred.xml`. The second command tells it to feed the contents of `fred.xml` into the program's standard input.

The results of doing so are as follows:

SOAP-style Formatting

As we discussed earlier, SOAP actually represents more or less the same data as Hammer, but uses a different way of mapping type and fieldname information. We're going to show here how the template methods we built into `Out` and `In` can be overridden by custom formatters to generate and read alternatively formatted XML.

The OutSOAP Class

```
package hammer;

public class OutSOAP extends Out {

  static { DEFAULT_ATTR=TYPE_ATTR; }
```

This static block overrides the assignment of the default attribute to "name" in Out, replacing it with "type". Now, calls to the tag generating methods will result in tags with a type attribute.

We implement the encoding by overriding the implementation methods. In each case, we have to check to see if the object we are writing out has a name, and if not, we must invent one. We use the type as a made-up name for anonymous elements such as the root element, and those found inside arrays.

```
    void primitiveImpl(String type, String name, String value,
                       String indent) {
    if (name==null) {
      openTag(indent, type, null);
      textContent(value);
      closeTag(type);
    } else {
      openTag(indent, name, type);
      textContent(value);
      closeTag(name);
    }
    System.out.println();
  }

  void nullReferenceImpl(String type, String name, String indent) {
    if (name==null) emptyTag(indent, type, null);
    else emptyTag(indent, name, type);
    System.out.println();
  }
  void aliasReferenceImpl(String type, String name,
                          String targetAlias, String indent) {
    if (name==null) emptyTag(indent, type, null, ALIAS_ATTR, targetAlias);
    else   emptyTag(indent, name, type, ALIAS_ATTR, targetAlias);
    System.out.println();
  }
  void arrayImpl(String type, String name, String length,
                 Class clazz, Object obj, String alias, String indent) {
    if (name==null) {
      openTag(indent, type, null, LENGTH_ATTR, length);
    System.out.println();
    componentDispatch(clazz, obj, alias, indent+SPACER);
      closeTag(indent,type);
    System.out.println();
  } else {
      openTag(indent, name, type, LENGTH_ATTR, length);
    System.out.println();
    componentDispatch(clazz, obj, alias, indent+SPACER);
      closeTag(indent, name);
    System.out.println();
    }
  }
```

```
   void classInstanceImpl(String type, String name, Class clazz,
                          Object obj, String alias, String indent) {
  if (name==null) {
    openTag(indent, type, null);
  System.out.println();
  fieldDispatch(clazz, obj, alias, indent+SPACER);
    closeTag(indent,type);
  System.out.println();
  } else {
    openTag(indent, name, type);
  System.out.println();
  fieldDispatch(clazz, obj, alias, indent+SPACER);
    closeTag(indent, name);
  System.out.println();
  }
  }
}
```

Now, we need to make a simple change to our tester class as follows:

```
import hammer.*;

public class HammerSOAPTest {
    public static void main(String[] args) {
        Out out = new OutSOAP();

        Person fred = new Person("Fred", 34);
        Person george = new Person("George", 43);
        Person deborah = new Person("Deborah", 28);

        george.setFriends(new Person[] {deborah, fred});
        fred.setFriends(new Person[] {george});
        deborah.setFriends(new Person[] {george});

        out.toXML(fred);
    }
}
```

Now, executing this test class results in this output:

As you can see, the elements that actually have names are now using them as tag names, rather than as attribute values.

The next challenge, then, is to read this differently formatted data back in.

The InSOAP Class

```
package hammer;
import org.xml.sax.*; //Attr, ContentHandler, Exceptions

public class InSOAP extends In {

  public void elementDispatch(String tagName, String nameAttr, Attributes atts) {
    String type = atts.getValue(TYPE_ATTR);
    if (nestedContainers.peek() instanceof ClassInstanceAsContainer)
      elementDispatchImpl(type, tagName, atts);  //type, name
    else elementDispatchImpl(tagName, null, atts); //for array, root
  }
}
```

This is even simpler than the OutSOAP class. We simply override elementDispatch(), and ignore the name attribute that is passed in (it will be empty). Instead, we simply extract the type attribute from the SAX Attributes object we've received, and then take a look to see if we're in a class. If we are, the contained elements will be named after the fields, if not, they will be named after the types. We then return control to the elementDispatchImpl() method. elementDispatchImpl() takes a type, a name (or null if there is no name), and an Attributes object. Having worked out whether the type is contained in the tag name or in the value of the type attribute, we can provide all this information.

A similar change to our test program allows us to test this inputter as well:

```
import hammer.*;

public class HammerInSOAPTest {
 public static void main(String[] args) {
  In in = new InSOAP();
  Person fred = (Person) in.fromXML();

  System.out.println(fred.toString());

 }
}
```

Now, running the two SOAP testers using redirection to direct output to and input from an intermediate file, we can get the result:

Evolution and Versioning

The world changes, while our specifications and standards, protocols and programs remain perfectly immutable, as they were when first created. However the world generally wins most of the time. Thus, even though it is the world that has changed, and not the software, the pragmatic view is that it is the software that changes; it is the software that decays.

On top of this, our understanding of complex problems changes as we learn more and understand them better, and this is the basis of iterative prototyping and evolutionary development. This gradual enlightenment is yet another cause for change, as we realize what a field really should be called, or that we don't need that one, or that a different implementation is more appropriate. This is no problem at all when we are writing for ourselves – but it is one fantastically huge headache when we are writing for the world; as we are when we use a lingua franca like XML.

One approach to managing change is to create an interface or format that remains constant, and isolates the underlying implementation, which can then freely change. By this approach, there are two things that can change: the implementation of the object and the format. We handle implementation changes as "evolution", and format changes as "versioning". The idea is to minimize different versions as much as possible, by trying to evolve our implementations so that they still fit into the previous version.

This interface – or layer – has another advantage of keeping all the information in one place, where it can be maintained comprehensively, without missing anything, and in a modular fashion, without cluttering up the rest of the code. If it specifies a mapping from which transformations in both directions are derived, then this is a form of code reuse, which lessens the chance of discrepancies between redundant systems. Putting all the persistent fields into one place also helps us to see the information all at once, and grasp it as a gestalt. Sometimes, it makes sense to group data fields close to the code that uses them in source code, and so the data supplies a unified different view of the field scattered through the source – including appropriate comments.

Of course, the primary benefit of a data layer is that it separates the object data and XML format, thus allowing them to vary independently. It is like a data version of the Adapter Design Pattern. A good generic example is the SAX `DefaultHandler` class, which implements a number of the handler interfaces, without any specific implementation. Programmers can then extend this class, implementing just the methods they need for the task in hand.

It does something more, too, something done by the `transient` keyword in serialization – it extracts or abstracts only the object data that we want to persist – for example, we might not want to save cached, computed, or incidental **run-time** information. Alternatively, we might want to persist this information separately – perhaps in a configuration file. That is, the one object might have its state separated into two different persistent stores. Note that caching can apply to derived, inferred or computed values, which have a canonical original to assure consistency – especially important if the XML may be hand-edited.

Abstract Data Layer (ADL)

Data layers are an essential part of XML-Object mapping – just as a stream of consciousness brain-dump is not particularly intelligible to readers, but some thought is required to select and present the information in a comprehensible manner. Databases have implicitly enforced this discipline for years; as indeed, has XML.

Object-oriented programming has delivered some important benefits. However, it has also created the illusion that data and code (objects) must always go together. But it isn't necessarily so. With the advent of XML, data comes into its own ever more strongly.

As further evidence that data is important in its own right, not necessarily bound up with code in objects, consider the more established data formats, like GIF, MP3, TCP/IP, e-mail headers, HTML, and even Word documents. There are many more such protocols, and they are resistant to change, because they have become part of the infrastructure. If you want to communicate broadly, you must speak the lingua franca; and these data formats are it. Once they reach critical mass in the community, the network effect means that they pretty much dominate everything – at times, even superior technology.

Data formats are very important; important to get right; and it is important to be able to switch to superior versions of the technology. For further support of the importance of data, consider the following quotes from *The Mythical Man Month* (Frederick P. Brooks Jr., Addison Wesley, ISBN 0-201835-95-9), which Eric Raymond picked up in his essay "The Cathedral and the Bazaar" (http://www.tuxedo.org/~esr/writings/cathedral-bazaar/):

> *"Show me your [code] and conceal your [data structures], and I shall continue to be mystified. Show me your [data structures], and I won't usually need your [code]; it'll be obvious."*

Brooks actually said "flowcharts" instead of code, and "tables" instead of data structures – Raymond updated it. Brooks also went on to say on the very last line of his book's Chapter 9:

> *"Representation is the essence of programming."*

An ADL Implementation

One way to create a data layer is with "getter" and "setter" (known to C++ programmers as accessor and mutator) methods, as in JavaBeans. However, this is massive overkill for what is needed. The essential problem is that we are using an API for data; but an API is about calling methods. It is about code, not data. This creates unnecessary overhead and awkwardness. It's basically wrong-headed, because it gives us the power to do many things that we don't want or need to do most of the time, and the power comes at a cost.

Specifically, an API of getters and setters allows us to do programmatic mappings. We can:

- ❏ Provide immediate range and constraint checking in the body of the methods, as soon as updates are made

- ❏ Calculate derived fields and cached versions thereof immediately when their basis changes.

- ❏ Distribute messages to synchronize with remote data stores

A subtle point is that all of these programmatic mappings need only occur when a value changes – that is, when a setter is invoked, but not when a getter is. Updates are more significant than reads. However, it is often possible to lazily defer these checks, calculations,and synchronizations until a getter requests the data. Thus, we could generally remove the programmatic burden on half of the API. An even lazier – and therefore more efficient – approach is to defer all these tasks until persistence time. That is, until the data is actually read or written; including communications to remote stores. Given the serial nature of XML, it will typically be dealt with as one big file or database CLOB (Character Large Object) rather than piecemeal – for the latter, we would really be talking about the fields of a relational database.

But there is something even more strange and unnatural about the getter and setter idea. Objects comprise data and code. APIs are for code. But getters and setters are using an API for data. What is missing is the equivalent of an API, but for data, and not for code.

Another problem with using an API: there is usually a strong relationship between a setter and a getter – they are the same mapping but in different directions. And yet we need to explicitly write code for both transformations, in violation of the fundamental directive of "code reuse".

However, an API does have some advantages: it is a view of code – one object can implement more than one API, and they can even end up doing the same things, just with a different appearance or front end. Consider the Adapter Design Pattern, which makes one API look like another, by forwarding the calls. Adapters can even be layered one atop the other, in an inelegant but effective way to cope with 'world-creep'.

The ADL we're going to implement here makes use of reflection APIs to map the real internal data members of a class to a well defined set of fields. This implementation of an Abstract Data Layer also uses Java interfaces, and so shares these advantages of APIs. Many ADLs can apply to the same object; but there are none of the problems of multiple inheritance, because it merely provides **views** of existing fields, rather than new fields altogether. As with APIs, it is also possible to add a new ADL to an existing class, by subclassing it, and implementing the ADL interface in the subclass.

What we are talking about here is the idea of being able to present different views of the data held in an object. We're going to do this by:

❑ Describing the view in an interface that extends the empty marker interface ADL

❑ Attaching the view to a class by stating that the class implements it

❑ Altering Hammer so that it is aware of ADL views

❑ Serializing the class with Hammer, which will use the view to interpret the data

❑ Deserializing the class using Hammer, to generate objects again

Of course, one interesting possibility this presents is that if we make two interfaces, both of which represent identical looking views of two different classes, Hammer can translate data from both classes to the same XML format – *and back*. This is the fundamental capability that will allow us to cope with evolution of classes, and much more besides.

The Person Class

Here is the original source code for our Person class, which does not have an abstract data layer:

```
public class Person {

    private int age;
    private Object name;
    private Person[] friends;

    public Person(String name, int age) {
        this.age=age;
        this.name=name;
    }

    public void setFriends(Person[] friends) {
this.friends=friends;
    }
```

```
public String toString() {
    StringBuffer s = new StringBuffer((String) name + ", " + age +
                                      " [friends: ");
    for (int i = 0; i < friends.length; i++) {
        s.append((String) friends[i].name);
    }
    s.append("]");
    return s.toString();
}
```

Let's define a data layer that describes the data the class currently exports. We first need our marker interface called ADL:

```
package hammer;

public interface ADL {}
```

This interface is extended by our data layer interfaces to tell Hammer that that is their function.

Next, we need a utility class called DataLayer:

```
package hammer;
import java.lang.reflect.*;

public class DataLayer {
    static public Field getField(Class clazz, String field) {
        Field f = null;
        try {
            f = MagicClass.getAnyField(clazz, field);
        } catch (Exception e) {
            e.printStackTrace();
        }
        return f;
    }
}
```

This simply provides a static method that accesses MagicClass, and traps any errors that might occur. We use this method to map elements of our data layer to the underlying implementation fields.

Here's a data layer interface:

```
import java.lang.reflect.Field;
import hammer.*;

public interface Person1 extends ADL {
    static final Field name = DataLayer.getField(Person.class, "name");
    static final Field age = DataLayer.getField(Person.class, "age");
    static final Field friends = DataLayer.getField(Person.class,
                                                    "friends");
}
```

As you can see, we simply declare a `static final Field` for each member of our data layer, and populate it with a reference to the underlying field that interests us.

Now, we simply need to change `Person` to reflect the existence of this new data layer:

```
public class Person implements Person1 {

    private int age;
    private Object name;
    private Person[] friends;

    // rest of methods as before

}
```

Now, what we want to happen is for Hammer to search among the interface ancestors of each class it encounters looking for interfaces that implement ADL. When it finds one, it will use the fields defined in that interface, rather than searching through and locating the fields itself, to serialize the object.

What happens if there's more than one ADL interface in the ancestor tree? Well, we can use the first one that we find, or we can introduce a way for the class to indicate which one should be used for serialization. We do this by use of a special attribute, `version`. By having a field called `version` in the object (it can be static or instance, and have any level of access control), we can allow the class designer, or the programmer at run-time, to choose which ADL view will be used by Hammer to serialize the object.

To do this, we'll need to make some changes. First, let's get serialization working, with a couple of new sections in `Out`. We'll make a new version of `Out` called `OutADL`. Apart from changing the class name, the first change is in the `fieldDispatch()` method.

```
void fieldDispatch(Class parentRunTimeType, Object obj,
                   String alias, String indent) {

Class[] interfaces = parentRunTimeType.getInterfaces();
int i;

boolean adl = false;

String version = null;
try {
    version = (String) MagicClass.getAnyField(parentRunTimeType,
                               VERSION_ATTR).get(obj);
} catch (NoSuchFieldException e) {
} catch (IllegalAccessException e) {
}
for (i=0; i<interfaces.length; i++) {
    if (ADL.class.isAssignableFrom(interfaces[i])) {
      if (version==null || interfaces[i].getName().equals(version)) {
        adl = true;
        break;
      }
    }
  }
}
```

This first new block of code is dedicated to discovering if the object in question has an ADL. First we look for a version attribute, but we don't panic if there is none. Then we try to find an ADL interface, and check to see if it matches our version specifier if we have one. The next part of the method is enclosed in an `if...else` block, one half for gathering data via the ADL interface, the other for gathering it the old-fashioned way.

```
if (adl) {
    Field[] f = interfaces[i].getDeclaredFields();
    AccessibleObject.setAccessible(f, true);
    for (int j=0; j<f.length; j++) {
        Field thisf = null;
        try {
            thisf = (Field)f[j].get(obj);
        } catch (IllegalAccessException e) { e.printStackTrace();
        }
        Class compileTimeType = thisf.getType();
        String fieldName = f[j].getName();  //we get the name from ADL
        Object fieldValue = null;
        try {
            thisf.setAccessible(true);
            fieldValue = thisf.get(obj);
        } catch (IllegalAccessException e) { e.printStackTrace(); }
        valueDispatch(compileTimeType, fieldName, fieldValue,
                    alias+"."+fieldName, indent);
    }
```

This first half handles retrieving data via the ADL. Using the `Field` objects contained in the fields of the ADL interface directly, it loops through calling `valueDispatch()` on each of them.

```
} else {
    Field[] fields = MagicClass.getAllFields(parentRunTimeType);
    for (i=0; i<fields.length; i++) {
    Field f = fields[i];
    if ((f.getModifiers() & STATIC_OR_TRANSIENT) != 0) continue;
    Class compileTimeType = f.getType();
    String fieldName = f.getName();
    Object fieldValue = null;
    try {
        fieldValue = f.get(obj);
    } catch (IllegalAccessException e) { e.printStackTrace(); }
    valueDispatch(compileTimeType, fieldName,
                fieldValue, alias+"."+fieldName, indent);
    }

    }

}
```

The second half remains unchanged, except for a slight alteration to take into account that the block is now embedded in an `if...else` statement.

The next thing to change is `classInstanceImpl()`. This needs to include a new attribute to store the version, so that decoders will know which ADL was used to obtain the view.

```
void classInstanceImpl(String type, String name, Class clazz,
                Object obj, String alias, String indent) {
```

```
        String version = null;
        try {
            version = (String) MagicClass.getAnyField(clazz, VERSION_ATTR).get(obj);
        } catch (NoSuchFieldException e) {
        } catch (IllegalAccessException e) {
        }
```

This block is new, and is devoted to finding out if the object has a `version` field.

```
        openTag(indent, type, name, VERSION_ATTR, version);
```

This line is altered, to include the new attribute as an extra attribute. The rest of the method is unchanged.

```
        System.out.println();
        fieldDispatch(clazz, obj, alias, indent+SPACER);

        closeTag(indent, type);
        System.out.println();
    }
```

And that's it – we now have an ADL-aware version of `Out`. Next we need to change some of the components used to deserialize. First, `In` itself. Let's again make a version of `In` called `InADL`. At the very end of `elementDispatchImpl()` we need to change the class instance dispatcher to read as follows:

```
//CLASS INSTANCE
    try {
        obj = MagicClass.newInstance(Class.forName(typeName));
    } catch (ClassNotFoundException e) { e.printStackTrace();
    }
    ((Container) nestedContainers.peek()).bind(name, obj);
    String version = atts.getValue(VERSION_ATTR);
    nestedContainers.push(new ADLClassInstanceAsContainer(obj, version));
    aliasTable.put(aliasStack.peek(), obj); //store
    }
```

As you can see, the important thing is to retrieve the version attribute, and then pass it on to the container. We need to create a new kind of class-instance container that's ADL-aware, so let's do that next:

```
package hammer;
import java.lang.reflect.*;

public class ADLClassInstanceAsContainer extends Container {
    Class containerClass;   //cache
    Class interfaceADL;
    boolean adl = false;
    public ADLClassInstanceAsContainer(Object container, String version) {
        super(container);
        containerClass = container.getClass();
        Class[] interfaces = containerClass.getInterfaces();
        for (int i=0; i<interfaces.length; i++) {
```

```
        if (ADL.class.isAssignableFrom(interfaces[i])) {
          if (version==null || interfaces[i].getName().equals(version)) {
            interfaceADL = interfaces[i];
            adl = true;
            break;
          }
        }
      }
    }
```

This loop is the mirror of the code we first added to Out: it is attempting to locate an ADL interface that matches the input data.

```
    public void bind(String fieldName, Object value) {
      if (adl) {
        try {
          Field f = interfaceADL.getDeclaredField(fieldName);
          f.setAccessible(true);
          f = (Field) f.get(container);
          f.set(container, value);
        } catch (NoSuchFieldException e) {  //eg: field evolved out
          e.printStackTrace();
        } catch (IllegalAccessException e) {  //eg: field evolved out
          e.printStackTrace();
        }
      } else {
```

Just like in Out, in the bind() method we simply split and do one of two things, according to whether ADL is available or not. This block handles binding if ADL is available. The alternative technique is just the same as before.

```
        try {
          MagicClass.getAnyField(containerClass, fieldName)
                          .set(container, value);
        } catch (NoSuchFieldException e) {  //eg: field evolved out
          e.printStackTrace();
        } catch (IllegalAccessException e) {  //eg: field evolved out
          e.printStackTrace();
        }
      }
    }
    public Class deriveValueType(String fieldName) {
      if (adl) {
        try {
          Field f = interfaceADL.getDeclaredField(fieldName);
          f.setAccessible(true);
          f = (Field)f.get(container);
          return f.getType();
        } catch (NoSuchFieldException e) {  //eg: field evolved out
          e.printStackTrace();
        } catch (IllegalAccessException e) {  //eg: field evolved out
          e.printStackTrace();
        }
      } else {
```

Similarly, we split the `deriveValueType()` method in two.

```
    try {
       return MagicClass.getAnyField(containerClass,
                       fieldName).getType();
    } catch (NoSuchFieldException e) {
       e.printStackTrace();
       System.exit(0);
    }
  }
  return null;
}
public String aliasAdd(String fieldName) {
  return "."+fieldName;
}
}
```

And that completes the deserialization logic for Hammer ADL. The other classes in the `hammer` package are all still needed.

Versions

Now, let's create a second view of the data in the `Person` class. This interface is a second ADL:

```
import java.lang.reflect.Field;
import hammer.*;

public interface Person2 extends ADL {
    static final Field cn = DataLayer.getField(Person.class, "name");
}
```

This version only picks out the internal 'name' field, an serializes it under the identifier 'cn', which is often used as an abbreviation for 'Common Name'.

Now, we need to edit the `Person` class to implement this new interface, and include a version attribute, like this:

```
public class Person implements Person1, Person2 {

  private String version = "Person1";

  private int age = 34;
  private Object name = "Fred";
  private Person[] friends = null;

  public void setVersion(String version) {
    this.version=version;
  }

  // rest of methods as before

}
```

All we need to do now is generate a new pair of test tools that work with the ADL versions of the classes. Here's the code that writes out XML:

```
public class HammerADLTest {
    public static void main(String[] args) {
        hammer.OutADL out = new hammer.OutADL();

        Person fred = new Person("Fred", 34);
        Person george = new Person("George", 43);
        Person deborah = new Person("Deborah", 28);

        george.setFriends(new Person[] {deborah, fred});
        fred.setFriends(new Person[] {george});
        deborah.setFriends(new Person[] {george});

        george.setVersion("Person2");

        out.toXML(fred);
    }
}
```

And here's the code that reads it in:

```
public class HammerADLInTest {
  public static void main(String[] args) {
    hammer.InADL in = new hammer.InADL();

    Person someone = (Person) in.fromXML();

    System.out.println(someone.toString());
  }
}
```

Now, compile up, and run:

```
java HammerADLTest > versions.xml
java HammerADLInTest < versions.xml
```

The result should be:

```
Command Prompt                                                    _ □ ×
K:\Hammer>java HammerADLTest > versions.xml

K:\Hammer>java HammerADLInTest < versions.xml
Fred, 34 [friends: George]

K:\Hammer>
```

This shouldn't come as much of a surprise. But let's take a look at the contents of versions.xml.

```
<Person version='Person1'>
 <java.lang.String name='name'>Fred</java.lang.String>
 <int name='age'>34</int>
 <ArrayOf-Person name='friends' length='1'>
  <Person version='Person2'>
   <java.lang.String name='cn'>George</java.lang.String>
  </Person>
 </ArrayOf-Person>
</Person>
```

We've got one `Person1`-type person, with all the data members from the `Person1` ADL, and in the `friends` array, George is represented by a `Person2`-type person, with only the `cn` attribute from the `Person2` ADL.

In spite of this variation in encoding, both Fred and George have made it into the `HammerADLInTest` program as `Person` objects (although George lost some data along the way – including Deborah). So Hammer has demonstrated its power at coping with different formats for the same class.

Class Evolution

But what about when the underlying class changes? Keep a hold of `versions.xml` from the last example, and let's see how we can import the data into a completely different `Person` class.

Save the current `Person.java`, `Person1.java`, and `Person2.java`, in a separate directory, and create a new `Person.java` class, like this:

```
public class Person implements Person1, Person2 {

    private String id;
    private int yearsOld;
    private float height;
    private Person[] colleagues;

    public Person(String id) {
        this.id = id;
    }

    public String toString() {
        String result= "ID: " + id + " (" + yearsOld + ", " +
                                            height + "ft)";
        for (int a=0; a < colleagues.length; a++) {
            result = result + "\n\t" + colleagues[a].id;
        }
        return result;
    }
}
```

As you can see, it represents fundamentally the same data, but it has evolved. We'll need to update the ADL to reflect the changes in the class. Here's `Person1`:

```
import java.lang.reflect.Field;
import hammer.*;

public interface Person1 extends ADL {
  static final Field name = DataLayer.getField(Person.class, "id");
  static final Field age = DataLayer.getField(Person.class, "yearsOld");
  static final Field friends = DataLayer.getField(Person.class,
                                               "colleagues");
  static final Field height = DataLayer.getField(Person.class, "height");
}
```

And `Person2`:

```
import java.lang.reflect.Field;
import hammer.*;

public interface Person2 extends ADL {
  static final Field cn = DataLayer.getField(Person.class, "id");
}
```

As you can see, all that really needs to be changed is which fields the ADL fields are mapped to. We can also safely add a new field to the ADL for `Person1`.

Now, we should be able to execute the `HammerADLInTest` program on our legacy `versions.xml` document, and this time see the following result:

OK – that's evolution of objects – but what about versioning? We say that versioning is evolution of the XML format.

If objects and XML are tightly tied in lockstep, this statement would be silly – for if one changes, the other must, too. But often, we only really want to change one... an abstract data layer allows us to keep them separated, so one can vary independently of the other (at least in some ways). If we vary the classes, but keep the XML the same, we have *evolution of classes*, as in the above. But if we vary the XML format instead, it is called *format versioning*. We have seen this with our use of two separate ADL interfaces.

Persistent Data Stores

Once we have converted objects into XML that can be stored as text, we need to actually store them somewhere so that they may persist. Three different types of store are considered here: files, relational databases, and directories. Despite the names, technically, all three are databases. Although there are other options, these are the most popular. How can we best use XML with these stores?

Files vs. Databases

What we mean by a flat file is usually that the file is written as a whole. Thus, to write an object graph, we simply output the entire XML document to a file. This is fine for small amounts of non-critical data.

However, this does not scale well with larger amounts of data: if we want to update only a small part of the data, we need to write out the entire document again. In contrast, a relational database allows specific parts of it to be accessed piecemeal – both for reading and writing.

There is also a problem for critical data, because if our program crashes half-way through writing the file (if there is a power failure), it is lost, and the previous version is also destroyed. We could make a back up of the previous version first, but this incurs an even greater performance overhead for large files. Basically, the persistence is too coarse-grained.

Relational databases have a number of sophisticated mechanisms for ensuring that critical data is not lost. Updates to the database can be logged before they are applied, so that if they fail, they can later be reapplied.

Atomic updates are also supported. This is when two or more transactions must all succeed, or all fail. A typical example is transfer of money between two accounts in a banking system. There are two updates – a withdrawal and a deposit – but if only one of them succeeds, then money would not have been conserved; that is, the sum would disappear if withdrawn but not deposited, and be doubled if it was deposited and not withdrawn. The solution is to say these two updates are a single "atomic" transaction – that is, one that is not divisible – which either fails (roll back) or succeeds (commit). These two phases, of beginning a transaction, and then possibly committing earns it the name "two-phase commit".

Concurrent access by many users is also desirable. We can prevent concurrent access on a flat file with a file lock, but again this is a very coarse-grained measure, as two users may be updating entirely different parts of the file. Relational databases allow much finer-grained locking, which minimizes the chance of different users blocking each other. This is yet another advantage made possible by the piecemeal of relational databases.

Directories

Directories are light-weight databases. They are accessed something like the directories of a file system, with paths to specific directories, which can contain things – like files. That is how they are presented, though the implementation can be quite different.

They are like databases in that each file has an associated key, which can be searched for. Because data is broken up, it is possible to read and write it piecemeal (like a database), rather than reading or writing the whole thing (like a file).

They are a "read mostly" system, as reading is much faster than writing, and relational databases are faster at both. Directories also tend to lack all the sophisticated integrity mechanisms of relational databases. However, they can be searched, and read and written concurrently, placing them between files and databases on all measures.

Summary

The chapter presents a simple and comprehensive XML format for XML-Object mapping, and source code that can be adapted for other formats, including an Abstract Data Layer for evolution and versioning.

XML-Object mapping is not just for persistence, but is an automatic method to bridge objects with XML, the lingua franca of the outside world, so that any application can read it, can do anything with it, and can write back to the original objects.

In addition to the graphical presentation of objects, as in the previous chapter, the object data can also be republished, it can interoperate with a relational database, it can be used for configuration and deployment, and it can even be an argument in method invocation to a remote service provider, in a wire protocol. However, this is only the beginning. The latter are covered in the following chapters – starting with wrapping up existing data as XML in order to republish it.

The Xerces Blue
butterfly, which became
extinct earlier this century,
and after which the Xerces XML
parser is named ...

17

XML and Databases

XML documents are often stored in a file system as text files. Storing XML documents in this fashion is quite popular because file handling is relatively safe and familiar. For a reasonably large system this becomes impractical and the only option is to store the documents in a database. Although in its simplest form a database can be used like a file system, this does not utilize its full potential. The main reasons for using a database are to retain the data in a form optimized for high intensity relational queries, and to exploit security and transaction infrastructures.

In this chapter, we'll examine several techniques for extracting information from a database as XML. We will look at the following techniques:

❑   Populating a resultset from a database and using it to generate SAX events

❑   Using Sun's JDBC Rowset classes

❑   Generating XML using Cocoon XSD pages with the ESQL "logicsheet"

Overview

The first technique we present views the data in the database as "virtual XML" by generating SAX event streams and DOM trees directly from database tables. With this technique, we do not need to convert information in the database into intermediate XML files in order to use them with other Java XML tools.

There are some situations, however, when we need XML data from a database in the form of character streams, for instance as a transmission format between distributed services. We can of course easily obtain this by adding a further step to the above mechanism. The early access release of Sun's JDBC Rowset implementation of the JDBC 2.0 Optional Extensions has a lot to offer in this respect. We'll be looking at some of the rowset classes in detail, and in particular how the WebRowSet can be used as a synchronizable data store, able to read and write itself as XML.

There are other situations, where the sole task is to present information in the database as web pages. The third technique shows how to use mechanisms available with the Cocoon architecture, developed by the Apache XML Project.

Storing XML Documents in a Database

Allowing access to the data in a database as XML also allows XML technology to be used with legacy databases. It is a fact of life that "legacy" systems will always be around. To add to that, regardless of a technology's strengths, we cannot start using it overnight; there is a migration period where a new technology solution must co-exist with legacy applications. Although XML offers a multitude of advantages, applications that utilize it must continue to work with information that exists in legacy data storage systems.

A typical enterprise computing system consists of several applications built around one or more databases. If a new XML-based application is added to the system, it must use the same database in order to ensure that new and legacy applications continue to view the same information.

Using a database as a primary storage mechanism for XML documents ensures that legacy applications co-exist with new XML-based applications. In fact, by making the data available in both XML and traditional form makes the question of legacy systems moot. As long as the store remains the same, adding an XML view to the database will keep systems working together. By making the data available in XML format we also enable gradual migration to XML.

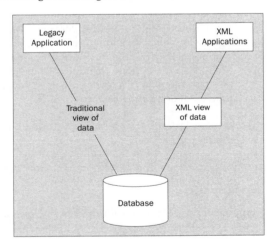

Of course a typical database excels when it comes to performance of search queries. A huge amount of research has gone into incorporating query-optimization algorithms, including various mechanisms. Using a database as the primary storage mechanism for XML documents allows us to leverage this advantage. XML on the other hand, offers the advantages of portability and wide availability of tools. Storing the data in a database and viewing it as XML offers the best of both worlds.

One method of storing XML documents in a database is to store them whole as a single binary or character entries in the database without deconstructing the document. This gives us the benefits of stability and access control, and even the optimized content location by query – at least at document level, further drilling down is not possible. However, in order to make the best use of databases we need to deconstruct the XML document and represent its infoset in a form the database can understand.

In order to do this though, we must define a mapping between each leaf element and a column in the database so that the database has access to the individual leaf elements within each document. Essentially, the data is stored in the traditional way, as values arranged in columns in database tables, and the mapping allows this data to be converted to and from its XML document format and its database structure. This approach is particularly suitable for data-centric XML documents due to their highly regular structure.

> *If we use object-relational database where a database column can support user-defined type (SQL3 data type), such as Oracle 8 and above, we could define a mapping between any XML elements – not just leaf elements – to database columns. Essentially, with object-relational database, we are not restricted to mapping only text nodes to database columns.*

Relational Data As Virtual XML

Once a mapping has been defined between the XML data and its format in the database, applications can query the database for relevant data and have it returned in XML form.

Alternatively, the structure of the XML document can directly mimic that of the database. Let's start by looking at a simple example. The following is a typical DTD for XML documents obtained from a particular database table:

```
<!ELEMENT table (row*)>
<!ELEMENT row (Id, Name, Languages)>
<!ELEMENT Id (#PCDATA)>
<!ELEMENT Name (#PCDATA)>
<!ELEMENT Languages (#PCDATA)>
```

In this case, the element names will correspond to the relevant columns in the database. For example, the following table:

ID	Name	Languages
1	James Gosling	Java
2	Dennis Ritchie	C
3	Bjarne Stroustrup	C++

This table can be mapped into the following XML file:

```
<?xml version="1.0"?>
<!DOCTYPE table SYSTEM "table.dtd">
<table>
  <row>
    <Id>
        1
    </Id>
    <Name>
        James Gosling
    </Name>
    <Languages>
```

```
                    Java
              </Languages>
        </row>
        <row>
          <Id>
                2
          </Id>
          <Name>
                Dennis Ritchie
          </Name>
          <Languages>
                C
          </Languages>
        </row>
        <row>
          <Id>
                3
          </Id>
          <Name>
                Bjarne Stroustrup
          </Name>
          <Languages>
                C++
          </Languages>
        </row>
    </table>
```

This technique takes two forms; the first is to create physical XML files that are passed to the application as an argument, whether as files in the file system or as character streams. The second is to make the XML data available as a SAX event stream or DOM object tree. These latter virtual XML documents present the data in the XML data to the application without requiring the application to load and parse the document first, thus saving on performance cost by eliminating this intermediate step.

> *In the remainder of the chapter, we use the term "physical XML document" to indicate an XML document stored in a file system. We use the term "virtual XML document" to indicate an XML document that does not exist in a physical form but that is presented to XML applications through XML APIs such as SAX and DOM.*

This first approach of translating query results into physical XML files offers a simple way to make database data available to XML tools, but it suffers from a performance cost. The second approach allows bypassing the creation of an XML file and parsing of that file thus resulting in a more efficient solution. In the diagram below, we see that the XML application is reading the virtual XML document, without needing to know that it is obtained as a rowset from the database:

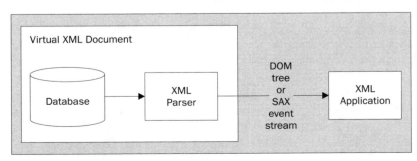

Most XML applications use either SAX or DOM parser to obtain and process XML documents. For example, XSLT processors such as Xalan from Apache, and XT from James Clark work with either a SAX event stream or DOM object tree or both. The concept behind using the database as virtual XML documents is that if we provide SAX and DOM API over the database, we can make these applications work with the database directly instead of going through an intermediate physical XML document.

> *An interesting aspect of using a database or similar storage as virtual XML documents is that, because no physical XML files are involved, the actual XML syntax becomes irrelevant. The interface between the database and XML applications is the SAX or DOM API. Yet another way to look at this technique is that we are abstracting the implementation of storing information: the APIs hide whether information is stored in XML files or a database.*

Although this chapter emphasizes use of a database as a source of virtual XML documents, the concept is more universally applicable. It is possible to view any kind of marked-up document as a virtual XML document. This kind of usage of XML API for non-XML documents can be a powerful way to look at XML technology, especially during migration to XML, where old applications continue to need documents in legacy format and XML tools need the same documents in XML format. In such cases, we can continue to store documents in legacy format, write SAX/DOM parsers that read the documents, and present it as a virtual XML documents to XML application.

Data Access Through the XML APIs

When a database does not offer XML as an output format, we will need to implement access to the database via the SAX or DOM API ourselves.

In this section, we will show how to use SAX and DOM parsers with a database as the document source. We can use them for integration with any tool that works with the SAX or DOM APIs. Our examples will use the JAXP and TrAX abstractions that we met first in Chapters 2 and 3.

Implementing the SAX Parser

We will begin by investigating what classes we would need to write to provide database access via SAX events. Although you should be able to follow the examples in the applications, familiarity with JDBC programming will help. For more information on JDBC refer to http://java.sun.com/products/jdbc.

The basic idea behind the SAX API is that the parser will generate events as it visits different parts of the document. The application that is using the SAX parser will install event handlers for each kind of event and take necessary action whenever it receives an event. To illustrate this idea further let's take another look at the example table presented earlier and see what events are generated for each part of table:

Database Location		Document Location	Event Generated
Start of table		`<table>`	`startDocument()` `startElement("table")`
First row		`<row>`	`startElement("row")`
	Id column	`<Id>`	`startElement("Id")`
		`1`	`character("1")`
		`</Id>`	`endElement("Id")`
	Name column	`<Name>`	`startElement("Name")`
		`James Gosling`	`character("James Gosling")`
		`</Name>`	`endElement("Name")`
	Language column	`<Languages>`	`startElement("Languages")`
		`Java`	`character("Java")`
		`</Languages>`	`endElement("Languages")`
		`</row>`	`endElement("row")`

The second row would be analogous, and then:

		`<row>`	`startElement("row")`
Third row	Id column	`<Id>`	`startElement("Id")`
		`3`	`character("2")`
		`</Id>`	`endElement("Id")`
	Name column	`<Name>`	`startElement("Name")`
		`Bjarne Stroustrup`	`character("Bjarne Stroustrup")`
		`</Name>`	`endElement("Name")`
	Languages column	`<Languages>`	`startElement("Languages")`
		`C++`	`character("C++")`
		`</Languages>`	`endElement("Languages")`
		`</row>`	`endElement("row")`
End of table		`</table>`	`endElement("table")` `endDocument()`

Thus we can view a database rowset as being able to generate a linear sequence of events, capable of being parsed into the XML document form we gave earlier. We'll next look at the rowset implementation that will be populated with our data and used to generate the events.

Rowsets

The JDBC 2.0 API (the extension package `javax.sql`) provides advanced features over the standard Java 2 `java.sql` package that are helpful in creating more robust and sophisticated applications. These include specifications for additional features such as datasources objects and connection pools. In addition, there are the JDBC 2.0 Optional Extensions, also in the package `javax.sql`, containing the Rowset interfaces.

Rowsets contain a set of rows from a resultset or other source of tabular data, like a file or spreadsheet. But rowset objects also follow the JavaBeans model for properties and event notification, so they are primarily intended for use as JavaBeans components in server-side applications.

The `javax.sql.RowSet` interface is an extension of the `java.sql.ResultSet` interface, and acts as a kind of wrapper for the standard features of resultsets, in addition to its data access JavaBeans features.

Rowset implementations can be classified into two broad categories:

❑ **Connected**
The rowset maintains a connection to a data source as long as it is in use.

❑ **Disconnected**
The rowset connects to a database only when it has to either populate itself with data or when it has to propagate changes in the data back to the database. The rest of the time, it does not have an open connection, which means that it does not require a JDBC driver or full JDBC API. This means that the footprint for the rowset is minimal. This feature is very helpful when passing the results retrieved from a data source across a network, or updating new data on a thin client.

We'll be using an early access implementation of the Optional Extensions, the `sun.jdbc.rowset` package that contains three implementations of `RowSet` as follows:

❑ `JdbcRowSet`
A connected rowset used to encapsulate a database connection as a JavaBeans component.

❑ `CachedRowSet`
A disconnected rowset that is particularly suited to storing the data from a `ResultSet` and propagating updates to the data back to the data store via methods such as `acceptChanges()` which reopen the connection if necessary. A `CachedRowSet` can also be (Java) serialized and sent between components in a distributed application.

❑ `WebRowSet`
An extension of `CachedRowSet` that adds the ability to populate itself from an XML character stream, and to write itself back to another stream, using methods such as `readXML(java.io.Reader)` and `writeXML(java.io.Writer)`.

We will use the first of these implementations in our JDBC SAX parser, and we'll talk more about the others later.

The JdbcRowSet Class

The `JdbcRowSet` is a connected rowset, in that it continually maintains its connection to the database. This means it is useful for creating an application that needs to continuously update the database, since it maintains the connection to the database even after updating or retrieving the results from database. The `JdbcRowSet` methods operate on its internal `ResultSet`, which in turn update or query the database. It provides a wrapper around a `ResultSet` object that makes it possible to use the `ResultSet` as a JavaBeans component.

The following example illustrates how `JdbcRowSet` is generally used:

```
JdbcRowSet jrowset = new JdbcRowSet();
jrowset.setCommand("SELECT book_name FROM library WHERE isbn = ?");
jrowset.setURL("jdbc:oracle:thin@dbserver:1521:database");
jrowset.setUsername("ribsao");
jrowset.setPassword("dj298");
jrowset.setString(1, "1-861004-04-2");
jrowset.execute();
```

The variable `jrowset` now represents an instance of `JdbcRowSet`. This is a thin façade around a `ResultSet` (which it extends through its implementation of `RowSet`) containing all the rows in the database table `library`, where the ISBN (International Standard Book Number) of the book is the identifier provided by the user (for example 1-861004-04-2). Data manipulation operations called on `jrowset` can now change the rows in the resultset, and propagate back to the database.

We'll now use this class to funnel data out of a database and into a stream of SAX events. As you'll recall from Chapter 2, an `org.sax.xml.InputSource` can be passed into the `parse()` method of an `org.sax.xml.XMLReader`. This is what we'll do with our virtual XML data. First we need to define an extension of `InputSource` that encapsulates the database as a source of XML.

The JDBCInputSource Class

The SAX API specifies that the `parse()` method of an `org.sax.xml.XMLReader` takes an XML document that is specified by an `InputSource` object. Now while an `InputSource` is sufficient when the XML document is specified by a character stream, file name, or URL, if we want to specify a database as the source of the XML we will need to extend `InputSource` to add the required support.

The purpose of the `JDBCInputSource` object is to encapsulate the information needed to connect to a database, and to encapsulate the data populating query to be performed. To simplify the implementation we will use the `JdbcRowSet` class from the RowSet Early Access Technology Release that we looked at above.

A `JdbcRowSet` is a wrapper around a `java.sql.ResultSet`. If it is desired not to be dependant on Sun's RowSet package, it is possible with a few simple modifications to use a `ResultSet` directly. You can look at one such implementation in my article at http://www.javaworld.com/javaworld/jw-01-2000/jw-01-dbxml.html.

Using a RowSet, however, opens up our implementation to be used with any tabular data format and not just a database as long as an implementation of RowSet for that format is available. Another advantage of using a RowSet is that allows the possibility of using disconnected RowSet implementations, such as CachedRowSet or WebRowSet. For more details on use of disconnected rowsets and their applications, please refer to the *"Disconnected Rowsets"* section later on.

We'll give full intructions on how to run the examples later. Here's our new JDBC input source object:

```
package sax;

import java.sql.*;
import javax.sql.RowSet;

import org.xml.sax.InputSource;

public class JDBCInputSource extends InputSource {

    private RowSet rowSet;
```

The constructor for the JDBCInputSource takes all the information needed to connect to a database. It first loads the given driver and then creates an internal JdbcRowSet object representing the data rows acquired from the sqlCommand argument:

```
public JDBCInputSource(String driver, String connectionURL,
                       String userName, String passwd,
                       String sqlCommand) throws SQLException,
                       ClassNotFoundException {
    super(connectionURL);

    Class.forName(driver);

    rowSet = new sun.jdbc.rowset.JdbcRowSet();
    rowSet.setUrl(connectionURL);
    rowSet.setUsername(userName);
    rowSet.setPassword(passwd);
    rowSet.setCommand(sqlCommand);
}
```

The method getRowSet() simply returns the rowSet member created in the constructor. Note that it uses no connection resources yet: the client must call the execute() method to populate it with data from the database before it can be used:

```
public RowSet getRowSet() {
    return rowSet;
}
}
```

JDBCSAXParser

We will now look into our implementation of SAX parser that works directly from relational data. We will implement the `org.xml.sax.XMLReader` interface.

```java
package sax;

import java.util.Locale;
import java.io.IOException;
import java.sql.*;
import javax.sql.RowSet;

import org.xml.sax.*;
import org.xml.sax.helpers.*;


public class JDBCSAXParser implements XMLReader {
```

None of our resulting XML data will have attributes, so we define a default empty attribute list to pass into our content handler methods:

```java
private static final Attributes noattrs = new AttributesImpl();
protected ContentHandler contenthandler = null;
```

The following store the tag names for the elements we will generate events for:

```java
protected static String tableMarker = "table";
protected static String rowMarker = "row";
```

The following methods implement the `XMLReader` interface's `parse()` methods. Because our parser cannot handle any other type of input source than `JDBCInputSource`, we throw a `SAXException` unless we are supplied with a `JDBCInputSource` object:

```java
public void parse(InputSource source) throws SAXException, IOException {
  if (!(source instanceof JDBCInputSource)) {
    throw new SAXException("JDBCSAXParser can work only with source "
                           + "of type JDBCInputSource");
  }
  parse((JDBCInputSource) source);
}

public void parse(String systemId) throws SAXException, IOException {
  throw new SAXException("JDBCSAXParser needs more information to "
                         + "connect to database");
}
```

We also provide a `parse()` method that takes a `JDBCInputSource` as its argument. The role of this method is to generate the top-level events, passing the event generation for the rest of the data to supplementary methods. The method checks if there is a content handler set and, if not, the method simply returns as there is no event listener to send events to.

If there is a handler installed, it fires a `startDocument()` event, followed by a `startElement()` event with the table marker `table` as the name of the element. It then gets the `RowSet` from the `JDBCInputSource`, calls `execute()` on it and for each row in the `RowSet` object, calls the `parseRow()` method. Finally, the `parse()` method calls `endDocument()` to signify the end of the event sequence:

```
public void parse(JDBCInputSource source)
        throws SAXException, IOException {
  if (contenthandler == null) {
    return;
  }
```

Refer to our large table a few pages back for the sequence of events that we are now about to generate. Note the use of `noattrs`. Our parser never uses attributes in any of the events fired. We take advantage of this fact and reuse a stock empty attribute list object for every `startElement()` event we fire:

```
try {
  contenthandler.startDocument();

  /* Note that we are not handling namespaces */
  contenthandler.startElement("", "", tableMarker, noattrs);

  RowSet rowSet = source.getRowSet();
```

Here we populate the rowset with the data arising from executing the SQL command that was used to initialize the rowset. We can then iterate through the rows, and launch the event generation process on each row:

```
  rowSet.execute();
  while (rowSet.next()) {
    parseRow(rowSet);
  }

  contenthandler.endElement("", "", tableMarker);
  contenthandler.endDocument();

  rowSet.close();
} catch (SQLException ex) {
  throw new SAXException(ex);
}
}
```

The `parseRow()` method's role is to fire events for the current row on the `RowSet` object passed as the argument, calling `parseColumn()` for each column in that row. It fires events for the current row by calling `startElement()` and `endElement()` with the row marker as the argument. Between this pair of events, we iterate over each column in the row and call the `parseColumn()` method on each:

```
public void parseRow(RowSet rowSet) throws SAXException, SQLException {
  contenthandler.startElement("", "", rowMarker, noattrs);

  ResultSetMetaData rsmd = rowSet.getMetaData();

  for (int numCols = rsmd.getColumnCount(), i = 1; i <= numCols; ++i) {
    parseColumn(rowSet, i);
  }
  contenthandler.endElement("", "", rowMarker);
}
```

The `parseColumn()` method handles leaf nodes in virtual XML documents. The method fires no event if it receives null data. The column label is used as the element name for the `startElement()` and `endElement()` methods. Sandwiched between these two event, a `character()` event is called with the column's data.

This method may be overridden in derived classes to enable special handling requirements. For example, one may override the method to allow a representation of null data, probably as empty elements whose names match the column labels in the database. Other reasons would be to provide formatting of column types such as date/time or currency.

```java
protected void parseColumn(RowSet rowSet, int columnIndex)
        throws SAXException, SQLException {

  String columnValue = rowSet.getString(columnIndex);

  if (columnValue == null) {
    return;
  }

  ResultSetMetaData rsmd = rowSet.getMetaData();
  String columnMarker = rsmd.getColumnLabel(columnIndex);
  char[] columnValueChars = columnValue.toCharArray();

  contenthandler.startElement("", "", columnMarker, noattrs);
  contenthandler.characters(columnValueChars, 0, columnValueChars.length);
  contenthandler.endElement("", "", columnMarker);
}
```

The rest of the methods implement the remaining part of `XMLReader` interface that involve accessing and mutating features, properties, and various specialized handlers:

```java
/*
 * Minimal support for handlers.
 * We make sure get(set(x)) = x.
 */
private EntityResolver er = null;
private DTDHandler dh = null;
private ErrorHandler eh = null;

public void setContentHandler(ContentHandler handler) {
  contenthandler = handler;
}
public void setEntityResolver(EntityResolver e) {
  er = e;
}
public void setDTDHandler(DTDHandler d) {
  dh = d;
}
public void setErrorHandler(ErrorHandler e) {
  eh = e;
}
```

```
   public ContentHandler getContentHandler() {
     return contenthandler;
   }
   public EntityResolver getEntityResolver() {
     return er;
   }
   public DTDHandler getDTDHandler() {
     return dh;
   }
   public ErrorHandler getErrorHandler() {
     return eh;
   }
```

```
   /*
    * Minimal support for features and properties.
    */
   public void setFeature(String feature, boolean b) {}
   public void setProperty(String property, Object o) {}
   public boolean getFeature(String feature) { return false;}
   public Object getProperty(String property) { return null; }
}
```

Implementing the DOM API

Although SAX is the API of choice for most applications due to its efficient event stream nature as opposed to holding the document in memory, there are situations where we need a DOM document instead. For example, consider a situation where we need to apply several stylesheets to produce multiple outputs. It may be more efficient to parse the input document, once to create a DOM tree and then perform several transformations on this tree, instead of parsing the document once for each transformation. Other cases where the DOM may be more appropriate is where an application needs random access to the structure of the document. We need to study the usage at hand and decide whether a SAX or DOM solution is more appropriate.

We will use our `JDBCSAXParser` to create the events necessary to create a DOM tree that corresponds to the `RowSet` received from the database. To accomplish this task we will use the JAXP and TrAX API to transform a SAX event stream into a DOM document:

```
package dom;

import java.io.IOException;

import org.w3c.dom.Document;
import org.xml.sax.*;
import javax.xml.parsers.*;

import javax.xml.transform.*;
import javax.xml.transform.dom.*;
import javax.xml.transform.sax.*;

import sax.*;
```

```
public class JDBCDOMParser {

    private static TransformerFactory tf = TransformerFactory.newInstance();

    public static Document createDocument(JDBCInputSource inputSource)
            throws SAXException, IOException,
                    TransformerConfigurationException, TransformerException,
                    ParserConfigurationException {
```

First we need to create a new instance of a DOM document builder:

```
DocumentBuilderFactory dbf = DocumentBuilderFactory.newInstance();
DocumentBuilder db = dbf.newDocumentBuilder();
```

Next we instantiate our `Source` and `Result`:

```
SAXSource ss = new SAXSource(new JDBCSAXParser(), inputSource);
DOMResult dr = new DOMResult(db.newDocument());
```

We then use the "null" transformer (that is, not created with a stylesheet processor) to perform the mapping:

```
Transformer t = tf.newTransformer();
t.transform(ss, dr);
return (Document) dr.getNode();
}
```

Note that it is the transformer that takes responsibility for setting the content handler on the parser.

As you can see there is not that much additional work to obtain a DOM document, once we have a SAX parser for our data. This approach makes it easy to create a DOM structure for legacy data sources that must work with XML-based applications as discussed earlier.

Note that our implementation parsers will work not just with a database but anything that can be represented by RowSet. This could include any data in tabular format. This particular attribute could be important for certain set of applications that do not store data in a standard database.

Using the SAX and DOM API with a Database

In this section, we look at an example of using SAX and DOM API for applying XSLT transformation on virtual XML documents obtained from a database directly without the need for an intermediate file or a byte stream.

Using the SAX API with a Database

The JDBCSAXTransformer is a simple utility program to demonstrate using virtual XML documents represented by relational data.

Our utility takes seven input arguments:

- ❏ JDBC driver class
- ❏ Connection URL of database
- ❏ User name to connect to database
- ❏ Password for that user
- ❏ SQL query command to obtain the data
- ❏ XSLT stylesheet file
- ❏ Output file name

First it creates our `JDBCInputSource` from the first five arguments, then it creates a `Transformer` from the XSLT stylesheet file argument. It performs the actual transformation and creates the output file by invoking `transform()` on the `Transformer` object:

```java
package transform;

import java.io.*;

import org.xml.sax.*;
import org.xml.sax.helpers.*;

import javax.xml.transform.*;
import javax.xml.transform.sax.*;
import javax.xml.transform.stream.*;

import sax.*;

public class JDBCSAXTransformer {
  public static void main(String[] argv) throws Exception {
    if (argv.length != 7) {
      System.out.println("Usage: transform.JDBCSAXTransformer driver "
                       + "connectionURL userName password sqlCommand "
                       + "xslFile outFile");
      System.exit(1);
    }

    JDBCInputSource dbis = new JDBCInputSource(argv[0], argv[1], argv[2],
                                              argv[3], argv[4]);
    String xslFile = argv[5];
    String outFile = argv[6];
```

This is how we create a transformer to do XSLT:

```java
Transformer transformer =
  TransformerFactory.newInstance()
    .newTransformer(new StreamSource(new File(xslFile)));

Source source = new SAXSource(new JDBCSAXParser(), dbis);
```

And this is how we turn the `Source` into a `Result`:

```
        transformer.transform(source, new StreamResult(new File(outFile)));
    }
}
```

Using the DOM API with a Database

Using the DOM API to apply stylesheet transformations on virtual documents may be useful when we want to apply several transformations on the same document. Using the SAX API in such cases will be inefficient in time, as it must parse the input source once for each transformation. DOM performs input document parsing only once and then we may use that DOM tree repeatedly. Of course DOM parsers will use more memory than SAX so this is a trade-off between processing power and memory space.

Implementing transformations using the DOM API is similar to that using the SAX API as described in the previous section. The only difference is we use `DOMSource` instead of `SAXSource`:

```
package transform;

import java.io.*;

import org.xml.sax.*;
import org.xml.sax.helpers.*;

import javax.xml.transform.*;
import javax.xml.transform.dom.*;
import javax.xml.transform.stream.*;

import dom.*;
import sax.*;

public class JDBCDOMTransformer {

    public static void main(String[] argv) throws Exception {
        if (argv.length != 7) {
            System.out.println ("Usage: transform.JDBCDOMTransformer driver " +
            "connectionURL userName password sqlCommand" + " xslFile outFile");
            System.exit(1);
        }

        JDBCInputSource dbis =
            new JDBCInputSource(argv[0], argv[1], argv[2],
                                argv[3], argv[4]);
        String xslFile = argv[5];
        String outFile = argv[6];

        Transformer transformer =
          TransformerFactory.newInstance()
            .newTransformer(new StreamSource(new File(xslFile)));

        Source source = new DOMSource(JDBCDOMParser.createDocument(dbis));
        transformer.transform(source, new StreamResult(new File(outFile)));
    }
}
```

Rowset Transforms Using SAX/DOM API

In this section we examine two XSLT stylesheets for transforming virtual XML documents. The first stylesheet performs a transformation to HTML suitable for displaying the data in a browser , the second one is simply an indentity transform.

Creating HTML Pages

To show how we can use our transformers together with a database, we use a simple, generic stylesheet that transforms any XML document in a specified table-like format to an HTML table:

```
<!-- createTable.xsl -->

<!-- A generic stylesheet for transforming a table-like structured XML
  document into an HTML table -->

<xsl:stylesheet version="1.0"
  xmlns:xsl="http://www.w3.org/1999/XSL/Transform">

<xsl:template match="/">
  <html>
  <head><title>Database table formatted as a HTML table</title></head>
  <body>
    <xsl:apply-templates/>
  </body>
  </html>
</xsl:template>
```

Use the first row to create table headers using "column-markers":

```
<xsl:template match="/*">
  <table>
```

For each column, check if it is the first row we are visiting. If so use the column name obtained using local-name() as column header:

```
    <xsl:for-each select="*[position() = 1]/*">
      <th>
      <xsl:value-of select="local-name()"/>
      </th>
    </xsl:for-each>

    <xsl:apply-templates/>

    </table>
  </xsl:template>
```

In the row-marker section we will wrap each row inside <tr> and </tr>:

```
<xsl:template match="/*/*">
  <tr>
  <xsl:apply-templates/>
  </tr>
</xsl:template>
```

For each column we wrap it inside a table data element (`<td>` and `</td>`):

```
<xsl:template match="/*/*/*">
  <td>
  <xsl:apply-templates/>
  </td>
</xsl:template>

</xsl:stylesheet>
```

In summary we can use this transform with any database table and our implementation of SAX or DOM API for database. This stylesheet is generic; you can of course write your own stylesheet that is specific to your application.

Setting Up and Running the Example

This section provides the set up required to compile and run the applications. You may need to adjust some of the steps to match your environment.

Setting the Classpath

You must add the following to your classpath:

- Add `jaxp.jar`, `crimson.jar`, and `xalan.jar` from your JAXP 1.1 installation.

- Add `rowset.jar` from Sun's rowset implementation, for instance the `rowset1.0ea4/rowset.jar` release currently available at http://developer.java.sun.com/developer/earlyAccess/crs/.

- Add the classpath for your database JDBC driver. For instance, the `classes12.zip` library for the `oracle.jdbc.driver.OracleDriver` is usually found in your `<ORACLE_HOME>/jdbc/lib` directory.

Compiling the Source

Issue the following command to compile the code we've been developing:

```
> javac sax\*.java dom\*.java transform\*.java
```

Creating a Sample Database Table

Issue the following command in your database's SQL shell:

```
create table creators (ID INTEGER, Name VARCHAR(64), Languages VARCHAR(64));
insert into creators VALUES ('1', 'James Gosling', 'Java');
insert into creators VALUES ('2', 'Dennis Ritchie', 'C');
insert into creators VALUES ('3', 'Bjarne Stroustrup', 'C++');
commit;
```

With an Oracle client installation you should have access to SQL*Plus:

```
Oracle SQL*Plus                                              _  □  X
File  Edit  Search  Options  Help

SQL*Plus: Release 8.1.6.0.0 - Production on Sat Mar 10 17:42:09 2001

(c) Copyright 1999 Oracle Corporation.  All rights reserved.


Connected to:
Oracle8i Enterprise Edition Release 8.1.6.0.0 - Production
With the Partitioning option
JServer Release 8.1.6.0.0 - Production

SQL> create table creators (ID INTEGER, Name VARCHAR(64), Languages VARCHAR(64));

Table created.

SQL> insert into creators VALUES ('1', 'James Gosling', 'Java');

1 row created.

SQL> insert into creators VALUES ('2', 'Dennis Ritchie', 'C');

1 row created.

SQL> insert into creators VALUES ('3', 'Bjarne Stroustrup', 'C++');

1 row created.

SQL> commit;

Commit complete.

SQL> |
```

Performing the Transformation

To run the demo of the transformation using our SAX parser, issue the following commands after substituting each parameter appropriate to your environment. For the database URL argument, please refer to the documentation provided by the JDBC driver you will be using:

```
> java transform.JDBCSAXTransformer <JDBC driver> <Database URL> <user> <password>
<SQL query command> <XSLT stylesheet file> <output file>
```

For example:

```
> java transform.JDBCSAXTransformer oracle.jdbc.driver.OracleDriver
jdbc:oracle:thin:@dbserver:1521:database scott tiger "SELECT * FROM creators"
createTable.xsl saxout.html
```

To run the transformation using the DOM parser, issue the following command:

```
> java transform.JDBCDOMTransformer <JDBC driver> <zDatabase URL> <user>
<password> <SQL query command> <XSLT stylesheet file> <output file>
```

For example, this would translate to something like:

```
> java transform.JDBCDOMTransformer oracle.jdbc.driver.OracleDriver
jdbc:oracle:thin:@dbserver:1521:database scott tiger "SELECT * FROM creators"
createTable.xsl domout.html
```

The following figure shows the browser view we created with our example database using either
`JDBCSAXTransformer` or `JDBCDOMTransformer`:

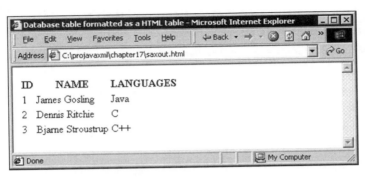

Creating Physical XML Documents

Sometimes we will be required to obtain real XML documents instead of virtual ones from a database.

One such instance is when a consumer of the XML document is on a different machine than where the
virtual XML document is produced. Using techniques such as RMI can be expensive in such cases. It
may be better, instead, to serialize the whole XML document at once and let the user parse this
document locally using a regular XML parser. Another situation where this may be needed is when the
XML needs to be passed on to tools that do not work with SAX or DOM API, or even Java.

We can perform the task of obtaining a real XML document from a virtual XML document through use
of the identity transformation stylesheet; just specify this stylesheet in the arguments for either the
`JDBCSAXTransformer` or `JDBCDOMTrasnformer`. The identity stylesheet defines a transformation
that produces an output document that is identical to the input document. For our purpose, the input is
a virtual XML document stored in the database and the output document is a physical XML file.
Identity transformations allows us to "copy" a virtual input document to a physical output document:

```
<!-- identityTransform.xsl -->

<xsl:stylesheet version="1.0"
  xmlns:xsl="http://www.w3.org/1999/XSL/Transform">

<!-- Stylesheet performing identity transformation on XML
  file. The output XML file is equivalent to input
  XML file
-->

<xsl:template match="@*|node()">
  <xsl:copy>
    <xsl:apply-templates select="@*|node()"/>
  </xsl:copy>
</xsl:template>

</xsl:stylesheet>
```

Performing the Identity Transformation

Performing the identity transformation is identical to performing the transformation to create the HTML pages described in the earlier section. The only difference is the use of `identityTransform.xsl` instead of `createTable.xsl`. The output of this transformation is an XML file that presents identical information obtained by the SQL command it was invoked with.

The output of either command is an XML file. For example, with our example the output is:

```
<?xml version="1.0" encoding="UTF-8"?>
<table><row><ID>1</ID><NAME>James
Gosling</NAME><LANGUAGES>Java</LANGUAGES></row><row><ID>2</ID><NAME>Dennis
Ritchie</NAME><LANGUAGES>C</LANGUAGES></row><row><ID>3</ID><NAME>Bjarne
Stroustrup</NAME><LANGUAGES>C++</LANGUAGES></row></table>
```

Another way of outputting XML data from a database is using a `WebRowSet`. We'll next have a look at the two `RowSet` implementations that we haven't covered, the `CachedRowSet` and the `WebRowSet`.

Disconnected Rowsets

We used the `JdbcRowSet` in our above implementation. Now we'll go on to talk about two other rowset types that are in the `sun.jdbc.rowset` package.

The CachedRowSet Class

A `CachedRowSet` is a disconnected rowset and makes use of the connection to its data source only briefly. It connects to a database whilst reading data to populate itself with rows, and then again while it is propagating changes back to its underlying database. The rest of the time, a `CachedRowSet` object is disconnected, and also remains disconnected whilst changes are being made to it. It provides a container for rows of data to be cached in memory, and even when `CachedRowSet` is disconnected from the database, it is scrollable, updatable and serializable. It should be explained that the entire database is read into memory, so it is not practicable to use it in cases where a huge amount of data needs to be retrieved from the database.

A `CachedRowSet` object is much leaner than a `ResultSet` object with the same data. So it is mostly suitable for sending data to a thin client, such as a PDA, where it would not be possible to use a JDBC driver due to resource limitations or security considerations. The `CachedRowSet` class provides a means to get new rows of data into the database and get changed rows out without the need to implement the full JDBC API. A `CachedRowSet` can also be used to augment the capabilities of a JDBC driver that doesn't provide full support for scrolling and updating.

Another major advantage of using a `CachedRowSet` is that it implements the `Serializable` interface and that the entire class is serializable. So after retrieving the results from the database, the entire `CachedRowSet` (which can be created in an Enterprise JavaBeans component) can be passed over the network from a server environment to a client running in a web browser, or to another remote server component.

The WebRowSet Class

This is the class that we are most concerned with in this chapter. WebRowSet is an extension of CachedRowSet, and when used in conjunction with classes like XmlReader and XMLWriter it provides the functionality to read and write a rowset in XML format. The format of an XML document written in this way is described in the DTD RowSet.dtd. The first part of this section will give a brief introduction on how to use the WebRowSet class. We will also look at how WebRowSet can generate and read XML data.

Using the WebRowSet Class

Being an extension of the CachedRowSet class, WebRowSet is essentially a disconnected rowset. Since Rowset objects follow the JavaBeans model for properties and event notification, this feature is very useful when the application using the current rowset needs to be notified of a change in the stored data model. The following example should shed a little more light on this idea.

Say a method informChanges() needs to be called in a CustSupport object whenever there is a change in a current auction price. Whenever the price for a particular item changes, this method will be used to inform the users who opted to be notified of this fact. Let's tackle this scenario using the WebRowSet class.

As part of this example, we need to tackle the following operations:

❑ Create a WebRowSet and set its properties

❑ Register a class called CustSupport as a listener to the rowset

❑ Implement the functionality to update the auction price using the current WebRowSet object

❑ Specify the rowset as a property of our Auction Application

Initializing a WebRowSet

The code for creating a WebRowSet object uses the default constructor as follows:

```
WebRowSet wbrset = new WebRowSet();
```

WebRowSet, being inherited from CachedRowSet, has lots of properties that can influence the current Rowset implementation. A rowset's properties include its command, concurrency, type, data source name, URL, user name, password, transaction isolation level, escape processing, maximum field size, maximum rows, query timeout, and type map. With get/set methods for all these properties as well as an event notification mechanism, rowset implementation makes an ideal JavaBean.

As part of the CustSupport implementation, the auction price at a particular time might also be required. So let's provide a scrollable facility to the current WebRowSet, by setting the scroll property to TYPE_SCROLL_INSENSITIVE. This is the default recommended scrolling type, and may not always be required, unless the vendor providing the implementation for WebRowSet has a different default for the scroll type value.

We also want to continually update the auction price for a particular item, so the concurrency type needs to be set to CONCUR_UPDATABLE. Once again, this is the recommended default and may not always require setting, unless the vendor providing implementation for WebRowSet has a different default value for concurrency type.

The following lines of code will make the `WebRowSet` object (`wbrset` in this instance) scrollable and updatable:

```
wbrset.setType(ResultSet.TYPE_SCROLL_INSENSITIVE);
wbrset.setConcurrency(ResultSet.CONCUR_UPDATABLE);
```

Next comes the task of setting the query to be executed. The table and the column being updated are `auction_list_table` and `auction_price` respectively. So our current `WebRowSet` will keep monitoring the `AUCTION_PRICE` column. Thus, the query string will be `"SELECT auction_price FROM auction_list_table"`.

Now the query to be executed is specified to `WebRowSet` as follows:

```
wbrset.setCommand("SELECT auction_price FROM auction_list_table");
```

Next comes the task of setting the data source name. There are two ways the data source location can be specified for `WebRowSet`.

The first is to use the method, `setUrl()`, with the data source URL as the parameter. When using this procedure, the JDBC driver that accepts the URL must be loaded before using the rowset to connect to a database. For instance, the following code will set it:

```
Class.forName("sun.jdbc.odbc.JdbcOdbcDriver");
wbrset.setUrl("jdbc:odbc:auctiondb");
```

Another way of specifying the database location is by calling the method `setDataSourceName()`. It can be set as follows:

```
wbrset.setDataSourceName("jdbc/auctiondb");
```

This is the preferred method to be used in most application servers. The parameter string specified to this method is a logical name, that the system administrator registered with the JNDI naming service as the name for the `auction` database. The main advantage of following this procedure is that if the entire project is installed on a different machine, and the code needs to connect to a different database with the same database schema but with a different data source name, then there is no code change required and the JNDI name can be bound to the new database. For example, on a different machine, the database URL may not be `auctiondb` and it could be `auctionData`. At this point all the system administrator has to do is register the JNDI name `jdbc/auctiondb` pointing to the `auctionData` data source URL.

The username and password for the data source are specified to `WebRowSet` as follows:

```
wbrset.setUserName("admins34jsfs");
wbrset.setPassword("getNew93434");
```

There is one last property that needs to be set for `WebRowSet`. Users only need to be notified when the auction price change is final and committed, so the transaction level needs to be set to `TRANSACTION_READ_COMMITTED`. The following line of code sets the rowsets property so that "dirty reads" will not be allowed:

```
wbrset.setTransactionIsolation(Connection.TRANSACTION_READ_COMMITTED);
```

717

Most of the other properties are optional for the purposes of our current example. If the SELECT statement needs to retrieve some custom-defined data types with custom mappings, then the type map property needs to be set.

Setting Up the Event Listener On a WebRowSet

The WebRowSet class, being a JavaBeans component, has the capability to participate in event notification. An object that has implemented the RowSetListener interface, and has been added to a rowset's list of listeners, will be notified when an event occurs on that rowset. Each listener's implementation of the RowSetListener methods defines what that object will do when it is notified that an event has occurred.

There are three possible **events** for a rowset:

❑ The cursor moves (this calls method cursorMoved())

❑ An individual row is updated, deleted, or inserted (this calls method rowChanged())

❑ The contents of the entire rowset are changed (calls method rowSetChanged())

In our current application, users need not be notified when the cursor location for the current rowset changes, so cursorMoved() can be ignored. When there are one or more changes in a row, then the rowChanged() method is called. CustSupport class needs to implement rowChanged() and needs to call informChanges() to inform the users that there is a change in the auction price.

The method rowSetChanged() is invoked when there is a whole rowset change, which in general happens only when there is a change in the query for data selection. CustSupport class also needs to implement the rowSetChanged() method and call informChanges().

The following line registers CustSupport as a listener for wbrset:

```
wbrset.addRowSetListener(custSupport);
```

After this line, CustSupport will be notified every time there's an event in wbrset.

Populating Data and Scrolling the WebRowSet

After setting all the properties as above, the next job is to populate the WebRowSet with results from the database. This is done by calling the execute() method on our current WebRowSet object. It's done as follows:

```
wbrset.execute();
```

When the execute() method is called, the following steps occur behind the scenes:

❑ A connection is made to the database using the data source name, user name and password

❑ The query, which has been set as the command string, is executed

❑ The rowset is filled with results returned from the query

After the execute() method is called, the current wbrset has the list of all auction prices, since the query was to retrieve all the auction prices from auction_list_table.

You can scroll through the entire rowset using the following code:

```
while(wbrset.next())  {
   System.out.println(wbrset.getFloat("auction_price") );
}
```

Since the scrolling property of wbrset has been set to TYPE_SCROLL_INSENSITIVE, it is possible to move the cursor in any direction and scroll from any location.

Updating the WebRowSet

The update and delete methods for WebRowSet have been copied from ResultSet and work the same way as in a ResultSet. Here are some examples, which should demonstrate how to perform update operations.

Suppose the user wants to change the auction price for the fourth item in the list to $38.23, instead of $30.23. This could be executed through entering the following commands:

```
wbrset.absolute(4);
wbrset.updateFloat("auction_price", 38.23f);
wbrset.updateRow();
```

This notifies CustSupport that there has been a change in the auction price for one of the items. CustSupport then compares its current auction prices and notifies users about the changes.

Next, if the user wants to change the price of the item on the fifth row to $43.92 instead of $37.82 then the following commands are executed:

```
wbrset.next(1);
wbrset.updateFloat("auction_price", 43.92 f);
wbrset.updateRow();
```

So far we have been updating values in a WebRowSet . Now it's time to update these values back into the database. In the case of ResultSet, if auto-commit was set to true then the values might have been updated into the database by now, when we executed the updateRow() method. But in the case of WebRowSet, since it is a disconnected rowset, the values are updated in the database only when acceptChanges() is called. So, in order to update the current WebRowSet values back into the database, the following code needs to executed:

```
wbrset.acceptChanges();
```

In order to use the optimistic concurrency control routine, the rowset maintains both its current value and its original value. Before updating changes back into the database, for each column rowset's writer component compares original values in the rowset with the value in the database. If the database has been changed, it will differ from the rowset 's original values, which means that there is a conflict. If such a conflict occurs, the rowset will not write any of its new values to the database.

For example, in the above scenario, the component checks that the current value in the database on the fifth row is $37.82, which was the original value before we updated the fifth row value to $43.92. If the value in the database matches the original, the new value of $43.92 is updated into fifth row. If it does not match, it is not updated.

Generating and Reading XML Files Using a WebRowSet

This is where the real functionality of the `WebRowSet` object comes into the picture. Up to this point, we have been trying to read data from the database, and then making changes which we write back into the database. This is quite similar to `ResultSet` operations, except that we have been working with a disconnected rowset.

> **CachedRowSet also provides most of the above functionality: recall it is the parent class of WebRowSet.**

Now, however, we are going to approach the real advantage of `WebRowSet`, which is that at any point after reading the data from a data source, and after the rowset has been initialized, `WebRowSet` can write the entire dataset to a `java.io.Writer` as an XML file. This means that even if the machine is brought down, the data is still safe in the XML file on the local hard disk. So, after a couple of hours when the machine is brought up or connected to a different server, it will be possible to read this XML file and re-initialize the `WebRowSet` object. If required, changes can be written to this `WebRowSet` object, as explained in the above section.

Generating the XML File from Query Results

This new `WebRowSet`, created from the XML file, can be used to update the data into a new database (that has the same column and table names), or update new data into the original database.

We will be looking at how this is done through the following code example. The code is divided into two parts to better explain the functionality we want. The first part generates the XML file after executing the query, and then the next part reads back the XML file and updates the database with the new data:

```
try {
    // This part will create a XML file after executing the
    // query provided in the command statement.

    WebRowSet wrs = new WebRowSet();
    wrs.setDataSourceName("jdbc/auctiondb");
    wrs.setUserName("admins34jsfs");
    wrs.setPassword("getNew93434");

    wrs.setCommand("SELECT auction_price FROM auction_list_table ");

    wrs.setType(ResultSet.TYPE_SCROLL_INSENSITIVE);
    wrs.setConcurrency(ResultSet.CONCUR_UPDATABLE);

    wrs.setTransactionIsolation(
        java.sql.Connection.TRANSACTION_READ_UNCOMMITTED);

    wrs.execute();

    // Column Mapping Variables

    int colMapping[] = {1,2};
    wrs.setKeyColumns(colMapping);

    java.io.FileWriter FW = new java.io.FileWriter("auctions.xml");
    wrs.writeXml(FW);
}

catch(Exception e) {
    e.printStackTrace();
}
```

Now we read back the XML file and update the new data to the database:

```
try {

    // This Part will read back the XML file and re-initialize the
    // WebRowSet Object

    java.io.FileReader FR = new java.io.FileReader("auctions.xml");
    WebRowSet wrs2 = new WebRowSet();
    wrs2.setDataSourceName("jdbc/auctiondb");
    wrs2.setUserName("admins34jsfs");
    wrs2.setPassword("getNew93434");
    wrs2.readXml(FR);

    // Making some changes to the new WebRowSet object
    // and updating new data back in the Database

    wrs2.absolute(4);
    wrs2.updateFloat("auction_price", 43.92 f);
    wrs2.updateRow();
    wrs2.acceptChanges();
}

catch(Exception e) {
    e.printStackTrace();
}
```

WebRowSet uses the internal classes XMLReader and XMLWriter to read and write XML files. XMLReader reads the XML file, parses the data and assists in recreating the WebRowSet object. While writing the data into the XML file, XMLWriter also saves the current configuration of the WebRowSet object, including the meta data information pertaining to the tables and columns (amongst other useful information), which may be required to regenerate the WebRowSet object from the XML file.

Before concluding this chapter, we'll look at another promising Java based technology for extracting XML content from database, the idea of the XSP page and ESQL logicsheet.

Cocoon and XSP

Cocoon is a publishing framework developed at Apache XML Project that uses XML technologies to deliver web content. The basic philosophy behind Cocoon publishing model is a complete separation of content from presentation: the XML forms the bare bones of the data, and all content information is added in using stylesheets.

You can download Cocoon from http://xml.apache.org/cocoon. The application is essentially a Java servlet running in a web container that intecepts requests for XML pages, applies any custom embedded processing instructions using its own libraries of parsers, "logicsheets", and transformers and then renders the output back to the requesting client.

One of the most interesting parts of the Cocoon framework is **eXtensible Server Pages (XSP)**. With XSP, it is possible to build web applications using just XML scripts. In many ways, XSP pages are like JavaServer Pages: both allow creation of dynamic content using a mixture of processing and display instructions, and both compile pages into binary code for faster execution.

XSP allows programmatic production of XML documents or fragments based on request parameters. It is possible to use XSP to create dynamic XML documents based on external sources such as databases. Just like JSP, it is possible to write customized tags to improve code reuse.

In this section, we'll give an illustration of using the ESQLtag library with XSP to create HTML pages directly out of a database without writing a single line of Java code. ESQL is a set of XSP tags that allows connecting and querying a database and obtaining the result in XML format. When we combine ESQL tags with the transformation capabilities of Cocoon, we can get HTML/WML/XML pages directly without requiring any procedural programming.

You can get detailed information on XSP from http://xml.apache.org/cocoon/xsp.html and on ESQL from http://xml.apache.org/cocoon/esql.html

```
<?xml version="1.0"?>
<?cocoon-process type="xsp"?>
<?cocoon-process type="xslt"?>
<?xml-stylesheet type="text/xsl" href="createTable.xsl"?>
<xsp:page
     xmlns:xsp="http://www.apache.org/1999/XSP/Core"
     xmlns:esql="http://apache.org/cocoon/SQL/v2">
  <table>
    <esql:connection>
      <esql:driver>oracle.jdbc.driver.OracleDriver</esql:driver>
      <esql:dburl>jdbc:oracle:thin:@dbserver:1521:database</esql:dburl>
      <esql:username>scott</esql:username>
      <esql:password>tiger</esql:password>
      <esql:execute-query>
        <esql:query>SELECT * FROM creators</esql:query>
        <esql:results>
          <esql:row-results>
            <row>
              <esql:get-columns/>
            </row>
          </esql:row-results>
        </esql:results>
      </esql:execute-query>
    </esql:connection>
  </table>
</xsp:page>
```

The above XSP page generates an identical document to the ones we created with our SAX and DOM parsers. Let's examine above the XSP code in more detail:

❑ First we use XML processing instructions to declare that we want XSLT post-processing of the document produced, and we would like to use createTable.xsl as the XSLT stylesheet.

❑ Then we declare that this page is an XSP page so that the Cocoon server can appropriately process it. We then put markup for the root element, <table> in our case.

❑ We then use the <esql:connection> tag and inside provide parameters required for connecting to our database.

❑ Next, we use the <esql:execute-query> tag and inside we specify the query string SELECT * FROM creators

❑ A row is obtained using the `<esql:row-results>` tag nested inside the `<esql:results>` tag.

❑ We then wrap the `<esql:get-columns>` tag inside the "row" element tag. The `<esql:columns>` tag produces columns for the current row wrapped inside a "column-name" element tag, just as we want.

❑ Before final presentation, the referenced stylesheet is applied.

You can replace the JDBC connection information, XSLT stylesheet, and `SELECT` query string to suit your needs. Cocoon also allows you to specify a stylesheet based on the output media. For example, you can use a different stylesheet for WAP devices, Netscape, and IE in the same XSP page. Cocoon will detect the media being served and apply an appropriate stylesheet automatically.

Summary

Databases are a viable storage medium for XML structures. Writing SAX and DOM parsers for databases is a relatively simple task and provides the ability to view database tables as virtual XML documents. Since most XML tools use a SAX or DOM parser as the interface to the document source, we can use the XML parser to connect such applications directly to the database without producing intermediate XML character streams.

We also looked at using the `WebRowSet` class to create XML documents directly out of a database with minimum code effort.

We considered a final technique, that of using a server pages technology such as XSP with the Cocoon architecture, to greatly simplify presenting information in a database to web clients.

The Xerces Blue
butterfly, which became
extinct earlier this century,
and after which the Xerces XML
parser is named ...

18

Configuration and Deployment

Configuration files are a persistence mechanism for the parameters of an application or component that tends to remain unchanged across multiple sessions. A simple application could start off by requiring simple command line parameters and environment variables, but as the application evolves, more and more configuration options become available and some of them migrate to configuration files. For complex applications, these files are vital, since they allow customization during and after deployment.

The first part of this chapter, *XML Descriptors in the Enterprise*, analyzes the use of XML for configuration files, called deployment descriptors by Java 2 Enterprise Edition (J2EE). The XML descriptors are compared with four different alternatives and some of the sections contain case studies:

❑ Simple text files (the **servlet descriptor** case)

❑ Binary files (rarely used)

❑ Serialized objects (the **EJB descriptor** case)

❑ User databases (the **user profiles** case)

In the second part, *Java Framework for XML Descriptors*, we'll show you how to implement an XML-based configuration solution and build a Java framework for managing XML descriptors. In particular, we'll answer the following questions:

❑ Where to locate the XML descriptors and how to create them

❑ How to build the structure of the XML descriptors and save them

❑ How to parse and query the XML descriptors

The third part of the chapter, *E-mail Application*, will present a Web application based on Java Server Pages (JSP) and JavaMail, which allows the users to send messages using an HTML form. The application's configuration parameters and the user profiles are stored in XML files. The users will be able to register, log in, send e-mails, edit options, and log out.

The table shows the tools we will use to build and run the examples:

❑ **Apache Xerces**
XML parser that implements the DOM, SAX and JAXP APIs
http://xml.apache.org/xerces-j/

❑ **Apache Xalan**
XSLT processor that supports the XPath standard
http://xml.apache.org/xalan-j/

❑ **Apache Ant**
XML-based make-like tool used to compile the code (optional)
http://jakarta.apache.org/ant/

❑ **Apache Tomcat**
Servlet engine used to run the e-mail application
http://jakarta.apache.org/tomcat/

❑ **Sun JavaMail**
Java extension that supports the SMTP, POP3 and IMAP standards
http://java.sun.com/products/javamail/

❑ **Sun JAF (Java Activation Framework)**
Java Activation Framework is used by JavaMail
http://java.sun.com/beans/glasgow/jaf.html

XML Descriptors in the Enterprise

On the client side, configuration files might (and should) remain unnoticed since most users prefer a GUI for setting their preferences. Advanced users might want to edit these files directly to quickly set their own preferences. Most development tools, including IDEs, use configuration files to store the user preferences, such as colors, fonts, keyboard mappings, etc.

On the server side, the configuration files are the most popular way for customizing an application or a component. They may be deployed together with the application, or they could be added later for providing contexts to the different instances of an application. A servlet engine, for example, can be instantiated multiple times on a shared server. Each instance will have its own configuration files and it can run multiple web applications with their own configuration files – these are called servlet descriptors. It should always be possible to make changes to these files at a later time via a remote administration application. The roles of the administration applications are to make the editing of the configuration files easier and, sometimes, to allow configuration changes without having to restart the applications or the servers.

XML for Configuration Files

As an application evolves, the configuration files need to store more and more information and their structure needs changing. The newest version should be able to read or import the old configuration files, and ideally, the old versions shouldn't crash when they have to deal with the new configuration files. XML is perfect for this job because of its extensibility. We can add new tags and the old parsing code should still work if it was designed properly, and we could also use namespaces to avoid name collisions.

The hierarchical structure of XML documents makes mapping to objects easy and natural. It is important to be able to place every piece of information or parameter within a context. Otherwise, we'll end up with a large number of global parameters. This would be a problem if our application were built from components, such as EJBs, JSPs or servlets.

It is easy to process XML files because there are standard parsing mechanisms such as SAX and DOM. This job could become even easier if we decide to use a tool that maps XML to objects automatically – there are all kinds of editors, utilities and APIs for XML. Some of them might require more processing power and memory resources than we would like, but on the other hand, there are alternatives. The variety of XML tools is amazing.

XML isn't the easiest method to use to store data, however. Developers might have to spend some time learning about all these tools. This would, however, decrease the maintenance costs. We won't have to reinvent a new file format for each version of our application. We'll just extend and improve the old one.

XML seems to be the right compromise for all kinds of file formats and especially for descriptors. It allows us to define a structure without ambiguities and still be able to extend it. It is tool friendly, but also human readable, and allows the use of different character encodings, which is important for internationalized applications.

XML Descriptors vs. Simple Text Files

Many applications store their configuration parameters in text files as name-value pairs. We'll compare this solution with the XML descriptors solution, and discuss the evolution of configuration mechanisms used by servlet engines.

Pros and Cons

It is very easy to edit the key-value pairs manually and the simple text files can be loaded and parsed with `java.util.Properties`. For complex applications, however, the management of these files is usually more difficult because it is hard to encode objects and arrays using key-value pairs. With XML, any configuration parameter is placed in a well-defined context, that is each element, except the root element, has a parent element.

Consider the following XML example:

```xml
<?xml version="1.0" encoding="UTF-8"?>
<demo attr1="value1" attr2="value2">
    <name attr="value">XML Descriptor</name>
    <array>
        <elem>first</elem>
        <elem>second</elem>
        <elem>third</elem>
    </array>
</demo>
```

The equivalent name-value pairs might look like this:

```
demo.attr1=value1
demo.attr2=value2
demo.name.attr=value
demo.name=XML Descriptor
demo.array.length=3
demo.array.1=first
demo.array.2=second
demo.array.3=third
```

This leads to a better structure of the descriptor. In addition, when we build internationalized applications, we'll benefit from XML's support for standard character encodings.

The Servlet Descriptor Case

The Servlet 2.0 and 2.1 engines use multiple properties files for servlet parameters, mappings, mime types, etc. For example, the `properties` configuration files of a simple web application might have the following structure:

`webapp.properties`	`welcomefiles=index.html,index.htm`

`servlets.properties`	`example.code=ExampleServlet`
	`example.initparams=param_1=value_1,`
	`param_2=value_2`

`mappings.properties`	`/example=example` `.ex=example`

`mime.properties`	`txt=text/plain`
	`htm=text/html`
	`html=text/html`
	`gif=image/gif`
	`jpg=image/jpeg`
	`jpeg=image/jpeg`

The Servlet 2.2 specification defines the XML **servlet descriptor**, which combines all of the configuration parameters into a single XML file called `web.xml`. It is easier to manage a single descriptor instead of four files.

The XML equivalent of the above examples would look like this:

```
<?xml version="1.0" encoding="ISO-8859-1"?>
<web-app>
    <welcome-file-list>
        <welcome-file>index.html</welcome-file>
        <welcome-file>index.htm</welcome-file>
    </welcome-file-list>
    <servlet>
        <servlet-name>example</servlet-name>
        <servlet-class>ExampleServlet</servlet-class>
        <init-param>
```

```
            <param-name>param_1</param-name>
            <param-value>value_1</param-value>
        </init-param>
        <init-param>
            <param-name>param_2</param-name>
            <param-value>value_2</param-value>
        </init-param>
    </servlet>
    <servlet-mapping>
        <servlet-name>example</servlet-name>
        <url-pattern>/example</url-pattern>
    </servlet-mapping>
    <servlet-mapping>
        <servlet-name>example</servlet-name>
        <url-pattern>*.ex</url-pattern>
    </servlet-mapping>
    <mime-mapping>
        <extension>txt</extension>
        <mime-type>text/plain</mime-type>
    </mime-mapping>

    <!-- And so on for the rest of the MIME mappings -->

</web-app>
```

`Properties` files are more compact, but the XML elements allow the creation of complex data structures when necessary. The Servlet 2.2 specification defines many other elements for tag libraries, security, error pages and session configuration. This would have required many other properties files. The Servlet 2.3 specification adds new elements for listeners and filters. It is much easier to define new tags and extend the hierarchical structure of the XML descriptors instead of devising new ways of coding the information into key-value pairs.

XML Descriptors vs. Binary Files

Configuration files are rarely encoded using a binary format, or any file format that isn't human readable.

Pros and Cons

Binary files require less disk space, they allow random access, and sometimes we don't want to let the users edit the configuration parameters manually. Unfortunately, the maintenance costs are much higher because we have to code parsers for all format versions. Debugging might also be harder because parsers built in-house for proprietary binary files usually don't match the error handling mechanisms implemented by the XML parsers. In addition, XML files are also human readable, so it is much easier to find out what is going on. During the development of the application we may lose our data samples after format changes, unless we code special utilities that convert the old files to the changed formats.

Disk space is usually not a problem because configuration files are generally quite small.
If we don't want to let users have access to the XML descriptors, we may encrypt them or use `java.util.zip.GZIPOutputStream` and `java.util.zip.GZIPInputStream`. We just have to wrap the input and output streams with the GZIP streams.

Fast random access remains the biggest advantage of binary files. This is very useful, for example, when we need to update a parameter frequently without having to rewrite the whole file. In this case, we could split the parameters in two categories: those parameters whose values tend to remain constant should be saved in XML files and the ones whose values are changed frequently could be stored in a binary data file.

729

XML Descriptors vs. Serialized Objects

The term "serialization" is often used when a structure is saved to an output stream. Without this operation, we cannot send objects over a network or save them to files. The reconstruction of the structure from an input stream is called "deserialization". For example, Apache Xerces includes a package that allows us to serialize a DOM tree to an XML file. The DOM parsing may be viewed as a deserialization process.

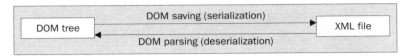

Java includes I/O APIs to serialize objects using a proprietary format. The Java classes just have to implement a marker interface called `java.io.Serializable` and their non-transient non-static fields must be serializable too. In addition, if a serializable class inherits a non-serializable class, the latter must have an accessible zero argument constructor. The rest is done automatically by the Java run-time. This solution is very easy-to-use but it has its disadvantages, as explained in the next section. Currently, XML is seen as an alternative to the proprietary format used by Java.

Pros and Cons

It is straightforward to read and write Java objects using `java.io.ObjectInputStream` and `java.io.ObjectOutputStream`. We just have to use the `readObject()` and `writeObject()` methods of these classes. There are also compatible changes that let us evolve our application. For example, we can add a new field to a class and still be able to read the objects that were serialized with the old version of the class. The new field will be initialized with a default value.

We cannot, however, remove or rename fields, change the class hierarchy, or move a serializable class from one package to another. Such changes are sometimes necessary in order to improve the design of the application. With XML, we can do all kinds of structural changes and will still be able to apply transformations in order to ensure compatibility. An important fact to remember is that XML files can be opened and changed easily, while the binary files created with Java serialization cannot be edited manually.

The EJB Descriptor Case

Remote Method Invocation (RMI) is a system introduced by JDK 1.1 for building distributed Java applications. Using RMI, a Java application can invoke methods of a remote object instantiated by a different Java Virtual Machine (JVM). This makes the communication between different JVMs much simpler than using TCP/IP sockets. With RMI, we still have to deal with thread synchronization and security issues, and we write code for saving the objects to files or databases. Enterprise Java Beans (EJB) are built on top of RMI and they add support for transactions, security and persistence. We just have to implement the business logic of our applications as classes that follow the patterns defined by the EJB specification. Then we use wizards to define the transactional attributes, security roles and other parameters. These wizards generate the EJB descriptors.

An example is included below:

```
<?xml version="1.0"?>

<!DOCTYPE ejb-jar PUBLIC
"-//Sun Microsystems, Inc.//DTD Enterprise JavaBeans 1.1//EN"
"http://java.sun.com/j2ee/dtds/ejb-jar_1_1.dtd">
```

```
<ejb-jar>
    <enterprise-beans>
        <entity>
            <description>
                Example of entity bean
            </description>
            <ejb-name>ProductBean</ejb-name>
            <home>ProductHome</home>
            <remote>Product</remote>
            <ejb-class>ProductBean</ejb-class>
            <persistence-type>Container</persistence-type>
            <prim-key-class>String</prim-key-class>
            <reentrant>False</reentrant>

            <cmp-field><field-name>name</field-name></cmp-field>
            <cmp-field><field-name>price</field-name></cmp-field>
            <cmp-field><field-name>color</field-name></cmp-field>
            <cmp-field><field-name>size</field-name></cmp-field>
        </entity>
    </enterprise-beans>

    <assembly-descriptor>
        <security-role>
            <description>
                The admin is allowed full access to the Product Bean.
            </description>
            <role-name>admin</role-name>
        </security-role>

        <method-permission>
            <role-name>admin</role-name>
            <method>
                <ejb-name>ProductBean</ejb-name>
                <method-name>*</method-name>
            </method>
        </method-permission>

        <container-transaction>
            <description>
                All methods require a transaction
            </description>
            <method>
                <ejb-name>ProductBean</ejb-name>
                <method-name>*</method-name>
            </method>
            <trans-attribute>Required</trans-attribute>
        </container-transaction>
    </assembly-descriptor>
</ejb-jar>
```

EJB 1.0-compliant application servers used serialized objects as EJB descriptors – the `javax.ejb.deployment` package was deprecated by EJB 1.1, which defines a specific XML format as a replacement.

What was the problem? The deprecated package contained two main descriptor classes (EntityDescriptor and SessionDescriptor extending the DeploymentDescriptor abstract class) and only two auxiliary classes (AccessControlEntry and ControlDescriptor). All EJB configuration information had to be coded using these five classes. The structural information was mixed with the application assembly information, blurring the demarcation of the roles defined by the EJB specification. To correct this, the class hierarchy should have been changed, which would have been an incompatible change. It wouldn't have been possible to read the descriptors serialized with the old classes. Yet, it would have been possible to define a new class hierarchy.

An XML solution was preferred instead of defining new classes within the javax.ejb.deployment package. In addition to the XML advantages explained in the earlier sections, such as extensibility and human readability, EJB descriptors need a rich hierarchical structure, such as that provided by lots of XML tags or Java classes. This is not a problem for an XML document, while a deep object tree makes the programming harder.

Look at the above EJB descriptor example, and think what the consequences of mapping each element to a Java class are, even if those that contain only character data are mapped to Strings. This would result in a large number of classes with only two or three properties. Next time the inheritance or containment tree must be changed, we would run into the same compatibility problem. Using XML, the descriptor's structure doesn't have to be coupled with any Java classes.

XML Profiles vs. User Databases

HTTP is a stateless protocol, meaning that there is no support for sessions and no data is maintained on the server side between the requests of the same client. This isn't a problem if we just want to publish static content. Many web applications, however, need to manage their user sessions. The Servlet API makes this easy and lets us maintain the session data in memory, but sometimes this isn't enough. We might need to create user accounts and let the users customize our application. In this case, the users' configurations must be made persistent. We could store them in a database or create an XML file for each user.

Pros and Cons

XML is much more extensible than the relational databases. The Web applications evolve very fast and need all kinds of changes. XML lets us define data structures very easily and extend them without breaking our Java code. With relational databases, we must design the tables and their relations very carefully. The changing of these relations may require a lot of recoding.

At any change of a parameter value, whether it's an attribute value or the character data of an element, the XML file has to be rewritten. This may not be a problem because the values of the configuration parameters tend to remain constant and they are stored in relatively small files.

The databases support transactions and are more reliable. If the computer crashes while an XML file is written, the data is lost. Therefore, when using XML we must implement some kind of primitive transactions manually and rely on the file system. For example, we could make a backup copy of an XML file before rewriting it. If something goes wrong, we would be able to restore it.

The databases use much less disk space, but the file system could be more scalable in this case. Searching for a user in a database can consume a lot of time, especially if the user data is stored in multiple tables that have to be joined. If each user has their own XML file, there is no need to do a search at the application level. The operating system still has to read the file allocation tables (FAT) and directory information, but this is very fast. One good idea is to create a, b, all the way through to z subdirectories within the main data directory. All users whose name starts with the appropriate letters should be stored in the directory they are associated with. This might help when we want to distribute the users across multiple servers.

The User Profiles Case

Suppose a web application needs to store the user preferences. Different types of users will share a common data structure, which will be extended with new elements specific to each user type. With databases, we'll have a different table for each type of user. In this hypothetical example, it is necessary to create multiple user tables because each user type has its own specific attributes. In addition, if the user data contains arrays and references to other objects after database normalization, we'll have lots of other tables that have to be joined in order to retrieve all the information relating to the user.

What happens when the type of a particular user changes? With XML, we just have to apply a transformation on a small file, which may involve the removal of some elements, adding of new ones, changing data or attribute values. With relational databases, we would have to delete a row from a user table, and add a new row to another user table, since each user type has its own table. Other tables might require updates too. For a large database, this may take more time than the simple rewriting of a small XML file (each user profile would be stored in a separate file).

If we just need to store a few user preferences, a relational database can be much faster than an XML-based solution. On the other hand, if the user profile is complex and has to be stored in a database consisting of multiple tables, XML could be a better solution. Instead of spreading a profile's data across multiple tables that have to be joined in the SQL statements, we could save each profile in a separate XML file.

There are cases when we cannot or don't want to use a database even if the user profiles are simple. For example, we might not want to make the presence of a database one of the requirements of our product. Also, on a shared server, other applications might overload the database and the use of XML would provide better performances in the production environment, even if a database were faster on the development platform.

The next part of this chapter presents a framework for handling XML descriptors. The last part contains an application that uses XML-based profiles.

Java Framework for XML Descriptors

When building enterprise applications, we divide the functionality of our applications into components, such as EJBs, Servlets and JSPs. The enterprise APIs, implemented by the J2EE application servers, act as a framework. In many cases, we need functionality that isn't standardized yet, but it isn't specific to our application either. This kind of functionality should be implemented as frameworks so that we can reuse it in future applications. A good framework should expose an easy-to-use API and hide the complexities of its activity.

In this second part of the chapter, we will:

- ❑ Define application configuration strategies
- ❑ Build XML utility classes for our framework
- ❑ Develop the framework for handling descriptors
- ❑ Present two simple examples

The following UML diagram depicts the relations between the classes presented in the next sections. The XPathUtils1 and XPathUtils2 classes extend the XMLUtils class, which is used by Descriptor. The CreateDemo and ShowDemo examples use only the Descriptor class.

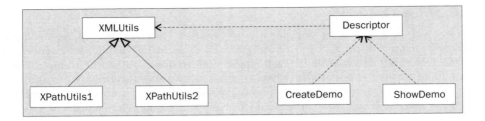

Application Configuration Strategies

What does it take to build an XML-based configuration solution? The previous sections compared the XML descriptors with various alternatives and analyzed the pros and cons. This section answers a few technical questions:

❑   Where to locate the XML Descriptors

❑   How to create the XML Descriptors

❑   How to parse the XML Descriptors

Where To Locate the XML Descriptors

When designing our own types of XML descriptors, we must decide where to place them. One possible solution is to package them together with the class files in a JAR archive. This should be considered only when the application or component doesn't have to modify the descriptor. Even though Java allows us to handle JAR files via the `java.util.jar` package, it isn't safe to open files that are also used by class loaders. Instead, the use of `getClass().getResourceAsStream(name)` is a good solution for getting files that are in the directories or archives found in the classpath.

The placing of the read-only descriptors in JAR files makes the deployment easier. In many cases, however, the application also needs to update the XML descriptors. In this case we could treat the configuration files as special data files and put them in their own directory. Keep in mind that our components might be instantiated multiple times and each instance will probably need its own descriptor. A desktop application might have to support multiple users. On the server side we'll have to deal with concurrent users and virtual servers. Instead of using the file system, read-write descriptors could also be stored in a database as BLOBs (Binary Large Objects), for more reliability.

How To Create the XML Descriptors

First of all, we must design the descriptor's structure. We have to choose the XML tags, their attributes and the general structure of the XML document. A DTD could be useful to formalize this structure, but it isn't absolutely necessary. A few descriptor examples might help us to determine if the descriptor's structure meets the requirements of our component or application.

The application will have to somehow manage the descriptor's data. It could be tempting to build a few Java classes to store that data in memory. These could even be generated automatically by a tool that takes as input the DTD of our descriptor. One such tool is Sun's JAXB, formerly Project Adelard. In this case the parsing and the serialization of the descriptor should be done automatically too. This solution, however, has a big disadvantage. Every time we change the descriptor's structure we would have to change the Java classes and recompile the application. We would develop the application faster but the maintenance costs might be higher.

Another solution is to handle the XML descriptor using DOM. To create a new descriptor we'll create a DOM instance. Then, we'll create the elements that store the configuration parameters. The data may also be stored as element attributes. It is harder to manipulate a DOM tree than our own data objects, but the descriptor's structure can be changed much easier. To simplify the development we'll build a few utility methods based on XPath, which is a language for addressing parts of an XML document. Instead of navigating through the DOM tree, we'll identify an XML element using a path similar to the absolute path of a file. Our examples won't have to deal with the DOM API. They will build the DOM tree in memory using our simple utilities, and then serialize the document to a file.

How To Parse the XML Descriptors

There are many ways to load and parse the XML files. We could map the XML elements to our own Java objects, using a tool like JAXB. A manual mapping would increase the maintenance costs because Java classes aren't as extensible as XML documents. We could use SAX and extract the information on the fly. This would be very fast, but SAX is a low-level API and not very easy to use. In addition, the saving of the XML descriptor would have to be implemented by our application, while in the DOM's case there are frameworks for serialization, such as the one included within Apache Xerces. Finally, we could use DOM, and then extract the information we need with XPath. The DOM trees tend to be memory-expensive, but this isn't a problem for the configuration files because they are usually small.

We'll use the JAXP interface to parse the XML descriptors. After getting the DOM tree, we'll use the XPath implementation provided by Apache Xalan to access the DOM nodes easier. We'll build a `Descriptor` class that will allow us to create and use XML descriptors without calling the DOM APIs. Before that, we'll implement a few XML utilities that will isolate our descriptor utilities from the JAXP, Xerces and Xalan APIs.

The XMLUtils Class

The `XMLUtils` class described in this section implements all the functionality that depends on the JAXP API or Apache's API for XML serialization:

❏   Document creation

❏   DOM parsing

❏   DOM serialization

If we want to switch later to other APIs we'll have to change only this class. The code that calls the methods of the `XMLUtils` class doesn't know it is actually using the JAXP and Apache's serialization APIs. Both these APIs are implemented by Apache Xerces.

We are also going to use Xalan for its XPath implementation. When this chapter was written, two Java versions of Xalan were available: Xalan 1.2.2 and Xalan 2.0.0. We wanted to be able to use any of them. Therefore the `XMLUtils` class defines the XPath utilities as abstract methods. The *XPath Utilities* section will present the two implementations of the abstract methods, one for each supported Xalan version.

```
import java.io.*;

import javax.xml.parsers.DocumentBuilder;
import javax.xml.parsers.DocumentBuilderFactory;
import javax.xml.parsers.ParserConfigurationException;
```

```
import org.w3c.dom.Document;
import org.w3c.dom.DocumentType;
import org.w3c.dom.Node;
import org.w3c.dom.NodeList;
import org.xml.sax.ErrorHandler;
import org.xml.sax.EntityResolver;
import org.xml.sax.InputSource;
import org.xml.sax.SAXException;
import org.xml.sax.SAXParseException;

import org.apache.xml.serialize.OutputFormat;
import org.apache.xml.serialize.XMLSerializer;

public abstract class XMLUtils {
```

The XMLUtils class creates at initialization two JAXP factories for document builders, one for non-validating parsing and the other one for validating parsing:

```
protected static DocumentBuilderFactory factory
    = DocumentBuilderFactory.newInstance();
protected static DocumentBuilderFactory vfactory
    = DocumentBuilderFactory.newInstance();
static {
    factory.setValidating(false);
    vfactory.setValidating(true);
}
```

The createBuilder() method uses these factories to create document builders, whose error handlers will print any warnings and throw exceptions if parsing errors or fatal errors occur. The entity resolver will look for DTDs in the classpath. When we parse an XML file, we know its path and there is no problem locating a system DTD. The Descriptor class described in a later section can also search XML files in the classpath. In this case we get only an input stream. The parser would not be able to locate the external DTD without our own entity resolver that searches the DTD in the classpath too:

```
public static DocumentBuilder createBuilder(boolean validating) {
    try {
        DocumentBuilder builder = null;
        if (validating)
            builder = vfactory.newDocumentBuilder();
        else
            builder = factory.newDocumentBuilder();
        builder.setErrorHandler(new ErrorHandler() {
            public void warning(SAXParseException e)
                throws SAXException {
                System.err.println(e.getMessage());
            }

            public void error(SAXParseException e)
                throws SAXException {
                throw e;
            }
```

```
                    public void fatalError(SAXParseException e)
                        throws SAXException {
                        throw e;
                    }
                });
                builder.setEntityResolver(new EntityResolver() {
                    public InputSource resolveEntity(
                        String publicID, String systemID) {
                        if (publicID != null && publicID.endsWith(".dtd"))
                        {
                            InputStream in
                                = getClass().getResourceAsStream(publicID);
                            if (in != null)
                                return new InputSource(in);
                        }
                        return null;
                    }
                });
                return builder;
            } catch (ParserConfigurationException e) {
                throw new InternalError(e.getMessage());
            }
        }
```

The createEmptyDocument() method simply creates a new org.w3c.dom.Document instance. It uses the newDocument() method of the javax.xml.parsers.DocumentBuilder class:

```
    public static Document createEmptyDocument() {
        return createBuilder(false).newDocument();
    }
```

This parses an XML input stream and returns an org.w3c.dom.Document instance. It calls the parse() method of a JAXP document builder:

```
    public static Document parse(File file, boolean validating)
        throws IOException, SAXException {
        return createBuilder(validating).parse(file);
    }
```

This parses an XML input stream and returns a Document instance. We use this method when the XML descriptor is not located as a file. This is the case when we load the document as a classpath resource. The previous parse() variant should always be used when parsing XML files whose path is known.

```
    public static Document parse(InputStream in, boolean validating)
        throws IOException, SAXException {
        return createBuilder(validating).parse(in);
    }
```

We'll use the org.apache.xml.serialize.XMLSerializer class to save the Document instances to XML files. The serializer can be configured to indent the XML output. The setIndenting() method might set the maximum line width to 72, which is a default value. We set this width to 0 to disable the line wrapping. CRLF (carriage return line feed) will be used to separate the lines.

If at least one of either `publicID` or `systemID` is not `null`, we remove temporarily the document's `org.w3c.dom.DocumentType` node. Without this operation, the Apache's serialization API would simply ignore these parameters if the `DOCTYPE` node were present in the serialized DOM tree. It is important to know that the `serializer` can obtain the public id, the system id and the possible internal DTD subset from the `org.w3c.dom.DocumentType` node only if DOM Level 2 is supported.

We experience problems when we use internal DTDs even if Xerces supports DOM 2. Using Xerces 1.2.3 and 1.3.0, the `doc.getDoctype().getInternalSubset()` calls returned `null` when our XML files had internal DTDs. Because of this bug, the Apache's API for XML serialization can't get the internal DTD of a parsed document. Therefore the internal DTDs of the saved XML documents are lost. This causes problems when the XML documents are parsed next time using a validating parser. We could use internal DTDs without problems if we are just planning to read the XML descriptors. Also, we can avoid any inconvenience using only external DTDs. The application presented in the third part of the chapter does this for read-write XML files.

The `serialize()` method will traverse the document tree recursively and save the information stored within its nodes. For example, when the current node is an `Element` instance, the `serializer` will output a start tag with its attributes, then it will serialize recursively all child nodes which might contain elements, character data, etc, and, before returning the control to its caller, it will output the end tag.

This method serializes a given document to an output stream:

```
public static void serialize(Document doc,
    OutputStream out, boolean indenting,
    String publicID, String systemID) throws IOException {
    // Configure the output format
    OutputFormat format = new OutputFormat(doc);
    if (publicID != null || systemID != null)
        format.setDoctype(publicID, systemID);
    format.setIndenting(indenting);
    if (!indenting)
        format.setPreserveSpace(true);
    format.setLineWidth(0);
    format.setLineSeparator("\r\n");

    // Remove the document's doctype if necessary
    DocumentType doctype = null;
    Node afterDoctype = null;
    if (publicID != null || systemID != null) {
        NodeList list = doc.getChildNodes();
        for (int i = 0; i < list.getLength(); i++)
            if (list.item(i) instanceof DocumentType) {
                doctype = (DocumentType) list.item(i);
                if (i+1 < list.getLength())
                    afterDoctype = list.item(i+1);
                break;
            }
    }
    if (doctype != null)
        doc.removeChild(doctype);

    // Serialize the document
    XMLSerializer serializer = new XMLSerializer(out, format);
    serializer.asDOMSerializer();
    serializer.serialize(doc);
    // Restore the document's type if necessary
    if (doctype != null)
        if (afterDoctype != null)
```

```
                    doc.insertBefore(doctype, afterDoctype);
            else
                    doc.appendChild(doctype);
    }
```

Most methods of the XMLUtils class are static. The evalToString() and evalToNodeList() methods cannot be declared static because they are abstract methods. The *XPath Utilities* section will describe the subclasses that implement these methods. Both methods evaluate an XPath string and they return the result as a string or as a node list.

For example, the character data contained by an element can be obtained with string(elemPath/text()) where elemPath is the absolute location path of the element, for instance, /book/chapter[3]/section[5]/title. We could also get the value of an attribute with something like string(elemPath@attrName/text()).

This evaluates an XPath string and returns the result as a string. The root element of the document is used as the context node of the evaluation:

```
public abstract String evalToString(Document doc, String str)
    throws SAXException;
```

The following evaluates an XPath string and returns the result as a NodeList. The root element of the document is used as the context node of the evaluation:

```
public abstract NodeList evalToNodeList(Document doc, String str)
    throws SAXException;
```

As we noted above, we had to write two implementations of the abstract XPath utilities. In order to select one of them, we need to determine the available version of the Xalan processor. Xalan 1 does not contain the org.apache.xpath.XPathAPI class, which was introduced by Xalan 2. If this class is loaded successfully, we assume that a Xalan 2-compatible version is available. Otherwise we try to use Xalan 1. The XPathUtils1 and XPathUtils2 classes are presented in the *XPath Utilities* section:

```
protected static Class utilsClass = null;
static {
    // Test if the XPathAPI is available
    boolean useXPathAPI = true;
    try {
        Class.forName("org.apache.xpath.XPathAPI");
    } catch (ClassNotFoundException e) {
        useXPathAPI = false;
    }

    // Load the class
    String className = useXPathAPI
        ? "XPathUtils2"
        : "XPathUtils1";
    try {
        utilsClass = Class.forName(className);
    } catch (ClassNotFoundException e) {
        e.printStackTrace();
    }
}
```

The `getImpl()` method will return a new instance of the utilities class that is loaded dynamically. If the implementation class isn't found or it cannot be instantiated, an `InternalError` is thrown:

```
public static XMLUtils getImpl() {
    if (utilsClass == null)
        throw new InternalError(
            "Don't have an XMLUtils implementation");
    try {
        // Return a new instance of the utils class
        return (XMLUtils) utilsClass.newInstance();
    } catch (Exception e) {
        e.printStackTrace();
        throw new InternalError(
            "Couldn't instantiate the XMLUtils implementation");
    }
}
```

XPath Utilities

The XPath standard doesn't define any API. Therefore, any XPath processor will come up with its own API. Worse, different versions of the same processor might contain incompatible changes in the absence of a standard XPath API. This is the case with Xalan 1 and 2. Since the latter is a new release, we will concentrate most of our efforts on this new version. However, our e-mail application will be compatible with both versions, and you shall see how this is managed later on in the chapter. The utilities implemented by the `XPathUtils1` (Xalan 1) and `XPathUtils2` (Xalan 2) classes can evaluate an XPath to:

❑   A Java string
❑   A list of DOM nodes

The XPathUtils2 Class - Using Xalan 2

Xalan 2 renamed all its packages and some of its classes. For example `org.apache.xalan.xpath.XObject` became `org.apache.xpath.objects.XObject`. In an attempt to help those who already built applications based on Xalan 1, Apache included a `xalanj1compat.jar` file within Xalan 2, which should help the porting and even the running of some of the old applications, especially for those who use Xalan for its main XSLT functionality. The compatibility JAR file doesn't help us since the XPath low-level APIs of Xalan 1 weren't available. It is easy, however, to port our code to Xalan 2 because we don't have to deal with the low-level APIs anymore. We used the `org.apache.xpath.XPathAPI` class.

```
import org.w3c.dom.Document;
import org.w3c.dom.Node;
import org.w3c.dom.NodeList;
import org.xml.sax.SAXException;

import javax.xml.transform.TransformerException;

import org.apache.xpath.XPathAPI;
import org.apache.xpath.objects.XObject;

public class XPathUtils2 extends XMLUtils {
```

Our first method evaluates an XPath string and returns the result as an XObject:

```
protected XObject eval(Document doc, String str)
        throws SAXException, TransformerException {
   Node root = doc.getDocumentElement();
   return XPathAPI.eval(root, str);
}
```

This evaluates an XPath string and returns the result as a String. The root element of the document is used as the context node of the evaluation:

```
public String evalToString(Document doc, String str) throws SAXException {
   try {
      return eval(doc, str).str();
   } catch (TransformerException e) {
      throw new SAXException(e);
   }
}
```

The following evaluates an XPath string and returns the result as a NodeList. The root element of the document is used as the context node of the evaluation:

```
public NodeList evalToNodeList(Document doc,
                                String str) throws SAXException {
   try {
      return (NodeList) eval(doc, str).nodeset();
   } catch (TransformerException e) {
      throw new SAXException(e);
   }
}
```

The Descriptor Class

The Descriptor class is our framework's core and it can be used to:

- ❑ Create a new descriptor
- ❑ Fill it with data
- ❑ Save it to a file

It can also be used to:

- ❑ Load an existent descriptor
- ❑ Parse the descriptor
- ❑ Extract information from the descriptor

All methods operate on the same org.w3c.dom.Document instance. To make them tread safely they are preceded by the synchronized keyword. The methods use the XMLUtils class for any operation that isn't defined by the DOM standard. Therefore, the Descriptor class doesn't depend on JAXP, Xerces or Xalan:

```
import java.io.*;
import java.util.*;

import org.w3c.dom.CharacterData;
import org.w3c.dom.Document;
import org.w3c.dom.Element;
import org.w3c.dom.Node;
import org.w3c.dom.NodeList;
import org.w3c.dom.Text;
import org.xml.sax.SAXException;

public class Descriptor {
    private XMLUtils utils;
    private Document doc;
```

In order to create a new descriptor, we need an `org.w3c.dom.Document` instance, which can be obtained with the static `createDocument()` method. The new document, created with `XMLUtils.createEmptyDocument()`, will also have a root element with the given name:

```
public static Document createDocument(String rootName) {

    // Create the document
    Document doc = XMLUtils.createEmptyDocument();

    // Create the root element
    Node root = doc.createElement(rootName);

    // Add the root element to the document
    doc.appendChild(root);

    // Return the new document
    return doc;
}
```

The `Descriptor()` constructor, which takes the `Document` instance as parameter, gets a new `XMLUtils` object with `XMLUtils.getImpl()`. This is an instance of `XPathUtils1` or `XPathUtils2`, depending on the available version of Xalan. The constructor also verifies if the document has a root element and throws an exception if this requirement isn't met:

```
public Descriptor(Document doc) {
    this.utils = XMLUtils.getImpl();
    this.doc = doc;

    // Check the existence of the root element
    Node root = doc.getDocumentElement();
    if (root == null) {
        throw new IllegalArgumentException("Document without root element");
    }
}
```

The structure of an XML file is given by its elements. Descriptors usually have a well-defined structure. For this reason, XPath seems to be a good tool for managing an XML descriptor. Any element can be identified with its absolute path. For example, `/rootName` is the path of the root element; `/rootName/childName` is the path of an element contained directly by the root element; `/rootName/childName/grandChildName` is the path of an element contained by a root's child, and so on.

If we know the path of an element, we can use the getElement() method to get the
org.w3c.dom.Element instance. This method calls the evalToNodeList() method of the
XMLUtils instance, gets the first node of the returned list, and casts it to org.w3c.dom.Element. The
caller of the getElement() method is responsible for passing a valid absolute path of an element:

```
public synchronized Element getElement(String elemPath)
       throws SAXException {

  // Get the list of nodes
  NodeList list = utils.evalToNodeList(doc, elemPath);

  // Get the first node of the list
  Node node = (list.getLength() > 0) ? list.item(0) : null;

  // Cast the Node object to Element
  if (node instanceof Element) {
    return (Element) node;
  } else {
    throw new IllegalArgumentException(elemPath
                          + " isn't the path of an element");
  }
}
```

Sometimes, a parent element contains a few elements with the same name. In this case, we may use indices
like this /rootName/childName[1]/grandChildName[3]. Note that 1 is the index of the first
element among a group of elements with the same name and parent. The getElementCount() method
returns the number of elements with a given name contained by a parent element. It uses the same
evalToNodeList() method of the XMLUtils instance and returns the length of the obtained node list:

```
public synchronized int getElementCount(String parentPath, String elemName)
       throws SAXException {

  // Build the XPath string
  String path = parentPath + '/' + elemName;

  // Get the list of elements
  NodeList list = utils.evalToNodeList(doc, path);

  // Return the element count
  return list.getLength();
}
```

We can use the DOM API to build a descriptor. The addElement() method takes the absolute path of
a parent element and the name of the element we want to create. It uses getElement() to obtain the
parent Element object, creates the new element and appends it to its parent:

```
public synchronized void addElement(String parentPath,
                         String elemName) throws SAXException {

  // Get the parent element
  Element parent = getElement(parentPath);

  // Create the element
  Element elem = doc.createElement(elemName);

  // Append the created element to its parent
  parent.appendChild(elem);
}
```

The following removes an existent element from the DOM tree:

```
public synchronized void removeElement(String elemPath)
        throws SAXException {

  // Get the element
  Element elem = getElement(elemPath);

  // Get the element's parent
  Node parent = elem.getParentNode();

  // Remove the element
  if (parent != null) {
    parent.removeChild(elem);
  }
}
```

After creating an element, we may call `addData()` to store some character data within the element. This method creates a text node with the given data and appends it to the existent element:

```
public synchronized void addData(String elemPath,
                                 String data) throws SAXException {

  // Get the element
  Element elem = getElement(elemPath);

  // Create the text node
  Text text = doc.createTextNode(data);

  // Append the text node to the element
  elem.appendChild(text);
}
```

The following removes the character data contained by an element:

```
    public synchronized void removeData(String elemPath) throws SAXException {

  // Get the element
  Element elem = getElement(elemPath);

  // Get the character data nodes
  NodeList list = elem.getChildNodes();
  Vector v = new Vector();
  for (int i = 0; i < list.getLength(); i++) {
    Node node = list.item(i);
    if (node instanceof CharacterData) {
      v.add(node);
    }
  }
  for (int i = 0; i < v.size(); i++) {
    elem.removeChild((Node) v.get(i));
  }
}
```

Data can also be stored as the values of the attributes of the elements. The `addAttribute()` method can be used to add an attribute to an existent element. If the attribute already exists, this method would update the attribute's value:

```
public synchronized void addAttribute(String elemPath, String attrName,
                                      String attrValue) throws SAXException {

  // Get the element
  Element elem = getElement(elemPath);

  // Add the attribute
  elem.setAttribute(attrName, attrValue);
}
```

The following removes an attribute of an element:

```
public synchronized void removeAttribute(String elemPath, String attrName)
         throws SAXException {

  // Get the element
  Element elem = getElement(elemPath);

  // Add the attribute
  elem.removeAttribute(attrName);
}
```

After building a descriptor, we can save it to a file using the `save()` method, which calls the `serialize()` method of the `XMLUtils` class. See the *XMLUtils Class* section for more details:

```
public synchronized void save(File file, boolean indenting,
                              String publicID,
                              String systemID) throws IOException {
  OutputStream out = new BufferedOutputStream(new FileOutputStream(file));
  try {

    // Serialize the document
    XMLUtils.serialize(doc, out, indenting, publicID, systemID);
  }
  finally {
    out.close();
  }
}
```

If we want to preserve the original DOCTYPE of the document, if there is one, we can use the following variant of the `save()` method:

```
public synchronized void save(File file,
                              boolean indenting) throws IOException {
  save(file, indenting, null, null);
}
```

Three different `Descriptor()` constructors can be used to load a descriptor from a file, classpath resource or input stream, and parse its content. The constructors use the `parse()` method of the `XMLUtils` class. See the *XMLUtils Class* section for more details.

This parses an XML file and constructs a descriptor object:

```
public Descriptor(File file,
                    boolean validating) throws IOException, SAXException {
   this.utils = XMLUtils.getImpl();

   // Parse the file
   doc = XMLUtils.parse(file, validating);
}
```

The following parses an XML resource and constructs a descriptor object. The resource must be in classpath:

```
public Descriptor(String name,
                    boolean validating) throws IOException, SAXException {
   this.utils = XMLUtils.getImpl();
   InputStream in = getClass().getResourceAsStream(name);
   if (in == null) {
      throw new FileNotFoundException(name);
   }
   try {

      // Parse the resource
      doc = XMLUtils.parse(in, validating);
   }
   finally {
      in.close();
   }
}
```

The next constructor parses an XML input stream:

```
public Descriptor(InputStream in,
                    boolean validating) throws IOException, SAXException {
   this.utils = XMLUtils.getImpl();

   // Parse the input stream
   doc = XMLUtils.parse(in, validating);
}
```

After parsing a descriptor, we'll want to extract the information from the DOM tree. The `getData()` method gets the character data contained by an element using the `evalToString()` method of the `XMLUtils` instance. The XPath processor will receive the `string(elemPath/text())` string for evaluation, where `elemPath` is the absolute path of the element:

```
public synchronized String getData(String elemPath) throws SAXException {
   return utils.evalToString(doc, "string(" + elemPath + "/text())");
}
```

The getAttribute() method passes elemPath/@attrName to getData() in order to get the value of an attribute of an element. Therefore, the XPath string that must be evaluated is string(elemPath/@attrName/text()):

```
public synchronized String getAttribute(String elemPath, String attrName)
        throws SAXException {

    // Build the path of the attribute
    String path = elemPath + '/' + '@' + attrName;

    // Return the value of the attribute
    return getData(path);
}
```

In case we have a group of elements with the same name and parent, we can obtain their character data using getArray(), which calls getData() for each arrayPath/elemName[index] path, where arrayPath is the absolute path of the parent element:

```
public synchronized String[] getArray(String arrayPath, String elemName)
        throws SAXException {

    // Get the number of elements
    int length = getElementCount(arrayPath, elemName);

    // Create the string array
    String array[] = new String[length];
    for (int i = 0, j = 1; i < length; i++, j++) {

        // Build the path of the current element
        String path = arrayPath + '/' + elemName + '[' + j + ']';

        // Get the character data of the current element
        array[i] = getData(path);
    }

    // Return the string array containing the character data
    return array;
}
}
```

Examples

This section uses the Descriptor class to create a descriptor file and then to extract information from it.

This code is already available, pre-compiled, in the code download for this chapter, under /ProJavaXML/ Chapter18/. You should copy this file to your root directory (in the examples below, this is C:). When the whole distribution is copied, we can set about making the necessary alterations for it to run upon our systems.

Using Ant To Compile the Code

Ant is a Java program that automates the process of compiling and manipulating source code structures. It is a platform independent tool intended to replace the make utilities. You can obtain a copy of Ant from the Jakarta Apache Project at (http://jakarta.apache.org/ant/index.html).

It is very simple to set up and run:

- ❑ Add Ant's `bin` directory to your `PATH` variable
- ❑ Make sure the `JAVA_HOME` environment variable is set
- ❑ Make sure the `ANT_HOME` environment variable is set − `ANT_HOME` is the directory that you have extracted your Ant distribution into, for instance `C:\ant`.

With Ant's bin directory in your classpath, you should be able to run it from any directory that contains a `build.xml` file. For the purposes of this installation, we will run the examples from `C:\projavaxml\chapter18`.

You should already have downloaded the tools listed at the beginning of the chapter, now, before we can compile the classes, you will need to set up the following classpath. We'll make use of a parameterized `setclasspath.bat` batch file as follows:

```
if "%1" == "x1" set xalan=C:\xalan-j_1_2_2\xalan.jar
if "%1" == "x2" set xalan=C:\xalan-j_2_0_0\build\xalan.jar

set classpath=.;%xalan%;C:\xerces-1_3_0\xerces.jar
```

These paths will naturally vary according to precisely where these files are on your computer.

The next step is to edit the `build.xml` file, which should be in your `projavaxml\chapter18` directory. In order to use Jakarta Ant for compiling the examples, you'll have to set the proper Xalan, JavaMail and JAF paths. Remove one of `<property>` tags if you don't have both Xalan versions.

The root element of the `build.xml` file is `<project>` and contains properties and targets. The name of the project is `"Demo"`, the default target is `"main"` and the base directory is the current directory:

```
<?xml version="1.0" encoding="UTF-8"?>
<project name="Demo" default="main" basedir=".">
```

Each property has a name and a value. We define four properties to indicate the class directories of Xalan 1 and Xalan 2, and the jar files of JavaMail and Java Activation Framework (edit as necessary):

```
<property name="xalan1" value="C:/xalan-j_1_2_2"/>
<property name="xalan2" value="C:/xalan-j_2_0_0/bin"/>
<property name="xerces" value="C:/xerces-1_3_0/xerces.jar"/>
<property name="javamail" value="C:/javamail-1.2/mail.jar"/>
<property name="jaf" value="C:/jaf1.0.1/activation.jar"/>
```

We now define Ant "targets" which are the basic unit of work. The targets sit in a hierarchy defined by the (optional) `depends` attribute in the `target` tag. The execution of the `main` target will trigger the execution of x1 and x2. These two targets will be executed only if the `xalan1` and `xalan2` properties, respectively, are defined. Each target contains Ant "tasks". There is a set of built-in tasks and you may define your own. See Ant's documentation for details. The `javac` task is a built-in task that uses the Java compiler:

```
    <target name="demo" depends="x2,x1"/>

      <target name="x2" if="xalan2">
        <javac
         srcdir="./demo" destdir="webapps/config/WEB-INF/classes"
         classpath=".;${xalan2}/xalan.jar;${xerces};${javamail};${jaf}">
           <exclude name="**/XPathUtils1.java"/>
        </javac>
      </target>

      <target name="x1" if="xalan1">
        <javac
         srcdir="./demo" destdir="webapps/config/WEB-INF/classes"
         classpath= ".;${xalan1}/xalan.jar;${xerces};${javamail}:${jaf}">
           <exclude name="**/XPathUtils2.java"/>
        </javac>
      </target>


    <!-- We won't use this till later -->
    <target name="email" depends="demo">
        <javac srcdir="./email"
            destdir="webapps/config/WEB-INF/classes"
            classpath=".;${xalan1}/xalan.jar;${xerces};${javamail}:${jaf}">
            <exclude name="**/XPathUtils2.java"/>
        </javac>
    </target>

  </project>
```

To compile, simply type ant x1, ant x2, or just ant demo in the directory containing build.xml. The output should resemble the following:

The build.bat Script

If you do not wish to install Ant, then you can use the build.bat script provided with the code download for this chapter.

Running the Examples

The CreateDemo application must be run first since it generates the demo.xml file used by ShowDemo. The following simple script will use our setclasspath batch file to run the example. Note that since we have compiled the classes to our webapp directory, we'll need to add that directory to our classpath as well:

```
@echo off

if "%1" == "x1" call setclasspath x1
if "%1" == "x2" call setclasspath x2

set classpath=%classpath%;./webapps/config/WEB-INF/classes

java CreateDemo
java ShowDemo
```

Now we can simply call run x1 or x2 to run the example with either Xalan 1 or Xalan 2:

The CreateDemo Class

When designing the structure of an XML document, we must choose the names of the tags and their attributes, which means we must decide if data is best stored as an attribute or as character data within an element. It is also important to define the containment relations between the XML elements. In the case of this simple example, the names of the XML tags, the character data, the names and values of the attributes are trivial, so that we can focus on the API calls of the framework presented in the previous section.

The `CreateDemo` example:

- Builds a new XML descriptor whose root element is named `demo`
- Sets the `attr1` and `attr2` attributes of the root element
- Creates a child element `name` with some character data and an attribute
- Creates three nested elements: `level1`, `level2` and `level3`
- Creates an `array` element that will contain three elements with character data
- Saves the XML descriptor to a `demo.xml` file in the current directory
- Prints the content of `demo.xml`

```java
import java.io.*;

public class CreateDemo {

  public static void main(String args[]) {
    String fileName = "demo.xml";
    try {
      Descriptor descriptor =
        new Descriptor(Descriptor.createDocument("demo"));
      descriptor.addAttribute("/demo", "attr1", "value1");
      descriptor.addAttribute("/demo", "attr2", "value2");

      descriptor.addElement("/demo", "name");
      descriptor.addAttribute("/demo/name", "attr", "value");
      descriptor.addData("/demo/name", "XML Descriptor");

      String path = "/demo";
      for (int i = 1; i <= 3; i++) {
        String tag = "level" + i;
        descriptor.addElement(path, tag);
        path += "/" + tag;
      }
      descriptor.addData(path, "abc");

      descriptor.addElement("/demo", "array");

      descriptor.addElement("/demo/array", "elem");
      descriptor.addData("/demo/array/elem[1]", "first");

      descriptor.addElement("/demo/array", "elem");
      descriptor.addData("/demo/array/elem[2]", "second");

      descriptor.addElement("/demo/array", "elem");
      descriptor.addData("/demo/array/elem[3]", "third");

      descriptor.save(new File(fileName), true);

      // Output the file's content
      System.out.println();
      BufferedReader reader = new BufferedReader(new FileReader(fileName));
      try {
```

```
         String line = null;
         while (true) {
           line = reader.readLine();
           if (line == null) {
             break;
           }
           System.out.println(line);
         }
       }
       finally {
         reader.close();
       }
       System.out.println();
     } catch (Exception e) {
       e.printStackTrace();
     }
   }
 }
```

The ShowDemo Class

The ShowDemo example loads the demo.xml descriptor as a classpath resource and extracts its
information: character data and attribute values. We could have loaded the descriptor as a file too. The
file's data is obtained with the getAttribute(), getData() and getArray() methods of the
Descriptor class:

```
public class ShowDemo {

  public static void main(String args[]) {
    String resourceName = "demo.xml";
    try {
      Descriptor descriptor = new Descriptor(resourceName, false);
      System.out.println();

      System.out.println("Demo attr1: "
                         + descriptor.getAttribute("/demo", "attr1"));
      System.out.println("Demo attr2: "
                         + descriptor.getAttribute("/demo", "attr2"));
      System.out.println();

      System.out.println("Demo name: " + descriptor.getData("/demo/name"));
      System.out.println("Demo name attr: "
                         + descriptor.getAttribute("/demo/name", "attr"));
      System.out.println();

      System.out
        .println("Level 123: "
                 + descriptor.getData("/demo/level1/level2/level3"));
      System.out.println();

      String array[] = descriptor.getArray("/demo/array", "elem");
      for (int i = 0, j = 1; i < array.length; i++, j++) {
        System.out.println("array[" + j + "]=" + array[i]);
      }
```

```
      System.out.println();
   } catch (Exception e) {
     e.printStackTrace();
   }
 }
}
```

E-mail Application

This third part of the chapter describes a web application that uses XML-based user profiles and an XML configuration file that can be modified from the command line. The user profiles can be edited using an HTML form. The list of the application's main capabilities is included below:

- ❏ Register new user
- ❏ Login user
- ❏ Send an e-mail message
- ❏ Edit user options
- ❏ Logout user

The following table contains the XML files, Java classes and JSP pages of the application:

web.xml or conf/server.xml	The application's servlet descriptor used by the servlet engine or application server. web.xml normally resides in \WEB-INF\, server.xml resides in TOMCAT_HOME\conf\ and allows the web application to operate from its home directory outside of Tomcat by means of a virtual directory.
EmailConfig.dtd	DTD for the configuration file of the application. This file is placed in WEB-INF\classes.
EmailConfig.xml	The configuration file of the application. This file is placed in WEB-INF\classes.
EmailAdmin.java	Extracts the configuration parameters from the EmailConfig.xml and allows the changing of their values from the command line.
EmailUser.dtd	DTD for the user profiles. This file is placed in WEB-INF\classes and WEB-INF\users.
EmailUser.xml	Template for the user profiles. This file is placed in WEB-INF\classes.
UserBean.java	Maintains data about users and also implements the logic for managing the users.
login.jsp	Builds the login form and handles the data submitted with this form
EmailBean.java	Maintains data about an email message and also implements the routine for sending e-mail messages.

Table continued on following page

header.jsp	Included within the `email.jsp` and `options.jsp` pages.
email.jsp	Builds the e-mail form and handles the data submitted with this form.
options.jsp	Builds the options and registration forms and handles the data submitted with these forms
register.jsp	New users will request this page in order to register. The request is forwarded to the `options.jsp` page which will handle the registration process.
logout.jsp	This page invalidates the user's session and shows a logout message.

For managing the XML files, the application uses the framework presented in the second part of this chapter. The `Descriptor` class provides the functionality for:

❑ Locating, loading and parsing the XML files

❑ Creating new XML files

❑ Updating existent XML files

The application also contains a few HTML forms generated by JSP pages – I used a design pattern created for one of my products (Devsphere Mapping Framework). A JSP page assumes that its HTML form is requested for the first time if the HTTP method is GET. In this case the generated form may be empty or it may contain default values. If the HTTP method is POST, the form data is validated and stored to a JavaBean object that acts as data model.

If the submitted form data is valid and complete, the HTTP request could be forwarded to another page. If some user errors occurred during validation, such as unfilled form fields, the HTML form is returned to the user for refilling. In this case the error messages are included and the values of the valid fields are preserved. The mapping framework mentioned above performs most of these operations automatically. For more information about this design pattern, you can visit www.Devsphere.com.

Deploying the Web Application

We'll run our Web application using Apache Tomcat 3.2.1 and deploy our application manually. Other application servers or servlet engines may provide deployment wizards.

The application's main directory must contain the JSP pages and the WEB-INF subdirectory. In a production environment, you normally wouldn't publish the source code of the Java classes. For development and testing, however, it is convenient to place the Java code, the JSP pages and the .bat files into the same directory, especially for a relatively small application like this. The class files were placed in WEB-INF\classes, which is added automatically to the classpath by the servlet engine. The subdirectories of WEB-INF also contain the XML files of the application. This is a good location for them because the content of WEB-INF may not be accessed over the network using the HTTP protocol.

Supposing that the application's directory is C:\projavaxml\chapter18\, we have to add the following lines to the conf\server.xml file of the Tomcat installation, within the `<ContextManager>` element:

```
<Context path="/projavaxml/chapter18/config"
    docBase="C:/projavaxml/chapter18/webapps/config"
    debug="9" reloadable="true">
</Context>
```

The application's servlet descriptor, which Tomcat needs, is already placed in the download `WEB-INF` directory. The `login.jsp` file is declared as the initial page of the application:

```
<?xml version="1.0" encoding="UTF-8"?>
<web-app>
    <welcome-file-list>
        <welcome-file>login.jsp</welcome-file>
    </welcome-file-list>
</web-app>
```

In addition, the following files must be added to Tomcat's classpath:

`xerces.jar`	Apache Xerces XML parser, also containing Apache's API for XML serialization
`xalan.jar`	Apache Xalan XSLT processor, whose XPath support is needed by our application
`mail.jar`	JavaMail standard extension used to send e-mail messages
`activation.jar`	Java Activation Framework used by JavaMail

You need to add Xerces, Xalan, JavaMail and JAF to the classpath at the beginning of the `bin\tomcat.bat` file of your Tomcat installation:

```
set CP=%CP%;C:\xalan-j_2_0_0;C:\xerces-1_3_0\xerces.jar;C:\javamail-
1_2\mail.jar;C:\jaf-1.0.1\activation.jar
```

On Unix machines, you would have to edit the equivalent `bin\tomcat.sh` file.

There are specific issues to discuss when deploying Web applications that use XML. The main problem is that almost any application server already has an XML parser since it needs to handle servlet descriptors and other kinds of XML-based descriptors. In many cases, that XML parser doesn't provide the features you need. You might have to replace it with your preferred XML parser, but sometimes this isn't possible.

Tomcat 3.2.1 uses the Sun's reference implementation of JAXP 1.0, which supports only DOM Level 1. (Note that JAXP 1.1 supports DOM Level 2.) If we just add Xerces to the classpath, we'll use Sun's parser because Tomcat places its XML parser at the beginning of the classpath variable. We still have to add `xerces.jar` to the classpath though, because we use Apache's serialization API. If we also add Xalan 1 to the classpath, everything works fine. Note that we use only the XPath support of Xalan. If we want to use Xalan 2, whose XPath implementation needs the JAXP 1.1 and DOM 2 APIs, we'll have to replace Sun's parser, Crimson, with Xerces.

We can do this, by editing the `bin\tomcat.bat` file of Tomcat 3.2.1 and replacing the `set CP=%CP%;%CLASSPATH%` line with `set CP=%CLASSPATH%;%CP%`. This way, `xerces.jar` will be present in the classpath before Crimson. In conclusion, we can use Tomcat 3.2.1 with Xalan 2 if we replace Tomcat's XML parser with Xerces.

In some production environments this is not possible, however. For example, the J2EE reference implementation also includes Tomcat, but you cannot remove the proprietary parser from the J2EE server. Even on a Tomcat server, some legacy applications could be based on Xalan 1, which is not 100% compatible with Xalan 2, even thought the latter provides some backward compatibility support. For these kinds of reasons, our framework supports both Xalan 1 and Xalan 2.

Compiling the Application

Recall that we included an extra Ant target to compile the E-mail application files into the web application folder. Call `ant email` now to deploy these files:

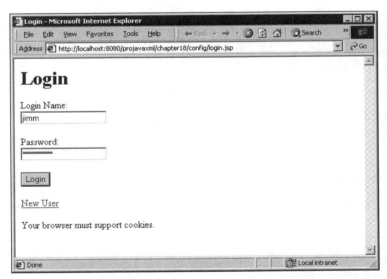

After deployment and restarting Tomcat, you should be able to open a browser and request an URL like this:

```
http://localhost:8080/projavaxml/chapter18/config/login.jsp
```

The Web browser must have the cookie support enabled:

The EmailConfig.dtd File

This is the DTD for the configuration file of the application. The root element, `<config>`, must contain three other elements: `<config-dir>`, `<users-dir>` and `<mail-host>`. These three elements must contain character data. The roles of all these elements are explained in the next two sections:

```
<?xml version="1.0" encoding="UTF-8"?>
<!ELEMENT config (config-dir, users-dir, mail-host)>
<!ELEMENT config-dir (#PCDATA)>
<!ELEMENT users-dir (#PCDATA)>
<!ELEMENT mail-host (#PCDATA)>
```

This file is placed in the WEB-INF/classes directory.

The EmailConfig.xml File

This is the configuration file for the application and it will be searched for in classpath with the Descriptor class. The XMLUtils class will use the public name of the DTD to search the EmailConfig.dtd file in CLASSPATH.

The root element contains three elements that represent the application's configuration parameters:

❑   The directory of this configuration file

❑   The directory used to maintain the user profiles

❑   The name of the SMTP host used to send e-mail messages

```
<?xml version="1.0" encoding="UTF-8"?>
<!DOCTYPE config PUBLIC "EmailConfig.dtd" "EmailConfig.dtd">
<config>
    <config-dir>webapps/config/WEB-INF/classes</config-dir>
    <users-dir>webapps/config/WEB-INF/users</users-dir>
    <mail-host>mail.company.com</mail-host>
</config>
```

This file is placed in the WEB-INF/classes/ directory, which is the default configuration directory of this application.

The EmailAdmin Class

This class extracts the configuration parameters from the EmailConfig.xml file using the Descriptor class, whose constructor takes the name of the XML descriptor as parameter. The true value of the second parameter of the Descriptor() constructor tells the framework to use a validating parser. This way, we know that all configuration parameters were present:

```
import org.xml.sax.SAXException;

import java.io.*;

public class EmailAdmin {
  private static Descriptor descriptor;
  private static String configDir, usersDir, mailHost;
  static {
    try {
      descriptor = new Descriptor("EmailConfig.xml", true);
      configDir = descriptor.getData("/config/config-dir");
      usersDir = descriptor.getData("/config/users-dir");
```

```
      mailHost = descriptor.getData("/config/mail-host");
   } catch (IOException e) {
     throw new InternalError(e.getMessage());
   } catch (SAXException e) {
     throw new InternalError(e.getMessage());
   }
}
```

This returns the directory of the configuration files:

```
public static String getConfigDir() {
   return configDir;
}
```

This returns the directory of the user files:

```
public static String getUsersDir() {
    return usersDir;
}
```

This returns the name of the SMTP host:

```
public static String getMailHost() {
    return mailHost;
}
```

The EmailAdmin class can also be used as a standalone application. Its main() method iterates over the command line arguments and replaces the existent values of the configuration parameters with the values from the command line, which must be preceded by the -c, -u and -h switches. Any subset of these three parameters can be specified in the command line in any order. The XML file is updated using the save() method of the Descriptor object. The second argument of this call is false because the descriptor's content had been already indented when it was loaded and parsed:

```
public static void main(String args[]) {
  if (args.length == 0) {
    System.out
      .println("java EmailAdmin -c configDir -u usersDir -h mailHost");
  } else {
    try {
      for (int i = 0; i < args.length - 1; i += 2) {
        if (args[i].equals("-c")) {
          configDir = args[i + 1];
          descriptor.removeData("/config/config-dir");
          descriptor.addData("/config/config-dir", configDir);
        } else if (args[i].equals("-u")) {
          usersDir = args[i + 1];
          descriptor.removeData("/config/users-dir");
          descriptor.addData("/config/users-dir", usersDir);
        } else if (args[i].equals("-h")) {
          mailHost = args[i + 1];
          descriptor.removeData("/config/mail-host");
          descriptor.addData("/config/mail-host", mailHost);
```

```
            }
          }
          File file = new File(configDir, "EmailConfig.xml");
          String dtd = "EmailConfig.dtd";
          descriptor.save(file, false, dtd, dtd);
        } catch (SAXException e) {
          e.printStackTrace();
        } catch (IOException e) {
          e.printStackTrace();
        }
      }
      System.out.println("config-dir: " + configDir);
      System.out.println("users-dir: " + usersDir);
      System.out.println("mail-host: " + mailHost);
    }
  }
```

Normally, you won't have to change the configuration directory or the users' directory, but you'll probably have to change the name of the SMTP host using a command like this: admin x2 -h another.company.com.

The admin.bat file is included with the source code and sets the classpath before launching EmailAdmin. You need to provide a variable x1 or x2 to indicate the Xalan version used:

```
@echo off

if "%1" == "x1" call setclasspath x1
if "%1" == "x2" call setclasspath x2

set classpath=%classpath%;./webapps/config/WEB-INF/classes

java EmailAdmin %2 %3 %4 %5 %6 %7 %8 %9
```

After changing the value of a configuration parameter, you have to restart the Web application.

The EmailUser.dtd File

We use an external DTD for the users' profiles. The `EmailUser.dtd` file must be stored twice, in the configuration directory and in the users' directory, since XML files from these two directories declare it as external DTD. The root element, `<user>`, must contain four other elements: `<name>`, `<email>`, `<display>` and `<password>`. The `<display>` element must contain two other elements: `<rows>` and `<columns>`. All elements, except `<user>` and `<display>`, must contain only character data. The roles of all these elements are explained in the next section:

```
<?xml version="1.0" encoding="UTF-8"?>
<!ELEMENT user (name, email, display, password)>
<!ELEMENT name (#PCDATA)>
<!ELEMENT email (#PCDATA)>
<!ELEMENT display (rows, columns)>
<!ELEMENT rows (#PCDATA)>
<!ELEMENT columns (#PCDATA)>
<!ELEMENT password (#PCDATA)>
```

This file is placed in `WEB-INF\classes` and `WEB-INF\users`.

The EmailUser.xml File

This file is used as a template for the user profiles. When a new user must be registered, the `EmailUser.xml` file is loaded from the configuration directory, filled with the user's options and then saved in the users' directory. A similar procedure is followed to change the user's options. See the following sections for more details. The login names are used as file names for the user profiles:

```
<?xml version="1.0" encoding="UTF-8"?>
<!DOCTYPE user SYSTEM "EmailUser.dtd">
<user>
    <name/>
    <email/>
    <display>
        <rows/>
        <columns/>
    </display>
    <password/>
</user>
```

A user profile will look like this:

```
<?xml version="1.0" encoding="UTF-8"?>
<!DOCTYPE user SYSTEM "EmailUser.dtd">
<user>
    <name>some one</name>
    <email>someone@company.com</email>
    <display>
        <rows>10</rows>
        <columns>60</columns>
    </display>
    <password>someone</password>
</user>
```

The data contained by <name> and <email> is used to build the **From** header of the e-mail messages. The <rows> and <columns> elements grouped by <display> are used to customize the HTML form, which lets the user compose e-mail messages. The data of the <password> element is used to authenticate the user.

The UserBean Class

This maintains data about users and also implements the logic for managing the users. It is marked with java.io.Serializable in order to conform to the JavaBeans specification and also provides get and set methods for its properties: loginName, name, email, rows, columns and password:

```
import org.xml.sax.SAXException;

import java.io.*;

public class UserBean implements java.io.Serializable {
   public static final int DEFAULT_ROWS = 10;
   public static final int DEFAULT_COLUMNS = 60;
   private String loginName;
   private String name;
   private String email;
   private int rows;
   private int columns;
   private String password;
```

The constructor of this class sets the default values of the properties:

```
public UserBean() {
   setName("");
   setEmail("");
   setRows(UserBean.DEFAULT_ROWS);
   setColumns(UserBean.DEFAULT_COLUMNS);
   setPassword("");
}
```

A UserBean instance is created for each user of the web application. This instance is accessed as a session bean within the JSP pages. Since a user can open multiple windows of the same browser instance and request JSP pages of this application, the same UserBean instance can be accessed from concurrent threads. In order to make it thread safe, all its methods were declared synchronized.

The login() method gets the users' directory, a login name and a password as parameters. The login name and the password must neither be null nor empty strings. In addition, a file whose name coincides with the given login name, must exist within the users' directory. If all these conditions are met, the Descriptor class is used to parse the XML user profile. The true value of the second parameter of the Descriptor() constructor tells the framework to use a validating parser. This way, we know that all the user's options are present. If the password loaded from the XML file isn't the same as the password passed as parameter, the login() method returns the Incorrect password message. Otherwise, the user's options are extracted from the XML profile using the getData() method of Descriptor. The rows and columns options must be converted to numeric values using Integer.parseInt(). Default values are used if the numeric conversions fail:

```
public synchronized String login(String usersDir, String loginName,
                                 String password) {
  if (loginName == null || loginName.length() == 0) {
    return "Missing login name";
  }
  if (password == null || password.length() == 0) {
    return "Missing password";
  }
  File file = new File(usersDir, loginName);
  if (!file.exists()) {
    return "Unknown user";
  }
  try {
    Descriptor user = new Descriptor(file, true);
    if (!password.equals(user.getData("/user/password"))) {
      return "Incorrect password";
    }
    name = user.getData("/user/name");
    email = user.getData("/user/email");
    try {
      rows = Integer.parseInt(user.getData("/user/display/rows"));
    } catch (NumberFormatException e) {
      rows = DEFAULT_ROWS;
    }
    try {
      columns = Integer.parseInt(user.getData("/user/display/columns"));
    } catch (NumberFormatException e) {
      columns = DEFAULT_COLUMNS;
    }
    this.loginName = loginName;
    this.password = password;
  } catch (IOException e) {
    return e.getMessage();
  } catch (SAXException e) {
    if (e.getException() != null) {
      return e.getException().toString();
    }
    return e.getMessage();
  }
  return null;
}
```

A user profile must be saved when the options are updated, and also the profile of a new user must be saved after registration. The save() method takes the users' directory and the configuration directory as parameters. First of all, it uses our framework to load and parse the EmailUser.xml template from the configuration directory. This template is filled with the values of the properties of this object: name, email, rows, columns and password. In the end, the user's profile is saved in the users' directory to an XML file whose name coincides with the user's login name. The second argument of the save() call is false because the template's content had been already indented when it was loaded and parsed. The EmailUser.dtd file is used as external DTD:

```
public synchronized String save(String usersDir, String configDir) {
  try {
    Descriptor user = new Descriptor(new File(configDir, "EmailUser.xml"),
                                     true);
    user.addData("/user/name", name);
    user.addData("/user/email", email);
    user.addData("/user/display/rows", Integer.toString(rows));
    user.addData("/user/display/columns", Integer.toString(columns));
    user.addData("/user/password", password);
    File file = new File(usersDir, loginName);
    user.save(file, false, null, "EmailUser.dtd");
  } catch (IOException e) {
    return e.getMessage();
  } catch (SAXException e) {
    if (e.getException() != null) {
      return e.getException().toString();
    }
    return e.getMessage();
  }
  return null;
}
```

The next method updates the user options, whose new values are taken as parameter variables. During the validation of the new values, error messages are collected to a `StringBuffer`. For a successful update, all new values must be non-null non-empty strings. In addition, the `rowsStr` and `columnsStr` parameters must have numeric values. The user profile is saved if no error has occurred and the value of the `loginName` property isn't `null`:

```
public synchronized String update(String usersDir, String configDir,
                                  String name, String email,
                                  String rowsStr, String columnsStr,
                                  String password) {
  StringBuffer buf = new StringBuffer();
  if (name != null && name.length() > 0) {
    setName(name);
  } else {
    buf.append("Missing name<BR>");
  }
  if (email != null && email.length() > 0) {
    setEmail(email);
  } else {
    buf.append("Missing email<BR>");
  }
  if (rowsStr != null && rowsStr.length() > 0) {
    try {
      int rows = Integer.parseInt(rowsStr);
      if (rows > 0) {
        setRows(rows);
      } else {
        buf.append("Invalid rows<BR>");
      }
    } catch (NumberFormatException e) {
      buf.append("Invalid rows<BR>");
    }
```

```
    } else {
      buf.append("Missing rows<BR>");
    }
    if (columnsStr != null && columnsStr.length() > 0) {
      try {
        int columns = Integer.parseInt(columnsStr);
        if (columns > 0) {
          setColumns(columns);
        } else {
          buf.append("Invalid columns<BR>");
        }
      } catch (NumberFormatException e) {
        buf.append("Invalid columns<BR>");
      }
    } else {
      buf.append("Missing columns<BR>");
    }
    if (password != null && password.length() > 0) {
      setPassword(password);
    } else {
      buf.append("Missing password<BR>");
    }
    if (buf.length() > 0) {

      // Remove the last <BR>
      buf.setLength(buf.length() - 4);
      return buf.toString();
    } else {
      if (getLoginName() != null) {
        return save(usersDir, configDir);
      }
      return null;
    }
  }
}
```

The following method registers a new user, whose options are passed as parameters, along with the users' directory, the configuration directory and the login name. During the registration, any error message is added to a `StringBuffer`. For a successful registration, the login name must be non-null, non-empty, composed only from letters and digits and it must be new, of course. (The registration fails if the login name is already in use.) In addition, the user's options, which are passed to the `update()` method, must be valid too. The user profile is saved if no error has occurred:

```
public synchronized String register(String usersDir, String configDir,
                                    String loginName, String name,
                                    String email, String rowsStr,
                                    String columnsStr, String password) {
  StringBuffer buf = new StringBuffer();
  if (loginName != null && loginName.length() > 0) {
    for (int i = 0; i < loginName.length(); i++) {
      char ch = loginName.charAt(i);
      if (!Character.isLetterOrDigit(ch)) {
        buf.append("Invalid login name: ");
        buf.append(loginName);
        loginName = null;
        break;
```

```
        }
      }
      if (loginName != null && new File(usersDir, loginName).exists()) {
        buf.append("Existent user: ");
        buf.append(loginName);
        loginName = null;
      }
    } else {
      buf.append("Missing login name");
    }
    String updateMsg = update(usersDir, configDir, name, email, rowsStr,
                              columnsStr, password);
    if (updateMsg != null) {
      if (buf.length() > 0) {
        buf.append("<BR>");
      }
      buf.append(updateMsg);
    }
    if (buf.length() > 0) {
      return buf.toString();
    } else {
      if (loginName != null) {
        setLoginName(loginName);
        return save(usersDir, configDir);
      }
      return null;
    }
  }
}
```

This gets the login name:

```
public synchronized String getLoginName() {
    return this.loginName;
}
```

This sets the login name:

```
public synchronized void setLoginName(String value) {
    this.loginName = value;
}
```

This gets the name of the user:

```
public synchronized String getName() {
    return this.name;
}
```

This sets the name of the user:

```
public synchronized void setName(String value) {
    this.name = value;
}
```

This gets the user's e-mail address:

```
public synchronized String getEmail() {
    return this.email;
}
```

This sets the user's e-mail address:

```
public synchronized void setEmail(String value) {
    this.email = value;
}
```

This gets the number of rows used in the e-mail form for the text area:

```
public synchronized int getRows() {
    return this.rows;
}
```

This sets the number of rows used in the e-mail form for the text area:

```
public synchronized void setRows(int value) {
    this.rows = value;
}
```

This gets the number of columns used in the e-mail form for the text area and input fields:

```
public synchronized int getColumns() {
    return this.columns;
}
```

This sets the number of columns used in the e-mail form for the text area and input fields:

```
public synchronized void setColumns(int value) {
    this.columns = value;
}
```

This gets the user's password:

```
public synchronized String getPassword() {
    return this.password;
}
```

This sets the user's password:

```
public synchronized void setPassword(String value) {
    this.password = value;
}
}
```

The Login JSP

The `login.jsp` page builds the login form and handles the data submitted with this form.

The first line declares the scripting language and the classes used by the Java code:

```
<%@ page language="java" import="UserBean, EmailAdmin" %>
```

The options of each user are maintained by a `UserBean` instance, across the whole user's session. If the user has already accessed pages of this application and has requested this login page without logging out first, the `UserBean` session bean already exists. This object must be removed from the `session` object, which is an instance of `javax.servlet.http.HttpSession`, using the `removeValue()` method. This way, the user can login again, perhaps with a different name:

```
<% session.removeValue("userBean"); %>
```

With the previous line, we ensured that the current session doesn't have a `UserBean` instance. The next line creates such an instance, makes it available to the following Java code as a local variable called `userBean` and also binds this object to the current session using the `userBean` ID:

```
<jsp:useBean id="userBean" scope="session" class="UserBean"/>
```

The next Java scriptlet handles the form data if the HTTP method is `POST`. The users' directory is obtained using the `EmailAdmin` class, introduced in the previous section. This directory is translated to a system path using the `application.getRealPath()` call. The login name and the password are obtained using `request.getParameter()` calls. If the `login()` method of the `userBean` object returns no error message, the user is redirected to the e-mail page, presented in a later section. Since the `response.sendRedirect()` call needs an absolute URL, we get the absolute URL of the current request using `HttpUtils.getRequestURL(request)` and then we replace `login.jsp` with `email.jsp`:

```
<%
    String message = null;
    if (request.getMethod().toUpperCase().equals("POST")) {
        String usersDir = EmailAdmin.getUsersDir();
        if (!usersDir.startsWith("/"))
            usersDir = "/" + usersDir;
        usersDir = application.getRealPath(usersDir);
        String loginName = request.getParameter("loginName");
        String password = request.getParameter("password");
        message = userBean.login(usersDir, loginName, password);
        if (message == null) {
            // Redirect to email.jsp
            StringBuffer url = HttpUtils.getRequestURL(request);
            int i = url.length() - 1;
            while (i >= 0 && url.charAt(i) != '/') i--;
            url.setLength(i+1);
            url.append("email.jsp");
            response.sendRedirect(url.toString());
        }
    }
%>
```

The login form contains two input fields for the login name and password and a link to the registration form. Any message returned by a login failure is inserted just above this form:

```
<HTML>
<HEAD><TITLE>Login</TITLE></HEAD>
<BODY>

<H1>Login</H1>

<P><B><%= message == null ? "" : message %></B></P>

<FORM METHOD="POST">
<P>Login Name:<BR>
<INPUT TYPE="TEXT" NAME="loginName" SIZE="20">
</P>
<P>Password:<BR>
<INPUT TYPE="PASSWORD" NAME="password" SIZE="20">
</P>
<P>
<INPUT TYPE="SUBMIT" VALUE="Login">
</P>
</FORM>
<P><A HREF="register.jsp">New User</A></P>
<P>Your browser must support cookies.</P>
</BODY>
</HTML>
```

The login form is shown above, and should be the first form we see as we point our web browser at our web application's address.

The EmailBean class

This class maintains data about an e-mail message and also implements the routine for sending e-mail messages. It is marked with `java.io.Serializable` in order to conform to the JavaBeans specification and also provides get and set methods for its properties: to, cc, bcc, subject and content:

```
import javax.mail.Message;
import javax.mail.Session;
import javax.mail.Transport;
import javax.mail.internet.InternetAddress;
import javax.mail.internet.MimeMessage;

import java.util.Date;
import java.util.Properties;

public class EmailBean implements java.io.Serializable {
  private String to;
  private String cc;
  private String bcc;
  private String subject;
  private String content;
```

The constructor calls the `clear()` method to initialize all fields with empty strings:

```
public EmailBean() {
  clear();
}
```

This clears the values of the fields:

```
public void clear() {
  to = "";
  cc = "";
  bcc = "";
  subject = "";
  content = "";
}
```

The `send()` method takes a `UserBean` object and e-mails the message on behalf of the given user. It uses Sun's implementation of the JavaMail API to:

❑   Get the default mail session

❑   Construct the e-mail message

❑   Send the e-mail message

The mail session has nothing to do with the HTTP session used by the JSP pages. The `javax.mail.Session` class used below collects properties used by the JavaMail API. The only property we need to set is `mail.smtp.host` whose value is obtained using the `EmailAdmin` class introduced in a previous section. The default mail session is shared by all users of our application, and possibly by other applications running within the same JVM.

Once we have the mail `session` object, we can create an instance of the `javax.mail.internet.MimeMessage` class, set the From address, set the To, CC and BCC recipients and finally, set the subject, content and date of the message.

The `Transport.send(msg)` call will send the message via the SMTP host whose name was obtained from the configuration file of our application:

```
public String send(UserBean userBean) {
  try {

    // Get the default session
    Properties props = new Properties();
    props.put("mail.smtp.host", EmailAdmin.getMailHost());
    Session session = Session.getDefaultInstance(props, null);

    // Construct the e-mail message
    Message msg = new MimeMessage(session);
    msg.setFrom(new InternetAddress(userBean.getEmail(),
                                    userBean.getName()));
    if (to.length() > 0) {
      msg.setRecipients(Message.RecipientType.TO,
                        InternetAddress.parse(to, false));
    }
```

```
      if (cc.length() > 0) {
        msg.setRecipients(Message.RecipientType.CC,
                          InternetAddress.parse(cc, false));
      }
      if (bcc.length() > 0) {
        msg.setRecipients(Message.RecipientType.BCC,
                          InternetAddress.parse(bcc, false));
      }
      msg.setSubject(subject);
      msg.setText(content);
      msg.setSentDate(new Date());

      // Send the message
      Transport.send(msg);
    } catch (Exception e) {
      return e.getMessage();
    }
    return null;
  }
```

This gets the to e-mail address:

```
      public String getTo() {
          return this.to;
      }
```

This sets the to e-mail address:

```
      public void setTo(String value) {
          if (value == null)
              value = "";
          this.to = value;
      }
```

This gets the cc e-mail address:

```
      public String getCc() {
          return this.cc;
      }
```

This sets the cc e-mail address:

```
      public void setCc(String value) {
          if (value == null)
              value = "";
          this.cc = value;
      }
```

This gets the bcc e-mail address:

```
      public String getBcc() {
          return this.bcc;
      }
```

This sets the bcc e-mail address:

```
public void setBcc(String value) {
    if (value == null)
        value = "";
    this.bcc = value;
}
```

This gets the subject of the message:

```
public String getSubject() {
    return this.subject;
}
```

This sets the subject of the message:

```
public void setSubject(String value) {
    if (value == null)
        value = "";
    this.subject = value;
}
```

This gets the content of the message:

```
public String getContent() {
    return this.content;
}
```

This sets the content of the message:

```
public void setContent(String value) {
    if (value == null)
        value = "";
    this.content = value;
}
}
```

The Header JSP

The header.jsp page is never invoked directly by users. Instead it is included within the email.jsp and options.jsp pages presented in the next sections.

The first line declares the scripting language and the only class used by the Java code:

```
<%@ page language="java" import="UserBean" %>
```

The next line gets the UserBean session object created and initialized by the login.jsp page. A reference to this object is made available to the following Java code as a local variable called userBean:

```
<jsp:useBean id="userBean" scope="session" class="UserBean"/>
```

Then we show the name and the e-mail address of the user:

```
<P><%= userBean.getName() %> - <%= userBean.getEmail() %></P>
```

The simple navigation bar of the application provides links to email.jsp, options.jsp and logout.jsp:

```
<P>
<A HREF="email.jsp">Email</A>   
<A HREF="options.jsp">Options</A>   
<A HREF="logout.jsp">Logout</A>
</P>
```

The Email JSP

The email.jsp page builds the e-mail form and handles the data submitted with this form.

The first line declares the scripting language and the classes used by the Java code:

```
<%@ page language="java" import="EmailBean, UserBean" %>
```

The next line gets the UserBean session object created and initialized by the login.jsp page. A reference to this object is made available to the following Java code as a local variable called userBean:

```
<jsp:useBean id="userBean" scope="session" class="UserBean"/>
```

If the user requests the email.jsp directly, without going through the login process, the user is redirected to the login page presented in a previous section. Since the response.sendRedirect() call needs an absolute URL, we get the absolute URL of the current request using HttpUtils.getRequestURL(request) and then we replace email.jsp with login.jsp:

```
<%
if (userBean.getLoginName() == null) {
    // Redirect to login.jsp
    StringBuffer url = HttpUtils.getRequestURL(request);
    int i = url.length() - 1;
    while (i >= 0 && url.charAt(i) != '/') i--;
    url.setLength(i+1);
    url.append("login.jsp");
    response.sendRedirect(url.toString());
}
%>
```

The next line creates an EmailBean object, whose reference is made available to the following Java code as a local variable called emailBean. Such an object is created for each request of email.jsp, no matter if the HTTP method is GET or POST:

```
<jsp:useBean id="emailBean" scope="request" class="EmailBean"/>
```

If the HTTP method is POST, the next Java scriptlet gets the values of the request parameters and sets the properties of the EmailBean instance. Then it tries to send the e-mail message to its recipients using the emailBean.send(userBean) call. If no error message is returned the properties of the bean object are cleared. Otherwise, their values are preserved so that the user can correct the error without having to refill the whole form:

```
<%
    String message = null;
    if (request.getMethod().toUpperCase().equals("POST")) {
        emailBean.setTo(request.getParameter("to"));
        emailBean.setCc(request.getParameter("cc"));
        emailBean.setBcc(request.getParameter("bcc"));
        emailBean.setSubject(request.getParameter("subject"));
        emailBean.setContent(request.getParameter("content"));
        message = emailBean.send(userBean);
        if (message == null) {
            message = "The message was sent";
            emailBean.clear();
        }
    }
%>
```

The HTML markup produced by this JSP will contain the application's header, a possible error message and an HTML form that lets the user compose a message. The size of the input fields is given by userBean.getColumns(). The number of rows and columns of the text area are set to userBean.getRows() and userBean.getColumns(). This way, the user may customize the look of this page. The values of the form elements are set to the properties of the EmailBean instance, so that they can be preserved after failing to send a message due to an error reported by JavaMail and shown at the beginning of the page.

```
<HTML>
<HEAD><TITLE>Email</TITLE></HEAD>
<BODY>

<H1>Email</H1>

<jsp:include page="header.jsp" flush="true"/>

<P><B><%= message == null ? "" : message %></B></P>

<FORM METHOD="POST">
<TABLE>
    <TR>
        <TD>TO:</TD>
        <TD><INPUT TYPE="TEXT" NAME="to"
            SIZE="<%= userBean.getColumns() %>"
            VALUE="<%= emailBean.getTo() %>"></TD>
    </TR>
    <TR>
        <TD>CC:</TD>
        <TD><INPUT TYPE="TEXT" NAME="cc"
            SIZE="<%= userBean.getColumns() %>"
            VALUE="<%= emailBean.getCc() %>"></TD>
    </TR>
```

```
        <TR>
            <TD>BCC:</TD>
            <TD><INPUT TYPE="TEXT" NAME="bcc"
                SIZE="<%= userBean.getColumns() %>"
                VALUE="<%= emailBean.getBcc() %>"></TD>
        </TR>
        <TR>
            <TD>Subject:</TD>
            <TD><INPUT TYPE="TEXT" NAME="subject"
                SIZE="<%= userBean.getColumns() %>"
                VALUE="<%= emailBean.getSubject() %>"></TD>
        </TR>
        <TR>
            <TD> </TD>
            <TD><TEXTAREA NAME="content"
                ROWS="<%= userBean.getRows() %>"
                COLS="<%= userBean.getColumns() %>"
                ><%= emailBean.getContent() %></TEXTAREA></TD>
        </TR>
        <TR>
            <TD> </TD>
            <TD><INPUT TYPE="SUBMIT" VALUE="Send"><TD>
        </TR>
    </TABLE>
    </FORM>
    </BODY>
    </HTML>
```

The e-mail form will look like this:

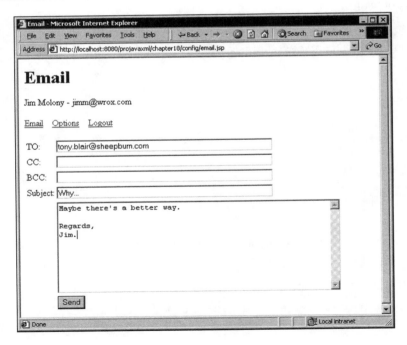

The Options JSP

The `options.jsp` page builds the options and registration forms and handles the data submitted with these forms.

The first line declares the scripting language and the classes used by the Java code:

```
<%@ page language="java" import="UserBean, EmailAdmin" %>
```

The next line gets the `UserBean` session object created and initialized by the `login.jsp` page. A reference to this object is made available to the following Java code as a local variable called `userBean`:

```
<jsp:useBean id="userBean" scope="session" class="UserBean"/>
```

This page is also used as a registration form. The `register` flag will be `true` in this case:

```
<% boolean register = userBean.getLoginName() == null; %>
```

If the HTTP method is `POST`, the next scriptlet gets the users and configuration directories, and converts them to system paths using `application.getRealPath()`. Whether the application is registering a new user or it lets an existent user change its options, the request parameters are stored in local variables. Depending on the value of the `register` flag, one of the `register()` and `update()` methods of the `UserBean` session object is called. After that, the user is redirected to the e-mail page, presented in a previous section:

```
<%
    String message = null;
    String loginName = null;
    if (request.getMethod().toUpperCase().equals("POST")) {
        String usersDir = EmailAdmin.getUsersDir();
        if (!usersDir.startsWith("/"))
            usersDir = "/" + usersDir;
        usersDir = application.getRealPath(usersDir);
        String configDir = EmailAdmin.getConfigDir();
        if (!configDir.startsWith("/"))
            configDir = "/" + configDir;
        configDir = application.getRealPath(configDir);
        loginName = request.getParameter("loginName");
        if (!register && loginName != null && loginName.length() > 0)
            register = true;
        String name = request.getParameter("name");
        String email = request.getParameter("email");
        String rows = request.getParameter("rows");
        String columns = request.getParameter("columns");
        String password = request.getParameter("password");
        if (register)
            message = userBean.register(usersDir, configDir,
                    loginName, name, email, rows, columns, password);
        else
            message = userBean.update(usersDir, configDir,
                    name, email, rows, columns, password);
        if (message == null) {
```

```
                      // Redirect to email.jsp
                      StringBuffer url = HttpUtils.getRequestURL(request);
                      int i = url.length() - 1;
                      while (i >= 0 && url.charAt(i) != '/') i--;
                      url.setLength(i+1);
                      url.append("email.jsp");
                      response.sendRedirect(url.toString());
                  }
              }
      %>
```

The application's header is not included if a new user is registered. In this case, the HTML form contains an additional field called `loginName`. The form includes input fields for all properties of the `UserBean` class: `name`, `email`, `rows`, `columns` and `password`. The values of these properties are inserted as default values for the input fields. This way, the user doesn't have to retype all the options in case he/she wants to change only one option:

```
<HTML>
<HEAD><TITLE><%= register ? "Register" : "Options" %></TITLE></HEAD>
<BODY>

<H1><%= register ? "Register" : "Options" %></H1>

<% if (!register) { %>
<jsp:include page="header.jsp" flush="true"/>
<% } %>

<P><B><%= message == null ? "" : message %></B></P>

<FORM METHOD="POST">

<% if (register) { %>

<P>Login Name:<BR>
<INPUT TYPE="TEXT" NAME="loginName" SIZE="20"
    VALUE="<%= loginName == null ? "" : loginName %>">
<BR>Use only letters and digits
</P>

<% } %>

<P>Your Name:<BR>
<INPUT TYPE="TEXT" NAME="name" SIZE="40"
    VALUE="<%= userBean.getName() %>">
</P>

<P>Email Address:<BR>
<INPUT TYPE="TEXT" NAME="email" SIZE="40"
    VALUE="<%= userBean.getEmail() %>">
</P>

<P>Display:</P>
<BLOCKQUOTE>
```

```
<P>Rows:<BR>
<INPUT TYPE="TEXT" NAME="rows" SIZE="3"
    VALUE="<%= userBean.getRows() %>">
</P>

<P>Columns:<BR>
<INPUT TYPE="TEXT" NAME="columns" SIZE="3"
    VALUE="<%= userBean.getColumns() %>">
</P>

</BLOCKQUOTE>

<P>Password:<BR>
<INPUT TYPE="PASSWORD" NAME="password" SIZE="20"
    VALUE="<%= userBean.getPassword() %>">
</P>

<P>
<INPUT TYPE="SUBMIT"
    VALUE="<%= register ? "Register" : "Save Options" %>">
</P>

</FORM>
</BODY>
</HTML>
```

The options form will look like this:

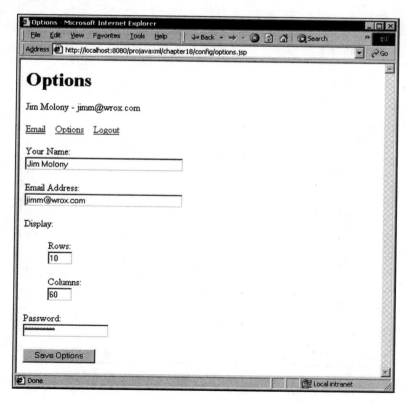

The Register JSP

New users will request this page in order to register. The login.jsp page provides a link to register.jsp:

The first line declares the scripting language, which is Java, of course:

```
<%@ page language="java" %>
```

We remove the user bean from the session object, just in case one has already used the application and wants to register as a new user:

```
<% session.removeValue("userBean"); %>
```

The request is forwarded to the options.jsp page, which will handle the registration process:

```
<jsp:forward page="options.jsp"/>
```

The registration form will look like this:

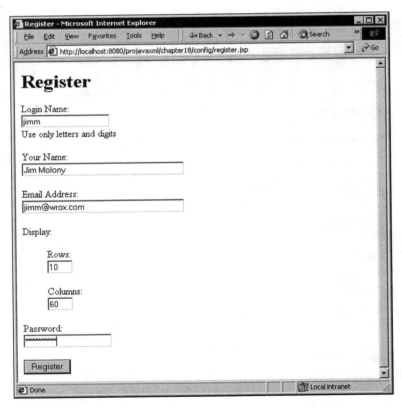

The Logout JSP

This page simply calls `session.invalidate()`, shows a logout message and provides a link to the login page in case the user wants to return to our application:

```
<%@ page language="java" %>
<% session.invalidate(); %>

<HTML>
<HEAD><TITLE>Login</TITLE></HEAD>
<BODY>

<H1>Logout</H1>

<P>Thank you for using the email application</P>

<P><A HREF="login.jsp">Return</A></P>

</BODY>
</HTML>
```

The logout page will look like this:

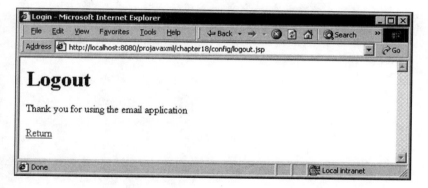

Summary

All descriptors used by J2EE are now based on XML. XML proves to be the best solution for storing configuration parameters because of its many advantages: extensibility, portability and human readability. This chapter has shown how to easily create and parse XML descriptors using DOM and XPath, and explanations have been offered as to why this is a good solution.

In this chapter, we developed a framework and used it for simple examples. Then we built a web application that uses XML-based user profiles. We studied the main configuration and deployment issues, their solutions, how others are using XML in this domain and how we can use our own XML descriptors and configuration files.

In the next chapter, we will be approaching the problem of protocols and communications.

The Xerces Blue
Butterfly, which became
extinct earlier this century,
and after which the Xerces XML
parser is named ···

19

XML Protocols and Communications

One vast application area for XML is in communications, more specifically in the area of application-level protocols – protocols that enable applications to talk to one another. In this chapter, we will explore how the developments in XML have had a great influence over the design of modern application protocols, and how XML has since evolved to be the language of choice for data encoding within these protocols.

Application protocols have evolved from the early, simple, fixed-purpose protocols (such as FTP, TELNET, or SMTP) to the current dynamically generated API-driven, mostly proprietary protocols that are used in the modern distributed computing world (Distributed COM, CORBA, RMI). Interoperability between dissimilar systems over the network, and the need to keep protocols simple to operate (and public pressure for true open definition) has prompted the protocol designers to take a step backwards and integrate XML. We will see what communications protocols are, how they work classically, and why these classic protocols are designed the way they are.

The design of robust, open, and interoperable XML-based application protocols does not have to remain within the realm of expert protocol designers. We will show you how you can leverage your XML knowledge to design application protocols for your very next project. We also include a detailed look at three examples of contemporary protocols that have XML at their core – all of which are extensible and can be applied immediately.

The best part is that we will be getting some hands-on experience of programming with each of these protocols using Java. We will be coding clients (consumers) and servers (listeners) for each of these protocols, to gain a solid appreciation for how they can work within Java systems today.

From here onwards we will refer to server-client communication. The server processes the client request and will usually return a value as a result of this process. The client in this case is the calling function or method, which requires some processing to be done from the server. Please note we will use function and method interchangeably henceforth as referring to a unit of processing.

What You Will Need

This chapter assumes that you're reasonably fluent in Java programming, understand basic web concepts such as HTTP and CGI, and have been following the chapters in this book thus far, and working on the examples. It will help if you've dabbled in Java network programming (sockets, RMI, CORBA, JINI, etc.) before, but it is not necessary.

In order to run the examples in this chapter you will need the following:

- ❏ The Java XMLRPC JARs, written by Hannes Wallenöfer, which can be downloaded from http://classic.helma.at/hannes/xmlrpc/. This download includes a small-footprint open source parser and an integrated RPC web server.

- ❏ You will need to have the Xerces XML parser, which can be found at http://xml.apache.org/xerces-j/index.html for those of you who have skipped ahead to this chapter.

- ❏ The latest Apache SOAP distribution, which may be found at http://xml.apache.org/soap/index.html.

- ❏ The last section of the book deals with the BXXP specification, about which further information can be found at http://www.bxxp.org. We will be using its SpaceKit to develop an application. We will cover downloading and installation of this package in more detail later.

In general, further instructions on downloading and installation will be provided as and when they are needed. Please note that the test machine is assumed to be a Windows NT PC. Unix users are usually more aware of their system setup and should therefore be able to map these instructions to their system without too much trouble.

In most cases we will refer to paths relative to the installation directory; in Tomcat's case this will be <TOMCAT_HOME>, whereas the installation directory for the JDK will be denoted by <JAVA_HOME>. The installation for the download code will be assumed to be in the root directory and will be referred to as \ProJavaXML\Chapter19; please add the path to this directory as appropriate.

All About Communications Protocols

Communications protocols are well-defined conventions that allow machines to communicate with each other (nowadays, mostly over the network). As developers, we benefit from communications protocols every single day. Our browsers use HTTP protocol daily. We may transfer files from a remote system using the FTP protocol. The entire Internet is working over the venerable TCP/IP protocol.

Java RMI uses either the JRMP or IIOP protocols, and the new wireless LAN card and point of presence are using the IEEE 802.11b protocol. Obviously, while all of these are examples of communications protocols, they are very different in nature. The unifying aspect that ties all of them together is the Open Systems Interconnect (OSI) seven layer model by the ISO (International Organization for Standardization).

The diagram below shows this layered model:

```
The OSI Layer Reference Model
┌─────────────────────────────┐
│      Application Layer       │
├─────────────────────────────┤
│      Presentation Layer      │
├─────────────────────────────┤
│        Session Layer         │
├─────────────────────────────┤
│       Transport Layer        │
├─────────────────────────────┤
│        Network Layer         │
├─────────────────────────────┤
│       Data Link Layer        │
├─────────────────────────────┤
│        Physical Layer        │
└─────────────────────────────┘
```

From the bottom up, these layers are as follows:

The **physical layer** describes how the bits are transmitted, while the **data link layer** is concerned with blocking, synchronization, and error and flow control. In some cases, this layer is combined with the physical layer to form a "media access" layer. The physical layer is determined by the actual physical hardware used in TCP/IP communications. For example, it may be Ethernet, token ring, serial line, or wireless.

The networking driver provides data link layer functionality on the physical medium and allows IP implementation to be completely independent of the underlying transmission medium. As developers, we are not often concerned with these layers, as they live in the province of the driver programmer. It is the remaining layers that begin to enter into our domain.

The **network layer** is built on top of the data link layer to provide an abstraction of the lower layers to a connection-based view; X.25 and IP are examples of this protocol. The network layer determines how a connection is made and destroyed between machines over the data link layer – potentially spanning multiple nodes over a network.

The **transport layer** implements the reliable transfer of data between the two endpoints on the network, and it addresses end-to-end error recovery and flow control. The **session layer**, meanwhile, provides an application-level view of the connection. For the sake of argument, we could say TCP sits somewhere between the session and transport layers.

The **presentation layer** decouples the **application layer** from dependence on specific structured data representations, which may mean translating the data into another format. Finally, the application layer interacts with users or services. HTTP, FTP, and SMTP are some examples of application layer protocols.

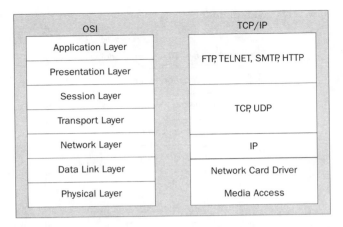

Each layer in the model is loosely coupled to the layer above and below it. The interface between the layers should be well specified, and layers can be replaced or re-implemented without requiring changes to the immediate neighboring layers.

Not all protocol stacks implement all seven layers of the OSI reference model. A committee-designed reference model, after all, is just that – a reference model. In the real world, the pragmatic protocol implementer has to worry about design issues such as performance degradation due to excessive layering, and also the purpose and intended applications of the final protocol stack. In practice, the functionality embodied in adjacent OSI layers is combined.

Communications Between Layers

According to the OSI model, each layer communicates only with the layer above it and below it. At whatever layer in the stack you are, though, it appears that the equivalent layers are communicating directly with each other. The diagram below illustrates this logical view of communications enabled by the model:

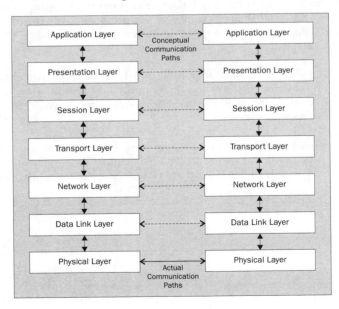

Conceptually, an application communicates directly with another application. In fact, of course, all of the layers below the application are working to make this happen. Each layer is virtually talking to its peer on the destination stack, and the layers below enable this.

Data Propagation – Frames and Headers

Because the OSI model was specified in a time when leased lines, direct line connection, and switching networks were in the mainstream of data communications, it was envisioned that data would be passed between the layer in frames. Each successive layer adds to the frame by appending its own header information.

The header information is meaningful to its counterpart at the destination communications stack. The diagram below illustrates this in action – notice that the lower layers increase the size of the actual data transmitted by appending their own headers.

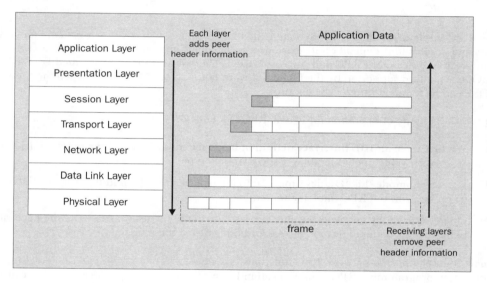

XML and Communications Protocols

Both the OSI model and TCP/IP protocol stack were designed long before applying XML to protocol design was conceived, and the current state of play is that in today's TCP/IP implementation, the application layer is actually a combination of the presentation and application layers. This is mainly due to:

❑ The slow development of open interoperable application-level protocols under the TCP/IP model

❑ The absence of a non-proprietary, universal way to represent structured data that can form the basis of a reasonable, useful and significantly generic presentation layer

Clearly, this second point is one of the main drivers behind the emergence of XML. In fact, now that XML is commonplace and is becoming better understood by the software design community, we see the emergence of a presentation layer protocol for applications. This is where the protocols covered in this chapter fit into the protocol stack.

XML's real usefulness is in the presentation and application layers of the OSI reference stack. XML's ability to express structured data in a machine-neutral way lends itself for deployment for the protocols in this layer.

We will now examine three mainstream examples of this application of XML. The first one we will look at is **XML-based Remote Procedure Calls** or **XMLRPC**.

Classic RPC

RPC enables software designers to make function or method calls across networks, which allows for rudimentary distributed applications over a network. Fundamentally, the RPC mechanism creates a new application -evel protocol for parts of an application to communicate with each other. Conceptually, an RPC call is identical in syntax to a local function call. To understand this further, we will need to delve deeper into RPC.

Today, RPC implementations are delivered as standard with most UNIX-based systems. In fact, many utilities and applications depend on its existence. RPC comes in many flavors – there are OS specific variants such as Sun's ONC RPC and Microsoft RPC. There is also the variant called DCE RPC. This is an X/Open standard supported by the Open Software Foundation (OSF), now called the Open Group (the OSF can be found at http://www.osf.org).

In all cases, the mode of operation for classic RPC is identical:

❑　We first write an **IDL (interface definition language)** description of the function, its arguments and return value, including their associated data types

❑　We now compile this IDL description into a language-specific binding using an IDL compiler (supplied with the RPC implementation)

❑　Once we have the language-specific classes, functions, or files we can write the necessary behavior for the functions or classes, for both sides of the interaction

Normally the relationship between RPC functions takes the form of a server-client interaction. Theoretically, programming RPC communication is equivalent to writing a local function call and implementing that function, excepting the generation of the IDL description. In practice, however, this is far from the truth. Because of transmission efficiency considerations, and differences in the ways that programming languages may alias variables, the typical RPC programmer has to be fully aware of how the underlying layer performs its task.

The RPC implementation takes the function call and marshals the arguments (packages them up in a form suitable for transmission over a network) passing them over the network to the server. The server then unmarshals the arguments and calls the function that implements the desired behavior; the return value is then subjected to the same marshaling – unmarshaling routine before being passed to the calling function.

The diagram below illustrates how classic RPC operates:

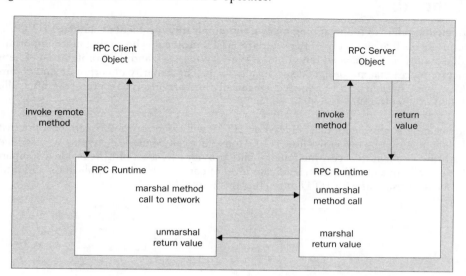

Because of the slightly different ways that each variant of RPC performs marshaling and unmarshaling, and also because of the use of different external data representations, dialects of RPC protocols are often not interoperable.

RPC operates in the same spirit as Java RMI. However, it differs from RMI in several key aspects:

❑   There is no object context – individual functions are called across the network as a remote API. RPC works over legacy C-based API, and there is no implicit way to retain state between calls; RMI accomplishes this naturally through the object context.

❑   There is no possibility of transferring behavior with data via RPC. Unlike RMI, the server cannot download additional classes from the client if it does not already have the code locally. RMI and Java allow us to program a class to call methods on that we have no previous knowledge of.

❑   Returning a call on the server side requires setting up the RPC server mechanism on both sides of the connection.

❑   The client and server can be implemented with totally different programming languages, on totally different operating systems

❑   There is no activation framework associated with RPC. If the server service is not already running, the call cannot be made (RMI can optionally bootstrap services across the network).

For more information on RMI please refer to Professional Java Server Programming J2EE Edition, *or alternatively look at the available material on* http://java.sun.com.

HTTP Tunneling

HTTP tunneling refers to the wrapping up of a communication protocol as standard HTTP. The ability to create protocols that sit on top of the standard HTTP protocol is becoming more important than ever. This is due mainly to the mass adoption of the World Wide Web and the proliferation of network infrastructure pieces that are designed specifically for it. The majority of corporate and commercial networks are now designed and optimized specifically for carrying HTTP protocol traffic, allowing any HTTP-based protocols to leverage their reach.

More importantly any protocol that is based on HTTP will safely travel through most pre-installed firewalls. The diagram below shows how HTTP tunneling can be used to create a web service that enables a browser client to access the functionality provided by a set of EJBs inside a company's firewall. Normally this would add a significant level of complexity to the application and introduce a potential security risk, but with HTTP tunneling this is avoided.

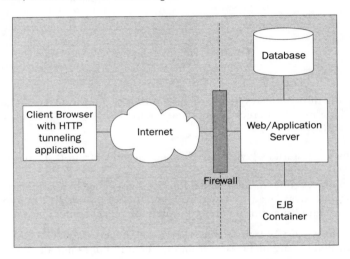

The XMLRPC Protocol

The XMLRPC protocol is designed to sit on top of the HTTP protocol. The interaction with applications is identical to that of a standard RPC:

❑ The client application makes a call

❑ The client stub marshals the call onto the transport as a message

❑ The server receives the message and unmarshals the call

❑ The server calls the function implementation

While XMLRPC is not an international standard, it is fast becoming the *de facto* standard for performing RPC-style operations over an HTTP tunnel.

> **Further information about XMLRPC (including the specification and the tools that you can use to put the technology into production use immediately) is available from: http://www.xmlrpc.com/**

Currently, toolkits are available for Java, C/C++, COM, PERL, PYTHON, TCL, PHP, LISP, BASIC, JavaScript, ASP and many other programming languages and environments. The wide availability of these programming toolkits makes this technology very accessible.

The Request Header Information

Since XMLRPC is typically tunneled through HTTP, XMLRPC defines very few additional requirements to a conventional HTTP POST operation. In fact, if an XMLRPC server is serving only XMLRPC traffic, there is no need to add additional header information. However, in most cases, a web server acts as a front-end for XMLRPC. In these cases, a URL can be specified that instructs the server to route the request. For example, here we are telling the web server to route the request to an application named \xmlrpc\ in the following POST header:

```
POST /xmlrpc HTTP/1.0
```

In Tomcat's case it will look for a web application called XMLRPC and failing that will check if there is a servlet in its root directory that maps to this URL. XMLRPC also requires several HTTP headers in order to operate correctly:

Header	Description
User-Agent	Describes the client
Host	Specifies the host and port
Content-Type	Must be text/xml
Content-Length	The content length in bytes

For example, here is a typical XMLRPC request header set when tunneled within an HTTP request:

```
POST /xmlrpc HTTP/1.0
User-Agent: Java1.3.0
Host: localhost:8081
Content-Type: text/xml
Content-length: 181
```

The Request Body

The body of an XMLRPC request is an XML document. The root element of the request is the <methodCall> element. The body of an XMLRPC response, naturally enough, is also an XML document. The root element of the response is the <methodResponse> element, which may have a different child element depending on the success or failure of the method call. A successfully called function will return a <methodReponse> whose child element is the <params> element while an error is denoted by the <fault> element.

789

A `<methodCall>` element is actually the XML encoding of the original procedure call. The most important aspect of this encoding is how the different types of arguments and return values are represented during the marshaling process. It is actually a rather straightforward way of implementing it. Each argument is encapsulated in an XML element whose tag name reflects the data type of the argument value.

Therefore:

```
<i4>3</i4>
```

represents an integer value of 3. And:

```
<string>This is a string.</string>
```

represents a string value.

The following table shows the available types for the XMLRPC protocol:

XMLRPC Data Type	Element	Java Data Type
integer, 32 bits	`<i4>` or `<int>`	`int`
string	`<string>` and by default	`String`
float number, double precision	`<double>`	`double`
boolean, '0' is false and '1' is true	`<boolean>`	`bool`
date – format is 20010801T22:22:00	`<dateTime.iso8601>`	Dependent on implementation
base 64 encoded binary	`<base64>`	Dependent on implementation

The `<dateTime>` does not have a time zone associated to it by default; this is implementation specific and you will need to refer to the specific documentation for further information.

The following XML document is a typical XMLRPC call. The example is equivalent to the following method call:

```
Rserver.processInput(41, "David James");
```

The corresponding XMLRPC request will have the following body:

```
<?xml version="1.0"?>
<methodCall>
  <methodName>RServer.processInput</methodName>
  <params>
    <param>
      <value>
        <i4>41</i4>
      </value>
    </param>
    <param>
      David James
    </param>
  </params>
</methodCall>
```

`<methodCall>` must have a `<methodName>` element as its child that contains the method name. The method name must be made up of upper case and lower case letters, numeric characters, underscores, dots, dashes, and colons only. It is up to the server to interpret this, so there is no reason why the value in `<methodName>` must map exactly to a function or method name. It may just as easily be a representation of a database query, to name but one possibility. Note that the second argument (or parameter) is not marked up and, by default, is assumed to be a string by XMLRPC.

Complex Data Types

XMLRPC also provides two complex data types, namely arrays and structures, as seen in C and C++. Languages that do not have structures will map this element to a language- (and often implementation-) specific format. Arrays can also be mapped to a language-specific data format in an implementation-specific way. For example, the java implementation that we will use in the example code for this section maps structure elements to `java.util.Hashtable` and RPC arrays to the `java.util.Vector` class.

Structures

Structures are defined inside a `<struct>` element with sub-elements called `<member>` indicating each field of the structure.

For instance, the following Java class:

```
public class myOwnDef {
    public int x;
    public int y;
    public bool finishFlag;
    public String name;
}
```

with values x=3, y=139, a finishFlag set to true, and name=Kim, will map to:

```
<struct>
  <member>
    <name>x</name>
    <value><i4>3</i4></value>
  </member>

  <member>
    <name>y</name>
    <value><i4>139</i4></value>
  </member>

  <member>
    <name>finishFlag</name>
    <value><boolean>1</boolean></value>
  </member>

  <member>
    <name>name</name>
    <value><string>Kim</string></value>
  </member>
</struct>
```

Structures can also have members that are themselves structures recursively. The specification does not define how null values should be represented and although this has been added in some implementations, this will obviously affect the platform/language independence of your application, especially in languages where a null value is not acceptable.

Arrays

To represent an array, we can use the `<array>` element in a similar way to the `<struct>` element, though with no named member. Here is the representation of an integer array:

```
<array>
  <data>
    <value><i4>234</i4></value>
    <value><i4>1</i4></value>
    <value><i4>15</i4></value>
  </data>
</array>
```

Which is equivalent to an array of three integer values, 234, 1, and 15, respectively. The RPC specifications do not specify that the values must be of the same data type, so we may freely mix data types.

The fault reporting for XMLRPC is layered on top of HTTP and does not trickle down as HTTP error codes do. That is, if there is no HTTP or lower level fault, the response always begins with:

```
200 OK
```

Application-level faults are reported via an XML element in the body of the response. As mentioned previously, a successful call will mean that a `<params>` child element is returned, and a single `<param>` child element is allowed for `<params>`. The `<value>` child element of the `<param>` element, of course, can be of any XMLRPC-supported data type.

The `<fault>` element contains a single `<value>` child element, and this value must contain a `<struct>` child element whose form matches that of the document below:

```
<?xml version="1.0"?>
<methodResponse>
  <fault>
    <value>
      <struct>
        <member>
          <name>faultCode</name>
          <value><int>4</int></value>
        </member>
        <member>
          <name>faultString</name>
          <value><string>Too many parameters.</string></value>
        </member>
      </struct>
    </value>
  </fault>
</methodResponse>
```

The first member variable of the fault structure is named `faultCode` and contains an implementation-specific error code, and the second is `faultString`, which contains a description of the error. You should note that although we have referred to them as the first and second arguments, XMLRPC does not consider members of a `<struct>` element to have precedence or order.

A Versatile Java XMLRPC Library

Having covered the surprisingly compact XMLRPC specification, you can see that it would be reasonably simple to create an implementation of the protocol using Java. However, several implementations already exist that are available to the XMLRPC development community.

One excellent implementation, supplying both client-side and server-side support, is a library from Hannes Wallenöfer. This implementation hides the IDL interface generation and compilation, mapping the method calls to XMLRPC at run-time. In this case the implementation maps the RPC data types as follows:

- ❏ `<dateTime.iso8601>` is mapped to the `java.util.Date` class
- ❏ The `<struct>` element is mapped to `java.util.HashTable`
- ❏ `<array>` maps to `java.util.Vector`
- ❏ `<base64>` maps to `byte[]`

Finally there is an additional element `<nil/>`, which is provided to represent the Java's `null` value. The latest version and documentation is located here:

http://classic.helma.at/hannes/xmlrpc

We will use this versatile library to implement our XMLRPC-based service and client, so you will need to download the latest release of this library from the URL above.

The system architecture for Hannes's library is illustrated in the figure below:

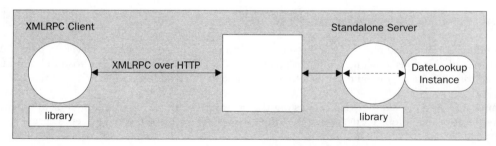

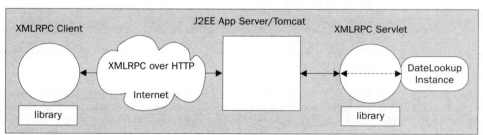

Notice that on the server side, you can use the simple standalone XMLRPC server that is supplied as part of the library, or you can opt to integrate it into another HTTP server's extension framework. For example, in J2EE, you can integrate Hannes's library with the servlet container. We will show how this can be accomplished with Tomcat – integration with any other commercial engine based on this reference will be similar. In other words, you can put XMLRPC to work for you in your J2EE application server today.

793

Installing the Library

The library comes in a ZIP file called xmlrpc-java.zip. At the time of writing, the latest version is 1.0 beta 4. To install the library, unzip the entire file into a path of your choice. In our case, we have placed it in the C:\ProJavaXML\Chapter19\ folder. You will need to set your classpath to include openxml-1.2.jar and xmlrpc.jar before running the examples as shown below:

```
set classpath=c:\ProJavaXML\Chapter19\xmlrpc-java\lib\openxml-
1.2.jar;c:\ProJavaXML\Chapter19\xmlrpc-java\lib\xmlrpc.jar;%classpath%;
```

You may need to change these values to reflect the path on your system.

> *The XMLRPC distribution works by default with the OpenXML parser from Exolab (an open source small-footprint XML parser). Version 1.2 of the parser is included with the XMLRPC distribution in the* openxml-1.1.jar *file that we have added to the classpath.*

Writing Our Own Standalone XMLRPC-Based Service

To begin, we will create an XMLRPC server that will use the standalone service provided by this library. To do this, we will need to be familiar with one key class in the library, helma.xmlrpc.WebServer, which implements a simple standalone web server for servicing XMLRPC requests.

There are several key methods in the helma.xmlrpc.WebServer class. To start the XMLRPC server running we must first call its constructor:

```
Webserver server = new Webserver(4505);
```

The argument is the local port to bind the server to, and in this case we start the server on port 4505. The constructor also accepts a second argument giving the IP address to bind to, if you wish to bind the server to an address in a multi-homed machine other than the default IP address associated with the localhost.

We must now add the handler that carries out the necessary work The first argument is of type string and represents a handler's name, which the client uses to locate the service. The server uses introspection to discover the methods to call.

```
server.addHandler("myhandler", myHandlerObject);
```

Finally, we would set up run conditions and call the server's run() command to begin listening for client requests, calling shutdown() to shut the server down.

The helma.xmlrpc.WebServer class also implements some simple security measures that allow us to specify IP addresses from which we wish to accept or deny requests. Users who want to handle the incoming XMLRPC requests at a lower level and do not want automatic invocation of class methods of a class instance can implement the helma.xmlrpc.XmlRpcHandler interface. Though these topics are beyond the scope of this chapter, interested readers are encouraged to explore these areas by examining the API documentation.

We will now go on to implement a server. First, we will create the class that contains the methods to be called remotely: the server object.

The simple `DateLookup` class has two methods. The `getServerDate()` method executes on the server and returns the current day and time as a string. The `addNumbers()` method adds two integers and returns the sum as an integer. While trivial in function, these methods will demonstrate how the various protocols perform method invocation, parameter passing, and return value processing. You will find the source code to `DateLookup.java` under the `\ProJavaXML\Chapter19\xmlrpc\server\` directory, and you should copy this `\xmlrpc\` directory under your own `\ProJavaXML\Chapter19\` directory, which you created under the root directory on your hard drive at the start of this chapter. This directory should contain the folders `server`, `client`, and `servlet`, but only `server` and `client` interest us in this particular example.

The content of the `server.java` file is presented below:

```java
import java.util.Calendar;

public class DateLookup {

  public String getServerDate() {
    return Calendar.getInstance().getTime().toString();
  }

  public int addNumbers(int i, int j) {
    return (i+j);
  }
}
```

Note that `DateLookup` has no reference to XMLRPC. As far as it is concerned its methods are being accessed locally. We can see how it is used to service XMLRPC requests by examining `XMLRPCHand`:

```java
import helma.xmlrpc.WebServer;
// import helma.xmlrpc.XmlRpc;

public class XMLRPCHand {

  public static void main(String[] argv) {
  //   XmlRpc.setDebug(true);
```

If you would like to see a trace of the SAX-based parsing, uncomment the two lines in the code above. This will switch the debug option for the server to `true`, and each XML element that is parsed by the XMLRPC implementation will be echoed as a trace message to the command line.

```java
    WebServer webServ = null;
    try {
      webServ = new WebServer (8008);
      System.out.println("Starting XMLRPC Server...");

      DateLookup myDateServ = new DateLookup();
      webServ.addHandler ("dserv", myDateServ);
```

We start the web server on port 8008, and associate the instance of `DateLookup` with a service name of `dserv`. The library will inspect the class and determine the methods that may be called remotely (its public members).

```
          System.out.println("Press any key to stop server");
          System.in.read();
      } catch (Exception e) {
          e.printStackTrace();
      }
      System.out.println("Shutting down...");
      webServ.removeHandler("dserv");
      webServ.shutdown();
      System.exit(0);
   }
}
```

This last section of code will wait for Enter to be pressed and will shut down once this input is detected. Compile these classes as usual, making sure that the relevant JAR files are in the classpath.

XMLRPC Client Application

In order to code an XMLRPC client with the Java library for XMLRPC, we will use the helma.xml.rpc.XmlRpcClient. This class provides support for cookies and proxies and essentially represents an RPC connection to the server. To use this class we simply instantiate it, giving it a URL as a string, as a URL object, or with a hostname and port; whichever version you use will depend on your system configuration. The syntax for these constructors is as follows:

```
XmlRpcClient(java.lang.String url)
XmlRpcClient(java.lang.String host, int port)
XmlRpcClient(java.net.URL url)
```

When you have an instance you can call the execute() method on the class. This is the method used to make the RPC call, and rather than working with IDL and language bindings, the call is built dynamically.

```
Object execute(java.lang.String methodName, java.util.Vector params)
                    throws XmlRpcException, java.io.IOException
```

The methodName argument should be of the form <service name>.<method> where <service name> is the name you have associated with the service handler on the server side. The params vector should carry arguments that match the signature of the method being called.

The execute() method generates an XMLRPC request and sends it along the HTTP tunneling transport. It then waits for the XMLRPC response before decoding the return value. The returned Object may be safely cast to the data type of the return value of the method being called. Any application-level exceptions are reported via the XmlRpcException, while lower level transport problems will throw a java.io.IOException and so we will need to declare or handle them in our class.

We are now ready to code the client application. Note that the same client application will work either for both the standalone XML RPC server we created earlier, or through an integrated Tomcat servlet such as the one we will create later. The only change required is the URL used to access the service. You can find XRClient.java in the source distribution under the \ProJavaXML\Chapter19\xmlrpc\client\ directory in the downloaded code for this chapter.

We will obtain the URL from the command line so that we can change it at will; however, there is a default URL provided, which is http://localhost:8008. This assumes that the server is on the local machine at port 8008 as defined in the previous example.

```
import java.util.Vector;
import helma.xmlrpc.XmlRpcClient;
// import helma.xmlrpc.XmlRpc;
public class XRClient  {

public static void main(String[] args) {
  String date;
  String serviceUrl;
  Integer returnValue;

  int arg1 = 3;
  int arg2 = 4;
```

The variables arg1 and arg2 hold the two integer arguments that we will be calling the remote addNumbers() method with:

```
if (args.length > 0) {
  serviceUrl = args[0];
}

if (serviceUrl == null) {
 serverUrl = "http://localhost:8008/";
}
```

We check to see if the user has supplied a URL to use; if not we use the default standalone server URL:

```
try {
    // XmlRpc.setDebug(true);
```

Again, uncomment the above lines if you want a trace of the SAX-based parsing that occurs with the returned value:

```
XmlRpcClient xmlrpc = new XmlRpcClient(serviceUrl);
```

Here we create an instance of the XmlRpcClient class, which we will use to make the call to the remote service:

```
Vector arguments = new Vector ();
date = (String) xmlrpc.execute("dserv.getServerDate", arguments);
System.out.println("The current server time is: " + date);
```

The first remote method we call, getServerDate(), has no input argument and so we can pass an empty Vector() element to represent a zero arguments array, but it does have to return a value of type String. Note how we cast the returned object to the expected string type. After printing out the returned server time, we are ready to call the addNumbers() method:

```
arguments.addElement(new Integer(int1));
arguments.addElement(new Integer(int2));
returnValue = (Integer)xmlrpc.execute("dserv.addNumbers", arguments);
System.out.println("The sum of " + arg1 + " and " + arg2 +
                   " is " + returnValue);
```

We place the two arguments in `Integer` wrappers, add them to `args` and then `execute()` the `addNumbers()` method with `args` as its argument:

```
        } catch (Exception e) {
            e.printStackTrace();
        }
    }
}
```

To compile the client, make sure that the classpath is still set up as for the server then enter the following at the command line:

```
javac XRClient.java
```

We're now ready to try out our standalone server with the client.

Testing Our XMLRPC System

Once again, we will need to make sure that the JAR files required to run the XMLRPC programs are included in the classpath. We can then start the XMLRPC standalone server. In the `\xmlrpc\server\` directory, run:

```
java XMLRPCHand
```

You should see a new console with a startup message similar to the screenshot below. To end the server session, we can simply press *Enter*.

Next, we can start the client and make the XMLRPC calls. Open a new command prompt window and change directory to the `\ProJavaXML\Chapter19\xmlrpc\client` directory. Run:

```
java XRClient
```

The default built-in URL for the server is fine, since we're running the client on the same machine as the standalone server. If you have two networked machines, you can relocate the server and add an argument to the command line as follows:

```
java XRClient http://<second machine host name>:8080
```

If everything is set up correctly, the HTTP tunneling XMLRPC call will be successful and the output in the client screen will be the same as that shown below:

Integrating XMLRPC into a J2EE Web Container

As well as using the standalone server, we can also integrate the server logic into a web container as a servlet. Here, we will integrate the XMLRPC service into Tomcat 3.2.1. The approach will be similar for any application server that supports the same servlet 2.0 standard. We have packaged the web application as follows:

```
\xmlrpc\
    \WEB-INF\
        web.xml
        \src\
            DataLookup.java
            XRServlet.java
        \classes\
            DataLookup.class
            XRServlet.class
                \lib\
```

The \xmlrpc\ folder is the root of the web container, so we need to create a subdirectory in it called \WEB-INF\ and create two subdirectories in that folder, \src\ and \classes\. The \src\ directory holds our java files, while \classes\ will hold the compiled class files. The compiler can place the class files in the correct class automatically or you may move resulting class files there yourself. \lib\ is a very important folder; we will need to place the JAR files for the XMLRPC java implementation here so that Tomcat can access them.

> *The basis for the above package is included in the code download under \ProJavaXML\ Chapter19\xmlrpc\servlet\webapps\ and is called \xmlrpc\. Copy the \xmlrpc\servlet\webapps\xmlrpc\ folder into \webapps\ directory in <TOMCAT_HOME>.*

It is a good idea to compile these files correctly outside the web container and then copy them in. We will also create web.xml in a moment, which defines how URLs map to servlets among other things. For more information please refer to Appendix H. You can find the code below in the \xmlrpc\WEB-INF\src\ directory of the code download for this chapter as XRServlet.java:

```java
import javax.servlet.*;
import javax.servlet.http.*;
import java.io.*;
import helma.xmlrpc.XmlRpcServer;

public class XRServlet extends HttpServlet {

    public XmlRpcServer xmlrpc;
    public DateLookup myDateServ;

    public void init(ServletConfig config) throws ServletException {

        xmlrpc = new XmlRpcServer ();
        myDateServ = new DateLookup();
        xmlrpc.addHandler ("dserv", myDateServ);
    }
```

When the `init()` methods are called we create an instance of the `DateLookup` class and register it with the XMLRPC server runtime. Notice that we're now using the `helma.xmlrpc.XmlRpcServer` class, which is a superclass of the `helma.xmlrpc.WebServer` that we have used earlier for the standalone server:

```
public void doPost(HttpServletRequest req, HttpServletResponse res)
    throws ServletException, IOException  {
  byte[] charAry = xmlrpc.execute (req.getInputStream());
```

We obtain a stream containing only the body of the HTTP POST request, without headers. This will be the XML document that contains the `<methodCall>` element. We than use the `execute()` method of the `XmlRpcServer` that takes an `InputStream` as an argument. This method will parse the XML document that is in the stream and invoke the corresponding registered handler to handle the incoming XMLRPC call.

It will also return a byte array that contains an XML document representing the return value from the call (contained in a `<methodResponse>` element). This byte array is ready to be bundled up and sent back to the client as an HTTP response:

```
    res.setContentType("text/xml");
    res.setContentLength (charAry.length);
    OutputStream output = res.getOutputStream();
    output.write (charAry);
    output.flush ();
  }
}
```

This last portion simply sends the byte array back as a response.

In order to successfully compile this servlet, `servlet.jar` will need to be in the classpath. The `servlet.jar` file is included in the `lib` directory of the Tomcat 3.2.1 distribution. If you have SUN's J2EE reference implementation installed, and are running under its environment, having the `j2ee.jar` file in your classpath is sufficient. We will also need to copy the `DateLookup.class` file into `<TOMCAT_HOME>\classes\` if this has not already been done.

Deploying the Servlet into the Servlet Engine

If you're using an applications server instead of Tomcat, you will most likely have a GUI-based deployment tool. Here, we will do the hard work manually. First, we must make sure that the servlet engine can find the classes necessary to run the XMLRPC library by placing the `xmlrpc.jar` and `openxml-1.2.jar` in the `\lib\` folder as previously mentioned.

Build the application, or copy the contents of `xmlrpc` from the download, into Tomcat's `webapps` directory. It will then be accessible by the URL http://localhost:8080/xmlrpc. One more thing we will do now, in the interests of stability, as we will continue to use Tomcat throughout the examples in this book. If we go into `<TOMCAT_HOME>` and create a new directory called `classes`, we can then be sure that if we put classes for our services into this directory, the classes contained in this directory will be in the server classpath. This should rule out possible classpath issues when we move on to our SOAP example.

So, we will now create `<TOMCAT_HOME>\classes` and save a copy of `DateLookup.class` into this folder.

One last requirement is that we must specify the `web.xml` file and store it in Tomcat's `\xmlrpc\WEB-INF` directory:

```xml
<?xml version="1.0" encoding="ISO-8859-1"?>

<!DOCTYPE web-app
    PUBLIC "-//Sun Microsystems, Inc.//DTD Web Application 2.2//EN"
    "http://java.sun.com/j2ee/dtds/web-app_2.2.dtd">

<web-app>
    <servlet>
        <servlet-name>
            dateserv
        </servlet-name>
        <servlet-class>
            XRServlet
        </servlet-class>
    </servlet>
</web-app>
```

Now, we are ready to try out this servlet-based XMLRPC service. Start Tomcat and when it has started up open a new command window and navigate to the `ProJavaXM\Chapter19\client\` folder. When you have done so start the client with the following URL:

```
java XRClient http://localhost:8080/xmlrpc/servlet/dateserv
```

If everything is working OK, the result will be exactly the same as before; however, we are now using a web server to act as a go-between:

SOAP

SOAP is the **Simple Object Access Protocol**. It is described in a W3C note, submitted to the W3C by Microsoft, IBM, and UserLand Software among others on May 8, 2000. The note describes the 1.1 version of the protocol, which at the time of writing is the most current one available and includes as one of its identified goals allowing DCOM and Object RPC calls to be made through HTTP tunneling via an HTTP POST request.

The essential idea behind SOAP 1.1 is similar to UserLand's XMLRPC. It also defines a protocol for remote method calls; however in contrast to XMLRPC, SOAP aspires to include many extensible features:

❑ SOAP specifies additional envelope information, to be included as part of the XML document being transmitted via the underlying transport, that describes the content, its intended recipient, and how it should be processed

❑ Although the 1.1 specifications only defines a concrete binding to HTTP, the SOAP does not couple tightly with HTTP, instead specifying a generic transport

801

❑ SOAP specifies at length how certain common complex data structures may be represented in its XML-based encoding – some examples are structures, arrays, array of structures, and sparsely populated arrays

❑ SOAP's operation model is a decentralized one, in which a message can be processed by many intermediaries before arriving at the final sink

❑ SOAP has specific features to accommodate conventions in classic RPC operations (in/out parameters, bounded array transmission, etc.)

The SOAP specification makes distinct references to four different aspects of the protocol:

❑ How it works with HTTP

❑ The envelope

❑ The encoding rules

❑ The RPC convention

We will examine each of these aspects in more detail below.

SOAP and HTTP

Although not required, SOAP 1.1 describes a binding of SOAP with HTTP, effectively tunneling through HTTP. This binding places SOAP messages within HTTP requests and responses. The interaction model is a request-response model in this case.

In addition:

❑ The Content-Type HTTP header must specify text/xml

❑ HTTP POST is the only request type defined

❑ A custom SOAPAction HTTP header is required to indicate the intent of the request

❑ A successful SOAP request is indicated by an HTTP response status code that indicates success, that is, 2nn, where nn is any number between 00 and 99

❑ An error response is indicated by a HTTP response with the status code 500 and the message Internal Server Error, together with a SOAP message containing a <Fault> element (which we will be looking at later)

SOAP messages carried in the body of HTTP requests and responses can contain additional header information (SOAP specific) beyond those carried in the HTTP headers.

The SOAP Envelope

A SOAP message consists of an XML document. The root element of the message is always the `<Envelope>` element. More specifically, the envelope tag together with all of its attributes should be from the standard SOAP envelope namespace:

```
<SOAP-ENV:Envelope
            xmlns:SOAP-ENV="http://schemas.xmlsoap.org/soap/envelope/">
```

The `<Envelope>` element can contain one optional `<Header>` child element, which must be the first immediate child. A `<Header>` element may contain multiple header entries. It is anticipated `<Header>` will be used to provide value-added processing between participants along the SOAP message path (such as transactions, for example, or custom authentication). The header entries must be namespace-qualified.

Following the `<Header>` element is a single `<Body>` element. This is the content of the message, intended for service consumption. `<Body>` can contain its own child elements, called body entries. Each body entry is independently encoded, and so may specify an `encodingStyle` attribute to indicate the encoding used.

SOAP only defines one type of body entry, called the SOAP `<Fault>`. The SOAP `<Fault>` element may occur only once within a `<Body>` element.

Note that the SOAP specification is very strict with regards to full namespace qualification, since a typical SOAP message may mix the use of several namespaces. Immediate children of `<Envelope>`, `<Header>`, and `<Body>` must all be namespace-qualified.

The SOAP Encoding Style

The encoding style portion of the SOAP specification is heavily reliant on XML Schemas, and weighted towards object graphs that are typically found in programming language data structures. In fact, the encoding is based on mapping between these items:

❑ An object graph – potentially an in-memory representation of a data structure in a programming language, database, etc

❑ An XML instance representing an instance of the object graph (for instance, XML-encoded serialization)

❑ An XML Schema describing the relationships and rules inherent in the object graph (serialization/deserialization constraints)

Let us take a look at a few simple examples of SOAP encoding, similar to our exploration of XMLRPC. Remember the namespace for all SOAP elements and attributes is the standard http://schemas.xmlsoap.org/soap/envelope/ namespace.

Encoding Simple Values

With assistance from the basic built-in data types of XML Schemas, simple types are encoded directly. For example, integers and strings are encoded as:

```
<count>32</count>
<motd>Welcome to Kentucky!</motd>
```

if we have a corresponding schema description:

```
<element name="count" type="int"/>
<element name="motd" type="SOAP-ENC:string">
```

Encoding Compound Values

Structures and arrays are called compound values. Structures are encoded by creating an element whose name is the struct's name and adding child elements whose name match their name in the struct. Each member is accessed by its name (the SOAP specification calls the name an **accessor**).

For example, a structure consisting of an integer and a string as members may be encoded as:

```
<viewfrequency>
   <count xsi:type="xsd:int">3</count>
   <motd xsi:type="xsd:string">Welcome to Texas!</motd>
</viewfrequency>
```

Wherea the namespaces qualifications are:

```
xmlns:xsi="http://www.w3.org/1999/XMLSchema-instance"
```

and

```
xmlns:xsd="http://www.w3.org/1999/XMLSchema"
```

The topic of SOAP encoding is a vast and complex one. What we have gained here is a basic understanding of how SOAP RPC works so we can begin to work with actual SOAP service and client samples. Readers who are interested in the subject of SOAP encoding are encouraged to review the exploration of XML object mapping in Chapter 6.

SOAP RPC Convention

According to SOAP 1.1 specifications, a method call is modeled as a struct with one accessor (member) for each parameter. The name of the struct is the name of the method, and each accessor is named and typed the same as the parameters of the method. These accessors appear in the same order as they are declared in the method. Therefore, the struct encoded above is equivalent to a method call of:

```
viewfrequency( 3, "Welcome to Texas!");
```

The response from a method call is also modeled as a struct, and any error returns a <Fault> element. The struct contains accessors representing the return value and any [out] or [in/out] parameters. What this means is that any changes made to the argument's values can be communicated back to the calling function – this is the classic RPC-specific implementation of pass by reference.

The first accessor of the return value struct is the return value – the name of the struct is not important. For example, this is a valid response from the call above – assuming it is returning a string value.

```
<viewfrequencyResponse>
    <return xsi:type="xsd:string">Move to Washington and do not pass GO!</return>
</viewfrequencyResponse>
```

To summarize, the history of SOAP is as follows; Microsoft has perfected an object-oriented variety of RPC called **Object RPC** or **ORPC**. It formed the inter-component communications protocol for the DCOM/COM+ technology. The added value is the object context associated with the remote call.

In the same way as XMLRPC, the ORPC binary standard can be expressed in terms of XML and what we end up with is SOAP.

Working with Apache SOAP

Apache SOAP started life at the IBM software research laboratory, Alphaworks, as SOAP4J. Now the Apache XML Project at http://xml.apache.org has embraced SOAP4J, and the name has been officially changed to **Apache SOAP**.

The latest Apache SOAP project binary distribution is available for download, and indeed we will be downloading and installing it below in order to implement our example.

Apache SOAP requires the use of a sophisticated XML parser, one that can handle XML Schemas. XML Schemas typically require parsers with a fairly large footprint, and the OpenXML that we used with the XMLRPC java library is inadequate to the task. So we will go back to using Xerces for the SOAP examples.

As a reminder, if you have not already done so, you will need to download Apache SOAP version 2.0 distribution at this URL:

http://xml.apache.org/soap/index.html

> At the time of publication SOAP 2.1 had just been released. However, there was some lack of documentation features, and some inconsistencies with the stable SOAP 2.0 version, which means that for the purposes of this chapter (and the next), we recomment you use SOAP 2.0.

Implementing an Apache SOAP Web Service

Once you've downloaded Apache SOAP, you are ready to create your first SOAP web service. Unzip the zip file to a convenient location, say to the \ProJavaXML\Chapter19\ folder (This is assumed from now on), and follow these steps. Firstly, add soap.jar, which can be found in the \ProJavaXML\Chapter19\soap-2_0\lib to your classpath. You can do this by typing the following in to the command prompt before compiling and running any classes:

```
set classpath=c:\ProJavaXML\Chapter19\soap-2_0\lib\soap.jar;%classpath%
```

Copy the \soap\ folder, which can found at \ProJavaXML\Chapter19\soap-2_0\webapps, into Tomcat's \webapps\ directory. This will install Apache SOAP into Tomcat and deploy an administration deployment tool that we will use. This will also create a new web application called soap in Tomcat from which we will deploy our application.

Once again, this implementation for remote method invocation both hides the SOAP specifics from us and will automatically generate the necessary XML files for us. To show the possibilities provided with SOAP, we will implement a SOAP service that is available as an HTTP service using Tomcat 3.2.1.

Before we begin, we will need to make sure that `xerces.jar` and `soap.jar` are included in Tomcat's classpath before any other files. To do so, you will need to locate `tomcat.bat` (`tomcat.sh` for Unix) and add `xerces.jar` to the classpath before any other package.

The relevant section of `tomcat.bat` in Tomcat 3.2.1 is shown below, containing the classpath additions necessary to run the example:

```
REM ----- Set Up The Runtime Classpath ------------------------

:setClasspath

set CP=%TOMCAT_HOME%\classes

REM Add these lines for ProJavaXML soap application:
set CP=C:\xerces-1_3_0\xerces.jar;C:\ProJavaXML\Chapter19\soap-bin-2.0\soap-
2_0\lib\soap.jar;%CP%

set CP=C:\projavaxml\chapter19\soap\client;%CP%
```

This is all quite similar as regards `tomcat.sh`, simply add the `xerces.jar` file (and the others after it) before the JAR files in `${TOMCAT_HOME}/lib/` are added in the script. If Tomcat does not load the classes in the files first, you may find that Apache SOAP will not work.

Create a `\classes\` subdirectory of `\soap\WEB-INF\`. We will use `DateLookup` to implement our service. Make a copy of its class file to the `\classes\` directory in the `soap` web application's `\WEB-INF\` folder.

The structure of the `soap` web application will now be as follows:

```
\soap\
    web.xml
    \admin\
    \WEB-INF\
        \classes\
            DateLookup.class
            Descriptor.xml
```

`\admin\` contains JSP files and other resources that the Apache SOAP administrator requires, and they do not need to be listed here. Remember that we also have a copy of `DateLookup.class` in `<TOMCAT_HOME>\classes\`. The `web.xml` file is that provided by the SOAP implementation, and we will not need to change it for this application. We will develop `Descriptor.xml` in just a moment; it is a deployment descriptor for deploying services on Apache SOAP.

You can find the source code to the implementation in the `\ProJavaXML\Chapter19\soapcode\` directory of the downloaded source code (if you wish, you may copy the contents of the `\soapcode\WEB-INF\` directory to the newly created `\soap\WEB-INF\` folder in Tomcat's webapps directory rather than building the application by hand).

The beauty of the Apache SOAP implementation is that we need almost nothing special on the service side of the equation.

Deploying Your Web Service

As mentioned, to deploy your SOAP Service, you need to create a deployment descriptor. In this case, we do not mean `web.xml`, although this new file will serve the identical function of providing system specific deployment information.

Here is `Descriptor.xml`, which we've simply placed in the `C:\ProJavaXml\Chapter19` directory:

```
<?xml version="1.0"?>
<isd:service
    xmlns:isd="http://xml.apache.org/xml-soap/deployment"
    id="urn:wrox-date-service">
  <isd:provider type="java"
                scope="Application"
                methods="getServerDate addNumbers">
    <isd:java class="DateLookup"/>
  </isd:provider>
</isd:service>
```

The file specifies the class that the service should use for RPC invocation. We have also specified the methods that are remotely callable here, as whitespace delimited method names. The Apache SOAP deployment tool takes care of the rest.

There are two ways to deploy the application; the first is through the command line. Open a command window in the `C:\ProJavaXml\Chapter19` directory (which is where we are going to deploy the application from, and which is where we have placed both the `DateLookup` class and `Descriptor.xml` in this instance). Now run the following:

```
java org.apache.soap.server.ServiceManagerClient
http://localhost:8080/soap/servlet/rpcrouter deploy Descriptor.xml
```

This will deploy the application. You can also deploy a SOAP service via a JSP-based web administration application, which we will look at next. Once deployment is successful, the deployment information is kept in a file called `DeployedServices.ds` in the web application root directory; in this case this will be the `<TOMCAT_HOME>\bin\` directory. The next time Apache SOAP starts up, it will read this file to determine what to deploy.

The Apache SOAP Service Administration Web Application

Apache SOAP includes a JSP-based service manager for SOAP. Once you have Apache SOAP installed, and Tomcat is up and running, you can access this service manager through a browser via the URL:

http://localhost:8080/soap/admin/

If everything is working, you should see a user interface similar to the one shown below:

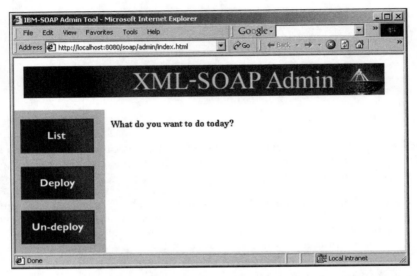

Select the List option and you will be presented with a list of deployed services, probably only ours, which will be shown as `urn:wrox-date-service`.

If you wish to try the graphical deployment administrator, you will first need to un-deploy the application by selecting Un-deploy and choosing the `wrox-date-service` once more. We are now ready to deploy the application once more. Select Deploy, and you should see the following screen:

We can fill in the details required to deploy our application. In the ID box enter the value urn:wrox-date-service. SOAP commonly uses URNs to define application IDs, which it prefixes with urn:. We have chosen to follow that custom. The **Scope** of the request should be set to Application.

We list the methods that are to be made available, these being getServerDate and addNumbers, delimited by whitespace. Our provider is a Java provider, thus we can leave this as is. This will tell the SOAP implementation how to map between SOAP calls and method calls.

Many of the remaining options are not relevant to us; however, there is one step left, we should specify the class name for our provider. Enter DateLookup and leave the **Static?** option as No. If you scroll down to the bottom of this page, you should find a **Deploy** button there. Press it to deploy the application and you should get a message confirming successful deployment.

Creating a Client for the Web Service

To create the client for our web service, we will need to be familiar with a few classes in the Apache SOAP library.

The org.apache.soap.rpc.Call class represents the RPC call that will be made. It contains all the information necessary to make the remote call and provide the return value (or <fault>) back to the client. Here are some of its frequently used methods, which it inherits from the org.apache.soap.rpc.RPCMessage class:

```
void setTargetObjectURI(String targetURI)
void setMethodName(String methodName)
void setEncodingStyleURI(String encodingStyleURI)
void setParams(Vector params)
```

These mutators have the following functions:

❑ setTargetObjectURI() sets the name of the requested service; for our example this would be urn:wrox-date-service

❑ setMethodName() should be passed a string that represents the method being called; SOAP also allows the payload to use alternative encoding

❑ setEncodingSyleURI() specifies the encoding; in our case, we will be using the SOAP-specified object serialization encoding org.apache.soap.Constants.NS_URI_SOAP_ENC.

❑ setParams() sets the arguments with a Vector of org.apache.soap.rpc.Parameter objects, one for each argument

The key method in this object is the following:

```
org.apache.soap.rpc.Response invoke(java.net.URL serverURL,
                                    java.lang.String SOAPActionURI)
    throws SOAPException;
```

This method invokes the remote call (in other words, marshals the call through the HTTP tunnel), and provides the return value in a Response object. SOAPActionURI is specified by SOAP, but not used in the Apache SOAP RPC router scenario and so we will pass a null. Any exception received during the invocation will be mapped to a SOAPException – interested readers should examine the API documentation for details.

The org.apache.soap.rpc.Response class holds the response from the remote call.

```
boolean generatedFault()
```

This method returns true if a fault is returned by the remote service. We can retrieve the nature of the error in more detail by calling the getFault() method.

```
Fault getFault()
```

If there is no fault, getReturnValue() will retrieve the return value supplied by the remote service. It is in the form of an org.apache.soap.rpc.Parameter object, which we will cover next.

```
Parameter getReturnValue()
```

org.apache.soap.rpc.Parameter is used to package any arguments on the client side for remote calling and is also used in obtaining the return value after invoking the remote service. It has one constructor, which takes the name of the parameter, data type, value, and encodingStyleURI in string form. It also has accessor/mutator pairs for the Type, Name, Value and EncodingSyleURI parameters.

The client code is located in the \ProJavaXML\Chapter19\soapcode\client\ directory of the code download distribution, in the SPClient.java file. You will notice that it is significantly more involved than the trivial service implementation. Most of the work involves the packing of an instance of the org.apache.soap.rpc.Call object and calling invoke() on it.

```
import java.net.URL;
import java.util.Vector;

import org.apache.soap.Fault;
import org.apache.soap.rpc.Call;
import org.apache.soap.rpc.Response;
import org.apache.soap.rpc.Parameter;
```

```
public class SPClient {

  public static void main(String[] args) throws Exception {

    //These are the numbers we will add together on the remote system.
    int x = 3;
    int y = 4;

    URL myURL = null;
    Response resp = null;
    // each method call will be build up in the Call class
    Call call = null;

    // the list of parameters is a vector
    Vector params = null;

    // this is the provided SOAP encoding type
    String encodingStyleURI = org.apache.soap.Constants.NS_URI_SOAP_ENC;

    if (args.length > 0) {
      myURL = new URL(args[0]);
    }
    if (myURL == null) {
      myURL = new URL("http://localhost:8080/soap/servlet/rpcrouter");
    }
```

The default URL points to a server hosting the RPC router running on the same machine as the client. To override this, we can supply any other URL on the command line.

We can now begin, so we set the encoding of the message to the standard SOAP encoding and specify the target service to be the urn:wrox-date-service that we have deployed earlier.

```
    // Build the call.
    call = new Call();
    call.setTargetObjectURI("urn:wrox-date-service");
    call.setMethodName("getServerDate");
    call.setEncodingStyleURI(encodingStyleURI);

    params = new Vector();
    call.setParams(params);
```

Finally, we build the Call() instance for calling the getServerData() remote method. Notice that params is empty in this case since there is no input argument for the method.

```
    resp = call.invoke(myURL, null);
    if (!resp.generatedFault()) {
      Parameter result = resp.getReturnValue();
      System.out.println("The current server time is: " + result.getValue());

    } else {
      Fault fault = resp.getFault();

      System.out.println("Ouch, the call failed: ");
      System.out.println("  Fault Code   = " + fault.getFaultCode());
      System.out.println("  Fault String = " + fault.getFaultString());
    }
```

We invoke the remote call, and either print out the fault returned or the actual returned value. Calling the `addNumbers()` method is similar, except that we need to create two new `Parameter` objects that hold the integers 3 and 4, to be added together remotely:

```
call = new Call();
call.setTargetObjectURI("urn:wrox-date-service");
call.setMethodName("addNumbers");
call.setEncodingStyleURI(encodingStyleURI);

params.addElement(new Parameter("i", Integer.class, new Integer(x), null));
params.addElement(new Parameter("j", Integer.class, new Integer(y), null));

call.setParams(params);
```

Finally, as long as there is no error, we invoke the remote call and retrieve the returned value as an integer type value. If a fault is returned to us we print out an error message, a fault code, and a string description:

```
resp = call.invoke(myURL, "" );
if (!resp.generatedFault()) {
  Parameter result = resp.getReturnValue();
  String sum = ((Integer)result.getValue()).toString();

  System.out.println("The sum of " + x + " and " + y + " is " + sum);

} else {
  Fault fault = resp.getFault();
  System.out.println("Ouch, the call failed: ");
  System.out.println("  Fault Code   = " + fault.getFaultCode ());
  System.out.println("  Fault String = " + fault.getFaultString ());
  }
 }
}
```

Compile the class and we are ready to try it out. Tomcat is particularly sensitive to the location of files on your classpath, and matters are further complicated because we are running both the servlet and the client on one machine in this example. If you try to run the above example and find it returns a `BadTargetObjectURI` fault code, then it may well be that the position of `soap.jar` in your classpath hierarchy is confusing Tomcat's class loader. Check to make sure that the client classes are in Tomcat's classpath, and then try again.

We will assume that you are using Tomcat 3.2.1 and that the client can be found in `C:\ProJavaXML\Chapter19\soapcode\client`. Please correct this as required.

Testing the Web Service

Assuming that Tomcat is still running, if it is not please start it, you can simply type invoke the client as follows:

```
java SPClient
```

If everything is working, you should see a similar output to the output from the previous XMLRPC example:

```
C:\WINNT\system32\cmd.exe

C:\ProJavaXML\Chapter19\soapcode\client>java SPClient
The current server time is: Wed Mar 07 22:23:04 GMT+00:00 2001
The sum of 3 and 4 is 7

C:\ProJavaXML\Chapter19\soapcode\client>
```

Watching the Action in the Tunnel

While we were testing out the XMLRPC system and the Apache SOAP system, you may have been thinking that it might be nice to actually see what sort of XML-based interchange is happening between the client and service. And of course, having this ability would enable us to better learn about the protocols involved and more effectively debug problematic situations.

So it happens that one of the most useful tools you will find included with the Apache SOAP distribution is an HTTP tunnel monitor. It is a utility that allows you to see what is being transmitted between the client and service pair in text format. The diagram below shows how this utility works architecturally. Any traffic you sent originally to the destination port will now be routed through the tunnel port. The utility will print out the traffic on one of its GUI windows before routing the data.

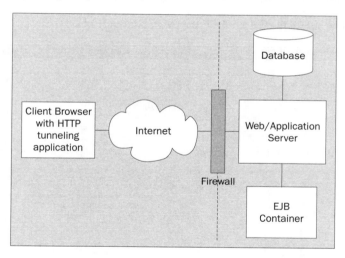

Assuming that you have soap.jar in your classpath, you can run the tool by using the command line:

```
> java org.apache.soap.util.net.TcpTunnelGui TunnelPort host DestinationPort
```

where TunnelPort is the port number you are using for the HTTP tunnel (any free port will do here – we will use 8081), host is your host name (in this instance, localhost will do) and DestinationPort is the port we are tunneling from (which in this example, is 8080).

The following window will appear:

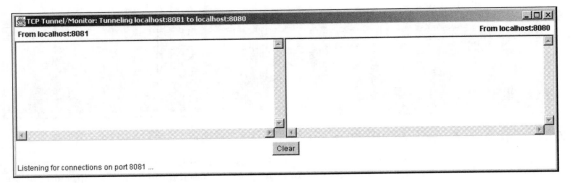

The left hand window represents any communications from the client, while the right hand side represents the responses to those communications.

We will have to adjust the URL that the client uses to access the service. This change will move the port from the actual service destination port to the tunnel port specified in the command line. In our case, we issue this command line in the `\ProJavaXML\Chapter19\soapcode\client\` directory:

```
java SPClient http://localhost:8081/soap/servlet/rpcrouter
```

The screenshot below shows the output from the tunnel monitor:

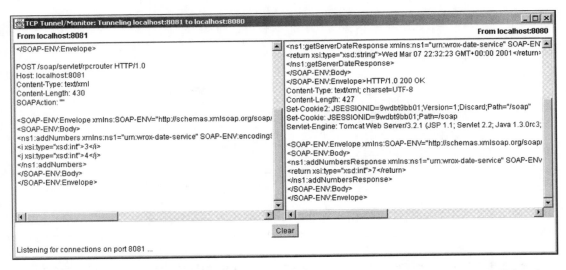

On the client side, we see the outgoing requests. Notice that each one begins with the HTTP headers, revealing the URL requested, including the host, port, and path, and the SOAP action type – here it is "", an empty string:

```
POST /soap/servlet/rpcrouter HTTP/1.0
Host: localhost:8081
Content-Type: text/xml; charset=utf-8
Content-Length: 378
SOAPAction: ""
```

```
<SOAP-ENV:Envelope xmlns:SOAP-ENV="http://schemas.xmlsoap.org/soap/envelope/"
xmlns:xsi="http://www.w3.org/1999/XMLSchema-instance"
xmlns:xsd="http://www.w3.org/1999/XMLSchema">
<SOAP-ENV:Body>
<ns1:getServerDate xmlns:ns1="urn:wrox-date-service" SOAP-
ENV:encodingStyle="http://schemas.xmlsoap.org/soap/encoding/">
</ns1:getServerDate>
</SOAP-ENV:Body>
</SOAP-ENV:Envelope>


POST /soap/servlet/rpcrouter HTTP/1.0
Host: localhost:8081
Content-Type: text/xml
Content-Length: 430
SOAPAction: ""


<SOAP-ENV:Envelope xmlns:SOAP-ENV="http://schemas.xmlsoap.org/soap/envelope/"
xmlns:xsi="http://www.w3.org/1999/XMLSchema-instance"
xmlns:xsd="http://www.w3.org/1999/XMLSchema">
<SOAP-ENV:Body>
<ns1:addNumbers xmlns:ns1="urn:wrox-date-service" SOAP-
ENV:encodingStyle="http://schemas.xmlsoap.org/soap/encoding/">
<i xsi:type="xsd:int">3</i>
<j xsi:type="xsd:int">4</j>
</ns1:addNumbers>
</SOAP-ENV:Body>
</SOAP-ENV:Envelope>
```

From the server side, we can see the response, which again includes the HTTP header. The return code 200 indicates a successful response:

```
HTTP/1.0 200 OK
Content-Type: text/xml; charset=utf-8
Content-Length: 469
Set-Cookie2: JSESSIONID=amuppzuxg1;Version=1;Discard;Path="/soap"
Set-Cookie: JSESSIONID=amuppzuxg1;Path=/soap
Servlet-Engine: Tomcat Web Server/3.2.1 (JSP 1.1; Servlet 2.2; Java 1.3.0rc3;
Windows 2000 5.0 x86; java.vendor=Sun Microsystems Inc.)


<SOAP-ENV:Envelope xmlns:SOAP-ENV="http://schemas.xmlsoap.org/soap/envelope/"
xmlns:xsi="http://www.w3.org/1999/XMLSchema-instance"
xmlns:xsd="http://www.w3.org/1999/XMLSchema">
<SOAP-ENV:Body>
<ns1:getServerDateResponse xmlns:ns1="urn:wrox-date-service" SOAP-
ENV:encodingStyle="http://schemas.xmlsoap.org/soap/encoding/">
<return xsi:type="xsd:string">Wed Mar 07 22:32:23 GMT+00:00 2001</return>
</ns1:getServerDateResponse>
</SOAP-ENV:Body>
</SOAP-ENV:Envelope>HTTP/1.0 200 OK
Content-Type: text/xml; charset=UTF-8
Content-Length: 427
Set-Cookie2: JSESSIONID=9wdbt9bb01;Version=1;Discard;Path="/soap"
Set-Cookie: JSESSIONID=9wdbt9bb01;Path=/soap
Servlet-Engine: Tomcat Web Server/3.2.1 (JSP 1.1; Servlet 2.2; Java 1.3.0rc3;
Windows 2000 5.0 x86; java.vendor=Sun Microsystems Inc.)
```

```
<SOAP-ENV:Envelope xmlns:SOAP-ENV="http://schemas.xmlsoap.org/soap/envelope/"
xmlns:xsi="http://www.w3.org/1999/XMLSchema-instance"
xmlns:xsd="http://www.w3.org/1999/XMLSchema">
<SOAP-ENV:Body>
<ns1:addNumbersResponse xmlns:ns1="urn:wrox-date-service" SOAP-
ENV:encodingStyle="http://schemas.xmlsoap.org/soap/encoding/">
<return xsi:type="xsd:int">7</return>
</ns1:addNumbersResponse>
</SOAP-ENV:Body>
</SOAP-ENV:Envelope>
```

If we wished we could also monitor the traffic caused by the XMLRPC application; however, this exercise is left to the reader.

BXXP – An XML Protocol Construction Set

BXXP is the **Blocks eXtensible eXchange Protocol** (pronounced BEEP, thanks to a recent BXXP community poll). It is an IETF (Internet Engineering Task Force) draft from the Network Working Group, created by Dr. Marshall T. Rose of Invisible Worlds. It is a generic framework for building application-level protocols. In particular, it is designed to support connection-oriented protocols with asynchronous interactions; and it has the ability to multiplex multiple independent channels over one single connection.

Unlike XMLRPC or SOAP, BXXP does not deal with HTTP tunneling or facilitate RPC. Instead, it is a foundation toolkit for building your very own application protocol. One way to think of BXXP is that it is to protocols what Swing is to UI. BXXP allows you to leverage the best practices of expert protocol designers, learned the hard way through experience, in your very own customized application protocol. This is the design goal and objective of BXXP.

How does BXXP achieve this? It provides support in six of the vital design areas that an application protocol designer typically needs to consider. These areas are tabulated below:

Design Area	BXXP Implementation
Framing	To delimit messages that are passed between applications, BXXP uses **octect** counting – where a length is transmitted in the header, in the same way that HTTP does.
Encoding	BXXP uses MIME, but the default is text/xml, so the message body can contain an XML-encoded message.
Error Reporting	BXXP uses a standard 3-digit error code with support for a localized text string.
Multiplexing	BXXP supports multiple independent simultaneous channels over which applications can communicate.
User Authentication	BXXP supports the use of **Simple Authentication and Security Layer (SASL)** for user authentication.
Transport Security	BXXP will support the use of **Transport Level Security (TLS)**, or SASL can be used.

Note how the design of BXXP stays clear of making any application-level decisions for the protocol designer. For example, it does not favor one type of MIME encoding over another, nor does it have the locked step request/response interaction typical of RPC and HTTP. In fact, BXXP can be used in a non client-server environment (for example, peer-to-peer networks, where a client can also be server).

One question now comes to mind – can we put XMLRPC or SOAP, two application-level protocol instances, over BXXP? The answer is: not in their current state of specification.

The current XMLRPC specification is dependent on HTTP as its underlying transport. If we simply use the XML encoding scheme specified by XMLRPC and decouple it from the transport, we can indeed carry XMLRPC traffic in a BXXP network. The current SOAP 1.1 specification maps to HTTP as its transport (for instance, in the use of custom headers and support for RPC interactions) – however, future versions of XMLRPC and SOAP may decouple further the relationship between the messages and their transport, allowing BXXP to serve as their foundation.

BXXP Details

BXXP relies on a session layer protocol, such as TCP, to work. The two applications that are connected via BXXP are called peers.

In general, this is the sequence of events that occur so BXXP peers may talk to each other:

❑   A session is established between the BXXP peers

❑   The BXXP peers exchange the profiles that they support

❑   One of the peers initiates the creation of a channel (conditional on common profile support)

❑   The BXXP peers communicate through the newly created channel

Profiles are descriptions of allowable messages and their semantics – they are denoted by URIs. Note that BXXP allows peers to create multiple independent channels on the same session. In the case of TCP/IP being used as the transport, this means that we only need to open one single connection to create as many "channels" as we want. This action is called multiplexing.

Once a channel is created between the peers, they can exchange messages according to their profiles.

BXXP Framing

Here is an example BXXP message:

```
MSG 0 1 . 66 135
Content-Type: application/BXXP+xml

<start number='1'>
  <profile uri='http://xml.wrox.com/profiles/DATE'>
  </profile>
</start>
END
```

Let's look at how a BXXP message is framed. The first and last lines are called the **frame header** and **frame trailer** respectively. Everything between the header and the trailer is called the **payload** of the message.

If we look at the frame header, we can see that MSG indicates this is a request message. It can also be:

Message Type	Description
RPY	A positive reply to a MSG message, usually returned after the server successfully performed some work.
ERR	A negative reply to a MSG, indicating an error.
ANS	A server may return multiple ANS replies in response to a MSG; the last one will be a NUL message. ANS messages are also used to provide flow control for large message payloads.

If we look back to our example message, we see a string of numbers following the MSG in the frame header.

❑ The first number is the **channel number**, 0.

❑ The next is the **message number**, 1.

❑ This is followed by a **more indicator**, which flags whether more messages might be expected. No more is represented by ".", while "*" means there will be more messages in that block.

❑ Next is a **sequence number**, 66 in this case.

❑ Finally, there is a **size of message number**, 135 octets.

Note that the message number is always unique for any one channel (among all messages pending reply on that channel). The sequence number is a number used to ensure synchronization between BXXP peers. On any particular channel, the sequence number starts with 0 and increases by the size of the payload with each message. For example, the first message sent on channel 1 will have sequence number 0, and if that message has a size of 66, the second message sent on the channel will have sequence number 66.

A BXXP may decide to segment a large block of data into multiple messages. The "more" indicator can indicate that there are more to come for a RPY.

BXXP Channel Management

The only channel active initially in a session is the **channel management channel**: channel 0, which will then remain open as long as the session is open, and will be used exclusively for channel management and control. Upon connection, the BXXP peers will send each other a RPY message that contains a <greeting> element. The <greeting> element can contain a <profile> child element indicating the profiles supported by the peer. It can also contain attributes associated with optional features in profile and/or localization information. This is message 0 for both peers.

To create a channel, the BXXP must send a <start> message on channel 0. The number parameter indicates the channel number. Here is an example for channel 1:

```
MSG 0 1 . 34 188
Content-Type: application/BXXP+xml

<start number='1'>
        <profile uri='http://xml.wrox.com/profiles/DATE'>
        </profile>
</start>
END
```

This message is an attempt to start channel number 1, supporting the DATE profile. The BXXP peer initiating the channel creation is called the **initiator**. The peer receiving the channel creation <start> message is called the **listener**. The listener should examine the profile on the proposed channel, and can then either respond with a positive reply (RPY) containing the profile supported, or a negative reply (ERR). Upon receipt of a positive reply, the initiator considers the channel open and can start sending messages on the channel to the listener.

To close a channel, the BXXP peer sends a close message on channel 0. The <close> message also indicates the channel referred to by the value of its number parameter:

```
MSG 0 1 . 45 122
Content-Type: application/BXXP+xml

<close number='1' code='200'/>
END
```

The BXXP receiving a close message can reply with positive reply (RPY) with an <ok/> element in the payload, or negative reply (ERR). The channel is considered closed only upon the receipt of a positive reply (RPY). A <close> message with number='0' is considered an attempt to close the BXXP session (closing the channel management channel itself – channel 0). Optionally, the number can be omitted, which will achieve the same result.

All BXXP peers support up to 256 channels in addition to the channel management channel 0. The actual usage will depend on the application using BXXP.

Our DATE Custom Profile

We will now define the DATE custom profile that will allow us to continue the theme of this chapter by implementing the getServerTime() and addNumber() methods using BXXP. A profile is simply a specification of the message that may be sent and its semantics.

The profile is identified by a URI, in this case: http://xml.wrox.com/profiles/DATE

There are two type of messages supported by this profile:

❑ A MSG with a null payload that will cause the listener to return a RPY with the current server time in its payload

❑ A MSG with a payload of two integer numbers, separated by a space, that will cause the listener to return the sum of the two numbers in its payload

Now, we are ready to implement the BXXP version of our RPC service.

Java SpaceKit for BXXP

The **Java SpaceKit for BXXP** is a Java library for developers interested in finding out more about BXXP. It is designed, written, and maintained by Frank Morton from Invisible Worlds. The SpaceKit for BXXP is as much a work-in-progress as the BXXP protocol is itself. Therefore, getting a 'workable' copy to experiment with will require some patience – this is generally true of evolving protocols that are not supported by a major commercial interest. You can find everything you want to know about BXXP, together with projects and the toolkit using the latest specification at: http://www.bxxp.org.

The only way currently to get the most updated version of the SpaceKit is via direct CVS access. The author, Frank Morton, continues to develop and check in his code regularly on the CVS server.

The file you want to pick up is `spacekit.jar`. You can access the CVS tree without your own CVS client by going through the web interface to CVS.

Using a CVS Client

If you're already using the CVS client, or if the web interface does not work for you, you can use a CVS client to find the server location:

```
:pserver:anonymous@www.bxxp.org:/projects/spacekit-java
```

The password is 'guest' and the said JAR file would be under `jars` folder

HTTP Download

If you wish to download the distribution via HTTP, you will need to download the entire version archive. You can find this as a link at the bottom of the BXXP SpaceKit for Java page.

Which Version Do We Use?

If you're writing all of the agents (whether client-server or peer) in the application yourself, you can probably use any version of the SpaceKit to build your project. However, if you need to talk to agents written by others, it is best to use the latest version of the SpaceKit since it usually tracks the changes in the BXXP draft as they are made. At the time of writing the latest version is 1.3.2.

To "install" the SpaceKit, simply make sure you put it into your classpath. We have put the JAR file in the `Chapter19` folder again. The best way to test your installation of the SpaceKit is to try:

```
java org.bxxp.spacekit.example.SpacePing sqa.invisible.net
```

This will "ping" the server at Invisible Worlds using a BXXP-level connect. The `sqa.invisible.net` server is up most of the time, and serves as a listener for many of the protocols support by the SpaceKit. Be aware, however, that some firewalls may make performing this utility difficult if not impossible. If the `SpacePing` is successful, you should see the ping reply:

```
echo: Ping
sink: <null />
```

One caveat: the actual path to the `SpacePing` utility and several other classes has moved around different packages quite a bit. It will likely move again in future releases of the SpaceKit. The best way to determine, given a specific download of the SpaceKit, where you may find `SpacePing`, is to enter (Unix only):

```
jar tvf spacekit.jar | grep SpacePing
```

and look for the actual path of the utility. Alternatively, you can examine the JAR file via a Win32 utility such as WinZip, or examine the revision history over the Web via CVS.

Creating a Custom BXXP Module

A BXXP module is the application logic that implements the listener side behavior of a specific profile. In an RPC analogy, it is the remote procedure implementation. The key to writing a BXXP module is to extend `org.bxxp.spacekit.bxxp.SpaceModuleThread`. This inherits from `Thread`, which implements the `Runnable` interface. Your core logic will be in the `run()` method.

You can find the source code to `SMDateOp.java` in the `Chapter19\bxxp\module` distribution directory in the downloaded source code for this chapter:

```
import java.util.Calendar;
import java.util.StringTokenizer;
import org.bxxp.spacekit.bxxd.SpaceBxxd.*;
import org.bxxp.spacekit.util.SpaceException;
import org.bxxp.spacekit.bxxp.SpaceTimeout;

public class SMDateOp extends org.bxxp.spacekit.bxxp.SpaceModuleThread {

  public void run() {
    try {
      if(isStart()) {
        start("");
        return;
      }
```

As per the BXXP specification, we respond with a start message if we receive a start message. If the message length is zero, our profile indicates that this is a request for the server time; we return a reply that includes the date:

```
      // if no arguments, this must be request for the time at the server
      if (message.toString().length() == 0)  {
        String servDate =  Calendar.getInstance().getTime().toString();
        reply(servDate);
        log("server date returned");
```

Our service includes only two methods so if it is not the date request it must be calculating the sum of two numbers. We check that there are two arguments provided with the request and if there are not we return an error:

```
      // request to add two numbers
      } else {
        StringTokenizer myTz = new StringTokenizer(message.toString()," ");
        if (myTz.countTokens() != 2)
          error(1000,"invalid add number call request");
```

821

We can now scan the message for the numbers to add and return the sum as a string.

```
          } else {
            try {
              int a = Integer.parseInt(myTz.nextToken());
              int b = Integer.parseInt(myTz.nextToken());
              reply("" + (a+b));
              log("addition performed and returned");
            } catch (NumberFormatException ex) {
            error(1000,"request arguments not numbers");
            }
          }
        }
    } catch(SpaceTimeout e) {
      fatal(e);
    } catch(SpaceException e) {
      fatal(e);
    }
  }
}
```

Obviously, we could have defined the procedure calls as an XML element, similar to XMLRPC's <methodCall> element. That would, however, have unnecessarily complicated the logic of the server, and obscured the BXXP-specific operations.

To compile the module, assuming that spacekit.jar is still in your classpath, use the command line:

```
javac SMDateOp.java
```

Writing a BXXP Client

In the BXXP client, we will be sending messages with the protocol according to our profile. The end result will be equivalent to the RPC calls we've made in the XMLRPC and SOAP examples. The file should be stored in the Chapter19\bxxp\client directory.

```
import org.bxxp.spacekit.bxxd.SpaceBxxd.*;
import org.bxxp.spacekit.util.*;
import org.bxxp.spacekit.bxxp.*;

public class SMClient {

  public static void main(String[] argv) {
    SpaceConnection connection = null;
    int x = 3;
    int y = 4;

    try {
      connection = new SpaceConnection("localhost",8080);
      SpaceReply greeting = connection.connect(true);
```

First, we create a connection with the server. By default, we will connect to the service at port 8080. Note the `true` flag indicates that we will wait until the connection is opened:

```
SpaceChannel channel =
        connection.getChannel("http://xml.wrox.org/profiles/DATE");
```

Next we open a channel that will support our custom profile, which we have called DATE. This will be successful only if the server supports such a profile on the port:

```
SpaceReply dateStart = channel.start(true);
```

As required by BXXP, the first message we send on this channel is the start message. Next, we make a call to obtain the server date and time:

```
SpaceReply myReply = channel.message("",true);
System.out.println("The current server time is: " + myReply.toString());
```

This is done via a message of zero length, as specified in our profile. The returned server date is then printed on the console:

```
myReply = channel.message("" + x + " " + y,true);
```

Next, we send a string with the two numbers to be added separated by a blank space. According to our DATE profile, this will trigger the `addNumber()` functionality:

```
System.out.println("The sum of " + x + " and " + y + " is " +
                        myReply.toString());
```

Finally, we print out the sum from the server:

```
    } catch(NullPointerException e) {
        System.err.println("java SMClient");
    } catch(SpaceTimeout e) {
        System.err.println(e.toString());
    } catch(SpaceException e) {
        System.err.println(e.toString());
    } finally {
        if(connection != null) {
            connection.close();
        }
    }
  }
}
```

To compile the client enter the command line:

```
javac SMClient.java
```

Running the Application

We will build into the application the ability to monitor the BXXP traffic with the tunnel monitor from the Apache SOAP distribution from the start. So our service will run on port 8082 and the monitor will connect requests to port 8080:

The BXXP service is implemented in `org.bxxp.spacekit.bxxd.SpaceBxxd`. This class expects a home directory to be specified, in which it will keep logging information. We have chosen to structure this home directory much like a web application. Our BXXP home folder structure looks like the following:

```
\BxxpHome\
    \config\
        bxxp.config
    \module\
        SpaceModule.java
    \logs\
        bxxd.log
```

The `\config\` directory contains configuration files. Note that it is not necessary to store the configuration files here, we have done this for convenience's sake. The `\module\` folder contains Java classes that service requests; this folder will need to be added to the classpath in order for the BXXP server to be able to load them.

The configuration file takes the relative address of a log file, which it will create if it does not exist. To test our application we will need to start up the BXXP service with our module running. We will first write the configuration file, called `bxxd.config`, supplied in the download for this chapter in the `\ProJavaXML\Chapter19\bxxp\config\` directory. Here are its contents:

```xml
<?xml version="1.0"?>
<!DOCTYPE config PUBLIC "-//Blocks//DTD BXXD CONFIG//EN"
                        "http://xml.resource.org/blocks/bxxd/config.dtd">

<config>
  <bxxd port="8082">
    <parameter name="homeDirectory"
                value="c:/projavaxml/chapter19/bxxp/" />
    <parameter name="logFile"
                value="logs/bxxd.8082.log" />
    <parameter name="debugLevel"
                value="none" />

    <profile uri="http://xml.wrox.com/profiles/DATE"
             module="SMDateOp">
    </profile>
  </bxxd>
</config>
```

The port parameter specifies the port to listen to. You may need to change the `homeDirectory` value to your system's requirement. The log file we will name after the port that is being listened to (`bxxd.8082.log`). This file also informs the service of the profile-to-module mapping.

Remember that in order to start the service we must make sure that:

❏   spacekit.jar is in the classpath

❏   The path to the module, SMDateOp.class, is also in the classpath

Starting from the \bxxp\config\ directory, we can start the service:

```
java org.bxxp.spacekit.bxxd.SpaceBxxd -standalone -portno 8082 bxxd.config
```

Once the server is running, we can start the tunnel monitor. This time we will make a bridge from port 8080 to port 8082, which is being used by the BXXP server.

Making sure that soap.jar is in your classpath, use this command line to start the tunnel monitor:

```
java org.apache.soap.util.net.TcpTunnelGui 8080 localhost 8082
```

With the tunnel monitor up and running, open a new window and navigating to the \ProJavaXML\Chapter19\bxxp\client\ directory, start the client:

```
java SMClient
```

Your client should obtain the server date and successfully add the two numbers. Output should be similar to the following, which should be familiar by now:

```
C:\ProJavaXML\chapter19\bxxp\client>java SMClient
The current server time is: Fri Mar 02 03:50:34 GMT+00:00 2001
The sum of 3 and 4 is 7

C:\ProJavaXML\chapter19\bxxp\client>
```

Examining BXXP Traffic Using Tunnel Monitor

Looking at the capture in the tunnel monitor for the client side, we can see in detail how BXXP works. You should be able to identify:

❏   Session establishment, a <greeting> message

❏   Create channel 1, the <start> message

❏   Get server time call with the DATE profile, a MSG with empty payload

❏   Add number call, DATE profile, a MSG with two integer to add as payload

❏   Close session, a <close> message

Here is the trace from the tunnel monitor:

```
RPY 0 0 . 0 66
Content-Type: application/beep+xml

<greeting localize='en-us'/>END
SEQ 0 127 65407
MSG 0 1 . 66 131
Content-Type: application/beep+xml
```

```
<start number='1'>
<profile uri='http://xml.wrox.org/profiles/DATE'>
</profile>
</start>
END
SEQ 0 224 65407
MSG 1 1 . 0 38
Content-Type: application/beep+xml

END
SEQ 1 60 65407
MSG 1 1 . 38 41
Content-Type: application/beep+xml

3 4END
SEQ 1 87 65407
MSG 0 1 . 197 58
Content-Type: application/beep+xml

<close code='200' />END
SEQ 0 268 65407
```

From the listener side, we can see:

❑   Session established with a <greeting> message

❑   Positive reply to create channel 1, returning profile supported as payload

❑   Getting server time call on channel 1, a RPY with server date as payload

❑   Added number call on channel 1, RPY with sum of two numbers as payload

❑   Received close session message, RPY with <ok/> as payload

Here is the tunnel monitor trace:

```
SEQ 0 66 65407
RPY 0 0 . 0 127
Content-Type: application/beep+xml

<greeting localize='en-us'><profile uri='http://xml.wrox.org/profiles/DATE'
/></greeting>END
SEQ 0 197 65407
RPY 0 1 . 127 97
Content-Type: application/beep+xml

<profile uri='http://xml.wrox.org/profiles/DATE'></profile>END
SEQ 1 38 65407
RPY 1 1 . 0 60
Content-Type: text/xml

Fri Mar 02 03:50:34 GMT+00:00 2001END
SEQ 1 79 65407
RPY 1 1 . 60 27
Content-Type: text/xml

7END
SEQ 0 255 65407
RPY 0 1 . 224 44
Content-Type: application/beep+xml

<ok />END
```

Examining BXXP Logs

During execution, the BXXP server will not output to the console. You can find status messages in the log file. The BXXP server logs information in a file under the log directory specified in the bxxp.config file; we can find our log in the bxxp.8082.log. Here is the content indicating the call had been successful:

```
03/02 03:50:19 info   8082        start
03/02 03:50:19 info   8082        listen
03/02 03:50:34 info   8082        connect 127.0.0.1
03/02 03:50:34 info   8082        listen
03/02 03:50:34 info   8082        connect 127.0.0.1
03/02 03:50:34 info   8082        greeting <greeting localize='en-us'/>
03/02 03:50:34 info   8082        localize en-us
03/02 03:50:34 info   8082.0.1    profile http://xml.wrox.org/profiles/DATE
03/02 03:50:34 info   8082.0.1    module SMDateOp
03/02 03:50:34 info   8082.0.1    start
03/02 03:50:34 info   8082.1.1    profile http://xml.wrox.org/profiles/DATE
03/02 03:50:34 info   8082.1.1    module SMDateOp
03/02 03:50:34 info   8082.1.1    start
03/02 03:50:34 info   8082.1.1    profile http://xml.wrox.org/profiles/DATE
03/02 03:50:34 info   8082.1.1    module SMDateOp
03/02 03:50:34 info   8082.1.1    start
03/02 03:50:34 info   8082.1.1    server date returned
03/02 03:50:34 info   8082        disconnect 127.0.0.1
03/02 03:50:34 info   8082.1.1    addition performed and returned
```

Comparing and Contrasting XML Protocols

Below is a relative comparison of the various features of the XML protocols that we have covered in this chapter, with observations on the strengths and weaknesses of each protocol. This also provides suggestions on when they should be used.

XMLRPC

XMLRPC is a lightweight, quick, easy, and workable implementation for remote invocation of functionality through HTTP tunneling.

Some of its features are as follows:

❑   HTTP Tunneling is integral to this protocol

❑   RPC Handling is integral to this protocol

❑   Disconnected Operations are not currently possible

❑   Specifications are very easy to understand

❑   It is very easy to program – this was one of the original design goals

❑   Protocol traffic is readily understandable and a human operator would find it easy to decipher unencrypted traffic flow if no specification was available

❑   General protocol efficiency is not a design criterion

❑   It is not possible to multiplex many channels – a new connection must be opened for each new channel

❑   It does not support decentralized, multi-agents "processing path", unlike SOAP; there can only be one server servicing a client.

❑   It is a fixed protocol instance – it has no ability to host other protocols

❑   There is no directly specified security and authentication, but many implementations provide authenticated services

❑   Request and response bodies are both XML documents

SOAP

This is the key infrastructure protocol for Microsoft's new .NET effort. It's a little heavyweight for general RPC use, but will be key to interoperability with Microsoft technologies moving forward into the future.

Its features include:

❑   SOAP supports HTTP tunneling as a transport binding, but only the one specified by 1.1 specifications

❑   It supports RPC handling as a service and the encoding in specification 1.1 caters for this

❑   It will potentially support disconnected operations if transport operates in a disconnected fashion; Apache SOAP can use SMTP for this

❑   It is not easy at all to understand the specifications – it has a complex encoding scheme with heavy reliance on complex schemas; binding to protocols other than HTTP is not specified.

❑   It is not very easy to program at the current state of development

❑   In terms of ability for a human operator to decipher unencrypted traffic flow if no specification is available, with SOAP simple cases will be decipherable and moderate-to-complex cases will require machine assistance

❑   General protocol efficiency was not a design criterion

❑   Multi-channels and multiplexing are not currently supported and new connections are required for new channels

❑   Mention is made in the specifications of decentralized, multi-agents "processing path" support and extending the attributes on the envelope possibly supports this; however, no details have been supplied with the 1.1 specifications

❑   The ability to host other protocols is not directly applicable, although the SOAP 1.1 specification is loose enough that different implementations may look like different protocols

❑   Security and authentication are not directly specified, but implementations have flexibility to implement security measures at several levels

❑   The envelope, request, and response are all XML documents; embedded encoding may or may not be wholly XML-based as per the 1.1 specification

BXXP

In summary, this is a generic, efficient, Internet-grade protocol construction set for cases where you have control over both ends of the connection and the XMLRPC model of interaction may be insufficient for your needs. Its features include:

- ❏ It has no direct relationship to HTTP tunneling
- ❏ It can readily create new profiles/modules to handle RPC
- ❏ It does not support disconnected operations
- ❏ It is easy to understand the specifications
- ❏ In terms of ease of programming, it is moderately difficult
- ❏ In terms of ability for a human operator to decipher unencrypted traffic flow, this will depend on the application-level protocol, but the BXXP portion should be easily understandable
- ❏ General protocol efficiency is a key design criterion
- ❏ Multi-channels and multiplexing are key design criteria, and one connection supports multiple channels
- ❏ Decentralized, mutli-agents "processing path" support is not part of the BXXP protocol, but application-level protocols can support this behavior
- ❏ BXXP is a construction kit for efficient XML protocols and the ability to host other protocols is a key design goal
- ❏ Security and authentication are an integral part of the protocol foundation, which is well-specified and completely extensible
- ❏ Protocol profile negotiation, channel management, and payload are all XML-based

Summary

In this chapter, we looked at three different types of protocols with a particularly affinity for transmitting XML documents. We also sampled them through building applications that incorporated them.

It is evident from the above that all three of the XML-based protocols have a place in our distributed design practice. They are designed with very different goals in mind, and as a result each services a slightly different audience.

XML and advanced parsing technologies have enabled protocol designers to easily create robust application protocols that facilitate distributed computing over the connected Internet. Applying XML to the structures that are part of the protocol enables third parties to observe and interface to legacy systems, even without the co-operation of the system.

Using XML as the mechanism to express structured data exchanged within these protocols enables heterogeneous machines, operating systems, and computing devices to all participate on an equal basis in the distributed computing world.

The Xerces Blue
butterfly, which became
extinct earlier this century,
and after which the Xerces XML
parser is named ...

20

XML and Messaging

Although there is no generally accepted definition of a message, it is typical to think of it in the most general sense as an information packet, which is used to transfer knowledge or request actions between participating nodes. A message can take many forms and can be used for many purposes. A message may contain some information such as a calendar time or a stock quote, or a message may contain a request to obtain some remote service according to some protocol.

In any messaging system, we must think of a message, rather than a chunk of bytes, as the unit of information transfer. We use many messaging systems commonly in day-to-day life. For example, we use e-mail, post-it notes, body language, books, fragrances, lectures, etc. to transfer information or request services.

In this chapter we will study how to use XML for messaging using a Java Message Service (JMS) provider. We will add the ability for messages to be routed to a web service via a "message to HTTP" bridge server. In the process we will cover:

❑ The two broad mechanisms for transporting messages: peer-to-peer systems and messaging middleware-based systems

❑ Publish/Subscribe (Pub/Sub) and Point-to-Point (PTP) domains for middleware-based messaging

❑ Some scenarios in a large distributed enterprise computing environments and how we can combine the advantages of XML with messaging

❑ Constructing a transport mechanism using JMS for the Apache-SOAP 2.0 implementation running on the Tomcat web server; then present a modified version of the example in the previous chapter to use this transport mechanism

Messaging and XML Overview

Messaging is getting an increasing focus for enterprise communication. It is increasingly evident that messaging is a valid answer to many problems encountered in traditional client-server type of communication. There is also an increasing support for messaging through standardization of messaging APIs such as Java Messaging Service (JMS). Further support for making messaging part of enterprise communication can be seen in the EJB 2.0 specification where the Message-Driven Bean, a type of simplified Enterprise JavaBean controlled through container-managed messaging software rather than directly by the client, is a new type of bean in addition to the familiar session and entity beans.

As seen in the rest of the book XML has many diverse uses. It is used in web-publishing systems, as persistence storage format, as a configuration and deployment description format, and with RPC protocols such as XML-RPC and SOAP.

An obvious question arises: Does the combination of messaging and XML make sense? The answer is a resounding "yes". New emerging standards such as ebXML and Java API for XML Messaging (JAXM) exclusively focus on combining these two technologies. Understanding how combining messaging and XML together brings advantages of the both worlds together for creating a reliable, scalable, fault-tolerant communication infrastructure is the focus of this chapter.

Mechanisms for Transporting Messages

Broadly speaking, there are two kinds of mechanism for transporting messages: the one that involves direct communication between interested parties and the other one that requires intermediate agent to facilitate communication. The direct communication mechanism is also called peer-to-peer communication. This kind of communication requires peers to know each other's physical address details, such as machine IP address and port number.

The other kind involves the use of messaging middleware. Transporting messages using messaging middleware can be further classified into one-to-many communication that uses a publish/subscribe paradigm and one-to-one communication that uses queue-based communication. Either of these approaches involves an abstract concept of message destination rather that using physical destination such as machine IP address and port number.

Peer-to-Peer Communication

The most common way to transfer a message is using peer-to-peer approach, where one peer plays the role of server and the other of client. To communicate they establish a connection and exchange messages over that connection. Communication between peers is direct; it does not involve an intermediate agent or facilitator. An example of such a mechanism is getting a web page from a web server. The browser sends a GET message to the server and server replies with a message that includes the content of the document sought.

This sort of peer-to-peer-based mechanism can transfer messages from point A to point B. However, it requires additional support if transaction, reliability, or persistence services are needed. Additional steps are also needed if there is more than one consumer for a message. Peer-to-peer mechanisms also suffer from scalability problems. When a system consists of hundreds of nodes, the resource requirement (memory, CPU power, and threads/processes) grows exponentially.

Messaging Service-Based Communication

A messaging service-based approach involves middleware that takes the responsibility of facilitating transfer of messages between different nodes. In this approach, nodes do not communicate to each other directly but only to the middleware. Nodes also need not know each other's physical address (for instance, their IP addresses and port numbers). Although most implementations of messaging middleware involve the use of a central server or set of central servers, the messaging paradigm itself does not impose this. It is possible, for example, to use a connection-less protocol such as UDP as an underlying protocol to implement the messaging service, in which case we can use broadcasting or multicasting of messages to reduce network traffic.

Messaging service-based communication has two basic paradigms: Publish/Subscribe and Point-to-Point.

Publish/Subscribe Messaging

A Publish/Subscribe (Pub/Sub) messaging system supports an event driven-model, where consumers and producers participate in the transmission of messages. Producers **publish** events, while consumers **subscribe** to events of interest. Producers associate messages with a specific **topic**, and the messaging system routes messages to consumers based on the topics the consumers registered an interest in.

Publish-subscribe networking is a messaging model that simplifies programming in applications that must distribute data in one-to-many and many-to-many patterns. In this model, applications communicate by sending information tagged with a topic – a user-provided name. Nodes in the system have roles of publisher and subscriber. Publishers publish information they know under some known topic and subscribers subscribe to topics they need to know. Publishers and subscribers do not need to know about each other, or about the destinations or the origins of the messages.

Pub/Sub networking scales well, makes the application modular because each node implements a specific and limited aspect of the system, and is well-suited to dynamic networks; for example, adding/removing publishers does not disrupt the information flow. Publish-subscribe eases application programming in three ways: publishers need to know only about the topics they publish on; subscribers need to know only about the topics they want to subscribe to; and it eliminates the need for establishing and managing information about the network itself.

Pub/Sub messaging naturally enables many-to-many communication. It thus enables the use of connection-less underlying protocols (UDP) and multicasting for achieving efficient communication and scalability. The use of a connectionless underlying protocol also addresses the issue of a central server being the single point-of-failure even where clustering technology is not employed.

In real life, we use the Pub/Sub communication paradigm all the time. For example, we subscribe to news groups we are interested in, mailing lists we are interested in, and so on. In each case, once subscribed we automatically get messages whenever a new message, which should interest us, is available.

Point-to-Point Messaging

In Point-to-Point (PTP) messaging, the destination of a message is called a **queue**. The messaging system maintains queues of messages. Producers send messages to a specified queue and the messaging system routes messages to a consumer of that queue. In some senses, point-to-point messaging is peer-to-peer communication with an extra level of indirection: the producers and consumers do not know about each other directly but only though the queue they are accessing. A good example of this paradigm is e-mail; the sender only knows about the recipient's e-mail address and not the machine the receiver will be using to read e-mail. The difference between Pub/Sub and PTP communication is that in the former, the middleware will deliver each message to all the subscribers for each destination (topic) whereas in the latter, it will deliver to only one consumer of that destination (queue). If there is more than one consumer for a queue, the middleware will choose, depending on implementation, one consumer and deliver the message to it. In other words, in PTP messaging, the middleware removes a message as soon as a consumer reads it effectively making the communication one-to-one.

Pub/Sub and PTP messaging lend themselves to different types of scenario. In general, Pub/Sub is more suitable for read-only service requests such as querying stock quotes. Because read-only requests do not affect the state of the server, if multiple subscribers get and fulfill that request, there is no effect on the state of the system. Pub/Sub is also a valid choice for implementing "idempotent" requests that change state of the system. Idempotency is a mathematical term describing operations that have the same effect however many times they are performed. An example of an idempotent operation is saving a document: if we save the document more that once, the result is no different from saving it once.

In Pub/Sub messaging, all subscribers to a topic will receive a message published on that topic. If multiple subscribers affect the state of the system in non-idempotent ways, the result will be as if the operation was invoked as many times as there are subscribers. For these reasons, point-to-point is a better choice for implementing non-idempotent service requests such as charging to a credit card. In the point-to-point domain, if multiple consumers exist for a queue, messaging middleware will ensure that only one of the consumers will get the message.

Distributed Enterprise Application Scenarios

In this section, we will examine a few cases in a typical large enterprise where applications need to transfer messages between its nodes. We will consider an e-commerce enterprise system that accepts customer orders, processes payment information, and ships the order. We will look into a few scenarios and solutions using simple peer-to-peer-based solutions to each. We will use the same scenarios later to explain how use of messaging middleware helps to simplify the architecture.

Consider a large enterprise providing e-commerce facilities to its customers. Because of the high stakes involved, there are some critical requirements that the architecture must satisfy:

- ❑ **Redundancy** – The system must include some amount of redundancy to accommodate node failures. Consequently, the system must use multiple servers for each role, such as credit card processing. A node can contact any of the servers fulfilling the desired role to get its job done. If one such node fails, other nodes in the same role should continue to let the system run without any noticeable interruptions. For example, an order-processing server can use any of the credit card-processing servers.

- ❑ **Load balancing** – The system must balance load between nodes in the same role. The system must try to use servers in such a way that throughput of the overall system is maximized.

❑   **Transactions** – Order processing must appear to have taken place atomically. In other words, order processing must be performed in the context of a transaction. The system must roll back the whole request if any of the steps fail. The unfulfilled request must leave system in the same state (except for appropriate logging etc. as if that request had never arrived).

If the node cannot deliver any of the messages, it must abandon the entire order processing. In other words, the system must perform distribution of all the messages as a part of a transaction. For example, order processing involves sending messages to several servers: credit card approval server, inventory management server, supply-chain management server, packaging and delivery server.

❑   **Delivery guarantee** – Failure or delayed delivery of certain kinds of message should not disrupt the main processing logic. However, the system must save all such failed requests and attempt to resend then at a later time. The system should also be able to differentiate between duplicate requests, to avoid charging a customer twice, or shipping an item twice. Because the system may need to deliver these kinds of messages to more than one node, the system must keep track of all the nodes that did not receive a message for some reason.

For example, consider a server in the packaging department that shows a list of unfulfilled deliveries. If such a server is up, it is desirable that it receives the message as soon as possible so that the packaging department can make earlier deliveries or at least schedule their deliveries. However, if such a server is down, it is not catastrophic; the system must accept customer orders. Whenever the server comes back online, the order-processing server will send the entire queue of unsent messages, perhaps in chunks to avoid overwhelming the order-processing node.

A Peer-to-Peer Example

Let's consider how we can use a peer-to-peer communication mechanism to achieve the above requirements. We will analyze each requirement and suggest a solution using peer-to-peer communication. Each requirement could be satisfied in a variety of ways, and the one suggested here might well not be optimal in all scenarios:

❑   **Redundancy** – Each node that needs to use credit-card processing services must be aware of all such servers. It then can contact a server from the list to use the service. If it realizes that the server it is using has failed, it must contact the next server to get its job done and so on.

❑   **Load balancing** – A client could periodically query each server's load and its maximum capacity. It can then sort its list of servers to call into an appropriate order. Another possibility is to monitor the time taken by each request and use the server with the quickest response time. Another possible solution is for servers to reject requests when their load is near its capacity.

❑   **Transactions** – Each node must perform its operations inside a transaction context. If any request fails, it must roll back the whole process. If all requests succeed the order processing node must send a "commit" message to all nodes it cooperated with during that transaction.

❑   **Delivery guarantee** – There are a few solutions to this problem using peer-to-peer-based messaging. One solution could be as follows. The packaging department's server could use a pull model instead of push, in which it will periodically query for new orders to ship. The other possibility is the order-processing server could periodically try to send new orders. This would add extra responsibility to the order server as it needs to keep track of which server received the message and which failed to receive so that it can resend it later. In either case, the order-processing server must take responsibility to store messages until delivered. This would necessitate a reliable persistence mechanism, such as a database, in case of sudden failure.

The node must tag each persisted message with information about the servers that require this message. For example, in addition to going to the packaging department's server, it may be required that a message be sent to a mailing server so that it can compose and send a confirmation e-mail to the customers, to the packaging department, and so on. Handling each node that is interested in a message can become complex to manage.

Although satisfying each individual requirement is already complex enough, the complexity grows even further when we consider requirements in conjunction. Consider, for example, the redundancy and transaction requirements. When a node fails, we store the message for it along with the address for the failed node. When eventually some other node comes back fulfilling the same role, we need to deliver the message to this new node instead of the original address.

The Need for MOM

In this section, we explain why we need **message-oriented middleware** (MOM). This is important because it's easy to understand the "how" part of messaging APIs, such as JMS, but effectively using messaging in an enterprise environment requires a good understanding of the "why" part.

Before we go into the need for MOM further, lets briefly look at kinds of MOMs available today. Most of the MOMs support either Publish/Subscribe messaging or PTP messaging or both. The most important set of MOMs from Java developers' point of view are the ones that implement the JMS API. These included FioranoMQ from Fiorano, SpiritWave from Push Technologies, SwiftMQ from IIT GmbH, and MQSeries from IBM. The latest J2EE 1.3 reference implementation also contains a JMS server which we will use in our example later.

We can summarize the requirements presented in the previous section as: **reliability**, **transaction management**, and **scalability**.

Meeting all three goals with a peer-to-peer based messaging solution is tricky. A quick glance at the above scenarios makes it clear that the order-processing server has to handle many issues apart from just the order-processing business logic. Firstly, the order-processing server needs to know about every other server in the system and the roles they perform. It also needs to know about any changes in configuration such as the addition of new server, changes in roles performed, changes in their capacity, and any failures of those nodes. It needs to also take responsibility for transaction management, and handle persistence and repeated attempts at delivery for failed messages. Scalability, an implicit requirement to any solution, is also harder to achieve, because adding a node is made more difficult by the need for all other nodes in the system to be informed.

Message-oriented-middleware comes to the rescue, helping with each of these problems. Now, let's consider solutions using MOM to each of the scenarios we listed before. We will use PTP as the communications backbone of the system. Each service will be available on a well-known queue. For example, the credit-processing service will be available on queue named `credit-processing`. Those who wish to process a credit card payment will send a message containing the required information to the `credit-processing` queue. A credit-card-processing server will receive this message and will reply with another message containing information such as purchase status, and confirmation number. For more concrete implementation details of this approach, see *"Marrying SOAP to JMS"* later in the chapter.

A typical system using this approach will use more than one node providing all critical services to introduce certain amount of redundancy. For example, there will be two or more nodes providing credit card processing service on the queue `credit-processing`.

❑ **Redundancy** – This implies that the system must use one-to-many communication. Having multiple servers providing the same service on the same queue satisfies the requirement of redundant nodes. The rest is taken care of by MOM. None of the nodes that need this service need to be aware of the presence of multiple servers; they just need to know what queue relates to which service.

Under normal circumstances, all nodes will serve requests based on their load. If one of the nodes fails, the others will continue to serve all the requests. In either case, no other nodes need to know about this change of scenario, except that they may experience increased response time due to the higher load on one server. If the failed node comes back online later, or some other new node offering same service joins the network, no other nodes will need to know about the change, except that they may notice an improved system response. In other words, use of MOM enables hot swapping of nodes in the system.

❑ **Load balancing** – Having multiple servers providing the message-oriented service also satisfies the requirement of automatic load balancing. With multiple service providers present, only the MOM needs to know about them and their capacity. MOM could incorporate a process that could, for example, use response time for each service provider as the criteria for dispatching the next request. The one that works fastest gets to do more work.

❑ **Transactions** – Using MOM that provides transaction services, such as those defined in the JMS API, satisfies the requirement of processing every order within a transaction. Applications need to send messages in the context of a transaction; MOM will take care of sending messages to all its consumers as an atomic operation.

❑ **Delivery guarantee** – MOM that provides persistent destinations for messaging clients solves this requirement. MOM takes care of storing such durable messages and delivers them when a consumer comes back online. If a new node joins the system, MOM will automatically deliver messages to the new node as it only cares about the logical destination – the queue a subscribing node is interested in – and not the actual address of any node.

It is evident from the solution above that because MOM takes on the responsibility of providing services needed, the components using messaging are much easier to write and maintain. This way each component developer can concentrate on business logic and not on providing extraneous services.

With the proposed architecture, using messaging as the base, nodes in the system do not know about each other directly, but only though the abstract destination such as topic or queue. Nodes requiring service do not care which node ultimately serves the request. This characteristic makes it possible to replace a node with another one providing the same services without the rest of the system knowing about it. In such a system with redundant nodes, failed nodes do not interrupt the operation of the system as a whole.

Although the focus of this chapter is XML messaging using Java, it is worth noting that one may architect an environment where some nodes use other languages than Java. The use of XML, as opposed to some adhoc text or binary format, provides a uniform communication protocol that is language neutral. The system may in theory replace a node programmed in one language with another node programmed in another language with no impact on the rest of the system.

XML in Messaging

XML documents contain structured information. For example, an XML document could describe an order, or an inventory. We can use messaging to transport these documents from one node to another.

Service Request and Response

Traditionally, RPC-like mechanisms such as CORBA or RMI are used to invoke services across a network. A server registers objects under a well-known name with an object registry, then clients who need to use services provided by such an object first locate the object by name using the object registry, which hands a proxy for the remote object to the client. Proxy objects relay calls to the real object over the network using some remote method invocation protocol such as the Internet Inter Orb Protocol (IIOP) or Java Remote Method Protocol (JRMP).

These protocols, due to their complexity, make it hard to communicate through a firewall. XML comes into play here. XML-based remote method protocols are easy for a firewall to inspect and make it possible to establish communication between a client and a server across firewall.

Additionally, protocols such as IIOP and JRMP are connection oriented. They assume a stream-oriented connection between the communicating parties. This makes it harder to use multicasting to improve scalability. Using a message-oriented approach enables the use of multicasting using connectionless protocols such as UDP.

XML-RPC and Simple Object Access Protocol (SOAP), which we looked at in the previous chapter, are examples of these XML-based remote method invocation protocols. These protocols specify an XML message format for invoking a method on a remote object and the response to such requests.

We can use XML-based RPC protocols along with messaging as a transport mechanism. Such a combination transfers requests and responses as text-messages using MOM. XML-based RPC protocols when combined with the messaging paradigm provide several advantages over those using traditional transports. Loosely speaking, messaging-based RPC mechanisms offer all the benefits of messaging itself:

- ❑ **Fault tolerance** – In messaging, the destination is only symbolic; you can simply add a node to the system that provides the same services, and pull off the serving nodes without the client noticing a difference.

- ❑ **Load balancing** – With Pub/Sub as the messaging paradigm for message-based RPC, if more than one service provider exists on network, MOM will automatically route requests among the service providers.

It is not necessary to use XML-based messages to take advantage of the benefits offered by the messaging paradigm. One could easily use, for example, arbitrary text or binary messages to invoke remote services. However, the use of XML makes it possible to take advantage of ubiquitous support tools such as XML parsers and transformers, which makes it easier to construct real-world applications. Many emerging standards for e-commerce communication are using XML. Using XML for messaging enables us to use those standards and avoid re-inventing the wheel, ensure compliance with them, and opens the door for interpretability with tools using those standards. XML also makes the protocol more firewall-friendly because it allows you to strictly specify the vocabulary for messages, which means you can ensure that nodes written in disparate programming languages are all working from the same standard communication medium.

The JMS API

JMS (Java Messaging Service) is an API from Sun Microsystems to provide asynchronous, transacted message production, distribution, and delivery. It specifies an API for PTP and Pub/Sub communication. In this section, we will elaborate only the Pub/Sub part of JMS; the point-to-point API is nearly identical. The following table shows respective interfaces for Publish/Subscribe and PTP messaging:

Publish/Subscribe API	Queue-based API	Description
Topic	Queue	Represents the message destination
TopicConnectionFactory	QueueConnectionFactory	A factory for obtaining connections to destinations
TopicConnection	QueueConnection	Represents the connection to the provider
TopicSession	QueueSession	Stores session details specific to the connection
TopicPublisher	QueueSender	Defines methods for publishing and sending messages within the session context
TopicSubscriber	QueueReceiver	Defines methods for subscribing to and receiving messages through a session context
TopicRequestor	QueueRequestor	Simulates Request/Reply messaging
TemporaryTopic	TemporaryQueue	Temporary destinations created by the client
No equivalent	QueueBrowser	For preselecting messages prior to delivery

Application developers can use either event-based message notification or write code that blocks, waiting for messages. With the event-based notification, the middleware notifies the subscribers when a message is received. With blocking I/O styled programming, applications poll the middleware for new messages. JMS provides the ability for nodes to request pattern-based subscriptions; that is, subscribers can specify SQL-based patterns on message headers for the destinations they are interested in receiving.

JMS also provides an API for client-server communication using the publish-subscribe model. With the client-server mechanism, a client can ask the network for a service and any node providing that service can reply to the request made.

JMS also specifies a durable subscription API. The API requires the middleware to store messages for the topics subscribed by durable subscription to be stored in some persistent storage so that these messages can be delivered even after network problems or crashes.

JMS provides a standard API making it possible to switch from one compliant JMS provider to another without requiring to change in the software that uses it. The JMS does not, however, specify the on-the-wire format for messages. Because of this, it is not guaranteed that a message from one JMS middleware will be accepted by other JMS middleware on a system. In other words JMS does not guarantee inter-operability between messaging middleware from different vendors.

JMS API for Point-to-Point Messaging

> All the objects we discuss with relation to the JMS API belong to the package
> `javax.jms`. The JAR file `jms.jar` can be obtained from http://java.sun.com/jms.

The JMS API uses the factory design pattern extensively to allow vendors to create objects of classes optimized for their middleware. The QueueConnectionFactory class is the factory for creating QueueConnection objects, which in turn acts as a factory for creating QueueSession objects. QueueSession is the factory for Queue, QueueSender, QueueReceiver, and Message.

Senders create QueueSender objects and send messages using the send() method. There are two ways to receive messages: asynchronously and synchronously. With asynchronous style, receivers create QueueReceiver objects and set a message listener on it. The middleware calls the method onMessage() on the message listener to notify it of the arrival of a new message on the queue. With synchronous style, receivers create QueueReceiver object and call receive() methods on them with an optional timeout parameter. The receive() method blocks until a message is received if no timeout is specified or in case a timeout value is specified, that much time passes without receiving a message.

Each JMS message consists of a header and a body part. The type of message determines the kind of body part it can carry. A JMS message can be of any of the five types: TextMessage, ByteMessage, ObjectMessage, StreamMessage, and MapMessage. The following table shows the main usage of these message types:

Message Type	Used to Transfer
TextMessage	Text-based information such as XML documents
ByteMessage	Raw bytes of data such as images
ObjectMessage	Java serializable objects
StreamMessage	Stream of Java primitives
MapMessage	Key/value pairs such as properties

Every JMS message has a header (in principle like an e-mail header), which is essentially a map with key of String type and value of any Java primitive type or object of any primitive wrapper type (Integer, Boolean etc.). Senders use message headers to send additional routing content, which the receivers and the middleware use. JMS reserves header entries with the prefix JMSX and JMS_.

Request/Reply Messaging with JMS

To provide services using JMS as the transport, we must be able to create a request/reply kind of mechanism. A request is sent to a server as a message, and it replies back with message. The JMS API provides the needed support to perform such operation.

The QueueRequestor class provides a basic Request/Reply mechanism. The most important method in the QueueRequestor class is request(), which takes a request message object as an argument and returns a reply message. QueueRequestor relies on the use of the TemporaryQueue class, which represents a unique queue that is valid only for the duration of QueueConnection that created it and can be consumed only by that QueueConnection. The QueueRequestor works as follows:

- The constructor creates a sender for the queue passed as an argument. It also creates a temporary queue and a receiver for that temporary queue.

- The request() method sets the outgoing message's JMSReplyTo header field using the setJMSReplyTo() method of the temporary queue created by the constructor. It then sends the message and blocks on the receiver using the receive() method.

- The replier node, on receiving the message, creates a response message. It sends that message on the queue specified in the incoming message's JMSReplyTo header field.

- The requestor node that is blocked on the temporary queue's receiver, receives the reply message and the receive() call unblocks, returning the response message.

The QueueRequestor class performs the minimum work to get job done. It does not provide timeout functionality, nor reuse of session objects. You can easily write your own custom QueueRequestor, if such additional functionality is required.

Another class provided by the JMS API is TopicRequestor, which differs from QueueRequestor only in that it uses a topic as its destination instead of a queue.

Queue requestors and topic requestors are at the heart of implementing an RPC-like mechanism using XML messages.

Example using JMS

In this section, we examine with simple code how we can use JMS to send or receive message and perform Request/Reply style communication. Although we talk about first about the Point-to-Point (PTP) domain, the API for Pub/Sub communication is identical; just replace "queue" with "topic", "send" with "publish", and "receiver" with "subscriber". But note, it is only the API – and not the behavior – that is similar between PTP and Pub/Sub messaging.

> The code in the chapter shows how to use point-to-point messaging model. But you should be easily able to port this code to use Pub/Sub model for providing the same functionality. Depending upon the nature of your problem, one may fit better than the other.

Node Initialization

Each JMS node, sender or receiver, must perform some initialization before it can send or receive any message. It is typical to use Java Naming and Directory Interface (JNDI) to obtain the administered objects, such as `QueueConnectionFactory` and `Queue` from the provider. The typical node initialization steps are

- ❑ Create the JNDI `javax.jndi.InitialContext` object suitable for connecting to the messaging provider, or other context in which messaging objects have been bound.

- ❑ Look up a `QueueConnectionFactory` from the initial context object using the its JNDI name. Typically, `QueueConnectionFactory` and `Queue` are "administered objects"; the administrator creates and names them and clients simply obtain a reference to them using their JNDI name.

- ❑ Create a `QueueConnection` using the `QueueConnectionFactory.createQueueConnection()` method on the queue connection factory.

- ❑ Create a `QueueSession` using `QueueConnection.createQueueSession()` method with the queue connection object as parameter.

The following sequence diagram formalizes these steps:

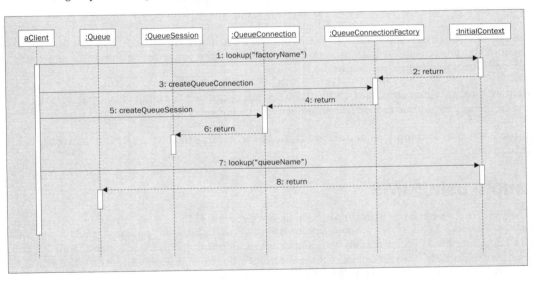

Sending a Message

Sending a message involves the following steps:

- ❑ Create a `QueueSender` using the `QueueSession.createQueueSender()` method on `QueueSession` object that was created earlier with our queue looked up from JNDI as a parameter on the queue session object.

- ❑ Create a `Message` object and set its message content.

- ❑ Send the message using the `QueueSender.send()` method with the message object as the parameter.

Again, let's take a look at the diagram to formalize this:

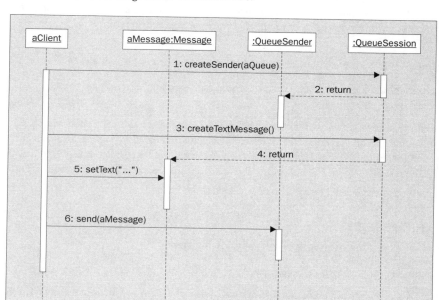

Example Sender

Here is an example program to illustrate these steps:

```
import javax.jms.*;
import javax.naming.*;

public class Sender {
  public static void main(String args[]) throws Exception {
    InitialContext ic = new InitialContext();
```

First we retrieve the administered objects, QueueConnectionFactory and Queue from the InitialContext:

```
QueueConnectionFactory qcf =
  (QueueConnectionFactory) ic.lookup("QueueConnectionFactory");

Queue queue = (Queue) ic.lookup("stock");
ic.close();

QueueConnection queueConnection = qcf.createQueueConnection();
queueConnection.start();
```

Next we create a QueueSession section using the QueueConnection.createQueueSession() method. We create the session in non-transacted mode (the first argument) and auto-acknowledgement mode (the second argument). With auto-acknowledgement, the middleware takes care of acknowledging reception of each message. If we chose Session.CLIENT_ACKNOWLEDGE instead, we would have to explicitly acknowledge receipt using the Message.acknowledge() method.

Another choice using Pub/Sub is to use `Session.DUPS_OK_ACKNOWLEDGE`, *where we are instructing the session that the receiver can tolerate duplicate message delivery and the middleware need not spend extra processing to ensure no duplicate message is delivered.*

```
    QueueSession queueSession = queueConnection.createQueueSession(false,
            Session.AUTO_ACKNOWLEDGE);
    QueueSender sender = queueSession.createSender(queue);

    TextMessage message = queueSession.createTextMessage("SUNW");
    sender.send(message);

    queueSession.close();
    queueConnection.close();
  }
}
```

Receiving a Message

Asynchronously receiving messages involves following steps:

❑   Create a `QueueSession` as before.

❑   Create a `QueueReceiver` using the `QueueSession.createReceiver()` method with required queue as a parameter on the queue session object.

❑   Create a `MessageListener` and set it as message listener to the receiver using the `QueueReceiver.setMessageListener()` method.

❑   The middleware will call the `MessageListener.onMessage()` method of this message listener object every time it receives a message for that queue (but may also route it to another consumer; recall that in the PTP domain, there can only be one final consumer of a message).

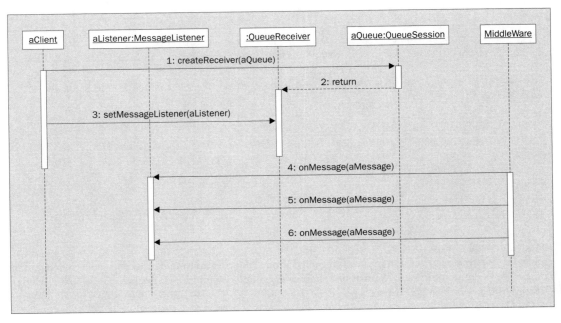

Example Receiver

Here is the code for the example receiver:

```
import javax.jms.*;
import javax.naming.*;

public class Receiver {
  public static void main(String args[]) throws Exception {
    InitialContext ic = new InitialContext();
    QueueConnectionFactory qcf =
      (QueueConnectionFactory) ic.lookup("QueueConnectionFactory");

    Queue queue = (Queue) ic.lookup("stock");
    ic.close();

    QueueConnection queueConnection = qcf.createQueueConnection();
    queueConnection.start();
    QueueSession queueSession = queueConnection.createQueueSession(false,
            Session.AUTO_ACKNOWLEDGE);
    QueueReceiver receiver = queueSession.createReceiver(queue);

    receiver.setMessageListener(new MessageHandler());
  }
}
```

```
class MessageHandler implements MessageListener {
  public void onMessage(Message msg) {
    try {
      TextMessage request = (TextMessage) msg;
      System.out.println("Request: " + request.getText());
    } catch (JMSException ex) {
      ex.printStackTrace();
    }
  }
}
```

Running the Sender/Receiver Example

> The latest 1.3 reference implementation of J2EE contains JMS server. We will use it for all our examples. You can download it from
> **http://developer.java.sun.com/developer/earlyAccess/j2ee**

This section provides instructions to run the example messaging application we've been discussing. The instructions here are provided for the JMS server bundled with the J2EE 1.3beta reference implementation. You will need to take corresponding steps if you want to use some other JMS server. Similarly, the instructions assume that you are running the example on a Windows machine. If you are running on a UNIX machine instead, you will need to adjust the path names accordingly.

Setting Up the Environment

You must set the following environment variables. For more detailed information, please see doc\guides\jms\html\client.fm.html under the J2EE installation directory:

Environment variable	Value
JAVA_HOME	Directory where JDK1.3 is installed
J2EE_HOME	Directory where J2EE reference implementation is installed
CLASSPATH	Include <J2EE_HOME>\lib\j2ee.jar and <J2EE_HOME>\lib\locale
PATH	Include <J2EE_HOME>\bin

Set up Administered Objects

To create, delete, or query administered objects, you need to use the j2eeadmin program. To create a queue named stock and a queue connection factory called QueueConnectionFactory issue the following commands:

```
> j2eeadmin -addJmsDestination stock queue
> j2eeadmin -addJmsConnectionFactor
```

You may want to verify the addition of the new queue object by issuing the following command:

```
> j2eeadmin -listJmsDestination
```

You should see the following:

Run the receiver:

Run the sender in a new window:

Requesting a Service

Requesting the service involves the following steps:

- ❏ Create a `QueueRequestor`.

- ❏ Call the `request()` method with the message containing the request as a parameter. This call will be blocked until it receives a reply, unless the timeout parameter was supplied. In this case it will return if there is no message within the time specified by the timeout parameter.

- ❏ When a reply is received, the `receive()` method will return the reply message.

The following diagram shows the sequence of events:

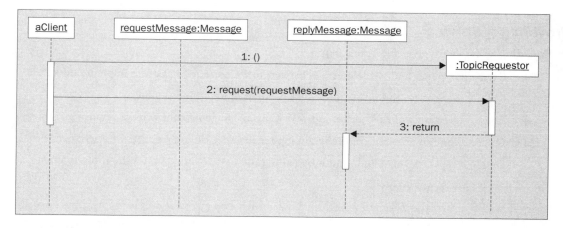

Example Requestor

Here is the code for the example requestor:

```java
import javax.jms.*;
import java.io.*;
import java.net.*;
import javax.naming.*;

public class Requestor {
  public static void main(String args[]) throws Exception {
    try {
      InitialContext ic = new InitialContext();
      QueueConnectionFactory qcf =
        (QueueConnectionFactory) ic.lookup("QueueConnectionFactory");
```

```
        Queue queue = (Queue) ic.lookup("stock");
        ic.close();

        QueueConnection queueConnection = qcf.createQueueConnection();
        queueConnection.start();
        QueueSession queueSession = queueConnection.createQueueSession(false,
                Session.AUTO_ACKNOWLEDGE);
        QueueRequestor requestor = new QueueRequestor(queueSession, queue);

        TextMessage request = queueSession.createTextMessage();
        request.setText("SUNW");
```

Note that here the code blocks until it receives a reply:

```
        TextMessage reply = (TextMessage) requestor.request(request);

        System.out.println("Reply: " + reply.getText());

        queueSession.close();
        queueConnection.close();
    } catch (JMSException ex) {
        ex.printStackTrace();
    }
  }
}
```

Providing a Service

Providing a service involves following steps:

❑ Create a receiver and set its message listener to a `MessageListener` implementation.

❑ Create a sender for the `null` queue – also called unidentified sender.

❑ The middleware will call `onMessage()` of this message listener when a request arrives.

❑ Obtain the reply-to queue of the incoming message by calling `getJMSReplyTo()`.

❑ Create a reply message and send it by calling the `send()` method on the reply-to queue.

Here's how it looks sequentially:

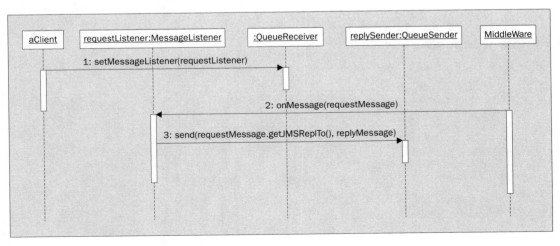

Example Service

Here is the example code for the service:

```java
import javax.jms.*;
import java.io.*;
import javax.naming.*;

public class Replier {
  public static void main(String args[]) throws Exception {
    try {
      InitialContext ic = new InitialContext();
      QueueConnectionFactory qcf =
        (QueueConnectionFactory) ic.lookup("QueueConnectionFactory");

      Queue queue = (Queue) ic.lookup("stock");
      ic.close();

      QueueConnection queueConnection = qcf.createQueueConnection();
      QueueSession queueSession = queueConnection.createQueueSession(false,
            Session.AUTO_ACKNOWLEDGE);
      QueueReceiver queueSub = queueSession.createReceiver(queue);
      queueConnection.start();

      queueSub.setMessageListener(new RequestHandler(queueSession, queue));
      System.out.println("Ready to serve requests");
    } catch (JMSException ex) {
      ex.printStackTrace();
    }
  }
}
```

```java
class RequestHandler implements MessageListener {
  private QueueSession queueSession;
  private QueueSender replier;

  RequestHandler(QueueSession queueSession,
                 Queue queue) throws JMSException {
    this.queueSession = queueSession;
    replier = queueSession.createSender(null);
  }

  public void onMessage(Message msg) {
    try {
      TextMessage request = (TextMessage) msg;
      Queue replyQueue = (Queue) msg.getJMSReplyTo();
      TextMessage reply = queueSession.createTextMessage();
      reply.setText("199.99");
      replier.send(replyQueue, reply);
    } catch (Exception ex) {
      ex.printStackTrace();
    }
  }
}
```

Running the Request/Reply Example

Before running this example, please follow the instructions on setting up the environment above. Now run the requestor:

```
Command Prompt

C:\projavaxml\chapter20>javac Requestor.java

C:\projavaxml\chapter20>java -Djms.properties=%J2EE_HOME%\config\jms_client.prop
erties Requestor
Java(TM) Message Service 1.0.2 Reference Implementation (build b10)
Reply: 199.99

C:\projavaxml\chapter20>
```

Run the service:

```
Command Prompt - java -Djms.properties=C:\j2sdkee1.3\config\jms_client.properties Replier

C:\projavaxml\chapter20>javac Replier.java

C:\projavaxml\chapter20>java -Djms.properties=%J2EE_HOME%\config\jms_client.prop
erties Replier
Java(TM) Message Service 1.0.2 Reference Implementation (build b10)
Ready to serve requests
```

This completes our introduction to JMS messaging. Now we'll get to the heart of the chapter and show how a web service can be hidden behind a JMS messaging façade.

Marrying SOAP to JMS

In the previous chapter *"XML Protocol and Communications"*, we saw details of the SOAP protocol and how to use Apache SOAP to work over HTTP. The Apache-SOAP implementation is designed such that we can use transport of our choice to transfer SOAP requests and replies. It also bundles implementation for two transports: HTTP and SMTP. In this section, we will develop a JMS transport mechanism for the Apache-SOAP implementation. Once we have such transport, we could use it to implement, for example, the credit-card processing discussed earlier in the chapter using a MOM that supports JMS transport.

As seen in the preceding chapter, SOAP specifies request and reply messages in XML format. We, therefore, can use any transport, including JMS, that can transfer text messages. Using the JMS as a SOAP transport combines the benefits of XML format with the benefits of JMS. The result is a simple, standardized, firewall-friendly, fault-tolerant, vendor-neutral, language-neutral RPC solution.

In this section, we will describe a JMS transport using the open source Java SOAP solution, Apache SOAP 2.0. It can be downloaded from http://xml.apache.org.

Apache SOAP through JMS

In this section, we discuss the architecture of ApacheSOAP 2.0 from the perspective of using JMS as the underlying transport mechanism.

The core classes we need to understand are the `Call` and `Response` objects, and the `SOAPTransport` interface. To create a request, you create a new `Call` object; set its properties, such as remote objects identifier, the method to invoke, and the arguments to the method. You also set the transport mechanism to use by calling the `setSOAPTransport()` method on the `Call` object. You then call the `invoke()` method, which returns a `Response` object that contains the result of the method invocation.

To simplify the implementation, we will use the implementation for processing requests provided by the HTTP-SOAP server. We simply create a bridge that accepts JMS request messages and relays them to the HTTP-SOAP server. The following class diagram illustrates some of the main relationships:

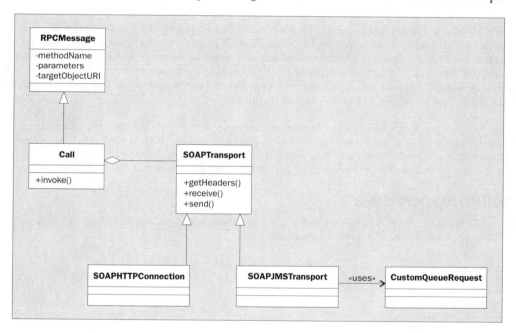

The JMS Transport

The `org.apache.soap.transport.SOAPTransport` interface, which is an abstraction of the transport layer that's carrying the messages, is defined as follows:

```
package org.apache.soap.transport;

import java.net.URL;
import java.io.BufferedReader;
import java.util.Hashtable;
import org.apache.soap.*;
import org.apache.soap.encoding.*;

public interface SOAPTransport {
```

This method is used to request that an envelope be sent:

```
public void send (URL sendTo, String action, Hashtable headers,
                  Envelope env, SOAPMappingRegistry smr)
   throws SOAPException;
```

This returns a buffered reader to receive back the response:

```
public BufferedReader receive ();
```

This returns access to the headers generated by the protocol:

```
public Hashtable getHeaders ();
}
```

We will now look at our implementation for a SOAP transport using JMS. Most of the work occurs inside the send() method of SOAPJMSTransport. This method first obtains the text message that represents the SOAP request. Then it uses a CustomQueueRequestor, which is similar in functionality to QueueRequestor except for its support of the timeout feature and reuse of session objects. The implementation of CustomQueueRequestor is explained later in this section, in particular how it sends this request to the desired queue and waits for a reply.

Internally, CustomQueueRequestor creates a temporary queue, sets the JMSReplyTo property of the outgoing message to this temporary queue, and sends the message. It then adds itself as a receiver to the temporary queue, and returns when that receiver receives a message. Once a reply message is received, it sets the responseReader member of SOAPJMSTransport that wraps the reply message string.

The SOAPTransport Class

Here is the code for the SOAPJMSTransport, an implementation of SOAPTransport that allows us to use JMS to transport SOAP request and replies:

```
package transport;

import java.io.*;
import java.net.URL;
import java.util.*;
import org.apache.soap.*;
import org.apache.soap.encoding.*;
import org.apache.soap.transport.SOAPTransport;

import javax.naming.*;
import javax.jms.*;

public class SOAPJMSTransport implements SOAPTransport {
  private QueueSession queueSession;
  private Queue queue;
  private boolean newSessionForEachRequest;
  private int requestTimeout;

  private QueueConnection queueConnection;

  private Hashtable responseHeaders = new Hashtable();
  private BufferedReader responseReader;
```

First, we implement the constructor. The constructor will take four arguments: the `String` name of the connection factory, the `String` name of the queue to send the message on, a `boolean` value indicating whether to create a new session for each request, and an `int` value for the timeout, in milliseconds:

```
public SOAPJMSTransport(String connectionFactoryName, String queueName,
                        boolean newSessionForEachRequest,
                        int requestTimeout) throws NamingException,
                        JMSException {

  InitialContext ic = new InitialContext();

  QueueConnectionFactory qcf =
    (QueueConnectionFactory) ic.lookup(connectionFactoryName);

  queue = (Queue) ic.lookup(queueName);
  ic.close();

  queueConnection = qcf.createQueueConnection();
  queueConnection.start();
  this.newSessionForEachRequest = newSessionForEachRequest;
  this.requestTimeout = requestTimeout;
}

public SOAPJMSTransport(String connectionFactoryName, String queueName)
        throws NamingException, JMSException {
  this(connectionFactoryName, queueName, true, 0);
}
```

Next, we implement the `send()` method in the `SOAPTransport` interface. It first marshals the SOAP envelope `env` so that we can obtain string representations of the request we need to make. It then creates a `QueueSession` if needed. We then create a `TextMessage` called `requestMsg` with the marshaled enevelope as the constructor argument, and set its header to match the `headers` argument passed. Next, we create a `CustomQueueRequestor` object, and call the `request()` method with the `requestMsg` argument. When this method returns, we extract the message from the returned value and set `responseReader` to point to its content:

```
public void send(URL sendTo, String actionURI, Hashtable headers,
                 Envelope env,
                 SOAPMappingRegistry smr) throws SOAPException {
  try {
    StringWriter payloadSW = new StringWriter();
    env.marshall(payloadSW, smr);

    if (queueSession == null) {
      queueSession = queueConnection.createQueueSession(false,
            Session.AUTO_ACKNOWLEDGE);
    }

    TextMessage requestMsg =
      queueSession.createTextMessage(payloadSW.toString());
    requestMsg.setStringProperty(Constants.HEADER_SOAP_ACTION,
                                 (actionURI != null)
                                 ? ('\"' + actionURI + '\"') : "");
```

```
         // Assume all headers are of string type...
         if (headers != null) {
           for (Enumeration keys = headers.keys();
                keys != null && keys.hasMoreElements(); ) {
             Object key = keys.nextElement();
             requestMsg.setStringProperty(key.toString(),
                                          headers.get(key).toString());
           }
         }

         CustomQueueRequestor queueRequestor =
           new CustomQueueRequestor(queueSession, queue, requestTimeout,
                                    newSessionForEachRequest);
         TextMessage replyMsg =
           (TextMessage) queueRequestor.request(requestMsg);

         responseReader =
           new BufferedReader(new StringReader(replyMsg.getText()));

         responseHeaders.clear();
         for (Enumeration keys = replyMsg.getPropertyNames();
              keys != null && keys.hasMoreElements(); ) {

           // JMS message's property keys are Strings
           String key = keys.nextElement().toString();
           String value = replyMsg.getStringProperty(key);
           if (value != null) {
             responseHeaders.put(key, value);
           }
         }

         queueRequestor.close();

         if (newSessionForEachRequest) {

           // so that we will create a new one next time
           queueSession = null;
         }
       } catch (Exception e) {
         throw new SOAPException(Constants.FAULT_CODE_CLIENT, e.getMessage(),
                                 e);
       }
     }
```

The `responseReader` is set to point to a buffered reader created from the message body received in `send()` method. The `receive()` method, therefore, simply returns that member so that caller can extract and decode the SOAP response envelope:

```
    public BufferedReader receive() {
      return responseReader;
    }
```

Similar to the `receive()` method, `getHeaders()` returns the `responseHeaders` member that was set by the `send()` method.

```
    public Hashtable getHeaders() {
        return responseHeaders;
    }
  }
```

The CustomQueueRequestor Class

Here is our `CustomQueueRequestor` version of a queue requestor that supports timeouts and reuses session objects for efficiency:

```
package transport;

import javax.jms.*;

public class CustomQueueRequestor {

  QueueSession session;
  TemporaryQueue tempQueue;
  QueueSender sender;
  QueueReceiver receiver;

  long timeout;
  boolean closeSessionOnDelete;

  public CustomQueueRequestor(QueueSession session, Queue queue,
                              long timeout,
                              boolean closeSessionOnDelete) throws
      JMSException {
    this.session = session;
    this.timeout = timeout;
    this.closeSessionOnDelete = closeSessionOnDelete;

    tempQueue = session.createTemporaryQueue();
    sender = session.createSender(queue);
    receiver = session.createReceiver(tempQueue);
  }

  public CustomQueueRequestor(QueueSession session,
                              Queue queue) throws JMSException {
    this(session, queue, 0, true);
  }

  public Message request(Message message) throws JMSException {
    message.setJMSReplyTo(tempQueue);
    sender.send(message);

    // JMS specifies that receive(0) should block forever.
    // However, atleast with swiftMQ, it returns immediately if
    // timeout value is zero.
    if (timeout == 0) {
      return receiver.receive();
    } else {
      return (receiver.receive(timeout));
    }
  }
}
```

```
      public void close() throws JMSException {
        sender.close();
        receiver.close();
        tempQueue.delete();
        if (closeSessionOnDelete) {
          session.close();
        }
      }
   }
}
```

The JMS to HTTP Bridge

The JMS2HTTPBridge class is responsible for accepting JMS service requests on specified queues, creating an HTTP GET request, forwarding it to an HTTP server, and getting back a response from the HTTP server. It then assembles it as a JMS message, and sends it back to the client:

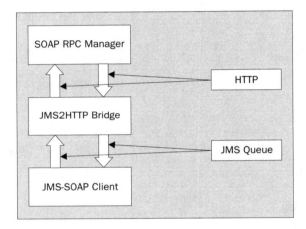

Here is the code:

```
package server;

import java.net.URL;
import java.util.Hashtable;

import org.apache.soap.util.net.*;
import org.apache.soap.util.IOUtils;
import org.apache.soap.Constants;

import javax.naming.*;
import javax.jms.*;

public class JMS2HTTPBridge {
  QueueSession queueSession;
  QueueSender replySender;
  URL httpSOAPForwardingURL;
```

```
    public JMS2HTTPBridge(URL httpSOAPForwardingURL,
                          String connectionFactoryName,
                          String[] queueNames) throws NamingException,
                          JMSException {
      this.httpSOAPForwardingURL = httpSOAPForwardingURL;

      InitialContext ictx = new InitialContext();
      QueueConnectionFactory qcf =
        (QueueConnectionFactory) ictx.lookup(connectionFactoryName);

      QueueConnection qc = qcf.createQueueConnection();

      queueSession = qc.createQueueSession(false, Session.AUTO_ACKNOWLEDGE);

      for (int queuesLen = queueNames.length, i = 0; i < queuesLen; ++i) {
        Queue queue = (Queue) ictx.lookup(queueNames[i]);
        QueueReceiver requestSubsciber = queueSession.createReceiver(queue);
        requestSubsciber.setMessageListener(new MessageHandler());
      }

      replySender = queueSession.createSender(null);

      qc.start();
      ictx.close();
      System.out.println("Ready to serve requests...\n");
    }
```

```
    public static void main(String[] args) throws Exception {
      if (args.length < 3) {
        System.err.println("Usage: java server.JMS2HTTPBridge "
                          + "httpForwardingURL "
                          + "connectionFactoryName queue1 queue2 ...");
        System.exit(1);
      }

      String[] queueNames = new String[args.length - 2];
      for (int queuesLen = queueNames.length, i = 0; i < queuesLen; ++i) {
        queueNames[i] = args[i + 2];
      }

      new JMS2HTTPBridge(new URL(args[0]), args[1], queueNames);
    }
```

The following method is called by our internal MessageHandler class:

```
    private String forwardMessage(TextMessage msg) throws JMSException {
      String actionURI = msg.getStringProperty(Constants.HEADER_SOAP_ACTION);

      /* forward the content to the HTTP listener as an HTTP POST */
      Hashtable headers = new Hashtable();
      if (actionURI != null) {
        headers.put(Constants.HEADER_SOAP_ACTION, actionURI);
      }
```

```
String payload = null;
try {
   HTTPUtils.Response response = HTTPUtils.post(httpSOAPForwardingURL,
            headers, Constants.HEADERVAL_CONTENT_TYPE, msg.getText());
   int contentLength = response.contentLength;

   // no content length; read the stream
   if (contentLength == -1) {
      payload = IOUtils.getStringFromReader(response.content);
   } else {    // read contentLength chars
      char[] payloadChars = new char[contentLength];
      int offset = 0;
      while (offset < contentLength) {
         offset += response.content.read(payloadChars, offset,
                                    contentLength - offset);

      }
      payload = new String(payloadChars);
   }
} catch (Exception e) {
   e.printStackTrace();
}
return payload;
}
```

```
public class MessageHandler implements MessageListener {
   public void onMessage(Message msg) {
      try {
         TextMessage request = (TextMessage) msg;
         TextMessage reply = queueSession.createTextMessage();
         reply.setText(forwardMessage(request));
         Queue replyToQueue = (Queue) msg.getJMSReplyTo();
         replySender.send(replyToQueue, reply);
      } catch (JMSException ex) {
         ex.printStackTrace();
      }
   }
}
}
```

Example Using JMS Transport

In this example, we will create an SPClientJMS program similar in principle to the one from the previous chapter. The only important difference we need to make is to set the transport mechanism of the Call to a SOAPJMSTransport object, which we implemented earlier:

```
import java.io.*;
import java.net.*;
import java.util.*;
import org.apache.soap.util.xml.*;
import org.apache.soap.*;
import org.apache.soap.rpc.*;
import org.apache.soap.transport.SOAPTransport;
```

```
    import transport.*;

    public class SPClientJMS {
      public static void main(String[] args) throws Exception {
        if (args.length != 2 && (args.length != 3 ||!args[0].startsWith("-"))) {
          System.err.println("Usage: java SPClientJMS [-encodingStyleURI]"
                             + " connectionFactoryName queueName ");
          System.exit(1);
        }

        // Process the arguments.
        int offset = 3 - args.length;
        String encodingStyleURI = args.length == 3 ? args[0].substring(1)
                                 : Constants.NS_URI_SOAP_ENC;
        String connectionFactoryName = args[1 - offset];
        String queueName = args[2 - offset];

        SOAPTransport jmsTransport = new SOAPJMSTransport(connectionFactoryName,
                 queueName);

        // Build the call.
        Call call = new Call();
```

We now set transport of the call object to the `jmsTransport` we just created:

```
        call.setSOAPTransport(jmsTransport);
```

Note that this is the URI of the SOAP service that we deployed in the previous chapter. We will refresh ourselves later on how to deploy it:

```
        call.setTargetObjectURI("urn:wrox-date-service");
        call.setMethodName("getServerDate");
        call.setEncodingStyleURI(encodingStyleURI);
        Vector params = new Vector();
        call.setParams(params);

        Response resp = call.invoke(null, "");
        if (resp.generatedFault()) {
          Fault fault = resp.getFault();
          System.out.println("Ouch, the call failed: ");
          System.out.println("  Fault Code   = " + fault.getFaultCode());
          System.out.println("  Fault String = " + fault.getFaultString());
        } else {
          Parameter result = resp.getReturnValue();
          System.out.println("The current server time is: "
                             + result.getValue());
        }
        System.exit(0);
      }
    }
```

Running the Example

Before running this example, please make sure that you follow the instructions provided in the previous chapter for running the SPClient example, illustrating the use of SOAP over the HTTP protocol. Once you can run that program successfully, please follow our earlier instructions for setting up JMS on the J2EE server.

Adding Administered Object

For running this example, we first need to create a queue and bind it to the name date. Then we need to deploy the SOAP service, if we already haven't done so. We then can start the JMS2HTTP bridge that forwards requests received over the JMS queue to HTTP and sends back the reply received over HTTP.

Compiling and Running the Server

Check your Tomcat startup file tomcat.bat to ensure that the web server has access to the DateLookup class in its classpath. You could copy over, download, or create DateLookup.java in your working directly and add a path C:\projavaxml\chapter20 for instance, or copy over the class file to <TOMCAT_HOME>\classes, which is normally added to Tomcat's classpath. Also, ensure that Tomcat has access to Xerces and SOAP:

```
REM In tomcat.bat
set CP=%CP%;C:\xerces-1_3_0\xerces.jar
set CP=%CP%;C:\soap-2_0\lib\soap.jar
REM set CP=%CP%;C:\projavaxml\chapter20
set CP=%CP%;%TOMCAT_HOME%\classes
```

Check that you have the context directive for the SOAP RPC router webapp set up in Tomcat's conf\server.xml:

```
<Context
    path="/soap"
    docBase="C:/soap-2_1/webapps/soap"
    debug="1"
    reloadable="true">
</Context>
```

Then start Tomcat. Compile the server and transport classes and re-deploy the service with Descriptor.xml if necessary:

```
<isd:service xmlns:isd="http://xml.apache.org/xml-soap/deployment"
             id="urn:wrox-date-service">
  <isd:provider type="java"
                scope="Application"
                methods="getServerDate addNumbers">
    <isd:java class="DateLookup"/>
  </isd:provider>
</isd:service>
```

Then run the JMS to HTTP bridge:

```
Command Prompt - java -Djms.properties=C:\j2sdkee1.3\config\jms_client.properties server.JMS2H...  _ □ X

C:\projavaxml\chapter20>echo %classpath%
.;C:\soap-2_0\lib\soap.jar;C:\xerces-1_3_0\xerces.jar;C:\j2sdkee1.3\lib\j2ee.jar
;C:\j2sdkee1.3\lib\locale

C:\projavaxml\chapter20>javac transport\*.java server\*.java

C:\projavaxml\chapter20>java org.apache.soap.server.ServiceManagerClient http://
localhost:8080/soap/servlet/rpcrouter deploy Descriptor.xml

C:\projavaxml\chapter20>java org.apache.soap.server.ServiceManagerClient http://
localhost:8080/soap/servlet/rpcrouter list
Deployed Services:
        urn:wrox-date-service

C:\projavaxml\chapter20>j2eeadmin -addJMSDestination date queue
C:\projavaxml\chapter21>start j2ee -verbose

C:\projavaxml\chapter20>java -Djms.properties=%J2EE_HOME%\config\jms_client.prop
erties server.JMS2HTTPBridge http://localhost:8080/soap/servlet/rpcrouter QueueC
onnectionFactory date
Java(TM) Message Service 1.0.2 Reference Implementation (build b10)
Ready to serve requests...
```

Next, compile and run the client:

```
Command Prompt                                                                  _ □ X

C:\projavaxml\chapter20>javac SPClientJMS.java

C:\projavaxml\chapter20>java -Djms.properties=%J2EE_HOME%\config\jms_client.prop
erties SPClientJMS QueueConnectionFactory date
Java(TM) Message Service 1.0.2 Reference Implementation (build b10)
The current server time is: Sat Mar 03 20:09:50 GMT+00:00 2001

C:\projavaxml\chapter20>
```

Summary

We studied two broad mechanisms for transporting messages: peer-to-peer and MOM-based messaging. The use of MOM makes it easier to satisfy the complex needs of an enterprise communication system. We also studied the two main paradigms for messaging-based systems: Publish/Subscribe and Point-to-Point. We looked at the suitability of one over another. We then looked at JMS API and examples of sending messages over a queue and requesting and providing a service using the API. Last, we examined using JMS as a transport with SOAP to provide an RPC-like mechanism using messaging.

So the motto of the chapter is that the use of messaging paradigms for communication offers significant advantages in terms of scalability, automatic load balancing, and reliability. We also get the benefit of simplifying node programming to concentrate on the business logic, and not the nitty-gritty of the communication layers. Combining JMS and XML adds the advantages of XML portability and international recognition to messaging. Using an XML-based transport enables us to create distributed applications that can exploit HTTP to cross firewalls.

In the next chapter we look at the kind of enterprise applications in a typical B2B scenario where these kinds of loosely-coupled web-friendly designs are highly advantageous.

The Xerces Blue
Butterfly, which became
extinct earlier this century,
and after which the Xerces XML
Parser is named ...

21

B2B Marketplaces

E-Business is a broad term used to describe a variety of electronic business transactions. The message traffic generated by the various programs and systems that participate in these electronic transactions is collectively known as B2B messaging. This chapter will introduce B2B messaging using XML and illustrate how some specific message types, such as electronic catalogs and purchase orders, are used in electronic marketplaces.

The future projections for XML B2B messaging have fueled a great deal of interest in the potential for electronic marketplaces. An **Electronic Marketplace** is an application or web site that allows buyers to search and purchase against several supplier catalogs simultaneously. These marketplaces provide aggregated views of supplier catalogs, providing a single point of procurement against multiple underlying vendors.

Introduction to B2B Messaging

An **Electronic Catalog** is an electronic listing of a supplier's products. Typically provided by the supplier in an XML or **comma-separated variable (CSV)** format, the marketplace aggregates and indexes the catalogs for the buyers who subscribe to it. Currently, there is no industry standard for catalogs. Each marketplace chooses (or develops) its own catalog format for the suppliers to provide. Suppliers wishing to participate in a marketplace must create catalogs in the format chosen by the marketplace.

In addition, the relatively recent introduction of XML to this arena means that most marketplaces use a comma-delineated format like the Catalog Interchange Format (CIF). The richer content that can be made available with XML, however, means that suppliers that provide their content in XML will be ahead of the game in the months to come, hence the high level of activity in this area.

Because each marketplace tends to choose its own catalog format, suppliers have to create a new version of their catalogs for each marketplace they choose to participate in. Having said this, it isn't quite as bad as it sounds – there are several new marketplaces opening up each day, but there really are a manageable number of catalog formats. Many of the marketplaces are standardizing on either **Commerce XML** (cXML), the format put forward by Ariba, Inc, or **XML Commerce Business Language** (xCBL), which the Commerce One marketplace uses.

Ultimately, the solution lies in providing an XML view of your data and transforming that data into the desired format automatically through the use of stylesheets. That means that as new standards emerge, the work involved in adding another "view" of your data will be much reduced. Unfortunately, one thing that cannot be provided for by generating static catalogs, in whatever format, is time critical information such as sale discounts, or inventory information.

The work involved in conforming their data into the required format can make suppliers reluctant to join the mêlée. Additionally, pricing models and availability are sometimes considered proprietary information by a supplier – and could conceivably change with each buyer relationship. Suppliers work very hard to establish relationships with their buyers – so to become 'just another vendor' in the marketplace model is something they work to avoid.

For these reasons, several suppliers have not chosen to follow this general trend towards marketplaces. Instead, many such suppliers choose to put up their own electronic storefronts – allowing buyers to interact directly with their B2B partners using a B2C (Business to Consumer) model. An **Electronic Storefront** is a web site that exposes a supplier's catalog and allows customers to purchase directly from that catalog. These storefronts can be quite comprehensive, and in many cases will access the available inventory and back-office systems of the supplier directly.

In order to address this new model, and the previously mentioned suppliers' issues, several marketplaces are now offering the ability for a buyer to leave the marketplace and go directly to the supplier's site for product information, availability, and configuration. In this situation, a URL is included in the product description in the catalog and is provided to the buyer when an item is hit in a search. When a buyer accesses a supplier's URL, an XML message is sent to the storefront of the supplier, identifying the incoming client as one from the marketplace.

The supplier's site then manages the purchasing experience directly, and the orders are routed back through the marketplace. This concept, of allowing a buyer to leave the marketplace to shop directly on a participating supplier's site, is known as **Punch Out** in cXML (In xCBL it is known as RoundTrip). Each marketplace has its own name for it, but Punch Out is rapidly becoming an e-business slang term to represent the ability to leave the marketplace and return.

Marketplaces, therefore, allow a buyer to make a purchase that generates a single purchase order that may in fact, in the background, create several purchase orders with several suppliers. These purchase orders are passed on to the suppliers through their preferred order method (usually this is via e-mail, fax, or an XML document delivered to a specific URL).

Marketplaces do more than just aggregate catalogs, or facilitate Punch Out requests. For buyers, marketplaces offer the ability to map users into buying accounts with budget controls, and approval chains. They also manage the messaging between the suppliers and buyers, and can consolidate purchases against several different supplier catalogs.

For more information on the marketplace vendors mentioned above, visit the marketplace web sites at Ariba Inc. (http://www.ariba.com) and Commerce One (http://www.commerceone.com).

Architecture of Electronic Marketplaces

Let's look a little further at what an electronic marketplace B2B messaging application might look like. Architecturally, they can take several forms, but a common theme is a large relational database for a data store. Add on to this an application server tier, to handle the message routing and aggregation tasks, and a web server tier to serve the various requests. Lastly, a client tier provides the UI and communication.

As we have seen, Marketplaces are often hosted by a third party, such as the Ariba Commerce Services Network (ACSN), or they can be hosted directly by the buyer – who assumes responsibility for loading catalogs and managing supplier content. The graphic below depicts the architecture of a hosted marketplace.

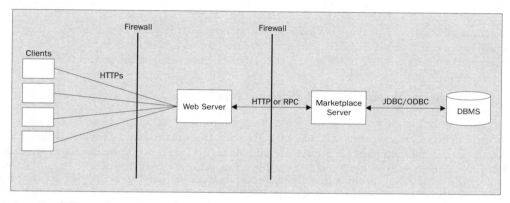

This is quite different from the traditional model, where the buyer would host a **Local Catalog** on a purchasing application that can be hooked into the buyer's ERP (Enterprise Resource Planning) systems to track purchasing activities.

If marketplaces are to survive, however, both sets of users must have access to equal toolsets. While buyer applications have had much investment, catalog creation tools are scarce, and so buyers are finding their choice limited to those companies that are willing to risk investment in this nascent market. Several initiatives are underway to simplify e-commerce for both buyers and suppliers; a few of them are discussed in the next section.

E-Business XML Initiatives

Several new marketplace initiatives are announced each month in trade magazines and corporate press releases (see http://www.oasis-open.org/cover/ for some examples). Many are very specific, aiming only at a specific vertical market, such as auto parts. Others are very generic – open to any supplier wishing to participate.

Each of these new marketplaces either develops its own catalog format, and tells suppliers who wish to participate to deliver their catalogs in its format – or picks some industry standard to define its catalog format and develops a system around it. There seems to be as many of the 'build-it-my-way' initiatives as there are those that use a standard.

There are also new 'standards' being developed every day, making it that much harder to determine which is the most appropriate to use. This section attempts to review some of the standards that have been developed to date. These were chosen for inclusion here due to the companies involved in their creation, ease of use, or just because they are doing something different or new. Doubtless by the time this book is printed there will be several additional activities to look into.

Commerce XML (cXML)

The Commerce Extensible Markup Language (cXML) is owned and maintained by Ariba Inc, and is evolving with the input from numerous companies. Several companies including Harbinger, Office Depot, and Sterling Commerce have adopted and implemented cXML. It was designed to represent the paper-based documents that have always been used in business, and specifically in commerce applications. As such, you will find some very intuitive, straightforward document types.

It has document types for supplier profiles, electronic catalogs, purchase orders, and various messages for status requests. It is probably one of the best DTDs to work with if you're just getting your feet wet with e-business. I found it to be the simplest form of e-business-type XML, and the easiest to learn.

There are several documents available to assist you in understanding the document types and the technical support at Ariba is excellent. For a copy of the complete specification, visit http://www.ariba.com or http://cXML.org. A tutorial in cXML follows in the next section.

XML Common Business Library (xCBL)

XML Common Business Library (xCBL) is an all-encompassing XML application that attempts to completely define all transactions that may take place in electronic business activities. It has a more thorough element set than cXML, in that it includes elements for reporting statistics and forecasting, as well as auctioning and direct quotes. It has a highly compartmentalized model, with several entities that are reused throughout the specification. This compartmentalized model allows for some very elegant data modeling activities – but also adds a great deal of complexity to an implementation. Commerce One has implemented xCBL as itsdefined message format.

The best place to look for information on xCBL is its web site http://www.xcbl.org, which contains the latest information on the DTDs/Schemas as they evolve. Another great source of information regarding xCBL and its usage in Commerce One is the Commerce One web site http://www.commerceone.com.

Rosetta Net

Rosetta Net provides a framework for e-commerce through technical dictionaries aimed at a particular industry. In addition, they define Partner Interface Processes known as PIPs. They have mostly been directed at facilitating supply chain management in the microelectronics and manufacturing supply industries. PIPs define how networked applications between business entities would interoperate to facilitate collaboration between businesses.

Before a PIP is defined, a business model documents and attempts to understand how the participants do business currently. Once that is done, the current business model is re-engineered to specify the desired levels of collaboration between the various partners. The Rosetta Net approach more closely resembles a registry for businesses to identify and define their data elements, and the business processes that act on them.

Visit http://www.RosettaNet.org for more information on the Rosetta Net specifications.

Universal Description, Discovery, and Integration (UDDI)

The Universal Description, Discovery and Integration (UDDI) initiative consists of a series of specifications that provide a way for businesses to publish information about their own web services and discover information about offerings from other businesses. UDDI consists of a business registry that a business can participate in by submitting an XML file to describe its web services. Several organizations have come together to participate and manage the UDDI specifications as they evolve including IBM, Microsoft Corporation, and Ariba Inc.

UDDI consists of an XML Schema for SOAP messages, and an API specification. It is an attempt to complement and formalize access to the various marketplaces that are out there today. It provides users with the ability to locate potential trading partners through sites that use UDDI registries.

For more information on this new and growing effort, please visit the UDDI web site at http://www.uddi.org. You may also find information on the Ariba (http://www.ariba.com), Microsoft (http://www.microsoft.com), and IBM (http://www.ibm.com) web sites.

BizTalk Framework

BizTalk is a schema for passing e-business documents between partners in an e-commerce relationship. The BizTalk Framework is a specification to provide addressing capabilities and identify transmission and processing actions to take place on the included document. BizTalk is schema based, and requires a **BizTalk Framework Compliant** (BFC) server in order to process BizTalk coded documents. It includes schemas for addressing and transporting documents, and then provides a single <Body> </Body> tag to contain the actual XML message (or messages) to convey.

For more information on the BizTalk Framework or the BizTalk server, please visit the BizTalk web site at http://www.BizTalk.org or Microsoft's site at http://Microsoft.com/biztalk.

Electronic Business XML Initiative (ebXML)

The ebXML initiative is a joint effort between the United Nations Center for Trade Facilitation and Electronic Business (UN/CEFACT) and the Organization for Advancement of Structured Information Standards (OASIS). It is primarily a working group pulled together to standardize the XML activities around e-business. There are several working groups approaching the problem from different sides.

The Technical Architecture Requirements group has already released the ebXML Technical Architecture Specification available for review online at http://www.ebXML.org. There are also groups for Business Processes, Core Components, Transport/Routing and Packaging, and several others.

An ebXML Initiative White Paper defines the vision of ebXML to "create a single global electronic marketplace where enterprises of any size and in any geographical location can meet and conduct business with each other through the exchange of XML-based messages". The interest and activity around ebXML is high – several companies from all over the world are participating in the working groups. It does appear to be pulling together several ideas from already existing efforts. It will have a registry of businesses and services, similar to Rosetta Net, and will provide transport and enveloping capabilities like BizTalk. It will have DTDs and Schema definitions to describe business document types like cXML and xCBL.

For more information on ebXML, please visit the ebXML web site at http://www.ebxml.org or Robin Cover's XML Cover Pages at http://xml.coverpages.org.

Commerce XML – a Tutorial

The cXML specification is a good example of a concise and intuitive application of e-commerce-based XML. By studying the message types available, one can get a fairly complete understanding of what is happening in the e-commerce arena. It comprises a single DTD that lays out the various document types needed for a complete e-business solution.

The following list illustrates the many document types available in the cXML standard:

- ❑ Contract
- ❑ GetPendingRequest
- ❑ GetPendingResponse
- ❑ Index
- ❑ OrderRequest
- ❑ OrderResponse
- ❑ ProfileRequest
- ❑ ProfileResponse
- ❑ PunchOutOrderMessage
- ❑ PunchOutSetupRequest
- ❑ PunchOutSetupResponse
- ❑ StatusUpdateRequest
- ❑ StatusUpdateResponse
- ❑ SubscriptionChangeMessage
- ❑ SubscriptionContentRequest
- ❑ SubscriptionContentResponse
- ❑ SubscriptionListRequest
- ❑ SubscriptionListResponse
- ❑ Supplier
- ❑ SupplierChangeMessage
- ❑ SupplierDataRequest
- ❑ SupplierDataResponse
- ❑ SupplierListRequest
- ❑ SupplierListResponse

A single cXML application may or may not implement all of the above listed document types. As a developer, you will typically be working either with the supplier documents, or the buyer documents – or possibly (as a marketplace developer) creating the various request/response documents and adding routing envelopes, but it is unlikely that you will have to deal with all three at once.

Attempting to understand and work with the entire framework is rather daunting. With that in mind, we will break out the cXML standard in the same way we did for the discussion on marketplaces – by looking at it from the perspective of the players involved.

This tutorial will illustrate the minimum set of documents needed to participate in a cXML marketplace.

A note about the following examples: Although all the documents refer to the same DTD, they each have a different document type declaration. The DOCTYPE tag is used to tell the parser where to find the rules (DTD) to validate this document. Typically the DOCTYPE tag must contain the name of the root element in the XML instance. In the case of the following examples, specific DOCTYPE tags were used for each document type (rather than using the cXML document type) because the root elements in the documents are not the cXML element, but rather the specific document elements.

The Supplier Documents

The supplier wishing to participate in a cXML marketplace must generate at a minimum three documents: a supplier profile, an electronic catalog, and a contract pricing file. The minimum list of supplier documents is listed below:

- ❏ Contract
- ❏ Index
- ❏ OrderResponse
- ❏ Supplier

Additionally, if the supplier wishes to fully participate in the XML messaging offered by the marketplace, they must also be able to receive and parse OrderRequest documents (discussed in the section *Buyer Documents* below).

We will begin with a supplier profile. The profile provides basic contact information. The Index provides product descriptions and is the main electronic catalog format for cXML. The Contract file allows for contract pricing for specific buyers.

Supplier

The Supplier document provides the basic contact information about a supplier, and specifies their preferred order method. The following data shows what information will be conveyed in the Supplier document:

```
AJ Soap Company
This is a small soap manufacturing company
01234598 (company ID)

Main Office
Deliveries to:
  Adam SoapGuy
  55 Main Street
  Anytown, CA 2000
  United States
  800-555-1212
  Fax: 800-555-1213
  adam@ajsoaps.com
```

```
Fax Orders To: 800 555-1213
Email Orders To: orders@ajsoaps.com


Order/Business Contact:
  Joany Soapmaker
  55 Main Street
  Anytown, CA 2000
  800-555-1213
  jsoapmaker@ajsoaps.com

Corporate URL:  http://www.ajsoaps.com
Online Store:  http://buy.ajsoaps.com
```

An example of this data as a supplier document is listed below – this supplier document is typically used to identify a supplier to a marketplace. This information is also passed on to buyers so they know how to contact and interact with suppliers:

```xml
<?xml version="1.0" encoding="UTF-8"?>
<!DOCTYPE Supplier SYSTEM
                "http://xml.cXML.org/schemas/cXML/1.1.008/cXML.dtd">

<Supplier corporateURL="http://www.ajsoaps.com"
         storeFrontURL="http://buy.ajsoaps.com">
  <Name xml:lang="en-US">AJ Soap Company</Name>
  <Comments xml:lang="en-US">
    This is a small soap manufacturing company
  </Comments>

  <SupplierID domain="DUNS">01234598</SupplierID>
  <SupplierLocation>

    <Address>
      <Name xml:lang="en-US">Main Office</Name>

      <PostalAddress>
        <DeliverTo>Adam SoapGuy</DeliverTo>
        <Street>55 Main Street</Street>
        <City>Anytown</City>
        <State>CA</State>
        <PostalCode>20000</PostalCode>
        <Country isoCountryCode="US">United States</Country>
      </PostalAddress>

      <Email>adam@ajsoaps.com</Email>
      <Phone name="Office">
        <TelephoneNumber>
          <CountryCode isoCountryCode="US">1</CountryCode>
          <AreaOrCityCode>800</AreaOrCityCode>
          <Number>5551212</Number>
        </TelephoneNumber>
      </Phone>
```

```
        <Fax name="Order">
          <TelephoneNumber>
            <CountryCode isoCountryCode="US">1</CountryCode>
            <AreaOrCityCode>800</AreaOrCityCode>
            <Number>5551213</Number>
          </TelephoneNumber>
        </Fax>

        <URL>http://www.ajsoaps.com</URL>
      </Address>

    <OrderMethods>

      <OrderMethod>
        <OrderTarget>
          <Email>orders@ajsoaps.com</Email>
        </OrderTarget>
      </OrderMethod>

      <OrderMethod>
        <OrderTarget>
          <Fax>
            <TelephoneNumber>
              <CountryCode isoCountryCode="US">1</CountryCode>
              <AreaOrCityCode>800</AreaOrCityCode>
              <Number>5551213</Number>
            </TelephoneNumber>
          </Fax>
        </OrderTarget>
      </OrderMethod>

      <Contact>
        <Name xml:lang="en-US">Joany Soapmaker</Name>

        <PostalAddress>
          <Street>123 Main Street</Street>
          <City>Anytown</City>
          <State>CA</State>
          <PostalCode>20000</PostalCode>
          <Country isoCountryCode="US">United States</Country>
        </PostalAddress>

        <Email>jsoapmaker@ajsoaps.com</Email>

        <Phone name="Office">
          <TelephoneNumber>
            <CountryCode isoCountryCode="US">1</CountryCode>
            <AreaOrCityCode>800</AreaOrCityCode>
            <Number>5551212</Number>
          </TelephoneNumber>
        </Phone>

      </Contact>
    </OrderMethods>
  </SupplierLocation>
</Supplier>
```

This simple example, `supplier.xml`, shows a supplier's basic information and order methodology.

In this case, the preferred order method is via e-mail or fax. The basic elements needed to convey the supplier information are the `<Name>`, `<SupplierID>`, `<Address>`, and `<OrderMethods>`. Additional order methods available are phone, URL, and other.

If you are developing supplier documents for the Ariba Network – it can generate the supplier file for you from the same information supplied when you register as an Ariba Supplier.

Index

The Index file represents an electronic catalog in cXML. This is the main file that provides the product information to potential buyers as basic line-item information. There are elements to specify the product information, as well as elements to aid in the searching and indexing of the catalog content.

An example of a basic Index file is listed below:

```xml
<?xml version="1.0" encoding="UTF-8"?>
<!DOCTYPE Index SYSTEM "http://xml.cXML.org/schemas/cXML/1.1.008/cXML.dtd">
<Index>
  <SupplierID domain="Internal">029</SupplierID>
  <Comments xml:lang="en-US">AJ Soaps Basic Catalog</Comments>

  <IndexItem>
    <IndexItemAdd>
      <ItemID>
        <SupplierPartID>1</SupplierPartID>
      </ItemID>

      <ItemDetail>
        <UnitPrice>
          <Money currency="USD">3.00</Money>
        </UnitPrice>
        <Description xml:lang="en-US">Basic Vanilla Hand Soap</Description>
        <UnitOfMeasure>EA</UnitOfMeasure>
        <Classification domain="SM">10B</Classification>
        <URL>http://www.ajsoaps.com</URL>
      </ItemDetail>

      <IndexItemDetail>
        <LeadTime>5</LeadTime>
      </IndexItemDetail>
    </IndexItemAdd>
  </IndexItem>

  <IndexItem>
    <IndexItemAdd>
      <ItemID>
        <SupplierPartID>2</SupplierPartID>
      </ItemID>

      <ItemDetail>
        <UnitPrice>
          <Money currency="USD">3.00</Money>
        </UnitPrice>
```

```
        <Description xml:lang="en-US">Peppermint Body Soap</Description>
        <UnitOfMeasure>EA</UnitOfMeasure>
        <Classification domain="SM">10A</Classification>
        <URL>http://www.ajsoaps.com</URL>
      </ItemDetail>

      <IndexItemDetail>
        <LeadTime>5</LeadTime>
      </IndexItemDetail>

    </IndexItemAdd>
  </IndexItem>

  <IndexItem>
    <IndexItemAdd>
      <ItemID>
        <SupplierPartID>12</SupplierPartID>
      </ItemID>

      <ItemDetail>
        <UnitPrice>
          <Money currency="USD">12.00</Money>
        </UnitPrice>
        <Description xml:lang="en-US">Variety Soaps 5 Pack</Description>
        <UnitOfMeasure>EA</UnitOfMeasure>
        <Classification domain="SM">1000</Classification>
        <URL>http://www.ajsoaps.com</URL>
      </ItemDetail>

      <IndexItemDetail>
        <LeadTime>5</LeadTime>
      </IndexItemDetail>
    </IndexItemAdd>
  </IndexItem>

  <IndexItem>
    <IndexItemAdd>
      <ItemID>
        <SupplierPartID>22</SupplierPartID>
      </ItemID>

      <ItemDetail>
        <UnitPrice>
          <Money currency="USD">30.00</Money>
        </UnitPrice>
        <Description xml:lang="en-US">Basic Vanilla Hand Soap</Description>
        <UnitOfMeasure>DZ</UnitOfMeasure>
        <Classification domain="UNSPSC">1002</Classification>
        <URL>http://www.ajsoaps.com</URL>
      </ItemDetail>

      <IndexItemDetail>
        <LeadTime>10</LeadTime>
      </IndexItemDetail>
    </IndexItemAdd>

  </IndexItem>
</Index>
```

The above XML file represents a cXML catalog with four line-items in it. This is the most basic form an electronic catalog can take in cXML. The Index file consists of a 'header' section (for lack of a better term) that specifies certain things about the catalog as a whole. The information specific to a catalog is the supplier ID (or list of suppliers contributing to the catalog).

Note that the `<SupplierID>` element has an attribute `domain`. This attribute gives the supplier ID context. An internal numbering scheme can be used – or, in the case of Ariba, a formally recognized external numbering scheme can be used. Ariba uses Data Universal Numbering System (DUNS) IDs to track suppliers in its system.

The `<Comments>` element provides a simple description of the catalog itself. Several suppliers have more than one catalog they offer – so this provides them a place to give a general description for the catalog (for example "Spring Sale Catalog"). `<supplierID>` is the only required element in the first part of the Index file, as `<Comments>` is optional.

The DTD below is a mini DTD for building Index files. It illustrates the required and optional tags available to developers generating electronic catalogs for cXML marketplaces. Its best to look at the DTD when you're trying to figure out what is required and what is optional. The cXML DTD is straightforward, but fairly large, so it's good to have a DTD viewing tool (OpenText Corporation's Near & Far designer is a great tool for this, look it up at http://www.opentext.com).

When I began developing Index files, I created a mini DTD that contained only the elements needed for the Index document type. (I do this often if I'm working with large DTDs – it simplifies the development and validation process).

The full cXML DTD is available at http://www.cXML.org. I recommend that you take a look at that as well, as that is the one to validate against.

```
<!ENTITY % string "CDATA">
<!ENTITY % uri "CDATA">
<!ENTITY % URL "%uri;">
<!ENTITY % nmtoken "CDATA">
<!ENTITY % isoCurrencyCode "%nmtoken;">
<!ENTITY % number "CDATA">
<!ENTITY % xmlLangCode "%nmtoken;">

<!ELEMENT Index (SupplierID+, Comments?, SearchGroup*, IndexItem+)>
<!ELEMENT SupplierID (#PCDATA)> <!-- string -->
<!ATTLIST SupplierID domain %string; #REQUIRED>

<!ELEMENT Comments ( #PCDATA | Attachment )* >
<!ATTLIST Comments xml:lang %xmlLangCode; #IMPLIED>
<!ELEMENT Attachment (URL)>

<!ELEMENT SearchGroup (Name, SearchAttribute+)>
<!ELEMENT Name (#PCDATA)> <!-- string -->
<!ATTLIST Name xml:lang %xmlLangCode; #REQUIRED>

<!ELEMENT SearchAttribute EMPTY>
<!ATTLIST SearchAttribute
    name %string; #REQUIRED
    type %string; #IMPLIED>
```

```
<!ELEMENT IndexItem (IndexItemAdd+ | IndexItemDelete+ | IndexItemPunchout+)>
<!ELEMENT IndexItemDelete (ItemID) >
<!ELEMENT IndexItemAdd (ItemID, ItemDetail, IndexItemDetail)>
<!ELEMENT ItemID (SupplierPartID, SupplierPartAuxiliaryID?)>
<!ELEMENT SupplierPartID (#PCDATA)> <!-- string -->
<!ELEMENT SupplierPartAuxiliaryID ANY>

<!ELEMENT ItemDetail (UnitPrice, Description+, UnitOfMeasure,
                      Classification+, ManufacturerPartID?,
                      ManufacturerName?, URL?, Extrinsic*)>
<!ELEMENT UnitPrice (Money)>
<!ELEMENT Money (#PCDATA)>
<!ATTLIST Money
    currency            %isoCurrencyCode;   #REQUIRED
    alternateAmount     %number;            #IMPLIED
    alternateCurrency   %isoCurrencyCode;   #IMPLIED>

<!ELEMENT Description ( #PCDATA | ShortName )* >
<!ATTLIST Description xml:lang %xmlLangCode; #REQUIRED>

<!ELEMENT ShortName (#PCDATA)>
<!ELEMENT UnitOfMeasure (#PCDATA)>
<!ELEMENT Classification (#PCDATA)>
<!ATTLIST Classification domain %string; #REQUIRED>

<!ELEMENT ManufacturerPartID (#PCDATA)>

<!ELEMENT ManufacturerName (#PCDATA)>
<!ATTLIST ManufacturerName xml:lang %xmlLangCode; #IMPLIED>

<!ELEMENT URL (#PCDATA)>
<!ATTLIST URL name %string; #IMPLIED>

<!ELEMENT Extrinsic ANY>
<!ATTLIST Extrinsic name  %string;  #REQUIRED>

<!ELEMENT IndexItemDetail (LeadTime, ExpirationDate?, EffectiveDate?,
                          SearchGroupData*, TerritoryAvailable*)>

<!ELEMENT TerritoryAvailable (#PCDATA)>

<!ELEMENT SearchGroupData (Name, SearchDataElement+)>

<!ELEMENT SearchDataElement EMPTY>
<!ATTLIST SearchDataElement
    name %string; #REQUIRED
    value %string; #REQUIRED
>

<!ELEMENT LeadTime (#PCDATA)>

<!ELEMENT ExpirationDate (#PCDATA)>

<!ELEMENT EffectiveDate (#PCDATA)>
<!ELEMENT IndexItemPunchout (ItemID, PunchoutDetail)>
<!ELEMENT PunchoutDetail (Description+, URL, Classification+,
                         ManufacturerName?, ManufacturerPartID?,
                         ExpirationDate?, EffectiveDate?,
                         SearchGroupData*, TerritoryAvailable*)>
```

875

Several of the elements described in the DTD above are not included in the basic example provided, which mostly includes those related to the `<SearchGroup>` and `<SearchGroupData>` elements. A `<SearchGroup>` element provides additional search capabilities to the catalog. If a procurement application supports the use of `<SearchGroup>` elements, it will enable the users of that catalog to search the catalog based on the contents of the `<SearchGroupData>` elements, in addition to the standard full text search of the description and various ID fields.

In the basic example listed above, each item that appears in the Index file has the following form:

```
<IndexItem>
  <IndexItemAdd>
    <ItemID>
      <SupplierPartID>2</SupplierPartID>
    </ItemID>

    <ItemDetail>
      <UnitPrice>
        <Money currency="USD">3.00</Money>
      </UnitPrice>
      <Description xml:lang="en-US">Peppermint Body Soap</Description>
      <UnitOfMeasure>EA</UnitOfMeasure>
      <Classification domain="SM">10A</Classification>
      <URL>http://www.ajsoaps.com</URL>
    </ItemDetail>

    <IndexItemDetail>
      <LeadTime>5</LeadTime>
    </IndexItemDetail>
  </IndexItemAdd>
</IndexItem>
```

`<IndexItem>` is the container element for all information about a line-item in a catalog. It contains information about the item itself, as well as an indicator that flags if this is an item to be added to or deleted from a catalog. The `<IndexItemAdd>` element indicates that this is a new element to be added. The `<IndexItemDelete>` element indicates that this item is to be removed (in which case the only data really necessary is the item number). We can use the `<IndexItemPunchout>` element to specify the user should execute a URL and visit the supplier's purchasing site directly.

Once the item type is identified – the remaining information is supplied. In all cases, an `<ItemID>` element is provided to uniquely identify the item. `<ItemID>` is a container element for the `<SupplierPartID>` element, which is a unique item key. If it is not possible to identify an item uniquely with the `<SupplierPartID>` (as is sometimes the case in catalogs with several suppliers, who may use similar cataloging systems) then the `<SupplierPartAuxiliaryID>` can be used to create that unique key.

Once the part ID is specified, the remaining information needed for an item is the unit price, the part description, unit of measure, and a classification of the item. The `<Classification>` element is used to group items into similar categories. Search engines use it to narrow the full text searches that are used against the catalogs.

A required element on the `<classification>` element is the domain attribute. This specifies the classification scheme used. In many cases, United Nations Standard Product and Service Codes (UNSPSC) coding is used here. Non-standard coding may be used instead, but this must be identified in the domain attribute, and must be understood by anyone who is receiving the catalog.

The last required bit of information needed for this item is the lead-time ("How soon can I receive this item if I order it?").

The information discussed above is the very minimum required to generate a basic cXML catalog. In creating a simple Index file, a supplier is able to define their product offering and with the supplier file, specify preferred ordering methods.

cXML Index files vary from the simple ones (such as that discussed above) to the very complex, providing searching support through the use of Search Groups and/or Punch Out services.

Contract

The contract file allows suppliers to overlay information about a specific item or items in their catalog for specific buyers. Contract files are typically used to adjust costing information of previously supplied catalogs. In many cases, a supplier actually generates different catalogs for each of the buyers they do business with, rather than creating Contract files.

The logic used to generate pricing models is dependent upon the specifics of the relationship with each of the buyers, and in many cases, can include complex queries into an ERP system. If a supplier intends to automate the order processing steps, it behoves them to attempt to create contract-pricing files. The logic needed to create the correct pricing for the Contract file will be similar to the logic needed to automate a check of an order against the same system.

The simplest form of a Contract file would include the supplier ID and the item IDs with new pricing information. The example listed below shows two of the four items from the previous catalog updated with a new price, and a URL for viewing the latest sale products.

```xml
<?xml version="1.0" encoding="UTF-8"?>
<!DOCTYPE Contract SYSTEM "http://xml.cXML.org/schemas/cXML/1.1.008/cXML.dtd">

<Contract effectiveDate="2001-01-01T14:32:20-08:00"
          expirationDate="2001-06-01T12:00:00-08:00">
  <SupplierID domain="Internal">029</SupplierID>

  <Comments xml:lang="en-US">
    AJSoaps Contract Pricing File
  </Comments>

  <ItemSegment>
    <ContractItem>
      <ItemID>
      <SupplierPartID>1</SupplierPartID>
      </ItemID>
      <UnitPrice>
        <Money currency="USD">1.50</Money>
      </UnitPrice>
      <Extrinsic name="URL">http://www.ajsoaps.com/SaleProducts</Extrinsic>
    </ContractItem>

    <ContractItem>
      <ItemID>
        <SupplierPartID>2</SupplierPartID>
      </ItemID>
      <UnitPrice>
        <Money currency="USD">1.50</Money>
      </UnitPrice>
    </ContractItem>
  </ItemSegment>

</Contract>
```

The Contract file gives suppliers more control to directly price their products based on the relationships negotiated with their buyers. Rather than uploading an entirely new catalog, listing all the previously loaded product descriptions and lead-time data, the Contract file provides a very succinct update model that can be controlled by the supplier. The use of the `<ItemSegment>` element allows suppliers to specify exactly which buyers are to see which pricing. An optional attribute named `segmentKey` allows suppliers to come up with pre-agreed strings to represent buyers or classes of buyers. When `segmentKey` is not specified (as in the above example), the contract pricing applies to all buyers accessing the catalog.

Once suppliers have provided their contact information, product catalog, and any pricing modifications, they are ready to participate in the cXML marketplace. Now they sit back and wait for the buyers to search their data and send them order requests. An order request is a document that closely mimics a purchase order. This document will come to the supplier from the cXML application (or Ariba buyer or marketplace). Once an order request is received, the supplier is to respond with an order response.

OrderResponse

The `OrderResponse` document serves as a receipt for an `OrderRequest`. Typically it only needs to indicate the `OrderRequest` payload ID and a status for the receipt. An order response example is provided below: the payload ID must match the payload ID on the order request.

```
<?xml version="1.0" encoding="UTF-8"?>
<!DOCTYPE cXML SYSTEM "http://xml.cXML.org/schemas/cXML/1.1.008/cXML.dtd">
<cXML payloadID="987654321@cxml.ajsoaps.com" xml:lang="en-US"
      timestamp="2000-09-12T19:29:09-05:00">
  <Response>
    <Status code="200" text="OK"/>
  </Response>
</cXML>
```

The status code in this example is based on HTTP – it is a simple OK response from the server. Any errors in transmission of the `OrderRequest` would be reflected in these status code and text attributes. The `OrderResponse` serves no purpose other than to let the transmitter of the `OrderRequest` know that the `OrderRequest` was received. Any issues with the content of the `OrderRequest` message must be handled via different means.

Because the documents discussed in this section are the very minimum set needed to participate in a cXML marketplace, there are several additional document types that are not discussed here. These additional document types were primarily to facilitate Punch Out and/or a variety of status and request for information messages.

The Buyer Documents

Buyers wishing to participate in a cXML marketplace must be capable of receiving and parsing the supplier documents. There are buying applications available today that handle this for the buyers. Most of the development work that has been taking place in the past few years has been on the buyer applications. The buyer only really has to communicate a single document type in order to accomplish a successful purchase within a marketplace. That document type is the `OrderRequest`.

OrderRequest

The OrderRequest document is the cXML form of a purchase order. It consists of a header and a body. It has a child element, <OrderRequestHeader>, which contains elements for a purchase order number, the date of the order, the total amount of the purchase, and the bill-to information. The body consists of a listing of the items being ordered.

The example provided below lists a minimal set of information needed to convey a valid cXML purchase order to a supplier.

```
<?xml version="1.0" encoding="UTF-8"?>
<!DOCTYPE OrderRequest SYSTEM "http://xml.cXML.org/schemas/cXML/1.1.008/cXML.dtd">
<OrderRequest>
  <OrderRequestHeader orderID="PO12345" orderDate="2000-06-19" type="new">
    <Total>
      <Money currency="USD">34.95</Money>
    </Total>

    <BillTo>
      <Address>
        <Name xml:lang="en">Al's Soap Shop</Name>

        <PostalAddress name="foo">
          <Street>123 Maple Lane</Street>
          <City>Mays Landing</City>
          <State>NJ</State>
          <PostalCode>08317</PostalCode>
          <Country isoCountryCode="US">United States</Country>
        </PostalAddress>
      </Address>
    </BillTo>

    <Shipping trackingDomain="FedEx" trackingId="1234567890">
      <Money currency="USD">3.00</Money>
      <Description xml:lang="en-us">FedEx 2-day</Description>
    </Shipping>

    <Tax>
      <Money currency="USD">1.95</Money>
      <Description xml:lang="en">NJ Sales Tax</Description>
    </Tax>

    <Payment>
      <PCard number="1234567890123456" expiration="2004-06-30"/>
    </Payment>
  </OrderRequestHeader>

  <ItemOut quantity="10" requestedDeliveryDate="2000-07-12">
    <ItemID>
      <SupplierPartID>1</SupplierPartID>
    </ItemID>

    <ItemDetail>
      <UnitPrice>
        <Money currency="USD">3.00</Money>
      </UnitPrice>
      <Description xml:lang="en">Basic Vanilla Hand Soap</Description>
      <UnitOfMeasure>EA</UnitOfMeasure>
      <Classification domain="SPSC">12345</Classification>
      <ManufacturerPartID>1</ManufacturerPartID>
```

```
        <ManufacturerName>AJ Soaps</ManufacturerName>
        <URL>www.ajsoaps.com</URL>
     </ItemDetail>

     <Comments xml:lang="en-US">
        Monthly order of Basic Vanilla Soap.
     </Comments>
   </ItemOut>
</OrderRequest>
```

This simple `OrderRequest` illustrates ordering a single item from the catalog with a quantity of ten. There is one `ItemOut` for each item ordered, which provides the information needed for the supplier to fulfill the order. This includes similar item information to that found in the Index (catalog) file supplied by the supplier. The information supplied by the `OrderRequest` is equivalent to a purchase order. Suppliers receive an `OrderRequest` and respond immediately with an `OrderResponse`, which serves to acknowledge receipt of the order.

There are other buyer documents that are part of the cXML standard, but this is the main document created by buyers. For a complete discussion of the cXML buyer documents, refer to the cXML web site (http://www.cXML.org).

Creating Electronic Catalogs

After looking at the syntax for a cXML catalog (an Index file), lets now look at a simple program that can generate a catalog from a few tables in a Microsoft Access database. The following program queries a database that contains two tables. The first table, `CatalogData`, contains information specific to the catalog as a whole, it represents the data that ends up in the first part of the Index file (which I have called the header for lack of a better term) and has the following form:

CatalogID	Description	SupplierID	Currency	Language	Effective Date	Expiration Date	Territory
AJ-1	AJ Soaps Everyday Catalog for 2001	123456	USD	EN-US	01/01/2001	01/01/2002	US

The second table, `Products`, contains the minimum information necessary about the products themselves to generate a valid cXML catalog:

ItemID	Product Name	Description	Price	UOM	Code	Supplier ID
1	Basic Vanilla Soap	All natural vegetable oil based soap. Free of dyes, with a light vanilla scent to accent the bath.	$3.00	EA	5313160800	123456
2	Serenity	Lavender-scented all natural vegetable soaps	$3.00	EA	5313160817	123457
3	Passion	A soap to incite the senses and bring out the wild side.	$3.00	EA	5313160829	123458

The program below will connect to the access database through JDBC. It will then use basic java techniques to create the catalog file, and then parse the created document against the DTD to check its validity (by using DOM).

Before we begin, we will need to set up the database as an ODBC source on the system. The database is available as soap.mdb in the code download. On Windows 2000 select Start | Settings | Control Panel and from the control panel choose Administrative Tools choose Data Sources (ODBC):

Select the System DSN tab from the tabbed window that opens. This will make the database available to all users, if you wish to make the database only available for the current login, choose User DSN and set the DSN as for a System DSN, as shown below. Now select the Add... button and choose Microsoft Access Driver (*.mdb). This should now look like the following:

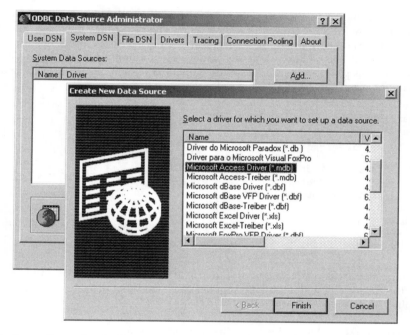

Select Finish. Enter Soaps for the Data Source Name, choose the Select button, and navigate to the location of the soaps.mdb file on your system. Select OK and that will set up the database.

The basic steps that we must take in order to generate a catalog are:

- ❏ Connect to the data source
- ❏ Query the catalog table to get the header information and the supplier ID
- ❏ Generate the Index file header from the catalog data
- ❏ Query the product table to get item information for the supplier ID
- ❏ Generate the Item information from the product data
- ❏ Parse the generated file to ensure it is valid XML

We have chosen to implement this in a JSP file. If you are not familiar with JSP, rest assured, sufficient explanations are provided for you to follow. Note that this is not the optimal design, and in addition, much important error checking is not included.

As a brief introduction, JSP allows us to embed java scriptlets and calls to JavaBeans inside content. A JSP container (or server) compiles the JSP file into a servlet, which it then runs. Java code is embedded within <% %> pairs. Any content outside this will be treated as text and output directly to the output stream; in this case, this is the connection to the client represented by the response object.

In order to show the differences between code and output that is not processed during editing these pages, the background for code is gray, while the content that will be output has a white background.

In this case we are using JSP to allow us to template the XML catalog document. We define the XML document and then use JSP to insert the necessary data using calls to the database. The first statement is a **page directive**, an instruction to the JSP container that allows us to set various page properties. Page directives are delimited by <%@ and %>. In this case we use it to import the required classes, set "Java" as the language for this page, and set the response content type to "text/xml". We then begin the XML page with the usual declaration:

```
<?xml version="1.0" encoding= "UTF-8" ?>
  <%@ page
    import="java.sql.DriverManager,
            java.sql.ResultSet,
            java.sql.Connection,
            java.sql.Statement,
            java.sql.SQLException"

    language="Java"
    contentType="text/xml;charset=ISO-8859-1"
%>
```

In order to define page-wide variables, we declare them inside "<%!" and "%>". We begin by defining variables for the catalog (these describe the supplier), the dates that the catalog is valid from and until, and the supplier ID. We also define the JDBC URI.

We will run two queries on the database: the first will retrieve supplier information, the second retrieves a result set of every product in the database.

```
<%!
  String dbURL = "jdbc:odbc:Soaps";
  String expireDate = null;
  String effectiveDate = null;
  String supplierID = null;
  String supplierDescr = null;

  ResultSet supplierInfo = null;
  ResultSet productInfo = null;
%>
```

We now begin our first scriptlet. We load the JDBC ODBC driver and attempt to connect to the Soaps database and, if this fails, exit the program, printing out an error message to client and server:

```
<%

  // Load the jdbc driver
  Class.forName("sun.jdbc.odbc.JdbcOdbcDriver");

  // create a connection to the database
  Connection dbConnection = DriverManager.getConnection(dbURL);
  if (dbConnection == null) {
    %>
      <errorMessage>
        Could not connect to Database. Terminating...
      </errorMessage>");
    <%
    System.out.println("Could not connect to Database. Terminating...");
    return;
  }
```

If we are successful in connecting, we create a statement and run a query to return all data from the CatalogData table; the result set returned should hold the supplier information:

```
  Statement query = dbConnection.createStatement();

  // query the CatalogData table for the supplier information needed
  supplierInfo = query.executeQuery("select * from CatalogData");

  if (supplierInfo == null) {
    %>
      <errorMessage>No Catalog Data Found</errorMessage>
    <%
    System.out.println("No Catalog Data found...");
    return;
  }
```

We extract the supplier ID and description, and the effective date and expiration date information from the result set, storing them in the corresponding variables.

```
  if (supplierInfo.next()) {
    supplierID = supplierInfo.getString("SupplierID");
    expireDate = supplierInfo.getString("ExpirationDate");
    effectiveDate = supplierInfo.getString("EffectiveDate");
    supplierDescr = supplierInfo.getString("Descr");
  }
```

We can now query the database for the product information.

```
  // now query the Products table to get the item information
  String qstring = "select * from Products where SupplierID='" +
                    supplierID + "'";
  productInfo = query.executeQuery(qstring);
```

```
    if (productInfo == null) {
    %>
        <errorMessage>No Product Data found...<errorMessage>
    <%
    System.out.println("No Product Data found...");
    return;
    }
%>
```

We can now begin to construct the document. Notice that up until now we have not specified a DTD; the error messages returned to the client in case of database problems do not match the cXML DTD and so we only include them when a successful connection is established and the required data is available. We now declare the DTD and open the Index document and output the supplier ID and description:

```
<!DOCTYPE Index SYSTEM "http://xml.cXML.org/schemas/cXML/1.1.008/cXML.dtd">
<Index>
  <SupplierID domain="DUNS">
    <%=supplierID%>
  </SupplierID>

  <Comments xml:lang="en-US">
    <%=supplierDescr%>
  </Comments>
```

Finally, we iterate through each product, outputting its details:

```
<%
  // list products
  while (productInfo.next()) {
      //build the IndexItem elements for the catalog
%>
      <IndexItem>
        <IndexItemAdd>
          <ItemID>
            <SupplierPartID>
              <%=productInfo.getString("ItemID")%>
            </SupplierPartID>
          </ItemID>

          <ItemDetail>
            <UnitPrice>
              <Money currency="USD">
                <%=productInfo.getString("Price")%>
              </Money>
            </UnitPrice>

            <Description xml:lang="en-US">
              <%=productInfo.getString("Descr")%>
            </Description>

            <UnitOfMeasure>
              <%=productInfo.getString("UOM")%>
            </UnitOfMeasure>
```

```
        <Classification domain="UNSPSC">
          <%=productInfo.getString("Code")%>
        </Classification>
      </ItemDetail>

      <IndexItemDetail>
        <LeadTime>30</LeadTime>
        <ExpirationDate>
          <%=expireDate%>
        </ExpirationDate>

        <EffectiveDate>
          <%=effectiveDate%>
        </EffectiveDate>

        <TerritoryAvailable>US</TerritoryAvailable>
      </IndexItemDetail>
    </IndexItemAdd>
  </IndexItem>
<%
  } // end while
%>
```

and close the Index document:

```
  </index>
```

Save this file as `CatalogCreator.jsp`. Of course, there are other ways to achieve this, including using DOM, however we chose not to use DOM to create the catalog document. This is because it is much less taxing on the computer memory (and on the maintenance coders) to leave DOM out of the creation process when generating certain types of XML files, especially those that will never be seen directly by humans. We use DOM once we've generated our catalog file, however, to parse and validate its structure.

As we work through the results set for the `Products` data, you can see that some of the attributes have been hard coded (such as currency on the `Money` tag). These too could be placed into the database, queried and, added as we build the document.

We can test this program in Tomcat, by creating a new web application called B2B. It should have the usual web application structure including a `WEB-INF` sub folder, which contains the following (empty) `web.xml` file:

```
<?xml version="1.0" encoding="ISO-8859-1"?>

<!DOCTYPE web-app
  PUBLIC "-//Sun Microsystems, Inc.//DTD Web Application 2.2//EN"
  "http://java.sun.com/j2ee/dtds/web-app_2_2.dtd">

<web-app>
</web-app>
```

The structure of the web application, which should be placed in Tomcat's /webbapps/ folder is as follows:

```
/b2b/
      CatalogCreator.jsp
      /WEB-INF/
            web.xml
```

Having made sure that the database system DSN is set up correctly, the following URL entered into a browser should return the document:

http://localhost:8080/b2b/CatalogCreator.jsp

This assumes that Tomcat has been set up as per Appendix H. This will return the document for AJ Soaps:

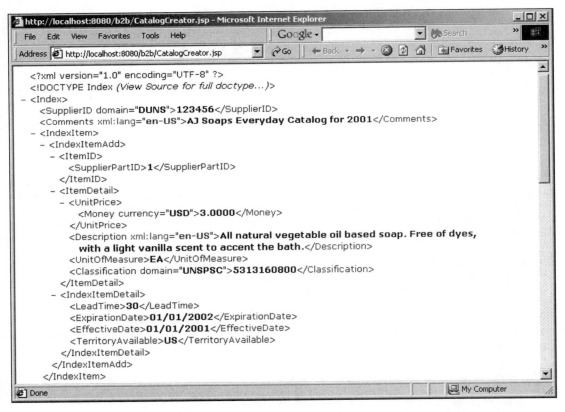

To save this file, choose File | Save As and enter Catalog.xml choosing text as the format. We will need this file later.

Parsing OrderRequest Documents

OrderRequests come to suppliers via e-mail usually, but can also be written so that they are sent to and processed by a web server. In any case, once a supplier has an OrderRequest, they must respond with an OrderResponse and then fill the order given. The OrderResponse does not convey any information to the buyer other than that the order was received. Any discrepancies in the order itself are handled via other means.

The simple program below will parse an OrderRequest document. The data gleaned from the OrderRequest will also be used to check against the database to determine if the inventory has sufficient stock to fill the order. If it does not, a message to that effect will be output.

We could set this program up to be run against any new orders coming into a supplier. It could also be set up to generate an e-mail notification, or something more elegant than a command-line message. The file name of the request is given as a command-line option:

```
import java.io.File;
import javax.xml.parsers.DocumentBuilder;
import javax.xml.parsers.DocumentBuilderFactory;

import org.w3c.dom.Document;
import org.w3c.dom.NodeList;
import org.w3c.dom.Node;

import java.sql.DriverManager;
import java.sql.Connection;
import java.sql.Statement;
import java.sql.ResultSet;

public class ProcessOrder {
  public static void main(String args[]) throws Exception {
    // get order request filename from command line
    if (args.length != 1) {
      System.out.println("No filename given...");
      System.exit(1);
    }
```

We instantiate a DocumentBuilderFactory, set parsers returned from its factory method to validate documents, and instantiate a document builder from it. doc is our XML document, rootNode represents the documents root node. We now create a file and use the document builder to load the file, setting rootNode to the root node for the document:

```
DocumentBuilderFactory xdocBuilderFactory =
                              DocumentBuilderFactory.newInstance();
xdocBuilderFactory.setValidating(true);
DocumentBuilder xdocBuilder = xdocBuilderFactory.newDocumentBuilder();

Document doc;
Node rootNode;

File xmlFile = new File(args[0]);

System.out.println("Parsing XML Document...");
doc = xdocBuilder.parse(xmlFile);
rootNode = doc.getDocumentElement();
```

We check that the root node for the document is an `OrderRequest`, which serves as simple error checking. In order to check the order, we will need to connect to the database, and this takes the same form as in the JSP file above:

```
if (!(rootNode.getNodeName()).equals("OrderRequest")) {
  System.out.println("Invalid XML document type");
  System.exit(1);
}
// connect to the database
// Load the jdbc driver
Class.forName("sun.jdbc.odbc.JdbcOdbcDriver");

// create a connection to the database
Connection dbConnection =
                DriverManager.getConnection("jdbc:odbc:Soaps");
if (dbConnection == null) {
  System.out.println("Could not connect to Database. Terminating...");
  System.exit(1);
}

Statement query = dbConnection.createStatement();
```

Now that the initialization has been done, we can get on with checking the order. We use the `getElementsByTagName()` method for the document to return a node list of the `ItemOut` elements. `ItemOutNode` represents the current `ItemOut` node being processed, `children` represents a node list of the item's children. `quantity` and `itemID` are self-evident as are `rs` and `query`. The basis for the program is quite simple:

We iterate through each item, first normalizing it to remove excess whitespace and extract the value of the quantity attribute:

```
NodeList itemOutNodes = doc.getElementsByTagName("ItemOut");

Node ItemOutNode = null;
Node supplierIDNode = null;
String itemID = null;
String quantity = null;
ResultSet rs;

int itemCount = itemOutNodes.getLength();
for (int i = 0; i < itemCount; i++) {
  ItemOutNode = itemOutNodes.item(i);

  ItemOutNode.normalize();
  quantity = ItemOutNode.getAttributes()
                     .getNamedItem("quantity")
                     .getNodeValue();
```

We need to get the item ID value. Let's see an extract from an order to refresh our mind on where this value is:

```
<?xml version="1.0" encoding="UTF-8"?>
<!DOCTYPE OrderRequest SYSTEM "http://xml.cXML.org/schemas/cXML/1.1.008/cXML.dtd">
<OrderRequest>
  <OrderRequestHeader orderID="PO12345" orderDate="2000-06-19" type="new">

...<!-- rest of document header here -->
```

```
<ItemOut quantity="10" requestedDeliveryDate="2000-07-12">
  <ItemID>
    <SupplierPartID>1</SupplierPartID>
  </ItemID>
```

In order to extract the SupplierPartID we must extract a node list of all the SupplierPartID elements that are in the item currently being processed, which should be exactly one. We extract the first node (item zero), and use the getFirstChild() method to get the text node that represents the value inside this element. In order to retrieve the text nodes value we call the getNodeValue() method; we now have the item's ID, which we can use to check inventory levels on the database:

```
// get the child nodes from the ItemOut element
Node supplierIDNode =
            ((Element)ItemOutNode).getElementsByTagName("SupplierPartID")
                                  .item(0);
    itemID = itemIDNode.getFirstChild().getNodeValue();
```

We now query the database to see if there is enough in stock to cover the order. The database table, Stock is as follows:

ItemID	QuantityOnHand
1	22
2	7
3	45

The ItemID translates to the SupplierPartID element value in an OrderRequest. The QuantityOnHand column represents unit values. The query to run against this table therefore is very simple. Assuming that the result set returned in not empty, we move the cursor to the value returned in the result set and attempt to parse the value in it.

The quantityDesired variable represents the ordered number of items, which we check against the QuantityOnHand, returning an appropriate message if there is not enough stock. Otherwise, we indicate that there is sufficient stock with another small message:

```
rs = query.executeQuery("select QuantityOnHand from Stock where" +
                        " ItemID = '" + itemID + "'");
if (rs != null) {
  if (rs.next()) {
    int quantityOnHand = rs.getInt("QuantityOnHand");
    int quantityDesired = Integer.parseInt(quantity, 10);
    if (quantityDesired > quantityOnHand) {
      System.out.println("Insufficient quantities on hand to fill " +
                         "this order for item #: "+itemID);
    } else {
      System.out.println("There is sufficient stock for your order");
    }
  }
  } else {
    System.out.println("No Inventory Data found - Possible invalid" +
                       " Item ID...");
    System.exit(1);
  } // end else
  } // end if (rs!= null)
} // end for
}
```

Notice that the program assumes that a `<SupplierID>` element is present and not the optional `<SupplierPartAuxiliaryID>`.

This was a simple example; it only checked for availability and did not subsequently process the order any further. Suppliers typically have more complicated processes going on to fulfill the orders, and they usually employ third-party software tools to aid in the workflow of the order processing. There are a few companies out there that provide complete supplier solutions – not only catalog creation but also back-end order processing.

Electronic Data Interchange (EDI)

Electronic Commerce has been around for years, and prior to the introduction of XML, companies relied almost solely on Electronic Data Interchange (EDI) to simplify and standardize their transactions. It is still uncertain as to whether either of those goals were achieved by EDI. Even bearing this mind, EDI has a solid foothold in the e-commerce space. It will undoubtedly be around for several years to come, as many of the global Fortune 1000 companies have implemented an EDI system for their e-business. EDI, however, poses a very expensive and not-so-straightforward problem for businesses wishing to conduct business with any of these large EDI-enabled companies. For companies just getting into the e-commerce market, it makes sense for them to move directly into XML for their message format. This leaves the problem of communicating with the businesses that have implemented EDI.

There are several options available to companies wishing to transact business with others who have chosen EDI. These options range from consulting services that create custom EDI to XML mappings of each of the message formats that are required, to software translation engines that allow users to map their XML element sets into the various EDI document formats. The software translation engines all work in quite similar ways – the user specifies a mapping between the XML format and the specific EDI format document. A list of some of the XML/EDI translation tools would include Sterling Commerce's Gentran Server (http://www.sterlingcommerce.com), GE Global Exchange Services Application Integrator (http://www.gegxs.com), and XML Solutions (www.xmlsolutions.com). This list is not all-inclusive, the point is that there are several options out there for folks trying to talk to EDI systems. These tools can be expensive, however, so it is best to let the marketplace handle the XML/EDI translations for you. For instance, Ariba allows users to specify EDI format messages as outputs if desired.

Security Considerations

Popular question from developers trying to figure out how to participate in electronic marketplaces are: "What about security? What do I have to be worried about when thinking of how to get the data safely to the intended site(s)? How does one prove they are who they say they are? And how do I know the data I've sent has actually been received?"

In addition, suppliers don't especially want the world seeing the pricing files they are sending to specific buyers. Buyers don't want suppliers to know their specific buying habits from another supplier.

The short answer to these questions is HTTPS. Most of the electronic marketplaces are SSL-enabled web sites. They use a username/password combination to identify members, and they use certificates and trusted pipes for communicating files across the Internet. For suppliers who provide their catalogs directly to the buyers, FTP is usually used. As far as the catalogs go, most suppliers are still providing their catalogs in **CIF (Catalog Interchange Format)** or some other CSV format. These catalogs are also supplied directly to the buyer via a trusted FTP login, or they are provided to the marketplace network through a secure web site. There is an acceptance procedure within the buying organization whenever a catalog is received. It has to check the catalog content and pricing against its own contracts and buying parameters.

Orders are handled a little differently – a vast majority of orders coming from marketplaces are currently transmitted via e-mail. For those orders coming directly from the marketplace as an XML order, the marketplace usually delivers the XML files via HTTPS to a web server waiting to receive them. Approved purchasers are handled through the marketplace – so the assumption tends to be that when an order is received, it is valid and from an authorized buying agent.

Summary

This chapter has been an introduction to B2B messaging through a look at electronic marketplaces. The electronic marketplace is a good example of a B2B messaging application because of the diverse kinds of messages that must be created and routed. Suppliers to marketplaces must develop electronic catalogs, supplier data information files, and contract pricing files. In addition, they must be able to receive electronic purchase orders. Buyers must be able to collect electronic marketplaces, search them, and find what they are looking for. They then must create purchase orders to go to the supplier for fulfillment.

There is much speculation regarding the marketplace model and whether it will succeed or fail as a viable commerce platform. While buyer systems have had a considerable amount of investment, suppliers find themselves a little behind in the race, lacking the tools and expertise to assist them in catalog creation, and find difficulty in managing the electronic contract terms that factor into the pricing and availability information that is generated for a specific catalog for a specific buyer.

Until the suppliers are supported with tools to assist their catalog generation, the marketplaces will continue to be an interesting research project and not much more. It will be worthwhile to watch for new supplier applications over the next few years.

There are several initiatives underway to define and implement a standard means of communicating business messages. Several of these initiatives were discussed in this chapter, and include Commerce XML (cXML), XML Commerce Business Language (xCBL), Rosetta Net, and others. We looked at electronic catalogs, and learned how to generate them in Java using data from an Access Database. We also learned how to parse OrderRequests, the cXML version of a purchase order, and check it against a database to see if the inventory was in stock. Each of these activities will be required in one form or another if you want to participate in electronic marketplaces.

This was an introduction to B2B Messaging with XML and Java. I hope this chapter has given you enough to whet your appetite on electronic marketplaces. I think that whatever turns the technology takes in the next few years, the experience gained by getting in there and working with Java, B2B Messages, and XML will prepare you for whatever 'next best thing' comes along.

The Xerces Blue
utterfly, which became
xtinct earlier this century,
nd after which the Xerces XML
arser is named ...

22

Web Services

So far over the course of this book, we have developed a number of client-server applications, often built over HTTP, in which the communication between the client and the server is in XML. However, in each case, the infrastructure for the client-server program has been *specific* to that individual application. Each side of the application is very tightly linked to the other; the client knows how to format an XML document that the server understands, and it knows how to encode the document into a protocol to transmit it to the server. The server expects a certain kind of document, and after processing, knows how to format a response that the client is expecting, and again, how to encode it within a protocol to send it back to the client. The client then knows how to extract the data it wants from this response.

This kind of procedure is fine when the development of client and server are tightly integrated. Perhaps the same developer or team is developing both – they can decide on exactly how the client-server protocol will work and then go right ahead and implement it. Or, in a B2B environment, perhaps, developers working in different companies will be writing the two endpoints for the interaction. Setting out a strong documentation procedure and ensuring that specifications are adhered to, exerts control over both endpoints.

Let's take an example. A company distributing a piece of software that plays audio CDs might strike a deal with a record company to provide information on their servers about recording artists, track listings, and so on, so that when you insert a CD into your CD-ROM drive, the information is downloaded to your player and displayed on screen. Let's further imagine they choose to use XML for the client-server communication in this system. The CD playing software would have to gather data from the CD that uniquely identifies it (a serial number, the number of tracks, their exact length, and so on).

An XML data structure would then be defined that described exactly how this data is transmitted, in terms of element structure, as well as additional details like character representations of non-character data. Then the format for transmitting CD details (allowing for all the different kinds of details required for different CDs – from an album by a single artist, to an orchestral recording, etc.) would need to be decided. Further, they would have to decide what protocol to use (HTTP would be the obvious choice, particularly since the software might well find itself being used behind a firewall), and exactly how to wrap the CD details inside an HTTP request. Once this was all decided, the client and server could be coded up.

Using XML might well help this development team internally. It provides them with any number of tools for parsing and manipulating the data involved in the exchange, as well as validation, which allows them to check that the client-server contract is being maintained. They will find the system easy to debug, and they will also be able to integrate changes to the protocol with the next version of the player software, should the need arise.

But from the perspective of the user, the data exchange format is irrelevant. Once the data has arrived in the application, the rich metadata, and descriptive formatting of the XML that the client received from the server has been lost – the data is extracted by the client and presented to us through the GUI of the player software. The user is at the mercy of the GUI designer as to whether it is possible to extract any of that information to insert into their CD catalog database, or whatever they may wish to do with it.

It seems a shame, in this scenario, that there is a source of machine-readable, richly formatted data about CDs available across a publicly accessible protocol, but that it is limited in use to just this one piece of CD playing software. It's possible, of course, for other people to reverse-engineer the protocol and make their own clients, or for other companies to enter into a deal with the original developers, and license the protocol for their own software. In this situation, they would receive a lot of human-readable documentation, and then have to set out to code their own clients up against the protocol's specification. This actually creates a barrier that discourages others from making use of a source of information that is readily available, and which the company could charge them for the privilege of using. Why not set out to make this internal product into a publicly sellable service?

What's interesting about this scenario is that the company who developed the CD player has now had to become a publisher of information, which isn't really one of their core business competencies. They would much rather be concentrating on getting out the next version of their CD playing software than on ensuring that the track listing for Meat Loaf's last album is spelled correctly.

Therefore, what if some business, whose specialty was aggregating data from many sources together and publishing it, were to take on the role of publishing the CD data. There would be a good chance that they'd do a better job of it than the CD player developers, and this would then allow the CD player developers to get on with writing the next version.

However, if the new data publishing company followed the same proprietary path as the original software developers (arbitrarily deciding how to encode the data their service handles and provides), then anyone else wishing to use that CD data service would have the same problem as we discussed before.

But what if instead, they published a machine-readable definition of how any client could interact with the service on the Internet? Instead of providing human-readable documentation that necessitates programmers developing clients from the ground up, this machine-readable documentation enables much of the client code to be generated automatically. This is what web services are all about.

It allows the client code to be easily updated if the interface to the service is changed, and it allows client developers to concentrate on adding value to the data they obtain from the service, by presenting it well, or aggregating it with other information.

The web services model also allows the content provider to charge for use of the service. Several models are possible:

❑ **Pay-per-use**
Micro payments can be used to charge the end user every time the service is accessed.

❑ **Subscription**
The end user must subscribe to the service in order to be allowed to use it.

❑ **Licensing**
Client developers must pay for a license to develop a client to the service. They can then embed a certificate into their client software that certifies it was developed by a licensee.

Of course, many web services could be offered for free. Current web services standards do not specifically enforce any payment schemes, leaving the implementation of such systems up to individual service developers. The use of secure SSL layered protocols, however, is already possible, so such schemes are technically perfectly feasible.

Many web sites already publish free information that people often want to process in some way not offered by the human-readable interface. For example, search engine results, flight times, or the current list of Fortune 100 companies. By exposing such information via a web service, existing information providers give end users more power to make use of the data and services the site has to offer. In addition, web services provide an excellent opportunity for companies that maintain large internal pools of information, which isn't very human-readable, to publish that information in a form that is usable outside the company.

Web Services Standards

Web services are based on standard ways of representing interfaces, and standard ways of accessing services.

So the question then is, how are these standards being developed? Web services standardization is being led initially by Microsoft, IBM, and B2B specialists Ariba, and is focused currently on developing standards for the following purposes:

❑ **Discovery** – locating the web service you are looking for

❑ **Description** – defining the interface to the web service

❑ **Invocation** – accessing the service through the known interface

The aim is not to provide separate protocols to perform each of these tasks, but rather to provide an interlocking collection of protocols that provide a number of different means for performing each of these tasks. This recognizes that some web service clients will already know more about the service they are looking for than others, and so will have different requirements.

So, for example, in the discovery space, there is the **Universal Description, Discovery, and Integration protocol (UDDI)**, which provides a means for clients to access a central repository to look up services by type, or by provider. Another protocol is Disco, which is intended for use in an intranet environment, and which allows a client to find out the details of all the services published locally. We briefly covered UDDI in the last chapter and we will discuss it further later in this chapter.

For description, a number of standards have been developed. IBM originally proposed NASSL (The Network Accessible Service Specification Language) and WDS (which stands for 'Well-Defined Service'). Microsoft also developed SDL (the Service Description Language), and SCL (the SOAP Contract Language). These have generally been superceded by the development of **WSDL**, the **Web Services Description Language**, since it provides facilities equivalent to all of them.

In the invocation layer, there are many ways a service might be accessed. Web services, in spite of the name, do not have to respond only to HTTP requests: SMTP mail is also a common means for activating a service. SOAP provides an encoding that can be applied to this layer, but web services are also capable of handling simple HTTP GET or POST requests, without complex SOAP formatted bodies.

Sun Microsystems announced in early 2001 an initiative called **Sun ONE**, or 'Open Network Environment' (http://www.sun.com/software/sunone/), and depends on pushing Java forward as a platform for web services (which Sun call 'open, smart web services'). However, Sun has not yet committed support for any particular family of standards.

Sun has also announced an intention to develop Java APIs for XML-based remote procedure calls, and for looking up services in XML registries – two more JAX* family APIs: **JAX/RPC (Java API for XML Remote Procedure Calls)** and **JAXR (Java API for XML Registries)**. These should wrap up implementations of web services standards, such as SOAP and UDDI, behind the familiar Java-style abstraction layer. These APIs remain, for now, fairly distant.

IBM, on the other hand, has already developed a suite of early-access tools for web services development, some of which have been released as open source products, and some of which are proprietary products, intended ultimately to form part of the IBM WebSphere platform. IBM DeveloperWorks has a web services zone at http://www.ibm.com/developerworks/webservices/, which will link you to three of their key tools, currently all hosted in AlphaWorks:

❑ **The Web Services Toolkit (WSTK)**
http://www.alphaworks.ibm.com/tech/webservicetoolkit. This toolkit provides all IBM's tools for web service description, deployment, discovery, and invocation, together with utilities for automatically generating web services based on existing classes or EJBs.

❑ **The WSDL Toolkit**
http://www.alphaworks.ibm.com/tech/wsdltoolkit. This is one of the elements of the WSTK, and possibly the most useful component. This toolkit provides utilities for automatically generating services and clients based on WSDL interface definitions.

❑ **The Web Services Development Environment (WSDE)**
http://www.alphaworks.ibm.com/tech/wsde. This is a complete development environment for web services, providing integrated GUI tools for web service creation. The WSTK complements the functionality of the WSDE by providing graphical deployment and discovery facilities.

In this chapter, we will principally be making use of the WSTK toolkit. We will look at how to install and configure the WSDL tools later on in the chapter.

We'll also need a Tomcat installation, and Apache SOAP, which you will already have in place from earlier in the book if you have been following the material in order. Details on installing the SOAP server on Tomcat can be found in Chapter 19.

IBM's tools support the following standards:

- ❑ **UDDI: Universal Description, Discovery, and Integration protocol**
  UDDI is a protocol for talking to registries that hold information about available services. UDDI defines the way you register services, discover services, and contact services once you've discovered them.

- ❑ **WSDL: Web Services Description Language**
  An XML-formatted language that defines the ways you can contact a web service, and describes the message formats you should use to do so.

- ❑ **SOAP: Simple Object Access Protocol**
  We've met SOAP before. It is probably the most powerful tool for accessing a web service, since it can model complex object data types easily, and therefore maps most cleanly onto remote procedure calls.

> **As these tools are only early-access, the full potential of their functionality has not been realized. This has imposed some limitations on the examples in this chapter.**

Before we look at how to use these standards to provide web services, let's set up an example where web services would be an ideal solution.

A Web Services Scenario

Let us imagine, for a moment, a traditional supermarket chain called WroxMart. Like most supermarkets, it makes use of a large database of products, associating each item with price information, stock and availability details, a barcode number, and much more. The overall data model for such a supermarket is obviously extremely complex.

Now, WroxMart wants to provide some high tech value-added facilities to its customers. They install recipe information points, which can provide customers with ideas for recipes they could make using the food they have just bought. In order to simplify things, the recipe database will be housed at the supermarket's data-center, rather than on-site at the store. In order to simplify the networking and hardware components for the kiosks, they are connected to the store LAN behind a local firewall. Let's think about how such a system could be constructed.

The first thing to do is work out how the kiosks will know what the customer has just bought. Luckily, the store has a customer loyalty card scheme, which means each customer has a card uniquely identifying them. When they go to the checkout, their card identifies the customer, and the details of which products they have bought can be cached in a record associated with that customer's ID. Then, at the kiosk, by inserting their card, the kiosk can identify them and retrieve the locally cached list.

Now, the kiosk has to contact the central recipe service, saying what food the customer has bought, and retrieve a recipe. The only problem is that what the customer will have bought (things like '2 WroxMart own 16oz. Prime Beef Fillets - SPECIAL OFFER') are not the sorts of thing that actually crop up on recipes. So, it makes sense to do some sort of lookup first that maps the barcode numbers for individually packaged, branded, specific food items to simple, quantified generic food ingredients ('beef fillet, 2x'). This allows the kiosk to aggregate, for example, three separate packets of two chicken breast fillets into simply six chicken breast fillets. Then it can send a simple list of available ingredients to the recipe server and expect a recipe in response.

So, we have a requirement for two services:

❏ A service that takes a barcode number and returns a quantity and a food identifier (some sort of URI scheme for defining food would be needed to uniquely identify generic food types, something like `http://food.wrox.com/pepper/chilli/jalapeno`)

❏ A service that takes a set of food identifiers and quantities, and returns a recipe suggestion.

Why implement these as web services? After all, we're talking about developing a set of kiosks in stores, so we'll have control of both endpoints. But, thinking about the possibilities offered by publishing this information as a web service, we can see that there are many other possible clients for the service:

❏ Our online store could make use of the same services to provide recipe ideas while people are shopping online.

❏ A software company could develop a diet program for home computers, which comes with a barcode scanner. By scanning in your weekly shopping when you get home, it could make use of our barcode-to-foodgroup converter to work out nutritional values for the different items you have bought. By using the recipe service, it could select recipes based on their nutritional value and suggest them to you.

❏ We could make a deal with a manufacturer of Internet-refrigerators (such things do exist), to build a barcode scanner into the door that keeps track of what items you have, and provides recipe ideas via a screen on the door.

OK, so it needs some work, but it provides some ideas for how web services are particularly likely to have an impact in the future, as Internet-connected appliances and networked devices become more common. Consider a television that accesses the Internet Movie Database through a web service, combined with a TV listings service, and provides you with film recommendations for the evening. If there's nothing on, it accesses the web service for your local video store and checks what they have in stock.

By publishing information as web services, the prospect for client software to act smarter, by collecting information from wherever it's available, and combining it with other information, leads to some very interesting possibilities in the upcoming era of media convergence.

Describing a Web Service with WSDL

In distributed computing, the problem of how to describe the interface a particular component exposes so that remote developers can write code that accesses it has been an issue from the start. The Object Management Group (OMG) solved this problem for the distributed component architecture they developed, CORBA, by developing a language called IDL (Interface Definition Language). IDL provides a language-neutral way of describing the method signatures of methods on a component, including information about what parameters a method accepts, what type of data it returns, and what exceptions it might throw.

WSDL is the IDL of web services. It is how we describe the interfaces our service presents to the world. A WSDL file simply makes a neutral declaration of the existence of one or more web services, and describes the ways a client can interact with those services.

Naturally, it's formatted in XML. A WSDL service definition applies several levels of abstraction around what will ultimately be a simple method call to our service application. This makes the language look extremely complicated, but it's not as frightening as it first appears.

We're going to define the following layers:

- ❑   The **types** of data that the service operates on

- ❑   What **messages** our service understands or can send

- ❑   How these in and out messages combine into **operations**

- ❑   What **protocols** our service will bind to

- ❑   Which operations can be performed via what protocol – WSDL calls this combination a **port**

- ❑   Finally, we can collect together a list of ports which constitute a **service**

A WSDL file can contain multiple service definitions. Although it would probably have been possible to describe these layered definitions in terms of deeply nested XML tags (a service consisting of one or more ports, each consisting of a protocol and a set of operations, each operation containing messages, and so on), WSDL instead takes the route of defining the types first, then defining the messages with references to the types, then defining operations with reference to messages, and so on.

The reasoning behind this is that it allows us to simply reuse a single type definition throughout the document, reuse a single operation across several services, and so on, which a strictly contained hierarchy would prevent us from doing easily.

WSDL Documents

A WSDL document's root element is <definitions>, reflecting the fact that all WSDL does is *define* elements of the service. Along with all the core elements of a WSDL document, the root element belongs to the namespace http://schemas.xmlsoap.org/wsdl/, so it's best to declare this as a default namespace attribute in the <definitions> element.

WSDL makes a slightly unusual use of namespaces (similar to the way schemas use them) as part of its system of internal references. The root element should also declare namespace prefixes for two XML namespaces specific to the WSDL document:

- ❑   One of them is a schema namespace, representing the namespace for the types used by the services the document describes. In our examples (and most of the examples you'll find elsewhere), this namespace is given the prefix xsd1.

- ❑   Another namespace, usually associated with the URL of the WSDL document itself, is called the 'this namespace' namespace, and is used to qualify references to definitions made within the document. By convention, it is assigned the prefix tns.

In addition to this, any binding scheme we choose to use will also make use of its own namespace. In some cases we will also want to declare the namespace for W3C schema definitions – we'll see when this is necessary later on.

As well as the namespace declarations, the root element may optionally contain either, or both, of the following attributes:

❑ A `targetNamespace` attribute, again pointing to the 'this namespace' URI. This tells the WSDL processor which namespace to assign the names for things we define to.

❑ A `name` attribute, containing an optional short name for the service(s) presented in the WSDL document.

The start of a WSDL document that will only use the SOAP binding scheme, will look like the following:

```
<?xml version="1.0"?>
<definitions       name="MyFirstWebService"
        targetNameSpace="http://wrox.com/services/first.wsdl"
            xmlns:tns="http://wrox.com/services/first.wsdl"
            xmlns:xsd1="http://wrox.com/services/first.xsd"
            xmlns:soap="http://schemas.xmlsoap.org/wsdl/soap/"
            xmlns:xsd="http://www.w3.org/1999/XMLSchema"
                xmlns="http://schemas.xmlsoap.org/wsdl/">
```

Optional attributes are shown here in italics, and the bold section marks the binding-scheme-specific line. This line will be replaced, or supplemented by, other namespace declarations according to what protocols we want our service to be available across. The WSDL specification defines two other binding schemes:

Binding Scheme	Namespace URI
HTTP	http://schemas.xmlsoap.org/wsdl/http/
MIME	http://schemas.xmlsoap.org/wsdl/mime/

Notice which namespaces are those linked to the WSDL standard: only the binding namespaces and the default namespace. The others are specific to this service definition, so we are free to make up our own names within these two namespaces. To recap, we will be using these two namespaces as follows:

❑ `tns`: for naming the parts of our service which we define in the WSDL document

❑ `xsd1`: for naming the data types our service can handle

So, the next question is, what can go inside the `<definitions>` element? All the child elements are defined as optional in the schema, but obviously you must define at least one service in order for the file to be of any use. In turn, this places requirements on what else we must declare. But, strictly in terms of the schema, it can contain:

❑ Zero or more `<import>` elements, to import schemas that qualify a previously declared namespace

❑ A single optional `<types>` element, in which we define types for use in our service

❑ Zero or more `<message>` elements; each `<message>` element describes a group of data types that make up a message the service understands or can generate

❑ Zero or more `<portType>` elements, which describe a set of operations (message exchanges) the service can perform

- ❏ Zero or more `<binding>` elements, which describe how operations are mapped onto an underlying protocol

- ❏ Zero or more `<service>` elements, which define the ports making up a service in terms of their `portType` and `bindings`

It's also possible to include an optional `<documentation>` element, which can contain mixed content (HTML, for example) that documents your service.

We'll take a look now at each of these above elements in turn, starting with the `<import>` and `<types>` elements.

In order to follow much of the following sections, you will need to have a familiarity with schemas. You may wish to refer to Chapter 5 for a refresher.

Types

Types are defined using the W3C Schema typing mechanism. Generally, you will define the types for the `xsd1` namespace using one of two techniques: a `<types>` element that contains an embedded schema, or an `<import>` element that references an external schema document. In either case, the schema itself will be identical.

> **Note that the current WSDL tools for Java from IBM are not able to handle complex types, so compatible WSDL definitions will generally not require any type definitions at all: by simply declaring the W3C XML Schema namespace, you can reference simple schema types directly, without having to declare or import them. Future versions of the WSDL processing tools, however, should support complex types, so we shall discuss them here.**

Let's imagine for a moment, that we are developing the second WroxMart web service we talked about earlier – a recipe search engine. Let's say the key component in this service is a method call, which takes a list of ingredients and their quantities as its input, and returns a list of recipes as its output. These are both complex datatypes, but certainly not beyond a simple object model or the XML data model. Let's look at some hypothetical schema definitions for these datatypes.

First of all, we have the usual preamble for the schema, introducing the schema namespace, and naming the `targetNamespace`, to which all the types and elements defined in this schema will belong:

```
<?xml version="1.0"?>
<xsd:schema          xmlns:xsd="http://www.w3.org/1999/XMLSchema"
             xsd:targetNamespace="http://wrox.com/services/recipes">
```

You might notice that the schema namespace we are using is the somewhat outdated `http://www.w3.org/1999/XMLSchema`. This is the schema namespace understood by the IBM WSDL tools, so we will stick with it here.

Then we create the first of our complex types, this one representing a quantity. We'll allow for several different measurements in which ingredients might be available. The `<xsd:choice>` model specifies that one of the contained types is valid as the content for an element of type `QuantityType`:

```
<xsd:complexType name="QuantityType" mixed="false">
  <xsd:choice>
    <xsd:element name="Kilograms" type="xsd:decimal"/>
    <xsd:element name="Liters" type="xsd:decimal"/>
    <xsd:element name="Packets" type="xsd:int"/>
    <xsd:element name="Items" type="xsd:int"/>
  </xsd:choice>
</xsd:complexType>
```

This basically defines quantities as being in Kilograms, Liters, Packets, and Items. Our second complex type associates a quantity (of type `QuantityType`) with one of our ingredient URIs. We'll use this to specify how much of an ingredient we have available, as well as how much of an ingredient is required in a recipe. The `<xsd:all>` content model specifies that both of the contained elements must be found inside an element of this type, but does not require that they appear in a particular sequence:

```
<xsd:complexType name="QualifiedIngredientType">
  <xsd:all>
    <xsd:element name="Ingredient" type="xsd:string"/>
    <xsd:element name="Quantity" type="QuantityType"/>
  </xsd:all>
</xsd:complexType>
```

Now we are ready to specify our first element type, a list of available ingredients. This provides the structure for a message to the web service requesting suitable recipes:

```
<xsd:element name="AvailableIngredientsList">
  <xsd:complexType>
    <xsd:all>
      <xsd:element name="AvailableIngredient"
                   type="QualifiedIngredientType"
                   minOccurs="0"
                   maxOccurs="unbounded"/>
    </xsd:all>
  </xsd:complexType>
</xsd:element>
```

We specify a second element type, representing a recipe returned by the server. A recipe has a title (telling us what the recipe is for), a list of ingredients consisting both food identifiers and quantities, optional elements telling us the preparation and cooking times and how many people we can cater for with these recipe quantities, and finally a set of instructions explaining how the recipe is actually made. We use the `<xsd:sequence>` content model for this type, which requires that the contained elements appear in the order specified:

```
<xsd:element name="Recipe">
  <xsd:complexType>
    <xsd:sequence>
      <xsd:element name="Title" type="xsd:string"/>
```

```
        <xsd:element name="RequiredIngredientsList">
          <xsd:complexType>
            <xsd:all>
              <xsd:element name="RequiredIngredient"
                           type="QualifiedIngredientType"
                           maxOccurs="unbounded"/>
            </xsd:all>
          </xsd:complexType>
        </xsd:element>

        <xsd:element name="PreparationTime"
                     type="xsd:timeDuration"
                     minOccurs="0"/>
        <xsd:element name="CookingTime"
                     type="xsd:timeDuration"
                     minOccurs="0"/>
        <xsd:element name="Serves" type="xsd:int" minOccurs="0"/>

        <xsd:element name="Instructions" type="xsd:string"/>
      </xsd:sequence>
    </xsd:complexType>
  </xsd:element>
```

Finally, we close the schema element:

```
  </xsd:schema>
```

Now, just to help you visualize the types we have defined here, let's take a look at what an XML representation of them might look like. A quick snippet from a sample ingredient list would look like this:

```
<?xml version="1.0"?>
<AvailableIngredientsList
     xmlns:xsi="http://www.w3.org/1999/XMLSchema-instance"
     xsi:noNamespaceSchemaLocation="http://wrox.com/services/recipes.xsd">
  <AvailableIngredient>
    <Ingredient>http://food.wrox.com/chicken/fillet/breast</Ingredient>
    <Quantity>
      <Items>4</Items>
    </Quantity>
  </AvailableIngredient>

  <AvailableIngredient>
    <Ingredient>http://food.wrox.com/lettuce/iceberg</Ingredient>
    <Quantity>
      <Items>1</Items>
    </Quantity>
  </AvailableIngredient>

  <AvailableIngredient>
    <Ingredient>http://food.wrox.com/pepper/chilli/jalapeno</Ingredient>
    <Quantity>
      <Items>4</Items>
    </Quantity>
  </AvailableIngredient>
</AvailableIngredientsList>
```

And a recipe might look like:

```xml
<?xml version="1.0" encoding="UTF-8"?>
<Recipe
        xmlns:xsi="http://www.w3.org/1999/XMLSchema-instance"
        xsi:noNamespaceSchemaLocation="http://wrox.com/services/recipes.xsd">
   <Title>Chicken Grill</Title>
   <RequiredIngredientsList>
     <RequiredIngredient>
       <Ingredient>http://food.wrox.com/chicken/fillet/breast</Ingredient>
       <Quantity>
          <Items>2</Items>
       </Quantity>
     </RequiredIngredient>
   </RequiredIngredientsList>
   <Serves>1</Serves>
   <Instructions>Grill chicken breasts until golden brown</Instructions>
</Recipe>
```

Note that the actual way that the data types are encoded within any interaction with the web service may well differ from these simple forms, but that these describe the data model that will be transmitted. The actual concrete format for the type depends on the way the message is bound to a protocol, which we will come to later on.

Now, how do we build these types into a WSDL document? If you remember, we have two choices: First, we can take the `<xsd:schema>` element and simply embed it in the WSDL document, inside a `<types>` element. We can, as we saw when looking at the `<definitions>` element, put the xsd: namespace declaration into that element rather than the `<xsd:schema>` element itself. This would result in the elements being nested roughly as follows:

```xml
<?xml version="1.0"?>
<definitions xmlns:tns="http://wrox.com/services/recipes.wsdl"
             xmlns:xsd1="http://wrox.com/services/recipes"
             xmlns:soap="http://schemas.xmlsoap.org/wsdl/soap/"
             xmlns:xsd="http://www.w3.org/1999/XMLSchema"
                xmlns="http://schemas.xmlsoap.org/wsdl/">
   <types>
     <xsd:schema xsd:targetNamespace="http://wrox.com/services/recipes">
       ...
     </xsd:schema>
   </types>

</definitions>
```

Notice that the targetNamespace declared in the schema element matches the namespace we declared for xsd1, our local type namespace. This tells the schema processor that the types defined in this schema are part of that namespace, and we can refer to them later on using that namespace prefix.

A word about choosing namespace URI's. In this case, we've chosen to use a URL, a good source of globally unique identifiers, since hopefully only the entity that owns the domain will allocate URI's that use this domain. So, in this case, we use the http URI scheme. It would be good practice, when publishing a service that uses a URI such as this, to make sure there was a viewable resource explaining the purpose of the URI at that location, but there is no reason why we have to – the URI can point to a non-existent resource.

> *The RDDL standard has recently been proposed to provide a standard way of providing resources at URL locations, when the URL is used as a URI. The most common alternative to using the http URI scheme is to use the urn (universal resource name) scheme, in which we simply provide a string after the urn: scheme identifier that we hope will uniquely identify our namespace. For more information on URIs, take a look at the W3C's URI FAQ at http://www.w3.org/2000/06/uriqa3934.html.*

The alternative technique, including the schema by reference, is actually much simpler:

```
<?xml version="1.0"?>
<definitions xmlns:tns="http://wrox.com/services/recipes.wsdl"
             xmlns:xsd1="http://wrox.com/services/recipes"
             xmlns:soap="http://schemas.xmlsoap.org/wsdl/soap/"
             xmlns="http://schemas.xmlsoap.org/wsdl/">

    <import namespace="http://wrox.com/services/recipes"
            location="http://wrox.com/services/recipes.xsd"/>

</definitions>
```

Notice here we don't actually have to declare the xsd namespace at all. Again, we tell the WSDL interpreter to associate the types it imports with the xsd1 namespace by referencing the same URI in our namespace attribute. The location attribute is used to specify the actual location of the file containing the schema.

So, we've now got a collection of types in our xsd1 namespace. The next step in WSDL is to construct the messages that the types will be transmitted in.

Messages

A message is a collection of zero or more parts, each part being a piece of data conforming to a defined type. Messages will form things like the parameters and return values to methods on our web service. <message> elements are placed immediately inside the root <definitions> element, and have a name attribute, which we must provide so we can refer to them later on. This is a name in the tns namespace, so it must be unique across this document. They contain zero or more <part> elements.

> *Not all of the services described by a WSDL document necessarily take the form of a remote procedure call, so our use of the terms 'parameter' and 'return value' might be a little misleading. We'll be implementing services that offer RPC functionality here, but the WSDL generalization of these concepts as 'messages' is important when considering other forms of web service operation.*

<part> elements represent a single parameter, return type, or equivalent. They possess both a name (which must be unique within the enclosing <message> element), and a type, defined by referencing a schema type. There are two attributes that can be used for this purpose: element, used to refer to a schema defined element type, and type, used to refer to a simple or complex type directly. This is probably better demonstrated than explained, so let's look at some possible messages:

```
<message name="ParameterlessMessage"/>
```

An empty message element, like the one above, can be used to invoke a method that takes no parameters, while the following:

```
<message name="IntegerMessage">
  <part name="a" type="xsd:int"/>
</message>
```

consists of a single integer called a. Note the use of the xsd namespace inside the type parameter. If all we need to specify in our messages are simple types such as this, we do not need to declare our own types namespace, and do not need either a <types> or an <import> element to generate complex types. We can add all of the type information to our messages in this way, by referencing the W3C Schema default data types.

Here is a more complex message:

```
<message name="ComplexMessage">
  <part name="recipe" element="xsd1:Recipe"/>
  <part name="recipeid" type="xsd:int"/>
</message>
```

This message, as you can see, consists of two separate parts, one a complex type from our schema definitions, one a simple integer.

Our WSDL document will contain several messages, which typically represent all of the possible ways methods can be invoked upon the service, and all the possible responses. For our recipe service, we might simply add the following two message types:

```
<message name="RecipeRequest">
  <part name="ingredients" element="xsd1:AvailableIngredientsList"/>
</message>

<message name="RecipeResponse">
  <part name="recipe" element="xsd1:Recipe"/>
</message>
```

Operations

Having defined the message types, we need to build them into interactions: the service will respond with message B when sent message A, or whatever. These sets of interactions are referred to by WSDL as **operations**. We define operations within an element called <portType>, which represents a collection of operations that might be available on several ports, but is always available as a set.

WSDL describes four types of operation, as follows:

- **One-way** – The service receives a message
- **Request-response** – The service receives a message, and sends the originator a reply
- **Solicit-response** – The service sends a message, and expects a reply
- **Notification** – The service sends a message

An operation is defined using an `<operation>` element, which has a mandatory `name` attribute. Again, this name will join the `tns` namespace, so must be unique in that context.

The four types are described in an `<operation>` element by the presence and ordering of `<input>` and `<output>` elements. One-way operations only have a single `<input>` element, request-response operations have an `<input>` followed by an `<output>`, and so on. Both `<input>` and `<output>` elements simply have to specify the name of the message as defined earlier as the value for their `message` attribute, qualified by the appropriate namespace prefix. So, the operation we have been building towards with our recipe service would look like this:

```
<portType name="RecipeRequestPort">
  <operation name="RequestPossibleRecipe">
    <input  message="tns:RecipeRequest"/>
    <output message="tns:RecipeResponse"/>
  </operation>
</portType>
```

This is actually now the complete specification of an interface: we know the names of all the possible operations we can perform within this interface, and we also know what messages we are allowed to send, and what we can expect to receive back, when operating through this interface. The rest of the WSDL file is concerned now with describing how to access a specific instance of a service that implements this interface.

This is important because the tools we will be using to build client and server classes around this interface definition use the name we give this interface as their name, and they use the operation names as method names.

Bindings

So, we've declared now that there is a type of port, called a `RecipeRequestPort`, which will return a `RecipeResponse` when sent a `RecipeRequest`. We've also explained exactly what data structures those messages represent. What we haven't done is explained how the request and response will actually be made. To do this, we need to create a **binding**.

A binding specifies the on-the-wire representations that make up each operation on a `portType`. It does not tie the operations to any particular physical address, it simply specifies how you build the messages that make up the operation and what protocol you transmit them on.

You can specify any number of bindings for a given `portType`. Each binding is defined using a `<binding>` element, which has a `name` parameter, specifying a unique name for the binding in the `tns` namespace, and a `type` parameter, which specifies the `portType`'s name. The content of the `<binding>` element is mostly specific to the protocol to which the `portType` is being bound, but the overall structure is as follows.

Any binding for the `portType` we defined above will be structured as follows:

```
<binding type="RecipeRequestPort" name="RecipeRequestBinding">
  < ... binding details ... >
  <operation name="RequestPossibleRecipe">
    < ... binding details ... >
    <input>
```

```
      < ... binding details ... >
   </input>
   <output>
      < ... binding details ... >
   </output>
  </operation>
</binding>
```

First, elements relating to the type of binding to be used are included, which set some overall
parameters for all operations on the `portType`. Then there is an `<operation>` element for each
`<operation>` in the original `<portType>` definition, identified by the name attribute, which should
match the original. This element can also contain binding-specific elements relating to the operation as
a whole, then it contains the same ordering of `<input>` and/or `<output>` elements, which contain
binding-specific elements explaining how the message should be transmitted.

SOAP Binding

The most common binding is probably SOAP over HTTP, certainly for request-response type
operations. The binding is specified using three basic elements, all of which belong to the
`http://schemas.xmlsoap.org/wsdl/soap/` namespace that we mapped to the `soap:`
prefix in the root element:

❑   `<soap:binding>`
    SOAP can be layered over HTTP, SMTP, even FTP, and this element is used to specify the
    underlying transport the SOAP messages will use, and the default style (an RPC call, or a raw
    encoded document) of the SOAP message to be used. It is placed in the `<binding>` element
    before any `<operation>` elements.

❑   `<soap:operation>`
    For a SOAP-over-HTTP binding, this element must be included in each `<operation>`
    element, and specifies the value for the `SOAPAction` header of the HTTP request. This URI
    identifies the name of the SOAP service that will process the request. Apache SOAP's
    `rpcrouter` servlet maps these URI values to classes.

❑   `<soap:body>`
    This element appears inside both the `<input>` and `<output>` elements, where it is used to
    specify exactly how the messages that they represent should be encoded in the body of the
    SOAP message. The details of SOAP encodings are somewhat beyond the scope of this
    chapter, but we'll demonstrate the most common options here.

Let's build a binding for our recipe request:

```
<binding type="RecipeRequestPort" name="SOAPrpcRecipeRequest">
  <soap:binding transport="http://schemas.xmlsoap.org/soap/http"
                style="rpc"/>
  <operation name="RequestPossibleRecipe">
    <soap:operation soapAction=""/>
    <input>
      <soap:body use="literal"/>
    </input>
    <output>
      <soap:body use="literal"/>
    </output>
  </operation>
</binding>
```

First of all, in the empty `<soap:binding>` element, we nominate a transport mechanism, in this case HTTP, using a URI that uniquely identifies the underlying protocol:

```
<binding type="RecipeRequestPort" name="SOAPrpcRecipeRequest">
  <soap:binding transport="http://schemas.xmlsoap.org/soap/http"
                style="rpc"/>
```

By stating that our service supports the `http://schemas.xmlsoap.org/soap/http` transport, we are specifying the exact way that SOAP messages should be embedded into HTTP requests and responses. We also choose one of two possible styles, `rpc` (the other option is `document`).

RPC (remote procedure call) messages consist of sets of parameters, and results, from procedure calls, and are wrapped in SOAP elements that describe them as such. Document-style operations simply transfer each part of the message as a separate SOAP document, within a SOAP envelope. The difference is more semantic than anything else, since the same data is transmitted regardless. So, already we have explained that the service will understand RPC formatted SOAP messages sent over HTTP, according to the `http://schemas.xmlsoap.org/soap/http` transport scheme.

Next, we have to include a `<soap:operation>` element:

```
<operation name="RequestPossibleRecipe">
  <soap:operation soapAction=""/>
```

This is used to specify the value for the `SOAPAction` HTTP header, and is compulsory. The `SOAPAction` header is used to specify a service that should handle the request, together with the service URI and the actual method name. However, the Apache-SOAP implementation ignores the `SOAPAction` header, relying on the service URI and method names to match a request to a particular service. For this reason, for our purposes an empty string will suffice.

Finally, in both the `<input>` and `<output>` elements, we specify how the parts that make up each message should be encoded in the SOAP envelope:

```
<input>
  <soap:body use="literal"/>
</input>
<output>
  <soap:body use="literal"/>
</output>
```

SOAP specifies several encoding schemes that can be used to represent data conforming to abstract types within the SOAP envelope. In this case, however, we have specified (using schema types) the exact elements that each part consists of (an `<AvailableIngredientsList>` element, and a `<Recipe>` element). For this reason, there is nothing to be left to the SOAP processor: we've encoded the data for it. This is why we specify the value `literal` for our `use` attribute. The client should simply place the element specified inside the SOAP envelope as-is.

If we had, when building our messages, created parts that conformed only to abstract schema types, rather than concrete elements, we would have to specify `use="encoded"`, and then specify a SOAP encoding scheme. In this case, we must specify the scheme to be used in an `encodingStyle` attribute, containing a URI identifying the scheme to be used. The standard SOAP encoding scheme is identified by the URI `http://schemas.xmlsoap.org/soap/encoding/`.

We would also have to specify a namespace that the generated elements should belong to (this doesn't have to be the same namespace that the types come from) using a `namespace` attribute. Any client or server involved in this communication would need to know the encoding style and the namespace in order to encode or decode data according to the WSDL specification. Such an element might look like this:

```
<soap:body           use="encoded"
           encodingStyle="http://schemas.xmlsoap.org/soap/encoding/"
               namespace="http://wrox.com/services/recipes"/>
```

Ports

All that remains now is to take this abstract port definition and attach it to a physical address, or port. `<port>` elements are specified inside a `<service>` element within the root. A service may provide any number of ports, conforming to any port type. It may provide the same port type on more than one binding (this represents alternative methods of accessing the same service).

A `<service>` element has a single compulsory attribute: a name, which again must be unique within the `tns` namespace. It contains any number of `<port>` elements, which each have a `name` (unique within the service), and a reference to a `binding` name in the `tns` namespace as attributes. Each port will contain elements from the binding-specific namespace (fore example a `<soap:address>` element) that specify addressing details in the form needed by that particular binding. So, the final definition for our recipe service would look like this:

```
<service name="WroxRecipeService">
  <port name="SOAPRecipePort" binding="tns:SOAPrpcRecipeRequest">
    <soap:address location="http://wrox.com/soap/servlet/rpcrouter"/>
  </port>
</service>
```

The Complete Document

That completes the service definition, which is shown here in its complete form:

```
<?xml version="1.0"?>
<definitions xmlns:tns="http://wrox.com/services/recipes.wsdl"
             xmlns:xsd1="http://wrox.com/services/recipes"
             xmlns:soap="http://schemas.xmlsoap.org/wsdl/soap/"
                xmlns="http://schemas.xmlsoap.org/wsdl/">

  <import namespace="http://wrox.com/services/recipes"
          location="http://wrox.com/services/recipes.xsd"/>


  <message name="RecipeRequest">
    <part name="ingredients" element="xsd1:AvailableIngredientsList"/>
  </message>

  <message name="RecipeResponse">
    <part name="recipe" element="xsd1:Recipe"/>
  </message>
```

```
    <portType name="RecipeRequestPort">
      <operation name="RequestPossibleRecipe">
        <input   message="tns:RecipeRequest"/>
        <output message="tns:RecipeResponse"/>
      </operation>
    </portType>

    <binding type="RecipeRequestPort" name="SOAPrpcRecipeRequest">
      <soap:binding transport="http://schemas.xmlsoap.org/soap/http"
                          style="rpc"/>
      <operation name="RequestPossibleRecipe">
        <soap:operation soapAction=""/>
          <input>
            <soap:body use="literal"/>
          </input>
          <output>
            <soap:body use="literal"/>
          </output>
      </operation>
    </binding>

    <service name="WroxRecipeService">
      <port name="SOAPRecipePort" binding="tns:SOAPrpcRecipeRequest">
        <soap:address location="http://wrox.com/soap/servlet/rpcrouter"/>
      </port>
    </service>

</definitions>
```

As we mentioned earlier, since this service relies on complex types being used within messages, we won't be able to use IBM's tools to process this WSDL file. Let's now go on to look at the other web service for WroxMart and use what we've learned to build a WSDL file that will work, and implement the barcode lookup service.

Developing a Web Service

The barcode lookup service has to provide general food identification information in response to a request containing a barcode identifier. There are two pieces of information of interest: what type of food the barcode relates to, and the quantity. For our purposes (since IBM's tools prevent us from transmitting that as a complex type containing both pieces of information), we will implement these as two separate operations on the service.

We'll model two operations: one that accepts a barcode and returns a UFI (Unique Food Identifier – a URI describing a type of food), and one that accepts a barcode and returns a quantity. We'll send all the pieces of data as strings, for maximum flexibility.

When we've developed the WSDL file, we're going to use IBM's WSDL toolkit to create an actual web service implementation and client. We'll deploy the service on Apache SOAP and Tomcat.

> *Set aside a working directory for the code for this example, such as*
> *C:\projavaxml\Chapter22\wsdl\. We'll use this directory path throughout this section –*
> *if you're using a different one, you should substitute appropriately.*

Defining the Interface

The interface will be defined, naturally, using WSDL. First, let's get the namespace-declaration marathon out of the way:

```xml
<?xml version="1.0" encoding="UTF-8"?>
<definitions targetNamespace="urn:wroxBarCodeLookup"
             xmlns:tns="urn:wroxBarCodeLookup"
             xmlns:soap="http://schemas.xmlsoap.org/wsdl/soap/"
             xmlns:xsd="http://www.w3.org/1999/XMLSchema"
             xmlns="http://schemas.xmlsoap.org/wsdl/">
```

Since we aren't using complex types, we don't need any `<type>` or `<import>` elements.

Now, we need to define messages that represent the arguments and return values for our methods. Both methods take a barcode as their sole argument, so we simply define a message called `BarCodeRequest` that will be used for both of these:

```xml
<message name="BarCodeRequest">
  <part name="code" type="xsd:string"/>
</message>
```

Notice how we specify the type, using a qualified type from the old W3C Schema namespace. The responses from the two methods are conceptually different (even though the types are the same). We model these using two further message types:

```xml
<message name="FoodTypeResponse">
  <part name="foodtype" type="xsd:string"/>
</message>

<message name="QtyResponse">
  <part name="quantity" type="xsd:string"/>
</message>
```

Now we define the interface to our service using a `<portType>` element. This defines the two operations, one to request a food type, and one to request a quantity. Both are request-response operations, so have an `<input>` followed by an `<output>` element:

```xml
<portType name="BarCodeLookupPort">
  <operation name="RequestFoodType">
    <input message="BarCodeRequest"/>
    <output message="FoodTypeResponse"/>
  </operation>

  <operation name="RequestQuantity">
    <input message="BarCodeRequest"/>
    <output message="QtyResponse"/>
  </operation>
</portType>
```

Now we must perform the binding for each operation to the chosen schema. We're using SOAP RPC again here:

```
<binding type="BarCodeLookupPort" name="SOAPrpcBarCodeLookup">
  <soap:binding transport="http://schemas.xmlsoap.org/soap/http"
                  style="rpc"/>
  <operation name="RequestFoodType">
    <soap:operation soapAction=""/>
    <input>
      <soap:body use="encoded"
        encodingStyle="http://schemas.xmlsoap.org/soap/encoding/"
          namespace="urn:wroxBarCodeLookup"/>
    </input>
    <output>
      <soap:body use="encoded"
        encodingStyle="http://schemas.xmlsoap.org/soap/encoding/"
          namespace="urn:wroxBarCodeLookup"/>
    </output>
  </operation>
```

As we defined our message parts in terms of abstract types, this time we have to specify how they will be encoded. We use the default SOAP encoding style. We have to do the same for both operations:

```
  <operation name="RequestQuantity">
    <soap:operation soapAction=""/>
    <input>
      <soap:body       use="encoded"
              encodingStyle="http://schemas.xmlsoap.org/soap/encoding/"
                namespace="urn:wroxBarCodeLookup"/>
    </input>
    <output>
      <soap:body       use="encoded"
              encodingStyle="http://schemas.xmlsoap.org/soap/encoding/"
                namespace="urn:wroxBarCodeLookup"/>
    </output>
  </operation>
</binding>
```

Finally, we can complete the WSDL file with the `<service>` element. You should include the address for a genuine SOAP server in the location attribute: if you are running this example on a single test machine, with Tomcat on the default port, you should use `http://localhost:8080/soap/servlet/rpcrouter`:

```
<service name=" WroxBarcodeService">
  <port name="SOAPBarcodePort" binding="SOAPrpcBarCodeLookup">
    <soap:address location="http://localhost:8080/soap/servlet/rpcrouter"/>
  </port>
</service>
```

And we complete the WSDL file with a closing `<definitions>` element:

```
</definitions>
```

You should save this file in your working directory as `BarcodeService.wsdl`.

Setting Up a Web Services Environment

We're now going to set up our web services system. We'll assume Tomcat 3.2.1 is already installed and working (See Appendix H for details if you don't have Tomcat set up). As well as Tomcat, we'll be using IBM's Web Services Toolkit 2.2. Download `wstk22.zip` from http://www.alphaworks.ibm.com /tech/webservicestoolkit. This includes the following components that we'll be using:

- ❑ Apache SOAP 2.0
- ❑ IBM WSDL Toolkit 1.1

Unzip the `wstk22.zip` file directly into your working directory. It should unpack the contents of the distribution into `C:\projavaxml\Chapter22\wsdl\wstk-2.2`. You should set up an environment variable on your system called `WSTK_HOME` containing the path to this directory (we'll refer to it later as `%WSTK_HOME%`).

Configuring Tomcat

In your Tomcat home directory (the directory called `jakarta-tomcat-3.2.1`), create a directory called `classes\`. Edit your `tomcat.bat` file (in Tomcat's `bin` directory), and add the following:

```
rem ----- Set Up The Runtime Classpath ------------------------------------

:setClasspath
set CP=%WSTK_HOME%\lib\xerces.jar;
set CP=%CP%;%WSTK_HOME%\soap\lib\soap.jar
set CP=%CP%;%WSTK_HOME%\soap\lib\mail.jar
set CP=%CP%;%WSTK_HOME%\soap\lib\activation.jar;
set CP=%CP%;%WSTK_HOME%\lib\jmxc.jar
set CP=%CP%;%WSTK_HOME%\lib\jmxx.jar;
set CP=%CP%;%WSTK_HOME%\lib\jlog.jar
set CP=%CP%;%TOMCAT_HOME%\classes
```

> Note that you will need to do this even if Xerces is in your system classpath. The version that ships with this distribution is required to ensure full compatibility. You may find that **Xerces.jar** is already the first line in the **setClasspath** section as a result of previous chapter, in which case you will need to delete the previous reference and replace it with this one.

Installing SOAP

If you have already installed SOAP onto your system, from Chapter 19, it is probably in your interest to reinstall the one provided with the WSTK, as there are differences between them. To do this, you need to copy the contents of the `%WSTK_HOME%\soap\webapps` directory into your Tomcat's `webapps` directory. You can now start up Tomcat in the usual way (run `startup.bat`). You should find that pointing your browser to http://localhost:8080/soap/ results in you seeing the Apache SOAP welcome screen. To verify that SOAP is working, run the admin client, and click on List. If you do not receive an error, then SOAP is working fine.

Setting Up the Environment

You will need to make use of many classes from various JAR files in the WSTK distribution. For this reason, you may find it useful to write a batch file that sets up your classpath for working with the WSTK. The following setenv.bat should work:

```
@echo off
set CLASSPATH=.;%WSTK_HOME%\lib\bsf.jar;%WSTK_HOME%\lib\xalan.jar
set CLASSPATH=%CLASSPATH%;%WSTK_HOME%\soap\lib\soap.jar
set CLASSPATH=%CLASSPATH%;%WSTK_HOME%\soap\lib\mail.jar
set CLASSPATH=%CLASSPATH%;%WSTK_HOME%\soap\lib\activation.jar
set CLASSPATH=%CLASSPATH%;%WSTK_HOME%\wsdl-toolkit\lib\wsdl.jar
set CLASSPATH=%CLASSPATH%;%WSTK_HOME%\lib\xerces.jar
set CLASSPATH=%CLASSPATH%;%JAVA_HOME%\lib\tools.jar
```

Running this batch file on the command-line before running any WSTK programs, or compiling or running any client-side code we develop, should ensure that all necessary classes are available. Now we're ready to work.

Building the Service

Change to your working directory (C:\projavaxml\Chapter22\wsdl, or wherever you saved the BarCodeService.wsdl file). Now, we are going to invoke the WSDL toolkit's service generator, using the commands:

```
> set
> java com.ibm.wsdl.Main -in BarCodeService.wsdl -target server
```

If the environment is configured correctly, and there are no typos in the WSDL file (mistyped URIs being the main source of errors in this process), you should see the following:

As you can see, this program has generated what it calls a 'skeleton' – a Java source file that contains the bare bones of an implementation of the service. It has, helpfully, compiled this class for us, although since we need to edit the source to add actual functionality to the service, this is maybe not so helpful after all, and we will probably want to delete the .class file that has been created. It has also generated a deployment descriptor for us.

The skeleton class (which has been formatted for readability) looks like this:

```
public class BarCodeLookupPortService {
  public synchronized
  java.lang.String RequestFoodType(java.lang.String code) {
    return null;
  }

  public synchronized
  java.lang.String RequestQuantity(java.lang.String code) {
    return null;
  }
}
```

To be honest, we could probably have coded that ourselves. But using the WSDL toolkit means that we have a class whose methods are guaranteed to match those defined in the WSDL document, and a matching deployment descriptor that can be used to deploy the service to the SOAP server. First off, let's add some functionality to the service:

```
public class BarCodeLookupPortService {

  private java.util.HashMap barcodes;

  public BarCodeLookupPortService() {
    barcodes=new java.util.HashMap(6);
    barcodes.put("47389283",
      new String[]{"http://food.wrox.com/beef/steak/fillet", "2"});
    barcodes.put("38293273",
      new String[]{"http://food.wrox.com/pepper/chilli/jalapeno", "4"});
    barcodes.put("64734738",
      new String[]{"http://food.wrox.com/banana", "5"});
    barcodes.put("09485973",
      new String[]{"http://food.wrox.com/chocolate/plain", "0.2kg"});
    barcodes.put("16374637",
      new String[]{"http://food.wrox.com/wine/chardonnay/oaked", "0.751"});
    barcodes.put("74873648",
      new String[]{"http://food.wrox.com/fish/salmon/steak", "3"});
  }

  public synchronized
  java.lang.String RequestFoodType(java.lang.String code) {
    return (((String[])barcodes.get(code))[0]);
  }

  public synchronized
  java.lang.String RequestQuantity(java.lang.String code) {
    return (((String[])barcodes.get(code))[1]);
  }

}
```

All we do is add a constructor, which initializes a HashMap with a set of barcodes and values. The method bodies are filled in with simple accesses to the hash map (complicated by the need to do some awkward casting, as usual when dealing with Java collections).

Now, we need to save this file, and recompile it. Assuming that you used setenv.bat, just compile using:

```
> javac BarCodeLookupPortService.java
```

Then move the new BarCodeLookupPortService.class file to the classes folder we created in Tomcat's directory. This makes it available to the SOAP servlet, which can now use the class to service requests it receives.

Now all we need to do is tell Apache SOAP that the service exists, and that this class is the one it should use. As we saw, the WSDL toolkit has created a DeploymentDescriptor.xml file for us, containing the following:

```
<isd:service xmlns:isd="http://xml.apache.org/xml-soap/deployment"
                id="urn:wroxBarCodeLookup">
  <isd:provider type="java" scope="Application"
             methods="RequestFoodType RequestQuantity">
    <isd:java class="BarCodeLookupPortService" static="false"/>
  </isd:provider>
</isd:service>
```

This descriptor is in the format Apache SOAP understands, and we can use the SOAP administration client to deploy the service. We do so using this command, which should all be entered on one line:

```
> java org.apache.soap.server.ServiceManagerClient
  http://localhost:8080/soap/servlet/rpcrouter deploy DeploymentDescriptor.xml
```

If all goes well, there is no output at all. The classpath we set earlier should be sufficient for this to work. This tells the SOAP server to associate the URI in the descriptor (urn:wroxBarCodeLookup) with the Java class BarCodeLookupPortService.

Now we need to write a client. Fortunately, the WSDL toolkit also caters for this requirement, and simply using the same tool as before, but without the -target switch, creates a client proxy that contains all of the code needed to access the service:

```
> java com.ibm.wsdl.Main -in BarCodeService.wsdl
```

This will then give the following output:

This time, we don't want to edit the proxy, but a look at the source code will be instructive. The proxy generated looks like this:

```java
import java.net.*;
import java.util.*;
import org.apache.soap.*;
import org.apache.soap.encoding.*;
import org.apache.soap.rpc.*;
import org.apache.soap.util.xml.*;

public class BarCodeLookupPortProxy
{
  private Call call = new Call();
  private URL url = null;
  private String SOAPActionURI = "";
  private SOAPMappingRegistry smr = call.getSOAPMappingRegistry();

  public BarCodeLookupPortProxy() throws MalformedURLException
  {
    call.setTargetObjectURI("urn:wroxBarCodeLookup");
    call.setEncodingStyleURI("http://schemas.xmlsoap.org/soap/encoding/");
    this.url = new URL("http://localhost:8080/soap/servlet/rpcrouter");
    this.SOAPActionURI = "";
  }

  public synchronized void setEndPoint(URL url)
  {
    this.url = url;
  }

  public synchronized URL getEndPoint()
  {
    return url;
  }
```

The first thing to note about the class is that its constructor can throw a MalformedURLException, which we need to be aware of when instantiating the proxy. The code generator has also added two methods that allow us to set or retrieve the URL at which the proxy is pointing (although it has picked out the URL we specified in the WSDL script as its initial setting). The next part of the class is the meat of the proxy implementation:

```java
  public synchronized
  java.lang.String RequestFoodType(java.lang.String code)
      throws SOAPException {

    if (url == null) {
      throw new SOAPException(Constants.FAULT_CODE_CLIENT,
      "A URL must be specified via " +
      "BarCodeLookupPortProxy.setEndPoint(URL).");
    }
```

```
        call.setMethodName("RequestFoodType");
        Vector params = new Vector();
        Parameter codeParam = new Parameter("code",
                                            java.lang.String.class,
                                            code,
                                            null);
        params.addElement(codeParam);
        call.setParams(params);
        Response resp = call.invoke(url, SOAPActionURI);

        // Check the response.
        if (resp.generatedFault()) {
          Fault fault = resp.getFault();

          throw new SOAPException(fault.getFaultCode(), fault.getFaultString());

        } else {
          Parameter retValue = resp.getReturnValue();
          return (java.lang.String)retValue.getValue();
        }
      }
    }
  }
```

We've omitted the second method definition since it is almost identical to the first. As you can see, the code generator has done all the hard work for us, creating a SOAP `Call` object, populating its fields and then sending it. It's all been wrapped up inside a simple method called `RequestFoodType()` that takes a string containing a barcode as an argument, and returns a string containing the UFI.

Notice that the method can throw a `SOAPException` if something goes wrong, so we'll need to be prepared to catch one of those.

Let's quickly code up a client that can make use of this proxy:

```
public class BarCodeClient {

  public static void main(String[] args) {

    try {

      BarCodeLookupPortProxy blpp = new BarCodeLookupPortProxy();
      System.out.println("Food type: " + blpp.RequestFoodType(args[0]));
      System.out.println("Quantity:  " + blpp.RequestQuantity(args[0]));

    } catch (Exception e) {
      e.printStackTrace();
    }
  }
}
```

This client, when run from the command line, will simply take the first argument from the `args` list and submit it as a parameter to each of the methods the proxy makes available, printing the result.

Try running the client using the numbers we specified as barcodes in the server's hashtable definition, and you should see results like the following:

```
Command Prompt                                                              _ □ X
C:\ProJavaXML\Chapter22\wsdl>java BarCodeClient 16374637
Food type: http://food.wrox.com/wine/chardonnay/oaked
Quantity:  0.751

C:\ProJavaXML\Chapter22\wsdl>java BarCodeClient 38293273
Food type: http://food.wrox.com/pepper/chilli/jalapeno
Quantity:  4

C:\ProJavaXML\Chapter22\wsdl>
```

We've now got a working web service client and server.

Going the Other Way

As we've seen, we can generate web service skeletons, and client proxies, from WSDL documents, using the IBM WSDL toolkit. But the WSTK includes some other tools that allow us to create a service from java files that we've already coded, saving us from having to try to write WSDL to describe the interface. The **Web Service Creation Wizard** is a GUI tool, which builds WSDL files based on Java classes and EJBs. To start the Service Wizard, run the serviceWizard.bat file in the %WSTK_HOME%\bin directory for the WSTK toolkit.

Firstly, you're asked if you want to build your service from a class or an EJB. For now, select Class, and click Next. You're presented with the following screen:

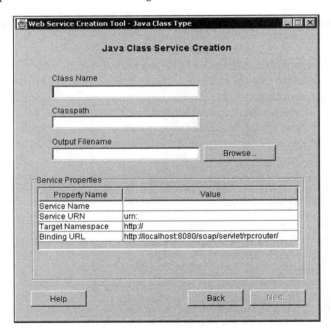

Fill in the name of our service class (BarCodeLookupPortService), and give the path to the directory that contains it. The wizard fills in the rest of the details:

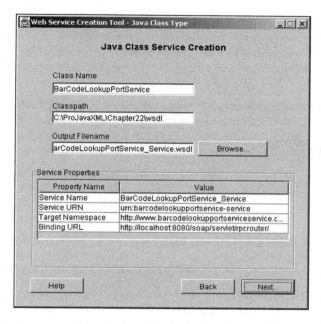

Click Next. The following screen lists all of the methods the class has (including those it inherits). You need to choose the two methods that make up our service – in this case RequestFoodType and RequestQuantity:

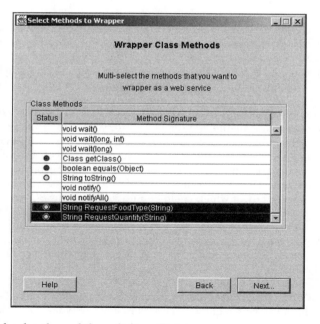

Click Next..., check the details, and then click on Finish.

The wizard will do a little working, and after a moment will output three files to the wizard's working directory (`%WSTK_HOME%\bin`). Beside the deployment descriptor, one of these files is called `BarCodeLookupPortService_Service-interface.wsdl`, and the other is `BarCodeLookupPortService_Service-impl.wsdl`. The interface file does most of the work defining the messages, `portType` and binding. The `impl` file imports the interface file's `tns` namespace into its own, and then simply defines the service element. This separation allows the impl file to be changed to reflect changes in server configuration (implementation issues), while the interface file remains unchanged unless the service's interface changes.

If you take a look at the definitions in the interface file, however, you should see the similarities in structure and definition to the WSDL file we used originally to generate the service in the first place.

This is a powerful little tool. By allowing us to take existing business logic components, whether they're simple classes or Enterprise JavaBeans, and automatically expose an interface to them as a web service, this enables us to create powerful web services, integrated directly into our business systems, almost immediately, and without having to write any additional code at all.

The Web Service Lifecycle

Web service classes, as we've seen, are basically a very simple implementation of the interface declared in the WSDL document. RPC messages are mapped into method parameters and return values, and operations are mapped into method names. The class inherits no functionality from a superclass. We haven't had to write `init()` or `destroy()` methods. In our barcode service, we wrote a constructor that created several entries in a hash table, but when is this constructor called? Every time our service is accessed? How is the web service's lifecycle managed on the server? When is the class instantiated? How many instances are created? How can we write a web service that manages resources, such as database connections, when we don't know when the service is created or destroyed?

The key is in an attribute of the deployment descriptor's `<provider>` element, called `scope`. All of the services we have looked at so far have a scope value of `Application`. The other two possible scope values are `Session` and `Request`. If you have any experience with JavaServer Pages, these might sound familiar (and you might be wondering if there's such a thing a `Page` scope web service: there isn't), but applying the concepts to the way our web services function is a little tricky.

The important thing to realize is that our web services are managed ultimately by a servlet – the `RPCRouterServlet` class that is mapped to the `soap/servlet/rpcrouter` URL we've been using. `RPCRouterServlet` actually handles all of the lifecycle issues of our web services. Of course, servlets have their own lifecycle – `init()`, `service()`, and `destroy()` – which is managed by the servlet container. Servlet containers are allowed to instantiate multiple objects belonging to the same servlet class, and can hand any request for that servlet to any of those instances. So, there could be several `RPCRouterServlet` objects, any of which could end up handling our SOAP requests.

So, the RPC router servlet never assumes that the instance handling a request for one web service is the only servlet that will ever handle requests for that service. It therefore stores instances of web service classes (such as our `BarCodeLookupPortService`) in one of three places, depending on which of the three scope values we mentioned before: `Application`, `Session`, or `Request`, is specified in that service's deployment descriptor. Instances of application-scope web services are stored in the servlet's web-application context (as a `ServletContext` attribute). Instances with session-scope are stored in the servlet's `HTTPSession` object. Instances with request scope are instantiated by the servlet while it handles the request, and only stored in local variables, so disappear when the servlet has finished handling the request.

If you aren't familiar with servlet contexts and sessions, you can think of them as two hash tables maintained by the servlet container. There is one context hash table for each web application in the container, so the RPCRouterServlet has access to the SOAP web application context. This context exists for as long as the servlet engine exists, and an object registered with the web application context will be available in the context of any call made to any servlet.

There is one session hashtable for each active HTTP session within a web application. A session is defined by a session key, which is used to identify multiple requests from the same client. The normal mechanism for this is to use a session cookie: the server tells the client to set a cookie with a particular name, containing that session key. As with all cookies, the client sends this key back to the server each time it makes another request. By associating this session key with a hashtable, the servlet engine makes it possible for servlets to have access to a separate object store for each of their clients. Instances of objects stored in a session are available to any servlet within the web application that is accessed by a client giving the same session key: the client has its own private instance on the server.

Unfortunately, sessions require some support from the client: the Set-Cookie header from the server needs to be understood, and the client needs to store cookies for all the servers it accesses. It then needs to set a Cookie header on subsequent HTTP requests to the server. In the Apache SOAP implementation, all of this would be the responsibility of the Call object – unfortunately, the implementation of Call doesn't understand cookies, so we don't have a client that works with session-scoped services.

Demonstrating Scope

We can see how scope actually affects our application by including these debugging lines in our web service class. These lines will allow us to see exactly when the service does what – when the constructor is activated, and when each method is called:

```
public class BarCodeLookupPortService {

  private java.util.HashMap barcodes;

  public BarCodeLookupPortService() {
    System.out.println("LookupPortservice instantiated");
    barcodes=new java.util.HashMap(6);
    barcodes.put("47389283",
      new String[]{"http://food.wrox.com/beef/steak/fillet", "2"});
    barcodes.put("38293273",
      new String[]{"http://food.wrox.com/pepper/chilli/jalapeno", "4"});
    barcodes.put("64734738",
      new String[]{"http://food.wrox.com/banana", "5"});
    barcodes.put("09485973",
      new String[]{"http://food.wrox.com/chocolate/plain", "0.2kg"});
    barcodes.put("16374637",
      new String[]{"http://food.wrox.com/wine/chardonnay/oaked", "0.75l"});
    barcodes.put("74873648",
      new String[]{"http://food.wrox.com/fish/salmon/steak", "3"});
  }

  public synchronized
  java.lang.String RequestFoodType(java.lang.String code) {
    System.out.println("LookupPortservice handling request for food type");
    return (((String[])barcodes.get(code))[0]);
  }
}
```

```
    public synchronized
    java.lang.String RequestQuantity(java.lang.String code) {
        System.out.println("LookupPortservice handling request for quantity");
        return (((String[])barcodes.get(code))[1]);
    }

}
```

Now, compile this class, and put the .class file in Tomcat's classes directory. Stop Tomcat and start it again (this will flush out any instances from the application context).

Now run the client again with the following line:

> **java BarCodeClient 16374637**

You should see the following output appear on Tomcat's console window:

```
LookupPortservice instantiated
LookupPortservice handling request for food type
LookupPortservice handling request for quantity
```

When our client calls the first method on the proxy class, the proxy sends a request to the server for the urn:WroxBarcodeService web service. The RPC router servlet identifies the service associated with this URI, by looking through the deployment descriptors that have been registered with it. It checks the deployment descriptor's scope setting (which in this case was Application), looks in the appropriate place (in this case, the application context) to see if there is an instance of the appropriate class there. It doesn't find one, so it creates one: we see the line appear to say the service has been instantiated.

Now the RPC router can call the method on the instantiated object, and we see the message appear saying the method has been called.

The second request is handled in exactly the same way: the RPC router looks in the context for an instance of the class, and this time finds one, so it uses it. No object is instantiated.

If you run the client again, you'll see the following:

```
LookupPortservice handling request for food type
LookupPortservice handling request for quantity
```

The constructor isn't called since the servlet is using the instance it created the last time the service was activated.

Request Scope

Now, edit the deployment descriptor file as follows:

```
<isd:service xmlns:isd="http://xml.apache.org/xml-soap/deployment"
                id="urn:wroxBarCodeLookup">
    <isd:provider type="java" scope="Request"
            methods="RequestFoodType RequestQuantity">
        <isd:java class="BarCodeLookupPortService" static="false"/>
    </isd:provider>
</isd:service>
```

All we've done is change the scope to Request. Now, we need to run the deployment utility again with the same command:

```
> java org.apache.soap.server.ServiceManagerClient
http://localhost:8080/soap/servlet/rpcrouter deploy DeploymentDescriptor.xml
```

We don't need to change the class file, or the client at all. This change will simply alter the way the RPC router manages the lifecycle of the service. This time when you run the client (having restarted Tomcat), you will see the following on Tomcat's console:

```
LookupPortservice instantiated
LookupPortservice handling request for food type
LookupPortservice instantiated
LookupPortservice handling request for quantity
```

Before each method call is handled, the servlet creates a new instance of the service. It does not check the servlet context to see if there is already an instance available – it's still there, in the application context, but that instance is not used – it uses a separate instance for every request.

Session Scope

It is possible to extend the SOAP Call class and implement cookie functionality (the details of such an implementation are beyond the scope of this chapter), enabling you to make use of session scope services.

If the Call object remembers any cookies it is asked to set using instance variables, then it will be able to participate in the same session for as long as the object exists – for as long as the client proxy holds onto its instance of the Call object. Since the proxy creates a single Call object in its constructor and then uses that to generate all the requests it needs to make, there will be one session for each proxy instance. If we were to deploy our service with session scope, and then run the client a couple of times, we'd see this output on the Tomcat console:

```
LookupPortservice instantiated
LookupPortservice handling request for food type
LookupPortservice handling request for quantity
LookupPortservice instantiated
LookupPortservice handling request for food type
LookupPortservice handling request for quantity
```

Each time the client is run, when it makes its first request it is not part of a session. The servlet container generates a new Session object and session key to associate with this new client. When the RPC router servlet looks up the service URI and discovers it is a session-scoped service, it looks in the Session object to see if there is an instance already. Since the Session object is new, there isn't one, so it creates an instance (we see the constructor report that it was called), and then calls the method on it.

When it sends the response back, there is a Set-cookie header attached to the HTTP message, giving the session key. Our modified Call object remembers this session ID. When the proxy invokes the second method, it uses the same Call object. This time, the Call object notices that it has a cookie for the host of this service, and includes the session key in a Cookie header on the HTTP request.

When this arrives on the server, the servlet container recognizes the session key in the HTTP header, and retrieves the same Session object. When the RPC router servlet identifies that the service requested is session scoped, it looks in the Session object for an instance, and this time finds one. So no constructor is called, and we see it call the method immediately.

However, when the client program exits, the proxy object disappears, and with it the instance of the `Call` object which knows the session key. So, when the client is run again, the process begins again from the beginning, with a new session key, and a new `Session` object on the server.

Incidentally, if you deploy a service with `Session` scope and access it with a client which doesn't support any form of client-side state, such as the `Call` object from the SOAP distribution, then its behavior will be identical to that if it had been deployed with `Request` scope: the servlet container treats each request as the first in a new session, since it has no way to associate the requests.

So, now that we've established how the web service's lifecycle is managed, we can draw a sequence diagram to illustrate what happens when we run `BarCodeClient`, with the service deployed to application scope:

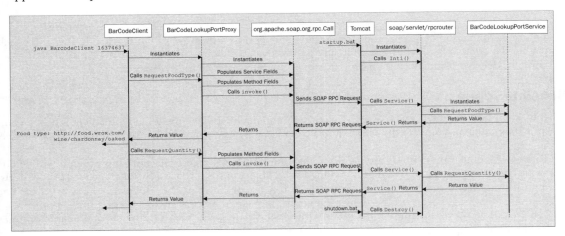

The three objects shown on the left are the client-side of the operation, and the three on the right are the server-side.

We start off by starting up Tomcat, which we then show instantiating and initializing the RPC router. This can happen at startup, or when the servlet is first accessed. Whatever, we're showing it as happening before we run our client.

We then execute the client. We can see it creates a proxy instance, which instantiates a SOAP `Call` object. It sets the parameters on the call that will be common to all requests (the server and target service URI). Then the client is able to call the first of the proxy's methods, at which point it will begin the process of making a SOAP call. It sets the request-specific parameters on the `Call` object: the method name and method parameters, and then invokes the call.

The `Call` object marshals the request data into an XML-formatted SOAP envelope (using various helper methods included in the client-side Apache-SOAP implementation), and sends it as the body of an HTTP POST request to the server port, addressed to the RPC router servlet.

Tomcat receives the request, identifies the target servlet, unpacks the HTTP request data and forwards it as a `ServletRequest` to the servlet's `service()` method. As usual for HTTP servlets, this is intercepted by the implementation in `HttpServlet`, and forwarded to the RPC servlet's `doPost()` method as an `HttpServletRequest`.

The servlet examines the SOAP envelope to determine the target service URI. It matches this to a deployment descriptor, and works out whether the service is request, session or application scope. Finding that it's application scope, it looks in the context for an instance, fails to find one, and so instantiates our service object. It is then able to call the method on it. It wraps up the response in a SOAP envelope and sends it back to our client as the body of the HTTP response.

The `Call` object unwraps the response envelope, and makes it available to the proxy, which pulls out the message, and returns it as the return-value from the method call our client made. The client then prints this value, and starts the process off again with a second method call.

Scaling Web Services

So, the two options we have in deploying a web service (assuming session scope is, for the moment, not possible) either give us a single instance of our web service class across all invocations by all users, or a new instance created on each invocation. Neither of these options sounds particularly scalable. If multiple clients access the RPC router servlet at the same time, requesting our service, then Tomcat will place each of those requests onto its own service thread. How do these different scopes affect the way our service has to handle threads? Let's look at each of them separately.

Request Scope

In a request-scoped service, a new instance of the class is created within each service thread, and then once the constructor has returned, the same thread is used to access the required method. The object reference is thrown away when the servlet has finished with it, so the object will be thrown on the garbage-collection pile. Obviously, if your service also creates a lot of other objects in the course of its brief life, all of those instances will be thrown away as well.

So, request scope is not suited to situations where a lot of expensive resources are needed – resources that take up a lot of memory, or take a while to create. Having said that, it is possible to access shared resources from a request-scoped service object, by employing, for example, the Singleton design pattern. By coding a 'singleton' resource manager, we can obtain a reference to the singleton within each of our request instances, and use that to access database connection pools, or EJBs. The singleton will have to be careful about how it copes with multiple threads accessing it simultaneously.

Application Scope

In an application-scope service, a single instance is created. Several service threads might reach our service simultaneously, and execute the service method within this single service instance at the same time. We need to be aware of this, since it means we can't rely on, for example, an instance variable for storing any sort of state information, or on storing any request-specific resources at all in instance variables.

One thread might store a value temporarily with a view to reading it back later on, and another thread in the meantime can come along and change the value stored. For this reason, we need to be careful how we manage synchronization to ensure our services are thread-safe. The service-class skeletons generated by the WSTK declare all of their methods as `synchronized`, meaning that only one client thread can execute in that method at a time. (However, different threads can access different methods within the class.)

To develop larger scale web applications, we don't want to do too much processing within a method that operates under these circumstances. If there is a single instance of our class across the entire web application, and its methods are all `synchronized`, then all requests for a particular method will be processed linearly. If the service is requesting a lot of external resources, such as database connections, or EJBs, then this system is going to grind to a halt very quickly indeed.

The solution is to remove method-scope synchronization, allowing multiple concurrent request threads to operate inside the single instance at the same time. Instead, we need to make use of method-scoped variables to store temporary state. However, if we do all the work for the service within the method, we might as well deploy our service with request scope. Again we can employ resource managers that are generated in our service's constructor, and accessed by service threads as they pass through the request methods.

Scalability Conclusions

Essentially, if we're prepared to get our head around the multi-threading issues, application-scoped services actually make it possible for us to build more scalable applications. We can build applications that share resources much more easily, and we can also have less objects being created and destroyed in the course of handling each request. Of course, this still leaves us having to code our own thread-safe resource manager. Or does it?

This is where EJBs come in. An EJB home interface is almost exactly the resource manager we need. We can use it to obtain remote interfaces to EJBs for use in our application, and then farm out our heavy-duty business logic to them. Their container-managed pooling and resource sharing will enable our web services to handle many more simultaneous connections. So, by obtaining the home interface for a bean in our web service's constructor, all the service threads can use it to obtain the remote interface to a bean.

Session-scope services promise to provide some additional scalability benefits. Resources related to a specific client can be stored in the service's instance variables, and most of the service's activity can quite happily be `synchronized`, since the client will most often not make multiple simultaneous requests.

Locating Web Services

We've now talked a great deal about how we write web services, how we describe them, and how we deploy them. We've not talked at all about how we find them. Web services represent a World Wide Web for computers – a system of web sites whose content is consumed by applications, not people. SOAP represents the computer equivalent of a web surfer filling out a form on a web page and clicking Submit. Web services provide the same sort of functionality as humans find in interactive web sites, but in a machine-readable form.

The way applications will surf the web of web services is very similar to the way people use the human-readable web. There are two main ways people locate a web site offering a service they're interested in. Either they type the address right into a browser's address bar, because they already know that a particular site offers the service they want, or they go to a search engine, and run a query. Web services are exactly the same.

Up until now, however, we've simply written programs that behave in the first way: they go where they're told and access the service there. Probably the most useful web service for humans is the Internet search engine, so one of the first defined web services to be developed for computers is **Universal Description, Discovery, and Integration (UDDI)**, a search engine for web services.

Most search engines have a pretty simple interface that looks something like this:

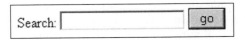

So, when confronted with a search engine homepage, people normally find it easy to work out what to do. Computers, who aren't as good at interpreting things that just look fairly similar (they won't necessarily be able to identify the purpose of a particular text box, because they can't associate it with the surrounding visual clues: they only have clues embedded in HTML, which is not designed to help them), need to have a well-defined interface they can work to. UDDI is basically a description of such an interface for a computer to use. Although it hasn't actually been codified as a WSDL document, UDDI is specified as a SOAP-activated web service. The idea is that there should be a number of sites offering the UDDI service, so that UDDI-aware programs can use them to locate and access web services.

Luckily, we don't need a WSDL document to generate a UDDI proxy, because IBM's UDDI4J extension to the WSTK includes one already (it has to handle some quite complex datatypes, so the current WSDL Toolkit wouldn't be able to generate a proxy anyway).

So how do the programs find these UDDI services in the first place? Unfortunately, there's no broadcast discovery system (such as that employed by Jini), so programs will have to know where to go. This again follows the same model as the part of the Web that is for human consumption – everybody who uses the Web on a regular basis has a favorite search engine. Most of us tend to have a shortcut to it on our desktop, or in our browser's bookmarks. Similarly, the intention is that a few simple configuration parameters (the URL for a UDDI service) should be all that's needed, and UDDI clients will be able to use that as their 'favorite' search engine. Knowing this one address should enable the program to find everything else it might need.

UDDI

UDDI is being developed as an open standard, hosted at http://www.uddi.org/, by IBM, Microsoft, and Ariba (the same combination as the WSDL specification). The following web sites host these companies' UDDI operations:

❑   http://uddi.microsoft.com/

❑   http://www.ibm.com/services/uddi/

❑   http://uddi.ariba.com/

In addition to offering the option to search UDDI registries hosted at these locations, you'll find links to resources and tutorials on all of these sites.

We'll be using the IBM UDDI4J client API, which is included in the WSTK we've already been using, but we'll also need to set up a local UDDI registry. The extension to the WSTK required to do this can be downloaded from the IBM WSTK page at http://www.alphaworks.ibm.com/tech/webservicetoolkit, and is called `wstkuddi22.zip`. In addition, the registry requires an IBM DB2 database to operate.

You can download a free personal edition of DB2 from IBM – installation details are included in the WSTK documentation, at %WSTK_HOME%\doc\Install.htm#LocalUDDI. This will set up a servlet on your Tomcat installation, which will handle UDDI queries.

The UDDI Data Model

UDDI defines services in terms of a service provider, which it describes as a **business entity**.

> **A business entity describes a provider of services, in terms of the name of the company, various unique identifiers, and more general categorizations of what kinds of service the company offers.**

Unique identifiers are designed to allow a business partner to locate a specific company about which they know quite a lot of real-world information, but for which they have no web service information. General categories are designed to allow a search to be narrowed down to companies within a particular industry, or geographical region: essentially, to allow white-pages searches to be made on the services registered in a UDDI server.

Business entities offer what UDDI calls **business services**. A business service is a collection of physical web services, grouped together to provide a logical service grouping, such as 'purchasing', or 'information services'. An entity can offer any number of services.

The actual web services are located and described by **binding templates**. A binding template describes where the web service is located, and provides information on how to access it. A binding template includes information such as the protocol on which the service can be accessed, and allows us to access WSDL or equivalent definitions for how we should interact with the service.

Descriptive information about all of these data types (the three key types in UDDI), such as what type of business a company is, or what type of service it offers, or what interface should be used to activate a service, is stored in metadata objects which UDDI calls a **TModel**.

UDDI offers two kinds of search operations: one, which is a general search for a type or class of entity, service, or template, that is a 'find-type' search, and another, which retrieves complete detailed information on a specific entity, service, or template, that is a 'get-type' search. The UDDI documentation refers to get searches as drill-down searches.

To get some idea of what the difference is between a business service and a binding template, let's take a look at IBM's public UDDI registry on http://www.ibm.com/services/uddi/find.htm. By opting to find a business, we can enter a search term to locate businesses in the registry by name. This, for example, is the services entry for IBM itself (you'll have to run a search to find a Business Name of IBM to get to this page):

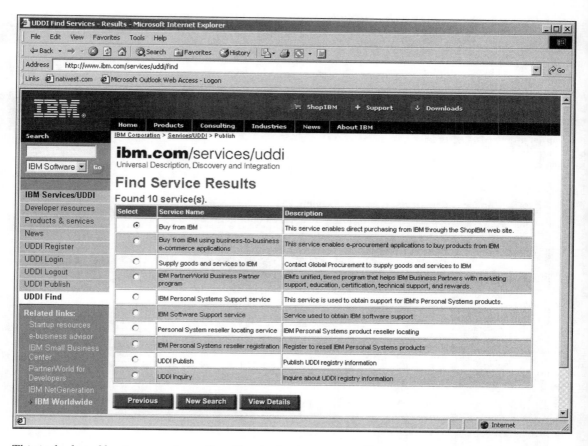

This is the list of business services offered by the business entity, IBM. If we select one of these services and select View Details, we can see the binding templates:

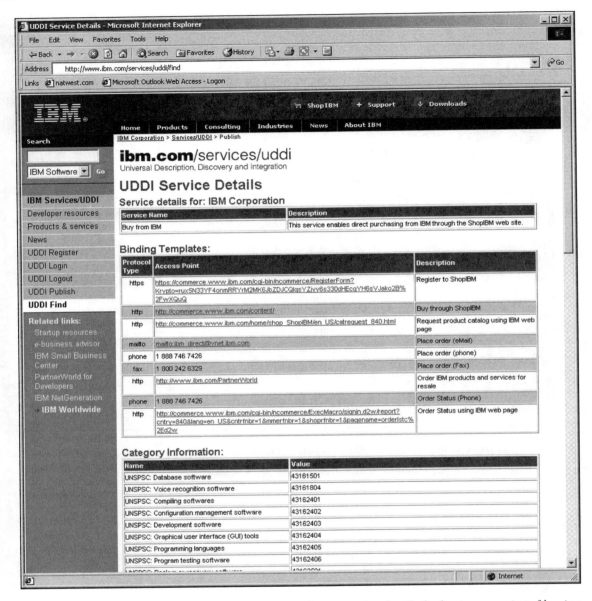

As you can see, there are nine different binding templates associated with the business service of buying from IBM. As well as services related directly to ordering goods or services, we can see order tracking services, catalog request services, and registration services.

These services, you may notice, aren't really machine-usable. UDDI can be used to provide lookup services such as this for human-readable resources as well.

At the bottom of the screen, we can see the start of a set of metadata, describing what types of services IBM offers via its purchasing interfaces. **UNSPSC** stands for Universal Standard Products and Services Classification, a United Nations standards effort, which provides a numerical index value for just about everything it is possible to sell, literally from abaca fibers (11121807) to zoonotic disease prevention and control services (85111509), via aircraft carriers (25111702), frozen crustaceans (50191607) and population census services (93141601). There are well over 10000 UNSPSC numbers in all.

UNSPSC is one classification system used by UDDI registries to represent service types – the other is NAICS (North American Industry Classification System), which is generally more concerned with the types of companies than the types of products. It runs to about 1800 classifications, across the slightly more prosaic range from abrasive product manufacturing (32791) to zoos and botanical gardens (71213).

This should give us some idea of the sorts of searches it will be possible to conduct on a UDDI registry, and what sort of data we will need to provide when we register a service. So, without further ado, let's go ahead and set up a UDDI registry, and register WroxMart with it.

The WSTK UDDI Registry

The WSTK UDDI registry comes in the `wstkuddi22.zip` file, and is one of the optional packages, which you can download from the WSTK download page. You need to unzip it in exactly the same directory you unzipped WSTK into, since it installs files into the same directory hierarchy. If you get it right, there'll be a `uddi` directory inside your `wstk-2.2` folder, containing a `scripts` directory and a `webapp` directory.

Now, before we can install the UDDI service, we need to set up DB/2. You can download the personal edition from http://www-4.ibm.com/software/data/db2/udb/downloads.html. You need to follow the DB/2 installation instructions to the letter, as included in the WSTK installation documentation, and the Readme files that come with the DB/2 download. Pay particular attention to the requirement that you set up a user account on your system called `wstkAdmin` with the password `wstkAdmin` before you start, and make sure you read the DB/2 instructions regarding the necessary user privileges required to install DB/2 successfully.

> *You don't actually need to know anything about DB/2's administration to run these examples, but it will be worthwhile familiarizing yourself with the basic tools.*

Once DB/2 is installed, you can set up the UDDI servlet and database. You need to run a DB/2 Command Window (a special DB/2 command prompt – you'll find it available in your **Start** menu on Windows), navigate to your WSTK installation and run the `loadDatabase` script from the WSTK's `uddi\scripts` directory. This will generate all the necessary tables, and populate them with data where appropriate.

From an ordinary (DOS or UNIX shell) command prompt, you should run the `serverConfigure` script from the `%WSTK_HOME%\bin` directory. Tell it the location of your Tomcat distribution, and your Tomcat's `server.xml` will be edited as necessary to access the UDDI servlet.

You also need to edit `wstk.properties` in `%WSTK_HOME%\lib`, to tell the WSTK tools to use your newly configured local UDDI registry. Change the server hostname to read as shown here:

```
server.hostname=localhost
server.port=8080
```

In the section listing UDDI registry names, uncomment only the `uddi.registry.name` which says `demohost8080`, as follows:

```
#Only one of the following lines should be uncommented to select which UDDI
repository you want the demos to access.
# Default UDDI registry name
#uddi.registry.name=ibmtest
#uddi.registry.name=ibmpublic
uddi.registry.name=demohost8080
#uddi.registry.name=localhost80
#uddi.registry.name=mstest
#uddi.registry.name=mspublic
```

You then need to change the reference to `demohost:8080` to a URL for `localhost:8080`, as follows:

```
# WSTK Local UDDI Registry - demohost:8080
uddi.inquiry.demohost8080=http://localhost:8080/uddi/servlet/uddi
uddi.publish.demohost8080=http://localhost:8080/uddi/servlet/uddi
uddi.userid.demohost8080=wstkDemo
uddi.cred.demohost8080=wstkPwd
```

The rest of the file can remain as it is.

That should complete setting up the UDDI registry. To run Tomcat, ensuring all necessary files are on the classpath, you need to check that TOMCAT_HOME and WSTK_HOME point to the correct directories, and then use the following commands:

```
> <WSTK_HOME>\bin\wstkenv -env -tomcat
> <TOMCAT_HOME>\bin\startup
```

Writing a UDDI Client

The UDDI4J distribution contains one key class for writing UDDI clients: `com.ibm.uddi.client.UDDIProxy`. Once it has been set up with the correct endpoints to access a UDDI registry's inquiry and publish interfaces, the `UDDIProxy` simply presents all of the methods a UDDI registry has, and allows us to call them locally. Behind the scenes, just like our WSDL proxy classes before, it translates the calls into SOAP requests for services on the UDDI server.

The proxy's methods fall into five main groups:

❑ Methods concerned with connecting to the server – setting the UDDI registry's URLs, or obtaining authentication

❑ Methods concerned with finding objects in the registry that take a general set of criteria, and which return a list of identifiers of matching objects

❑ Methods concerned with getting objects from the registry, which take a specific identifier and return an individual object

❑ Methods concerned with saving objects into the registry, either to create new entries or update existing ones

❑ Methods concerned with deleting objects from the registry

We'll consider first the methods in the first category, connection methods, and then we'll look at the UDDI operations we can perform using the other four sets of methods.

Connecting to the UDDI Server

The first category really only contains three methods we'll be using:

- ❑   setInquiryURL(String url)
- ❑   setPublishURL(String url)
- ❑   com.ibm.uddi.response.AuthToken getAuthToken(String username, String password)

The inquiry URL is the URL of the service that handles find and get requests. The publish URL handles save and delete operations – operations which, naturally, require some sort of authentication. When using a public UDDI repository, this will normally be an https URL. Using our private UDDI registry, both URLs will be http://localhost:8080/uddi/servlet/uddi. Both of the URL setter methods can throw a java.net.MalformedURLException, so we'll need to catch and handle this.

An AuthToken is simply a class wrapping a UID that is returned by the registry when we send valid authentication criteria, which we can then extract and send along with requests to save or delete data in the registry, to avoid us having to send our user ID and password every time. Our server has been set up with the default user account, username wstkAdmin, password wstkAdmin.

So, in order to make use of a UDDIProxy, all our code will begin like this:

```
UDDIProxy proxy = new UDDIProxy();
try {
  proxy.setInquiryURL("http://localhost:8080/uddi/servlet/uddi");
  proxy.setPublishURL("http://localhost:8080/uddi/servlet/uddi");
} catch (java.net.MalformedURLException e) {
  e.printStackTrace();
}
```

All subsequent UDDI operations can throw a com.ibm.uddi.UDDIException, and some can throw an org.apache.soap.SOAPException if something goes wrong with the SOAP transport layer (such as an unsupported encoding being used by the client or server, such that they can't actually communicate), so we should wrap all operations in a try...catch block. UDDIExceptions contain a lot of details, and a wrapped com.ibm.uddi.response.DispositionReport, which we can retrieve to find out details of the UDDI failure. So, a typical UDDI client will wrap its UDDI operations with a block looking something like this:

```
try {

  // UDDI operations here

} catch (UDDIException e) {

  DispositionReport dr = e.getDispositionReport();
  System.out.println("UDDI: [" + e.getFaultCode() + "] "
                                + e.getMessage());
  if (dr!=null) {
    System.out.println("Disposition report:" +
    "\n  operator:" + dr.getOperator() +
    "\n  generic:" + dr.getGeneric() +
    "\n  errno:"   + dr.getErrno() +
    "\n  errCode:" + dr.getErrCode() +
    "\n  errInfoText:" + dr.getErrInfoText());
  }
  e.printStackTrace();
```

```
    } catch (SOAPException e) {

      System.out.println("SOAP: [" + e.getFaultCode() + "] "
                                    + e.getMessage());
      e.getRootException().printStackTrace();

    } catch (Exception e) {

      // Catch anything else unexpected
      e.printStackTrace();

  }
```

If we plan on performing any updates to the registry, we also need to obtain an `AuthToken`. This is done using the following code, inside our main UDDI `try` block:

```
AuthToken token = proxy.get_authToken("wstkAdmin", "wstkAdmin");
```

UDDI Operations

The last four method types all have very recognizable signatures, which begin with `find_`, `get_`, `save_` or `delete_`, followed by the name of the type of object you want to perform the action on (`binding`, `business`, `service`, or `tModel`, or, in the case of `get_` methods, `bindingDetail`, `businessDetail`, `serviceDetail`, or `tModelDetail`). There are usually several overloaded versions of each method, each taking a different combination of arguments to specify which particular object we want to operate on.

> The current version of the UDDI local registry has some problems handling entities other than businesses, thanks to a missing class called **ExceptionMessages**, so we'll simply be working with business entities here. The same principles apply to registering the other three entity types.

To store a business entity, we first construct a Business Entity object, and add various properties to it. We then place the entity in a vector, and call a version of the `save_business()` method. Here is an example that we can use to register WroxMart as a business entity with the local UDDI registry:

```
import com.ibm.uddi.client.*;
import com.ibm.uddi.datatype.*;
import com.ibm.uddi.datatype.binding.*;
import com.ibm.uddi.datatype.business.*;
import com.ibm.uddi.datatype.service.*;
import com.ibm.uddi.datatype.tmodel.*;
import com.ibm.uddi.request.*;
import com.ibm.uddi.response.*;
import com.ibm.uddi.util.*;
import com.ibm.uddi.*;
import java.util.*;
import org.apache.soap.SOAPException;

public class AddBusiness {

  public static void main(String[] args) {
```

```
    UDDIProxy proxy = new UDDIProxy();
    try {
      proxy.setInquiryURL("http://localhost:8080/uddi/servlet/uddi");
      proxy.setPublishURL("http://localhost:8080/uddi/servlet/uddi");
    } catch (java.net.MalformedURLException e) {
      e.printStackTrace();
    }

    try {

      AuthToken token = proxy.get_authToken("wstkAdmin", "wstkAdmin");

      BusinessEntity wroxMart = new BusinessEntity("", args[0]);

      Vector entities = new Vector();
      entities.add(wroxMart);

      BusinessDetail bd = proxy.save_business(token.getAuthInfoString(),
                                              entities);
      wroxMart = (BusinessEntity)bd.getBusinessEntityVector().elementAt(0);

      System.out.println(wroxMart.getBusinessKey());

    } catch (UDDIException e) {
      DispositionReport dr = e.getDispositionReport();
      System.out.println("UDDI: [" + e.getFaultCode() + "] "
                              + e.getMessage());
      if (dr!=null) {
        System.out.println("Disposition report:" +
        "\n  operator:" + dr.getOperator() +
        "\n  generic:"  + dr.getGeneric() +
        "\n  errno:"    + dr.getErrno() +
        "\n  errCode:"  + dr.getErrCode() +
        "\n  errInfoText:" + dr.getErrInfoText());
      }
      e.printStackTrace();
    } catch (SOAPException e) {
      System.out.println("SOAP: [" + e.getFaultCode() + "] "
                              + e.getMessage());
      e.getRootException().printStackTrace();
    } catch (Exception e) {
      // Catch anything else unexpected
      e.printStackTrace();
    }


  }


}
```

The first highlighted block of code is the extensive set of import statements. This listing should cover us for most UDDI client coding.

Next, we simply get hold of an instance of the UDDI proxy, as discussed before, and set the endpoints to the local UDDI service. Inside the main UDDI try block, we then obtain an AuthToken, and we can start building our business entity – at the start of the second highlighted block of text.

We create a new business entity using a constructor, which takes two strings as arguments. The first is the business key, a unique identifier of the entity within the registry. By specifying the key of an existing business entity here, we can overwrite it with our new details. We want to create a new entry, so we specify an empty string. The second is the business name. We pass in the first command-line argument as a parameter.

Next we create a `Vector`, and add our entity to it. Most of the save operations allow you to save several entities of the same type at once, so take a `Vector` as an argument.

Now we can call the `save_business()` method. It takes two arguments: the first is a string, into which we pass our authentication credentials, and the second is our vector containing a single business entity.

What's returned is a `BusinessDetails` object, which contains a vector of business entities, matching those we submitted but with additional details filled in by the server (such as the business key).

We extract the vector, and pull out the first item from it. We can then print out information from it. Here, we just print out the business key.

When you compile and execute this client (use the same command prompt you used to set up Tomcat's environment, since it will have the necessary files on the classpath – otherwise you'll need to add the `uddi4j.jar` file to your classpath), you should see the following sort of result:

```
C:\WINNT\System32\cmd.exe

C:\projavaxml\Chapter22\uddi>setenv

C:\projavaxml\Chapter22\uddi>javac AddBusiness.java

C:\projavaxml\Chapter22\uddi>java AddBusiness WroxMart
FF3C7A2B-00E4-FFA8-2D64-C0A800B5AA77

C:\projavaxml\Chapter22\uddi>_
```

The key returned will almost certainly be different when you run this code. We can use this key to amend the company's details, delete it, or to add services that the company provides.

Let's now perform a search operation. Copy the previous source file into a file called `FindBusiness.java`, and change the class name to `FindBusiness`. Change the contents of the main `try` block to:

```
// Code same until here

try {
        BusinessList bl = proxy.find_business(args[0], null, 1);

        BusinessInfos info = bl.getBusinessInfos();
        Vector infoVector=info.getBusinessInfoVector();

        if (infoVector.isEmpty()) {
          System.out.println("No matching businesses found");
        } else {
          BusinessInfo foundBusiness = (BusinessInfo)infoVector.elementAt(0);

          System.out.println("Found a business called: " +
                             foundBusiness.getNameString());
```

```
        BusinessDetail bd =
            proxy.get_businessDetail(foundBusiness.getBusinessKey());
        BusinessEntity foundEntity =
            (BusinessEntity)bd.getBusinessEntityVector().elementAt(0);

        System.out.println("Details:"
        + "\n  Registered by: " + foundEntity.getAuthorizedName()
        + "\n  Operator: "       + foundEntity.getOperator()
        + "\n  Name: "         + foundEntity.getNameString());
    }
  } catch (UDDIException e) {

// Rest of code as before
```

What's happening this time is we are first performing a general get-type search, and then drilling down using the returned business key to get details about the business we have found.

First of all, we call the proxy's `find_business()` method. This takes three arguments: a search string (the search will match any business whose name begins with the search string), a `FindQualifiers` object to narrow down the search (we pass in `null`), and an integer indicating the maximum number of results we are prepared to handle. We're only expecting to get one result, so that's all we ask for.

The results come back as `BusinessInfo` objects, wrapped in traditional UDDI style, in a vector, contained in a `BusinessInfos` object. That object itself is further contained inside the returned `BusinessList`. We spend the next few lines of code unwrapping this package to extract the vector. We then check to see if it contains any results at all, and report a failure if there's nothing in the vector. If it isn't empty, we must have a match, so we extract it.

A `BusinessInfo` object contains a small amount of information about a business entity, enough to enable us to decide if it is the business we're interested in before we download its complete business profile. At this point, we print out the name of the business we found, and then we start our drill-down search on the business.

We call the proxy again, this time using the `get_businessDetail()` method. This takes a single argument: a business key. We extract the key from the `BusinessInfo` object. The `BusinessDetail` object that is returned is the same as the one we got back when we registered our business. The technique for extracting a `BusinessEntity` from it is the same. We can then print out some details from the `BusinessEntity` object.

Here are two runs of this class, one successful search, and one failed:

UDDI Summary

We've just had a taste of how we can use UDDI4J's `UDDIProxy` class to communicate with a UDDI registry. The details of the UDDI standard are a little too complex to go into in depth here, but there is excellent technical documentation available from http://www.uddi.org/, and the three UDDI partners listed earlier. You should take a look at the UDDI Data Structures reference, and the UDDI API specification. In conjunction with UDDI4J's JavaDocs, you should find enough information to work out how to interact with a UDDI registry. Once you have a working program, you can let it loose on the public UDDI registries hosted by Microsoft, IBM, and Ariba. If you want to test out publishing functionality before you run your code against the real public servers, you can make use of the test servers hosted by both IBM and Microsoft, at these addresses:

❑   http://www.ibm.com/services/uddi/testregistry/

❑   http://test.uddi.microsoft.com/

Summary

Web services represent a path towards true cross-platform interoperability. Imagine programming in an IDE that makes use of UDDI and WSDL to discover web services anywhere on the Internet, and provide you with automatically generated client proxy stubs to access them. Writing an application that makes purchases, or aggregates information, from any number of distant sources, becomes as easy as making use of a local class. This functionality will be partly implemented in Microsoft's Visual Studio.NET, meaning .NET programmers will be able to make use of your web services. Similarly, IBM has produced its Web Services Development Environment to provide this sort of functionality to Java programmers. Sun's ONE announcement of February 2001 talks about integrating the APIs for accessing web services into the Java platform.

At the beginning of this chapter, we talked about how the client-server systems in the rest of the book are tightly coupled, relying on agreement over every detail of the underlying protocols and how the data to be transmitted would be structured. In the course of this chapter, we've developed several web service descriptions, and also looked at UDDI – how do these actually help us get away from this tight coupling?

Simply put, they abstract our code away from the decisions about how the communication will be performed. Our client simply called methods on an automatically generated client object; it knew nothing of the underlying communication protocols. Our service simply implemented the necessary methods; it too knew nothing of the underlying communication. They simply understand the datatypes and message operations defined in the WSDL. Everything else the WSDL document described (how the messages should map onto XML, how the XML should be transmitted on the wire, what protocol the transmission should be handled by) is simply implemented by the automatically generated code.

UDDI allows our clients to become totally divorced from the service. The client might simply need to know the name of the service it was looking to use, in order to look up its location, obtain the WSDL definition of the service, generate a proxy, and communicate with the service. Simply changing the service's entry in the UDDI registry could enable the same client code to talk to the same server code using SOAP over SMTP (e-mail), or XML over HTTP POST, or any future protocol. Provided that the interface definition remained unchanged, the same proxy could use any actual communication method.

By providing these ways for a client to discover the current, local, or most suitable way to use a web service, allowing it to recover gracefully if it discovered the service was no longer accessible the way it thought it was, we reduce significantly the amount of knowledge required by the client at compile-time, and allow it to act more like a person does. If you went to your favorite search engine, and found the search terms textbox had moved, you'd still be able to get the search results you wanted. Web services have the potential to offer this flexibility to computer programs as well.

Web services have the capacity to change the sort of applications we can put the Internet to, and they make programming applications that make use of code on distant servers extremely simple.

The Xerces Blue
butterfly, which became
extinct earlier this century,
and after which the Xerces XML
parser is named ...

XML-Related Standards

You will find gathered in this appendix a reference guide to some of the XML standards that we have covered in this book. We reserve XSLT for its own Appendix G, but here we will cover the core details of:

- ❑ **XLink** and **XPointer** – we used these in Chapter 9
- ❑ **XPath** – covered in Chapters 7, 8, and 18
- ❑ **XML Schemas** – we introduced this in Chapter 5 and covered them in Chapters 6, 10, 22, and elsewhere

XLink

The namespace for XLink is:

http://www.w3.org/1999/xlink

Simple Links

The following section describes all of the attributes necessary to describe simple links, and how elements with these attributes must be associated together.

xlink:type = "simple"

Required. An element must be declared with this attribute to indicate the presence of a simple link. The element with this attribute should be rendered as the linked element by the rendering engine.

Attribute: `href`	Optional. The URI of the remote resource. For simple links, this URI is the "destination" of the link.
Attribute: `role`	Optional. Used to describe the function of a remote resource in a machine-readable fashion. It may be qualified with a namespace. For simple links, this attribute is descriptive only.
Attribute: `title`	Optional. Used to provide a human-readable description of a remote resource's function. A rendering engine might use this value to indicate a link to other information.
Attribute: `show`	Optional. Used to define *how* the rendering engine should show the content of the remote resource. Legal values are: `new` – Creates a new context in which the remote resource is to be rendered (by, for example, opening a new browser window). `replace` – Renders the content in place of the resource being navigated from. `embed` – Embed the content of the remote resource at the location of the link in the current resource. `undefined` – The rendering engine may choose how the remote resource is to be rendered.
Attribute: `actuate`	Optional. Indicates *when* the remote resource is to be rendered. Legal values are: `onLoad` – The remote resource should be navigated to when the current resource is loaded and its contents rendered immediately. `onRequest` – The remote resource should be navigated to only when the user requests that the navigation should happen. `undefined` – The rendering engine may decide when the remote resource's content is to be actuated.

Extended Links

The following section describes all of the attributes necessary to describe extended links, and how elements with these attributes must be associated together.

xlink:type = "extended"

Required. An element must be declared with this attribute to indicate the presence of an extended link. The element with this attribute should be rendered as the linked element by the rendering engine.

Attribute: `role`	Optional. Used to describe the function of a link in a machine-readable fashion. It may be qualified with a namespace. For extended links, this attribute is descriptive only.
Attribute: `title`	Optional. Used to provide a human-readable description of an extended link's function. A rendering engine might use this value to control the way the extended link is rendered.

xlink:type = "locator"

Optional. An element declared with this type must be a child of an element with xlink:type = extended. This element type describes a remote resource that participates in the extended link.

Attribute: href	Required. The URI of the remote resource that is participating in the link.
Attribute: role	Optional. Used to describe the function of a remote resource in a machine-readable fashion. It may be qualified with a namespace. For remote resources, this attribute is also used to govern the definition of arcs between linked resources – see the xlink:type = "arc" element for more information.
Attribute: title	Optional. Used to provide a human-readable description of a remote resource's function. A rendering engine might use this value to control the way the extended link is rendered.

xlink:type = "arc"

Optional. An element declared with this type must be a child of an element with xlink:type = "extended". This element type describes traversal rules between the resources that participate in the extended link.

Attribute: role	Optional. Used to describe the function of a traversal path in a machine-readable fashion. It may be qualified with a namespace. For arcs, this information is descriptive only.
Attribute: title	Optional. Used to provide a human-readable description of a traversal path. A rendering engine might use this value to control the way the extended link is rendered.
Attribute: show	Optional. Used to define *how* the rendering engine should show the content of the target resource when the link is traversed. Legal values are: new – Creates a new context in which the target resource is to be rendered (by, for example, opening a new browser window). replace – Renders the content in place of the resource being navigated from. embed – Embeds the content of the target resource at the location of the link in the current resource. undefined – The rendering engine may choose how the target resource is to be rendered.

Table continued on following page

Attribute: `actuate`	Optional. Indicates *when* the target resource is to be rendered. Legal values are:
	`onLoad` – The target resource should be navigated to when the current resource is loaded and its contents rendered immediately.
	`onRequest` – The target resource should be navigated to only when the user requests that the navigation should happen.
	`undefined` – The rendering engine may decide when the target resource's content is to be actuated.
Attribute: `from`	Optional. Indicates the role of the starting resource. Any resource participating in the extended link with a role matching the role specified in the `from` attribute of this arc will be treated as a starting resource for traversal using this arc's definition. If this attribute is not supplied, all participating resources are assumed to be valid starting resources for this arc.
Attribute: `to`	Optional. Indicates the role of the target resource. Any resource participating in the extended link with a role matching the role specified in the `to` attribute of this arc will be treated as a target resource for traversal using this arc's definition. If this attribute is not supplied, all participating resources are assumed to be valid target resources for this arc.

xlink:type = "resource"

Optional. An element declared with this type must be a child of an element with `xlink:type = "extended"`. This element type describes a local resource that participates in the extended link.

Attribute: `role`	Optional. Used to describe the function of a local resource in a machine-readable fashion. It may be qualified with a namespace. For local resources, this attribute is also used to govern the definition of arcs between linked resources – see the `xlink:type = "arc"` element for more information.
Attribute: `title`	Optional. Used to provide a human-readable description of a local resource. A rendering engine might use this value to control the way the extended link is rendered.

xlink:type = "title"

Optional. An element declared with this type must be a child of an element with `xlink:type = "extended"`, `xlink:type = "arc"`, or `xlink:type = "locator"`. This element type describes additional title information about the link, arc, or locator. It has no attributes.

XPointer

Syntax

XPointers may be defined using full XPointer syntax or "bare" syntax.

The full syntax for XPointer is:

```
Full_document_URL#xpointer(XPath_expression)
```

The "bare" syntax for XPointer allows an ID to be specified without the XPointer prefix. So, the XPointer:

```
#chapter1
```

is equivalent to:

```
#xpointer(id("chapter1"))
```

More than one XPointer expression may be included – each one is evaluated, from left to right, and if any succeed for a node, then that node is included in the result. For example:

```
#xpointer(id("chapter1"))xpointer(id("chapter2"))
```

will include both chapter1 and chapter2.

XPointer Extensions to XPath

The point Location Type

XPath defines a new type of location, called a point. It does not necessarily correspond directly to a node; rather, it defines a location within the document. It may represent the location preceding any individual character in text content, or preceding or following any node in the document.

The range Location Type

XPath defines another new type of location, called a range. A range is defined as all of the structure and content between two points (see the definition of the point location type, above).

New Node Tests

point()	Matches any location in the location set (analogous to a node set for pure XPath) that is a point.
range()	Matches any location in the location set that is a range.

New Operators

`to`	Returns a range between the start point of the covering range of the first operand and the end point of the covering range of the second operand.

New Functions

`location-set string-range(location-set string number? number?)`	Returns a set of range locations for each non-overlapping incidence of the `string` argument found in the string values of the members of the `location-set` argument. If the third argument is provided, it is the position of the start point of the range relative to the location of the matched string. If the fourth argument is provided, it is the number of characters to be returned in each range (if not provided, only the matched string is returned in the range).
`location-set range(location-set)`	Returns a set of ranges that are covering ranges for each location specified in the argument `location-set`.
`location-set range-inside(location-set)`	Returns a set of ranges that are covering ranges for the contents of each location specified in the argument `location-set` (but not necessarily the location itself).
`location-set start-point (location-set)`	Returns a set of points that correspond to the start point of the covering ranges, for each location in the argument `location-set`.
`location-set end-point(location-set)`	Returns a set of points that correspond to the end point of the covering ranges, for each location in the argument `location-set`.
`location-set here()`	Returns a location set containing a single element node that contains or bears the XPointer itself.
`location-set origin()`	Returns a location set corresponding to the source link of a traversal. This function is only meaningful if XPointer is being used in conjunction with some link traversal mechanism such as XLink.
`boolean unique()`	Returns true if the current context size is 1.

XPath Reference

An XPath expression contains one or more "location steps", separated by slashes. Each location step has the following form:

```
axis-name::node-test [predicate]*
```

In other words, there is an axis name, then two colons, then a node test and finally zero or more predicates in brackets. A predicate is an expression. It exists of values, operators and other XPath expressions. We will show a list of valid axes and a list of valid node tests.

The XPath axis contains a part of the document, defined from the perspective of the "context node". The node test makes a selection from the nodes on that axis. By adding predicates, it is possible to select a subset from these nodes. If the expression in the predicate returns true, the node remains in the selected set, otherwise it is removed. XPath defines a set of functions for use in predicates. These are listed in the appendix as well.

Axes

ancestor

Contains the parent node, the parent's parent node, etc., all the way up to the document root.

Primary node type:	element

ancestor-or-self

This is identical to the ancestor axis, but includes the context node itself.

Primary node type:	element

attribute

Contains all attributes on the context node.

Primary node type:	attribute

child

Contains all direct children of the context node.

Primary node type:	element
Shorthand:	(default axis)

descendant

This refers to all children of the context node, including all children's children recursively.

Primary node type:	element
Shorthand	//

descendant-or-self

This is identical to the descendant axis, but includes the context node itself.

Primary node type:	element

following

Contains all nodes that come after the context node in the document order.

Primary node type:	element

following-sibling

Contain all siblings (children of the same parent node) of the context node that come after the context node in document order.

Primary node type:	element

namespace

Contains all valid namespaces that can be used on the context node. This includes the default namespace and the XML namespace, which are automatically declared in any document.

Primary node type:	namespace

parent

Contains only the direct parent node of the context node.

Primary node type:	element
Shorthand:	. .

preceding

Contains all nodes that come before the context node in the document order.

Primary node type:	element

preceding-sibling

Contains all siblings (children of the same parent node) of the context node that come before the context node in document order.

Primary node type:	element

self

Contains only the context node itself.

Primary node type:	element
Shorthand:	.

Node Tests

*

Returns true for all nodes of the primary type of the axis.

comment()

Returns true for all comment nodes.

literal-name()

Returns true for all nodes of that name. If the node test is 'PERSON', it returns true for all nodes of name 'PERSON'.

node()

Returns true for all nodes, except attributes and namespaces.

processing-instruction(name?)

Returns true for all processing instruction nodes. If a name is passed, returns true only for processing instruction nodes of that name.

text()

Returns true for all text nodes.

Functions

boolean boolean(object)

Converts anything passed to it into a Boolean value (true or false).

Parameter: object	Numbers are true if they are not zero or NaN (not a number). Strings are true if their length is non-zero. Node sets return true if they are not empty.

number ceiling(number)

Rounds a passed number up to the nearest integer, for example 2.2 becomes 3.

Parameter: number	The number to be rounded.

string concat(string, string+)

Concatenates all strings passed.

Parameter 1: `string`	The first string.
Parameters 2 +: `string`	All subsequent strings.

boolean contains(string, string)

Returns true if the first passed string contains the second passed string.

Parameter 1: `string`	The string to be searched.
Parameter 2: `string`	The search string.

number count(node-set)

Returns the number of nodes in the passed node set.

Parameter: `node-set`	The node set that is to be counted.

boolean false()

Only returns `false`.

number floor(number)

Rounds a passed number down to the nearest integer, for example 2.8 becomes 2.

Parameter: `number`	The number to be rounded.

node-set id(string)

Returns the element, identified by the passed identifier. Note that this will only work in validated documents.

Parameter: `string`	The ID value.

boolean lang(string)

Returns true if the language of the context node is the same as the passed language identifier. The language of the context node can be set using the `xmllang` on it or any of its ancestors.

Parameter: `string`	Language identifier. `lang('en')` returns true for English language nodes.

number last()

Returns the index number of the last node in the current context node set.

string local-name(node-set?)

Returns the local part of the name of the first node (in document order) in the passed node set. The local part of an xsl:value-of element is 'value-of'.

Parameter (opt): node-set	If no node set is specified, the current context node is used.

string name(node-set?)

Returns the name of the passed node. This is the fully qualified name, including the namespace prefix.

Parameter (opt): node-set	If no node set is specified, the current context node is used.

string namespace-uri(node-set?)

Returns the full URI that defines the namespace of the passed node.

Parameter (opt): node-set	If no node set is specified, the current context node is used.

string normalize-space(string?)

Returns the whitespace-normalized version of the passed string. This means that all leading and trailing whitespace gets stripped and all sequences of whitespace get combined to one single space.

Parameter (opt): string	If no string is passed, the current node is converted to a string.

boolean not(boolean)

Returns the inverse from the passed value.

Parameter: boolean	true or false.

number number(object?)

Converts the passed value to a number. String values are converted according to the IEE 754 standard, Boolean values are converted to 1 or 0, node sets are first converted to string values and then to the numerical equivalent.

Parameter (opt): object	If nothing is passed, the current context node is used.

number position()

Returns the position of the current context node in the current context node set.

number round(number)

Rounds a passed number to the nearest integer (up or down), i.e. 2.5 becomes 3 and 2.4 becomes 2.

Parameter: number	The number to be rounded.

boolean starts-with(string, string)

Returns true if the first passed string starts with the second passed string.

Parameter 1: string	The string to be checked.
Parameter 2: string	The substring that must be searched.

string string(object?)

Converts the passed object to a string value.

Parameter (opt): object	If nothing is passed, the result is an empty string.

number string-length(string?)

Returns the number of characters in the passed string.

Parameter: object	If nothing is passed, the current context is converted to a string.

string substring(string, number, number?)

Returns the substring from the passed string starting at the first numeric value, with the length specified by the second numeric value. If no length is passed, the substring runs to the end of the passed string.

Parameter 1: string	The string that will be used as the source for the substring.
Parameter 2: number	Start location of the substring.
Parameter 3 (opt): number	Length of the substring.

string substring-after(string, string)

Returns the string following the first occurrence of the second passed string inside the first passed string. The return value of substring-after('2000/2/22', '/') would be '2/22'.

Parameter 1: string	The string that serves as the source.
Parameter 2: string	The string that is searched in the source string.

string substring-before(string, string)

Returns the string part preceding the first occurrence of the second passed string inside the first passed string. The return value of `substring-before('2000/2/22', '/')` would be '2000'.

Parameter 1: `string`	The string that serves as the source.
Parameter 2: `string`	The string that is searched for in the source string.

number sum(node-set)

Sums the values of all nodes in the set when converted to a number.

Parameter: `node-set`	The node set containing all values to be summed.

string translate(string, string, string)

Translates characters in a string to other characters. The strings to translate from and to are specified by the second and third parameters respectively. So `translate('A Space Odissei', 'i', 'y')` would result in A Space Odyssey, and `translate('abcdefg', 'aceg', 'ACE')` results in AbCdEf. The final g gets translated to nothing, because the third string has no counterpart for that position in the second string.

Parameter 1: `string`	String to be translated character by character.
Parameter 2: `string`	String defining which characters must be translated.
Parameter 3: `string`	String defining what the characters from the second string should be translated to.

boolean true()

Always returns `true`.

A Few Examples of XPath Expressions

Select all descendent elements from the root:

```
/descendent::*
```

Select ancestor elements of the context node that are named `Chapter`:

```
ancestor::Chapter
```

Select nodes that have more than two direct children with the name `Skip`:

```
/descendant::node()[count(child::Skip) < 2]
```

Select all `Student` elements whose name attribute starts with an A (using shorthand notation):

```
//Student[starts-with(@name, 'A']
```

XML Schema Data types

In this section, we'll go through the details of XML Schema data types. XML Schemas provide two basic kinds of data types:

- **Primitive data types** – those that are not defined in terms of other types
- **Derived data types** – types that are defined in terms of existing types

There are three W3C documents of interest: XML Schema Part 0: Primer, XML Schema Part 1: Structures, and XML Schema Part 2: Data types *[all 7 April 2000], at* http://www.w3.org/TR/xmlschema-0, http://www.w3.org/TR/xmlschema-1, *and* http://www.w3.org/TR/xmlschema-2, *respectively. Together, these comprise the W3C candidate recommendation of XML Schema, as of the 24th October 2000.*

XML Schema is based on XML 1.0, but also requires the use of Namespaces in XML *[14 January 1999], available at* http://www.w3.org/TR/REC-xml-names.html.

Primitive Types

The following are the primitive data types that are built into XML Schema:

- `string` – a finite-length sequence of UCS characters
- `boolean` – a two-state "true" or "false" flag
- `float` – a 32-bit single-precision floating-point number
- `double` – a 64-bit double-precision floating-point number
- `decimal` – a decimal number of arbitrary precision
- `timeDuration` – a duration of time
- `recurringDuration` – a recurring duration of time
- `binary` – text-encoded binary data
- `uriReference` – a standard Internet URI
- `ID` – equivalent to the XML 1.0 `ID` attribute type
- `IDREF` – equivalent to the XML 1.0 `IDREF` attribute type
- `ENTITY` – equivalent to the XML 1.0 `ENTITY` attribute type
- `NOTATION` – equivalent to the XML 1.0 `NOTATION` attribute type
- `QName` – a legal `QName` string (name with qualifier), as defined in *Namespaces in XML*

Let's take a closer look at these.

string

A set of finite-length sequences of UCS characters, as defined in ISO 10646 and Unicode. Value and lexical spaces are identical. This data type is ordered by UCS code points (integer character values). For example:

```
<an_element>This sentence is a legal string literal with élan.</an_element>
```

Built-in derived types: CDATA.

boolean

A binary value. True may be represented as "true" or "1" (one), and false may be either "false" or "0" (zero).

```
<an_element flag1="true" flag2="1" />    <!-- two flags, equivalent values -->
<an_element flag3="false" flag4="0" />   <!-- ditto -->
```

This data type is not ordered, and there are no built-in derived types.

decimal

An arbitrary precision decimal number, with values in the range $i \times 10^n$, where i and n are integers (with n being the scale of the value space). This data type is ordered by numeric value.

It's represented by a finite-length sequence of decimal digits separated by a period (.) as a decimal indicator, and an optional leading sign (+ or -). If the sign is omitted, it's assumed to be a plus. The representation is further constrained by the scale and precision facets. Leading and/or trailing zeroes are optional. For example, each of the following is a valid decimal:

```
<an_element num1="-1.23" num2="3.1416" num3="+042" num4="100.00" />
```

Built-in derived type: integer.

float

An IEEE single-precision 32-bit floating-point number as specified in IEEE 754-1985.

> *The* IEEE Standard for Binary Floating-Point Arithmetic (IEEE 754-1985) *is available at http://standards.ieee.org/reading/ieee/std_public/description/busarch/754-1985_desc.html. (Someone needs to talk to these people about using simpler and more reasonable URLs!)*

The value space includes all values $m \times 2^e$, where m is an integer whose absolute value is less than 2^{24}, and e is an integer between -149 and 104, inclusive. There are also five special values in a float's value space: positive and negative zero (represented as "0" and "-0"), positive and negative infinity ("INF" and "-INF"), and not-a-number ("NAN"). This data type is ordered by numeric value.

The lexical representation is a mantissa (which must be a decimal number) optionally followed by the character **E** or **e**, followed by an exponent (which must be an integer). If the **E/e** and exponent are omitted, an exponent value of 0 (zero) is assumed. For example:

```
<an_element num1="-1E4" num2="3.1416" num3="12.78e-1" num4="NAN" />
```

There are no built-in derived types.

double

An IEEE double-precision 64-bit floating-point number as specified in IEEE 754-1985.

The value space includes all values **m** × **2 ^ e**, where **m** is an integer whose absolute value is less than **2 ^ 53**, and **e** is an integer between **-1075** and **970**, inclusive. There are also the same five special values as defined for the `float` type. This data type is ordered by numeric value.

The lexical representation is the same as the `float` type. For example:

```
<an_element num1="-1E666" num2="3.1416" num3="12.78e-1040" num4="INF" />
```

There are no built-in derived types.

timeDuration

A duration of time, with a countably infinite value space, as specified in ISO 8601.

> **ISO 8601:Representations of dates and times, 1988-06-15** *is one of the few ISO standards that are available on the WWW (at http://www.iso.ch/markete/8601.pdf). Ordering information for the new draft and its corrections are at http://www.iso.ch/cate/d15903.html and http://www.iso.ch/cate/d15905.html.*

The lexical representation is the ISO 8601 extended format: P*n*Y*n*M*n*DT*n*H*n*M*n*S. The upper-case letters P, Y, M, D, T, H, M, and S in this format are called designators. The "P" stands for "period" (as in a duration of time) and is required to be the first character of any `timeDuration` string. The recurring "*n*" represents number, so *n*Y is the number of years, *n*M the number of months, *n*D of days, T is the date/time separator, *n*H is hours, the second *n*M is minutes, and *n*S is seconds. Seconds may be any decimal number of arbitrary precision.

For example:

```
<an_element duration="P12Y10M2DT0H40M27.87S" />
```

This represents a `timeDuration` of 12 years, 10 months, 2 days, 0 hours, 40 minutes, and 27.87 seconds.

Truncated lexical representations of this format are allowed provided they conform to the following:

❑ Lowest order items may be omitted. If so, their value is assumed to be zero.

❑ The lowest order item may have a decimal fraction of arbitrary precision.

❑ If any of the number values equals zero, the number and its corresponding designator may be omitted. However, at least one number and its designator must always be present.

❑ The designator **T** must be absent if all time items are omitted.

❑ The leading designator **P** must always be present.

For example:

```
<an_element duration="P12Y10M2DT40M27.87S" />
```

represents the same `timeDuration` as the previous example – except here we're using one of the truncated forms (hours have been omitted).

An optional preceding minus sign (-) is also allowed, to indicate a negative duration; if the sign is omitted, a positive duration is assumed.

One more example: the durations in the first line below are all legal (meaning 500 years, 42 months, 1 year + 6 months + 2 hours, and 42 days + 1 hour + 57 minutes, respectively), while the subsequent two lines are both *illegal*:

```
<an_element d1="P500Y" d2="P42M" d3="P1Y6MT2H" d4="P42DT1H57M" />
<an_element d="P-1347M" />        <!-- minus sign must precede the P -->
<an_element d="P1Y2MT" />         <!-- T must be omitted in this case -->
```

There are no built-in types derived from `timeDuration`.

recurringDuration

A `timeDuration` that recurs with a specific `timeDuration` starting from a specific origin. The value space is countably infinite. (See also §5.5.3.2 of ISO 8601.)

The lexical representation is the ISO 8601 extended format `CCYY-MM-DDThh:mm:ss.sss`. The `CC` represents the century, `YY` the year, `MM` the month and `DD` the day. The `T` is the date/time separator. The `hh`, `mm`, and `ss.sss` represent hours, minutes and seconds respectively. Additional digits may be used to increase the precision of the fractional seconds, and additional digits can be added to `CC` to accommodate year values greater than 9999. An optional preceding minus sign (–) is allowed to indicate a negative duration; if the sign is omitted, a positive duration is assumed.

The basic string may be immediately followed by a `Z` to indicate Coordinated Universal Time (UTZ).

> *UTZ is the internationally-accepted apolitical term for the world's base time zone on the Zero Meridian, commonly-known in Anglo-countries as Greenwich Mean Time.*

A local time zone offset (the difference between the local time zone and UTZ) may also be indicated by adding another string with the format: `±hh.mm`, where `hh` and `mm` are defined as above, and the sign may be either plus or minus. The two time zone options (UTZ and local) are mutually exclusive

The primary purpose, and only legal use, of `recurringDuration` is as a base type for some derived date/time type. This derived type must specify both the duration and period constraining facets. This primitive data type *may not be used directly in a schema* – though it may be used indirectly via a derived type.

Built-in derived types: `recurringDate`, `recurringDay`, `time`, `timeInstant`, and `timePeriod` (all of these, except the first, use truncated versions of the above lexical representation).

The two required facets are specified using the same lexical format as `timeDuration`. These facets specify the length of the duration (`duration`) and after what duration it recurs (`period`). If `duration`'s value is zero, it means that the duration is a single instant of time. If the `period` is zero, the duration doesn't recur, in other words there's only a single occurrence.

binary

Some arbitrary binary data, which is a set of finite-length sequences of binary octets (8-bit bytes). This data type is not ordered.

The lexical representation of this data type depends upon the choice of encoding facet (see its description in the previous section). For example:

```
<an_element encoding="hex">312D322D33</an_element>
```

This example shows the hex encoding of the ASCII string "1-2-3".

There are no built-in derived types.

This type *may not be used directly in a schema* – it may only be used indirectly via a derived type.

uriReference

An absolute or relative Uniform Resource Identifier (URI) Reference that may have an optional fragment identifier. This data type is not ordered.

The lexical representation of this data type is the set of strings that match the URI-reference production in Section 4 of RFC 2396. For example:

```
<an_element link="http://www.w3.org" />        <!-- HTTP -->
<an_element link="ftp://ftp.is.co.za/rfc/rfc2396.txt" />  <!-- FTP -->
<an_element link="mailto://sales@wrox.com" />    <!-- email -->
<an_element link="telnet://melvyl.ucop.edu" />   <!-- Telnet -->
```

ID

A data type that is equivalent to the ID attribute type as defined in the XML 1.0. This data type is not ordered, and the following validity constraints apply:

❑   The value of the ID string must uniquely identify its associated element

❑   It must be used once, and only once, in a document instance

The lexical representation of this data type is any NCName string (name without colon), as defined in *Namespaces in XML*. For example:

```
<an_element its_id="AGENT_ID_007" />
```

There are no built-in derived types.

IDREF

A data type that is equivalent to the IDREF attribute type as defined in the XML 1.0 recommendation. The value of the IDREF string must match the value of an element or attribute of type ID, somewhere within the same document instance. This data type is not ordered.

The lexical representation of this data type is any NCName string (name without colon), as defined in *Namespaces in XML*. For example:

```
<an_element codename="AGENT_ID_007" />
```

Built-in derived type is: IDREFS.

For compatibility with XML 1.0 DTDs, this data type should only be used for attributes.

ENTITY

A data type that's equivalent to the ENTITY attribute type as defined in the XML 1.0 recommendation, with a value space that's scoped to a specific document instance. The ENTITY value must match an unparsed entity name that's declared in the schema. This data type is not ordered.

The lexical representation of this data type is any NCName string (name without colon), as defined in *Namespaces in XML*.

Built-in derived type: ENTITIES.

For compatibility with XML 1.0 DTDs, this data type should only be used for attributes.

NOTATION

A data type that's equivalent to the NOTATION attribute type as defined in the XML 1.0 recommendation, with a value space that is scoped to a specific document instance. The NOTATION value must match a notation name that is declared in the schema. This data type is not ordered.

The lexical representation of this data type is any NCName string (name without colon), as defined in *Namespaces in XML*.

There are no built-in derived types.

For compatibility with XML 1.0 DTDs, this data type should only be used for attributes.

QName

A qualified name, as defined in *Namespaces in XML*. Each qualified name is comprised of a pair of names, separated by the namespace delimiter (:) character, the namespace name (which is a uriReference), and the local name (which is an NCName). This data type is not ordered.

The lexical representation of this data type is any legal QName string (name with qualifier). For example:

```
<a_ns_name:an_element_name> .. </a_ns_name:an_element_name>
```

There are no built-in derived types.

Constraining Facets for Primitive Types

The usable constraining facets for each of the 14 primitive data types are:

	length	min Length /max Length	pattern	enumeration	min/max Exclusive/ Inclusive	scale, precision	encoding	duration, period
string	X	X	X	X	X			
boolean			X					
float			X	X	X			
double			X	X	X			
decimal			X	X	X	X		
timeDuration			X	X	X			
recurringDuration			X	X	X			X (*req*)
binary	X	X	X	X			X (*req*)	
uriReference	X	X	X	X				
ID	X	X	X	X	X			
IDREF	X	X	X	X	X			
ENTITY	X	X	X	X	X			
NOTATION	X	X	X	X	X			
QName	X	X	X	X	X			

*Those facets labeled **req** are always required for any derived types based on this base data type.*

Built-in Derived Types

The following are the derived data types that are built-in to XML Schema:

❑ CDATA – representing white space normalized strings

❑ Token - represents tokenized strings

❑ language – a natural language identifier, as defined by RFC 1766

❑ NMTOKEN, NMTOKENS - represent NMTOKEN and NMTOKENS from the XML 1.0 recommendation (2nd edition)

- ❏ ENTITIES - represent the ENTITIES attribute type from the XML 1.0 recommendation (2nd edition)

- ❏ IDREFS - represent the IDREFS attribute type from the XML 1.0 recommendation (2nd edition)

- ❏ Name – a legal XML 1.0 name

- ❏ NCName – a legal XML 1.0 "non-colonized" name, as defined in *Namespaces in XML*

- ❏ integer – an integer number

- ❏ negativeInteger – an integer number with a value < 0

- ❏ positiveInteger – an integer number with a value > 0

- ❏ nonNegativeInteger – an integer number with a value ≥ 0

- ❏ nonPositiveInteger – an integer number with a value ≤ 0

- ❏ byte – an integer number with a value in the range -128 to +127 (inclusive)

- ❏ short – an integer number with a value in the range -32,768 to +32,767 (inclusive)

- ❏ int – an integer number with a value in the range -2,147,483,648 to +2,147,483,647 (inclusive)

- ❏ long – an integer number with a value in the range -9,223,372,036,854,775,808 to +9,223,372,036,854,775,807 (inclusive)

- ❏ unsignedByte – a non-negative integer number with a value in the range 0 to +255 (inclusive)

- ❏ unsignedShort – a non-negative integer number with a value in the range 0 to +65,535 (inclusive)

- ❏ unsignedInt – a non-negative integer number with a value in the range: 0 to +4,294,967,295 (inclusive)

- ❏ unsignedLong – a non-negative integer number with a value in the range 0 to +18,446,744,073,709,551,615 (inclusive)

- ❏ year – a Gregorian calendar year

- ❏ month – a Gregorian calendar month

- ❏ century – a Gregorian calendar century (a year without the two rightmost digits)

- ❏ date – a Gregorian calendar date (a single day)

- ❏ recurringDate – a Gregorian calendar date that recurs once every year

- ❏ recurringDay – a Gregorian calendar date that recurs once every month

- ❏ time – an instant of time that recurs every day

- ❏ timeInstant – a specific instant in time

- ❏ timePeriod – a specific period of time with a given start and end

Let's look at examples of some of these data types:

CDATA

CDATA represents white space normalized strings. CDATA value space is the set of strings that do not contain the characters:

❏ carriage-return (#xD)

❏ line-feed (#xA)

❏ tab (#x9)

CDATA lexical space is the set of strings that do not contain the characters:

❏ newline (#xD)

❏ tab (#x9)

The base type of CDATA is string, and the only data type derived from it is token

token

token represents tokenized strings.

The value space is the string-set that do not contain the characters:

❏ linefeed (#xA)

❏ tab (#x9)

❏ leading or trailing spaces (#x20)

Also, they must not have any internal sequences of two or more spaces. The lexical space is the string-set that doesn't contain the characters:

❏ line-feed

❏ tab

❏ leading or trailing spaces

Also, they must not have any internal sequences of two or more spaces.

language, NMTOKEN, and Name can be derived from this data type

language

A natural language identifier, as defined by RFC 1766.

```
<LanguageOfOrigin>en-GB</LanguageOfOrigin>
<an_element xml:lang="en-US" > ... </an_element>
```

The first of these two examples shows an element that has its content constrained to be the language data type. The second exploits a little-known attribute defined in the XML 1.0 REC, which uses the same type of values.

NMTOKEN, NMTOKENS

NMTOKEN represents the NMTOKEN attribute type from XML 1.0 (2nd edition). The value space and lexical space of NMTOKEN are the set of tokens, and set of strings (respectively) that match the NMTOKEN production in the above XML version. The base type of NMTOKEN is token.

The only data type derived from NMTOKEN is NMTOKENS.

NMTOKENS represents the NMTOKENS attribute type from the above XML version. The value space of NMTOKENS is the set of finite-length sequences of NMTOKENs. The lexical space of NMTOKENS is the set of whitespace-separated tokens, each of which is in the lexical space of NMTOKEN.

The Itemtype of NMTOKENS is NMTOKEN.

For compatibility, NMTOKEN and NMTOKENS should be used only on attributes (as per terminology (§1.4)

ENTITIES

ENTITIES represents the ENTITIES from XML 1.0 (2nd edition), value space equal to the set of finite-length sequences declared as unparsed in a DTD (and is scoped to a specific instance document), and lexical space equal to the set of whitespace separated-tokens in the lexical space of NMTOKEN.

The Itemtypeof ENTITIES is ENTITY.

For compatibility, ENTITIES should be used only on attributes, as per Terminology (§1.4)

IDREFS

IDREFS represents the IDREFS attribute type from XML 1.0 (2nd ed), with value space equal to the set of finite-length sequences of IDREFs that have been used in an XML document (and scoped to a specific instance document), and lexical space equal to the set of whitespace separated tokens, each of which is in the lexical space of IDREF.

The Itemtype of IDREFS is IDREF.

For compatibility, IDREFS should be used only on attributes, as per Terminology (§1.4)

name, NCName

Respectively a legal XML 1.0 name and a legal XML 1.0 "non-colonized" name, as defined in *Namespaces in XML*.

```
<somens:an_element_name> ... </somens:an_element_name>
<an_element_name> ... </an_element_name>
```

Both of the above examples are legal XML names that conform to the name data type. The first is also a QName, that is a namespace-qualified name. The latter is a non-qualified ("non-colonized") name that conforms to the NCName data type, a more restrictive version of name.

integer, negativeInteger, positiveInteger, nonNegativeInteger, nonPositiveInteger

These five data types are all integers, but `negativeInteger`, `positiveInteger`, `nonNegativeInteger`, `nonPositiveInteger` are constrained to specific (but open-ended) ranges of values. The difference between a `negativeInteger` and a `nonPositiveInteger` (or `positiveInteger` and `nonNegativeInteger`) is that the latter also includes zero in its value space.

byte, short, int, long

These four data types are all `integer` types, and are all constrained to finite ranges of values.

unsignedByte, unsignedShort, unsignedInt, unsignedLong

These four data types are all `nonNegativeInteger` types, and are also constrained to finite ranges of values (as shown in the above table).

century, year, month, date

These four data types are all derived from another derived data type, the `timePeriod` type. They represent Gregorian calendar dates based upon the formats defined in §5.2.1 of ISO 8601, as shown in the following examples:

```
<Century>19</Century>
<Year>2525</Year>
<Month>08</Month>
<Date>31</Date>
```

Note that the names of the elements are also just examples – the correlation between these names and the data type names is strictly illustrative. Dates in XML are always represented using numbers, in the form "YYYY-MM-DD", where "YYYY" is the year, "MM" is the month, and "DD" is the day of the month. This minimizes any confusion based upon language or cultural differences.

The `century` data type is used to represent the leftmost digits of the year (underlined in the preceding format example). It is important to note that this is not the commonly used ordinal century (for example the 1900s were known as the "20th century" – strictly speaking this century was the years 1901-2000, since there is no year 0 in the Gregorian calendar). Rather, a `century` is the two (or more) leftmost digits of a `year`, up to and including the hundreds digits ("19" is the `century` of the `year` "1999").

A `year` or `century` may be preceded by a minus sign (-) to indicate years BCE (Before Common Era). Additional digits may be added to the left of these to represent years before -9999 BCE and after 9999 CE.

recurringDate, recurringDay

These two data types are derived from the `recurringDuration` primitive type. The former must always be represented in the truncated date form of "--MM-DD", the latter as "---DD".

```
<AnnualAppointment>--04-15</AnnualAppointment>
<MonthlyAppointment>---10</MonthlyAppointment>
```

The above examples show the date/day of two different appointments: the first on the 15th of April, the second on the 10th of every month.

time, timeInstant, timePeriod

These three data types are derived from the `recurringDuration` primitive type. The first two use similar formats. A `time` always uses the 24-hour clock in the form "`HH:MM:SS.SSS±HH:MM`", where "`HH`" is hours (0-24), "`MM`" is minutes, "`SS.SSS`" is seconds. The fractional seconds and the decimal point are optional, as is the "`±HH:MM`", which is used to show the difference between local time zone and UTZ (also known as GMT). Data of the `timeInstant` type must always include the full date, as well as the time-of-day.

```
<TheTimeNowIs>20:14:57+07:00</TheTimeNowIs>
<ThisInstantIs>2000-05-28T20:14:57+07:00</ThisInstantIs>
<Duration>P12Y10M2DT0H40M27.87S</Duration>
```

The `timePeriod` type uses same representation as its base type, `recurringDuration`. See its definition in the **Primitive Types** section above (the above example uses the same value as the examples in that section, only this time it's shown as the content of an element rather than the value of an attribute).

Constraining Facets for Derived Types

The usable constraining facets for each of the built-in derived data types are:

	length	min Length /max Length	pattern	enumeration	min/max Exclusive/ Inclusive	scale, precision	duration, period
CDATA	X	X	X	X			
token	X	X	X	X			
language	X	X	X	X	X		
Name	X	X	X	X	X		
NCName	X	X	X	X	X		
integer			X	X	X	X	
negativeInteger			X	X	X	X	
positiveInteger			X	X	X	X	
nonNegativeInteger			X	X	X	X	
nonPositiveInteger			X	X	X	X	
byte			X	X	X	X	
short			X	X	X	X	
long			X	X	X	X	

Table continued on following page

	length	min Length /max Length	pattern	enumeration	min/max Exclusive/ Inclusive	scale, precision	duration, period
int			X	X	X	X	
unsignedByte			X	X	X	X	
unsignedShort			X	X	X	X	
unsignedLong			X	X	X	X	
unsignedInt			X	X	X	X	
year			X	X	X		X
month			X	X	X		X
century			X	X	X		X
date			X	X	X		X
recurringDate			X	X	X		X
recurringDay			X	X	X		X
time			X	X	X		X
timeInstant			X	X	X		X
timePeriod			X	X	X		X
IDREFS	X	X		X			
NMTOKEN	X	X	X	X	X		
NMTOKENS	X	X		X			
ENTITIES	X	X		X			

The Xerces Blue
butterfly, which became
extinct earlier this century,
and after which the Xerces XML
parser is named ...

The Simple API for XML

This appendix contains the specification of the SAX interface, versions 1.0 and 2.0, much of which is explained in Chapter 2. It is based on the definitive specification to be found on http://www.megginson.com/SAX/index.html.

The classes and interfaces are described in alphabetical order. Within each class and interface, the constructors and methods are also listed alphabetically. Deprecated classes and interfaces from SAX 1.0 are indicated throughout, and their respective replacements in SAX 2.0 are described.

The SAX distribution also includes four other "helper classes":

- ❏ DefaultHandler is an empty implementation of the EntityResolver, DTDHandler, ContentHandler, and ErrorHandler interfaces and is used as a convenience class. By inheriting from it, we can implement only the methods in these interfaces that interest us, rather than having to implement empty methods for every possibility.

- ❏ ParserAdapter wraps a SAX1 parser and converts it into a SAX2 XMLReader although you should note that skipped entities will not be reported as there is no facility for this in SAX 1.0

- ❏ XMLReaderAdapter converts an XMLReader into a (SAX1) Parser.

- ❏ XMLReaderFactory is a class that enables you to load an XMLReader identified by the org.xml.sax.driver run-time parameter. In this book, JAXP's SAXParserFactory is the preferred tool for this job.

The documentation of these helper classes is not included here as their use is fairly self-explanatory. For this, and for SAX sample applications, see the SAX distribution available from http://www.megginson.com/.

SAX 1.0

All the classes and interfaces listed here in SAX 1.0 belong to the `org.xml.sax` package.

Classes

HandlerBase (deprecated)

```
public class HandlerBase extends Object implements EntityResolver, DTDHandler,
DocumentHandler, ErrorHandler
```

Note that this class works with the deprecated `DocumentHandler` interface. It has been replaced by the SAX2 `org.xml.sax.helpers.DefaultHandler` class.

This class provides default implementations of most of the methods that would otherwise need to be implemented by the application. If you write classes in your application as subclasses of `HandlerBase`, you need only code those methods where you want something other than the default behavior. Note that the use of this class is optional.

InputSource

```
public class InputSource extends Object
```

An `InputSource` object represents a container for the XML document or any of the external entities it references. It provides three ways of supplying input to the parser: a System Identifier (or URL), a `Reader` (which delivers a stream of Unicode characters), or an `InputStream` (which delivers a stream of uninterpreted bytes). This class allows a SAX application to encapsulate information about an input source in a single object, which may include a public identifier, a system identifier, a byte stream (possibly with a specified encoding), and/or a character stream. There are two places that the application will deliver this input source to the parser: as the argument to the `Parser.parse` method, or as the return value of the `EntityResolver.resolveEntity` method.

The SAX parser will use the `InputSource` object to determine how to read XML input. If there is a character stream available, the parser will read that stream directly; if not, the parser will use a byte stream, if available; if neither stream is available, the parser will attempt to open a URI connection to the resource identified by the system identifier.

An `InputSource` object belongs to the application: the SAX parser shall never modify it in any way (it may modify a copy if necessary).

Constructors

Signature	Description
public InputStream getByteStream()	Return the byte stream for this input source, or null if none was supplied. The getEncoding() method will return the character encoding for this byte stream, or null if unknown.
public Reader getCharacterStream()	Return the character stream for this input source, or null if none was supplied.
public String getEncoding()	Return the character encoding for a byte stream or URI, null if none was supplied.
public String getPublicId()	Return the public identifier for this input source, or null if none was supplied.
public String getSystemId()	Get the system identifier for this input source. The getEncoding method will return the character encoding of the object pointed to, or null if unknown.
public InputSource()	Zero-argument default constructor.
public InputSource(InputStream byteStream)	Create a new input source with a byte stream. Can use setSystemId() to provide a base for resolving relative URIs, setPublicId() to include a public identifier, and/or setEncoding() to specify the object's character encoding. ❑ byteStream: The raw byte stream containing the document.
public InputSource(Reader characterStream)	Create a new input source with a character stream. Can use setSystemId() to provide a base for resolving relative URIs, and setPublicId() to include a public identifier. The character stream shall not include a byte order mark.
public InputSource(String systemId)	Create a new input source with a system identifier. Can use setPublicId() to include a public identifier as well, or setEncoding() to specify the character encoding, if known. If the system identifier is a URL, it must be fully resolved. ❑ systemId: The system identifier (URI).
public void setByteStream (InputStream byteStream)	Set the byte stream for this input source. If the application knows the character encoding of the byte stream, it should set it with the setEncoding() method. If there is also a character stream specified, the SAX parser will ignore this, but it will use a byte stream in preference to opening a URI connection itself. ❑ byteStream: A byte stream containing an XML document or other entity.

Table continued on following page

Signature	Description
`public void setCharacterStream(Reader characterStream)`	Set the character stream for this input source. If there is a character stream specified, the SAX parser will ignore any byte stream and will not attempt to open a URI connection to the system identifier. ❑ `characterStream`: The character stream containing the XML document or other entity.
`public void setEncoding(String encoding)`	Set the character encoding, if known. ❑ `encoding`: A string describing the character encoding.
`public void setPublicId (String publicId)`	Set the public identifier for this input source. The public identifier is always optional: if the application writer includes one, it will be provided as part of the location information. ❑ `PublicId`: The public identifier as a string.
`public void setSystemId (String systemId)`	Set the system identifier for this input source. This is optional if there is a byte stream or a character stream, but it is still useful to provide one, since the application can use it to resolve relative URIs and can include it in error messages and warnings. If the application knows the character encoding of the object pointed to by the system identifier, it can register the encoding using the `setEncoding()` method. ❑ `systemId`: The system identifier as a string.

SAXException

```
public class SAXException extends Exception
```

This class is used to represent an error detected during processing either by the parser or by the application. A parser writer or application writer can subclass it to provide additional functionality. If the application needs to pass through other types of exceptions, it must wrap those exceptions in a SAXException or an exception derived from a SAXException. If the parser or application needs to include information about a specific location in an XML document, it should use the SAXParseException subclass.

Constructors

Signature	Description
`public Exception getException()`	Return the embedded exception, or `null` if there is none.
`public String getMessage()`	Return an error or warning message for this exception. If there is an embedded exception, and if the SAXException has no detail message of its own, this method will return the detail message from the embedded exception.

Signature	Description
`public SAXException (Exception e)`	Create a new `SAXException` wrapping an existing exception. The existing exception will be embedded in the new one, and its message will become the default message for the `SAXException`. ❑ e: The exception to be wrapped in a `SAXException`.
`public SAXException (String message)`	Create a new `SAXException`. ❑ message: The error or warning message.
`public SAXException (String message, Exception e)`	Create a new `SAXException` from an existing exception. The existing exception will be embedded in the new one, but the new exception will have its own message. ❑ message: The detail message. ❑ e: The exception to be wrapped in a `SAXException`.
`public String toString()`	Convert this exception to a string and return the string version.

SAXParseException

```
public class SAXParseException extends SAXException
```

This exception class represents an error or warning condition detected by the parser or by the application. In addition to the basic capability of SAXException, a SAXParseException allows information to be retained about the location in the source document where the error occurred. Note that although the application will receive a SAXParseException as the argument to the handlers in the ErrorHandler interface, the application is not actually required to throw the exception; instead, it can simply read the information in it and take a different action.

Constructors

Signature	Description
`public int getColumnNumber()`	Return an integer representing the column number of the end of the text where the exception occurred, or -1 if none is available.. The first column in a line is position 1.
`public int getLineNumber()`	Return an integer representing the line number of the end of the text where the exception occurred, or -1 if none is available.
`public String getPublicId()`	Return a string containing the public identifier of the entity where the exception occurred, or `null` if none is available.
`public String getSystemId()`	Return a string containing the system identifier of the entity where the exception occurred, or `null` if none is available. Note that the term "entity" includes the top-level XML document.

Table continued on following page

Signature	Description
`public SAXParseException (String message, Locator locator)`	Create a new SAXParseException from a message and a Locator. Useful when an application is creating its own exception from within a DocumentHandler callback. ❑ message: The error or warning message. ❑ locator: The Locator object for the error or warning.
`public SAXParseException (String message, Locator locator, Exception e)`	Wrap an existing exception in a SAXParseException. Useful when an application is creating its own exception from within a DocumentHandler callback, and needs to wrap an existing exception that is not a subclass of SAXException. ❑ message: The error or warning message, or null to use the message from the embedded exception. ❑ locator: The Locator object for the error or warning. ❑ e: Any exception.
`public SAXParseException (String message, String publicId, String systemId, int lineNumber, int columnNumber)`	Create a new SAXParseException. Useful for parser writers. If the system identifier is a URL, the parser must resolve it fully before creating the exception. ❑ message: The error or warning message. ❑ publicId: The public identifier of the entity that generated the error or warning. ❑ systemId: The system identifier of the entity that generated the error or warning. ❑ lineNumber: The line number of the end of the text that caused the error or warning. ❑ columnNumber: The column number of the end of the text that caused the error or warning.
`public SAXParseException (String message, String publicId, String systemId, int lineNumber, int columnNumber, Exception e)`	Create a new SAXParseException with an embedded exception. Most useful for parser writers who need to wrap an exception that is not a subclass of SAXException. If the system identifier is a URL, the parser must resolve it fully before creating the exception. ❑ message: The error or warning message, or null to use the message from the embedded exception. ❑ publicId: The public identifier of the entity that generated the error or warning. ❑ systemId: The system identifier of the entity that generated the error or warning. ❑ lineNumber: The line number of the end of the text that caused the error or warning. ❑ columnNumber: The column number of the end of the text that caused the error or warning. ❑ e: Another exception to embed in this one.

Interfaces

AttributeList (deprecated)

```
public interface AttributeList
```

Note that this interface has been replaced by the SAX2 Attributes *interface, which includes Namespace support.*

An AttributeList is a collection of attributes appearing on a particular element's start tag. The Parser supplies the DocumentHandler with an AttributeList as part of the information available on the startElement() event. The instance provided will return valid results only during the scope of the startElement() invocation – the parser is entitled to recycle the object. To save a persistent copy of the attribute list, use the SAX1 AttributeListImpl helper class. An AttributeList includes only attributes that have been specified or defaulted: #IMPLIED attributes will not be included.

Methods

Signature	Description
public int getLength()	Return the number of attributes in this list. The number of attributes may be zero.
public String getName(int index)	Return the name of an attribute in this list by position, or null if there is no attribute with that index. If the attribute name has a namespace prefix, the prefix will still be attached.
	❏ index: The index of the attribute in the list (starting at 0).
public String getType(int index)	Return the type of an attribute in the list (by position). The attribute type is one of the strings "CDATA", "ID", "IDREF", "IDREFS", "NMTOKEN", "NMTOKENS", "ENTITY", "ENTITIES", or "NOTATION"; null will be returned if there is no attribute at that position.
	❏ index: The index of the attribute in the list (starting at 0).
public String getType(String name)	Return the type of an attribute in the list (by name). The return value is the same as the return value for getType(int). If the attribute name has a namespace prefix in the document, the application must include the prefix here.
	❏ name: The name of the attribute.
public String getValue(int index)	Return the value of an attribute in the list (by position), or null if there is no such attribute. If the attribute value is a list of tokens (IDREFS, ENTITIES, or NMTOKENS), the tokens will be concatenated into a single string separated by whitespace.
	❏ index: The index of the attribute in the list (starting at 0).
public String getValue(String name)	Return the value of an attribute in the list (by name), or null if there is no such attribute. The return value is the same as the return value for getValue(int). If the attribute name has a namespace prefix in the document, the application must include the prefix here.
	❏ name: The name of the attribute.

DocumentHandler (deprecated)

```
public interface DocumentHandler
```

Note that this interface has been replaced by the SAX2 ContentHandler interface, which includes Namespace support.

Receive notification of general document events: if a class wishes to be informed of basic parsing events, it implements this interface and registers an instance with the SAX parser. The parser uses the instance to report basic document-related events like the start and end of elements and character data. Every SAX application is likely to include a class that implements this interface, either directly or by subclassing the supplied class HandlerBase.

Methods

Signature	Description
public void characters(char[] ch, int start, int length) throws SAXException	Receive notification of character data. Parser calls this method to report each chunk of character data. SAX parsers may return all contiguous character data in a single chunk, or they may split it into several chunks. Note that some parsers will report whitespace using the ignorableWhitespace() method rather than this one. ❑ ch: The characters from the XML document. ❑ start: The start position in the array. ❑ length: The number of characters to read from the array.
public void endDocument() throws SAXException	Receive notification of the end of a document. The SAX parser will invoke this method only once for each document, and it will be the last method invoked during the parse.
public void endElement(String name) throws SAXException	Receive notification of the end of an element. The SAX parser will invoke this method at the end of every element in the XML document; there will be a corresponding startElement() event for every endElement() event. If the element name has a namespace prefix, the prefix will still be attached to the name. ❑ name: The element type name.
public void ignorableWhitespace (char[] ch, int start, int length) throws SAXException	Receive notification of ignorable whitespace in element content. Validating parsers must use this method to report each chunk of ignorable whitespace. Parsers may return all contiguous whitespace in a single chunk, or they may split it into several chunks; however, all of the characters in any single event must come from the same external entity, so that the Locator provides useful information. ❑ ch: The characters from the XML document. ❑ start: The start position in the array. ❑ length: The number of characters to read from the array.

Signature	Description
public void processingInstruction (String target, String data) throws SAXException	Receive notification of a processing instruction. The parser will invoke this method once for each processing instruction found: note that processing instructions may occur before or after the main document element. This method is not used to report an XML declaration or a text declaration. ❑ target: The processing instruction target. ❑ data: The processing instruction data, or null if none was supplied.
public void setDocumentLocator (Locator locator)	Receive an object for locating the origin of SAX document events. Parsers may supply a Locator by invoking this method before invoking any of the other methods in the DocumentHandler interface. The Locator allows the application to determine the end position of any document-related event, even if the parser is not reporting an error. The application will use this information for reporting its own errors. ❑ locator: An object that can return the location of any SAX document event.
public void startDocument() throws SAXException	Receive notification of the beginning of a document. The SAX parser will invoke this method only once for each document, before any other methods in this interface or in DTDHandler (except for setDocumentLocator).
public void startElement (String name, AttributeList atts) throws SAXException	Receive notification of the beginning of an element. The parser will invoke this method at the beginning of every element in the XML document; there will be a corresponding endElement() event for every startElement() event. All of the element's content will be reported, in order, before the corresponding endElement() event. If the element name has a namespace prefix, the prefix will still be attached. ❑ name: The element type name. ❑ atts: The attributes attached to the element, if any.

DTDHandler

```
public interface DTDHandler
```

This interface should be implemented by the application in order to receive notification of events related to the DTD. SAX does not provide full details of the DTD, but this interface makes it possible to access notations and unparsed entities referenced in the body of the document. The HandlerBase class provides a default implementation of this interface, which simply ignores the events.

Methods

Signature	Description
public void notationDecl (String name, String publicId, String systemId) throws SAXException	Receive notification of a notation declaration event. The parser will call this method to notify the application that it has encountered a notation declaration. ❏ name: The notation name. ❏ publicId: The notation's public identifier, or null if none was given. ❏ systemId: The notation's system identifier, or null if none was given.
public void unparsedEntityDecl (String name, String publicId, String systemId, String notationName) throws SAXException	Receive notification of an unparsed entity declaration event. The parser calls this method when it encounters a declaration of an unparsed entity. Note that the notation name corresponds to a notation reported by the notationDecl() event. ❏ name: The unparsed entity's name. ❏ publicId: The entity's public identifier, or null if none was given. ❏ systemId: The entity's system identifier (it must always have one). ❏ notationName: The name of the associated notation.

EntityResolver

```
public interface EntityResolver
```

This is the basic interface for resolving entities. When the XML document contains references to external entities, the URL will normally be analyzed automatically by the parser: the relevant file will be located and parsed where appropriate. This interface allows an application to override this behavior and is most useful for applications that build XML documents from databases or other specialized input sources, or for applications that use URI types other than URLs.

When the parser needs to obtain an entity, it calls this interface, which can respond by supplying any InputSource object. If a SAX application needs to implement customized handling for external entities, it must implement this interface and register an instance with the SAX parser using the parser's setEntityResolver method. The parser will then allow the application to intercept any external entities (including the external DTD subset and external parameter entities, if any) before including them.

The application can also use this interface to redirect system identifiers to local URIs or to look up replacements in a catalog (possibly by using the public identifier). The HandlerBase class implements the default behavior for this interface, which is simply always to return null (to request that the parser use the default system identifier).

Methods

Signature	Description
```public InputSource resolveEntity (String publicId String systemId) throws SAXException, IOException```	Allow the application to resolve external entities by returning an `InputSource` object that describes the new input source, or `null` to request that the parser open a regular URI connection to the system identifier. This method can be used to redirect external system identifiers to secure and/or local URIs, to look up public identifiers in a catalogue, or to read an entity from a database or other input source. ❑ `publicId`: The public identifier of the external entity being referenced, or `null` if none was supplied. ❑ `systemId`: The system identifier of the external entity being referenced.

ErrorHandler

```
public interface ErrorHandler
```

Basic interface for SAX error handlers. If a SAX application needs to implement customized error handling, it must implement this interface and then register an instance with the SAX parser using the parser's setErrorHandler method. The parser will then report all errors and warnings through this interface. Note that there is no requirement that the parser continue to provide useful information after a call to fatalError. The HandlerBase class provides a default implementation of this interface, ignoring warnings and recoverable errors and throwing a SAXParseException for fatal errors. An application may extend that class rather than implementing the complete interface itself.

Methods

Signature	Description
```public void error (SAXParseException exception) throws SAXException```	Receive notification of a recoverable error. After invoking this method it should still be possible for the application to process the document through to the end. If the application cannot do so, then the parser should report a fatal error. ❑ `exception`: The error information encapsulated in a SAX parse exception.
```public void fatalError (SAXParseException exception) throws SAXException```	Receive notification of a non-recoverable error. After the parser has invoked this method the application must assume that the document is unusable, and should continue (if at all) only for the sake of collecting additional error messages. ❑ `exception`: The error information encapsulated in a SAX parse exception.
```public void warning (SAXParseException exception) throws SAXException```	Receive notification of a warning. SAX parsers will use this method to report conditions that are not errors or fatal errors. The default behavior is to take no action. After invoking this method it should still be possible for the application to process the document through to the end. ❑ `exception`: The warning information encapsulated in a SAX parse exception.

Locator

```
public interface Locator
```

Interface for associating a SAX event with a document location. This interface provides methods that the application can use to determine the current position in the source XML document. If a SAX parser provides location information to the SAX application, it does so by implementing this interface and then passing an instance to the application using the document handler's `setDocumentLocator` method. The application can use the object to obtain the location of any other document handler event in the XML source document. Note that the results returned by the object will be valid only during the scope of each document-handler method.

Methods

Signature	Description
public int getColumnNumber()	Return the column number where the current document event ends, or -1 if none is available. Note that this is the column number of the first character after the text associated with the document event. The first column in a line is position 1.
public int getLineNumber()	Return the line number where the current document event ends, or -1 if none is available. Note that this is the line position of the first character after the text associated with the document event. In practice some parsers report the line number and column number where the event starts.
public String getPublicId()	Return a string containing the public identifier for the current document event, or null if none is available.
public String getSystemId()	Return a string containing the system identifier for the current document event, or null if none is available. If the system identifier is a URL, the parser must resolve it fully before passing it to the application.

Parser (deprecated)

```
public interface Parser
```

Note that this interface has been replaced by the SAX2 XMLReader interface, which includes Namespace support.

Basic interface for SAX parsers. An application parses an XML document by creating an instance of a Parser (that is, a class that implements this interface) and calling one of its parse() methods. This interface allows applications to register handlers for different types of events and to initiate a parse from a URI, or a character stream. All SAX parsers must implement this interface and also implement a zero-argument constructor (though other constructors are also allowed). SAX parsers are reusable but not re-entrant: the application may reuse a Parser object (possibly with a different input source) once the first parse has completed successfully, but it may not invoke the parse() methods recursively within a parse.

Methods

Signature	Description
`public void parse (InputSource source) throws SAXException, IOException`	Parse an XML document. This method can be used to instruct the SAX `Parser` to begin parsing an XML document from any valid input source (a character stream, a byte stream, or a URI). Applications may not invoke this method while a parse is in progress (they should create a new `Parser` instead for each additional XML document). Once a parse is complete, an application may reuse the same `Parser` object, possibly with a different input source. ❑ `source`: The input source for the top-level of the XML document.
`public void parse (String systemId) throws SAXException, IOException`	Parse an XML document from a system identifier (URI). This method is a shortcut for the common case of reading a document from a system identifier. If the system identifier is a URL, it must be fully resolved by the application before it is passed to the parser. ❑ `systemId`: The system identifier (URI). Note that this method is the exact equivalent of the following: `parse(new InputSource(systemId));`
`public void setDocumentHandler (DocumentHandler handler)`	Allow an application to register a document event handler. If the application does not register a document handler, all document events reported by the SAX parser will be silently ignored (this is the default behavior implemented by `HandlerBase`). Applications may register a new or different handler in the middle of a parse, and the SAX parser must begin using the new handler immediately. ❑ `handler`: The document handler.
`public void setDTDHandler (DTDHandler handler)`	Allow an application to register a DTD event handler. If the application does not register a DTD handler, all DTD events reported by the SAX parser will be silently ignored (this is the default behavior implemented by `HandlerBase`). Applications may register a new or different handler in the middle of a parse, and the SAX parser must begin using the new handler immediately. ❑ `handler`: The DTD handler.
`public void setEntityResolver (EntityResolver resolver)`	Allow an application to register a custom entity resolver. If the application does not register an entity resolver, the SAX parser will resolve system identifiers and open connections to entities itself (this is the default behavior implemented in `HandlerBase`). Applications may register a new or different entity resolver in the middle of a parse, and the SAX parser must begin using the new resolver immediately. ❑ `resolver`: The object for resolving entities.

Table continued on following page

983

Signature	Description
public void setErrorHandler (ErrorHandler handler)	Allow an application to register an error event handler. If the application does not register an error event handler, all error events reported by the SAX parser will be silently ignored, except for fatalError, which will throw a SAXException (this is the default behavior implemented by HandlerBase). Applications may register a new or different handler in the middle of a parse, and the SAX parser must begin using the new handler immediately. ❑ handler: The error handler.
public void setLocale(Locale locale) throws SAXException	Allow an application to request a locale for errors and warnings. SAX parsers are not required to provide localization for errors and warnings; if they cannot support the requested locale, however, they must throw a SAX exception. Applications may not request a locale change in the middle of a parse. ❑ locale: A Java Locale object.

Classes and Interfaces new in SAX 2.0

SAX 2.0 added the following classes and interfaces to the org.xml.sax package:

Classes

SAXNotRecognizedException

```
public class SAXNotRecognizedException extends SAXException
```

Exception class for an unrecognized identifier. An XMLReader will throw this exception when it finds an unrecognized feature or property identifier; SAX applications and extensions may use this class for other, similar purposes.

Constructors

Signature	Description
public SAXNotRecognizedException (String message)	Construct a new exception with the given message. ❑ message: The text message of the exception.

Methods inherited from class org.xml.sax.SAXException:

❑ getException()

❑ getMessage()

❑ toString()

SAXNotSupportedException

```
public class SAXNotSupportedException extends SAXException
```

Exception class for an unsupported operation. An `XMLReader` will throw this exception when it recognizes a feature or property identifier, but cannot perform the requested operation (setting a state or value). Other SAX2 applications and extensions may use this class for similar purposes.

Constructors

Signature	Description
`public SAXNotSupportedException (String message)`	Construct a new exception with the given message. ❑ `message`: The text message of the exception.

Methods inherited from class `org.xml.sax.SAXException`:

❑ `getException()`

❑ `getMessage()`

❑ `toString()`

Interfaces

Attributes

```
public interface Attributes
```

Interface for a list of XML attributes: this interface allows access to a list of attributes in three different ways: by attribute index, by Namespace-qualified name, and by qualified (prefixed) name. The list will not contain attributes that were declared `#IMPLIED` but not specified in the start tag.
The order of attributes in the list is unspecified, and will vary from implementation to implementation. It will also not contain attributes used as namespace declarations (xmlns*) unless the http://xml.org/sax/features/namespace-prefixes feature is set to `true` (it is `false` by default). If this feature or the http://xml.org/sax/features/namespaces feature is `false`, access by qualified names and namespace-qualified names may not be available.

Note that this interface replaces the now-deprecated SAX1 `AttributeList` interface, which does not contain namespace support. In addition to namespace support, it adds the `getIndex()` methods.

Methods

Signature	Description
`public int getIndex (String qName)`	Look up and return the index of an attribute by XML 1.0 qualified name, or -1 if it does not appear in the list. ❑ `qName`: The qualified (prefixed) name.

Table continued on following page

Signature	Description
`public int getIndex(String uri, String localPart)`	Look up and return the index of an attribute by namespace name, or -1 if it does not appear in the list.
	❑ `uri`: The namespace URI, or the empty string if the name has no namespace URI.
	❑ `localName`: The attribute's local name.
`public int getLength()`	Return the number of attributes in the list. Once you know the number of attributes, you can iterate through the list.
`public String getLocalName (int index)`	Look up and return an attribute's local name by index, or the empty string if namespace processing is not being performed, or `null` if the index is out of range.
	❑ `index`: The attribute index (zero-based).
`public String getQName(int index)`	Look up and return an attribute's XML 1.0 qualified name by index, or the empty string if none is available, or `null` if the index is out of range.
	❑ `index`: The attribute index (zero-based).
`public String getType(int index)`	Look up and return an attribute's type by index, or `null` if the index is out of range. The attribute type is one of the strings "CDATA", "ID", "IDREF", "IDREFS", "NMTOKEN", "NMTOKENS", "ENTITY", "ENTITIES", or "NOTATION". If the parser has not read a declaration for the attribute, or if the parser does not report attribute types, then it must return the value "CDATA". For an enumerated attribute that is not a notation, the parser will report the type as "NMTOKEN".
	❑ `index`: The attribute index (zero-based).
`public String getType(String qName)`	Look up an attribute's type by XML 1.0 qualified name and return as a string, or `null` if the attribute is not in the list or if qualified names are not available. See `getType(int)` for a description of the possible string types.
	❑ qName: The XML 1.0 qualified name.
`public String getType(String uri, String localName)`	Look up an attribute's type by namespace name and return as a string, or `null` if the attribute is not in the list or if namespace processing is not being performed. See `getType(int)` for a description of the possible string types.
	❑ `uri`: The namespace URI, or the empty string if the name has no namespace URI.
	❑ `localName`: The local name of the attribute.
`public String getURI(int index)`	Look up an attribute's namespace URI by index. Returns the namespace URI of the attribute referenced by `index`, or an empty string if none is available, or `null` if the index is out of range.
	❑ `index`: The attribute index (zero-based).

Signature	Description
`public String getValue(int index)`	Look up an attribute's value by index and return as a string, or `null` if the index is out of range. If the attribute value is a list of tokens (`IDREFS`, `ENTITIES`, or `NMTOKENS`), the tokens will be concatenated into a single string with each token separated by a single space. ❑ index: The attribute index (zero-based).
`public String getValue(String qName)`	Look up an attribute's value by XML 1.0 qualified name and return as a string, or `null` if the attribute is not in the list or if qualified names are not available. See `getValue(int)` for a description of the possible values. ❑ qName: The XML 1.0 qualified name.
`public String getValue(String uri, String localName)`	Look up an attribute's value by namespace name and return as a string, or `null` if the attribute is not in the list. See `getValue(int)` for a description of the possible values. ❑ uri: The namespace URI, or the empty String if the name has no namespace URI. ❑ localName: The local name of the attribute.

ContentHandler

```
public interface ContentHandler
```

Receive notification of the logical content of a document. This is the main interface that most SAX applications implement, either directly or by subclassing the supplied class `HandlerBase`. If the application needs to be informed of basic parsing events, it implements this interface and registers an instance with the SAX parser using the `setContentHandler` method. The parser uses the instance to report basic document-related events like the start and end of elements and character data. The order of events in this interface is very important, and mirrors the order of information in the document itself. For example, all of an element's content (character data, processing instructions, and/or subelements) will appear, in order, between the `startElement` event and the corresponding `endElement` event.

Note that this interface is similar to the now-deprecated SAX1 `DocumentHandler` interface, but it adds support for namespaces and for reporting skipped entities (in non-validating XML processors).

Methods

Signature	Description
public void characters (char[] ch, int start, int length) throws SAXException	Receive notification of character data. The Parser will call this method to report each chunk of character data. SAX parsers may return all contiguous character data in a single chunk, or they may split it into several chunks; however, all of the characters in any single event must come from the same external entity so that the Locator provides useful information. Note that some parsers will report whitespace in element content using the ignorableWhitespace method rather than this one (validating parsers *must* do so). ❏ ch: The characters from the XML document. ❏ start: The start position in the array. ❏ length: The number of characters to read from the array.
public void endDocument() throws SAXException	Receive notification of the end of a document. The SAX parser will invoke this method only once, and it will be the last method invoked during the parse. The parser shall not invoke this method until it has either abandoned parsing (because of an unrecoverable error) or reached the end of input.
public void endElement(String namespaceURI, String localName, String qName) throws SAXException	Receive notification of the end of an element. The SAX parser will invoke this method at the end of every element in the XML document; there will be a corresponding startElement event for every endElement event. For information on the names, see startElement (below). ❏ namespaceuri: The namespace URI, or the empty string if the element has no namespace URI or if namespace processing is not being performed. ❏ localName: The local name (without prefix), or the empty string if namespace processing is not being performed. ❏ qName: The qualified XML 1.0 name (with prefix), or the empty string if qualified names are not available.
public void endPrefixMapping (String prefix) throws SAXException	End the scope of a prefix-URI mapping. See startPrefixMapping (below) for details. This event will always occur after the corresponding endElement event, but the order of endPrefixMapping events is not otherwise guaranteed. ❏ prefix: The prefix that was being mapping.

Signature	Description
`public void ignorableWhitespace (char[] ch, int start, int length) throws SAXException`	Receive notification of ignorable whitespace in element content. Validating Parsers must use this method to report each chunk of whitespace in element content; non-validating parsers may also use this method if they are capable of parsing and using content models. SAX parsers may return all contiguous whitespace in a single chunk, or they may split it into several chunks; however, all of the characters in any single event must come from the same external entity, so that the `Locator` provides useful information. ❏ `ch`: The characters from the XML document. ❏ `start`: The start position in the array. ❏ `length`: The number of characters to read from the array.
`public void processingInstruction (String target, String data) throws SAXException`	Receive notification of a processing instruction. The Parser will invoke this method once for each processing instruction found (processing instructions may occur before or after the main document element). A SAX parser must never report an XML declaration or a text declaration using this method. ❏ `target`: The processing instruction target. ❏ `data`: The processing instruction data, or `null` if none was supplied. The data does not include any whitespace separating it from the target.
`public void setDocumentLocator (Locator locator)`	Receive an object for locating the origin of SAX document events. If a SAX parser supplies a `Locator`, it does so by invoking this method before any other method in the `ContentHandler` interface. The `Locator` allows the application to determine the end position of any document-related event, even if the parser is not reporting an error. Note that the `Locator` will return correct information only during the invocation of the events in this interface. The application should not attempt to use it at any other time. ❏ `locator`: An object that can return the location of any SAX document event.
`public void skippedEntity (String name) throws SAXException`	Receive notification of a skipped entity. The Parser will invoke this method once for each entity skipped. Non-validating processors may skip entities if they have not seen the declarations. All processors may skip external entities, depending on the values of the http://xml.org/sax/features/external-general-entities and the http://xml.org/sax/features/external-parameter-entities properties. ❏ `name`: The name of the skipped entity. If it is a parameter entity, the name will begin with %, and if it is the external DTD subset, it will be the string `[dtd]`.

Table continued on following page

Signature	Description
`public void startDocument() throws SAXException`	Receive notification of the beginning of a document. The SAX parser will invoke this method only once, before any other methods in this interface or in `DTDHandler` (except for `setDocumentLocator`).
`public void startElement(String namespaceURI, String localName, String qName, Attributes atts) throws SAXException`	Receive notification of the beginning of an element. The Parser will invoke this method at the beginning of every element in the XML document; there will be a corresponding `endElement` event for every `startElement` event. All of the element's content will be reported, in order, before the corresponding `endElement` event.
	This event allows up to three name components for each element: the Namespace URI, the local name, and the qualified (prefixed) name. Any or all of these may be provided, depending on the values of the http://xml.org/sax/features/namespaces and the http://xml.org/sax/features/namespace-prefixes properties. The Namespace URI and local name are required when the namespaces property is `true` (the default), and are optional when the namespaces property is `false` (if one is specified, both must be). The qualified name is required when the namespace-prefixes property is `true`, and is optional when the namespace-prefixes property is `false` (the default).
	Note that the attribute list provided will contain only attributes with explicit values (specified or defaulted): `#IMPLIED` attributes will be omitted. The attribute list will contain attributes used for namespace declarations (`xmlns*` attributes) only if the http://xml.org/sax/features/namespace-prefixes property is `true` (it is `false` by default).
	❑ `namespaceuri`: The namespace URI, or the empty string if the element has no namespace URI or if namespace processing is not being performed.
	❑ `localName`: The local name (without prefix), or the empty string if namespace processing is not being performed.
	❑ `qName`: The qualified name (with prefix), or the empty string if qualified names are not available.
	❑ `atts`: The attributes attached to the element. If there are no attributes, it shall be an empty `Attributes` object.

Signature	Description
public void startPrefixMapping (String prefix, String uri) throws SAXException	Begin the scope of a prefix-URI namespace mapping. The information from this event is not necessary for normal namespace processing: the SAX XML reader will automatically replace prefixes for element and attribute names when the http://xml.org/sax/features/namespaces feature is true (the default). There are cases, however, when applications need to use prefixes in character data or in attribute values, where they cannot safely be expanded automatically; the start/endPrefixMapping event supplies the information to the application to expand prefixes in those contexts itself, if necessary. Note that start/endPrefixMapping events are not guaranteed to be properly nested relative to each other: all startPrefixMapping events will occur before the corresponding startElement event, and all endPrefixMapping events will occur after the corresponding endElement event, but their order is not otherwise guaranteed. There should never be start/endPrefixMapping events for the "xml" prefix, since it is predeclared and immutable. ❏ prefix: The namespace prefix being declared. ❏ uri: The namespace URI the prefix is mapped to.

XMLFilter

```
public interface XMLFilter extends XMLReader
```

Interface for an XML filter. This interface is like the reader, except it is used to read documents from another XML reader rather than a primary source like a document or database. Filters can modify a stream of events as they pass on to the final application. Note that the XMLFilterImpl helper class provides a convenient base for creating SAX2 filters, by passing on all EntityResolver, DTDHandler, ContentHandler, and ErrorHandler events automatically.

Methods

Signature	Description
public XMLReader getParent()	Returns the parent filter, or null if none has been set. This method allows the application to query the parent reader (which may be another filter).
public void setParent (XMLReader parent)	Set the parent reader. This method allows the application to link the filter to a parent reader (which may be another filter). The argument may not be null. ❏ parent: The parent reader.

XMLReader

```
public interface XMLReader
```

Interface for reading an XML document using callbacks. This is the interface that an XML parser's SAX2 driver must implement, which allows an application to set and query features and properties in the parser, to register event handlers for document processing, and to initiate a document parse. All SAX interfaces are assumed to be synchronous: the parse methods must not return until parsing is complete, and readers must wait for an event-handler callback to return before reporting the next event.

Note that this interface replaces the (now deprecated) SAX1 parser interface. The XMLReader interface contains two important enhancements over the old Parser interface: it adds a standard way to query and set features and properties, and it adds Namespace support, which is required for many higher-level XML standards.

Methods

Signature	Description
public ContentHandler getContentHandler()	Return the current content handler, or null if none has been registered.
public void getDTDHandler()	Return the current DTD handler, or null if none has been registered.
public EntityResolver getEntityResolver()	Return the current entity resolver, or null if none has been registered.
public ErrorHandler getErrorHandler()	Return the current error handler, or null if none has been registered.
public boolean getFeature(String name) throws SAXNotRecognizedException, SAXNotSupportedException	Look up the value of a feature and return the current state (true or false). The feature name is any fully-qualified URI. It is possible for an XMLReader to recognize a feature name but to be unable to return its value; this is especially true in the case of an adapter for a SAX1 Parser, which has no way of knowing whether the underlying parser is performing validation or expanding external entities. ❑ name: The feature name, which is a fully-qualified URI.
public Object getProperty(String name) throws SAXNotRecognizedException, SAXNotSupportedException	Look up and return the current value of a property. The property name is any fully-qualified URI. It is possible for an XMLReader to recognize a property name but to be unable to return its state; this is especially true in the case of an adapter for a SAX1 Parser. ❑ name: The feature name, which is a fully-qualified URI.

Signature	Description
`public void parse(InputSource input) throws SAXException, IOException`	Parse an XML document. The application can use this method to instruct the XML reader to begin parsing an XML document from any valid input source (a character stream, a byte stream, or a URI). Applications may not invoke this method while a parse is in progress and once a parse is complete, an application may reuse the same `XMLReader` object, possibly with a different input source. During the parse, the `XMLReader` will provide information about the XML document through the registered event handlers. This method is synchronous: it will not return until parsing has ended. If a client application wants to terminate parsing early, it should throw an exception. ❑ input: The input source for the top-level of the XML document.
`public void parse(String systemId) throws SAXException, IOException`	Parse an XML document from a system identifier (URI). If the system identifier is a URL, it must be fully resolved by the application before it is passed to the parser. ❑ systemId: The system identifier (URI).
`public void setContentHandler (ContentHandler handler) throws NullPointerException`	Allow an application to register a content event handler. If the application does not register a content handler, all content events reported by the SAX parser will be silently ignored. Applications may register a new or different handler in the middle of a parse, and the SAX parser must begin using the new handler immediately. ❑ handler: The content handler.
`public void setDTDHandler(DTDHandler handler) throws NullPointerException`	Allow an application to register a DTD event handler. If the application does not register a DTD handler, all DTD events reported by the SAX parser will be silently ignored. Applications may register a new or different handler in the middle of a parse, and the SAX parser must begin using the new handler immediately. ❑ handler: The DTD handler.
`public void setEntityResolver (EntityResolver resolver) throws NullPointerException`	Allow an application to register an entity resolver. If the application does not register an entity resolver, the `XMLReader` will perform its own default resolution. Applications may register a new or different resolver in the middle of a parse, and the SAX parser must begin using the new resolver immediately. ❑ resolver: The entity resolver.

Table continued on following page

Signature	Description
`public void setErrorHandler (ErrorHandler handler) throws NullPointerException`	Allow an application to register an error event handler. If the application does not register an error handler, all error events reported by the SAX parser will be silently ignored; however, normal processing may not continue. Applications may register a new or different handler in the middle of a parse, and the SAX parser must begin using the new handler immediately. ❑ `handler`: The error handler.
`public void setFeature(String name, boolean value) throws SAXNotRecognizedException, SAXNotSupportedException`	Set the state of a feature. The feature name is any fully-qualified URI. It is possible for an XMLReader to recognize a feature name but to be unable to set its value (especially in the case of an adapter for a SAX1 Parser, which has no way of affecting whether the underlying parser is validating). All XMLReaders are required to support setting http://xml.org/sax/features/namespaces to `true` and http: //xml.org/sax/features/namespace-prefixes to `false`. Some feature values may be available only in specific contexts, such as before, during, or after a parse. ❑ `name`: The feature name, which is a fully-qualified URI. ❑ `value`: The requested state of the feature (`true` or `false`).
`public void setProperty ( String name, Object value) throws SAXNotRecognizedException, SAXNotSupportedException`	Set the value of a property. The property name is any fully-qualified URI. It is possible for an XMLReader to recognize a property name but to be unable to set its value; this is especially true in the case of an adapter for a SAX1 parser. XMLReaders are not required to recognize setting any specific property names, though a core set is provided with SAX 2.0. Some property values may available only in specific contexts, such as before, during, or after a parse. This method is also the standard mechanism for setting extended handlers. ❑ `name`: The feature name, which is a fully-qualified URI. ❑ `value`: The requested value for the property.

The Xerces Blue
butterfly, which became
extinct earlier this century,
and after which the Xerces XML
parser is named ...

C

The W3C Document Object Model

This appendix contains the specifications of the Document Object Model, much of which is explained in Chapter 3. It is based on the definitive specifications which can be found on http://www.w3.org/DOM/.

The packages, classes, and interfaces are described in alphabetical order. Within each class, the constructors, fields, and methods are also listed alphabetically.

org.w3c.dom Package

Classes

DOMException

```
public class DOMException extends RuntimeException
```

DOM operations raise exceptions when an operation is impossible to perform; in other cases the DOM methods return specific error values. Note that implementations may raise other exceptions under certain circumstances.

Constructors

Signature	Description
`public DOMException (final short code, String message)`	Constructs an exception with the specified descriptive detail message. ❏ `code`: Integer indicating type of error. ❏ `message`: Descriptive message.

Fields

Field	Description
`public short code`	Indicates the type of error that the DOM implementation is reporting.
`public static final short DOMSTRING_SIZE_ERR`	Specified range of text does not fit into a String.
`public static final short HIERARCHY_REQUEST_ERR`	A node is inserted somewhere it doesn't belong.
`public static final short INDEX_SIZE_ERR`	Index or size is negative, or greater than the allowed value.
`public static final short INUSE_ATTRIBUTE_ERR`	An attempt to add an attribute that is already in use elsewhere.
`public static final short INVALID_CHARACTER_ERR`	An invalid character is specified.
`public static final short NO_DATA_ALLOWED_ERR`	Data is specified for a node that does not support data.
`public static final short NO_MODIFICATION_ALLOWED_ERR`	An attempt to modify an object where modifications are not allowed.
`public static final short NOT_FOUND_ERR`	An attempt to reference a node in a context where it does not exist.
`public static final short NOT_SUPPORTED_ERR`	The implementation does not support the type of object requested.
`public static final short WRONG_DOCUMENT_ERR`	A node is used in a different document from the one that created it.

Interfaces

Attr

```
public interface Attr extends Node
```

The `Attr` interface represents an attribute in an `Element` object, the allowable values of which are defined in a document type definition. `Attr` objects inherit the `Node` interface but, since they are not actually child nodes of the element they describe, the DOM does not consider them part of the document tree. Thus, the `Node` attributes `parentNode`, `previousSibling`, and `nextSibling` have a `null` value for `Attr` objects. `Attr` nodes may not be immediate children of a `DocumentFragment`, but they can be associated with `Element` nodes contained within a `DocumentFragment`.

The effective value can be explicitly assigned to an attribute; otherwise, if there is a declaration for this attribute, the default value of the declaration is the attribute's effective value. The attribute does not exist on this element in the structure model until its effective value has been added. Note that the `nodeValue` attribute on the `Attr` instance can also be used to retrieve the string version of the attribute's value(s).

Child nodes of the `Attr` node provide a representation in which entity references are not expanded. These child nodes may be either `Text` or `EntityReference` nodes.

Methods

Signature	Description
`public String getName()`	Returns the name of this attribute.
`public boolean getSpecified()`	If this attribute was explicitly given a value in the original document, this is `true`; otherwise, it is `false` (or the attribute does not appear in the structure model of the document).
`public String getValue() throws DOMException`	The value of the attribute is returned as a string. Character and general entity references are replaced with their values. On setting, this creates a `Text` node with the unparsed contents of the string such that any markup is instead treated as literal text.
`public void setValue(String value)`	Assigns the value of the `value` property.
`public Element getOwnerElement()`	The `Element` node this attribute is attached to or `null` if this attribute is not in use.

CDATASection

```
public interface CDATASection extends Text
```

CDATA sections are used to escape blocks of text containing characters that would otherwise be regarded as markup. The only delimiter that is recognized in a CDATA section is the "]]>" string that ends the CDATA section. CDATA sections cannot be nested. Their primary purpose is for including material such as XML fragments, without needing to escape all the delimiters. The DOMString attribute of the Text node holds the text that is contained by the CDATA section. The CDATASection interface inherits from the CharacterData interface through the Text interface. Adjacent CDATASection nodes are not merged by use of the normalize method of the Element interface. Because no markup is recognized within a CDATASection, character numeric references cannot be used as an escape mechanism when serializing.

CharacterData

```
public interface CharacterData extends Node
```

The CharacterData interface extends a Node with a set of attributes and methods for accessing character data in the DOM. This set is defined here rather than on each object that uses these attributes and methods. No DOM objects correspond directly to CharacterData, though Text and others do inherit the interface from it. All offsets in this interface start from 0. Text strings in the DOM are represented in UTF-16 (as a sequence of 16-bit units).

Methods

Signature	Description
public void appendData(String arg) throws DOMException	Appends the string to the end of the character data of the node. Upon success, data provides access to the concatenation of data and the DOMString specified. ❑ arg: The DOMString to append.
public void deleteData(final int offset, final int count) throws DOMException	Removes a range of 16-bit units from the node. Upon success, data and length reflect the change. If the sum of offset and count exceeds length then all 16-bit units from offset to the end of the data are deleted. ❑ offset: The offset from which to start removing. ❑ count: The number of 16-bit units to delete.
public String getData() throws DOMException	The character data of the node that implements this interface. The DOM implementation may not put arbitrary limits on the amount of data that may be stored in a CharacterData node. Implementation limits may mean that the entirety of a node's data may not fit into a single DOMString, in which case the user may call substringData to retrieve the data in appropriately sized pieces.
public int getLength()	The number of 16-bit units that are available through data and the substringData method below. This may have the value zero (CharacterData nodes may be empty).

Signature	Description
`public void insertData(final int offset, String arg) throws DOMException`	Inserts a string at the specified character offset. ❑ `offset`: The character offset at which to insert. ❑ `arg`: The `DOMString` to insert.
`public void replaceData(final int offset, final int count, String arg) throws DOMException`	Replaces the characters starting at the specified 16-bit unit offset with the specified string. If the sum of `offset` and `count` exceeds `length`, then all 16-bit units to the end of the data are replaced. ❑ `offset`: The offset from which to start replacing. ❑ `count`: The number of 16-bit units to replace. ❑ `arg`: The `DOMString` with which the range must be replaced.
`public void setData(String data)`	Assigns the value of the `data` property.
`public String substringData(final int offset, final int count) throws DOMException`	Extracts a range of data from the node. Returns the specified substring. If the sum of `offset` and `count` exceeds the `length`, then all 16-bit units to the end of the data are returned. ❑ `offset`: Start offset of substring to extract. ❑ `count`: The number of 16-bit units to extract.

Comment

```
public interface Comment extends CharacterData
```

This interface inherits from `CharacterData` and represents the content of a comment (all the characters between the starting "`<!--`" and ending "`-->`").

Document

```
public interface Document extends Node
```

The `Document` interface represents the entire document and is the root of the document tree, providing the primary access to the document's data. Since elements, text nodes, comments, processing instructions, etc. cannot exist outside the context of a `Document`, the `Document` interface also contains the methods needed to create these objects. The `Node` objects created have an `ownerDocument` attribute, which associates them with the `Document` within whose context they were created.

Methods

Signature	Description
public Attr createAttribute(String name) throws DOMException	Creates a new Attr object with the nodeName attribute set to name, and localName, prefix, and namespaceURI set to null. ❑ name: The name of the attribute. To create an attribute with a qualified name and namespace URI, use the createAttributeNS method.
public Attr createAttributeNS(String namespaceURI, String qualifiedName) throws DOMException	Creates an attribute of the given qualified name and namespace URI. ❑ namespaceURI: The namespace URI of the attribute to create. ❑ qualifiedName: The qualified name of the attribute to instantiate.
public CDATASection createCDATASection(String data) throws DOMException	Creates a new CDATASection node whose value is the specified string. ❑ data: The data for the CDATASection contents.
public Comment createComment(String data)	Creates a new Comment node given the specified string. ❑ data: The data for the node.
public DocumentFragment createDocumentFragment()	Creates an empty DocumentFragment object.
public DocumentType getDoctype()	The Document Type Declaration associated with this document. Returns null for XML documents without a document type declaration.
public Element createElement(String tagName) throws DOMException	Creates a new element with the nodeName attribute set to tagName, and localName, prefix, and namespaceURI set to null. ❑ tagName: The name of the element type to instantiate (case-sensitive). To create an element with a qualified name and namespace URI, use the createElementNS method.
public Element createElementNS(String namespaceURI, String qualifiedName) throws DOMException	Creates a new element of the given qualified name and namespace URI. ❑ namespaceURI: The namespace URI of the element to create. ❑ qualifiedName: The qualified name of the element type to instantiate.

Signature	Description
public EntityReference createEntityReference(String name) throws DOMException	Creates a new EntityReference object. If the referenced entity is known, the child list of the EntityReference node is made the same as that of the corresponding Entity node. If any descendant of the Entity node has an unbound namespace prefix, the corresponding descendant of the created EntityReference node is also unbound. ❑ name: The name of the entity to reference.
public ProcessingInstruction createProcessingInstruction (String target, String data) throws DOMException	Creates a new ProcessingInstruction node given the specified name and data strings. ❑ target: The target part of the processing instruction. ❑ data: The data for the node.
public Text createTextNode(String data)	Creates a Text node given the specified string. ❑ data: The data for the node.
public Element getDocumentElement()	This is a convenience attribute that allows direct access to the child node that is the root element of the document.
public Element getElementById(String elementId)	Returns the Element whose ID is given by elementId. Returns null if no such element exists. Behavior is not defined if more than one element has this ID. The DOM implementation must have information indicating which attributes are of type ID. Attributes with the name "ID" are not of type ID unless so defined. Implementations that do not know whether attributes are of type ID or not are expected to return null. ❑ elementId: The unique ID value for an element.
public NodeList getElementsByTagName(String tagname)	Returns a NodeList of all the Elements with a given tag name in the order in which they would be encountered in a preorder traversal of the Document tree. ❑ tagname: The name of the tag to match on. The special value "*" matches all tags.
public NodeList getElementsByTagNameNS (String namespaceURI, String localName)	Returns a NodeList object containing all the Elements with a given local name and namespace URI in the order in which they would be encountered in a preorder traversal of the Document tree. ❑ namespaceURI: The namespace URI of the elements to match on. The special value "*" matches all namespaces. ❑ localName: The local name of the elements to match on. The special value "*" matches all local names.

Table continued on following page

Signature	Description
`public DOMImplementation getImplementation()`	The `DOMImplementation` object that handles this document. A DOM application may use objects from multiple implementations.
`public Node importNode(Node importedNode, final boolean deep) throws DOMException`	Imports a node from another document to this document. The returned node has no parent (`parentNode` is `null`). The source node is not altered or removed from the original document; this method creates a new copy of the source node. ❑ `importedNode`: The node to import. ❑ `deep`: If `true`, recursively import the subtree under the specified node; if `false`, import only the node itself, as explained above. This does not apply to `Attr`, `EntityReference`, and `Notation` nodes.

DocumentFragment

```
public interface DocumentFragment extends Node
```

`DocumentFragment` is a "lightweight" `Document` object. In order to extract a portion of a document's tree or to create a new fragment of a document it is necessary have an object that can hold such fragments. A `Node` is suitable for this purpose. Various operations, such as inserting nodes as children of another `Node`, may take `DocumentFragment` objects as arguments; this results in all the child nodes of the `DocumentFragment` being moved to the child list of this node. When a `DocumentFragment` is inserted into a `Document` the children of the `DocumentFragment` (not the `DocumentFragment` itself) are inserted into the `Node`. This makes the `DocumentFragment` very useful when the user wishes to create nodes that are siblings; the `DocumentFragment` acts as the parent of these nodes so that the user can use the standard methods from the `Node` interface, such as `insertBefore` and `appendChild`.

DocumentType

```
public interface DocumentType extends Node
```

Each Document has a `doctype` attribute whose value is either `null` or a `DocumentType` object. The `DocumentType` interface in the DOM Core provides an interface to the list of entities that are defined for the document. The DOM Level 2 doesn't support editing `DocumentType` nodes.

Methods

Signature	Description
`public String getName()`	The name of DTD (specifically, the name immediately following the `DOCTYPE` keyword).
`public NamedNodeMap getEntities()`	A `NamedNodeMap` containing the general entities, both external and internal, declared in the DTD. Parameter entities are not contained and duplicates are discarded. The DOM Level 2 does not support editing entities, therefore they cannot be altered in any way.

Signature	Description
`public String getInternalSubset()`	The internal subset as a string.
`public NamedNodeMap getNotations()`	A `NamedNodeMap` containing the notations declared in the DTD. Duplicates are discarded. Every node in this map also implements the `Notation` interface. The DOM Level 2 does not support editing `notations`.
`public Element getOwnerElement()`	The `Element` node this attribute is attached to or `null` if this attribute is not in use.
`public String getPublicId()`	The public identifier of the external subset.
`public String getSystemId()`	The system identifier of the external subset.

DOMImplementation

```
public interface DOMImplementation
```

The `DOMImplementation` interface provides a number of methods for performing operations that are independent of any particular instance of the DOM.

Methods

Signature	Description
`public Document createDocument (String namespaceURI, String qualifiedName, DocumentType doctype) throws DOMException`	Creates a new XML `Document` object of the specified type with its document element. ❑ `namespaceURI`: The namespace URI of the document element to create, or `null`. ❑ `qualifiedName`: The qualified name of the document element to be created. ❑ `doctype`: The type of document to be created or `null`. When `doctype` is not `null`, its `Node.ownerDocument` attribute is set to the document being created.
`public DocumentType createDocumentType (String qualifiedName, String publicId, String systemId) throws DOMException`	Creates a new empty `DocumentType` node with `Node.ownerDocument` set to `null`. ❑ `qualifiedName`: The qualified name of the document type to be created. ❑ `publicId`: The external subset public identifier. ❑ `systemId`: The external subset system identifier.

Table continued on following page

Signature	Description
`public boolean hasFeature(String feature, String version)`	Test if the DOM implementation implements a specific feature. Returns `true` if the feature is implemented in the specified version, `false` otherwise.
	❑ `feature`: The name of the feature to test (case-insensitive). To avoid possible conflicts, as a convention, names referring to features defined outside the DOM spec. should be made unique by reversing the name of the Internet domain name of the person (or the organization) who defines the feature and use this as a prefix, for example, the W3C SYMM Working Group defines the feature `"org.w3c.dom.smil"`.
	❑ `version`: This is the version number of the feature to test, for example, in Level 2, this is the string "2.0". If the version is not specified, supporting any version of the feature causes the method to return `true`.

Element

```
public interface Element extends Node
```

The `Element` interface represents an element in a document. Elements may have attributes associated with them and, since the `Element` interface inherits from `Node`, the generic `Node` interface `attributes` may be used to retrieve the set of all attributes for an element. There are methods on the `Element` interface to retrieve either an `Attr` object by name or an attribute value by name. Where an attribute value may contain entity references, an `Attr` object should be retrieved to examine the possibly fairly complex subtree representing the attribute value. In DOM Level 2, the method `normalize()` is inherited from the `Node` interface where it was moved.

Methods

Signature	Description
`public String getAttribute(String name)`	Retrieves the `Attr` value by name, or the empty string if that attribute does not have a specified or default value.
	❑ `name`: The name of the attribute to retrieve.
`public Attr getAttributeNode (String name)`	Retrieves an attribute node by specified name (nodeName), or returns `null` if there is no such attribute.
	❑ `name`: The name (nodeName) of the attribute to retrieve.
	To retrieve an attribute node by qualified name and namespace URI, use the `getAttributeNodeNS` method.
`public Attr getAttributeNodeNS (String namespaceURI, String localName)`	Retrieves an `Attr` node by local name and namespace URI, or `null` if there is no such attribute.
	❑ `namespaceURI`: The namespace URI of the attribute to retrieve.
	❑ `localName`: The local name of the attribute to retrieve.

Signature	Description
`public String getAttributeNS(String namespaceURI, String localName)`	Retrieves an attribute value as a string by local name and namespace URI, or `null` if that attribute does not have a specified or default value. This is different from `getAttribute`, which never returns `null`. ❑ `namespaceURI`: The namespace URI of the attribute to retrieve. ❑ `localName`: The local name of the attribute to retrieve.
`public NodeList getElementsByTagName (String name)`	Returns a `NodeList` of all descendant `Element` nodes with a given tag name, in the order in which they would be encountered in a preorder traversal of the `Element` tree. ❑ `name`: The name of the tag to match on. The special value `"*"` matches all tags.
`public NodeList getElementsByTagNameNS (String namespaceURI, String localName)`	Returns a `NodeList` of all the `Elements` with a given local name and namespace URI in the order in which they would be encountered in a preorder traversal of the `Document` tree, starting from this node. ❑ `namespaceURI`: The namespace URI of the elements to match on. The special value `"*"` matches all namespaces. ❑ `localName`: The local name of the elements to match on. The special value `"*"` matches all local names.
`public String getTagName()`	The name of the element. Note that this is case-preserving.
`public boolean hasAttribute(String name)`	Returns `true` when an attribute with a given name is specified on this element or has a default value, `false` otherwise. ❑ `name`: The name of the attribute to look for.
`public boolean hasAttributeNS(String namespaceURI, String localName)`	Returns `true` when an attribute with a given local name and namespace URI is specified on this element or has a default value, `false` otherwise. ❑ `namespaceURI`: The namespace URI of the attribute to look for. ❑ `localName`: The local name of the attribute to look for.
`public void removeAttribute(String name) throws DOMException`	Removes an attribute by name. If the removed attribute is known to have a default value, an attribute immediately appears containing the default value as well as the corresponding namespace URI, local name, and prefix when applicable. ❑ `name`: The name of the attribute to remove. To remove an attribute by local name and namespace URI, use the `removeAttributeNS` method.

Table continued on following page

Signature	Description

`public Attr`
`removeAttributeNode`
`(Attr oldAttr)`
`throws DOMException`
	Removes and returns the specified attribute node. If the removed `Attr` has a default value it is immediately replaced. The replacing attribute has the same namespace URI and local name, as well as the original prefix, when applicable.
	
	❑ `oldAttr`: The `Attr` node to remove from the attribute list.

`public void`
`removeAttributeNS`
`(String`
`namespaceURI, String`
`localName) throws`
`DOMException`
	Removes an attribute by local name and namespace URI. If the removed attribute has a default value it is immediately replaced. The replacing attribute has the same namespace URI and local name, as well as the original prefix.
	
	❑ `namespaceURI`: The namespace URI of the attribute to remove.
	
	❑ `localName`: The local name of the attribute to remove.

`public void`
`setAttribute(String`
`name, String value)`
`throws DOMException`
	Adds a new attribute. If an attribute with that name is already present in the element, its value is changed to be that of the value parameter.
	
	❑ `name`: The name of the attribute to create or alter.
	
	❑ `value`: Value to set in string form.
	
	To assign an attribute value that contains entity references, the user must create an `Attr` node plus any `Text` and `EntityReference` nodes, build the appropriate subtree, and use `setAttributeNode` to assign it as the value of an attribute. To set an attribute with a qualified name and namespace URI, use the `setAttributeNS` method.

`public Attr`
`setAttributeNode`
`(Attr newAttr)`
`throws DOMException`
	Adds a new attribute node. If the `newAttr` attribute replaces an existing attribute, the replaced `Attr` node is returned, otherwise `null` is returned.
	
	❑ `newAttr`: The `Attr` node to add to the attribute list.
	
	To add a new attribute node with a qualified name and namespace URI, use the `setAttributeNodeNS` method.

`public Attr`
`setAttributeNodeNS`
`(Attr newAttr)`
`throws DOMException`
	Adds a new attribute. If the `newAttr` attribute replaces an existing attribute with the same local name and namespace URI, the replaced `Attr` node is returned, otherwise `null` is returned.
	
	❑ `newAttr`: The `Attr` node to add to the attribute list.

Signature	Description
public void setAttributeNS (String namespaceURI, String qualifiedName, String value) throws DOMException	Adds a new attribute. If an attribute with the same local name and namespace URI is already present on the element, its prefix is changed to be the prefix part of the `qualifiedName`, and its value is changed to be the `value` parameter. ❏ namespaceURI: The namespace URI of the attribute to create or alter. ❏ qualifiedName: The qualified name of the attribute to create or alter. ❏ value: The value to set in string form. To assign an attribute value that contains entity references, the user must create an `Attr` node plus any `Text` and `EntityReference` nodes, build the appropriate subtree, and use `setAttributeNodeNS` or `setAttributeNode` to assign it as the value of an attribute.

Entity

```
public interface Entity extends Node
```

This interface represents an entity, either parsed or unparsed, in an XML document. The nodeName attribute that is inherited from Node contains the name of the entity. An XML processor may choose to completely expand entities before the structure model is passed to the DOM; in this case there will be no EntityReference nodes in the document tree. Note that the DOM Level 2 does not support editing Entity nodes; if a user wants to make changes to the contents of an Entity, every related EntityReference node has to be replaced in the structure model by a clone of the Entity's contents, and then the desired changes must be made to each of those clones instead. All the descendants of an Entity node are read-only. An Entity node does not have any parent. If the entity contains an unbound namespace prefix, the namespaceURI of the corresponding node in the Entity node subtree is null. The same is true for EntityReference nodes that refer to this entity, when they are created using the createEntityReference method of the Document interface.

Methods

Signature	Description
public String getPublicId()	The public identifier associated with the entity, if specified. If the public identifier was not specified, this is null.
public String getSystemId()	The system identifier associated with the entity, if specified. If the system identifier was not specified, this is null.
public String getNotationName()	For unparsed entities, the name of the notation for the entity. For parsed entities, this is null.

EntityReference

```
public interface EntityReference extends Node
```

`EntityReference` objects may be inserted into the structure model when an entity reference is in the source document, or when the user wishes to insert an entity reference. Note that character references and references to predefined entities are considered to be expanded by the processor so that characters are represented by their Unicode equivalent rather than by an entity reference. As with the `Entity` node, all descendants of the `EntityReference` are read-only.

NamedNodeMap

```
public interface NamedNodeMap
```

Objects implementing the `NamedNodeMap` interface are used to represent collections of nodes that can be accessed by name. Note that `NamedNodeMap` does not inherit from `NodeList` and is not maintained in any particular order. Objects contained in an object implementing `NamedNodeMap` may also be accessed by an ordinal index, but this is simply to allow convenient enumeration of the contents of a `NamedNodeMap`, and does not imply that the DOM specifies an order to these `Nodes`.

Methods

Signature	Description
`public int getLength()`	The number of nodes in this map. The range of valid child node indices is 0 to `length-1` inclusive.
`public Node getNamedItem(String name)`	Retrieves a node with the specified nodeName, or `null` if it does not identify any node in this map. ❑　name: The nodeName of a node to retrieve.
`public Node getNamedItemNS(String namespaceURI, String localName)`	Retrieves a node with the specified local name and namespace URI, or `null` if it does not identify any node in this map. ❑　namespaceURI: The namespace URI of the node to retrieve. ❑　localName: The local name of the node to retrieve.
`public Node item(final int index)`	Returns the node at the indexth position in the map, or `null` if that is not a valid index. ❑　index: Index into this map.
`public Node removeNamedItem(String name) throws DOMException`	Removes and returns a node specified by name. ❑　name: The nodeName of the node to remove.
`public Node removeNamedItemNS (String namespaceURI, String localName) throws DOMException`	Removes and returns a node specified by local name and namespace URI. ❑　namespaceURI: The namespace URI of the node to remove. ❑　localName: The local name of the node to remove.

Signature	Description
`public Node setNamedItem(Node arg) throws DOMException`	Adds a node using its `nodeName` attribute. If the new `Node` replaces an existing node the replaced `Node` is returned, otherwise `null` is returned. As the `nodeName` attribute is used to derive the name which the node must be stored under, multiple nodes of certain types (those that have a "special" string value) cannot be stored as the names would clash. ❑ `arg`: A node to store in this map. The node will later be accessible using the value of its `nodeName` attribute.
`public Node setNamedItemNS(Node arg) throws DOMException`	Adds a node using its `namespaceURI` and `localName`. If the new `Node` replaces an existing node the replaced `Node` is returned, otherwise `null` is returned. ❑ `arg`: A node to store in this map. The node will later be accessible using the value of its `namespaceURI` and `localName` attributes.

Node

```
public interface Node
```

The `Node` interface is the primary data type for the entire DOM. It represents a single node in the document tree. While all objects implementing the `Node` interface expose methods for dealing with children, not all objects implementing the `Node` interface may have children. For example, `Text` nodes may not have children, and adding children to such nodes results in a `DOMException` being raised. The attributes `nodeName`, `nodeValue`, and `attributes` are included as a mechanism to get at node information without casting down to the specific derived interface. In cases where there is no obvious mapping of these attributes for a specific `nodeType` (for example, `nodeValue` for an `Element` or `attributes` for a `Comment`), this returns `null`. Note that the specialized interfaces may contain additional and more convenient mechanisms to get and set the relevant information.

Methods

Signature	Description
`public Node appendChild(Node newChild) throws DOMException`	Adds and returns the node `newChild` to the end of the list of children of this node. If the `newChild` is already in the tree, it is first removed. ❑ `newChild`: The node to add. If it is a `DocumentFragment` object, the entire contents of the document fragment are moved into the child list of this node.
`public Node cloneNode(final boolean deep)`	Returns a duplicate of this node. The duplicate node has no parent (`parentNode` returns `null`). ❑ `deep`: If `true`, recursively clone the subtree under the specified node; if `false`, clone only the node itself (and its attributes, if it is an `Element`).

Table continued on following page

1011

Signature	Description
`public NamedNodeMap getAttributes()`	A `NamedNodeMap` containing the attributes of this node (if it is an `Element`) or `null` otherwise.
`public NodeList getChildNodes()`	A `NodeList` that contains all children of this node. If there are no children, this is a `NodeList` containing no nodes. The content of the returned `NodeList` is "live" (it is not a static snapshot of the content of the node).
`public Node getFirstChild()`	The first child of this node. If there is no such node, this returns `null`.
`public Node getLastChild()`	The last child of this node. If there is no such node, this returns `null`.
`public String getLocalName()`	Returns the local part of the qualified name of this node. For nodes created with a DOM Level 1 method, such as `createElement` from the `Document` interface, it is `null`.
`public String getNamespaceURI()`	The namespace URI of this node, or `null` if it is unspecified.
`public Node getNextSibling()`	The node immediately following this node. If there is no such node, this returns `null`.
`public String getNodeName()`	The name of this node (depending on its type).
`public short getNodeType()`	A code representing the type of the underlying object, as defined above.
`public String getNodeValue() throws DOMException, DOMException`	The value of this node (depending on its type). When it is defined to be `null`, setting it has no effect.
`public Document getOwnerDocument()`	The `Document` object associated with this node (also the `Document` object used to create new nodes). `Null` when this node is a `Document` or a `DocumentType` that is not used with any `Document` yet.
`public Node getParentNode()`	The parent of this node. All nodes, except `Attr`, `Document`, `DocumentFragment`, `Entity`, and `Notation` may have a parent. However, if a node has just been created and not yet added to the tree, or if it has been removed from the tree, this is `null`.
`public String getPrefix() throws DOMException`	The namespace prefix of this node, or `null` if it is unspecified.
`public Node getPreviousSibling()`	The node immediately preceding this node. If there is no such node, this returns `null`.
`public boolean hasAttributes()`	Returns `true` if this node (if it is an element) has any attributes, `false` otherwise.

Signature	Description
`public boolean hasChildNodes()`	This is a convenience method to allow easy determination of whether a node has any children. Returns `true` if the node has any children and `false` if the node has no children.
`public Node insertBefore(Node newChild, Node refChild) throws DOMException`	Inserts and returns the node `newChild` before the existing child node `refChild`. If `refChild` is `null`, inserts `newChild` at the end of the list of children. If `newChild` is a `DocumentFragment` object, all of its children are inserted, in the same order, before `refChild`. If the `newChild` is already in the tree, it is first removed. ❑ `newChild`: The node to insert. ❑ `refChild`: The reference node.
`public void normalize()`	Puts all `Text` nodes in the full depth of the subtree underneath this `Node`, including attribute nodes, into a "normal" form where only markup separates `Text` nodes. In cases where the document contains `CDATASections`, the normalize operation alone may not be sufficient, since XPointers do not differentiate between `Text` nodes and `CDATASection` nodes.
`public Node removeChild(Node oldChild) throws DOMException`	Removes and returns the child node indicated by `oldChild` from the list of children, and returns it. ❑ `oldChild`: The node being removed.
`public Node replaceChild(Node newChild, Node oldChild) throws DOMException`	Replaces and returns the child node `oldChild` with `newChild` in the list of children, and returns the `oldChild` node. If `newChild` is a `DocumentFragment` object, `oldChild` is replaced by all of the `DocumentFragment` children, which are inserted in the same order. If the `newChild` is already in the tree, it is first removed. ❑ `newChild`: The new node to put in the child list. ❑ `oldChild`: The node being replaced in the list.
`public void setNodeValue(String nodeValue)`	Assigns the value of the `nodeValue` property.
`public void setPrefix(String prefix)`	Assigns the namespace prefix of the node.
`public boolean supports(String feature, String version)`	Tests whether the DOM implements a specific feature that is supported by this node. Returns `true` if the specified feature is supported on this node, `false` otherwise. ❑ `feature`: The name of the feature to test. This is the same name as can be passed to the method `hasFeature` on `DOMImplementation`. ❑ `version`: This is the version number of the feature to test. In Level 2, version 1, this is the string "2.0". If the version is not specified, supporting any version of the feature will cause the method to return `true`.

NodeList

```
public interface NodeList
```

The `NodeList` interface provides the abstraction of an ordered collection of nodes, without defining or constraining how this collection is implemented. The items in the `NodeList` are accessible via an integral index, starting from 0.

Methods

Signature	Description
`public int getLength()`	The number of nodes in the list. The range of valid child node indices is 0 to `length-1` inclusive.
`public Node item(final int index)`	Returns the node at the indexth position in the `NodeList`, or `null` if that is not a valid index.item in the collection. ❑ index: Index into the collection.

Notation

```
public interface Notation extends Node
```

This interface represents a notation declared in the DTD. A notation either declares, by name, the format of an unparsed entity, or is used for formal declaration of processing instruction targets. The `nodeName` attribute inherited from `Node` is set to the declared name of the notation. The DOM Level 1 does not support editing `Notation` nodes; they are therefore read-only. A `Notation` node does not have any parent.

Methods

Signature	Description
`public String getPublicId()`	The public identifier of this notation (`null` if unspecified).
`public String getSystemId()`	The system identifier of this notation (`null` if unspecified).

ProcessingInstruction

```
public interface ProcessingInstruction extends Node
```

The `ProcessingInstruction` interface is used as a way to keep processor-specific information in the text of the document.

Methods

Signature	Description
`public String getData() throws DOMException`	The content of this processing instruction. (Defined from the first non-whitespace character after the target to the character immediately preceding the `?>` .)
`public String getTarget()`	The target of this processing instruction. (Defined as being the first token following the markup that begins the processing instruction.)
`public void setData(String data)`	Assigns the value of the `data` property.

Text

```
public interface Text extends CharacterData
```

The `Text` interface inherits from `CharacterData` and represents the textual content (termed character data) of an `Element` or `Attr`.

Methods

Signature	Description
`public Text splitText(final int offset) throws DOMException`	Breaks this node into two nodes at the specified `offset`, keeping both in the tree as siblings. This node then only contains all the content up to the `offset` point. A new node of the same type, which is inserted as the next sibling of this node, contains all the content at and after the `offset` point. When the `offset` is equal to the length of this node, the new node has no data.
	❑ `offset`: The 16-bit unit offset at which to split, starting from 0.

org.w3c.dom.events Package

Classes

EventException

```
public class EventException extends RuntimeException
```

Event operations may throw an `EventException` as specified in their method descriptions.

Constructors

Signature	Description
`public EventException(final short code, String message)`	Constructs an exception with the specified descriptive detail message. ❑ code: Integer indicating type of error. ❑ message: Descriptive message.

Fields

Field	Description
`public short code`	Indicates the type of error that the implementation is reporting.
`public static final short UNSPECIFIED_EVENT_TYPE_ERR`	The Event's type was not specified by initializing the event before the method was called. Specification of the Event's type as `null` or an empty string will also trigger this exception.

Interfaces

DocumentEvent

```
public interface DocumentEvent
```

The DocumentEvent interface provides a mechanism by which the user can create an Event of a type supported by the implementation. It is expected that the DocumentEvent interface will be implemented on the same object as implements the Document interface in an implementation which supports the Event model.

Methods

Signature	Description
`public Event createEvent(String eventType) throws org.w3c.dom.DOMException`	Returns the newly created Event. ❑ eventType: The eventType parameter specifies the type of Event interface to be created.

Event

```
public interface Event
```

The Event interface is used to provide contextual information about an event to the handler processing the event. An object that implements the Event interface is generally passed as the first parameter to an event handler. More specific context information is passed to event handlers by deriving additional interfaces from Event, which contains information directly relating to the type of event they accompany. These derived interfaces are also implemented by the object passed to the event listener.

Methods

Signature	Description
public boolean getBubbles()	The bubbles property indicates whether or not an event is a bubbling event. If the event can bubble the value is true, else the value is false.
public boolean getCancelable()	The cancelable property indicates whether or not an event can have its default action prevented. If the default action can be prevented the value is true, else the value is false.
public org.w3c.dom.Node getCurrentNode()	The currentNode property indicates the Node whose EventListeners are currently being processed.
public short getEventPhase()	The eventPhase property indicates which phase of event flow is currently being evaluated.
public EventTarget getTarget()	The target property indicates the EventTarget to which the event was originally dispatched.
public long getTimeStamp()	The timeStamp specifies the time (in milliseconds relative to the epoch) at which the event was created. Note that some systems may not provide this information therefore the value of timeStamp may not be available for all events, in which case a value of 0 will be returned.
public String getType()	The type property represents the event name as a string property (must be an XML name).
public void initEvent(String eventTypeArg, final boolean canBubbleArg, final boolean cancelableArg)	The initEvent method is used to initialize the value of an Event created through the DocumentEvent interface. This method may only be called before the Event has been dispatched via the dispatchEvent method, though it may be called multiple times during that phase if necessary. If called multiple times the final invocation takes precedence. ❑ eventTypeArg: Specifies the event type. This type may be any event type currently defined in this specification or a new event type (must be an XML name). Any new event type must not begin with any upper, lower, or mixed case version of the string "DOM". ❑ canBubbleArg: Specifies whether or not the event can bubble. ❑ cancelableArg: Specifies whether or not the event's default action can be prevented.
public void preventDefault()	If an event is cancelable, the preventDefault method is used to signify that the event is to be canceled, meaning any default action normally taken by the implementation as a result of the event will not occur.
public void stopPropagation()	The stopPropagation method is used prevent further propagation of an event during event flow. If this method is called by any EventListener the event will cease propagating through the tree.

EventListener

```
public interface EventListener
```

The EventListener interface is the primary method for handling events. Users implement the EventListener interface and register their listener on an EventTarget using the AddEventListener method. The users should also remove their EventListener from its EventTarget after they have completed using the listener.

Methods

Signature	Description
public void handleEvent (Event evt)	This method is called whenever an event occurs of the type for which the EventListener interface was registered. ❏ evt: The Event contains contextual information about the event. It also contains the stopPropagation and preventDefault methods, which are used in determining the event's flow and default action.

EventTarget

```
public interface EventTarget
```

The EventTarget interface is implemented by all Nodes in an implementation that supports the DOM Event Model. The interface allows registration and removal of EventListeners on an EventTarget and dispatch of events to that EventTarget.

Methods

Signature	Description
public void addEventListener (String type, EventListener listener, final boolean useCapture)	This method allows the registration of event listeners on the event target. If an EventListener is added to an EventTarget that is currently processing an event, the new listener will not be triggered by the current event. If multiple identical EventListeners are registered on the same EventTarget with the same parameters the duplicate instances are discarded and do not cause the EventListener to be called twice. ❏ type: The event type for which the user is registering. ❏ listener: The listener parameter takes an interface implemented by the user, which contains the methods to be called when the event occurs. ❏ useCapture: If true, indicates that the user wishes to initiate capture. After initiating capture, all events of the specified type will be dispatched to the registered EventListener before being dispatched to any EventTargets beneath them in the tree.

Signature	Description
public boolean dispatchEvent (Event evt) throws EventException	This method allows the dispatch of events into the event model. The return value of dispatchEvent indicates whether any of the listeners that handled the event called preventDefault. If preventDefault was called the value is false, else the value is true. The target of the event is the EventTarget on which dispatchEvent is called. ❑　evt: Specifies the event type, behavior, and contextual information to be used in processing the event.
public void removeEvent Listener (String type, EventListener listener, final boolean useCapture)	This method allows the removal of event listeners from the event target. If an EventListener is removed from an EventTarget while it is processing an event, it will complete its current actions but will not be triggered again during any later stages of event flow. If an EventListener is removed from an EventTarget that is currently processing an event, the removed listener will still be triggered by the current event. ❑　type: The event type of the EventListener being removed. ❑　listener: Indicates the EventListener to be removed. ❑　useCapture: Specifies whether the EventListener being removed was registered as a capturing listener or not.

MutationEvent

```
public interface MutationEvent extends Event
```

The MutationEvent interface provides specific contextual information associated with Mutation events.

Methods

Signature	Description
public String getAttrName()	Indicates the name of the changed Attr node in a DOMAttrModified event.
public String getNewValue()	Indicates the new value of the Attr node in DOMAttrModified events, and of the CharacterData node in DOMCharDataModified events.
public String getPrevValue()	Indicates the previous value of the Attr node in DOMAttrModified events, and of the CharacterData node in DOMCharDataModified events.
public org.w3c.dom.Node getRelatedNode()	Used to identify a secondary node related to a mutation event.

Table continued on following page

Signature	Description
`public void initMutationEvent (String typeArg, final boolean canBubbleArg, final boolean cancelableArg, org.w3c.dom.Node relatedNodeArg, String prevValueArg, String newValueArg, String attrNameArg)`	This method is used to initialize the value of a `MutationEvent` created through the `DocumentEvent` interface. This method may only be called before the `MutationEvent` has been dispatched via the `dispatchEvent` method, though it may be called multiple times during that phase if necessary. If called multiple times, the final invocation takes precedence. ❏ `typeArg`: Specifies the event type. ❏ `canBubbleArg`: Specifies whether or not the `Event` can bubble. ❏ `cancelableArg`: Specifies whether or not the `Event`'s default action can be prevented. ❏ `relatedNodeArg`: Specifies the `Event`'s related `Node`. ❏ `prevValueArg`: Specifies the `Event`'s `prevValue` property. ❏ `newValueArg`: Specifies the `Event`'s `newValue` property. ❏ `attrNameArg`: Specifies the `Event`'s `attrName` property.

org.w3c.dom.ranges Package

Classes

RangeException

```
public class RangeException extends RuntimeException
```

Range operations may throw a `RangeException` as specified in their method descriptions.

Constructors

Signature	Description
`public RangeException (final short code, String message)`	Constructs an exception with the specified descriptive detail message. ❏ `code`: Integer indicating type of error. ❏ `message`: Descriptive message.

Fields

Field	Description
public short code	Indicates the type of error that the implementation is reporting.
public static final short BAD_BOUNDARYPOINTS_ERR	The boundary-points of a Range do not meet specific requirements.
public static final short INVALID_NODE_TYPE_ERR	The container of a boundary-point of a Range is being set to either a node of an invalid type or a node with an ancestor of an invalid type.

Interfaces

DocumentRange

```
public interface DocumentRange
```

Methods

Signature	Description
public Range createRange()	This interface can be obtained from the object implementing the Document interface using binding-specific casting methods. The initial state of the Range returned from this method is such that both of its boundary-points are positioned at the beginning of the corresponding Document, before any content. The Range returned can only be used to select content associated with this Document, or with DocumentFragments and Attrs for which this Document is the ownerDocument.

Range

```
public interface Range
```

The Event interface is used to provide contextual information about an event to the handler processing the event. An object that implements the Event interface is generally passed as the first parameter to an event handler. More specific context information is passed to event handlers by deriving additional interfaces from Event, which contains information directly relating to the type of event it accompanies. These derived interfaces are also implemented by the object passed to the event listener.

Methods

Signature	Description
public DocumentFragment cloneContents() throws DOMException	Duplicates the contents of a Range, returning a DocumentFragment containing content equivalent to this Range.

Table continued on following page

Signature	Description
`public Range cloneRange() throws DOMException`	Produces and returns a new Range whose boundary-points are equal to the boundary-points of the Range.
`public void collapse(boolean toStart) throws DOMException`	Collapses a Range onto one of its boundary-points. ❏ toStart: If true, collapses the Range onto its start; if false, collapses it onto its end.
`public short compareBoundaryPoints (short how, Range sourceRange) throws DOMException`	Compares the boundary-points of two Ranges in a document, returning -1, 0, or 1 depending on whether the corresponding boundary-point of the Range is respectively before, equal to, or after the corresponding boundary-point of sourceRange. ❏ how: A code representing the type of comparison. ❏ sourceRange: The Range on which this current Range is compared to.
`public void deleteContents() throws DOMException`	Removes the contents of a Range from the containing document or document fragment without returning a reference to the removed content.
`public void detach() throws DOMException`	Called to indicate that the Range is no longer in use and that the implementation may relinquish any resources associated with this Range.
`public DocumentFragment extractContents() throws DOMException`	Moves the contents of a Range from the containing document or document fragment to a new DocumentFragment.
`public boolean getCollapsed() throws DOMEXCEPTION`	True if the Range is collapsed
`public Node getCommonAncestor Container() throws DOMException`	The deepest common ancestor container of the Range's two boundary-points.
`public Node getEndContainer() throws DOMException`	Node within which the Range ends.
`public int getEndOffset() throws DOMException`	Offset within the ending node of the Range.
`public Node getStartContainer() throws DOMException`	Node within which the Range begins.
`public int getStartOffset() throws DOMException`	Offset within the starting node of the Range.

Signature	Description
public void insertNode(Node newNode) throws DOMException, RangeException	Inserts a node into the Document or DocumentFragment at the start of the Range. If the container is a Text node, this will be split at the start of the Range and the insertion will occur between the two resulting Text nodes. If the node to be inserted is a DocumentFragment node, the children will be inserted rather than the DocumentFragment node itself. ❑ newNode: The node to insert at the start of the Range.
public void selectNode(Node refNode) throws RangeException, DOMException	Select a node and its contents. ❑ refNode: The node to select.
public void selectNodeContents (Node refNode) throws RangeException, DOMException	Select the contents within a node. ❑ refNode: The node to select from.
public void setEnd(Node refNode, int offset) throws RangeException, DOMException	Sets the attributes describing the end of the Range. ❑ refNode: The refNode value (must be different from null). ❑ offset: The endOffset value.
public void setEndAfter(Node refNode) throws RangeException, DOMException	Sets the end of a Range to be after a node. ❑ refNodeRange: Ends after refNode.
public void setEndBefore(Node refNode) throws RangeException, DOMException	Sets the end position to be before a node. ❑ refNodeRange: Ends before refNode.
public void setStart(Node refNode, int offset) throws RangeException, DOMException	Sets the attributes describing the start of the Range. ❑ refNode: The refNode value. This parameter must be different from null. ❑ offset: The startOffset value.
public void setStartAfter(Node refNode) throws RangeException, DOMException	Sets the start position to be after a node. ❑ refNodeRange: Starts after refNode.
public void setStartBefore(Node refNode) throws RangeException, DOMException	Sets the start position to be before a node. ❑ refNodeRange: Starts before refNode.

Table continued on following page

Signature	Description
public void surroundContents (Node newParent) throws DOMException, RangeException	Reparents the contents of the Range to the given node and inserts the node at the position of the start of the Range. ❑ newParent: The node to surround the contents with.
public String toString() throws DOMException	Returns the contents of a Range as a string that contains only data characters (no markup).

org.w3c.dom.traversal Package

Interfaces

DocumentTraversal

```
public interface DocumentTraversal
```

DocumentTraversal contains methods that create iterators and tree-walkers to traverse a node and its children in document order (depth first, pre-order traversal, which is equivalent to the order in which the start tags occur in the text representation of the document).

Methods

Signature	Description
public NodeIterator createNodeIterator (org.w3c.dom.Node root, final int whatToShow, NodeFilter filter, final boolean entityReference Expansion)	Create a new NodeIterator over the subtree rooted at the specified node. ❑ root: The node that will be iterated together with its children. The iterator is initially positioned just before this node. ❑ whatToShow: This flag specifies which node types may appear in the logical view of the tree presented by the iterator. These flags can be combined using OR. ❑ filter: The Filter to be used with this TreeWalker, or null to indicate no filter. ❑ entityReferenceExpansion: The value of this flag determines whether entity reference nodes are expanded.

Signature	Description
`public TreeWalker createTreeWalker (org.w3c.dom.Node root, final int whatToShow, NodeFilter filter, final boolean entityReference Expansion) throws org.w3c.dom. DOMException`	Create a new `TreeWalker` over the subtree rooted at the specified node. ❑ root: The node that will serve as the root for the `TreeWalker` (must not be `null`). ❑ whatToShow: This flag specifies which node types may appear in the logical view of the tree presented by the iterator. These flags can be combined using OR. ❑ filter: The `Filter` to be used with this `TreeWalker`, or `null` to indicate no filter. ❑ entityReferenceExpansion: The value of this flag determines whether entity reference nodes are expanded.

NodeFilter

```
public interface NodeFilter
```

Filters are objects that know how to "filter out" nodes. If a `NodeIterator` or `TreeWalker` is given a filter, it applies the filter before it returns the next node. If the filter says to accept the node, the iterator returns it; otherwise, the iterator looks for the next node and pretends that the node that was rejected was not there. The DOM does not provide any filters. `Filter` is just an interface that users can implement to provide their own filters. One filter may be used with a number of different kinds of iterators, encouraging code reuse.

Methods

Signature	Description
`public short acceptNode (org.w3c.dom.Node n)`	Test whether a specified node is visible in the logical view of a `TreeWalker` or `NodeIterator`. Returns a constant to determine whether the node is accepted, rejected, or skipped. This function will be called by the implementation of `TreeWalker` and `NodeIterator`; it is not intended to be called directly from user code. ❑ n: The node to check to see if it passes the filter or not.

NodeIterator

```
public interface NodeIterator
```

`NodeIterators` are used to step through a set of nodes. The set of nodes to be iterated is determined by the implementation of the `NodeIterator`. DOM Level 2 specifies a single `NodeIterator` implementation for document-order traversal of a document subtree. Instances of these iterators are created by calling `DocumentTraversal.createNodeIterator()`.

Methods

Signature	Description
`public void detach()`	Detaches the iterator from the set that it iterated over, releasing any computational resources and placing the iterator in the INVALID state.
`public boolean getExpandEntity References()`	The value of this flag determines whether the children of entity reference nodes are visible to the iterator. If `false`, they will be skipped over.
`public NodeFilter getFilter()`	The filter used to screen nodes.
`public org.w3c.dom.Node getRoot()`	The root node of the Iterator, as specified when it was created.
`public int getWhatToShow()`	This attribute determines which node types are presented via the iterator. The available set of constants is defined in the `NodeFilter` interface.
`public org.w3c.dom.Node nextNode() throws org.w3c.dom. DOMException`	Returns the next `Node` in the set being iterated over and advances the position of the iterator in the set; `null` if there are no more members in that set.
`public org.w3c.dom.Node previousNode() throws org.w3c.dom. DOMException`	Returns the previous `Node` in the set being iterated over and moves the position of the iterator backwards in the set; `null` if there are no more members in that set.

TreeWalker

```
public interface TreeWalker
```

`TreeWalker` objects are used to navigate a document tree or subtree using the view of the document defined by its `whatToShow` flags and any filters that are defined for the `TreeWalker`. Nodes that are siblings in the `TreeWalker` view may be children of different, widely separated nodes in the original view.

Methods

Signature	Description
`public org.w3c.dom.Node firstChild()`	Moves the `TreeWalker` to the first visible child of the current node, and returns the new node. If the current node has no visible children, returns `null`, and retains the current node.
`public org.w3c.dom.Node getCurrentNode() throws org.w3c.dom. DOMException`	The node at which the `TreeWalker` is currently positioned. The value must not be `null`.

Signature	Description
`public boolean getExpandEntity References()`	The value of this flag determines whether the children of entity reference nodes are visible to the `TreeWalker`. If `false`, they will be skipped over.
`public NodeFilter getFilter()`	The filter used to screen nodes.
`public org.w3c.dom.Node getRoot()`	The root node of the `TreeWalker`, as specified when it was created.
`public int getWhatToShow()`	This attribute determines which node types are presented via the `TreeWalker`.
`public org.w3c.dom.Node lastChild()`	Moves the `TreeWalker` to the last visible child of the current node, and returns the new node. If the current node has no visible children, returns `null`, and retains the current node.
`public org.w3c.dom.Node nextNode()`	Moves the `TreeWalker` to the next visible node in document order relative to the current node, and returns the new node. If the current node has no next node, returns `null`, and retains the current node.
`public org.w3c.dom.Node nextSibling()`	Moves the `TreeWalker` to the next sibling of the current node, and returns the new node. If the current node has no visible next sibling, returns `null`, and retains the current node.
`public org.w3c.dom.Node parentNode()`	Moves to the closest visible ancestor node of the current node and returns the new parent node; `null` if the current node has no parent in the `TreeWalker`'s logical view.
`public org.w3c.dom.Node previousNode()`	Moves the `TreeWalker` to the previous visible node in document order relative to the current node, and returns the new node. If the current node has no previous node, returns `null`, and retains the current node.
`public org.w3c.dom.Node previousSibling()`	Moves the `TreeWalker` to the previous sibling of the current node, and returns the new node. If the current node has no visible previous sibling, returns `null`, and retains the current node.
`public void setCurrentNode (org.w3c.dom.Node currentNode)`	Assigns the `CurrentNode`.

The Xerces Blue
butterfly, which became
extinct earlier this century,
and after which the Xerces XML
parser is named ...

D

The Transformation API for XML

This appendix contains the specifications of the javax.xml.transform Package. It is based on the definitive specifications which can be found on http://java.sun.com/xml/jaxp-docs-1.1/docs/api/.

The packages, classes, and interfaces are described in alphabetical order. Within each class, the constructors, fields, and methods are also listed alphabetically.

The javax.xml.transform Package

Classes

OutputKeys

```
public class OutputKeys extends Object
```

Provides string constants that can be used to set output properties for a Transformer, or to retrieve output properties from a Transformer or Templates object. Properties in this class are read-only.

Fields

Signature	Description [XSL Specification]
public static final String CDATA_SECTION_ELEMENTS	[cdata-section-elements = expanded names] cdata-section-elements specifies a whitespace delimited list of the names of elements whose text node children should be output using CDATA sections.
public static final String DOCTYPE_PUBLIC	[doctype-public = string] See the documentation for the DOCTYPE_SYSTEM property for a description of what the value of the key should be.
public static final String DOCTYPE_SYSTEM	[doctype-system = string] doctype-public specifies the public identifier to be used in the document type declaration. doctype-system specifies the system identifier to be used in the document type declaration.
public static final String ENCODING	[encoding = string] encoding specifies the preferred character encoding that the Transformer should use to encode sequences of characters as sequences of bytes. The value of the attribute (case-insensitive) must only contain characters in the range #x21 to #x7E (printable ASCII characters). The value should either be a charset registered with the Internet Assigned Numbers Authority (IANA), or start with X-.
public static final String INDENT	[indent = "yes" | "no"] indent specifies whether the Transformer may add more whitespace when outputting the result tree; the value must be yes or no.
public static final String MEDIA_TYPE	[media-type = string.] media-type specifies the media type of the data that results from outputting the result tree. The charset parameter should not be specified explicitly; instead, when the top-level media type is text, a charset parameter should be added according to the character encoding actually used by the output method.
public static final String METHOD	[method = "xml" | "html" | "text" | expanded name] The method attribute identifies the overall method that should be used for outputting the result tree. Other non-namespaced values may be used, such as "xhtml". If any of the method values are not accepted and are not namespace qualified, then Transformer.setOutputProperty or Transformer.setOutputProperties will throw an IllegalArgumentException.
public static final String OMIT_XML_DECLARATION	[omit-xml-declaration = "yes" | "no"] This specifies whether the XSLT processor should output an XML declaration; the value must be yes or no.

Signature	Description
`public static final String STANDALONE`	[`standalone` = "yes" | "no"] Specifies whether the Transformer should output a standalone document declaration; the value must be `yes` or `no`.
`public static final String VERSION`	[`version` = `nmtoken`] Specifies the version of the output method. When the output method is "`xml`", the version value specifies the version of XML to be used for outputting the result tree. The default value for the `xml` output method is 1.0.

Transformer

```
public abstract class Transformer extends Object
```

An instance of this abstract class can transform a source tree into a result tree. An instance of this class can be obtained with the `TransformerFactory.newTransformer` method. This instance may then be used to process XML from a variety of sources and write the transformation output to a variety of sinks. An object of this class may not be used in multiple threads running concurrently. Different Transformers may be used concurrently by different threads. A Transformer may be used multiple times. Parameters and output properties are preserved across transformations.

Constructors

Signature	Description
`protected Transformer()`	Default constructor is protected on purpose.

Methods

Signature	Description
`public abstract void clearParameters()`	Clear all parameters set with `setParameter`.
`public abstract ErrorListener getErrorListener()`	Get the current error event handler in effect for the transformation, which should never be `null`.
`public abstract Properties getOutputProperties()`	Get a copy of the set of the output properties in effect for the transformation. The properties returned should contain properties set by the user, and by the stylesheet, and the default properties are specified by the XSL Transformations (XSLT) W3C Recommendation. The properties that were specifically set by the user or the stylesheet should be in the base Properties list.

Table continued on following page

Signature	Description
`public abstract String getOutputProperty (String name) throws IllegalArgumentException`	Get the string value of output property that is in effect for the transformation, or null if no property was found. The property specified may be a property that was set with setOutputProperty, or it may be a property specified in the stylesheet. ❑ name: A non-null String that specifies an output property name, which may be namespace qualified.
`public abstract Object getParameter(String name)`	Get a parameter that was explicitly set with setParameter or setParameters, or null if a parameter with the given name was not found. This method does not return a default parameter value, which cannot be determined until the node context is evaluated during the transformation process.
`public abstract URIResolver getURIResolver()`	Get an object that implements the URIResolver interface in document(), or null.
`public abstract void setErrorListener (ErrorListener listener) throws IllegalArgumentException`	Set the error event listener in effect for the transformation. ❑ listener: The new error listener.
`public abstract void setOutputProperties (Properties oformat) throws IllegalArgumentException`	Set the output properties for the transformation. These properties will override properties set in the Templates with xsl:output. If argument to this function is null, any properties previously set are removed, and the value will revert to the value defined in the templates object. ❑ oformat: A set of output properties that will be used to override any of the same properties in affect for the transformation.
`public abstract void setOutputProperty(String name, String value) throws IllegalArgumentException`	Set an output property that will be in effect for the transformation. ❑ name: A non-null String that specifies an output property name, which may be namespace qualified. ❑ value: The non-null string value of the output property.
`public abstract void setParameter(String name, Object value)`	Add a parameter for the transformation. ❑ name: The name of the parameter, which may begin with a namespace URI in curly braces ({}). ❑ value: The value object. This can be any valid Java object. It is up to the processor to provide the proper object coercion or to simply pass the object on for use in an extension.

Signature	Description
`public abstract void setURIResolver (URIResolver resolver)`	Set an object that will be used to resolve URIs used in `document()`. If the resolver argument is `null`, the URIResolver value will be cleared, and the default behavior will be used. ❑ `resolver`: An object that implements the URIResolver interface, or `null`.
`public abstract void transform(Source xmlSource, Result outputTarget) throws TransformerException`	Process the source tree to the output result. ❑ `xmlSource`: The input for the source tree. ❑ `outputTarget`: The output target.

TransformerConfigurationException

```
public class TransformerConfigurationException extends TransformerException
```

Indicates a serious configuration error.

Constructors

Signature	Description
`public TransformerConfiguration Exception()`	Create a new `TransformerConfigurationException` with no detail mesage.
`public TransformerConfiguration Exception(String msg)`	Create a new `TransformerConfigurationException` with the `String` specified as an error message. ❑ `msg`: The error message for the exception.
`public TransformerConfiguration Exception(String message, SourceLocator locator)`	Create a new `TransformerConfigurationException` from a message and a `Locator`. This is especially useful when an application is creating its own exception from within a `DocumentHandler` callback. ❑ `message`: The error or warning message. ❑ `locator`: The locator object for the error or warning.
`public TransformerConfiguration Exception(String message, SourceLocator locator, Throwable e)`	Wrap an existing exception in a `TransformerConfigurationException`. ❑ `message`: The error or warning message, or `null` to use the message from the embedded exception. ❑ `locator`: The locator object for the error or warning. ❑ `e`: Any exception.

Table continued on following page

Signature	Description
`public TransformerConfiguration Exception(String msg, Throwable e)`	Create a new `TransformerConfigurationException` with the given `Exception` base cause and detail message. ❑ `msg`: The detail message. ❑ `e`: The exception to be encapsulated in a `TransformerConfigurationException`.
`public TransformerConfiguration Exception(Throwable e)`	Create a new `TransformerConfigurationException` with a given `Exception` base cause of the error. ❑ `e`: The exception to be encapsulated in a `TransformerConfigurationException`.

TransformerException

```
public class TransformerException extends Exception
```

This class specifies an exceptional condition that occured during the transformation process.

Constructors

Signature	Description
`public TransformerException (String message)`	Create a new `TransformerException`. ❑ `message`: The error or warning message.
`public TransformerException (String message, SourceLocator locator)`	Create a new `TransformerException` from a message and a `Locator`. This constructor is useful when an application is creating its own exception from within a `DocumentHandler` callback. ❑ `message`: The error or warning message. ❑ `locator`: The locator object for the error or warning.
`public TransformerException(String message, SourceLocator locator, Throwable e)`	Wrap an existing exception in a `TransformerException`. ❑ `message`: The error or warning message, or null to use the message from the embedded exception. ❑ `locator`: The locator object for the error or warning. ❑ `e`: Any exception.

Signature	Description
`public TransformerException (String message, Throwable e)`	Wrap an existing exception in a `TransformerException`. This is used for throwing processor exceptions before the processing has started. ❑ message: The error or warning message, or `null` to use the message from the embedded exception. ❑ e: Any exception.
`public TransformerException (Throwable e)`	Create a new `TransformerException` wrapping an existing exception. ❑ e: The exception to be wrapped.

Methods

Signature	Description
`public Throwable getCause()`	Returns the cause of this exception, or `null` if the cause is nonexistent or unknown. (The cause is the throwable that caused this exception to get thrown.)
`public Throwable getException()`	This method retrieves an exception (a `Throwable` object) that this exception wraps, or `null`.
`public String getLocationAsString()`	Get the location information as a string, or `null` if there is no location information.
`public SourceLocator getLocator()`	Retrieves an instance of a `SourceLocator` object that specifies where an error occured or `null` if none was specified.
`public String getMessageAndLocation()`	Get the error message with location information appended.
`public Throwable initCause(Throwable cause) throws IllegalArgumentException, IllegalStateException`	Initializes the cause of this throwable to the specified value. (The cause is the throwable that caused this exception to get thrown.) This method can be called only once. It is generally called from within the constructor, or immediately after creating the throwable. If this throwable was created with `TransformerException(Throwable)` or `TransformerException(String,Throwable)`, this method cannot be called at all. ❑ cause: the cause (which is saved for later retrieval by the `getCause()` method). Note that a `null` value indicates that the cause is nonexistent or unknown.
`public void printStackTrace()`	Print the trace of methods from where the error originated. This will trace all nested exception objects, as well as this object.

Table continued on following page

1035

Signature	Description
public void printStackTrace(PrintStream s)	Print the trace of methods from where the error originated. This will trace all nested exception objects, as well as this object. ❏ s: The stream where the dump will be sent to.
public void printStackTrace(PrintWriter s)	Print the trace of methods from where the error originated. This will trace all nested exception objects, as well as this object. ❏ s: The writer where the dump will be sent to.
public void setLocator(SourceLocator location)	The method setLocator sets an instance of a SourceLocator object that specifies where an error occured. ❏ location: A SourceLocator object, or null to clear the location.

TransformerFactory

```
public abstract class TransformerFactory extends Object
```

A TransformerFactory instance can be used to create Transformer and Template objects. The system property that determines which Factory implementation to create is named "javax.xml.transform.TransformerFactory". This property names a concrete subclass of the TransformerFactory abstract class. If the property is not defined, a platform default is used.

Constructors

Signature	Description
protected TransformerFactory()	Default constructor is protected on purpose.

Methods

Signature	Description
public abstract Source getAssociatedStylesheet (Source source, String media, String title, String charset) throws TransformerConfiguration Exception.	Get the stylesheet specification(s) associated via the xml-stylesheet processing instruction in the form of a Source object suitable for passing to the TransformerFactory. It is possible to return several stylesheets, in which case they are applied as if they were a list of imports or cascades in a single stylesheet. ❑ source: The XML source document. ❑ media: The media attribute to be matched. May be null, in which case the prefered templates will be used. ❑ title: The value of the title attribute to match. May be null. ❑ charset: The value of the charset attribute to match. May be null.
public abstract Object getAttribute(String name) throws IllegalArgument Exception	Retrieves the value of specific attributes on the underlying implementation. ❑ name: The name of the attribute.
public abstract ErrorListener getErrorListener()	Get the current error event handler for the TransformerFactory, which should never be null.
public abstract boolean getFeature(String name)	Look up and return the value of a feature (true or false). The feature name is any absolute URI. ❑ name: The feature name, which is an absolute URI.
public abstract URIResolver getURIResolver()	Get the object (the URIResolver that was set with setURIResolver) that is used by default during the transformation to resolve URIs used in document(), xsl:import, or xsl:include.
public static TransformerFactory newInstance() throws TransformerFactory ConfigurationError	Obtain a new instance of a TransformerFactory (never null). This static method creates a new factory instance and uses the DocumentBuilderFactory system property.
public abstract Templates newTemplates(Source source) throws Transformer ConfigurationException	Process the Source into a Templates object, which is a compiled representation of the source. Returns a Templates object capable of being used for transformation purposes (never null). The Templates object may be used concurrently across multiple threads allowing the TransformerFactory a detailed performance optimization of transformation instructions, without penalizing run-time transformation. ❑ source: An object that holds a URL, input stream, etc.

Table continued on following page

Signature	Description
public abstract Transformer newTransformer(Source source) throws TransformerConfiguration Exception	Create a new `Transformer` object that performs a transformation in a single thread (never `null`). ❑ source: An object that holds a URI, input stream, etc.
public abstract Transformer newTransformer (Source source) throws TransformerConfiguration Exception	Process the `Source` into a `Transformer` object, which is returned and may be used to perform a transformation in a single thread (never `null`). Care must be given not to use this object in multiple threads running concurrently. Different `TransformerFactories` can be used concurrently by different threads. ❑ source: An object that holds a URI, input stream, etc.
public abstract void setAttribute(String name, Object value) throws IllegalArgumentException	Allows the user to set specific attributes on the underlying implementation. An attribute in this context is defined to be an option that the implementation provides. ❑ name: The name of the attribute. ❑ value: The value of the attribute.
public abstract void setErrorListener (ErrorListener listener) throws IllegalArgumentException	Set the error event listener for the `TransformerFactory`, which is used for the processing of transformation instructions, and not for the transformation itself. ❑ listener: The new error listener.
public abstract void setURIResolver (URIResolver resolver)	Set an object that is used by default during the transformation to resolve URIs used in `xsl:import`, or `xsl:include`. ❑ resolver: An object that implements the `URIResolver` interface, or `null`.

TransformerFactoryConfigurationError

```
public class TransformerFactoryConfigurationError extends Error
```

Thrown when a problem with configuration with the Transformer Factories exists. This error will typically be thrown when the class of a transformation factory specified in the system properties cannot be found or instantiated.

Constructors

Signature	Description
public TransformerFactory ConfigurationError()	Create a new `TransformerFactoryConfigurationError` with no detail mesage.

Signature	Description
`public TransformerFactory ConfigurationError (Exception e)`	Create a new `TransformerFactoryConfigurationError` with a given `Exception` base cause of the error. ❑ e: The exception to be encapsulated in a `TransformerFactoryConfigurationError`.
`public TransformerFactory ConfigurationError (Exception e, String msg)`	Create a new `TransformerFactoryConfigurationError` with the given `Exception` base cause and detail message. ❑ e: The exception to be encapsulated in a `TransformerFactoryConfigurationError`. ❑ msg: The detail message.
`public TransformerFactory ConfigurationError (String msg)`	Create a new `TransformerFactoryConfigurationError` with the `String` specified as an error message. ❑ msg: The error message for the exception.

Methods

Signature	Description
`public Exception getException()`	Returns the actual exception (if any) that caused this exception to be raised, or `null` if there is none.
`public String getMessage()`	Returns the message (if any) for this error. If there is no message for the exception then the message of the encapsulated exception (if any) will be returned.

Interfaces

ErrorListener

```
public interface ErrorListener
```

To provide customized error handling, implement this interface and use the `setErrorListener` method to register an instance of the implmentation with the Transformer. The Transformer then reports all errors and warnings through this interface. If an application does not register an `ErrorListener`, errors are reported to `System.err`. For transformation errors, a Transformer must use this interface instead of throwing an exception: it is up to the application to decide whether to throw an exception for different types of errors and warnings. Note however that the Transformer is not required to continue with the transformation after a call to `fatalError`. Transformers may use this mechanism to report XML parsing errors as well as transformation errors.

Methods

Signature	Description
`public void error(TransformerException exception) throws TransformerException`	Receive notification of a recoverable error. After invoking this method, the transformer must continue to try to provide normal transformations. If no other errors are encountered, it should still be possible for the application to process the document through to the end. ❑ `exception`: The error information encapsulated in a transformer exception.
`public void fatalError(Transformer Exception exception) throws TransformerException`	Receive notification of a non-recoverable error. After invoking this method, the transformer must continue to try to provide normal transformations. If no other errors are encountered, it should still be possible for the application to process the document through to the end, but there is no guarantee that the output will be useable. ❑ `exception`: The error information encapsulated in a transformer exception.
`public void warning(Transformer Exception exception) throws TransformerException`	Receive notification of a warning. Transformers can use this method to report conditions that are not errors or fatal errors (default behaviour is to take no action). After invoking this method, the Transformer must continue with the transformation. and it should still be possible for the application to process the document through to the end. ❑ `exception`: The warning information encapsulated in a transformer exception.

Result

```
public interface Result
```

An object that implements this interface contains the information needed to build a transformation result tree.

Fields

Signature	Description
`public static final String PI_DISABLE_OUTPUT_ESCAPING`	The name of the processing instruction that is sent if the result tree disables output escaping. Normally, result tree serialization escapes & and < (and possibly other characters) when outputting text nodes. This ensures that the output is well-formed XML. However, it is sometimes convenient to be able to produce output that is almost, but not quite well-formed XML. If a processing instruction is sent with this name, serialization should be output without any escaping.

Signature	Description
`public static final String PI_ENABLE_OUTPUT_ESCAPING`	The name of the processing instruction that is sent if the result tree enables output escaping at some point after having received a `PI_DISABLE_OUTPUT_ESCAPING` processing instruction.

Methods

Signature	Description
`public String getSystemId()`	Returns the system identifier that was set with `setSystemId`, or `null` if `setSystemId` was not called.
`public void setSystemId (String systemId)`	Sets the system identifier for this `Result`. If the `Result` is not to be written to a file, the system identifier is optional. The application may still want to provide one, however, for use in error messages and warnings, or to resolve relative output identifiers. ❑ `systemId`: The system identifier as a URI string.

Source

```
public interface Source
```

An object that implements this interface contains the information needed to act as source input (XML source or transformation instructions).

Methods

Signature	Description
`public String getSystemId()`	Returns the system identifier that was set with `setSystemId`, or `null` if `setSystemId` was not called.
`public void setSystemId (String systemId)`	Sets the system identifier for this `Source`. The system identifier is optional if the source does not get its data from a URL, but it may still be useful to provide one. The application can use a system identifier, for example, to resolve relative URIs and to include in error messages and warnings. ❑ `systemId`: The system identifier as a URL string.

SourceLocator

```
public interface SourceLocator
```

This interface is primarily for the purposes of reporting where an error occurred in the XML source or transformation instructions.

Methods

Signature	Description
`public int getColumnNumber()`	Return the column number where the current document event ends, or -1 if none is available. Note that the return value is an approximation of the column number in the document entity or external parsed entity (for the sake of error reporting) where the markup that triggered the event appears.
`public int getLineNumber()`	Return the line number where the current document event ends, or -1 if none is available. Note that the return value is an approximation of the column number in the document entity or external parsed entity (for the sake of error reporting) where the markup that triggered the event appears.
`public String getPublicId()`	Return a string containing the public identifier for the current document event, or `null` if none is available. The return value is the public identifier of the document entity or of the external parsed entity in which the markup that triggered the event appears.
`public String getSystemId()`	Return a string containing the system identifier for the current document event, or `null` if none is available. The return value is the system identifier of the document entity or of the external parsed entity in which the markup that triggered the event appears. If the system identifier is a URL, the parser must resolve it fully before passing it to the application.

Templates

```
public interface Templates
```

An object that implements this interface is the run-time representation of processed transformation instructions. `Templates` must be threadsafe for a given instance over multiple threads running concurrently, and may be used multiple times in a given session.

Methods

Signature	Description
`public Properties getOutputProperties()`	Get the static properties for `xsl:output` (never `null`). The object returned will be a clone of the internal values which can be mutated without mutating the `Templates` object, and then handed in to `Transformer.setOutputProperties`. The properties returned should contain properties set by the stylesheet. The default properties are specified by the XSL Transformations (XSLT) W3C Recommendation. The properties that were specifically set by the stylesheet should be in the base `Properties` list, while the XSLT default properties that were not specifically set should be in the "default" `Properties` list.

Signature	Description
`public Transformer newTransformer() throws TransformerConfiguration Exception`	Create a new transformation context for this `Templates` object returning a valid (non-`null`) instance of a `Transformer`.

URIResolver

```
public interface URIResolver
```

An object that implements this interface that can be called by the processor to turn a URI used in `document()`, `xsl:import`, or `xsl:include` into a `Source` object.

Methods

Signature	Description
`public Source resolve(String href, String base) throws TransformerException`	Called by the processor when it encounters an xsl:include, xsl:import, or document() function. Returns a Source object, or `null` if the href cannot be resolved.
	❑ `href`: An href attribute, which may be relative or absolute.
	❑ `base`: The base URI in effect when the href attribute was encountered.

The javax.xml.transform.dom Package

Classes

DOMResult

```
public class DOMResult extends Object implements Result
```

Acts as a holder for a transformation result tree, in the form of a DOM tree. If no output DOM source is set, the transformation will create a `Document` node as the holder for the result of the transformation, which may be retrieved with `getNode`.

Constructors

Signature	Description
`public DOMResult()`	Zero-argument default constructor.
`public DOMResult (Node node)`	Use a DOM node to create a new output target. The node should be a `Document` node, a `DocumentFragment` node, or an `Element` node (a node that accepts children).
	❑ `node`: The DOM node that will contain the result tree.

Table continued on following page

Signature	Description
public DOMResult(Node node, String systemID)	Create a new output target with a DOM node. The node should be a Document node, a DocumentFragment node, or an Element node (a node that accepts children). ❑ node: The DOM node that will contain the result tree. ❑ systemID: The system identifier that may be used in association with this node.

Fields

Signature	Description
public static final String FEATURE	If TransformerFactory.getFeature returns true when given this value as an argument, the Transformer supports Result output of this type.

Methods

Signature	Description
public Node getNode()	Returns the node that will contain the result DOM tree. If no node was set via setNode, the node will be set by the transformation, and may be obtained from this method once the transformation is complete.
public String getSystemId()	Returns the system identifier that was set with setSystemId, or null if setSystemId was not called.
public void setNode(Node node)	Sets the node that will contain the result DOM tree. In practice, the node should be a Document node, a DocumentFragment node, or an Element node (that is, a node that accepts children). ❑ node: The node to which the transformation will be appended.
public void setSystemId (String systemId)	Sets the systemID that may be used in association with the node. ❑ systemId: The system identifier as a URI string.

DOMSource

```
public class DOMSource extends Object implements Source
```

Acts as a holder for a transformation Source tree in the form of a DOM tree.

Constructors

Signature	Description
`public DOMSource()`	Zero-argument default constructor. If no DOM source is set, the Transformer will create an empty source `Document` using `DocumentBuilder.newDocument`.
`public DOMSource(Node n)`	Create a new input source with a DOM node. The operation will be applied to the subtree rooted at this node. ❑ n: The DOM node that will contain the `Source` tree.
`public DOMSource(Node node, String systemID)`	Create a new input source with a DOM node, and with the system ID also passed in as the base URI. ❑ node: The DOM node that will contain the `Source` tree. ❑ systemID: Specifies the base URI associated with node.

Fields

Signature	Description
`public static final String FEATURE`	If `TransformerFactory` returns `true` when given this value, the Transformer supports `Source` input of this type.

Methods

Signature	Description
`public Node getNode()`	Get the node that represents a `Source` DOM tree.
`public String getSystemId()`	Get the base ID (URL or system ID) from where URLs will be resolved for this DOM tree.
`public void setNode (Node node)`	Set the node that will represents a `Source` DOM tree. ❑ node: The node that is to be transformed.
`public void setSystemId (String baseID)`	Set the base ID (URL or system ID) from where URLs will be resolved. ❑ baseID: Base URL for this DOM tree.

Interfaces

DOMLocator

```
public interface DOMLocator
```

Indicates the position of a node in a source DOM, intended primarily for error reporting. To use a DOMLocator, the receiver of an error must downcast the SourceLocator object returned by an exception. A Transformer may use this object for purposes other than error reporting, for instance, to indicate the source node that originated a result node.

Methods

Signature	Description
public Node getOriginatingNode()	Returns the node that is the location for the event.

The javax.xml.transform.sax Package

Classes

SAXResult

```
public class SAXResult extends Object implements Result
```

Acts as a holder for a transformation Result.

Constructors

Signature	Description
public SAXResult()	Zero-argument default constructor.
public SAXResult (ContentHandler handler)	Create a SAXResult that targets a SAX2 ContentHandler. ❑ handler: Must be a non-null ContentHandler reference.

Fields

Signature	Description
public static final String FEATURE	If TransformerFactory.getFeature returns true when given this value, the Transformer supports Result output.

Methods

Signature	Description
public ContentHandler getHandler()	Returns the ContentHandler that is to be the output.
public LexicalHandler getLexicalHandler()	Returns a SAX2 LexicalHandler for the output, or null.
public String getSystemId()	Returns the system identifier that was set with setSystemId, or null if setSystemId was not called.
public void setHandler(Content Handler handler)	Sets the target to be a SAX2 ContentHandler. ❑ handler: Must be a non-null ContentHandler reference.

Signature	Description
public void setLexicalHandler (LexicalHandler handler)	Sets the SAX2 LexicalHandler for the output (required to handle XML comments). If the lexical handler is not set, an attempt should be made by the transformer to cast the ContentHandler to a LexicalHandler. ❑ handler: A non-null LexicalHandler for handling lexical parse events.
public void setSystemId(String systemId)	Sets the systemID that may be used in association with the ContentHandler. ❑ systemId: The system identifier as a URI string.

SAXSource

```
public class SAXSource extends Object implements Source
```

Acts as a holder for SAX-style Source.

Constructors

Signature	Description
public SAXSource()	Zero-argument default constructor. If this constructor is used, and no other method is called, the Transformer assumes an empty input tree, with a default root node.
public SAXSource(InputSource inputSource)	Create a SAXSource, using a SAX InputSource. The Transformer or SAXTransformerFactory creates a reader via XMLReaderFactory (if setXMLReader is not used), sets itself as the reader's ContentHandler, and calls reader.parse(inputSource). ❑ inputSource: An input source reference that must be non-null and that will be passed to the parse method of the reader.
public SAXSource (XMLReader reader, InputSource inputSource)	Create a SAXSource, using an XMLReader and a SAX InputSource. The Transformer or SAXTransformerFactory will set itself to be the reader's ContentHandler, and then will call reader.parse(inputSource). ❑ reader: An XMLReader to be used for the parse. ❑ inputSource: A SAX input source reference that must be non-null and that will be passed to the reader parse method.

Fields

Signature	Description
`public static final String FEATURE`	If `TransformerFactory.getFeature` returns `true` when given this value as an argument, the Transformer supports `Source` input of this type.

Methods

Signature	Description
`public InputSource getInputSource()`	Returns a valid `InputSource` reference, or `null`.
`public String getSystemId()`	Returns the Base URL for the `Source`, or `null`.
`public XMLReader getXMLReader()`	Returns a valid `XMLReader` or `XMLFilter` reference, or `null`.
`public void setInputSource(Input Source inputSource)`	Set the SAX `InputSource` to be used for the `Source`. ❑ `inputSource`: A valid `InputSource` reference.
`public void setSystemId(String systemId)`	Sets the system identifier for this `Source`. If an input source has already been set, it will set the system ID or that input source, otherwise it will create a new input source. System identifier is optional if there is a byte stream or a character stream, but it is still useful to provide one, since the application can use it to resolve relative URIs and can include it in error messages and warnings. ❑ `systemId`: The system identifier as a URI string.
`public void setXMLReader(XMLReader reader)`	Set the `XMLReader` to be used for the `Source`. ❑ `reader`: A valid `XMLReader` or `XMLFilter` reference.
`public static InputSource sourceToInputSource (Source source)`	Returns a SAX `InputSource` object from a TrAX `Source` object, or `null` if `Source` can not be converted. ❑ `source`: Must be a non-null `Source` reference.

SAXTransformerFactory

```
public abstract class SAXTransformerFactory extends TransformerFactory
```

This class extends `TransformerFactory` to provide SAX-specific factory methods. It provides two types of `ContentHandlers`, one for creating Transformers, the other for creating `Templates` objects. If an application wants to set the `ErrorHandler` or `EntityResolver` for an `XMLReader` used during a transformation, it should use a `URIResolver` to return the `SAXSource` which provides (with `getXMLReader`) a reference to the `XMLReader`.

Constructors

Signature	Description
`protected SAXTransformerFactory()`	The default constructor is protected on purpose.

Fields

Signature	Description
`public static final String FEATURE`	If `TransformerFactory.getFeature` returns `true` when given this value as an argument, the `TransformerFactory` returned from `TransformerFactory.newInstance` may be safely cast to a `SAXTransformerFactory`.
`public static final String FEATURE_XMLFILTER`	If `TransformerFactory.getFeature` returns `true` when given this value as an argument, the `newXMLFilter(Source src)` and `newXMLFilter(Templates templates)` methods are supported.

Methods

Signature	Description
`public abstract TemplatesHandler newTemplatesHandler() throws Transformer ConfigurationException`	Returns a non-null reference to a `TransformerHandler`, that may be used as a `ContentHandler` for SAX parse events.
`public abstract TransformerHandler newTransformerHandler() throws Transformer ConfigurationException`	Returns a non-null reference to a `TransformerHandler`, that may be used as a `ContentHandler` for SAX parse events. The transformation is defined as an identity (or copy) transformation.
`public abstract TransformerHandler newTransformerHandler (Source src) throws Transformer ConfigurationException`	Returns a `TransformerHandler` object that can process SAX `ContentHandler` events into a `Result`, based on the transformation instructions specified by the argument. ❑ src: The `Source` of the transformation instructions.
`public abstract TransformerHandler newTransformerHandler (Templates templates) throws Transformer ConfigurationException`	Returns a `TransformerHandler` object that can process SAX `ContentHandler` events into a `Result`, based on the `Templates` argument. ❑ templates: The compiled transformation instructions.
`public abstract XMLFilter newXMLFilter(Source src) throws Transformer ConfigurationException`	Create an `XMLFilter` object that uses the given `Source` as the transformation instructions, or `null` if this feature is not supported. ❑ src: The `Source` of the transformation instructions.
`public abstract XMLFilter newXMLFilter (Templates templates) throws Transformer ConfigurationException`	Returns an `XMLFilter` object based on the `Templates` argument, or `null` if this feature is not supported. ❑ templates: The compiled transformation instructions.

Interfaces

TemplatesHandler

```
public interface TemplatesHandler extends TemplatesHandler
```

A SAX `ContentHandler` that may be used to process SAX parse events (parsing transformation instructions) into a `Templates` object. Note that `TemplatesHandler` does not need to implement `LexicalHandler`.

Methods

Signature	Description
public String getSystemId()	Returns the `systemID` that was set with `setSystemId`.
public void setSystemId(String systemID)	Sets the base ID (URI or system ID) for the `Templates` object created by this builder. This must be set in order to resolve relative URIs in the stylesheet and must be called before the `startDocument` event. ❑ `baseID`: Base URI for this stylesheet.
public Templates getTemplates()	When a `TemplatesHandler` object is used as a `ContentHandler` for the parsing of transformation instructions, it creates and returns a `Templates` object, which the caller can get once the SAX events have been completed.

TransformerHandler

```
public interface TransformerHandler extends ContentHandler, LexicalHandler,
DTDHandler
```

A `TransformerHandler` listens for SAX `ContentHandler` parse events and transforms them to a `Result`.

Methods

Signature	Description
public String getSystemId()	Returns the `systemID` that was set with `setSystemId`.
public Transformer getTransformer()	Gets the `Transformer` associated with this handler (required in order to set parameters and output properties).
public void setResult (Result result) throws IllegalArgumentException	Enables the user of the TransformerHandler to set the `Result` for the transformation. ❑ `result`: A Result instance, should not be `null`.
public void setSystemId (String systemID)	Sets the base ID from where relative URLs will be resolved. ❑ `systemID`: Base URI for the source tree.

The javax.xml.transform.stream Package

Classes

StreamResult

```
public class StreamResult extends Object implements Result
```

Acts as a holder for a transformation result, which may be XML, plain Text, HTML, or some other form of markup.

Constructors

Signature	Description
public StreamResult()	Zero-argument default constructor.
public StreamResult (File f)	Construct a StreamResult from a File. ❏ f: Must a non-null File reference.
public StreamResult (OutputStream outputStream)	Construct a StreamResult from a byte stream. ❏ outputStream: A valid OutputStream reference.
public StreamResult (String systemId)	Construct a StreamResult from a URL. ❏ systemId: Must be a String that conforms to the URI syntax.
public StreamResult (Writer writer)	Construct a StreamResult from a character stream. ❏ writer: A valid Writer reference.

Fields

Signature	Description
public static final String FEATURE	If TransformerFactory.getFeature returns true when given this value as an argument, the Transformer supports Result output of this type.

Methods

Signature	Description
public OutputStream getOutputStream()	Returns the byte stream that was set with setOutputStream, or null if setOutputStream or the ByteStream constructor was not called.
public String getSystemId()	Returns the system identifier that was set with setSystemId, or null if setSystemId was not called.

Table continued on following page

Signature	Description
`public Writer getWriter()`	Returns the character stream that was set with `setWriter`, or `null` if `setWriter` or the `Writer` constructor was not called.
`public void setOutputStream(Output Stream outputStream)`	Set the `ByteStream` that is to be written to. ❑ `outputStream`: A valid `OutputStream` reference.
`public void setSystemId(File f)`	Set the `systemId` from a `File` reference. ❑ `f`: Must a non-null `File` reference.
`public void setSystemId(String systemId)`	Set the `systemID` that may be used in association with the byte or character stream, or, if neither is set, use this value as a writeable URI (probably a file name). ❑ `systemId`: The system identifier as a URI string.
`public void setWriter(Writer writer)`	Set the writer that is to receive the result. ❑ `writer`: A valid `Writer` reference.

StreamSource

```
public class StreamSource extends Object implements Source
```

Acts as a holder for a transformation `Source` in the form of a stream of XML markup.

Constructors

Signature	Description
`public StreamSource()`	Zero-argument default constructor. If this constructor is used, and no other method is called, the transformer will assume an empty input tree, with a default root node.
`public StreamSource(File f)`	Construct a `StreamSource` from a `File`. ❑ `f`: Must a non-null `File` reference.
`public StreamSource (InputStream inputStream)`	Construct a `StreamSource` from a byte stream. ❑ `inputStream`: A valid `InputStream` reference to an XML stream.
`public StreamSource (InputStream inputStream, String systemId)`	Construct a `StreamSource` from a byte stream. This constructor allows the `systemID` to be set in addition to the input stream, which allows relative URIs to be processed. ❑ `inputStream`: A valid `InputStream` reference to an XML stream. ❑ `systemId`: Must be a `String` that conforms to the URI syntax.

Signature	Description
public StreamSource(Reader reader)	Construct a StreamSource from a character reader. ❑ reader: A valid Reader reference to an XML character stream.
public StreamSource (Reader reader, String systemId)	Construct a StreamSource from a character reader. ❑ reader: A valid Reader reference to an XML character stream. ❑ systemId: Must be a String that conforms to the URI syntax.
public StreamSource (String systemId)	Construct a StreamSource from a URL. ❑ systemId: Must be a String that conforms to the URI syntax.

Fields

Signature	Description
public static final String FEATURE	If TransformerFactory.getFeature returns true when passed this value as an argument, the Transformer supports Source input of this type.

Methods

Signature	Description
public InputStream getInputStream()	Returns the byte stream that was set with setByteStream, or null if setByteStream or the ByteStream constructor was not called.
public String getPublicId()	Returns the public identifier that was set with setPublicId, or null if setPublicId was not called.
public Reader getReader()	Returns the character stream that was set with setReader, or null if setReader or the Reader constructor was not called.
public String getSystemId()	Returns the system identifier that was set with setSystemId, or null if setSystemId was not called.
public void setInputStream(Input Stream inputStream)	Set the byte stream to be used as input. Normally, a stream should be used rather than a reader, so that the XML parser can resolve character encoding specified by the XML declaration. If this Source object is used to process a stylesheet, normally setSystemId should also be called, so that relative URL references can be resolved. ❑ inputStream: A valid InputStream reference to an XML stream.

Table continued on following page

Signature	Description
`public void setPublicId (String publicId)`	Set the public identifier for this `Source`. Note that the public identifier is always optional. If the application writer includes one, it will be provided as part of the location information. ❏ `publicId`: The public identifier as a string.
`public void setReader (Reader reader)`	Set the input to be a character reader. ❏ `reader`: A valid `Reader` reference to an XML `CharacterStream`.
`public void setSystemId(File f)`	Set the system ID from a `File` reference. ❏ `f`: Must a non-null `File` reference.
`public void setSystemId (String systemId)`	Set the system identifier for this `Source`. Note that the system identifier is optional if there is a byte stream or a character stream, but it is still useful to provide one, since the application can use it to resolve relative URIs and can include it in error messages and warnings (the parser will attempt to open a connection to the URI only if there is no byte stream or character stream specified). ❏ `systemId`: The system identifier as a URL string.

The Xerces Blue
butterfly, which became
extinct earlier this century,
and after which the Xerces XML
parser is named ...

E

JAXP 1.1 API

The javax.xml.parsers Package

This appendix contains the specification of JAXP 1.1 API. It is based on the definitive specification to be found on http://java.sun.com/xml/jaxp-docs-1.1/docs/api.

This package provides classes allowing the processing of XML documents. Two types of pluggable parsers are supported:

- ❑   SAX (Simple API for XML)
- ❑   DOM (Document Object Model)

Below is a summary of the Classes, Exceptions, and Errors:

- ❑   `DocumentBuilder` - Defines the API to obtain DOM `Document` instances from an XML document.

- ❑   `DocumentBuilderFactory` – Defines a factory API that enables applications to obtain a parser that produces DOM object trees from XML documents.

- ❑   `SAXParser` – Defines the API that wraps an `org.xml.sax.XMLReader` implementation class.

- ❑   `SAXParserFactory` – Defines a factory API that enables applications to configure and obtain a SAX-based parser to parse XML documents.

- ❑   `ParserConfigurationException` – Indicates a serious configuration error.

- ❑   `FactoryConfigurationError` – Thrown when a problem with the configuration of parser factories exists.

Included here is a class-by-class breakdown in which the classes are described in alphabetical order. Within each class, the constructors and methods are also listed alphabetically.

Classes

DocumentBuilder

```
public abstract class DocumentBuilder extends Object
```

Defines the API to obtain DOM Document instances from an XML document. Using this class, an application programmer can obtain an org.w3c.dom.Document from XML. An instance of this class can be obtained from the DocumentBuilderFactory.newDocumentBuilder() method. Once an instance of this class is obtained, XML can be parsed from the following input sources: input streams, files, URLs, and SAX InputSources.

Methods

Signature	Description
public abstract DOMImplementation getDOMImplementation()	Obtains a new instance of a DOMImplementation object.
public abstract boolean isNamespaceAware()	Indicates whether or not this parser is configured to understand namespaces.
public abstract boolean isValidating()	Indicates whether or not this parser is configured to validate XML documents.
public abstract Document newDocument()	Obtains a new instance of a DOM Document object to build a DOM tree with.
public Document parse(File f) throws SAXException, IOException	Parses the content of the given file as an XML document and return a new DOM Document object. ❑ f: The file containing the XML to parse
public abstract Document parse(InputSource is) throws SAXException, IOException	Parses the content of the given input source as an XML document and return a new DOM Document object. ❑ is: InputSource containing the content to be parsed.
public Document parse(InputStream is) throws SAXException, IOException	Parses the content of the given InputStream as an XML document and return a new DOM Document object. ❑ is: InputStream containing the content to be parsed.
public Document parse(InputStream is, String systemId) throws SAXException, IOException	Parses the content of the given InputStream as an XML document and return a new DOM Document object. ❑ is: InputStream containing the content to be parsed. ❑ systemId: Provides a base for resolving relative URIs.

Signature	Description
`public Document parse(String uri) throws SAXException, IOException`	Parses the content of the given URI as an XML document and return a new DOM `Document` object. ❑ uri: The location of the content to be parsed.
`public abstract void setEntityResolver (EntityResolver er)`	Specifies the `EntityResolver` to be used to resolve entities present in the XML document to be parsed. Setting this to `null` will result in the underlying implementation using its own default implementation and behavior.
`public abstract void setErrorHandler (ErrorHandler eh)`	Specifies the `ErrorHandler` to be used to resolve entities present in the XML document to be parsed. Setting this to `null` will result in the underlying implementation using its own default implementation and behavior.

DocumentBuilderFactory

```
public abstract class DocumentBuilderFactory extends Object
```

Defines a factory API that enables applications to obtain a parser that produces DOM object trees from XML documents.

Methods

Signature	Description
`public abstract Object getAttribute (String name) throws Illegal ArgumentException`	Allows the user to retrieve specific attributes on the underlying implementation, returning the value of the attribute. ❑ name: The name of the attribute.
`public boolean isCoalescing()`	Indicates (`true` or `false`) whether or not the factory is configured to produce parsers that convert CDATA nodes to `Text` nodes and appends it to the adjacent (if any) `Text` node.
`public boolean isExpandEntity References()`	Indicates (`true` or `false`) whether or not the factory is configured to produce parsers that expand entity reference nodes.
`public boolean isIgnoringComments()`	Indicates (`true` or `false`) whether or not the factory is configured to produce parsers that ignore comments.
`public boolean isIgnoringElement ContentWhitespace()`	Indicates (`true` or `false`) whether or not the factory is configured to produce parsers that ignore ignorable whitespace in element content.
`public boolean isNamespaceAware()`	Indicates (`true` or `false`) whether or not the factory is configured to produce parsers that are namespace aware.
`public boolean isValidating()`	Indicates (`true` or `false`) whether or not the factory is configured to produce parsers that validate the XML content during parse.

Table continued on following page

Signature	Description
`public abstract DocumentBuilder newDocumentBuilder() throws Parser Configuration Exception`	Creates a new instance of a `DocumentBuilder` using the currently configured parameters.
`public static DocumentBuilderFactory newInstance()`	Obtains a new instance of a `DocumentBuilderFactory`. This static method creates a new factory instance based on a System property setting or uses the platform default if no property has been defined. The system property that controls which Factory implementation to create is named `"javax.xml.parsers. DocumentBuilderFactory"`. This property names a class that is a concrete subclass of this abstract class. If no property is defined, a platform default will be used. Once an application has obtained a reference to a `DocumentBuilderFactory` it can use the factory to configure and obtain parser instances.
`public abstract void setAttribute(String name, Object value) throws IllegalArgument Exception`	Allows the user to set specific attributes on the underlying implementation. ❑ `name`: The name of the attribute. ❑ `value`: The value of the attribute.
`public void setCoalescing (boolean coalescing)`	Specifies that the parser produced by this code will convert CDATA nodes to `Text` nodes and append it to the adjacent (if any) text node. By default the value of this is set to `false`. ❑ `coalescing`: True if the parser produced will convert CDATA nodes to `Text` nodes and append it to the adjacent (if any) text node; `false` otherwise.
`public void setExpandEntity References (boolean expandEntityRef)`	Specifies that the parser produced by this code will expand entity reference nodes. By default the value of this is set to `true`. ❑ `expandEntityRef`: True if the parser produced will expand entity reference nodes; `false` otherwise.
`public void setIgnoringComments (boolean ignoreComments)`	Specifies that the parser produced by this code will ignore comments. By default the value of this is set to `false`.
`public void setIgnoringElement ContentWhitespace (boolean whitespace)`	Specifies that the parsers created by this factory must eliminate whitespace in element content when parsing XML documents. Only whitespace which is directly contained within element content that has an element-only content model, will be eliminated. Note that this setting requires the parser to be in validating mode. By default the value of this is set to `false`. ❑ `whitespace`: True if the parser created must eliminate whitespace in the element content when parsing XML documents; `false` otherwise.

Signature	Description

`public void`
`setNamespaceAware`
`(boolean awareness)`
	Specifies that the parser produced by this code will provide support for XML namespaces. By default the value of this is set to `false`.
	
	❑ `awareness`: `True` if the parser produced will provide support for XML namespaces; `false` otherwise.

`public void`
`setValidating (boolean`
`validating)`
	Specifies that the parser produced by this code will validate documents as they are parsed. By default the value of this is set to `false`.
	
	❑ `validating`: `True` if the parser produced will validate documents as they are parsed; `false` otherwise.

SAXParser

```
public abstract class SAXParser extends Object
```

Defines the API that wraps an `XMLReader` implementation class. In JAXP 1.0, this class wrapped the `Parser` interface, however `XMLReader` replaces this interface. For ease of transition, this class continues to support the same name and interface as well as supporting new methods. This static method creates a new factory instance based on a system property setting or uses the platform default if no property has been defined. An instance of this class can be obtained from the `SAXParserFactory.newSAXParser()` method. Once an instance of this class is obtained, XML can be parsed from the following of input sources: `InputStreams`, `Files`, `URLs`, and SAX `InputSources`.

The system property that controls which Factory implementation to create is named `"javax.xml.style.TransformFactory"`. This property names a class that is a concrete subclass of this abstract class. If no property is defined, a platform default will be used.

Methods

Signature	Description

`public abstract Parser`
`getParser() throws`
`SAXException`
	Returns the SAX parser that is encapsulated by the implementation of this class.

`public abstract Object`
`getProperty(String name)`
`throws SAXNot`
`RecognizedException, SAX`
`NotSupportedException`
	Returns the particular value of the property requested in the underlying implementation of `XMLReader`.
	
	❑ `name`: The name of the property to be retrieved.

`public abstract XMLReader`
`getXMLReader() throws`
`SAXException`
	Returns the XMLReader that is encapsulated by the implementation of this class.

`public abstract boolean` `isNamespaceAware()`	Indicates (`true` or `false`) whether or not this parser is configured to understand namespaces.
`public abstract boolean` `isValidating()`	Indicates (`true` or `false`) whether or not this parser is configured to validate XML documents.

Table continued on following page

Signature	Description
`public void parse(File f, DefaultHandler dh) throws SAXException, IOException`	Parses the content of the file specified as XML using the specified `DefaultHandler`. ❑ f: The file containing the XML to parse. ❑ dh: The SAX Handler to use.
`public void parse(File f, HandlerBase hb) throws SAXException, IOException`	Parses the content of the file specified as XML using the specified `HandlerBase`. Use of the `DefaultHandler` version of this method is recommended as the `HandlerBase` class has been deprecated in SAX 2.0. ❑ f: The file containing the XML to parse. ❑ hb: The SAX `HandlerBase` to use.
`public void parse(InputSource is, DefaultHandler dh) throws SAXException, IOException`	Parses the content given `InputSource` as XML using the specified `DefaultHandler`. ❑ is: The `InputSource` containing the content to be parsed. ❑ dh: The SAX `DefaultHandler` to use.
`public void parse(InputSource is, HandlerBase hb) throws SAXException, IOException`	Parses the content given `InputSource` as XML using the specified `HandlerBase`. Use of the `DefaultHandler` version of this method is recommended as the `HandlerBase` class has been deprecated in SAX 2.0. ❑ is: The `InputSource` containing the content to be parsed. ❑ hb: The SAX HandlerBase to use.
`public void parse(InputStream is, DefaultHandler dh) throws SAXException, IOException`	Parses the content of the given `InputStream` instance as XML using the specified `DefaultHandler`. ❑ is: `InputStream` containing the content to be parsed. ❑ dh: The SAX `DefaultHandler` to use.
`public void parse(InputStream is, DefaultHandler dh, String systemId) throws SAXException, IOException`	Parses the content of the given `InputStream` instance as XML using the specified `DefaultHandler`. ❑ is: `InputStream` containing the content to be parsed. ❑ dh: The SAX `DefaultHandler` to use. ❑ systemId: The `systemId` which is needed for resolving relative URIs.

Signature	Description
public void parse(InputStream is, HandlerBase hb) throws SAXException, IOException	Parses the content of the given InputStream instance as XML using the specified HandlerBase. Use of the DefaultHandler version of this method is recommended as the HandlerBase class has been deprecated in SAX 2.0. ❑ is: InputStream containing the content to be parsed. ❑ hb: The SAX HandlerBase to use.
public void parse(InputStream is, HandlerBase hb, String systemId) throws SAXException, IOException	Parses the content of the given InputStream instance as XML using the specified HandlerBase. Use of the DefaultHandler version of this method is recommended as the HandlerBase class has been deprecated in SAX 2.0. ❑ is: InputStream containing the content to be parsed. ❑ hb: The SAX HandlerBase to use. ❑ systemId: The systemId which is needed for resolving relative URIs.
public void parse(String uri, DefaultHandler dh) throws SAXException, IOException	Parses the content described by the giving Uniform Resource Identifier (URI) as XML using the specified DefaultHandler. ❑ uri: The location of the content to be parsed. ❑ dh: The SAX HandlerBase to use.
public void parse(String uri HandlerBase hb) throws SAXException, IOException	Parses the content described by the giving Uniform Resource Identifier (URI) as XML using the specified HandlerBase. Use of the DefaultHandler version of this method is recommended as the HandlerBase class has been deprecated in SAX 2.0. ❑ uri: The location of the content to be parsed. ❑ hb: The SAX HandlerBase to use.
public abstract void setProperty(String name, Object value) throws SAXNotRecognizedException, SAXNotSupportedException	Sets the particular property in the underlying implementation of XMLReader. ❑ name: The name of the property to be set. ❑ value: The value of the property to be set.

SAXParserFactory

```
public abstract class SAXParserFactory extends Object
```

Defines a factory API that enables applications to configure and obtain a SAX based parser to parse XML documents.

Methods

Signature	Description
public abstract boolean getFeature(String name) throws ParserConfigurationException, SAXNotRecognizedException, SAXNotSupportedException	Returns the particular value of the property requested in the underlying implementation of XMLReader. ❑ name: The name of the property to be retrieved.
public boolean isNamespaceAware()	Indicates (true or false) whether or not the factory is configured to produce parsers that are namespace aware.
public boolean isValidating()	Indicates (true or false) whether or not the factory is configured to produce parsers which validate the XML content during parse.
public static SAXParserFactory newInstance()	Obtains a new instance of a SAXParserFactory. This static method creates a new factory instance based on a System property setting or uses the platform default if no property has been defined. The system property that controls which Factory implementation to create is named "javax.xml.parsers. SAXParserFactory". This property names a class that is a concrete subclass of this abstract class. If no property is defined, a platform default will be used. Once an application has obtained a reference to a SAXParserFactory it can use the factory to configure and obtain parser instances.
public abstract SAXParser newSAXParser() throws ParserConfigurationException, SAXException	Creates a new instance of a SAXParser using the currently configured factory parameters.
public abstract void setFeature(String name, boolean value) throws ParserConfigurationException, SAXNotRecognizedException, SAXNotSupportedException	Sets the particular feature in the underlying implementation of XMLReader. ❑ name: The name of the feature to be set. ❑ value: The value of the feature to be set.

Signature	Description
`public void setNamespaceAware (boolean awareness)`	Specifies that the parser produced by this code will provide support for XML namespaces. By default the value of this is set to `false`. ❑ `awareness`: `True` if the parser produced by this code will provide support for XML namespaces; `false` otherwise.
`public void setValidating(boolean validating)`	Specifies that the parser produced by this code will validate documents as they are parsed. By default the value of this is set to `false`. ❑ `validating`: `True` if the parser produced by this code will validate documents as they are parsed; `false` otherwise.

Exceptions

ParserConfigurationException

```
public class ParserConfigurationException extends Exception
```

Indicates a serious configuration error.

Constructors

Signature	Description
`public ParserConfigurationException()`	Creates a new `ParserConfigurationException` with no detail message.
`public ParserConfigurationException (String msg)`	Creates a new `ParserConfigurationException` with the `String` specified as an error message. ❑ `msg`: The error message for the exception.

FactoryConfigurationError

```
public class FactoryConfigurationError extends Error
```

Thrown when a problem with configuration of the parser factories exists. This error will typically be thrown when the class of a parser factory specified in the system properties cannot be found or instantiated.

Constructors

Signature	Description
public FactoryConfigurationError()	Creates a new FactoryConfigurationError with no detail message.
public FactoryConfigurationError (Exception e)	Creates a new FactoryConfigurationError with a given Exception base cause of the error. ❑ e: The exception to be encapsulated in a FactoryConfigurationError.
public FactoryConfigurationError (Exception e, String msg)	Creates a new FactoryConfigurationError with the given Exception base cause and detail message. ❑ e: The exception to be encapsulated in a FactoryConfigurationError ❑ msg: The detail message.
public FactoryConfigurationError (String msg)	Creates a new FactoryConfigurationError with the String specified as an error message. ❑ msg: The error message for the exception.

Methods

Signature	Description
public Exception getException()	Returns the actual exception (if any) that caused this exception to be raised, or null if there is none.
public String getMessage()	Returns the message (if any) for this error. If there is no message for the exception and there is an encapsulated exception then the message of that exception will be returned. Else the name of the encapsulated exception will be returned.

The Xerces Blue
Butterfly, which became
extinct earlier this century,
and after which the Xerces XML
parser is named ...

JDOM

JDOM, the subject of Chapter 4, is an alternative API to the W3C's DOM, for representing XML documents as in-memory objects. Developed as an open source project and hosted at http://www.jdom.org/, JDOM tries to present a more Java-friendly approach to the task of mapping XML document structures into Java objects.

This documentation is based on the API of JDOM beta 6, the most recent version at the time of going to press. For information on changes to the JDOM API in subsequent releases, refer to the JDOM website.

The org.jdom Package

Classes

Attribute

```
public class Attribute extends Object implements Serializable, Cloneable
```

Attribute models an XML attribute.

Constructors

Signature	Description
`public Attribute(String name, String value)`	Creates a new `Attribute` with the specified name and value, in the default 'no-namespace' namespace.
	❑ name: name of attribute.
	❑ value: value for new attribute.
`public Attribute(String name, String value, Namespace namespace)`	Creates a new `Attribute` within the specified namespace, with the given name and value.
	❑ name: name of attribute.
	❑ value: value for new attribute.
	❑ namespace: a JDOM `Namespace` object to which the attribute will belong.
`public Attribute(String name, String prefix, String uri, String value)`	Creates a new `Attribute` within the specified namespace, using the specified prefix, with the given name and value.
	❑ name: name of attribute.
	❑ prefix: prefix for attribute.
	❑ uri: URI for namespace this attribute is in.
	❑ value: value for new attribute.

Methods

Signature	Description
`public boolean getBooleanValue() throws DataConversionException`	Returns the value of the attribute as a boolean value.
`public double getDoubleValue() throws DataConversionException`	Returns the value of the attribute as a double precision floating point number.
`public float getFloatValue() throws DataConversionException`	Returns the value of the attribute as a `float`.
`public int getIntValue() throws DataConversionException`	Returns the value of the attribute as an `int`.
`public long getLongValue() throws DataConversionException`	Returns the value of the attribute as a long integer.
`public String getName()`	Retrieves the local name of the attribute.
`public Namespace getNamespace()`	Returns a JDOM `Namespace` object representing the attribute's namespace.

Signature	Description
`public String getNamespacePrefix()`	Gets the namespace prefix of the attribute. If the attribute has no namespace, an empty `String` is returned.
`public String getNamespaceURI()`	Returns the URI of the namespace this attribute belongs to, or an empty string if the attribute does not have a namespace.
`public Element getParent()`	Returns the parent of this attribute. If there is no parent, returns `null`.
`public String getQualifiedName()`	Gets the qualified name of the attribute, including any namespace prefix that is present.
`public final String getSerializedForm()`	Returns a `String` containing the attribute as it should be written into an XML document.
`public String getValue()`	Returns the attribute's value.
`public Attribute setValue(String value)`	Sets the value of the attribute. Returns a reference to the modified attribute, to allow chaining of operations. ❑ `value`: value for the attribute.

CDATA

```
public class CDATA extends Object implements Serializable, Cloneable
```

CDATA defines behavior for an XML CDATA section, modeled in Java. Methods allow the user to obtain the text of the CDATA.

Constructors

Signature	Description
`public CDATA(String text)`	Creates the CDATA with the supplied text. ❑ `text`: String content of CDATA.

Methods

Signature	Description
`public final String getSerializedForm()`	Returns the CDATA in XML format, usable in an XML document.
`public String getText()`	Returns the textual data within the CDATA.
`public void setText(String text)`	Sets the value of the CDATA. ❑ `text`: String text for CDATA.

Comment

```
public class Comment extends Object implements Serializable, Cloneable
```

Comment defines an XML comment, modeled in Java.

Constructors

Signature	Description
public Comment(String text)	Creates a comment containing the specified text. ❑ text: comment text.

Methods

Signature	Description
public Document getDocument()	Returns the Document which contains this comment, or null if it is not a currently a member of a Document.
public Element getParent()	Returns the element which contains this comment. If there is no parent, returns null.
public final String getSerializedForm()	Returns the comment in XML format.
public String getText()	Returns the text of the comment.
public Comment setText (String text)	Sets the text of the comment. ❑ text: new comment text.

DataConversionException

```
public class DataConversionException extends JDOMException
```

DataConversionException is thrown when a requested XML value is requested to be converted and conversion fails.

Constructors

Signature	Description
public DataConversionException(String name, String dataType)	Creates an Exception indicating that the specified attribute does not exist for the current element. ❑ name: String name of XML attribute being searched for. ❑ dataType: String name of data type being converted to.

DocType

```
public class DocType extends Object implements Serializable, Cloneable
```

DocType represents an XML DOCTYPE declaration.

Constructors

Signature	Description
public DocType (String elementName)	Creates a new DocType for the specified root element, but doesn't associate a DTD. ❑ elementName: name of root element.
public DocType (String elementName, String systemID)	Creates a new DocType for the specified root element using the indicated external DTD. ❑ elementName: name of root element. ❑ systemID: system ID of referenced DTD.
public DocType (String elementName, String publicID, String systemID)	Creates a new DocType for the specified root element, using the indicated external DTD. ❑ elementName: name of root element. ❑ publicID: public ID of referenced DTD. ❑ systemID: system ID of referenced DTD.

Methods

Signature	Description
public String getElementName()	Returns the root element name.
public String getPublicID()	Returns the public ID of an externally referenced DTD, or an empty String if none is referenced.
public final String getSerializedForm()	Returns the DocType in XML format.
public String getSystemID()	Returns the system ID of an externally referenced DTD, or an empty String if none is referenced.
public DocType setPublicID(String publicID)	Sets the public ID to refer to the given external DTD.
public DocType setSystemID(String systemID)	Sets the system ID to refer to the given external DTD.

Document

```
public class Document extends Object implements Serializable, Cloneable
```

Document defines behavior for an XML Document in JDOM.

Constructors

Signature	Description
public Document (Element rootElement)	Creates a new Document, with the supplied Element as the root element, and no DocType declaration. ❑ rootElement: Element for document root.
public Document (Element rootElement, DocType docType)	Create a new Document, with the supplied Element as the root element and the supplied DocType declaration. ❑ rootElement: Element for document root. ❑ docType: DocType declaration.

Methods

Signature	Description
public DocType getDocType()	Returns the DocType declaration for this Document, or null if none exists.
public Element getRootElement()	Returns the root Element for this Document, or null if the root element hasn't been set yet.
public Document setDocType(DocType docType)	Sets the DocType declaration for this Document. ❑ docType: DocType declaration.
public Document setRootElement (Element rootElement)	Sets the root Element for the Document. ❑ rootElement: Element to be the new root.

Element

```
public class Element extends Object implements Serializable, Cloneable
```

Element is the class which represents an XML element in JDOM.

Constructors

Signature	Description
public Element(String name)	Creates an Element which belongs to no namespace. ❑ name: name of element.
public Element(String name, Namespace namespace)	Creates a new Element with the given name, belonging to the specified namespace. ❑ name: name of element. ❑ namespace: JDOM Namespace object representing the element's namespace.

Signature	Description
`public Element(String name, String uri)`	Creates an `Element` with the given name, and specifies the URI of the namespace the element belongs to. ❑ `name`: name of element. ❑ `uri`: URI for element's namespace.
`public Element(String name, String prefix, String uri)`	Creates an `Element` with the given name, and specifies the prefix and URI of the namespace the `Element` should be in. ❑ `name`: name of element. ❑ `uri`: URI for element's namespace. ❑ `prefix`: Namespace prefix element should use.

Methods

Signature	Description
`public Element addAttribute (Attribute attribute)`	Adds an attribute to this element. Any existing attribute with the same name and namespace URI is removed. ❑ `attribute`: `Attribute` to add.
`public Element addAttribute (String name, String value)`	Adds an attribute to this element with the given name and value. To add attributes in namespaces use `addAttribute(Attribute)`. ❑ `name`: name of the attribute to add. ❑ `value`: value of the attribute to add.
`public Element addContent (CDATA cdata)`	Adds a CDATA section as content to this element. ❑ `cdata`: CDATA to add.
`public Element addContent (Comment comment)`	Adds a comment as content to this element. ❑ `comment`: `Comment` to add.
`public Element addContent (Element element)`	Adds element content to this element. ❑ `element`: `Element` to add.
`public Element addContent (Entity entity)`	Adds entity content to this element. ❑ `entity`: `Entity` to add.
`public Element addContent (ProcessingInstruction pi)`	Adds a processing instruction as content to this element. ❑ `pi`: `ProcessingInstruction` to add.

Table continued on following page

Signature	Description
`public Element addContent (String text)`	Adds text content to this element. It does not replace the existing content as does `setText()`. ❏ text: String to add.
`public void addNamespaceDeclaration (Namespace additionalNamespace)`	Adds a namespace declaration to this element. This is specifically for adding namespace declarations to the element not relating directly to itself. ❏ additionalNamespace: Namespace to add.
`public List getAdditionalNamespaces()`	Returns any namespace declarations on this element that exist, excluding the namespace of the element itself, which can be obtained through `getNamespace()`.Null if there are no additional declarations.
`public Attribute getAttribute(String name)`	Returns the attribute for this element with the given name and not within a namespace. ❏ name: name of the attribute to return.
`public Attribute getAttribute(String name, Namespace ns)`	Returns the attribute for this element with the given name and within the given Namespace. ❏ name: name of the attribute to return. ❏ ns: Namespace to search within.
`public List getAttributes()`	Returns the complete set of attributes for this element, as a List of Attribute objects in no particular order, or an empty list if there are none.
`public String getAttributeValue (String name)`	Returns the attribute value for the attribute with the given name and not within a namespace, null if there is no such attribute, and the empty string if the attribute value is empty. ❏ name: name of the attribute whose value to be returned.
`public String getAttributeValue (String name, Namespace ns)`	Returns the attribute value for the attribute with the given name and within the given Namespace, null if there is no such attribute, and the empty string if the attribute value is empty. ❏ name: name of the attribute whose value is to be returned. ❏ ns: Namespace to search within.
`public Element getChild (String name)`	Returns the first child element within this element with the given local name and not belonging to a namespace. Null if no elements exist for the specified name and namespace. ❏ name: local name of child element to match.

Signature	Description
`public Element getChild(String name, Namespace ns)`	Returns the first child element within this element with the given local name and belonging to the given namespace. `Null` if no elements exist for the specified name and namespace. ❑ name: local name of child element to match. ❑ ns: Namespace to search within.
`public List getChildren()`	Returns a `List` of all the child elements nested directly within this element, as `Element` objects. If this target element has no nested elements, an empty `List` is returned.
`public List getChildren(String name)`	Returns a `List` of all the child elements nested directly within this element with the given local name and not belonging to a namespace, returned as `Element` objects. If this target element has no nested elements with the given name outside a namespace, an empty `List` is returned. ❑ name: local name for the children to match.
`public List getChildren(String name, Namespace ns)`	Returns a `List` of all the child elements nested directly within this element with the given local name and belonging to the given Namespace, returned as `Element` objects. If this target element has no nested elements with the given name in the given Namespace, an empty `List` is returned. ❑ name: local name for the children to match. ❑ ns: Namespace to search within.
`public String getChildText(String name)`	This convenience method returns the textual content of the named child element, or returns an empty `String` ("") if the child has no textual content. `Null` if the child does not exist. ❑ name: the name of the child.
`public String getChildText(String name, Namespace ns)`	This convenience method returns the textual content of the named child element, or returns `null` if there's no such child. ❑ name: the name of the child. ❑ ns: the namespace of the child.
`public String getChildTextTrim (String name)`	This convenience method returns the trimmed textual content of the named child element, or `null` if there is no such child. See `getTextTrim()` for details of text trimming. ❑ name: the name of the child.

Table continued on following page

Signature	Description
`public String getChildTextTrim(String name, Namespace ns)`	This convenience method returns the trimmed textual content of the named child element, or returns `null` if no such child exists. See `getTextTrim()` for details of text trimming. ❑ name: the name of the child. ❑ ns: the namespace of the child.
`public Element getCopy(String name)`	Returns a copy of this `Element`, with a given name, and not in a namespace. ❑ name: name of new copy.
`public Element getCopy(String name, Namespace ns)`	Returns a copy of this `Element`, with a given name, and in the specified `Namespace`. ❑ name: name of new copy. ❑ ns: JDOM `Namespace` to put copy in.
`public Document getDocument()`	Retrieves the owning `Document` for this `Element`, or `null` if not currently a member of a `Document`.
`public List getMixedContent()`	Returns all content for the `Document`.
`public String getName()`	Returns the (local) name of the `Element`, without any namespace prefix, if one exists.
`public Namespace getNamespace()`	Returns this `Element`'s `Namespace` object.
`public Namespace getNamespace(String prefix)`	Returns the `Namespace` in scope on this element for the given prefix. It returns `null` if there is no `Namespace` with the given prefix at this point in the document. ❑ prefix: namespace prefix to look up.
`public String getNamespacePrefix()`	Returns the namespace prefix of the `Element`, if one exists. Otherwise, an empty `String` is returned.
`public String getNamespaceURI()`	Returns the URI mapped to this `Element`'s prefix. An empty `String` is returned if no mapping is found.
`public Element getParent()`	Returns the parent of this `Element`, or `null` if there is no parent. This should be used in tandem with `isRootElement` to determine this.
`public List getProcessingInstructions()`	Returns the list of `ProcessingInstructions` for this `Document` located at the document level.

Signature	Description
public List getProcessingInstructions (String target)	Returns the processing instructions for this `Document` located at the document level which correspond to the supplied target. ❑ target: `String` target of PI to return.
public ProcessingInstruction getProcessingInstruction (String target)	Returns the first processing instruction for this `Document` located at the document level for the supplied target, or `null` if no such processing instruction exists. ❑ target: `String` target of PI to return.
public String getQualifiedName()	Returns the full name of the `Element` in the form `[namespacePrefix]:[localName]`. If no namespace prefix exists for the `Element`, the local name is returned.
public final String getSerializedForm()	Returns the `Document` in XML format, usable as an XML document.
public String getText()	Returns the textual content directly held under this element, including all text within this single element, whitespace, and CDATA sections (if they exist). If no textual value exists for the element, an empty `String` ("") is returned.
public String getTextTrim()	Returns the textual content of this element with all surrounding whitespace removed and internal whitespace normalized to a single space. If no textual value exists for the element, or if only whitespace exists, the empty string is returned.
public boolean hasMixedContent()	Indicates whether the element has mixed content or not (whether an element contains both textual and element data). When this evaluates to `true`, `getMixedContent` should be used for getting element data.
public boolean isRootElement()	Returns a `boolean` value indicating whether this `Element` is a root `Element` for a JDOM `Document`. Should be used with `getParent` to determine if an `Element` has no "attachments" to parents.
public boolean removeAttribute (String name)	Removes the attribute with the given name and not within a namespace. ❑ name: name of attribute to remove.
public boolean removeAttribute (String name, Namespace ns)	Removes the attribute with the given name and within the given Namespace. ❑ name: name of attribute to remove. ❑ ns: namespace URI of attribute to remove.

Table continued on following page

Signature	Description
`public boolean removeAttribute (String name, String uri)`	Removes the attribute with the given name and within the given namespace URI. ❑ name: name of attribute to remove. ❑ uri: namespace URI of attribute to remove.
`public boolean removeChild(String name)`	Removes the first child element with the given local name and not belonging a namespace. Returns `true` if a child was removed. ❑ name: the name of child elements to remove.
`public boolean removeChild(String name, Namespace ns)`	Removes the first child element with the given local name and belonging to the given namespace. Returns `true` if a child was removed. ❑ name: the name of the child element to remove. ❑ ns: Namespace to search within.
`public boolean removeChildren()`	Removes all child elements. Returns `true` if any were removed.
`public boolean removeChildren(String name)`	Removes all child elements with the given local name and belonging to no namespace. Returns `true` if any were removed. ❑ name: the name of child elements to remove.
`public boolean removeChildren(String name, Namespace ns)`	Removes all child elements with the given local name and belonging to the given namespace. Returns `true` if any were removed. ❑ name: the name of child elements to remove. ❑ ns: Namespace to search within.
`public boolean removeContent (Comment comment)`	Removes the specified `Comment`. ❑ comment: Comment to delete.
`public boolean removeContent (Element element)`	Removes the specified `Element`. ❑ element: Element to delete.
`public boolean removeContent (Entity entity)`	Removes the specified `Entity`. ❑ entity: Entity to delete.
`public boolean removeContent(Processing Instruction pi)`	Removes the specified `ProcessingInstruction` (PI). ❑ pi: ProcessingInstruction to delete.
`public boolean removeProcessingInstruction (String target)`	This will remove the first PI with the specified target. ❑ target: String target of PI to remove.

Signature	Description
`public Element setAttributes (List attributes)`	Sets all the attributes for this element to be those in the given `List`; all existing attributes are removed. ❑ `attributes`: `List` of attributes to set.
`public Element setChildren(List children)`	Sets the content of the element to be the `List` of `Element` objects within the supplied `List`. All existing element and non-element content of the element is removed. ❑ `children`: `List` of `Element` objects to add.
`public Document setMixedContent (List content) throws IllegalAddException`	Sets all content for the `Document`. The `List` may contain only objects of type `Element`, `Comment`, and `ProcessingInstruction`, and only one `Element` that becomes the root. ❑ `content`: the new mixed content.
`public Element setMixedContent (List mixedContent)`	Sets the content of the element. The `List` should contain only objects of type `String`, `Element`, `Comment`, `ProcessingInstruction`, and `Entity`. Passing a `null` `List` simply clears the existing content.
`public Document setProcessingInstructions (List pis)`	Sets the PIs for this `Document` to those in the `List` supplied (removing all other PIs). ❑ `pis`: `List` of PIs to use.
`public Element setText(String text)`	Sets the content of the element to be the text given. All existing text content and non-text context is removed. If this element should have both textual content and nested elements, use `setMixedContent` instead. Setting a `null` text value is equivalent to setting an empty string value. ❑ `text`: new content for the element.

Entity

```
public class Entity extends Object implements Serializable, Cloneable
```

`Entity` defines an XML entity in Java.

Constructors

Signature	Description
`public Entity(String name)`	Creates a new `Entity` with the supplied name. ❑ `name`: `String` name of element.

Methods

Signature	Description
public Entity addChild (Element element)	Adds an Element as a child of this Entity. ❑　element: Element to add as a child.
public Entity addChild (String s)	Adds a String as a child of this Entity and returns the modified Entity. ❑　s: String to add as a child.
public Entity addText (String text)	Adds text to the content of this Entity and returns the modified Entity. ❑　text: String to add as content.
public List getChildren()	Returns a List of all the XML elements nested directly within this Entity, each in Element form. If the Entity has no nested elements an empty list will be returned.
public String getContent()	Returns the actual textual content of this Entity. This will include all text within this single element, including CDATA sections if they exist. If no textual value exists for the Entity an empty String is returned.
public Document getDocument()	This retrieves the owning Document for this Entity, or null if not currently a member of a Document.
public List getMixedContent()	Returns the content of the entity. This should be used when the hasMixedContent evaluates to true. When there is no mixed content, it returns a List with a single String (when only data is present) or a List with only elements (when only nested elements are present).
public String getName()	Returns the name of the Entity.
public Element getParent()	Returns the parent of this Entity. Null if there is no parent.
public final String getSerializedForm()	Returns the Comment in XML format, usable in an XML document.
public int hashCode()	Returns a probably unique hash code for the Namespace. If two namespaces have the same URI, they are equal and have the same hash code, even if they have different prefixes.
public boolean hasMixedContent()	This will indicate whether the entity has mixed content or not. Mixed content is when an element contains both textual and element data within it. When this evaluates to true, getMixedContent should be used for getting element data.

Signature	Description
public Entity setChildren(List children)	Sets the children of this Entity to the Elements. All existing children of this Entity are replaced. ❑ children: List of Elements to add.
public Entity setContent (String textContent)	Sets the textual content of the Entity. If this Entity has both textual content and nested elements, setMixedContent should be used instead. ❑ textContent: String content for Entity.
public Entity setMixedContent (List mixedContent)	Returns the content of the element. This should be used when the hasMixedContent evaluates to true. When there is no mixed content, it returns a List with a single String (when only data is present) or a List with only elements (when only nested elements are present).

IllegalAddException

```
public class IllegalAddException extends IllegalArgumentException
```

IllegalAddException is thrown when an Element or Attribute is added to a JDOM construct illegally.

Constructors

Signature	Description
public IllegalAdd Exception(Document base, Comment added, String reason)	Creates an Exception indicating that the addition of the Comment supplied as content to the supplied document is not allowed. ❑ base: document that the PI couldn't be added to. ❑ added: PI that could not be added. ❑ reason: cause for the problem.
public IllegalAddException (Document base, Element added, String reason)	Creates an Exception indicating that the addition of the Element supplied as a child of the document is not allowed.
public IllegalAddException (Document base, Processing Instruction added, String reason)	Creates an Exception indicating that the addition of the ProcessingInstruction supplied as content to the supplied document is not allowed. ❑ base: document that the PI couldn't be added to. ❑ added: PI that could not be added. ❑ reason: cause for the problem.

Table continued on following page

Signature	Description
public IllegalAdd Exception(Element base, Attribute added, String reason)	Creates an Exception indicating that the addition of the Attribute supplied to the Element supplied is illegal. ❏ base: Element that Attribute couldn't be added to. ❏ added: Attribute that could not be added. ❏ reason: cause for the problem.
public IllegalAdd Exception(Element base, Comment added, String reason)	Creates an Exception indicating that the addition of the Comment supplied as content to the supplied element is not allowed. ❏ base: element that the comment couldn't be added to. ❏ added: comment that could not be added. ❏ reason: cause for the problem.
public IllegalAdd Exception (Element base, Element added, String reason)	Creates an Exception indicating that the addition of the Element supplied as a child of the supplied parent is not allowed. ❏ base: Element that the child couldn't be added to. ❏ added: Element that could not be added. ❏ reason: cause for the problem.
public IllegalAdd Exception (Element base, Entity added, String reason)	Creates an Exception indicating that the addition of the Entity supplied as content to the supplied element is not allowed. ❏ base: element that the entity couldn't be added to. ❏ added: entity that could not be added. ❏ reason: cause for the problem.
public IllegalAdd Exception(String reason)	Creates an Exception with the specified error message.

IllegalDataException

```
public class IllegalDataException extends IllegalArgumentException
```

IllegalDataException is thrown when illegal text is supplied to a JDOM construct.

Constructors

Signature	Description
public IllegalDataException (String data, String construct)	Creates an Exception indicating that the specified data is illegal for the construct it was supplied to. ❑ data: String data that breaks rules. ❑ construct: String construct that data is illegal for.
public IllegalDataException (String data, String construct, String reason)	Creates an Exception indicating that the specified data is illegal for the construct it was supplied to. ❑ data: String data that breaks rules. ❑ construct: String construct that data is illegal for. ❑ reason: String message or reason data is illegal.

IllegalNameException

```
public class IllegalNameException extends IllegalArgumentException
```

IllegalNameException is thrown when a name is supplied in construction of a JDOM construct which breaks XML naming conventions.

Constructors

Signature	Description
public IllegalNameException (String name, String construct)	Creates an Exception indicating that the specified name is illegal for the construct it was supplied to. ❑ name: String name that breaks rules. ❑ construct: String name of JDOM construct that name was supplied to.
public IllegalNameException (String name, String construct, String reason)	Creates an Exception indicating that the specified name is illegal for the construct it was supplied to. ❑ name: String name that breaks rules. ❑ construct: String name of JDOM construct that name was supplied to. ❑ reason: String message or reason name is illegal.

IllegalTargetException

```
public class IllegalTargetException extends IllegalArgumentException
```

IllegalTargetException is thrown when a target is supplied in construction of a JDOM ProcessingInstruction with a name that breaks XML naming conventions.

Constructors

Signature	Description
public IllegalTargetException (String target)	Creates an Exception indicating that the specified target is illegal for the ProcessingInstruction it was supplied to. ❑ target: String target that breaks rules.
public IllegalTargetException (String target, String reason)	Creates an Exception indicating that the specified target is illegal for the ProcessingInstruction it was supplied to. ❑ target: String target that breaks rules. ❑ reason: String message or reason target is illegal.

JDOMException

```
public class JDOMException extends Exception
```

This Exception subclass is the top level Exception that JDOM classes can throw. Its subclasses indicate specific problems that can occur using JDOM, but this single Exception can be caught to handle all JDOM specific problems.

Constructors

Signature	Description
public JDOMException()	Creates an Exception.
public JDOMException (String message)	Creates an Exception with the given message. ❑ message: String message indicating the problem that occurred.
public JDOMException (String message, Throwable rootCause)	Creates an Exception with the given message and wraps another Exception. This is useful when the originating Exception should be held on to. ❑ message: String message indicating the problem that occurred. ❑ rootCause: Exception that caused this to be thrown.

Methods

Signature	Description
public String getMessage()	Returns the message for the Exception. If there is a root cause, the message associated with the root Exception is appended.
public Throwable getRootCause()	Returns the root cause Throwable, or null if one does not exist.

Signature	Description
public void printStackTrace()	Prints the stack trace of the Exception. If there is a root cause, the stack trace of the root Exception is printed after it.
public void printStackTrace (Print Stream s)	Prints the stack trace of the Exception to the given PrintStream. If there is a root cause, the stack trace of the root Exception is printed right after.
public void printStackTrace (Print Writer w)	Prints the stack trace of the Exception to the given PrintWriter. If there is a root cause, the stack trace of the root Exception is printed right after.

Namespace

```
public final class Namespace extends Object
```

Namespace defines both a factory for creating XML namespaces, and a namespace itself.

Fields

Signature	Description
public static final Namespace NO_NAMESPACE	Defines a Namespace for when not in a namespace.

Methods

Signature	Description
public boolean equals(Object ob)	Tests for equality; two Namespaces are equal if and only if their URIs are byte-for-byte equals and their prefixes are equal. ❑ ob: Object to compare to this Namespace.
public static Namespace getNamespace (String uri)	Retrieves (if in existence) or creates (if not) a Namespace for the supplied URI, and makes it usable as a default namespace (no prefix is supplied). ❑ uri: String URI of new Namespace.
public static Namespace getNamespace (String prefix, Element context)	Retrieves the Namespace for the supplied prefix in the specified context. Null if the prefix is not mapped within that element. ❑ prefix: String prefix of the existing Namespace. ❑ context: Element against which this prefix is resolved.

Table continued on following page

Signature	Description
`public static Namespace getNamespace (String prefix, String uri)`	Retrieves (if in existence) or creates (if not) a Namespace for the supplied prefix and URI. Note that the prefix of an XML namespace is both non-normative and not an intrinsic part of the Namespace and it is possible that the supplied uri is already attached to a Namespace, and a different prefix is used by it. In such a case, the existing Namespace is returned, with the different prefix, and the supplied prefix is ignored. This is perfectly legal XML namespace behavior. ❑ prefix: String prefix to map to Namespace. ❑ uri: String URI of new Namespace.
`public String getPrefix()`	Returns the prefix mapped to this Namespace.
`public String getURI()`	Returns the namespace URI for this Namespace.
`public String toString()`	Returns a String representation of this Namespace.

ProcessingInstruction

```
public class ProcessingInstruction extends Object implements Serializable,
Cloneable
```

ProcessingInstruction models an XML processing instruction modeled in Java. Methods allow the user to obtain the target of the PI as well as its data. The data can always be accessed as a String, and where appropriate can be retrieved as name/value pairs.

Constructors

Signature	Description
`public ProcessingInstruction (String target, Map data)`	Creates a new ProcessingInstruction with the specified target and data. ❑ target: String target of PI. ❑ data: Map data for PI, in name/value pairs.
`public ProcessingInstruction (String target, String data)`	Creates a new ProcessingInstruction with the specified target and data. ❑ target: String target of PI. ❑ data: String data for PI.

Methods

Signature	Description
`public String getData()`	Gets the raw data from all instructions.

Signature	Description
public Document getDocument()	Returns the Document containing the processing instruction (PI), or null if it is not a currently a member of a Document.
public Element getParent()	Gets the element containing this ProcessingInstruction. Null if there is no parent.
public final String getSerializedForm()	Returns the PI in XML format.
public String getTarget()	Gets the target of the PI.
public String getValue(String name)	Returns the value for a given instruction name within the PI. If no instruction of that name is found for this PI, an empty String will result. ❑ name: name of instruction to look up.
public boolean removeValue (String name)	Removes the instruction with the specified name. Returns a boolean indicating whether the requested instruction was removed.
public ProcessingInstruction setData(Map data)	Sets the name/value pairs within the passed Map as the pairs for the data of this PI and returns the modified PI.
public ProcessingInstruction setData(String data)	Sets the raw data for the PI. ❑ data: PI data.
public ProcessingInstruction setValue(String name, String value)	Adds or replaces the specified name-value pair to the PI. ❑ name: name of pair. ❑ value: value for pair.

Verifier

```
public final class Verifier extends Object
```

Verifier handles XML checks on names, data, and other verification tasks for JDOM.

Methods

Signature	Description
public static final String checkAttributeName (String name)	Checks the supplied name to see if it is valid for use as a JDOM Attribute name. ❑ name: String name to check.
public static final String checkCDATASection (String data)	This will ensure that the data for a CDATA section is appropriate. ❑ data: String data to check.

Table continued on following page

Signature	Description
`public static final String checkCharacterData (String name)`	Checks the supplied string to see if it only contains characters allowed by the XML 1.0 specification. ❑ name: String value to check.
`public static final String checkCommentData (String data)`	This will ensure that the data for a Comment is appropriate. ❑ data: String data to check.
`public static final String checkElementName (String name)`	Checks the supplied name to see if it is valid for use as a JDOM Element name. ❑ name: String name to check.
`public static final String checkNamespacePrefix (String prefix)`	Checks the supplied name to see if it is valid for use as a JDOM Namespace prefix. ❑ prefix: String prefix to check.
`public static final String checkNamespaceURI (String uri)`	Checks the supplied name to see if it is valid for use as a JDOM Namespace URI. ❑ uri: String URI to check.
`public static final String checkProcessingInstruct ionTarget (String target)`	Checks the supplied name to see if it is valid for use as a JDOM processing instruction target. ❑ target: String target to check.
`public static boolean isXMLCharacter (final char c)`	Determines (true or false) whether a specified character is a character according to production 2 of the XML 1.0 specification. ❑ c: char to check for XML compliance.
`public static boolean isXMLCombiningChar (final char c)`	Determines (true or false) whether a specified character is a combining character according to production 87 of the XML 1.0 specification. ❑ c: char to check.
`public static boolean isXMLDigit (final char c)`	Determines (true or false) whether a specified Unicode character is a digit according to production 88 of the XML 1.0 specification. ❑ c: char to check for XML digit compliance.
`public static boolean isXMLExtender (final char c)`	Determines (true or false) whether a specified character is an extender according to production 88 of the XML 1.0 specification. ❑ c: char to check.
`public static boolean isXMLLetter (final char c)`	Determines (true or false) whether a specified character is a letter according to production 84 of the XML 1.0 specification. ❑ c: char to check for XML name compliance.

Signature	Description

`public static boolean`
`isXMLLetterOrDigit`
`(final char c)`
	Determines (`true` or `false`) whether a specified character is a letter or digit according to productions 84 and 88 of the XML 1.0 specification.
	
	❑ c: char to check.

`public static boolean`
`isXMLNameCharacter`
`(final char c)`
	Determines (`true` or `false`) whether a specified character is a name character according to production 4 of the XML 1.0 specification.
	
	❑ c: char to check for XML name compliance.

`public static boolean`
`isXMLNameStartCharacter`
`(final char c)`
	Determines (`true` or `false`) whether a specified character is a legal name start character according to production 5 of the XML 1.0 specification. Note that this production does allow names to begin with colons which the Namespaces in XML Recommendation disallows.
	
	❑ c: char to check for XML name start compliance.

The org.jdom.adapters Package

Classes

AbstractDOMAdapter

```
public abstract class AbstractDOMAdapter extends Object implements DOMAdapter
```

This class defines wrapper behavior for obtaining a DOM `Document` object from a DOM parser.

Methods

Signature	Description

`public abstract`
`Document`
`createDocument() throws`
`IOException`
	Creates and returns an empty `Document` object based on a specific parser implementation.

`public Document`
`getDocument`
`(File filename,`
`final boolean validate)`
`throws IOException`
	Creates a new `Document` from an existing `InputStream` by letting a DOM parser handle parsing using the supplied stream.
	
	❑ filename: File to parse.
	
	❑ validate: boolean to indicate if validation should occur.

Table continued on following page

Signature	Description
`public abstract Document getDocument (InputStream in, final boolean validate) throws IOException`	Creates a new `Document` from an existing `File` by using a DOM parser ❑ in: `InputStream` to parse. ❑ validate: `boolean` to indicate if validation should occur.

CrimsonDOMAdapter

```
public class CrimsonDOMAdapter extends AbstractDOMAdapter
```

This class defines wrapper behavior for obtaining a DOM `Document` object from the Apache Crimson DOM parser.

Methods

Signature	Description
`public Document createDocument() throws IOException`	Creates and returns an empty `Document` object based on a specific parser implementation.
`public Document getDocument(InputStream in, final boolean validate) throws IOException`	Creates a new `Document` from an existing `InputStream` by letting a DOM parser handle parsing using the supplied stream. ❑ in: `InputStream` to parse. ❑ validate: `boolean` to indicate if validation should occur.

OracleV1DOMAdapter

```
public class OracleV1DOMAdapter extends AbstractDOMAdapter
```

This class defines wrapper behavior for obtaining a DOM `Document` object from the Oracle Version 1 DOM parser.

Methods

Signature	Description
`public Document createDocument() throws IOException`	Creates and returns an empty `Document` object based on a specific parser implementation.
`public Document getDocument(InputStream in, final boolean validate) throws IOException`	Creates a new `Document` from an existing `InputStream` by letting a DOM parser handle parsing using the supplied stream. ❑ in: `InputStream` to parse. ❑ validate: `boolean` to indicate if validation should occur.

OracleV2DOMAdapter

```
public class OracleV2DOMAdapter extends AbstractDOMAdapter
```

This class defines wrapper behavior for obtaining a DOM Document object from the Oracle Version 2 DOM parser.

Methods

Signature	Description
public Document createDocument() throws IOException	Creates and returns an empty Document object based on a specific parser implementation.
public Document getDocument(InputStream in, final boolean validate) throws IOException	Creates a new Document from an existing InputStream by letting a DOM parser handle parsing using the supplied stream. ❑ in: InputStream to parse. ❑ validate: boolean to indicate if validation should occur.

ProjectXDOMAdapter

```
public class ProjectXDOMAdapter extends AbstractDOMAdapter
```

This class defines wrapper behavior for obtaining a DOM Document object from a Sun Project X DOM parser.

Methods

Signature	Description
public Document createDocument() throws IOException	Creates and returns an empty Document object based on a specific parser implementation.
public Document getDocument(InputStream in, final boolean validate) throws IOException	Creates a new Document from an existing InputStream by letting a DOM parser handle parsing using the supplied stream. ❑ in: InputStream to parse. ❑ validate: boolean to indicate if validation should occur.

XercesDOMAdapter

```
public class XercesDOMAdapter extends AbstractDOMAdapter
```

This class defines wrapper behavior for obtaining a DOM Document object from an Apache Xerces DOM parser.

Methods

Signature	Description
`public Document createDocument() throws IOException`	Creates and returns an empty `Document` object based on a specific parser implementation.
`public Document getDocument(InputStream in, final boolean validate) throws IOException`	Creates a new `Document` from an existing `InputStream` by letting a DOM parser handle parsing using the supplied stream. ❑ in: `InputStream` to parse. ❑ validate: `boolean` to indicate if validation should occur.

XML4JDOMAdapter

```
public class XML4JDOMAdapter extends AbstractDOMAdapter
```

This class defines wrapper behavior for obtaining a DOM `Document` object from an IBM XML4J DOM parser.

Methods

Signature	Description
`public Document createDocument() throws IOException`	Creates and returns an empty `Document` object based on a specific parser implementation.
`public Document getDocument(InputStream in, final boolean validate) throws IOException`	Creates a new `Document` from an existing `InputStream` by letting a DOM parser handle parsing using the supplied stream. ❑ in: `InputStream` to parse. ❑ validate: `boolean` to indicate if validation should occur.

Interfaces

DOMAdapter

```
public interface DOMAdapter
```

This interface defines wrapper behavior for obtaining a DOM `Document` object from a DOM parser.

Methods

Signature	Description
`public Document createDocument() throws IOException`	Creates and returns an empty `Document` object based on a specific parser implementation.

Signature	Description
`public Document getDocument(File filename, final boolean validate) throws IOException`	Creates a new `Document` from a given filename by letting a DOM parser handle parsing from the file. ❑ `filename`: file to parse. ❑ `validate`: `boolean` to indicate if validation should occur.
`public Document getDocument(InputStream in, final boolean validate) throws IOException`	Creates a new `Document` from an existing `InputStream` by letting a DOM parser handle parsing using the supplied stream. ❑ `in`: `InputStream` to parse. ❑ `validate`: `boolean` to indicate if validation should occur.

The org.jdom.input Package

Classes

BuilderErrorHandler

```
public class BuilderErrorHandler extends Object implements ErrorHandler
```

Methods

Signature	Description
`public void error (SAXParseException exception) throws SAXException`	Called in response to an error that has occurred, this method indicates that a rule was broken, typically in validation, but that parsing could reasonably continue. The implementation of this method here is to rethrow the exception. ❑ `exception`: `SAXParseException` that occurred.
`public void fatalError (SAXParseException exception) throws SAXException`	Called in response to a fatal error, this method indicates that a rule has been broken that makes continued parsing almost certainly impossible. The implementation of this method here is to rethrow the exception. ❑ `exception`: `SAXParseException` that occurred.
`public void warning (SAXParseException exception) throws SAXException`	Called when a warning has occurred, this method indicates that while no XML rules were broken, something appears to be incorrect or missing. The implementation of this method here is a "no op". ❑ `exception`: `SAXParseException` that occurred.

DOMBuilder

```
public class DOMBuilder extends Object
```

DOMBuilder builds a JDOM tree from a pre-existing DOM. The class can be used to build from files, streams, etc, but other builders like SAXBuilder can perform the task faster because they don't create a DOM tree first.

Constructors

Signature	Description
`public DOMBuilder()`	Creates a new DOMBuilder which will attempt to first locate a parser via JAXP, then will try to use a set of default parsers. The underlying parser will not validate.
`public DOMBuilder(final boolean validate)`	Creates a new DOMBuilder which will attempt to first locate a parser via JAXP, then will try to use a set of default parsers. The underlying parser will or will not validate, depending on the given parameter. ❑ `validate: boolean` indicating if validation should occur.
`public DOMBuilder(String adapterClass)`	Creates a new DOMBuilder using the specified DOMAdapter implementation as a way to choose the underlying parser. The underlying parser will not validate. ❑ `adapterClass: String` name of class to use for DOM building.
`public DOMBuilder(String adapterClass, final boolean validate)`	Creates a new DOMBuilder using the specified DOMAdapter implementation as a way to choose the underlying parser. The underlying parser will or will not validate, according to the given parameter. ❑ `adapterClass: String` name of class to use for DOM building. ❑ `validate: boolean` indicating if validation should occur.

Methods

Signature	Description
`public Document build(Document domDocument)`	Builds and returns a JDOM tree from an existing DOM tree. ❑ `domDocument: Document` object.
`public Element build(Element domElement)`	Builds and returns a JDOM Element from an existing DOM Element ❑ `domElement: Element` object.

Signature	Description
public Document build(File file) throws JDOMException	Builds and returns a document from the supplied filename by constructing a DOM tree and reading information from the DOM to create a JDOM document (useful for debugging). ❑ file: File to read from.
public Document build(InputStream in) throws JDOMException	Builds and returns a document from the supplied input stream by constructing a DOM tree and reading information from the DOM to create a JDOM document (useful for debugging). ❑ in: InputStream to read from.
public Document build(URL url) throws JDOMException	Builds and returns a document from the supplied URL by constructing a DOM tree and reading information from the DOM to create a JDOM document (useful for debugging). ❑ url: URL to read from.
public void setValidation(final boolean validate)	Sets validation for the builder. ❑ validate: boolean indicating whether validation should occur.

SAXBuilder

```
public class SAXBuilder extends Object
```

SAXBuilder builds a JDOM tree using SAX.

Constructors

Signature	Description
public SAXBuilder()	Creates a new SAXBuilder which will attempt to locate a parser via JAXP and use a set of default SAX Drivers. The underlying parser will not validate.
public SAXBuilder(final boolean validate)	Creates a new SAXBuilder which will attempt to locate a parser via JAXP and use a set of default SAX Drivers. The underlying parser will or will not validate, according to the given parameter. ❑ validate: boolean indicating if validation should occur.
public SAXBuilder(String saxDriverClass)	Creates a new SAXBuilder using the specified SAX parser. The underlying parser will not validate. ❑ saxDriverClass: String name of SAX Driver to use for parsing.

Table continued on following page

Signature	Description
`public SAXBuilder(String saxDriverClass, final boolean validate)`	Creates a new SAXBuilder using the specified SAX parser. The underlying parser will or will not validate according to the given parameter. ❑ `saxDriverClass`: `String` name of SAX Driver to use for parsing. ❑ `validate`: `boolean` indicating if validation should occur.

Methods

Signature	Description
`public Document build(File file) throws JDOMException`	Builds and returns a `Document` object from the supplied filename. ❑ `file`: `File` to read from.
`public Document build(InputStream in) throws JDOMException`	Returns a `Document` object from the supplied input stream. ❑ `in`: `InputStream` to read from.
`public Document build(InputStream in, String systemId) throws JDOMException`	Builds and returns a `Document` object from the supplied input stream. ❑ `in`: `InputStream` to read from. ❑ `systemId`: base for resolving relative URIs.
`public Document build(Reader characterStream) throws JDOMException`	Builds and returns a `Document` object from the supplied Reader. ❑ `in`: `Reader` to read from.
`public Document build(Reader characterStream, String SystemId) throws JDOMException`	Builds and returns a `Document` object from the supplied Reader. ❑ `in`: `Reader` to read from. ❑ `systemId`: base for resolving relative URIs.
`public Document build(String systemId) throws JDOMException`	Builds and returns a `Document` object from the supplied URI. ❑ `systemId`: URI for the input.
`public Document build(URL url) throws JDOMException`	Builds and returns a `Document` object from the supplied URL. ❑ `url`: URL to read from.
`public void setDTDHandler (DTDHandler dtdHandler)`	Sets custom `DTDHandler` for the `Builder`. ❑ `dtdHandler`: `DTDHandler`.
`public void setEntityResolver (EntityResolver entityResolver)`	Sets custom `EntityResolver` for the `Builder`. ❑ `entityResolver`: `EntityResolver`.

Signature	Description
public void setErrorHandler (ErrorHandler errorHandler)	Sets custom ErrorHandler for the Builder. ❑ errorHandler: ErrorHandler.
public void setValidation(final boolean validate)	Sets validation for the builder. ❑ validate: boolean indicating whether validation should occur.
public void setXMLFilter(XMLFilter xmlFilter)	Sets custom XMLFilter for the Builder. ❑ xmlFilter: XMLFilter.

The org.jdom.output Package

Classes

DOMOutputter

```
public class DOMOutputter extends Object
```

Takes a JDOM tree and outputs to a DOM tree.

Constructors

Signature	Description
public DOMOutputter()	Creates a new DOMOutputter which will attempt to first locate a DOM implementation to use via JAXP If JAXP does not exist or there is a problem, it will fall back to the default parser.
public DOMOutputter (String adapterClass)	Creates a new DOMOutputter using the specified DOMAdapter implementation as a way to choose the underlying parser. ❑ adapterClass: String name of class to use for DOM output.

Methods

Signature	Description
public Attr output (Attribute attribute)	This converts the JDOM Attribute parameter to a DOM Attr, returning the DOM version. ❑ attribute: Attribute to output.

Table continued on following page

Signature	Description
public Document output (Document document)	This converts the JDOM Document parameter to a DOM Document, returning the DOM version. ❑ document: Document to output.
public Element output (Element element)	This converts the JDOM Element parameter to a DOM Element, returning the DOM version. ❑ element: Element to output.

SAXOutputter

```
public class SAXOutputter extends Object
```

SAXOutputter takes a JDOM tree and fires SAX2 events. Most ContentHandler callbacks are supported. Both ignorableWhitespace and skippedEntity have not been implemented. The setDocumentLocator callback has been implemented, but the locator object always returns –1 for getColumnNumber and getLineNumber. The EntityResolver callback resolveEntity has been implemented for DTDs. DTDHandler callbacks have not been implemented yet because, at this point, it is not possible to access notations and unparsed entity references in a DTD from a JDOM tree. The ErrorHandler callbacks have not been implemented since they are supposed to be invoked when the document is parsed. However, the document has already been parsed in order to create the JDOM tree.

Constructors

Signature	Description
public SAXOutputter(Content Handler contentHandler)	Creates a SAXOutputter with the specified ContentHandler. ❑ contentHandler: contains callback methods for ContentHandler.
public SAXOutputter (ContentHandler contentHandler, ErrorHandler errorHandler, DTDHandler dtdHandler, EntityResolver entityResolver)	Creates a SAXOutputter with the specified SAX2 handlers. At this time, only ContentHandler and EntityResolver are supported. ❑ contentHandler: contains callback methods for ContentHandler. ❑ errorHandler: contains callback methods for ErrorHandler. ❑ dtdHandler: contains callback methods for DTDHandler. ❑ entityResolver: contains callback methods for EntityResolver.

Methods

Signature	Description
public void output (Document document)	This will output the JDOM Document, firing off the SAX events that have been registered. ❑ document: JDOM Document to output.
public void setContentHandler (ContentHandler contentHandler)	Sets the ContentHandler. ❑ contentHandler: contains callback methods for ContentHandler.
public void setDTDHandler (DTDHandler dtdHandler)	Sets the DTDHandler. ❑ dtdHandler: contains callback methods for DTDHandler.
public void setEntityResolver (EntityResolver entityResolver)	Sets the EntityResolver. ❑ entityResolver: contains callback methods for EntityResolver.
public void setErrorHandler (ErrorHandler errorHandler)	Sets the ErrorHandler. ❑ errorHandler: contains callback methods for ErrorHandler.

XMLOutputter

```
public class XMLOutputter extends Object implements Cloneable
```

XMLOutputter takes a JDOM tree and formats it to a stream as XML using typical document formatting. The XML declaration and processing instructions are always on their own lines. Empty elements are printed as <empty/> and text-only contents are printed as <tag>content</tag> on a single line. Constructor parameters control the indent amount and whether new lines are printed between elements; other parameters are configurable through the set* methods. For compact machine-readable output create a default XMLOutputter and call setTrimText(true) to strip any whitespace that was preserved from the source.

There are output(...) methods to print any of the standard JDOM classes, including Document and Element, to either a Writer or an OutputStream. Note that using your own Writer may cause the outputter's preferred character encoding to be ignored (for encodings other than UTF8, use of the method that takes an OutputStream is recommended). The methods outputString(...) are for convenience only; for top performance you should call output(...) and pass in your own Writer or OutputStream if possible.

Constructors

Signature	Description
public XMLOutputter()	Creates an XMLOutputter with no additional whitespace (indent or new lines) added; the whitespace from the element text content is fully preserved.

Table continued on following page

Signature	Description
public XMLOutputter (String indent)	Creates an XMLOutputter with the given indent added but no new lines added; all whitespace from the element text content is also included.
	❑ indent: the indent String, usually some number of spaces.
public XMLOutputter (String indent, final boolean newlines)	Creates an XMLOutputter with the given indent that prints new lines only if newlines is true; all whitespace from the element text content is included as well.
	❑ indent: the indent String, usually some number of spaces.
	❑ newlines: true indicates new lines should be printed, else new lines are ignored (compacted).
public XMLOutputter (String indent, final boolean newlines, String encoding)	Creates an XMLOutputter with the given indent and new lines printing only if newlines is true, and encoding format encoding.
	❑ indent: the indent String, usually some number of spaces.
	❑ newlines: true indicates new lines should be printed, else new lines are ignored (compacted).
	❑ encoding: set encoding format.
public XMLOutputter (XMLOutputter that)	Creates an XMLOutputter with all the options as set in the given XMLOutputter.
	❑ that: the XMLOutputter to clone.

Methods

Signature	Description
public void output(CDATA cdata, OutputStream out)	Prints out a CDATA.
	❑ cdata: CDATA to output.
	❑ out: OutputStream to write to.
public void output(CDATA cdata, Writer out)	Prints out a CDATA.
	❑ cdata: CDATA to output.
	❑ out: Writer to write to.
public void output(Comment comment, OutputStream out)	Prints out a Comment.
	❑ comment: Comment to output.
	❑ out: OutputStream to write to.

Signature	Description
`public void output (Comment comment, Writer out)`	Prints out a `Comment`. ❏ comment: `Comment` to output. ❏ out: `Writer` to write to.
`public void output (Document doc, Writer out) throws IOException`	This will print the `Document` to the given `Writer`. Note that using your own `Writer` may cause the outputter's preferred character encoding to be ignored. For encodings other than UTF8, use of the method that takes an `OutputStream` is recommended. ❏ doc: `Document` to format. ❏ out: `Writer` to write to.
`public void output (Element element, OutputStream out)`	Prints out an `Element`, including its `Attributes`, and its value, and all contained (child) elements etc. ❏ element: `Element` to output. ❏ out: `Writer` to write to.
`public void output (Element element, Writer out)`	Prints out an `Element`, including its `Attributes`, and its value, and all contained (child) elements etc. ❏ element: `Element` to output. ❏ out: `Writer` to write to.
`public void output (Entity entity, OutputStream out)`	Prints out an `Entity`. ❏ entity: `Entity` to output. ❏ out: `OutputStream` to write to.
`public void output (Entity entity, Writer out)`	Prints out an `Entity`. ❏ entity: `Entity` to output. ❏ out: `Writer` to write to.
`public void output (ProcessingInstruction pi, OutputStream out)`	Prints out a `ProcessingInstruction`. ❏ pi: `ProcessingInstruction` to output. ❏ out: `OutputStream` to write to.
`public void output (ProcessingInstruction pi, Writer out)`	Prints out a `ProcessingInstruction`. ❏ pi: `ProcessingInstruction` to output. ❏ out: `Writer` to write to.

Table continued on following page

Signature	Description
`public void output (String string, OutputStream out)`	Prints out a `String`. Performs the necessary entity escaping and whitespace stripping. ❑ string: `String` to output. ❑ out: `OutputStream` to write to.
`public void output (String string, Writer out)`	Prints out a `String`. Perfoms the necessary entity escaping and whitespace stripping. ❑ string: `String` to output. ❑ out: `Writer` to write to.
`public void outputElementContent (Element element, Writer out)`	This will handle printing out an `Element`'s content only (not including tag and attributes). ❑ element: `Element` to output. ❑ out: `Writer` to write to. ❑ indent: `int` level of indention.
`public String outputString (Document doc)`	Returns a string representing a document using an internal `StringWriter`. Note that a `String` is Unicode and may not match the outputter's specified encoding. ❑ doc: `Document` to format.
`public String outputString (Element element)`	Returns a string representing an element. Note that a `String` is Unicode and may not match the outputter's specified encoding. ❑ element: `Element` to format.
`public int parseArgs (String args, final int i)`	Returns `int` index of first parameter that was not understood. Parse command-line arguments of the form: `-omitEncoding -indentSize 3...`
`public void setEncoding (String encoding)`	Sets encoding. ❑ encoding: encoding format to be set.
`public void setExpandEmptyElements (final boolean expandEmptyElements)`	Sets whether empty elements are expanded from `<tagName>` to `<tagName></tagName>`. ❑ expandEmptyElements: `boolean` indicating whether or not empty elements should be expanded.
`public void setIndent (final boolean doIndent)`	Sets the indent on or off. If setting on, will use the value of `STANDARD_INDENT` (usually two spaces). ❑ doIndent: if `true`, sets indenting on; if `false`, sets indenting off.

Signature	Description
`public void setIndent (String indent)`	Sets the indent `String` to use (usually a `String` of empty spaces). If you pass `null`, or the empty string (`""`), then no indentation will happen. Default is none (`null`). ❑ `indent`: `String` to use for indentation.
`public void setIndentLevel (final int indentLevel)`	Sets the initial indentation level. This can be used to output a document (or element) starting at a given indent level, so it is not always flush against the left margin. Default is 0. ❑ `indentLevel`: the number of indents to start with.
`public void setIndentSize(final int indentSize)`	Sets the size of the indent `String`. ❑ `indentSize`: `int` number of spaces in indentation.
`public void setLineSeparator (String separator)`	Sets the new-line separator. The default is `\r\n`. Note that if the "newlines" property is `false`, this value is irrelevant. Call `setLineSeparator(System.getProperty ("line.separator"))` to make it output the system default line ending string. ❑ `separator`: `String` line separator to use.
`public void setNewlines (final boolean newlines)`	Sets newlines. ❑ `newlines`: `true` indicates new lines should be printed, else new lines are ignored (compacted).
`public void setOmitEncoding(final boolean omitEncoding)`	Sets whether the XML declaration (`<?xml version="1.0" encoding="UTF-8"?>`) includes the encoding of the document. ❑ `omitEncoding`: `boolean` indicating whether or not the XML declaration should indicate the document encoding.
`public void setPadText (final boolean padText)`	Ensure that text immediately preceded by or followed by an element will be "padded" with a single space. Default is `false`. ❑ `padText`: `boolean` if `true`, pad string-element boundaries.
`public void setSuppressDeclaration (final boolean suppressDeclaration)`	Sets whether the XML declaration (`<?xml version="1.0"?>`) will be suppressed or not. It is common to suppress this in uses such as SOAP and XML-RPC calls. ❑ `suppressDeclaration`: `boolean` indicating whether or not the XML declaration should be suppressed.
`public void setTrimText (final boolean trimText)`	Sets whether the text is output verbatim (`false`) or with whitespace stripped as per `Element.getTextTrim()`. Default is `false`. ❑ `trimText`: `boolean` `true`=>trim the whitespace, `false`=>use text verbatim.

The Xerces Blue
butterfly, which became
extinct earlier this century,
and after which the Xerces XML
parser is named ...

G

XSLT Reference

This reference appendix describes the elements and functions that are part of XSLT. We covered this in Chapters 7 and 8. For the XPath functions that can also be used with XSLT, see Appendix A.

The XSLT 1.0 specification became a W3C recommendation on 16 November 1999. Version 1.1 was a working draft at the time of writing, as were the requirements for version 2.0. Both the attributes on XSLT elements and the parameters of XSLT functions can be of several types. At the end of this appendix, you will find a list of the types used in the elements and functions of XSLT.

Elements

The XSLT stylesheet is itself an XML document, using a number of special elements in its own namespace. This namespace is http://www.w3.org/1999/XSL/Transform, but in this appendix (and the rest of this book) we simply use the prefix xsl.

For each element we give a short description of its use, describe the **attributes** that can or must be used on the element, and indicate **where** in the stylesheet the element can occur (as a child of which other elements).

<xsl:apply-imports>

For calling a template from an imported stylesheet that was overruled in the importing stylesheet. This is normally used if you want to add functionality to a standard template that you imported using <xsl:import>.

Can contain:	No other elements
Can be contained by:	`<xsl:attribute>`, `<xsl:comment>`, `<xsl:copy>`, `<xsl:document>`, `<xsl:element>`, `<xsl:fallback>`, `<xsl:for-each>`, `<xsl:if>`, `<xsl:message>`, `<xsl:otherwise>`, `<xsl:param>`, `<xsl:processing-instruction>`, `<xsl:template>`, `<xsl:variable>`, `<xsl:when>`

<xsl:apply-templates>

Used to pass the context on to another template. The `select` attribute specifies which nodes should be transformed now; the processor decides which templates will be used.

select (optional)	Expression describing which nodes in the source document should be transformed next. Defaults to `child::*`.	
	Type:	node-set-expression
	Attribute Value Template:	no
mode (optional)	By adding a `mode` attribute, the processor will transform the indicated source document nodes using only templates with this same `mode` attribute. This allows us to process the same source node in different ways.	
	Type:	qname
	Attribute Value Template:	no
Can contain	`<xsl:sort>`, `<xsl:with-param>`	
Can be contained by	`<xsl:attribute>`, `<xsl:comment>`, `<xsl:copy>`, `<xsl:document>`, `<xsl:element>`, `<xsl:fallback>`, `<xsl:for-each>`, `<xsl:if>`, `<xsl:message>`, `<xsl:otherwise>`, `<xsl:param>`, `<xsl:processing-instruction>`, `<xsl:template>`, `<xsl:variable>`, `<xsl:when>`	

<xsl:attribute>

Generates an attribute in the destination document. It should be used in the context of an element (either a literal, `<xsl:element>`, or some other element that generates an element in the output). It must occur before any text or element content is generated.

name (required)	The name of the attribute.	
	Type:	qname
	Attribute Value Template:	yes
namespace (optional)	The namespace (the default uses the namespace of the element the attribute is placed on)	

	Type:	uri-reference
	Attribute Value Template:	yes
Can contain:	`<xsl:apply-imports>`, `<xsl:apply-templates>`, `<xsl:call-template>`, `<xsl:choose>`, `<xsl:copy>`, `<xsl:copy-of>`, `<xsl:fallback>`, `<xsl:for-each>`, `<xsl:if>`, `<xsl:message>`, `<xsl:number>`, `<xsl:text>`, `<xsl:value-of>`, `<xsl:variable>`	
Can be contained by:	`<xsl:attribute-set>`, `<xsl:copy>`, `<xsl:document>`, `<xsl:element>`, `<xsl:fallback>`, `<xsl:for-each>`, `<xsl:if>`, `<xsl:message>`, `<xsl:otherwise>`, `<xsl:param>`, `<xsl:template>`, `<xsl:variable, xsl:when>`	

<xsl:attribute-set>

Used to define a set of attributes that can then be added to an element as a group by specifying the `<xsl:attribute-set>` element's name attribute value in the `use-attribute-sets` attribute on the `<xsl:element>` element.

name (required)	Name that can be used to refer to this set of attributes.	
	Type:	qname
	Attribute Value Template:	no
use-attribute-sets (optional)	For including an existing attribute set in this attribute set.	
	Type:	qnames
	Attribute Value Template:	no
Can contain:	`<xsl:attribute>`	
Can be contained by:	`<xsl:stylesheet>`, `<xsl:transform>`	

<xsl:call-template>

Used to call a template by name. Causes no context switch (change of context node) as `<xsl:apply-templates>` and `<xsl:for-each>` do. The template you call by name will still be processing the same context node as your current template. This element can be used to reuse the same functionality in several templates.

name (required)	Name of the template you want to call.	
	Type:	qname
	Attribute Value Template:	no
Can contain:	`<xsl:with-param>`	

Table continued on following page

Can be contained by:	`<xsl:attribute>`, `<xsl:comment>`, `<xsl:copy>`, `<xsl:document>`, `<xsl:element>`, `<xsl:fallback>`, `<xsl:for-each>`, `<xsl:if>`, `<xsl:message>`, `<xsl:otherwise>`, `<xsl:param>`, `<xsl:processing-instruction>`, `<xsl:template>`, `<xsl:variable>`, `<xsl:when>`

<xsl:choose>

For implementing the `choose/when/otherwise` construct. Compare to `Case/Select` in Visual Basic or `switch` in C and Java.

Can contain:	`<xsl:otherwise>`, `<xsl:when>`
Can be contained by:	`<xsl:attribute>`, `<xsl:comment>`, `<xsl:copy>`, `<xsl:document>`, `<xsl:element>`, `<xsl:fallback>`, `<xsl:for-each>`, `<xsl:if>`, `<xsl:message>`, `<xsl:otherwise>`, `<xsl:param>`, `<xsl:processing-instruction>`, `<xsl:template>`, `<xsl:variable>`, `<xsl:when>`

<xsl:comment>

For generating a `comment` node in the destination document.

Can contain:	`<xsl:apply-imports>`, `<xsl:apply-templates>`, `<xsl:call-template>`, `<xsl:choose>`, `<xsl:copy>`, `<xsl:copy-of>`, `<xsl:fallback>`, `<xsl:for-each>`, `<xsl:if>`, `<xsl:message>`, `<xsl:number>`, `<xsl:text>`, `<xsl:value-of>`, `<xsl:variable>`
Can be contained by:	`<xsl:copy>`, `<xsl:document>`, `<xsl:element>`, `<xsl:fallback>`, `<xsl:for-each>`, `<xsl:if>`, `<xsl:message>`, `<xsl:otherwise>`, `<xsl:param>`, `<xsl:template>`, `<xsl:variable>`, `<xsl:when>`

<xsl:copy>

Generates a copy of the context node in the destination document. Does not copy any children or attributes.

`use-attribute-sets` (optional)	For adding a set of attributes to the copied node.	
	Type:	qnames
	Attribute Value Template:	no

Can contain:	`<xsl:apply-imports>`, `<xsl:apply-templates>`, `<xsl:attribute>`, `<xsl:call-template>`, `<xsl:choose>`, `<xsl:comment>`, `<xsl:copy>`, `<xsl:copy-of>`, `<xsl:document>`, `<xsl:element>`, `<xsl:fallback>`, `<xsl:for-each>`, `<xsl:if>`, `<xsl:message>`, `<xsl:number>`, `<xsl:processing-instruction>`, `<xsl:text>`, `<xsl:value-of>`, `<xsl:variable>`
Can be contained by:	`<xsl:attribute>`, `<xsl:comment>`, `<xsl:copy>`, `<xsl:document>`, `<xsl:element>`, `<xsl:fallback>`, `<xsl:for-each>`, `<xsl:if>`, `<xsl:message>`, `<xsl:otherwise>`, `<xsl:param>`, `<xsl:processing-instruction>`, `<xsl:template>`, `<xsl:variable>`, `<xsl:when>`

<xsl:copy-of>

Copies a full tree, including attributes and children, to the destination document. If multiple nodes are matched by the `select` attribute, all of the sub-trees are copied. If you have an XML fragment stored in a variable, `<xsl:copy-of>` is the handiest element to send the variables content to the output.

`select` (required)	XPath expression leading to the nodes to be copied.	
	Type:	expression
	Attribute Value Template:	no
Can contain:	No other elements	
Can be contained by:	`<xsl:attribute>`, `<xsl:comment>`, `<xsl:copy>`, `<xsl:document>`, `<xsl:element>`, `<xsl:fallback>`, `<xsl:for-each>`, `<xsl:if>`, `<xsl:message>`, `<xsl:otherwise>`, `<xsl:param>`, `<xsl:processing-instruction>`, `<xsl:template>`, `<xsl:variable>`, `<xsl:when>`	

<xsl:decimal-format>

Declares a decimal-format, which controls the interpretation of a format pattern used by the `format-number()` function. This includes defining the decimal separator and the thousands separator.

name (optional)	The name of the defined format.	
	Type:	qname
	Attribute Value Template:	no
`decimal-separator` (optional)	The character that will separate the integer part from the fraction part. Default is a dot (.).	
	Type:	char
	Attribute Value Template:	no

Table continued on following page

grouping-separator (optional)	The character that will separate the grouped numbers in the integer part. Default is a comma (,).
	Type: char
	Attribute Value Template: no
infinity (optional)	The string that should appear if a number equals infinity. Default is the string 'Infinity'
	Type: string
	Attribute Value Template: no
minus-sign (optional)	The character that will be used to indicate a negative number. Default is minus (-).
	Type: char
	Attribute Value Template: no
NaN (optional)	The string that should appear if a number is Not a Number. Default is the string 'NaN'
	Type: string
	Attribute Value Template: no
percent (optional)	Character that will be used as the percent sign. Default is %.
	Type: char
	Attribute Value Template: no
per-mille (optional)	Character that will be used as the per-thousand sign. Default is the Unicode character #x2030, which looks like ‰.
	Type: char
	Attribute Value Template: no
zero-digit (optional)	The character used as the digit zero. Default is 0.
	Type: char
	Attribute Value Template: no
digit (optional)	The character used in a pattern to indicate the place where a leading zero is required. Default is 0.
	Type: char
	Attribute Value Template: no

pattern-separator (optional)	The character that is used to separate the negative and positive patterns (if they are different). Default is semicolon (;).
	Type: char
	Attribute Value Template: no
Can contain:	No other elements
Can be contained by:	`<xsl:stylesheet>`, `<xsl:transform>`

`<xsl:document>`

Switches the target of the result tree to another document. All output nodes instantiated within the `<xsl:document>` element will appear in the document indicated by the href attribute. All other attributes are identical to the attributes on `<xsl:output>`. Note that this element is not part of the XSLT 1.0 specification; it is an XSLT 1.1 extension.

method (optional)	xml is default
	html will create empty elements like ` ` and use HTML entities like `&agrave;`
	text will cause no output escaping to happen at all (no entity references in output.)
	Type: xml|html|text|qname-but-not-ncname
	Attribute Value Template: yes
version (optional)	The version number that will appear in the XML declaration of the output document.
	Type: token
	Attribute Value Template: yes
encoding (optional)	The encoding of the output document.
	Type: string
	Attribute Value Template: yes
omit-xml-declaration (optional)	Specifies if the resulting document should contain an XML declaration (`<?xml version="1.0"?>`)
	Type: yes|no
	Attribute Value Template: yes
standalone (optional)	Specifies whether the XSLT processor should output a standalone document declaration.
	Type: yes|no
	Attribute Value Template: yes

Table continued on following page

`doctype-public` (optional)	Specifies the public identifier to be used in the DTD
	Type: string
	Attribute Value Template: yes
`doctype-system` (optional)	Specifies the system identifier to be used in the DTD
	Type: string
	Attribute Value Template: yes
`cdata-section-elements` (optional)	Specifies a list of elements that should have their content escaped by using a CDATA section instead of entities.
	Type: qnames
	Attribute Value Template: yes
`indent` (optional)	Specifies addition of extra whitespace for readability
	Type: yes|no
	Attribute Value Template: yes
`media-type` (optional)	To specify a specific MIME type while writing out content.
	Type: string
	Attribute Value Template: yes
Can contain:	`<xsl:apply-imports>`, `<xsl:apply-templates>`, `<xsl:attribute>`, `<xsl:call-template>`, `<xsl:choose>`, `<xsl:comment>`, `<xsl:copy>`, `<xsl:copy-of>`, `<xsl:document>`, `<xsl:element>`, `<xsl:fallback>`, `<xsl:for-each>`, `<xsl:if>`, `<xsl:message>`, `<xsl:number>`, `<xsl:processing-instruction>`, `<xsl:text>`, `<xsl:value-of>`, `<xsl:variable>`
Can be contained by:	`<xsl:copy>`, `<xsl:document>`, `<xsl:element>`, `<xsl:fallback>`, `<xsl:for-each>`, `<xsl:if>`, `<xsl:message>`, `<xsl:otherwise>`, `<xsl:param>`, `<xsl:template>`, `<xsl:variable>`, `<xsl:when>`

<xsl:element>

Generates an element with the specified name in the destination document.

name (required)	Name of the element (this may include a prefix bound to a namespace in the stylesheet)
	Type: qname
	Attribute Value Template: yes
namespace (optional)	To overrule the namespace that follows from the prefix in the name attribute (if any).
	Type: uri-reference
	Attribute Value Template: yes
use-attribute-sets (optional)	To add a predefined set of attributes to the element.
	Type: qnames
	Attribute Value Template: no
Can contain:	`<xsl:apply-imports>`, `<xsl:apply-templates>`, `<xsl:attribute>`, `<xsl:call-template>`, `<xsl:choose>`, `<xsl:comment>`, `<xsl:copy>`, `<xsl:copy-of>`, `<xsl:document>`, `<xsl:element>`, `<xsl:fallback>`, `<xsl:for-each>`, `<xsl:if>`, `<xsl:message>`, `<xsl:number>`, `<xsl:processing-instruction>`, `<xsl:text>`, `<xsl:value-of>`, `<xsl:variable>`
Can be contained by:	`<xsl:copy>`, `<xsl:document>`, `<xsl:element>`, `<xsl:fallback>`, `<xsl:for-each>`, `<xsl:if>`, `<xsl:message>`, `<xsl:otherwise>`, `<xsl:param>`, `<xsl:template>`, `<xsl:variable>`, `<xsl:when>`

<xsl:fallback>

Can be used to specify actions to be executed if the action of its parent element is not supported by the processor.

Can contain:	`<xsl:apply-imports>`, `<xsl:apply-templates>`, `<xsl:attribute>`, `<xsl:call-template>`, `<xsl:choose>`, `<xsl:comment>`, `<xsl:copy>`, `<xsl:copy-of>`, `<xsl:document>`, `<xsl:element>`, `<xsl:fallback>`, `<xsl:for-each>`, `<xsl:if>`, `<xsl:message>`, `<xsl:number>`, `<xsl:processing-instruction>`, `<xsl:text>`, `<xsl:value-of>`, `<xsl:variable>`

Table continued on following page

Can be contained by:	`<xsl:attribute>`, `<xsl:comment>`, `<xsl:copy>`, `<xsl:document>`, `<xsl:element>`, `<xsl:fallback>`, `<xsl:for-each>`, `<xsl:if>`, `<xsl:message>`, `<xsl:otherwise>`, `<xsl:param>`, `<xsl:processing-instruction>`, `<xsl:template>`, `<xsl:variable>`, `<xsl:when>`

<xsl:for-each>

For looping through the node selected by the XPath expression in the `select` attribute. The context is shifted to the current node in the loop.

`select` (required)	Expression that selects the nodes to loop through.	
	Type:	node-set-expression
	Attribute Value Template:	no
Can contain:	`<xsl:apply-imports>`, `<xsl:apply-templates>`, `<xsl:attribute>`, `<xsl:call-template>`, `<xsl:choose>`, `<xsl:comment>`, `<xsl:copy>`, `<xsl:copy-of>`, `<xsl:document>`, `<xsl:element>`, `<xsl:fallback>`, `<xsl:for-each>`, `<xsl:if>`, `<xsl:message>`, `<xsl:number>`, `<xsl:processing-instruction>`, `<xsl:sort>`, `<xsl:text>`, `<xsl:value-of>`, `<xsl:variable>`	
Can be contained by:	`<xsl:attribute>`, `<xsl:comment>`, `<xsl:copy>`, `<xsl:document>`, `<xsl:element>`, `<xsl:fallback>`, `<xsl:for-each>`, `<xsl:if>`, `<xsl:message>`, `<xsl:otherwise>`, `<xsl:param>`, `<xsl:processing-instruction>`, `<xsl:template>`, `<xsl:variable>`, `<xsl:when>`	

<xsl:if>

Executes the contained elements only if the test expression returns true (or a filled node set).

`test` (required)	The expression that is tested. If it returns true or a non-empty node-set, the content of the `<xsl:if>` element is executed.	
	Type:	boolean-expression
	Attribute Value Template:	no

Can contain:	`<xsl:apply-imports>`, `<xsl:apply-templates>`, `<xsl:attribute>`, `<xsl:call-template>`, `<xsl:choose>`, `<xsl:comment>`, `<xsl:copy>`, `<xsl:copy-of>`, `<xsl:document>`, `<xsl:element>`, `<xsl:fallback>`, `<xsl:for-each>`, `<xsl:if>`, `<xsl:message>`, `<xsl:number>`, `<xsl:processing-instruction>`, `<xsl:text>`, `<xsl:value-of>`, `<xsl:variable>`
Can be contained by:	`<xsl:attribute>`, `<xsl:comment>`, `<xsl:copy>`, `<xsl:document>`, `<xsl:element>`, `<xsl:fallback>`, `<xsl:for-each>`, `<xsl:if>`, `<xsl:message>`, `<xsl:otherwise>`, `<xsl:param>`, `<xsl:processing-instruction>`, `<xsl:template>`, `<xsl:variable>`, `<xsl:when>`

<xsl:import>

Imports the templates from an external stylesheet document into the current document. The priority of these imported templates is very low, so if a template in the importing document is implemented for the same pattern, it will always prevail over the imported template. The imported template can be called from the overriding template using `<xsl:apply-imports>`.

`href` (required)	Reference to the stylesheet to be imported.	
	Type:	uri-reference
	Attribute Value Template:	no
Can contain:	No other elements	
Can be contained by	`<xsl:stylesheet>`, `<xsl:transform>`	

<xsl:include>

Includes templates from an external document as if they where part of the importing document. This means that templates from the included stylesheet have the same priority as they would have had if they were part of the including stylesheet. An error occurs if a template with the same `match` and `priority` attributes exists in both the including and included stylesheets.

`href` (required)	Reference to the stylesheet to be imported.	
	Type:	uri-reference
	Attribute Value Template:	no
Can contain:	No other elements	
Can be contained by:	`<xsl:stylesheet>`, `<xsl:transform>`	

<xsl:key>

Can be used to create index-like structures that can be queried from the key() function. It is basically a way to describe name/value pairs inside the source document (like a Dictionary object in VB, a Hashtable in Java, or an associative array in Perl). However, in XSLT, more than one value can be found for one key and the same value can be accessed by multiple keys.

name (required)	The name that can be used to refer to this key.	
	Type:	qname
	Attribute Value Template:	no
match (required)	The pattern defines which nodes in the source document can be accessed using this key. In the name/value pair analogy, this would be the definition of the value.	
	Type:	pattern
	Attribute Value Template:	no
use (required)	This expression defines what the key for accessing each value would be. Example: if an element PERSON is matched by the match attribute and the use attribute equals "@name", the key() function can be used to find this specific PERSON element by passing the value of its name attribute.	
	Type:	expression
	Attribute Value Template:	no
Can contain:	No other elements	
Can be contained by:	<xsl:stylesheet>, <xsl:transform>	

<xsl:message>

To issue error messages or warnings. The content of the element is the message. What the XSLT processor does with the message depends on the implementation. You could think of displaying it within a message box or logging to the error log.

terminate (optional)	If terminate is set to yes, the execution of the transformation is stopped after issuing the message.	
	Type:	yes|no
	Attribute Value Template:	no
Can contain:	<xsl:apply-imports>, <xsl:apply-templates>, <xsl:attribute>, <xsl:call-template>, <xsl:choose>, <xsl:comment>, <xsl:copy>, <xsl:copy-of>, <xsl:document>, <xsl:element>, <xsl:fallback>, <xsl:for-each>, <xsl:if>, <xsl:message>, <xsl:number>, <xsl:processing-instruction>, <xsl:text>, <xsl:value-of>, <xsl:variable>	

Can be contained by	`<xsl:attribute>`, `<xsl:comment>`, `<xsl:copy>`, `<xsl:document>`, `<xsl:element>`, `<xsl:fallback>`, `<xsl:for-each>`, `<xsl:if>`, `<xsl:message>`, `<xsl:otherwise>`, `<xsl:param>`, `<xsl:processing-instruction>`, `<xsl:template>`, `<xsl:variable>`, `<xsl:when>`

<xsl:namespace-alias>

Used to make a certain namespace appear in the destination document without using that namespace in the stylesheet. The main use of this element is in generating new XSLT stylesheets.

`stylesheet-prefix` (required)	The prefix for the namespace that is used in the stylesheet	
	Type:	prefix|#default
	Attribute Value Template:	no
`result-prefix` (required)	The prefix for the namespace that must replace the aliased namespace in the destination document.	
	Type:	prefix|#default
	Attribute Value Template:	no
Can contain:	No other elements	
Can be contained by:	`<xsl:stylesheet>`, `<xsl:transform>`	

<xsl:number>

For outputting the number of a paragraph or chapter in a specified format. It has very flexible features, to allow for different numbering rules.

`level` (optional)	The value `single` counts the location of the nearest node matched by the `count` attribute (along the ancestor axis) relative to its preceding siblings of the same name. Typical output: chapter number.	
	The value `multiple` will count the location of all the nodes matched by the `count` attribute (along the ancestor axis) relative to their preceding siblings of the same name. Typical output: paragraph number of form 4.5.3.	
	The value `any` will count the location of the nearest node matched by the `count` attribute (along the ancestor axis) relative to their preceding nodes (not only siblings) of the same name. Typical output: bookmark number	
	Type:	single|multiple|any
	Attribute Value Template:	no

Table continued on following page

count (optional)	Specifies the type of node that is to be counted	
	Type:	pattern
	Attribute Value Template:	no
from (optional)	Specifies the starting point for counting	
	Type:	pattern
	Attribute Value Template:	no
value (optional)	Used to specify the numeric value directly instead of using `level`, `count` and `from`.	
	Type:	number-expression
	Attribute Value Template:	no
format (optional)	How to format the numeric value to a string (1 becomes 1, 2, 3, ...; a becomes a, b, c,)	
	Type:	string
	Attribute Value Template:	yes
lang (optional)	Language used for alphabetic numbering	
	Type:	token
	Attribute Value Template:	yes
letter-value (optional)	Some languages have traditional orders of letters specifically for numbering. These orders are often different from the alphabetic order	
	Type:	alphabetic|traditional
	Attribute Value Template:	yes
grouping-separator (optional)	Character to be used for group separation.	
	Type:	char
	Attribute Value Template:	yes
grouping-size (optional)	Number of digits to be separated. grouping-separator=";" and grouping-size="3" causes: 1;000;000	
	Type:	number
	Attribute Value Template:	yes
Can contain:	No other elements	

Can be contained by:	`<xsl:attribute>`, `<xsl:comment>`, `<xsl:copy>`, `<xsl:document>`, `<xsl:element>`, `<xsl:fallback>`, `<xsl:for-each>`, `<xsl:if>`, `<xsl:message>`, `<xsl:otherwise>`, `<xsl:param>`, `<xsl:processing-instruction>`, `<xsl:template>`, `<xsl:variable>`, `<xsl:when>`

<xsl:otherwise>

Content is executed if none of the `<xsl:when>` elements in an `<xsl:choose>` is matched.

Can contain:	`<xsl:apply-imports>`, `<xsl:apply-templates>`, `<xsl:attribute>`, `<xsl:call-template>`, `<xsl:choose>`, `<xsl:comment>`, `<xsl:copy>`, `<xsl:copy-of>`, `<xsl:document>`, `<xsl:element>`, `<xsl:fallback>`, `<xsl:for-each>`, `<xsl:if>`, `<xsl:message>`, `<xsl:number>`, `<xsl:processing-instruction>`, `<xsl:text>`, `<xsl:value-of>`, `<xsl:variable>`
Can be contained by:	`<xsl:choose>`

<xsl:output>

Top level element for setting properties regarding the output style of the destination document. The `<xsl:output>` element basically describes how the translation from a created XML tree to a character array (string) happens.

`method` (optional)	`xml` is default	
	`html` will create empty elements like ` ` and use HTML entities like `&agrave;`.	
	`text` will cause no output escaping to happen at all (no entity references in output.)	
	Type:	xml|html|text|qname-but-not-ncname
	Attribute Value Template:	no
`version` (optional)	The version number that will appear in the XML declaration of the output document.	
	Type:	token
	Attribute Value Template:	no
`encoding` (optional)	The encoding of the output document.	
	Type:	string
	Attribute Value Template:	no

Table continued on following page

`omit-xml-declaration` (optional)	Specifies if the resulting document should contain an XML declaration (`<?xml version="1.0"?>`)	
	Type:	yes|no
	Attribute Value Template:	no
`standalone` (optional)	Specifies whether the XSLT processor should output a standalone document declaration	
	Type:	yes|no
	Attribute Value Template:	no
`doctype-public` (optional)	Specifies the public identifier to be used in the DTD	
	Type:	string
	Attribute Value Template:	no
`doctype-system` (optional)	Specifies the system identifier to be used in the DTD	
	Type:	string
	Attribute Value Template:	no
`cdata-section-elements` (optional)	Specifies a list of elements that should have their content escaped by using a CDATA section instead of entities	
	Type:	qnames
	Attribute Value Template:	no
`indent` (optional)	Specifies the addition of extra whitespace for readability	
	Type:	yes|no
	Attribute Value Template:	no
`media-type` (optional)	To specify a specific MIME type while writing out content	
	Type:	string
	Attribute Value Template:	no
Can contain:	No other elements	
Can be contained by:	`<xsl:stylesheet>`, `<xsl:transform>`	

<xsl:param>

Defines a parameter in a `<xsl:template>` or `<xsl:stylesheet>`.

`name` (required)	Name of the parameter
	Type: qname
	Attribute Value Template: no
`select` (optional)	Specifies the default value for the parameter
	Type: expression
	Attribute Value Template: no
Can contain:	`<xsl:apply-imports>`, `<xsl:apply-templates>`, `<xsl:attribute>`, `<xsl:call-template>`, `<xsl:choose>`, `<xsl:comment>`, `<xsl:copy>`, `<xsl:copy-of>`, `<xsl:document>`, `<xsl:element>`, `<xsl:fallback>`, `<xsl:for-each>`, `<xsl:if>`, `<xsl:message>`, `<xsl:number>`, `<xsl:processing-instruction>`, `<xsl:text>`, `<xsl:value-of>`, `<xsl:variable>`
Can be contained by:	`<xsl:stylesheet>`, `<xsl:transform>`

<xsl:preserve-space>

Allows you to define which elements in the source document should have their whitespace content preserved. See also `<xsl:strip-space>`.

`elements` (required)	In this attribute you can list the elements (separated by whitespace) for which you want to preserve the whitespace content.
	Type: tokens
	Attribute Value Template: no
Can contain:	No other elements
Can be contained by:	`<xsl:stylesheet>`, `<xsl:transform>`

<xsl:processing-instruction>

Generates a processing instruction in the destination document.

`name` (required)	The name of the processing instruction (the part between the first question mark and the first whitespace of the processing instruction)
	Type: ncname
	Attribute Value Template: yes

Table continued on following page

Can contain:	`<xsl:apply-imports>`, `<xsl:apply-templates>`, `<xsl:call-template>`, `<xsl:choose>`, `<xsl:copy>`, `<xsl:copy-of>`, `<xsl:fallback>`, `<xsl:for-each>`, `<xsl:if>`, `<xsl:message>`, `<xsl:number>`, `<xsl:text>`, `<xsl:value-of>`, `<xsl:variable>`
Can be contained by:	`<xsl:copy>`, `<xsl:document>`, `<xsl:element>`, `<xsl:fallback>`, `<xsl:for-each>`, `<xsl:if>`, `<xsl:message>`, `<xsl:otherwise>`, `<xsl:param>`, `<xsl:template>`, `<xsl:variable>`, `<xsl:when>`

<xsl:sort>

Allows specifying a sort order for `<xsl:apply-templates>` and `<xsl:for-each>` elements. Multiple `<xsl:sort>` elements can be specified for primary and secondary sorting keys.

select (optional)	Expression that indicates which should be used for the ordering	
	Type:	string-expression
	Attribute Value Template:	no
lang (optional)	To set the language used while ordering (in different languages the rules for alphabetic ordering can be different)	
	Type:	token
	Attribute Value Template:	yes
data-type (optional)	To specify alphabetic or numeric ordering	
	Type:	text|number|qname-but-not-ncname
	Attribute Value Template:	yes
order (optional)	Specifies ascending or descending ordering	
	Type:	ascending|descending
	Attribute Value Template:	yes
case-order (optional)	Specifies if upper case characters should order before or after lower case characters. Note that case insensitive sorting is not supported	
	Type:	upper-first|lower-first
	Attribute Value Template:	yes
Can contain:	No other elements	
Can be contained by:	`<xsl:apply-templates>`, `<xsl:for-each>`	

\<xsl:strip-space\>

Allows you to define which elements in the source document should have their whitespace content stripped. See also \<xsl:preserve-space\>.

elements (required)	Specifies which elements should preserve their whitespace contents.
	Type: tokens
	Attribute Value Template: no
Can contain:	No other elements
Can be contained by:	\<xsl:stylesheet\>, \<xsl:transform\>

\<xsl:stylesheet\>

The root element for a stylesheet. Synonym to \<xsl:transform\>.

id (optional)	A reference for the stylesheet.
	Type: id
	Attribute Value Template: no
extension-element-prefixes (optional)	Allows you to specify which namespace prefixes are XSLT extension namespaces (like msxml)
	Type: tokens
	Attribute Value Template: no
exclude-result-prefixes (optional)	Namespaces that are only relevant in the stylesheet or in the source document, but not in the result document, can be removed from the output by specifying them here.
	Type: tokens
	Attribute Value Template: no
version (required)	Version number
	Type: number
	Attribute Value Template: no
Can contain:	\<xsl:attribute-set\>, \<xsl:decimal-format\>, \<xsl:import\>, \<xsl:include\>, \<xsl:key\>, \<xsl:namespace-alias\>, \<xsl:output\>, \<xsl:param\>, \<xsl:preserve-space\>, \<xsl:strip-space\>, \<xsl:template\>, \<xsl:variable\>
Can be contained by:	No other elements

<xsl:template>

Defines a transformation rule. Some templates are built-in and don't have to be defined. Refer to Chapter 3 for more information about writing templates.

match (optional)	Defines the set of nodes on which the template can be applied
	Type: pattern
	Attribute Value Template: no
name (optional)	Name to identify the template when calling it using `<xsl:call-template>`
	Type: qname
	Attribute Value Template: no
priority (optional)	If several templates can be applied (through their match attributes) on a node, the priority attribute can be used to make a certain template prevail over others
	Type: number
	Attribute Value Template: no
mode (optional)	If a mode attribute is present on a template, the template will only be considered for transforming a node when the transformation was started by an `<xsl:apply-templates>` element with a mode attribute with the same value
	Type: qname
	Attribute Value Template: no
Can contain:	`<xsl:apply-imports>`, `<xsl:apply-templates>`, `<xsl:attribute>`, `<xsl:call-template>`, `<xsl:choose>`, `<xsl:comment>`, `<xsl:copy>`, `<xsl:copy-of>`, `<xsl:document>`, `<xsl:element>`, `<xsl:fallback>`, `<xsl:for-each>`, `<xsl:if>`, `<xsl:message>`, `<xsl:number>`, `<xsl:processing-instruction>`, `<xsl:text>`, `<xsl:value-of>`, `<xsl:variable>`
Can be contained by:	`<xsl:stylesheet>`, `<xsl:transform>`

<xsl:text>

Generates a text string from it's content. Whitespace is never stripped from an `<xsl:text>` element.

disable-output-escaping (optional)	If set to yes, the output will not be escaped: this means that a string `'<'` will be written to the output as `'<'` instead of `&lt;`. This means that the result document will not be a well-formed XML document anymore
	Type: yes|no
	Attribute Value Template: no

Can contain:	No other elements
Can be contained by:	`<xsl:attribute>`, `<xsl:comment>`, `<xsl:copy>`, `<xsl:document>`, `<xsl:element>`, `<xsl:fallback>`, `<xsl:for-each>`, `<xsl:if>`, `<xsl:message>`, `<xsl:otherwise>`, `<xsl:param>`, `<xsl:processing-instruction>`, `<xsl:template>`, `<xsl:variable>`, `<xsl:when>`

<xsl:transform>

Identical to `<xsl:stylesheet>`

`id` (optional)	A reference for the stylesheet	
	Type:	id
	Attribute Value Template:	no
`extension-element-prefixes` (optional)	Allows you to specify which namespace prefixes are XSLT extension namespaces (like `msxml`)	
	Type:	tokens
	Attribute Value Template:	no
`exclude-result-prefixes` (optional)	Namespaces that are only relevant in the stylesheet or in the source document, but not in the result document, can be removed from the output by specifying them here.	
	Type:	tokens
	Attribute Value Template:	no
`version` (required)	Version number	
	Type:	number
	Attribute Value Template:	no
Can contain:	`<xsl:attribute-set>`, `<xsl:decimal-format>`, `<xsl:import>`, `<xsl:include>`, `<xsl:key>`, `<xsl:namespace-alias>`, `<xsl:output>`, `<xsl:param>`, `<xsl:preserve-space>`, `<xsl:strip-space>`, `<xsl:template>`, `<xsl:variable>`	
Can be contained by:	No other elements	

<xsl:value-of>

Generates a text string with the value of the expression in the `select` attribute.

`select` (required)	Expression that selects the node-set that will be converted to a string
	Type: string-expression
	Attribute Value Template: no
`disable-output-escaping` (optional)	You can use this to output < instead of < to the destination document. Note that this will cause your destination to become invalid XML. Normally used to generate HTML or text files.
	Type: yes|no
	Attribute Value Template: no
Can contain:	No other elements
Can be contained by:	`<xsl:attribute>`, `<xsl:comment>`, `<xsl:copy>`, `<xsl:document>`, `<xsl:element>`, `<xsl:fallback>`, `<xsl:for-each>`, `<xsl:if>`, `<xsl:message>`, `<xsl:otherwise>`, `<xsl:param>`, `<xsl:processing-instruction>`, `<xsl:template>`, `<xsl:variable>`, `<xsl:when>`

<xsl:variable>

Defines a variable with a value. Note that in XSLT, the value of a variable cannot change– you can instantiate a variable using `<xsl:variable>`, but it cannot be changed afterwards. Refer to Chapter 4 for more information on the use of variables.

`name` (required)	Name of the variable
	Type: qname
	Attribute Value Template: no
`select` (optional)	Value of the variable (if the `select` attribute is omitted, the content of the `<xsl:variable>` element is the value)
	Type: expression
	Attribute Value Template: no
Can contain:	`<xsl:apply-imports>`, `<xsl:apply-templates>`, `<xsl:attribute>`, `<xsl:call-template>`, `<xsl:choose>`, `<xsl:comment>`, `<xsl:copy>`, `<xsl:copy-of>`, `<xsl:document>`, `<xsl:element>`, `<xsl:fallback>`, `<xsl:for-each>`, `<xsl:if>`, `<xsl:message>`, `<xsl:number>`, `<xsl:processing-instruction>`, `<xsl:text>`, `<xsl:value-of>`, `<xsl:variable>`

Can be contained by:	`<xsl:attribute>`, `<xsl:comment>`, `<xsl:copy>`, `<xsl:document>`, `<xsl:element>`, `<xsl:fallback>`, `<xsl:for-each>`, `<xsl:if>`, `<xsl:message>`, `<xsl:otherwise>`, `<xsl:param>`, `<xsl:processing-instruction>`, `<xsl:stylesheet>`, `<xsl:template>`, `<xsl:transform>`, `<xsl:variable>`, `<xsl:when>`

<xsl:when>

Represents one of the options for execution in a `<xsl:choose>` block.

`test` (required)	Expression to be tested	
	Type:	boolean-expression
	Attribute Value Template:	no
Can contain:	`<xsl:apply-imports>`, `<xsl:apply-templates>`, `<xsl:attribute>`, `<xsl:call-template>`, `<xsl:choose>`, `<xsl:comment>`, `<xsl:copy>`, `<xsl:copy-of>`, `<xsl:document>`, `<xsl:element>`, `<xsl:fallback>`, `<xsl:for-each>`, `<xsl:if>`, `<xsl:message>`, `<xsl:number>`, `<xsl:processing-instruction>`, `<xsl:text>`, `<xsl:value-of>`, `<xsl:variable>`	
Can be contained by:	`<xsl:choose>`	

<xsl:with-param>

Used to pass a parameter to a template using `<xsl:apply-templates>` or `<xsl:call-template>`. The template called must have a parameter of the same name defined using `<xsl:param>`.

`name` (required)	Name of the parameter	
	Type:	qname
	Attribute Value Template:	no
`select` (optional)	XPath expression selecting the passed value	
	Type:	expression
	Attribute Value Template:	no
Can contain:	No other elements	
Can be contained by:	`<xsl:apply-templates>`, `<xsl:call-template>`	

Functions

Within expressions in an XSLT stylesheet, you can use all the XPath functions we saw in Appendix A and also a number of special XSLT functions. These functions are described here.

Each function is described by a line of this form:

return-type function-name *(parameters)*

For each parameter, we display the type (`object`, `string`, `number`, `node-set`) and where necessary a symbol indicating if the parameter is optional (?) or can occur multiple times (+). The type `object` means that any type can be passed.

If an expression is passed as a parameter, it is first evaluated and (if necessary) converted to the expected type before passing it to the function.

node-set current *( )*

Returns the current context node-set, outside the current expression. For MSXML2 you can use the `context()` function as a workaround. `context(-1)` is synonymous to `current()`

node-set document *(object, node-set?)*

To get a reference to an external source document.

object	If of type String, this is the URL of the document to be retrieved. If a node-set, all nodes are converted to strings and all these URLs are retrieved in a node-set.
node-set	Represents the base URL from where relative URLs are resolved.

boolean element-available *(string)*

To query availability of a certain extension element.

string	Name of the extension element.

string format-number *(number, string1, string2?)*

Formats a numeric value into a formatted and localized string.

number	The numeric value to be represented.
string1	The format string that should be used for the formatting.
string2	Reference to a `<xsl:decimal-format>` element to indicate localization parameters.

boolean function-available *(string)*

To query availability of a certain extension function.

string	Name of the extension function.

node-set generate-id (*node-set?*)

Generates a unique identifier for the specified node. Each node will cause a different ID, but the same node will always generate the same ID. You cannot be sure that the IDs generated for a document during multiple transformations will remain identical.

node-set	The first node of the passed node-set is used. If no node-set is passed, the current context is used.

node-set key (*string, object*)

To get a reference to a node using the specified <xsl:key>.

string	The name of the referenced <xsl:key> .
object	

object system-property (*string*)

To get certain system properties from the processor.

string	The name of the system property. Properties that are always available are xsl:version, xsl:vendor and xsl:vendor-url.

node-set unparsed-entity-url (*string*)

Returns the URI of the unparsed entity with the passed name.

string	Name of the unparsed entity.

Inherited XPath Functions

Check Appendix A for information on the XPath functions.:

boolean()	ceiling()	concat()	contains()
count()	false()	floor()	id()
lang()	last	local-name()	name()
namespace-uri()	normalize-space()	not	number()
position()	round()	starts-with()	string()
string-length()	substring()	substring-after()	substring-before()
Sum()	translate()	true()	

Types

These types are used to specify the types of the attributes for the XSLT elements given in the tables above.

`boolean`	Can have values `true` and `false`.
`char`	A single character.
`expression`	A string value, containing an XPath expression.
`id`	A string value. Must be an XML name. The string value can be used only once as an `id` in any document.
`language-name`	A string containing one of the defined language identifiers. American English = EN-US.
`name`	A string value that conforms to the name conventions of XML. That means: no whitespace, should start with either a letter or an underscore.
`names`	Multiple name values separated by whitespace.
`namespace-prefix`	Any string that is defined as a prefix for a namespace.
`ncname`	A name value that does not contain a colon.
`node`	A node in an XML document. Can be of several types, including: element, attribute, comment, processing instruction, text node, etc.
`node-set`	A set of nodes in a specific order. Can be of any length.
`node-set-expression`	A string value, containing an XPath expression that returns nodes.
`number`	A numeric value. Can be either floating point or integer.
`object`	Anything. Can be a string, a node, a node-set, anything.
`qname`	Qualified name: the full name of a node. Made up of two parts: the local name and the namespace identifier.
`qnames`	A set of qname values, separated by whitespace.
`string`	A string value.
`token`	A string value that contains no whitespace.
`tokens`	Multiple token values separated by whitespace.
`uri-reference`	Any string that conforms to the URI specification.

The Xerces Blue
butterfly, which became
extinct earlier this century,
and after which the Xerces XML
parser is named ···

Installing Tomcat

In this appendix we will discuss the basics of installing and configuring Tomcat 3.2.1, which supports JSP 1.1 and Servlet 2.2.

Installing Tomcat 3.2.1

Whilst there are many Servlet and JSP engines available (as of this writing, Sun's "Industry Momentum" page at http://java.sun.com/products/jsp/industry.html lists nearly 40), we have chosen to focus our attention on Tomcat 3.2.1. Tomcat is produced by the Apache Software Foundation's Jakarta project, and is freely available at http://jakarta.apache.org/tomcat/.

Since Tomcat is primarily used by programmers, its open-source development model is of particular benefit as it brings the developers and users close together. If you find a bug, you can fix it and submit a patch; if you need a new feature, you can write it yourself, or suggest it to the development team.

Tomcat is also the reference implementation of the JSP and Servlet specifications, version 4.0 supporting the latest Servlet 2.3 and JSP 1.2 versions (version 3.2.1 is the current version of the Servlet 2.2/JSP 1.1 reference implementation). Many of the principal developers are employed by Sun Microsystems, who are investing considerable manpower into ensuring that Tomcat 4.0 provides a high-quality, robust web container with excellent performance.

Currently, Tomcat 4.0 is in Beta Release and so we recommend that you install 3.2.1 unless you have particular need for the latest versions of the JSP and Servlet specifications.

Basic Tomcat Installation

These steps describe installing Tomcat 3.2.1 on a Windows 2000 system, but the steps are pretty generic – the main differences between platforms will be the way in which environment variables are set.

❑   You will need to install the Java 2 Standard Edition software development kit, if you have not already done so; JDK 1.3 can be downloaded from http://java.sun.com/j2se/1.3/.

❑   Download the Tomcat 3.2.1 release from http://jakarta.apache.org/builds/jakarta-tomcat/release/v3.2.1/bin/ – the file will be called something like jakarta-tomcat-3.2.1.zip. (Other archive formats are available which will be more suitable if you are on a Unix-type platform.)

❑   Unzip the file you downloaded into a suitable directory. On a Windows machine, unzipping into C:\ will create a directory named C:\jakarta-tomcat-3.2.1 containing the Tomcat files.

❑   Create TOMCAT_HOME and JAVA_HOME environment variables pointing to the directories where you installed the Tomcat and Java 2 SDK files. Typical values are C:\jakarta-tomcat-3.2.1 for TOMCAT_HOME and C:\jdk1.3 for JAVA_HOME.

Under Windows 2000, environment variables are set using the System control panel. On the Advanced tab, click on the Environment Variables... button. In the resulting dialog box, add TOMCAT_HOME and JAVA_HOME as system variables:

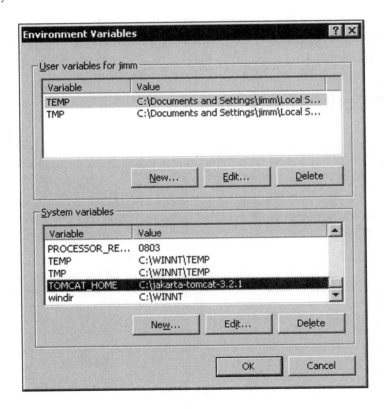

These environment variables allow Tomcat to locate both its own files (using TOMCAT_HOME), and the Java 2 SDK components it needs, notably the Java compiler, (using JAVA_HOME).

If you are using Windows 98, you can set the environment variables by editing the C:\autoexec.bat file. Add the following lines:

```
set TOMCAT_HOME= C:\jakarta-tomcat-3.2.1
set JAVA_HOME=C:\jdk1.3
```

Under Windows 98 you will also need to increase the environment space available, by right-clicking on your DOS prompt window, selecting **Properties**, going to the **Memory** tab, and setting the initial environment to 4096 bytes.

Start Tomcat by running the startup.bat batch file (startup.sh on Unix-type systems), which can be found in the <TOMCAT_HOME>\bin directory (in other words, the bin directory inside the directory where Tomcat is installed).

We now have Tomcat up and running, using its internal web server (on port 8080). Point your web browser at http://localhost:8080/; you should see the default Tomcat home page:

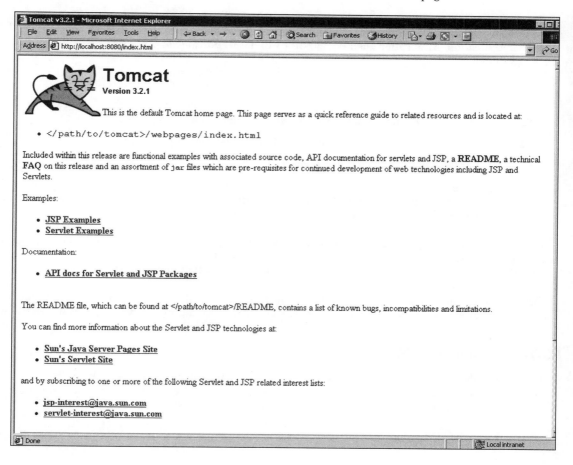

Spend some time exploring the examples and documentation provided with Tomcat.

❑ To shut down Tomcat, run the `shutdown.bat` batch file (`shutdown.sh` on Unix-type systems), again from the `%TOMCAT_HOME%\bin` directory.

The Tomcat Directory Structure

Looking inside our Tomcat installation directory we find a few text files, and seven directories:

❑ `bin` contains Windows batch files and Unix shell scripts for starting and stopping Tomcat, and for other purposes, together with various JAR files (Java library files) needed by Tomcat. Notable among these is `servlet.jar`, which contains the classes defined by the Servlet 2.2 and JSP 1.1 specifications. You will need to have `servlet.jar` listed in your `CLASSPATH` environment variable when compiling classes (for example, Servlets) that use these APIs.

❑ `conf` contains Tomcat's configuration files, notably `server.xml` (used to configure the server – which hostname and port number to use, which web applications to deploy, etc.) and the server-wide `web.xml`.

> Note that settings in the server-wide `web.xml` file (located in `%TOMCAT_HOME%\conf`) apply to the whole server, but that this behavior is not mandated by the Servlet specification. Applications making use of it will not be portable to other servlet containers.

❑ `doc` contains Tomcat's documentation.

❑ `lib` is populated with various JAR files (library files) required by Tomcat.

❑ `logs` is where Tomcat places its log files. Logging is configured in `server.xml`.

❑ `src` contains the source code for Tomcat.

❑ `webapps` is the location where Tomcat looks for web applications to deploy. Any `.war` file placed here, or any expanded web application directory structure stored within the directory, will automatically be deployed when Tomcat starts up.

The URL path under which the application is deployed will correspond to the name of the `.war` file or directory; for example, if you place a `myapplication.war` file or a `myapplication` directory within webapps, Tomcat will automatically deploy it as http://localhost:8080/myapplication/.

The automatic deployment settings may not suit your application, in which case you may prefer to store the application outside the `webapps` directory and configure it as desired using `server.xml` as shown below.

Tomcat Configuration

The Tomcat documentation has improved considerably from earlier versions, and should be your first stop if you need to configure Tomcat in any way. However, there are a few steps that are sufficiently common that we cover them here.

Deploying a Web Application

There are two ways to tell Tomcat to deploy a web application:

❑ You can deploy an application simply by placing a `.war` file or an expanded web application directory structure in the `%TOMCAT_HOME%\webapps` directory. You may deploy the applications developed in Chapters 12 and 13 in this way using the appropriate files provided in the code download.

❑ However, the default settings may not be suitable for your application, and if you are building the application by hand, it will be necessary to edit `%TOMCAT_HOME%\conf\server.xml` and add a `<Context>` element for your application.

The default `server.xml` file is well commented, and you should read these to familiarize yourself with the contents of this file. Various additional elements, not shown or described here but included in the default `server.xml`, provide for logging and other similar functionality.

The relevant structure of `server.xml` is as follows:

```
<Server>
  <ContextManager>
  </ContextManager>
</Server>
```

At the top level is a `<Server>` element, representing the entire Java Virtual Machine. A `<Context>` element is used to define an individual web application. Any number of these may be placed within the `ContextManager` element. The following is an extract from the `web.xml` file:

```
<Context
  path="/projavaxml/chapterXX/app"
  docBase="C:/projavaxml/chapterXX/webapps/app"
  debug="9"
  reloadable="true">
</Context>
```

The attributes of the `<Context>` element are:

❑ `path` determines the URL prefix where the application will be deployed. In the example above, the application will be found at `http://localhost:8080/examples/`.

❑ `docBase` specifies the whereabouts of the `.war` file or expanded web application directory structure for the application. Since a relative file path is specified here, Tomcat will look in its webapps directory (this was configured in the `<Host>` element, above) but an absolute file path can also be used.

❑ `debug` specifies the level of debugging information that will be produced for this application.

❑ `reloadable` specifies whether the container should check for changes to files that would require it to reload the application. When deploying your application in a production environment, setting its value to `"false"` will improve performance, as Tomcat will not have to perform these checks.

Getting Help

If you need help with Tomcat, and this appendix and the documentation just haven't helped, your first port of call should be the Tomcat web site, http://jakarta.apache.org/tomcat/. There are two mailing lists dedicated to Tomcat issues:

❑ tomcat-user, for Tomcat's users – this is where you can ask questions on configuring and using Tomcat. The Tomcat developers should be on hand to help out as necessary.

❑ tomcat-dev, which is where the developers themselves lurk. If you decide to get stuck in with contributing to improving Tomcat itself, this is where the action is.

The Xerces Blue
Butterfly, which became
extinct earlier this century,
and after which the Xerces XML
Parser is named ...

Index

A Guide to the Index

The index is arranged hierarchically, in alphabetical order, with symbols preceding the letter A. Most second-level entries and many third-level entries also occur as first-level entries. This is to ensure that users will find the information they require however they choose to search for it.

R

p2p.wrox.com
The programmer's resource centre

A unique free service from Wrox Press
with the aim of helping programmers to help each other

Wrox Press aims to provide timely and practical information to today's programmer. P2P is a list server offering a host of targeted mailing lists where you can share knowledge with your fellow programmers and find solutions to your problems. Whatever the level of your programming knowledge, and whatever technology you use, P2P can provide you with the information you need.

ASP — Support for beginners and professionals, including a resource page with hundreds of links, and a popular ASP+ mailing list.

DATABASES — For database programmers, offering support on SQL Server, mySQL, and Oracle.

MOBILE — Software development for the mobile market is growing rapidly. We provide lists for the several current standards, including WAP, WindowsCE, and Symbian.

JAVA — A complete set of Java lists, covering beginners, professionals,and server-side programmers (including JSP, servlets and EJBs)

.NET — Microsoft's new OS platform, covering topics such as ASP+, C#, and general .Net discussion.

VISUAL BASIC — Covers all aspects of VB programming, from programming Office macros to creating components for the .Net platform.

WEB DESIGN — As web page requirements become more complex, programmer sare taking a more important role in creating web sites. For these programmers, we offer lists covering technologies such as Flash, Coldfusion, and JavaScript.

XML — Covering all aspects of XML, including XSLT and schemas.

OPEN SOURCE — Many Open Source topics covered including PHP, Apache, Perl, Linux, Python and more.

FOREIGN LANGUAGE — Several lists dedicated to Spanish and German speaking programmers, categories include .Net, Java, XML, PHP and XML.

How To Subscribe

Simply visit the P2P site, at **http://p2p.wrox.com/**

Select the 'FAQ' option on the side menu bar for more information about the subscription process and our service.

wrox

PROGRAMMER TO PROGRAMMER™

Wrox writes books for you. Any suggestions, or ideas about how you want information given in your ideal book will be studied by our team. Your comments are always valued at Wrox.

Free phone in USA 800-USE-WROX
Fax (312) 893 8001

UK Tel. (0121) 687 4100   Fax (0121) 687 4101

Professional Java XML - Registration Card

Name _____

Address _____

_____

_____

_____

City_____ State/Region _____

Country_____ Postcode/Zip _____

E-mail _____

Occupation _____

How did you hear about this book? _____

☐ Book review (name) _____

☐ Advertisement (name) _____

☐ Recommendation _____

☐ Catalog _____

☐ Other _____

Where did you buy this book? _____

☐ Bookstore (name)_____ City _____

☐ Computer Store (name)_____

☐ Mail Order _____

☐ Other _____

What influenced you in the purchase of this book?

☐ Cover Design

☐ Contents

☐ Other (please specify) _____

How did you rate the overall contents of this book?

☐ Excellent   ☐ Good

☐ Average   ☐ Poor

What did you find most useful about this book? _____

What did you find least useful about this book? _____

Please add any additional comments. _____

What other subjects will you buy a computer book on soon? _____

What is the best computer book you have used this year?

Note: This information will only be used to keep you updated about new Wrox Press titles and will not be used for any other purpose or passed to any other third party.

401X

Check here if you DO NOT want to receive support for this book ▮ 401X

wrox
PROGRAMMER TO PROGRAMMER

NB. If you post the bounce back card below in the UK, please send it to:

Wrox Press Ltd., Arden House, 1102 Warwick Road,
Acocks Green, Birmingham B27 6BH. UK.

———— *Computer Book Publishers* ————

BUSINESS REPLY MAIL
FIRST CLASS MAIL   PERMIT#64   CHICAGO, IL

POSTAGE WILL BE PAID BY ADDRESSEE

WROX PRESS INC.,
29 S. LA SALLE ST.,
SUITE 520
CHICAGO IL 60603-USA